W-X-Y-Z Volume 21

The World Book Encyclopedia

World Book, Inc.
a Scott Fetzer company

Chicago

The World Book Encyclopedia

World Book, Inc.
233 North Michigan Avenue
Chicago, IL 60601

www.worldbook.com

Library of Congress Cataloging-in-Publication Data

The World Book encyclopedia.
        p. cm.
    Includes bibliographical references and index.
    ISBN 0-7166-0105-2
      1. Encyclopedias and dictionaries. I. World Book, Inc.

AE5 .W55 2005
031—dc22

                                                    2004007545

Printed in the United States of America

05 5 4 3 2 1

Ww

W is the 23rd letter of our alphabet. The letter developed from a symbol used by the Semites, who once lived in Syria and Palestine. They named it *waw,* meaning *hook,* and adapted an Egyptian *hieroglyphic* (picture symbol). The Romans, who took it from the Greeks, gave it a V shape. They first pronounced it as we pronounce *w,* but later pronounced it as *v.* During the 1000's, French scribes doubled the *v,* as *vv,* in order to write the Anglo-Saxon letter *wen,* for which they had no letter in their alphabet. The VV was also written in a rounded form as UU. It later came to be called "double U" in English. See **Alphabet**.

Uses. *W* or *w* is about the 19th most frequently used letter in books, newspapers, and other printed material in English. *W* is used to abbreviate *west.* In military titles, *W* often stands for *women* or *women's,* as in *WAC* for *Women's Army Corps.* In electricity, *w* is used for *watt.* In chemistry *W* is the symbol for the element tungsten.

Pronunciation. In English, *w* is pronounced by rounding the lips and raising the tongue toward the velum, or soft palate, in preparation for a vowel sound to follow. The velum is closed, and the vocal cords vibrate. *W* is silent in words such as *wrong* and *answer.* It rarely occurs in Scandinavian languages or in French and other Romance languages, except for a few words from other tongues. In German, it usually has the sound of *v.* See **Pronunciation**.   Marianne Cooley

---

Development of the letter W

The ancient Egyptians drew this symbol of a supporting pole about 3000 B.C. The Semites adapted the symbol and named it *waw,* their word for *hook.*

The Phoenicians used this symbol of a hook in their alphabet about 1000 B.C.

The Greeks changed the symbol and added it to their alphabet about 600 B.C. They called their letter *upsilon.*

The Romans gave the letter V its capital shape about A.D. 114.

Medieval scribes used VV as a letter about 1000. VV was also written UU, and the letter became known as "double U."

The **small letter w** came into use along with the capital during the 1000's. By the 1500's, the small letter had developed its present shape.

1000   Today

Special ways of expressing the letter W

International
Morse Code

Braille

International
Flag Code

Semaphore Code

Sign Language
Alphabet

Common forms of the letter W

Handwritten letters vary from person to person. *Manuscript* (printed) letters, *left,* have simple curves and straight lines. Cursive letters, *right,* have flowing lines.

Roman letters have small finishing strokes called *serifs* that extend from the main strokes. The type face shown above is Baskerville. The italic form appears at the right.

Sans-serif letters are also called *gothic letters.* They have no serifs. The type face shown above is called Futura. The italic form of Futura appears at the right.

Computer letters have special shapes. Computers can "read" these letters either optically or by means of the magnetic ink with which the letters may be printed.

Wabash River, *WAW bash,* is the best-known river in Indiana. It is 475 miles (764 kilometers) long. The Wabash rises in western Ohio and flows northwest into Indiana. It turns near Huntington and flows west and southwest until it joins the Ohio River in the southwestern corner of Indiana. The Wabash forms part of the boundary between Indiana and Illinois (see **Indiana** [physical map]). The Wabash and its branches drain most of Indiana and a large area of Illinois. The river is mentioned in several songs, including Indiana's state song, "On the Banks of the Wabash, Far Away."

Indians used the Wabash as a transportation route as early as the 1300's. By the 1700's, the Wabash was an important transportation route for French traders and colonial settlers. In the 1850's, a new railroad system linked the major cities along the Wabash, and river transportation declined.   Michael E. Sullivan

Waco, *WAY koh* (pop. 113,726; met. area pop. 213,517), is a city in central Texas. It lies on the Brazos River, about 100 miles (160 kilometers) south of Dallas. For location, see **Texas** (political map).

Waco's industries include candy manufacturing and systems modification and modernization for military and commercial aircraft. The surrounding area produces cotton, dairy foods, grains, hay, livestock, poultry, and vegetables. Waco is the home of Baylor University, the largest Baptist university in the world.

Waco was founded in 1849 on the site of a deserted Waco Indian village and was named for that tribe. That

Baylor University
Baylor University's main campus is located in Waco. Pat Neff Hall houses the university's administrative offices.

same year, settler Shapley P. Ross established a ferry service across the Brazos River. The ferry made Waco an important gateway to the West. Construction of a suspension bridge over the Brazos in 1870 and the arrival of the railroad in 1871 encouraged the city's growth. Waco is the seat of McLennan County and has a council-manager form of government. In 1993, a 51-day stand-off took place between federal law enforcement agents and a cult called the Branch Davidians at the cult's compound near Waco (see **Reno, Janet**).   Barbara Elmore

Wager is a bet, or anything which is risked on the outcome of an event or the answer to a question. Money or other property may be wagered, or it may be agreed that the loser of the bet shall do a certain thing. Laws do not enforce the payment of wagers, except in certain countries and states where that kind of gambling is lawful.   Dwight Chuman

See also **Gambling; Lottery.**

Wages and hours. Wages are the price paid for work. They are usually figured by the hour or by the week.

Wages are the main source of income for most people in the United States. Wages may be classified as *money wages* and *real wages.* Money wages are the actual amount of money a worker receives from an employer. Real wages represent the amount of goods and services workers can buy with their money wages. The prices of goods and services may change sharply over time. As a result, economists must compare real wages to determine how the ability of workers to buy changes. Such comparisons adjust for changing prices.

Real-wage comparisons are especially important over long periods of time. During such periods, money wages may increase sharply even though real wages may increase little or even decline. For example, from 1985 to 1995, money wages increased by 33 percent while real wages actually declined by about 5 percent. Thus, workers could buy more goods and services with their average weekly wages in 1985 than in 1995.

The growth of real wages over time is much more important than the growth of money wages because real-wage levels determine the purchasing power of workers. A main contributing factor in the growth of real wages over time is growth in productivity. When more goods and services are produced without an increase in the cost of production, prices stay low, and wages can buy more. The growth in productivity is measured by the workers' average *output per worker-hour.* Output per worker-hour measures the amount of goods and services an average worker produces in one hour. Output per worker-hour increases as workers become more skilled, and as machinery, tools, and factories become more efficient.

From 1909 to 1950, output per worker-hour in the United States rose an average of 2 percent annually. From 1950 to 1969, it increased at an average annual rate of 2.8 percent. However, from 1969 to 1989, the growth slowed to an average rate of 1 percent yearly. In 1980, 1982, 1989, and 1990, worker productivity actually declined. Since 1990, average worker productivity per hour has risen an average of about 2 percent a year.

Since the 1940's, employers have spent an increasing percentage of their labor costs on *fringe benefits,* rather than *take-home pay* for the worker. The most popular

Wages and hours in the United States

Average weekly gross wages (before social security and income tax deductions) have increased greatly since 1940. Factoring out inflation by showing wages in constant dollars reveals that wages peaked in the 1970's, then leveled off. Average weekly working hours fell at the beginning of the 1900's, increased during World War II, then stabilized at about 40 hours per week. Figures apply only to production workers in manufacturing industries, a benchmark for measuring changes in wages and hours.

Average weekly wages

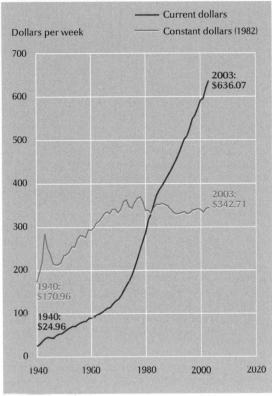

Average weekly hours

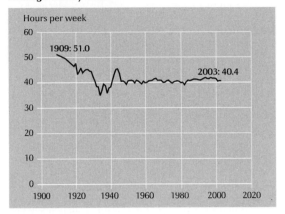

Average weekly wages

Year	Current dollars	Constant dollars (1982)
1940	$ 24.96	$170.96
1945	44.20	236.36
1950	58.32	233.12
1955	75.70	270.86
1960	89.72	291.30
1965	107.53	328.84
1970	133.33	331.67
1975	190.79	341.92
1980	288.62	337.17
1985	386.37	350.29
1990	441.86	331.98
1995	509.26	329.40
1998	557.12	338.06
2000	590.65	338.87
2003	636.07	342.71

Source: U.S. Bureau of Labor Statistics.

fringe benefits include pension plans, medical and dental insurance, paid holidays, and paid sick time. Employers usually consider benefits as a substitute for wages, rather than as an additional contribution to the workers.

Hours. Before the Industrial Revolution, most people worked on farms where the workday ran from sunrise to sunset. Factory operators tried to enforce the same hours during the Industrial Revolution of the 1700's and early 1800's, despite the difference in working conditions and the type of work. Gradually, the 10-hour day and the 6-day week became the normal working period in U.S. and European factories.

Labor began its demands for an 8-hour day in the mid-1800's. But the 8-hour day did not become common in the United States until after World War I. During the 1930's, the 5-day, 40-hour workweek came into general practice in the United States. This practice has changed little through the years. By the early 1980's, the average workweek was 35 hours. Flexible work scheduling, called *flextime* or *flexitime,* began in West Germany in 1967 and spread to the United States during the 1970's. Flextime workers may choose their own daily work hours, within certain limits, as long as they work the re-

quired number of hours per week. Most flextime systems require all employees to be present during a period called the *core hours.*   Paul L. Burgess

Related articles in *World Book* include:

Child labor
Cost of living
Labor, Department of
Labor movement

Minimum wage
Profit sharing
Unemployment insurance

Wagner, *WAG nuhr,* **Honus,** *HOH nuhs* (1874-1955), is often considered baseball's greatest shortstop. Wagner played for the Pittsburgh Pirates from 1900 to 1917. He led the National League in batting eight years, including four seasons in a row. He batted .300 or higher in a league record 17 consecutive seasons. His lifetime batting average was .329. Wagner led the league

Culver

Honus Wagner

in stolen bases five times. Wagner holds the National League record for most triples with 252. He also ranks second in major league putouts by a shortstop.

Wagner was born in Mansfield (now Carnegie), Pa. His given and family name was John Peter Wagner. He was called *Honus,* a nickname for *Johannes,* the German form of John. Wagner began his major league career with the Louisville Colonels in 1897. He was elected to the National Baseball Hall of Fame in 1936.   Jack Lang

Wagner, *VAHG nuhr,* **Richard** (1813-1883), was a great German composer who fundamentally changed European musical, literary, and theatrical life. Wagner believed that the theater should be the center of a community's culture rather than merely a place of entertainment. He finally built his own theater and founded Europe's oldest summer music festival. He intended this festival and the ideal conditions it offered to performing artists to serve as a model for other theaters.

Wagner wrote his own opera *librettos* (texts), basing his mature works on episodes from history and from medieval myths and legends. In the music of his earlier works, he used elements of the German, French, and Italian operatic styles of his time. He reached a climax in *Lohengrin,* which brought these diverse elements to intense, expressive unity. After *Lohengrin,* Wagner developed a new musical language. Composers like Mozart tended to compose operas that were divided into a series of separate musical pieces or "numbers." Wagner moved to a freer chain of many melodic ideas (called motives) and keys, using new ways to blend them into the vast dimensions of his musical dramas.

Early career. Wagner was born in Leipzig on May 22, 1813. Early in life, he showed a flair for the theater and might have become a great actor if he had not decided to become a musician. From 1833 to 1839, he was an opera conductor in German cities. He wrote his first complete opera, *The Fairies* (1834), in the German romantic style. He abandoned this style in his next opera, *The Ban on Love* (1835), based on Shakespeare's *Measure for Measure.* In 1836, he married Minna Planer, an actress. It was a stormy marriage and they lived apart in the last years before her death in 1866.

Wagner's next project was *Rienzi,* an opera in the imposing style called French grand opera. He interrupted his work on *Rienzi* after hearing a performance of Beethoven's ninth symphony in Paris in 1839. This renewed his faith in German music and inspired his first masterpiece, *A Faust Overture* for orchestra (1840). Wagner no longer had complete faith in *Rienzi.* But he completed it anyway, because a successful production in Paris would ensure his reputation as an opera composer all over Europe. The opera was not produced, however, and Wagner ran out of money. In 1841, he finished *The Flying Dutchman,* returning to the German romantic style. It was first performed in 1843.

His fortunes revived in 1842 with an offer to conduct *Rienzi* at the Dresden opera house. In Dresden, Wagner composed *Tannhäuser* (1845) and *Lohengrin* (1848), two great treatments of the romantic view of medieval chivalry.

Meanwhile, social revolution brewed in Germany. Wagner was convinced that musicians were treated unjustly and that the organization and operation of the theaters were poor. His resentment led to his participation

in an unsuccessful revolution in 1849. A warrant was issued for his arrest and he fled to Switzerland. He was not allowed to return to Germany for 12 years.

Later career. During his first years in Switzerland, Wagner wrote no music. Instead, he examined his own philosophy of art and life and wrote on social, religious, and artistic problems. He also began to expand the libretto for his greatest creation, *The Ring of the Nibelung.* He began work on the music for this cycle of four operas in 1853. He finished *The Rhine Gold (Das Rheingold)* in 1854, *The Valkyrie (Die Walküre)* in 1856, and the first two acts of *Siegfried* by 1857. Then he composed another work he had been planning, *Tristan and Isolde.* He did not compose the third act of *Siegfried* until 1869.

Historical Pictures Service
Richard Wagner

Tristan, completed by 1859, is a landmark in music because of the intensely *chromatic* style which reflects the ambiguity in the relationship between Tristan and Isolde. This style greatly increased the expressive nature of Wagner's melodies and harmonies. *Tristan* is a unique conception for the stage. It deals less with external events or actions than with the powerful emotional lives of the characters, what Wagner called an "interior drama."

Getting *Tristan* produced was Wagner's chief concern after 1859. *Tannhäuser,* in a revised version, was performed unsuccessfully in Paris in 1861. Debts piled up, and he constantly faced financial ruin. In 1864, King Ludwig II of Bavaria came to his rescue. Wagner became the king's adviser in Munich, and *Tristan* was produced there in 1865. Meanwhile, Wagner had started work on his only mature comedy, *The Mastersingers of Nuremberg (Die Meistersinger von Nürnberg).* He finished it in Switzerland in 1867. In 1874, he concluded the entire *Ring* cycle with the completion of *The Twilight of the Gods (Die Götterdämmerung).* About 1864, Wagner fell in love with Cosima von Bülow, the married daughter of composer Franz Liszt. Cosima became his mistress, and they were married in 1870.

Wagner's music made a great impression on King Ludwig's romantic imagination. The composer used the king's admiration for his work to further his own ambitions. With the king's aid, Wagner built a theater in Bayreuth in which to perform the *Ring.* The first festival was held there in 1876. He composed his last work, the opera *Parsifal* (1882), to be performed in this theater.

Wagner's philosophy. Wagner tried to find a new way of combining music and drama in the theater. He believed the basic error in opera was that music had become the sole end. Drama served merely as an excuse for musical display. Wagner aimed at a work in which all the various elements in operatic composition were in perfect harmony and directed toward a single artistic end.

Wagner considered the orchestra the greatest artistic achievement of his time, and wanted to take greater advantage of its expressive possibilities. Wagner did not believe the orchestra should accompany a vocal line with repeated chords like a "monstrous guitar." He thought it could be given a more elaborate musical texture in which the vocal line would be one independent strand. His use of recurrent motives permitted continuous music throughout an act, with no breaks until the end. Wagner disliked "operatic" acting, and insisted that singers use only movements required by the music.

In addition to his opera texts, Wagner wrote criticism, *polemics* (literary arguments), and theoretical works. His most important writings outline and defend the principles of his mature music dramas. Wagner wrote passionately on many scientific, political, and religious topics. Wagner's arguments, however, were sometimes illogical and cruel. For example, his dislike of the German-Jewish composer Giacomo Meyerbeer led Wagner to write an attack on Judaism in music. Wagner had conflicting feelings about Jews, and many people have considered him anti-Semitic. Despite his controversial personal life, Wagner's works have placed him in the ranks of the world's greatest composers.   Thomas A. Bauman

See also **Opera** (Richard Wagner; The opera repertoire).

Additional resources

Deathridge, John, and others, eds. *Wagner Handbook.* Harvard Univ. Pr., 1992.
Holman, J. K. *Wagner's Ring.* Amadeus Pr., 1996.
Magee, Bryan. *The Tristan Chord: Wagner and Philosophy.* Henry Holt, 2001.
Millington, Barry, ed. *The Wagner Compendium.* Schirmer Bks., 1992.

Wagner, *WAG nuhr,* **Robert Ferdinand** (1877-1953), was a United States statesman. He served in the New York legislature and showed special interest in welfare questions. Wagner was justice of the Supreme Court of New York from 1919 to 1926. From 1927 to 1949, he represented New York in the U.S. Senate. A Democrat, he sponsored the National Industrial Recovery Act; the National Labor Relations Act, or "Wagner Act"; the Social Security Act; and the Housing Act of 1937. Wagner was born on June 8, 1877, in Nastatten, near Wiesbaden, Germany. His son, Robert F. Wagner, Jr., served as mayor of New York City from 1954 to 1965.   Alonzo L. Hamby

Wagner Act. See National Labor Relations Act.
Wagon. The wheel and the wagon were developed at the same time. This was at least 5,500 years ago, when people first discovered that they could pull sledges

more easily if they fitted the sledges with wheels of solid wood.

The Mesopotamians were probably the earliest people to use wagons. The use of wagons spread quickly through much of Europe and central Asia. The Scythians wandered the plains of southeastern Europe as early as 700 B.C., carrying their possessions on two-wheeled carts covered with reeds. The Greeks and the Romans developed chariots that were lighter and faster than Egyptian chariots. The four-wheeled coach was developed in Germany during the Middle Ages.

English governors of the American Colonies introduced the first wagons in North America. Stagecoaches began to run over colonial roads about the time of George Washington. The *prairie schooner* (covered wagon), first built by the German farmers of Pennsylvania, was used in the development of the American West. Farm wagons carried crops to market until the early 1900's.   Robert C. Post

See also **Chuck wagon; Conestoga wagon; Pioneer life in America** (The wagon train); **Stagecoach; Transportation** (pictures).

Wagon train. See **Pioneer life in America** (The wagon train); **Western frontier life in America** (Transportation).
Wahoo is a fish that lives in warm parts of the Atlantic, Indian, and Pacific oceans. In American waters, it is found from Florida to Venezuela in the Atlantic Ocean, and from Mexico to Ecuador and the Hawaiian Islands in the Pacific. The wahoo is known as *peto* in Latin America and as *ono* in Hawaii. The wahoo has a long body with a pointed snout and a long fin on the back. The back is dark blue and the sides are silver with wavy bars. Wahoos can grow to a length of more than 8 feet (2.4 me-

WORLD BOOK illustration by Colin Newman, Linden Artists Ltd.

The wahoo is an excellent game and food fish that lives in the warm waters of all oceans. It is an active swimmer.

ters) and can weigh more than 180 pounds (82 kilograms).   Gary T. Sakagawa

Scientific classification. The wahoo belongs to the mackerel family, Scombridae. It is *Acanthocybium solandri.*

Detail of the Bayeux Tapestry (late 1100's);
William the Conqueror Center,
Bayeux, France (Giraudon)

A wagon of the Middle Ages was used to carry weapons into battle.

Brown Brothers

The Conestoga wagon carried pioneers westward over the Allegheny Mountains from the early 1700's until about 1850. It was drawn by a team of four to six horses.

Wailing Wall. See Western Wall.

Wainwright, Jonathan Mayhew (1883-1953), was an American general whose courage made him a hero of World War II. After General Douglas MacArthur was ordered to leave the Philippines and go to Australia in March 1942, Wainwright remained in command of the American and Filipino forces on Bataan Peninsula and Corregidor. He was forced to surrender in May 1942, and was held a prisoner for three years by the Japanese. Wainwright was released in 1945, and participated in the surrender ceremony of the Japanese delegates aboard the U.S.S. *Missouri* in Tokyo Bay. On his return to the United States, Wainwright became a full general and received the Medal of Honor.

AP/Wide World
Jonathan M. Wainwright

Wainwright was born on Aug. 23, 1883, in Walla Walla, Washington, and graduated from the United States Military Academy in 1906. He became a cavalry officer and served in the Philippines in 1909 and 1910. During World War I, Wainwright served on the general staff of the 82nd Division in France. After World War II, he commanded the Fourth Army. He retired in 1947.

Maurice Matloff

See also **Bataan Peninsula**.

Waite, *wayt,* **Morrison Remick** (1816-1888), served as chief justice of the United States from 1874 until his death. In the Granger Cases, his opinions upheld the power of state governments to regulate business (see **Granger Cases**). This doctrine later lost favor when the Supreme Court developed broad powers to enforce the 14th Amendment. But the doctrine of broad power to regulate business was revived in the 1930's.

Waite was born on Nov. 29, 1816, in Lyme, Connecticut. He graduated from Yale University. In 1871, he was an American delegate to the Geneva Tribunal of Arbitration, which considered the *Alabama* claims (see **Alabama** [ship]). He helped found the Republican Party.

Jerre S. Williams

Wake is the custom of watching over a dead person before burial. Some form of the custom has been practiced in all parts of the world. But the practice is no longer used as widely in Western society as in earlier times. In the traditional wake, family and friends gathered at the dead person's home. The custom probably began because of a concern over occasional errors made in the determination of death. It is also likely that some early people believed that the presence of the living would ward off the evil spirits that might possess a body prior to disposal.   Richard A. Kalish

Wake Island is a United States possession in the west-central Pacific Ocean (see **Pacific Islands** [map]). It is a triangular atoll made up of three small coral islets, Wake, Peale, and Wilkes. The islets cover a land area of about 3 square miles (8 square kilometers). They have about 100 people, all of whom are U.S. citizens. With a curving reef, they enclose a lagoon that is less than 4 square miles (10 square kilometers) in area. Wake's vegetation consists mainly of shrubs and bushes.

Spaniards probably sighted Wake when they explored the Pacific in the late 1500's. The British schooner *Prince William Henry* landed there in 1796. In 1841, Lieutenant Charles Wilkes of the United States Exploring Expedition surveyed Wake with the aid of the naturalist Titian Peale. They found no indication that the atoll had ever been inhabited. Wake Island became an unincorporated territory of the United States in 1898. The United States claimed Wake because it lay on the cable route from San Francisco to Manila. In 1935, Wake became a base for Pacific air traffic.

Wake Island was the site of an early World War II battle. For two weeks in December 1941, a force of 400 U.S. Marines and about 1,000 civilians fought off a Japanese invasion. But the Japanese captured Wake in late December 1941. The Japanese garrison on Wake surrendered at the end of the war, in 1945.

Today, Wake is used primarily for emergency stopovers for airplanes and ships. The United States National Weather Service and the United States National Oceanographic and Atmospheric Administration have research and monitoring units on the atoll.   Robert C. Kiste

Waksman, *WAKS muhn,* **Selman Abraham** (1888-1973), was an American bacteriologist who made important contributions to soil microbiology and to the development of antibiotics. He received the 1952 Nobel Prize for physiology or medicine for the discovery of the antibiotic *streptomycin* (see **Streptomycin**).

Waksman studied a group of soil microbes known as *actinomycetes.* He examined the effects of these microbes on the fertility of soil and on the development of *humus* (organic matter in soil). In 1939, he began testing actinomycetes for antibiotic activity. He and his co-workers tested about 10,000 of the microbes before they discovered streptomycin in 1943.

Waksman was born on July 22, 1888, in Priluka, near Kiev, Ukraine (then a part of the Russian Empire). He moved to the United States in 1910 and joined the faculty of Rutgers University in 1918. From 1949 to 1958, he directed the Rutgers Institute of Microbiology.

Kenneth R. Manning

Wal-Mart Stores, Inc., is the largest retail company in the world. The company has more than 3,300 stores in the United States and about 1,200 stores in other countries. Its stores include Wal-Mart discount stores, which sell general merchandise; Wal-Mart Supercenters, which sell groceries in addition to general merchandise and also operate specialty shops and restaurants; and Sam's Club, the largest warehouse club in the United States, which sells deeply discounted products for personal and business use to club members. Sam's Club operates more than 500 clubs and has more than 45 million members. Wal-Mart and Sam's Club also sell merchandise through company Web sites.

Sam Walton, a retail merchant, along with his brother, James Lawrence Walton, founded Wal-Mart. The Waltons opened the first Wal-Mart store in Rogers, Arkansas, in 1962. In 1968, the chain of stores expanded outside Arkansas. Wal-Mart began trading stock as a publicly held company in 1970. The first Sam's Club opened in Midwest City, Oklahoma, in 1983.

Critically reviewed by Wal-Mart Stores, Inc.

Walachia. See Romania (History).

Walata, *wah LAH tah,* was a leading trading city in West Africa from the late 1000's to the 1500's. Copper, swords, and other goods were traded there for gold and sometimes for slaves. Today, Walata is a small town in Mauritania called *Oualata.*

During the 1000's, Muslim traders from the south settled in Walata. The city became part of the Mali Empire in the 1300's. The Tuareg of the south seized and occupied Walata in 1433. In the late 1400's, it became part of the Songhai Empire. After that empire fell, various peoples ruled Walata.   Leo Spitzer

Walcott, Derek (1930-   ), a West Indian poet and playwright, won the 1992 Nobel Prize for literature. His work explores such themes as the Caribbean experience from colonial slavery to independence, and the nature of the Caribbean's post-colonial identity—a mixture of different cultures and traditions. Walcott's writings reflect his rich racial heritage and cultural background, both African and European. Walcott writes his works in English.

Walcott's first commercially published collection of poetry was *In a Green Night: Poems, 1948 1960* (1962). His other verse includes *Another Life* (1973), a long narrative poem; *The Star-Apple Kingdom* (1979); *The Fortunate Traveller* (1981); and *The Arkansas Testament* (1987). *Omeros* (1990) is an epic poem that describes the poet's inner struggle to find a balance between personal and collective memories.

Walcott's plays include *Dream on Monkey Mountain* (1967), *Remembrance* (1977), *Pantomime* (1978), and *Odyssey: A Stage Version* (1992). They focus on the human struggle against hypocrisy, exploitation, and authority. Derek Alton Walcott was born in Castries, Saint Lucia.   Julie Minkler

Wald, George (1906-1997), an American biochemist, determined how chemical changes in the retina enable a person to see. He shared the 1967 Nobel Prize for physiology or medicine.

Wald analyzed the *pigment* (coloring matter) of *rods,* the cells in the retina that respond to dim light. He found that light causes certain changes in *retinene,* a chemical in the pigment. These changes trigger a nerve impulse that transmits to the brain an image of what is seen. Wald discovered that the body makes retinene from vitamin A. This discovery explained why a deficiency of vitamin A reduces vision at night.

Wald was born in New York City and earned a Ph.D. at Columbia University. He joined the faculty of Harvard University in 1934. He was an outspoken opponent of the Vietnam War (1957-1975).   Eric Howard Christianson

Wald, Lillian D. (1867-1940), founded the first visiting nurse program in the United States that was not affiliated with a religious group. Her contacts with the poor in New York City in the depression of 1892-1893 inspired her to found the Nurses' Settlement, later known as the Henry Street Settlement. It became a model for public school nursing programs in the United States. She also worked with the founder of the first "ungraded" class for mentally retarded children.

Wald and social reformer Florence Kelley were the first to suggest to President Theodore Roosevelt the idea of a national children's bureau to study the needs of children. Congress set up the Children's Bureau as an agency of the U.S. government in 1912. In addition, Wald was active in the American Union Against Militarism, and her views were highly respected by President Woodrow Wilson and others who worked for peace. Lillian Wald was born in Cincinnati.   Elizabeth Fee

Henry Street Settlement Archives
Lillian D. Wald

Waldenses, *wahl DEHN seez,* are members of a Christian religious group. The group was founded by Peter Waldo, a wealthy merchant of Lyon, France. In 1173, Waldo left his wife, gave his fortune to the church and charity, and began preaching in the streets of Lyon. His message of poverty and religious devotion attracted many followers, who were called the *poor men of Lyon.* Pope Alexander III and the Archbishop of Lyon approved of the Waldenses. But the succeeding pope and archbishop forbade the Waldenses to preach because they were not priests and their teachings differed from those of the church. For example, they denied the pope's authority and the existence of purgatory. In 1184, Pope Lucius III excommunicated the Waldenses.

Many Waldenses adopted the doctrines of the Reformation, which took place during the 1500's. There are now about 50,000 Waldenses in Europe and North and South America. Their headquarters are in Rome.
Eugene TeSelle

Waldheim, *VALT hym,* **Kurt,** *koort* (1918-   ), is an Austrian diplomat who served as secretary-general of the United Nations (UN) from 1972 to 1982. He replaced U Thant of Burma. As secretary-general, Waldheim carried out several difficult peacekeeping missions. He failed to stop a war between China and Vietnam in 1979, though the fighting ended that same year. In 1980, Waldheim could not get the release of American hostages held in Iran. The Americans were freed in 1981. He also failed to end the Iran-Iraq war that began in 1980. A UN-arranged cease-fire halted the fighting in 1988, six years after he had stepped down as secretary-general.

From 1986 to 1992, Waldheim served as president of Austria, a largely ceremonial position. His campaign for the presidency was marked by controversy when records surfaced concerning his possible involvement in Nazi atrocities during World War II. The documents showed that Waldheim had been a German army officer in units that killed thousands of Yugoslav patriots and assisted in the deportation of thousands of Greek Jews to concentration camps during the 1940's. Waldheim denied involvement in these actions.

Waldheim was born near Vienna. He attended the Vienna Consular Academy and earned a law degree at the University of Vienna. Waldheim entered the Austrian foreign service in 1945. He became permanent Austrian observer at the UN in 1955 and headed Austria's first delegation to the UN that same year. From 1964 to 1968, and again in 1970 and 1971, he served as Austria's representative at the UN. He was Austria's foreign minister from 1968 to 1970.   R. E. Herzstein

See also **United Nations** (The Secretariat [picture]).

The Welsh countryside includes rugged mountains, green valleys, and picturesque villages. Snowdon, which is the highest peak in Wales, rises behind this village in the northwest. About one-fifth of the Welsh people live in rural areas.

Colin Molyneux, Bruce Coleman Ltd.

Wales is one of the four major political divisions that make up the United Kingdom of Great Britain and Northern Ireland. England, Northern Ireland, and Scotland are the other divisions of the United Kingdom, which is often called the U. K. or Britain. Cardiff is the capital and largest city of Wales.

Wales lies on the west coast of the island of Great Britain. It takes up about a tenth of the island. Wales has a wealth of scenic beauty. Its landscape includes low, broad mountains and deep, green valleys. Wales is bordered by extensions of the Atlantic Ocean on the north, west, and south, and by England on the east. Most of the Welsh people live in towns, cities, and industrial areas of southern Wales. The rest of Wales is mainly rural.

The Welsh take great pride in their heritage. Although Wales has been united with England for more than 400 years, the Welsh have kept alive their own language, literature, and traditions. The Welsh name for Wales is *Cymru* (pronounced *KUM ree*).

This article describes the people, geography, and economy of Wales. It also traces the history of Wales up to 1536, when the country was united with England. For a discussion of the United Kingdom as a whole, of the relation of Wales to the other British political divisions, of the government of the United Kingdom, and of British history, see **United Kingdom.**

Government

The United Kingdom is both a parliamentary democracy and a constitutional monarchy. Wales elects 40 of the 659 members of the House of Commons, the main governing body of the United Kingdom. In 1999, the United Kingdom granted Wales its own government, transferring many powers from the central government to the new government.

The National Assembly for Wales meets in Cardiff. It consists of 60 members, who serve four-year terms. Most members are elected directly by the Welsh voters, but some are elected by *proportional representation.* This system gives a political party a share of seats in parliament according to its share of the total votes cast in an election.

The first secretary leads the Welsh government with the help of a cabinet. The first secretary is usually the leader of the political party that controls the most seats

Facts in brief

Capital: Cardiff.
Official languages: Welsh and English.
Area: 8,015 mi² (20,758 km²). *Greatest distances*—north-south, 137 mi (220 km); east-west, 116 mi (187 km). *Coastline*—614 mi (988 km).
Elevation: *Highest*—Snowdon, 3,561 ft (1,085 m) above sea level. *Lowest*—sea level, along the coast.
Population: *Estimated 2004 population*—2,919,000; population density, 364 per mi² (141 per km²); distribution, 78 percent urban, 22 percent rural. *2001 census*—2,903,085.
Chief products: *Agriculture*—barley, cabbage, cattle, cauliflower, hay, oats, potatoes, sheep. *Manufacturing*—aluminum, chemicals, electrical and electronic equipment, iron, motor vehicle and airplane parts, petroleum products, plastics, steel, synthetic fibers, tin plate. *Mining*—coal, limestone, slate.

in the Assembly. Assembly members who head the various government departments make up the cabinet. A secretary of state for Wales still sits in the United Kingdom's cabinet, though most of the secretary's power has been transferred to the National Assembly for Wales.

The National Assembly for Wales cannot make laws or alter taxation. The British Parliament makes laws both for the whole of the United Kingdom and for England and Wales. The Welsh government administers programs such as education, health, and transportation.

Local government in Wales is carried out by 22 unitary authorities, which are directly responsible to the Welsh cabinet. Each unitary authority is supervised by an elected council. The unitary authorities are responsible for matters such as housing, recreation, and roads. Local government is financed by a mixture of *council tax* (local taxes) and grants from the national government.

People

Population. Most of the people of Wales live in the industrialized and formerly industrialized areas of southern Wales. The growth in these areas took place in the 1600's and during the Industrial Revolution, a period of rapid industrialization that began in the 1700's. At that time, people came to the region from rural Wales and from England. Cardiff, Newport, and Swansea grew as ports to serve the coal and iron industries.

Ancestry. Some Welsh are descended from prehistoric peoples from continental Europe who colonized Wales thousands of years ago. Many others trace their ancestry to such later settlers as the Celts, Romans, Anglo-Saxons, Vikings, Normans, and English.

Language. Wales has two official languages, Welsh and English. Either language may be used in the courts or for government business. Some newspapers are published partly or only in Welsh, and many radio and television programs are broadcast in both languages.

Welsh is still the daily language in many sections of western and northern Wales. In some parts of these areas, more than three-fourths of the people speak Welsh. Overall, however, the number of Welsh-speaking people has declined since 1901, when half the population spoke Welsh, to less than one-fifth today.

Welsh is one of the oldest languages in Europe. It is derived from ancient Celtic and has been influenced by each group of settlers. The letters *j, k, q, v, x,* and *z* are not used in modern Welsh. The letter *y* is always a vowel, and the letter *w* is usually used as one.

Certain letter combinations are considered part of the Welsh alphabet. They include the double letters *dd, ff,* and *ll.* The combination *dd* is pronounced like the *th* in *they.* The letter *f* sounds like the English *v,* and *ff* sounds like *f.* The *ll* sound is made by placing the tongue in the position for *l* and then trying to pronounce an *h.*

Way of life

In general, the way of life in Wales is similar to that in the rest of the Western world. For example, many people relax in the evenings by watching television. In Wales, as in the United Kingdom as a whole, the *pub* (public house) is an important part of social life. A number of older customs also survive. On March 1, the feast of Saint David, the patron saint of Wales, people throughout the land wear the traditional Welsh symbols of the leek and daffodil.

City life. About four-fifths of the Welsh people live in urban areas. Many urban dwellers live on the outskirts of cities in large public housing developments, some of which have fallen into disrepair. Welsh metal-processing industries have declined since the 1950's, leading to increased unemployment in Welsh cities. Urban areas have also experienced a rise in crime, overcrowding, and other social problems.

In the steep-sided coal-mining valleys of southern Wales, many townspeople live in *row houses.* These houses have the same design and are attached in a row.

Rural life. Approximately a fifth of the Welsh people live in rural areas. Welsh farms are small, and most are owned by the people who live on them. Many rural people live in stone cottages.

An older Welsh way of life has lasted in rural areas, especially where the Welsh language is the primary one. Ties to religion and to families tend to be stronger in these areas. However, many people fear that age-old customs may soon be lost. Rural housing has become scarce, and farming has become less profitable over the years. As a result, more and more young people have migrated to the cities to look for employment and housing. As the young people leave the countryside, they tend to abandon the old values and traditions.

Food and drink. Most Welsh cooking is simple and uses local ingredients. Many Welsh people enjoy roast Welsh lamb served with mint sauce. Other favorite dishes include *cawl,* a clear broth with vegetables, and

The flag of Wales features a red dragon on a white and green background. The dragon has been a Welsh symbol for nearly 2,000 years.

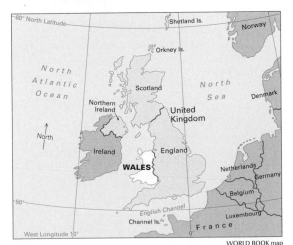

WORLD BOOK map

Wales is bordered by extensions of the Atlantic Ocean on the north, west, and south, and by England to the east.

Wales

WORLD BOOK map

Legend	
National boundary	Railroad
Unitary authority boundary	⊛ National capital
Expressway	★ Administrative center
Other road	• Other city or town

Key to numbered unitary authorities

1 Blaenau Gwent
2 Bridgend
3 Caerphilly
4 Cardiff
5 Merthyr Tydfil
6 Neath Port Talbot
7 Newport
8 Rhondda Cynon Taff
9 Torfaen

Wales map index

Unitary authorities*

Blaenau Gwent	70,058	.D	4
Bridgend	128,650	.E	4
Caerphilly	169,521	.D	4
Cardiff	305,340	.E	4
Carmarthenshire	173,635	.D	3
Ceredigion	75,384	.C	3
Conwy	109,597	.A	3
Denbighshire	93,092	.A	4
Flintshire	148,565	.A	4
Gwynedd	116,838	.B	3
Isle of Anglesey	66,828	.A	2
Merthyr Tydfil	55,983	.D	4
Monmouthshire	84,879	.D	5
Neath Port Talbot	134,471	.D	3
Newport	137,017	.E	5
Pembrokeshire	112,901	.D	2
Powys	126,344	.C	4
Rhondda Cynon Taff	231,952	.E	4
Swansea	223,293	.E	3
Torfaen	90,967	.D	4
Vale of Glamorgan	119,293	.E	4
Wrexham	128,477	.A	4

Cities and towns†

Aberystwyth	C	3
Barry	E	4
Bridgend	E	4
Caernarfon	A	3
Caerphilly	E	4
Cardiff	E	4
Carmarthen	D	3
Colwyn Bay	A	3
Cwmbran	E	4
Llandrindod Wells	C	4
Llanelli	E	3
Merthyr Tydfil	D	4
Milford Haven	D	2
Mold	A	4
Monmouth	D	5
Newport	E	5
Pontypridd	E	4
Rhondda	E	4
Swansea	E	3
Wrexham	A	4

Physical features

Anglesey (island)	A	3
Bala Lake	B	4
Berwyn Mountains	B	4
Black Mountains	D	4
Cambrian Mountains	C	3
Cardigan Bay	C	2
Conwy, River	A	4
Dee, River	A	4
Gower Peninsula	E	3
Lleyn Peninsula	B	2
Menai Strait	A	3
St. George's Channel	D	1
Severn, River	C	4
Snowdon (peak)	A	3
Snowdonia	A	3
Tywi, River	D	3
Usk, River	D	4
Wye, River	D	4

*Refer to key in upper left corner of map for unitary authorities in southern Wales.
†The government of the United Kingdom does not report populations for individual cities and towns.
Source: 2001 census.

Welsh rarebit, which consists of melted cheese and butter served on toast. *Laver bread* is made from seaweed and oatmeal. Tasty Welsh cakes and cheeses are also popular. Beer is a traditional Welsh drink, and many pubs sell locally brewed beer. Ale is especially popular.

Recreation. Rugby football is the most popular sport in Wales. The Welsh rugby team competes internationally. Almost every town and village has its own team. Another popular sport is *football,* the game Americans call soccer. Cricket is also played widely in Wales.

In rural areas, many people fish, and some hunt wild duck. Snowdonia National Park and Brecon Beacons National Park have rugged terrain that is excellent for climbing and other mountain sports. Many people visit Pembrokeshire Coast National Park to hike along its coastal cliffs and admire its scenery.

Education. Wales and England have the same school system. In Wales, it is supervised by the Welsh Office Education Department and by local authorities.

All Welsh children from the ages of 5 to 16 must attend school, and they must study Welsh either as a first or a second language. Children attend primary school until the age of 11. Then they typically enter high school. Many students leave high school at age 16. Others go on to technical colleges or other forms of further education. Those who stay in high school until the age of 18 or 19 may study at a university, college, or other school of higher education anywhere in the United Kingdom.

Wales has one university, the University of Wales. It was founded in 1893 and has about 25,000 students. It consists of colleges at Aberystwyth, Bangor, Cardiff, and Swansea. The university also includes the College of Medicine in Cardiff and St. David's University College in Lampeter, near Carmarthen.

Religion. Most Welsh people are Protestants. The Methodist and Anglican churches are the largest Protestant churches in Wales. Others include the Baptist, Presbyterian, and United Reformed churches.

The Church of England became the official Welsh church in 1536. But by 1811, so many people had joined the Methodist Church that it formally separated from the Church of England and became a separate denomination. The Welsh Church Act of 1914 declared that the Church of England was no longer the official church of Wales. The act went into effect in 1920.

Religion has traditionally been important in Welsh life, but it has become less so since the mid-1900's. However, the choral tradition it fostered survives, notably with some famous male choirs.

The arts. Wales is a land of poets and singers. The traditions of Welsh literature and music are among the oldest in Europe and date back more than 1,000 years to the *bards* (poet-singers) of the Middle Ages.

The most notable of early Welsh poets were Taliesin and Aneirin. Aneirin composed a poem called the *Gododdin* about the year 600. In it, he described the adventures of a band of noble warriors. Eleven Welsh stories written in the 1000's and known today as *The Mabinogion* rank among the most important works of medieval European literature. During the 1100's, Geoffrey of Monmouth composed poetry about the legendary King Arthur. Dafydd ap Gwilym, the greatest Welsh poet of the Middle Ages, wrote about love and nature during the 1300's.

The publication in 1588 of the complete translation of the Bible into Welsh ranks as one of the most important events in the history of Welsh literature. This Bible helped preserve the Welsh language and establish standards for written Welsh.

Many poets and other writers continued to use the Welsh language in the 1600's, 1700's, and 1800's, but other Welsh authors turned to English. Dylan Thomas, who wrote in English, became the most celebrated Welsh poet of the 1900's.

The *eisteddfod (eye STEHTH vahd)*, a popular Welsh tradition, is a festival of poetry and music in which performers compete. Its origins date back to the Middle Ages, but the modern form began at the end of the 1700's. Annual eisteddfods, or *eisteddfodau,* are held throughout the land. The largest is the Royal National Eisteddfod. This festival is held in various cities and towns, alternately between northern and southern Wales.

Wales has a rich tradition of choral music that developed in the 1700's at a time of religious revival. The Welsh National Opera has also become world famous.

The land

Wales occupies a broad peninsula on the west coast of the island of Great Britain. It is bounded on the east by England and on the south by the Bristol Channel. St. George's Channel on the west and the Irish Sea on the north separate Wales from Ireland. For information about the climate of Wales, see the *Climate* section of **United Kingdom.**

Surface features. Most of Wales consists of mountains and upland plateaus. The Cambrian Mountains cover about two-thirds of the land. In northern Wales, the mountains are steep and rugged. The highest peak in Wales, 3,561-foot (1,085-meter) Snowdon (called *Yr Wyddfa* in Welsh), rises in the northwest. It is part of the Snowdonia range *(Eryri* in Welsh).

In central and southern Wales, the Cambrian range becomes flatter and forms large plateaus cut deeply by valleys. On the plateaus are forests, pastures, grassy plains, *moors* (open wasteland), and *bogs* (swamplands). Many small lakes and waterfalls dot the mountain and plateau regions.

Coastal plains and river valleys cover about a third of Wales. Low, narrow plains stretch along the south and west coasts.

Rivers and coastline. The longest rivers in Wales are the Severn and the Wye. Both rise near Aberystwyth, flow eastward into England, and then turn south and empty into the Bristol Channel. The Severn stretches for 220 miles (354 kilometers) and is the longest river in Britain. The River Dee forms part of the boundary between Wales and England. The Rivers Dyfi, Teifi, and Tywi drain the west coast of Wales.

The Welsh coastline is 614 miles (988 kilometers) long. Much of it is irregular and lined with cliffs. Many natural bays and harbors lie along the coast.

Queen Street in Cardiff, a popular shopping area, features an outdoor mall, *left.* Cardiff is the capital and largest city of Wales. It is also the Welsh cultural, economic, and industrial center.

A colorful procession announces an *eisteddfod* in Bargoed, a town in southern Wales. An eisteddfod is a Welsh festival of poetry and music in which performers compete.

A large island, Anglesey *(Ynys Mon* in Welsh), lies off the northwest coast. The Menai Strait separates the island from the mainland.

Economy

Coal mining and metal processing became the chief industries of Wales during the Industrial Revolution. Today, however, the economy of Wales depends more on service industries and manufacturing.

Service industries are the largest employers in the cities and towns of Wales. Leading Welsh service industries include banking, insurance, finance, and business services; education; health and welfare services; public administration; and the retail and wholesale trades. Tourism is increasing in both urban and rural areas.

Manufacturing. Major steelworks operate at Llanwern, near Newport, and at Port Talbot. A large plant for producing tin plate is at Llanelli, and aluminum is smelted in Anglesey. Other products manufactured in Wales include automobile parts, chemicals, electronic and electrical equipment, plastics, and synthetic fibers.

Agriculture. Livestock production ranks as the leading agricultural activity in Wales. Farmers raise beef and dairy cattle in the lowlands, and southwest Wales is the center of the Welsh dairy industry. Farmers in the uplands raise sheep for meat and wool. The main crops grown in Wales include barley, oats, and potatoes.

Mining. Coal mining was once the most important industry in Wales. But since the mid-1940's, it has declined steadily, chiefly due to falling demand. The largest coal field lies in the south between Kidwelly and Cwmbran. Oil refineries operate at Milford Haven and Pembroke.

Transportation and communication. An extensive system of well-paved roads covers Wales. Expressways run along part of the northern coast and between the Severn Bridge and southern Wales. High-speed trains connect northern and southern Wales with London, and additional rail lines crisscross the land. Cardiff-Wales Airport is the only international airport in Wales.

Welsh television viewers can choose among two British Broadcasting Corporation channels, two independent channels, and dozens of cable and satellite channels. One of the independent channels, Sianel Ped-war Cymru, broadcasts programs in Welsh and English. The *Western Mail,* a daily newspaper published in Cardiff, is distributed throughout Wales.

History

Prehistoric people occupied caves in northeastern Wales more than 200,000 years ago. About 4000 B.C., people from the European continent migrated to Wales. These people brought farming to Wales and introduced such new tools as stone axes and flint arrowheads to the region. They also built huge monuments called *megaliths.* About 2000 B.C., people from central and eastern Europe settled in Wales, where they raised crops and made bronze tools. By the mid-600's B.C., the Celts had arrived from central Europe. They introduced the use of iron into Wales and built defended settlements called *hill forts* throughout the region.

The Romans conquered Wales between about A.D. 50 and 78. They controlled the region for over 300 years and built roads, walls, and cities throughout Wales.

Struggles against the Anglo-Saxons. The Romans left Britain in the early 400's. Soon afterward, Angles, Jutes, and Saxons from the European mainland invaded the island. By about 700, they had conquered all of southern Britain except Wales and Cornwall. In the late 700's, Offa, ruler of the Anglo-Saxon kingdom of Mercia, built a boundary between Mercia and Wales, possibly to keep out Welsh raiders. The boundary, called *Offa's Dyke,* consists of a ditch and earthen wall from the River Dee to the River Severn.

The Welsh remained independent for the next several hundred years by fighting off the Anglo-Saxons and the Vikings. However, the Welsh were not politically united but were divided into tribes headed by chieftains.

Revolts against England. William the Conqueror and his Norman armies won control of England in 1066. William gave the lands along the border between Wales and England to Norman barons in order to control the Welsh. These borderlands were called the *Marches,* and the barons were known as *marcher lords.* The marcher lords built castles on their lands and gradually expanded their estates. They soon controlled most of central and southern Wales. However, the Normans never conquered the heartland of Wales. During the 1100's, the Welsh regained much of their land from the barons.

During the 1200's, Llywelyn ap Iorwerth, also known as Llywelyn the Great, won control of northern Wales. His grandson Llywelyn ap Gruffydd was acknowledged as Prince of Wales by King Henry III of England in 1267. In return, Llywelyn recognized Henry as his king.

Important dates in Wales

A.D. 50-78 Roman armies conquered Wales.
1282 English troops killed Llywelyn ap Gruffydd, Prince of Wales, during the Welsh revolt that ended in 1283.
1301 King Edward I of England gave the title Prince of Wales to his son.
1400-1410 Owen Glendower (Owain Glyn Dwr) revolted against English rule.
1485 Henry Tudor, a Welsh nobleman, became King Henry VII of England.
1536 King Henry VIII united Wales and England.
(For later dates, see **England** [History]; **United Kingdom** [History].)

After Henry died in 1272, Llywelyn refused to accept Henry's son Edward I as his king. Edward I's armies attacked him in 1277. Fighting again broke out in 1282, and Llywelyn was slain in a battle with English troops. After Llywelyn's death, the Welsh revolt collapsed.

In 1284, Edward I issued the Statute of Rhuddlan. This order placed the conquered Welsh lands directly under English control and divided them into counties under the control of English sheriffs. To ensure control over Wales, Edward built a number of powerful castles, including those at Caernarfon (also spelled *Caernarvon*) and Harlech. In 1301, Edward I gave the title Prince of Wales to his son Edward, who later became Edward II. Since then, nearly all English and British monarchs have given the title to their oldest son.

During the 1300's, the Welsh grew increasingly dissatisfied with English rule. In 1400, Owen Glendower *(Owain Glyn Dwr* in Welsh), a Welsh prince, led a revolt against the English. By 1404, he had driven them out of much of Wales. But by 1410, the English had regained control. Glendower's struggles against the English—despite his final defeat—made him a hero of many Welsh people.

Union with England. In 1485, Henry Tudor, a Welsh nobleman, became King Henry VII of England. The Welsh people then gradually began to accept the idea of uniting with England. In 1536, Henry VIII, the son of Henry VII, joined the two countries under a single government by the first Act of Union. The English government passed a second Act of Union in 1543.

Through the years since England and Wales were united, Wales has struggled—and managed—to maintain a distinct language and culture. For example, the publication of the Welsh Bible in 1588 helped set standards for written Welsh. The Society for the Promotion of Christian Knowledge, founded in 1699, assisted in the publication of Welsh religious books and sought to establish schools throughout Wales. Nevertheless, the history of Wales became closely bound to the history of England and, later, of Britain. For the history of England and the United Kingdom, see **England** (History); **United Kingdom** (History).   D. Q. Bowen and Rodney Barker

Related articles in *World Book* include:

Biographies

Bradley, Francis H.	Geoffrey of Monmouth	Owen, Robert
Charles, Prince	mouth	Thomas, Dylan
David, Saint	Lawrence, T. E.	Williams, Emlyn
Diana, Princess of Wales	Lloyd George, David	

Other related articles

Bard	Llanfairpwllgwyngyll
Bristol Channel	Mythology (Welsh myths)
Cardiff	Prince of Wales
Celts	Severn, River
Irish Sea	Swansea

Outline

I. Government
   A. National Assembly   B. Local government
      for Wales
II. People
   A. Population   B. Ancestry   C. Language
III. Way of life
   A. City life   C. Food and drink
   B. Rural life   D. Recreation

   E. Education   G. The arts
   F. Religion
IV. The land
   A. Surface features   B. Rivers and coastline
V. Economy
   A. Service industries   D. Mining
   B. Manufacturing   E. Transportation and com-
   C. Agriculture   munication
VI. History

Questions

What is an *eisteddfod?*
What are the powers of the National Assembly for Wales?
From what ancient language is Welsh derived?
What are the largest Protestant churches in Wales?
Who became the most famous Welsh poet of the 1900's?
What is *cawl? Laver bread? Welsh rarebit?*
What are the two official languages of Wales?
In what part of Wales do most people live?
What is the leading agricultural activity in Wales?
Who were the *marcher lords?*

Additional resources

Davies, John. *A History of Wales.* 1994. Reprint. Penguin, 1995.
Hestler, Anna. *Wales.* Benchmark Bks., 2001. Younger readers.
Turvey, Roger. *The Welsh Princes.* Longman Pub. Group, 2002.

Wałęsa, *vah WEHN sah,* **Lech,** *lehk* (1943-   ), was president of Poland from 1990 to 1995. Prior to his election, Wałęsa had been an important labor leader.

In 1980, Wałęsa was chosen as provisional head of Solidarity—an organization composed of about 50 Polish trade unions. His negotiations with Poland's government that year led to the government's recognition of Solidarity. This action marked the first time a Communist country recognized a labor organization that was independent of the country's Communist Party. Wałęsa was elected chairman of Solidarity in 1981. The movement faced growing hostility from Poland's Communist Party and the Soviet Union. In December 1981, Poland's govern-

© B. Bisson, Sygma

Lech Wałęsa

ment established martial law and suspended Solidarity's activities. Wałęsa and hundreds of other union leaders were imprisoned. In October 1982, the government outlawed Solidarity. Wałęsa was released in November. The other prisoners were freed over the next several years.

The government ended its ban on Solidarity in 1989. Also in 1989, it allowed elections for a new parliament. The elections were the freest ones in Poland since the country became a Communist state in 1945. Almost every candidate who was endorsed by Wałęsa and Solidarity won a seat in Parliament (see **Poland** [Free elections]). After Wałęsa was elected president in 1990, he resigned as chairman of Solidarity.

Wałęsa was born on Sept. 29, 1943, in Popow, north of Warsaw. In 1967, he became an electrician at the shipyards in Gdańsk. There, Wałęsa began taking part in the workers' rights movement. Wałęsa won the 1983 Nobel Peace Prize for his efforts to prevent violence while trying to gain workers' rights.   Janusz Bugajski

Walker, Alice (1944-   ), is an African American
writer. In her novels, short stories, poetry, and essays,
Walker writes about black and white people living in
America and Africa in differing economic circumstances. She uses a variety of narrative forms and levels
of diction to create vivid, memorable, and larger-than-
life characters. Her novel *The Color Purple* (1982) won
the 1983 Pulitzer Prize for fiction.

Walker creates joyous communities of blacks in
which women, not men, are the powerful figures. Unlike
some other black writers, Walker seldom blames white
culture for the tragic events in the lives of her black
characters. She has been criticized for this view. But she
also has been praised for expressing a positive philosophy about being black and female.

Walker's novels include *The Third Life of Grange
Copeland* (1970), *Meridian* (1976), *The Temple of My Familiar* (1989), *Possessing the Secret of Joy* (1992), and *By
the Light of My Father's Smile* (1998). Her poetry is collected in *Once: Poems* (1968) and *Revolutionary Petunias
& Other Poems* (1973). Some of her short fiction has
been published in *In Love & Trouble: Stories of Black
Women* (1973). She became a major figure in feminism—
which she called *womanism*—through such writings as
In Search of Our Mothers' Gardens: Womanist Prose
(1983) and *Living by the Word* (1988). These collections of
essays, speeches, and letters focus on Walker's experiences as a black woman in America, and on racial and
class inequality.

Alice Malsenior Walker was born in Eatonton, Georgia. She was the youngest of eight children of black
sharecroppers.   Linda Wagner-Martin

Walker, David (1785-1830), was an African American
abolitionist who wrote a famous antislavery pamphlet.
This pamphlet, called *An Appeal to the Colored Citizens
of the World* (1829), urged American slaves to fight for
their freedom. Its publication marked the beginning of
the radical antislavery movement in the United States.
The *Appeal* was the strongest attack on slavery made up
to that time by a black writer.

Walker was born a free man in Wilmington, North
Carolina. His father had been a slave, and his mother a
free woman. Walker educated himself. In 1827, he settled in Boston and opened a second-hand clothing business. He became a leader in Boston's Colored Association, which opposed slavery. He wrote for *Freedom's
Journal,* the first black newspaper in the United States.
Walker died under mysterious circumstances, report-
edly of poisoning. Many abolitionists believed he was
murdered.   Otey M. Scruggs

Walker, James John (1881-1946), served as Democratic mayor of New York City from 1926 to 1932. Handsome and fun-loving, he came to symbolize the Roaring
Twenties. In 1932, Governor Franklin D. Roosevelt asked
Walker to explain corruption in the city's affairs. Investigation showed that Walker had been more careless than
crooked, but his reputation was injured, and he resigned. Walker, who was known as Jimmy, was born in
New York City.   James S. Olson

Walker, Leroy Pope (1817-1884), served as the first
Confederate secretary of war, from February to September 1861, during the American Civil War. Walker raised
200,000 troops and bought war equipment from abroad.
He resigned after the Confederate Congress and Con-

federate President Jefferson Davis became dissatisfied
with his management of the war department.

Walker was born in Huntsville, Alabama. He served in
the Alabama House of Representatives several times between 1843 and 1853. He was House speaker from 1847
to 1850. In 1875, Walker was president of a convention
that wrote a new Alabama constitution.   Michael Perman

Walker, Madam C. J. (1867-1919), is generally regarded as the first African American woman to become a
millionaire. She operated
a successful cosmetics
company, the Madam C. J.
Walker Manufacturing
Co., during the early
1900's.

Madam Walker was
born near Delta, Louisiana.
Her given name was Sarah
Breedlove. She was or-
phaned at the age of 7 and
raised by her older sister.
In 1881, Sarah married a
man named Moses
McWilliams. Her husband
died in 1887, leaving her

Madam C. J. Walker

with one daughter. In 1905, while working as a washer-
woman in St. Louis, Missouri, she developed and started
selling a line of hair care products. In 1905, Sarah moved
to Denver, Colorado, where she met and married
Charles J. Walker, a newspaperman.

Sarah Walker began demonstrating and selling her
hair care products door-to-door in African American
communities. She trained women to establish their own
businesses for selling her hair products and other cosmetics. These "Walker Agents" dressed in white blouses
and long black skirts. They became well-known throughout the black communities of the United States and the
Caribbean. In 1910, Walker moved to Indianapolis,
where she established a manufacturing plant.

Walker increased her wealth through real estate in-
vestments. She was a philanthropist who gave gener-
ously to causes that aided African Americans. She willed
two-thirds of her estate to charitable and educational institutions.   Alton Hornsby, Jr.

Walker, Mary Edwards (1832-1919), was the only
woman to receive the Medal of Honor, the highest military award given by the United States government. She
was a pioneer woman physician and a supporter of the
women's rights movement of the late 1800's.

Walker served as a surgeon with the Union Army during the American Civil War. In 1864, she was captured
and held for four months in a Confederate prison. She
was released in exchange for a Confederate officer. In
1865, she was awarded the Medal of Honor for her medical treatment of Union soldiers.

Walker helped lead a movement aimed at ending the
social restrictions on women's dress. She believed that
women should wear whatever they wished and became
known for wearing trousers. She also campaigned to
give women the vote. Walker wrote several books on
the role of women in society, including *Hit* (1871) and
Unmasked, or the Science of Immorality (1878).

Walker was born in Oswego, New York, and graduated from Syracuse Medical College. In 1917, a federal re-

view board revoked Walker's Medal of Honor, claiming she had never served in the Union Army. The Army restored the award in 1977. Miriam Schneir

Walker, Sarah Breedlove. See Walker, Madam C. J.

Walker, William (1824-1860), was an American *filibuster* (military adventurer). He tried to conquer parts of Mexico and, later, made himself ruler of Nicaragua. In 1853, he gathered a company of soldiers and tried to conquer Lower California and the state of Sonora, both in Mexico. He failed, and United States officials arrested him for violating neutrality laws. He was freed, and in 1855 led a successful revolution in Nicaragua. He ruled as president in 1856 and 1857 but then was forced to leave by Nicaraguans and other Central Americans.

Walker tried to regain power in Nicaragua in 1860 but was captured and executed in Honduras. He was born in Nashville, Tennessee. Helen Delpar

Walkie-talkie is a two-way radio that provides quick voice communication over short distances. Many people use walkie-talkies, including firefighters, construction workers, and military personnel. Unlike many other two-way communication devices, a walkie-talkie cannot *transmit* (send) and receive signals at the same time.

Walkie-talkies include handheld models and citizens band (CB) radios. Most handheld models can transmit and receive any of 14 channels. Their transmitter signal strength provides a maximum range of about 2 miles (3.2 kilometers). Inexpensive handheld models sold as toys operate on only one channel. Their maximum range is about 1,200 feet (370 meters). CB radios can transmit and receive any of 40 channels. They can transmit up to about 4 miles (6.4 kilometers). See **Citizens band radio.**

Some types of walkie-talkies require a license to operate. They can transmit greater distances than other types of walkie-talkies. Police and emergency personnel use walkie-talkies that transmit over the *private land mobile radio service.* Ordinary citizens can obtain a license to operate over the *general mobile radio service.*

Development of walkie talkies took place in the 1930's and 1940's. Backpack and handheld models were used extensively by U.S. military forces during World War II (1939-1945). Patrick D. Griffis

See also **Radio** (Two-way communication).

Walking, as a competitive sport, is a race between two or more people, or against time. Walking races are also called *race-walking.* Most races are held at distances ranging from 1 mile to 50,000 meters. In one event, the winner is decided by which competitor covers the greatest distance in two hours.

Competitive walkers developed a method of walking called the "heel-and-toe." A long stride lands the foot on the heel and swings the walker forward to put weight quickly on the toe. The toe acts as a springboard for the next stride. At least part of one foot must always be on the ground and the leg must be completely straight, or *locked,* momentarily during each step. A nonracer walks 1 mile (1.6 kilometers) in 15 to 20 minutes. A heel-and toe expert can do it in $6\frac{1}{2}$ minutes.

The walking contest was popular in England for centuries before it was introduced in the United States in the 1870's. At one time, U.S. contestants competed in six-day marathons on indoor tracks. Michael Takaha

Walkingstick is an insect that looks like a twig. The strange appearance of this insect hides it from its ene-

WORLD BOOK illustration by Oxford Illustrators Limited

The common walkingstick resembles a twig.

Edward S. Ross

A long, slender walkingstick, shown here hanging from a twig, is well hidden from its enemies. Walkingsticks eat leaves and sometimes damage trees.

mies. There are several species of these insects in the United States. The common walkingstick of the eastern United States has long legs and a slender body that is 2 to 3 inches (5 to 8 centimeters) long. Unlike most insects, a walkingstick has no wings. It may be brown or green. It eats leaves, and sometimes harms trees. The female usually drops her eggs on the ground. The young are neglected, and few survive. Several of the larger, tropical species of walkingsticks are popular in zoos and can be raised in captivity. See also **Leaf insect.**
  Betty Lane Faber

Scientific classification. Walkingsticks form the walkingstick family, Phasmidae. The scientific name for the common walkingstick is *Diapheromera femorata.*

Wall Street is a short, narrow street in New York City. With Broad and New streets, it forms a triangle where the New York Stock Exchange and many great commercial houses and banks are located (see **New York City** [map]). The district is the heart of United States banking and business and a worldwide symbol of finance. See also **New York City** (Settlement). Roger G. Ibbotson

Wallaby. See Kangaroo.

Wallace, Alfred Russel (1823-1913), was a British naturalist and explorer. He independently developed the same principle of *natural selection* as did British naturalist Charles R. Darwin. Natural selection is a process by which historical changes occur in species of plants and animals. The changes occur because of higher survival rates of individuals with hereditary traits that make them better suited to their environment. This process is the basis of evolution. Wallace also established the principles of *animal geography*—the study of the geographical distribution of animal species.

From 1848 to 1852, Wallace explored the Amazon Basin with British naturalist Henry Walter Bates. Wallace traveled to the East Indies in 1854 and remained there eight years collecting data. He found that the mammals of the Malay Archipelago are divided by an imaginary line into two groups of species. This line became known as *Wallace's Line.* Species that are west of the line are more closely related to mammals of Asia, and those that are east of the line are closer relatives of mammals of Australia.

Wallace was born in Usk, Wales, on Jan. 8, 1823. He wrote *The Malay Archipelago* (1869) and *Geographical Distribution of Animals* (1876).   G. J. Kenagy

See also **Evolution; Natural selection; Bates, Henry Walter.**

Wallace, George Corley (1919-1998), an American political leader, ran unsuccessfully for president in 1968, 1972, and 1976. He was elected governor of Alabama four times, in 1962, 1970, 1974, and 1982. Wallace gained national attention in the early 1960's for his strong support of states' rights and his opposition to school integration.

Wallace was born Aug. 25, 1919, in Clio, Alabama, and graduated from the University of Alabama Law School in 1942. After serving three years in the Army Air Forces, he began a career in politics. A Democrat, he served in the Alabama Legislature from 1947 to 1953. Wallace served as a state judge from 1953 to 1958. He ran for governor in 1958 and lost. Four years later, he won.

Wallace opposed federal involvement in what he considered state problems, especially school integration. At his inauguration as governor in 1963, he pledged: "Segregation now, segregation tomorrow, and segregation forever."

Wallace denounced federal court orders to end school segregation. His "stand in the doorway" at the University of Alabama in 1963, in which he opposed the enrollment of two black students, made him a hero to opponents of integration. Actually, many schools in Alabama became integrated during Wallace's first term as governor.

Wallace's wife, Lurleen, ran for governor in 1966 because at that time Alabama law prohibited Wallace from serving two terms in a row. But, most people understood that he would continue to act as governor. Mrs. Wallace won the gubernatorial election, but she died in office in 1968.

In 1968, Wallace was nominated as the presidential candidate of the American Independent Party (later called the American Party). He lost the election to Republican Richard M. Nixon and ran third behind Hubert H. Humphrey, the Democratic nominee. Wallace failed to achieve his goal of a deadlock in the Electoral College, which would have given him bargaining power to decide who became president. However, he received almost 10 million votes. He carried five states and received 46 electoral votes. Wallace's running mate was retired Air Force General Curtis E. LeMay. See **American Party.**

In 1971, Wallace married Cornelia Ellis Snively, a niece of former Alabama Governor James E. Folsom. The couple were divorced in 1978. In 1981, Wallace married Lisa Taylor, a country music singer. The marriage ended in divorce in 1987.

Wallace was the victim of an attempted assassination in May 1972, during his campaign for the 1972 Democratic presidential nomination. He was shot and seriously wounded in Laurel, Maryland, by Arthur H. Bremer. Bremer, a 21-year-old man from Milwaukee, was convicted of the shooting and was sentenced to 53 years in prison. The shooting left Wallace's legs paralyzed. He did not win the Democratic nomination. Wallace also sought, and failed to win, the Democratic nomination in 1976.

In a speech in 1978 and on later occasions, Wallace stated that his opposition to integration had been wrong, and he apologized for his actions. During the 1982 race for governor, he stressed his intention to help all needy Alabamians. He received strong support from black voters. Wallace retired from politics in 1987.

David S. Broder

Wallace, Henry Agard (1888-1965), served as vice president of the United States from 1941 to 1945 under President Franklin D. Roosevelt. He was also secretary of agriculture from 1933 to 1940 and secretary of commerce in 1945 and 1946.

In 1948, Wallace was the presidential nominee of the Progressive Party, which was a third party that opposed President Harry S. Truman's foreign policies. Wallace was also an expert on plant culture. During the 1920's, he developed a successful hybrid seed corn and founded Pioneer Hi-Bred, which became a major seed company.

Brown Bros.

Henry A. Wallace

Wallace was one of the most controversial figures of the New Deal and Fair Deal periods (see **New Deal**). He urged adoption of the Agricultural Adjustment Act, a New Deal plan designed to solve the farm problem by government planning. Wallace was not renominated for the vice presidency in 1944 because many Democrats did not like his social idealism and internationalism. In 1946, President Truman asked Wallace to resign as secretary of commerce because of his outspoken criticism of the "get-tough" policy of the United States toward the Soviet Union.

Wallace was an active administrator in the U.S. war effort during World War II. Roosevelt appointed him chairman of the Supply Priorities and Allocation Board in 1941 and chairman of the Board of Economic Warfare in 1942. Wallace also participated in decisions leading to the development of the atomic bomb.

Wallace was born on Oct. 7, 1888, in Adair County, Iowa. He graduated from Iowa State College (now Iowa State University). When his father, Henry Cantwell Wallace, became U.S. secretary of agriculture in 1921, young Wallace took his place as editor of the family magazine, *Wallace's Farmer.*   Alonzo L. Hamby

Wallace, Lew (1827-1905), was an American author, diplomat, lawyer, and military leader. He is best known for his historical novel *Ben-Hur* (1880), which tells of the rise of Christianity in the Roman Empire.

Lewis Wallace was born in Brookville, Indiana. He was an officer in the Mexican War (1846-1848). He later practiced law and was elected to the Indiana Senate in 1856. Wallace rose to the rank of major general in the Union Army during the American Civil War (1861-1865). In 1862, his troops captured Fort Donelson, Tennessee, weakening Confederate defenses. Wallace's bravery in delaying the advance of Confederate General Jubal A. Early's troops at Monocacy River helped prevent the capture of Washington, D.C., in 1864.

Wallace was a member of the court in 1865 that tried those involved in the assassination of President Abraham Lincoln. From 1878 to 1881, Wallace was governor of the territory of New Mexico. He was United States minister to Turkey from 1881 to 1885.   Ronald T. Curran

Wallace, Sir William (1272?-1305), was a Scottish patriot who led a revolt against King Edward I of England. The story of his life has stirred the national pride of Scots for more than 600 years.

In 1296, King Edward drove out the king of Scotland and stationed English soldiers in the country. Wallace, known for his strength and courage, became the leader of bands of Scottish patriots who carried on a bitter war against the invaders. The English raised an army and advanced against Wallace. He defeated them in the battle of Stirling Bridge in 1297. At that point, King Edward hurried home from France and led a great army against the rebels. His heavily armored soldiers defeated the rebels at Falkirk in 1298. Wallace escaped and carried on the fight in the mountains. In 1305, he was captured and executed for treason.   John Gillingham

Wallboard is a kind of board made of gypsum and paper or of fibers of wood, cane, or other materials. It is used to cover large areas such as walls and ceilings. Wallboard gives protection against fire and weather, and insulation against heat and cold. It absorbs sound and also serves as a decoration. Wallboard is made in sheets $\frac{1}{10}$ inch to 3 inches (2.5 to 76 millimeters) thick. It is made in sections up to 8 feet (2.4 meters) wide and 20 feet (6 meters) long. A wall that has its surface covered with wallboard is called a *drywall.* A type of wallboard called *plasterboard,* often sold under the trade name *Sheetrock,* has a core of gypsum sandwiched between layers of heavy paper.

Fiberboard is made from wood or cane fiber pressed into sheets. The fibers may be loosely compressed, leaving air spaces for good heat insulation and sound absorption. The surface is usually fibrous, but some is veneered with paper-thin sheets of decorative woods. Fiberboard is used for interior surfaces and also for outside wall sheathing.

Hardboard is a kind of wallboard also used in making furniture. It is made by heating specially treated masses of wood fibers with small amounts of adhesive and placing them under pressure to form a dense, hard board. *Tempered board* is made by further treatment of hardboard with chemicals and heat to improve durability.

George H. Kyanka

Wallenberg, Raoul (1912-   ?   ), a Swedish businessman and diplomat, helped save about 100,000 Hungarian Jews from being killed by the Nazis in 1944, during World War II. He often risked his life, and later won worldwide admiration for his heroic efforts.

Wallenberg was born in Kapptsta, near Stockholm. He was a member of a prominent family of bankers and industrialists. He visited Hungary on business in the early 1940's, during World War II. Wallenberg became increasingly disturbed by the campaign of Nazi leader Adolf Hitler to kill all the Jews of Europe. In 1944, Wallenberg came to the attention of the World Jewish Congress and the American War Refugee Board. He accepted their invitation to head a program in Hungary to save the Jews remaining there.

The Swedish government appointed Wallenberg to serve as a diplomat in Budapest, Hungary's capital. He issued Swedish passports to about 20,000 Jews, allowing them to claim the protection of the neutral Swedish government. He also sheltered Jews in houses he bought or rented with his own money or money from the groups that had sent him. Wallenberg, a Lutheran, was assisted by Roman Catholic and other non-Jewish leaders.

Adolf Eichmann, a Nazi official who directed the sending of Jews to concentration camps, ordered Wallenberg to stop interfering with German plans for the Jews. Wallenberg refused. Eichmann tried to have Wallenberg assassinated, but the attempt failed. In the final days before the liberation of Budapest by Soviet soldiers, Wallenberg persuaded the Nazis to cancel a plan to kill 70,000 Jews who were forced to live in a *ghetto* (segregated area) of the city.

In January 1945, Soviet forces took Wallenberg into custody. They apparently believed he was an American spy. In 1957, the Soviet government reported that Wallenberg had died of a heart attack in prison in 1947. Later inquiries failed to clarify the circumstances of his death. In 1981, the United States Congress made Wallenberg an honorary U.S. citizen.   Abraham Cooper

Wallenstein, *WAHL uhn STYN* or *VAHL uhn SHTYN,* **Albrecht Wenzel Eusebius von,** *AHL brehkt VEHN tsuhl oy ZAY bee US fuhn* (1583-1634), a Bohemian general, played an important role in the Thirty Years' War (1618-1648). He was the inspiration for *Wallenstein* (1798-1799), a tragedy by the German playwright Friedrich Schiller.

Wallenstein was born in Bohemia. His father was a Protestant nobleman. Wallenstein became a Roman Catholic and fought for Holy Roman Emperor Rudolf II, a Catholic, against the Turks.

Bohemian Protestants began the Thirty Years' War by rebelling against the Catholic Habsburg family, which ruled Bohemia as part of the Holy Roman Empire. Wallenstein remained loyal to the Holy Roman Empire and raised a small army for Emperor Ferdinand II. Ferdinand rewarded him with the title Duke of Friedland. Wallenstein, who had been made a general, recruited troops and led them in battles in Germany and Bohemia.

Wallenstein believed he was destined to play a great political role. His goal was a huge European empire that would dominate the Turks and western Europe. The Catholic princes resented his great ambition and power, and the emperor was alarmed by his intrigues with Swedish and German Protestant leaders. The emperor ordered his arrest, or death, and officers loyal to the emperor murdered him.   Charles W. Ingrao

See also **Thirty Years' War.**

Waller, Fats (1904-1943), was an American jazz pianist, songwriter, and entertainer. He became one of the most accomplished pianists in the history of jazz, though in his day he was known primarily as an entertainer.

Many of Waller's songs have lively, witty lyrics. His first songs were published in 1923. Later, he started working with Andy Razaf, an American lyricist who wrote the words for some of Waller's most popular songs. Their compositions include "Ain't Misbehavin' " (1929), "Blue Turning Grey Over You" (1930), "Honeysuckle Rose" (1929), and "Jitterbug Waltz" (1942).

Waller made several hundred recordings, many of them with a small band that he led from 1934 until his death. He sang on many of these records. Waller weighed almost 300 pounds (140 kilograms). Thomas Wright Waller was born in New York City.   Paul F. Wells

See also **Jazz** (The 1920's).

Wallflower is a fragrant plant that bears clusters of golden or maroon flowers. It blooms in spring and is a *perennial,* which means it lives for two years or more. It is called *wallflower* because its stems often grow on or over walls or cliffs, particularly limestone cliffs. Wallflowers originated in southern Europe but now grow

© Kent and Donna Dannen, Photo Researchers
Wallflowers have clusters of colorful blossoms.

well in England and many parts of the United States. They are also called *gillyflowers.*   Theodore R. Dudley

Scientific classification. The wallflower is in the mustard family, Brassicaceae or Cruciferae. Its scientific name is *Cheiranthus cheiri.*

Walloons are a group of people who live in southern Belgium. The region they inhabit is called Wallonia. It consists of the provinces of Hainaut, Liège, Luxembourg, Namur, and the southern half of Brabant (see **Belgium** [political map]). The Walloons make up about 30 percent of the Belgian population.

Walloons trace their original heritage to the Belgae, a Celtic people, who were conquered by the Romans in the 50's B.C. In the A.D. 200's to 400's, a Germanic tribe called the Franks invaded the region. In Wallonia, the Romanized inhabitants largely absorbed the Franks. The area to the north, now called Flanders, was more thinly populated, and many people fled. The Franks became dominant. Today, the people of Flanders are called Flemings.

During the 1700's, Wallonia became one of Europe's most wealthy industrial regions. The Walloon cities of Liège and Charleroi became centers for coal mining and

steelmaking. During the 1800's, the Belgians built extensive networks of canals and railroads in Wallonia. They also developed an advanced banking system.

Language and cultural differences have created friction between the Walloons and the Flemings. The Walloons speak French. The Flemings speak Dutch.

When Belgium became independent in 1830, the Walloons largely controlled the government. They made French the only official language of the country. The Flemings then began a movement to gain recognition of their own language and culture. Dutch became an official language of Belgium during the late 1800's.

Conflicts between the Walloons and the Flemings continued during the 1900's. In 1980, the Belgian government granted limited self-rule to Flanders and Wallonia.

Janet L. Polasky

See also **Belgium** (People); **Flemings.**

Wallpaper is decorative paper used to cover inside walls. Many wall coverings made of other materials—for example, burlap, linen, manufactured fibers, plastics, and thin sheets of wood—are also considered wallpaper. A special paste, brushed onto the undecorated side of wallpaper, makes it stick to a wall. Manufacturers sell most wallpaper in rolls of sheets that measure about 30 feet (9.1 meters) long and $2\frac{1}{4}$ feet (69 centimeters) wide.

Most people use wallpaper to make a room more attractive. Wallpaper also provides practical advantages. For example, it hides cracks, stains, and other flaws on walls. Paper made of plaster reinforced with plant fibers can be used to cover brick, concrete blocks, or rough plaster. Wallpaper made of a plastic material called *vinyl* can be scrubbed with a mild detergent and water. Many apartment dwellers and people who frequently redecorate use *strippable wallpaper,* which can be peeled off easily without damaging the wall.

Scholars believe the first wallpaper was made in England, France, or the Netherlands during the 1500's. Artists designed patterned wallpaper as a cheaper substitute for the *tapestries* (woven wall hangings) that had decorated European palaces for centuries. Craftworkers painted designs on the paper by hand or printed them from carved blocks of wood. The Chinese began to make wallpaper in the early 1600's. They painted birds, flowers, and landscapes on rectangular sheets of rice paper. In the 1700's, the French decorated wallpaper with Chinese objects and patterns. This popular style became known as *chinoiserie.*

Wallpaper was first produced in the United States in Philadelphia in 1739. In 1947, vinyl-covered wallpaper was introduced. Prepasted paper, which sticks to a wall when the paper is moistened with water, was developed in the 1950's.   Howard A. Rickspoone

See also **Interior design.**

Walnut is the name of a type of tree valued for its nuts and wood. Several species of walnut trees grow in the United States. Two of these are native to the East—the *black walnut* and the *butternut,* also called the *white walnut.* Another species, the *English walnut* or *Persian walnut,* was brought to the United States from southern Europe. It is grown commercially in California and Oregon. Black and English walnut trees provide high-quality wood for furniture.

English walnut trees produce walnuts that have the greatest commercial value. They are large, spreading

The English walnut tree may grow up to 100 feet (30 meters) tall. The nuts of the English walnut tree have greater commercial value than those of any other variety.

Grant Heilman

trees that grow up to 100 feet (30 meters) tall. They have gray bark, large leaflets, and soft wood. They have been grown commercially in Europe since ancient times.

The English walnut tree bears clusters of small flowers called *catkins*. The flowers may be cross-pollinated or self-pollinated. After flowering, the tree produces walnuts. The nuts have thin shells and taste mild and sweet. They contain mostly fats and some proteins.

The nuts of the English walnut tree, *above,* have thin shells and a mild flavor.

Debbie Dean

Growers typically plant English walnut trees at least 60 feet (18 meters) apart. But several varieties may be planted closer together. English walnut trees thrive in deep, well-drained soil. After the nuts ripen, they are shaken from the trees, hulled, and dried. The nuts are taken to packing houses and are sorted and sized. They may be packaged either in the shell or shelled. The poorer grades of nuts are used to make walnut oil.

Growers once left walnut shells that fell to the ground as waste. Today, the shells are collected and used in glues and plastics. They are also used to make solutions for cleaning and polishing metal surfaces.

China leads the world in the production of walnuts. Other major walnut-growing countries include the United States, Iran, and Turkey. The U.S. walnut industry is centered in the area around Stockton, California. In addition, several hardy varieties of English walnut trees are grown in the Midwest and the East. But growers usually do not plant large orchards of these varieties. English walnut trees do not grow well in the South.

Black walnut trees grow in forests from Massachusetts to Florida and west to Texas. They are hardy trees grown mainly for their lumber. The nuts also are harvested and sold. They have a distinctive, rich flavor, but their shell is hard and thick. They are usually shelled before they are sold. Growers have also developed a few thin-shelled varieties of these nuts. Black walnut wood is

dark purplish-brown, with a fine grain and luster. It is valuable for interior finishing, furniture, and gunstocks. This wood is becoming rare.   Richard A. Jaynes

Scientific classification. Walnuts belong to the walnut family, Juglandaceae. The English walnut is *Juglans regia.* The black walnut is *J. nigra,* and the butternut is *J. cinerea.*

See also **Butternut; Tree** (Familiar broadleaf and needleleaf trees [picture]).

Walnut Canyon National Monument is in central Arizona. It contains 800-year-old cliff-dwelling ruins in shallow caves. It was established in 1915. For its area, see **National Park System** (table: National monuments).

Walpole, Horace (1717-1797), was an English letter writer and author. Even at a time when personal letters were considered a minor art form, Walpole's huge correspondence is remarkable. His witty letters provide an entertaining documentary of life in English high society. They report social and political gossip and express Walpole's opinions on literature and the arts.

As a scholar fascinated by medieval life, Walpole greatly influenced the Gothic revival of the late 1700's. He transformed Strawberry Hill, his house in Twickenham, into a miniature Gothic castle. He built a printing press nearby, and published many of his own writings. His most influential literary work is *The Castle of Otranto* (1764). This tale of terror and the supernatural was the first of what became known as Gothic novels.

Walpole was born in London. He was the youngest son of Sir Robert Walpole, the first prime minister of England. Horace Walpole served in Parliament from 1741 to 1768. In 1791, he succeeded to the family title as the fourth Earl of Orford.   Martin C. Battestin

Walpole, Hugh Seymour (1884-1941), was one of the most popular British novelists in the early 1900's. His finest novels are probably the *Herries Chronicles* (1930-1933), a series of four historical novels set in England in the 1700's. The series includes *Rogue Herries, Judith Paris, The Fortress,* and *Vanessa.* Walpole wrote over 30 other novels on a variety of subjects. In *The Dark Forest* (1916) and *The Secret City* (1919), he described his World War I experiences with the Red Cross in Russia. *The Cathedral* (1922) is based on his experiences as a clergyman's son. *Portrait of a Man with Red Hair* (1925) is a horror story about a brutal murderer.

Walpole was born in Auckland, New Zealand, and was sent to school in England at the age of 5. King George VI knighted him in 1937, and he became known as Sir Hugh Walpole.   Sharon Bassett

Walpole, Sir Robert (1676-1745), the first Earl of Orford, was the most influential politician in the United Kingdom during the first half of the 1700's. He became the country's first prime minister, though the title was not official then. Walpole became famous for his ability to transact government business. He also supported the United Kingdom's Kings George I and George II of the German House of Hanover against the Stuart family's claims to the British throne (see **Stuart, House of**).

Walpole entered Parliament in 1701 and by 1708 was secretary at war. He showed ability, but he lost his offices when the Tories replaced the Whigs in 1710-1711. He then became the leader of the opposition in the House of Commons. The new government convicted Walpole of graft and sent him to prison in 1712. But he returned to Parliament in 1713.

After George I became king in 1714, Walpole's political stature increased. He served as first lord of the treasury from 1715 to 1717. For the next few years, he attacked the government and built up his influence in the House of Commons. In 1721, Walpole again became first lord of the treasury and chancellor of the exchequer. For the next 21 years, he was the most powerful person in Britain. His primary goal was to end the political instability that had plagued Britain in the late 1600's and early 1700's by helping the Whigs dominate the government. Walpole worked to control the House of Commons using his debating skill, his power and influence, and his constant attendance in the House.

Eventually, grievances against Walpole's rule led to growing opposition to him among Tories and some Whigs. For example, Walpole worked to prevent war with Spain at a time when demand for such a war was growing in Britain. He knew that war would threaten his power and encourage supporters of the Stuarts. But war broke out with Spain in 1739 and with France in 1741, and Walpole's hold on the House of Commons declined. His loss of a majority in the House and his failing health caused him to resign in 1742. But Walpole was almost immediately made Earl of Orford, and he influenced policies in the House of Lords until his death.

Walpole was born on Aug. 26, 1676, in Houghton, in the county of Norfolk, and was educated at Eton College and Cambridge University. He died on March 18, 1745. His youngest son was the author Horace Walpole.

J. C. D. Clark

See also **United Kingdom** (History).

Walpurgis Night, *vahl PUR gihs,* is the eve of May Day, when German people celebrate the feast of Saint Walpurgis. According to legend, witches gather on this night and celebrate their Sabbath on mist-covered Brocken, the highest peak in the Harz Mountains.

Walrus is a sea animal that lives in parts of the Arctic, North Atlantic, and North Pacific oceans. It has two ivory tusks, and its four feet are flattened into flippers. The flippers make the walrus a good swimmer.

During the winter and spring, walruses drift along on large floating fields of ice. In summer, some may rest on shore. A walrus spends much time in the water seeking clams, its favorite food. It uses its tongue to form a vacuum to suck clams into its mouth and to suck the flesh from the shell. A walrus has bristles on its upper lip that are sensitive to touch and probably help it find food.

Scientists classify the walrus as a kind of large seal. An adult male grows about 12 feet (3.7 meters) long and weighs up to 3,000 pounds (1,400 kilograms). Adult females measure about 8 feet (2.4 meters) in length and weigh up to 2,750 pounds (1,250 kilograms).

The walrus is the only seal with tusks. The tusks—its upper canine teeth—point downward and may grow as long as 39 inches (99 centimeters). A walrus defends itself from polar bears with its tusks. It also uses them as hooks when climbing onto ice. Walruses do not normally attack people. However, an angry, wounded walrus can injure a hunter or damage a boat with its tusks.

Walruses spend most of their time in herds. During the mating season, male walruses make unusual bell-like sounds underwater. These "songs" attract females and drive away other males. Walruses are mammals. A female walrus usually has one calf every other year and

© Leonard Lee Rue III, Tom Stack & Assoc.

The walrus has long tusks that it uses mainly for defense. Its thick hide helps it survive in its cold environment.

cares for her young for about two years. Twins are rare. Baby walruses are grayish-brown, and adults are rusty-brown. Some walruses live as long as 40 years.

Some Inuit (sometimes called Eskimos) hunt walruses, mainly for meat. Traditionally, the Inuit used the walrus hides to make shelters or boats and burned the oil from walrus blubber for heat and light.　　John K. B. Ford

Scientific classification. The walrus is in the order Pinnipedia. It forms the walrus family, Odobenidae. Its scientific name is *Odobenus rosmarus.*

See also **Seal.**

Walt Disney Company is a leading American entertainment company. It operates theme parks and resorts, produces and distributes motion pictures, and runs a broadcast television network and several cable television channels. It also sells publications, videocassettes, videodiscs, and merchandise based on the Walt Disney name and characters (see **Disney, Walt**).

The company owns and operates Disneyland Resort in Anaheim, California, which opened as Disneyland in 1955, and Walt Disney World Resort near Orlando, Florida. Walt Disney World opened in 1971 with the Magic Kingdom, a theme park similar to Disneyland. Today, in addition to the Magic Kingdom, this resort includes EPCOT (Experimental Prototype Community of Tomorrow) Center, which features futuristic technology and cultural exhibits; Disney-MGM Studios Theme Park, a movie studio with exhibits and shows; and Animal Kingdom, which displays hundreds of animals in re-creations of a jungle, savanna, and other habitats. Today, Disneyland Resort includes two theme parks—the original Disneyland Park and Disney's California Adventure, which celebrates the state's varied regions.

The Walt Disney Company financed Celebration, Florida, a planned community that opened in 1995. The company's international operations include Tokyo Disney Resort, which opened in 1983, and Disneyland Resort Paris, which opened as Disneyland Paris Theme Park in 1992. The Walt Disney Company also owns a professional sports team, the Anaheim Mighty Ducks of the National Hockey League.

The Walt Disney Company has four motion-picture units. Walt Disney Pictures creates family entertainment films. Touchstone Pictures and Hollywood Pictures produce films that appeal to adult audiences. Miramax Films makes motion pictures by independent filmmakers. The company's Buena Vista Music Group produces recorded music under several labels. The Walt Disney Company also owns ABC, Inc., which operates the ABC television network, and the Disney ABC Cable Networks Group, which operates the cable TV channels ABC Family, the Disney Channel, SOAPnet, and Toon Disney.

Walt Disney founded the company as Walt Disney Productions in 1938. It changed its name in 1986 to the Walt Disney Company. Company headquarters are in Burbank, California.

Critically reviewed by the Walt Disney Company

See also **California** (Visitor's guide); **Florida** (Visitor's guide); **Graves, Michael** (picture); **Orlando.**

Walter, *VAHL tuhr,* **Bruno,** *BROO noh* (1876-1962), was a leading orchestra and symphony conductor of the 1900's. He was noted for the warmth and insight of his musical interpretations, especially in works by Wolfgang Mozart, Ludwig van Beethoven, and Franz Schubert. He was also noted for his support of the music of his friend Gustav Mahler. Walter was an accomplished pianist and often accompanied singers in recitals.

Walter was born on Sept. 15, 1876, in Berlin, where he received his musical education. His real name was Bruno Walter Schlesinger. At the age of 18, he became an assistant to Mahler, director of the Hamburg Opera. Their association continued until Mahler died in 1911.

While still a young man, Walter became one of the most celebrated conductors in central Europe. He moved to the United States in 1939. Walter often conducted the New York Philharmonic Orchestra from 1941 to 1957 and the Metropolitan Opera from 1941 to 1959. He wrote an autobiography, *Themes and Variations* (1946). He died on Feb. 17, 1962.   Martin Bernheimer

Walter, Thomas Ustick, *YOO stihk* (1804-1887), an American architect, became noted for his buildings in the Greek Revival style. He is known chiefly as the architect of the United States Capitol from 1851 to 1865. He added the Senate and House wings, and the large cast-iron dome, painted to resemble stone. Walter was born on Sept. 4, 1804, in Philadelphia. With architect Richard Upjohn, he founded the American Institute of Architects in 1857. He died on Oct. 30, 1887.   Leland M. Roth

Walter Reed Army Medical Center, in Washington, D.C., provides care for active-duty and retired military personnel and their families. It also conducts scientific research and trains doctors in advanced methods. It covers 113 acres (46 hectares) in Washington and also includes 118 acres (48 hectares) in Forest Glen and 22 acres (9 hectares) in Glenhaven, both in Maryland. Major activities of the center are the treatment facility, the Walter Reed Army Institute of Research, and the Armed Forces Institute of Pathology. The center was named for Major Walter Reed, an Army surgeon who helped conquer typhoid fever and yellow fever (see **Reed, Walter**).

Critically reviewed by the Walter Reed Army Medical Center

Walther von der Vogelweide, *VAHL tuhr fawn duhr FOH guhl vv duh* (1170?-1230?), was perhaps the greatest of the medieval *minnesingers* (love poets). Walther was born in Austria, and he lived during the period when the elegance and grace of aristocratic culture flourished. He was a poet in the court of Vienna but apparently had to leave when his patron died. He then moved from court to court until, late in life, he received a grant of land from German Emperor Frederick II.

Walther's love poetry differed from the conventions of courtly *minnesang,* which celebrated a hopeless love for some high-born lady. Walther praised the love for a village girl. He also raised poems of political commentary to a high art. His large and varied poetic production shows originality. His technique ranges from simple to highly complex forms.   James F. Poag

Walton, Ernest Thomas Sinton (1903-1995), an Irish physicist, shared the 1951 Nobel Prize in physics with Sir John Cockcroft. They discovered jointly the transmutations of atomic nuclei by artificially accelerated particles in 1932. They constructed the first of the controlled particle accelerators, producing 500,000 volts. Their experiments confirmed Albert Einstein's theory that mass and energy are equivalent.

Walton was born on Oct. 6, 1903, in Dungarvan. He died on June 25, 1995.   Robert H. March

See also **Cockcroft, Sir John Douglas.**

Walton, George (1741-1804), a Georgia signer of the Declaration of Independence, was governor and chief justice of Georgia several times. In 1775, he became secretary of Georgia's provincial congress and president of the colony's council of safety. Walton served in the Continental Congress from 1776 to 1781. He fought in the defense of Savannah in 1778 and was captured by the British. He was a United States senator in 1795 and 1796. Walton was born near Farmville, Virginia. He died on Feb. 2, 1804.   Gary D. Hermalyn

Walton, Izaak (1593-1683), was an English author best known for his book on fishing, *The Compleat Angler.* The work is a classic example of a *pastoral* (about rural life) book in English literature. *The Compleat Angler* was first published in 1653 and went through four revisions during the author's lifetime. The book is written as a dialogue, primarily between Piscator, a fisherman, and Venator, a hunter. *The Compleat Angler* combines practical information about fish and fishing with songs, poems, and descriptions of country life and the English countryside. Walton also gained fame for his biographies, notably of the poets John Donne (1640, revised edition 1658) and George Herbert (1670); the clergymen Richard Hooker (1665) and Robert Sanderson (1678); and the diplomat and author Sir Henry Wotton (1651).

Walton was born on Aug. 9, 1593, in Stafford and became a wealthy London hardware merchant. He also became a friend of a number of famous men, including Donne and playwright Ben Jonson. Walton died on Dec. 18, 1683.   Steven N. Zwicker

See also **Izaak Walton League of America.**

Walton, Sam (1918-1992), an American businessman, was the founder of Wal-Mart Stores. Walton revolutionized U.S. retailing. For example, he built relatively large stores that concentrated on selling a wide variety of merchandise at low prices; yet he located his stores in small cities and rural areas, rather than in large cities. He also created a distribution system that can usually resupply his stores within one day rather than two weeks—the typical period at other retailers.

Samuel Moore Walton was born on March 29, 1918, in Kingfisher, Oklahoma. He worked his way through the University of Missouri by delivering newspapers and waiting on tables. After graduating from the university in 1940, he worked as a management trainee in Des Moines, Iowa, with the J. C. Penney Company.

In 1945, with the help of a loan from his father-in-law,

Walton acquired his first store, a Ben Franklin franchise in Newport, Arkansas. In 1962, with his brother, James Lawrence Walton, he opened the first Wal-Mart Discount City store, in Rogers, Arkansas. Today, Wal-Mart ranks as the nation's largest retailer. The company has over 2,500 Wal-Mart stores throughout the United States and more than 600 in other countries. It also operates about 500 Sam's Club stores in the United States. Walton died on April 5, 1992.   John C. Schmeltzer

See also **Wal-Mart Stores, Inc.**

Walton, Sir William (1902-1983), was an English composer whose works are noted for their strong sense of melody and form. Walton was a slow and deliberate composer who produced a relatively small body of works. Most of his compositions are instrumental and many follow the symphonic form.

Walton's first major composition was *Façade* (1922), a chamber work set to poems by his friend Edith Sitwell. Walton's other important works include two symphonies and concertos for viola, violin, and cello. He wrote *Sinfonia Concertante* (1927, revised 1943) for piano and orchestra. Among Walton's other orchestral compositions are *Troilus and Cressida* (1954), *Partita* (1958), *Variations on a Theme by Hindemith* (1963), *The Bear* (1967), and *Improvisations on an Impromptu of Benjamin Britten* (1970). Walton composed marches, chamber music, and music for radio, television, and films. *Belshazzar's Feast* (1931), an oratorio, is his most famous vocal composition. In addition, Walton wrote two operas and the popular "Crown Imperial" (1937), a coronation march.

William Turner Walton was born on March 29, 1902, in Oldham. He received his first musical training from his father, a music teacher. Walton later studied at Oxford University. He was knighted in 1951. He died on March 8, 1983.   Stewart L. Ross

Waltz is a ballroom dance in $\frac{3}{4}$ time characterized by its swift gliding turns. The dance was enormously popular throughout the 1800's. The term *waltz* also refers to the music that accompanies this dance. The waltz has been danced in two distinct styles, the *three-step* and the *two-step*. In Europe, especially in Vienna, the dancers waltzed much faster than they waltzed in North America.

The waltz developed rapidly in the last years of the 1700's. It emerged from a group of south German and Austrian dances involving the turning motion of the dancers in a close embrace position. The popularity of waltzes among young people led some authorities to outlaw the dance because it was thought to be immoral for couples to dance so closely.

Many composers of the 1800's and 1900's wrote waltzes for listening rather than for dancing. Leading composers of *concert waltzes* included members of the Strauss family (see **Strauss, Johann, Jr.**). Waltz music and dancing also appear in many operas, operettas, and ballets.   Patricia W. Rader

See also **Ballroom dancing; Dance** (picture: The romantic waltz).

Walvis Bay is a part of Namibia that was formerly a district of South Africa. It lies in west-central Namibia along the Atlantic Ocean. For location, see **Namibia** [map]). Walvis Bay covers 434 square miles (1,124 square kilometers). Its largest city, also called Walvis Bay, is Namibia's chief port.

Portuguese sailors were the first white people to see the Walvis Bay area. They landed there in 1487, but black Africans had settled in the area long before. Walvis Bay came under British rule in 1878 as part of the Cape Colony. In 1910, the Cape Colony became one of the four colonies that formed South Africa. From 1922 through 1977, South Africa administered Walvis Bay as part of Namibia, then called South West Africa. In 1978, South Africa began to govern Walvis Bay directly.

South Africa kept Walvis Bay after Namibia became independent in 1990. But Namibian leaders sought to make the district part of their country. In 1994, South Africa turned the district over to Namibia.   Robert I. Rotberg

Wampum is an Algonquian Indian word for purple or white beads made from shells. The beads were made mainly by North American Indians living near the Atlantic coast. The Indians decorated their clothing and other possessions with wampum. They also used it to keep records.

The Indians carved white beads from the shells of sea snails called *whelks* and purple beads from the shells of hard-shell clams. Manufacturing the beads required patience and skill because the shells were brittle and the beads were tiny. The beads were about $\frac{1}{8}$ inch (3 millimeters) in diameter and about $\frac{1}{4}$ inch (6 millimeters) long. The Indians drilled a fine hole in each bead. They then used the holes to string the beads or to sew them onto fabrics or animal skins.

The Indians often wove thousands of beads into wampum belts. They exchanged the belts as pledges to keep treaties and to assure friendships. The Indians recorded events on their belts by arranging beads in designs. In many cases, the colors of the beads had meanings. White often represented health, peace, and riches. Purple often meant grief or sympathy.

The Algonquian Indians made the first wampum about 1600. European fur traders exchanged wampum from coastal tribes for the furs of inland Indians. Dutch and English colonists, who had few metal coins, adopted wampum as money. However, wampum began to lose its value during the mid-1600's, when new metal coins began to appear. During the 1700's, colonists made wampum themselves for use in the fur trade with Great Plains and Northwest Coast Indians.   Lynn Ceci

See also **Indian, American** (picture); **Money** (picture).

Wandering Jew is a legendary figure who is condemned to wander throughout the world until the *Second Coming* of Jesus Christ. The most popular version of the legend of the Wandering Jew developed during the early 1600's in Germany. It tells of a Jewish shoemaker named Ahasuerus who cursed Jesus while Jesus was carrying His cross to the Crucifixion. As punishment, Jesus ordered Ahasuerus to wander throughout the world until Jesus would return to the earth. Ahasuerus thus became the Wandering Jew and the living witness of Jesus's Crucifixion.

According to legend, the Wandering Jew appears at various times and places and describes events that have happened since the time of Jesus. Since the 1600's, many writers have used the legend as the framework for political and social commentary, especially because the character had observed so much of world history. The legend of the Wandering Jew has also been used to promote prejudice against Jews.   Richard R. Ring

Townsend P. Dickinson, Photo Researchers

A wandering-jew's attractive leaves and graceful flowers make it a favorite ornamental plant.

Wandering-jew is the common name of three species of plants in the spiderwort family. Two species have long, green leaves and purple flowers and are common greenhouse or garden plants. The other species is grown as a house plant for the beautiful, silvery sheen of its leaves. In strong sunlight, the leaves show white or cream stripes above and reddish-purple beneath.

Wandering-jew plants grow in the southern United States, Central America, and South America. The plant's name refers to the legend of the Jew who was doomed to wander the earth forever because he mocked Jesus as He carried the cross. Wandering-jew plants seem to wander all over and live indefinitely.   Robert A. Kennedy

Scientific classification. Wandering-jew plants belong to the spiderwort family, Commelinaceae. The scientific names for the garden species are *Tradescantia albiflora* and *T. fluminensis*. The other species is *Zebrina pendula*.

Wang Wei (699-759) was a Chinese painter and poet known especially for his skill as a landscape artist. He painted beautiful *monochromatic* landscapes, which use shades, tones, and tints of a single color. Records tell of Wang Wei's many paintings on the walls of temples and palaces. He also painted on silk and probably on paper. None of his wallpaintings has survived, and only a few

other existing paintings are said to be his. However, much of Wang Wei's poetry has been saved.

Wang Wei lived during the Tang dynasty (618-907), generally regarded as the golden age of Chinese civilization. He lived in the capital, Chang-an (now Xi'an), where he earned a high government office. Wang Wei also produced beautiful Chinese *calligraphy* (handwriting) and was a skilled musician. He has come to be recognized as a genius who brought painting, poetry, and calligraphy together into a unified art.   Robert A. Rorex

Wankel engine. See Rotary engine.

Wapiti. See Elk.

War is the organized use of violence between independent political groups. Since the dawn of civilization, there have been many kinds of wars. *International wars* involve the use of force between countries. *Civil wars* are violent conflicts between different political communities within the same country. Violence between a government and a substantial opposition group within the country is called a *violent rebellion* or *revolutionary war*. *Cold wars* are conducted through diplomatic, economic, and psychological means but not with direct force.

Throughout history, wars have caused great suffering and hardship. Many international organizations work to prevent wars from occurring and to resolve them quickly once they start.

Why wars occur

Most wars result from a combination of causes. Three of the most common causes are conflicts over resources, clashing ideologies, and struggles over power.

Conflicts over resources are the most basic and enduring causes of war. Resources include land, minerals, energy sources, and important geographical features. The field of *geopolitics* examines the importance of geography and territory to a country's identity, wealth, and behavior. Examples of conflicts over resources are numerous. In the Crimean War (1853-1856), the United Kingdom, France, and the Ottoman Empire fought against Russia for control of the area around the Black Sea. The Persian Gulf War of 1991 resulted in large part from Iraq's attempt to seize Kuwait's oil reserves.

Clashing ideologies can also lead to war. *Ideologies* are sets of ideas that define different communities. Reli-

Detail of *Clearing After Snowfall Along the River* (1500's), an ink painting on paper; Honolulu Academy of Arts, Gift of Robert Lehman, 1960

A landscape in the style of Wang Wei shows this early Chinese artist's mastery of *monochromatic* painting. This technique uses shades, tones, and tints of a single color.

gious teachings are often central to a society's ideology. Sometimes, these teachings are hostile toward those of neighboring communities. In these cases, religious wars can erupt. From 1096 to the late 1200's, for example, Christians from Europe waged war on Muslim rulers in Palestine as part of the series of military expeditions known as the Crusades. Ideological conflicts can also involve political concepts. An example of such a conflict was the Cold War between Communist and non-Communist nations in the latter half of the 1900's.

Struggles over power. Power involves the ability to control other people or to control the outcome of a situation. War often results when one country seeks to expand its power at the expense of others. In some cases, a decline in the strength of a powerful nation may prompt a *war of opportunity*, in which rival nations try to take advantage of the nation's weakened state. In other cases, one or more nations may act together to stop the increasing power of a rival country. The ancient Greek historian Thucydides described the Peloponnesian War (431-404 B.C.) in terms of power. As the power of Athens grew, he said, other cities joined together to stop it. Although power may be valued for its own sake, both resources and ideologies are closely connected to power.

Waging war

Wars are complex events that involve the preparation of large numbers of soldiers and the involvement of much equipment and weaponry. Large wars place extreme stress on a society's population and economy. Several factors influence a nation's ability to wage war.

Population plays an important role in war operations. A country must have a large supply of young people to fight in its military. When people leave to fight in a war, others must step in to replace them in the national economy. People are injured and killed in wars, and a country may rapidly reduce its best human resources.

Industrial and financial resources are also important to a war effort. Supplying and equipping a modern army requires a great deal of money. For centuries, rulers borrowed money to pay for their wars. Today's governments have broad powers to collect taxes and so are better able to pay for wars out of tax revenue.

Information and intelligence. Learning an enemy's secrets can be crucial to success. *Espionage* is the act of acquiring information through spying. Modern technology allows for much better communication between commanders and troops, but it also creates opportunities for espionage. During World War II (1939-1945), for example, U.S. intelligence experts broke the Japanese military code, which enabled them to surprise and destroy most of the Japanese fleet in the Battle of Midway.

Today, computers and other advanced technological instruments influence all aspects of warfare, from strategic planning to weapon design. Satellites provide images of territories and troops around the world.

Organization and control are crucial in conducting an efficient war effort. Military organizations are typically *hierarchical*—that is, they consist of levels of higher and lower ranks. In modern democracies, the top military leaders take direction from civilian political leaders, who provide the strategic goals of the war effort. In other systems of government, the military may cooperate less with political leadership. In some cases, the military

itself is a nation's political leadership. Generally, these militaries are less restrained in their use of force.

Ethical and legal aspects of war

Beginning in the Middle Ages, scholars and statesmen began to think seriously about the moral and legal aspects of waging war. Roman Catholic theologians developed a concept of *just war* to describe circumstances where war could be fought without breaking Christian rules against killing. Modern legal considerations originated with the Peace of Westphalia, at the end of the Thirty Years' War (1618-1648). This treaty between European nations established individual countries' rights to territory and self-government.

The basic rules of warfare. There are certain behavioral guidelines that combatants should obey during times of war. Violations of these rules are called *war crimes.* The rules of warfare apply in three main areas.

First, nonfighting civilians should be treated differently from military and political leaders and combat troops. Militaries should try to minimize the amount of harm done to civilians. The second area involves the treatment of prisoners of war. In the modern era, prisoners should receive humane treatment. When hostilities end, prisoners should be returned home. The third area addresses the use of weapons. Several international treaties prohibit the use of specific kinds of weapons during war. These mainly include chemical and biological weapons. The use of nuclear weapons is highly controversial, but some countries refuse to abandon them.

Changes in the rules of war have occurred mostly in the 1900's. War crimes issues were central to the Hague Conventions of 1899 and 1907 and the Geneva Conventions of 1864, 1906, 1929, 1949, and 1977.

In World War II, Nazi Germany exterminated millions of European Jews and others whom Adolf Hitler regarded as racially inferior or politically dangerous. These actions prompted new legal concepts of *crimes against humanity.* The most serious crime against humanity is *genocide,* the deliberate and systematic mistreatment or extermination of a national, racial, religious, or cultural group. Other crimes against humanity include using civilians for slave labor or for inhumane medical experiments. These new concepts developed during trials of Nazi leaders at Nuremberg, Germany.

Recent developments. In the early 1990's, ethnic wars in Bosnia-Herzegovina and in Rwanda left hundreds of thousands of civilians killed. The United Nations (UN) convened court sessions to try the nations' leaders for their violence against civilians of other ethnic groups. By 2000, UN courts had charged several top political and military leaders with war crimes.

How wars end

Wars can end in several different ways. Traditionally, the side with the greatest military power wins, but, in some cases, a militarily "weaker" side can gain an advantage. Wars often end with negotiated settlements that seek peaceful relationships between nations.

Superior force and resources typically determine the winner of a war. In some cases, the losing side is virtually crushed or taken over by the overwhelming victors. In the third Punic War (149-146 B.C.), for instance, Rome destroyed Carthage and took survivors as slaves.

Popular support. A persistent smaller opponent may not win a war outright, but it may prevent the stronger side from winning. One of the most important resources that a militarily weaker side can possess is the commitment and support of its people. During the most intense periods of the Vietnam War (1957-1975), the United States had vastly superior military resources but unsteady public support. As a result, the U.S. government withdrew troops and negotiated a peace agreement.

Stalemates. When parties in a war are evenly balanced, the sides may fight to a *stalemate* (draw). A negotiated settlement, bargained directly or through a third party, can result. The settlement may not differ much from the conditions that existed before the war. For instance, during the war between Iran and Iraq (1980-1988), neither side managed to gain a lasting advantage. After eight years of fighting, they reached a truce that restored the original conditions.

A stalemate can also result in a more beneficial settlement. During the 1980's, El Salvador experienced a violent internal war between socialist guerrillas and the conservative government. In 1992, the parties negotiated an arrangement that set the country on the path toward true democracy.

Effects of war

Wars typically have many long-lasting consequences. Some of the most important include the loss of life, the building and collapsing of nations, the creation of refugees, and lingering scars and hatred.

Loss of life is the most dramatic consequence of war. A major war can leave thousands dead and many more wounded. World War II caused about 17 million military deaths, and even more civilian deaths. Even after a war has ended, people may continue to die as a result of the war. Abandoned land mines are particularly dangerous in such countries as Cambodia and Angola, where thousands remain buried in fields and near roads.

The building and collapsing of nations. Victory in war can establish new world powers. Defeat can cause nations to collapse. New countries can also develop in the aftermath. The aftermath of World War I, for instance, saw the establishment of the United States as the most powerful country in the world; the collapse of the Austro-Hungarian, Ottoman, and Russian empires; and

the creation of Czechoslovakia, Turkey, and Yugoslavia.

Refugees are an increasingly common consequence of war today. Civil wars frequently cause mass migrations of civilians as they try to escape violence. Refugees may remain inside their own country if the territory is large enough. Often, however, they cross borders, creating pressing demands on the receiving countries and international aid agencies. Both world wars created millions of displaced people and refugees.

Scars of war. Individuals, especially children, bear the scars of war in many ways. Soldiers' deaths create orphans and widows. Adults may suffer disabling physical injuries. Additionally, people who experience or witness extreme violence in wartime may develop emotional or psychological problems. Warring groups also experience lingering anger and hatred.

Preventing war

Philosophers and diplomats have sought ways to prevent war for centuries. Some proposals have called for the transformation of governments into types less inclined to go to war. Other proposals have suggested new ways to structure relationships between nations.

The League of Nations. World War I prompted the creation of an international organization called the League of Nations. The League sought to give its members *collective security,* in which the security of each member would be guaranteed by the protection of all. In principle, wars between League members would be avoided by the pledge that all member nations would respond to an attack on any one member. The League proved too weak, however, to stop rising aggression in the years leading up to World War II.

The United Nations. The destruction of World War II brought government officials together once again to form a new international organization, the United Nations. The UN formed a Security Council of the world's major powers aimed at preventing wars or stopping them quickly.

The UN's first major challenge came when the United States and the Soviet Union became involved in the Cold War. Although the two countries did not fight directly, their ideological differences caused them to take part in smaller conflicts in other parts of the world. The UN's attempts to prevent war were therefore frustrated.

In 1991, 39 nations joined a UN effort led by the United States to reverse Iraq's occupation of Kuwait. The UN also provided assistance in the settlement of civil wars in Angola, El Salvador, and Guatemala. However, the UN and other organizations were less effective in ending the wars that tore apart Yugoslavia in the 1990's.

The history of warfare

Ancient times. Most scholars believe that warfare emerged in human history between 8,000 and 6,000 B.C. At this time, the development of settled agricultural civilizations created both riches and scarcity. Tribes fought against tribes, and families fought against families. Warrior social classes and armies formed to protect wealth and to expand into new areas. Warfare was common in ancient Greece and Rome, where political units called *city-states* competed for power. Each city-state was an independent state consisting of a city and the region surrounding it. Soldiers fought these wars with weap-

Wars involving the United States

Wars		U.S. military deaths	U.S. war costs
Revolutionary War			
in America	(1775-1783)	25,324	$101,100,000
War of 1812	(1812-1815)	2,260	$90,000,000
Mexican War	(1846-1848)	13,283	$71,400,000
American			
Civil War	(1861-1865)		
Union forces		360,222	$3,183,000,000
Confederate forces		260,000*	$2,000,000,000
Spanish-American			
War	(1898)	2,446	$283,200,000
World War I	(1914-1918)	116,516	$18,676,000,000
World War II	(1939-1945)	405,399	$263,259,000,000
Korean War	(1950-1953)	36,516	$67,386,000,000
Vietnam War	(1957-1975)	58,000*	$150,000,000,000*
Persian Gulf War	(1991)	305	$61,000,000,000
Iraq War	(2003-)**		

*Estimate. **Final figures not available.

ons that typically included swords, shields, and spears. For centuries, war remained relatively unchanged.

Technological advancements eventually shaped the ways of war. In medieval Europe, rulers created fortified cities and castles to defend their domains. Rivals developed tools for the destruction of defensive walls. Sometimes, innovations in arms or organization allowed smaller armies to defeat larger ones. For instance, at the Battle of Agincourt (1415), a small English army used its trained archers to defeat a much larger French force.

By the 1400's, Europeans began using firearms. The power and range of guns and cannons dwarfed those of older weapons. European conquests in the Americas, Africa, and Asia after 1500 offer vivid examples.

The Industrial Revolution of the 1700's and 1800's further changed the face of warfare. Rifles with remarkable accuracy replaced muskets. New techniques of industrial production and transportation enabled large armies to receive better supplies and to move more quickly. Additionally, mass production enabled armies to equip more soldiers than ever before.

The world wars. In World War I, nations moved large numbers of troops to the battlefronts by train and steamship. Each side used long-range cannons to bombard enemy troops. The improved technology of the rapid-fire machine gun helped soldiers to guard positions more effectively. The destructive technologies of each side were evenly matched, however, and thousands of soldiers died in single battles.

By World War II, the warring nations made extensive use of two innovations from World War I, the airplane and the submarine. The Allied nations largely destroyed such cities as Dresden, Germany, and Tokyo with air attacks. German submarines sank hundreds of troop and cargo ships in the Atlantic Ocean. World War II also saw the invention and first use of nuclear weapons. The United States dropped atomic bombs on the Japanese cities of Hiroshima and Nagasaki, destroying most of each city.

The Cold War era. The astonishing power of nuclear weapons dramatically transformed warfare. As the Cold War competition between the United States and the Soviet Union intensified, each country rushed to build more powerful weapons. But by the early 1960's, the United States and the Soviet Union reached a point of *nuclear deterrence*. In other words, they recognized that a war between them would most likely result in two losers and no winner. As a result, an actual war between the two countries never broke out.

The war against terrorism. On Sept. 11, 2001, terrorist attacks in the United States killed about 3,000 people. United States President George W. Bush called the attacks "acts of war." After the attacks, the United States formed an international coalition and led a military campaign against international terrorist groups in Afghanistan and other nations. Because the terrorist networks were secretive and widespread, the conflict lacked many features of conventional warfare between nations.

Recent developments. In March 2003, a U.S.-led coalition began military action against the Iraqi regime of Saddam Hussein. United States officials argued that Iraq supported terrorist organizations and concealed illegal weapons programs. The coalition's invasion of Iraq led to the fall of Hussein's government in April.

Today, nuclear weapons remain a danger among several medium-sized nations engaged in sharp conflicts with their neighbors. Many people also fear that dictatorial leaders could use nuclear weapons.

Among new forms of war that seem likely in the coming decades is *cyberwar* (war through computer-based attacks). The rapid expansion of computer networks in business, government, and military organizations has created new vulnerabilities.   William B. Vogele

Related articles in *World Book* include:

Wars

Anglo-Boer Wars	French and Indian wars	Revolutionary War in America	Spanish Civil War
Arab-Israeli conflict	Hundred Years' War	Russo-Japanese War	Succession wars
Chinese-Japanese wars	Indian wars	Russo-Turkish wars	Thirty Years' War
Civil War, American	Iraq War		Vietnam War
	Korean War	Seven Weeks'	War of 1812
Cold War	Mexican War	War	Wars of the
Crimean War	Peasants' War	Seven Years'	Roses
Crusades	Peloponnesian War	War	World War I
Franco-Prussian War	Persian Gulf War of 1991	Spanish-American War	World War II
	Punic Wars		

Other related articles

Air force	Embargo	Navy
Amphibious warfare	Espionage	Neutrality
Army	Geneva Conventions	Nuclear weapon
Blockade	Geopolitics	Peace
Bomb	Guerrilla warfare	Prisoner of war
Censorship	Guided missile	Propaganda
Chemical-biological-radiological warfare	Hostage	Psychological warfare
Contraband	International law	Reparations
Diplomacy	Jihad	Submarine
Draft, Military	Jingoism	Truce
	Marine	Underground
	Military science	Weapon

Additional resources

Brogan, Patrick. *World Conflicts*. 3rd ed. Scarecrow, 1998.
Keegan, John. *War and Our World*. 1998. Reprint. Vintage Bks., 2001.
Kohn, George C. *Dictionary of Wars*. Rev. ed. Facts on File, 1999.
Parker, Geoffrey, ed. *The Cambridge Illustrated History of Warfare*. 1995. Reprint. Cambridge, 2000.

War, Department of. See Air Force, Department of the; Army, Department of the.

War aces. See Ace.

War Between the States. See Civil War, American.

War correspondent is one of the most dramatic news reporting jobs. A reporter on a war front runs the risk of being killed or wounded. War correspondents have covered fighting in all parts of the world.

Perhaps the first efforts to give readers fast, accurate war news were made by George W. Kendall, founder of the *New Orleans Picayune*. Kendall set up a system of messengers to speed news of the Mexican War (1846-1848) back to the United States. During the American Civil War (1861-1865), correspondents for newspapers in both the North and South sent reports from the field by telegraph, often giving eyewitness accounts.

Richard Harding Davis was one of the first roving war correspondents to become well known. He covered the Spanish-American War (1898) and other major conflicts. During World War I (1914-1918) and World War II (1939-1945), U.S. correspondents were free to move with the troops. But they had to submit their reports to government censors. Ernie Pyle's descriptions of World War II endeared him to U.S. readers. During the Korean War (1950-1953), Marguerite Higgins of the *New York Herald Tribune* became the first woman to win the Pulitzer Prize for war correspondence.

The Vietnam War (1957-1975) was the first war to receive widespread television coverage. Some correspondents, such as David Halberstam of *The New York Times,* raised questions about U.S. involvement in the war in their reports. These reports led to heated debates over the degree to which U.S. correspondents should be free to criticize national policy during a war.

When the United States invaded Grenada in 1983, it set up a *press pool* system of coverage. This restricted the number of correspondents allowed to enter the combat area or to interview participants and required these correspondents to share their information. The United States also set up a pool during the Persian Gulf War of 1991. In 2003, during the Iraq War, about 600 *embedded journalists* reported on the war while moving with U.S. and British military units.   Maurine H. Beasley

See also **Davis, Richard Harding; Pyle, Ernie.**

War crime is a military violation of the rules of warfare. Since World War II (1939-1945), the term has referred to any crime, atrocity, or persecution committed during the course of a war. For thousands of years, numerous rules and customs have governed the conduct of warfare. These rules developed partly from the customs of chivalry and diplomacy and partly from the desire to limit the destruction of war. Many people throughout history have been tried for war crimes.

Since the late 1800's, most nations have signed international treaties and agreements establishing rules of war. The rules deal with fair treatment of war prisoners, outlawing of gas and germ warfare, and humane treatment of civilians in areas occupied by military forces. The Geneva Conventions and the Hague Conventions are the most famous of these agreements. The first Geneva Convention was adopted in 1864; the first Hague Convention, in 1899. See **Geneva Conventions.**

World War I. After World War I (1914-1918), the Treaty of Versailles required Germany to turn over about 900 people for trial by the Allies as war criminals. Germany held its own trials instead. Only 13 of the 900 were tried. Those convicted received light sentences.

World War II. In 1943, during World War II, the Allies set up the United Nations War Crimes Commission in London. The commission collected evidence and made lists of war criminals. After the war, trials took place in Nuremberg, Germany, and Tokyo, Japan. The defendants were charged with starting wars of conquest, violating the rules of war, and crimes against humanity. However, except for several high-ranking German and Japanese officials, few people were tried and convicted of war crimes. See **Nuremberg Trials.**

From 1945 to 1950, the Allies held many other war crimes trials in Europe and East Asia. Some countries that had been occupied by German or Japanese troops held their own trials of officers and occupation officials. West Germany also tried a number of Germans for war crimes. Some of these trials continued into the 1980's.

For years after World War II, Israeli agents sought Adolf Eichmann, a former German officer believed responsible for deporting Jews to Nazi extermination camps. In 1960, the agents found Eichmann in Argentina. The agents took him to Israel, where a court found him guilty of war crimes, crimes against Jews, and crimes against humanity. He was hanged.

New accords involving the treatment of civilians emerged after World War II. The Universal Declaration of Human Rights, adopted by the United Nations (UN) General Assembly in 1948, set forth basic rights for all people. In addition, new provisions were added to the Geneva Conventions in 1949 and again in 1977. A number of other human rights agreements also contributed to the further prosecution of war criminals.

The Korean War. During the Korean War (1950-1953), the United States accused the Chinese and North Korean forces of war crimes against UN troops and South Korean civilians. In 1953, the UN General Assembly expressed "grave concern" over these reports. However, the war ended without any war crimes trials.

The Vietnam War. Beginning in 1965, the United States sent troops to Vietnam to aid South Vietnam against the Communist Viet Cong forces and the North Vietnamese. As the fighting grew heavier, each side accused the other of violating the rules of war. The United States and South Vietnam charged North Vietnam with violating the Geneva Conventions.

In 1969, news reports charged that in March 1968, U.S. troops had massacred hundreds of civilians in and around the hamlet of My Lai. As a result, U.S. courts-martial tried several officers and enlisted men for war crimes. One man, Lieutenant William L. Calley, Jr., was found guilty of murder and sentenced to prison.

Wars in Iraq. The United States accused Iraq of war crimes—including murder, torture, and the mistreatment of prisoners of war—during the Persian Gulf War of 1991 and the Iraq War, which began in 2003. In 2004, an Iraqi court charged Saddam Hussein, the former president of Iraq, with using chemical weapons, illegally invading Kuwait, and carrying out several other crimes while he was president.

Also in 2004, the U.S. government began investigating reports that U.S. soldiers had abused Iraqi prisoners during the Iraq War. Photographs taken at Abu Ghraib, a U.S.-run prison in Iraq, showed prisoners being threatened, beaten, and humiliated by U.S. soldiers. The photos led to criminal charges against several soldiers.

The United Nations and war crimes. In 1947, the UN set up the International Law Commission to develop a code of international laws, including those governing war crimes. But the UN has not yet adopted such a code.

In the 1990's, the UN began holding trials of people accused of war crimes in civil wars in Rwanda and in the lands that made up Yugoslavia before that country began to break up in 1991. The International Criminal Tribunal for the Former Yugoslavia, established by the UN in 1993, has indicted many suspected war criminals. In 2001, the UN brought war crimes charges against Slobodan Milošević, former president of Yugoslavia, in connection with conflicts in Bosnia-Herzegovina, Croatia, and the Serbian province of Kosovo.

In 1998, the UN approved a treaty calling for the creation of the International Criminal Court, a permanent UN body for trying war crimes and other offenses. The court began operations in 2003.   Tom Mockaitis

See also **International Criminal Court.**

Detail of *Perry's Victory on Lake Erie*, (about 1813), an engraving by A. Lawson, after a painting by Thomas Birch, New-York Historical Society, New York City, Olds Collection

The Battle of Lake Erie in 1813 was won by U.S. naval forces under Master-Commandant Oliver H. Perry. During the battle, Perry was rowed from his sinking ship to another vessel, *above*.

War of 1812

War of 1812. The War of 1812 was in many ways the strangest war in United States history. It could well be named the War of Faulty Communication. Two days before war was declared, the British government stated that it would repeal the laws which were the chief reason for fighting. If there had been telegraphic communication with Europe, the war might well have been avoided. Speedy communication would also have prevented the greatest battle of the war, which was fought at New Orleans 15 days after a treaty of peace had been signed.

The chief United States complaint against the British was interference with shipping. But New England, the great shipping section of the United States, bitterly opposed the idea of going to war. The demand for war came chiefly from the West and South.

It is strange also that the war, fought for freedom of the seas, began with the invasion of Canada. In addition, the treaty of peace that ended the war settled none of the issues over which it had supposedly been fought.

Another oddity was that the young United States was willing to risk war against powerful Great Britain. Finally, add that both sides claimed victory in the War of 1812, and it becomes clear that the whole struggle was a confused mass of contradictions.

Causes of the war

Napoleon Bonaparte, head of the French government after 1799 and emperor after 1804, had made himself the master of continental Europe. Except for one short breathing spell (1801-1803), Great Britain had been fighting France since 1793. Napoleon had long hoped to invade and conquer Britain, but in 1805 his navy was destroyed at the battle of Trafalgar. This forced Napoleon to give up the idea of taking an army across the English Channel. So he set out instead to ruin Great Britain by destroying British trade. Napoleon's Berlin and Milan decrees (1806-1807) were an attempt to shut off Great Britain from all trade with Europe. Great Britain, in turn, issued a series of Orders in Council which declared a blockade of French ports and of ports in Europe and elsewhere that were under French control. See **Continental System; Milan Decree; Order in Council.**

The British and French blockades had disastrous effects on United States shipping. Before 1806, the United States was getting rich on the European war. United States ships took goods to both Great Britain and France, and the value of trade carried increased fourfold from 1791 to 1805. Now the picture had suddenly changed. A United States ship bound for French ports had to stop first at a British port for inspection and payment of fees. Otherwise the British were likely to seize the ship. But Napoleon ordered neutral ships not to stop at British ports for inspection, and he also announced that he would order his forces to seize any United States ships which they found had obeyed the British Orders in Council.

The British navy controlled the seas. So the easiest thing for United States vessels was to trade only with other neutrals, with Great Britain, or under British license. A few adventurous spirits ran the British blockade for the sake of huge profits they could make, and continued the risky trade with continental Europe. The United States complained of both French and British policies as illegal "paper blockades," because neither side could really enforce such an extensive blockade. See **Blockade** (Paper blockade).

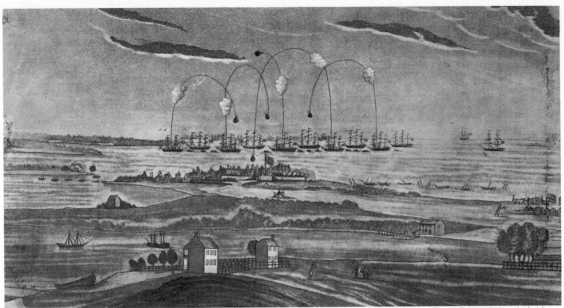

Detail of *A View of the Bombardment of Fort McHenry . . .* (about 1817), an aquatint engraving by J. Bower, The Peale Museum, Baltimore, Maryland, The Hambleton Collection

Bombs burst in the air over Fort McHenry in 1814 during a British attack on the Baltimore area. Francis Scott Key wrote "The Star-Spangled Banner" after watching this battle.

Impressment of seamen. The British navy was always in need of seamen. One reason for this need was that hundreds of deserters from the British navy had found work on United States ships. The British government claimed the right to stop neutral ships on the high seas, remove sailors of British birth, and *impress,* or force, them back into British naval service. The United States objected strongly to this practice, partly because many native-born Americans were impressed "by mistake" along with men who had actually been British seamen. See **Jefferson, Thomas** (The struggle for neutrality).

In June 1807, Captain James Barron of the frigate *Chesapeake* refused to let the British search his ship for deserters. The British frigate *Leopard* fired on the *Chesapeake,* removed four men whom the British called deserters, and hanged one of them. Anti-British feeling in the United States rose sharply. President Thomas Jefferson ordered all British naval vessels out of American harbors. Four years later, the British apologized for the incident and paid for the damage done, but the bitterness remained.

American reaction. The United States tried several times to get the British to change their policy toward neutral shipping and toward impressment. In April 1806, the United States Congress passed a Non-Importation Act, which barred British goods from American markets. The act was not put into continuous operation until December 1807. By that time, the *Chesapeake* incident had taken place and sterner measures were believed to be necessary. Also in December 1807, Congress passed the Embargo Act. This act prohibited exports from the United States and forbade American ships from sailing into foreign ports.

The embargo did not produce anything like the results Congress desired. Overseas trade nearly stopped,

Detail of *Washington,* an engraving by an unknown artist, from *The Stationer's Almanack,* London, 1815 (Library of Congress)

The British captured Washington, D.C., in 1814, *above.* They burned the Capitol, the White House, and other buildings.

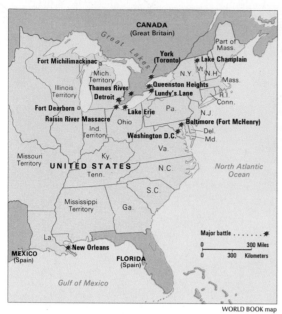

WORLD BOOK map

The War of 1812 was fought mainly in the northern United States and southern Canada. This map shows where the major land and water battles took place.

almost ruining New England shipowners and putting many sailors out of work. Shipyards closed, and goods piled up in warehouses. The embargo also hurt Southern planters, who normally sold tobacco, rice, and cotton to Great Britain. Opponents of the embargo described its effects on the United States by spelling the word backward. They called the embargo the "O-Grab-Me" act. Even with the hardships the embargo caused for the United States, it failed as a policy. The British and the French were intent on winning the European war at all costs, and so both refused to yield to American pressure.

After 14 months, Congress gave up the embargo and tried a new device for hurting British and French commerce. It passed the Non-Intercourse Act in March 1809, permitting American ships to trade with any countries but Great Britain and France. The act also opened American ports to all but British and French ships. But this plan also failed.

In 1810, Congress passed Macon's Bill No. 2, which removed all restrictions on trade. The law went on to say that if either Great Britain or France would give up its orders or decrees, the United States would restore nonintercourse rules against the other nation, unless it also agreed to change its policy.

Macon's Bill really helped Napoleon, who was eager to get the United States into the war against Great Britain. He pretended to repeal his Berlin and Milan decrees so far as they applied to United States ships. President James Madison shut off all trade with Great Britain. In the summer of 1811, further attempts were made to reach an agreement with the British. But these attempts failed, and in November, Madison advised Congress to get ready for war.

The War Hawks. A group of young men known as "War Hawks" dominated Congress during this period.

Henry Clay of Kentucky and John C. Calhoun of South Carolina were the outstanding leaders of the group. Clay was then Speaker of the House of Representatives. Like Clay and Calhoun, most of the War Hawks came from Western and Southern states, where many of the people were in favor of going to war with Great Britain.

The people of New England generally opposed going to war because they feared that war with Great Britain would wipe out entirely the New England shipping trade which had already been heavily damaged. Another reason New England opposed war was because many New Englanders sympathized with Great Britain in its struggle against Napoleon.

Some historians have argued that a leading motive of the War Hawks was a desire for expansion. The people of the Northwest were meeting armed resistance in their attempt to take more land from the Indians, and they believed that the Indians had considerable British support. Friction between Westerners and Indians climaxed in November 1811 at the Battle of Tippecanoe near what is now Lafayette, Ind. Indians attacked an American army, and British guns were found on the battlefield. A desire to eliminate British aid to the Indians may have inspired some Westerners to seek an invasion of Canada, Britain's main possession in North America. But most Westerners favored such an invasion chiefly because of a deep resentment over long-lasting British insults at sea.

The main concerns of Congress were maritime rights, national honor, and the country's obligation to respond to foreign threats. The Federalists in Congress strongly opposed going to war. But the Democratic-Republicans believed that war was the only solution to America's dilemmas. They hoped a successful invasion of Canada would force Britain to change its policies. See **Democratic-Republican Party.**

Progress of the war

Declaration of war. On June 1, 1812, President Madison asked Congress to declare war against Great Britain. He gave as his reasons the impressment of United States seamen and the interference with United States trade. He charged also that the British had stirred up Indian warfare in the Northwest. Congress declared war

Important dates in the War of 1812

1812 (June 18) The United States declared war on Great Britain.

1812 (Oct. 13) British forces won the Battle of Queenston Heights in Canada.

1813 (April 27) The Americans captured York (now Toronto), the capital of Upper Canada. They later burned some public buildings.

1813 (Sept. 10) American forces under Master-Commandant Oliver Hazard Perry won the Battle of Lake Erie.

1813 (Oct. 5) The Americans won the Battle of the Thames River in Moraviantown, an Indian village in Canada.

1814 (Aug. 24) British troops invaded Washington, D.C., and burned the Capitol and the White House.

1814 (Sept. 11) American forces won the Battle of Lake Champlain.

1814 (Dec. 24) The Americans and the British signed a peace treaty in Ghent, Belgium.

1815 (Jan. 8) American forces won the Battle of New Orleans. News of the peace treaty did not reach the United States until after this battle.

on June 18, 1812. Two days earlier, the British foreign minister had announced that the Orders in Council would be repealed, but word of this announcement did not reach America until after the war had begun. Because President Madison asked for the declaration of war, many Federalists blamed him for the conflict, calling it "Mr. Madison's war."

Attitude of the nation. Congress had known for seven months that war was likely to come, but no real preparations had been made. There was little money in the U.S. treasury. The regular Army had less than 10,000 troops, and very few trained officers. The Navy had fewer than 20 seagoing ships.

To make matters worse, a large minority, both in Congress and in the country, was opposed to war. The declaration of war had passed by a vote of only 79 to 49 in the House, and 19 to 13 in the Senate. New England, the richest section in the country, bitterly opposed the war, and interfered with its progress by withholding both money and troops.

The war at sea. At sea, the United States depended primarily on *privateers*—that is, armed ships owned by private people and hired by the government to fight. This was because the tiny regular American navy was dwarfed by the massive British fleet. Several single-ship U.S. victories against British ships improved American morale but had no permanent effect on the naval struggle.

A British blockade was clamped on the United States coast, and United States trade almost disappeared. Because duties on imports were the chief source of federal revenue, the U.S. treasury drifted further and further into debt.

The only American naval victories that directly affected the course of the war were those won by Oliver Hazard Perry on Lake Erie, on Sept. 10, 1813, and by Thomas Macdonough on Lake Champlain, on Sept. 11, 1814. But United States naval vessels and privateers did considerable damage to British commerce, taking about 1,500 prize ships in all.

Land campaign of 1812. The American plan of attack called for a three-way invasion of Canada. Invasion forces were to start from Detroit, from the Niagara River, and from the foot of Lake Champlain.

At Detroit, General William Hull led about 2,000 troops across the Detroit River into Canada. The British commander, General Sir Isaac Brock, drove Hull's forces back into Detroit, surrounded them, and captured both the city and Hull's entire army. The British and Indians also captured Michilimackinac and Fort Dearborn (Chicago).

On the Niagara River, a United States force occupied Queenston Heights on the Canadian side. This force was defeated and captured when New York militia units refused to come to its support.

At Lake Champlain, the third United States army advanced from Plattsburgh, N.Y., to the Canadian frontier. Here, too, the militia refused to leave United States territory, and the army marched back again to Plattsburgh. Thus the first attempt to invade Canada failed completely.

Campaigns of 1813. In January 1813, an American army advancing toward Detroit was defeated and captured at Frenchtown on the Raisin River. In April, York

(now Toronto), the capital of Upper Canada, was captured by United States troops and held for a short time. Some of the public buildings were burned.

Perry's destruction of the British fleet on Lake Erie forced the British to pull out of Detroit, and much of the Michigan Territory came under United States control. General William Henry Harrison was able to take his army across the lake and defeat the retreating British at the Battle of the Thames.

In the autumn, General James Wilkinson and General Wade Hampton undertook a campaign against Montreal. This attempt failed, and the United States armies retreated into northern New York. In December, the British crossed the Niagara River, captured Fort Niagara, and burned Buffalo and neighboring villages.

Campaigns of 1814. By 1814, Napoleon had been defeated in Europe. Great Britain was then able to send over 15,000 troops to Canada, thus ending all American hopes of conquest. But the United States had at last built up a well-trained and disciplined army on the New York frontier. Under the able leadership of Major General Jacob Brown and Brigadier General Winfield Scott, this army crossed the Niagara River from Buffalo in July and defeated the British at the Battle of Chippewa. But soon after that, the Americans were turned back at the Battle of Lundy's Lane. After holding Fort Erie in Canada for several months, United States troops finally withdrew to the American side. This was the last attempt to invade Canada. Meanwhile, nearly 11,000 British troops had moved into New York by way of Lake Champlain. The troops retreated hastily when the destruction of the British fleet on the lake threatened their supply lines back to Canada.

Another British army, under General Robert Ross, was escorted by a fleet to Chesapeake Bay, scattered the United States troops at the Battle of Bladensburg, occupied Washington, D.C., and set fire to the Capitol, the White House, and other public buildings. Both the British army and the British fleet were driven back at Baltimore. This engagement inspired Francis Scott Key to write "The Star-Spangled Banner" (see **Star-Spangled Banner**).

"The needless battle." The Battle of New Orleans was the last engagement of the war. It was fought on Jan. 8, 1815. Like the declaration of war, this battle might have been prevented if there had been speedy communication. A treaty of peace had been signed at Ghent, Belgium, 15 days before the battle took place, but the treaty was not ratified by the United States until a month later.

The British had sent an army of more than 8,000 men to capture New Orleans. There were several possible routes to the city, but the British army chose to march straight toward the entrenchments that had been prepared by General Andrew Jackson. American artillery and sharpshooting riflemen killed or wounded about 1,500 British soldiers, including the commanding officer, General Sir Edward Pakenham. The Americans lost few men in the battle.

Treaty of Ghent. The British public was tired of war and especially of war taxes, and an increasing number of Americans feared disaster if the war continued. Commissioners of the two countries met at Ghent, Belgium, in August 1814.

The Battle of New Orleans was fought 15 days after the United States and Great Britain had signed a peace settlement. Word of the treaty had not reached New Orleans in time to prevent the fighting. Although the American victory had no effect on the outcome of the war, it gave the United States increased political standing in Europe.

The British at first insisted that the United States should give up certain territory on the northern frontier, and set up a large permanent Indian reservation in the Northwest. But American victories in the summer and fall of 1814 led the British to drop these demands. A treaty was finally signed in Ghent on Dec. 24, 1814, and ratified on Feb. 17, 1815. By the terms of this treaty, all land that had been captured by either party was to be given up. Everything was to be exactly as it was before the war, and commissions from both of the countries were to settle any disputed points about boundaries. Nothing whatever was said in the treaty about impressments, blockades, or the British Orders in Council, although they supposedly had caused the war.

Results of the war

The United States had faced near disaster in 1814. But the victory at New Orleans and what seemed to be a successful fight against Britain increased national patriotism and helped to unite the United States into one nation.

The war settled none of the issues over which the United States had fought. But most of these issues faded out during the following years. In the long period of peace after 1815, the British had no occasion to make use of impressments or blockades. Indian troubles in the Northwest were practically ended by the death of the chief Tecumseh and by the rapid settlement of the region. The United States occupied part of Florida during the war, and was soon able to buy the rest of it from Spain.

One indirect result of the War of 1812 was the later election to the presidency of Andrew Jackson and of William Henry Harrison. Both of these men won military fame which had much to do with their elections. Another indirect result was the decline of Federalist power. New England leaders, most of them Federalists, met in secret in Hartford, Conn., to study ways to protest the conduct of the war. Their opponents accused them

of plotting treason, and the Federalists never recovered (see **Hartford Convention**).

Chief battles of the war

The War of 1812 was not an all-out struggle on either side. The United States was ill-prepared for the war militarily. Britain, which could devote only part of its resources to the conflict, viewed the war as just an annoying part of its struggle with Napoleon.

The chief battles of the war are described below.

Lake Champlain (Sept. 11, 1814). The British had four ships and about a dozen rowing galleys on Lake Champlain to protect the flank of General Sir George Prevost's army. Prevost was advancing against Plattsburgh on the west shore of the lake. Master-Commandant Thomas Macdonough commanded the American fleet of 4 ships and 10 rowing galleys. Macdonough anchored his ships across the mouth of Plattsburgh Bay, so the British had to approach him head on. He also arranged the anchors and cables of his flagship, the *Saratoga,* so he could turn the ship about to bring a fresh broadside to bear on the enemy at a critical point in the fighting. As a result of his careful planning, the entire British fleet surrendered.

Lake Erie (Sept. 10, 1813). At Erie, Pa., Master-Commandant Oliver Hazard Perry had built two fine brigs, each carrying 20 guns. In addition, he had under his command a smaller brig captured from the British, and six small schooners, each armed with one or two heavy guns. With these nine ships, Perry blockaded the British fleet of six ships at the western end of the lake. The British came out to fight, and at first had the advantage. When Perry's flagship, the *Lawrence,* was disabled, he transferred in a small boat to the *Niagara,* which had suffered little damage in the battle. He went on to defeat the British fleet and capture it. Perry reported his victory to General Harrison in the famous words, "We have met the enemy and they are ours."

Lundy's Lane (July 25, 1814). This battle took place on Canadian soil, about 1 mile (1.6 kilometers) from Niagara

Falls. The battle began when General Winfield Scott was advancing toward Queenston with about 1,000 men and came upon about 2,800 British troops. The American General Jacob Brown had some 2,700 men in Chippewa, about 3 miles (4.8 kilometers) away. The fighting began at about 5 o'clock in the afternoon. Before darkness fell, General Brown had arrived on the field with reinforcements. The battle raged until midnight, and the losses were heavy.

Each side claimed victory in the battle. The Americans drove the British from their position and captured the chief British battery, but the British later retook the field and recaptured the guns. The battle of Lundy's Lane is remembered for brave fighting on both sides.

New Orleans (Jan. 8, 1815). This battle has already been described under the heading *"The needless battle."* It had no effect on the outcome of the war, but it helped to bring about a surging American nationalism. It also brought fame to General Andrew Jackson.

Queenston Heights (Oct. 13, 1812). This battle ended the second American attempt to invade Canada. General Sir Isaac Brock, the British commander, had about 1,500 men scattered along 34 miles (55 kilometers) of the Niagara River. The Americans, under Generals Stephen Van Rensselaer and Alexander Smyth, numbered more than 6,000. The Americans tried to cross the Niagara River from a point opposite Queenston Heights, 7 miles (11 kilometers) below Niagara Falls. About 400 Americans got across the river and were attacked by a force under Brock. Brock was fatally wounded in the battle.

Later in the day, after both sides had received reinforcements, the British drove the invaders down to the river bank. Here the U.S. troops stopped, because they could not get back across the stream. The entire American force of about 900 surrendered. The British victory was clouded by the death of General Brock, who was one of the finest officers in either army. A monument to his memory stands on the battlefield.

Raisin River (Jan. 22, 1813) took place in Frenchtown (now Monroe, Michigan) on the Raisin River. A detachment of Kentucky troops, sent to drive the British from Frenchtown, was defeated and captured by the British and Indians. After the battle the British departed with the able-bodied American prisoners, leaving the wounded Americans behind with the Indians. The Indians killed wounded prisoners.

Thames River (Oct. 5, 1813), also known as the Battle of Moraviantown, was the direct result of Perry's naval victory on Lake Erie. The British had to abandon Detroit. British troops withdrew from Detroit and crossed into Canada. The British were accompanied by 600 Indians under their chief, Tecumseh. After the British had entered Canada, about 3,000 United States troops under General Harrison pursued them for several days.

The British finally halted near Moraviantown, on the Thames River in Kent County, Ontario, and offered battle. British General Proctor and many of his men fled soon after the first volley, but Tecumseh died on the battlefield. The death of Tecumseh, the leading Indian chief, broke the league of Indian tribes that had been allied to the British and practically ended the cooperation of the British and Indians on the northwestern frontier. A court-martial later publicly reprimanded General Proctor and suspended him. Reginald Horsman

Related articles in *World Book* include:

Biographies

Brock, Sir Isaac	Key, Francis Scott
Decatur, Stephen	Lawrence, James
Forten, James	Macdonough, Thomas
Harrison, William Henry	Madison, James (Events leading to war)
Hull, Isaac	
Hull, William	Perry, Oliver H.
Jackson, Andrew (Jackson the soldier)	Scott, Winfield
	Secord, Laura I.

Other related articles

Constitution (ship)	Hartford Convention
Ghent, Treaty of	Star-Spangled Banner

Outline

I. **Causes of the war**
    A. Impressment of seamen
    B. American reaction
    C. The War Hawks
II. **Progress of the war**
    A. Declaration of war   E. Campaigns of 1813
    B. Attitude of the nation   F. Campaigns of 1814
    C. The war at sea   G. "The needless battle"
    D. Land campaign   H. Treaty of Ghent
        of 1812
III. **Results of the war**
IV. **Chief battles of the war**

Questions

Why might the War of 1812 be called the War of Faulty Communication?
What was *impressment?* Why did Americans object to it?
Who were the War Hawks?
What two U.S. naval victories affected the course of the war?
When and by whom were these historic words written: "We have met the enemy and they are ours"?
When was the Capitol burned by the British?
What famous American patriotic song was written during the battle of Baltimore?
What battle is known as "The needless battle"? Why?

Additional resources

Berton, Pierre F. D. *Flames Across the Border.* 1981. Reprint. Penguin, 1988. *The Invasion of Canada.* 1980. Reprint. 1988.
Elting, John R. *Amateurs, to Arms! A Military History of the War of 1812-1815.* 1991. Reprint. Da Capo, 1995.
Heidler, David S. and Jeanne T., eds. *Encyclopedia of the War of 1812.* ABC-Clio, 1997.
Hickey, Donald R. *The War of 1812.* Univ. of Ill. Pr., 1989.
Stefoff, Rebecca. *The War of 1812.* Benchmark Bks., 2001. Younger readers.
Suthren, Victor. *The War of 1812.* McClelland, 1999.

War of Secession. See Civil War.

War of the American Revolution. See Revolutionary War in America.

War on Poverty. See Johnson, Lyndon Baines (The national scene).

War Powers Resolution is a United States law designed to balance military powers of the president and Congress. The law, passed in 1973, is popularly known as the War Powers Act. According to Section 4(a)(1) of the resolution, the president must inform Congress within 48 hours if U.S. forces are sent into a hostile area without a declaration of war. The forces may remain no longer than 60 days unless Congress approves the president's action or declares war. The president may extend this deadline an additional 30 days.

The resolution was created as a result of actions taken by Presidents Lyndon B. Johnson and Richard M. Nixon during the Vietnam War (1957-1975). Johnson and Nixon sent troops into battle even though Congress did not specifically approve such an action or declare war.

The resolution's 90-day limit has never been applied because no President who has ordered troops into combat areas since 1973 has referred to Section 4(a)(1) of the resolution. Instead, the Presidents have referred to their constitutional authority as commander in chief.

Congress took its first major action under the resolution in 1983 after U.S. Marines in Lebanon were attacked. President Ronald Reagan reported the situation. But he disagreed with Congress that the resolution's 90-day limit had been triggered because he did not mention Section 4(a)(1) in his report. Congress later passed a law allowing the troops to remain in Lebanon for 18 months.

Louis Fisher

Warbeck, Perkin (1474?-1499), became one of the most famous "pretenders" in European history. He appeared in Ireland in 1491 to challenge King Henry VII of England. Warbeck claimed to be Richard, the younger son of the former Yorkist king of England, Edward IV. Richard and his brother, Edward V, had been imprisoned in the Tower of London by their uncle, Richard III, in 1483 and were never heard from again. Warbeck's claim to the throne was supported by a number of people who were dissatisfied with King Henry, by many followers of the House of York in England, and by several European princes who were Henry's enemies.

Warbeck tried to invade England from 1495 to 1497,

but he was captured in 1497 and imprisoned. When he tried to escape, Henry had him hanged. There is convincing evidence that Warbeck was a Flemish commoner, not royalty.   Ralph A. Griffiths

Warble fly is a type of large, hairy fly that resembles a bumble bee. Warble flies belong to a group of flies called *bot flies* (see **Bot fly**). The *larvae* (young) of warble flies live under the skin of animals. The *cattle warble,* or *heel fly,* usually lays its eggs on the hairs of the feet or legs of cattle. The larvae, called *cattle grubs,* work their way through the skin of the animal. Under the skin of the back, the larvae cause painful swellings, called *warbles.*

E. W. Cupp

Scientific classification. Warble flies are in the order Diptera. They make up the family Hypodermatidae. The scientific name for the cattle warble is *Hypoderma lineatum.*

WORLD BOOK illustration by Oxford Illustrators Limited

Adult warble fly

Warbler is the popular name of a group of small migratory songbirds. These birds are also known as *wood-warblers.* They live in the Americas from the tropics to

Yellow warbler
Dendroica petechia
Found from Canada to northern South America
Body length: $4\frac{1}{2}$ to $5\frac{1}{4}$ inches (11.4 to 13.3 centimeters)

Blackburnian warbler
Dendroica fusca
Found from Canada to northern South America
Body length: $4\frac{1}{2}$ to $5\frac{1}{2}$ inches (11.4 to 14.0 centimeters)

Yellow-rumped warbler
Dendroica coronata
Found in North and Central America
Body length: 5 to 6 inches (12.7 to 15.2 centimeters)

Hooded warbler
Wilsonia citrina
Found in Eastern and Midwestern United States and in Central America
Body length: 5 to 6 inches (12.7 to 15.2 centimeters)

Black-and-white warbler
Mniotilta varia
Found from Canada to northwestern South America
Body length: $4\frac{1}{2}$ to $5\frac{1}{2}$ inches (11.4 to 14.0 centimeters)

WORLD BOOK illustrations by Albert Earl Gilbert

the far north. Most of them are about $5\frac{1}{2}$ inches (14 centimeters) long. Warblers are hard to see because they are small and they keep close to the foliage of trees and bushes. Their feathers are of many beautiful colors. People enjoy the quick movements and abrupt, high-pitched songs of the warblers.

Many warblers spend the winter in South America and Central America, and migrate through the United States late in the spring. In May, they begin to appear in woods, in city parks, and in trees near buildings. Many species go on farther north for their nesting. Some warblers go as far north as the Hudson Bay and the Yukon Territory in Canada, but others nest in the Southern States.

Warblers build their nests in trees and bushes or on the ground. The nests are usually cup-shaped, and loosely built of twigs and grasses woven together, but some are compact structures of plant down. The female warbler lays from three to six eggs, which are whitish with brownish markings at the larger end.

Many kinds of warblers have fine singing voices. Others sing only weak, lisping notes. There are more than 150 species and subspecies of warblers. Some of the better-known ones are the *yellow warbler,* the *black-and-white warbler,* and the *yellow-rumped warbler.* Yellow warblers are quite common in city parks. The black-and-white warbler likes to creep along the branches of trees. The yellow-rumped warbler has four yellow patches on its head, rump, and breast.

Another well-known warbler is the *American redstart.* It is colored a striking black with salmon markings, and looks somewhat like a small oriole. The redstart is one of the most active and graceful of American warblers. The *Blackburnian warbler* has a bright orange throat. Two other warblers are named for their colors. They are the *black-throated green warbler* and the *black-throated blue warbler.* The *ovenbird* has a dull orange stripe on its head, a white breast marked with black, and an olive-green back. It is named for its ovenlike nest.

Warblers help farmers by killing insects that destroy fruits and strip trees of their leaves. Warblers search in tiny cracks in the bark and in fruit buds for insects that might escape larger birds. 　　　Sandra L. Vehrencamp

Scientific classification. Warblers make up the subfamily Parulinae in the family Emberizidae. The scientific name for the black-and-white warbler is *Mniotilta varia.* The American redstart is *Setophaga ruticilla.* The ovenbird is *Seiurus aurocapillus.* The yellow warbler is *Dendroica petechia,* and the yellow-rumped is *D. coronata.* The Blackburnian warbler is *D. fusca,* the black-throated green is *D. virens,* and the black-throated blue is *D. caerulescens.*

See also **Bird** (pictures: Birds of forests and woodlands; Birds' eggs); **Ovenbird; Redstart; Yellowthroat.**

Ward is a word that once had much the same meaning as the word *guard.* The relationship between the two words may be seen in two of the present meanings of *ward* that are described below.

In law, a ward is a person who needs to be guarded or protected, and so the court has appointed a guardian for the ward. Most wards are *minors* (people under legal age). Spendthrifts or people who are mentally unsound, however, may be legally considered wards. A guardian's duty is to protect the ward's interests and act in the place of a parent (*in loco parentis*).

In politics, a ward is a political division of a city. The early use of this name started when cities were divided into wards so that they might be guarded more easily. But today cities are divided into wards chiefly to simplify city government and city elections. For purposes of government, each ward elects one or two *aldermen.* The aldermen help govern the city and look after the ward. 　　　Carlfred B. Broderick

See also **Guardian.**

Ward, Aaron Montgomery (1844-1913), an American businessman, pioneered in the mail-order business in the United States. As a traveling salesman in the Midwest, he conceived the idea of buying merchandise in large quantities from manufacturers for cash and selling it directly to farmers for cash.

Ward was born on Feb. 17, 1844, in Chatham, New Jersey. In 1872, he and his partner, George R. Thorne, began in the mail-order business in a livery-stable loft with $2,400 capital and a single-sheet catalog listing a few dry goods items. When Ward died, annual sales had risen to $40 million. 　　　William H. Becker

Ward, Artemus, *AHR tuh muhs* (1834-1867), was the pen name of Charles Farrar Browne, one of the most important American humorists of the 1800's. Ward's subjects varied from current events to general human weaknesses, all of which he treated in a light manner. He was largely responsible for the widespread use among humorists of intentionally misspelled words for comic effect. Ward also popularized comic lecturing.

Ward was born on April 26, 1834, in Waterford, Maine. His most famous works are the Artemus Ward letters, which describe the fictional adventures of a traveling showman. These letters first appeared in the Cleveland *Plain Dealer* in 1858. In 1866, Ward moved to London, where he enjoyed great popularity. He died there of tuberculosis at the age of 33. 　　　David B. Kesterson

Ward, Barbara (1914-1981), was a British economist and journalist. She became known for her books about the problems of economic development in developing nations. Ward argued for a more even distribution of the world's economic resources between the industrial and the developing countries. To achieve these goals, she favored international cooperation and programs to control population growth.

Barbara Mary Ward was born on May 23, 1914, in York, England. She attended schools in Paris and in Germany before entering Oxford University in England in 1932. She graduated in 1935.

Ward joined the staff of *The Economist,* an influential weekly British newspaper, in 1939. In 1950, she married Sir Robert G. A. Jackson, an Australian economist and United Nations official. She received the title Dame Commander of the Order of the British Empire in 1974. In 1976, she was made a life *peeress* (member of the nobility) with the title Baroness Jackson of Lodsworth.

Ward wrote numerous books and essays. Her major works include *The Rich Nations and the Poor Nations* (1962), *Nationalism and Ideology* (1967), *The Lopsided World* (1968), *The Home of Man* (1976), and *Progress For a Small Planet* (1979). 　　　Daniel R. Fusfeld

Ward, Joseph (1838-1889), was a noted clergyman and educator, and a leader in South Dakota's drive for statehood. In 1879, he helped form a group that worked for South Dakota's statehood.

Ward became a Congregational minister in 1869, and

became a missionary in Yankton, then capital of the Dakota Territory. Because of his missionary work, some people call him the *Father of Congregationalism in Dakota.* In 1881, he helped establish Yankton College, a private school associated with the Congregational Church. He served as president and professor of philosophy at Yankton until his death.

Ward was born in Perry Centre, New York. A statue of him represents South Dakota in the United States Capitol in Washington, D.C.　　Richard A. Bartlett

Ward, Lynd Kendall (1905-1985), was an American artist. His reputation as a wood engraver was established with the publication of *God's Man* (1929) and five other novels in woodcut. They were the first such novels without text to be published in the United States. His works also appear in water color, oil, and lithography. He wrote and illustrated *The Biggest Bear* (1952), a children's book that received the Caldecott Medal in 1953. Ward and his wife, May McNeer, received the 1975 Regina Medal. Ward was born in Chicago. He graduated from Columbia University.　　Marilyn Fain Apseloff

Warhol, *WAWR hawl,* **Andy** (1930?-1987), was an American artist best known for his images of common objects or famous people. Warhol's style made him a leading figure of the Pop Art movement in the 1960's.

Warhol created most of his pictures with a mechanical stencil process called *silk-screen printing.* The process gives his work a mass-produced and impersonal appearance. Warhol often derived his subject from advertising or the mass media. He isolated and simplified these images, sometimes enlarging them in a series

Acrylic and silk-screen enamel painting on canvas (1962); Leo Castelli Gallery, New York City

An Andy Warhol painting shows repeated images of movie star Marilyn Monroe. Many of Warhol's works deal with familiar subjects in a style that looks mass-produced and impersonal.

tinted with various colors. He often repeated them many times in a single picture.

Warhol's most familiar subjects are probably commercial products, such as soup cans and soft-drink bottles. He often worked in series, variously treating themes that some people have considered a catalog of the preoccupations of the time. These subjects included disasters, such as newspaper images of death and destruction. His subjects also included celebrities, notably movie stars Elizabeth Taylor and Marilyn Monroe and Chinese political leader Mao Zedong. Warhol also produced a significant body of film work.

Warhol was born in Pittsburgh. After graduating from the art school of the Carnegie Institute of Technology in 1949, he moved to New York City. There he became a successful commercial artist before achieving recognition as a painter about 1962.　　Charles C. Eldredge

See also **Pop art; Screen printing.**

Warm-blooded animal is an animal that almost always has about the same body temperature, regardless of the temperature of its surroundings. Birds and mammals, including human beings, are warm-blooded animals. Nearly all other kinds of animals are cold-blooded. Scientists refer to warm-blooded animals as *endothermic* or *homeothermic.*

The body of a warm-blooded animal produces heat by burning food. Shivering and physical activity also generate body heat. Young warm-blooded animals and some adult small mammals have heat-producing organs, called *brown fat,* on their neck, chest, and back.

A layer of fat beneath the skin, plus a covering of hair, fur, or feathers, helps keep a warm-blooded animal warm. The animal's body can also conserve heat by reducing the flow of blood to the limbs and to uncovered skin. The body becomes cooler by such means as panting and sweating.　　James Edward Heath

See also **Bird** (The respiratory system); **Cold-blooded animal; Mammal; Temperature, Body.**

Warner, Pop (1871-1954), was one of the most influential coaches in the history of American college football. His many contributions to the game include the single-wing and double-wing formations, the screen pass, and the practice of numbering plays.

Warner was born in Springville, New York. His real name was Glenn Scobey Warner. He attended Cornell University. There, he acquired the nickname "Pop" because he was older than the average student. He was captain of Cornell's 1894 football team. After briefly practicing law, Warner began coaching at Georgia in 1895. He later coached at Cornell, the Carlisle (Pennsylvania) Indian Industrial School, Pittsburgh, Stanford, and Temple. He retired in 1938 with a career record of 313 victories, 106 losses, and 32 ties.　　Bob Carroll

Warner, Seth (1743-1784), was an American soldier in the Revolutionary War (1775-1783). He is chiefly remembered for his role in forming and leading the famed regiment of Green Mountain Boys. His greatest contribution to winning the war was his timely arrival to help reinforce the colonial troops at the Battle of Bennington on Aug. 16, 1777. His support of John Stark clinched a decisive victory for the American forces. In recognition of his services, Warner was appointed a brigadier general in 1778. He was born in Roxbury, Connecticut. See also **Green Mountain Boys.**　　James H. Hutson

Warrant, *WAHR uhnt,* is a document authorizing a person to do something. A *search warrant* authorizes a law officer to search a house or other premises for goods held illegally. A *bench warrant* authorizes a law officer to arrest and bring before the court a person charged with a crime, misdemeanor, or contempt of court. Other warrants certify or guarantee the quality and validity of things.   George T. Felkenes

See also **Arrest; Search warrant; Wiretapping.**

Warren, Earl (1891-1974), served as chief justice of the United States from 1953 to 1969. He won recognition as a liberal and influential presiding officer during the most revolutionary period in Supreme Court history. In 1954, he wrote the opinion for the unanimous ruling by the Supreme Court outlawing racial segregation in the public schools. He wrote the 1964 decision that states must apportion both houses of their legislatures on the basis of equal population. Also in 1964, he was chairman of a presidential committee that investigated the assassination of President John F. Kennedy (see **Warren Report**). In 1966, Warren wrote the decision that required police officers to advise suspects of their rights before questioning them.

Warren was born in Los Angeles, and received his law degree from the University of California. He served as attorney general of California from 1939 to 1943, and as governor of California from 1943 to 1953. Warren was the Republican nominee for Vice President in 1948.

Wide World

Earl Warren

Warren submitted his resignation as chief justice in June 1968, but did not leave office. He remained on the court because a Senate filibuster prevented a vote on the nomination of associate justice Abe Fortas to succeed him as chief justice. Warren later agreed to remain in office until the end of the Supreme Court's term in mid-1969.   Bruce Allen Murphy

Warren, Joseph (1741-1775), was a leading Massachusetts statesman in the period before the Revolutionary War. He was among the first to die for the patriot cause when he was killed at the Battle of Bunker Hill. He spoke and wrote frequently for the colonial cause after 1765, and he helped draft some key Massachusetts protests against the British enactments. Warren's selection in 1775 as president of the Provincial Assembly and his election as major general in the Massachusetts forces reflected the respect he won. Warren was born in Roxbury, Mass. He studied at Harvard College.

James H. Hutson

Warren, Mercy Otis (1728-1814), was a colonial American writer. Her most important work was the three-volume *History of the Rise, Progress, and Termination of the American Revolution* (1805). She had helped encourage prorevolutionary feeling by satirizing the British colonial government in the plays *The Adulateur* (published in 1773) and *The Group* (published in 1775). Both were widely read but apparently not performed.

Warren had extensive knowledge of political affairs and was a close friend of many leaders of the revolution, who included her brother, James Otis, and her husband, James Warren. Mercy Otis Warren expressed her political convictions even when they were unpopular. For example, she opposed ratification of the U.S. Constitution because she felt it gave too much power to the federal government. She favored increased safeguards for individual liberties and equal opportunities for women in education and public affairs. Warren was born in Barnstable, Mass.   Samuel Chase Coale

Warren, Robert Penn (1905-1989), was an American novelist, poet, and literary critic. Warren won the 1947 Pulitzer Prize for fiction for *All the King's Men* (1946), which describes the rise and fall of a ruthless Southern politician. Warren won the 1958 Pulitzer Prize for poetry for his collection *Promises: Poems 1954-1956,* published in 1957. He also won the 1979 Pulitzer Prize for poetry for his collection *Now and Then: Poems 1976-1978,* published in 1978. Warren served as the first poet laureate of the United States in 1986 and 1987.

In addition to *All the King's Men,* Warren's major novels include *World Enough and Time* (1950), *The Cave* (1959), and *Meet Me in the Green Glen* (1971). These books reflect the author's Southern heritage. They also emphasize the interaction of past and present, and what Warren believed is each person's struggle to determine his or her identity. Warren's poetry explores the themes of time, the individual, and the nature of evil. His long poem *Brother to Dragons* (1953) is typical of his verse. Warren also co-edited, with the critic Cleanth Brooks, two influential textbooks—*Understanding Poetry* (1938) and *Understanding Fiction* (1943). Warren was born in Guthrie, Ky.   Noel Polk

Warren Report is a summary of events related to the assassination of United States President John F. Kennedy in Dallas, Tex., on Nov. 22, 1963. Issued by the Warren Commission in September 1964, it concluded that Lee Harvey Oswald, acting alone, shot Kennedy from a window on the sixth floor of the Texas School Book Depository building. The report also said that Jack Ruby acted alone in killing Oswald on Nov. 24, 1963, in a Dallas jail. The report found no evidence of a conspiracy involving Oswald and Ruby. It criticized the U.S. Secret Service and Federal Bureau of Investigation (FBI), and it asked for better measures in the future to protect the President.

The commission was appointed on Nov. 29, 1963. President Lyndon B. Johnson named Earl Warren, chief justice of the United States, to head the commission. The other members were Senator Richard B. Russell, Democrat of Georgia; Senator John S. Cooper, Republican of Kentucky; Representative T. Hale Boggs, Democrat of Louisiana; Representative Gerald R. Ford, Republican of Michigan; Allen W. Dulles, former director of the U.S. Central Intelligence Agency (CIA); and John J. McCloy, former adviser to President Kennedy. During 10 months, the commission took testimony from 552 witnesses.

After the Warren Report was issued, other investigations criticized the report's findings. During the late 1970's, a special committee of the U.S. House of Representatives reexamined the evidence. It concluded that Kennedy "was probably assassinated as a result of a conspiracy." See **Kennedy, John F.** (The assassination controversy).   James I. Lengle

Additional resources

Galanor, Stewart. *Cover-Up.* Kestrel, 1998.
Meagher, Sylvia. *Accessories After the Fact.* 1967. Reprint. Random Hse., 1992.

Wars of succession. See **Succession wars.**

Wars of the Roses were a series of civil wars in England in the 1400's. Two branches of the royal Plantagenet family fought for the English throne. Each side had a rose as its symbol. The House of York had long used a white rose as its emblem. The House of Lancaster became identified with a red rose.

A number of factors helped lead to the wars—disputes between the two houses, the defeat of English forces in France, the weakness and corruption of England's government, and the existence of powerful, warlike nobles. The wars began in 1455 with the Battle of St. Albans, near London.

At that time, King Henry VI of the House of Lancaster held the throne. His grandfather Henry IV had seized power in 1399. Richard, Duke of York, claimed that Henry VI had no right to be king. Richard was killed at the Battle of Wakefield in 1460. But in 1461, his oldest son was proclaimed King Edward IV. Soon after being proclaimed king, Edward crushed the Lancastrians at the Battle of Towton, near York.

In 1470, the forces of Lancaster drove Edward from England and brought back Henry VI. Edward returned seven months later, defeated the Lancastrian forces at the battles of Barnet (near London) and Tewkesbury, and regained the throne. The House of York ruled until 1485, when King Richard III was killed in the Battle of Bosworth Field, near Leicester, and Henry Tudor, a kinsman of the House of Lancaster, became King Henry VII. Many historians have considered this battle as the war's end.

In 1486, Henry married Elizabeth, daughter of Edward IV, uniting the houses of Lancaster and York and founding the Tudor dynasty. Some Yorkists continued to oppose Henry. But a lack of funds on both sides, weariness of war, and firm government soon ended the fighting. One further engagement, the Battle of Stoke, occurred near Newark in 1487. This battle was easily won by Henry VII over Yorkist rebels. Some scholars view it as the true final engagement of the wars.   Ralph A. Griffiths

See also **England** (The Wars of the Roses); **Lancaster; Tudor, House of; York.**

Warsaw, *WAWR saw* (pop. 1,653,300), is the capital and largest city of Poland. Its name in Polish is *Warszawa.* The city is a center of business, culture, and industry. It lies in east-central Poland, on both banks of the Vistula River. For location, see **Poland** (political map).

Warsaw has been a capital throughout much of its history. But Prussia, Russia, and Germany have each controlled the city at various times. During World War II (1939-1945), German troops occupied Warsaw. The city was almost completely destroyed during the war but rebuilt itself from the ruins.

The city. Warsaw covers 174 square miles (450 square kilometers). The Vistula River divides the city. The left bank section lies west of the river, and the right bank section lies east of it. The center of Warsaw and most of the residential areas are on the left bank.

The city has many high-rise housing developments and office buildings. It has spacious parks, and fine libraries, museums, and theaters. Modern hospitals, schools, and government buildings stand near churches and palaces built in the Middle Ages. The huge Palace of Culture and Science, a gift from the Soviet Union in 1954, stands in a modern part of Warsaw. The city's educational and research institutions include the University of Warsaw and the headquarters of the Polish Academy of Science. The city's monuments include the Column of King Sigismund, built in 1644. This monument honors the king who moved the Polish capital from Kraków, in what is now southern Poland, to Warsaw.

The Poles rebuilt many of Warsaw's historic buildings damaged in World War II. Rebuilt landmarks include the Cathedral of St. John and the city walls, both dating from the 1300's. Warsaw's opera house, also reconstructed after the war, is one of the largest in the world.

Numerous cultural events take place in the capital. Each fall, the Festival of Contemporary Music attracts musicians from throughout Europe. Every five years, pianists from many parts of the world play in Warsaw's Frédéric Chopin International Piano Competition.

The people. Almost all the people of Warsaw are Poles. The great majority are Roman Catholics, and religion plays an important role in their lives. Religious festivals, such as the Corpus Christi procession in May or June, rank as major events.

Economy. Warsaw is the leading business city and one of the chief railroad hubs in eastern Europe. The city has long been a center of trade, and it is also an important industrial center. Warsaw's major industries include food processing and the manufacture of automobiles, electronic equipment, and textiles. Thousands of its citizens work in agencies of the Polish government.

History. As early as the A.D. 900's, a small Slavic settlement existed in the area that is now Warsaw. During the late Middle Ages, from the 1200's to the 1500's, Warsaw was the home of the dukes of Mazovia. Mazovia entered the Polish kingdom in the 1500's, and King Sigismund III moved the capital from Kraków to Warsaw in 1596. Swedish forces invaded Poland in the mid-1600's and destroyed much of Warsaw in 1656. But Warsaw remained the capital of Poland until 1795. That year, Austria, Prussia, and Russia divided Poland among themselves, and Prussia took over Warsaw.

From 1807 to 1813, the city was the capital of the Duchy of Warsaw, a state created by the French emperor Napoleon. After Napoleon's defeat in eastern Europe, Russia gained control of Warsaw. The Poles rebelled against the Russians in 1830 and 1863, but these uprisings failed. In the late 1800's, the Russians tightened control over Warsaw. World War I (1914-1918) brought an end to Russian rule. Germany controlled Warsaw from 1915 to 1918, when Poland again became independent.

World War II brought the almost total destruction of Warsaw. In 1939, the Germans captured the city in a three-week siege that caused great damage. Warsaw surrendered to the Germans, but the city became the heart of the Polish underground resistance movement.

The people of Warsaw suffered greatly during the German occupation. The Nazis staged mass arrests and public executions. They forced many people to leave Warsaw. They confined about 500,000 Jews to a section

Downtown Warsaw has wide streets lined with modern office buildings, apartments, and stores. The city is Poland's capital and a leading center of business and industry in eastern Europe. Warsaw also has numerous libraries, museums, theaters, and historic landmarks.

© Gregory Wrona, Panos Pictures

called the *ghetto*. Many Jews died of hunger or disease or were executed by the Nazis. In April 1943, thousands of Jews revolted. However, the Nazis killed or sent to death camps all of the 60,000 Jews still remaining in the ghetto.

By the summer of 1944, Soviet armies had pushed the Germans out of the Soviet Union and had reached the outskirts of Warsaw. On Aug. 1, 1944, the people of Warsaw rose against the Germans. At first, the Poles seized large parts of the city. But the nearby Soviet troops did not come to their aid, and the Poles soon weakened. In spite of massive German counterattacks, the Poles held on to areas on the left bank of the Vistula. They finally surrendered on October 3. The Germans evacuated all the people from the left bank. They burned and dynamited the buildings and destroyed what remained of Warsaw. About 200,000 residents died in the uprising. On Jan. 17, 1945, Soviet forces entered the city. They set up a Polish Communist government centered in Warsaw.

World War II severely reduced the city's population. But after the war, the population increased so rapidly that serious housing shortages developed. The government built many housing projects and restricted the flow of new residents into Warsaw.

The period of Communist control came to an end in 1989. In that year, non-Communist candidates were allowed to run for legislative seats, and Poland held its freest elections since World War II. Janusz Bugajski

See also **Poland** (picture).

Warsaw Pact was a treaty that held most Eastern European nations in a military command under tight Soviet control. Albania, Bulgaria, Czechoslovakia, East Germany, Hungary, Poland, Romania, and the Soviet Union signed the treaty in Warsaw in May 1955. They claimed they signed the treaty as a response to the creation of the North Atlantic Treaty Organization (NATO), a defense alliance formed by the United States and its European allies. NATO was formed in 1949. Albania withdrew from the Warsaw Pact in 1968.

Soviet control of its Warsaw Pact allies declined sharply in 1989 and 1990. This decline occurred as a result of Communist parties being driven from power in peaceful revolutions in Poland, Hungary, East Germany, and Czechoslovakia. In 1990, Hungary declared that it would no longer participate in military operations associated with the pact. Hungary also announced its intention to withdraw from the Warsaw Pact by the end of

1991. Poland and Czechoslovakia announced plans to withdraw from the pact as well. In addition, East Germany's membership in the pact ended in 1990, when the country became part of a united Germany. In 1991, the leaders of the six nations remaining in the Warsaw Pact formally agreed to dissolve the pact. Stuart D. Goldman

Warship is a naval combat ship. Some kinds of warships fight enemy aircraft, surface ships, and submarines. They are heavily armed with such weapons as guns, missiles, rockets, and torpedoes. Others serve as bases for planes or helicopters. Still others transport troops, weapons, and equipment to landing areas.

Warships range in size from small vessels with only a few crew members to large aircraft carriers that carry nearly 6,000. Most warships have radar to detect enemy aircraft and surface ships and sonar to locate submarines. Electronic intercept equipment can detect radio and radar transmissions from enemy ships and aircraft.

From ancient times until the 1600's, warships and cargo ships were almost identical. Warships gradually became specialized vessels for military use.

Kinds of warships

Large modern navies have many kinds of warships that are designed for certain combat operations. The United States Navy uses six principal types. These types are (1) aircraft carriers, (2) amphibious warfare ships, (3) cruisers, (4) destroyers, (5) frigates, and (6) submarines. Many fleets also include small warships called *small combatants*.

Aircraft carriers are the largest and most powerful warships. They serve as bases for bomber and fighter planes. They also carry antisubmarine aircraft, helicopters, and small numbers of other kinds of planes. Aircraft carriers have few defensive weapons, and so they depend on other warships for protection.

A carrier has a large, flat flight deck with equipment that enables planes to take off and land without a long runway. The aircraft are launched by four catapults, each of which can put a plane into the air every 30 seconds. The landing area of the flight deck has steel wires across it. A hook attached to the bottom of each plane catches onto a wire, bringing the aircraft to a quick stop.

The powerful radars of an aircraft carrier not only detect enemy planes but also guide the carrier's own aircraft. Short-range radars are used to detect enemy missiles. They also help the crew keep track of nearby ships at night and navigate the carrier near shore.

A warship in action. The aircraft carrier U.S.S. *Constellation* tests a missile for use against enemy ships. Members of the crew watch the test from the ship's flight deck. Aircraft carriers are the largest and most powerful type of warship.

Aircraft carriers are about 1,100 feet (335 meters) long and can carry from 85 to 95 planes. Carriers travel at speeds of over 30 knots (nautical miles per hour).

Amphibious warfare ships land troops, weapons, and vehicles on beaches held by the enemy. Some of these ships remain far from shore and use small amphibious landing craft or helicopters to land the troops and cargo. Such ships have closed-off areas at sea level called *docking wells.* The docking wells are flooded and opened into the sea so that landing craft can float out through them.

Some amphibious warfare ships serve chiefly as helicopter carriers. They resemble small aircraft carriers but do not have the launching and landing equipment needed for conventional planes. These ships carry from 20 to 30 helicopters, as well as troops and small vehicles. The ships also can serve as bases for *V/STOL aircraft.* V/STOL's can take off and land vertically or on a very short runway. Other amphibious warfare ships have command and communications facilities to coordinate air, shore, and surface operations.

Amphibious warfare ships measure up to 800 feet (245 meters) long and travel at speeds of about 20 knots. They carry few defensive weapons.

Cruisers escort aircraft carriers and defend them against air and submarine attacks. Modern cruisers are called *guided missile cruisers.* They carry supersonic missiles that can be fired at aircraft that are from 15 to 85 miles (25 to 135 kilometers) from the ship. Cruisers also have antisubmarine rockets and torpedoes for use against enemy submarines. Some cruisers carry one or

two helicopters. After an enemy submarine has been detected by sonar, the helicopters pinpoint its location and attack it with torpedoes or depth bombs. Some cruisers also carry 5-inch guns. Modern cruisers are about 570 feet (175 meters) long and travel at speeds of more than 30 knots.

Destroyers are used chiefly to defend aircraft carriers, amphibious ships, and merchant ships. They also perform various independent missions, such as bombarding enemy shores and conducting search and rescue operations at sea.

Modern destroyers have 5-inch guns, short-range antiaircraft missiles, and antisubmarine weapons. They also carry one or two helicopters to attack submarines. Destroyers range in length from about 375 to 560 feet (115 to 170 meters). They can reach speeds of 30 to 33 knots.

Frigates are used primarily to defend amphibious ships and merchant ships against enemy submarines. Frigates carry torpedoes, nuclear depth charges, and other antisubmarine weapons. They also have a helicopter for locating and attacking submarines. In addition, most of these warships carry missiles and one or two guns for defense against air and surface attacks. Modern frigates measure up to 445 feet (135 meters) long. They travel at speeds of 27 to 30 knots.

Some navies have small frigates called *corvettes* to patrol coastal waters. Corvettes measure about 150 feet (45 meters) long. The U.S. Navy does not use corvettes.

Submarines search out and attack enemy submarines and surface ships. Some can also fire missiles at enemy cities and military bases. Modern submarines have nuclear power systems that enable them to remain underwater for months at a time. The U.S. Navy has two principal kinds of submarines, *attack submarines* and *ballistic missile submarines.*

Attack submarines have large sonars for detecting submarines and surface ships from long distances. They carry torpedoes that are fired from tubes inside the hull. In addition, these tubes carry mines that are laid off an enemy coast. Antiship missiles can be fired from torpedo tubes or, on some submarines, from a special launching tube. Attack submarines range in length from about 250 to 360 feet (75 to 110 meters). Some can travel underwater at speeds of more than 30 knots.

Ballistic missile submarines carry long-range missiles that can hit targets up to 4,000 miles (6,400 kilometers) away. These submarines are designed chiefly to attack enemy cities. They also carry torpedoes for defense against enemy surface ships and submarines. Ballistic missile submarines measure from about 380 to 550 feet (115 to 170 meters) long. They reach speeds of more than 20 knots underwater.

Small combatants include such ships as minesweepers, missile boats, and patrol boats. Minesweepers locate and remove underwater explosives. Missile boats carry guided missiles that can attack enemy surface ships from 10 to 60 miles (15 to 95 kilometers) away. Patrol boats guard rivers and coastal waters.

Small combatants are generally operated near coasts. The U.S. Navy has few of these ships because it conducts chiefly long-range ocean operations.

History

Ships have been used in combat for at least 3,000 years. Until the 1600's, however, there were few differences between warships and cargo ships. Any ship that fought in combat might also transport goods or carry explorers on long voyages.

Early warships. The ancient Greek and Roman navies used long, narrow wooden ships called *galleys.* These vessels were powered by oarsmen, who sat in one or more rows on each side. Galleys also had a rectangular sail called a *square sail,* which was used in a favorable wind. The bow ended in a long, sharp point that was rammed into the hull of an enemy ship.

During the A.D. 700's, the Vikings of northern Europe developed the *long ship.* It was powered by rowers and a square sail but weighed only about half as much as a galley. Long ships were strong and seaworthy, and they helped the Vikings control the seas until the 1000's.

Southern Europeans continued to use galleys in battle but gradually stopped attacking by ramming enemy ships. Instead, the rowers maneuvered their galley close to an enemy ship and then boarded it.

By the 1500's, most warships carried guns, and so battles no longer were fought aboard ship. Navies began to use warships as floating gun platforms and replaced galleys with larger, more heavily armed ships.

The age of sailing ships. During the 1500's, Europeans began to build large, heavy sailing ships designed for long ocean voyages by explorers. Such ships included *galleons,* which were also used as warships.

The Spanish Navy built large galleons that sailed high on the water. English galleons were smaller, lower, and easier to maneuver. In 1588, the Spanish Navy tried to invade England. The Spaniards called their fleet the "Invincible Armada" because they were sure it could not be defeated. But the English defeated the Spaniards, partly because their galleons were more maneuverable.

After Spain's defeat, navies began to build specialized fighting ships. These vessels included *capital ships,* an important type of warship during the 1600's and 1700's. Capital ships were fairly easy to maneuver and large enough to carry more than 100 guns. They became known as *ships of the line* because they could serve in the line of battle.

Warships of the 1800's. In 1814, Robert Fulton, an American artist and inventor, built the first steam-powered warship. Navies then began to use warships driven by steam, but the vessels were also powered by sails until the mid-1800's.

Naval guns that fired explosive shells, rather than solid cannon balls, were developed in the 1820's. The shells could easily tear huge holes in the sides of wooden ships. Therefore, navies began to build iron vessels and also *ironclad* ships. The hulls of these vessels were made of wood or iron, and were covered with thick plates of iron. Ironclads could withstand attack far better than wooden ships could. The first battle between these new types of warships occurred in 1862, during the American Civil War. The North's iron *Monitor* fought the South's ironclad *Merrimack* (then called the *Virginia*) at Hampton Roads, Virginia. Neither ship won, but the battle marked the beginning of the age of steel ships. It was also one of the first battles between ships powered only by steam.

Rotating gun turrets were invented in the mid-1800's, and the *Monitor* was the first ship in the U.S. Navy to use them. They enabled guns to be turned in various directions and ended the need for extensive maneuvers by warships. Heavy rifles became standard armament on combat vessels and greatly improved the range and accuracy of naval gunfire.

The birth of the modern battleship. In 1906, the British Navy introduced the *Dreadnought,* the first modern battleship. It was the forerunner of the massive battleships that ruled the seas for more than 35 years. The *Dreadnought* was more powerfully armed and more heavily armored than any earlier warship.

During the early and mid-1900's, navies improved the basic design of the *Dreadnought* to make battleships larger and faster. Better communications methods developed within the ships increased the efficiency of their command. The battleship became the chief combat warship, and nations measured their power in the world by the number of battleships in their navies.

Warships in the two world wars. Battleships were the most powerful warships during World War I (1914-1918). However, the German Navy proved that submarines were also highly effective warships. German submarines, called *U-boats,* sank thousands of Allied merchant ships. These deadly attacks soon led to the development of various antisubmarine ships. After the war, sonar detection equipment was introduced.

Radar was perfected shortly before World War II began in 1939. It enabled warships to locate enemy aircraft and ships at night, through clouds, and at great distances. Improved *gun directors* were developed at

The development of warships

Ships have been used in battle since ancient times. But warships and cargo ships were almost identical until the 1600's, when navies began to build vessels designed only for combat. Today, large navies have many kinds of warships. Each type performs specific functions in battle. These illustrations show the development of some major warships from the 200's B.C. to modern times.

WORLD BOOK illustrations by George Suyeoka

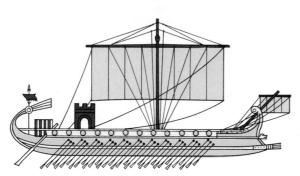

Roman galley (200's B.C.)
About 180 feet (55 meters) long

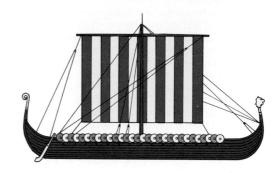

Viking long ship (about A.D. 1000)
About 80 feet (24 meters) long

Galleon (1500's)
About 140 feet (43 meters) long

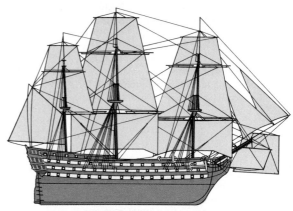

Ship of the line (1700's)
About 220 feet (67 meters) long

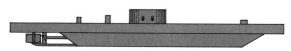

U.S. Civil War iron ship (1860's)
About 170 feet (52 meters) long

U.S. Civil War ironclad ship (1860's)
About 270 feet (82 meters) long

about the same time. They quickly tracked moving aircraft and directed gunfire at them. Gun directors were used with *proximity fuzes,* which exploded a shell as it neared its target and eliminated the need for a direct hit.

Aircraft became the most effective military weapons of World War II. The importance of battleships declined, and navies began to concentrate on building aircraft carriers. They also built large numbers of cruisers and destroyers to protect the carriers and installed antiaircraft weapons on all warships.

The U.S. Navy built thousands of amphibious warfare ships during World War II. One type, the *landing ship—tank (LST)*, carried tanks and landed them on enemy beaches. Other amphibious warfare ships carried

troops, landing craft, and military supplies. Still others used guns, mortars, and rockets to bombard enemy beaches before invasions.

Warships in the nuclear age. After World War II ended in 1945, the U.S. Navy began to develop nuclear-powered warships. It launched the first nuclear-powered submarine, the *Nautilus,* in 1954. The *Nautilus* could travel much faster than the diesel-powered submarines then in use. Its nuclear power system also enabled the submarine to travel hundreds of thousands of miles underwater without refueling. Shortly after the *Nautilus* went to sea, the Soviet Union completed its first nuclear submarine. The navies of Great Britain, France, and China have also built nuclear submarines.

WORLD BOOK illustrations by George Suyeoka and Kim Downing

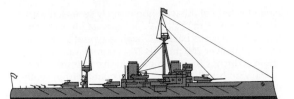

Dreadnought battleship (early 1900's)
About 500 feet (150 meters) long

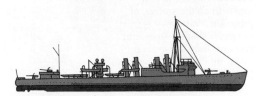

World War I destroyer (early 1900's)
About 300 feet (90 meters) long

World War II battleship (1940's)
About 500 feet (150 meters) long

World War II submarine (1940's)
About 300 feet (90 meters) long

Amphibious assault ship (currently in service)
About 840 feet (255 meters) long

Coastal minesweeper (1950's)
About 150 feet (45 meters) long

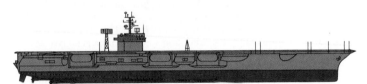

Aircraft carrier (currently in service)
About 1,000 feet (300 meters) long

Missile boat (1970's)
About 130 feet (40 meters) long

Guided-missile destroyer (currently in service)
About 470 feet (140 meters) long

Attack submarine (currently in service)
About 350 feet (110 meters) long

Powerful, long-range guided missiles also increased the capabilities of warships. These missiles can be launched from almost every kind of warship. In the late 1950's, the United States Navy developed the first submarine that could launch ballistic missiles while submerged.

During the 1960's, the U.S. Navy built the first nuclear-powered surface ships. In the 1970's, U.S. warships began to use gas turbine engines. These engines operated almost as effectively in surface ships as did nuclear power systems, and they cost much less. In the 1980's, the U.S. Navy modernized and reactivated several World War II battleships. All of these ships were decommissioned during the 1990's. Norman Polmar

Related articles in *World Book* include:

Kinds of ships

Aircraft carrier	Destroyer	Missile boat
Amphibious ship	Frigate	Privateer
Battleship	Galleon	PT boat
Cruiser	Galley	Submarine

Famous warships

Alabama	Constellation	Graf Spee	Monitor and
Bismarck	Constitution	Maine	Merrimack

Other related articles

Depth charge	Navy	Sonar
Guided missile	Navy, United States	Torpedo
Mine warfare	Radar	V/STOL

Wart is a hard, rough growth on the surface of the skin. Warts may appear in many shapes, sizes, and places. They can even appear on the lips or tongue. On moist parts of the body, such as the genitals, warts may grow into masses like tiny cauliflowers. Warts that grow on the sole of the foot look like corns and make walking painful. Warts on the face may form little beardlike projections.

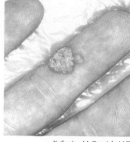

Katherine M. Ozanich, M.D.

Warts are hard, rough growths on the skin. They may appear on the hands, face, or other areas.

Warts result from infection by certain viruses. The viruses live in cells of the surface layer of the skin and do not infect the underlying tissue. The thickened surface layer forms folds into which little blood vessels grow. If a wart is scratched open, the virus may spread by contact to another part of the body or to another person.

More than 65 types of wart viruses can infect human beings. These viruses do not infect animals, and animal wart viruses do not infect people. Contrary to superstition, touching the skin of a toad will not cause warts.

Warts are common in children, and they usually affect the hands, arms, and legs. Most such warts disappear by the time the individual reaches age 20. Later in life, the appearance of many warts may be a sign of decreased immunity in patients with cancer or the human immunodeficiency virus (HIV, the virus that causes AIDS).

Many warts go away without treatment, perhaps because the body develops immunity to the virus. Physicians often remove warts by heating them with an electric needle or with a laser, or by freezing the wart tissue. Such treatments often require a local anesthetic to decrease the pain. Home remedies that apply chemicals to the skin often do not remove all the wart tissue, and the wart grows back in the same place. Paul R. Bergstresser

Wart hog is an African pig with large, curved tusks protruding from its huge, flattened head. These tusks may be as much as 2 feet (61 centimeters) long. Between the tusks and the eyes are three pairs of large "warts" from which the hog gets its name. The coarsely grained,

Leonard Lee Rue III, Tom Stack & Assoc.

The wart hog is named for the "warts" on its head.

pale gray hide of the wart hog is thinly sprinkled with stiff, brownish-gray hairs. A thin mane of long, bristly hair hangs over its back and head. A typical large boar may weigh over 200 pounds (91 kilograms) and measure about 30 inches (76 centimeters) high at the shoulder.

The wart hog lives in dry, sandy country from southern Africa northward to the region just south of the Sahara desert. It prefers open forest with plenty of thickets for protection. The wart hog travels in small family groups. Old boars, however, usually live by themselves. The sow may produce as many as six to eight young at a time. Ordinarily, only half that number are born at one time. Wart hogs often enlarge and use burrows made by other animals. They eat roots, plants, birds' eggs, and even small mammals. Duane A. Schlitter

Scientific classification. The wart hog belongs to the pig family, Suidae. Its scientific name is *Phacochoerus aethiopicus.*

Warwick, *WAWR ihk* or *WAWR wihk* (pop. 85,808), is Rhode Island's second largest city and a commercial center. Only Providence has more people. Warwick lies on Greenwich Bay, in east-central Rhode Island. For its location, see **Rhode Island** (political map). Warwick, Providence, and Fall River form a metropolitan area with 1,188,613 people.

Warwick is the home of the Warwick Musical Theater. Its industries produce textiles and metal products. Warwick is the headquarters for a division of an insurance company. The Theodore Francis Green State Airport, Rhode Island's largest airport, is in Warwick. Narragansett Bay, a popular sailing and fishing area, is nearby. Warwick received its city charter in 1931. It has a mayor-council form of government. Stanford E. Demars

Warwick, *WAWR ihk,* **Earl of** (1428-1471), was a famous English soldier and statesman. He is known as the *Kingmaker* and has been called *Last of the Barons.*

Warwick was one of the most powerful men in England during the Wars of the Roses. These wars were fought between two branches of the English royal family—the House of Lancaster and the House of York. The conflict began when nobles of the House of York came together in an attempt to overthrow King Henry VI, who was of the House of Lancaster.

Warwick helped command the victorious York army at the Battle of St. Albans in 1455. In 1460, Warwick won the Battle of Northampton, capturing King Henry VI. But later in the year the Yorkists were defeated at Wakefield. The Duke of York was captured and killed. Warwick became head of the Yorkists as guardian of his cousin, Prince Edward.

Another battle was fought at St. Albans in 1461, and Warwick was defeated. But he boldly proclaimed Edward, the Duke of York, King Edward IV of England. Later in 1461, Edward and Warwick decisively defeated the Lancastrians in the Battle of Towton. But Edward and Warwick soon quarreled. In 1470, an army led by Warwick invaded England from France and forced King Edward to flee. Warwick then restored Queen Margaret and Henry VI to the throne. But in 1471, Warwick met Edward in battle again, at Barnet, and was killed. Warwick's given and family name was Richard Neville.

John Gillingham

Warwick, Guy of. See Guy of Warwick.

Wasatch Range, *WAW sach,* is a mountain range that extends about 160 miles (257 kilometers) between southern Idaho and central Utah. Its western face, known as the Wasatch Front, forms the western edge of the Rocky Mountains and the eastern rim of the Great Basin (see **Utah** [terrain map]). Most Utahns live just west of the range.

The range's average elevation is 10,000 feet (3,000 meters). The highest peak, Mount Nebo, rises 11,928 feet (3,636 meters) in the southern part of the range. Vegetation includes sagebrush and grasses at the lower levels and aspen, fir, mahogany, maple, and spruce trees at higher elevations. Little vegetation grows above 10,500 feet (3,200 meters). Annual snowfall usually ranges from 200 inches (510 centimeters) to well over 510 inches (1,397 centimeters). Most of the range is managed as national forestland. Camping, hiking, and skiing are popular recreational activities.   Dale J. Stevens

See also **Salt Lake City** (picture).

Washakie, *WAHSH uh kee* (1804?-1900), was a chief of the eastern Shoshone Indians in Utah and Wyoming. He was known for his friendliness toward white people and for his relentless warfare against his Indian enemies.

In the 1840's, Washakie furnished aid to many immigrants moving west over the Oregon Trail. In the 1850's, he aided Mormon settlers in the Utah Territory. In 1876, he sent Shoshone warriors to General George Crook to serve as scouts against the Sioux Indians. Washakie spent his later years negotiating for lands and rights for his people on the Wind River Reservation in Wyoming. He renounced many Indian customs and joined the Protestant Episcopal Church.   Jerome A. Greene

Wyoming State Museum
Washakie

Washing machine is a machine that quickly washes clothes, linens, and other items. Before its invention, people spent hours doing their laundry by hand. Some people soaked their clothes in streams and then beat them with rocks to get out the dirt. Later, people scrubbed their laundry on washboards. People in some parts of the world still use such methods.

Most washing machines work automatically. The operator simply puts in laundry, pours in detergent, and sets the controls. One set of controls determines whether the machine uses hot, warm, or cold water. The water enters the machine through hoses connected to hot and cold water pipes. The operator also sets controls to select the length of washing and rinsing time and the amount of water that enters the machine. The machine, which is powered by an electric motor, then operates automatically. Many automatic washing machines have special features, such as filters that remove lint, and dispensers for bleach and fabric softener.

Most automatic washers have an inner tub that is surrounded by an outer tub. The washing takes place in the inner tub, which is called the *basket.* After the laundry has been washed and rinsed, the basket begins to spin rapidly. The spinning removes most of the water from the various items and throws it into the outer tub. The water is then pumped out of the machine through a drain hose.

There are two types of automatic washers, *agitator machines* and *tumbler machines.* Most automatic washers are agitator machines. The operator of an agitator machine puts in laundry by lifting the lid. Inside the machine, a cone-shaped device called an *agitator* is mounted in the center of the basket. Most agitators have several projections called *fins.* As the agitator rotates, it continually reverses direction. This action moves the laundry through the water and forces water through the items. A tumbler machine is loaded through a door on the front of the machine. The basket revolves, and the laundry tumbles through the water.

One of the first mechanical washers was patented about 1860 by Hamilton E. Smith of Philadelphia. A crank on this machine turned paddles inside, pushing the laundry through the water. An electric-powered washer was invented in 1910, and an automatic washing machine was introduced in 1937.   Evan Powell

How an agitator washing machine works

Hot- and cold-water inlet hoses

Controls

Agitator

Inner tub

Outer tub

Drain hose

Drain pump

Drain outlet hose to sewer

Drive mechanism

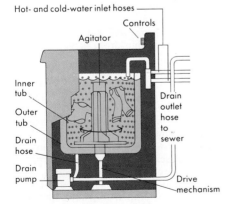

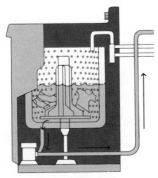

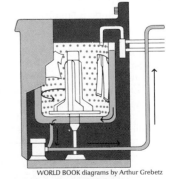

WORLD BOOK diagrams by Arthur Grebetz

Washing begins after water fills the tubs. The action of the agitator moves the laundry and forces water through it.

Rinsing occurs after the wash water is pumped out of the tubs. After the rinsing process, the rinse water is pumped out.

Spin drying. As the inner tub spins, excess water from the laundry goes into the outer tub. The water is then pumped out.

Seattle, the largest city in Washington, is an important manufacturing and trade center of the Pacific Northwest. Mount Rainier, Washington's highest peak, rises southeast of the city.

Washington   *The Evergreen State*

Washington is the only state of the United States named for one of the nation's Presidents. It was named in honor of George Washington. The state lies on the Pacific Coast in the northwestern part of the country. Its location makes it a gateway for land, sea, and air travel to Alaska and to Asian countries across the Pacific Ocean.

Washington is famous for scenery of breathtaking beauty and sharp contrasts. High mountains rise above evergreen forests and sparkling coastal waters. The junglelike forests of the Olympic Peninsula in the west are among the rainiest places in the world. But the flat semidesert land that lies east of the Cascade Mountains stretches for long distances without a single tree.

Snow-covered peaks tower above the foothills and lowlands around them. Mount Rainier, the highest mountain in the state, appears to "float" on the horizon

The contributors of this article are Ronald Reed Boyce, Professor at the School of Social and Behavioral Sciences at Seattle Pacific University; and Robert C. Carriker, Professor of History at Gonzaga University.

southeast of Seattle and Tacoma. On a clear day, persons in the Seattle area can also see Mount Baker to the north, the Olympic Mountains to the west, and the Cascades to the east. Lodges and chair lifts in the mountains attract thousands of tourists and skiers.

Washington's coastline has several bays and inlets that make excellent harbors. Ships from all parts of the world dock at Bellingham, Seattle, Tacoma, and other ports on Puget Sound. Washington also has important shipping centers on the Pacific Ocean and the Columbia River. Washington fishing fleets catch salmon, halibut, and other fishes in the chilly waters off the northern Pacific Coast. The state is famous for seafoods, especially chinook and sockeye salmon.

Washington's nickname, the *Evergreen State*, comes from its many firs, hemlocks, pines, and other evergreen trees. Washington has large areas of thick forests, especially on the western slopes of the Cascades. The state produces large amounts of lumber, pulp and paper, and other wood products. The state's nickname also suggests the lush green lowlands found in western Washington. A mild, moist climate makes this region excellent

Rain forests in Olympic National Park, with moss-covered trees and thick undergrowth, look like tropical jungles.

A. D. Lodwick, Black Star

Interesting facts about Washington

WORLD BOOK illustrations by Kevin Chadwick

One of the world's foremost aircraft and spacecraft manufacturers, the Boeing Company, has assembly and research facilities in Washington. Boeing produced the booster rocket for the Apollo/Saturn 5 moon landing of 1969; the lunar roving vehicle, which transported astronauts and equipment on the moon; and the Mariner 10 spacecraft, which flew by Mercury and Venus in 1974.

Boeing aircraft and spacecraft

The first municipal monorail service in the United States began operating in Seattle in 1962. It was built to connect the World's Fair with downtown Seattle.

The city of George, Washington, has streets named after varieties of cherries, such as Bing and Maraschino avenues.

First monorail

Father's Day, first celebrated on June 19, 1910, was originated by Sonora Louise Smart Dodd of Spokane.

The greatest snowfall in North America in one season occurred at Rainier Paradise Ranger Station. A total of 1,122 inches (2,850 centimeters) fell from July 1971 through June 1972.

---

for dairy farming and for growing flower bulbs.

East of the Cascades, farmers raise livestock and wheat on large ranches. They grow fruits and vegetables in fertile, irrigated river valleys such as the Okanogan, Wenatchee, and Yakima. Apples produced in these areas are a Washington specialty. Washington leads the states in apple production.

Giant dams on the Columbia River and its tributaries capture water for irrigation and power. The largest dam, Grand Coulee, is one of the engineering wonders of the world. Irrigation water is transforming the Columbia Basin, where farmers raise large crops of vegetables on land that once was dry and bare.

High-technology manufacturing and services play an important part in Washington's economy. The Boeing Company, a leading producer of commercial airliners and spacecraft, has several assembly and research facilities in King and Snohomish counties. Microsoft Corporation, the world's largest computer software developer, has its headquarters in Redmond.

Olympia is the capital of Washington. Seattle is the state's largest city.

Antje Gunnar, Bruce Coleman Inc.

The San Juan Islands, which lie near Canada's Vancouver Island, are noted for their scenic beauty. Vacation resorts on the islands attract many visitors.

Washington in brief

Symbols of Washington

The state flag, first adopted in 1923, bears the state seal. The flag's green field stands for Washington's forests. The seal, first adopted in 1889, has a likeness of George Washington, for whom the state was named. The first seal used a postage stamp for the likeness of Washington. Both the flag and seal were readopted in 1967 when a portrait for the seal by Gilbert Stuart, an American artist, was approved by the state legislature.

State flag

State seal

Washington (brown) ranks 20th in size among all the states and is the smallest of the Pacific Coast States (yellow).

The state capitol, called the Legislative Building, is in Olympia. Olympia has been the state capital since Washington became a state in 1889.

General information

Statehood: Nov. 11, 1889, the 42nd state.
State abbreviations: Wash. (traditional), WA (postal).
State motto: *Alki* (An Indian word for *Bye and Bye*).
State song: "Washington, My Home." Words and music by Helen Davis.

Land and climate

Area: 68,126 mi² (176,446 km²), including 1,545 mi² (4,001 km²) of inland water but excluding 2,511 mi² (6,503 km²) of coastal water.
Elevation: *Highest*—Mount Rainier, 14,410 ft (4,392 m) above sea level. *Lowest*—sea level along the coast.
Coastline: 157 mi (253 km).
Record high temperature: 118 °F (48 °C) in Grant County on July 24, 1928, and at Ice Harbor Dam on Aug. 5, 1961.
Record low temperature: −48 °F (−44 °C) at Mazama and at Winthrop on Dec. 30, 1968.
Average July temperature: 66 °F (19 °C).
Average January temperature: 30 °F (−1 °C).
Average yearly precipitation: 38 in (97 cm).

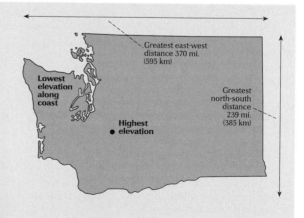

Greatest east-west distance 370 mi. (595 km)

Lowest elevation along coast

Greatest north-south distance 239 mi. (385 km)

Highest
● elevation

Important dates

1775	**1792**	**1810**	**1846**

George Vancouver surveyed the coast of Washington and Puget Sound.

A treaty between the United States and Britain established Washington's boundary at the 49th parallel.

Bruno Heceta and Juan Francisco de la Bodega y Quadra of Spain made the first landing by Europeans at Washington.

A British-Canadian fur-trading post was established near present-day Spokane.

State bird
Willow goldfinch

State flower
Coast rhododendron

State tree
Western hemlock

People

Population: 5,894,121
Rank among the states: 15th
Density: 87 per mi^2 (33 per km^2), U.S. average 78 per mi^2 (30 per km^2)
Distribution: 82 percent urban, 18 percent rural

Largest cities in Washington

Seattle	563,374
Spokane	195,629
Tacoma	193,556
Vancouver	143,560
Bellevue	109,569
Everett	91,488

Source: 2000 census.

Population trend

Millions

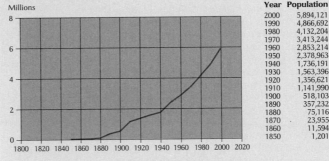

Year	Population
2000	5,894,121
1990	4,866,692
1980	4,132,204
1970	3,413,244
1960	2,853,214
1950	2,378,963
1940	1,736,191
1930	1,563,396
1920	1,356,621
1910	1,141,990
1900	518,103
1890	357,232
1880	75,116
1870	23,955
1860	11,594
1850	1,201

Source: U.S. Census Bureau.

Economy

Chief products

Agriculture: apples, beef cattle, flower bulbs, milk, timber, wheat.
Manufacturing: transportation equipment, computer and electronic products, food products, paper products, wood products.
Mining: sand and gravel, coal.

Gross state product

Value of goods and services produced in 2000: $219,938,000,000. *Services* include community, business, and personal services; finance; government; trade; and transportation, communication, and utilities. *Industry* includes construction, manufacturing, and mining. *Agriculture* includes agriculture, fishing, and forestry.

Source: U.S. Bureau of Economic Analysis.

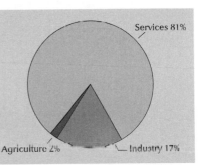

Services 81%
Agriculture 2%
Industry 17%

Government

State government

Governor: 4-year term
State senators: 49; 4-year terms
State representatives: 98; 2-year terms
Counties: 39

Federal government

United States senators: 2
United States representatives: 9
Electoral votes: 11

Sources of information

For information about tourism, write to: Office of Trade and Economic Development, Tourism, P.O. Box 42500, Olympia, WA 98504-2500. The Web site at www.experiencewashington.com also provides information.
For information on the economy, write to: Office of Trade and Economic Development, Business Development, P.O. Box 42500, Olympia, WA 98504-2500.
The state's official Web site at access.wa.gov also provides a gateway to much information on Washington's economy, government, and history.

The Northern Pacific Railroad linked Washington and the East.

1883   **1889**   **1942**   **1980**

Grand Coulee Dam was completed.

Washington became the 42nd state on November 11.

Mount St. Helens volcano erupted, causing 57 deaths and enormous damage in southwestern Washington.

Population. The 2000 United States census reported that Washington had 5,894,121 people. The state's population had increased 21 percent over the 1990 census figure, 4,866,692. According to the 2000 census, Washington ranks 15th in population among the 50 states.

About 83 percent of the people of Washington live in metropolitan areas (see **Metropolitan area**). About two-fifths of Washington's people live in the Seattle metropolitan area in the western part of the state. Washington has nine metropolitan areas entirely or partly within the state. For the names and populations of these areas, see the *Index* to the political map of Washington.

Most of the larger Washington cities are in the western part of the state along Puget Sound. Seattle, the state's largest city, is in this region. It serves as an important shipping and manufacturing center. Tacoma, an industrial and port city, is about 28 miles (45 kilometers) south of Seattle. Vancouver, which is part of the Portland (Oregon)-Vancouver metropolitan area, is one of the fastest-growing cities in the United States.

Most of the cities in eastern Washington developed as centers for farm trade, lumbering, or mining. Spokane, the largest eastern city, is an important railroad, manufacturing, grain, and financial center. The "Tri-Cities" of Richland, Pasco, and Kennewick in south-central Washington grew in size and importance after World War II (1939-1945). During the war, the Hanford nuclear energy center was established nearby.

More than 7 percent of the state's residents are of Hispanic origin. Asian Americans make up over 5 percent of the population. African Americans account for about 3 percent. Washington has more than 90,000 American Indians. Many of them live on the state's 27 reservations.

Population density

Most of the larger cities in Washington are located in the western part of the state along Puget Sound. About 40 percent of the people live in the Seattle metropolitan area.

Persons per sq. mi.	Persons per km²
More than 100	More than 40
25 to 100	10 to 40
10 to 25	4 to 10
Less than 10	Less than 4

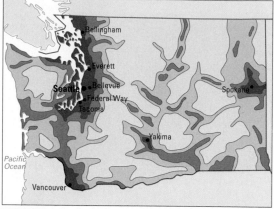

WORLD BOOK map; based on U.S. Census Bureau data.

The state's largest population groups include people of German, English, Irish, Norwegian, French, Swedish, Scottish, and Italian descent. Ten percent of the state's residents were born in other countries. The largest groups have come from East Asia, Canada, and Mexico.

Schools. The first school in Washington opened at Old Fort Vancouver in 1832. It was established for the

Joel W. Rogers, Earth Images

An Indian worker shovels herring into a loading net in Bellingham. More than 90,000 American Indians live in Washington. Many of them live on the state's 27 reservations.

Pacific Science Center

The Pacific Science Center, in Seattle, features exhibits of modern science. These children are experimenting with one of the center's many scientific demonstrations.

children of employees of the Hudson's Bay Company, a British trading firm. In the 1830's, missionaries began teaching Indians in eastern Washington near present-day Spokane and Walla Walla. These early teachers included Marcus Whitman and his wife, Narcissa, and Cushing Eells, Henry Spalding, and Elkanah Walker. In 1859, Whitman College, Washington's first private institution of higher learning, was founded in Walla Walla. The state's first public university, the University of Washington, was founded in 1861. A statewide public school system began in 1895. A law passed that year provided state financial support for Washington's schools.

An elected state superintendent of public instruction and a State Board of Education supervise Washington's public school system. Children ages 8 to 18 must attend school. For the number of students and teachers in Washington, see **Education** (table).

Libraries. Washington's oldest library, the State Library in Olympia, began in 1853 as the Territorial Library. Today, in addition to public libraries in many cities, county and regional library systems also exist. The State Library serves state government as well as public libraries and citizens. The Seattle Public Library has collections on the Pacific Northwest and Seattle's history. Many Washington colleges and universities also include outstanding libraries. The University of Washington libraries have major collections on Pacific Northwest history, the lumber industry, architecture, and other topics.

Museums. The Burke Museum of Natural History and Culture on the campus of the University of Washington features exhibits on the natural and cultural history of the Pacific Northwest. Museums with relics of Washington history include the Northwest Museum of Arts and Culture in Spokane, the Washington State Historical Society in Tacoma, the Museum of History and Industry in Seattle, and the State Capital Museum in Olympia.

The Seattle Art Museum has a fine collection of Asian art and works by Pacific Northwest artists. The Frye Art Museum in Seattle displays American and European paintings. The Maryhill Museum of Art in Goldendale has an excellent collection of items of European royalty. The Pacific Science Center in Seattle has exhibits on modern science. Seattle's Museum of Flight has an outstanding collection of items related to aviation history.

David R. Frazier

Washington State University is in Pullman. Bryan Hall, *shown here,* houses the university's philosophy department and is the center of a program for international students.

Universities and colleges

This table lists the universities and colleges in Washington that grant bachelor's or advanced degrees and are accredited by the Northwest Association of Schools and Colleges.

Name	Mailing address
Antioch University Seattle	Seattle
Argosy University	Seattle
Bastyr University	Kenmore
Central Washington University	Ellensburg
City University	Bellevue
Cornish College of the Arts	Seattle
DeVry University	*
Eastern Washington University	Cheney
Evergreen State College	Olympia
Gonzaga University	Spokane
Henry Cogswell College	Everett
Heritage College	Toppenish
Northwest College	Kirkland
Pacific Lutheran University	Tacoma
Puget Sound, University of	Tacoma
St. Martin's College	Lacey
Seattle Pacific University	Seattle
Seattle University	Seattle
Trinity Lutheran College	Issaquah
Walla Walla College	College Place
Walla Walla Community College	Walla Walla
Washington-Seattle, University of	Seattle
Washington State University	Pullman
Western Washington University	Bellingham
Whitman College	Walla Walla
Whitworth College	Spokane

* Campuses at Bellevue and Federal Way.

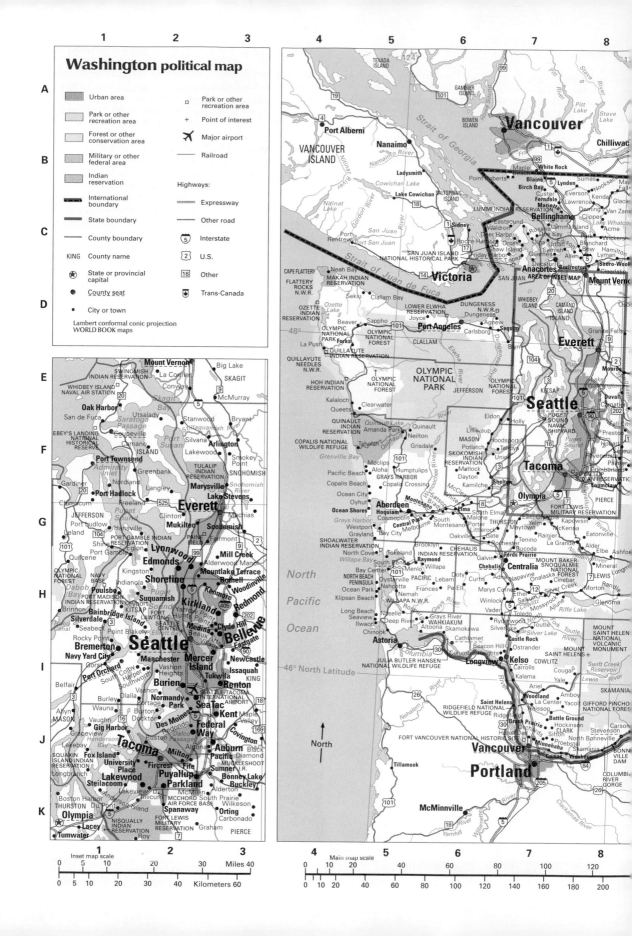

Washington political map

Legend:

- Urban area
- Park or other recreation area
- Forest or other conservation area
- Military or other federal area
- Indian reservation
- International boundary
- State boundary
- County boundary
- KING County name
- ⊛ State or provincial capital
- ● County seat
- • City or town

- □ Park or other recreation area
- + Point of interest
- ✈ Major airport
- ━ Railroad

Highways:
- Expressway
- Other road
- ⑤ Interstate
- ② U.S.
- 16 Other
- Trans-Canada

Lambert conformal conic projection
WORLD BOOK maps

Inset map scale
0 5 10 20 30 Miles 40
0 5 10 20 30 40 Kilometers 60

Main map scale
0 10 20 40 60 80 100 120
0 10 20 40 60 80 100 120 140 160 180 200

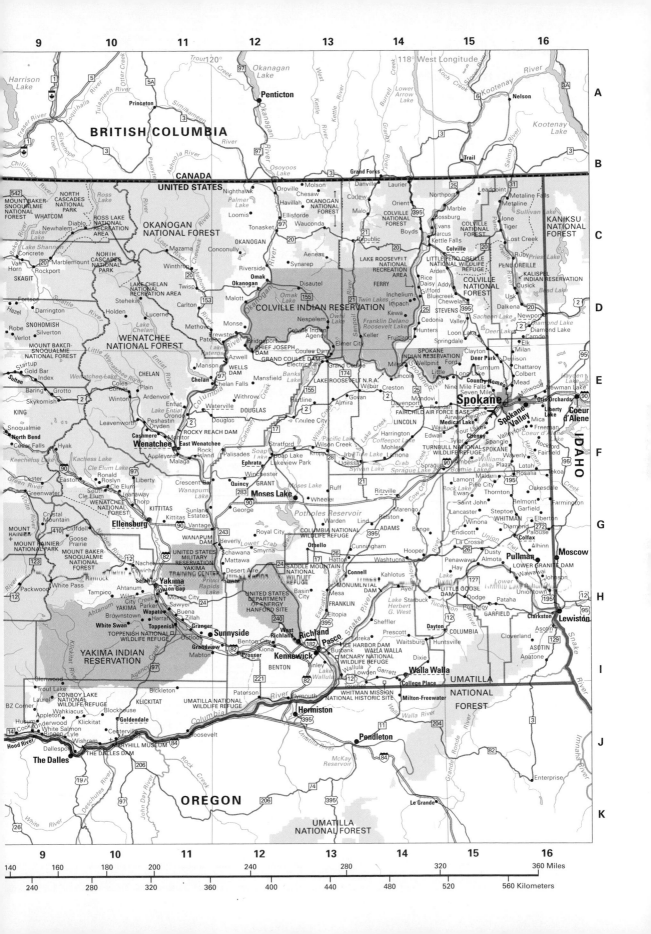

Washington map index

*Does not appear on map; key shows general location.
†Census designated place—unincorporated, but recognized as a significant settled community by the U.S. Census Bureau.
‡The city of Spokane Valley, when incorporated in 2003, absorbed the communities marked by §.

°County seat.
Places without population figures are unincorporated.
Source: 2000 census.

James P. Rowan

Tacoma, Washington's third largest city, rises behind shipyards on Puget Sound. Washington ranks as a leading shipbuilding center. Seattle and Bremerton also have major shipyards.

Washington is a paradise for people who enjoy the outdoors. Its richly diverse environment offers a wide variety of warm- and cold-weather activities, including camping, fishing, boating, and hunting. Every winter and spring, skiers flock to the slopes of Mount Spokane and areas in the Cascade Range such as Crystal Mountain, Mission Ridge, Mount Baker, Mount Rainier, Snoqualmie Pass, Stevens Pass, and White Pass. In summer, rugged mountains and wilderness areas attract hikers and mountain climbers.

Washington's many annual events include Indian festivals, flower exhibitions, sports competitions, and regional fairs. Perhaps the outstanding annual event is Seafair, held in Seattle from mid-July through early August. This show features parades, water carnivals, and hydroplane races on Lake Washington.

Owen Blauman, Seattle Seafair

Hydroplane race at the Seattle Seafair

Places to visit

Following are brief descriptions of some of Washington's many interesting places to visit:

Grand Coulee Dam, 92 miles (148 kilometers) west of Spokane, is the largest concrete dam in the United States (see **Grand Coulee Dam**).

Lewis and Clark Interpretive Center, near Ilwaco, features maps and paintings illustrating the Lewis and Clark expedition between Missouri and the Pacific Coast.

Maryhill Museum, near Goldendale, is an art museum in an elaborate mansion built in 1926 by multimillionaire Samuel Hill. The gray stone structure stands on a high bluff overlooking the scenic Columbia River Gorge.

Mount St. Helens National Volcanic Monument consists of 110,000 acres (44,500 hectares) of land set aside by the Forest Service. The monument includes Mount St. Helens and nearby areas that were damaged by the effects of the volcano's eruptions. There also is a visitors center.

Point Defiance Park, in Tacoma, has a zoo, an aquarium, an Oriental garden, and replicas of an old fort and a logging camp.

Seattle Center includes the Pacific Science Center from Century 21, a world's fair held in 1962. The Space Needle, a tower 605 feet (184 meters) high, is in the area. It has an observation deck. A monorail links the center and downtown Seattle.

National parks and forests. Washington has three national parks—Mount Rainier, North Cascades, and Olympic. These parks include some of the country's most scenic areas. Part of Klondike Gold Rush National Historical Park is in Washington.

The other part is in Alaska. Washington has eight national forests. Six of them lie entirely within the state. They are Okanogan, Gifford Pinchot, Mount Baker-Snoqualmie, Wenatchee, Olympic, and Colville. Kaniksu National Forest is shared by Washington, Idaho, and Montana. Umatilla National Forest, in the Blue Mountains, lies in both Washington and Oregon. Several areas in Washington's national forests are set aside as national wilderness areas, to be preserved in their natural condition. For the area and chief features of each national park, see **National Park System**. See also the separate articles on the national parks.

National historic sites. Whitman Mission National Historic Site marks the spot of the Indian mission founded by Marcus Whitman and his wife in 1836. It was also the scene of the Indian massacre of 1847 in which the Whitmans and others lost their lives. The place became a national monument in 1936, and a historic site in 1963. See **Whitman Mission National Historic Site**. Fort Vancouver National Historic Site was the western headquarters of the Hudson's Bay Company from 1825 to 1849. Established in 1948 as a national monument, the area became a national historic site in 1961. Ebey's Landing National Historical Reserve, on Whidbey Island, has forts built in the 1890's and 1940's.

State parks. Washington has over a hundred developed parks and historic and geologic sites under the administration of the state parks and recreation commission. The park system includes several undeveloped tracts. For information on state parks, write to Director, Washington State Parks and Recreation Commission, 7150 Cleanwater Lane, Olympia, WA 98504.

Annual events

January-May

International Boat Show in Seattle (January); Northwest Bach Festival in Spokane (January); Annual Gray Whale Migration in Westport and Ocean Shores (March); Daffodil Festival in Tacoma (March); Tacoma Dome Boat Show in Tacoma (April); Apple Blossom Festival in Wenatchee (late April and early May); Lilac Festival in Spokane (May); Rhododendron Festival in Port Townsend (late May).

June-August

Outboard Hydroplane Races in Electric City (June); Toppenish Indian Pow Wow in Toppenish (July 3-4); Pacific Northwest Arts and Crafts Fair in Bellevue (July); King County Fair in Enumclaw (July); Omak Stampede and Suicide Race (August).

September-December

Ellensburg Rodeo (early September); Western Washington State Fair in Puyallup (September); Autumn Leaf Festival in Leavenworth (late September and early October); Yule Log Festival in Poulsbo (December).

Cindy McIntyre, West Stock

Japanese Garden at Point Defiance Park in Tacoma

Crystal Mountain ski area

Don Mason, West Stock

© Steve Balum, Bruce Coleman Inc.

Ruby Beach at Olympic National Park

Land regions. Washington has six main land regions: (1) the Olympic Mountains, (2) the Coast Range, (3) the Puget Sound Lowland, (4) the Cascade Mountains, (5) the Columbia Plateau, and (6) the Rocky Mountains.

The Olympic Mountains region lies in the northwest corner of the state. It is bordered by the Strait of Juan de Fuca on the north and the Pacific Ocean on the west. Most of the region lies within Olympic National Park. The rugged snow-capped Olympic Mountains are one of the wildest parts of the United States. Some areas of these mountains have never been explored. The chief industry in the region is logging in the foothills of the mountains.

The Coast Range region covers the southwestern corner of Washington and extends southward into Oregon. The Willapa Hills, which overlook Willapa Bay, are the chief land feature of this region in Washington. Logging and lumber milling are the region's most important economic activities. Many people also work in fishing and dairying.

The Puget Sound Lowland region is wedged between the Olympic Mountains on the west and the Cascade Mountains on the east. It extends northward into British Columbia and southward into Oregon. The valley of the Chehalis River is also part of the region. The valley extends westward to the Pacific Ocean between the Willapa Hills on the south and the Olympic Mountains on the north.

Puget Sound, a huge bay almost completely enclosed by land, covers the north-central part of the lowland region. The Strait of Juan de Fuca connects Puget Sound with the Pacific Ocean. Narrow, twisting branches of the sound extend far inland. These branches reach south to the cities of Tacoma and Olympia.

About three-fourths of Washington's people live on the lowland plain. The plain has about three-fifths of the state's cities, and most of its factories and sawmills.

The Cascade Mountains region, east of the Puget Sound Lowland, separates the western section of the state from the eastern section. The Cascade Mountains of Washington are part of a long mountain range that stretches southward from British Columbia into northern California. The peaks of several volcanoes rise above the main chain of mountains. Most of these volcanoes

are inactive. However, Mount St. Helens in southwestern Washington erupted violently in 1980. Its elevation is 8,364 feet (2,549 meters).

Mount Rainier, the highest point in the state and one of the highest mountains in the United States, is a long-quiet volcano. It rises 14,410 feet (4,392 meters). Other high peaks include Mount Adams (12,307 feet, or 3,751 meters); Mount Baker (10,778 feet, or 3,285 meters); and Glacier Peak (10,541 feet, or 3,213 meters). All these mountains have glaciers and permanent snowfields on their upper slopes. Farther down the slopes, and on the lower mountains, are magnificent forests. Tall Douglas-fir trees grow on the rainy western slopes. Most of the forested area lies within national forests.

The Columbia Plateau covers most of central and southeastern Washington. This great basin lies from 500 to 2,000 feet (150 to 610 meters) or more above sea level, and is surrounded by a rim of higher lands. It makes up part of the largest lava plateau in the world. The basin was formed by lava which flowed out of cracks in the earth's crust thousands of years ago.

Interesting features of the Columbia Plateau are its *coulees* and *scablands,* especially in the Big Bend region. This area lies south and east of a great bend in the Columbia River. Coulees are trenchlike dry canyons with steep walls. They were formed thousands of years ago, when glaciers blocked the Columbia River. Rushing streams of river water and melting ice cut new channels across the lava plateau. After the glacial period ended,

Land regions of Washington

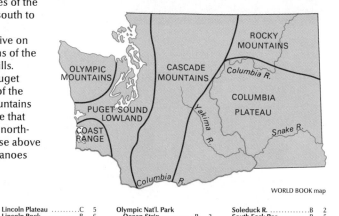

WORLD BOOK map

Map index

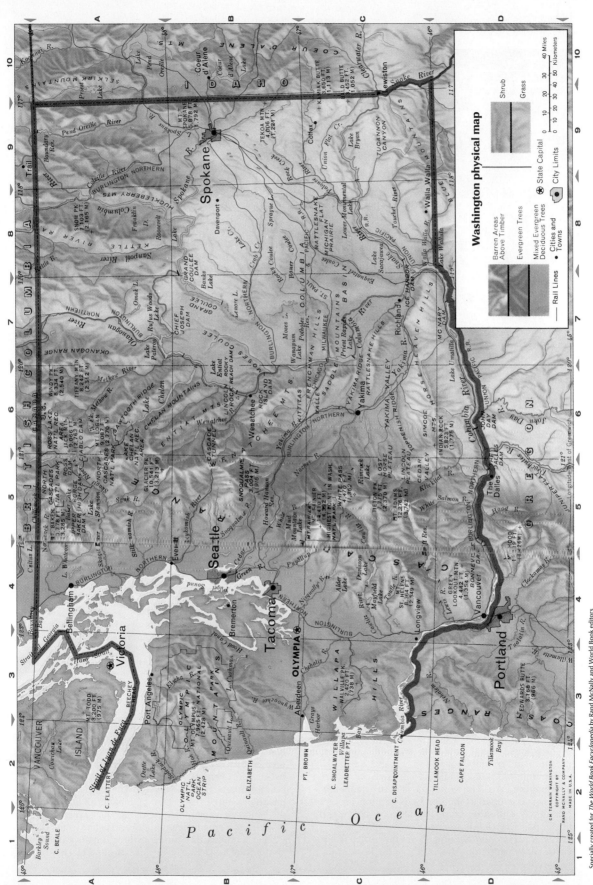

Washington physical map

Barren Areas
Above Timber

Evergreen Trees

Mixed Evergreen
Deciduous Trees

Shrub

Grass

Rail Lines

⊛ State Capital

● Cities and
Towns

⬡ City Limits

0   10   20   30   40 Miles
0 10 20 30 40 50 Kilometers

Specially created for *The World Book Encyclopedia* by Rand McNally and World Book editors

CM TERRAIN WASHINGTON
COPYRIGHT BY
RAND McNALLY & COMPANY
MADE IN U.S.A.

Pacific Ocean

BRITISH COLUMBIA

IDAHO

OREGON

Spokane

Seattle

Tacoma

OLYMPIA

Portland

Vancouver

Victoria

Bellingham

Doug Wilson, Black Star

Washington apples are famous throughout the United States. The state is the nation's leading producer of apples. Most are grown in the irrigated valleys of central Washington.

the Columbia settled into its present course. The other streams dried up, leaving empty canyons. Grand Coulee and Moses Coulee are the chief dry canyons. Scablands are areas where patches of hard lava rock lie on the surface of the plateau.

The Wenatchee, Yakima, Snake, Walla Walla, and other irrigated river valleys in the Columbia Plateau region contain fertile cropland. Much of the desertlike Columbia Basin is good for growing crops when the land is irrigated. The Yakima Valley in south-central Washington is one of the most productive farm areas in the nation. Farmers there raise beef and dairy cattle, and grow large crops of hops and orchard fruits.

Another important part of the Columbia Plateau is the Palouse country in the southeast. Much of Washington's valuable wheat crop is grown on the gently rolling hills of the Palouse. The deep, fertile soils of this region hold moisture and permit dry farming.

The Blue Mountains in the southeastern corner of Washington extend into Oregon. They are neither as high nor as rugged as the Cascades. Farmers grow grains, hay, and other crops in the larger valleys, and the slopes serve as summer pastures for livestock.

The Rocky Mountains cut across the northeastern corner of Washington. The branch of the Rockies in

Washington is also called the Columbia Mountains. These mountains consist of several ridges with valleys in between. The Columbia River and its branch, the Okanogan, are the main rivers in the region. Minerals found in this area include clay, copper, gold, lead, limestone, magnesite, silver, and zinc.

Coastline. Washington's general coastline measures 157 miles (253 kilometers). Its *tidal shoreline* measures 3,026 miles (4,870 kilometers). This measurement includes the shoreline along the Strait of Juan de Fuca, along Puget Sound, and around the islands in Puget Sound. These islands include Bainbridge, Camano, Fidalgo, Vashon, Whidbey, and the more than 170 islands of the San Juan group. Puget Sound has many good protected harbors, but other parts of Washington's coast have few natural ports. The lack of other ports makes Puget Sound's harbors highly valuable.

Rivers, waterfalls, and lakes. The mighty Columbia River, one of the longest rivers in the United States, flows through Washington for more than 700 miles (1,100 kilometers). It enters the state at the eastern end of the border with British Columbia. Then it makes a giant southward curve through central Washington. At the Washington-Oregon border it makes a sharp turn to the west and flows to the Pacific Ocean. The river forms most of the boundary between the two states. The Columbia drains more than half of Washington. Many dams on the Columbia and its tributaries control floods and provide water for irrigation and power. The Snake River, which flows into the Columbia in south-central Washington, is the second longest river in the state. Other tributaries of the Columbia River in eastern and central Washington include the Colville, Methow, Okanogan, Pend Oreille, Sanpoil, Spokane, Wenatchee, and Yakima rivers.

Many rivers of western Washington, including the Skagit, Skykomish, and Puyallup, flow from the mountains into Puget Sound. These rivers furnish water for many cities, and provide power for industry. Some of them contain large numbers of salmon and other kinds of fishes that travel upstream to lay their eggs. Logging companies use the rivers to float logs to sawmills. Other important rivers include the Chehalis, which flows into the Pacific Ocean at Grays Harbor, and the Cowlitz, which flows into the Columbia River near Longview. Parts of many rivers in western Washington are named for Indian tribes that dominated those areas during the years of white settlement.

Many of the state's rivers break into falls and rapids in mountainous areas. The chief waterfalls include Cascade, Fairy, Horseshoe, Klickitat, Ladder Creek, Metaline, Nooksack, Palouse, Rainbow, Snoqualmie, Spokane, and White River.

A number of lakes were formed around Puget Sound when glaciers scooped out the land and water filled the hollow places. Some were formed when soil and rock pushed by the glaciers dammed river valleys. The largest and best known of these glacial lakes are Washington, Sammamish, and Whatcom. Other freshwater lakes include Ozette, Crescent, and Quinault, all on the Olympic Peninsula west of Puget Sound. The Cascade Mountains area has many beautiful lakes. The largest is Lake Chelan, 51 miles (82 kilometers) long, on the eastern slope. Franklin D. Roosevelt Lake, formed by Grand Coulee Dam, covers 130 square miles (337 square kilometers) and is the state's largest lake.

Plant and animal life. Forests cover more than half of Washington. In the western part of the state, important softwood trees include the Douglas-fir, Sitka spruce, western hemlock, and western redcedar. In the eastern section, softwoods include the Douglas-fir, lodgepole pine, ponderosa (western yellow) pine, and western larch. Common hardwoods include alder, aspen, cottonwood, and maple. Many kinds of plants grow in Washington because of the great variety of climates and elevations. Rare wild flowers bloom in mountain meadows. Colorful lupine, brown-eyed Susan, and goldenrod grow in fields and along roads. Flowering plants such as the western rhododendron and the western dogwood brighten the forests and hillsides.

Game animals found in Washington include bears and four kinds of deer—elks, Columbian black-tailed deer, mule deer, and western white-tailed deer. Washington also has many small fur-bearing animals, such as beavers, martens, minks, muskrats, and western bobcats. The state's game birds include pheasants, quail, ruffed grouse, sage grouse, wild ducks, and wild geese.

Fishes in Washington's many freshwater rivers and lakes include grayling, cutthroat trout, rainbow trout, steelhead trout, and whitefish. Huge sturgeon have been caught in the Columbia and Snake rivers. Saltwater fishes include cod, flounder, halibut, and salmon. Crabs, oysters, and several kinds of clams live in the coastal waters.

Climate. Western Washington has a milder climate than any other region in the United States that is as far north. Westerly winds from the Pacific Ocean help keep the summers pleasantly cool and the winters relatively warm. Seattle's temperature averages about 66° F. (19° C) in July and 41° F. (5° C) in January.

Eastern Washington has warmer summers and colder winters than western Washington. Spokane, near the Idaho border, has an average temperature of 70° F. (21° C) in July and 25° F. (−4° C) in January.

The state's highest temperature, 118° F. (48° C), occurred in Grant County on July 24, 1928, and at Ice Harbor Dam in southeastern Washington on Aug. 5, 1961. The lowest, −48° F. (−44° C), occurred at Mazama and at Winthrop in the northeast on Dec. 30, 1968.

Moist winds from the Pacific Ocean bring much rain to western Washington. By the time the winds reach eastern Washington, they have lost much moisture. As a result, the east has a much drier climate than the west. *Precipitation* (rain, melted snow, and other forms of moisture) averages over 135 inches (343 centimeters) a year in parts of the Olympic Peninsula. But Washington's central plateau receives only 6 inches (15 centimeters). Much of this area is semidesert.

Snowfall in Washington averages about 5 inches (13 centimeters) a year along the coast. Mount Rainier receives 50 to 75 inches (130 to 191 centimeters) on its lower slopes and over 500 inches (1,300 centimeters) on its higher slopes. In 1970-1971, Paradise Ranger Station on Mount Rainier recorded the nation's heaviest snowfall for one winter—1,027 inches (2,609 centimeters).

Average monthly weather

	Seattle						Spokane					
	Temperatures				Days of rain or snow		Temperatures				Days of rain or snow
	F°		C°				F°		C°		
	High	Low	High	Low			High	Low	High	Low	
Jan.	43	31	6	−1	19	Jan.	30	20	−1	−7	17
Feb.	48	34	9	1	16	Feb.	36	23	2	−5	12
Mar.	52	37	11	3	17	Mar.	46	30	8	−1	13
Apr.	58	40	14	4	13	Apr.	56	37	13	3	7
May	65	45	18	7	10	May	66	44	19	7	9
June	70	50	21	10	11	June	72	51	22	11	8
July	75	53	24	12	6	July	82	57	28	14	4
Aug.	74	53	23	12	6	Aug.	81	55	27	13	4
Sept.	68	49	20	9	8	Sept.	71	48	22	9	5
Oct.	59	44	15	7	16	Oct.	58	39	14	4	10
Nov.	50	38	10	3	18	Nov.	42	30	6	−1	12
Dec.	45	34	7	1	20	Dec.	34	24	1	−4	16

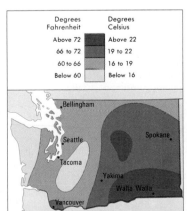

Average January temperatures

Winds from the Pacific Ocean keep western Washington's winters relatively warm. Eastern Washington is the coldest.

Degrees Fahrenheit	Degrees Celsius
Above 40	Above 4
32 to 40	0 to 4
24 to 32	−4 to 0
Below 24	Below −4

Average July temperatures

The eastern part of the state has the warmest summers. Ocean winds keep the coast pleasantly mild in summertime.

Degrees Fahrenheit	Degrees Celsius
Above 72	Above 22
66 to 72	19 to 22
60 to 66	16 to 19
Below 60	Below 16

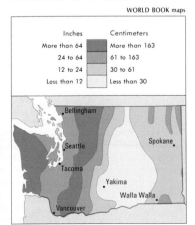

Average yearly precipitation

Washington has wide variations in precipitation. The west has a rainy climate. The central area is the driest.

WORLD BOOK maps

Inches	Centimeters
More than 64	More than 163
24 to 64	61 to 163
12 to 24	30 to 61
Less than 12	Less than 30

Washington has a diverse economy. The state's leading economic activity is community, business, and personal services. Chief among these services is the creation of computer software. Washington is closer to Asian ports than most other parts of the country, so foreign trade plays a significant role. The manufacture of aircraft and the processing of farm and forest products are also major parts of the state's economy.

Natural resources. Washington's many natural resources include a plentiful water supply, large timber reserves, and fertile soils.

Water is one of Washington's most important resources. Melted snow from the mountains feeds the rivers of western Washington and provides water for industry, electric power, irrigation, and home use. The Columbia River ranks among the nation's greatest sources of hydroelectric power, and it and its tributaries are valuable sources of water in central and eastern Washington. Inlets and bays that lie in the Puget Sound region and along the coast encourage shipping, commercial fishing, and pleasure boating.

Forests cover about 22 million acres (8.9 million hectares) in Washington. About 80 percent of the state's forests is of commercial value. In the west, where the rainfall is heaviest, the Douglas-fir is the leading timber tree. Sitka spruce, western hemlock, and western redcedar are also common. The Douglas-fir is also the chief timber tree in the drier eastern section. Ponderosa pine, western larch, and lodgepole pine also grow there. The eastern forests lie chiefly along the slopes of the Cascades, in the northeastern highlands, and in the Blue Mountains. The most common Washington hardwoods include alder, aspen, cottonwood, and maple.

The state government, the U.S. government, and many private companies work to conserve Washington's valuable timber resources. They use a variety of harvesting methods, including cutting only some of the trees to allow for natural reseeding. However, most harvested areas are replanted with seedlings grown in private and government tree nurseries.

Soils. Washington's best soils for agriculture are the silts and sands of the river valleys and of the irrigated dry lands east of the Cascades. The soils of the Palouse region in southeastern Washington, especially in Whitman County, were built up from fine materials carried by winds from the west. The Puget Sound area and most of the high mountain areas have rocky soils.

Minerals. Washington has the only large coal deposits on the Pacific Coast. The largest coal fields lie in western Washington, especially in Lewis County. Magnesite deposits occur near Chewelah. Gold deposits are found on the eastern slopes of the Cascades and in the Okanogan Mountains. Lead and zinc occur mainly in northeastern Washington. Clay, limestone, and sand and gravel occur in many areas. The state also has deposits of barite, copper, diatomite, gypsum, olivine, peat, pumice, silver, soapstone, talc, and tungsten.

Service industries account for the largest part of Washington's *gross state product*—the total value of all goods and services produced in a state in a year. Most of these industries are concentrated in the state's metropolitan areas.

The community, business, and personal services industry is Washington's leading service industry in terms

Production and workers by economic activities

Economic activities	Percent of GSP* produced	Employed workers Number of people	Employed workers Percent of total
Community, business, & personal services	24	1,073,100	30
Finance, insurance, & real estate	18	267,200	8
Wholesale & retail trade	17	762,500	22
Government	13	547,800	15
Manufacturing	12	371,200	10
Transportation, communication, & utilities	9	168,100	5
Construction	5	214,300	6
Agriculture	2	143,400	4
Mining	†	5,400	†
Total	100	3,553,000	100

*GSP = gross state product, the total value of goods and services produced in a year.
†Less than one-half of 1 percent.
Figures are for 2000.
Source: *World Book* estimates based on data from U.S. Bureau of Economic Analysis.

of the gross state product. This group employs more people than any other economic activity in the state. These services include enterprises such as private health care, computer programming and engineering companies, and law firms. The Seattle-Tacoma area has many companies that specialize in creating computer software, including Microsoft Corporation, the world's largest developer and publisher of software. In the 1990's, the Seattle area became a home to many new companies that focus on products that support e-commerce, business conducted via the Internet.

Finance, insurance, and real estate rank second among Washington's service industry groups. Seattle is the state's top financial center. The city is the home of a major banking company, Washington Mutual, and a major insurance firm, Safeco. Real estate is an important part of the economy because of the large sums of money involved in the buying and selling of homes and other property.

Wholesale and retail trade ranks next among Washington's service industries in terms of the gross state product. The wholesale trade of automobiles and parts, computers and other office equipment, groceries, industrial supplies, and construction materials is especially important. Much of the wholesale trade involves goods shipped through ports along Puget Sound. Major types of retail establishments include grocery stores, discount stores, and restaurants. Seattle is the home of several major retailers, including Nordstrom, a large retail clothing company; Starbucks, a large gourmet coffee vendor; REI, a leading sportswear company; and Amazon.com, an important online retailer.

Government ranks fourth among the state's service industries. Government services include public schools and hospitals, and military bases. Fort Lewis, the largest United States Army post on the Pacific Coast, is located between Olympia and Tacoma. The U.S. Air Force operates an Air Combat Command base near Spokane. The U.S. Department of Energy runs the Hanford Site, a nuclear energy center near Richland. The Hanford Site is the focus of one of the world's largest environmental cleanup projects. Washington's public school system employs many people. Washington's government offices are based in Olympia, the state capital.

Transportation, communication, and utilities rank fifth among the state's service industries. Alaska Air Group, a major U.S. transportation company, has its headquarters in Seattle. Washington is also home to many companies that specialize in cellular telephone systems and personal communications services. More information about transportation and communication appears later in this section.

Manufacturing. Products made in Washington have a *value added by manufacture* of about $35 billion a year. Value added by manufacture represents the increase in value of raw materials after they become finished products.

Transportation equipment is Washington's leading product in terms of value added by manufacture. Washington is a leading center of the aircraft and space industry. The Boeing Company leads the nation in producing commercial airliners. The company has several assembly and research facilities in King and Snohomish counties and employs more workers than any other manufacturer in the state. Washington is also a leading shipbuilding center. It has major shipyards at Bremerton, Seattle, and Tacoma. The Puget Sound Naval Shipyard at Bremerton is one of the largest naval shipyards on the Pacific Coast.

Computer and electronic products are Washington's second-ranked manufactured goods. Computer microchips and equipment for telephones and wireless communications are important parts of this sector. Medical equipment and navigational instruments are the leading types of scientific instruments made in the state.

Third among Washington's manufactured goods are food products. Food-processing activities include milling flour; coffee and tea manufacturing; potato processing; packing fish and meats; canning, freezing, and preserving fruits, vegetables, and berries; and producing butter, cheese, milk, wine, breakfast foods, and bakery goods.

Ranking next among the state's manufactured items are paper products and wood products. Weyerhaeuser, a company that ranks among the leading makers of forest products, is headquartered in Tacoma. Several other large forest products companies have operations in Washington. Many areas in the western part of the state have factories that manufacture paper and wood products. The state's other manufactures include fabricated metal products, machinery, and refined petroleum.

Agriculture. Farmland covers about a third of Washington's land area. The state has about 39,000 farms. Farmers produce good crops both by dry farming methods and by irrigation. The chief irrigated regions are in the Columbia Basin and in the valleys of the Okanogan, Snake, Spokane, Walla Walla, Wenatchee, and Yakima rivers. The state has about 13,000 irrigated farms.

Timber is the most valuable agricultural product in Washington. Washington is one of the leading states in the harvesting of timber. Douglas-fir and western hemlock are the state's most valuable timber trees.

Wheat is Washington's most valuable field crop. Farmers in eastern Washington grow some spring wheat and a large amount of winter wheat. Washington leads the nation in the production of hops, used in making beer. The state ranks second only to Idaho in the production of potatoes, which are grown mainly in Grant and other counties of south-central Washington. Washington also ranks among the leading producers of asparagus, carrots, green peas, and onions, and of barley and other grains. It also produces dry beans, dry peas, sweet corn, and hay.

Washington grows more apples than any other state. People throughout the country enjoy such famous kinds of Washington apples as the Red Delicious, Golden Delicious, Granny Smith, and Fuji.

Washington is also the top pear-growing state. The state ranks high in the production of apricots, berries, cherries, grapes, and plums and prunes. Most fruit is

Economy of Washington

This map shows the economic uses of land in Washington and where the state's leading farm, mineral, and forest products are produced. Major manufacturing centers are shown in red.

- ☐ Mostly cropland
- ☐ Cropland mixed with grazing land and forest
- ☐ Grazing land mixed with cropland
- ☐ Forest land
- ☐ Mostly unproductive land with alpine vegetation
- ☐ Urban areas
- ● Manufacturing center
- • Mineral deposit

WORLD BOOK map

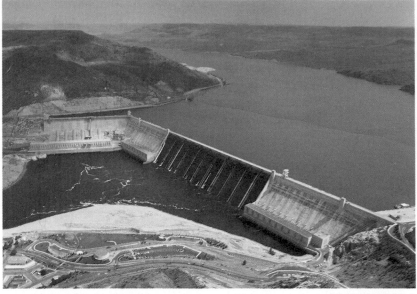

Grand Coulee Dam, the largest concrete dam in the United States, lies on the Columbia River in northeastern Washington. The dam has three power plants and is one of the world's greatest sources of water power.

© Tim Heneghan, West Stock

grown in central Washington's irrigated valleys.

Flower bulbs are also an important Washington crop. The state is one of the world's chief producers of iris, tulip, and daffodil bulbs. Washington growers also produce alfalfa seed, grass seed, and mint.

Milk and beef cattle are by far the most important livestock products in Washington. Most of the dairy farms are in the western part of the state. Beef cattle are raised chiefly on ranches in eastern Washington. The state's other livestock products include eggs and *broilers* (chickens between 5 and 12 weeks old).

Mining. Washington's leading mined products are coal, cement, crushed stone, gold, and sand and gravel. Coal mines lie south of Olympia. Cement and sand and gravel are mined near the largest cities. Crushed stone is mined in Okanogan and Stevens counties. Chelan and Ferry counties have gold mines. Washington's other mined products include clays, gypsum, and silver.

Fishing. Washington has an annual fish catch valued at more than $100 million. The state has won fame for its seafoods, especially chinook and sockeye salmon. The Washington fish catch also includes chum, coho, and pink salmon; clams; cod; crabs; flounder; halibut; herring; oysters; rockfish; shrimp; steelhead; and tuna.

Electric power. Washington leads the nation in hydroelectric power production. The state produces about 80 percent of its power from hydroelectric plants. Most of the rest comes from nuclear plants and plants that burn coal or natural gas.

Grand Coulee Dam, the largest concrete dam in the world, is also one of the world's greatest sources of water power. Other large dams on the Columbia River include Bonneville, Chief Joseph, John Day, McNary, Priest Rapids, Rock Island, Rocky Reach, The Dalles, and Wanapum. There are also many dams on the Snake River and several smaller rivers.

Transportation facilities in Washington help link the United States with Asia and western Canada. They also provide a means for shipping the state's goods to major markets in other states, which lie far away.

The Seattle-Tacoma International Airport is one of the busiest airports in the Western states. Spokane has the state's second busiest airport.

About 20 rail lines provide freight service in Washington. Passenger trains serve about 30 Washington cities. In 1883, the Northern Pacific Railroad began transcontinental service to Tacoma. The Cascade Tunnel, 7.8 miles (12.5 kilometers) long, was completed in 1929. It is the longest railroad tunnel in the United States.

Washington has about 80,000 miles (129,000 kilometers) of roads and highways. Two floating concrete pontoon bridges cross Seattle's Lake Washington. The longest one has a floating portion that is 7,518 feet (2,291 meters) long. The structure is the longest concrete pontoon bridge in the United States. The Tacoma Narrows Bridge, one of the nation's longest suspension bridges, crosses a part of Puget Sound.

Anacortes, Everett, Seattle, Tacoma, and several other Puget Sound cities are important seaports. Oceangoing ships enter Puget Sound through the Strait of Juan de Fuca. The vessels bring products from Asia, South America, and other parts of the world. Longview and Vancouver on the Columbia River and Grays Harbor on the Pacific Ocean are also major ports. The Port of Seattle and the Port of Tacoma are growing rapidly as *container ports.* These ports service *container ships*—ships that carry goods in metal containers the size of railroad cars.

An artificial waterway, the Lake Washington Ship Canal, cuts across Seattle. It connects Lake Washington and Lake Union with Puget Sound. The Seattle fishing fleet, many pleasure boats, and some ocean vessels travel up the canal to landlocked harbors. An extensive, state-owned ferry system links the San Juan Islands and the mainland. Privately owned ferries link Seattle to cities in British Columbia.

Communication. Washington's first newspaper, the *Columbian,* began in Olympia in 1852. Today, Washington has about 200 newspapers, including about 25 dailies. Washington newspapers with the largest circulations are the *Seattle Post-Intelligencer,* the *Seattle Times, The* (Spokane) *Spokesman-Review,* and *The* (Tacoma) *News-Tribune.* In addition, Washington publishers issue approximately 175 periodicals.

Washington's first commercial radio broadcast was made from Everett in 1920 by station KFBL (now KRKO). KING-TV, the state's first television station, began operating in Seattle in 1948. Today, Washington has about 190 radio stations and 25 television stations. Cable television systems and Internet providers serve many areas.

Government

Constitution. Washington is governed under its original Constitution, adopted in 1889. Amendments to the Constitution may be proposed by the state Legislature, or by a constitutional convention. A constitutional convention may be called by a majority of the legislators with the approval of a majority of the voters. All amendments must be approved by two-thirds of the legislators in both houses, and then by a majority of the voters in a statewide election.

Executive. The governor and lieutenant governor of Washington serve four-year terms. The governor has the power to appoint more than 350 lesser state officials. The governor may also fill vacancies that occur in elective executive offices and among the Superior Court of Appeals and Supreme Court judges. The governor may choose to veto bills that have been passed by the Legislature. The governor also has the power to veto individual sections in any bill without killing the whole bill.

Other top state officials in Washington are the secretary of state, treasurer, auditor, attorney general, superintendent of public instruction, commissioner of public lands, and insurance commissioner. These officials serve four-year terms. They may be reelected to an unlimited number of terms in office. The superintendent of public instruction is elected by *nonpartisan* (no-party) ballot.

Legislature consists of a 49-member Senate and a 98-member House of Representatives. By law, the House of Representatives cannot have fewer than 63 members or more than 99. The number of senators cannot be more than one-half or less than one-third of the number of representatives.

The state has 49 legislative districts. Voters in each district of the state elect one senator and two representatives. Senators serve four-year terms. Representatives serve two-year terms.

Regular legislative sessions begin on the second Monday in January each year. The law limits these sessions to 60 days in even-numbered years and 105 days in odd-numbered years. The governor has the power to call special sessions of no more than 30 days. The Legislature can also vote to call a special session.

Courts. The highest court in Washington is the state Supreme Court. It has nine justices elected to six-year terms. The state's voters elect three Supreme Court justices in each general election, every two years. The justices elect one of their number to serve as chief justice.

The next highest court is the state court of appeals. This court is divided into three geographic regions. Altogether, it has 22 judges elected to six-year terms. Other courts include district and superior courts, headed by judges elected to four-year terms.

Local government. A 1948 amendment to the Washington Constitution gave counties the right to choose their own form of county government. In most of Washington's 39 counties, a three-member board of commissioners has both executive and lawmaking powers. The commissioners are elected to four-year terms. Other county officials include the prosecuting attorney, sheriff, clerk, assessor, auditor, treasurer, and coroner. In addition, Washington's counties may have a health officer, relief administrator, and other officials.

Washington has nearly 300 incorporated cities and towns. The state Constitution provides that any city with 20,000 or more residents may have *home rule.* That is, the city may choose its own system of local government. Ten Washington cities have home rule. Some have a council-manager form of government, some a commission system of government, and some a mayor-council form. The majority of smaller cities in Washington are run by a mayor and a city council.

Revenue. The state government receives about three-fifths of its *general revenue* (income) from state taxes. Most of the rest comes from federal grants and other United States government programs. Washington's main source of tax revenue is a general retail sales tax. Retail sales taxes total approximately half of state taxes. Other important sources of tax revenue include taxes on property, motor fuels, motor vehicle licenses, stock transfers, public utilities, and tobacco products. Washington does

The governors of Washington

	Party	Term
Elisha P. Ferry	Republican	1889-1893
John McGraw	Republican	1893-1897
John Rogers	Democratic-Populist	1897-1901
Henry McBride	Republican	1901-1905
Albert E. Mead	Republican	1905-1909
Samuel G. Cosgrove	Republican	1909
Marion E. Hay	Republican	1909-1913
Ernest Lister	Democrat	1913-1919
Louis F. Hart	Republican	1919-1925
Roland H. Hartley	Republican	1925-1933
Clarence D. Martin	Democrat	1933-1941
Arthur B. Langlie	Republican	1941-1945
Monrad C. Wallgren	Democrat	1945-1949
Arthur B. Langlie	Republican	1949-1957
Albert D. Rosellini	Democrat	1957-1965
Daniel J. Evans	Republican	1965-1977
Dixy Lee Ray	Democrat	1977-1981
John D. Spellman	Republican	1981-1985
Booth Gardner	Democrat	1985-1993
Mike Lowry	Democrat	1993-1997
Gary Locke	Democrat	1997-

not levy state taxes on personal or corporate income.

Politics. In the 1912 presidential election, Washington supported the Progressive Party. In other elections, the state has supported Republicans and Democrats an equal number of times. For the state's voting record in presidential elections since 1892, see **Electoral College** (table).

Voters of farm areas and suburbs have generally favored Republicans. People in the cities of western Washington have usually supported the Democrats.

History

Indian days. Many Indians lived in the Washington region before white people came. Tribes of the plateau Indian group lived on the plains and in river valleys east of the Cascades. These included the Cayuse, Colville, Nez Perce, Okanogan, Spokane, and Yakima. The coastal Indians lived west of the Cascade Mountains. These tribes included the Chinook, Clallam, Clatsop, Nisqually, Nooksack, and Puyallup. They lived mainly on salmon and other fish and clams. In addition, they gathered wild fruits and vegetables.

Discovery and exploration. The first white people to see the Pacific Northwest were probably Spanish and English explorers who sailed northward along the coast from California during the 1500's. After the mid-1700's, Russian fur traders settled in what is now Alaska. The Spaniards feared that the Russians would move to occupy the region farther south. To prevent this expansion, Spain sent several expeditions to establish Spanish rights to the area. In 1775, Bruno Heceta and Juan Francisco de la Bodega y Quadra were the first Europeans to land on Washington soil, near present-day Point Grenville. They claimed the region for Spain.

The first English explorer to reach the area was Captain James Cook, in 1778. He did not touch the coast or, because of stormy weather, see much of it. Captain George Vancouver, another English explorer, made a survey of Puget Sound and Georgia Gulf in 1792. Vancouver named the sound for Peter Puget, one of his officers. The United Kingdom (U.K.) based its claim to the region on the explorations of Cook and Vancouver.

Captain Robert Gray, an American, headed a fur-trading expedition sent by a Boston company. Gray sailed into the harbor that now bears his name. In 1792, he reached the mouth of the Columbia River. Gray's arrival at the Columbia became a basis for American claims to the region. In 1805, the explorers Meriwether Lewis and William Clark crossed the Rocky Mountains. They reached the Columbia River and followed it to the Pacific Ocean. Their voyage gave the United States a second claim to the Northwest. Between 1807 and 1811, the British strengthened their claim when David Thompson, a Canadian explorer and geographer, traveled down the Columbia to the Pacific.

Settlement. During the early 1800's, British and American fur traders both operated in the region. In 1810, the Canadian North West Company established Spokane House near present-day Spokane for the purpose of trading with the Indians. In 1811, a company sent by the American trader John Jacob Astor set up a fur-trading post at Astoria, in present-day Oregon. Astor's group also founded Fort Okanogan, the first United States settlement established on land that now lies within the state of Washington.

During the War of 1812 between the United States and the United Kingdom, Astor's company gave up its trading posts. After the war, the two countries could not agree on a boundary line to separate their territories west of the Rocky Mountains. They signed a treaty in 1818 permitting citizens of both countries to trade and settle in the region, which was called the Oregon Country. John McLoughlin of the Hudson's Bay Company, a British trading firm, completed Fort Vancouver (now Vancouver) on the Columbia River in 1825.

During the 1840's, many Americans settled in the Oregon Country. The boundary dispute between the United States and the United Kingdom reached a climax during the presidential campaign of 1844. James K. Polk partially based his campaign on the claim that all the region south of latitude 54° 40' belonged to the United States (see **Fifty-Four Forty or Fight**). In 1846, President Polk signed a treaty with the United Kingdom which set the boundary line at the 49th parallel, Washington's present northern border. The U.K. kept Vancouver Island.

Territorial days. A bill creating the Oregon Territory, of which Washington was a part, passed Congress in 1848. General Joseph Lane was appointed governor. In 1853, President Millard Fillmore signed a bill creating the Washington Territory. This region included the present state of Washington, northern Idaho, and western Montana. The capital was established at Olympia. Fillmore appointed Isaac Ingalls Stevens as the first governor of the new territory. Stevens sought treaties with the Indians, in order to put them on reservations and free more territory for white settlers. The coastal Indians signed the treaties. But Stevens's efforts in 1855 to sign treaties with the plateau Indians led to war. Kamiakin, a Yakima Indian chief, led the warring tribes. The fighting ended in 1858, soon after the Indians lost a battle near Four Lakes. Treaties were ratified in 1859.

In 1859, when Oregon became a state, the Washington Territory was expanded to include parts of what are now Idaho and Wyoming. Washington received its present boundaries in 1863, when the Idaho Territory was established. Rising numbers of settlers streamed into Washington after 1860, partly because of gold discoveries in Idaho, Oregon, and British Columbia. But there were no major gold strikes in Washington.

Statehood. The completion of a railroad connection with the East in 1883 brought many settlers. President Benjamin Harrison proclaimed the territory as the 42nd state on Nov. 11, 1889. Elisha P. Ferry, former governor of the territory, was elected Washington's first state governor. Olympia remained the capital.

Between 1890 and 1900, parts of the desertlike lands of eastern Washington were reclaimed by irrigation. Large numbers of wheat ranchers and fruit growers came to the state. By 1900, much of the open cattle range had been replaced by wheat fields and fruit orchards. Lumbering, fishing, and mining also increased rapidly, and shipping to the Far East and Alaska became

Historic Washington

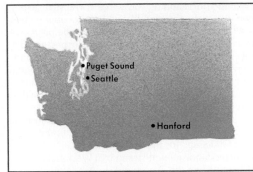

Captain George Vancouver, an English explorer, surveyed the coast of Washington and Puget Sound in 1792.

"Fifty-Four Forty or Fight" was the cry during the presidential campaign of 1844. But the boundary between Washington and Canada was fixed at latitude 49° by the 1846 Treaty of Oregon.

A nuclear energy center was built by the federal government at Hanford in 1943. The center helped make the first atomic bombs. In the 1960's, the facility began producing electricity.

Lewis and Clark reached the Pacific in the autumn of 1805 after crossing the Rockies and descending the Snake and Columbia rivers. Thomas Jefferson had commissioned them to explore the upper Louisiana Territory.

The Space Needle was built for Century 21, a world's fair held in Seattle in 1962. The observation tower rises 605 feet (184 meters).

Important dates in Washington

WORLD BOOK illustrations by Kevin Chadwick

1775 Bruno Heceta and Juan Francisco de la Bodega y Quadra of Spain became the first Europeans to land on Washington soil.

1792 Robert Gray sailed into Grays Harbor and the Columbia River. George Vancouver surveyed the coast of Washington and Puget Sound.

1805 Lewis and Clark reached Washington and the Pacific Ocean.

1810 A British-Canadian fur-trading post was established near present-day Spokane.

1818 Britain and the United States agreed to a joint occupation of the Oregon region, which included Washington.

1846 A treaty between the United States and Britain established Washington's boundary at the 49th parallel.

1853 Congress created the Washington Territory.

1855-1858 Indian wars raged in the Washington Territory.

1883 The Northern Pacific Railroad linked Washington and the East.

1889 Washington became the 42nd state on November 11.

1909 The Alaska-Yukon-Pacific Exposition was held in Seattle.

1942 Grand Coulee Dam was completed.

1962 Century 21, a world's fair, was held in Seattle.

1964 The Columbia River Treaty of 1961 and related agreements received final approval from the U.S. and Canadian governments.

1974 Expo '74, a world's fair, was held in Spokane.

1980 Mount St. Helens volcano erupted, causing 57 deaths and enormous damage in the southwestern part of Washington.

1996 Gary Locke of Washington became the first person of Chinese ancestry to be elected governor of a U.S. state.

a leading activity. The shipping industry added to the wealth of the ports and railway centers. The state also profited greatly by the Klondike and Alaska gold rush of 1897-1898 (see **Alaska** [The gold rush]). Seattle profited most as the chief supply center for the prospectors, but all of western Washington increased in population and prosperity. Farmers in eastern Washington also profited.

The early 1900's. In 1909, the Alaska-Yukon-Pacific Exposition was held in Seattle to celebrate the growth of the port of Seattle. After the United States entered World War I in 1917, Washington's economy boomed as it provided needed forest products, agricultural commodities, and ships for the war effort.

Organized labor gained strength in Washington during the war. When the war ended in 1918, labor unions feared their position would weaken. To protest industry's power, about 60,000 workers in Seattle walked off their jobs in February 1919 in the nation's first general strike. The Great Depression during the 1930's brought great reductions in many industries. Food processing remained Washington's only stable industry. Other industries that kept producing on a small scale included metalworking and aircraft construction. These activities, along with construction work on the Bonneville and Grand Coulee dams, helped the state regain some prosperity in the late 1930's.

The mid-1900's. During World War II (1939-1945), Washington industries produced aircraft and ships. Expansion occurred in truck and railroad car construction, the wood products industry, and agriculture. In 1943, the government built a nuclear energy center, the Hanford Works, in southeastern Washington. The center helped make the first atomic bombs. In the 1960's, it began to produce electricity. It later became known as the Hanford Site of the U.S. Department of Energy.

Many Washington cities grew as a result of the construction and expansion of military bases. Thousands of people who came to the state to work in defense plants stayed after the war to build new careers in the aluminum and aircraft industries. The importance of forest products and agriculture declined in Washington after World War II. However, farms in the central part of the state benefited from Columbia River irrigation projects. These projects resulted from the construction of a number of federal dams on the river. Development of the Columbia River also led to the growth of inland ports and an increase in river shipping. In 1964, the United States and Canada approved a cooperative plan for hydroelectric and river-control projects on the Columbia and connecting streams.

In 1962, Century 21, a world's fair held in Seattle, helped promote tourism, an important industry in the state. The fairgrounds and buildings and the 605-foot (184-meter) Space Needle observation tower remain as a year-round civic and tourist center. Seattle and its suburbs spent $130 million in a nine-year project to clean up polluted Lake Washington and Elliott Bay, two major recreation areas. In 1968, Seattle-area voters approved a $333-million improvement program called "Forward Thrust." Plans included a $118-million expansion of park and recreational facilities.

In the late 1960's, industry and population increased rapidly in Seattle and the Puget Sound area. An important reason for the expansion was the growth of the

Boeing Company. Boeing Company, a major military airplane builder in wartime, expanded into both the commercial jet and aerospace industries. At one time, nearly 10 per cent of the work force in Washington was employed in jet aircraft and related businesses.

Recent developments. The state's attempt to meet increasing needs for electric power suffered a major setback in the 1970's and early 1980's. During this period, the Washington Public Power Supply System (WPPSS) worked to build five nuclear power plants. But the project became burdened with cost overruns. In 1983, WPPSS defaulted on 2\frac{1}{4}$ billion in municipal bonds and, having completed only two plants, ceased construction. WPPSS was the most expensive civil works project in history. Its default also was the largest of its kind.

Washington was hit by a natural disaster on May 18, 1980, when the volcanic eruption of Mount St. Helens in the southwestern part of the state resulted in 57 deaths

Douglas Miller, West Stock

The eruption of Mount St. Helens in southwestern Washington on May 19, 1980, spread volcanic ash over a wide area. The volcanic eruption caused billions of dollars of damage.

and billions of dollars in damage. The eruption caused floods and forest fires and spread a thick layer of ash over a wide area. In 1982, Congress created the Mount St. Helens National Volcanic Monument. It is the first such monument in the United States.

During the late 1900's, state officials increased efforts to attract more industries to Washington. Interest in the state's highly skilled labor force helped draw several electronics companies. During the 1980's, telecommunications, biotechnology, and computer software companies hired more workers. Expansion by Boeing, Microsoft Corporation, and Weyerhaeuser Paper greatly aided Washington's economy in the 1990's.

State officials became more concerned about the deaths of salmon at Washington hydroelectric facilities. The dams on the Columbia and Snake rivers provide *fish ladders* (ascending pools of water) to allow adult salmon to swim upstream, where the fish *spawn* (repro-

duce). But many young salmon, as they travel downstream to the Pacific Ocean, die in the electric turbines at these dams. During the 1990's, the U.S. Army Corps of Engineers conducted studies for the purpose of coming up with a way to eliminate this threat to the young salmon. In 2002, the corps presented a plan that would redirect river water to flow around some of the dams.

In the late 1900's, the state faced problems of a weak timber industry and declining agricultural prices. But the state's greatest challenge centered on the cleanup of nuclear waste leaking from aging underground tanks at the Hanford Site. Radioactive liquid waste had polluted the nearby Columbia River. In 1989, state and federal officials began a cleanup plan that continued into the early 2000's. In 1996, state voters elected Gary Locke governor. The son of Chinese immigrants, Locke became the first person of Chinese ancestry to be elected governor of a U.S. state.   Ronald Reed Boyce and Robert C. Carriker

Study aids

Related articles in *World Book* include:

Biographies

Foley, Thomas Stephen
Joseph, Chief
Landes, Bertha Knight
Puget, Peter
Ray, Dixy Lee

Vancouver, George
Wainwright, Jonathan M.
Whitman, Marcus
Whitman, Narcissa

Cities

Olympia
Seattle
Spokane

Tacoma
Vancouver

History

Chinook Indians
Fifty-Four Forty or Fight
Lewis and Clark expedition
Nootka Indians
Oregon (Exploration and settlement)
Oregon Territory
Western frontier life in America

National parks and historic sites

Mount Rainier National Park
North Cascades National Park
Olympic National Park
Whitman Mission National Historic Site

Physical features

Bonneville Dam
Cascade Range
Coast Ranges
Columbia River
Grand Coulee Dam

Mount Rainier
Mount Saint Helens
Olympic Mountains
Puget Sound
Snake River

Outline

I. People
  A. Population
  B. Schools
  C. Libraries
  D. Museums
II. Visitor's guide
  A. Places to visit
  B. Annual events
III. Land and climate
  A. Land regions
  B. Coastline
  C. Rivers, waterfalls, and lakes
  D. Plant and animal life
  E. Climate
IV. Economy
  A. Natural resources
  B. Service industries
  C. Manufacturing
  D. Agriculture

E. Mining
F. Fishing
G. Electric power
V. Government
  A. Constitution
  B. Executive
  C. Legislature
  D. Courts
VI. History

H. Transportation
I. Communication

E. Local government
F. Revenue
G. Politics

Questions

On what grounds did both England and the United States claim the region that is now Washington?
Where is the longest railroad tunnel in the United States?
Why does western Washington have a mild climate?
What is Washington's most valuable field crop?
In what ways does Washington benefit from the dams in the Columbia River system?
How does the state protect its forest resources?
What is the Space Needle?
In what region do most of Washington's people live?
What is the largest concrete dam in the United States?
What are *coulees*? What are *scablands*?

Additional resources

Level I
Blashfield, Jean F. *Washington.* Children's Pr., 2001.
Powell, E. S. *Washington.* 2nd ed. Lerner, 2001.
Stefoff, Rebecca. *Washington.* Benchmark Bks., 1999.
Wright-Frierson, Virginia. *A North American Rain Forest Scrapbook.* Walker, 1999.

Level II
Brokenshire, Doug. *Washington State Place Names from Alki to Yelm.* Caxton Printers, 1993.
Ficken, Robert E., and LeWarne, C. P. *Washington.* Univ. of Wash. Pr., 1988.
Kirk, Ruth, and Alexander, Carmela. *Exploring Washington's Past.* Rev. ed. Univ. of Wash. Pr., 1995. Historical guide book.
Mapes, Lynda. *Washington.* Voyageur Pr., 1999. A book of photographs.
Stein, Julie K. *Exploring Coast Salish Prehistory.* Univ. of Wash. Pr., 2000.
Stratton, David H., ed. *Spokane and the Inland Empire.* Wash. State Univ. Pr., 1991.
Strickland, Ron. *Whistlepunks & Geoducks: Oral Histories from the Pacific Northwest.* 1990. Reprint. Oregon State Univ. Pr., 2001.
Tabor, Rowland W., and Haugerud, R. A. *Geology of the North Cascades.* Mountaineers, 1999.

Robert H. Glaze, Artstreet

The United States Capitol, in Washington, D.C., is the place where Congress makes the nation's laws. Tourists flock to this magnificent building to enjoy its beauty and to see Congress in action.

Washington, D.C.

Washington, D.C., is the capital of the United States and the headquarters of the U.S. government. It is one of the nation's most beautiful and historic cities and the site of many of its most popular tourist attractions.

Washington serves the American people as a symbol of the country's unity, history, and democratic tradition. Every year, millions of tourists from all parts of the United States and many other countries visit Washington. They tour such government buildings as the Capitol, where Congress meets; the White House, where the president lives and works; and the Supreme Court, where the justices of the nation's highest court hear cases. Tourists also visit the city's many famous monuments, memorials, and museums.

Washington lies on the Potomac River in the eastern part of the United States, between Maryland and Virginia. It is the only American city or town that is not part of a state. Washington also differs from most American cities because it has no factories or traditional manufacturing enterprises. It was founded to house the federal government.

Washington was the first city in the United States to be designed before it was built. The nation's first president, George Washington, chose the site in 1791, and he hired Pierre Charles L'Enfant, a French engineer, to plan the city. The federal government moved there from Philadelphia in 1800. The city's commissioners named the city for George Washington and called the larger area the *District of Columbia.* The city now covers the entire district, and it is sometimes called simply *D.C.*

The Constitution of the United States gave Congress the power to govern Washington. For much of the city's history, its leaders were appointed by the president. In 1973, Congress granted Washingtonians the right to

Facts in brief

Population: *City*—572,059. *Metropolitan area*—4,923,153. *Consolidated metropolitan area*—7,608,070.

Area: *City*—68 mi² (177 km²). *Metropolitan area*—6,511 mi² (16,863 km²), excluding inland water. *Consolidated metropolitan area*—9,578 mi² (24,807 km²), excluding inland water.

Altitude: 25 feet (7.6 meters) above sea level.

Climate: *Average temperatures*—January, 37 °F (3 °C); July, 78 °F (26 °C). *Average annual precipitation* (rainfall, melted snow, and other forms of moisture)—50 in (127 cm). For the monthly weather in Washington, D.C., see **Maryland** (Climate).

Government: Federal District under the authority of Congress. Mayor and city council, elected to four-year terms, run the local government.

Founded: Site chosen, 1791. Became capital, 1800.

elect their local officials. However, Washington does not have a voting representative in Congress. Many Washington residents feel it is unjust for them to be required to pay federal taxes and not have a congressional vote.

Visitor's guide

Most of Washington's tourist attractions are in the area the city's people call the *monumental core.* This area stretches from the U.S. Capitol to the Potomac River along a narrow park called the Mall. It extends several blocks on either side of the Mall. This section of the article describes the main features of the monumental core. The two-page map provides an overview of it. The last part of this section mentions interesting sights in other parts of the city and its suburbs.

Many of Washington's points of interest also have separate articles in *World Book.* See the list of *Related articles* at the end of this article.

Capitol Hill rises 88 feet (26.8 meters) near the center of Washington. Pierre L'Enfant chose the hill as the site for the U.S. Capitol. In addition to the Capitol, several large government buildings stand on the hill. They include congressional office buildings, the Library of Congress, the Supreme Court, and the conservatory of the U.S. Botanic Garden. Union Station and the Folger Shakespeare Library are also on Capitol Hill.

United States Capitol is the place where members of Congress meet to propose and adopt legislation. The Capitol ranks among the nation's most magnificent buildings. Tall Corinthian columns and an enormous dome beautify its white marble exterior. The bronze Statue of Freedom 19 $\frac{1}{2}$ feet (5.94 meters) high stands on top of the dome. The Capitol, including the statue, rises nearly 300 feet (91 meters) above ground.

The Capitol has 540 rooms. Many of them contain beautiful paintings, sculptures, and wall carvings that portray events and people important in American history. These artworks and the bustle of lawmakers and their staff members help convey to visitors a strong sense of purpose and patriotism. Visitors may attend sessions of Congress to hear the debates and watch democracy in action.

Congressional office buildings. Six large buildings as well as several smaller annexes provide office space for the members of Congress. The Dirksen, Hart, and Russell Senate office buildings are north of the Capitol. The Cannon, Longworth, and Rayburn House of Representatives office buildings are south of the Capitol. The members of Congress welcome visits to their offices by the people they represent.

Library of Congress holds more than 100 million items and research materials in more than 450 languages. It serves as a legislative and research library for Congress and as a center for scholars. It is the copyright agency of the United States and the national library. It is housed in three buildings east of the Capitol—the Jefferson, Adams, and Madison buildings.

Highlights of the library's collection include American Civil War photographs by Mathew Brady, two copies of Abraham Lincoln's Gettysburg Address handwritten by Lincoln, and a Gutenberg Bible printed in the 1450's. The library also owns more than 6,000 books that once belonged to Thomas Jefferson. Jefferson sold his private library to the Library of Congress in 1815. It replaced the

library's original collection, which was destroyed by British soldiers in August 1814 during the War of 1812.

Supreme Court stands directly east of the Capitol. In this building, the nine justices of the Supreme Court of the United States decide on the constitutionality of laws, government practices, and the decisions of lower courts. The building's white marble exterior resembles a Greek temple. The room where the justices hear cases is decorated with long red drapes, copper gates, and marble columns. Visitors may attend sessions of the court, which begin each year on the first Monday of October and usually end in June.

United States Botanic Garden is southwest of the Capitol. It exhibits more than 10,000 varieties of plants, including many rare species.

Union Station, north of the Capitol, is Washington's railroad station, a subway stop, and the headquarters for Amtrak. The huge 1907 building is also a popular tourist attraction. Its many shops, restaurants, motion-picture theaters, and special exhibits and other events attract millions of visitors every year.

Folger Shakespeare Library, east of the Capitol, houses the world's most important collection of works by and about English playwright William Shakespeare. Only scholars may do research in the library, but exhibits of rare books and manuscripts are open to the public. The Folger presents productions of Shakespeare's plays at a small theater in the library.

The Mall is a narrow park 2 miles (3 kilometers) long that stretches west from the Capitol to the Lincoln Memorial. It serves as the nation's "front yard." The Mall is the location of a number of Smithsonian museums and important memorials. It is also the site of many festivals, demonstrations, and public celebrations.

Smithsonian museums. The Smithsonian Institution is a government corporation that operates cultural, educational, and scientific facilities throughout Washington. It was established by an act of Congress in 1846 and fund-

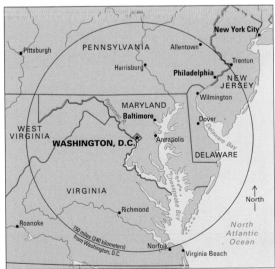

WORLD BOOK map

Washington, D.C., the capital of the United States, lies between Maryland and Virginia on the Potomac River. It is the only American city or town that is not part of a state.

Milt & Joan Mann

The Capitol's Great Rotunda, or room under its dome, has many paintings and sculptures. These artworks portray events and people important in American history.

Milt & Joan Mann

The Supreme Court Building resembles a Greek temple. In a courtroom inside, the Supreme Court justices make legal decisions that may affect the lives of every American.

ed by James Smithson, a British scientist who had never visited the United States. Smithson left his fortune to the nation for the "increase and diffusion of knowledge." The Smithsonian's buildings on the mall are listed here in alphabetical order.

The Arthur M. Sackler Gallery specializes in Asian art.

The Arts and Industries Building includes the Discovery Theater, changing special exhibitions, and administrative offices.

The Freer Gallery of Art is noted for its collection of American paintings of the 1800's and 1900's, particularly the works of James McNeill Whistler. The Freer also has an important collection of Asian art.

The Hirshhorn Museum and Sculpture Garden features modern paintings and sculpture.

The National Air and Space Museum has the world's largest collection of historic aircraft and spacecraft. Its exhibits include the plane of the Wright brothers, in which Orville Wright made the first successful flight; the *Spirit of St. Louis,* in which Charles Lindbergh made the first solo flight across the Atlantic Ocean; and the Apollo 11 spacecraft, in which American astronauts traveled to the moon.

The National Museum of African Art is dedicated to the preservation of African art and culture.

The National Museum of American History houses the Star-Spangled Banner, the flag that inspired Francis Scott Key to write the national anthem. The museum has exhibits on the presidents and first ladies of the United States and numerous collections related to American popular culture.

The National Museum of the American Indian focuses on presenting the historical and contemporary cultures

War memorials stand on the Mall. The Vietnam Veterans Memorial has two adjoining black granite walls, *left.* They are inscribed with the names of all Americans who died in the Vietnam War. The National World War II Memorial includes 56 pillars that represent the District of Columbia and the states and territories of the war period. They surround a pool and plaza, *left below.* The Korean War Veterans Memorial features stainless steel sculptures of Korean War troops, *right below.*

Wally McNamee, Woodfin Camp, Inc.

© Tim Sloan, AFP/Getty Images

© Karen A. McCormack

and cultural achievements of Native Americans.

The National Museum of Natural History, one of the world's most popular museums, features skeletons of dinosaurs, a gem collection that includes the Hope Diamond, and an insect zoo.

The Smithsonian Institution Building, known as the *Castle,* was the Smithsonian's original building. The red sandstone castlelike structure is a replica of Norman architecture of the 1100's. Once a museum, the building now houses administrative offices, the Smithsonian Information Center, and the burial place of James Smithson.

Also on the Mall is the National Gallery of Art, one of the world's leading art museums. It is affiliated with the Smithsonian Institution but is governed by its own board of trustees.

Several Smithsonian museums are in other parts of Washington. The Anacostia Museum is a center for the preservation of African American art and culture. The National Portrait Gallery displays a collection of paintings of important people in American history. The National Postal Museum focuses on the history of American postal delivery and stamp design. The Smithsonian American Art Museum includes collections of American art from the 1700's to the present. The Renwick Gallery of the Smithsonian American Art Museum features American crafts.

The National Zoological Park is also part of the Smithsonian Institution. The zoo houses rare pandas and thousands of other animals.

Washington Monument is a towering, slender, white marble *obelisk* (pillar) dedicated to the memory of George Washington. The tallest structure in Washing-

ton, it rises 555 feet 5 $\frac{1}{8}$ inches tall (169.29 meters). From the top, visitors can see much of the Washington area.

Lincoln Memorial is a white marble monument that honors Abraham Lincoln. On the outside, 36 Doric columns, one for each state in the Union at the time of Lincoln's death, support the roof. Inside is a majestic marble sculpture of Lincoln seated in a chair. Quotations from Lincoln's writings appear on the interior walls.

The National World War II Memorial honors those who served in World War II (1939-1945). Fifty-six small pillars representing the District of Columbia and the states and territories of the war period surround a granite plaza and sunken pool. A curved wall is covered with gold stars representing those who died in the war.

The Vietnam Veterans Memorial, east of the Lincoln Memorial, is dedicated to those who served in the Vietnam War (1957-1975). It includes two black granite walls on which are inscribed the names of all Americans who died in the war or who remain classified as missing in action. Many visitors leave flowers or other remembrances of their loved ones who served in Vietnam. The memorial also includes two bronze sculptures, one of three servicemen and the other of battlefield nurses.

The Korean War Veterans Memorial, east of the Lincoln Memorial, is a monument to those who served in the Korean War (1950-1953). It features 19 large stainless steel sculptures of American servicemen and a black granite wall that reflects the sculptures. The wall has engraved images of about 2,500 nurses, mechanics, and other military personnel who served in Korea.

The Tidal Basin. The Jefferson Memorial and the Roosevelt Memorial stand near the Tidal Basin, a lagoon that adjoins the Mall south of the Washington Monu-

Monuments to four American presidents stand in the capital. The Jefferson Memorial, *left above,* and the Roosevelt Memorial, *below,* are in a beautiful setting among Japanese cherry trees at the edge of the Tidal Basin. On the Mall are the towering Washington Monument, *center above,* the city's tallest structure, and the majestic Lincoln Memorial, *right above,* with its famous Lincoln statue.

ment. The Tidal Basin is surrounded by more than 3,000 Yoshino cherry trees, a gift from the mayor of Tokyo, Japan, in 1912 to memorialize Japanese-American friendship. Since 1934, the blossoming of the trees in late March or early April each year has been celebrated with the Cherry Blossom Festival.

Jefferson Memorial, on the south side of the Tidal Basin, is dedicated to Thomas Jefferson. The design of the circular white marble building is based on the Classical style of architecture. Jefferson introduced the style to the United States when he designed and built his own home, Monticello. A bronze statue of Jefferson and quotations from his writings are inside the monument.

Franklin Delano Roosevelt Memorial, which stands on the west side of the Tidal Basin, honors Franklin D. Roosevelt. It is also called the *Roosevelt Memorial* or the *FDR Memorial.* It includes four outdoor "rooms," each dedicated to one of Roosevelt's four terms as president. The monument spreads out over $7\frac{1}{2}$ acres (3 hectares). Sculptures depict the Great Depression and other events of Roosevelt's presidency.

North of the Mall stand a number of massive office buildings, along or near Pennsylvania Avenue. This broad, treelined street crosses the city from southeast to northwest and connects the Capitol with the White House. It is sometimes known as "America's Main Street," and it serves as Washington's main parade route. Major demonstrations take place on the street as well as races to fund medical research.

The White House ranks as the most important building in this area. Some of the other buildings house offices of the executive branch of the federal government. Several national and international organizations have their headquarters near the federal buildings. These include the American Red Cross, Daughters of the American Revolution (DAR), the National Academy of Sciences, the International Monetary Fund, the Organization of American States, and the World Bank. Also nearby is a major tourist attraction, Ford's Theatre.

White House, at 1600 Pennsylvania Avenue NW, has served as the home and office of every United States president except George Washington. The building is constructed of white sandstone and stands in an 18-acre (7.3-hectare) park. Five of its 132 rooms are open to the public. These rooms—the Blue, East, Green, and Red rooms and the State Dining Room—are decorated with magnificent art and elegant furnishings. The president's offices and family quarters are not open to tourists.

Two parklike areas border the White House grounds. Lafayette Square lies to the north, and the Ellipse lies to the south. Blair House, a mansion on the west side of Lafayette Square, serves as a guesthouse for high-ranking international officials visiting the president. President Harry S. Truman lived in Blair House from 1948 to 1952, while the White House was being renovated.

Executive branch buildings. The Old Executive Office Building is west of the White House, and the New Executive Office Building is north of it. The employees of the Office of Management and Budget and other presidential staff members work in these buildings. The Department of the Treasury is directly east of the White House.

Several large office buildings for the executive branch stand close together on the south side of Pennsylvania Avenue between the White House and the Capitol. This group of buildings is called *Federal Triangle* because it consists of federal government buildings grouped in a triangle. Federal Triangle includes the Department of Commerce, Department of Justice, Federal Trade Commission, Internal Revenue Service, National Archives, and U.S. Customs Service. The Department of Labor and the Federal Bureau of Investigation (FBI) lie north of Pennsylvania Avenue. The departments of State and Interior are southwest of the White House, in a neighborhood known as Foggy Bottom.

Most popular with tourists are the National Archives and the FBI facilities. The Archives stores government documents. It displays three of the most important documents in American history—the Declaration of Independence, the Constitution of the United States, and the Bill of Rights. The FBI tour includes a demonstration of agents taking target practice.

Ford's Theatre is the playhouse where Abraham Lincoln was shot. It stands $1\frac{1}{2}$ blocks north of Pennsylvania Avenue, between the Capitol and the White House. The theater, which still offers live performances of touring dramas and musicals, houses a collection of items related to Lincoln's life and death. Petersen House, the house where Lincoln died, stands across the street from the theater.

South of the Mall stand several government office buildings. They include the offices of the United States Postal Service and of six executive departments—Agriculture, Education, Energy, Health and Human Services, Housing and Urban Development, and Transportation.

The Bureau of Engraving and Printing, also known as the *Mint,* is south of the Mall. This popular tourist attraction is the place where government workers engrave and print the nation's paper money.

Next door to the Mint is the U.S. Holocaust Memorial Museum. This museum honors the millions of Jews and others murdered by the Nazis during World War II.

Other points of interest draw visitors to other parts of Washington and its suburbs.

John F. Kennedy Center for the Performing Arts borders the Potomac River near the Lincoln Memorial. It has three large theaters and two smaller spaces that host dramas, ballets, operas, symphonies, and films.

Watergate, a complex north of the Kennedy Center, includes condominiums, offices, a hotel, and shops. Watergate became internationally famous in 1972 when campaign workers for President Richard M. Nixon, a Republican, were caught breaking into Democratic political headquarters there. The break-in marked the start of a major American political scandal that led to Nixon's resignation from office.

Other Washington museums. The Corcoran Gallery of Art, which specializes in American art, was founded in 1869. It was Washington's first art museum. The Phillips Collection includes American and European paintings from the 1700's to the present. The National Museum of Women in the Arts exhibits the work of women artists of all periods and nationalities. The Textile Museum exhibits textiles dating from 3000 B.C. to the present. Woodrow Wilson House, the home that the 28th president lived in after he left office, is a national historic landmark.

Robert H. Glaze, Artstreet

The White House has served as the home and office of every United States president with the exception of George Washington. This picture shows the south side of the White House.

Washington, D.C.

This map of west-central Washington shows many of the city's main points of interest in blue and keys them with a number to the map index, *below*.

American Art Portrait Gallery Building **1** B 4
Arthur M. Sackler Gallery **2** C 5
Blair House **3** C 1
Bureau of Engraving and Printing **4** D 4
Bureau of Indian Affairs **5** D 2
Cannon House Office Building **6** B 8
Corcoran Gallery of Art **7** D 2
Department of Agriculture **8** D 5
Department of Commerce **9** C 3
Department of Education **10** C 7
Department of Energy **11** C 5
Department of Health and Human
  Services **12** C 7
Department of Housing and Urban
  Development **13** C 6
Department of Justice **14** C 4
Department of Labor **15** B 6
Department of State **16** D 1
Department of the Interior **17** D 2
Department of the Treasury **18** C 2
Department of Transportation **19** C 7
Department of Veterans Affairs **20** C 2
Dirksen and Hart Senate Office
  Buildings **21** A 7
Executive Office Buildings **22** C 1
Federal Aviation Administration **23** C 6
Federal Bureau of Investigation **24** C 4
Federal Reserve System **25** D 1
Federal Trade Commission **26** B 5
Folger Shakespeare Library **27** A 8
Ford's Theatre **28** B 4
Franklin Delano Roosevelt Memorial **66** E 3
Freer Gallery of Art **29** C 5
General Services Administration **30** D 1

Government Printing Office **31** A 5
Hirshhorn Museum and Sculpture
  Garden **32** C 5
House Office Buildings (see 6, 39, and 51) —
Internal Revenue Service **33** C 4
Jefferson Memorial **34** E 5
Korean War Veterans Memorial **67** E 2
Library of Congress Thomas Jefferson
  Building **35** B 8
Library of Congress John Adams
  Building **36** B 8
Library of Congress James Madison Memorial
  Building **37** B 8
Lincoln Memorial **38** E 1
Longworth House Office Building **39** B 8
Martin Luther King Memorial Library **40** B 3
National Aeronautics and Space
  Administration **41** C 6
National Air and Space Museum **42** C 6
National Archives Building **43** C 5
National Gallery of Art **44** B 6
National Museum of African Art **45** C 5
National Museum of American History **46** C 4
National Museum of Natural History **47** C 4
National Museum of the American Indian **69** C 6
National Museum of the Building Arts (Pension
  Building) **48** B 5
National Portrait Gallery (housed in number 1) —
National World War II Memorial **70** D 3
Office of Personnel Management **49** D 1
Old Post Office Building **50** C 4
Rayburn House Office Building **51** B 7
Renwick Gallery **52** C 1
Ronald Reagan Building **68** C 3

Russell Senate Office Building **53** A 7
Senate Office Buildings (see 21 and 53) —
Smithsonian American Art Museum (housed in
  number 1) —
Smithsonian Arts and Industries
  Building **54** C 5
Smithsonian Institution Building
  (administrative offices) **55** C 5
Smithsonian Museums (see 1, 29, 32,
  42, 44, 45, 46, 47, 52, and 54) —
Supreme Court Building **56** A 8
Union Station **57** A 6
United States Botanic Garden **58** B 7
United States Capitol **59** B 7
United States Customs Service (housed in
  number 68) —
United States Holocaust Memorial
  Museum **61** D 4
United States Postal Service **62** D 6
Vietnam Veterans Memorial **63** E 1
Washington Monument **64** D 3
White House **65** C 2

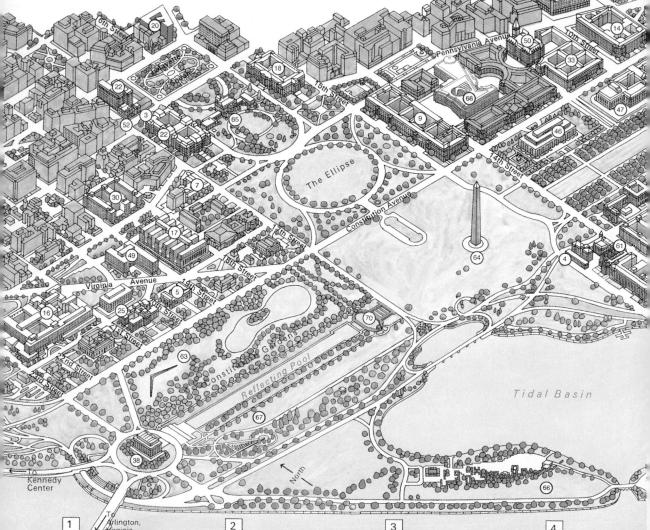

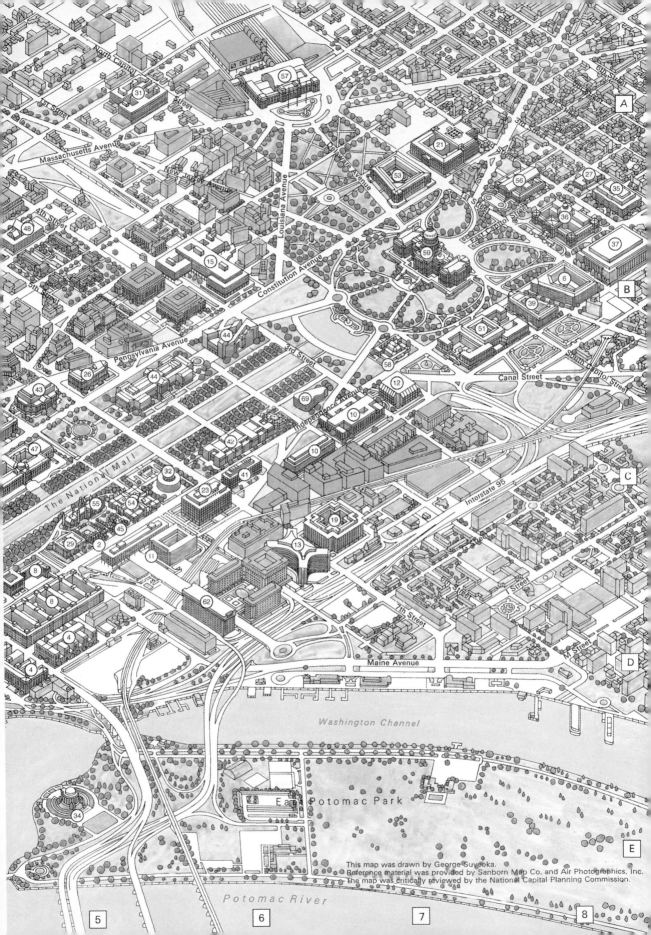

This map was drawn by George Suyeoka.
Reference material was provided by Sanborn Map Co. and Air Photographics, Inc.
The map was critically reviewed by the National Capital Planning Commission.

Jack Rottier, National Parks Service

Ford's Theatre was the scene of the assassination of Abraham Lincoln. The president was sitting in a box seat behind the flags when he was shot. The box overlooks the stage.

Milt & Joan Mann

The Bureau of Engraving and Printing makes the nation's paper money. The employee shown here is inspecting large sheets of newly printed $1 bills.

The Pentagon, the headquarters of the Department of Defense, is the world's largest office building. It covers 29 acres (11.7 hectares) in Arlington, Virginia, across the Potomac from Washington.

Arlington National Cemetery, which lies northwest of the Pentagon in Arlington, contains the graves of thousands of men and women who served in the U.S. armed forces. It includes the Tomb of the Unknowns, where three unidentified servicemen who died in action are buried. They represent all the unidentified members of the armed forces who gave their lives for their country. The cemetery also includes the graves of President William Howard Taft; President John F. Kennedy; Kennedy's wife, Jacqueline; and Kennedy's brother Senator Robert F. Kennedy.

The Marine Corps War Memorial, also known as the *Iwo Jima Memorial,* is just north of Arlington Cemetery. It features one of America's most famous monuments, a dramatic bronze sculpture of five marines and a Navy medical corpsman raising the American flag on the island of Iwo Jima during World War II.

Mount Vernon, the home of George Washington, is in northern Virginia, about 15 miles (24 kilometers) south of Washington. The first president's grave is there.

Architectural styles. Many visitors enjoy the rich and varied architecture of the city's buildings and monuments. Many structures, including the Capitol, Supreme Court, and Lincoln Memorial, are built in the Neoclassical style or the Greek Revival style. These building styles were derived from the traditions of ancient Greece and Rome.

Washington National Cathedral, an Episcopal church at Massachusetts and Wisconsin Avenues NW, was built in the Gothic style of medieval Europe. The National Shrine of the Immaculate Conception, at 4th Street and Michigan Avenue NE, has elements of Byzantine and Romanesque architecture. The Islamic Center on Massachusetts Avenue NW is an outstanding example of Muslim architecture.

Many buildings in Georgetown, a neighborhood west of the White House, provide examples of colonial American residential architecture. Other sections of the city have fine examples of many other historic and modern styles of architecture. However, no building in Washington may be built taller than the 13-story Washington Monument. As a result, Washington, unlike most other large cities, has no skyscrapers.

The city

Washington, D.C., lies along the northern bank of the Potomac River. The state of Maryland borders Washington on the northwest, northeast, and southeast. Virginia lies across the Potomac River to the southwest. Suburban communities of Maryland and Virginia surround Washington.

Pierre L'Enfant's city plan created a large grid, with the U.S. Capitol at its heart. The city is divided into four *quadrants* (fourths of a circle) by the streets that extend directly north, south, east, and west of the Capitol— North Capitol Street, South Capitol Street, East Capitol Street, and the Mall. The quadrants are Northwest (NW), Southwest (SW), Northeast (NE), and Southeast (SE). All four quadrants have the same basic street pattern. Streets that run north-south are numbered, beginning at

Paul S. Conklin

Arlington National Cemetery includes the gravesites of President John F. Kennedy and his wife, Jacqueline, *foreground*. Thousands of armed forces veterans are buried there. The cemetery is in Arlington, Virginia.

for its beautiful old houses, many of which date from the late 1700's and early 1800's. Northwest includes a wide range of high-income, middle-income, and lower-income housing. It also includes five of the city's leading universities—American, George Washington, Georgetown, and Howard universities and the University of the District of Columbia.

Northeast lies between North Capitol and East Capitol streets. It covers about one-fourth of the city. Much of Northeast is residential, with large sections of lovely middle- and upper-middle-class housing as well as some lower-income areas. In this quadrant are the Kenilworth Aquatic Gardens, the National Arboretum, and Gallaudet University, a university for students who are deaf or hearing-impaired. This section also has an extensive complex of buildings owned by the Roman Catholic Church. The church's holdings include Catholic University, the National Shrine of the Immaculate Conception, five colleges, and the Franciscan Monastery. The Anacostia River cuts through Northeast.

Southeast is the area between East Capitol and South Capitol streets. It covers just under one-fourth of the city's area. Southeast includes the Washington Navy Yard and the extensive grounds of St. Elizabeth's Hospital. It also includes Fort Dupont Park and other parks established where forts stood during the American Civil War (1861-1865). There is an important commercial district on Pennsylvania Avenue SE. It includes Eastern Market, an old-fashioned farmers' market where locally grown fresh fruits, vegetables, and flowers are sold. The Anacostia River flows through the heart of Southeast. The area south of the river is primarily residential, with mostly middle-class and low-income neighborhoods.

Southwest is the city's smallest quadrant, extending from South Capitol Street west to the Potomac River. It covers less than one-eighth of the district's land area. Al-

the Capitol. The east-west streets are letters of the alphabet, beginning at the Capitol.

Overlaid onto the grid are 50 diagonal avenues, each named for a U.S. state. The avenues closest to the Capitol are named for the original 13 states, and those farther away are named for the states that joined the Union later. Where two or more avenues intersect there is a circle. Many of the circles have lovely parks.

Northwest includes that part of Washington between North Capitol Street and the Potomac River. It covers about the half the city's area and is its largest section. Northwest is also Washington's main center of cultural, economic, and government activity.

Northwest Washington holds the White House, a large number of federal office buildings, half the Smithsonian museums, and most of the foreign embassies. Washington's main commercial and retail districts also lie in Northwest. North of the commercial area, Rock Creek Park winds through Northwest Washington in a north-south direction. The official residence of the vice president of the United States is near the park, on the grounds of the Naval Observatory on Massachusetts Avenue NW.

Large residential areas lie east and west of Rock Creek Park. Georgetown, which is west of the park, is the part of the district that was settled the earliest. It is famous

James H. Pickerell

The Marine Corps War Memorial shows servicemen raising the American flag on Iwo Jima during World War II. Located in Arlington, it is a famous tribute to the American war effort.

most all of Southwest has been rebuilt since the 1950's as part of a major urban renewal program. As a result, the housing stock in Southwest is considerably newer than in other parts of the city. Southwest also holds a substantial number of government office buildings, half the Smithsonian museums, Fort Lesley J. McNair, the National War College, and the sprawling Bolling Air Force Base.

Metropolitan area. The Washington metropolitan area includes the District of Columbia, six cities in northern Virginia that are not part of a county—Alexandria, Fairfax, Falls Church, Fredericksburg, Manassas, and Manassas Park—and 18 counties in Maryland, Virginia, and West Virginia. The metropolitan areas of Washington; Baltimore, Maryland; and Hagerstown, Maryland, form the Washington-Baltimore Consolidated Metropolitan Area.

Washington's suburbs include cities and towns as well as large open areas of hills, woods, and farms. However, increases in population and the spread of the suburbs has begun to threaten remaining open spaces.

Paul S. Conklin

Row houses line many of the residential streets of Washington, D.C. Large numbers of the city's residents live in neighborhoods similar to the one shown here.

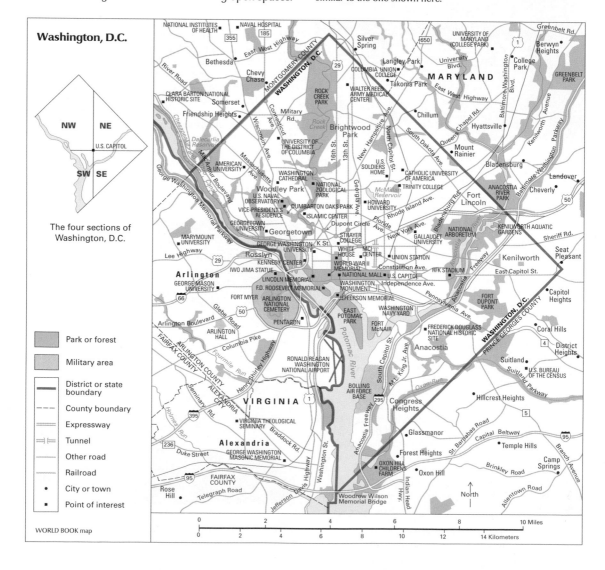

WORLD BOOK map

Milt & Joan Mann

Georgetown, a neighborhood in Northwest Washington, has fine examples of colonial American residential architecture. The area was first settled in the mid 1700's

James H. Pickerell

Single-family houses line a curving street in Bethesda, Maryland, a Washington suburb. Large numbers of people in the Washington area live in suburbs and commute to the city.

The suburbs are under the jurisdiction of the states or counties in which they are located.

In the Washington area, as in other metropolitan areas, large numbers of people who live in the suburbs work in the city. However, beginning in the mid-1900's, a number of *belt cities* have sprouted around the Washington suburbs.

The first of the belt cities were Beltsville and Greenbelt in Maryland. These cities grew up around the National Agricultural Center. In Virginia, substantial suburban centers later developed at Tysons Corner, around high technology and telecommunications firms; around the Pentagon in Arlington; and around Dulles Airport in Loudoun County. Development also took place along the I-270 corridor in Montgomery County, Maryland, the site of the National Institutes of Health, Bethesda Naval Hospital, and numerous biomedical research organizations. A number of federal agencies have moved to these suburban areas, fueling further population growth.

Two of the most famous *new towns* in the United States—Columbia, Maryland, and Reston, Virginia—are near Washington. Begun in the early 1960's, these two communities were carefully planned before they were built (see **City planning** [Building new communities]).

People

Population. About 60 percent of the people of Washington, D.C., are African Americans. Non-Hispanic whites make up about 28 percent of the city's population. Hispanics, who may be of any race, account for about 8 percent of the people. Asians and American Indians make up about 4 percent of the population.

The suburbs remain primarily white, though a number of African Americans moved to the suburbs in the late 1900's. Also during the late 1900's, many refugees from countries torn by war and political turmoil settled in Washington and its suburbs. They included many people of Southeast Asian and Hispanic origins. Some of these newcomers live close together, creating interesting ethnic neighborhoods. These residents as well as the staffs of the many embassies and international organizations help give Washington a cosmopolitan flavor.

Housing. About half of Washington's residents live in one- or two-family houses, and about half in apartments or condominiums. Approximately 40 percent own their homes. The lack of sufficient housing remains one of the most crucial problems facing the Washington area.

Education. About 71,000 students are enrolled in 146 public schools in D.C. Nearly 85 percent of the students are African American, 9 percent are Hispanic, and 5 percent white. Thousands of students attend private schools in the city.

The District of Columbia Board of Education governs the public school system. The board has nine members, and they serve four-year terms. Voters elect five of the board's members, and the mayor appoints four members. The board members appoint a superintendent to administer the system. The public schools are funded by local taxes.

Washington's numerous accredited colleges and universities include American, Catholic, Gallaudet, George Washington, Georgetown, and Howard universities, and the University of the District of Columbia. Howard University is one of the country's largest predominantly black colleges and has a long history of producing im-

Paul S. Conklin

A soccer game on the Ellipse provides recreation for a group of Washington young people. The Washington Monument rises above the trees in the background.

portant African American leaders. Catholic University is the national university of the Roman Catholic Church in the United States.

Washington does not have a comprehensive state university. Under legislation passed by Congress, high school graduates who are residents of the district are eligible to attend any state university in the United States and pay in-state tuition.

Social problems. Like all major cities, Washington faces a variety of social problems, including poverty and crime. Due to rapid population growth, the area also struggles with the need for more housing, schools, highways, and Potomac River crossings.

Overall, the people of Washington have a high standard of living. However, thousands of people who live in the city and suburbs do not share in the wealth. Approximately 15 percent of all the families in the city and about 5 percent of the families in the suburbs have incomes that classify them as poor by U.S. government standards. Unemployment is low, but there are shortages of qualified workers in several sectors of the economy.

Since the 1990's, crime rates have been rising in the suburbs and dropping in the city. Washington crime receives more nationwide publicity than that of any other city because the federal government is located there.

Cultural life and recreation. The museums, government buildings, parks, monuments, libraries, and theaters described in the *Visitor's guide* help make Washington a leading cultural and recreational center. Residents as well as tourists enjoy these opportunities.

Washington also has many cultural and recreational facilities used chiefly by its residents. These include the

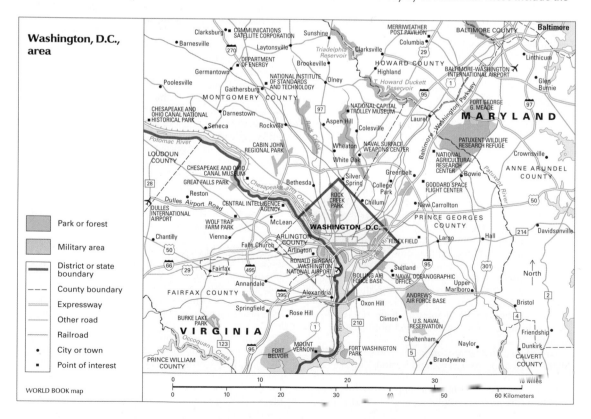

Washington, D.C., area

Park or forest

Military area

District or state boundary

County boundary

Expressway

Other road

Railroad

• City or town

▪ Point of interest

WORLD BOOK map

Universities and colleges

This table lists the universities and colleges in Washington, D.C., that grant bachelor's or advanced degrees and are accredited by the Middle States Association of Colleges and Schools.

Name	Founded
American University	1893
Catholic University of America	1887
Corcoran College of Art and Design	1890
District of Columbia, University of the	1976
Dominican House of Studies	1902
Gallaudet University	1864
George Washington University	1821
Georgetown University	1789
Howard University	1867
Joint Military Intelligence College	1962
National Defense University	1976
Southeastern University	1879
Strayer University	1892
Trinity College	1897
Washington Theological Union	1969
Wesley Theological Seminary	1882

public library system. The system's main library is the Martin Luther King, Jr., Memorial Library at 9th and G Streets NW. The city has an increasing number of professional acting companies. Its main theaters include the Arena Stage, the Shakespeare Theatre, the National Theater, Ford's Theatre, and the John F. Kennedy Center for the Performing Arts. The National Symphony Orchestra, the Washington Opera, the Washington Ballet, touring companies of Broadway productions, and the American Film Institute entertain audiences in the performance

spaces at the Kennedy Center.

Washington has about 150 parks. Many residents enjoy boating on the Potomac River or in nearby Chesapeake Bay. Local sports teams include the Washington Redskins of the National Football League, the Washington Wizards of the National Basketball Association, and the Washington Capitals of the National Hockey League.

Economy

Washington's economy thrives on tourism and the activities of the federal government. The city's many attractions, which include the largest concentration of museums in the world, draw millions of tourists each year. The federal government is the largest employer in Washington and its surrounding area. It also generates a substantial portion of Washington's private economic activity. Since the late 1900's, however, the local economy has diversified considerably. The city still depends primarily on service industries. But leading employers outside of government and tourism now include business, finance, and trade associations; health care; higher education; information technology and telecommunications; and the communications industry.

Government. The federal government employs about 185,000 people in Washington and another 120,000 in the surrounding metropolitan area. The best-known and most important government employees include the president of the United States, the president's Cabinet officers and advisers, the members of Congress, and the Supreme Court justices. Those key policymakers account for only a tiny portion of Washington's government workers, however. Most government employ-

The Folger Shakespeare Library's theater resembles the theaters of William Shakespeare's time. It provides a setting for concerts and lectures as well as productions of Shakespeare's plays.

Cameramann International, Ltd.

Government workers jam Pennsylvania Avenue on their way to and from work. The federal government is the largest employer in the Washington area.

ees staff the departments and agencies of the executive branch. They carry out the daily operations of the government, on which individual citizens depend.

Washington is one of the nation's few cities with little manufacturing employment. The primary manufacturing industry in the city is printing and publishing, most of which is done by the federal government. Government printing makes Washington one of the nation's leading publishing centers. Its departments and agencies produce pamphlets and books on thousands of subjects, ranging from census information to farming advice.

Other service industries. The federal government remains the leading employer in Washington. But many people work in a variety of other service industries.

Business, finance, and trade associations employ more than 130,000 people. Many businesses and private organizations have offices in Washington so that they can closely observe and interact with the federal government. This sector of the economy includes law firms; accounting, banking, and financial organizations; labor unions; and trade associations. Perhaps the best-known workers in this category are *lobbyists,* people who work to influence the government on behalf of their members or clients.

Health care employs about 40,000 workers. Hospitals in Washington include Children's Hospital National Medical Center; Columbia Hospital for Women; St. Elizabeth's Hospital, which provides care for people with mental illnesses; and a major Veterans Administration

hospital. The city also has hospitals associated with medical schools at Howard, George Washington, and Georgetown universities. The presence of these schools and of the National Institutes of Health in Bethesda, Maryland, has attracted a large concentration of biomedical and genetic research organizations to Washington and the suburbs of Montgomery County, Maryland.

Tourism is important to Washington's economy. The city hosts millions of tourists each year. They come to see the United States government in action. They also come to visit the many museums, historic sites, and monuments and to enjoy the city's cultural activities. Hotels, motels, restaurants, and other tourist-related businesses employ about 60,000 people in Washington.

Higher education is an important part of the Washington economy. More than 100,000 students from every U.S. state and more than 150 countries are enrolled in the city's colleges and universities. Institutions of higher education employ about 45,000 people.

Information technology and telecommunications firms employ thousands of people in Washington and make up an important part of the area's economy. Telecommunications firms with headquarters in the Washington area have particularly influenced growth in the northern Virginia suburbs.

Communication. The city has two daily newspapers, *The Washington Post* and *The Washington Times,* and a number of radio and television stations. All of the nation's major television networks and metropolitan newspapers have Washington bureaus. In addition, newspeople from all over the world are stationed in Washington to provide first-hand accounts of events that will affect the lives of people in their countries.

USA Today, a national daily newspaper, is published in Washington. United Press International, one of the world's leading wire services, is headquartered in the capital. About 600 periodicals are published there, including *National Geographic, U.S. News & World Report, The New Republic,* and the *National Journal.*

Transportation. The Washington area has an extensive public transportation system. About half of the people who work in the metropolitan area use public transportation to get to and from work. The Washington Area Metropolitan Transit Authority, known as *Metro,* operates a bus service and a subway system that serve the city and its suburbs. The 103-mile (166-kilometer) subway system was completed in 2000. Commuter rail lines connect Washington with cities and towns in neighboring Maryland and Virginia.

About half of the area's workers use automobiles to get to and from their jobs. Washington is served by one of the country's most extensive highway systems. The system includes six major interstate highways and a large network of roads and bridges. Increases in population, however, have put a severe strain on Washington roads and highways. Traffic congestion has become one of the most difficult problems facing the region.

Union Station lies two blocks north of the U.S. Capitol. Amtrak provides passenger rail service from the station to all major cities on the East Coast and to many cities in the West. Union Station is the southernmost destination for the high-speed Amtrak trains that serve the Northeast. The station is the terminal for local commuter trains, and it has a Metro subway stop.

Three major airports handle Washington's commercial air traffic. Ronald Reagan National Airport lies just across the Potomac River in Arlington, Virginia. Dulles International Airport, also in Virginia, is 25 miles (40 kilometers) west of Washington. Baltimore-Washington International Airport is in Maryland, about 30 miles (48 kilometers) northeast of Washington.

Local government

Washington's system of local government is different from that of all other American cities. As in most cities, local citizens elect a mayor and city council to make laws and carry out government functions. However, the federal government has veto power and final authority in all matters relating to Washington.

Washington's mayor serves a four-year term. The mayor appoints the heads of city agencies and departments and four members of the board of education.

Washington's City Council has 13 members. Five members are elected by the city as a whole. One member is elected from each of Washington's eight wards. The members are elected to four-year terms. The council passes local laws, and the mayor may sign or veto their legislation. However, all city laws are subject to veto by the U.S. Congress. Congress and the U.S. Office of Management and Budget must approve the city's budget each year.

Washington's city government gets about two-thirds of its revenue from taxes, including property, sales, and local income taxes. The federal government makes an annual payment to the city in lieu of property taxes on the land occupied by government offices.

Washington's present system of local government was established by an act of Congress in 1973 and approved by the voters in 1974. For 100 years before that time, the people of Washington had almost no voice in their government. The president, rather than the people, chose the three commissioners who made up the government. See the *History* section of this article for details on Washington's former system of local government.

For the District of Columbia's electoral votes and voting record in presidential elections since 1964, see **Electoral College** (table).

History

Early days. Historians believe that Indians first lived in what is now the Washington, D.C., area about 12,000 years ago. Captain John Smith, the English soldier who helped establish the colony at Jamestown, Virginia, explored the Potomac River in 1608. At that time, he found a well-established settlement of Nacotchtank Indians, a group that spoke the Algonquin language. The Indians initially welcomed English trade and alliances, but conflicts over property ownership led to bloody battles. The Nacotchtank then abandoned their villages and retreated into the forests.

By 1660, a few wealthy and powerful English colonists began to acquire land along the Potomac River for tobacco cultivation. They established large plantations that were worked by slaves forcibly transported from Africa. In 1740, a tobacco inspection station and warehouse were established on the Maryland side of the Potomac River. In 1751, the community that grew up around the inspection station was named George Town (later

Washington's flag was adopted in 1938. Its design is based on George Washington's coat of arms.

The city seal, adopted in 1871, shows Justice placing a wreath on a statue of George Washington.

spelled Georgetown). By 1791, when it became part of the area chosen as the capital, Georgetown was one of the nation's leading tobacco ports and trading centers.

Choosing the capital. Several different cities served as the nation's capital during the early years of American independence. In 1783, Congress decided that the country should have a permanent center of government. It was difficult for the members of Congress to agree on a location because they realized that the area where the capital was placed would gain wealth and political influence. Representatives from the Northern states wanted the capital to be in Philadelphia. Southerners felt that the economic interests of the Northern states were too different from their own, and they wanted the capital in a state where slavery was legal.

Alexander Hamilton and Thomas Jefferson worked out a compromise. Hamilton, who was serving as the U.S. secretary of the treasury, was concerned about stabilizing the national economy. He felt that Congress should agree to pay the debts that some Northern states still owed due to their participation in the Revolutionary War in America (1775-1783). Jefferson, the secretary of state, was from Virginia, a state that had already paid all its war debts. Jefferson agreed to support Hamilton's proposal if Hamilton would agree to locating the capital in a Southern city. Their compromise resulted in Congress passing the Residence Act of 1790.

The act gave President George Washington the power to choose a spot for the capital. Washington selected an area of 100 square miles (259 square kilometers) on the Potomac River between the mouth of the Eastern Branch (now known as the Anacostia River) and Conocheague Creek, 70 miles (113 kilometers) upstream. The site Washington chose was only a few miles north of his home at Mount Vernon, Virginia.

The president's choice, made in 1791, included the land north of the Potomac that is now occupied by the city as well as an area south of the Potomac River. The land north of the Potomac, which belonged to the state of Maryland, included the port of Georgetown. The land south of the Potomac, which belonged to Virginia, had a well-established tobacco port of its own, Alexandria. The states of Maryland and Virginia turned over the territory to the federal government.

Building the city. George Washington hired Pierre Charles L'Enfant, a French engineer, to create a plan for the physical layout of the city. L'Enfant's plan dealt only with the area between the Anacostia River and Georgetown, and extended north only to what is now Florida Avenue. Georgetown, Alexandria, and Washington County (the land north of Florida Avenue) remained separate, with their own local governments. The entire plan centered around the placement of the U.S. Capitol on Jenkins Hill, which L'Enfant called "a pedestal awaiting a monument." L'Enfant's plan is discussed in more detail earlier in this article, in the section *The City.*

President Washington had to persuade the people who owned the land designated as the capital to donate their property to the U.S. government. Because L'Enfant had difficult relationships with the local landowners and government officials, Washington had to fire him before his work was completed. But two surveyors, Andrew Ellicott and Benjamin Banneker, laid out the streets and lots according to L'Enfant's plan. Ellicott was a veteran of the Revolutionary War. Banneker was a free African American scientist and mathematician.

President Washington appointed three commissioners to direct the construction and affairs of the new capital city. When the federal government moved to its new home in 1800, the commissioners named the city *Washington,* after the president who had played such a key role in the city's establishment. They called the entire area the *District of Columbia.*

Slow beginnings. The Constitution of the United States gave Congress the power to govern Washington. In 1802, Congress established a local government. The City Council members were elected by local residents, but the mayor was appointed by the president. In 1820, the citizens of Washington were granted the right to elect their own mayor. But they were not permitted to vote for members of Congress or the president.

In August 1814, during the War of 1812, British soldiers invaded Washington and burned most of the public buildings, including the Capitol, White House, Library of Congress, and the Navy Yard. Members of Congress threatened to move the Capitol to a less vulnerable location, but Washingtonians persuaded them to stay. Workers completed the reconstruction of the government buildings in 1819.

The predictions that Washington would become an important commercial and industrial center did not come true right away. Once the Baltimore and Ohio Railroad was completed from Baltimore to Cumberland, Maryland, the city could no longer compete economically with Baltimore and other long-established cities, such as Boston, New York, Philadelphia, and Charleston. Lacking economic growth, Washington remained a small city. By the 1840's, there were still only about 50,000 residents, and much of the land in the District of Columbia remained undeveloped. In 1846, Congress returned to Virginia the land south of the Potomac River.

The issue of slavery. The presence of slavery in the capital of freedom remained a difficult issue and the subject of much argument. Slaves helped construct the U.S. Capitol, the White House, other federal buildings, and city streets. By 1830, free blacks outnumbered slaves in the District of Columbia. Washington's City Council repeatedly tried to prohibit local slavery and the slave trade, but pro-slavery congressmen blocked their every attempt. In the mid-1800's, Washington became the focus of the abolition movement. The Underground Railroad, an informal system that helped slaves escape, was active in both the city and Georgetown.

The Compromise of 1850 abolished the buying and selling of slaves in the District of Columbia. In 1862, sev-

eral months before President Abraham Lincoln issued the Emancipation Proclamation, slavery was abolished there. The district conducted the nation's only compensated emancipation. Slaveowners who were willing to swear a loyalty oath to the U.S. government were paid an average of $300 for each of their slaves.

The Civil War. Washington's main periods of growth have mostly been associated with times of crisis, such as wars and depressions. During such times, the role of the federal government has expanded to deal with the country's problems, resulting in increased employment opportunities in the capital city.

The American Civil War (1861-1865) was the first crisis that caused Washington to expand. During the war, the city's population nearly doubled, from about 60,000 to 120,000. The Union stationed thousands of troops in Washington to protect the city from Confederate attack. Large numbers of people flocked to the city to participate in the war effort. In addition, thousands of escaping slaves, known as "contrabands," poured into Washington from the South. Most of them settled near Union military camps. After Lincoln issued the Emancipation Proclamation, the number of black refugees increased. The enormous population growth led to a severe housing shortage. Public facilities, such as water and sewerage systems, could not handle the increased demands.

Congress began a major rebuilding and expansion program in Washington after the war. The program solved the city's physical needs. But it indirectly led to an end of the people's right to choose their local government leaders.

Territorial government abolished. In 1871, Congress established a territorial government for the district, headed by a governor appointed by the president. But the territorial government was dominated by Alexander "Boss" Shepherd, the head of the Board of Public Works. Shepherd directed a massive program of con-

Detail from an engraving by Andrew Ellicott (1792); Library of Congress, Geography and Map Division

Pierre L'Enfant's plan for Washington showed the location of the Capitol, White House, and Mall. President George Washington hired L'Enfant, a French engineer, to plan the city.

Pennsylvania Avenue in 1827 was a quiet dirt road. The Capitol, *background,* had a different dome and was smaller than it is today. The present Capitol design dates from the 1850's.

View of the Capitol at Washington, D.C., a hand-tinted engraving by C. J. Bentley after a painting by W. H. Bartlett; from *American Scenery,* published in 1840 by George Virtue

struction and improvements that transformed Washington into a beautiful modern city. However, Shepherd vastly overspent his budget, and he came under criti cism for his procedures for awarding contracts. He was accused of favoritism and dishonesty.

In 1874, a congressional committee investigated the Board of Public Works and discovered that the territorial government was nearly $19 million in debt. In their dismay at what they saw as sloppy business practices, the members of Congress abolished the territorial government. They replaced it with a panel of three commissioners. The president appointed the commissioners, who had absolute control over district affairs.

Georgetown and Washington County lost their independent existence and became part of the city of Washington. Even the street names were changed in George town to conform to the L'Enfant plan. Washington became the only American city in which the people did not elect their local officials.

Continued growth. In 1917, when the United States entered World War I, another period of enormous growth began. Again, the government needed new workers to help direct the war effort as well as the businesses and services to support them. The city's population increased from about 350,000 when the country entered the war to more than 450,000 in 1918, when the war ended. Shortages developed in housing, office space, and public facilities. The public school system was particularly hard-hit. Overcrowded classrooms held as many as 60 students. A number of new neighborhoods developed in what had previously been the farmland and countryside of Washington County.

During the Great Depression of the 1930's, jobs became scarce in all parts of the country except Washington. The federal government undertook numerous projects designed to end the Depression, and thousands of new government jobs were created. Washington's population grew from about 485,000 to 665,000 between 1930 and 1940. The participation of the United States in World War II accelerated Washington's growth during

the 1940's. The district's population peaked at more than 800,000 in 1950.

Population changes. The city's population began to decline during the 1950's. However, the population of the surrounding suburbs increased. The city's popula tion decline began with school desegregation in 1954. At that time, many white families moved to the suburbs. Since about 1955, African Americans have made up the majority of the city's population. However, since the 1970's, many of the city's African Americans have also moved to the suburbs.

Between 1950 and 1980, the population of the Washington metropolitan area grew faster than that of any other large city. It increased from about 1 $\frac{1}{2}$ million to more than 3 million. By 2000, the metropolitan population rose to nearly 5 million.

Government changes. After World War II, many Washingtonians began demanding the right to partici pate in government. Congress and the states passed a constitutional amendment that allowed Washingtonians to vote in presidential elections for the first time in 1964.

In 1967, President Lyndon B. Johnson reorganized the district's government by executive order. A mayor and nine-member City Council replaced the three-member board of commissioners. The mayor and council members were appointed by the president. Johnson named as mayor Walter E. Washington, a former District of Columbia housing administrator. Washington became the first African American to head a major U.S. city.

In 1970, Congress passed legislation permitting Washington to have a delegate in the U.S. House of Representatives. The delegate may vote in committees but not in votes of the full House of Representatives. Many Washingtonians feel this is unjust. They argue that they pay federal income taxes but have no voice in the legislative process that determines those taxes.

In 1973, Congress granted Washingtonians the right to elect local officials for the first time in 100 years. In 1974, city voters elected Walter E. Washington, who had held the post as an appointee since 1967. The mayor and the City Council took responsibility for oversight of the city's 14 local government departments.

In the 1970's, many Washingtonians began to support a movement to make the District of Columbia a state. In a 1980 election, a majority of Washington's voters supported statehood and, two years later, chose the name New Columbia for the proposed state. The statehood petition was sent to the U.S. Congress for approval in 1983. In 1992, the U.S. House of Representatives approved statehood, but the Senate declined to vote on the issue. Statehood bills were introduced in both houses of Congress in 1993, but neither passed.

The city faced a financial crisis in 1995. As a result, Congress seized control of the district government and created a Financial Control Board to run the city. The president appointed the board members. Control of some city functions was restored to local elected officials in 1999, and control of the rest was restored by 2001. The operations of the board created renewed local support for the movement to make the district a state.

On Sept. 11, 2001, terrorists crashed a hijacked commercial airplane into the Pentagon Building, near Washington, D.C. In related incidents that day, two more hijacked planes crashed into the twin 110-story towers of the World Trade Center in New York City, and a fourth hijacked plane crashed in Pennsylvania. Part of the Pentagon was destroyed and, in New York, both towers of the World Trade Center collapsed to the ground. About 3,000 people were killed. The terrorist attack was the worst in U.S. history.   Jane Donovan

Related articles in *World Book* include:

Arlington National Cemetery
Banneker, Benjamin
Botanic Garden, United States
Capitol, United States
Corcoran Gallery of Art
Folger Shakespeare Library
Franklin Delano Roosevelt
　Memorial
Freer Gallery of Art
Georgetown University
Hirshhorn Museum and
　Sculpture Garden
Holocaust Memorial Museum, United States
Jefferson Memorial
Kelly, Sharon Pratt
Kennedy Center for the Performing Arts
Korean War Veterans
　Memorial
Latrobe, Benjamin H.
L'Enfant, Pierre C.
Library of Congress
Lincoln Memorial

Mount Vernon
National Air and Space
　Museum
National Archives and
　Records Administration
National Gallery of Art
National Museum of African
　Art
National Museum of American History
National Museum of Natural
　History
National Zoological Park
Pentagon Building
Smithsonian Institution
Statuary Hall
Supreme Court of the U.S.
Unknown Soldier
Vietnam Veterans Memorial
Washington National
　Cathedral
Washington Monument
White House

Outline

I. **Visitor's guide**
　A. Capitol Hill
　B. The Mall
　C. The Tidal Basin
　D. North of the Mall
　E. South of the Mall
　F. Other points of interest
II. **The city**
　A. Northwest
　B. Northeast
　C. Southeast
　D. Southwest
　E. Metropolitan
　　area
III. **People**
　A. Population
　B. Housing
　C. Education
　D. Social problems
　E. Cultural life and recreation
IV. **Economy**
　A. Government
　B. Other service industries
　C. Communication
　D. Transportation
V. **Local government**
VI. **History**

Questions

Why is Washington's local government unusual?
What is the Tidal Basin?
What have been the chief causes of the city's growth?
Why does Washington have no skyscrapers?
Which presidents are buried in Arlington National Cemetery?
Why did Congress have a hard time deciding where to locate the capital? Who planned the physical layout of Washington?
What are Washington's *quadrants?*
Why may Washington residents pay in-state tuition at any state university?
What avenue is known is "America's Main Street?"

Additional resources

Benedetto, Robert, and Donovan, Jane. *Historical Dictionary of Washington, D.C.* Scarecrow, 2002.
Stein, R. Conrad, and Kent, Deborah. *Washington, D.C.* Children's Pr., 1999. Younger readers.

Washington, Booker T. (1856-1915), was the most influential African American leader and educator of his time. He became prominent largely because of his role as founder and head of Tuskegee Institute, a vocational school for blacks in Tuskegee, Alabama.

Washington advised two presidents—Theodore Roosevelt and William Howard Taft—on racial problems and policies. He also influenced the appointment of several blacks to federal office, especially during Roosevelt's administration. Washington described his rise from slavery to national prominence as an educator in his best-selling autobiography, *Up from Slavery* (1901).

Early life. Booker Taliaferro Washington was born a slave on April 5, 1856. His birthplace was Hales Ford, Virginia, near Roanoke. After the U.S. government freed all slaves in 1865, his family moved to Malden, West Virginia. There, Washington worked in coal mines and salt furnaces. From 1872 to 1875, he attended the Hampton Institute, an industrial school for blacks in Hampton, Virginia. He became a teacher at the institute in 1879.

Booker T. Washington National Monument

Booker T. Washington, a black leader and educator, founded Tuskegee Institute and headed the school from 1881 to 1915.

Washington based many of his educational theories on his training at Hampton.

Educator. In 1881, Washington founded and became principal of Tuskegee Normal and Industrial Institute. He started this school in an old abandoned church and a shanty. The school's name was later changed to Tuskegee Institute (now Tuskegee University). The school taught specific trades, such as carpentry, farming, and mechanics, and trained teachers. As it expanded, Washington spent much of his time raising funds. Under Washington's leadership, the institute became famous as a model of industrial education. The Tuskegee Institute National Historic Site, established in 1974, includes Washington's home, student-made college buildings, and the George Washington Carver Museum.

Washington believed that blacks could benefit more from a practical, vocational education rather than a college education. Most blacks lived in poverty in the rural South, and Washington felt they should learn skills, work hard, and acquire property. He believed that the development of work skills would lead to economic prosperity. Washington predicted that blacks would be granted civil and political rights after gaining a strong economic foundation. He explained his theories in *Up from Slavery* and in other publications.

Racial leader. In the late 1800's, more and more blacks became victims of lynchings and *Jim Crow* laws that segregated blacks (see **Jim Crow**). To reduce racial conflicts, Washington advised blacks to stop demanding equal rights and to simply get along with whites. He urged whites to give blacks better jobs.

In a speech given in Atlanta, Georgia, in 1895, Washington declared: "In all things that are purely social we can be as separate as the fingers, yet one as the hand in all things essential to mutual progress." This speech was often called the *Atlanta Compromise* because Washington accepted inequality and segregation for blacks in exchange for economic advancement. The speech was widely quoted in newspapers and helped make him a prominent national figure and black spokesman.

Washington became a shrewd political leader and advised not only presidents, but also members of Congress and governors, on political appointments for blacks and sympathetic whites. He urged wealthy people to contribute to various black organizations. He also owned or financially supported many black newspapers. In 1900, Washington founded the National Negro Business League to help black business firms.

Throughout his life, Washington tried to please whites in both the North and the South through his public actions and his speeches. He never publicly supported black political causes that were unpopular with Southern whites. However, Washington secretly financed lawsuits opposing segregation and upholding the right of blacks to vote and to serve on juries.

Opposition to Washington came chiefly from W. E. B. Du Bois, a historian and sociologist. Du Bois criticized Washington's educational and political philosophy and practices. Du Bois supported higher education for talented African Americans who could serve as leaders. He feared that the success of Washington's industrial school would limit the development of true higher education for blacks. Du Bois accepted the need for industrial training. However, he believed that African

Americans should also have the opportunity to obtain a college education.

Du Bois attacked Washington's compromising views on political and civil rights. Du Bois felt that blacks must openly strive for their rights. He criticized what he regarded as Washington's surrender of rights and human dignity for economic gain. Du Bois also attacked some ways that Washington used his power. By controlling many black newspapers, for example, Washington made it difficult for differing views to be published. And because he was acclaimed as the foremost black leader, Washington helped determine what racial policies and practices were "acceptable." Du Bois outlined his criticisms in his book *The Souls of Black Folk* (1903).

By 1910, Washington's influence had started to decline as Du Bois and others began new movements. These movements led to the creation of such organizations as the National Association for the Advancement of Colored People (NAACP) and the National Urban League. Washington died on Nov. 14, 1915.   Raymond W. Smock

See also **African Americans** (The rise of new black leaders); **Du Bois, W. E. B.; Niagara Movement; Tuskegee University.**

Additional resources

Harlan, Louis R. *Booker T. Washington.* 2 vols. 1972, 1983. Reprint. Oxford, 1975, 1986.
Troy, Don. *Booker T. Washington.* Child's World, 1999. Younger readers.
Washington, Booker T. *Up from Slavery.* 1901. Reprint. Available in many editions.

Washington, Denzel (1954-   ), is a leading African American actor who has gained fame for his intelligent performances in challenging roles. He won the 2001 Academy Award as best actor for his portrayal of a corrupt policeman in *Training Day.* Washington was the second African American actor to win the best actor award. Sidney Poitier was the first in 1963.

Washington was born on Dec. 28, 1954, in Mount Vernon, New York. He graduated from Fordham University in 1977 and studied acting at the American Conservatory Theatre in San Francisco. He started his acting career on the stage in New York City, appearing in both Shakespearean and modern plays. Washington made his motion-picture debut in 1981 in *Carbon Copy.* From 1982 to 1988, he was featured in the television dramatic series "St. Elsewhere."

Washington won the 1989 Academy Award as best supporting actor for his performance as a black soldier during the American Civil War in *Glory.* Washington's other notable motion pictures include *A Soldier's Story* (1984), *Cry Freedom* (1987), *Mo' Better Blues* (1990), *Mississippi Masala* (1991), *Malcolm X* (1992), *The Pelican Brief* (1993), *Philadelphia* (1993), *Crimson Tide* (1995), *Courage Under Fire* (1996), *The Siege* (1998), *The Bone Collector* (1999), *The Hurricane* (1999), and *Remember the Titans* (2000).

Louis Giannetti

AP/Wide World

Denzel Washington

**1st President of
the United States 1789-1797**

Washington
1st President
1789-1797
No political
party

John Adams
2nd President
1797-1801
Federalist

John Adams
Vice President
1789-1797

Oil painting on canvas (1796) by Gilbert Stuart; jointly owned by the National Portrait Gallery, Smithsonian Institution, and the Museum of Fine Arts, Boston

Washington, George (1732-1799), won a lasting place in American history as the "Father of the Country." For nearly 20 years, he guided his country much as a father cares for a growing child.

In three important ways, Washington helped shape the beginning of the United States. First, he commanded the Continental Army that won American independence from Great Britain in the Revolutionary War. Second, Washington served as president of the convention that wrote the United States Constitution. Third, he was elected the first President of the United States.

Most Americans of his day loved Washington. His army officers would have tried to make him king if he had let them. From the Revolutionary War on, his birthday was celebrated each year throughout the country.

Washington lived an exciting life in exciting times. As a boy, he explored the wilderness. When he grew older, he helped the British fight the French and Indians. Several times he was nearly killed. As a general, he suffered hardships with his troops in the cold winters at Valley Forge, Pa., and Morristown, N.J. He lost many battles, but led the American army to final victory at Yorktown, Va. After he became President, he successfully solved many problems in turning the plans of the Constitution into a working government.

Washington went to school only until he was about 14 or 15. But he learned to make the most of all his abilities and opportunities. Washington's remarkable patience and his understanding of others helped him win people to his side in times of hardship and discouragement.

There are great differences between the United States of Washington's day and that of today. The new nation was small and weak. It stretched west only to the Mississippi River and had fewer than 4,000,000 people. Most people made their living by farming. Few children went to school. Many men and women could not read or write. Transportation and communication were slow. It took Washington 3 days to travel about 90 miles (140 kilometers) from New York City to Philadelphia, longer than it now takes to fly around the world. There were only 11 states in the Union when Washington became President and 16 when he left office.

Many stories have been told about Washington. Most are probably not true. So far as we know, he did not chop down his father's cherry tree, then confess by saying: "I cannot tell a lie, Pa." He probably never threw a stone across the Rappahannock River. But such stories show that people were willing to believe almost anything about his honesty and his great strength. One of Washington's officers, Henry "Light Horse Harry" Lee, summed up the way Americans felt and still feel about Washington: "First in war, first in peace, and first in the hearts of his countrymen."

Washington the man

Washington's appearance caused admiration and respect. He was tall, strong, and broad-shouldered. As he grew older, cares lined his face and gave him a somewhat stern appearance. Perhaps the best description of Washington was written by a friend, George Mercer, in 1760:

"He may be described as being straight as an Indian, measuring 6 feet 2 inches in his stockings, and weighing 175 pounds . . . A large and straight rather than a prominent nose; blue-gray penetrating eyes . . . He has a clear though rather colorless pale skin which burns with the sun . . . dark brown hair which he wears in a queue . . .

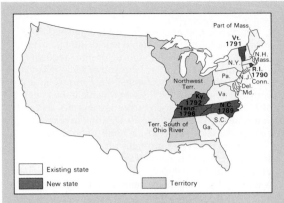

When Washington became president in 1789, 11 states had ratified the Constitution. When he left office in 1797, the Union had 16 states.

The U.S. flag adopted in 1795 recognized the addition of Vermont and Kentucky to the Union. It served as the nation's flag until 1818.

The world of President Washington

The French Revolution began in 1789. In one of the first major acts of rebellion, French citizens captured the Bastille, a royal fortress and hated symbol of oppression.
The first U.S. census was begun in August 1790, and took 18 months to complete. It counted 3,929,214 people.
The Industrial Revolution in the United States made a big advance in 1790, when Samuel Slater established the nation's first water-powered cotton mill in Pawtucket, R. I.
Plans for a permanent national capital moved forward when President Washington selected a site on the Potomac River in 1791. Construction of the White House began the next year.
The Bill of Rights became law in 1791. These first 10 amendments to the U.S. Constitution guaranteed basic liberties.
The New York Stock Exchange was established in 1792.
Eli Whitney's cotton gin, patented in 1794, revolutionized the economy of the South. The device led to mass production of cotton and increased the demand for slave labor.
General Anthony Wayne defeated the Indians in 1794 in the Battle of Fallen Timbers. A treaty signed the following year opened a huge tract of land in Ohio to white settlers.
The first important turnpike in the United States was completed in 1795 between Philadelphia and Lancaster, Pa. Other toll roads built in the 1790's encouraged development in New England and the Middle Atlantic region.
The first smallpox vaccination was given by English physician Edward Jenner in 1796. It represented a major advance in the battle against this dread disease.

WORLD BOOK map

His mouth is large and generally firmly closed, but which from time to time discloses some defective teeth … His movements and gestures are graceful, his walk majestic, and he is a splendid horseman."

Washington set his own strict rules of conduct, but he also enjoyed having a good time. He laughed at jokes, though he seldom told any.

One of the best descriptions of Washington's character was written after his death by Washington's fellow Virginian Thomas Jefferson:

"His mind was great and powerful … as far as he saw, no judgment was ever sounder. It was slow in operation, being little aided by invention or imagination, but sure in conclusion. …

"Perhaps the strongest feature in his character was prudence, never acting until every circumstance, every consideration, was maturely weighed; refraining if he saw a doubt, but, when once decided, going through with his purpose, whatever obstacles opposed.

"His integrity was most pure, his justice the most inflexible I have ever known …

"He was, indeed, in every sense of the words, a wise, a good and a great man. … On the whole, his character was, in its mass, perfect … it may truly be said, that

Important dates in Washington's life

1732   (Feb. 22) Born in Westmoreland County, Virginia.
1749   Became official surveyor for Culpeper County, Virginia.
1751   Went to Barbados Island, British West Indies.
1753   Carried British ultimatum to French in Ohio River Valley, as a major.
1754   Surrendered Fort Necessity in the French and Indian War, as a colonel.
1755   (July 9) With General Edward Braddock when defeated by French and Indians.
1755-1758   Commanded Virginia's frontier troops, as a colonel.
1759   (Jan. 6) Married Mrs. Martha Dandridge Custis.
1774   Elected delegate to First Continental Congress.
1775   Elected delegate to Second Continental Congress.
1775   (June 15) Elected commander in chief of Continental Army.
1781   (Oct. 19) Victory at Yorktown.
1787   (May 25) Elected president of the Constitutional Convention.
1789   Elected first President of the United States.
1792   Reelected President of the United States.
1796   (Sept. 19) Published *Farewell Address,* refusing a third term.
1798   (July 4) Commissioned lieutenant general and commander in chief of new United States Army.
1799   (Dec. 14) Died at Mount Vernon at age 67.

David R. White, StockFile

A memorial mansion stands on the site of George Washington's birthplace on Pope's Creek in Westmoreland County, Virginia. The original house burned down in 1779.

never did nature and fortune combine more perfectly to make a man great . . ."

Early life (1732-1746)

Family background. George Washington inherited much more than a good mind and a strong body. Washington belonged to an old colonial family that believed in hard work, in public service, and in worshiping God. The Washington family has been traced back to 1260 in England. The name at that time was de Wessington. It was later spelled Washington. Sulgrave Manor in England is regarded as the home of George Washington's ancestors (see **Sulgrave Manor**).

George's great-grandfather, John Washington (1632-1677), came to live in America by accident. He was mate on a small English ship that went aground in the Potomac River in 1656 or 1657. By the time the ship was repaired, he had decided to marry and settle in Virginia. He started with little money. Within 20 years he owned more than 5,000 acres (2,000 hectares), including the land that later became Mount Vernon. Lawrence Washington (1659-1698), the eldest son of John, was the grandfather of George.

Washington's parents. George's father, Augustine Washington (1694-1743), was Lawrence's youngest son. After iron ore was discovered on some of his land, he spent most of his time developing an ironworks. He had four children by his first wife, Jane Butler. She died in 1729. In March 1731, he married Mary Ball (1709?-1789), who became George's mother.

Mary Ball did not have a very happy childhood. Her father and mother both died before she was 13. Although she had inherited property from her mother, she spent all her life worrying about money. After her son George became a man, she wrote him many letters asking for money even though she did not always need it.

Augustine and Mary Ball Washington had six children. Besides George, there were: Betty (1733-1797), Samuel (1734-1781), John Augustine (1736-1787), Charles (1738-1799), and Mildred (1739-1740).

Boyhood. George Washington was born on Pope's Creek Plantation in Westmoreland County, Virginia, on February 22, 1732 (February 11, on the Old Style Calendar then in use; see **Calendar**). When George was about 3 years old, his family moved to the large, undeveloped plantation that was later called Mount Vernon. It lay about 50 miles (80 kilometers) up the Potomac River in Virginia and was then called Little Hunting Creek Farm. George's only playmates at the plantation were his younger sister and brothers. No neighbors lived close by. But George probably had fun exploring the nearby woods and helping out in farm work. He saw little of his father, who made many trips to his ironworks, about 30 miles (48 kilometers) away.

In 1738, when George was nearly 7, his father decided to move closer to the ironworks. He bought the 260-acre (105-hectare) Ferry Farm which lay on the Rappahannock River across from Fredericksburg, Va.

Education. George probably began going to school in Fredericksburg soon after the family moved to Ferry Farm. No accurate records have been found that tell who his teachers were. Altogether, he had no more than seven or eight years of school. His best subject was arithmetic. He wrote his lessons in ink on heavy paper.

His mother or a teacher then sewed the paper into notebooks.

George studied enough history and geography to know something of the outside world. But he never learned as much about literature, foreign languages, and history as did Thomas Jefferson or James Madison. They had the advantage of much more formal education.

By the time he ended his schoolwork at the age of 14 or 15, George could keep business accounts, write clear letters, and do simple figuring. During the rest of his life he kept diaries and careful accounts of his expenses.

George's father had probably planned to send him to school in England because there were few schools in Virginia. But Augustine Washington died when George was only 11, and the plans came to nothing. After his father's death, George's mother did not like to have him away from home for long. George was to inherit Ferry Farm when he reached 21. Meanwhile, he, his younger sister and brothers, and the farm were left in the care of his mother.

Plantation life. Growing up at Ferry Farm, young George helped manage a plantation worked by 20 black slaves. He was observant and hard-working. He learned how to plant and produce tobacco, fruit, grains, and vegetables. He saw how many things a plantation needed to keep operating, such as cloth and iron tools. He also developed his lifelong love for horses. At the same time, Washington enjoyed the life of a young Virginia country gentleman. He had boyhood romances and wrote love poems. He became a good dancer. And he enjoyed hunting, fishing, and boating on the river.

Development of character. As a youth, Washington was sober, quiet, attentive, and dignified. His respect for his elders and his dependability made him admired. He experienced the hardships of colonial life on the edge of the wilderness. He learned that life was difficult. This helped make him become strong and patient.

As a schoolboy, Washington copied rules of behavior in an exercise book, perhaps at the suggestion of his mother or a teacher. Following are some of these rules in his own spelling, capitalization, and punctuation:

Turn not your Back to others especially in Speaking, Jog not the Table or Desk on which Another reads or writes, lean not upon any one.

Use no Reproachfull Language against any one neither Curse nor Revile.

Play not the Peacock, looking every where about you, to See if you be well Deck't, if your Shoes fit well, if your Skokings Sit neatly, and Cloths handsomely.

While you are talking, Point not with your Finger at him of Whom you Discourse nor Approach too near him to whom you talk especially to his face.

Be not Curious to Know the Affairs of Others neither approach those that Speak in Private.

It's unbecoming to Stoop much to ones Meat Keep your Fingers clean & when foul wipe them on a Corner of your Table Napkin.

George Washington's admiration for his half brother Lawrence (1718-1752) also influenced his development. Lawrence had been educated in England. He had the polish of a young English gentleman. From 1740 to 1742, Lawrence had gone to South America as a Virginia volunteer captain in a brief war between Great Britain and Spain. Lawrence took no part in the actual fighting. But he returned to Virginia with many war stories. These tales excited George's imagination. George became a

and hunt for food. By the time he returned to Mount Vernon, he felt he had grown into a man.

Professional surveyor. In July 1749, Washington was appointed official surveyor for Culpeper County. In November, Lord Fairfax allowed him to make a short surveying trip on his own to the Allegheny Mountains.

Washington lived at Mount Vernon for part of that winter. His surveying work paid him well. It was one of the few occupations in which a person could expect to be paid in cash. Most other business in Virginia was carried on with payments in tobacco. Washington kept track in his account book of small loans he made to his relatives and friends. He also wrote down winnings and losses at playing cards and billiards.

During the next three years, Washington made more and more surveys as settlers moved into the Shenandoah Valley. He carefully saved his money. When he saw a particularly good piece of land, he bought it. By 1752, he owned about 2,300 acres (930 hectares).

Only foreign trip. In 1751, George Washington made his only trip away from the shores of America. Lawrence Washington had become seriously ill. He decided to sail to the warm climate of Barbados Island in the British West Indies for his health. He asked George to go along.

The brothers arrived at the island in November. George's diary shows he was interested in comparing farming methods on the island with those of Virginia. Two weeks after arriving, George became ill with smallpox. He carried a few pox scars on his face the rest of his life. A week after recovering, George decided to return to Virginia while Lawrence remained in the tropics.

George was now 20. He fell in love with 16-year-old Betsy Fauntleroy, the daughter of a Richmond County planter and shipowner. George proposed to her at least twice. Each time he was refused. He sadly wrote that she had given him a "cruel sentence."

In early June 1752, Lawrence Washington suddenly returned home. He died of tuberculosis before the end of the month. Lawrence left Mount Vernon to his wife for as long as she lived, then to his daughter. He provided that the estate should go to George if his daughter died with no children of her own. He also left George an equal share of his land in the Shenandoah Valley with his other three brothers.

Early military career (1753-1758)

At the age of 20, George Washington had no experience or training as a soldier. But Lawrence's war stories had interested him in military affairs. He applied to the governor for a commission in the militia. In December 1752, he was commissioned as a major and put in charge of training militia in southern Virginia. Washington probably prepared for his new duties by reading books on military drills and tactics.

Messenger to the French. In October 1753, Washington learned that Robert Dinwiddie, the acting governor of Virginia, planned to send a message to the French military commander in the Ohio River Valley. Dinwiddie intended to warn the French that they must withdraw their troops from the region. Both the French and the British wanted the Ohio River Valley for fur trading, and British speculators wanted to invest in land there. Washington volunteered to carry the message. Dinwiddie gave him the task.

Library of Congress

Washington became a surveyor when he was a teen-ager. He earned enough to support himself and to buy many acres of land. He made several survey trips to the Virginia wilderness.

frequent visitor to the fashionable new house that Lawrence had built at Mount Vernon.

Lawrence decided that 14-year-old George should join the British Royal Navy. George wanted to go, but he needed his mother's permission. No matter how much he argued, she would not let him go. She asked advice of her half brother, Joseph Ball. He suggested somewhat jokingly that rather than let George become a sailor, it would be better to apprentice him to a *tinker*, a mender of pots and pans.

Washington the surveyor (1747-1752)

After teen-aged George Washington gave up hopes of becoming a sailor, he became interested in exploring the frontier. Becoming a surveyor and marking out new farms in the wilderness would give him a chance to seek adventure and earn money. He enjoyed mathematics, and he easily picked up an understanding of fractions and geometry. Then he took his father's old set of surveying instruments out of storage. At 15, he began studying to be a surveyor.

On one of his frequent visits to Mount Vernon, George met Lord Fairfax, the largest property owner in Virginia. Fairfax was a cousin of Lawrence Washington's wife. He owned more than 5 million acres (2 million hectares) of land in northern Virginia. These lands extended to the Allegheny Mountains and included much of the Shenandoah Valley.

First expedition. Lord Fairfax began planning an expedition to survey his western lands. James Genn, an expert surveyor, was put in charge of the expedition. Sixteen-year-old George Washington was invited to go along. The boy persuaded his mother to let him make his first long trip away from home.

The month-long expedition set out on horseback in March 1748. Washington learned to sleep in the open

In mid-November, Washington set out on the dangerous trip. With him went Christopher Gist, a frontier guide; an interpreter; and four frontiersmen. Washington's party traveled north into western Pennsylvania. Sometimes the men covered as much as 20 miles (32 kilometers) in a day. They stopped at an Indian village near the site of present-day Pittsburgh, Pa. There, three Indian chiefs agreed to accompany the party to visit the French. The Indians gave George the name *Conotocarious,* which meant Towntaker.

Early in December, Washington reached French headquarters at Fort Le Boeuf, just south of present-day Erie, Pa. The French commander rejected Dinwiddie's warning. He said that his orders were to take and hold the Ohio River Valley. He gave Washington a letter to carry back to the British. Washington experienced many hardships and dangers on the return trip to Virginia. It was late December and bitterly cold. Snow lay deep on the ground. Once Washington nearly drowned trying to cross the Allegheny River on a raft.

On Jan. 16, 1754, Washington reached Williamsburg, Va., and delivered the French reply to Dinwiddie. Washington urged Dinwiddie to build a fort where the Ohio and Allegheny rivers joined (the site of present-day Pittsburgh). He also drew a detailed map of the region. Before the end of the month, Dinwiddie ordered a force of frontiersmen to build the fort. The governor had unknowingly taken the first step toward the French and Indian War, which was to spread to many other countries. This war was known in Canada and Europe as the Seven Years' War.

First military action. The 22-year-old Washington was promoted to lieutenant colonel. He received orders to enlist troops to man the new fort. He found Americans resentful because the Virginia government refused to pay them as much as regular British soldiers. Washington himself angrily threatened to resign because his pay was lower than that of a lieutenant colonel in the regular British army. Perhaps for the first time he realized that American colonists were treated unfairly. It also may have been the first time he thought of himself as an American rather than as an Englishman.

Washington set out with about 160 poorly trained soldiers in April 1754. He was still 100 miles (160 kilometers) from the fort when he learned the French had captured it. Washington decided to move on toward the fort, which the French had named Fort Duquesne.

On May 28, 1754, Washington's men fired the first shots of the war. He surprised a group of French troops, killed 10, wounded 1, and took 21 prisoners. Only one of Washington's men was killed. Washington described his feelings in the short fight: "I heard bullets whistle and believe me there is something charming in the sound."

Surrender of Fort Necessity. Washington's men built a fort about 60 miles (97 kilometers) south of Fort Duquesne. They completed it in June and named it Fort Necessity. Meanwhile, Washington had been promoted to the rank of colonel.

Early in June, about 180 Virginia soldiers arrived to reinforce Fort Necessity. Some friendly Indians also joined Washington's forces. But no food arrived. On June 14, just as the last food was being eaten, a company of about 100 British regular army troops arrived. They brought with them some vitally needed supplies.

On July 3, the French attacked Fort Necessity. Washington had fewer than 400 men. Many of the troops were sick, and all of them were hungry. The French fired from behind trees and rocks. About 30 of Fort Necessity's defenders were killed and 70 wounded. A rainstorm turned the battlefield into a sea of mud. As night fell, the young colonel had few men, little food, and no dry gunpowder. His position was hopeless. About midnight, Washington agreed to surrender Fort Necessity. The French let him march out of the fort and return to Virginia with his men and guns.

A discouraged Washington returned to Williamsburg two weeks later. The colonists did not blame the young colonel for losing the fort. They praised Washington and his men for their bravery.

In October, Washington again visited Williamsburg. He was shocked when Dinwiddie told him he had orders from London not to allow colonial officers to have ranks above captain. Washington wanted a military career, but he angrily resigned, rather than be lowered from the rank of colonel to captain.

Washington had inherited Ferry Farm from his father, but he did not wish to go there to live with his mother. Instead, he rented Mount Vernon from the widow of his half brother Lawrence. He agreed to pay a rent of 15,000 pounds (6,800 kilograms) of tobacco a year.

Braddock's defeat. In March 1755, Washington received a message from Major General Edward Braddock. The British general invited Washington to help him in a new campaign against the French at Fort Duquesne. Washington agreed to serve without pay as one of Braddock's aides. He believed this was an excellent opportunity to learn from an experienced general.

Braddock assembled his forces at Fort Cumberland, Md., about 90 miles (140 kilometers) southeast of Fort Duquesne. On June 7, the troops started across the rough country. Washington was upset by the slow march. He wrote in a letter: "They were halting to level every mole hill, and to erect bridges over every brook; by which means we were 4 days getting 12 miles."

During the second week of the march, Washington became seriously ill with a high fever. He was forced to remain behind in camp for two weeks. He warned Braddock to be careful of "the mode of attack which, more than probably, he would experience from the Canadian French, and their Indians."

On July 9, the British had nearly reached Fort Duquesne. After making two dangerous crossings of the Monongahela River, Braddock ordered his long column to march forward. Wearing bright red uniforms, the British soldiers looked as though they were parading before the king. Washington was not yet well, but he had rejoined the army and rode his horse with pillows tied to the saddle. Braddock was confident that the French now would wait at their fort for his attack. What happened next was later described by Washington:

"We were attacked (very unexpectedly I must own) by about 300 French and Indians; our numbers consisted of about 1300 well armed men, chiefly regulars, who were immediately struck with such a deadly panic, that nothing but confusion and disobedience of orders prevailed amongst them.

". . . the English soldiers . . . broke and ran as sheep before the hounds . . . The general (Braddock) was

During the French and Indian War, Washington served as an aide to British General Edward Braddock. Braddock was killed in July 1755, after leading his troops to defeat near Fort Duquesne. Washington is shown above reading the burial service over Braddock's body.

wounded behind the shoulder, and into the breast; of which he died three days after . . .

"I luckily escaped without a wound, though I had four bullets through my coat and two horses shot under me . . ."

With Braddock's defeat and death, Washington was released from service. He rode home to Mount Vernon. Shortly after, in a letter to one of his brothers, he summed up his military career thus far:

"I was employed to go a journey in the winter (when I believe few or none would have undertaken it) and what did I get by it? My expenses borne! I then was appointed with trifling pay to conduct a handful of men to the Ohio. What did I get by this? Why, after putting myself to a considerable expense in equipping and providing necessaries for the campaign—I went out, was soundly beaten, lost them all—came in, and had my commission taken from me, or in other words, my command reduced, under pretense of an order from home . . . I have been on the losing order ever since I entered the service . . ."

Frontier commander. The French encouraged the Indians to attack English settlers. In August 1755, Dinwiddie persuaded Washington to accept a new commission as colonel. Washington would take command of Virginia's colonial troops to defend the colony's 350-mile (563-kilometer) western frontier.

Many of the Virginians recruited by Washington and his officers were homeless men. Sometimes Washing-

ton had less than 400 of the 1,500 men that he was supposed to have. Often he had to call the militia to help him. But the militia would not stay with him very long, and many of the militiamen did not even have weapons.

Washington constantly urged that a new attack be made on Fort Duquesne. The British finally decided in 1758 to attack Fort Duquesne again. An advance British force of 800 men again was ambushed by the French and Indians. More than 300 British soldiers were killed. When the main army, including Washington, finally reached the fort in late November, the French had burned it and retreated toward Canada.

Washington returned to Virginia to hang up his sword. He was now the most famous American-born soldier. He knew how to train other soldiers and how to run an army. More important, he had shown courage and patience in leading his men.

The peaceful years (1759-1773)

At the age of 26, Washington turned to seeking happiness as a country gentleman and to building a fortune. During the next 16 years, he became known as a skilled farmer, an intelligent businessman, a popular legislator, a conscientious warden of the Church of England, and a wise county court judge.

Marriage. On Jan. 6, 1759, Washington married Mrs. Martha Dandridge Custis (see **Washington, Martha Custis**). She was a widow, eight months older than George. The marriage probably took place in New Kent County,

Washington married Mrs. Martha Dandridge Custis, a wealthy Virginia widow, in 1759. He became a loving stepfather to Martha's two children, "Patsy" and "Jackie."

Virginia, at the bride's plantation home, which was called the *White House*. Her first husband had left a fortune of about 18,000 acres (7,300 hectares) of land and £30,000. This was divided equally among the widow and her two children, John "Jackie" Parke Custis (1754-1781) and Martha "Patsy" Parke Custis (1756-1773). Washington became a loving stepfather to the children. He and Martha had no children of their own.

Legislator. After a six-week honeymoon at the White House, Washington took his new family to Williamsburg. There he served for the first time in the colonial legislature. He had been elected to the House of Burgesses in 1758, while still on the frontier. Although he had not personally campaigned, he had paid bills for his friends to entertain voters during the campaign.

During the next 15 years, Washington was reelected time after time to the legislature. He seldom made speeches and did not put any important bills before the legislature. More important, he learned the process of representative government. He saw the difficulties in getting a law passed. The experience gave him patience in later years when he had to deal with Congress during the Revolutionary War and as President. He also became acquainted with Thomas Jefferson, Patrick Henry, and other Virginia leaders.

Farmer and landowner. Washington brought his wife and children to Mount Vernon in April 1759. He found it badly run down by the neglect of his overseers.

In 1761, Washington inherited Mount Vernon because his half brother Lawrence's widow and daughter had both died. He began to buy farms that lay around the estate. He also bought western lands for future development. In 1770, Washington made a trip west as far as the present town of Gallipolis, Ohio, searching for good land to buy. By 1773, he owned about 40,000 acres (16,000 hectares). Washington also controlled the large Custis estate of his wife and her children. He rented much of his land to tenant farmers.

Washington was a careful businessman. He did his own bookkeeping and recorded every penny of expense or profit. His ledgers tell us when he bought gifts for his family, and what prices he received for his crops.

As a large landowner, Washington had to supervise many different activities. He wanted to learn more about farming, so he bought the latest books on the subject. When he discovered he could not grow the best grade of tobacco at Mount Vernon, he switched to raising wheat. He saw the profit in making flour, so he built his own flour mill. Large schools of fish swam in the Potomac River, and Mount Vernon became known for the barrels of salted fish it produced. Washington experimented with tree grafting to improve his fruit orchards.

Social life at Mount Vernon revolved around receiving visitors. Many people came there for pleasure as well as for business. The men often joined Washington in his favorite sport, fox hunting. Both men and women enjoyed dining and playing cards in the beautiful rooms of the mansion. Washington often visited other plantations. Several times a year, he went to such towns as Williamsburg and Alexandria, Va., and Annapolis, Md., to attend plays and dances, watch horse races, and shop.

The coming revolution (1774-1775)

The American colonists in the late 1760's and early 1770's grew angrier and angrier at the taxes placed on them by Great Britain. As a legislator and as a leading landowner, Washington was deeply concerned as relations with Great Britain worsened. During this time his knowledge of colonial affairs increased. He read many newspapers and political pamphlets and often discussed the growing crisis with his neighbor, George Mason, a leading statesman of the time (see **Mason, George**).

Lord Botetourt, the British governor, dismissed the Virginia legislature in 1769 because the representatives had protested the taxation imposed by the British Townshend Acts. Washington met with other legislators in a Williamsburg tavern. He presented a plan that he and

Mason had discussed for forming an association to boycott imports of British goods. The plan was quickly adopted.

Washington became one of the first American leaders to consider using force to "maintain the liberty of the colonies." He wrote Mason in April 1769: ". . . That no man should scruple, or hesitate a moment to use arms in defense of so valuable a blessing, on which all the good and evil of life depends, is clearly my opinion; yet Arms I would beg leave to add, should be the last . . . resort."

In 1774, the British closed the port of Boston as punishment for the Boston Tea Party. Virginia legislators who protested were dismissed by Governor Lord Dunmore. Again the representatives met as private citizens. They elected seven delegates, including Washington, to attend the First Continental Congress in Philadelphia. Washington wrote: ". . . shall we supinely sit and see one province after another fall a prey to despotism?"

First Continental Congress. The Continental Congress met in September 1774. There, Washington had his first chance to meet and talk with leaders of other colonies. The members were impressed with his judgment and military knowledge. Washington made no speeches and he was not appointed to any committees. But he worked to have trade with Great Britain stopped by all the colonies. The trade boycott was approved by the Congress. Then Congress adjourned.

In March 1775, representatives from each Virginia county met in a church in Richmond, Va. Washington and the others heard Patrick Henry's famous speech in which he said: "Give me liberty or give me death!" But

Washington's quiet common sense impressed people as much as Henry's dramatic words did. The representatives again elected Washington to attend the Second Continental Congress in Philadelphia. See **Continental Congress.**

Elected commander in chief. By the time Washington left Mount Vernon to attend the Second Continental Congress, the Battles of Lexington and Concord already had been fought in Massachusetts. The Congress opened on May 10, 1775. For six weeks the delegates to the Congress debated and studied the problems facing the colonies. The majority, including Washington, wanted to avoid war. At the same time, they feared they could not avoid it.

To express his desire for action, Washington began wearing his red and blue uniform of the French and Indian War. He was appointed to one military committee after another. He was asked to prepare a defense of New York City, to study ways to obtain gunpowder, to make plans for an army, and to write army regulations.

Then, on June 14, Congress called on Pennsylvania, Maryland, and Virginia to send troops to aid Boston, which had been placed under British military rule. John Adams, who in later years would be Washington's Vice President and successor as President, rose to discuss the need of electing a commander in chief. Adams praised Washington highly and said his popularity would help unite the colonies. Many New England delegates believed a northerner should be made commander in chief. But the following day Washington was elected unanimously.

Washington had not sought the position. He particu-

A View of Mount Vernon, oil painting on canvas (about 1790) by an unknown artist of the American School; National Gallery of Art, Washington, D.C., gift of Edgar William and Bernice Chrysler Garbisch

Washington's estate at Mount Vernon included an impressive mansion overlooking the Potomac River, and about 7,600 acres (3,075 hectares) of farmland and forests. Washington brought his family to Mount Vernon in 1759. He died there in 1799, two years after leaving the presidency.

John Adams Proposing Washington for Commander-in-Chief (Second Continental Congress, Philadelphia, June 15, 1775), oil painting on canvas (1913) by John Ward Dunsmore; Fraunces Tavern Museum, Sons of the Revolution in the State of New York, New York City

Washington became commander in chief of the colonial army at the Second Continental Congress in 1775. John Adams, *center,* proposed Washington, *standing far right,* for the position. The delegates elected him unanimously. He accepted reluctantly and refused pay for his services.

larly wanted to make everyone understand he did not want the $500 monthly pay that had been voted. He said he would keep track of his expenses, and would accept nothing else for his services. His acceptance speech, on June 16, was presented with modesty.

"I beg it may be remembered by every gentleman in the room," Washington said, "that I this day declare with the utmost sincerity, I do not think myself equal to the command I am honored with."

"First in war" (1775-1783)

"These are the times that try men's souls," Thomas Paine wrote during the Revolutionary War. "The summer soldier and the sunshine patriot, will in this crisis, shrink from the service of their country. . . ."

During the eight years of war, Washington's soul was tried many times both by "summer soldiers," who did not care to fight in winter, and by "sunshine patriots," who were friendly to the American cause only when things went well. Only his strong will to win made it possible for Washington to overcome his many discouragements.

The following sections describe the most important problems that Washington overcame to win the Revolutionary War. For an account of the main battles, see the article **Revolutionary War in America.**

Symbol of independence. To most Americans of his time, Washington became the chief symbol of what they were fighting for. The colonists had been brought up to respect the British king. They did not easily accept the idea of independence. The Congress that approved the Declaration of Independence on July 4, 1776, was not elected by the people, but by the legislatures of the states. And the legislatures were elected only by property owners. As a result, some people who did not own property and had no vote viewed independence with suspicion. Thousands of *Loyalists,* as British sympathizers were called, refused to help the fight for independence in any way.

Although many people did not especially wish for independence and did not trust Congress, they came to believe in Washington. They sympathized with him for the misery he shared with his soldiers. They cheered his courage in carrying on the fight.

"Washington retreats like a General and acts like a hero," the *Pennsylvania Journal* said in 1777. "Had he lived in the days of idolatry, he had been worshiped as a god." That same year, the Marquis de Lafayette wrote to Washington: ". . . if you were lost for America, there is nobody who could keep the army and the Revolution for six months."

Discouragement. Praise did not keep Washington from feeling discouraged. Often he believed he could not hold out long enough to win. Following are several comments he wrote throughout the war.

1776—"Such is my situation that if I were to wish the

Library of Congress

The Battle of Trenton in December 1776 ended in a resounding victory for the patriots. Washington led his troops across the icy Delaware River and launched a successful surprise attack against the Hessians.

bitterest curse to an enemy on this side of the grave, I should put him in my stead with my feelings. . . ."

1779—". . . there is every appearance that the Army will infallibly disband in a fortnight."

1781—". . . it is vain to think that an Army can be kept together much longer, under such a variety of sufferings as ours has experienced."

The army. Throughout the war, Washington seldom commanded more than 15,000 troops at any one time. He described his soldiers as "raw militia, badly officered, and with no government." There were two kinds of troops: (1) soldiers of the Continental Army, organized by Congress, and (2) militia, organized by the states.

Washington had trouble keeping soldiers in the Continental Army. At the beginning of the war, Congress let soldiers enlist for only a few months. Toward the end of the war, Washington convinced Congress that enlistments had to be longer. When their enlistments were up, the soldiers of the Continental Army went home. Sometimes a thousand men marched off at once.

Washington often had to plan battles for certain dates, because if he waited longer the soldiers' enlistments would be up. For example, Washington attacked the Hessian (German) troops at Trenton, N.J., on Dec. 26, 1776, for this reason. His army had shrunk to only about 5,000 men and the enlistments of most of his soldiers would be up at the end of December. The victory at Trenton inspired many of his soldiers to reenlist.

From time to time, Washington asked the states to call out their militia to help in a particular battle. The militia included storekeepers, farmers, and other private citizens. They were poorly trained and did not like being called from their homes to fight. The militia complained so much that troops of the Continental Army called them "long faces." Washington's army was defeated many times because the militia turned and ran when they saw redcoated British soldiers.

Desertion by his soldiers was another one of Washington's major problems. Many soldiers enlisted only to collect bonuses offered by Congress. At some times, as many men deserted each day as were enlisted. Washington authorized harsh punishment for deserters. He

had some hanged. Dangerous mutinies also occurred.

"We are, during the winter, dreaming of independence and peace, without using the means to become so," a concerned Washington wrote in 1780. "In the spring, when our recruits should be with the Army and in training, we have just discovered the necessity of calling for them, and by the fall, after a distressed, and inglorious campaign for want of them, we begin to get a few men, which come in just in time enough to eat our provisions. . . ."

From the time Washington took command to the end of the war, he had to put up with many incompetent officers. Congress sometimes appointed the generals without asking Washington's advice. The states appointed the lower-ranking officers in the Continental Army and all of the militia officers. Most officers were chosen for political reasons. Some generals, such as Charles Lee and Horatio Gates, believed they should have been chosen commander in chief. They sometimes ignored Washington's orders. In the winter of 1777-1778, a few army officers and members of Congress hoped that Washington might be replaced by Gates. This group became known as the *Conway cabal.* It was named for the foreign-born general Thomas Conway, who had criticized Washington sharply (see **Cabal**). But there was no organized movement against Washington. Congress continued to support him.

Shortage of supplies. Washington's troops lacked food, clothing, ammunition, and other supplies throughout the war. If the British had attacked the Americans around Boston in 1775, Washington could have issued only enough gunpowder for nine shots to each soldier. He had to give up Philadelphia to the British in 1777 because he could not risk losing the few supplies he had. The army repeatedly ran out of meat and bread. Sometimes hundreds of troops had to march barefoot in the snow because they had no shoes.

"The want of clothing, added to the misery of the season," Washington wrote in the winter of 1777-1778 at Valley Forge, Pa., "has occasioned (the soldiers) to suffer such hardships as will not be credited but by those who have been spectators."

In the winter of 1779-1780 at Morristown, N.J., Major General Nathanael Greene described Washington's army: "Poor fellows! They exhibit a picture truly distressing—more than half naked and two thirds starved. A country overflowing with plenty are now suffering an Army, employed for the defense of everything that is dear and valuable, to perish for want of food."

Winning the war. From the beginning of the war, Washington knew the powerful British navy gave the enemy a great advantage. The ships of the British could carry their army anywhere along the American coast. Washington's tiny, ragged army could not possibly defend every American port.

On the other hand, Washington knew from his experience in the French and Indian War that the British army moved slowly on land. He also knew it could be beaten. He proved that he could stay one jump ahead of the British by quick retreats. Meanwhile, Washington waited and prayed for the French to send a large fleet of warships to America. He hoped then to trap the British while the French navy prevented them from escaping.

Washington's prayers came true at Yorktown, Va.

Granger Collection

Winter at Valley Forge was a period of great suffering for the Continental Army. Washington and the French General Marquis de Lafayette led their discouraged troops through several months of hardships, including bitter cold, inadequate shelter, and shortages of food and clothing.

There, on Sept. 28, 1781, he surrounded Lord Cornwallis' army. The French fleet prevented the British from escaping by ship. Washington began attacking on October 6. On October 19, Cornwallis and 8,000 men surrendered.

Turning down a crown. After Cornwallis surrendered, the British lost interest in continuing the war. Peace talks dragged on in Paris for many months.

In May 1782, Colonel Lewis Nicola sent a document to Washington on behalf of his officers. It complained of injustices the army had suffered from Congress. It suggested that the army set up a monarchy with Washington as king. Washington replied that he read the idea "with abhorrence." He ordered Nicola to "banish these thoughts from your mind."

In November 1783, word finally arrived that the Treaty of Paris had been signed two months earlier. The last British soldiers went aboard ships at New York City on November 25. That same day Washington led his troops into the city. About a week later, on December 4, he said good-by to his officers at Fraunces Tavern. On his way home to Virginia, he stopped at Annapolis, Maryland, where Congress was meeting. He returned his commission as commander in chief, saying "... I resign with satisfaction the appointment I accepted with diffidence."

"First in peace" (1784-1789)

Washington, now 51 years old, reached Mount Vernon in time to spend Christmas, 1783, with Martha. The war had aged him. He now wore glasses. As he had told his officers: "I have grown gray in your service and now find myself growing blind."

For the next five years, Washington lived the life of a Virginia planter. Many guests and visitors dropped in at Mount Vernon. His entertainment expenses were large. In 1787, he wrote: "My estate for the last eleven years has not been able to make both ends meet."

Washington believed strongly in the future development of the West. This made him search for more land to buy. In 1784, he made a 680-mile (1,090-kilometer) trip on horseback through the wilderness to visit his land holdings southwest of Pittsburgh. He helped promote two companies interested in building canals along the Potomac and James rivers. He took part in plans to drain the Dismal Swamp in southern Virginia.

Washington also widened his interest in farming. In many ways his farm methods were ahead of the times. He began breeding mules. He introduced rotation of crops to his farms. He began using waste materials from his fishing industry as fertilizer. He also took steps to prevent soil erosion.

Constitutional Convention. In 1786, Washington wrote: "We are fast verging to anarchy and confusion." In Massachusetts, open revolt broke out (see **Shays's Rebellion**). Finally, the states agreed to call a meeting in 1787 to consider revising the weak Articles of Confederation (see **Articles of Confederation**). Washington was elected unanimously to head the Virginia delegates. A huge welcome greeted him when he arrived in Philadelphia in May. All the bells in the city were rung. The Constitutional Convention opened on May 25. The delegates elected Washington president of the convention.

Debate on the proposed constitution went on throughout the hot summer. Washington wrote: "I see no end to my staying here. To please all is impossible

. . ." As president, Washington took little part in the debates, but helped hold the convention together. The convention finally reached agreement in September. See **Constitution of the United States**.

Elected President. By the summer of 1788, enough states had approved the Constitution to allow for the reorganization of the government. Throughout the country, people linked Washington's name directly to the new Constitution. They took it for granted that he would be chosen as the first President. But Washington had many doubts as to whether he should accept the position. He wrote: ". . . If I should receive the appointment, and if I should be prevailed upon to accept it, the acceptance would be attended with more diffidence and reluctance than I ever experienced before in my life."

In February 1789, members of the first Electoral College met in their own states and voted (see **Electoral College**). Each elector voted for two candidates. The candidate who received the most votes became President, and the runner-up became Vice President. Washington was elected President with a total of 69 votes—the largest number possible—from the 69 electors. John Adams was elected Vice President with 34 votes.

First Administration (1789-1793)

Washington's journey from Mount Vernon to New York City was the parade of a national hero. Every town and city along the way held a celebration.

Inauguration Day was April 30, 1789. The 57-year-old Washington rode in a cream-colored coach to Federal Hall at Broad and Wall streets. Washington walked upstairs to the Senate Chamber, then out onto a balcony. Thousands watched as Washington raised his right hand and placed his left hand on an open Bible. Solemnly he repeated the presidential oath of office given by Robert R. Livingston of New York. Washington added the words, "So help me God!" and kissed the Bible. Cannons fired a 13-gun salute. Then President Washington walked back to the Senate Chamber and delivered his inaugural address.

Life in the Executive Mansion. The house of Samuel Osgood on Cherry Street in New York City was the first Executive Mansion. In February 1790, Washington moved to a larger house on Broadway. When Congress later made Philadelphia the capital, the Washingtons moved into the home there of financier Robert Morris. It was the finest house in the city.

The Washingtons entertained a great deal. They had a large staff of servants and slaves. The President held two afternoon receptions each week so he could meet the hundreds of people who wanted to see him. Every Friday night, Mrs. Washington held a formal reception. These affairs ended at 9 p.m. because, she said, the President "always retires at 9 in the evening." Each year on

Detail of *George Washington Addressing the Constitutional Convention,* oil painting on canvas (1856) by Junius Brutus Stearns; Virginia Museum of Fine Arts, Richmond

Washington presided over the Constitutional Convention that was held in Philadelphia in 1787 to write a constitution for the United States. Although he participated little in the discussions, he helped keep the convention together for months of debate before agreement was reached.

Library of Congress

The future President learned of his election from Charles Thomson, secretary of Congress, at Mount Vernon.

Vice President and Cabinet

Vice President	*John Adams
Secretary of state	*Thomas Jefferson
	*Edmund Randolph (1794)
	*Timothy Pickering (1795)
Secretary of the treasury	*Alexander Hamilton
	*Oliver Wolcott, Jr. (1795)
Secretary of war	*Henry Knox
	*Timothy Pickering (1795)
	*James McHenry (1796)
Attorney general	*Edmund Randolph
	William Bradford (1794)
	Charles Lee (1795)

*Has a separate biography in *World Book.*

his birthday, Washington gave a ball at which dancing lasted until well after midnight.

Martha Washington's two young grandchildren, Eleanor Parke Custis and George Washington Parke Custis, came to live with the Washingtons in the early 1780's. Their father, John Custis, had died during the Revolutionary War and their mother had remarried.

Martha Washington was described in a letter by Abigail Adams, wife of the Vice President: "She is plain in her dress, but that plainness is the best of every article. … Her hair is white, her teeth beautiful, her person rather short. … Her manners are modest and unassuming, dignified and feminine. …"

The Washingtons made many trips home to Mount Vernon during the next eight years. The President sometimes stayed there as long as three months when Congress was not in session.

New precedents of government. "I walk on untrodden ground," Washington said as he began the new responsibilities of his office. "There is scarcely any part of my conduct that may not hereafter be drawn into precedent."

Washington believed strongly in the constitutional provision that the executive, legislative, and judicial branches of the government should be kept as separate as possible. He thought the President should not try to influence the kinds of laws that Congress passed. But he believed that if he disapproved of a bill, he should let Congress know by vetoing it. Washington regarded the duties of his office largely as administering the laws of Congress and supervising relations with other countries.

In 1789, at the beginning of Washington's presidency, 11 of the original 13 colonies had ratified the Constitution. North Carolina accepted the Constitution in November 1789, and Rhode Island in 1790. Three other states joined the Union while Washington was in office—Vermont in 1791, Kentucky in 1792, and Tennessee in 1796.

On July 4, 1789, Washington received the first important bill passed by the new Congress. It provided income to run the government by setting taxes on im-

ports. He signed it with no comment.

By September, Congress had established three executive departments to help run the government: the Department of Foreign Affairs (now Department of State), the Department of War, and the Department of the Treasury. Congress provided for an Attorney General and a continuation of the Post Office. It also adopted the Bill of Rights and established a system of federal courts.

Cabinet. In September, Washington began making important appointments. He chose men whom he knew and could trust:

Chief justice of the United States—John Jay, who had been secretary of foreign affairs under the Articles of Confederation.

Secretary of state—Thomas Jefferson, who had served with Washington in Virginia's legislature.

Secretary of war—Henry Knox, Washington's chief of artillery during the Revolutionary War.

Secretary of the treasury—Alexander Hamilton, who had been one of Washington's military aides.

Attorney general—Edmund Randolph, former governor of Virginia and a member of the Constitutional Convention. He had been Washington's friend for many years.

During his first Administration, Washington relied

Library of Congress

Washington took the oath of office as first President of the United States on the balcony of Federal Hall in New York City. His second inauguration took place in Philadelphia.

Granger Collection

Washington gave an inaugural address in the Senate Chamber of Federal Hall after taking the oath of office. He thus established a tradition that every other President has followed.

heavily on the advice of Hamilton and James Madison, a congressman from Virginia. At first, Washington did not call his department heads together as a group. Instead, he asked them to give him written opinions or to talk with him individually. Washington allowed his department heads to act independently. He did not try to prevent Hamilton, Jefferson, or the others from influencing Congress. Toward the end of his first Administration, he began calling the group together for meetings. In 1793, Madison first used the term *cabinet* to refer to the group (see **Cabinet**).

Finances. Washington's new government had millions of dollars in debts which the Congress of the Articles of Confederation had been unable to pay. Hamilton drew up a plan to straighten out the finances. There was much argument, but finally the plan passed in July 1790. The law provided that the national government would assume the wartime debts of the states. It also called for borrowing $12 million from other countries and for paying interest on the public debts.

New national capital. Congress approved a bill in July to transfer the government to Philadelphia until 1800. After that, the capital would be moved to a federal district to be located on the Potomac River. The President took up residence in Philadelphia in November 1790. During the next several years, Washington devoted much time to the plans for the new national capital, which came to bear his name.

Constitutional debate. Hamilton obtained passage in 1791 of a bill setting up the First Bank of the United States (see **Bank of the United States**). Washington had

to decide whether the government had powers under the Constitution to charter such a corporation. Jefferson and Randolph believed that the bill was unconstitutional. They said such powers were not mentioned in the Constitution. Hamilton argued that the government

Granger Collection

Washington's Cabinet consisted of four men that he knew and trusted. This picture shows Washington with, *left to right,* Secretary of War Henry Knox, Secretary of the Treasury Alexander Hamilton, Secretary of State Thomas Jefferson, and Attorney General Edmund Randolph.

could use all powers except those denied by the Constitution. Washington, who believed in a strong national government, took the side of Hamilton and signed the law.

First veto by Washington of congressional legislation was made in April 1792. The first census of the United States had shown that the population was 3,929,214, including 697,000 slaves. Congress then passed a bill in March to raise the number of U.S. representatives from 67 to 120. Washington believed the bill was unconstitutional because some states would have greater representation in proportion to population than other states. Many people thought the bill favored Northern States over Southern States. Congress failed to override Washington's veto, and then revised the bill to provide for a House of 103 members.

Rise of political parties. Washington was disturbed as he saw that Jefferson and Hamilton were disagreeing more and more with each other. Men and newspapers who supported Hamilton's views of a stronger and stronger national government called themselves *Federalists* (see **Federalist Party**). The Federalists became the party of the Northern States and of banking and manufacturing interests. Those who favored Jefferson's ideas of a strict interpretation of the Constitution in defending states' rights became known as *Anti-Federalists,* or *Democratic-Republicans* (see **Democratic-Republican Party**). The Democratic-Republicans mainly represented

Unfinished portrait of Martha Washington (1796) by Gilbert Stuart; Jointly owned by the National Portrait Gallery, Smithsonian Institution, and the Museum of Fine Arts, Boston

Martha Washington handled her duties as first lady with grace and dignity, though she said she felt like a "state prisoner" in the role. She was 65 years old when this portrait was painted.

The Republican Court by Daniel Huntington; The Brooklyn Museum, Gift of the Crescent-Hamilton Athletic Club

The Washingtons entertained a great deal in the executive mansions they occupied in New York and Philadelphia. Martha Washington held a formal reception each Friday evening, *above*. These gatherings ended at 9 p.m., when, according to the first lady, the President always retired.

Quotations from Washington

The following quotations come from some of George Washington's speeches and writings. His famous Farewell Address was prepared with the assistance of Alexander Hamilton, among others.

Discipline is the soul of an army. It makes small numbers formidable; procures success to the weak, and esteem to all.
Letter of instructions to the captains of the Virginia Regiments, July 29, 1757

I am embarked on a wide ocean, boundless in its prospect and from whence, perhaps, no safe harbor is to be found.
Written in 1775, a few days before going to Boston as commander in chief of the Revolutionary forces

The time is now near at hand which must probably determine, whether Americans are to be freemen or slaves . . . The fate of unborn millions will now depend, under God, on the courage and conduct of this army—our cruel and unrelenting enemy leaves us no choice but a brave resistance, or the most abject submission . . . We have therefore to resolve to conquer or die.
General orders to the Continental Army, July 2, 1776

It is too probable that no plan we propose will be adopted. Perhaps another dreadful conflict is to be sustained. If, to please the people, we offer what we ourselves disapprove, how can we afterwards defend our work? Let us raise a standard to which the wise and honest can repair.
Remarks at the Constitutional Convention, 1787

Liberty, when it begins to take root, is a plant of rapid growth.
Letter to James Madison, March 2, 1788

The preservation of the sacred fire of liberty, and the destiny of the republican model of government, are justly considered as deeply, perhaps as finally staked, on the experiment entrusted to the hands of the American people.
First Inaugural Address, April 30, 1789

To be prepared for war is one of the most effectual means of preserving peace.
First Annual Address, presented to both houses of Congress, Jan. 8, 1790

If the laws are to be so trampled upon, with impunity, and a minority . . . is to dictate to the majority there is an end put, at one stroke, to republican government.
Response to the Whiskey Rebellion, 1794

. . . The basis of our political systems is the right of the people to make and to alter their constitutions of government. But the constitution which at any time exists, 'till changed by an explicit and authentic act of the whole People, is sacredly obligatory upon all. . . .

. . . Let me now . . . warn you in the most solemn manner against the baneful effects of the spirit of party . . . It agitates the Community with ill founded jealousies and false alarms, kindles the animosity of one part against another, foments occasionally riot and insurrection.

. . . Of all the dispositions and habits which lead to political prosperity, religion and morality are indispensable supports.

. . . Promote . . . institutions for the general diffusion of knowledge . . . it is essential that public opinion should be enlightened.

. . . Observe good faith and justice towards all Nations. Cultivate peace and harmony with all . . . nothing is more essential than that permanent, inveterate antipathies against particular Nations and passionate attachments for others should be excluded . . . The nation, which indulges toward another an habitual hatred, or an habitual fondness, is in some degree a slave. It is a slave to its animosity or to its affection, either of which is sufficient to lead it astray from its duty and its interest.

. . . 'Tis our true policy to steer clear of permanent Alliances, with any portion of the foreign world . . . Taking care always to keep ourselves, by suitable establishments, on a respectably defensive posture, we may safely trust to temporary alliances for extraordinary emergencies . . . There can be no greater error than to expect, or calculate upon real favors from nation to nation.
Farewell Address, published in the *American Daily Advertiser*, a Philadelphia newspaper, Sept. 19, 1796

---

the Southern States and the farmers.

Washington attempted to favor neither party. He tried to bring Hamilton and Jefferson into agreement and tried to discourage the growth of political parties.

Reelection. In 1792, Washington began to make plans for retirement. In May, he asked Madison to help him prepare a farewell address. Madison did so, but he urged Washington to accept reelection as President. Hamilton, Knox, Jefferson, and Randolph each asked Washington to continue as President. Perhaps one of the strongest arguments came from Jefferson, who wrote: "Your being at the helm will be more than an answer to every argument which can be used to alarm and lead the people in any quarter into violence or secession. North and South will hang together if they have you to hang on."

Members of the Electoral College cast their votes in December 1792. Their ballots were counted on Feb. 13, 1793, and Washington again was elected President with the largest number of votes possible—132. Adams received 77 votes and was again the runner-up and Vice President.

Second Administration (1793-1797)

Washington's second inauguration took place in Congress Hall in Philadelphia on March 4, 1793. The 61-year-old Washington faced greater problems during his second Administration than during his first.

Neutrality proclamation. Word came in April 1793 that a general war had begun in Europe. England, Spain, Austria, and Prussia were all fighting against the new French republic. Although the United States had signed an alliance with the French king in 1778, Washington wanted to "maintain a strict neutrality." Jefferson, who favored the recent French Revolution, did not want to issue a neutrality statement. Hamilton believed neutrality was necessary.

Washington ordered Attorney General Randolph to write up a statement. On April 22, the President signed the Neutrality Proclamation which called for "conduct friendly and impartial" to all the warring nations. It also forbade American ships from carrying war supplies to the fighting countries.

Relations with France. The United States decision to stay out of the European war pleased the English, but it angered the French. Leaders of the French Revolution believed the United States should stand by its alliance of 1778 with King Louis XVI. But the revolutionaries had beheaded the king who made the alliance. This posed a delicate point in international law, and Washington had no precedents to guide him. He finally decided to be cool and formal in receiving Edmond Genêt, the new minister appointed by the French republic.

Genêt seemed determined to draw Americans into the war on the side of France. He tried secretly to win Democratic-Republicans to the French cause during the spring and summer of 1793. This upset Washington. The President's patience gave out when Genêt tried to outfit warships in American ports and send them to sea against the British.

After a stormy Cabinet meeting in July 1793, Washington asked France to recall Genêt because he endangered American neutrality. Genêt was stripped of his power, but was allowed to stay in the United States. The neutrality crisis of 1793 passed, and the United States remained at peace.

Whiskey Rebellion. In 1794, Washington proved that the government could enforce federal laws in the states. Farmers in four counties in western Pennsylvania had refused to pay federal taxes on manufacturing whiskey. They armed themselves and attacked federal officials. Washington raised nearly 13,000 troops and sent them to western Pennsylvania. By November 1794, the rebellion had been crushed and the ringleaders arrested.

Relations with Britain. Washington worried as relations with Great Britain grew worse. British warships stopped American ships carrying food supplies to France and seized their cargoes. They sometimes took seamen off the American ships and forced them into the British navy. British troops refused to give up western frontier forts they were supposed to have surrendered under terms of the treaty of 1783. The British also were stirring up Indian fighting on the western frontier. In an effort to settle problems with Britain, Washington sent Chief Justice John Jay to London in 1794.

In March 1795, Washington received a copy of a treaty Jay had signed on Nov. 19, 1794. Earlier copies had been lost in the mail. Most of the treaty had to do with regulation of trade between America and Britain. It also called for British troops to give up the frontier forts in 1796. But it contained no agreement that British ships would stop waylaying American ships and taking seamen. See **Jay Treaty**.

Washington called a special session of the Senate in June to study the treaty. Federalists supported the Jay Treaty because it insured continuing trade with Britain. The Democratic-Republicans violently opposed the treaty because they believed it would harm France. The Federalists controlled the Senate, so the treaty was ratified by a vote of 20 to 10, except for one section. This section opened trade with the British West Indies to United States ships, but it also severely restricted this trade. Washington could not make up his mind whether or not to sign the treaty. He went home to Mount Vernon to think about it.

At Mount Vernon, the President received word of riots in many cities protesting the Jay Treaty. A mob in New York City stoned Hamilton. A Philadelphia mob broke windows at the British embassy.

Cabinet scandal. Washington returned to Philadelphia on Aug. 11, 1795. He learned that the British had captured a French diplomatic message which seemed to indicate that Edmund Randolph, who was now secretary of state, was a traitor. Washington read a translation of the French message. He believed that Randolph might have sold secrets to the French.

Without saying anything to Randolph about his suspicions, Washington called a Cabinet meeting to discuss the Jay Treaty. At the meeting, Randolph argued against signing the treaty as long as Britain continued to seize American ships. Washington became convinced Randolph was in the pay of France, so he signed the treaty.

As soon as the Jay Treaty had been delivered to the British embassy, Washington called in Randolph and showed him the French message. Randolph denied his guilt, but resigned. He swore he would prove his innocence. Randolph later published a book in which he declared that he had never betrayed his country.

Washington now suffered the bitterest criticism of his career. He was accused by Democratic-Republican newspapers of falling victim to a Federalist plot in signing the Jay Treaty. It was even suggested that he should be impeached because he had overdrawn his $25,000 salary. Washington's feelings were badly hurt.

Public opinion of Washington began to improve when he was able to announce a few months later that a treaty had been negotiated with Spain opening up the Mississippi River to trade. Agreement also had been reached with the pirates of the Barbary States to release American prisoners and to let American ships alone for a payment of $800,000 ransom, plus $24,000 tribute each year. Peace treaties also had been signed with Indian tribes on the frontier.

Farewell Address. Washington, who believed the office of President should be above political attack, had become tired of public office. The new House of Representatives had a large Democratic-Republican majority and was unfriendly to Washington. He also felt himself growing old.

In May 1796, Washington dusted off the draft of his *Farewell Address* that he and James Madison had worked on four years earlier. He sent it to Jay and to Hamilton for their suggestions. Finally, in September, the much-edited address, all in Washington's handwriting, was ready. He gave it to the editor of the *American Daily Advertiser,* a Philadelphia newspaper, which published it on September 19.

In the election campaign that followed, Washington favored John Adams, the Federalist candidate for President. But Washington did not take an active part in the campaigning. The Democratic-Republican candidate was Thomas Jefferson. When the Electoral College met, it gave 71 votes to Adams and 68 to Jefferson. Under the existing constitutional provision, Adams became President and Jefferson Vice President.

At the inauguration in March 1797, Adams sensed Washington's relief at retirement. Adams wrote to his wife: "He seemed to me to enjoy a triumph over me. Methought I heard him say, 'Ay! I am fairly out and you fairly in! See which of us will be the happiest!' "

"First in the hearts of his countrymen" (1797-1799)

Washington was 65. He happily went home to Mount Vernon. Friends said he looked even older. But he did not lose touch with public affairs. Almost every day visitors dropped in to see him. On July 31, 1797, he wrote: "Unless someone pops in unexpectedly—Mrs. Washington and myself will do what has not been done within the last twenty years by us—that is to set down to dinner by ourselves."

The Washingtons had no children of their own, but they raised Martha's children from her first marriage. Then they cared for two of her grandchildren, whose father died during the Revolutionary War. This painting shows the Washingtons with the grandchildren, George and Eleanor.

The Washington Family, oil painting on canvas (1796) by Edward Savage; National Gallery of Art, Washington, D.C., Andrew W. Mellon Collection

He described his daily routine in a letter:

"I begin . . . with the sun . . . if my hirelings are not in their places at that time I send them messages expressive of my sorrow for their indisposition . . . breakfast (a little after seven o'clock . . .). This over, I mount my horse and ride round the farms . . . The usual time of sitting at table; a walk, and tea, brings me within the dawn of candlelight . . . I resolve that . . . I will retire to my writing table and acknowledge the letters I have received; but when the lights are brought, I feel tired, and disinclined to engage in this work."

Managing the several farms which made up the more than 7,600 acres (3,075 hectares) of Mount Vernon took much of his time. He made frequent trips to watch construction in the new city of Washington, D.C., which then was called the Federal City.

Recall to duty. While Washington enjoyed his retirement, relations between the United States and France grew worse. The government decided to raise an army for defense. President Adams asked Washington's help. On July 4, 1798, Washington was commissioned as "Lieutenant General and Commander in Chief of the armies raised or to be raised."

He went to Philadelphia for a few weeks in November to help plan the new army. He had dinner one night in debtors' prison with financier Robert Morris, in whose Philadelphia home he had lived while President. Morris had gone to prison because he could not pay his debts.

During his last year of life, Washington wrote many letters to the various men he chose as generals for the new army. Federalist leaders asked if he would consider running for a third term as President. He said no. Washington also was saddened by the deaths of friends and relatives. Patrick Henry died on June 6, 1799, and Washington's last living brother, Charles Washington, died on Sept. 20, 1799.

Death. On December 12, Washington wrote his last letter. It was to Alexander Hamilton. In it he discussed the importance of establishing a national military academy. After finishing the letter, Washington went for his daily horseback ride around Mount Vernon. The day was cold, with snow turning into rain and sleet. Washington returned after about five hours and sat down to dinner without changing his damp clothes. The next day, he awoke with a sore throat. He went for a walk. Then he made his last entry in his diary, noting down the weather: "Morning Snowing & abt. 3 Inches deep . . . Mer. 28 at Night." These were his last written words.

Between 2 and 3 a.m. on Dec. 14, 1799, Washington awakened Martha. He had difficulty speaking and was quite ill. But he would not let her send for a doctor until dawn. James Craik, who had been his friend and doctor since he was a young man, hurried to Mount Vernon. By the time he arrived, Washington already had called in an overseer and had about a cup of blood drained from his veins. Craik examined Washington and said the illness was "inflammatory quinsy." Craik bled Washington again. Present-day doctors believe the illness was a streptococcal infection of the throat.

Two more doctors arrived in the afternoon. Again Washington was bled. Late in the afternoon he could hardly speak, but told the doctors: "You had better not take any more trouble about me; but let me go off quietly; I cannot last long."

About 10 p.m. on December 14, Washington whispered: "I am just going. Have me decently buried, and do not let my body be put in the vault in less than two days after I am dead. Do you understand me?" His secretary answered: "Yes, sir." Washington said: " 'Tis well." He felt for his own pulse. Then he died.

On December 18, Washington was given a military funeral. His body was laid to rest in the family tomb at Mount Vernon. Throughout the world, people were saddened by his death. In the United States, thousands of people wore mourning clothes for months.

No other American has been honored more than

Washington. The nation's capital, Washington, D.C., was named for him. There, the giant Washington Monument stands. The state of Washington is the only state named after a president. Many counties, cities, towns, streets, bridges, lakes, parks, and schools bear his name. Washington's portrait appears on postage stamps, on the $1 bill, and on the quarter.

After the siege of Boston in 1776, the Massachusetts legislature in a resolution had said: "… may future generations, in the peaceful enjoyment of that freedom, the exercise of which your sword shall have established, raise the richest and most lasting monuments to the name of Washington." The legislators foresaw the place he would hold forever in the hearts of Americans.

At his death, Washington held the title of lieutenant general, then the highest U.S. military rank. But through the years, he was outranked by many U.S. Army officers. In 1976, Congress granted Washington the nation's highest military title, General of the Armies of the United States. This action confirmed him as the senior general officer on the Army rolls.   Philander D. Chase

Related articles in *World Book* include:

Adams, John
Braddock, Edward
Brother Jonathan
Cabinet
Constitution of the U.S.
French and Indian wars
Genêt, Edmond Charles Édouard
George Washington Birthplace National Monument
Hamilton, Alexander
Jefferson, Thomas
Knox, Henry
Lafayette, Marquis de
Masonry (picture)
Mount Rushmore National Memorial
Mount Vernon
President of the U.S.
Randolph, Edmund
Revolutionary War in America
Sculpture (American sculpture; picture)
Stamp collecting (picture)
Stuart, Gilbert Charles
Sulgrave Manor
Valley Forge
Virginia (picture)
Washington, D.C.
Washington, Martha Custis
Washington Monument
Washington's Birthday
Whiskey Rebellion

Outline

I. Washington the man
II. Early life (1732-1746)
  A. Family background
  B. Washington's parents
  C. Boyhood
  D. Education
  E. Plantation life
  F. Development of character
III. Washington the surveyor (1747-1752)
  A. First expedition
  B. Professional surveyor
  C. Only foreign trip
IV. Early military career (1753-1758)
  A. Messenger to the French
  B. First military action
  C. Surrender of Fort Necessity
  D. Braddock's defeat
  E. Frontier commander

V. The peaceful years (1759-1773)
  A. Marriage   C. Farmer and landowner
  B. Legislator   D. Social life
VI. The coming revolution (1774-1775)
  A. First Continental Congress
  B. Elected commander in chief
VII. "First in war" (1775-1783)
  A. Symbol of independence
  B. Discouragement
  C. The army
  D. Shortage of supplies
  E. Winning the war
  F. Turning down a crown
VIII. "First in peace" (1784-1789)
  A. Constitutional Convention
  B. Elected President
IX. First Administration (1789-1793)
  A. Inauguration day
  B. Life in the Executive Mansion
  C. New precedents of government
  D. Cabinet
  E. Finances
  F. New national capital
  G. Constitutional debate
  H. First veto
  I. Rise of political parties
  J. Reelection
X. Second Administration (1793-1797)
  A. Neutrality proclamation D. Relations with Britain
  B. Relations with France   E. Cabinet scandal
  C. Whiskey Rebellion   F. Farewell Address
XI. "First in the hearts of his countrymen" (1797-1799)
  A. Recall to duty
  B. Death

Questions

Why is Washington called the "Father of His Country"?
When did Washington first notice that the British treated Americans as second-class citizens?
How did Washington react to his first sound of bullets in war?
What was Washington referring to when he said: "I went out, was soundly beaten, lost them all …"?
How did Washington acquire Mount Vernon?
When and why did Washington make his only trip outside of America?
Why did his presidential receptions usually end at 9 p.m.?
As a farmer, how was Washington ahead of his time?
How did Washington show the Second Continental Congress that he was ready to defy Britain?
Who praised Washington as "First in war, first in peace, and first in the hearts of his countrymen"?

Additional resources

Brookhiser, Richard. *Founding Father: Rediscovering George Washington.* Free Pr., 1996.
Harness, Cheryl. *George Washington.* National Geographic Soc., 2000. Younger readers.
Marrin, Albert. *George Washington and the Founding of a Nation.* Dutton, 2001.
Rhodehamel, John H. *The Great Experiment: George Washington and the American Republic.* Yale, 1998.

Washington, Harold (1922-1987), won election as the first African American mayor of Chicago in 1983. Washington, a Democrat, defeated Republican Bernard E. Epton, a former state representative. Washington received about 52 percent of the total vote. He won support from about 99 percent of Chicago's black voters and 18 percent of its white voters, including Hispanics. At that time, blacks made up about 40 percent of the city's population. Washington was reelected in April 1987. He had a fatal heart attack on Nov. 25, 1987.

Washington was the first black mayoral nominee of Chicago's Democratic Party. He became the nominee by defeating Mayor Jane M. Byrne and Cook County State's Attorney Richard M. Daley in a primary election.

Washington was born on April 15, 1922, in Chicago. His father was a lawyer and a Methodist minister. Washington graduated from Roosevelt University in 1949 and from the Northwestern University School of Law in 1952. He became a lawyer in 1953.

Washington served in the Illinois House of Representatives from 1965 to 1976 and in the Illinois Senate from 1976 to 1980. He represented Illinois's First Congressional District in the United States House of Representatives from 1981 to 1983.   Basil B. Talbott, Jr.

Washington, Martha Custis (1731-1802), was the wife of George Washington. When he took office as the first president in 1789, she became America's first first lady.

Martha Washington was born on June 2, 1731, near Williamsburg, Virginia. Her father, Colonel John Dandridge, was a wealthy landowner. Martha had no formal schooling. Until she married Washington, she had never traveled beyond Virginia. At the age of 17, she married Daniel Parke Custis, a wealthy Virginia planter 13 years older than she. They had four children, two of whom died in childhood. The other two died before Washington became president. The death of Custis in 1757 made Martha one of the richest women in Virginia.

No one knows when Martha Custis first met George Washington. They may have met at a neighbor's home in Williamsburg early in 1758. Washington was then a colonel in the militia. She was eight months older than he. They were married on Jan. 6, 1759.

Washington called his wife by her childhood nickname, "Patsy." During the Revolutionary War, she traveled long distances to share his hardships. Mrs. Washington joined him at his camp at Valley Forge, Pennsylvania, during the winter of 1777-1778. She also spent the harsh winters of 1778-1779 and 1779-1780 with him in camp at Morristown, New Jersey. She organized a women's sewing circle and mended clothes for the troops.

As first lady, Mrs. Washington managed the president's home with dignity and grace. But she did not enjoy being first lady. She said she felt like a "state prisoner." Many people called her "Lady Washington." But Mrs. Washington dressed so plainly that people often mistook her for the family maid.

After Washington's death in 1799, she continued to live at Mount Vernon, their estate. Shortly before she died on May 22, 1802, she burned the letters Washington had written her. Mrs. Washington was buried at Mount Vernon.   Kathryn Kish Sklar

See also **Washington, George.**

Washington, Mount. See Mount Washington.

Washington, Treaty of, was signed on May 8, 1871, by the United States and the United Kingdom in Washington, D.C. It led to the settlement of several disputes that had arisen during the American Civil War (1861-1865) or soon afterward. The chief issue consisted of U.S. demands that the British pay for damages caused during the war by the *Alabama* and other British-built warships. The United Kingdom had sold the ships to the Confederacy. The U.S. demands became known as the *Alabama* Claims. The treaty also dealt with a dispute over whether the United States or British-ruled Canada owned the San Juan Islands in Puget Sound, in what is now the state of Washington. In addition, the treaty resolved a disagreement over fishing rights in territorial waters off the coasts of the United States and Canada.

The Treaty of Washington established guidelines for the settlement of the *Alabama* Claims. It also referred the claims to a special court of arbitration in Geneva, Switzerland. In 1872, the court ruled that the United Kingdom should pay the United States $15 $\frac{1}{2}$ million.

The treaty referred the San Juan Islands dispute to the German Emperor Wilhelm I, who upheld the U.S. claim to the islands. The treaty also granted fishing rights to the United States in territorial waters along Canada's east coast. The United Kingdom gained similar rights in U.S. waters north of the 39th parallel.   Michael Perman

See also **Alabama** (ship); **Fish, Hamilton.**

Washington, University of, is a coeducational state-supported research university in Seattle. It has colleges of architecture and urban planning, arts and sciences, education, engineering, forest resources, and ocean and fishery sciences. The university also has a graduate school and schools of business administration, dentistry, law, librarianship, medicine, nursing, pharmacy, public affairs, public health and community medicine, and social work. It grants bachelor's, master's, and doctor's degrees.

The University of Washington was founded in 1861 in what is now downtown Seattle. The school moved to its present location along Lake Washington in 1895.

Critically reviewed by the University of Washington

Washington Conference was a meeting held in Washington, D.C., to discuss naval disarmament and certain problems involving east Asia. It took place from November 1921 to February 1922. Nations represented were Belgium, China, France, Italy, Japan, the Netherlands, Portugal, the United Kingdom, and the United States. It led to one of the few successful disarmament agreements in modern times.

Three major treaties resulted from the conference. The Five-Power Naval Limitation Treaty, adopted by France, Italy, Japan, the United Kingdom, and the United States, ended a growing build-up of major warships among these nations. It resulted in destruction of *capital ships* (battleships) and a 10-year prohibition on construction of more battleships. The Four-Power Treaty, signed by France, Japan, the United Kingdom, and the United States, recognized each nation's possession of certain islands in the Pacific Ocean. The Nine-Power Treaty was signed by all the countries at the conference. Its chief purpose was to guarantee the independence of China. The treaty was observed until 1931, when Japan invaded Manchuria, a region in northeastern China.

Thomas H. Buckley

Washington Monument is a great obelisk built in honor of George Washington. It stands in Washington, D.C., near the Potomac River, about halfway between the Capitol and the Lincoln Memorial.

The monument has the shape of the obelisks of ancient Egypt, but it is several times larger than they were. It is 555 feet 5 $\frac{1}{8}$ inches (169.29 meters) high, and measures 55 feet 1 $\frac{1}{2}$ inches (16.9 meters) along each of its four sides at the bottom. The sides slant gradually inward as they rise to the base of the *pyramidion* (small pyramid) which tops the pillar. At this point, each side of the pillar is 34 feet 5 $\frac{1}{2}$ inches (10.5 meters) long. The pyramidion

© James P. Blair, Corbis

Washington National Cathedral is an Episcopal church in Washington, D.C. The church is designed in the style of medieval Gothic cathedrals with pointed arches and spires.

rises 55 feet (16.8 meters). The walls of the monument are 15 feet (4.6 meters) thick at the bottom and 18 inches (46 centimeters) thick at the top. They are covered with white marble from Maryland. The stones covering the pyramidion are 7 inches (18 centimeters) thick. A cap of cast aluminum protects the tip.

Inside, the monument is hollow. The inner walls are set with 193 carved memorial stones, many of historic interest. The stones were presented by individuals, societies, cities, states, and other countries.

Visitors may take an elevator to an observation area at the top of the monument. From there, the view of Washington, D.C., is impressive. The elevator that takes visitors back to the ground slows down at certain levels to allow people to see some of the commemorative stones set in the walls.

Some people planned a memorial to Washington while he was still alive, but he objected to the expense. In 1833, the Washington National Monument Society began raising funds for a monument. A design by Robert Mills had already been accepted in part. The government approved the project, and the cornerstone was laid on July 4, 1848, with the same trowel that Washington had used to lay the cornerstone of the Capitol in 1793. But engineers found the ground too soft, so they moved the site to the north.

Many people donated stones. Pope Pius IX sent a marble block from the Temple of Concord in Rome. One night in 1854, a group believed to be Know-Nothings, or members of the American Party, stole this block (see **Know-Nothings**). This act shocked the public, and contri-

butions almost stopped. In 1855, Congress agreed to give some financial aid to the project. But Know-Nothings broke into the society's offices and claimed possession of the monument.

In 1876, Congress voted to finish the project at government expense. Work began on Aug. 17, 1880. It was completed on Dec. 6, 1884. The monument was dedicated on Feb. 21, 1885, and opened to the public on Oct. 9, 1888. It is maintained as a national memorial by the National Park Service. Renovations in the late 1990's included adding a ground-floor museum with exhibits on George Washington and the monument.

Critically reviewed by the National Park Service

See also **Washington, D.C.** (picture).

Washington National Cathedral, also called the National Cathedral, is an Episcopal church in Washington, D.C. Its official name is the Cathedral Church of Saint Peter and Saint Paul.

The building is laid out in the form of a Latin cross (see **Cross**). It is 525 feet (160 meters) long and 275 feet (84 meters) wide at its widest point. It is English Gothic in style, with pointed arches and vaulted ceilings. The cathedral is noted for its rich stone carvings and beautiful stained-glass windows. Stones from historic buildings and shrines in all parts of the world were used in building it. The *Gloria* tower of the cathedral contains a large carillon with 53 bells and a 10-bell English peal.

Work on the cathedral began in 1907, and services have been held in some of its chapels since 1912. The building was consecrated in 1990. President Woodrow Wilson is among the well-known people buried in the cathedral.   J. William Rudd

Washington State University is a coeducational, state-controlled land-grant institution with a main campus in Pullman, Washington. Branch campuses include the Tri-Cities campus in Richland and campuses in Spokane and Vancouver.

The university has colleges of agriculture and home economics, business and economics, education, engineering and architecture, nursing, pharmacy, sciences and arts, and veterinary medicine, as well as a graduate school. It was founded in 1890.

Critically reviewed by Washington State University

Washington's Birthday is celebrated as a federal holiday on the third Monday in February. It honors the first president of the United States. George Washington was born on Feb. 22, 1732, according to the calendar we now use. But by the Old Style Calendar then in use, his birth date was February 11. People first celebrated the anniversary in the late 1700's, some on the 11th and some on the 22nd. Today, some states also honor Abraham Lincoln and other presidents on the third Monday in February and call the holiday *Presidents' Day*. See also **Presidents' Day.**

Washita River. See Ouachita River.

Washoe Indians, *WAHSH oh* or *WAW shoh,* also spelled *Washo,* live in California and Nevada near Lake Tahoe. Traditionally, Washoe territory extended from the western slope of the Sierra Nevada to areas as far east as Pyramid Lake in Nevada. Washoe territory included Honey Lake and the upper valleys of the Truckee, Carson, and West Walker rivers (see **Nevada** [terrain map]).

The Washoe lived primarily in small camps. They built

Some kinds of wasps There are more than 17,000 species of true wasps. These drawings show three species that live in North America. The scientific name of each species appears in italics.

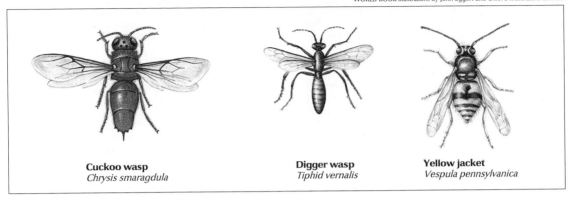

Cuckoo wasp
Chrysis smaragdula

Digger wasp
Tiphid vernalis

Yellow jacket
Vespula pennsylvanica

dome-shaped houses of poles and thatch in summer and cone-shaped homes of bark slabs in winter. For food, they fished, hunted deer and rabbits, and gathered plants, berries, and such seeds as pine nuts and acorns. Each spring, the Washoe gathered along the shores of Lake Tahoe, which they considered a sacred place.

The discovery of gold and silver around Virginia City, Nevada, in 1859 brought numerous white settlers to Washoe lands. The settlers cut down many of the trees that had provided seeds eaten by the Washoe. Game became scarce, and the whites restricted fishing. As a result, most Washoe began living in poverty at the fringes of white settlements. In the early 1900's, a number of Washoe reservations were set up in California and Nevada. The tribe has established housing, agricultural, and other development projects on the reservations.

Victoria D. Patterson

Wasp is any of a large number of insects closely related to bees and ants. There are more than 17,000 species of true wasps. They are characterized by a narrowing of the abdomen into a thin "wasp waist," and by the presence of a sting in the female.

Wasps are most common in regions with tropical or warm climates. Only a few species live in cold regions. About 3,800 species are found in the United States and Canada. Most wasps have wings and fly. However, the females of a few species, called *velvet ants,* lack wings. The majority of wasps are yellow, reddish, bluish-black, or black in color. Some are black and white, black and yellow, or black and red. Others have stripes of black and a bright color across the body.

Scientists divide wasps into two groups: (1) solitary and (2) social. Each group has different nesting habits. Among solitary wasps, the female does all the work of nesting by herself. Common solitary wasps include mud daubers, cuckoo wasps, and digger wasps. Social wasps have a social system in which members of the community help build and maintain the nest. Hornets and yellow jackets are two common kinds of social wasps.

Body. A wasp's body has three parts: (1) a head, (2) a thorax, and (3) an abdomen. On each side of its head, a wasp has two *compound* eyes made up of many tiny lenses. Two antennae between the eyes serve mainly as organs of smell and touch. A wasp's mouthparts are designed for chewing food and for sucking up liquids.

The thorax is the middle part of a wasp's body. The insect's wings and legs are connected to the thorax. Wasps have four wings and six legs.

A wasp's abdomen contains organs of digestion and reproduction. Female wasps have a sting hidden near the end of the abdomen. Solitary wasps use their sting to paralyze prey. Social wasps also use their sting to defend their nest against intruders. Attached to a wasp's sting are glands that produce poison. The poison of social wasps contains chemical compounds that irritate higher animals. People who are especially sensitive to these poisonous compounds can die from being stung.

Life cycle. Wasps develop in four stages: (1) egg, (2) larva, (3) pupa, and (4) adult. The egg of a wasp hatches into a wormlike larva, also called a *grub.* The larva reaches its full size in 7 to 20 days, depending on the species and the weather. It then spins a covering known as a *cocoon.* Most solitary wasps that live in cool climates spend the winter in the cocoon. Most social wasps stay in the cocoon about two weeks. While in the cocoon, the larva becomes a pupa, a stage during which the insect changes dramatically into an adult. At the end of the pupal stage, the adult breaks out of the cocoon.

Social wasps most commonly mate in the fall. The female hibernates during winter in a protected place and

Wasp nests vary in form and in the building materials used. Polistes wasps build open paper nests, such as the one shown above. Mud daubers construct nests of mud. A cross section of a mud dauber nest, *right,* shows the tube-shaped cells where the offspring hatch and grow.

emerges in the spring to start a nest. Female solitary wasps hibernate as larvae and mate in the spring, after they have become adults. Female social wasps and female solitary wasps store *sperm* (male sex cells) in a sac near the end of the abdomen. When a female wasp lays an egg, she may fertilize it with sperm. Fertilized eggs become female wasps, while unfertilized eggs become males. Mated female social wasps may live up to a year. All other types of wasps usually live two months or less.

Food. Adult wasps feed mainly on the nectar of flowers. They prey on other insects and on spiders chiefly to provide food for developing offspring. Most species of wasps hunt a particular kind of prey. For example, one species of sphecid wasp preys on cockroaches. Another wasp species, the bee wolf, preys on honey bees.

In most species of solitary wasps, the female paralyzes a prey by stinging it. She then puts it in a nest and lays an egg on it. The larva that hatches from the egg feeds on the prey. A few solitary wasps and most social wasps capture a prey and immediately eat it. Later, they *regurgitate* (spit up) the food to their larvae.

Nests. Wasps are talented nest-builders. Most solitary wasps dig nesting burrows in the ground. Some of these wasps nest above the ground in hollow twigs or abandoned beetle burrows. They separate the chambers for each offspring with bits of grass, stone, or mud. Other solitary wasps build nests completely of mud.

Most social wasps make their nests of paper. The female produces the paper by chewing up plant fibers or old wood. She spreads the paper in thin layers to make cells in which she lays her eggs. Some species of wasps, including a group called *Polistes,* build open nests with a single comb of cells. Other species, such as hornets and yellow jackets, construct nests of many cells enclosed by a paper covering with a single entrance. The nests may be suspended from trees, or they may be built underground in abandoned rodent burrows. A few kinds of social wasps build delicate mud nests.

Group life. Solitary wasps do not live in groups. In most species, the male and female get together only to mate. The female maintains the nest and provides food for her offspring. Soon after emerging from the cocoon, each of the offspring leaves the nest and seeks a mate.

Social wasps live in organized communities consisting largely of members of the same family. In the spring, the mated female, called the *queen,* builds the first cells of the nest and lays eggs. Her first offspring are small females, most of which stay unmated and cannot reproduce. These females, called *workers,* enlarge and defend the nest and care for new larvae. The queen continues to lay eggs until late summer. Her last offspring include males and larger females that can reproduce. Among some species, the queen may be joined by other queens, usually her sisters. If the founding queen dies, one of the other queens will take over her position.

Some social wasps that live in tropical climates establish new communities by *swarming.* Swarming occurs when a nest becomes overcrowded. One or more of the young queens leave the nest with several workers. Huddled together, the wasps fly to another location and build a new nest.   H. Jane Brockmann

Scientific classification. Wasps belong to the order Hymenoptera. True wasps make up the division Aculeata in the suborder Apocrita.

See also **Hornet; Insect** (pictures: The compound eyes of a wasp; A fierce battle); **Yellow jacket.**

Wassermann, *WAH suhr muhn* or *VAHS uhr MAHN,* **August von,** *OW goost fuhn* (1866-1925), was a German bacteriologist and immunologist. He became well known for the development of an important blood test used to diagnose syphilis called the *Wassermann test.* The test, announced in 1906, became a model for later research on blood tests to determine the presence of antibodies to viruses and other disease agents. Today, the Wassermann test has been largely replaced by other tests for syphilis.

Wassermann was born on Feb. 21, 1866, in Bamberg, Germany. During the 1890's, Wassermann became noted for his research on cholera and diphtheria immunity. He discovered that people possess varying amounts of resistance to diseases. After 1900, Wassermann helped develop diagnostic tests for tuberculosis. In 1913, he became director of his own institute of experimental therapy.   John Scarborough

Wasserstein, *WAH suhr steen,* **Wendy** (1950-   ), is an American dramatist whose most successful plays deal with feminist themes. Wasserstein is a skillful and subtle satirist. Her plays lean toward self-mocking humor, mixing comedy with serious overtones. Many of her works contain autobiographical elements.

Wasserstein's first major play was *Uncommon Women and Others* (1977), a comedy depicting a reunion of several graduates of Mount Holyoke women's college. *Isn't It Romantic* (1983) is the story of two women and their relationships with lovers and parents and their uncertain futures. *The Heidi Chronicles* (1988) won the 1989 Pulitzer Prize for drama. It traces the career of the central character as she faces her dreams, failures, and triumphs, especially as part of the women's movement. *The Sisters Rosensweig* (1992) is a comedy-drama about a woman banker who celebrates her 54th birthday with her two sisters, and their shared reflections about their lives. *An American Daughter* (1997) is a comedy-drama about the problems a woman faces after she is nominated to be surgeon general of the United States. *Old Money* (2000) is about wealthy New Yorkers living 100 years apart. She also wrote a children's book, *Pamela's First Musical* (1996). Wasserstein was born on Oct. 18, 1950, in the Brooklyn section of New York City.   Don B. Wilmeth

Waste disposal is the process of removing waste materials. People produce *gaseous waste,* such as carbon monoxide from cars; *liquid waste,* such as sewage; and *solid waste.* The many kinds of solid waste include paper and plastic products, bottles and cans, food scraps, and junked automobiles. Solid waste is also called *refuse, garbage, rubbish,* or *trash.* If not disposed of properly, it looks unattractive, smells bad, and contaminates the environment. It may also cause health hazards.

Solid waste from homes, offices, restaurants, and stores is called *municipal solid waste.* This article discusses how to dispose of such waste. Solid waste also comes from industries and farms. For information on these sources of waste, see the *World Book* article on **Environmental pollution.** See also the **Sewage** article for information on the disposal of waste matter from sinks and toilets.

Most cities and towns have waste-collecting departments or private firms that gather municipal solid waste from homes and other buildings. Trash haulers remove the waste in trucks. Disposing of municipal solid waste has become a serious problem because people produce more each year. Also, because few people want to live or work near a waste disposal site, it grows increasingly difficult to find locations for new sites.

Communities use three chief methods to process and dispose of municipal solid waste. These methods are (1) recycling and waste reduction, (2) incineration, and (3) land disposal. In the United States, about 30 percent of solid waste is recycled, 15 percent incinerated, and 55 percent buried in landfills. The United Kingdom disposes of about 75 percent of its solid waste in landfills.

Recycling and waste reduction help lessen the amount of waste that is burned in incinerators or buried in landfills. *Recycling* is the process of reusing materials instead of throwing them away. Commonly recycled materials include metals, glass, and paper. *Waste reduction* is the process of producing less waste. For example, people can reduce waste by buying items that last longer or have less packaging. See **Recycling.**

Incineration is the burning of waste products. Some large cities use incinerators because they do not have suitable areas nearby for land disposal sites. In the United States, Canada, and many European countries, incinerators must limit the amount of pollution they release. Incineration plants must properly handle the ash they produce and monitor the ash to ensure that it will not harm the environment. Most incineration plants use the heat from burning waste to produce steam, which can drive electric power generators or provide heat for buildings or industrial processes. See **Incinerator.**

Land disposal involves hauling garbage to an area owned by a community or a private firm. Such areas include open dumps, sometimes called *unsanitary landfills,* and properly operated *sanitary landfills.*

Open dumps provide a poor method of waste disposal because they harm the environment and cause human health risks. They can ruin an area's appearance and may produce bad odors. In addition, rain water that drains through refuse can carry harmful substances to nearby water. The burning of wastes at unregulated dumps can produce smoke and foul odors. Decomposing wastes produce a flammable gas called *methane,* and methane explosions can result. In many industrialized countries, it is illegal to create a new open dump. In the United States, the Environmental Protection Agency is working to phase out open dumps.

Sanitary landfills are designed to protect the environment by sealing off waste material. Each day, landfill operators pack the waste firmly and cover it with earth or specially manufactured materials. When a site fills up, the operator spreads it with dirt, sometimes after first covering it with a plastic membrane. Many communities then use such sites for recreational purposes.

Because of the limited water and oxygen in tightly packed and covered landfills, many waste materials *decompose* (break down) slowly. As materials decompose, they release gases into the air and compounds that dissolve into the water in the landfill. Landfill operators monitor and control the release of gases and water to prevent pollution. Modern landfills have liners of plastic or clay to hold in contaminated water. A drainage system pumps out rain water that collects in the landfill and transfers the water to a treatment plant for removal of contaminants.   Melody J. Hunt

See also **Energy supply** (Solid and liquid wastes); **Garbage disposer; Landfill; Nuclear energy** (Wastes and waste disposal); **Plastics** (Plastics and the environment).

Additional resources

Coffel, Steve. *Encyclopedia of Garbage.* Facts on File, 1996.
Cozic, Charles P., ed. *Garbage and Waste.* Greenhaven, 1997.

Wat Tyler's Rebellion, also called the Peasants' Revolt, was an uprising by English farm laborers in 1381. The peasants objected to the harsh conditions under which they lived, such as forced labor and heavy taxation. An unfair new tax touched off the uprising. A man named Wat Tyler, whose origins and occupation are unknown, dominated the movement for eight days.

Riots broke out in many parts of England. Mobs destroyed property and killed many tax collectors and wealthy people. On June 11, 1381, Tyler led thousands of angry peasants from Kent in a march on London. They and thousands of other peasants from Essex arrived outside the city walls on June 12. The leaders of the peasants demanded to see King Richard II. The king, who was only 14 years old, finally agreed to listen to their demands on June 14. The rebels demanded an end to serfdom, and a low rent on freed lands. They also called for a repeal of England's burdensome labor laws. The king agreed to their terms, and most of the mob disbanded. But Tyler and many rebels remained in the London area and killed more people, including Archbishop Simon Sudbury and England's treasurer, Robert Hales.

On June 15, Richard met with Tyler and the rebels again. At this meeting, Tyler was attacked and wounded after he seemed to threaten the king's life. Tyler died then or soon afterward. Upon seeing the attack on Tyler, the rebels moved against the king's party. But Richard courageously stopped their advance by riding out alone to meet them. He shouted that he was their true leader and that they should follow him. This action won the rebels' respect, and Richard led them out of the city. Richard later broke his promises to the rebels. However, the rebellion inspired other popular movements for freedom and equality in England.   George B. Stow

Watauga Association was a group of settlers who, in 1772, formed the first white community independent of colonial government in what is now the United States. The group had settled in 1769 on the Watauga River, in the northeast corner of present-day Tennessee. In 1771, they discovered that their land was not part of any colony's organized territory. As a result, in 1772, they drew up a constitution to govern themselves. This document was one of the first written constitutions in North America. In 1776, the Watauga land, then known as the Washington District, was annexed by North Carolina at the request of the Watauga community.

In 1784, North Carolina agreed to give its western lands, including the Washington District, to the federal government. The Wataugans feared that they would be left without state or federal protection. As a result, they set up the independent State of Franklin, which the U.S. government refused to recognize. North Carolina regained control of the area in 1788 and gave it to the U.S. government in 1789. The Wataugan land became part of Tennessee in 1796.   C. Edward Skeen

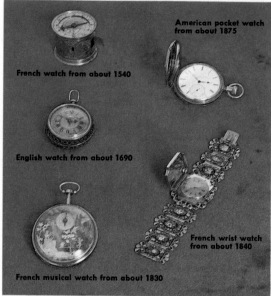

Time Museum, Rockford, Ill. (WORLD BOOK photo)

Some early watches are shown above. The French watch from about 1540 has only an hour hand. The English watch has a hairspring. The French musical watch tells time by playing a melody. The French wrist watch has a gold and enamel bracelet. The American pocket watch is enclosed in a hinged gold case.

Watch is a small, portable clock. People use watches to tell time and also wear or carry them as personal accessories. More than 60 million watches are sold in the United States annually.

Portable clocks were first used during the 1500's by town watchmen in Europe. As the watchmen made their rounds, they carried the portable clocks on straps around their necks. As other people began carrying timepieces, the name was shortened to watch.

Kinds of watches

Most modern watches are worn on the wrist. Before the 1920's, they were almost always carried in the pocket or purse. In the past, women sometimes used watches as decorative accessories, wearing them as necklaces, rings, or pins. Today's watches range from plain models costing less than $5 to ones decorated with precious stones that cost more than $50,000. Watches have traditionally displayed the time by means of hands pointing to numerals or markers on a dial. This method is known as *analog display.* Today, lighted numerals are also used to display time by a method called *digital display.*

Many watches give information in addition to the passing of hours and minutes. Most also show the passage of seconds. Many show the day of the week, the day of the month, and the year. Some watches sound an alarm at any desired time. Some novelty and special function watches show the wearer's pulse or body temperature. Some include electronic games or tiny calculators for solving mathematical problems.

How watches work

Every watch has two main parts, the *case* and the *movement,* or *works,* inside the case. The movement shows the time, provides power to run the watch, and regulates the speed of the watch. Watches differ according to how their movements perform these functions. This article divides watches into two groups—(1) mechanical watches and (2) electronic watches—based on how they are powered.

Mechanical watches are powered by a coiled spring called a *mainspring.* In many watches, the mainspring is wound by turning a knob, or *crown,* that is connected to a shaft inside the case. Other watches, called *self-winding watches,* contain a weight mechanism that winds the mainspring automatically when the watch is moved about. As the watch runs, the mainspring unwinds. The power that is supplied by the unwinding mainspring turns several tiny gear wheels that are connected in a series called the *train.* The hands of a watch are attached to individual gear wheels that turn at specific speeds. The speed of the gear wheels is partially determined by a mechanism that is called the *escapement.*

The escapement includes an *escape wheel,* a *balance wheel,* a *balance spring,* and a *pallet lever.* The escape wheel is connected to the train and turns when the watch runs. It also transmits energy to the balance wheel, which is the time base, or timekeeping device, of the watch. The balance spring, also called the *hairspring,* makes the balance wheel *oscillate* (swing back and forth) at a specific frequency. Most balance wheels oscillate 5 or 6 times a second. The pallet lever has two *pallets* (hooks)—one at either end—that catch on the escape wheel. Each oscillation of the balance wheel causes the pallet lever to swing, thus enabling the escape wheel briefly to escape the grip of the pallets. The escape wheel then turns slightly before the pallets again catch on it. This catching action stops the movement of the escape wheel and also produces the characteristic ticking sound of a mechanical watch. Each slight movement of the escape wheel is transmitted through the other wheels in the train to the hands of the watch. Because the oscillations of the balance wheel regulate the speed of the escape wheel, they are responsible for the accuracy of the timepiece.

Many mechanical watches have more than 100 parts. In the most expensive watches, some parts are finished by hand to assure accuracy and durability. In addition, the pallets and various other parts of such watches are made from tiny, hard jewels, such as natural or synthetic rubies, to reduce wear. Such timepieces contain 15 or more jewels.

One type of mechanical watch sold in the United States is called a *pin-lever watch.* In pin-lever watches, the parts are not finished by hand, and the pallets on the pallet lever are metal pins instead of jewels. These watches are inexpensive, but they wear out sooner than do finer watches. If a pin-lever watch is adjusted very carefully by a jeweler, it can be just as accurate as a more expensive jeweled watch.

Electronic watches contain tiny quartz crystals. Some are accurate to within 60 seconds a year. The time base for this type of watch is its vibrating quartz crystal. Most crystals vibrate 32,768 times a second. Quartz-based watches contain a battery-powered electronic integrated circuit on a tiny piece of silicon that is called a *chip.* This chip keeps the crystal vibrating, and it

A mechanical watch has hands that show the time on a dial. The movement of a mechanical watch, *far right*, includes a *mainspring,* which powers the watch. A *balance wheel* regulates the watch's speed. It moves the *pallet lever,* which allows the *escape wheel* to move slightly. This action moves a train of gears that turn the hands on the watch face.

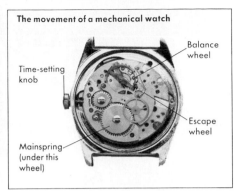

The movement of a mechanical watch

Balance wheel

Time-setting knob

Escape wheel

Mainspring (under this wheel)

A digital electronic watch displays the time in digits that form when electric current passes through patterns of liquid crystal. The movement of an electronic watch, *far right,* includes a *battery,* which makes a *quartz crystal* vibrate. An integrated circuit on a *circuit board* translates the vibrations into information for display on the face of the watch.

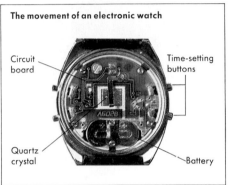

The movement of an electronic watch

Circuit board

Time-setting buttons

Quartz crystal

Battery

WORLD BOOK photos

translates the vibrations into electric impulses. In electronic analog watches, these impulses activate a tiny motor that moves the watch hands at the correct speeds.

Another electronic watch, the *solid-state watch,* also uses quartz as its time base. However, it has no moving parts. Instead, the circuits of a solid-state watch translate the time information directly into a *liquid crystal display* (LCD) on the watch face. Most LCD's show the time in the form of digits. In a digital LCD, a thin layer of liquid crystal is sandwiched between two layers of glass. Digital patterns are printed onto the glass with transparent conductive coatings. Normally, these patterns are invisible. However, when an electric charge is applied to the coatings, the liquid crystal becomes visible as a dark numeral. In analog LCD watches, the liquid crystal forms the pattern of watch hands, instead of digits, to indicate the time. A liquid crystal display requires little power from the battery and therefore appears continuously. But the display cannot be seen clearly in dim light. Some LCD watches have a light that can be turned on to illuminate the face.

History

Peter Henlein, a German locksmith, traditionally has been credited with making the first watch. In the early 1500's, Henlein invented a mainspring to power clocks. Until then, clocks had been driven by falling weights and had to remain stationary and stand upright for the weights to operate. Mainsprings enabled clockmakers to produce small, portable clocks. Watchmaking soon spread to England, France, and Switzerland.

The earliest watches were heavy and inaccurate. They weighed so much that they had to be suspended from a cord or chain and worn around the neck or hanging from a belt. Early watches had only an hour hand, and their cases were spherical or drum-shaped. Unusual shapes, including skulls and crosses, became popular during the mid-1600's.

Many watches had a minute hand by the late 1600's, but a hand for the seconds did not become common until the 1900's. The balance spring and escape lever mechanisms had been developed by the late 1700's.

During the late 1600's, watches became small and light enough to fit into a pocket of a jacket or vest. These *pocket watches* were the most popular style of watch for more than 200 years. Wrist watches became common in the late 1800's, but they were designed for women only. During World War I (1914-1918), soldiers realized that wrist watches were more convenient than pocket watches. As a result, wrist watches soon became accepted as accessories for men as well.

Electric analog watches, which were powered by a tiny battery, were introduced in the 1950's. Originally, these watches used a balance wheel as a time base. But later models contained a vibrating tuning fork that acted as a time base in much the same way as quartz crystals do in electronic watches. Quartz-based watches appeared in the early 1970's and, because of their accuracy, soon made earlier electric watches obsolete.

Milton C. Stevens

See also **Clock; Switzerland** (picture: Switzerland's watchmaking industry).

Watch Tower Bible and Tract Society. See Jehovah's Witnesses.

Cameramann International, Ltd. from Marilyn Gartman

Waterfalls flow over rocky cliffs.

Frederick Figall from Artstreet

A flood can cause enormous destruction of property.

© Robert Frerck, Woodfin Camp, Inc.

Waterways are used to transport bulky goods.

Water

Water is the most common substance on earth. It covers more than 70 percent of the earth's surface. It fills the oceans, rivers, and lakes, and is in the ground and in the air we breathe. Water is everywhere.

Without water, there can be no life. In fact, every living thing consists mostly of water. Your body is about two-thirds water. A chicken is about three-fourths water, and a pineapple is about four-fifths water. Most scientists believe that life itself began in water—in the salty water of the sea.

Ever since the world began, water has been shaping the earth. Rain hammers at the land and washes soil into rivers. The oceans pound against the shores, chiseling cliffs and carrying away land. Rivers knife through rock, carve canyons, and build up land where they empty into the sea. Glaciers plow valleys and cut down mountains.

Water helps keep the earth's climate from getting too hot or too cold. Land absorbs and releases heat from the sun quickly. But the oceans absorb and release the sun's heat slowly. So breezes from the oceans bring warmth to the land in winter and coolness in summer.

Throughout history, water has been people's slave—and their master. Great civilizations have risen where

Thomas M. Keinath, the contributor of this article, is Dean of the College of Engineering at Clemson University.

water supplies were plentiful. They have fallen when these supplies failed. People have killed one another for a muddy water hole. They have worshiped rain gods and prayed for rain. Often, when rains have failed to come, crops have withered and starvation has spread across a land. Sometimes the rains have fallen too heavily and too suddenly. Then rivers have overflowed their banks, drowning large numbers of people and causing enormous destruction of property.

Today, more than ever, water is both slave and master to people. We use water in our homes for cleaning, cooking, bathing, and carrying away wastes. We use water to irrigate dry farmlands so we can grow more food. Our factories use more water than any other material. We use the water in rushing rivers and thundering waterfalls to produce electricity.

Our demand for water is constantly increasing. Every year, there are more people in the world. Factories turn out more and more products, and need more and more water. We live in a world of water. But almost all of it—about 97 percent—is in the oceans. This water is too salty to be used for drinking, farming, and manufacturing. Only about 3 percent of the water in the world is *fresh* (unsalty). Most of this water is locked in ice that covers Antarctica, Greenland, and the waters of the north polar region. But there is still enough to meet people's needs.

There is as much water on the earth today as there was when dinosaurs inhabited the planet millions of years ago. Almost every single drop of water we use

Ice is the solid form of water.

© E. Schulthess, Black Star

Many people enjoy the recreational uses of water.

© Alexander Lowrey, Photo Researchers

Falling water from a dam produces energy.

Bureau of Reclamation

finds its way to the oceans. There, it is evaporated by the sun. It then falls back to the earth as rain. Water is used and reused over and over again. It is never used up.

Although the world as a whole has plenty of fresh water, some regions have a water shortage. Rain does not fall evenly over the earth. Some regions are always too dry, and others too wet. A region that usually gets enough rain may suddenly have a serious dry spell, and another region may be flooded with too much rain.

Some regions have a water shortage because the people have managed their supply poorly. People settle where water is plentiful—near lakes and rivers. Cities grow, and factories spring up. The cities and factories dump their wastes into the lakes and rivers, polluting them. Then the people look for new sources of water. Shortages also occur because some cities do not make full use of their supply. They have plenty of water but not enough storage tanks, treatment plants, and distribution pipes to meet the people's needs.

As our demand for water grows and grows, we will have to make better and better use of our supply. The more we learn about water, the better we will be able to meet this challenge.

This article tells broadly about water. It discusses water's importance to civilization and to life itself. It describes the nature of water. For a discussion of our water problems and how we use and abuse our water supply, see **Water pollution**. Separate articles, including **Climate**, **Conservation**, **Lake**, **Ocean**, **Rain**, and **River**, provide details about the broad subject of water.

Interesting facts about water

How much water is on the earth? There are about 326 million cubic miles (1.4 billion cubic kilometers) of water. There are over a million million (1,000,000,000,000) gallons of water per cubic mile (0.9 million million liters per cubic kilometer).

How much of the earth's water is fresh? Only about 3 per cent of the earth's water is fresh. About three-fourths of the earth's fresh water is frozen in icecaps and other glaciers. Glaciers contain as much water as flows in all the earth's rivers in about 1,000 years.

How much water do living things contain? All living things consist mostly of water. For example, the body of a human being is about 65 per cent water. An elephant is about 70 per cent water. A potato is about 80 per cent water. A tomato is about 95 per cent water.

How much water does a person take in over a lifetime? On the average, a person takes in about 16,000 gallons (60,600 liters) of water during his or her life.

What are the different forms of water? Water is the only substance on earth that is naturally present in three different forms—as a liquid, a solid (ice), and a gas (water vapor).

How much water does a person use every day? On the average, each person in the United States uses more than 100 gallons (380 liters) of water a day in the home.

What is the largest single use of water? The largest single use of water is by industry. It takes about 80 gallons (300 liters) of water to make the paper for one Sunday newspaper, and about 20 gallons of water per pound (170 liters per kilogram) of steel produced.

Can water ever be used up? Water is used and reused over and over again—it is never used up. Every glass of water you drink contains molecules of water that have been used countless times before.

Every plant, animal, and human being needs water to stay alive. This is because all the life processes—from taking in food to getting rid of wastes—require water. But people depend on water for more than just to stay alive. We also need it for our way of life. We need water in our homes—to brush our teeth, cook food, and wash dishes. We need water in our factories—to manufacture almost everything from automobiles to zippers. We need water for irrigation—to raise crops in regions that do not get enough rain.

Water in living things. Every *organism* (living thing) consists mostly of water. The human body is usually made up of 50 to 75 percent water. A mouse is about 65 percent water. An elephant and an ear of corn are about 70 percent water. A potato and an earthworm are about 80 percent water. A tomato is about 95 percent water.

All living things need a lot of water to carry out their life processes. Plants, animals, and human beings must take in *nutrients* (food substances). Watery solutions help dissolve nutrients and carry them to all parts of an organism. Through chemical reactions, the organism turns nutrients into energy, or into materials it needs to grow or to repair itself. These chemical reactions can take place only in a watery solution. Finally, the organism needs water to carry away waste products.

Every living thing must keep its water supply near normal, or it will die. Human beings can live without food for several weeks, but they can live without water for only about one week. If the body loses more than 20 percent of its normal water content, a person will die painfully. Human beings should take in about $2\frac{1}{2}$ quarts (2.4 liters) of water a day. This intake can be in the form of beverages we drink, or water in food.

Water in our homes. In our homes, we use far more water than the amount we need simply to stay alive. We require water for cleaning, cooking, bathing, and carrying away wastes. For many people, such water is a luxury. Millions of homes in Asia, Africa, and South America have no running water. The people must haul water up by hand from the village well, or carry it in jars from pools and rivers far from their homes.

The United States has more homes with kitchen faucets and flush toilets than any other country. On the average, every American uses more than 100 gallons (380 liters) of water a day in the home. It takes up to about 4 gallons (15 liters) of water to flush a toilet. It takes 20 to 30 gallons (76 to 114 liters) to take a bath, and each minute under a shower takes at least 5 gallons (19 liters). It takes more than 15 gallons (57 liters) of water to wash a day's dishes, and about 40 gallons (152 liters) to run an automatic washing machine.

Water for irrigation. Most of the plants that people raise need great quantities of water. For example, it takes 115 gallons (435 liters) of water to grow enough wheat to bake a loaf of bread. People raise most of their crops in areas that have plenty of rain. But to raise enough food for their needs, people must also irrigate dry areas. The rainfall that crops use to grow is not considered a water use, because the water does not come from a country's supply. Irrigation, on the other hand, is a water use because the water is drawn from a nation's rivers, lakes, or wells.

The water a nation uses for irrigation is important to its water supply because none of the water remains for reuse. Plants take in water through their roots. They then pass it out through their leaves into the air as a gas called *water vapor.* Winds carry away the vapor, and the liquid water is gone. On the other hand, nearly all the water used in our homes is returned to the water supply. The water is carried by sewer pipes to treatment plants, which return the water to rivers so it can be used again.

The United States uses about 140 billion gallons (530 billion liters) of water a day for irrigation. This is enough water to fill a lake 5 miles (8 kilometers) long, 1 mile (1.6 kilometers) wide, and 130 feet (40 meters) deep. About 40 percent of all the water used in the United States is used for irrigation. For a discussion of irrigation systems, see the article **Irrigation.**

Water for industry. Industry uses water in many ways. It uses water for cleaning fruits and vegetables before canning and freezing them. It uses water as a raw material in soft drinks, canned foods, and many other products. It uses water to air-condition and clean factories. But most of the water used by industry is for cooling. For example, water cools the steam used in producing electric power from fuel. It cools the hot gases produced in refining oil, and the hot steel made by steel mills.

About 38,000 gallons (144,000 liters) of water are required to make a ton of steel or a ton of paper. Manufacturers use about 7 gallons (27 liters) of water to refine 1 gallon (3.8 liters) of gasoline. It takes about 15 gallons (57 liters) of water to brew 1 gallon of beer.

In the United States, factories and steam-producing power plants draw about 160 billion gallons (600 billion liters) of water every day from wells, rivers, or lakes. This total accounts for 48 percent of all the water used in the country. Power plants use 80 percent of this water. In addition, many factories buy water from city water systems.

Although industry uses a lot of water, only 6 percent of it is consumed. Most of the water used for cooling is piped back to the rivers or lakes from which it is taken. The water consumed by industry is the water added to soft drinks and other products, and the small amount of water that turns to vapor in the cooling processes.

Water for power. People also use water to produce electric power to light homes and to run factories. Electric power stations burn coal or other fuel to turn water into steam. The steam supplies the energy to run machines that produce electricity. Hydroelectric power stations use the energy of falling water from waterfalls and dams to produce electricity. See **Water power; Electric power.**

Water for transportation and recreation. After people learned to build crude small boats, they began using rivers and lakes to carry themselves and their goods. Later, they built larger boats and sailed the ocean in search of new lands and new trade routes. Today, people still depend on water transportation to carry such heavy and bulky products as machinery, coal, grain, and oil. See **Transportation.**

People build most of their recreation areas along lakes, rivers, and seas. They enjoy water sports, such as swimming, fishing, and sailing. Many people also enjoy the beauty of a quiet lake, a thundering waterfall, or a roaring surf.

U.S. water budget

On the average, 4,200,000,000,000 gallons (15,900,000,000,000 liters) of precipitation fall on the United States every day. About 70 per cent of this moisture returns directly to the air by evaporation, or is used by plants where it falls. People use about 6 per cent of the precipitation.

WORLD BOOK diagram by Murrie-White & Associates, Inc.

Precipitation
returned to the air
by evaporation
or used where it falls
by plants
70%

Industrial use 3.12%

Irrigation use 2.46%

City use 0.42%

Precipitation returned
unused to the sea
24%

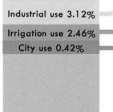

Canfield Beverage Co. (WORLD BOOK photo)

Soft drink manufacturing

Jones & Laughlin Steel Corporation

Cooling hot steel

© Robert P. Carr, Bruce Coleman Inc.

Irrigation for raising crops in dry areas

WORLD BOOK photo

Drinking

© George Hall, Woodfin Camp, Inc.

Fire fighting

The waters of the earth move continuously from the oceans, to the air, to the land, and back to the oceans again. The sun's heat evaporates water from the oceans. The water rises as invisible vapor, and falls back to the earth as rain, snow, or some other form of moisture. This moisture is called *precipitation*. Most precipitation drops back directly into the oceans. The remainder falls on the rest of the earth. In time, this water also returns to the sea, and the cycle starts again. This unending circulation of the earth's waters is called the *water cycle* or *hydrologic cycle*.

Because of nature's water cycle, there is as much water on earth today as there ever was—or ever will be. Water changes only from one form to another, and moves from one place to another. The water you bathed in last night might have flowed in Russia's Volga River last year. Or perhaps Alexander the Great drank it more than 2,000 years ago.

The waters of the earth. The earth has a tremendous amount of water, but almost all of it is in the oceans. The oceans cover about 70 per cent of the earth's surface. They contain about 97 per cent of all the water on earth, and are the source of most precipitation that falls to earth. Ocean water is too salty to be used for drinking, agriculture, or industry. But the salt is left behind during evaporation, and the precipitation that falls to earth is fresh water.

Only about 3 per cent of the water on earth is fresh water—and most of it is not easily available to people. It includes water locked in icecaps and other glaciers, more than 2 per cent of the earth's water. About half of 1 per cent of the earth's water is beneath the earth's surface. Rivers and lakes contain only about one-fiftieth of 1 per cent of the earth's water.

Water in the air. At one time or another, all the water on earth enters the air, or atmosphere, as water vapor. This vapor becomes the life-giving rain that falls to the earth. Yet, the atmosphere contains only one-thousandth of 1 per cent of the earth's water.

Moisture in the air comes mostly from evaporation. The sun's heat evaporates water from land, lakes, rivers, and, especially, the oceans. About 85 per cent of the vapor in the air comes from the oceans. Plants also add moisture. After plants have drawn water from the ground through their roots, they pass it out through their leaves as vapor in a process called *transpiration*. For example, a birch tree gives off about 70 gallons (260 liters) of water a day. Corn gives off about 4,000 gallons per acre (37,000 liters per hectare) daily. See **Evaporation; Leaf** (Transpiration).

Precipitation. Vapor is carried by the air moving over the earth. The moisture-filled air cools wherever it is forced up by colder air or by mountains or hills. As the air cools, the vapor *condenses* into droplets of liq-

The water cycle

This diagram traces the never-ending circulation of the earth's water as it makes its long journey from the oceans, to the air, to the land, and back to the oceans again.

WORLD BOOK diagram by George Suyeoka

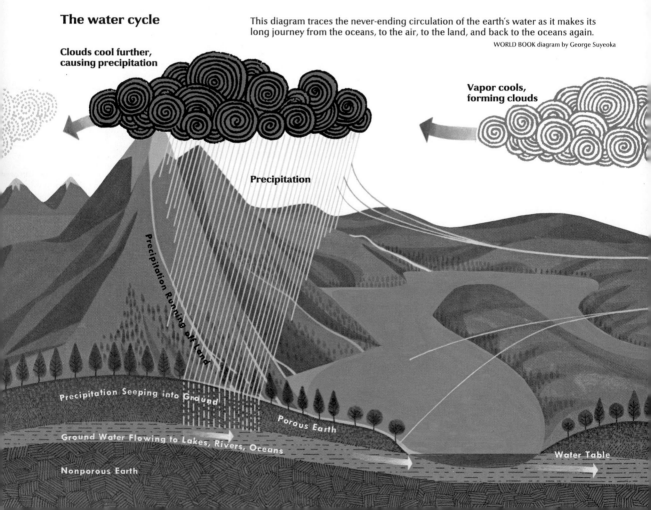

Clouds cool further, causing precipitation

Vapor cools, forming clouds

Precipitation

Precipitation Running off Land

Precipitation Seeping into Ground

Porous Earth

Ground Water Flowing to Lakes, Rivers, Oceans

Water Table

Nonporous Earth

uid water, forming clouds. The droplets fall to the earth as rain. If the vapor is chilled enough, it condenses into ice crystals, and falls as snow.

About 75 percent of the precipitation falls back directly on the oceans. Some of the rest of the precipitation evaporates immediately—from the surface of the ground, from rooftops, from puddles in the streets. Some of it runs off the land to rivers. From the rivers, it flows back to the sea. The rest of the precipitation soaks into the earth and becomes part of the *ground water* supply. Ground water moves slowly through the ground to the rivers and returns to the sea. This movement of ground water to rivers keeps the rivers flowing during periods without rain. See **Ground water; Rain; Snow; Weather.**

How water shapes the earth. Water changes the face of the earth as it moves through the great water cycle. Water wears down mountains, carves valleys, and cuts deep canyons. It also builds deltas and straightens coastlines.

During precipitation, some water falls on highlands and mountains. The force of gravity pulls the water downhill. As the water flows to lower levels, it *erodes* (wears away) the soil and rocks. In this way, after many thousands of years, mountains are worn down. The water that runs off the land during precipitation cuts small channels. The small channels drain into larger channels.

The larger channels drain into still larger ones, until finally the water empties into the main stream that runs to the sea. The water then flows to the sea carrying the materials it has eroded from the land. See **River.**

Some of the precipitation that falls is captured in mountain glaciers. As the glaciers slide down mountainsides, they cut the mountains into sharp and jagged peaks. See **Glacier.**

The ocean also changes the face of the land. As waves pound against the shore, they cut away land and leave steep cliffs. Much of the material the waves wear away from the land is carried far out to sea. Some of the material piles up near the shore in sand bars. For more information about how water shapes the earth, see the *World Book* articles **Earth** (Cycles on and in Earth); **Erosion.**

How water began. The question of how water began on earth is part of the question of how the earth itself began. Many scientists believe the earth was formed from materials that came from the hot sun. These materials included the elements that make up water.

As the earth cooled and grew solid, water was trapped in rocks in the earth's crust. The water was gradually released, and the ocean basins filled with water. Other scientists have other ideas about how the earth and water began. For a discussion of these ideas, see the article **Earth** (Earth's early development).

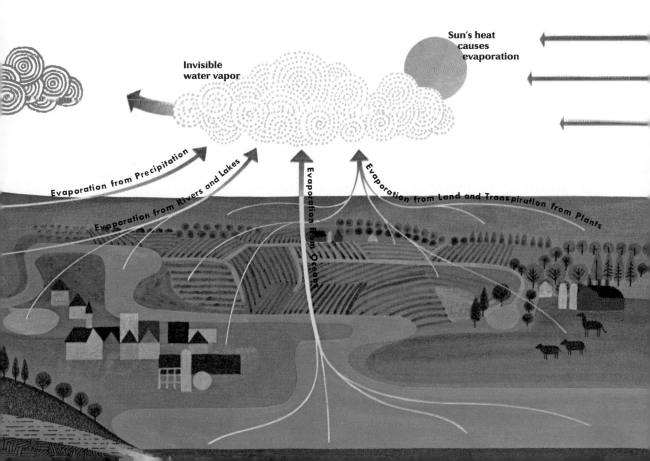

Invisible water vapor

Sun's heat causes evaporation

Evaporation from Precipitation

Evaporation from Rivers and Lakes

Evaporation from Ocean

Evaporation from Land and Transpiration from Plants

Shortages of fresh water have troubled people throughout history. Today, they trouble people more than ever because the demand for water is growing rapidly. Many people fear that the world does not have enough water to meet all our needs. Yet the world has—and always will have—the same amount of water it has always had. All the water we use passes through the great water cycle and can be used again and again.

The total amount of water on earth is enough for all our needs. However, the earth's water is distributed unevenly. Some regions suffer a constant *drought* (lack of rain). Other regions generally have plenty of water, but they may be struck by drought at times. In addition, people have created many water problems by mismanaging the supply.

World distribution of water. The earth has an enormous amount of water—about 326 million cubic miles (1.4 billion cubic kilometers) of it. In a cubic mile, there are more than a million million—1,000,000,000,000—gallons, or 3.8 million million liters. However, 97 per cent of this water is in the salty oceans, and more than 2 per cent is in glaciers and icecaps. The rest totals less than 1 per cent. Most of this water is underground, and the remainder includes the water in lakes, rivers, springs, pools, and ponds. It also includes rain and snow, and the vapor in the air.

A country's water supply is determined by its precipitation. In regions with plenty of precipitation year after year, there is plenty of water in lakes, rivers, and underground reservoirs.

The earth as a whole receives plentiful rain. If this rain fell evenly, all the land would receive 34 inches (86 centimeters) a year. But the rain is distributed unevenly. For example, over 400 inches (1,000 centimeters) drenches northeastern India every year. But northern Chile may not get rain for years.

Generally, the world's most heavily populated areas receive enough rain for their needs. These areas include most of Europe, Southeast Asia, the Eastern United States, India, and much of China. But about half the earth's land does not get enough rain. These dry areas include most of Asia, central Australia, most of northern Africa, and the Middle East.

The United States has plenty of water. It averages about 30 inches (76 centimeters) of rain annually. This total is large, but it is distributed unevenly. Over 135 inches (343 centimeters) soaks parts of western Washington each year, but Nevada averages only 9 inches (23 centimeters). Most states east of the Mississippi get 30 to 50 inches (76 to 130 centimeters) of precipitation a year—more than enough to grow crops. But large regions in the West get less than 10 inches (25 centimeters). There, only a small amount of grass and shrubs can grow without irrigation.

Canada's annual precipitation is also distributed unevenly. In the southeast, it ranges from 30 inches (76 centimeters) in central Ontario to 55 inches (140 centimeters) in eastern Nova Scotia. From 14 to 20 inches (36 to 51 centimeters) of precipitation falls in most of the Prairie Provinces. Parts of the west coast get over 100 inches (250 centimeters).

Water shortages. Many regions of the world have a constant water shortage because they never get enough rain. But even a region that normally has enough rain

may suddenly have a dry year or several dry years. The climates in regions that receive only light rainfall are especially changeable. Such regions can have a series of destructive dry years.

In the 1930's, one of the worst droughts in United States history struck the Southwest, an already dry region. Winds whipped the dry soil into gigantic dust storms, and most of the region became known as the *Dust Bowl.* Hundreds of farm families had to leave their homes. See **Dust Bowl**.

Periods of low rainfall alternate with periods of high rainfall from year to year and from place to place. In the 1980's, for example, drought struck the Midwestern and Southeastern United States, as well as parts of Argentina, Australia, Brazil, Ethiopia, Paraguay, Uruguay, and other countries. Meanwhile, floodwaters spilled over the land in the south-central United States and in parts of Bangladesh, China, India, and other countries.

Many regions have water shortages because the people have not prepared for a period of less than normal rainfall. These shortages could have been prevented if the people had built artificial lakes, storage tanks, and other facilities to carry them through a drought.

The United States is especially rich in water. But every year, a number of U.S. communities must ration their water. As a result, many people fear that the country is running out of water. The United States as a whole has as much water today as the land had when Christopher Columbus sailed to the New World. But rainfall patterns change. In addition, the demand for water is increasing faster in the United States than in any other country. More and more Americans want air conditioners, garbage disposers, automatic washers, and an extra bathroom. Industry also demands more water as production rises. When drought strikes, the effects can be severe.

During the 1960's, rainfall in the Northeastern United States fell below normal for several years. Many cities had to restrict the use of water. New York City suffered especially, because it is so heavily populated. To save water, people turned off their air conditioners and let their lawns wither. Restaurants tried not to serve water to customers. The city was declared a disaster area. New York City's troubles came about because the city did not have enough storage tanks, distribution lines, and other facilities to supply the city with water during a long period of light rainfall. The city improved its facilities after the drought.

Water management and conservation. Throughout history, people have attempted to increase their water supply by trying to "make rain." They have prayed to rain gods and performed rain dances (see **Rain dance**). They have sprayed the clouds with chemicals to make them release their moisture (see **Rainmaking**). People also have always looked to the sea as a source of water (see the section *Fresh water from the sea*). In many cases, however, people do not need more water than they already have. They only need to manage the supply better.

Many water problems in the United States have arisen because the country has had a plentiful and easily available water supply. Water has been cheap, and people have been careless and wasteful. In the past, they dumped untreated sewage and other wastes into rivers and lakes, spoiling the water (see **Water pollution**). In most U.S. cities, people pay about $1.25 per 1,000 gallons (3,800 liters) of water. In contrast, New York City charges many people a fixed fee for water based on the size of the house or apartment building they live in. The fee is the same no matter how much water a household uses. As a result, many people waste water. However, commercial buildings and large apartment buildings in New York City have water meters, and people pay for the water they use. The city has begun to install water meters in all homes and apartment buildings.

The supply of cheap, easily available water is shrinking in the United States. The development of new supplies will become more and more costly. It will then be cheaper to reuse water from existing supplies. Many industries reuse water. For example, most steel companies use a small amount of water over and over in a circulating cooling system.

Sewage, also called *wastewater,* can be treated and turned into usable water. Many communities in California, Florida, Texas, and other states irrigate crops with treated wastewater. Water reuse will become much more common in the future.

The unequal distribution of precipitation

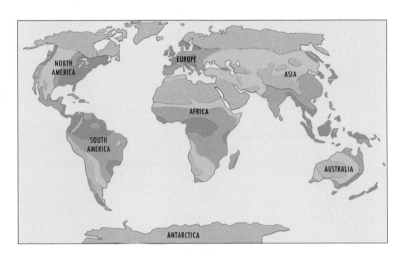

Always Enough Rain

Usually Enough Rain

Usually Not Enough Rain

Never Enough Rain

WORLD BOOK map

Artstreet

A tropical rain forest receives plentiful rainfall and remains green throughout the year.

Photri from Marilyn Gartman

A desert receives little rainfall, resulting in a dry landscape that can support little vegetation or animal life.

Artstreet

A drought occurs when a region receives less than normal rainfall over a long time, often leaving soil parched and cracked.

AP/Wide World

A mud slide can occur when a sudden downpour drenches an area that seldom receives large amounts of rain.

When you turn on a faucet, you expect clean, pure water to flow out. You also expect your city to have plenty of water for its industries, for fighting fires, and for cleaning streets. The job of supplying a modern city with water is tremendous. First of all, there must be sources of plentiful water to meet the demands of a growing city. Then, the water must be purified. Next, it must be piped into every house, office building, factory, and hotel in the city. Finally, the water must be piped away after it has been used.

Sources of supply. Cities can draw fresh water from only two sources: (1) rivers and lakes, or (2) the ground. Smaller cities, especially those with fewer than 5,000 people, remove water from underground supplies. Most larger cities obtain their water supplies from rivers or lakes.

Rivers and lakes. Most cities that depend on rivers for their water are located on small rivers—simply because most rivers are small. The amount of water in a river can vary from time to time, depending on the rainfall. During a dry spell, a river's water level may fall sharply. Then, a city may not have enough water.

For this reason, many cities that depend on rivers store water during rainy periods so they will always have an adequate supply. Some cities build a dam on the river and store water behind the dam in a reservoir. Other cities store water in a pond or a small lake. See **Reservoir.**

A city that obtains its water supply from a lake possesses a natural storage reservoir in the lake itself. Lakes are fed by rivers and by waters moving through the ground. During wet spells, a lake stores some of the extra water that it receives. This extra water enables the lake to supply the city with plenty of water during dry periods of little or no rainfall.

Ground water. Many cities are not near rivers or lakes that are large enough for their needs. Such cities use water that is stored underground. This water comes from rain that soaks into the ground. As the water trickles downward, it fills the spaces between grains of sand and pieces of gravel, and it settles into cracks and pores in rocks.

In time, the water trickles down to a layer of rock or other material that is watertight. The water collects above the watertight layer, and the materials above the layer become *saturated* (soaked). This saturated zone is called an *aquifer.* The upper limit of the aquifer is called the *water table.* Cities obtain underground water by drilling wells that reach below the water table and pumping up the water from the aquifer. See **Ground water; Well** (Water wells).

Uses of city water supplies. Most of the water that is supplied by public waterworks goes to people's homes. The waterworks also deliver large amounts of water to commercial users, for example hotels and restaurants; and to manufacturers. City water systems also provide water for fighting fires, cleaning streets, and sprinkling park lawns.

Another "use" of a city's water is waste. In many cities, homeowners pay a flat fee, no matter how much water they use. They do not have meters that measure the water they use. If their faucets leak, the water is wasted.

How Chicago treats its water

This diagram traces the eight-hour course of water as it flows through Chicago's main water purification plant. The water enters intake cribs (1) about $2\frac{1}{2}$ miles (4 kilometers) out in Lake Michigan, and flows through tunnels (2) under the lake into the plant's intake basin (3). Water can also enter the plant directly through a shore intake (4). Screens (5) keep out fish, plants, and trash. Pumps (6) lift the water about 20 feet (6 meters) above the lake level, so that it flows by gravity through the filtration processes. Alum, chlorine, lime, and other chemicals are added (7), and then thoroughly

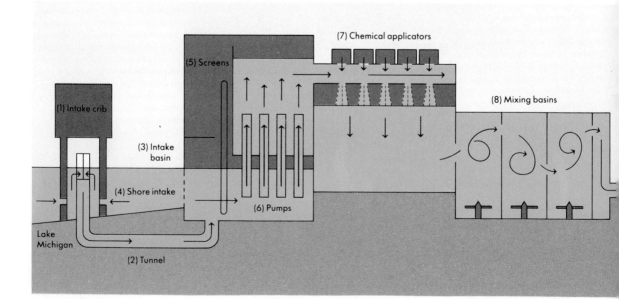

Artstreet

Chicago's main water purification plant is the largest water treatment plant in the world. It serves about 2.8 million people in Chicago and nearby suburbs, and can produce nearly 1½ billion gallons (5.7 billion liters) of water a day. The plant is on a 61-acre (25-hectare) artificially created peninsula that extends into Lake Michigan.

mixed with the water in mixing basins (8). Bacteria, silt, and other impurities stick to the alum, which sinks to the bottom of settling basins (9). The water then trickles through sand and gravel filters (10), which screen out any remaining impurities. The filtered water collects in clear wells (11), and then flows to reservoirs (12), where it receives a final treatment with chlorine, fluoride, and other chemicals. The purified water passes through tunnels (13) to pumping stations (14). The stations send the water through underground mains to homes, factories, and other buildings.

WORLD BOOK diagram by Zorica Dabich

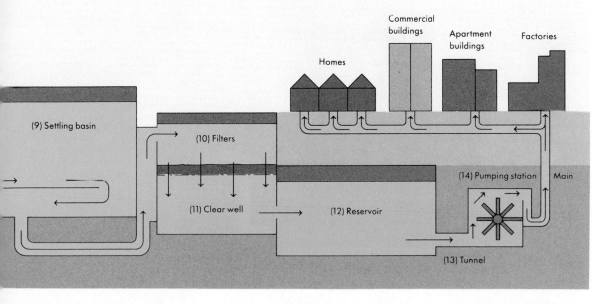

Water is also wasted through leaks in a city's underground pipes. Generally, water lost through leakage is 10 to 15 per cent of a city's water use. Chicago loses about 130 million gallons (490 million liters) of water daily through waste.

Purifying and treating water. People want drinking water that is free of bacteria, sparkling clear, and without an objectionable taste or odor. Water in its natural state seldom has these qualities. So after water is drawn from a source, it is piped into a treatment plant. The plant may put the water through one or several processes, depending on the quality of the untreated water, and on a city's standards. Many cities use three basic processes: (1) coagulation and settling, (2) filtration, and (3) disinfection.

Coagulation and settling. The *raw* (untreated) water flows into the treatment plant and is mixed with chemicals. Some of these chemicals are *coagulants.* The most widely used coagulant is a fine powder called *aluminum sulfate* or *alum.* In the water, the alum forms tiny, sticky globs called *flocs.* Bacteria, mud, and other impurities stick to the flocs. The water then passes into a *settling basin,* where the flocs settle to the bottom. Coagulation and settling remove most impurities.

Filtration. The water is then passed through a filter. The filter consists of a bed of sand, or of sand and coal, usually about $2\frac{1}{2}$ feet (76 centimeters) deep on top of a bed of gravel about 1 foot (30 centimeters) deep. As the water trickles down through the filter, any remaining particles are screened out. The water then flows to huge reservoirs for a final treatment that kills bacteria.

Disinfection kills disease-carrying bacteria. Most plants disinfect water by adding a substance called *chlorine.* Chlorine sometimes is added before coagulation and settling, and often after filtration. Most cities chlorinate their water, even if they do not treat it in any other way. See **Chlorine.**

Sally Wayland

A water tower is a part of the water system in many towns and cities. It provides storage and helps maintain water pressure.

Other processes are also used to remove unpleasant tastes or smells, or to give water special qualities. *Aeration* improves taste and odor. In this process, water is usually sprayed or trickled through the air. The oxygen in the air takes away the bad taste and odor. Many communities have water containing minerals that make it *hard.* Hard water requires lots of soap to make a lather. It also forms deposits on pipes and other equipment. Several processes can be used to *soften* the water (see **Water softening**). Some cities add *lime* or *soda ash* to their water to help prevent pipes from rusting. *Activated carbon* helps improve the taste and odor and remove

A small town water system

WORLD BOOK diagram by Zorica Dabich

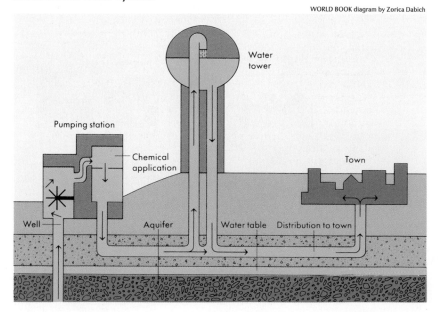

Water tower

Pumping station

Chemical application

Town

Well

Aquifer

Water table

Distribution to town

Most small U.S. towns get water by drilling wells and pumping up underground water. The water is chemically treated and then pumped to consumers. Most towns also pump water into tall water towers. When water is released from these towers, the force of gravity distributes it through the piping system.

toxic chemicals. Many communities add a substance called *fluoride* to their water to help reduce tooth decay (see **Fluoridation**).

Distributing water. The treated water flows to a pumping station, where it is pumped into large cast iron pipes called *water mains*. Water mains run beneath the streets. They carry water to every fire hydrant, and connect with smaller pipes that lead to every home, office building, factory, and restaurant. The pumping station sends the water into the mains under enough pressure to carry it to every faucet. This pressure is usually so high that you cannot hold back the water by putting your finger under a fully opened faucet.

Sometimes the demand for water may be too great for the pressure a pumping station can supply. Then, water may only trickle from the faucets. This can happen on a hot summer day when many people in the neighborhood are watering their lawns or filling backyard pools. The water pressure may also fall when fire fighters use a large amount of water to fight a fire.

Most cities pump water into elevated storage tanks to help keep their water pressure high at all times. The tanks are built on hills, or they are tall water towers. When water is released from these tanks, gravity pulls the water downward, giving it the pressure to rush through the water mains.

Disposing of used water. Most of the water in our homes is used to carry away wastes. This water, and the wastes it carries, is called *sewage*. Factories also use water to wash away such industrial wastes as acids and greases. In most U.S. cities, a piping system under the streets carries away the sewage from homes, factories, hotels, and other buildings. This system is called a *sewerage system*.

Sewage has a bad odor. But more important, it contains disease-producing bacteria. Most cities have treatment plants that clean sewage water and kill the bacteria in it. The treated water can then be returned to a river, stream, or lake. To learn how sewage is treated, see the **Sewage** article.

Almost all of the sewage in the United States undergoes some type of sewage treatment. Only a little of the sewage is dumped untreated into rivers. The dumping of untreated sewage causes serious problems for the environment and for cities downstream that take their water from the same rivers.

Fresh water from the sea

About 97 per cent of the water on earth is in the salty oceans. In their thirst for water, people have looked longingly throughout history at this endless supply. Some *brackish* (slightly salty) water is found inland. Today, more than ever, many people believe that desalting ocean water and brackish water holds the answer to the ever-increasing demand for fresh water in many areas.

The salt in seawater is mostly the same substance as common table salt. A person can safely drink water that contains less than $\frac{1}{2}$ pound of salt to 100 pounds of water, or 0.5 kilogram to every 100 kilograms. But seawater has about seven times this amount of salt. A person who drinks only seawater will eventually die. The body's cells will *dehydrate* (dry out) as they try to get rid of the excess salt from the seawater. Nor can people use seawater in agriculture or industry. It kills most crops, and quickly rusts most machinery.

People have found many ways to *desalinate* (remove the salt from) seawater and brackish water. Desalination offers hope of relieving water shortages near the seacoasts. However, desalination does not hold the answer to all of the earth's water problems. Even if the oceans contained fresh water, people would still have to face such problems as pollution, flood control, and water distribution.

The desalination processes used most commonly today are *distillation, reverse osmosis,* and *electrodialysis.* These processes produce fresh water from salt water.

Distillation is the oldest method of turning salt water into fresh water. Most ocean ships use it to obtain drinking water. Seawater can be distilled simply by boiling it in a teapot, and piping the steam into a cool bottle. The steam rises, leaving the salt behind. As the steam cools in the bottle, it condenses into fresh water.

Every day, the sun evaporates millions of tons of water from the ocean's surface. The water vapor then condenses and falls back to earth as fresh water. For centuries, people have copied nature and used the sun's heat to distill seawater. Two thousand years ago, Julius Caesar used solar distillation in Egypt to obtain drinking water for his soldiers.

Solar distillation can be done by filling a shallow basin with seawater and covering it with a transparent plastic dome, or a sloping sheet of glass. The salt water turns to vapor under the sun's heat. The vapor rises until it hits the underside of the dome or glass, where it condenses. The fresh water runs down into collecting troughs. This type of distillation produces little water. In one day, such a basin in a sunny climate can produce only about a pint of water per square foot (5 liters per square meter) of the basin's surface area. Solar distillation is not a commonly used method of distillation because it is expensive. The cost stems from the fact that this method requires the use of an enormous land area in order to produce sufficient quantities of water. Solar distillation also is less efficient in operation than other methods of distillation.

Most modern distillation plants use a process called *multistage flash distillation.* This is a type of the age-old method of boiling and condensation. In flash distillation, preheated seawater flows into a large chamber in which the pressure is low. The low pressure causes some of the water to *flash* (turn quickly) into steam. The steam is condensed into salt-free water. The seawater passes through several distillation chambers. Each of the chambers has a lower pressure than the previous chamber. Often, the final water is so pure that it is tasteless, and some salt must be tossed back in to give it flavor. The desalting plant at the United States naval base at Guantánamo Bay, Cuba, uses this process. It produces more than 1 million gallons (3.8 million liters) of fresh water a day.

Reverse osmosis is a widely used method for desalting seawater and brackish water. In normal osmosis, a less concentrated liquid flows through a membrane into a more concentrated liquid. Thus, if salt water and fresh water are separated in a chamber by a special semipermeable membrane, the fresh water will flow through the membrane into the salt water. However, if enough pressure is placed on the salt water, this normal flow pattern can be reversed. Fresh water will then be squeezed from the salt water as it passes through the membrane, leaving the salt behind. The reverse osmosis desalting process works in this way.

A desalting plant at Cape Coral, Fla., uses reverse osmosis. This plant can produce about 14 million gallons (53 million liters) of fresh water a day.

Electrodialysis is used chiefly to desalt brackish ground water and water from *estuaries* (river mouths). Electrodialysis is based on the fact that when salt is dissolved in water, it breaks up into *ions* (electrically charged particles) of sodium and chloride. Sodium ions carry a positive charge, and chloride ions carry a negative charge.

Electrodialysis uses a large chamber divided into many compartments by stacks of thin plastic membranes. Two types of membranes are used, and they are used in pairs. One type allows only positive ions to pass through it. The other lets only negative ions through. One of the end compartments contains a positive *electrode* (electrical pole). The other end compartment contains a negative electrode.

When an electric current is sent through the water, the negative ions are drawn through the membranes permeable to negative ions toward the positive electrode. The positive ions are drawn through the membranes permeable to positive ions toward the negative electrode. Thus, the salt in every other compartment is drawn off, leaving fresh water.

A desalting plant on Sanibel Island, Fla., uses the electrodialysis process. This plant produces about 2 million gallons (7.6 million liters) of fresh water daily.

Other desalting processes are also being studied. During the 1970's, several plants experimented with freezing as a method of desalination. When seawater freezes, the ice crystals produced are pure water in solid form. The salt is separated and trapped between the ice crystals. There are several freezing processes that may be used to desalt water. The main problem lies in separating the ice crystals from the salt. This is usually done by washing off the salt with fresh water. The ice is then melted and becomes fresh, liquid water. High costs and engineering problems have prevented the widespread commercial use of freezing as a desalting method.

The future of desalting. All methods of desalination are costly, largely because desalting plants use large amounts of energy, and energy is expensive to produce. In addition, plants must pay to dispose of the salt that is removed during the desalination process. It costs from about \$4 to about \$7 to produce 1,000 gallons (3,800 liters) of fresh water from seawater. The cost depends on such factors as the capacity of the treatment plant and its location. Desalting brackish water costs less than desalting seawater. Engineers and scientists are continuing to work on the development of less expensive methods of desalination.

The thousands of desalting plants around the world together produce more than $3\frac{1}{2}$ billion gallons (13 billion liters) of fresh water each day. A large facility, such as the plant in Al Jubayl, Saudi Arabia, can produce about 250 million gallons (950 million liters) of fresh water daily. Although desalting plants meet only a small part of the world's daily demand for fresh water, they are essential to millions of people.

Many desalting plants are small facilities that serve isolated military posts, oil-drilling crews in deserts, island resorts, and industrial plants. The largest number of plants are in the Middle East, where fresh water sources are scarce. As the cost for desalting water drops, more and more towns and cities may begin using desalted water.

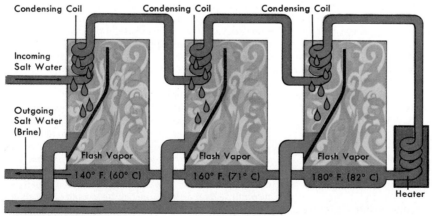

Condensing Coil   Condensing Coil   Condensing Coil

Incoming Salt Water

Outgoing Salt Water (Brine)

Flash Vapor   Flash Vapor   Flash Vapor

140° F. (60° C)   160° F. (71° C)   180° F. (82° C)

Heater

Outgoing Fresh Water

Flash distillation handles the greatest volume of water of all desalting processes. Incoming seawater is heated and then released into a low-pressure chamber. This causes part of the water to flash into steam, even though its temperature is below 212° F. (100° C). The steam condenses into fresh water on a condensing coil, which is cooled by incoming seawater. The remaining seawater passes through similar chambers, each at a successively lower pressure.

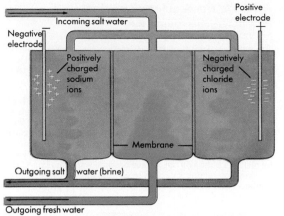

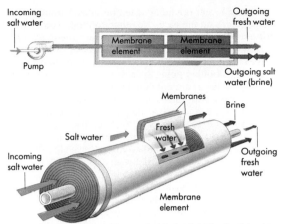

WORLD BOOK diagram by Murrie White & Associates, Inc.

Electrodialysis is based on the fact that when salt dissolves in water, it breaks up into negatively and positively charged ions. This diagram, showing three compartments of an electrodialysis unit, illustrates how the ions are drawn from the middle one.

WORLD BOOK illustration by J. Harlan Hunt, Koralik Associates

Reverse osmosis uses membranes through which salt water is pumped under pressure. Fresh water passes through the membranes, leaving the salt behind. A section of the membrane is lifted in the bottom diagram to show the inside of the membrane element.

What water is and how it behaves

Water is not only the most common substance on earth, it is also one of the most unusual. No other substance can do all the things that water can do. Water is an exception to many of nature's rules because of its unusual *properties* (qualities).

The chemistry of water. Water consists of tiny particles called *molecules.* A drop of water contains many millions of molecules. Each molecule, in turn, consists of even smaller particles called *atoms.* Water molecules consist of atoms of hydrogen and oxygen. Hydrogen and oxygen by themselves are gases. But when two atoms of hydrogen combine with one atom of oxygen, they form the chemical compound H_2O—water.

Even the purest water contains substances besides ordinary hydrogen and oxygen. For example, water contains very tiny portions of *deuterium,* a hydrogen atom that weighs more than the ordinary hydrogen atom. Water formed by a combination of deuterium and oxygen is called *heavy water* (see **Heavy water; Deuterium**). Water is a combination of several different substances, but these substances make up only a small fraction of it.

The properties of water. Water can be a solid, a liquid, or a gas. No other substance appears in these three forms within the earth's normal range of temperature. The molecules that make up water are always moving, and the form water takes depends on how fast they move. The molecules in solid water (ice) are far apart and almost motionless. The molecules in liquid water are close together and move about freely. The molecules in water vapor, a gas, move about violently and bump into one another.

Ice. Most substances contract as they grow colder. But when water is cooled, it contracts only until its temperature reaches 39° F. (4° C). Water expands when it becomes colder than 39° F. For this reason, when ice forms at 32° F. (0° C), it floats on liquid water. If water contracted upon freezing, any volume of ice would be heavier than an equal volume of liquid water. Ice would then sink. If ice sank, the earth would become a lifeless arctic desert. Each winter, more and more ice would pile up on the bottom of lakes, rivers, and oceans. In summer, the sun's heat could not reach deep enough to melt the ice. Water life would die. The hydrologic cycle would slow down. In time, all of the water would turn to solid ice, except perhaps for a thin layer of water over the ice during the summer.

The water molecule

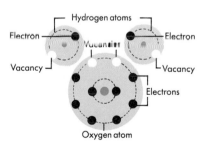

A water molecule is made up of two hydrogen atoms and one oxygen atom. Each hydrogen atom has room for another electron around its nucleus. The oxygen atom has room for two more electrons around its nucleus.

Water molecule

The two hydrogen atoms and one oxygen atom fill their empty spaces by sharing electrons. The resulting water molecule is an extremely tight structure because its atoms share electrons.

Liquid. Water is a liquid at temperatures found in most places on the earth. No other common substance is liquid at ordinary temperatures. In fact, the temperatures at which water is a liquid are unusual. Water is a liquid between 32° F. (0° C), its freezing point, and 212° F. (100° C), its boiling point. But substances with a structure like that of water are not liquid in this temperature range. These substances include gases with the formulas H_2Te, H_2Se, and H_2S. As their formulas show, they are closely related to water (H_2O). Each has two atoms of hydrogen, plus an atom of the elements tellurium, selenium, or sulfur. If water behaved like these close relatives, it would be a liquid between about −148° F. (−100° C) and −130° F. (−90° C). In that case, there would be no liquid water on earth because the earth's temperatures are far higher than −130° F.

Water weighs about 62.4 pounds per cubic foot (1 kilogram per liter). Scientists compare the weight of other substances with the weight of water to find the *specific gravity* of the other substances (see **Density**).

Vapor. If an uncovered glass of water stands for a few days, the water will gradually disappear because the water molecules are moving constantly. Those at the surface break free of those below and enter the air as vapor. The higher the temperature of the water, the faster it evaporates, because the water molecules move faster.

Water can also be turned into vapor by boiling it, and creating *steam.* It takes an enormous amount of heat to produce steam. Water boils at 212° F. (100° C). But when water reaches the boiling point, it does not immediately turn into steam. First there is a pause, during which the water absorbs additional heat without any rise in the temperature. This heat is called *latent heat.* More than five times as much heat is required to turn boiling water into steam as to bring freezing water to a boil. Thus, steam holds a great amount of latent heat energy. People use this energy to run machinery.

Water vapor in the air also holds a tremendous amount of latent heat energy. This energy is released when the vapor cools and condenses, and falls as rain. The high latent heat of water is related to water's remarkable heat capacity.

Heat capacity is the ability of a substance to absorb heat without becoming much warmer itself. Water has a greater heat capacity than any other substance except ammonia. To illustrate water's unusual heat capacity, imagine a pound of water, a pound of gold, and a pound of iron—all at −459.67° F. (−273.15° C). This is *absolute zero,* the temperature at which a substance supposedly contains no heat at all. If all three substances were heated and each absorbed the same amount of energy, the gold would melt at 2016° F. (1102° C). But the ice would still be at −300° F. (−184° C). When the iron began to melt at 2370° F. (1299° C), the ice would finally have reached 32° F. (0° C).

Surface tension is the ability of a substance to stick to itself and pull itself together. Water's surface tension is extremely high. A dripping faucet shows how water sticks to itself. As the water drips, each drop clings to the faucet, stretches, lets go, and then snaps into a tiny ball. Water molecules cling together so tightly that water can support objects heavier than itself. For example, a needle or a razor blade can float on water. Insects

A *World Book* science project
How detergents reduce the surface tension of water

The purpose of this project is to determine how various detergents reduce surface tension and how this ability is related to their cost. The ability to reduce surface tension is an important part of a detergent's cleaning action.

Surface tension makes the surface of water act like a film. This "film" can support a small, flat object, such as a button, that is actually too heavy to float. Surface tension also makes it hard for water to clean soiled materials, and so a detergent must reduce surface tension in order to work effectively. You can approximately measure a detergent's ability to reduce surface tension by resting a button on the surface of some water and counting the drops of detergent needed to weaken the "film" so that the button sinks.

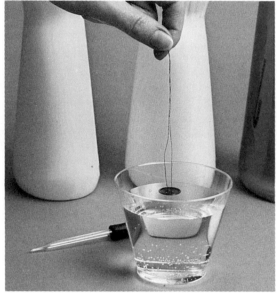

WORLD BOOK photo

Materials

- Glass or plastic container
- Stirring rod
- Several plastic buttons
- Short piece of thread
- Eyedropper

- Assorted brands of liquid dishwashing detergent
- Several quarts or liters of tap water at room temperature

can walk on water. Water can also stick to other substances, such as cloth, glass, and soil. By sticking to these substances, water wets them. See **Surface tension**.

Capillarity is the ability of a liquid to climb up a surface against the pull of gravity. You can see water's climbing ability in a glass of water. The water is higher around the edges, where it touches the glass. The capillarity of water helps it circulate through soil, and up through the roots and stems of plants. It also helps circulate blood, which is mostly water, throughout our bodies. See **Capillarity**.

Dissolving ability. Water can dissolve almost any substance. It dissolves the hardest rocks as it runs over the land and seeps through the ground. In time, it carries the dissolved materials to the oceans. Water also dis-

Procedure

1. Fill the container with 8 ounces (237 milliliters) of the water to be used in the tests.
2. Loop the thread through the holes of the button. Holding the thread, gently lower the button onto the surface of the water. If the button sinks, try other buttons until you find one that rests on the surface.
3. Remove the button and dry it thoroughly.
4. Using the eyedropper, place one drop of the first detergent to be tested in the container of water. Stir the solution thoroughly with the stirring rod.

5. Carefully lower the button and rest it on the water's surface. Remove the button and dry it thoroughly.
6. Repeat steps 4 and 5, adding a drop of detergent each time, until the button sinks when lowered onto the water. Keep track of the number of drops you add to the water.
7. After the button sinks, record the number of drops of detergent you added. Remove the button and rinse and dry it. Pour the water into the sink and rinse and dry the container thoroughly. Repeat all the steps for each of the detergents to be tested.

Organizing your information

1. For each detergent tested, divide the cost of the detergent in cents by the number of ounces or milliliters in an unopened bottle to find the *cost per unit quantity.*
2. Make a table that shows the following information for each detergent: the number of drops used in the test, the cost per unit quantity, and the *economic rating.* Calculate the economic rating by using this formula:

   number of drops $\times$ *cost per unit quantity = economic rating*

The economic rating provides a way of comparing the costs of using the detergents tested. The detergent with the smallest economic rating reduces surface tension most economically.

3. Prepare a series of graphs, such as the ones shown below, to illustrate the information in your table. Which detergent is most economical to use?

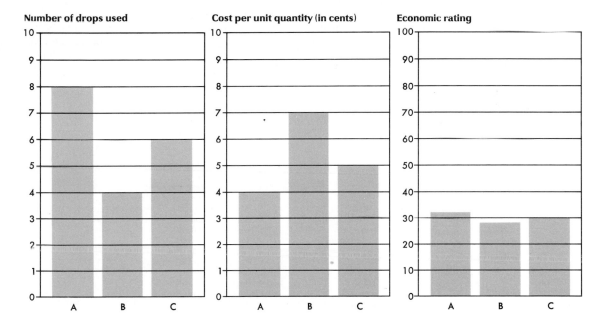

Number of drops used

Cost per unit quantity (in cents)

Economic rating

solves the nutrients that all living things need. Water dissolves and carries the nutrients in the soil to plants and to the cells within plants. Water also dissolves the food that people and animals eat, and then carries this food to the cells.

How water is held together. Water's unusual properties depend on the forces that hold it together. These forces are (1) chemical bonds and (2) hydrogen bonds.

Chemical bonds are the forces that hold the two hydrogen atoms and the one oxygen atom together in a water molecule. Each hydrogen atom has one electron whirling in orbit around its nucleus. But each of these atoms has room for two electrons. The oxygen atom has six electrons in its outer orbit, but it has room for eight. The hydrogen and oxygen atoms each fill their empty spaces by sharing their electrons. The two electrons

from the two hydrogen atoms enter the orbit of the oxygen atom. At the same time, two electrons from the oxygen atom fill the empty spaces in the two hydrogen atoms. The resulting water molecule is an extremely tight structure.

Hydrogen bonds are the forces that link water molecules together. Water molecules have a lopsided shape because the two hydrogen atoms bulge from one end of the oxygen atom. The hydrogen end of the water molecule has a positive electric charge. At the opposite end, the molecule has a negative charge. Water molecules link together because the positive and negative charges attract. The positive ends of water molecules attach to the negative ends of other water molecules, whose positive ends attach to the negative ends of still other water molecules.

Water and civilization. Water has been vital to the development and survival of civilization. The first great civilizations arose in the valleys of great rivers—in the Nile Valley of Egypt, the Tigris-Euphrates Valley of Mesopotamia, the Indus Valley of Pakistan and north-western India, and the Huang He Valley of China. All these civilizations built large irrigation systems, made the land productive, and prospered.

Civilizations crumbled when water supplies failed or were poorly managed. Many historians believe the Sumerian civilization of ancient Mesopotamia fell because of poor irrigation practices. Salt in irrigation water is left behind during evaporation and tends to build up in the soil. The accumulation can be avoided by washing the salt away with extra water. But if the land is not well drained, it becomes water-logged.

The Sumerians failed to achieve a balance between salt accumulation and drainage. As a result, the salt and excess water harmed their crops. Farm production gradually declined, and food shortages developed. With the collapse of agriculture, the Sumerian civilization fell.

The challenge of today, as in ancient times, is for people to make the best use of water. But the challenge is greater than ever before because more water is needed as the world's population increases. Scientists estimate that nearly 50 countries will face water shortages by 2025. Also, many people do not conserve water, and they pollute water and manage it poorly in other ways.

Countries are working together to try to solve water problems. The United Nations (UN) has been heavily involved in these efforts. In addition, groups of countries whose lands are drained by major rivers and seas have formed regional organizations to fight water pollution.

From 1965 through 1974, about 70 countries took part in the International Hydrological Decade, a UN program established to promote scientific research on water resources. In 1975, the UN founded the International Hydrological Programme (IHP) to continue the research. The IHP is a long-term program that is carried out in phases lasting three or more years. Each phase has a theme. For example, the theme of the fifth phase, for the years 1996 to 2001, is "Hydrology and Water Resources Development in a Vulnerable Environment."

In 1993, the UN General Assembly declared March 22 of each year as World Day for Water. Each year, the day's activities promote public awareness of issues related to the protection and use of fresh water.

One regional antipollution group is the International Commission for the Protection of the Danube River, which was established in 1998. Members of the commission include 12 nations whose lands are drained by the Danube River in Europe. The organization operates an early warning network for oil spills and other pollution alerts. One of the commission's main projects is to recommend plans for cleaning up the sources of the most severe pollution of the Danube.   Thomas M. Keinath

Study aids

Related articles in *World Book* include:

Forms of water

Artesian well	Glacier	Iceberg	Spring
Cloud	Ground water	Liquid	Steam
Dew	Hail	Mineral water	Waterfall
Fog	Heavy water	Rain	Waterspout
Frost	Humidity	Sleet	Well
Geyser	Ice	Snow	Whirlpool

Purification and distribution of water

Aqueduct	Fluoridation	Sanitation
Chlorine	Plumbing	Sewage
Dam	Pump	Water meter
Filter	Reservoir	Water softening

Other related articles

Boiling point	Eutrophication	Irrigation	Surface
Canal	Evaporation	Lake	tension
Capillarity	Flood	Nutrition	Thirst
Climate	Hydraulics	(Water)	Transportation
Conservation	Hydrography	Ocean	Water
(Water con-	Hydrology	Osmosis	pollution
servation)	Hydrolysis	Rainmaking	Water power
Deuterium	Hydroponics	River	Water wheel
Electric power	Hydrosphere	Salt	Weather
Erosion	Hydrotherapy		Wetland

Outline

I. Water in our daily lives
  A. Water in living things   E. Water for power
  B. Water in our homes   F. Water for transportation
  C. Water for irrigation   and recreation
  D. Water for industry
II. Nature's water cycle
  A. The waters of the earth
  B. Water in the air

  C. Precipitation
  D. How water shapes the earth
  E. How water began
III. The water supply problem
  A. World distribution of water
  B. Water shortages
  C. Water management and conservation
IV. City water systems
  A. Sources of supply
  B. Uses of city water supplies
  C. Purifying and treating water
  D. Distributing water
  E. Disposing of used water
V. Fresh water from the sea
  A. Distillation
  B. Reverse osmosis
  C. Electrodialysis
  D. Other desalting processes
  E. The future of desalting
VI. What water is and how it behaves
  A. The chemistry of water
  B. The properties of water
  C. How water is held together
VII. Water and the course of history

Questions

How much of the water on the earth is in the salty oceans?
What are some of the ways in which people use water?
How does water affect the earth's climate?
What are some reasons for water shortages? What can be done to conserve water?
Why would people die if they drank only seawater?
What are some ways in which water shapes the earth?
How much of the earth is covered with water?
Why would the earth become a lifeless arctic desert if ice did not float?
What is the *water,* or *hydrologic, cycle?*

Additional resources

Level I

Farndon, John. *Water.* Benchmark Bks., 2001.
Graham, Ian. *Water Power.* Raintree Steck-Vaughn, 1999.
Hooper, Meredith. *The Drop in My Drink: The Story of Water on Our Planet.* Viking Penguin, 1998.
McLeish, Ewan. *Keeping Water Clean.* Raintree Steck-Vaughn, 1998.
Wick, Walter. *A Drop of Water.* Scholastic, 1997.

Level II

Ball, Philip. *Life's Matrix: A Biography of Water.* Farrar, 2000.
Barzilay, Joshua I., and others. *The Water We Drink.* Rutgers, 1999.
De Villiers, Marq. *Water: The Fate of Our Most Precious Resource.* Houghton, 2000.
Lewis, Scott A. T*he Sierra Club Guide to Safe Drinking Water.* Sierra Club, 1996.
Outwater, Alice B. *Water: A Natural History.* Basic Bks., 1996.

Water beech. See Ironwood.

Water beetle is the name given to many separate families of beetles that live in the water. Typical water beetles are the *whirligigs,* the *predaceous diving beetles,* and the *giant water scavenger beetles.* Some of these water beetles live in the water all their lives. Others live in or near the water only in the *larval* (young) stage.

Whirligigs whirl on the top of the water. They have short *antennae* (feelers), long-clawed front legs, and paddle-shaped hind legs. Their eyes are divided into a lower pair and an upper pair. Whirligigs produce an applelike scent when handled. Predaceous diving beetles have long, threadlike antennae. Their hind legs are flat and fringed. Giant water scavenger beetles have short, stubby antennae. Predaceous diving and giant water scavenger beetles are fierce predators. These beetles eat small fish and insect larvae.

David J. Shetlar

WORLD BOOK illustration by Shirley Hooper, Oxford Illustrators Limited

Giant water scavenger

Scientific classification. Water beetles are in the order Coleoptera. Whirligig beetles belong to the family Gyrinidae, predaceous diving beetles to the family Dytiscidae, and giant water scavenger beetles to the family Hydrophilidae.

See also **Beetle** (pictures).

Water bird. For examples, see **Bird** (pictures: Birds of inland waters and marshes; Birds of the seacoasts) and also the lists of Swimming and diving birds and Wading birds in the *Related articles* section.

Water boa. See Anaconda.

Water boatman. See **Insect** (Beneficial insects); Water bug.

Water buffalo. Several kinds of wild oxen may be called water buffaloes. Some have been domesticated and are among the most useful of all farm animals. The water buffalo of India is one of the largest of wild cattle. The *bulls* (males) are often 5 to $6\frac{1}{2}$ feet (1.5 to 2 meters) tall, and their horns may spread 12 feet (3.7 meters) from tip to tip, measured along the curve. The horns of the bull sweep out and back to form almost a circle, and are three-sided. The Indian buffalo's hide is bluish black,

L. R. Dawson, Bruce Coleman Ltd.

The water buffalo has large curved horns. This Indian water buffalo is a farm animal used in Asian rice fields.

and is easy to see through its thin hair. Wild Indian buffaloes graze in herds of about 50 animals. Both wild buffaloes and domesticated buffaloes have a keen sense of smell.

Water buffaloes like to wallow in the mud and water much of the day. They are fierce when wild, and a water buffalo is said to be a match for a large lion or tiger.

The Indian buffalo has made rice farming possible on a large scale in Asia. This powerful animal can plow knee deep in mud. The Indian buffalo has also been taken to many other parts of the world, including Australia, Brazil, Egypt, Hungary, Indonesia, Italy, the Philippines, Spain, and the United States.

Buffalo hide is tough and thick, and makes good leather. The milk of the cow is nourishing, with more fat than the milk of domestic cows. It is used in India for making a liquid butter.

The *carabao* is a smaller water buffalo of the Philippines. It is also important in farming. A native wild buffalo on Mindoro Island is called the *tamarau.* Africa is the home of two types of wild buffalo that are not actually water buffaloes. These are the big Cape buffalo, which has flattened horns, and the smaller Congo buffalo of central Africa.   C. Richard Taylor

Scientific classification. Water buffaloes belong to the subfamily Bovinae of the bovid family, Bovidae. The scientific name for the Indian water buffalo is *Bubalus bubalis.*

See also **Buffalo.**

Water bug is the common name for insects that spend most of their lives in the water. Most kinds of water bugs inhabit freshwater ponds, slow-moving streams, or pools of standing water. A few kinds of water bugs live in salt water.

Water bugs may be divided into five groups. The five groups are *water boatmen, back swimmers, water scorpions, giant water bugs,* and *water striders.* Most water bugs measure $\frac{1}{8}$ to $1\frac{3}{4}$ inches (0.3 to 4.4 centimeters) long. Giant water bugs grow to $2\frac{1}{3}$ inches (6 centimeters) long.

Water boatmen have weakly developed mouthparts. They use their short forelegs to collect algae and other submerged particles of food. All other water bugs have biting, piercing, or sucking mouthparts that enable them to feed on other insects, tadpoles, small fish, and salamanders. All water bugs except water boatmen can cause painful bites.

Water boatmen and back swimmers have long, flat, hair-fringed back legs that they use like oars when they swim. Back swimmers swim on their backs. They are able to swim up beneath their prey, and they can stay underwater for several hours at a time. Water scorpions generally live on the bottom of ponds. A water scorpion has oval disks on its abdomen. The disks probably help the insect adjust to changes in water pressure and depth. Water striders have long, stiltlike back legs that enable them to dart across the water's surface. They do not actually swim.

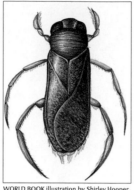

WORLD BOOK illustration by Shirley Hooper, Oxford Illustrators Limited
Water boatman

Scientific classification. Water bugs belong to the order Heteroptera in the class Insecta. Water boatmen are included in the family Corixidae; back swimmers, in the family Notonectidae; water scorpions, in the family Nepidae; giant water bugs, in the family Belostomatidae; and water striders, in the family Gerridae.   P. A. McLaughlin

Water chestnut is the common name for two very different kinds of aquatic plants. The *Chinese water chestnut* is a grasslike plant grown for its edible *corms* (underground stems). The other kind of water chestnut is a leafy, floating aquatic plant. It is also called the *water caltrop.*

The Chinese water chestnut has tube-shaped, leafless green stems that grow to about 5 feet (1.5 meters) high. It is cultivated in flooded fields similar to rice paddies. The small, rounded corms have a crispy white flesh and can be eaten raw, slightly boiled, broiled, pickled, or canned. They are a popular ingredient in Chinese foods. The Chinese water chestnut is native to China and is

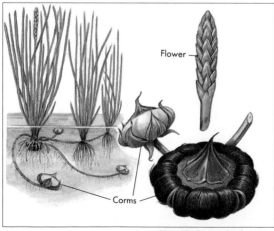

Flower

Corms

WORLD BOOK illustration by John F. Eggert

Chinese water chestnut, *above,* is a grasslike plant that is cultivated in flooded fields. Its edible underground stems, called *corms,* are a popular ingredient in Chinese foods.

widely cultivated in southern China and parts of the Philippines. The plant was introduced into the United States in 1934 and grows well along much of the Atlantic Coast.

Water caltrops bear nutlike fruits that are a delicacy throughout Asia. These plants grow chiefly in tropical and subtropical regions of Asia and Africa. They also can be found in some streams and lakes in the Eastern and Southern United States.

Scientific classification. The Chinese water chestnut belongs to the sedge family, Cyperaceae. It is *Eleocharis dulcis.* Water caltrops belong to the genus *Trapa* in the water chestnut family, Trapaceae.   Chien Yi Wang

Water clock, also called *clepsydra* (*KLEHP suh druh*), was an instrument that recorded time by measuring water escaping from a vessel. Egyptians were using water clocks about 1400 B.C. People used it long before modern clocks were invented.

The water clock consisted of a container with a scale of markings on its side. These were so arranged that, as the water ran out, the water left in the jar marked the time. Various improvements were made in the device, such as having a floating figure point to the hour. Another design caused the dripping water to turn a small wheel that was connected to the hands on the face of a dial. The water clock was used in Rome as early as 159 B.C. It was used in Athens to regulate the length of speeches in the law courts.   James Jespersen

Water color. See Painting (Materials and techniques).

Water conservation. See Conservation (Water conservation); Water (Water management).

Water cress. See Cress.

Water cycle. See Water (picture: The water cycle).

Water dog. See Mudpuppy.

Water flea is the common name of a group of tiny animals that live primarily in freshwater ponds and lakes. A few species of water fleas live in the ocean. Water fleas are a major source of food for many fish. Water fleas measure about $\frac{1}{125}$ to $\frac{3}{4}$ inch (0.2 to 18 millimeters) long. They received their name because their jerky swimming motions resemble the jumping of a flea. They swim by making a rowing movement with their *antennae* (feelers), which extend from the front of the head.

A water flea's body is covered by a transparent *carapace* (shell). The action of the heart and other organs can be seen through the carapace. As a result, water fleas are often used in scientific experiments to observe the effects of drugs on body organs. The water flea's head is not covered by the carapace. Water fleas use their four to six pairs of legs, called *appendages,* for filtering food particles from the water.

Scientific classification. Water fleas are in the phylum Arthropoda and the subphylum Crustacea.   P. A. McLaughlin

Water hyacinth is a plant that grows chiefly in the tropical regions of the world. It floats on lakes, rivers, and swamps and grows to a height of about 2 feet (61 centimeters) above the water. The water hyacinth has as many as 38 purple flowers grouped around the top of the stem.

Diseases and insects control the growth of water hyacinths in South America, where the plants first grew. But in the Southern United States and other regions where people have introduced the plant, there are no natural controls on its growth. In those regions, water hyacinths are a serious environmental problem because they grow so fast. The plants may double in number every 10 days. They form floating mats that can cover entire water surfaces and destroy the plant and animal life below. Plants need sunlight to live, and fish must have oxygen. The thick growth of water hyacinths blocks the sunlight, and the roots of the plants use up the oxygen in the water. In addition, boats cannot travel on waterways that are choked with water hyacinths.

Many scientists are exploring possible uses of water hyacinths. In the early 1970's, researchers began the experimental use of the plants to clean up polluted streams. Water hyacinths can absorb many chemicals—including sewage and industrial wastes—from the water in which the plants grow. Thus, polluted water might be purified by passing it through tanks that contain water hyacinths. Other people are studying the possibility of making cattle feed from dried water hyacinths.

Scientific classification. The water hyacinth belongs to the pickerelweed family, Pontederiaceae. It is *Eichhornia crassipes.*

James D. Mauseth

Water lily, also called *pond lily,* is the popular name for various beautiful water plants that grow in both temperate and hot climates. Water lilies send their long, stout leaf and flower stalks up from the mud bottom of clear, shallow water. Their narrow to round green leaves usually are seen floating on the surface of the water but may also be submerged. The flowers are usually raised above the water on long flower stalks. The

John L. Tveten

Water lilies grow in clear, shallow water in temperate and hot climates. The plants' beautiful flowers grow on long stalks that rise from the mud bottom.

white-flowered water lily is the most common. The flowers may be as large as 1 foot (30 centimeters) across. Some of the water lilies bloom during the day and others during the night. The water lily is the flower for the month of July.

Scientific classification. Water lilies belong to the water lily family, Nymphaeaceae. The most common white water lily of the Eastern United States is *Nymphia ordorata.*   Thomas B. Croat

See also **Flower** (picture: Flowers of woodlands and forests).

Badger Meter, Inc.

A water meter measures the volume of water that flows through a pipe. The meters above measure water in gallons, *left,* and in cubic feet, *right.* Water companies use such meters to measure water consumed in homes, factories, and businesses.

Water meter is a device that measures the volume of water that flows through a pipe or a large channel. The most widely known type of water meter turns numbers on a register that operates like an *odometer* (mileage recorder) of an automobile. This type is used by water companies to measure the water used in homes, factories, and business establishments.

In mild climates, such a home water meter is installed in a small box outside a house on the *service line* (pipe) leading to the street. In cold climates, the meter is installed inside a house—usually in the basement—to protect it from freeze-ups during winter. The meter is often connected to a register mounted outside the house so that the meter reader does not have to go inside.

The measuring chamber of a residential-type water meter usually contains a disk. Incoming water causes the disk to wobble. The amount of water that flows through the chamber determines how much the disk moves. The motion of the disk turns the numbers on the register. A large number of water meters use a magnetic coupling to transfer the disk's motion to the register. The register records the flow of water in cubic feet, gallons, or liters.

Other types of meters continuously register the flow of water on a chart-recording instrument. These meters are used in filtration plants, pumping stations, and industries.

The *venturi meter* and the *orifice meter* restrict the passage through which the water moves. They are used to measure the difference in water pressure to determine the amount of the flow.

The *magnetic flow meter* uses two electrodes mounted flush in the walls of a pipe, outside of which have been mounted powerful magnets. *Ions* (electrically charged atoms or groups of atoms) carried in the water pass through the magnetic field and generate voltage used by the meter to measure the water flow.

Electronic meters measure water flow by measuring changes in the wavelength of the sounds made by moving water. A variety of other devices are used to measure the flow of water in open channels, such as sewers and rivers.   Evan Powell

Water moccasin is a poisonous snake that lives in the southeastern United States. It is also called *moccasin snake* and *cottonmouth.* Water moccasins live in the area south of a line running from Cape Charles, Virginia, to the middle of the Alabama-Georgia boundary, then to

WORLD BOOK illustration by John F. Eggert

The water moccasin is one of several poisonous snakes in North America. It lives in southern swamps and bayous.

southern Illinois, and from there to the point where the Pecos River and the Rio Grande meet in Texas. Water moccasins rarely appear above this line.

The water moccasin is a pit viper, like the rattlesnake. It has a hollow, or pit, in the side of its head, between and slightly below the eye and nostril. Several harmless water snakes have a broad head like the moccasin, but they all lack the pit.

Adult water moccasins are about $3\frac{1}{2}$ feet (107 centimeters) long, though some grow to more than 5 feet (1.5 meters) long. They usually have broad dark bands across their bodies. Water moccasins feed on a wide variety of animals, including frogs, fish, small mammals, and birds. The young are born alive in the summer.

Water moccasins are most often seen in watery places, in the swampy backwaters of rivers and streams, and on marshy lake shores. Knowing this makes it easier for people to avoid the water moccasin. The bite of the water moccasin is highly dangerous and may be fatal. This snake is also called a cottonmouth because when threatened it throws back its head and flashes its white-lined mouth as a warning signal.   D. Bruce Means

Scientific classification. The water moccasin belongs to the family Viperidae. It is *Agkistrodon piscivorus.*

See also **Snake** (picture: Anatomy); **Viper.**

Water ouzel. See Dipper.

Water plant, also called *aquatic plant* or *hydrophyte,* is a name used for any plant that is specially adapted to live in water. Many botanists also consider the term *water plant* to include those plants that grow in water-saturated soils.

Water plants may be rooted in the mud and have their leaves and blossoms above or at the surface of the water. Some kinds grow completely underwater. Submerged water plants often have air bladders or large air pores in their stems and leaves that help the plants stand upright or stay afloat. Some of the best-known water plants are water lilies, sedges, and cattails. These plants often grow in lakes and ponds. Some biologists consider certain types of algae to be water plants. However, most scientists do not include algae in the plant kingdom. They classify algae in the kingdoms Protista and Prokaryotae.   David A. Francko

Related articles in *World Book* include:

Bladderwort	Bulrush	Cattail

Cress	Rush
Duckweed	Seaweed
Lotus	Water hyacinth
Papyrus	Water lily

Water pollution is one of the most serious environmental problems. It occurs when water is contaminated by such substances as human and other animal wastes, *toxic* (poisonous) chemicals, metals, and oils. Pollution can affect rain, rivers, lakes, oceans, and the water beneath the surface of the earth, called *ground water.*

Polluted water may look clean or dirty, but it all contains bacteria, viruses, chemicals, or other materials that can cause illness or death. Impurities must be removed before such water can be used safely for drinking, cooking, washing, or laundering. Some industries must clean the water before it can be used in their manufacturing processes.

Water pollution has become a serious problem in most countries. As a result, governments have passed laws limiting the amounts and kinds of wastes that can be dumped into water. Nations, states and provinces, cities and towns, and various industries have spent billions of dollars on research to reduce pollution and on the construction of water treatment plants. Nevertheless, pollution continues. In many parts of the world, cities and towns release untreated sewage into rivers, lakes, and coastal waters. Also, pollution that does not come from a direct point, such as a sewerage outlet or factory drain, is largely uncontrolled. These *nonpoint sources* of pollution include water that runs off construction sites and farmland, carrying soil particles and *nutrients* (nourishing substances) into streams and lakes. They also include water from lawns and gardens that may carry fertilizer and insecticide, and water from roads and parking lots that carries salt, oil, and grease.

Sources

There are three chief sources of water pollution. These sources are (1) industrial wastes, (2) sewage, and (3) agricultural chemicals and wastes.

Industrial wastes. United States industries discharge pollutants that include many toxic chemicals. Industries discharge much chemical waste directly into natural bodies of water. In addition, the burning of coal, oil, and other fuels by power plants, factories, and motor vehicles releases sulfur and nitrogen oxides into the air. These pollutants cause *acid rain,* which enters streams and lakes.

High levels of mercury have been found in fish far from industrial areas. The main sources of the mercury appear to be emissions to the atmosphere from coal-fired boilers, municipal incinerators, and smelters.

Some industries pollute water in yet another way. They use large quantities of water to cool certain equipment. Heat from the equipment makes the water hot. The industries then discharge the hot water into rivers and lakes, heating those bodies of water. Such heating that harms plants or animals is known as *thermal pollution.*

Sewage consists of human wastes, garbage, and water that has been used for laundering or bathing. Most of the sewage in the United States goes through treatment plants that remove solids and such dissolved substances as the nutrients nitrogen and phosphorus.

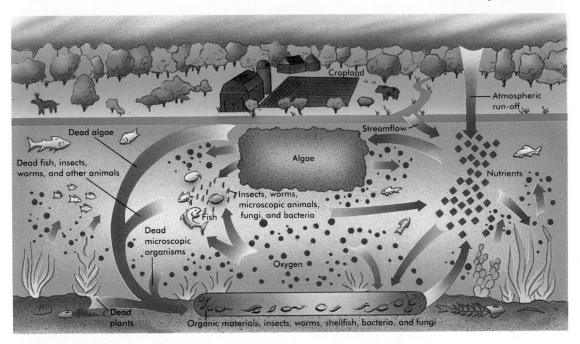

In a healthy water system, a cycle of natural processes turns waste material into useful substances. The bacteria of decay break down dead plants and animals and the body wastes of fish, releasing nitrates, phosphates, and other *nutrients* (chemicals needed for growth). Nutrients also enter the water from streams and other natural sources. Algae absorb the nutrients. Microscopic animals called *zooplankton* eat the algae, and fish eat the zooplankton. The fish produce body wastes and eventually die. Bacteria break down the wastes and dead fish, and the cycle continues.

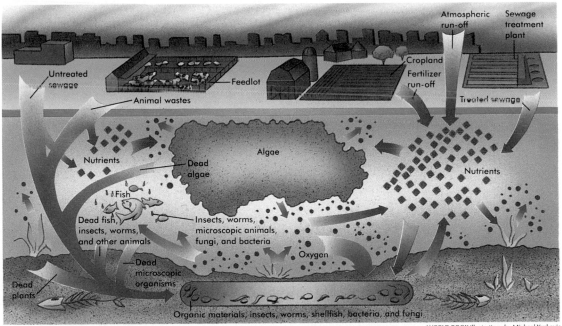

WORLD BOOK illustrations by Michael Yurkovic

Water pollution occurs when people upset the balance with excess nutrients from such sources as fertilizers and untreated sewage. This process is called *eutrophication*. The algae grow faster than the fish can eat them. As more algae grow, more also die. Bacteria in the water use up much oxygen consuming the excess dead algae. The oxygen level of the water drops, causing many aquatic plants and animals to die. As they decay, they consume still more oxygen. Without oxygen, the bacteria of decay can no longer function. Dead fish and other wastes sink to the bottom.

About 25 percent of U.S. households use *septic tank systems,* which pass the sewage through tanks and filter it through *leaching fields* into the land. Some sewage in the United States still goes untreated directly into waterways or the ocean. However, government regulations control the amount and the quality of the discharge.

Agricultural chemicals and wastes. Water from rain or melted snow flows from farmland into streams, carrying chemical fertilizers and pesticides that farmers have used on the land. Animal wastes also can cause water pollution, particularly from feed lots with many animals. Cattle, hogs, sheep, and poultry raised on feed lots do not distribute their wastes over widespread pastureland. Instead, much of their wastes runs off into nearby streams. Water used for irrigation also may be polluted by salt, pesticides, and toxic chemicals on the soil surface before it flows back into the ground.

Effects

Human illness. Water polluted with human and animal wastes can spread typhoid fever, cholera, dysentery, and other diseases. About 80 percent of the U.S. community water supplies are disinfected with chlorine to kill disease-causing germs. However, disinfection does not remove harmful chemical compounds, such as polychlorinated biphenyls (PCB's) and chloroform, or harmful metals, such as arsenic, lead, and mercury. The careless release of such toxic wastes, primarily into waste dumps, threatens ground water supplies. PCB's, chloroform, and pesticides have been found in some municipal drinking water. Scientists are concerned that drinking even small quantities of these substances over many years may have harmful effects.

Reduced recreational use. Pollution prevents people from enjoying some bodies of water for recreation. For example, odors and floating debris make boating and swimming unpleasant, and the risk of disease makes polluted water unsafe. Oil spilled from ships or offshore wells may float to shore. It can kill water birds, shellfish, and other wildlife. Water pollution also affects commercial and sport fishing. Fish can be killed by oil or by a lack of oxygen in the water, or they may die because of a reduction in the quantity and quality of their food supply. Industrial wastes also harm fish.

Disruption of natural processes. Various natural processes that occur in water turn wastes into useful or harmless substances. These processes use oxygen that is dissolved in the water. Water pollution upsets these processes, mainly by robbing the water of oxygen.

Mineralization is a natural process by which *aerobic* (oxygen-using) bacteria break down organic wastes into simpler substances. Some of these substances, such as phosphates and nitrates, are nutrients for plants. Normal quantities of these nutrients help support normal quantities of life in the water. When there are too many nutrients, however, a body of water may suffer from a process called *eutrophication.* The added nutrients may come from fertilizers draining off farmland or from detergents and other substances in sewage. An excess of nutrients causes the growth of higher-than-normal numbers of plants, such as pondweeds and duckweeds, plantlike organisms called *algae,* fish and other animals, and bacteria. As more grow, more also die and decay.

Because the decay process uses oxygen, the addition-

al decay uses up more of the oxygen in the water. Thus, less oxygen becomes available to support living things in the water.

Some types of game fish—such as salmon, trout, and whitefish—cannot live in water with reduced oxygen. Fish that need less oxygen, such as carp and catfish, will replace them. If all the oxygen in a body of water were to be used up, most forms of life in the water would die.

Thermal pollution can also reduce the amount of oxygen dissolved in water. In addition, the warmer-than-normal water can kill some kinds of plants and fish.

Control

Sewage treatment. The most efficient sewage treatment plants use three processes—*primary, secondary,* and *tertiary* treatment. Primary and secondary treatment can remove up to 95 percent of the waste in sewage. Tertiary treatment removes even more impurities. Many plants use primary and secondary processes, and some use tertiary processes as well. However, most treated sewage still contains nutrients and toxic chemicals because secondary processes cannot remove them all.

Pretreatment of wastes. Industries can reduce pollution by treating wastes to remove harmful chemicals before dumping the wastes into water. Industrial wastes can also be reduced by using manufacturing processes that recover and reuse polluting chemicals.

Drinking water standards. In 1974, the U.S. Congress passed the Safe Drinking Water Act to help protect the public water supply against pollution. This act authorized the Environmental Protection Agency (EPA) to establish uniform quality standards for over 200,000 public water systems. The standards were designed to reduce the amount of harmful bacteria, chemicals, and metals in drinking water. The EPA and the state governments began to enforce the standards in 1977.

In 1979, the EPA issued rules to limit the amount of chloroform and other related organic chemicals called *trihalomethanes* (THM) in the drinking water of large cities. These chemicals form at treatment plants when chlorine is added to drinking water to kill disease-causing bacteria and viruses. Extended exposure to high levels of THM's, especially chloroform, is thought to increase the risk of cancer in people.

In 1986, Congress amended the Safe Drinking Water Act to ban the use of lead solder in public water systems. In 1988, further changes in the law lowered the amount of lead allowable in drinking water and banned the use of lead solder in drinking water pipes for new homes. In 1996, the Safe Water Drinking Act was amended to further improve the quality of drinking water. Among the many changes were provisions to improve methods to detect and kill certain disease-causing microorganisms.   Gene E. Likens

Related articles in *World Book* include:

Tanker (Oil spills)   Thermal pollution

Additional resources

De Villiers, Marq. *Water.* Mariner Bks., 2001.
Donnelly, Andrew. *Water Pollution.* Child's World, 1998.
    Younger readers.
Markle, Sandra. *After the Spill: The Exxon Valdez Disaster, Then
    and Now.* Walker, 1999. Younger readers.
Simon, Paul. *Tapped Out: The Coming Crisis in Water and What
    We Can Do About It.* Welcome Rain, 1998.

Water polo is a sport in which two teams in a swimming pool attempt to score by throwing or pushing a hollow rubber ball into the goal of the opposing team. A player who does so scores one point for his or her team. Water polo is a rough sport because the players kick and wrestle or sometimes hold an opponent's head underwater. However, such actions are against the rules of the game.

Men's water polo is played in an area not less than 20 meters (66 feet) or more than 30 meters (98 feet) long. The width must be from 10 to 20 meters (33 to 66 feet). Women's water polo is played in an area no larger than 25 by 17 meters (82 by 56 feet). The goals are 3 meters (10 feet) wide and usually .9 meter (3 feet) above the water.

A water polo team consists of a goalie and six field players. The goalie can handle the ball with both hands. However, the field players may use only one hand at a time. Players move the ball by passing it or swimming with it. Each time a team gets the ball, it has 35 seconds to try to score. If the team does not shoot the ball at the goal within that period of time, the other team gets the ball.

If a player commits a minor foul, the other team is given three seconds to pass the ball without opposition. When a major foul is committed, the player must leave the game—without a substitute—for 20 seconds or until a goal is scored. An even more serious foul results in a *penalty throw,* in which an opposing player shoots at the goal from the 4-meter line with only the goalie defending it.

All water polo games are divided into four quarters. Men's water polo games are 28 minutes long and are split into 7-minute quarters. Women's water polo matches last 24 minutes and are divided into 6-minute quarters. Water polo originated in England during the 1870's.

Critically reviewed by United States Water Polo

Water power is a valuable source of energy. When such fuels as coal, oil, and even nuclear fuels are burned up as a source of energy, they cannot be reused. However, water that is used as a source of energy is not used up. The earth's constant flow of water can be harnessed in order to produce useful mechanical and electric power.

Wheels mounted on a frame over a river were the first devices used by people to harness water power. Blades around the outside of the wheels dipped into the river, and the flowing water striking the blades turned the wheels. The ancient Romans connected water wheels to grinding stones and used the power to mill grain.

During the Industrial Revolution, large water wheels were used to run the machinery in factories. The power was not completely reliable, however. Floodwaters created more power than was needed, and droughts left the factories without power. By the end of the 1800's, the steam engine had replaced water power in most factories.

The first water-powered plant for generating electric power was built in Appleton, Wisconsin, in 1882. This *hydroelectric plant* established water power as a major source of electricity. Hydroelectric power is now used all over the world.

Today, almost all water power is used to generate electric power. Many hydroelectric plants are combined with *thermal power plants*—that is, plants that use fuel in order to create energy. With this combination, the thermal plant can supply power if the hydroelectric plant is affected by drought. Hydroelectric plants are especially useful for producing electric power during periods when it is in great demand, because they can be turned on and off rapidly.

The mechanics of water power. Water flowing from a higher place to a lower place—as in a river, a waterfall, or a dam—is most often used to produce electric power. People use the effects of gravity (the attraction that the earth exerts on an object) pulling the water downward when they harness water for power. Thus, in the inch-pound system of measurement, a cubic foot of

Water polo is a rough sport played in a pool. Two teams try to score by throwing or pushing a hollow rubber ball into their opponent's goal.

water weighs 62.4 pounds. The pull of gravity then creates a pressure of 6,240 pounds per square foot at the base of a body of water 100 feet tall. If this water were released from a nozzle at the bottom of its source, the stream of water would travel at a speed of about 80 feet per second. The force of this stream striking the blades of a water wheel would cause the wheel to turn, producing useful mechanical energy.

Researchers are also developing several different technologies that can use waves to produce electric power. These technologies include devices that use the rise of waves to compress air that then turns a turbine, and floating devices that drive pistons as the water level rises and falls.

World water power production. The potential water power of the world is about $2\frac{1}{4}$ billion kilowatts of electric power. This is a very general estimate, because the flow of many large rivers has not been measured. Of this potential, about 600 million kilowatts is developed.

The United States has about a sixth of the world's developed power. Canada and Europe have most of the rest of the developed power. The potential of Asia, Africa, and Latin America is just beginning to be developed.

The world's largest hydroelectric power plant, the Itaipu plant of Brazil and Paraguay on the Paraná River, has a capacity of about 13 million kilowatts. The Guri power plant, on the Caroni River in Venezuela, can produce 10 million kilowatts. The Grand Coulee on the Columbia River in the United States has a capacity of about $7\frac{1}{2}$ million kilowatts, and the Sayano-Shushensk on the Yenisey River in Russia can produce about $6\frac{1}{2}$ million kilowatts.   Vijay P. Singh

Related articles. See the section on *Electric power* in state articles, such as **Arizona** (Electric power). See also:

Conservation	Electric power	Reservoir
Dam	Irrigation	Turbine

Water purification. See Water (City water systems).
Water safety. See Boating; Safety; Swimming.
Water-skiing is a popular sport in which a person wearing special skis is pulled over the water by a speeding motorboat. The skier holds on to a line attached to the boat. Millions of people throughout the world water-ski for recreation, and many compete in tournaments.

Water skis are wider than skis used on snow. They are made of fiberglass or various kinds of wood and are available in many lengths. The skier's feet fit into flexible *bindings,* which come off easily if the person falls, thus helping to prevent injury. A water-skier should always wear a life jacket for maximum safety.

The skier grasps a handle at one end of the towline, which measures about 75 feet (23 meters) long. The other end of the line is connected to the stern of the boat. A boat with a V-shaped hull is best for water-skiing because it pulls the skier on a straighter course than a flat-bottomed boat. The minimum speed for water-skiing is about 20 miles (32 kilometers) per hour. Experts are pulled at speeds of up to 100 miles (160 kilometers) per hour.

A water-skier starts from a dock or in the water. When the skier begins to move, the front end of the skis should be above the water. The person's back should be straight, the arms held straight ahead, and the knees

© Pierre Kopp, West Light

Water-skiing requires a good sense of balance but is easy to learn. Water-skiers wear life jackets for maximum safety.

slightly bent. Water-skiing is easy to learn and requires only a good sense of balance.

In the United States, water-skiing tournaments are held by the American Water Ski Association and by water-skiing clubs. These tournaments include competition in *jumping, slalom,* and *trick skiing.* In jumping, the skiers soar off a ramp in the water. The longest jump wins. The slalom involves skiing as fast as possible around a series of buoys. In trick skiing, water-skiers are judged on how well they perform jumps, turns, and other difficult maneuvers.

Critically reviewed by the American Water Ski Association

Water softening is a method of removing from water the minerals that make it hard. Hard water does not dissolve soap readily. It forms scale in pipes, boilers, and other equipment in which it is used. The principal methods of softening water are the lime soda process and the ion exchange process.

In the *lime soda process,* soda ash and lime are added to the water in amounts determined by chemical tests. These chemicals combine with the calcium and magnesium in the water to make insoluble compounds that settle to the bottom of the water tank.

In the *ion exchange process,* the water filters through minerals called *zeolites.* As the water passes through the filter, the sodium ions in the zeolite are exchanged for the calcium and magnesium ions in the water, and the water is softened. After household softeners become exhausted, a strong solution of *sodium chloride* (salt) is passed through the filter to replace the sodium that has been lost. The use of two exchange materials makes it possible to remove both metal and acid ions from water. Some cities and towns, however, prohibit or restrict the use of ion exchange equipment on drinking water, pending the results of studies on how people are affected by the consumption of the added sodium in softened water.   Evan Powell

Water sports. See Boating; Diving; Fishing; Rafting; Skin diving; Surfing; Swimming; Water-skiing.
Water supply. See Water.

Water table. See Ground water.
Water vapor. See Humidity.
Water wheel changes the energy of falling water into mechanical energy that can be used for running machinery. The best source of water power in nature is found in waterfalls and rapids in rivers. The water is directed into the wheel through a chute. The wheel is mounted on an axle, which is connected by belts or gearing with the machinery it is to operate.

There are two main types of water wheels, vertical and horizontal. The vertical wheels include the overshot and the undershot.

The overshot water wheel has many scooplike buckets around its edge. Water is delivered to the top of the wheel. The weight of the water falling into the buckets causes the wheel to turn. An overshot water wheel may have an efficiency of up to 80 percent. That is, it may turn as much as 80 percent of the energy of the water fed to it into mechanical energy. However, its use is limited to generating small amounts of power.

The undershot water wheel is built so the water strikes against blades at the bottom of the wheel. The power of the wheel depends on the speed of the water as it strikes the blades. The undershot wheel has such a low efficiency that it is rarely used.

Most modern water wheels are horizontal. A horizontal wheel rotates on a vertical shaft. It is driven by the force of the water striking the blades on one side of the wheel. Horizontal wheels are highly efficient if properly designed for the conditions of their use.

Historians believe the water wheel was developed in the 100's B.C. It was used mainly to grind grain. Later it was used for many kinds of mechanical operations. It was a major source of power until the development of the steam engine in the 1700's.   Vijay P. Singh

See also **Turbine** (Water turbines); **Water power.**
Water witch. See Grebe.

E. R. Degginger
This overshot water wheel in Virginia has been used to power a mill for grinding grain since the early 1800's.

Waterbury (pop. 107,271; met. area 228,984) is one of the largest cities in Connecticut. It lies along the Naugatuck River (see **Connecticut** [political map]). Products made in Waterbury include brass and copper products, buttons, watches and clocks, and machine-shop products. The city also has industries that provide health, financial, and insurance services. It is the home of Teikyo Post University (formerly Post College) and Naugatuck Valley Community-Technical College.

In 1802, Waterbury began manufacturing products made of brass. It later became first among the cities of the United States in production of brass products. It came to be called the *Brass Center of the World.* It manufactured such brass products as sheeting, screws and rivets, and ammunition casings. After World War II ended in 1945, Waterbury's production of brass goods began to decline dramatically. Brass products are now manufactured there only on a limited scale.

People in nearby Farmington bought the Waterbury area from Indians in 1674. They built a frontier outpost called Mattatuck there. The name became Waterbury when the town was incorporated in 1686. Waterbury received its city charter in 1853. A mayor and a board of aldermen head the government.   Robert D. Veillette

Waterfall is any sudden descent of a stream from a higher to a lower level. In wearing down its channel, a river uncovers certain layers of rock that are softer than others. If the hard rock is farther upstream than the soft, the channel below is worn more rapidly, and a waterfall results. Sometimes the hard ledge forms the edge of a vertical cliff, over which the water plunges.

If the volume of water is small, the fall may be called a *cascade.* If the volume of water is large, the fall is called a *cataract.* Famous cataracts include Niagara Falls on the Niagara River, which lies on the United States-Canada border; Victoria Falls on the Zambezi River in Africa; and Churchill Falls of the Churchill River in Labrador. Often, the term *cataract* is applied to a series of rapids or falls caused by the flow of the stream over a rapidly sloping rocky bed. Examples of these are the cataracts of the Nile and the Orinoco rivers. Cataracts that have small, gradual falls are termed *rapids.* Some noted rapids in North America are those in the St. Lawrence River and at Sault Ste. Marie, at the outlet of Lake Superior.

Small waterfalls are often of great height. These include the Upper Yosemite Falls in California at 1,430 feet (436 meters), and Sutherland Falls in New Zealand at 1,904 feet (580 meters). Other noted waterfalls include Niagara Falls; Montmorency Falls, near Quebec; Multnomah Falls, near the Columbia River, Oregon; and the Upper and Lower falls in Yellowstone National Park.

Falls usually occur in mountainous regions. But sometimes they are caused by the descent of streams from an upland to a lowland, as at the edge of a plateau. The line along which several rivers flowing into the same body of water descend is called the *fall line.*

The Fall Line of the eastern United States occurs where rivers flowing from the harder rocks of the Piedmont Region descend to the softer rocks of the Atlantic Coastal Plain. The waterfalls and rapids along the Fall Line provide a major source of waterpower and form a barrier to ships sailing westward. For this reason, the Fall Line helped determine the site of many Eastern cities, including Philadelphia; Baltimore; Washington, D.C.;

Famous waterfalls

Photographs of some of the world's most striking waterfalls appear below and on the opposite page. The tables below compare the heights of these falls and highlight some of their interesting facts and features.

© James Blank, West Stock

Niagara Falls, New York section

Gene Ahrens, Shostal
Multnomah Falls

© Charles Moore, Black Star
Yosemite Falls

© James Blank, West Stock
Yellowstone Lower Falls

C. G. Maxwell, FPG
Ribbon Falls

Famous waterfalls of North America

Name	Height In feet	In meters	Location	Interesting facts
Basaseachic	1,020	311	Mexico	Mexico's highest; fed by Piedra Volada Creek.
Bridalveil	620	189	California	One of many spectacular waterfalls in Yosemite National Park; its Indian name, Pohono, means *puffing wind.*
Della	1,443	440	British Columbia	Canada's highest; located on Vancouver Island.
Fairy	700	213	Washington	Fed by Stevens Creek in Mount Rainier National Park.
Multnomah	542	165	Oregon	Plunges a total of 620 feet (189 meters) from a creek on Larch Mountain into the Columbia River gorge.
Niagara (American)	176	54	New York	Also called the American Falls; the higher of the two waterfalls.
Niagara (Canadian)	167	51	Ontario	Also called Horseshoe Falls; about 85 percent of Niagara Falls's water flows over this section.
Ribbon	1,612	491	California	The longest uninterrupted falls in North America.
Takakkaw	833	254	British Columbia	In Yoho National Park. Cree Indian name means *magnificent.*
Vernal	317	97	California	Mist from powerful falls in Yosemite National Park keeps surrounding vegetation green the year around.
Yellowstone Lower Falls	308	94	Wyoming	Yellowstone River drops a total of over 400 feet (120 meters) before entering the Grand Canyon of the Yellowstone.
Yosemite Lower Falls	320	98	California	Of Yosemite's major waterfalls, the most accessible to visitors.
Yosemite Upper Falls	1,430	436	California	Snowmelt makes its tributary, Yosemite Creek, become a raging torrent in the spring; it dwindles to a trickle by late summer.

© Mark Boulton, Bruce Coleman Inc.

Victoria Falls on the Zambia-Zimbabwe border

© John Elk III, Wheeler Pictures

Gavarnie Falls

© Ray Manley, Shostal

Sutherland Falls

George de Steinheil, Shostal

Angel Falls

Kim Hart, Black Star

Vettisfoss

Famous waterfalls of the world

Name	Height In feet	In meters	Location	Interesting facts
Angel	2,648	807	Venezuela	Drops a world-record total of 3,212 feet (979 meters). Named for the American pilot Jimmy Angel, who first flew over it in 1935.
Cuquenàn	2,000	610	Venezuela	In Canaima National Park. Also spelled Kukenàn or Kukenaam.
Gavarnie	1,385	422	France	The falls, situated in the Pyrenees Mountains, drops into an enormous natural amphitheater.
Jog	830	253	India	Sharavathi River tumbles over a cliff and becomes four smaller waterfalls named Raja, Rani, Rocket, and Roarer.
Kaieteur	820	250	Guyana	Surrounded by virgin forest, this waterfall reaches nearly 330 feet (100 meters) wide in the rainy season.
Krimml	1,312	400	Austria	Located in Hohe Tauern National Park; fed by the Krimmler Ache, a tributary of the Upper Salzach River.
Mardalsfossen (Northern)	1,535	468	Norway	Name comes from Old Norse *Mar*, meaning either *horse* or *ocean; dal* meaning *valley;* and *fors* meaning *waterfall.*
Mardalsfossen (Southern)	2,149	655	Norway	Europe's highest; it falls at full strength from late June to late August. At other times hydroelectric plants restrict its flow.
Sutherland	815	248	New Zealand	Located on New Zealand's South Island; the falls drop a total of 1,904 feet (580 meters) from Lake Quill to the Arthur River.
Trümmelbach	1,312	400	Switzerland	A series of falls near the Swiss town of Lauterbrunnen.
Tugela	597	182	South Africa	One of a series of falls that drop a total of 3,000 feet (914 meters).
Vettisfoss	900	274	Norway	Set in Norway's Sogne Fjord region; fed by the Mörkedola River.
Victoria	355	108	Zambia-Zimbabwe border	The world's largest waterfall by water volume. Its local name, Mosi-oa-Tunya, means *smoke that thunders.*

Richmond, Virginia; Raleigh, North Carolina; and Augusta, Georgia. See **Fall line.**   James C. Walters

Related articles in *World Book* include:

Angel Falls	Iguaçu Falls	Sutherland Falls
Argentina (picture)	Minnehaha Falls	Takakkaw Falls
Brazil (picture)	Niagara Falls	Victoria Falls
Bridalveil Fall	Reversing Falls of	Wyoming (picture)
Cuquenán Falls	Saint John	Yosemite Falls
Ethiopia (picture)	Ribbon Falls	

Waterford (pop. 44,594) is a city in southeastern Ireland. It lies on the River Suir, about 10 miles (16 kilometers) from the point at which the river enters Waterford Harbour. For location, see **Ireland** (political map). Waterford is an industrial center and an important port for container ships. It is also a service and shopping area for southeastern Ireland.

The city's best-known industry is the manufacture of Waterford crystal glass. Waterford glassware was first manufactured in 1783, and it soon became known worldwide. Its production was ended in 1851 and was resumed in 1952. See **Glass** (picture: Waterford crystal jar). The city's other products include chemicals, electrical equipment, furniture, metal products, optical goods, and processed foods. Many of Waterford's modern factories are in an industrial area built in the 1960's.

Waterford was established by Viking raiders, who arrived there in the A.D. 800's. Norman invaders from England captured Waterford in 1170. During the late 1700's and early 1800's, the town prospered based on its export of agricultural products and its glassware industry.

Desmond A. Gillmor

Watergate was the name of the biggest political scandal in United States history. It included various illegal activities designed to help President Richard M. Nixon win reelection in 1972. Watergate resulted in Nixon's resignation from the presidency in 1974.

Watergate differed from most previous political scandals because personal greed apparently did not play an important role. Instead, Watergate represented an attack on one of the chief features of a democracy—free and open elections.

The Watergate activities included burglary, wiretapping, violations of campaign financing laws, sabotage, and the attempted use of government agencies to harm political opponents. The scandal also involved a cover-up of many of those actions. About 40 people were charged with crimes in the scandal and with related crimes. Most of these people were convicted by juries or pleaded guilty.

Watergate involved more high-level government officials than any previous political scandal. It led to the conviction on criminal charges in 1975 of former Attorney General John N. Mitchell and two of Nixon's top aides, John D. Ehrlichman and H. R. Haldeman. Also in 1975, former Secretary of Commerce Maurice H. Stans, a leader of Nixon's reelection campaign, pleaded guilty to Watergate criminal charges and was fined $5,000. Watergate also had resulted in the resignation of Attorney General Richard G. Kleindienst in 1973.

The break-in and cover-up. The scandal took its name from the Watergate complex of apartment and office buildings in Washington, D.C. On June 17, 1972, the police arrested five men for breaking into the Democratic Party's national headquarters there. One of the bur-

glars was James W. McCord, Jr., the security coordinator of the Committee for the Re-election of the President (CRP). The five men—along with G. Gordon Liddy, another CRP aide; and E. Howard Hunt, Jr., a White House consultant—were indicted for a number of crimes, including burglary and wiretapping. In January 1973, five of the seven, including Hunt, pleaded guilty. The other two—Liddy and McCord—were found guilty by a jury.

Nixon's press secretary had said repeatedly that the scandal involved no member of the White House staff. But the press found evidence that White House aides had helped finance sabotage and spying operations against candidates for the 1972 Democratic presidential nomination. Reporters Carl Bernstein and Bob Woodward of *The Washington Post* led the investigation.

Early in 1973, evidence was uncovered that tied several top White House aides to plans for the Watergate break-in or to concealment of evidence that implicated members of the Nixon administration. The evidence indicated that White House officials had tried to involve the Central Intelligence Agency and the Federal Bureau of Investigation in the cover-up. These officials falsely claimed that national security was involved.

On April 30, 1973, Nixon stated that he had no part in either planning the Watergate break-in or covering it up. He promised that the Department of Justice would appoint a special prosecutor to handle the case. In May, Archibald Cox, a Harvard Law School professor, was named to that position. Also in May, the Senate Select Committee on Presidential Campaign Activities began hearings on Watergate. Senator Sam J. Ervin, Jr., of North Carolina headed the committee. Former Presidential Counsel John W. Dean III became the chief witness against Nixon in the hearings. Dean admitted that he had played a major role in a White House cover-up and charged that Nixon knew of his activities. Dean also revealed administration plans to use the Internal Revenue Service and other government agencies to punish opponents whom the White House had placed on so-called enemies lists. Dean was later sentenced to a prison term of one to four years. After serving four months, his sentence was reduced to that time and he was released.

The tape controversy. In July, the Senate committee learned that Nixon had secretly made tape recordings of conversations in his White House offices since 1971. The committee and Cox believed the tapes could answer key questions raised in their investigations. They asked Nixon to supply them with certain tapes, but he refused to do so. Nixon argued that, as president, he had a constitutional right to keep the tapes confidential. In August, Cox and the committee sued Nixon to obtain the tapes. United States District Court Judge John J. Sirica decided to review the tapes himself and ordered Nixon to give them to him. Nixon appealed the order, but a U.S. court of appeals supported Sirica.

In October, Nixon offered to provide summaries of the tapes. But Cox declared that summaries would be unacceptable as evidence in court and rejected the offer. Nixon ordered Attorney General Elliot L. Richardson to fire Cox, but Richardson refused to do so and resigned. Deputy Attorney General William D. Ruckelshaus resigned after being ordered to dismiss Cox. Nixon then named Solicitor General Robert H. Bork acting attorney general, and Bork fired Cox. Leon Jaworski, a noted Texas attorney, later succeeded Cox.

The president's actions angered many Americans. In October, a number of members of the House of Representatives began steps to impeach him. Later in 1973, Nixon agreed to supply the tapes to Sirica. Then it was discovered that three key conversations were missing. The White House said that the tape-recording system failed to work properly during two of the talks and that the third had been accidentally erased.

In April 1974, Jaworski served Nixon with a *subpoena* (legal order) to furnish tape recordings and documents relating to 64 White House conversations. Jaworski said the materials contained evidence in the cover-up case. At the end of April, Nixon released 1,254 pages of edited transcripts of White House conversations. He said they told the full Watergate story.

Jaworski, however, insisted on receiving the original tapes and documents that he had requested. Nixon again claimed he had a constitutional right to protect confidential documents. Jaworski then sued the president in federal court. In July, the Supreme Court of the United States ordered Nixon to give Jaworski the materials. The Supreme Court ruled unanimously that a president cannot withhold evidence in a criminal case.

The cover-up trial. In March 1974, seven former officials of Nixon's administration or his 1972 reelection committee were indicted on charges of conspiracy in covering up the Watergate break-in. Among them were Domestic Council Chief Ehrlichman, White House Chief of Staff Haldeman, and Attorney General Mitchell.

The trial lasted from October 1974 to January 1975. Ehrlichman, Haldeman, and Mitchell were each convicted of conspiracy, obstruction of justice, and perjury, and sentenced to a prison term of from $2\frac{1}{2}$ to 8 years. The sentences were later reduced to 1 to 4 years.

The resignation of Nixon. The president suffered another major setback in July 1974, when the House Judiciary Committee recommended that he be impeached. The committee adopted three articles of impeachment for consideration by the full House of Representatives. The first article accused Nixon of obstructing justice in the scandal. The other two articles accused him of abusing presidential powers and illegally withholding evidence from the judiciary committee.

Nixon's chief defenders continued to argue that the president had committed no impeachable offense. But on August 5, Nixon released additional transcripts of taped White House conversations. The transcripts convinced most Americans that Nixon had authorized the Watergate cover-up at least as early as June 23, 1972—six days after the break-in. Nixon immediately lost almost all his remaining support in Congress. He resigned on August 9, and Vice President Gerald R. Ford took office as president that day. On September 8, Ford pardoned Nixon for all federal crimes that Nixon might have committed while serving as president.

Other effects of Watergate. In 1974, Congress approved reforms in the financing of federal election campaigns. Some reforms limit the amount of money contributors may give to candidates for president, vice president, and Congress. Other financial reforms require detailed reporting of both contributions and expenses. Many state legislatures limited contributions and spending in state election campaigns and adopted codes of ethics for all government employees.

Critically reviewed by J. Anthony Lukas

See also **Nixon, Richard M.** (The Watergate scandal); **Mitchell, John N.; Republican Party** (The Watergate scandal); **Washington, D.C.** (Watergate).

Additional resources

Bernstein, Carl, and Woodward, Bob. *All the President's Men.* 1974. Reprint. Simon & Schuster, 1999.

Cohen, Daniel. *Watergate.* Millbrook, 1998. Younger readers.

Emery, Fred. *Watergate.* 1994. Reprint. Touchstone, 1995.

Fremon, David K. *The Watergate Scandal in American History.* Enslow, 1998.

Genovese, Michael A. *The Watergate Crisis.* Greenwood, 1999.

Waterloo, Battle of, fought on June 18, 1815, was the final battle of the French military genius, Napoleon Bonaparte. It put an end to his political ambitions to rule Europe. His defeat was so crushing that, when a person suffers a disastrous reverse, we say the person has "met his (or her) Waterloo."

Napoleon returns to France. After abdicating in 1814, Napoleon was exiled to the island of Elba, off the coast of Italy. He spent less than a year there before he decided to return to rule France. He saw that the allies at the Congress of Vienna seemed unable to settle their differences, and he hoped to take advantage of this split to regain power.

But the allies joined forces against Napoleon as soon as they heard of his return to France. Napoleon marched north into Belgium to meet this threat. The British Duke of Wellington commanded the allied forces of Belgium, Britain, Hanover, and the Netherlands. Neither commander had good intelligence services. Napoleon was not in good health at the time, and failed to display his earlier energy and military grasp.

The battle took place at Waterloo, a small town near Brussels. The two armies were about equal in size. Napoleon had about 74,000 troops, and superior cavalry and artillery. Wellington had about 67,000 troops. He placed them in a strong defensive position. The French started a fierce attack against the allied lines on June 18. Wellington's troops resisted the French assaults.

Napoleon might have won at Waterloo if he had attacked earlier in the day. But he waited until noon because of a heavy rain the night before. This delay permitted Marshal Gebhard von Blücher to arrive with his Prussian troops to reinforce Wellington. The battle was a draw until the arrival of Blücher's forces. These forces helped turn the battle against the French.

Napoleon made one last effort to win the battle. He flung his best troops, the famous "Old Guard," against the enemy's lines. Three battalions of the Guard fought bravely. However, they were overwhelmed. The French troops then retreated from a fierce bayonet counterattack.

Both sides lost many killed and wounded in the battle. The French suffered about 40,000 casualties, and the allies about 23,000. After this defeat, Napoleon failed to gather a new army. He had no choice left but to abdicate a second time.   Eric A. Arnold, Jr.

See also **Blücher, Gebhard L. von; Napoleon I; Wellington, Duke of.**

Watermark is an identifying mark pressed into paper as it is formed by a papermaking machine. Usually, it is the mark left by wires bent into the watermark pattern and attached to the *dandy roll* of a Fourdrinier machine (see **Paper** [diagram: How paper is made from wood]). As the wire pattern comes into contact with the layer of wet pulp, a translucent impression is made, which can be seen when the finished paper is held in front of a light. A mark that looks like a watermark can also be produced chemically on finished paper. Watermarked paper is often used for important documents to help prevent counterfeiting.   Larry L. Graham

Watermelon is a large, sweet fruit. It has a smooth *rind* (hard outer skin) and juicy, edible flesh. Most watermelons possess seeds, but growers also produce seedless types. Watermelons may appear round, oval, oblong, or blocky in shape. The rind is striped or solid and can be various shades of green or grayish-green, with the stripes darker in color. The flesh of ripe watermelons may have white, yellow, orange, pink, or red coloring. People often classify watermelon *cultivars* (varieties) by weight. The smallest fruits weigh less than 12 pounds (5.4 kilograms). The largest weigh more than 32 pounds (14.5 kilograms), with record weights exceeding 250 pounds (113 kilograms).

Watermelons consist of about 93 percent water. Yet they provide a good source of vitamins A and C and of *lycopene,* a chemical that may help reduce the risk of cancer. People generally eat the watermelon fruit fresh. But they also eat the seeds, pickle the rind to make relish, and use the fruit in syrup and even cattle feed.

Watermelons grow on vines. The plants require a long growing season, usually maturing in 75 to 100 days. Growers plant the seeds about 4 feet (1.2 meters) apart in rows spaced about 6 to 8 feet (1.8 to 2.4 meters) from one another. In cold weather, seeds are often planted in a greenhouse first. They are then transplanted into fields after the danger of frost has passed. Growers also transplant all seedless cultivars of watermelons.

Watermelon vines, or *runners,* can grow 40 feet (12.2 meters) long or more. They produce slender, coiling *tendrils* and yellow blossoms. The tendrils attach themselves to objects in the field. Watermelon fruit develops

WORLD BOOK illustration by Kate Lloyd-Jones, Linden Artists
Watermelons are popular fruits with sweet, juicy flesh. The fruits develop from the yellow flowers of the watermelon plant after the blossoms are pollinated.

from pollinated flowers. When a watermelon ripens, the rind color becomes dull and the top of the fruit flattens slightly. Ripe watermelons make a dull, hollow thud when thumped.

A fungal disease called *Fusarium wilt* is the main disease of watermelon plants. The wilt fungus remains in the soil and may infect new plants for several years. Growers control wilt by rotating the watermelon crop to a different field each year, or by planting cultivars resistant to the disease. Watermelons also suffer from viruses, roundworms, insects, spider mites, and other pests. Farmers combat these problems with chemical pesticides and with pest-resistant cultivars.

The watermelon plant probably originated in western or southern Africa. China, which has cultivated the fruit for more than 1,000 years, ranks as the top watermelon-producing country. Other major producers include Turkey, Iran, and the United States..   Todd Wehner

Scientific classification. The watermelon plant belongs to the gourd family, Cucurbitaceae. It is *Citrullus lanatus.*

Waterproofing is a way of treating cloth, leather, wood, or other materials so that they will shed water. Many different chemical solutions are used in waterproofing. Nearly all of them work by forming a protective coating over the material to be waterproofed.

Materials which have pores are often soaked in solutions of rubber, linseed oil, paraffin, or some other substance which is itself waterproof. The solution fills the pores. Silicone and fluorocarbon finishes are widely used to waterproof clothing. Building materials are waterproofed with silicones (see **Silicone**).

In 1823, the Scottish chemist Charles Macintosh invented a water-resistant fabric made of cloth and rubber. A raincoat made of his protective material became commonly known as a *mackintosh.*   Howard L. Needles

Waters, Ethel (1900-1977), was a popular black American singer and actress. She gained recognition as a singer of both blues and popular songs. Waters starred in several Broadway musicals, including *Africana* (1927), *As Thousands Cheer* (1933), *At Home Abroad* (1935), and *Cabin in the Sky* (1940). She introduced a number of well-known songs during her stage career, including "I'm Coming Virginia," "Heat Wave," and "Taking a Chance on Love." She also appeared in dramatic roles, and won acclaim for her roles in the movie *Pinky* (1949) and the play *The Member of the Wedding* (1950).

Waters was born Oct. 31, 1900, in Chester, Pennsylvania. She began singing in nightclubs and in vaudeville at the age of 17. Waters wrote a highly praised autobiography, *His Eye Is on the Sparrow* (1951).   Gerald Bordman

Watershed. See Forestry (Water).

Waters, Muddy (1915-1983), was an influential rhythm and blues singer and guitarist. His music inspired many rock music performers, including Mick Jagger of the Rolling Stones and Elvis Presley.

Waters was born April 4, 1915, in Rolling Fork, Mississippi. His given and family name was McKinley Morganfield. He made his first recording in Mississippi in 1941. At that time, he performed country blues music, singing and accompanying himself on an *acoustic* (nonelectric) guitar. In 1943, Waters moved to Chicago, where an active blues scene offered new ideas and greater opportunities for work. He became the most important originator of urban blues music, which featured a blues singer with an electrically amplified guitar; a rhythm section of piano, bass, and drums; and a loud, aggressive style. He began to record commercially under the name Muddy Waters in 1947.

Waters's first hit, recorded in 1948, was "I Can't Be Satisfied." The greatest successes of Waters's career came during the 1950's and 1960's. They included "I'm Your Hoochie Coochie Man," "Got My Mojo Working," and "Tiger in Your Tank." Frank Tirro

Waterspout is a tornado that occurs over a lake or ocean. A waterspout begins when a center of low air pressure develops, causing winds to whirl. A thick, black, rotating cloud forms, with a rotating column of air extending beneath the cloud to the water's surface. The air column becomes visible as water vapor in the atmosphere condenses in the column and surface water is drawn up at the column's base.

Most waterspouts measure from about 20 to 200 feet

© Chesher, Photo Researchers

A waterspout's whirling column is a spectacular sight and may be dangerous. This waterspout occurred off Key West, Florida.

(6 to 60 meters) in diameter. They are usually associated with strong winds and can cause severe damage. Most waterspouts occur in the tropics. Most whirl counterclockwise in the Northern Hemisphere and clockwise in the Southern Hemisphere. Wayne M. Wendland

Waterton-Glacier International Peace Park is on the United States-Canadian boundary line between Montana and Alberta. It covers over 1 million acres (400,000 hectares) on the United States side, and over 130,000 acres (52,600 hectares) in Canada. The park unites Glacier National Park in Montana with Waterton Lakes National Park in Alberta. See also **Glacier National Park.** Critically reviewed by Glacier National Park

Watie, Stand (1806-1871), became the only Indian brigadier general in the Confederate Army. Born near Rome, Georgia, he moved to Oklahoma with the Cherokee Indians in 1838 and became a tribal leader. Watie entered the army after forming an alliance between the Cherokee and the Confederacy in 1861. He led a regiment of Cherokee volunteers called the Cherokee Mounted Rifles. In 1864, he was made a brigadier gen-

eral. Watie was one of the last Confederate officers to surrender. Michael D. Green

Watson, Homer (1855-1936), was a Canadian landscape painter. He became known for his direct, detailed paintings of the countryside around Doon, Ontario, near Kitchener, where he was born and spent much of his life. Many of Watson's paintings portray scenes of pioneer life or capture the various moods of nature.

From 1887 to 1890, Watson lived in England, where his work was popular. He returned there several times to exhibit his work. Watson was the first president of the Canadian Art Club, formed in 1907. He was president of the Royal Canadian Academy from 1918 to 1922.

David Burnett

Watson, James Dewey (1928-   ), is an American biologist. He shared the 1962 Nobel Prize for physiology or medicine with biologist Francis H. C. Crick and biophysicist Maurice H. F. Wilkins, both of Britain. In 1953, Watson and Crick, relying mainly on experimental data provided by Wilkins, devised a model of the molecular structure of *deoxyribonucleic acid* (DNA). DNA is the substance that makes up *genes,* the material in cells that determines the characteristics of an organism.

The *Watson-Crick model* shows that a DNA molecule forms a *double helix*—that is, it resembles a twisted ladder. Each "rung" consists of one of two pairs of chemicals, called *base pairs.* If the ladder is divided at the middle of each rung, the legs form two new ladders, each identical to the original ladder. The model thus suggested how genetic information is passed from one generation to the next. See **Heredity** (The chemistry of genes).

Watson was born in Chicago. He studied at the University of Chicago and Indiana University. In 1955, Watson joined the biology faculty at Harvard University. In 1968, he became director of the Cold Spring Harbor Laboratory on Long Island, New York. That same year, he published *The Double Helix,* an account of the discovery of the DNA structure. From 1988 to 1989, Watson was associate director for human genome research at the National Institutes of Health in Bethesda, Maryland. From 1989 to 1992, he was director of the agency's National Center for Human Genome Research (now the National Human Genome Research Institute). In that position, he helped launch a project to locate the genes and determine the sequences of chemical base pairs in the *human genome* (all the genes in a human cell).

Daniel J. Kevles

See also **Cell** (The 1900's; picture: A model of a DNA molecule); **Human Genome Project; Science** (picture).

Watson, John Broadus (1878-1958), was an American psychologist. In the early 1900's, he led a revolutionary movement in psychology called *behaviorism.* At that time, Watson claimed that psychology was not a true science because it was based on the examination of thought processes and feelings. He believed that psychology would become a true science only if it came to be based on directly observed behavior.

Watson thought that almost all behavior is a direct result of certain stimuli in a person's environment. His belief that the environment shapes an individual's behavior was so extreme that he claimed he could teach any healthy child any talent or skill. Although Watson generally opposed the notion of innate abilities, he did allow for three inborn emotions—fear, anger, and love.

Watson was attracted to the Russian physiologist Ivan P. Pavlov's description of behavior as a *conditioned reflex* (see **Pavlov, Ivan P.**). Watson used this idea as the chief model of behavior in his *Psychology from the Standpoint of a Behaviorist* (1919).

Watson's extreme views are not widely held today. But his work helped lead to the development of scientific psychology, particularly in the United States. Watson's behaviorism greatly influenced the American psychologist B. F. Skinner (see **Skinner, B. F.**). Watson was born in Greenville, South Carolina.   Phillip L. Rice

Watson, Thomas Edward (1856-1922), was one of the most important Southern leaders of the Populist Party in the United States. He was elected from Georgia to the U.S. House of Representatives as a Democrat in 1890. He then joined the new Populist Party, which represented the farmers (see **Populism**). The Populists nominated him for vice president in 1896 and for president in 1904 and 1908. Watson later became a Democrat again. In 1920, he was elected to the Senate. He often promoted racial and religious prejudice. He opposed U.S. involvement in World War I (1914-1918) and the League of Nations, a forerunner to the United Nations. Watson was born near Thomson, Georgia.   Robert W. Cherny

Watson, Thomas John (1874-1956), was an American industrialist. He worked for the National Cash Register Company (now NCR Corporation) for 15 years. In 1914, he was made president of a company that became International Business Machines Corporation (IBM) in 1924. Under Watson's leadership from 1914 to 1956, it became one of the world's most successful corporations. Watson was born in Campbell, New York.   William H. Becker

Watson-Watt, Sir Robert Alexander (1892-1973), a Scottish electronics engineer and inventor, helped develop radar. In 1919, he invented a crude form of radio direction finder while associated with the British weather bureau. In 1935, Watson-Watt began to develop ways to detect aircraft using radio waves. By 1940, he had helped to complete reliable radar stations along British shores. These stations played a crucial role in the Battle of Britain during World War II (1939-1945). Watson-Watt was born in Brechin, Scotland. He was knighted in 1942. See also **Radar** (The first uses of radar).   Joan L. Richards

Watt is a unit of *power* in the metric system. Power is the rate of producing or using energy. The symbol for the watt is W. The watt is commonly used to measure electric power, even in countries that have not adopted the metric system. An electric device uses 1 watt when 1 volt of electric potential drives 1 ampere of current through it. The number on a light bulb shows its power requirement in watts. For example, a light bulb operating at 100 volts and using 2 amperes consumes 200 watts (100 volts × 2 amperes). Often, power is measured in *kilowatts*. One kilowatt equals 1,000 watts.

The watt also is used to measure mechanical power. A machine requires a power of 1 watt if it uses 1 joule of energy in 1 second. The watt was named for the Scottish engineer and inventor James Watt.   Gregory Benford

See also **Ampere; Joule; Kilowatt; Watt, James**.

Watt, James (1736-1819), was a Scottish engineer whose improved engine design first made steam power practicable. Crude steam engines were used before Watt's time, but they burned large amounts of coal and produced little power. Their *reciprocating* (back-and-

forth) motion restricted their use to operating pumps. Watt made steam engines more efficient by inventing the *separate condenser.* This device changed steam back into water by cooling. Watt's later improvements made possible the wide application of steam engines, contributing much to the growth of modern industry.

Watt was born in Greenock, Scotland. He was the son of a shopkeeper and carpenter. When Watt was 18, he went to Glasgow and then to London to learn the trade of a mathematical instrument maker. In 1757, Watt became instrument maker at the University of Glasgow.

In 1763, Watt received a model of a Newcomen *atmospheric* steam engine to repair. Although he made it work, Watt was not satisfied with the way it operated and set about to improve it. He obtained advice from students and professors at the university and discovered the principle of the separate condenser. Watt patented his discovery in 1769.

In the Newcomen engines, steam filled the cylinder space under the piston. The steam was then condensed, leaving a vacuum into which the piston was pushed by atmospheric pressure. This meant alternately heating and chilling the cylinder.

Watt reasoned that because steam was an elastic vapor, it would fill any container into which it was admitted. If the steam-filled cylinder opened into a separate, chilled container, steam would move into the container and condense, producing the vacuum in the cylinder without having to chill it. Watt spent several years trying to develop an operating engine of the new design. In 1774, he obtained the support of Matthew Boulton, an energetic Birmingham manufacturer. The two organized a company to rent the design of the new engine and to supervise its construction and operation. The firm succeeded. In 1782, Watt patented the *double-acting* steam engine, which used steam pressure to push a piston both ways. He also developed the *parallel motion linkage* to transmit the reciprocating motion of the piston to a rocking device called a *working beam.* The working beam in turn transferred the motion to a crank and flywheel to produce rotary motion.

Watt also invented a throttle valve, a governor for regulating engine speed, and many other devices. He did

Illustration of 1788 engine; Granger Collection

James Watt's steam engine, developed during the late 1700's, led to the widespread use of steam power by industry.

scientific research in chemistry and metallurgy and was one of the first people to suggest that water is a compound, not an element.

Watt retired a wealthy and respected man in 1800. The power unit the watt is named in his honor (see **Watt**).　　J. P. Hartman

See also **Automation** (Early automation); **Horsepower; Industrial Revolution** (The steam engine); **Invention** (picture); **Steam engine** (History).

Additional resources

Champion, Neil. *James Watt*. Heinemann Lib., 2001. Younger readers.
Dickinson, Henry W. *James Watt*. Macmillan, 1936. A classic biography.
Sproule, Anna. *James Watt*. 1992. Reprint. Blackbirch Pr., 2001. Younger readers.

Watteau, *wah TOH,* **Antoine,** *an TWAHN* (1684-1721), a French painter, developed a style and subject matter that began the Rococo movement. Watteau's specialty was the small, intimate painting called the *fête galante* (elegant party) or *fête champetre* (country party). In these works, elegant young people wear shimmering satins and silks. They play music, dance, talk, and fall in love in rich, leafy garden settings. Watteau also painted portraits of characters from the French theater.

Watteau's popularity was part of a reaction against the large, cold academic paintings of serious subjects that dominated French art about 1700. When Watteau applied for admission to the Royal Academy of Painting and Sculpture, he was given the unprecedented honor of choosing his own subject matter for his admission picture. Watteau painted *The Island of Cythera* (1717). The painting shows lovers who have traveled to Cythera, the island of Aphrodite, the Greek goddess of love. They prepare to board boats to return to the everyday world. The scene reflects a mood of melancholy as the lovers leave their paradise with regretful backward glances. The painting appears in **Painting** (Rococo painting).

Jean Antoine Watteau was born on Oct. 10, 1684, in Valenciennes. He moved to Paris in 1702. As a youth, he worked for a patron, the collector Pierre Crozat. Later, Watteau became one of the first major painters to operate outside the patronage system and live by selling his works through a dealer.　　Ann Friedman

See also **Rococo**.

Wattmeter is an instrument used to measure electric power. The most commonly used type of wattmeter is called an *electrodynamic wattmeter.* This device has two coils of wire. A *fixed* coil is arranged to receive the current of the circuit to be measured. A *movable* coil, supported by jeweled pivots that permit it to turn, is arranged to receive a current proportional to the voltage of the circuit to be measured. When the circuit is energized, the magnetic fields produced by the currents make the movable coil try to turn so that its axis is parallel to the axis of the fixed coil. Springs stop it in a position that depends on the power in the circuit. A pointer shows the power in watts on a scale.　　Gregory Benford

Watts, Isaac (1674-1748), an English clergyman, wrote over 700 hymns and psalms. He also wrote theological treatises, volumes of sermons, and books on ethics, psychology, and teaching. He was considered one of the greatest preachers of his time. Watts's best hymns are noted for simplicity of poetic structure, apt use of fig-

ures of speech, and emotional vitality. Some of them still appear in most English hymnals. He wrote "Joy to the World," "O God, Our Help in Ages Past," "When I Survey the Wondrous Cross," and "There Is a Land of Pure Delight." He adapted many Old Testament psalms to a Christian viewpoint. Watts was born on July 17, 1674, in Southampton, England.　　Leonard W. Van Camp

See also **Hymn** (History).

Watts, J. C., Jr. (1957-   ), a Republican from Oklahoma, served as a member of the United States House of Representatives from 1995 to 2003. He was chairman of the House Republican Conference from 1999 to 2003. In that post, he dealt mainly with party organization. He was the first African American since the late 1800's to hold a House leadership post in the Republican Party.

Julius Caesar Watts, Jr., often called J. C., was born on Nov. 18, 1957, in Eufaula, Oklahoma. He graduated from the University of Oklahoma in 1981 and played professional football in Canada from 1981 to 1986. In 1990, he was elected to the Oklahoma Corporation Commission, which regulates gas and oil utilities. He became the first African American to win a statewide elective office in Oklahoma. Watts was ordained a Southern Baptist minister in 1993.　　Jackie Koszczuk

Watusi. See **Tutsi**.

Waugh, *waw,* **Evelyn,** *EEV lihn* (1903-1966), was an English author best known for his satirical novels about wealthy London society. He also wrote novels that combined comic satire with spiritual and religious themes.

In his novels, Waugh explored the pretentious and absurd qualities he saw in ambitious, upper middle-class English people. Waugh's characters were often only thinly disguised portraits of actual people who were well known in England during the mid-1900's. Waugh strongly believed that the upper classes should have special rights and privileges. But his novels reflect his belief that the behavior of the upper classes was sometimes heartless and superficial. Waugh's first satirical novel was *Decline and Fall* (1928). His other important satires include *Vile Bodies* (1930), *Black Mischief* (1932), and *A Handful of Dust* (1934).

Waugh converted to Roman Catholicism in 1930. The novels written after his conversion show an increasing concern with religious questions. Although Waugh continued to write such humorous satires as *The Loved One* (1948), he also wrote more serious, searching novels. The most famous is *Brideshead Revisited* (1945), a study of an aristocratic Catholic family. Waugh's other later novels include the autobiographical *The Ordeal of Gilbert Pinfold* (1957) and three related novels about World War II. These books are *Men at Arms* (1952), *Officers and Gentlemen* (1955), and *Unconditional Surrender* (American title *The End of the Battle,* 1961).

Waugh also wrote much nonfiction, including travel books, biographies, and essays. In his autobiography, *A Little Learning* (1964), he described his childhood and youth. Waugh's *Diaries* (1976) and *Letters* (1980), published after his death, are filled with gossip and personal opinion that is often malicious, snobbish, or prejudiced. *The Complete Stories of Evelyn Waugh* was published in 1999. Evelyn Arthur St. John Waugh was born on Oct. 28, 1903, in London. Alec Waugh (1898-1981), Evelyn's older brother, was a popular English novelist and travel writer.　　James Douglas Merritt

Waves are disturbances in water, air, or another substance, or in a field of force. Waves on water are perhaps the most familiar example, but sound and light also travel in waves. Waves carry energy from place to place and can also transmit information.

It is easy to generate a wave. If you throw a stone into a large, still pond, a series of disturbances will travel outward from the point where the stone enters the water. The disturbances will be expanding, ring-shaped waves, all with the same center—the entry point of the stone.

Energy produces the disturbances, and the disturbances carry energy. The movement of the stone from your hand to the water's surface carries both matter—

that is, the stone—and energy. As the stone penetrates the surface, energy carried by the stone displaces some water. The water closest to where the stone entered rises and then falls, producing a ring-shaped disturbance with the stone's entry point at its center. The falling water displaces other nearby water, causing another sequence of rising and falling, which in turn causes still others. As a result, a wave travels outward as an expanding ring. But the water closest to the stone's entry point has enough energy to rise and fall again several times. So a series of circular waves travel outward.

Another simple wave experiment involves a rope. Ask two people to hold the ends of the rope. When one person moves an end of the rope up and down sharply, en-

The shape of a wave

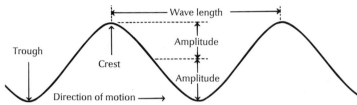

Many waves resemble hills and valleys. Scientists have various terms to describe waves. They call the hills *crests* and the valleys *troughs*. The *amplitude* is a measure of how much the medium carrying the wave rises or falls from its usual position. *Wavelength* is the distance between comparable points on two waves next to each other.

Solitary wave

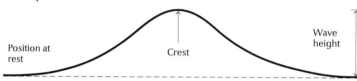

A solitary wave, or *soliton,* unlike an ordinary wave, consists of a single crest with no trough. A solitary wave also holds its shape much longer than an ordinary wave does. Solitary waves often form in shallow water channels.

Transverse wave

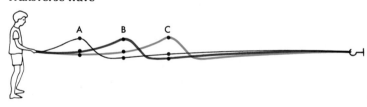

Transverse waves cause individual particles of the medium to move up and down while the wave moves forward. As a single wave moves down the rope away from the boy, the crest passes from point A to point B and then to point C. But the three points themselves do not move along the rope.

Standing wave

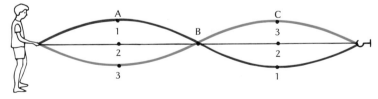

Standing waves do not move along the medium. Instead, they vibrate in a certain whole number of loops. To make two loops, the boy makes a wave with a wavelength equal to the length of the rope. Then he holds his end still. Points A and C on the loops move, but point B—between them—does not move.

Longitudinal wave

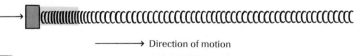

Longitudinal waves, also called *compressional waves,* cause individual particles of the medium to move back and forth. Unlike transverse waves, the particles move in the same direction the wave moves, not across the direction of wave motion. If one end of a stretched spring receives a sharp push, a longitudinal wave travels along the spring. The wave moves the spring's coils closer together when it passes along them. After it passes, the coils move farther apart again.

A *World Book* science project

The purpose of this project is to learn about the behavior of waves by studying water waves in a ripple tank. Wave behavior such as reflection, diffraction, and interference is shown in the photos taken of a homemade ripple tank. Experiment with various objects in the tank to see how they affect the motion of the waves.

To make a ripple tank, cut a strip of window screening to fit the inside edge of a baking dish. Then tape a layer of gauze inside the screening as shown. Fill the tank about one-third full of water and place the round stick near one end. Drop water from a medicine dropper or slightly lift one end of the tank and drop it to make waves. Two round-headed pins in a bar of soap will make waves that come from two points. Attach the soap to a yardstick or meter rule with rubber bands. Then set the soap over the tank so that the pins just touch the water when the yardstick or rule vibrates up and down.

Materials needed

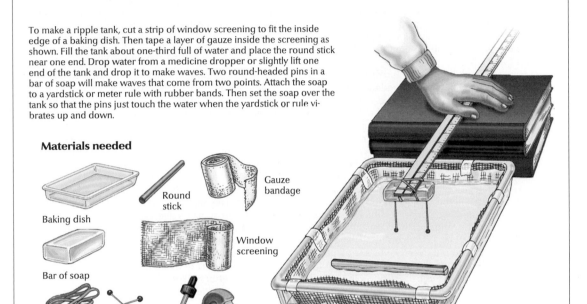

Baking dish

Round stick

Gauze bandage

Bar of soap

Window screening

Rubber bands

Round-headed pins

Medicine dropper

Adhesive tape

WORLD BOOK illustration by George Hamblin, Steven Edmund and C

Wave patterns in a ripple tank

Reflected waves form curved arches near the barrier that reflected them. The original waves form nearly complete circles near the top of the picture.

Curved diffracted waves in the top half of the picture resulted when parts of parallel waves passed through the small slit in the barrier.

Interfering waves cancel each other along the faint gray lines coming from the center. They strengthen themselves where the bright dashed lines occur.

WORLD BOOK photos

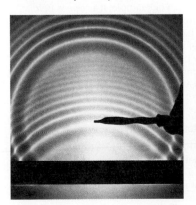

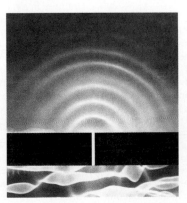

ergy moves from that person's hand and travels through the rope. The person at the other end will feel the incoming energy move his or her hand. As the energy passes through the rope, the rope moves up and down, but does not move forward.

Scientists call the material in which waves travel the *wave medium*. Water is the medium for water waves, and the rope is the medium for rope waves. Waves cause little overall displacement of their medium unless the disturbances become unusually large. For example, water waves travel horizontally across the surface of the water, but usually almost all the motion of the water itself is vertical.

Light waves and other kinds of electromagnetic waves are disturbances in a nonmaterial medium—*fields* of electric and magnetic force. In physics, a field is a region of space in which a particular kind of force can be felt. For example, a magnetic field is a region in which the force of magnetism can be felt. A magnet produces such a field in the space around itself.

Radio waves are another kind of electromagnetic wave. These waves can be controlled to carry information. Radio and television broadcasts and cellular telephone messages travel through the air on radio waves.

Waves may be one-, two-, or three-dimensional. Rope waves travel along the length of the rope and are one-dimensional. Water waves generated by a falling stone form circles that spread out over the surface of the pond. These waves are two-dimensional. Sound originates at a point and travels equally strongly in all directions. Sound waves are spherical and three-dimensional.

Types of waves

There are two main types of waves, longitudinal and transverse, depending on the motion of the medium. In *transverse waves*, the medium moves perpendicular to the direction in which the wave travels. For example, a rope wave is a transverse wave because the rope moves up and down while the wave moves from one end of the rope to the other. Light waves and other electromagnetic waves are also transverse waves.

Waves that travel in the same direction that the medium moves are *longitudinal waves*. Longitudinal waves require a medium that can be compressed. You can generate a longitudinal wave in a stretched spring by squeezing and then releasing a few coils at one end of the spring. Sound waves and some *seismic* (earthquake-generated) waves are longitudinal waves.

Measuring waves

Waves are usually measured by their amplitude, height, frequency, and wavelength. We can determine the size of a wave by measuring the maximum distance that the wave medium moves from its usual position. For example, as rope waves travel through a rope, the rope forms a wavy line. The highest point on the line is called the *wave crest,* and the lowest point is the *wave trough*. The vertical distance from the crest to the level of the rope at rest is the *wave amplitude*.

The distance from the usual position of the rope to the bottom of the trough may differ from the amplitude. When water waves move toward shore, for example, their crests become higher and sharper, while their troughs become shallower and wider. In this situation,

the size of a wave is measured by *wave height,* the vertical distance from the crest to the trough.

The number of waves that pass a given point in a given time is called the *frequency* of the series of waves. By moving the free end of the rope up and down faster, for example, we increase the frequency of the waves because more waves pass any point in a given time.

As the frequency is increased, the distance between the two adjacent wave crests or troughs is shortened. This distance is called *wavelength*. The shorter the wavelength, the higher the frequency.

How waves move

The simplest waves rise and fall with a fixed frequency and wavelength. Such waves are called *simple harmonic waves*. But most wave motions are combinations of several waves with different frequencies and wavelengths.

Combined waves are either *nondispersive* or *dispersive*. In a nondispersive wave, all the individual waves travel at the same speed, regardless of their frequency. Water waves in shallow water are nondispersive. Their speed depends only on the square root of the depth of the water. The higher this number is, the more rapid are the waves. In a dispersive wave, the individual waves travel at speeds that depend on their frequencies. The longer wavelengths tend to race ahead of the shorter ones, making the combined wave spread out. This spreading occurs in much the same way that a tight pack of racehorses spreads out as the faster horses pull out in front of the slower ones. Water waves in deep water are dispersive.

Other factors tend to compress waves. When ocean waves approach the shore, for example, the shallow bottom may slow down the waves and cause them to pile up, much as a loose pack of racehorses bunches up when the front-runners suddenly encounter rough terrain.

Under the right conditions, the effects of dispersion and compression balance out, producing an unusual wave called a *solitary wave* or *soliton*. A soliton has a single humplike crest but no trough. Solitons do not readily disperse, but instead keep their size and shape much longer than ordinary waves do. Solitons often form in shallow water channels.

Most waves, such as water waves, travel from one place to another. These waves are called *progressive waves*. Under certain conditions, however, waves can be trapped in a medium. For example, if a rope is held at both ends and plucked, the energy in the waves cannot leave the rope at either end. This trapping of waves results in patterns of vibration called *standing waves*. Standing waves vibrate at a certain frequency but do not move along the medium. The vibrations of guitar strings and violin strings are standing waves. Standing waves can also occur on a surface, such as a drumhead, or in an enclosed space, such as a pipe of a pipe organ.

Changes in wave motion

Wave motion changes when waves move from one medium to another and when one wave meets another.

Refraction and reflection. *Refraction* is a change in wave direction when waves pass from one medium into another. When waves leave one medium and enter another, some of the energy in the waves is reflected and some is transmitted to the new medium. The amount of energy reflected and transmitted depends on the *angle of incidence*—that is, the angle at which the incoming wave strikes the medium. It also depends on the density and other properties of the two mediums. The direction taken by the transmitted wave, called the *refracted wave,* also depends on the angle of incidence and the characteristics of the two mediums.

Diffraction is the spreading out of waves as they pass through an opening or by the edge of an obstacle. An expanding ring of water waves moves away from a stone dropped into a pond. As the ring becomes larger, any short part of the *wave front* (the outside edge of the ring) becomes a nearly straight line. But if the wave front passes through a small slit in a barrier, the wave coming out the other side will spread out from the slit in a curve.

Diffraction occurs because each point on the surface of a wave is the source of small, curved waves called *wavelets* that move outward in all directions. The wavelets along the front combine to make the straight-line wave front. But the slit allows only a few wavelets through. The wavelets on either side of the slit are blocked, so the wave front is no longer straight.

Interference. Where the crests of two waves with the same frequency pass the same point at the same time, the waves are said to be *in phase* with each other—that is, their crests and troughs coincide. The two waves combine to produce a single wave with a larger amplitude. The amplitude of the combined wave equals the sum of the amplitudes of the two original waves. Scientists say that *constructive interference* takes place.

If the crest of one wave passes a point at the same time as the trough of the other, however, the waves combine to produce a wave with a smaller amplitude. The amplitude of the combined wave equals the difference between the amplitudes of the original waves. *Destructive interference* occurs.   Philip L.-F. Liu

Related articles in *World Book* include:
Diffraction
Earthquake (How an earthquake spreads)
Electromagnetic waves
Hertz
Interference
Light (The nature of light)
Microwave
Ocean (Waves)
Polarized light
Radar (How radar works)
Radio (How radio programs are broadcast)
Reflection
Refraction
Shock wave
Short waves
Sound (The nature of sound)
Tsunami

WAVES. See Navy, United States (Women in the Navy).

Wax is a fatty substance that is widely used as a protective coating for various surfaces. It resists air, water, and chemical change. Most wax is solid at room temperature. It softens when heated. The word *wax* comes from the Anglo-Saxon word *weax,* meaning *beeswax.*

Manufacturers produce three chief kinds of wax: (1) mineral, (2) animal, and (3) vegetable. Most manufacturers blend two or more types of wax to give their product the desired qualities.

Mineral wax. Most wax comes from petroleum. Manufacturers chill and filter oil and then use various chemical processes to separate the wax from it. There are three major kinds of petroleum wax: (1) *paraffin wax,* (2) *microcrystalline wax,* and (3) *petrolatum.* These waxes differ in color, hardness, and melting point.

Petroleum wax resists moisture and chemicals and has no odor or taste. It serves as a waterproof coating for such paper products as milk cartons and waxed paper. Petroleum wax also is used in making polishes for automobiles, floors, and furniture. It does not conduct electric current, and so it can serve as an electric insulator. Manufacturers use petroleum wax molds in casting jewelry and machinery parts.

Most candles are made from paraffin wax. Microcrystalline wax is used mostly in making paper for packaging. Petrolatum, also called *petroleum jelly,* is used in making cosmetics and medicines.

Other mineral waxes include *montan wax,* obtained from coal; *ozokerite,* made from shale; and *peat wax,* made from peat. *Synthetic* (artificially made) wax comes from glycol, a chemical obtained from petroleum. These waxes are usually blended with petroleum wax.

Animal wax is used alone or is blended with petroleum wax in making candles, polishes, and other products. Bees produce *beeswax* in building honeycombs. *Wool wax* comes from a greasy coating on unprocessed wool. *Lanolin,* a form of wool wax, is used in making cosmetics.

Vegetable wax. Many plants have a natural wax coating that protects them from heat and moisture. *Carnauba wax,* the hardest and most widely used vegetable wax, coats the leaves of the carnauba palm tree. It remains solid in hot weather and is an important ingredient in automobile wax and other polishes. Other vegetable waxes include *bayberry wax, candelilla wax, Japan wax,* and *sugar cane wax.*   Richard F. Blewitt

Related articles in *World Book* include:
Beeswax   Paraffin
Candle   Petrolatum
Carnauba wax   Spermaceti
Painting (Encaustic painting)

Wax myrtle is a large, fragrant evergreen shrub or small tree found along the eastern coast of the United States. It grows from southern New Jersey to southern Florida and as far west as Texas. It also is found in the West Indies. The wax myrtle grows up to 35 feet (11 meters) tall and has small, greenish flowers. The 2- to 4-inch (5- to 10-centimeter) leaves are covered with tiny amber to brown dots. The wax myrtle is grown as an ornamental shrub and does best in damp soil.   Walter S. Judd

Scientific classification. The wax myrtle belongs to the bayberry or wax myrtle family, Myricaceae. Its scientific name is *Myrica cerifera.*

Waxwing is a silky-feathered, grayish-brown bird that is larger than a sparrow, with a conspicuous crest or topknot. The waxwing has a band of yellow across the end of its tail. It has red, waxlike drops on its wing feathers.

The *cedar waxwing* is the best known of these birds. It lives in most parts of North America, as far north as central Canada and Labrador. These birds eat berries and fruits, and insects. They build bulky nests, usually in a fruit or shade tree. Many cedar waxwings are found on

Cedar waxwings live in most parts of North America. They build bulky nests and eat berries, fruits, and insects.

Ken Carmichael, Animals Animals

the islands of Lake Superior and around the lakes of Ontario and northern Minnesota in the summer. The birds cannot sing, but produce a soft, high-pitched whistle. The female lays three to five eggs, which are a pale bluish or purplish gray, speckled with black, brown, or purple. See **Bird** (picture: Birds of forests and woodlands).

The *Bohemian waxwing* is a slightly larger bird. It has yellow marks on its wings and reddish-brown undertail feathers. This bird lives in the northern latitudes of the world. In winter, the Bohemian waxwing appears in the northwestern and central northern United States and northern Europe. The *Siberian waxwing* lives in southeastern Siberia and Japan.   Fred J. Alsop III

Scientific classification. Waxwings belong to the waxwing family, Bombycillidae. The cedar waxwing is *Bombycilla cedrorum;* the Bohemian, *B. garrulus,* and the Siberian, *B. japonica.*

See also **Bird** (How birds feed; picture: A Bohemian waxwing).

Wayne, Anthony (1745-1796), was an American officer in the Revolutionary War (1775-1783). He became known as "Mad Anthony" Wayne because of his reckless courage. He was the hero of the recapture of Stony Point, New York, a British post on the Hudson River, in 1779. Wayne commanded the attack, which was considered one of the most daring of the war.

Wayne was born on Jan. 1, 1745, in Chester County, Pennsylvania. He studied at a Philadelphia academy and eventually became a surveyor. A Philadelphia land company sent him to Nova Scotia in 1765 to oversee the surveying and settlement of land. He returned to Pennsylvania and served in the colonial assembly. When the war began in 1775, he raised a regiment for the Canadian campaign, and later com-

Pastel on paper (about 1796) by James Sharples, Sr.; Independence National Historical Park Collection, Philadelphia

"Mad Anthony" Wayne

manded the garrison at Ticonderoga.

In 1777, Wayne became a brigadier general and joined George Washington's army to take charge of the Pennsylvania line. He led a division at Brandywine, commanded the right wing at Germantown, and spent the winter with Washington at Valley Forge. Wayne led the advance attack at Monmouth the next year. In 1781, Wayne served with the Marquis de Lafayette against General Cornwallis, and took part in the siege of Yorktown. He later served in Georgia and South Carolina.

In 1783, Wayne became a brevet major general and then retired from the army. He represented Georgia in Congress in 1791, but the seat was declared vacant because of election irregularities. He returned to the army in 1791 as a major general and commander in chief. Wayne fought against a confederacy of Indian tribes in Ohio in 1794, defeating them at the Battle of Fallen Timbers. He made a treaty with the Indians in 1795 that secured a great tract of land for the United States. Wayne died at Presque Isle (now Erie, Pennsylvania) on Dec. 15, 1796.   Paul David Nelson

See also **Indian wars** (picture: Indian wars in America).

Wayne, John (1907-1979), an American motion-picture actor, became famous for his he-man roles. He starred in such Western films as *Red River* (1948) and in other action movies, including *Sands of Iwo Jima* (1949) and *The Quiet Man* (1952). He won an Academy Award for *True Grit* (1969). Wayne made over 150 movies.

Wayne was born Marion Robert Morrison on May 26, 1907, in Winterset, Iowa. He later used the middle name Mitchell, and at times may have used Michael. While attending the University of Southern California, he worked as a prop boy, and occasionally as an extra or stuntman. He played his first role in *Hangman's House* (1928). Wayne's first leading role was in *The Big Trail* (1930), a box office failure. He then worked mostly in low-budget Westerns until the late 1930's.

Warner Bros. Inc.

John Wayne

He became a star after director John Ford cast him in the classic Western movie *Stagecoach* (1939). His other notable films include *The Long Voyage Home* (1940), *The Spoilers* (1942), *She Wore a Yellow Ribbon* (1949), *The Searchers* (1956), *Rio Bravo* (1959), *The Comancheros* (1961), and *The Green Berets* (1968).   Rachel Gallagher

WCTU. See **Woman's Christian Temperance Union.**

Weakfish is a popular saltwater food and sport fish of the drum family. Dutch colonists of Manhattan Island named the weakfish, probably in reference to its soft flesh. The weakfish has a dark yellowish-green or bluish body with dark spots. It measures from 1 to 3 feet (30 to 90 centimeters) long or more. The weakfish is also called *squeteague* (pronounced *skwee TEEG)* or *gray sea trout.*

The weakfish lives along the Atlantic Coast of North America from Nova Scotia to Florida. It is usually found in shallow waters along open, sandy shores and in bays and estuaries. Weakfish often travel in large schools near the water's surface. Their food consists mainly of smaller fish, but includes crabs, shrimps, squids, and worms. Seatrouts are closely related to the weakfish and are often referred to as weakfish.

Scientific classification. The weakfish belongs to the drum family, Sciaenidae. The scientific name for the weakfish is *Cynoscion regalis.*   Tomio Iwamoto

Weapon. Weapons have played an important part in the history of humanity. They have helped people conquer vast areas of wilderness and defend their homes and families from enemies. Nations use weapons to carry on wars. They continue to develop new weapons that kill more and more people. Many people believe nuclear weapons are the greatest threat to humanity because of their destructive power.   Frances M. Lussier

Related articles in *World Book.* See **Firearm** and its list of *Related articles.* See also the following:

Explosives

Bomb	Detonator	Gunpowder	RDX
Bullet	Fragmentation	Nitroglycerin	Shrapnel
Cartridge	Fuse	Nuclear	TNT
Cordite	Grenade	weapon	Torpedo
Depth charge	Guncotton	PETN	

Other weapons

Ax	Catapult	Guided missile	Sling
Bayonet	Crossbow	Knife	Spear
Blowgun	Dagger	Mace	Sword
Boomerang	Flail	Rocket	Tomahawk
Bowie knife	Flame thrower		

Other related articles

Ammunition	Greek fire
Archery	Magazine
Arms control	Mine warfare
Arrowhead	Ordnance
Ballistics	Powder horn
Chemical-biological-	Shot tower
radiological warfare	

Weasel is a small furry animal that has a long, slender body and short legs. Weasels have alert black or dark brown eyes and small, rounded ears. They are found on every continent except Africa, Australia, and Antarctica. The *long-tailed weasel* grows from 12 to 18 inches (30 to 46 centimeters) long, and weighs up to 9 ounces (255 grams). The females are smaller and weigh 3 to 4 ounces (85 to 115 grams). The *ermine* is a type of small weasel. Male ermines grow from 9 to 13 inches (22 to 34 centimeters) long. The *least weasel* is the smallest flesh-eating animal in the world. It grows up to 10 inches (25 centimeters) long and weighs approximately 2 ounces (55 grams).

Most weasels have brownish, reddish-brown, or yellowish-brown fur on the back and sides, and white, yellowish, or tan fur on the underparts. In winter, the fur of weasels that live in cold climates changes to white, except for a black-tipped tail. The white fur provides camouflage in the snow. The black-tipped tail may catch the eye of an attacking predator, such as a hawk or owl, and cause the attacker to miss the weasel. Weasels found in Florida and the Southwestern United States sometimes have distinctive whitish or buff markings on the face.

Weasels have keen smell and vision. They are amazingly strong for their size and prey on mice and squirrels. They usually bite their victims on the neck or at the base of the skull. Weasels also eat earthworms, insects,

Bob and Clara Calhoun, Bruce Coleman Ltd.

A weasel is a small furry animal with a slender body and short legs. The *long-tailed* weasel is a common species in North America. During the winter, the long-tailed weasel has a coat of white fur, *above.* During the rest of the year, the animal's coat is brown, with light-colored fur on its underside, *below.*

frogs, lizards, rabbits, shrews, snakes, and birds. The weasel's slender body enables it to easily invade mouse burrows, rock crevices, and squirrel burrows. Weasels often raid chicken yards and kill more chickens than they need for food. As a result, many farmers dislike weasels even though they destroy farmyard pests. The weasel's chief enemies are great horned owls and people. Weasels, like skunks, discharge a foul-smelling liquid called *musk* when they are threatened or attacked.

Weasels live in a variety of environments. They make dens in rock piles, under tree stumps, and in abandoned rodent burrows. They sometimes catch food in their dens and make nests using the fur and feathers of their victims. Weasels are most active at night. Most females have four to eight young born at a time.

Scientific classification. Weasels belong to the weasel family, Mustelidae. The scientific name for the long-tailed weasel is *Mustela frenata.* The ermine is *M. erminea,* and the least weasel is *M. nivalis.*   Charles A. Long

Related articles in *World Book* include:

Badger	Mink	Sable
Ermine	Otter	Skunk
Ferret	Polecat	Tayra
Grison	Ratel	Wolverine
Marten		

The Weather Channel® (WORLD BOOK photo by Steven Spicer)

© Gordon Garradd, SPL from Photo Researchers

Weather affects people's lives every day. Weather reports and forecasts help people decide what to wear, plan trips and other outdoor activities, and even avoid dangers, such as lightning storms, *above*. A television weather reporter explains current conditions in Texas and Oklahoma to a nationwide audience, *left*.

Weather

Weather is the state of the atmosphere at some place and time. We describe the weather in many ways. For example, we may refer to the temperature of the air, whether the sky is clear or cloudy, how hard the wind is blowing, or whether it is raining or snowing. At any given time, the weather is fair in some places, while it rains or snows in others. In some places it is warm, and in others it is cold.

Earth is not the only planet with a variety of weather conditions. Every planet in the solar system except Mercury and perhaps Pluto has enough of an atmosphere to support weather systems. In addition, Titan, a moon of the planet Saturn, has such an atmosphere. Pluto is so far away that little is known about its atmosphere. The remainder of this article discusses the weather on Earth.

Joseph M. Moran, the contributor of this article, is Professor of Earth Sciences at the University of Wisconsin at Green Bay.

The weather affects our lives every day. For example, it can have an impact on what type of clothing we wear and how we spend our free time. Weather also affects agriculture, transportation, and industry. Freezing temperatures can damage citrus crops in Florida or Spain, causing a rise in the price of oranges at the grocery store. Winter snows often create hazardous driving conditions. Thick fog may slow traffic on the roads and cause delays at airports. Our use of air conditioning during heat waves and heating during cold weather means that utility companies must supply more power at those times. Severe weather, such as tornadoes, hurricanes, and blizzards, can damage property and take lives.

Because of weather's importance, *meteorologists* (scientists who study the atmosphere and the weather) have developed ways to forecast weather conditions. Forecasts for the next 12 to 24 hours are correct more than 80 percent of the time. Long-range forecasts for the next week or month are less accurate. These forecasts indicate general trends, such as whether or not temperatures are expected to be warmer or colder than normal.

Closely related to weather is climate. Climate is the

weather of a place averaged over a length of time. Scientists determine a region's climate by examining its vegetation, average monthly and annual temperature, and average monthly and annual precipitation. The earth's surface is a patchwork of climate zones. For example, in various parts of the earth, we find tropical rain forests; deserts; prairies; forests of cone-bearing trees; frozen, treeless plains; and coverings of glacial ice. Unlike weather changes, which can occur in minutes, climate changes generally take many years. See **Climate**.

What causes weather

Weather takes place in the atmosphere, the layer of air that surrounds the earth. Air is a mixture of gases and tiny suspended particles.

The most plentiful gas is nitrogen, which accounts for about 78 percent of the air we breathe. The second most plentiful gas is oxygen, at 21 percent. The remaining 1 percent consists of a variety of gases. In spite of their low concentrations, some of these gases play vital roles. For example, the atmosphere contains little *water vapor*—an invisible gas produced when water evaporates. Yet, without water vapor there would be no clouds, no rain, no snow, and no plants or animals.

Most of the tiny particles floating in the atmosphere are too small to be visible. They are solid or liquid and come from a number of sources, such as the wind erosion of soil, volcanic eruptions, and the release of pollutants by smokestacks and automobile tailpipes.

Most weather occurs in the lowest portion of the atmosphere, called the *troposphere*. The troposphere extends from Earth's surface up to an altitude of about 6 to 12 miles (10 to 19 kilometers). Three key factors that determine the weather in the troposphere are air temperature, air pressure, and humidity.

Air temperature is a measure of the energy of motion of the air's gas molecules. The factors most responsible for the heating and cooling of the atmosphere are radiation arriving from the sun and radiation flowing from the earth.

Weather terms

Air mass is a large volume of air that is relatively uniform in temperature and humidity.

Front is a narrow zone of transition between air masses that differ in temperature or humidity. Most changes in the weather occur along fronts.

High-pressure area is an area in which the weight of the atmosphere on the earth is relatively high. High-pressure areas usually have clear skies.

Humidity is a measure of the amount of water vapor in the air.

Low-pressure area is an area in which the weight of the atmosphere on the earth is relatively low. Low-pressure areas usually have cloudy skies.

Precipitation is moisture that falls from clouds in the form of rain, snow, sleet, or hail.

Temperature is a measure of the heat energy of the oxygen and other gases in the air.

Wind is the movement of air. Air tends to move from a high-pressure area to a low-pressure area. Winds are named for the direction from which they blow. For example, a north wind blows from the north.

The sun continually sends energy into space as electromagnetic radiation. One kind of solar radiation is visible light. The other forms of solar electromagnetic radiation are invisible to human beings. They include *infrared* (heat) rays and ultraviolet rays. About 30 percent of the solar electromagnetic radiation that reaches the atmosphere is reflected back into space, mostly by clouds. The atmosphere and the earth's surface absorb the remaining 70 percent, becoming warmer.

The warmed earth cools by radiating infrared rays. Some of this radiation travels directly into space. The atmosphere absorbs almost all the remainder as it streams off the surface of the planet. This absorption of radiation, known as the *greenhouse effect,* makes the air near the earth's surface about 59 Fahrenheit degrees (33 Celsius degrees) warmer than it would be otherwise.

The atmosphere also sheds heat energy by radiating infrared rays. Some of this infrared radiation flows down to the surface, while the remainder travels out into space.

Air temperature generally varies from day to night and from season to season because of changes in the amount of radiation heating the earth's atmosphere. For example, days usually are warmer than nights because the earth receives the heating rays of the sun only during the day. At night, infrared radiation from the planet streams off into space, and the air temperature drops.

Air temperature also changes with the seasons. Except near the equator, where temperatures remain fairly constant the year around, summers are warmer than winters. In the summer, the sun is higher in the sky, and days are longer. When the sun is higher above the horizon, the intensity of the sunlight striking the earth's surface increases. More hours of sunlight in summer also mean more solar heating.

Altitude also affects air temperature. Within the troposphere, the air temperature generally drops 3.5 Fahrenheit degrees per 1,000 feet of elevation (6.5 Celsius degrees per 1,000 meters of elevation). Thus, it is usually colder on top of a mountain than in the surrounding lowlands.

Air pressure is the weight per unit of area of a column of air that reaches to the top of the atmosphere. Air pressure always decreases with increasing altitude because as you move higher there is less and less air above you. Air pressure is, on average, highest at sea level and drops to about half its sea-level value at an average altitude of about 18,000 feet (5,500 meters).

Air pressure also changes from place to place across the earth's surface. Part of this change is due to differences in land elevation. Most of the remainder is caused by changes in air temperature. Cold air is relatively dense—that is, it has more air molecules per unit volume—and so it exerts relatively high pressure. Warm air is less dense and exerts relatively low pressure.

Regions where air pressure is relatively high usually experience fair weather, while regions where air pressure is relatively low experience cloudy, stormy weather. Generally, the weather stays fair or improves if air pressure rises. If the air pressure falls steadily, however, the weather may turn cloudy and rainy or snowy.

Air moves from areas where the air pressure is relatively high toward areas where the air pressure is relatively low. This movement of air is what we call wind.

Weather extremes around the world

Highest temperature recorded was 136 °F (58 °C) at Al Aziziyah, Libya, on Sept. 13, 1922. The highest temperature recorded in North America was 134 °F (57 °C) in Death Valley, California, on July 10, 1913.

Lowest temperature observed on the earth's surface was −128.6 °F (−89.2 °C) at Vostok Station in Antarctica, on July 21, 1983. The record low in the United States was −80 °F (−62 °C) at Prospect Creek, Alaska, on Jan. 23, 1971.

Highest air pressure at sea level was recorded at Agata, in Siberia in the Soviet Union (now Russia), on Dec. 31, 1968. The barometric pressure reached 32.01 inches (81.31 centimeters or 108.4 kilopascals).

Lowest air pressure at sea level was estimated at 25.69 inches (65.25 centimeters or 87.00 kilopascals), during a typhoon in the Philippine Sea on Oct. 12, 1979.

Strongest winds measured on the earth's surface were recorded at Mount Washington, New Hampshire, on April 12, 1934. For five minutes, the wind blew at 188 miles (303 kilometers) per hour. One gust reached 231 miles (372 kilometers) per hour.

Driest place on earth is Arica, Chile. In one 59-year period, the average annual rainfall was $\frac{3}{100}$ inch (0.76 millimeter). No rain fell in Arica for a 14-year period.

Heaviest rainfall recorded in 24 hours was 72.00 inches (182.88 centimeters) on Jan. 7-8, 1966, at Foc-Foc, on the island of Reunion, a part of France, in the Indian Ocean. The most rain in one year was at Cherrapunji, India. From August 1860 to July 1861, 1,401.78 inches (2,646.12 centimeters) fell. The wettest place is Mount Waialeale, on the island of Kauai in Hawaii, with an average annual rainfall of 460 inches (1,168 centimeters).

Heaviest snowfall recorded in North America in 24 hours—76 inches (193 centimeters)—fell at Silver Lake, Colorado, on April 14-15, 1921. The most snow recorded in North America in one winter—1,122 inches (2,850 centimeters)—fell at Rainier Paradise Ranger Station in Washington in 1971-1972.

Largest hailstone in the United States fell in Coffeyville, Kansas, on Sept. 3, 1970. The hailstone measured $17\frac{1}{2}$ inches (44.5 centimeters) in circumference, and it weighed $1\frac{2}{3}$ pounds (0.76 kilogram).

Source: *Weather and Climate Extremes*, U.S. Army Topographic Engineering Center.

Humidity is a measure of the amount of water vapor in the air. There is an upper limit to this amount. Air that contains its maximum amount of water vapor is described as *saturated.* The amount of water vapor the air can hold increases as the air temperature rises and decreases as the temperature falls. Thus, saturated warm air has more water vapor than saturated cold air.

Weather reports commonly describe the amount of water vapor in the air in terms of the *relative humidity.* Relative humidity compares the amount of water vapor in the air with the amount of water vapor at saturation. It is expressed as a percentage. If the relative humidity is 50 percent, the amount of water vapor in the air is half of what it would be if the air were saturated. Lowering the air temperature increases the relative humidity.

If the relative humidity is 100 percent, the air is saturated. When air becomes saturated, water vapor begins to condense into droplets of water. Condensation is the opposite of evaporation. It is a change from a gas to a liquid. If the air is cold enough, at saturation the water vapor develops into tiny ice crystals.

If condensation occurs on a cold surface such as the surface of an automobile window at night, dew or frost forms. Dew and frost do not fall from the sky like rain or snow. Rather, they form when air in contact with a relatively cold surface is chilled to saturation. The same process occurs when small drops of water appear on the outside of a cold soft-drink can on a hot summer day. The temperature to which air must be cooled to reach saturation and produce dew is known as the *dew point.*

When saturation occurs within the atmosphere, water vapor condenses into droplets (or develops into tiny ice crystals) that form clouds. A cloud that is in contact with the earth's surface is known as fog. Most clouds occur within the troposphere. Because air temperature drops with increasing altitude within the troposphere, high clouds are extremely cold and consist mostly of ice crystals. The crystals give these clouds a fuzzy appearance. Low clouds are warmer and generally are composed of droplets. These clouds appear to have sharper edges.

Clouds usually form where air moves upward. As air ascends, it encounters lower and lower pressure. Air responds to lower pressure by expanding. Whenever gases expand, they cool. As air cools, its relative humidity increases until it reaches saturation and clouds form.

Where air moves downward, clouds usually do not develop. Descending air is compressed, it warms up, and its relative humidity decreases. Saturation is not possible, and so clouds do not form.

Weather systems

Meteorologists classify weather systems according to their size and how long they last. The two largest and longest-lasting types of systems are *planetary-scale systems* and *synoptic-scale systems.* Planetary-scale systems are the belts of winds that circle the globe and may blow in the same direction for weeks at a time. Synoptic-scale systems cover a portion of a continent or ocean and last up to a week or so. The term *synoptic* comes from a Greek word meaning *a general view.*

Two briefer and smaller types of systems are *mesoscale systems* and *microscale systems.* Mesoscale systems may last an hour or less and are so small they may affect the weather of only part of a city. Examples include thunderstorms and sea breezes. Microscale systems, such as tornadoes, usually last only several minutes and affect an area not much larger than a few football fields.

Planetary-scale systems. Suppose that the earth did not rotate and that the noon sun was always directly above the equator. Air temperatures would be highest at the equator and decrease toward the poles. Cold air is denser than warm air. Thus, air pressure would be higher at the poles and lower at the equator. Because air moves from areas of high pressure to areas of low pressure, cold air would sweep toward the equator, where it would push the warm air upward. In the upper atmosphere, the warm air would move toward the poles, cool, and sink over the poles. Thus, the planetary-scale circulation of wind would consist of two huge cells, one in each hemisphere.

The real earth rotates. Rotation of the earth on its axis causes winds that blow long distances—thousands of miles or kilometers—to shift direction gradually. This shift is known as the *Coriolis effect,* which causes winds in the Northern Hemisphere to shift to the right and winds in the Southern Hemisphere to shift to the left. In

Cirrus clouds occur at heights that can exceed 35,000 feet (10,700 meters). The air is so cold at these altitudes that the clouds consist entirely of ice crystals.

© Joseph M. Moran

the Northern Hemisphere, for example, winds blowing southward shift to the west. Winds blowing northward shift to the east.

Rotation of the planet also causes winds near the earth's surface to split into three belts in each hemisphere. These three belts are (1) the trade winds, which blow near the equator, between 30° north latitude and 30° south latitude; (2) the *westerlies* (winds from the west), which blow in the middle latitudes between 30° and 60° north and south of the equator; and (3) the polar winds, which blow in the Arctic and Antarctic, from 60° latitude toward the poles.

Trade winds north of the equator blow from the northeast. South of the equator, they blow from the southeast. The trade winds of the two hemispheres meet near the equator, causing air to rise. Rising air cools, and its relative humidity therefore increases. Thus, a band of cloudy, rainy weather circles the globe near the equator.

Westerlies blow from the southwest in the Northern Hemisphere and from the northwest in the Southern Hemisphere. Westerlies and trade winds blow away from the 30° latitude belt. Over broad regions centered at 30° latitude, surface winds are light or calm, and air slowly descends. Air warms as it descends, and its relative humidity decreases, making clouds and precipitation unlikely. As a result, fair, dry weather characterizes much of the 30° latitude belt.

Polar winds are *easterlies* (winds from the east). They blow from the northeast in the Arctic and from the southeast in the Antarctic. In the Northern Hemisphere, the boundary between the cold polar easterlies and the mild westerlies is known as the *polar front.* A *front* is a narrow zone of transition, usually between a mass of cold air and a mass of warm air. Storms develop and move along the polar front, bringing cloudiness, rain, or snow.

Important seasonal changes take place in the earth's wind patterns. Wind belts shift toward the poles in spring and toward the equator in fall. For example, during the fall, the polar front in the Northern Hemisphere often moves from Canada down to the continental United States.

Planetary-scale winds control the direction of movement of smaller-scale weather systems. For example, in the tropics, trade winds generally steer hurricanes and other weather systems from east to west. In middle latitudes, westerlies move weather systems from west to east. The westerlies are particularly vigorous near the top of the troposphere and just over the polar front. This corridor of exceptionally strong winds is known as a *jet stream.* The jet stream of the polar front supplies energy to developing storms and then moves them rapidly along the front.

Synoptic-scale systems include air masses, fronts, lows, and highs. The movement of these systems causes the day-to-day changes in the weather of Europe, the continental United States, and other regions in the middle latitudes.

Air masses. An *air mass* is a huge volume of air covering thousands of square miles or kilometers that is relatively uniform in temperature and humidity. The properties of an air mass depend on where it forms. Air masses that develop at high latitudes are colder than air masses that form over low latitudes. Air masses that form over the ocean are relatively humid, and those that form over land are relatively dry. The four basic types of air masses are (1) cold and dry, (2) cold and humid, (3) warm and dry, and (4) warm and humid.

Across North America, warm air masses move north and northeastward, and cold air masses move south and southeastward. Maritime polar air, which is cool and humid, forms over the North Pacific and North Atlantic. This air mass brings low clouds and precipitation to the Pacific Northwest, New England, and eastern Canada. Continental polar air, which is dry and cold in winter and dry and mild in summer, forms in north-central Canada. Arctic air, which is dry and much colder than continental polar air, forms over the snow-covered regions north of about 60° latitude in the Northern Hemisphere. The movement of Arctic air to the south causes the bone-numbing cold waves that sweep across the Great Plains and Northeast in winter.

Most of the maritime tropical air that invades North America originates over the Gulf of Mexico and the tropical Atlantic. This warm, humid air mass brings oppressive summer heat waves to areas east of the Rocky Mountains. Continental tropical air forms over the deserts of Mexico and the southwest United States.

How air masses affect the weather

The weather in the Northern Hemisphere is greatly influenced by the movements of *air masses*. These enormous bodies of air form over areas in which the temperature is fairly constant. The air masses take on the temperature of these areas. As the masses move across great distances, they influence the weather below. Arctic air can cause dangerously cold weather as it sweeps south. Continental polar air is dry and cold in the winter and dry and mild in the summer. Maritime polar air masses, which are cool and humid, bring low clouds and precipitation to coastal areas. Warm and humid maritime tropical air can cause oppressive heat waves in the summer.

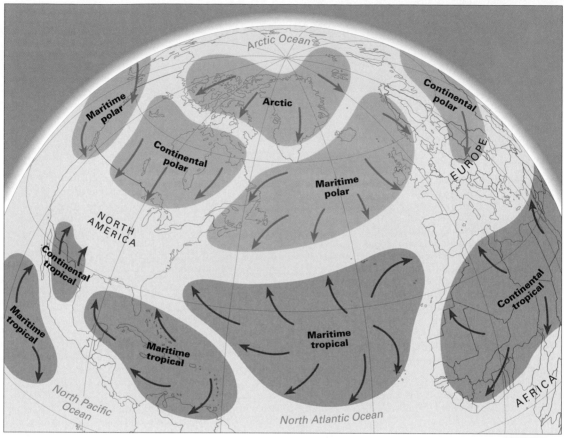

WORLD BOOK map

In summer, this hot, dry air mass surges over Texas and other parts of the American Southwest.

As an air mass travels from place to place, its temperature and humidity can change. For example, air over the Pacific Ocean west of North America is mild and humid. If that air mass moves eastward, it is forced up the slopes of the coastal mountain ranges. Air temperature drops, the relative humidity increases to saturation, clouds form, and rain or snow develops. As the air travels down the opposite slopes of the mountain ranges, the air temperature rises, the relative humidity decreases, and clouds thin out or vanish.

This process repeats with each mountain range the air mass encounters as it moves eastward. By the time it reaches the Western Plains, the air mass has become considerably drier and milder. This modified air mass, known as Pacific air, brings mild, dry weather to much of the central and eastern regions of the United States and Canada.

Fronts form where air masses meet. A front is a narrow zone of transition between air masses that differ in

temperature or humidity. In most cases, the air masses differ in temperature, so that the fronts are either warm or cold.

A *warm front* is the leading edge of an advancing warm air mass. Warm air is less dense than cold air, so warm air advances by riding up and over the retreating cold air. As the warm air ascends, its temperature drops, relative humidity increases, and clouds and perhaps precipitation form. In North America, clouds can extend hundreds of miles or kilometers to the north and northwest of a warm front. Rain or snow is usually light to moderate and may last 12 to 24 hours or longer.

A *cold front* is the leading edge of an advancing cold air mass. Cold air is denser than warm air, so that cold air advances by moving under and pushing up the retreating warm air. As warm air ascends, its temperature falls, relative humidity rises, and clouds and often precipitation develop. Clouds associated with a cold front typically form a narrow band along the front. Rain or snow falls in brief showers. If the cold front is fast-moving and well-defined by considerable temperature contrast across the front, thunderstorms are likely. Some of these thunderstorms could become severe and produce hail, torrential rains, or strong winds. Tornadoes also may develop from severe thunderstorms.

A front that stalls is known as a *stationary front.* The weather along a stationary front often consists of considerable cloudiness and light rain or snow.

Cold fronts move faster than warm fronts, so a cold front may catch up to and merge with a warm front. The warm air is lifted off the earth's surface, and the merged front is known as an *occluded front.* An occluded front sometimes moves very slowly and causes several days of considerable cloudiness and light precipitation.

Lows are areas of relatively low air pressure. The winds in a low pressure system bring contrasting air masses together to form fronts. For this reason, lows are sometimes described as the chief weather-makers of regions in the middle latitudes. Scientists use the term *cyclone* to refer to a synoptic-scale low-pressure area. They also use the term to mean a hurricane in some parts of the world.

Viewed from above in the Northern Hemisphere, surface winds in a low-pressure area blow in a counterclockwise and inward direction. Surface winds converging in the low cause air to rise, cool, and reach saturation. Clouds and precipitation usually develop. Air ascends mostly along fronts that develop as winds in the low bring cold and warm air masses together.

Lows generally travel from southwest to northeast across North America and may complete a journey from Colorado to New England in three or four days. As a rule, temperatures are lower to the left (north) of the path followed by the low-pressure area and higher to the right (south). In winter, the heaviest snows usually fall about 90 to 150 miles (150 to 250 kilometers) to the north and west of the moving low-pressure area.

Highs, also known as *anticyclones,* are areas of relatively high air pressure. A high, which brings fair weather, often follows in the wake of a low. Viewed from above in the Northern Hemisphere, surface winds in a high blow in a clockwise and outward direction. As winds blow out and away from a high, air descends near

The formation of fronts A *front* forms where air masses meet. An air mass is a huge volume of air that is relatively uniform in temperature and humidity. A front is a zone between masses that differ in temperature or humidity. In most cases, the temperatures differ, so the zones are either *cold fronts* or *warm fronts.*

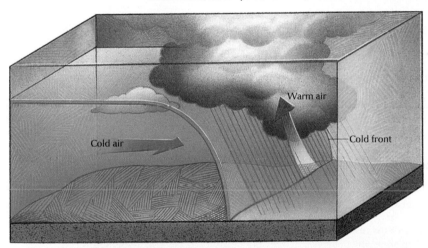

A cold front is the leading edge of a mass of cold air that advances into a region occupied by warm air. Cold air weighs more than warm air, so the cold air moves under the retreating warm air and pushes it upward. The rising warm air cools, so its relative humidity increases, often bringing precipitation. The diagram at the left represents a region about 300 miles (500 kilometers) long.

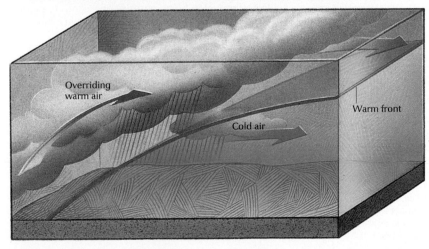

A warm front is the leading edge of a mass of warm air that advances into a region occupied by cold air. Warm air weighs less than cold air, so the warm air rides up and over the cold air. As the warm air rises, it cools, so its relative humidity increases, bringing clouds and precipitation. The diagram at the left represents a region about 900 miles (1,500 kilometers) long.

WORLD BOOK illustrations by Paul Turnbaugh

A supercell thunderstorm is a violent storm dominated by a single gigantic *cell*—a weather system made up of storm clouds and the winds associated with them. Rain and hail may fall for hours.

the center of the system. Descending air warms, and the relative humidity decreases.

Highs are either warm or cold. Warm highs form south of the polar front and are characterized by high temperatures and low relative humidities. Such highs are massive weather systems that extend from the earth's surface to the top of the troposphere. In the summer, a warm high sometimes stalls over North America. If the high remains stationary for several weeks, it creates a drought.

Cold highs form north of the polar front. They are shallow masses of cold, dry air that develop mostly in the winter over the snow-covered regions of northern Canada, Alaska, and Siberia. As cold highs move southeastward over Canada and into the continental United States, they bring fair but cold weather.

Mesoscale and microscale systems result from the development and movement of synoptic and planetary-scale systems. Mesoscale systems, which may last an hour or less and affect only part of a city, include thunderstorms and sea breezes. A tornado is an example of a microscale system, the smallest and briefest of significant weather systems.

Measuring the weather

Because no single country can constantly measure and report on conditions in every part of the atmosphere, the world's nations must cooperate to monitor the weather effectively. To this end, they founded the International Meteorological Organization in 1873, renaming it the World Meteorological Organization (WMO) in 1950. Members of the WMO participate in the worldwide observation of the atmosphere and in the exchange of weather data and forecasts. Weather observations come from many different sources, including land-based observation stations, radar systems, weather balloons, airplanes, ships, and satellites.

Land-based observation stations. About 10,000 land-based weather stations—also known as *surface stations*—monitor the weather worldwide. In the United States, the National Weather Service coordinates weather observations at about 1,000 land-based stations with information obtained from about 10,000 volunteer weather observers. The Atmospheric Environment Service of Canada operates a similar observation network.

Observation stations use a variety of instruments to monitor the state of the atmosphere. An electronic thermometer checks air temperature and registers the highest and lowest temperature of the day. A *hygrometer* measures the amount of water vapor in the air. A *barometer* shows the air pressure. A weather vane indicates the direction of the wind, and an anemometer monitors wind speed. Rain gauges measure rainfall or snowfall. For more information, see the separate articles on weather instruments in *World Book*.

Weather radar. Some observation stations use radar to track storms. Weather radar can operate in either a *reflectivity mode* or a *velocity mode*.

In the reflectivity mode, weather radar locates areas of rain or snow. The system sends out a radar signal, which consists of microwave energy pulses. If the radar signal encounters rain, snow, or hail, the falling precipitation reflects some of that signal back to the radar. The reflected radar signal, called a *radar echo,* appears as a blotch on a television-type screen. As the radar rotates, it generates a map of radar echoes that represents the pattern of precipitation surrounding the radar. In the reflectivity mode, weather radar can detect precipitation more than 250 miles (400 kilometers) away.

In the velocity mode, weather radar determines the circulation of air from the motion of raindrops, snowflakes, or dust particles. This radar is also known as Doppler radar because it uses the Doppler effect to calculate how the air in a weather system is moving.

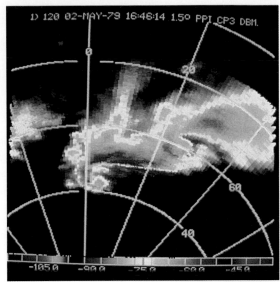

National Center for Atmospheric Research

A Doppler radar image is color-coded to indicate the speed and direction at which rain clouds and other masses of air are moving. Doppler radar can provide warning of severe weather.

The Doppler effect is the change in frequency of sound or radiation waves caused by the motion of the source of the waves relative to their observer. For example, the *pitch* (frequency) of a train whistle seems higher as a train approaches and lower as the train moves away. Similarly, as raindrops, snowflakes, or dust particles move through the atmosphere, the radar signals they reflect change in frequency. The radar monitors these frequency changes and then uses them to calculate the speed at which the drops, flakes, or particles are advancing or receding.

By enabling meteorologists to monitor the motion of air in a weather system, rather than merely track areas of precipitation, Doppler radar has improved their ability to provide advance warning for severe weather. For example, meteorologists can use Doppler radar to detect the development of a tornado before it descends from its parent thunderstorm and strikes the earth's surface. In the velocity mode, radar can detect the speed of precipitation or dust particles more than 120 miles (190 kilometers) away. A network of more than 150 Doppler radar stations across the United States called NEXRAD began operation in 1997 to improve the forecasting of severe weather.

Weather balloons, airplanes, and ships. To obtain information on the state of the atmosphere above the earth's surface, meteorologists routinely use an instrument package called a *radiosonde*. The radiosonde, which is carried aloft by a weather balloon, measures changes in temperature, pressure, and humidity. A small radio transmitter beams these data back to a weather station, where they are recorded by computer. At an altitude of about 19 miles (30 kilometers), the balloon bursts, and a parachute carries the instrument package back to the earth's surface.

Meteorologists use a special antenna to track a radiosonde and thereby measure wind speed and direction at different altitudes within the atmosphere. Such an observation is known as a *rawinsonde*. Radiosonde and rawinsonde observations are made every 12 hours.

Meteorologists sometimes use a *dropwindsonde* to obtain atmospheric measurements over the oceans. A dropwindsonde is a radiosonde attached to a parachute and dropped from an aircraft. As the instrument package falls toward the sea, it radios back to the aircraft measurements of temperature, pressure, and humidity.

Ships also report on weather conditions at sea. Some launch weather balloons, and others release special ocean buoys that record and transmit information about weather at sea level.

Weather satellites play a major role in worldwide weather observation. They monitor clouds associated with weather systems, track hurricanes and other severe weather systems, measure winds in the upper atmosphere, and obtain temperature measurements.

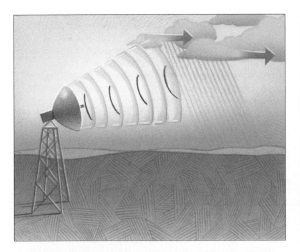

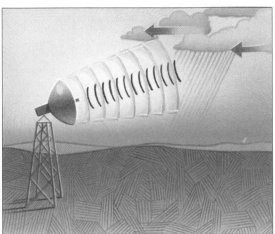

WORLD BOOK illustrations by Paul Turnbaugh

Doppler radar enables meteorologists to see how fast a storm is moving and in what direction. The radar sends out microwave pulses that bounce off raindrops or ice particles. The frequency of the pulses as they return to the antenna shows whether the storm is retreating, *left,* or advancing, *right.*

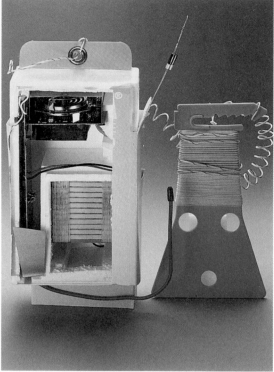

Weather instruments measure characteristics of the atmosphere that determine the weather. A weather balloon, *left,* carries aloft a package of instruments. One such package, a *radiosonde, above,* measures temperature, pressure, and humidity. A built-in radio transmitter sends the data to a weather station on the ground, where they are recorded by a computer.

Weather satellites offer significant advantages over the network of surface weather stations. They can observe weather over a broad and continuous field of view, whereas surface stations are widely spaced and may not observe some weather systems directly. Furthermore, satellites provide valuable data from the oceans, which cover about 70 percent of the globe. Land-based weather stations provide little information about these vast regions.

Sensors aboard weather satellites detect two types of radiation signals coming from the planet. One signal consists of reflected sunlight. These satellite images, which resemble black-and-white photographs of the planet, reveal cloud patterns.

The second signal recorded by weather satellites is infrared radiation (IR). The intensity of the infrared radiation emitted by an object depends on the object's temperature. For example, low clouds and fog, which are relatively warm objects, give off more intense infrared radiation than do high clouds, which are relatively cool. Thus, an IR image reveals not only cloud patterns but also cloud temperatures. Weather satellites can record IR images at any time—day or night—because objects continually emit infrared radiation.

There are two main types of weather satellites—*geostationary* and *polar-orbiting*. A geostationary satellite or-

bits about 22,300 miles (35,900 kilometers) above the equator and travels eastward at the same rate as the earth rotates. Thus, a geostationary satellite remains above the same point on the equator. Because geostationary satellites orbit at such a high altitude, they can record images that cover a wide area. For example, two of them cover most of the United States and Canada. Most satellite images shown on televised weather reports come from this type of satellite.

A polar-orbiting satellite follows a north-south path that takes it over the polar regions. Because the satellite does not rotate east as the earth does, the rotation of the earth causes the satellite to pass over different areas of the earth each orbit. Polar-orbiting satellites travel at a much lower orbit than geostationary satellites, and so they record more detailed images.

Weather forecasting

After meteorologists have gathered weather data from around the world, they can try to predict the development and movement of future weather systems. To forecast the weather, meteorologists use such tools as weather maps and mathematical models.

Weather maps. Meteorologists use weather observation data to create weather maps that represent the state of the atmosphere at a particular time. To capture

How to read a weather map

Maps like the one below appear in many daily newspapers and are based on government weather service reports. This map shows the weather conditions expected across the United States at a certain time of the day. It also predicts the high and low temperature for the day in various cities.

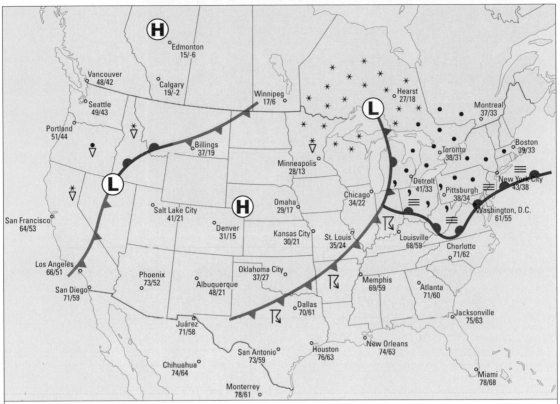

WORLD BOOK map

Weather map symbols

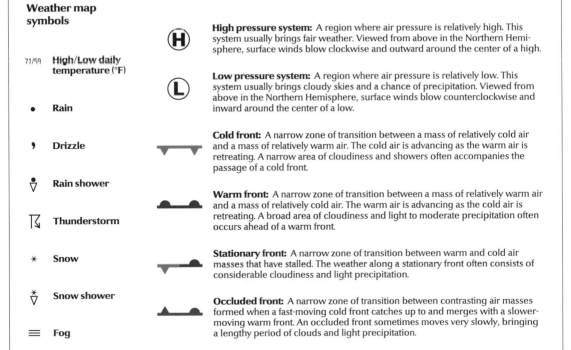

71/59 **High/Low daily temperature (°F)**

• **Rain**

❜ **Drizzle**

Rain shower

Thunderstorm

✳ **Snow**

Snow shower

≡ **Fog**

High pressure system: A region where air pressure is relatively high. This system usually brings fair weather. Viewed from above in the Northern Hemisphere, surface winds blow clockwise and outward around the center of a high.

Low pressure system: A region where air pressure is relatively low. This system usually brings cloudy skies and a chance of precipitation. Viewed from above in the Northern Hemisphere, surface winds blow counterclockwise and inward around the center of a low.

Cold front: A narrow zone of transition between a mass of relatively cold air and a mass of relatively warm air. The cold air is advancing as the warm air is retreating. A narrow area of cloudiness and showers often accompanies the passage of a cold front.

Warm front: A narrow zone of transition between a mass of relatively warm air and a mass of relatively cold air. The warm air is advancing as the cold air is retreating. A broad area of cloudiness and light to moderate precipitation often occurs ahead of a warm front.

Stationary front: A narrow zone of transition between warm and cold air masses that have stalled. The weather along a stationary front often consists of considerable cloudiness and light precipitation.

Occluded front: A narrow zone of transition between contrasting air masses formed when a fast-moving cold front catches up to and merges with a slower-moving warm front. An occluded front sometimes moves very slowly, bringing a lengthy period of clouds and light precipitation.

A hurricane approaches the Bahamas and Florida in this image taken from a weather satellite in orbit about 22,300 miles (35,900 kilometers) above the earth. Only satellites can provide images of the weather over vast expanses of the earth's surface, making satellites an essential part of modern storm detection.

National Oceanic and Atmospheric Administration

the three-dimensional nature of weather, they draw maps for conditions at the earth's surface and at various levels within the atmosphere. By examining a sequence of weather maps, forecasters can determine how the weather changes through time and then make predictions about the future state of the atmosphere.

Mathematical models. Since the mid-1950's, weather forecasters have used mathematical models of the atmosphere, processed by computers, to improve the accuracy of their predictions. A mathematical model of the atmosphere consists of a set of equations intended to approximate the atmospheric processes that drive the development and movement of weather systems. Mathematical models are based on scientific laws, and through the years scientists have developed increasingly sophisticated models. Improvements in computer technology have greatly enhanced meteorologists' ability to use mathematical models effectively because computers can process enormous amounts of observation data and perform a multitude of calculations extremely rapidly.

A mathematical model begins with the current state of the atmosphere, as determined by the most recent weather observations. The model uses these data to predict the state of the atmosphere for a specific time interval—for example, the next 10 minutes. Using this predicted state as a new starting point, the model then forecasts the state of the atmosphere for another 10-minute period. This process repeats over and over again until the model produces short-range weather forecasts for the next 12, 24, 36, and 48 hours.

The accuracy of weather forecasts generated by mathematical models declines steadily over time for two main reasons. First, the weather observation data initially fed into the model can never provide a complete picture of the present state of the atmosphere. Not all the data are reliable, due to both technical and human error, and data are missing from vast stretches of the atmosphere over the oceans. Second, mathematical models of the atmosphere are only approximations of the way the atmosphere actually works, and errors in the models tend to grow with each repetition.

Meteorologists understand the limitations of mathematical models. They base their forecasts on observations of how the weather has changed over the past several days and on their understanding of atmospheric processes. Experience and even intuition play important roles, along with the cautious interpretation of the output of mathematical models.

Meteorologists also use mathematical models to produce long-range weather forecasts, such as 6- to 10-day forecasts and monthly (30-day) and seasonal (90-day) outlooks. Long-range forecasts and outlooks typically are less accurate than short-range forecasts, but they can provide an indication of general trends, such as whether conditions will be wetter or drier than normal.

Reporting the weather

The National Weather Service of the United States and the Atmospheric Environment Service of Canada issue weather forecasts, watches, warnings, and advisories to the public through regional forecast offices. The public accesses this information through radio and television broadcasts, newspapers, and the Internet.

When hazardous weather threatens, forecasters issue outlooks, watches, warnings, and advisories. An outlook provides advance notice of a general weather trend. For example, the outlook for spring flooding due to expected snowmelt is usually available many weeks in advance. A weather watch is issued when hazardous weather is possible based on current or predicted atmospheric conditions. A weather warning applies when hazardous weather is taking place nearby. Watches and warnings are issued for severe thunderstorms, tornadoes, floods, hurricanes, and winter storms, such as blizzards and ice storms.

Weather advisories refer to expected weather hazards that are less serious than those covered by a warning. An example is a winter weather advisory.

Weather advisories are also issued for low wind chill temperatures and for a high heat index. *Wind chill* is a measure of the cooling power of a combination of low air temperature and strong winds. Even if the air temper-

(Text continued on page 170.)

A National Weather Service meteorologist works with computer images of weather patterns at the Weather Service control center near Washington, D.C.

Some kinds of storms   Storms are periods of strong wind accompanied by rain, snow, hail, or thunder and lightning. Violent storms can kill people and destroy property. The most common types of storms include (1) thunderstorms, (2) winter storms, (3) tornadoes, and (4) hurricanes.

A thunderstorm brings lightning, thunder, and rain.

A winter storm can be a blinding blizzard.

A tornado is a deadly, spinning funnel cloud.

A hurricane's swirling winds form over tropical seas.

A *World Book* science activity

A cloud in a bottle

This activity has two purposes: (1) to demonstrate that air warms when it is compressed and cools when it expands; and (2) to demonstrate that, if air cools sufficiently, water vapor in the air will condense to form a cloud.

What you need:

To carry out this activity, you will need a two-liter plastic soft-drink bottle, masking tape, matches, and a strip thermometer designed to mount on the outside of a home-aquarium tank. The thermometer is made of film and contains special materials called *liquid crystals* that indicate the temperature. It is available at aquarium-supply stores.

Caution:

This activity involves lighting a match, which can cause burns or fire. Do not use matches unless you have a responsible adult help you.

What to do:

1. Bend the thermometer into a half-circle, with the numbers facing outward. Use a short piece of the tape to join the ends of the thermometer, forming a "D." Preparing the thermometer in this way will enable you to read it easily when it is inside the bottle.

2. Put the thermometer inside the bottle and replace the cap. Let the bottle stand for two minutes. Record the temperature of the air inside it.

3. Squeeze the bottle—either between your hands or around the edge of a desk. After two minutes, again record the temperature. You will see that squeezing the bottle—thereby compressing the air in the bottle—increases the temperature of the air. If you squeeze hard enough, the temperature will rise about 2 Celsius degrees.

4. Release the bottle. It will pop back to almost its original shape. You may have to "help" it by pushing against large dents. Again, wait two minutes and record the temperature. The expansion of the air causes the temperature to fall back to its original value.

5. Pour about $\frac{3}{4}$ inch (2 centimeters) of water into the bottle and replace the cap. Swirl the water to wet all the inside of the bottle. Let the bottle stand for two minutes, then pour out the excess water. The bottle will now contain a large amount of *water vapor*—a clear, colorless gas resulting from evaporation.

6. Quickly turn the bottle upside down and squeeze it just a little. Light a match and quickly blow it out. While easing your grip on the bottle—enabling it to expand—allow smoke from the match to enter the bottle. Quickly put the cap back on the bottle. The bottle will now contain the ingredients needed to form a cloud: water vapor and tiny particles from the smoke on which the vapor can *condense* (turn into liquid droplets).

7. Water vapor will condense rapidly on the smoke particles, forming a cloud. The cloud will be a thin, foglike mist filling the bottle—rather than a separate object floating in the air inside the bottle.

8. Squeeze the bottle as you did at the beginning of the experiment. You will see the cloud vanish. Compressing the air raises the temperature of the air, increasing its ability to hold water vapor. As a result, water droplets in the cloud evaporate.

9. Release the bottle, enabling the bottle and the air inside it to expand. You will see the cloud reappear. The expansion of the air causes the temperature of the air to fall, decreasing its ability to hold water vapor. As a result, water vapor in the bottle condenses.

10. Quickly squeeze and release the bottle several times. The cloud will vanish and reappear each time.

11. You can "set the cloud free" by taking the cap off the bottle, then squeezing the bottle. The cloud will puff out of the top of the container.

WORLD BOOK illustrations by Yoshi Miyake

ature remains constant, the human body loses increasing amounts of heat to the environment as wind speed increases. At low wind chill temperatures, people need to take special precautions to prevent *frostbite* (the freezing of skin tissue) and *hypothermia* (a dangerous drop in body temperature).

Heat index is a measure of the stress produced by a combination of high air temperature and high relative humidity. During excessively hot and muggy weather, the human body may not be able to release sufficient heat to prevent *hyperthermia* (a dangerous rise in body temperature). High humidity reduces the rate at which perspiration evaporates from the skin's surface. The cooling that accompanies this evaporation represents one of the body's main ways to release heat.

Private weather forecasters provide weather information tailored to a special need. For example, prior to pouring concrete, a building contractor may consult a private forecaster to find out the probability of rainfall during specific hours of the day. Department stores may hire a private forecaster to advise them of prospects for hot summer weather to ensure the stores have enough air conditioners and fans in stock.

How people affect the weather

Human activities affect the weather both intentionally and unintentionally. For example, the construction of cities creates areas that are drier and warmer than the surrounding countryside. Cities are drier because they have storm sewer systems that quickly carry off rainwater and snowmelt.

Cities are warmer for several reasons. The use of storm drainage systems means that less solar radiation is used to evaporate water and more is used to heat the city surfaces and air. The brick, asphalt, and concrete surfaces of city buildings, sidewalks, and streets readily transmit the heat they absorb and so raise urban air temperatures even more. In addition, cities themselves generate heat from a number of sources, including motor vehicles and heating and air conditioning systems.

Large urban areas also affect the weather in the areas downwind of them. Smokestacks and automobile tailpipes in cities emit water vapor and tiny particles that stimulate the formation of clouds. Heat energy rising from a city also spurs the growth of clouds. Thus, the weather downwind from many large urban areas is cloudier and rainier than the weather upwind from those same areas.

Urban and industrial areas also produce air pollutants, such as carbon monoxide, nitrogen oxides, and hydrocarbons. Although improved controls on factories and motor vehicles have reduced considerably the amount of these gases released into the atmosphere, air quality problems persist. For example, many large cities still have problems with smog—a mixture of gases and tiny particles that reduces visibility and poses serious health hazards.

Smog and other air pollution problems are particularly serious in areas where winds are light and a *temperature inversion* occurs in the lower atmosphere. In a temperature inversion, warm air overlies cold air, so that the air temperature rises with increasing altitude, which is the opposite of the usual situation in the troposphere. Under such circumstances, smokestack and tailpipe

emissions do not rise and disperse, and so emissions may build up to unhealthy concentrations.

From time to time, scientists have tried to alter the weather. Most of these efforts—including attempts to modify hurricanes, suppress hailstorms, and clear fog—have not worked. Today, scientists focus their weather modification efforts primarily on *cloud seeding,* an attempt to stimulate the natural precipitation-forming process.

Most clouds do not produce rain or snow. This is because few clouds have just the right combination of tiny ice crystals and *supercooled water droplets* (droplets that remain liquid even at subfreezing temperatures). In such clouds, ice crystals grow at the expense of water droplets and eventually become snow crystals. If the temperature is below freezing all the way to the earth's surface, precipitation falls as snow. If the air temperature is above freezing, the snow crystals melt into raindrops.

Cloud seeding is intended to stimulate precipitation in clouds that do not have enough ice crystals. Scientists use a small aircraft to introduce into the clouds either dry ice or silver iodide crystals. Dry ice, which is frozen carbon dioxide, lowers the temperature so that cloud droplets freeze into ice crystals. Silver iodide crystals resemble ice crystals and cause supercooled water to form crystals of ice around them. When cloud seeding succeeds, precipitation is increased by perhaps as much as 20 percent.

Careers in weather

High school students interested in meteorology as a career should take college-preparatory classes, including courses in mathematics, computer science, physics, and chemistry. Most entry-level jobs in meteorology require at least a bachelor's degree, and many require a master's degree. A limited number of U.S. and Canadian colleges and universities offer degrees in meteorology, and the U.S. armed forces offer meteorological training as well.

Meteorologists specialize in a number of different areas. For example, research meteorologists study some subfield of meteorology, such as tropical weather systems. Regional forecasters prepare weather forecasts for portions of one or more states or provinces. Consulting meteorologists provide weather information tailored for specific industrial, business, or government needs. Broadcast meteorologists have skills in both meteorology and television or radio broadcasting. This type of meteorologist informs the public of current and expected weather conditions. Specialists called *synoptic meteorologists* analyze weather observations, interpret the output of computer models, and monitor weather systems. *Physical meteorologists* study the physical and chemical properties of the atmosphere. *Dynamic meteorologists* focus on creating models of atmospheric circulation.

Joseph M. Moran

Related articles in *World Book* include:

Storms

Blizzard	Hurricane	Squall
Cloudburst	Lightning	Storm
Cyclone	Rain	Thunder
Dust devil	Sandstorm	Tornado
Dust storm	Sleet	Typhoon
Hail	Snow	Waterspout

Other elements of weather

Air turbulence	Fog	Monsoon
Calms, Regions of	Frost	Norther
Chinook	Harmattan	Rainbow
Cloud	Horse latitudes	Sirocco
Dew	Humidity	Temperature
Drought	Ice	Trade wind
Foehn	Jet stream	Wind

Weather instruments

Anemometer	Radar (In weather	Satellite, Artificial
Balloon (Scientific	observation and	(Weather satel-
uses)	forecasting)	lites)
Barometer	Radiosonde	Thermocouple
Hygrometer	Rain gauge	Thermometer
Kite		Weather satellite
		Weather vane

Other related articles

Air	Flag (picture: Flags	Summer
Autumn	that talk)	Sunspot
Boating (picture:	Heat index	Troposphere
Warning sig-	Indian summer	Weather Service,
nals)	Isobar	National
Climate	Isotherm	Wind chill
Dew point	Meteorology	Winter
Dust	Rainmaking	World Meteoro-
Evaporation	Season	logical
	Spring	Organization

Outline

I. **What causes weather**
 A. Air temperature B. Air pressure C. Humidity
II. **Weather systems**
 A. Planetary-scale systems
 B. Synoptic-scale systems
 C. Mesoscale and microscale systems
III. **Measuring the weather**
 A. Land-based observation stations
 B. Weather radar
 C. Weather balloons, airplanes, and ships
 D. Weather satellites
IV. **Weather forecasting**
 A. Weather maps B. Mathematical models
V. **Reporting the weather**
VI. **How people affect the weather**
VII. **Careers in weather**

Questions

Why do winds in the Northern Hemisphere shift to the right?
What kind of weather system usually causes a drought?
What is the difference between weather and climate?
Where does the atmosphere get most of its heat?
What are some ways that cities affect the weather?
What kinds of weather information does weather radar provide?
In which part of the atmosphere does most weather occur?
How do cold fronts and warm fronts affect the weather?
How do the temperature and relative humidity of warm air
 change as the air ascends?
What is the *dew point?*

Additional resources

Level I
Burroughs, William J., and others, eds. *Weather.* Time-Life Bks.,
 1996.
Kahl, Jonathan D. *National Audubon Society First Field Guide:
 Weather.* Scholastic, 1998.
Maslin, Mark. *Storms.* Raintree Steck-Vaughn, 2000.
Oxlade, Chris. *Weather.* Raintree Steck-Vaughn, 1999.

Level II
Engelbert, Phillis. *The Complete Weather Resource.* 4 vols. UXL,
 1997-2000.
Resnick, Abraham. *Due to the Weather: Ways the Elements Affect Our Lives.* Greenwood, 2000.
Reynolds, Ross. *The Cambridge Guide to the Weather.* Cambridge, 2000.
Watts, Alan. *The Weather Handbook.* 2nd ed. Sheridan Hse.,
 1999.

Weather satellite is an instrument in orbit around the earth that is used to study and forecast the weather and climate. Weather satellites measure several forms of *electromagnetic radiation* (energy moving through space), including ultraviolet and visible light, infrared radiation, and microwave radiation. Measurements from satellites help scientists detect storms and provide scientists with information on atmospheric properties. These properties include temperature, humidity, precipitation, ozone concentration, and wind speed and direction.

In addition, weather satellites measure the earth's *radiation budget*, the total amount of electromagnetic radiation entering and leaving the earth's atmosphere. Measuring the radiation budget is essential to monitoring climate.

Most weather satellites travel in low-altitude orbits that cross the equator and both poles. These satellites orbit from 430 to 780 miles (700 to 1,250 kilometers) above the surface. They circle the earth about every 100

NOAA GOES by NASA-GSFC Lab for Atmospheres

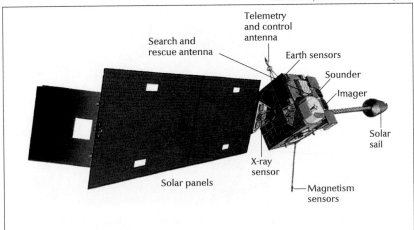

Telemetry
and control
antenna

Search and
rescue antenna

Earth sensors

Sounder

Imager

Solar
sail

X-ray
sensor

Solar panels

Magnetism
sensors

A weather satellite transmits information to the earth to help forecasters predict weather. Its major instruments include a sounder, which sends back temperature information and other data, and an imager, which transmits information in the form of pictures. The satellite shown here is a *geostationary satellite,* which remains in orbit above the same point on the earth.

minutes as the earth turns, viewing the entire surface twice each day. Other weather satellites are *geostationary,* remaining in orbit about 22,240 miles (35,790 kilometers) above the same point on the equator. Most weather-satellite images shown on television come from geostationary satellites.   Stanley Q. Kidder

See also **Satellite, Artificial.**

Weather Service, National, provides forecasts, watches, warnings, statements, observations, and records of the weather and certain water resources in the United States and its territories. It is a part of the National Oceanic and Atmospheric Administration (NOAA) of the U.S. Department of Commerce. The National Weather Service issues watches and warnings for hurricanes, tornadoes, severe thunderstorms, flash floods, winter storms, and other dangerous conditions. It measures rainfall and river levels to forecast navigation, flood, and water-supply conditions, and issues special weather information for airplane pilots and mariners. The National Weather Service records the climate of the United States and other countries, and studies ways to improve weather forecasting.

The agency's headquarters are in Silver Springs, Maryland. Regional offices are located in Bohemia, New York; Kansas City, Missouri; Fort Worth, Texas; Salt Lake City, Utah; Honolulu, Hawaii; and Anchorage, Alaska. About 300 weather stations in the United States and its possessions have full-time staffs. These stations generally take observations every hour. They observe weather conditions and issue local information and forecasts. The National Weather Service also has about 11,500 cooperative weather stations that gather climate information.

Weather reports pour into the National Meteorological Center (NMC), the Weather Service's central computer complex near Washington, D.C. Meteorologists at the NMC analyze the data and use the information to create computer models of the atmosphere. Forecasts are made with the aid of high-speed computers and the computer models. The forecasts and models are then sent to local National Weather Service offices and to private meteorologists. The Weather Service also exchanges weather information with other nations.

The National Severe Storms Forecast Center at Kansas City, Missouri, monitors the nation for conditions that may produce tornadoes or severe thunderstorms. The National Hurricane Center in Miami, Florida, provides forecasts, watches, and warnings of tropical storms threatening the East, West, and Gulf coasts of the United States. The National Hurricane Center in Honolulu provides such information for areas in the central Pacific Ocean.

Several federal agencies work with the Weather Service. For example, the Coast Guard gathers information about the weather from merchant ships. The Federal Aviation Administration helps gather weather information from pilots and airport stations, and it supplies weather reports to pilots.

The public receives weather forecasts, watches, reports, and warnings through newspapers, radio, television, and telephone. The Weather Service also broadcasts reports through its own radio program, NOAA Weather Radio (NWR). The public can tune into a local NWR station by using a special high-frequency receiver.

The U.S. public weather service began in 1870 as part of the Army Signal Service. In 1890, Congress organized the Weather Bureau under the Department of Agriculture. The president transferred the bureau to the Department of Commerce in 1940. In 1965, Congress made it part of the Environmental Science Services Administration, a branch of the Department of Commerce. The bureau was renamed the National Weather Service in 1970, when it became part of the National Oceanic and Atmospheric Administration.

Critically reviewed by the National Weather Service

See also **Heat index; Weather** (Measuring the weather; Reporting the weather).

Weather vane is a device that turns freely on an upright rod and points in the direction from which wind comes. It is also called a *wind vane* or *weathercock.* The weather vane is one of the oldest weather instruments and is often ornamental in shape.

The part of the vane which turns into the wind is usually shaped like an arrow. The other end is wide, so it will catch the smallest breeze. The breeze turns the arrow until it catches both sides of the wide end equally. Thus, the arrow always points into the wind. Below the arrow is a round plate on which the directions are marked. Some vanes, such as those used at weather stations, have electrical connections that record and display wind direction in a room that is far from the vane itself.   David D. Houghton

Weathering. See **Earth** (Earth's rocks; The rock cycle); **Soil** (How soil is formed).

Weaver is a type of small bird that usually weaves a hanging nest. There are about 290 kinds of weavers. They live in most parts of the world. The familiar *house sparrow* in the United States is a weaver. Weavers eat seeds and grain. They chatter continually. Most females and young weavers are plainly colored. But the males are generally brightly colored during the mating season.

Arthur Gloor, Animals Animals

A weaver builds a hanging nest by weaving grass and twigs together. Some of these nests have tunnel entrances.

The *sociable weaver* of South Africa builds an umbrella-shaped community roof of sticks and grass in a tree. The roof may be up to 25 feet (7.6 meters) long and 15 feet (4.6 meters) wide. The underside of the roof is divided into compartments, each occupied by a pair of birds. As many as 95 individual nests have been counted under one roof.

The *village weaver* of Africa tears palm leaves with its beak and then uses the shredded leaves to weave its nest. The *baya weaver* of India and Sri Lanka builds a flask-shaped nest with a long tunnel entrance.

Fred J. Alsop III

Scientific classification. Weavers are in the families Passeridae and Ploceidae. The house sparrow is *Passer domesticus,* and the sociable weaver is *Philetairus socius.* The village weaver is *Ploceus cucullatus,* and the baya is *Ploceus philippinus.*

See also **Bird** (picture: Birds of Africa).

Weaver, Robert Clifton (1907-1997), served as secretary of the Department of Housing and Urban Development under President Lyndon B. Johnson from 1966 through 1968. As head of the new department, Weaver became the first African American Cabinet member in United States history.

Weaver was born in Washington, D.C. He received B.S., M.A., and Ph.D. degrees from Harvard University. He began his government career in 1933 as adviser on black affairs in the Department of the Interior. Weaver was named New York deputy state housing commissioner in 1954. Appointed state rent administrator in 1955, he became the first black to attain New York state cabinet rank. From 1961 to 1966 he served as administrator of the federal Housing and Home Finance Agency. Weaver also served as chairman of the National Association for the Advancement of Colored People (NAACP). He received the Spingarn Medal in 1962. Weaver was president of Bernard M. Baruch College in New York City in 1969 and 1970. Carl T. Rowan

Weaving is the process of making cloth by crossing two sets of threads over and under each other. Many fabrics and most blankets, clothing, and rugs are woven. Weavers may use thread spun from such natural fibers as cotton, silk, and wool. Strong artificially made fibers, including nylon and Orlon, are also popular.

Narrow strips of almost any flexible material can also be woven. People learned to weave thousands of years ago with grasses, leafstalks, palm leaves, and thin strips of wood. Today, craftworkers throughout the world still use such fibers to weave baskets, hats, and other articles. Weaving also plays an important part in the manufacture of such products as screens, metal fences, and rubber tire cord.

Weaving ranks as a major industry in many countries. Weaving is also a popular craft. Artists exhibit and sell decorative woven items at art fairs, galleries, and museums. Many people design and weave colorful fabrics as a hobby.

Types of weaves

Weavers use three basic kinds of weaves: (1) the *plain weave,* or *tabby weave;* (2) the *twill weave;* and (3) the *satin weave.* More complex types of weaves are known as *fancy weaves.* All weaves consist of two sets of threads. One set, called the *warp,* stretches lengthwise on a loom or frame. To make cloth, the weaver repeatedly draws a set of crosswise threads called the *weft* over and under the warp. The weft is sometimes called the *woof* or the *filling.*

The plain weave, also called the *tabby weave,* is the simplest and most common type of weave. In the odd-numbered rows of this weave, a weft thread passes under the first warp thread, over the second, and so on. In the even-numbered rows, the weft passes over the first warp, under the second, and so on. This close weave produces a strong, flat-textured cloth that wears well. Plain-woven fabrics include gingham, muslin, and percale.

The *basket weave,* a variation of the plain weave, has a bulkier texture that resembles the weaves of a basket. The weft is drawn under two or more warp threads, then over the same number of threads, and so on. This method adds fullness to the weave.

The twill weave produces sturdy cloth that has raised diagonal lines. Each weft thread crosses two, three, or four warp threads at a time, creating extra width. This added width makes a decorative fabric that holds its shape despite repeated wear. Each row of weft threads follows the same pattern. But each row's pattern begins slightly to the right or left of the pattern in the

Some kinds of weaves

© Peter Gonzalez

The plain, or tabby, weave is the simplest type of weave. A *weft* (crosswise thread) passes under one *warp* (lengthwise thread), over the next, and so on.

The twill weave forms diagonal lines in fabric. The weft crosses several warps at once. Each row's pattern begins slightly left or right of that of the previous row.

The satin weave is used in making such luxurious fabrics as rayon, satin, and silk. Each weft spans up to 12 warps in creating a smooth, glossy finish.

previous row. This technique puts a series of diagonal lines in the fabric. The weaver may create unusual patterns by changing the direction of the weave and adding various colored threads.

Common twill fabrics include denim, flannel, gabardine, and serge. The twill weave produces strong, tightly-woven cloth used to make coats, work clothes, and men's suits.

The satin weave makes soft, luxurious fabrics, such as damask, sateen, and satin. The wefts of a satin weave can cover as many as 12 warps. The threads may interlace at such wide intervals that the diagonal line of the weave cannot be seen without a magnifying glass. Satin-weave cloth may snag easily. It is used to make such products as draperies and formal clothes.

Fancy weaves produce a variety of designs and textures in fabric. A *pile weave* has cut or looped weft yarns that extend above the fabric surface and provide a furry texture. Pile weaves include corduroy, terrycloth, velvet, and most carpet fabrics. A *double weave* binds two layers of cloth together for added strength and warmth. Blankets, coats, drapes, and upholstery fabrics may be double woven. A *gauze weave* is a loose, open weave that makes a sheer, lightweight fabric. The warp threads are arranged in pairs and twisted around the weft threads. Gauze-woven cotton, rayon, and silk make attractive curtains and lightweight clothing.

Weaving on a loom

How a loom works. Almost all looms have the same basic features and weave fabric in much the same way. On most looms, cloth is woven on a metal or wooden frame located at the front of the loom and parallel to the floor.

The weaver must thread the loom before weaving. A set of warp threads is wound onto a cylinder called the *warp beam* at the back of the loom. Each warp thread is then passed through one of two or more vertical frames called *harnesses*. The number of harnesses depends on the complexity of the weave. In the harnesses, each

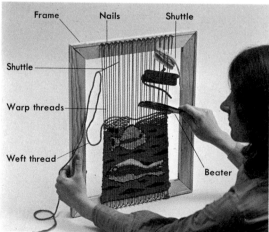

WORLD BOOK photo

A simple hand loom can be made from a picture frame. Nails hammered into the top and bottom of the frame hold the warp in place. This photograph shows a weaver using a comb as the beater. A needle and two pieces of cardboard serve as shuttles.

warp is threaded through a narrow opening in one of many strings or wires called *heddles*. The heddles hold the individual threads in place and prevent them from tangling. The warp threads then stretch over the weaving frame.

Next, the weaver winds the weft thread around a spool called the *bobbin*. The bobbin is held in an oblong metal or wood container called the *shuttle*. The shuttle serves as a needle that draws the weft thread over and under the warp. The weaving process begins when the weaver lifts the harness that holds the odd-numbered threads. This action creates a space called the *shed* through which the shuttle and weft then pass. Finally, the weaver lowers the first harness and pushes the newly woven row into place with a device called the *beater*, or *reed*. The beater is in a frame located in front of, and parallel to, the harnesses. It has comblike "teeth" made of steel wires that push each weft row compactly into place to tighten the weave.

To weave the next row, the weaver raises the second harness and passes the shuttle through the shed. The weaving of each row involves the same process. The finished cloth is wound around a bar called the *apron beam*, or *cloth beam*, at the front of the loom.

Kinds of looms. There are two basic types of looms, hand looms and power looms. A hand loom is any loom that is not power driven, such as a *table loom* or a *floor loom*.

A table loom is a compact, portable device that stands on a table or some other flat surface. Table looms of various sizes can weave cloth that measures from 8 to 36 inches (20 to 91 centimeters) wide. Table looms generally have from 2 to 8 harnesses, which the weaver controls by raising and lowering levers by hand. A table loom threads easily and costs less than most other kinds of looms. But weaving on a hand loom can be tiring because the weaver must put down the shuttle and operate the harnesses manually after every row.

Floor looms are large and stationary and measure from 20 inches (51 centimeters) to 5 feet (1.5 meters) wide. The weaver raises and lowers the harnesses of a floor loom by pressing foot pedals called *treadles*. This action frees the weaver's hands to pass the shuttle rhythmically through the sheds. Such rhythm adds speed and enjoyment to the weaving process.

Power looms produce millions of yards of textiles on factory assembly lines yearly. Looms run by steam, electricity, or water power have shuttles that refill automatically and can move as fast as 60 miles (97 kilometers) an hour. The beaters and harnesses on power looms move faster than the eye can follow.

Weaving without a loom

Artists and hobbyists have developed many ways to weave without a mechanical loom. In *paper weaving,* for example, strips of colored construction paper serve as the warps and wefts. The weaver interlaces the strips by hand to make place mats, wallhangings, and other decorative objects.

In *finger weaving,* or *Indian braiding,* several pieces of cord tied together at one end serve as the warp. A longer cord, also attached to the warp, is threaded over and under the lengthwise pieces to make belts and sashes. Some artists weave reeds, yarn, and other materials through flexible wire screens. The weaver can then bend the decorated wire into sculptural forms.

A loom made from a piece of cardboard can be used to weave yarn place mats, potholders, and purses. Evenly spaced notches cut at the top and bottom of the cardboard hold the warps in place. The weaver slips a stick under alternate warp threads to create a shed and passes a threaded needle through the shed.

History

Thousands of years ago, people discovered how to weave baskets from grasses. Historians do not know when the process of weaving cloth developed. But civilizations in central Europe, the Middle East, and Pakistan probably had learned to weave textiles by 2500 B.C. Ancient wallpaintings illustrate weaving techniques mastered by the Egyptians as early as 5000 B.C.

The Chinese learned to weave sometime between 2500 and 1200 B.C. They became famous for spinning silk thread that was woven into exquisite brocade and damask fabrics in Persia (now Iran) and Syria.

The Pueblo and other Indian tribes of what is now the southwestern United States began to weave cotton textiles during the A.D. 700's. The two-bar loom mounted in a frame was used in Europe by the 1200's. By the 1400's, the art of weaving had become highly developed in Europe. For example, skilled weavers in the city of Arras, in what is now France, produced beautiful tapestries that decorated castles and cathedrals.

The greatest improvements in machinery for weaving came during the Industrial Revolution, a period of rapid industrial growth in Europe during the 1700's and early 1800's. In 1785, an English inventor named Edmund Cartwright developed the first power loom (see **Cartwright, Edmund**). The French inventor Joseph M. Jacquard developed the Jacquard loom in 1801. It uses punched cards and other attachments that guide the threads in weaving complex patterns.

Today, many textile firms use high-speed looms that have many tiny shuttles called *darts* instead of a single large shuttle. The darts pick up weft yarns that lie beside the loom and pass them through the shed faster than other kinds of shuttles.   Dona Z. Meilach

Related articles in *World Book* include:

Basket making	Ireland (picture: Textile manu-
Beadwork	facturing)
Colonial life in America	Jacquard, Joseph M.
(Colonists at home; picture)	Rugs and carpets
Handicraft (picture)	Spinning jenny
Indian, American (pictures)	Tapestry
Industrial Revolution (The tex-	Textile
tile industry)	

Additional resources

Chandler, Deborah. *Learning to Weave.* Rev. ed. Interweave, 1995.
Hecht, Ann. *The Art of the Loom.* Rizzoli, 1990.
Held, Shirley E. *Weaving.* 3rd ed. Harcourt Brace Coll. Pubs., 1999.

Web. See Spider.

Web site is a collection of information at a specific address on the World Wide Web. The World Wide Web, also known as the Web, is a worldwide system of interconnected computer files that are linked to one another on the Internet. The Web enables the use of *multimedia,* which includes illustrations, animation, video, and sound files in addition to text.

The information on a Web site is arranged in separate displays called *pages.* A Web site can have hundreds or even thousands of pages. Web sites can be devoted to a single topic or can include a variety of topics, each spanning many pages. Parts of some sites are *interactive—* that is, they offer a range of different responses, depending on input from the user.

Web sites and pages are created using a simple programming language called HyperText Markup Language (HTML). Learning HTML can be easy, even for users with no programming experience. Many classrooms, including those in elementary schools, have created their own Web sites. Businesses, groups and institutions of all types, and even individuals have Web sites.

Many Web sites take advantage of the way information can be connected on the Web. Hypertext linkage enables users to move directly from a *link—*usually a highlighted word, phrase, or picture—to a body of related information at the same site or a different site. The user moves to the related information by using a mouse or other input device to position an electronic marker on the link and then clicking the device.

Because Web sites are collections of computer information, they reside in computers. Each Web site is identified and accessed by an address known as a *uniform resource locator* (URL). The URL indicates where on the Internet a Web site can be found.

Many *Internet service providers* (ISP's) and *online services,* two types of companies that provide access to the Internet, offer their subscribers software for building Web sites. The sites created with this software reside in computers operated by the companies. ISP's and online services also generate the sites' URL addresses and distribute those addresses to various Web indexes. These indexes provide access to Web sites for users throughout the world.   Keith Ferrell

See also Internet; World Wide Web.

Webb, Sidney and Beatrice, were British social reformers. The Webbs, husband and wife, were also noted historians of the labor movement that took place in the United Kingdom. Their activities led to reforms that aided the poor, strengthened the labor movement, and improved public education.

Sidney James Webb (1859-1947) was born in London. His father was a bookkeeper. In 1885, Sidney joined the Fabian Society, an organization of British socialists. Sidney remained one of the society's leaders for the rest of his life and helped make social research its chief interest.

Beatrice Webb (1858-1943) was born into a wealthy and socially prominent family on an estate near Gloucester. Her maiden name was Martha Beatrice Potter. Her interest in social research brought her into contact with Sidney Webb, and they were married in 1892.

Sidney entered politics as a member of the London County Council in 1892. In the council, he helped reshape education programs in London. The Webbs took the lead in founding the London School of Economics and Political Science in 1895. Beatrice's wealth enabled the couple to devote themselves to the study of the British labor movement. They wrote a number of pioneering books, notably *The History of Trade Unionism* (1894) and *Industrial Democracy* (1897).

From 1906 to 1909, Beatrice served on the Royal Commission on the Poor Law, which investigated poverty in the United Kingdom. She and Sidney wrote a minority report for the commission that called for legislation to guarantee a minimum standard of living for all citizens. In 1913, the Webbs established the *New Statesman,* a weekly periodical, to promote their socialist views.

Sidney became active in the Labour Party during World War I (1914-1918) and was elected to its executive committee. He prepared the statement in 1918 that first committed the party to socialism. In 1922, Sidney was elected to Parliament. He held Cabinet posts in Labour governments in 1924 and from 1929 to 1931.

During the 1920's and 1930's, Beatrice revised and edited the detailed diary she had kept since 1872. The resulting books, *My Apprenticeship* (1926) and *Our Partnership* (1948), form an eloquent record of the Webbs' productive careers.   Willard Wolfe

Weber, *WEHB uhr, VAY buhr,* or *WEE buhr,* is a unit used to measure a magnetic field. A *magnetic field* is the influence that a magnet or electric current creates in the region around it. You can picture a magnetic field by placing a sheet of paper on a bar magnet and sprinkling iron filings on the paper. The filings will line up to make loops, called magnetic field lines, that connect the poles of the magnet (see **Magnetism** [picture: A magnetic field]). The magnetic field is strong where the field lines are close together, as they are near the poles.

The weber measures *magnetic flux,* a quantity related to the number of magnetic field lines passing through an area that is perpendicular to the field. The more field lines that pass through a given area, the stronger the field. The total flux divided by the area gives the *field strength,* measured in a unit called the *tesla.* If the flux is 1 weber for every square meter of area, the magnetic field strength is 1 tesla.

The weber was named for the German physicist Wilhelm Weber. Its symbol is Wb.   Richard Wolfson

Weber, *VAY buhr,* **Carl Maria von** (1786-1826), was the first important composer of German romantic opera. This kind of opera is based on conflict between a mortal and a supernatural being.

Weber's most popular romantic opera is *Der Freischütz (The Free-Shooter,* 1821). This opera tells about a pact that a hunter makes with the devil to get magic bullets that will strike anything he chooses. An important romantic feature of *Der Freischütz* is its atmospheric settings. A major scene takes place in a frightening wild rocky place called the "Wolf's Glen." The rest of the story is set in a friendlier region inhabited by hunters and farmers. Weber's other operas include *Euryanthe* (1823) and *Oberon* (1826). His other works include the piano piece *Invitation to the Dance* (1819). Weber was born in Eutin, near Lübeck.   Carolyn Abbate

Weber, *VAY buhr,* **Max** (1864-1920), was a German sociologist and economist who helped establish the foundations of modern sociology. Weber considered *bureaucracy* to be the most important feature of modern society. Bureaucracy is a method of organization based on specialization of duties, action according to rules, and a stable order of authority. Weber also developed an *ideal type* method for studying society. This method studies the basic elements of social institutions and how these elements relate to one another.

In "The Protestant Ethic and the Spirit of Capitalism" (1904-1905), Weber developed a theory that certain Protestant religious beliefs promoted capitalism. He argued that the Calvinist belief in working hard and avoiding luxury promoted the expansion of business enterprise. According to Weber, the Calvinist doctrine of business success as a sign of spiritual salvation justified the desire for profits. Weber also wrote on other religions and their relationship to the social system.

Weber was born in Erfurt, Germany. He studied at the universities of Berlin, Göttingen, and Heidelberg. Important works by Weber translated into English include *From Max Weber: Essays in Sociology* and *The Theory of Social and Economic Organization.*   Daniel R. Fusfeld

See also **Bureaucracy; Protestant ethic.**

Weber, *WEHB ur,* **Max** (1881-1961), was a pioneer modern painter in America. He is best known for the abstract works he painted between 1912 and 1919. His later paintings move back toward representation, featuring figures with expressive gestures. Many of these later canvases deal with Jewish themes, reflecting his personal background.

Weber was born in western Russia and moved with his family to New York City when he was 10. He came under the influence of modern artists while painting and studying in Paris from 1905 to 1908. Weber's paintings began to receive favorable criticism in the late 1920's. In 1930, the Museum of Modern Art in New York City presented a one-man show of Weber's works. It marked the first time the museum devoted a show to one living American artist.   Charles C. Eldredge

Webern, *VAY buhrn,* **Anton** (1883-1945), was an Austrian composer best known for his works written in the 12-tone style. The *12-tone style* is a method of composition that uses 12 notes arranged in an order chosen by the composer. Such compositions, especially Webern's *Symphony* (1928), influenced many composers during the mid-1900's.

Webern's early work, the *Passacaglia* for orchestra (1908), was written in a traditional style. His *Five Movements for String Quartet* (1909) represents a transition leading to the adoption of his teacher Arnold Schoenberg's method of composing with 12 tones. More than half of Webern's music is for voice, though he never wrote an opera. His major works for solo voices and choir include *Das Augenlicht* (1935) and the First and Second Cantatas (1939, 1943). The cantatas are among the longest and most lyrical of his works, most of which last less than 10 minutes. Webern's music as a whole is marked by extreme delicacy of sound.

Anton Friedrich Wilhelm von Webern was born in Vienna, Austria. He was also a conductor and an expert in the history and theory of music.   Stewart L. Ross

Webster, Daniel (1782-1852), was the best-known American orator, and one of the ablest lawyers and statesmen of his time. He gained his greatest fame as the champion of a strong national government. For years after his death, students memorized thrilling lines from his speeches. Such words as "Liberty *and* Union, now and forever, one and inseparable!" inspired many Northern soldiers during the American Civil War (1861-1865).

Early career. Webster was born on Jan. 18, 1782, in Salisbury (now Franklin), New Hampshire, and graduated from Dartmouth College. He studied law in Boston and then became a successful lawyer in Portsmouth, New Hampshire. At the beginning of his career, Webster did not favor a strong national government. Instead, he stood for the rights of the states.

Portsmouth was a thriving seaport until President Thomas Jefferson's embargo and the War of 1812 destroyed most of its overseas trade. Siding with the local shipowners, Webster opposed trade restrictions and war. As a Federalist in the United States House of Representatives from 1813 to 1817, he objected to war taxes, and helped defeat a bill for drafting soldiers. He said that state governments should "interpose" to protect their citizens from the national government.

Webster moved to Boston in 1816. New spinning and weaving mills were springing up along New England streams where there was water power. In much of the Northeast, manufacturing came to be more important than shipping. The manufacturers desired a strong national government that could aid business.

As a friend and attorney of Northeastern businessmen, Webster changed his views on national power and states' rights. In the Dartmouth College case, he argued against New Hampshire's claim to control the college and won the verdict of the Supreme Court of the United States (see **Dartmouth College case**). In another famous case, he held that it was constitutional for the federal government to charter a national bank. Representing Massachusetts in the United States House of Representatives from 1823 to 1827, he insisted that a protective tariff was unconstitutional. But after his election to the United States Senate in 1827, he became the country's most eloquent tariff advocate.

The U.S. senator. The so-called "tariff of abominations," passed in 1828, led John C. Calhoun of South Carolina to develop the theory that a state could "nullify" federal laws, and refuse to obey them (see **Nullification**). Senator Robert Y. Hayne of South Carolina brilliantly de-

fended nullification in 1830, and Webster answered him with a famous speech declaring that the Constitution had created a single, unified nation (see **Hayne, Robert Young**). In 1832, when South Carolina tried to put nullification into effect, Webster gave strong support to President Andrew Jackson in resisting the attempt.

But Webster disagreed with Jackson on other issues, especially on the question of the Bank of the United States. When Jackson vetoed a bill for rechartering the bank, Webster did his best to save the institution, but failed (see **Bank of the United States**).

During his last years in the Senate, Webster opposed adding Texas to the Union and also opposed the war with Mexico. He feared that the country might break up because of a quarrel over territories in the West. Most Northerners wished to keep slavery from spreading into the new territories, but Southerners were ready to leave the Union if the spread of slavery was prevented. In a "Union-saving" speech, Webster favored the Compromise of 1850 and helped get it passed (see **Compromise of 1850**). Some Northerners denounced his willingness to give Southerners part of what they wanted.

Secretary of state. Webster served as secretary of state under Presidents William Henry Harrison and John Tyler, and then under President Millard Fillmore. Under Tyler, he negotiated the Webster-Ashburton Treaty which settled the Maine boundary dispute and avoided a war with the United Kingdom (see **Webster-Ashburton Treaty**). Under Fillmore, he befriended the Hungarian patriot Lajos Kossuth and spoke for Hungarian independence (see **Kossuth, Lajos**).

The man. Webster was a handsome, imposing man with deep-set, penetrating eyes, craggy brows, dark complexion, and a rich voice. After the founding of the Whig Party in the 1830's, Webster became one of its top leaders, along with his great rival, Henry Clay. His Whig friends thought he deserved to be president, and he ran as one of the party's three candidates in 1836. His later failures to become president made him bitter at the end of his life. A statue of him represents New Hampshire in Statuary Hall in the U.S. Capitol. Richard N. Current

Additional resources

Baxter, Maurice G. *One and Inseparable: Daniel Webster and the Union.* Harvard Univ. Pr., 1984.
Remini, Robert V. *Daniel Webster: The Man and His Time.* Norton, 1997.

Webster, John (1580?-1625?), an English playwright, is noted for two tragedies, *The White Devil* (completed about 1612) and *The Duchess of Malfi* (completed about 1613). Essentially, both plays deal with the common Elizabethan subject of revenge. But their power lies in the complexity of the characters' motives for acting as they do, the physical horror of the situations, and poetic dialogue which is second only to that of William Shakespeare. The plays show the world as corrupt and immoral. However, Webster used dramatic action to express the concern of all great tragic writers in the restoration of moral order.

Webster was born in London, but little is known of his life. He wrote or collaborated in writing more than a dozen plays and entertainments and his works were apparently popular with audiences. Albert Wertheim

Webster, Noah (1758-1843), was an American educa-

Detail of an oil painting on canvas (about 1850) by
G. P. A. Healy; Faneuil Hall, Boston (City of Boston Art Commission)

Daniel Webster, *right,* opposed Senator Robert Y. Hayne in a famous Senate debate in 1830 over states' rights. Webster rejected Hayne's view that a state could nullify federal laws.

tor and journalist who won fame for compiling *Webster's Dictionary.* This work was the finest English dictionary of its time. Its most recently revised form is *Webster's Third New International Dictionary.*

Webster was born in the village of West Hartford, Connecticut. He was descended from John Webster, governor of Connecticut in 1656, and from William Bradford, who governed Plymouth Colony for more than 30 years. Webster graduated from Yale College. He then studied law and was admitted to the bar at Hartford. But Webster practiced law only briefly.

While teaching school at Goshen, New York, in the 1780's, he compiled an elementary spelling book. He then compiled a grammar, and, finally, a reader for schoolchildren. Millions of copies of the speller were sold well into the 1900's and helped standardize spelling and pronunciation in the United States.

Webster campaigned for the first American copyright laws. He became an active member of the Federalist Party, and wrote many political pamphlets. In 1793, he became the editor of two Federalist newspapers. After 1803, he devoted most of his time to dictionary work.

In 1806, Webster published his first dictionary. He thought of it as a preliminary effort. His great dictionary, *An American Dictionary of the English Language,* appeared in two volumes in 1828. This work, which was enlarged for an edition in 1840, included 12,000 words and 40,000 definitions that had never before appeared in a dictionary. After his death, Webster's heirs sold the dictionary rights to the G. and C. Merriam Co. of Springfield, Massachusetts.   Bert Hitchcock

See also **Dictionary** (History).

Webster-Ashburton Treaty was an agreement between the United States and the United Kingdom. It settled a number of annoying disputes between the two countries. Secretary of State Daniel Webster signed the treaty for the United States and Lord Ashburton for the United Kingdom at Washington, D.C., in August 1842. The most important dispute settled was the fixing of the boundary line between Canada and the state of Maine. The United States received more than half of the disputed area of 12,000 square miles (31,100 square kilometers). The treaty also settled several minor disputes and provided for the mutual extradition of criminals. The negotiations provided opportunity for the peaceful discussion of problems arising from British efforts to suppress the African slave trade. The Webster-Ashburton Treaty was one of many instances in which the United States and the United Kingdom settled disputes without going to war.   Robert F. Dalzell, Jr.

Wedding. See Marriage.

Wedding anniversary. It is customary for married couples to celebrate their wedding anniversaries. The 10th, 25th, and 50th anniversaries generally receive special attention. A certain type of gift is appropriate for many anniversaries. For example, silver is given to a couple married for 25 years, and gold is given to a couple married for 50 years.

Invitations to an anniversary celebration may be simple, handwritten notes or formal, printed or engraved cards, depending on the number of guests expected. In early years of marriage, the couple usually hosts a party for close friends to celebrate the anniversary. In later years, their children and grandchildren may honor them with a party or send them on a cruise or a trip. Examples of traditional gifts are listed in the table below.
Letitia Baldrige

Wedekind, *VAY duh kihnt,* **Frank** (1864-1918), was a German playwright who savagely attacked the smugness, hypocrisy, and corruption he saw in middle-class morality. His characters are overdrawn and sometimes grotesque symbols of the individual's sexual freedom and physical vitality. They scorn the conformity of the middle class. The plays *Earth Spirit* (1894), *Pandora's Box* (1894), and *The Marquis von Keith* (1900) are variations on Wedekind's view of society. An earlier play, *Spring's Awakening* (1890-1891), established Wedekind's reputation as a controversial playwright. In this play, Wedekind says the torments of youth are caused by the cruelty and narrow-mindedness of the adult world.

Wedekind was born in Hanover and grew up in Switzerland. In 1912, he formed a theater company that toured Germany performing his plays.   Peter Gontrum

Wedge is a device that has two or more sloping surfaces that taper either to a sharp edge or to a point. Wedges are used to split or pierce materials, and to adjust the positions of heavy objects. Knives, chisels, axes, pins, needles, and nails are wedges. A wedge must overcome the resistance of friction as well as the resistance of the material it is being used on. The total resistance may be high enough to require heavy blows from a hammer to drive the wedge forward. See also **Machine** (picture: Six simple machines).

Wedgwood, Josiah. See Wedgwood ware.

Wedgwood ware is a type of pottery first made by the English potter Josiah Wedgwood about 1759. The term *Wedgwood ware* generally refers to Wedgwood's fine *creamware,* a cream-colored earthenware. In 1765, Queen Charlotte, wife of King George III, ordered a set of creamware tableware. She was so pleased with it that

Wedding anniversary gifts

First	Paper, plastics, furniture		**Thirteenth**	Lace
Second	Cotton, china		**Fourteenth**	Ivory, agate
Third	Leather, any leatherlike article		**Fifteenth**	Crystal, glass
Fourth	Linen, silk, synthetic silks		**Twentieth**	China or occasional furniture
Fifth	Wood and decorative accessories for the home		**Twenty-fifth**	Silver
Sixth	Iron		**Thirtieth**	Pearls or personal gifts
Seventh	Wool, copper, brass		**Thirty-fifth**	Coral, jade
Eighth	Bronze, electric appliances		**Fortieth**	Rubies, garnets
Ninth	Pottery, china, glass, crystal		**Forty-fifth**	Sapphires, tourmalines
Tenth	Tin, aluminum		**Fiftieth**	Gold
Eleventh	Steel		**Fifty-fifth**	Emeralds, turquoise
Twelfth	Linen, silk, nylon		**Sixtieth, Seventy-fifth**	Diamonds, diamondlike stones, gold

Dwight M. Beeson, the Wedgwood Society of New York

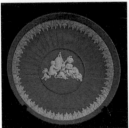

Wedgwood ware is a popular type of English pottery. The term generally refers to a cream-colored earthenware known as *creamware* or *Queen's Ware*. A type of stoneware called *jasper* often features white raised designs on a blue background. Both plates were created during the late 1700's.

Leonard S. Rakow, M.D., the Wedgwood Society of New York

she allowed Wedgwood to name the pottery *Queen's Ware*. It is still known and sold by that name.

In addition to Queen's Ware, Wedgwood made other kinds of pottery. They included *Egyptian black* or *black basalt*, a black stoneware; *rosso antico*, a red stoneware; and a stoneware called *jasper* that came in blue, green, lavender, pink, and yellow. Many of the jasper pieces had delicate raised designs, usually in white.

Wedgwood's pottery reflected the English taste for ancient Greek and Roman designs. He made copies of antique vases and sculptured ornaments, as well as chess sets, buttons, cameos for jewelry, and plaques to decorate furniture. Wedgwood also manufactured statuettes, flowerpots, and other practical or decorative objects. Wedgwood ware is still made today in Barlaston, near Stoke-on-Trent.   William C. Gates, Jr.

Wednesday, *WEHNZ dee* or *WEHNZ day,* is the English name for the fourth day of the week. This day gets its name from Woden, or Odin, the chief god in Teutonic mythology, to whom it was sacred. At the beginning of the Christian Era, the Germans called the day Woden's-day. Its name later changed to *Wednesday.* The first to name the days of the week after gods in mythology were the ancient Romans. They called the fourth day of the week after the god Mercury. From this name, the French called Wednesday *mercredi.* See also **Ash Wednesday; Odin; Week.**   Jack Santino

Weed is any plant that grows where people do not want it to grow. A plant may be considered a weed in one place but not in another. For example, a morning-glory in an alfalfa field is a weed pest, but a morning-glory in a garden is a lovely flower. Some plants, such as poison ivy and poison oak, are called weeds wherever they grow because they have no known use.

Many weeds are destructive. These species reduce both the quality and quantity of crops by competing with them for sunlight, water, and nourishing substances in the soil. Some types of weeds also shelter insects and diseases that damage nearby crops. Farmers in the United States spend more than $8 billion annually to control weeds. Nevertheless, the yearly loss due to weeds in crops totals about $10 billion. Weeds are usually considered unsightly in gardens, parks, and playgrounds. They interfere with transportation if allowed to grow unchecked along highways, railroad tracks, and waterways.

Some kinds of weeds, such as jimson weed and locoweed, are poisonous to human beings and other animals. Certain weeds, including nettles and poison ivy, produce severe skin reactions in most people. Ragweed pollen causes hay fever in many individuals.

Weeds can be beneficial in some cases. For example, they reduce soil erosion on land where cultivated plants do not grow. They also provide shelter and food for birds and other wildlife. A weed, such as quackgrass, may serve as food for livestock if other food is not available. People in some countries eat parts of dandelions, lamb's-quarters, and other weeds. Fireweed, one of many weeds used in making certain medicines, helps relieve pain. Other weeds, such as goldenrod and wild carrot, are attractive in gardens.

How weeds grow. Weeds are classified as *annuals, biennials,* and *perennials,* depending on how long they live. Annual weeds grow from seeds and live one year or less. There are two kinds of annual weeds, *summer annuals* and *winter annuals.* Summer annuals start to grow in spring and produce seeds before dying in fall. Winter annuals begin to grow in fall and produce roots and a group of leaves, called a *rosette,* before winter. The plant then remains inactive until spring, when it grows to maturity. Common annual weeds include crabgrass, dodder, and ragweed.

Biennial weeds grow from seeds and live about two years. They produce roots and a rosette during the first year and then remain inactive until spring. Biennials produce stems, flowers, and seeds during the second year. Examples of biennial weeds include burdock, poison hemlock, and wild parsnip.

Perennial weeds, which live longer than two years, grow from seeds or from other parts of a plant. New growth may start from the roots, bulbs, or stems if the upper part of a plant dies or is cut down. Most perennials are difficult to control because they have extremely deep root systems. Canada thistle, dandelion, and quackgrass are common perennial weeds.

Weeds may spread from one area to another in a variety of ways. Many weed seeds have special structures that enable them to travel great distances on wind currents. For example, the dandelion has a fluffy seed structure that can be blown for miles. Birds and other animals also scatter seeds of weeds. People spread weeds by means of seeds caught on farm and lawn equipment. In addition, weed seeds may be moved from one place to another in animal feed and among crop seeds.

Weed control. There are four general methods of weed control—*cultural, mechanical, biological,* and *chemical.* Cultural control is the use of efficient crop production to prevent weeds from growing. One such technique involves planting crop seeds that are free of weed seeds. Crop rotation helps keep weeds from adapting to a certain area. In small areas, a covering called a *mulch* is placed on the ground around plants to prevent weed growth. Common types of mulches include grass clippings, wood chips, and plastic sheets. See Mulch.

Mechanical control is the destruction of weeds manually or by machine. Farmers use a machine called a *cultivator* to dig up large weeds and cover smaller ones with soil. Tall weeds in pastures and on roadsides are controlled by mowing. Hoeing weeds or pulling them out of the ground by hand can be effective in small gardens, flower beds, and lawns.

Biological control involves the use of natural enemies of weeds growing in a specific area. For example, insects and other small animals that eat certain weeds may be put into a field where those weeds are growing. Bacteria and other organisms are used to spread diseases among specific species of weeds.

Chemical control is the use of chemical compounds called *herbicides*. Most herbicides are *selective*—that is, they kill weeds but do not harm crops. Herbicides must be used carefully to avoid harm to crops, human beings, and wildlife.   Harold D. Coble

Related articles in *World Book* include:

Amaranth	Glasswort	Milkweed	Sorrel
Beggarweed	Goldenrod	Mullein	Sowthistle
Bindweed	Grass	Nettle	Teasel
Brome	Hemlock	Parsnip	Thistle
Burdock	Herbicide	Pigweed	Toadflax
Canada thistle	Horsetail	Plantain	Tumbleweed
Cinquefoil	Jimson weed	Poison ivy	Velvetleaf
Cocklebur	Knotweed	Poison oak	Viper's bu-
Compass plant	Lamb's- quar-	Pokeweed	gloss
Dandelion	ters	Purslane	Water hy-
Dock	Lawn	Ragweed	acinth
Dodder	Locoweed	Sandbur	Wild carrot
Foxtail barley	Lupine	Solanum	

Weed, Thurlow (1797-1882), was an American journalist and political leader. He became a leader of the Whig and Republican parties, and was largely responsible for the election of two Whig presidents, William Henry Harrison and Zachary Taylor. His support of William H. Seward, U.S. secretary of state, led to Weed's appointment as a commissioner to England and France at the outset of the American Civil War (1861-1865). Weed was born at Cairo, New York, on Nov. 15, 1797. In 1830, he established the Albany (New York) *Evening Journal.*

Joseph P. McKerns

Week is a division of time which includes seven days. We do not know exactly how this division of time began, but the ancient Hebrews were among the first to use it. The book of Genesis in the Bible says that the world was created in six days and the seventh day, or Sabbath, was a day of rest and worship.

The ancient Egyptians named each day of the week for one of the planets, which they incorrectly believed included the sun and the moon. They considered the seventh day merely as a day of rest and play. Among the later Romans, the days of the week were named after the sun, the moon, and the five planets then known. Each day was considered sacred to the Roman god associated with that planet. The days were known as Sun's-day, Moon's-day, Mars'-day, and so on. This system was used about the beginning of the Christian Era. The English names for the days *Tuesday, Wednesday, Thursday,* and *Friday* were derived from the names of Norse gods.

James Jespersen

See also separate articles in *World Book* on each day of the week.

Weems, Mason Locke (1759-1825), was an American clergyman who became famous as a writer and traveling bookseller. An Episcopal priest, he was often called "Parson" Weems. He wrote the first popular biography of United States President George Washington, *The Life and Memorable Actions of George Washington* (about 1800). It includes many tales that Weems apparently invented, notably the one about the young Washington chopping down a cherry tree. Weems also wrote biographies of other leading Americans and several moral tracts. Weems was born in Anne Arundel County, Maryland, on Oct. 11, 1759.   Marcus Klein

Weevil, *WEE vuhl,* is the name of many kinds of beetles with a long snout. They are among the worst insect pests that attack farm crops. The cotton boll weevil, commonly called the *boll weevil,* is one of the most destructive insects in the United States. The name weevil is also given to the *grubs* (larvae) of these beetles. Both grubs and adult weevils cause damage.

Adult weevils are sometimes so small that they are hard to see. They have long snouts that may be longer than the rest of the body. These insects lay their eggs in the stalk, seed, or fruit of the plant. The grub then feeds on these plant parts, causing great damage.

Besides the boll weevil, there are other kinds that attack grain, fruit, clover, and alfalfa. The *granary weevil* is harmful to wheat and other seeds. It lays its eggs on the seed after it is stored, and the grubs burrow into the grain. The *rice weevil* destroys rice and other cereals in the same way. The *alfalfa weevil* first appeared in Salt Lake City about 1904. It has spread rapidly and causes great loss in alfalfa-growing regions every year. This insect is less than $\frac{1}{4}$ inch (6 millimeters) long and is grayish-brown to almost black. It came to the United States from southern Europe. In its native home it has many insect enemies that attack the weevil and its eggs, and keep it in check. The U.S. Department of Agriculture has imported large numbers of weevil enemies and spread them among the weevils to limit the damage to alfalfa.

There are also many kinds of fruit weevils. The *plum curculio* is the most important of the group that attacks apples, cherries, and plums. The wormlike larvae of these insects feed on the fruit, which falls off or spoils.

Ellis W. Huddleston

Scientific classification. Weevils belong to the weevil or snout-beetle family, Curculionidae.

See also **Beetle** (Kinds of beetles); **Boll weevil; Grain weevil.**

Weighing scale. See Scale, Weighing.

Weight is a measure of the heaviness of an object. The term *weight* has two general meanings. In science and technology, the weight of an object is the gravitational force on the object. When *weight* is used in this sense, the units of weight are units of force. In the International System of Units (SI), the modern metric system, the unit of force is the newton. In the inch-pound system customarily used in the United States, units of force include the ounce and the pound. One pound equals 4.448 newtons.

In commercial and everyday use, *weight* is used to mean *mass,* the amount of matter in an object. When people use *weight* in this sense, they measure it in pounds or *kilograms.* The kilogram is the SI's base unit of mass. One pound equals 0.454 kilogram.

The gravitational force on an object is related to the mass of the object by the equation $F = mg,$ where F is the force, m is the mass, and g is the acceleration due to gravity. At the surface of the earth, g is about 9.8 meters per second per second. A one-kilogram object therefore has a weight—in the sense of *gravitational force*—of about 9.8 newtons (2.2 pounds). On the moon, where the acceleration due to gravity is about 1.6 meters per second per second, the object would still have a mass of one kilogram, but its weight would be about 1.6 newtons (0.4 pound).   Michael Dine

See also Force; Gravitation; Mass.

Weight, Tables of. See Adolescent; Baby; Child; Growth.

Weight control is the process of maintaining a healthy body weight. In human beings, weight control usually involves regulating body fat. When people gain excess weight, most of the extra weight is body fat, and when people lose weight, most of the weight that is lost comes from body fat. The relationship between the amount of energy you obtain through food and the energy your body uses to maintain normal functions and to perform physical activity mainly determines how much body fat you will have.

Weight control is medically important because excess body fat is a major factor in many health problems. The condition of having an excessive amount of body fat is called *obesity.* Obese people have a higher risk of developing diabetes, *hypertension* (high blood pressure), and heart disease. See **Obesity.**

Energy supplied in food and burned by our bodies is measured in units called *kilocalories.* This term is often shortened to *calories* (see **Calorie**). Countries that use the metric system measure energy in *joules* instead of calories. One kilocalorie equals 4.184 joules. If you eat more calories than your body burns, most of the excess calories will be stored in your body as fat. If you eat fewer calories than your body burns, your body will burn stored fat for energy. For example, eating about 3,500 more calories than are burned will cause you to gain about 1 pound (0.45 kilogram) of fat. You will lose about 1 pound of fat if you consume 3,500 fewer calories than you use.

How body weight is determined

Food intake. Certain centers of the brain control the sensations associated with appetite, hunger, and fullness. These centers normally make people eat an amount of food that provides the right amount of energy for their needs. The *feeding centers* make people want to eat. The *satiety (suh TY uh tee)* centers act as a brake on the feeding centers, and they make people feel satisfied and stop eating.

The feeding and satiety centers are extremely complicated systems that are controlled by many chemicals in the brain. Many factors affect the production and release of these chemicals. These systems operate to determine food intake, including the amount and type of food that is eaten, how much body fat a person has,

blood sugar levels, and protein and fat metabolism. The systems can be affected by illness or emotions. Illness usually causes a decrease in appetite. Emotions can affect people's eating behaviors in different ways. For example, strong emotions, such as great disappointment, cause some people to eat more food and others to eat less food than they normally consume.

Energy expenditure. *Daily total energy expenditure* is the total amount of calories burned by a person's body in a day. It consists of three components: (1) resting energy expenditure, (2) the thermic effect of food, and (3) energy expended in physical activity. Resting energy expenditure is the energy used for normal body function, such as breathing and the beating of the heart, while the body is at rest. It accounts for about 70 percent of total energy expenditure. The thermic effect of food is the increase in energy expenditure that occurs after eating a meal because of the increased cellular activity required to digest food. It accounts for about 10 percent of total energy expenditure. Energy expended in physical activity is energy used in daily activities and exercise. It accounts for about 20 percent of total energy expenditure.

In general, the number of calories burned through resting energy expenditure is proportional to a person's weight. For example, a person who weighs 75 pounds (34 kilograms) will burn fewer calories at rest than a person who weighs 150 pounds (68 kilograms). A large person also burns more calories than a small person when engaged in weight-bearing activities, such as walking or running. In addition, the more vigorous the activity, the more calories are burned.

Energy balance. Consuming the same amount of calories that are expended maintains a constant body weight. Small, but consistent, differences between energy intake and energy expenditure over a long period can lead to major changes in body fat. For example, eating as few as 10 calories more than expended each day leads to an increase in weight of about 1 pound (0.45 kilogram) in one year or 30 pounds (14 kilograms) over 30 years.

Maintaining a healthy body weight

Many people who are not medically obese still weigh more than they would like. Several methods are available to help overweight and obese people lose weight. These methods include changing the diet to decrease calorie intake and increasing physical activity. Many methods involve behavior modification therapy to help people make lifestyle changes that are necessary to maintain a healthy weight. Although many obese people are able to lose weight initially, maintaining long-term weight loss is much more difficult to achieve. Physicians may prescribe certain drugs and even use surgery for people whose obesity is life threatening or who cannot reduce their weight through other methods.

Dieting is often the first step in any weight reduction program. The goal of a weight-reducing diet is to consume fewer calories than a person's daily total energy expenditure. For example, a person who eats 1,000 fewer calories a day than he or she uses will lose about 2 pounds (0.9 kilogram) a week. However, the foods in a reducing diet must provide a well-balanced selection of all the nutrients needed for good health. For a complete discussion of well-balanced diets, see **Nutrition.**

Diets for weight reduction vary. A very-low-calorie diet provides fewer than 800 calories per day, and a low-calorie diet provides 1,000 to 1,500 calories per day. For obese adults, a very-low-calorie diet will usually result in a loss of about 15 to 20 percent of a person's initial body weight within 12 to 16 weeks. A very-low-calorie diet is often difficult for people to maintain for long, and many people fail at such a diet and regain the weight they lost. Low-calorie diets usually produce a loss of about 8 percent of initial body weight after 16 to 26 weeks.

Health professionals commonly prescribe low-fat diets to help obese patients lose weight. Dietary fat contains 9 calories per gram compared with 4 calories per gram for carbohydrates and proteins. Thus, diets that limit dietary fat usually have fewer calories. Many people try to lose weight through diets that limit high-carbohydrate foods in favor of high-fat and high-protein foods. Most of these diets do not attempt to limit calories. However, many scientists are uncertain about the long-term effectiveness of low-carbohydrate diets.

Eating foods with a high water content, such as fruits, vegetables, and certain soups, can also help people lose weight. Such foods are called *low energy density foods.* These foods contain fewer calories per weight of food than dry foods, such as pretzels or crackers, or foods that contain a lot of fat, such as cheese or butter. A diet containing many low energy density foods results in fewer total calories consumed.

Prepackaged meals or liquid formula meal replacements can also help people lose weight. These products work by controlling portion size and calories. They also reduce food variety, which usually causes people to eat less.

Physical activity. Increasing physical activity is not an effective method for achieving initial weight loss, but is important in helping people keep weight off that is lost by dieting. However, an obese person—even one who is otherwise healthy—should not suddenly start a program of prolonged, strenuous exercise. An exercise program should be developed gradually to avoid dangerous strain on the heart or other parts of the body.

For example, a person may begin an exercise program by taking daily walks and gradually increasing the length each day. More demanding exercises can be added as a person becomes fitter and thinner. A person should build up to five to six hours of exercise per week. However, men over 40 years old, women over 50, and anyone with risk factors or symptoms of heart or lung disease should consult a physician before starting a vigorous exercise program.

Behavior modification therapy is used to help people make the lifestyle changes needed to lose weight and keep weight off. The goal is to identify and then modify habits that contribute to obesity. Behavior modification programs are usually conducted by psychologists or other trained personnel.

Behavior therapy for weight control usually includes keeping daily records of food intake and physical activity. People also must avoid situations that may prompt overeating. Social support, including assistance from family members and friends, to modify lifestyle is an important aspect of the therapy. Patients must also develop a relapse prevention plan to help recover from episodes of overeating or from regaining weight. Obese people who are treated with group behavior therapy usually lose about 9 percent of their initial weight in 20 to 26 weeks of treatment.

Drugs. Physicians may prescribe certain drugs as part

Energy equivalents of calories in some foods

This table shows the calories in some foods, and the minutes it would take a 150-pound (68-kilogram) person to use them up in various ways. A person half as heavy would need twice as long.

Food	Calories	Minutes of lying down	Minutes of walking (2½ mph)	Minutes of walking (4 mph)	Minutes of bicycle riding (9 mph)	Minutes of swimming	Minutes of running (7 mph)
Apple, large	125	83	34	23	20	14	14
Beans, green, canned, 1 cup	25	17	7	5	4	3	3
Bread and butter	100	67	27	18	16	11	11
Cake, yellow, with chocolate frosting, 1 piece	235	157	64	43	38	26	26
Carrot, grated, raw, 1 cup	45	30	12	8	7	5	5
Chicken potpie, 1 pie	545	363	149	99	87	60	60
Egg, fried	95	63	26	17	15	10	10
Ham, 2 slices	140	93	38	25	22	15	15
Hamburger sandwich	245	163	67	45	39	27	27
Ice cream, vanilla, ½ cup	135	90	37	25	22	15	15
Malted milk shake, 10 ounces	335	223	91	61	54	37	37
Milk, whole (3.3% fat), 1 cup	150	100	41	27	24	16	16
Milk, lowfat (2% fat), 1 cup	120	80	33	22	19	13	13
Pancake with syrup	121	81	33	22	19	13	13
Peas, green, canned, ½ cup	57	38	16	10	9	6	6
Pie, apple, ⅙ of pie	405	270	110	74	65	44	44
Pizza, cheese, 15-inch diameter, ⅛ of pizza	290	193	79	53	46	32	32
Pork chop, pan fried	335	223	91	61	54	37	37
Shrimp, french-fried, 7 medium	200	133	55	36	32	22	22
Spaghetti with tomato sauce and cheese	190	127	52	35	30	21	21
Steak, sirloin, 3 ounces	240	160	65	44	38	26	26
Strawberry shortcake	417	278	114	76	67	45	45

Energy equivalent values based on figures compiled by Robert E. Johnson, Professor Emeritus, University of Illinois.
Calorie content of food based on *Nutritive Value of Foods*, U.S. Dept. of Agriculture, 1985.

of a weight control program for carefully selected obese patients. Some drugs used to treat obesity act on brain centers that control appetite and, as a result, lead people to decrease food intake. Other drugs affect the intestine to decrease the absorption of dietary fat, thereby helping limit calorie intake. Drug treatment must be combined with a reduced calorie diet and regular physical activity to be most effective.

People using weight-loss drugs must be supervised by a physician to reduce the risk of medication side effects. Most patients using weight-loss drugs as part a weight control program lose about 10 percent of their body weight within 6 months. Researchers are continuing their efforts to develop safe and effective medications to help control weight.

Surgery. People who are obese face serious and life-threatening medical problems. Some extremely obese people require a surgical operation to reduce the size of their stomach to lose weight.

The most commonly performed weight-loss operation is called *gastric bypass surgery.* In this operation, a surgeon uses staples to close off the top of the stomach. This procedure reduces the size of the stomach to a small pouch. The upper portion of the small intestine is then attached to the pouch, bypassing a portion of the intestine. After surgery, the patient can eat only a small amount of food before becoming full. Patients usually lose about one-third of their body weight within 1 year, and they maintain the weight loss for many years.

Successful weight loss. Effective treatment for obesity considers the patient's willingness to undergo therapy and his or her ability to comply with treatment requirements. Successful treatment also may depend on a person's access to skilled caregivers and whether the patient can afford treatment. Obesity is a chronic condition that requires long-term, structured therapy for successful weight management. Support from physicians, caregivers, family, and friends and appropriate use of available treatments increase the chance for long-term weight-loss success.   Samuel Klein

See also **Diet; Obesity; Overeaters Anonymous; Physical fitness** (Health-related fitness).

Additional resources

Berg, Frances M. *Women Afraid to Eat: Breaking Free in Today's Weight-Obsessed World.* Healthy Weight Network, 2000.
Cassell, Dana K., and Gleaves, D. H. *The Encyclopedia of Obesity and Eating Disorders.* 2nd ed. Facts on File, 2000.
Drohan, Michele I. *Weight-Loss Programs.* Rosen Pub. Group, 1998.
Hensrud, Donald D., ed. *Mayo Clinic on Healthy Weight.* Kensington Pub., 2000.
Vogel, Shawna. *The Skinny on Fat: Our Obsession with Weight Control.* W. H. Freeman, 1999.

Weightlifting involves the lifting of weights attached to a barbell. People lift weights for exercise and to build their muscles. Weightlifting also serves as the basis of competitive sports called *weightlifting* and *powerlifting.* In these sports, athletes compete to determine who can lift the most weight. Such competitions match lifters with similar body weights. Athletes who participate in other sports sometimes lift weights to increase their strength and flexibility. Lifting weights is also a popular hobby for improving muscle tone and general health. Professional bodybuilders lift weights to improve their

© Douglas Kirkland, Sygma

A powerful weightlifter raises a heavy metal barbell over his head during competition in the Olympic Games.

muscular development. They exhibit their physiques in organized competitions. Judges decide which body-builder has the best body.

In the sport of weightlifting, there are two types of lifts—the *snatch* and the *clean and jerk.* In the snatch, lifters bend down and grasp the barbell. They then lift the bar in a quick motion, raising it above their head while squatting under it. In the clean and jerk, the lifter brings the bar to a resting position at the shoulders, then jerks the barbell over the head by thrusting out the arms and legs.

Participants are allowed three attempts on each lift. Weights are added to the barbell after each successful attempt. A panel of three referees determines whether each lift was properly executed. The lifter in each class who lifts the highest total wins. The total is the weight of the heaviest successful snatch added to the heaviest successful clean and jerk. Weightlifting is an event in the Summer Olympic Games.

In the sport of powerlifting, the three chief types of lifts are the *squat,* the *bench press,* and the *dead lift.* In the squat, lifters stand upright with the barbell resting on the rear of the shoulders. They then lower themselves to a squatting position, pause, and again rise to an upright position. In the bench press, lifters raise and lower the weight above their chest while lying on their back on a bench. In the dead lift, the barbell rests on the floor in front of the lifter. The competitor bends, grasps, then lifts it in one motion and straightens to a standing position, keeping the weight hanging at arm's length.

Critically reviewed by the United States Weightlifting Federation

See also **Bodybuilding; Olympic Games** (table).

Additional resources

Baechle, Thomas R., and Groves, B. R. *Weight Training: Steps to Success.* 2nd ed. Human Kinetics, 1998.
Roberts, Scott, and Weider, Ben. *Strength and Weight Training for Young Athletes.* Contemporary Bks., 1994.
Savage, Jeff. *Fundamental Strength Training.* Lerner, 1998. Younger readers.

Weights and measures are tools that we use to measure the physical properties of things. They are essential elements for trade and commerce, and they lie at the foundation of science and engineering.

A *measurement unit* is a precisely defined quantity that can be used to measure all other quantities of the same kind. For example, we can use the unit *meter* to measure any length or distance—the height of a person, the length of a swimming pool, or the distance to the moon.

A *measurement standard* is an object that uniquely defines or represents the size of a unit. One important standard is known as the *international prototype kilogram*. This standard is a particular weight that is made of an *alloy* (mixture) of the metals platinum and iridium. It is the standard for the *kilogram,* a unit of *mass* (amount of matter). All standard weights in the world, including those for pounds and ounces, are related to this one.

All countries enforce the uniform use of measurement standards within their borders. Inspectors check the accuracy of gasoline pumps to make sure that what is being sold as a liter or a gallon of gasoline is actually that much gasoline. Other officials check the scales used to weigh meat, fruits, and vegetables in grocery stores. Still others weigh samples of packaged foods and compare the weight with what is printed on the labels.

Measurement systems. Groups of units are organized into *measurement systems.* The most widely used measurement system is the modern metric system, which is known as the International System of Units. People commonly refer to this system by the initials SI, which stand for its name in French: *Système International d'Unités.*

Since about 1980, every technologically advanced nation but the United States has used SI for almost all measurements. In the United States, scientists and most engineers use SI. But for many commercial and everyday measurements, Americans use the *inch-pound system.* This system consists mainly of units that English people brought to what is now the United States. The English brought the units with them in the 1600's, when they began to settle along the Atlantic coast of North America.

Because of the source of the units, Americans often call them *English units.* Because the units have been used for so long in the United States, people there sometimes refer to them as *customary units.*

The inch-pound units are now defined in terms of SI units. In 1959, the United States and other English-speaking nations entered into an agreement that made the foot equal to exactly 0.3048 meter and the pound equal to exactly 453.59237 grams. However, for land surveying in the United States, an older definition of the foot is sometimes used. This foot, called the *U.S. survey foot,* is exactly $\frac{1,200}{3,937}$ meter long.

Representatives of countries throughout the world regulate SI. These delegates gather every four years at a General Conference on Weights and Measures. A permanent organization called the International Bureau of Weights and Measures (BIPM) operates under the authority of the General Conference. The BIPM, which is located in France, maintains the fundamental measurement standards of the SI. For example, the BIPM carefully preserves the international prototype kilogram. This organization also compares national prototype standards with the international standards.

In the United States, the National Institute of Standards and Technology, an agency of the Department of Commerce, maintains the country's primary measurement standards. That agency also compares other standards with the primary standards, and it conducts studies in precision measurement. Many different federal and state agencies carry out inspections to ensure fair measurements in commerce.

Conversion factors. Tables in this article define commonly used units in the SI and inch-pound systems. The tables also provide factors that are needed to convert from one system to the other. Suppose, for example, you wanted to convert a distance of 15 miles to kilometers. You would multiply 15 by 1.609, the number of kilometers that make up 1 mile: $15 \times 1.609 = 24.135$. You would then round this number to 24. So 15 miles equals 24 kilometers.

Almost all the conversion factors in the tables are giv-

Miscellaneous weights and measures

***Angstrom** is an old metric unit used to measure sizes of atoms and molecules and wavelengths of radiation. One angstrom equals $\frac{1}{10}$ nanometer or $\frac{1}{10,000,000}$ millimeter ($\frac{1}{254,000,000}$ inch). The angstrom is not a part of the modern metric system (SI).

Astronomical unit (AU) is the average distance from the earth to the sun—about 93 million miles (150 million kilometers).

***Barrel** is the name given to various units of liquid capacity. The barrel that is used internationally for petroleum products contains 42 United States gallons (159.0 liters).

***Carat,** used to weigh precious stones and pearls, equals 200 milligrams (0.0071 ounce). Some people confuse *carat* with *karat,* a measure of the purity of gold.

Cord is a measure of cut wood equal to 128 cubic feet or 3.625 cubic meters. A pile of wood 4 feet high, 4 feet wide, and 8 feet long is a cord.

***Furlong,** used mainly to measure distances in horse races, equals $\frac{1}{8}$ mile (201.2 meters).

Hand, used to measure horses from the ground to the withers, equals 4 inches (10.16 centimeters).

Imperial pint, used to measure the volume of beverages in the United Kingdom, equals 34.68 cubic inches (0.5683 liter). It also equals 1.201 of the pints used to measure liquids in the United States.

Karat is a measure used to express the proportion of pure gold in an alloy, one karat indicating a fraction of $\frac{1}{24}$. Thus, 24-karat gold is pure, and 18-karat gold alloy contains $\frac{18}{24}$ pure gold. Some people confuse *karat* with *carat,* used to weigh precious stones and pearls.

***Knot** is a speed of 1 nautical mile (1.151 statute miles or 1.852 kilometers) per hour.

Light-year is the distance light travels in space in a year. It is about 5.878 trillion miles (9.461 trillion kilometers).

Line, used to measure buttons, is $\frac{1}{40}$ inch (0.635 millimeter).

Load, of earth or gravel, equals 1 cubic yard (0.7646 cubic meter)

Micron is an old, non-SI metric unit equal to 1 micrometer.

Point is either of two units that specify the size of type. In the American Point System traditionally used in the printing industry, 1 point equals 0.01384 inch (0.3515 millimeter). In type that is set using modern computer programs, 1 point equals $\frac{1}{72}$ inch (0.3528 millimeter).

Skein is a unit used to measure yarn. There are 360 feet (109.7 meters) in a skein of cotton yarn.

Square, used to measure floor or roofing material, is an area of 100 square feet (9.290 square meters).

Stone, used in the United Kingdom to measure weight, especially of people, equals 14 pounds (6.350 kilograms).

---

*Has a separate article in *World Book.*

en in four *significant figures.* The significant figures are the digits that follow any zeroes at the beginning of a factor. For example, in the conversion factor 0.03937, used to convert millimeters to inches, the digits, 3, 9, 3, and 7 are significant figures.

The number of significant figures in a conversion factor indicates the precision of the factor—the larger the number of significant figures, the more precise the factor. A precision of four significant figures is sufficient for almost all practical purposes. The tables give factors for the teaspoon, the tablespoon, and the cup in fewer significant figures because people do not use those units for precise work. The factor for converting inches to centimeters is given in three figures because this conversion is exact.

Comparison of measurement systems. The metric system is easier to use than the inch-pound system. Indeed, the metric system was designed for ease of use, with simple relationships established among the units. By contrast, the inch-pound system is a combination of groups of units that developed separately. As a result, the inch-pound system involves a host of conversion factors that are difficult to use.

One feature that makes SI easy to use is the decimal relationship between the units for measuring a given property. For example, the base unit for the measure-

ment of length is the *meter.* A larger unit for measuring this property is the *dekameter,* which is 10 times as long as the meter. The *hectometer* is 10 times as long as the dekameter, and the *kilometer* is 10 times as long as the hectometer.

To convert from one of these units to another, merely shift the decimal point the appropriate number of places to the left or right. For example, to convert meters to kilometers, shift the decimal point three places to the left. The three decimal places represent the three factors of 10 by which the meter differs from the kilometer. Thus, 2,864 meters converts to 2.864 kilometers.

Another feature that makes SI easy to use is the simple relationship between groups of units that measure different properties. For example, 1 liter of water has a volume of 1,000 cubic centimeters and a mass of 1 kilogram.

In the inch-pound system, the unit that corresponds to the liter is the quart. But people in the United States use two kinds of quarts—one to measure "dry" products, such as strawberries, and the other for liquids. The quart used for dry measure has a volume of 67.20 cubic inches. The quart used for liquid measure has a volume of 57.75 cubic inches—and 1 quart of water weighs 2.086 pounds.

Development of units of measure. No one knows

Length and distance

	Inch-pound	Metric
1 inch (in.)*		=2.54 centimeters (cm)
1 foot (ft.)*	=12 in.	=30.48 cm
1 yard (yd.)*	=3 ft.	=0.9144 meter (m)
1 rod (rd.)*	=5 $\frac{1}{2}$ yd.	=5.029 m
1 statute mile (mi.)	=5,280 ft.	=1,609 m
1 fathom*	=6 ft.	=1.829 m
1 nautical mile	=1.151 statute mile	=1,852 m

*Has a separate article in *World Book.*

	Metric	Inch-pound
1 nanometer (nm)	=0.001 micrometer (µm)	
1 micrometer (µm)	=0.001 millimeter (mm)	
1 millimeter (mm)	=0.001 m	=0.03937 in.
1 centimeter (cm)*	=0.01 m	=0.3937 in.
1 decimeter (dm)	=0.1 m	=3.937 in.
1 meter (m)*		=39.37 in.
1 dekameter (dam)	=10 m	=32.81 ft.
1 hectometer (hm)	=100 m	=328.1 ft.
1 kilometer (km)	=1,000 m	=3,281 ft.
		=0.6213 mi.

*Has a separate article in *World Book.*

Surface or area

	Inch-pound	Metric
1 square inch (in.²)		=6.452 square centimeters (cm²)
1 square foot (ft.²)	=144 in.²	=929.0 cm²
1 square yard (yd.²)	=9 ft.²	=0.8361 square meter (m²)
1 acre (land measure)*	=43,560 ft.²	=4,047 m²
1 square mile (mi.²)	=640 acres	=2.590 square kilometers (km²)

*Has a separate article in *World Book.*

	Metric	Inch-pound
1 square millimeter (mm²)	=0.000001 m²	
1 square centimeter (cm²)	=0.0001 m²	=0.1550 in.²
1 square decimeter (dm²)	=0.01 m²	=15.50 in.²
1 square meter (m²)		=10.76 ft.²
1 square dekameter (dam²)	=100 m²	=1,076 ft.²
1 square hectometer (hm²)	=10,000 m²	=107,639 ft.²
1 hectare (land measure)	=10,000 m²	=2.471 acres
1 square kilometer (km²)	=1,000,000 m²	=0.3861 mi.²

who developed the first measurement units. But surely the need existed when tribes began to trade. Suppose two tribes regularly exchanged ropes for grain. The owners of the grain would want to know how long the ropes would be. The tribes would therefore need to agree on a unit of length. The owners of the ropes would want to know how heavy the grain was or how many baskets or pots it would fill. Thus, the two parties would also need a unit of weight or volume.

Early units. The earliest measurement units were probably units of length. These units almost certainly were related to parts of the body—the hand or foot, for example. Later, local leaders established a particular

stick of wood or a certain rod of metal as a standard. They made copies of this standard for commercial use and placed the primary standard in a temple or some other secure place. People based early units of weight on the heaviness of a given number of kernels of grain. They based units of volume on the capacity of baskets and, later, clay pots.

Ancient civilizations developed simple groups of standard units. In an old Hebrew system, for example, four finger widths made a *palm,* and six palms made a *cubit.* Not all cubits were the same, however. The Hebrew cubit was about 450 millimeters long. The cubit that the Egyptians used in building the Pyramids of Giza

Volume and capacity

Inch-pound volume

	Inch-pound	Metric
1 cubic inch (in.³)		=16.39 cubic centimeters (cm³)
1 cubic foot (ft.³)	=1,728 in.³	=28.32 cubic decimeters (dm³)
1 cubic yard (yd.³)	=27 ft.³	=0.7646 cubic meter (m³)

Metric volume and capacity

	Metric	Inch-pound
1 cubic centimeter (cm³)	=0.000001 m³	=0.06102 in.³
1 cubic decimeter (dm³)	=0.001 m³	=61.02 in.³
1 cubic meter (m³)		=35.31 ft.³
1 cubic dekameter (dam³)	=1,000 m³	=1,308 yd.³

Liter-based metric capacity

	Metric	Inch-pound
1 milliliter (mL)	=1 cm³ =0.001 liter (L)	=0.03381 fluid ounce (fl. oz.)
1 centiliter (cL)	=0.01 L	=0.3381 fl. oz.
1 deciliter (dL)	=0.1 L	=3.381 fl. oz.
1 liter (L)*	=1 dm³	=0.9081 dry quart =1.057 liquid quart
1 dekaliter (daL)	=10 L	=2.642 gallons
1 hectoliter (hL)	=100 L	=26.42 gallons
1 kiloliter (kL)	=1,000 L	=264.2 gallons =28.38 bushels =35.31 ft.³

Inch-pound liquid capacity

	Inch-pound	Metric
1 teaspoon	=1/6 fl. oz.	=5 mL
1 tablespoon	=1/2 fl. oz.	=15 mL
1 fluid ounce (fl. oz.)*		=29.57 mL
1 cup	=8 fl. oz.	=237 mL
1 pint*	=16 fl. oz.	=0.4732 L
1 quart*	=32 fl. oz.	=0.9464 L
1 gallon*	=4 quarts	=3.785 L

Inch-pound dry capacity

	Inch-pound	Metric
1 pint (dry)*		=0.5506 L
1 quart (dry)*	=2 pints	=1.101 L
1 peck*	=8 quarts	=8.810 L
1 bushel*	=4 pecks	=35.24 L

Shipping capacity

	Inch-pound	Metric
1 shipping ton, or 1 measurement ton, or 1 freight ton	=40 ft.³	=1.132 m³
1 displacement ton	=35 ft.³	=0.991 m³
1 register ton	=100 ft.³	=2.832 m³

*Has a separate article in *World Book.*

in about 2600 to 2500 B.C. was about 524 millimeters in length.

Inch-pound units. Some inch-pound units originated in the Roman Empire, which once included most of what is now England. The *mile,* for example, comes from *mille passus,* which means *thousand paces* in Latin, the language of the empire. Other inch-pound units reached England when Norman invaders from what is now France conquered England in 1066.

In the 1500's, a law signed by Queen Elizabeth I of England established many of the present relationships among the inch-pound units. Previously, the mile of 1,000 paces had been understood to be 5,000 feet. The new law established the statute mile of 5,280 feet. This change also made the mile equal to exactly 8 *furlongs.* The furlong was originally the length of a furrow that oxen could plow without resting. The change was convenient because the furlong was still widely used at the time. It is now used mainly to measure distances in horse races.

The British government simplified the standards for volume measurement in 1824. It established an *Imperial gallon,* defined as the volume occupied by 10 pounds of water. The new measures of the Imperial system were adopted throughout the British Empire, but not in the United States, which retained the old liquid and dry pints and quarts that had arrived with the colonists.

The metric system. In the 1600's and 1700's, a rise in international commerce and an increase in international contact among scientists created a need for a new system. Merchants and scientists wanted a system that would be widely agreed upon and easy to use. Various proposals were debated. Finally, in 1790, France's National Assembly, or parliament, asked the French Academy of Sciences to propose a system of measurement that would be suitable for adoption by the entire world. The work of the Academy resulted in the metric system adopted by France in 1795.

France required the French people to use the metric system in 1840. Soon after, other countries in Europe, Central America, and South America began to use the system. In 1875, 17 nations, included the United States, signed a document known as the Treaty of the Meter. That document established the International Bureau of Weights and Measures. It also ensured continuing international cooperation in the development of metric weights and measures.

By 1900, scientists throughout the world were using metric units, and most of the technologically advanced countries had adopted the metric system for everyday use. The main exceptions were the United States and the nations that were then part of the British Empire. But in 1965, the pressures of international commerce persuaded the United Kingdom to announce that it would convert to SI. New Zealand began conversion in 1969, Australia in 1970, and Canada in 1975.

In the United States, Presidents John Adams and Thomas Jefferson, whose terms ran from 1797 to 1809, had shown interest in the metric system. However, it was still little used at that time, even in France. The United States Congress took no action on the metric system until 1866, when it legalized use of the metric units. In 1893, the U.S. Office of Weights and Measures carefully compared the U.S. prototype standards with the metric standards in France. The Americans then defined the U.S. yard in terms of the meter and the U.S. pound in terms of the kilogram.

In 1975, the United States Congress passed the Metric Conversion Act, which called for a voluntary changeover to the metric system. A bill passed in 1988 declared that the metric system was "the preferred system of weights and measures for United States trade and commerce." However, the bill did not establish a timetable for conversion from inch-pound units, nor did it specify penalties for failing to convert.

In the early 2000's, international trade and other international business were becoming more important to the United States. The growth of this commerce increased

Weight and mass

Avoirdupois weight (mass)*

	Inch-pound	Metric
1 ounce (oz.)*		=28.35 grams (g)
1 pound (lb.)*	=16 oz.	=453.6 g
1 hundredweight (short)	=100 lb.	=45.36 kilograms (kg)
1 hundredweight (long)	=112 lb.	=50.80 kg
1 ton (short)*	=2,000 lb.	=907.2 kg
1 ton (long)	=2,240 lb.	=1,016 kg

Metric mass

	Metric	Inch-pound
1 milligram (mg)	=0.001 g	
1 gram (g)*		=0.03527 oz.
1 kilogram (kg)*	=1,000 g	=2.205 lb.
1 metric ton	=1,000 kg	=2,205 lb.
		=1.102 short tons
		=0.9842 long ton

Troy weight (mass)*

	Inch-pound	Metric
1 ounce (troy)*		=31.10 g
1 pound (troy)*	=12 ounces	=373.2 g

*Has a separate article in *World Book.*

the pressure to use metric units in the United States. In engineering and manufacturing, conversion to the metric system was proceeding steadily. More and more consumer products were being sold in metric packaging. Examples included all medicines, even aspirin and vitamins; wine and liquor; and many groceries and soft drinks.   Bruce B. Barrow

Related articles. See **Metric system** and its list of related articles. See also:

Area
Astronomy (Units of distance)
Calendar
Energy (Units of work and energy)
Force (Characteristics of force)
Heat (Temperature and heat)
International Bureau of Weights and Measures
League
Light (Measuring light)
Mass
Mathematics
Mile
National Institute of Standards
    and Technology
Navigation
Sound (The nature of sound)
Square measure
Surveying
Temperature
Testing
Time
Volume
Weight

Weill, *vyl* or *wyl,* **Kurt** (1900-1950), was a German composer famous for his music for the theater. Weill is noted for music he wrote for the plays of the German playwright Bertolt Brecht. The best-known work by Brecht and Weill is *The Threepenny Opera* (1928), which includes the popular song "Mack the Knife." They also wrote *Happy End* (1929), *The Rise and Fall of the City of Mahagonny* (1930), and *The Seven Deadly Sins* (1933).

Weill was born on March 2, 1900, in Dessau. He studied with the noted composers Engelbert Humperdinck and Ferruccio Busoni. He composed instrumental music and works for the stage before starting his collaboration with Brecht. Weill left Germany in 1933 after the Nazis came to power. He settled in the United States in 1935.

Weill's first two works in America were the experimental musical plays *Johnny Johnson* (1936) and *The Eternal Road* (1937). His first traditional musical comedy, *Knickerbocker Holiday* (1938), features the ballad "September Song." Weill's other musicals include *One Touch of Venus* (1943), *Street Scene* (1947), *Down in the Valley* (1948), and *Lost in the Stars* (1949).   Stewart L. Ross

Weimar Republic. See **Germany** (The Weimar Republic).

Weimaraner, *VY muh RAH nuhr* or *WY muh RAH nuhr,* is a hunting dog that originated in Weimar, Germany, in the 1800's. It was first bred to hunt big-game animals, such as deer and bears. Later, the dog became chiefly used to hunt game birds. Its gray coat, gray nose, and amber eyes give the dog a striking appearance. The dog has short fur and a tail cropped to be about 6 inches (15 centimeters) long when the dog is full grown. The Weimaraner weighs 60 to 80 pounds (27 to 36 kilograms) and is 24 to 28 inches (61 to 71 centimeters) high. It is intelligent, friendly, and obedient and makes an excellent pet. The dog is sometimes called the *gray ghost* because

of its color and its silent movements when hunting. See also **Dog** (picture: Sporting dogs).
            Critically reviewed by the Weimaraner Club of America

Weinberger, Caspar Willard (1917-   ), was a Republican government official who held two Cabinet posts. He served as secretary of defense under President Ronald Reagan from 1981 to 1987 and helped direct a major increase in U.S. military forces. Weinberger was secretary of health, education, and welfare under President Richard M. Nixon from 1973 to 1975.

Weinberger was born on Aug. 18, 1917, in San Francisco and graduated from Harvard University in 1938. He earned a law degree from the Harvard Law School in 1941. In 1952, he won election to the California Assembly. In 1968, he became California state finance director. Nixon named Weinberger chairman of the Federal Trade Commission in 1970. In 1972, Nixon appointed him director of the Office of Management and Budget. In 1989, he became publisher of *Forbes* magazine.

In 1992, Weinberger was charged with lying to Congress and government investigators and blocking their investigations about the Iran-contra affair. He was scheduled to stand trial in early 1993. But Weinberger declared that he was innocent of the charges, and in December 1992, President George H. W. Bush granted him a full pardon. See **Iran-contra affair; Reagan, Ronald W.** (The Iran-contra affair).   Charles Bartlett

Weisgard, Leonard (1916-2000), was an American artist and an illustrator of children's books. He won the Caldecott Medal in 1947 for his illustrations for *The Little Island* by Margaret Wise Brown, writing under the name Golden MacDonald. Weisgard illustrated over 20 other books by Brown and many picture books by other authors, including *The Courage of Sarah Noble* (1954) by Alice Dalgliesh. Weisgard wrote and illustrated over 20 books, including *My First Picture Book* (1953) and *The Plymouth Thanksgiving* (1967). He was born Dec. 13, 1916, in New Haven, Connecticut.   Jill P. May

Weismann, *VYS mahn,* **August,** *OW gust* (1834-1914), a German biologist, is known chiefly for his theories of heredity and evolution. He stressed the independence from the rest of the body of the *germ plasm,* his name for the factors of inheritance in the sex cells. He denied that acquired characteristics can be inherited. He located the germ plasm in the chromosomes, a prediction that was proved correct early in the 1900's. Weismann upheld the theory of natural selection and was one of the first German scientists to support the British scientist Charles Darwin.

In Weismann's later years, he devoted himself chiefly to theoretical studies, and wrote extensively on heredity and evolution. His major work, *The Germ Plasm,* appeared in 1892. Weismann was born on Jan. 17, 1834, in Frankfurt (am Main), Germany.   Alan R. Rushton

Weizmann, *VYTS mahn* or *WYTS muhn,* **Chaim,** *KY ihm* (1874-1952), served as Israel's first president from 1949 until his death. From 1920 to 1930 and from 1935 to 1946, Weizmann was president of the World Zionist Organization. This group worked to establish a national homeland in Palestine for Jews. Weizmann headed the Jewish delegation to the Paris Peace Conference in 1919, and worked there to have the League of Nations assign administration of Palestine to the United Kingdom. In 1917, the United Kingdom had issued the Balfour

Declaration, which supported the idea of a Jewish national homeland in Palestine (see **Balfour Declaration**).

Weizmann was born in Motol, Russia, and he was educated in Germany and Switzerland. He taught chemistry at Manchester University in England from 1904 to 1914. During World War I (1914-1918), Weizmann discovered an improved method of making acetone and butyl alcohol for explosives. This discovery aided Britain's war effort.　　Bernard Reich

Wide World Photos

Chaim Weizmann

Welding is a method of permanently joining two pieces of metal, usually by means of heat. Manufacturers use welding in making many products, including automobiles, home appliances, and furniture. Construction firms use it in erecting bridges, buildings, and other structures. The production of electronic equipment involves sophisticated microwelding processes.

There are more than 60 welding processes. Each process falls into one of three groups: (1) fusion welding, (2) solid-state bonding, and (3) brazing and soldering. However, some metallurgists do not consider brazing and soldering technically to be forms of welding.

Fusion welding uses heat to partially melt the metal surfaces that are to be joined. When the metal cools and hardens, the two pieces are connected by a welded joint that may be as strong as any other part of the metal.

Most fusion welding processes also use a *filler metal,* which is added to the weld in the form of a *welding rod* or a *consumable electrode.* The heat of the welding process melts the rod or electrode, which mixes with the melted base metal. The filler metal thus fills in the joint and strengthens it. The seam of hardened filler and base metal is called the *fusion zone.*

In most fusion welding processes, the heated metals must be shielded from hydrogen, nitrogen, and oxygen in the atmosphere. If the metals absorbed these gases, the weld could be weak or brittle. Shielding may be provided by spraying the metals during welding with an inactive gas, such as argon, carbon dioxide, or helium. Another method involves applying a nonmetallic *flux* to the metals before welding. The heat of welding melts the flux, which covers and protects the metals. A third way of shielding the metals is to weld in a vacuum.

There are a number of methods of fusion welding. They include the following.

Arc welding joins metals by using heat from an electric arc (see **Electric arc**). The welder uses an electrode holder, an electrode or welding rod, and a generator that produces an electric current. One type of arc welding, *shielded metal arc welding,* forms an electric arc between the metals and a flux-covered electrode. Heat from the electric arc melts the metal, the electrode, and the flux. In *submerged arc welding,* the electric arc is covered by powdered flux from a container attached to the welding tool. The arc forms between the metals and a consumable wire electrode that adds filler metal to the weld. The consumable wire electrode is fed continu-

ously through the welding tool from a coil.

Another type of arc welding is *gas tungsten arc welding.* In this process, an electric arc is directed between the metals and a bare wire electrode made from tungsten, which does not melt in the arc's heat. Argon or helium gas shields the metals. The welder must use a separate welding rod if filler metal is required. In *plasma arc welding,* argon or a similar gas is electrically heated until it forms an ionized gas called a *plasma.* An arc of plasma is directed on the metals to weld them, and a filler metal is supplied separately. The plasma arc also shields the metals. A plasma arc produces extremely high temperatures and can be used to weld metals that are difficult to join by other methods.

Resistance welding joins metals by means of the heat produced by resistance to the flow of an electric current. This process does not use filler metal or flux. The metals are clamped together, and electrodes apply pressure on opposite sides. An electric current passing through the electrodes meets resistance when it flows from one metal to the other. The resulting heat melts the metals and welds them together. In *resistance spot welding,* rod-shaped electrodes form spot welds along the metals. In *resistance-seam welding,* electrodes in the form of rollers create a continuous seam.

Gas welding uses heat from a gas torch to join two metals. The most common welding gas is acetylene mixed with oxygen (see **Acetylene**). If the job requires a filler metal, the welder dips a welding rod into the liquid metal between the pieces being joined. A flux may be applied to the metal before welding.

Other fusion welding processes include those that use electron beams and lasers to produce the energy necessary to join metals. These methods require complex, specialized equipment. See **Laser**.

Solid-state bonding uses pressure as well as heat to bond metal and other materials. Common methods of solid-state bonding include the following.

Deformation bonding joins metals partly by means of pressure great enough to deform the pieces. The pressure forces the surfaces so close together that a strong joint forms by atomic attraction. Methods of exerting pressure include *roll bonding, friction* or *inertia welding, explosive bonding,* and *ultrasonic bonding.* In most cases, deformation bonding also involves heating metals to temperatures just below their melting points, so

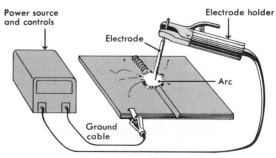

Power source and controls

Electrode holder

Electrode

Arc

Ground cable

Electrode cable

WORLD BOOK diagram

Arc welding joins metals by means of the heat produced by an electric arc. In shielded metal-arc welding, the arc forms between a flux-covered electrode and the metals to be welded.

Phil Degginger

A welder wears a mask with a special lens that protects the worker's eyes from the intense light of the welding process.

that atoms will move to the joint and fill in any gaps.

Diffusion bonding resembles deformation bonding but uses pressure insufficient to noticeably deform pieces. Diffusion bonding is especially suitable for joining unusual or reactive materials.

Brazing and soldering use a melted filler metal to join unusually close-fitting parts. The filler metal and a special flux are applied to the parts, which are then heated in an oven or with a gas torch. The temperature is too low to melt the parts. But the filler metal melts into the joint and welds the parts together. Brazing uses such fillers as brass, bronze, or a silver alloy. Soldering uses lead-tin alloys or other metals with comparatively lower melting points. See **Solder.**   Donald R. Askeland

Welfare refers to government programs that provide money, medical care, food, housing, and other necessities for needy people. Welfare is also called *public assistance.* People who receive welfare include children, the aged, the blind, the disabled, and others who cannot adequately provide for themselves and their families.

Public assistance differs from other government assistance programs called *social insurance,* or *social security.* Social insurance programs provide benefits to people whether or not they are poor. Social insurance programs are funded mainly by special payroll taxes on workers and their employers. Such programs include old-age, survivors, disability, and health insurance; unemployment insurance; and workers' compensation.

Welfare around the world

All nations have some type of welfare. But countries differ in how much they spend on welfare as compared to social insurance, and in how much they spend on welfare relative to the size of their overall economy.

Most European countries provide for their needy mainly through national programs that benefit all their citizens. These countries have welfare programs, but they also have universal programs that provide free medical and hospital care, family allowances, and retirement pensions. European countries typically spend a larger share of their economy on welfare and social insurance than other countries do. The Scandinavian countries, in particular, have such comprehensive programs that they are said to be *welfare states.* For more

information on such programs, see the *Social welfare* section of the articles on **Norway** and **Sweden.**

Canada, Australia, New Zealand, and the United Kingdom, like the United States, provide a larger share of aid through public assistance than do the continental West European nations. But these nations have more generous welfare systems than the United States does, spending a larger share of their economy on aid to the poor.

East Asian countries, such as Japan, South Korea, and Singapore, rely more on privately funded welfare. Much of this aid is provided by employers and families themselves. Therefore, government spending on welfare in those nations is low by international standards.

Less developed countries in Africa, Latin America, and Asia have lower overall budgets for welfare than other nations. South Africa has one of the better-developed social welfare systems, with a particularly comprehensive health care system. Many countries in Latin America have well-developed welfare systems, with Uruguay traditionally having a particularly generous system. The East Asian countries and the Philippines have some of the strongest welfare systems in Asia. The South Asian countries, in particular India and Sri Lanka, provide smaller benefits and serve fewer recipients.

Welfare in the United States

Federal and state governments in the United States serve the needy through a number of public assistance programs. Most people receive help through (1) Medicaid, (2) cash aid programs, and (3) the Food Stamp Program. Welfare mainly helps people who live below the *poverty line,* an income level established by the federal government. The poverty line is adjusted annually to account for inflation. For the poverty line for families of various sizes, see **Poverty** (table).

Medicaid provides free medical care to needy people. Each state administers its own Medicaid program, and eligibility criteria vary from state to state. About a third of all Medicaid expenses are for the aged. Most of these expenses pay for nursing home care. Medicaid is funded mostly by the federal government, and the states pay the rest.

Cash aid programs provide money to poor people who cannot support themselves or their dependents. Temporary Assistance to Needy Families (TANF) provides aid to families with children. Most families that qualify have just one parent in the home, usually a woman. But benefits may also be available to two-parent families if both parents are unemployed. Much of the funding for TANF comes from the federal government. The states provide the rest of the money and administer the program. The size of payments varies from state to state. The program requires most recipients of cash aid to start working within two years after they begin receiving aid. In addition, most families can receive no more than five years of cash assistance during the lifetime of the head of the family.

Supplemental Security Income for the Aged, Blind, and Disabled (SSI) provides aid to needy people who are at least 65 years old, or are blind or disabled. The federal government finances and administers SSI programs in most states, but some states supplement the federal payment and administer their own programs.

The Food Stamp Program helps low-income households buy more and better food than they could otherwise afford. Participating households receive a plastic card resembling a credit card that can be loaded with a monetary value. The value varies depending on the family's size, income, and expenses. Cooperating grocery stores accept the card for food purchases only. Funds are then electronically transferred to the stores from special accounts for each family. Before the use of the cards, participants used coupons called *food stamps* to make their purchases.

Other welfare programs include public housing and energy assistance. Public housing provides low-cost rental apartments in government-owned buildings. Other federal housing programs give cash allowances to help low-income families rent privately owned housing. Energy assistance, which is federally financed but administered by the states, helps people pay fuel bills.

The federal government also finances and administers nutrition programs for low-income families. These programs furnish free food supplements for pregnant mothers and young children, and free or low-cost school lunches. The federal government also provides financial aid to college students from needy families.

The Internal Revenue Service finances and administers the Earned Income Tax Credit (EITC), a federal program. It reduces income taxes for low-income individuals and families with dependent children. Unlike other programs, it assists people living above the poverty line.

Finally, state and local governments fund and administer their own general assistance programs. These programs provide financial aid for needy people who do not qualify for other welfare. People waiting to receive assistance from other programs also may get temporary emergency aid from general assistance.

Criticism of the welfare system

Criticism of the welfare system ranges over a number of economic and social issues. Some people criticize welfare programs for not providing enough benefits to eliminate poverty. Spending on welfare would have to increase greatly to eliminate poverty, and many people believe the cost of welfare is already too high.

Many critics of the welfare system charge that providing a steady income to needy people encourages idleness. Actually, most welfare benefits go to elderly, blind, and disabled people and mothers with young children. But welfare does discourage some recipients from seeking employment, especially if they cannot get much more money from a job than they can get from benefits. Welfare discourages other recipients from working harder by reducing benefits if their income increases.

Many people say the welfare system is too complex and costly to administer. In the United States, for example, each program has its own eligibility requirements and ways of calculating benefits, and these rules vary from state to state. Public officials collect detailed information about applicants to determine their eligibility. This process is time-consuming and costly. It may also make recipients feel ashamed or embarrassed, particularly if welfare caseworkers treat them harshly.

Some welfare recipients cheat by not reporting income. But most welfare fraud comes from suppliers of services to welfare recipients. Some physicians, pharmacists, and others have overcharged for services.

Welfare programs also may affect family stability. Unhappy marriages may break up partly because cash aid is more readily available to families with only one parent. In addition, some people believe that welfare causes higher birth rates, with welfare mothers deliberately having children to increase their benefits. But statistics show that there is no relationship between birth rates and cash aid programs. The availability of cash aid may enable needy parents to raise their children themselves rather than give them up for adoption or foster care.

History

In early times, governments seldom took responsibility for relieving poverty. Charity to needy people came from relatives and neighbors. Religious groups gave the poor shelter, medical care, and financial help.

Early welfare laws treated the poor harshly. For example, the Statute of Laborers, passed in England in 1349, prohibited charity because it might encourage idleness. In 1601, Parliament passed the Act for the Relief of the Poor, also known as the Elizabethan Poor Law. This law made local government units called *parishes* responsible for their own poor.

Early welfare laws recognized two forms of assistance—*outdoor relief* and *indoor relief.* Outdoor relief was given to the needy in their own homes. To get indoor relief, however, the poor had to live in institutions known as *poorhouses, workhouses,* or *almshouses.* The terrible conditions in most such institutions discouraged all but the most desperate from seeking relief.

Early welfare in the United States resembled the English system. Local governments were responsible for aiding the poor. But the American Colonies, and later the states, sometimes helped provide aid. The first federal welfare programs, begun after the Revolutionary War in America (1775-1783), provided pensions to war veterans. During the American Civil War (1861-1865), these pensions were expanded to cover soldiers' widows and orphans. In the early 1900's, responsibility for providing welfare benefits shifted from local to state governments. During these years, states enacted programs to aid dependent children and the aged.

The Great Depression of the 1930's, an economic slump that brought joblessness and poverty to millions, led to a dramatic shift from state to federal responsibility. The Social Security Act of 1935 established federal assistance programs for dependent children, the blind, and the elderly, as well as old-age and unemployment insurance programs.

Since 1960. Several new welfare programs were created during the 1960's as part of the War on Poverty program of President Lyndon B. Johnson, including the Food Stamp Program and Medicaid. Existing programs also received more funding. The SSI and EITC programs began in the mid-1970's. But welfare benefits did not increase as fast as inflation during the 1970's, and Congress reduced benefits in the 1980's and 1990's.

Congress also gradually changed the nature of aid for dependent children. When federal cash aid for such children began in 1935, most poor single mothers were widows, and the aid was designed to enable them to stay home with their children. But by the 1980's, most poor single mothers were divorced or separated, or had never married. During the 1960's, Congress passed laws providing incentives for welfare mothers to find jobs. Laws since the late 1960's also increased the power of the federal government to require fathers of children receiving cash aid to provide financial support.

Congress made major changes in the U.S. welfare system in 1996, when it passed the Personal Responsibility and Work Opportunity Reconciliation Act. The 1996 act replaced Aid to Families with Dependent Children (AFDC), the main federal program for helping children in poor families, with Temporary Assistance to Needy Families (TANF). Under AFDC, the government had required the states to provide aid to families who had an income below a certain level. Under TANF, the government gives cash payments directly to the states and allows each state to determine who gets cash assistance. The act requires states to reduce benefits for most recipients if they do not start working within two years and to cut off benefits for most families after five years.

Since passage of the 1996 legislation, welfare caseloads have fallen, and more single mothers have gone to work. The 1996 changes were only partly responsible, however. The U.S. economy boomed during the late 1990's, creating more and better jobs for people formerly on welfare.

Irwin Garfinkel and Jane Waldfogel

Related articles in *World Book* include:

Food Stamp Program	Housing (Public housing)	New Deal
Great Society	Medicaid	Social security
		Welfare state

Additional resources

Erlbach, Arlene. *Everything You Need to Know If Your Family Is on Welfare.* Rosen Pub. Group, 1998.
Katz, Michael B. *The Price of Citizenship: Redefining America's Welfare State.* Metropolitan Bks., 2001.

Welfare state is a term sometimes applied to a country in which the government assumes major responsibility for providing for the financial needs of the people. Welfare state governments help furnish medical care, housing, and child support, as well as aid to the poor. Communist countries, such as China and Cuba, provide most goods and services for the people. But the term *welfare state* is generally applied to non-Communist countries with basically capitalistic economic systems.

The concept of the welfare state was developed in Europe during the 1800's. The movement was a response to *laissez faire* economic policies, which say governments should not interfere with economic matters. Critics charged that laissez faire capitalism failed to solve many economic and social problems, such as poverty and unemployment.

The first welfare states developed in the mid-1900's. The Great Depression of the 1930's created a need for increased welfare, and governments responded by expanding welfare programs and creating new ones. After World War II ended in 1945, governments in Western Europe continued to expand welfare as part of a promise to citizens for a better future. The programs of the United Kingdom, Sweden, and Norway grew so large that these nations became known as *welfare states.* The expansion of welfare systems soon spread to other parts of the world. The oil-rich Middle Eastern country of Kuwait is one of the most extensive welfare states.

The United States and Canada expanded welfare during the Great Depression and after World War II. But they have fewer programs than most industrialized countries and are generally not called welfare states.

A chief feature of the welfare state is *social security*, a system of insurance under government control. All workers pay taxes to finance benefits for those who cannot work due to disease, disability, unemployment, old age, or death. Some economists argue that increased welfare spending is bad for economic growth and will cause the failure of welfare states.

Related articles in *World Book* include:

Communism	Sweden (Social welfare)
Kuwait (introduction)	United Kingdom (The welfare
Laissez faire	state)
Norway (Social welfare)	Welfare
Social security	

Well is a hole in the earth from which a fluid is withdrawn. Water wells are the most common type. Oil and

Kinds of water wells

Water wells may be dug, driven, bored, or drilled. Dug wells can be constructed with hand tools or power tools. They measure up to 50 feet (15 meters) deep and have the greatest diameter of any water well. Driven wells consist of a series of pipes with a point at one end. The point is driven into the ground to a depth of up to 50 feet (15 meters). Bored wells, which are constructed with tools called *augers,* may be up to 100 feet (30 meters) deep. Drilled wells are constructed with special well-drilling equipment. They measure up to 1,000 feet (300 meters) deep.

WORLD BOOK diagrams by Arthur Grebetz

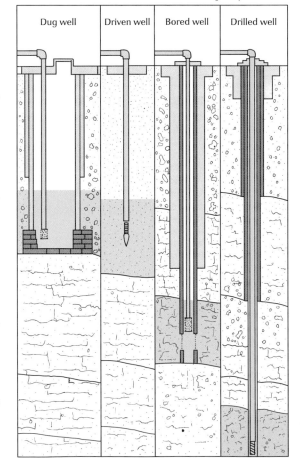

| Dug well | Driven well | Bored well | Drilled well |

natural gas wells are also common. Mining companies also pump steam and hot water down wells to remove salt and sulfur from deep in the ground.

Scientists and engineers use *seismographs* and other equipment to locate underground deposits of oil or water (see **Seismograph**). They then determine at what rate they can take these materials out of the ground. They also decide how much they can remove without damaging the natural resources.

Water wells. The underground water that flows into wells is called *ground water* (see **Ground water**). Most of this water comes from rain that soaks into the ground and slowly moves down to the *ground water reservoir,* an area of soil and rock saturated with water. The top of this zone is the *water table,* the level at which water stands in a well that is not being pumped.

In damp places, the water table may lie just below the surface. It is easily reached by digging. A dug well is usually lined with bricks, stone, or porous concrete to keep the sides from caving in. In drier places, the water table may be hundreds of feet or meters down. It may be necessary to drill the well and sink pipes. Power-driven pumps usually draw the water out of deep wells.

In some areas, underground water moving down from the slopes of hills and mountains becomes trapped under watertight layers of clay or shale. Wells drilled through these layers in valleys and plains run into water under pressure. Such wells are called *flowing artesian wells.* See **Artesian well.**

Many people depend on wells for their water supply, especially in rural areas. Underground water is usually pure, because soil makes a good filter. This water generally contains dissolved minerals. A well that taps water with a high mineral content is called a *mineral well.*

Water wells should be located so that they do not collect poisons or disease germs. A well should be at least 100 feet (30 meters) from a cesspool and should never be located so that sewage drains toward it. Water from a well sunk through limestone may be dangerous because water runs through crevices and caves in limestone without being filtered. It is also important that surface water does not drain into a well.

Oil and natural gas wells. Oil and natural gas are lighter than water. Because of this, they would normally float upward and escape from the ground. But oil and gas become trapped beneath thick beds of rock in areas called *reservoirs.* Wells penetrate deep into the earth to reach these reservoirs and bring the oil and gas to the surface. *Wildcat wells* are drilled in search of reservoirs. A *production well* is drilled into a proven field.

Drilling oil and gas wells is a highly developed science. Workers who drill deep wells must have many years of training and experience. See **Gas** (From well to user; picture); **Petroleum** (Drilling for petroleum).

Ronald W. Falta and David S. Snipes

Welland Ship Canal is one of Canada's greatest engineering projects. It forms an important part of the St. Lawrence Seaway. The canal provides a navigable waterway 27 miles (44 kilometers) long between Lakes Ontario and Erie. The only natural connection between the two lakes is the Niagara River. But falls and rapids make much of the river useless as a commercial waterway.

The Welland Canal extends from Port Weller on Lake Ontario to Port Colborne on Lake Erie. Lake Erie is about

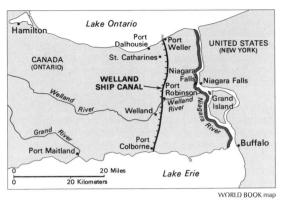

WORLD BOOK map

Location of the Welland Ship Canal

326 feet (99 meters) higher than Lake Ontario, so ships are raised and lowered by a series of eight locks.

The project to connect Lakes Ontario and Erie was completed in 1829. The original canal, built by a private company with help from government loans, cost about $7,700,000. It extended from Port Dalhousie, just west of Port Weller, on Lake Ontario to Port Robinson on the Welland River. From Port Robinson, southbound ships sailed east along the Welland to the Niagara River, then south along the Niagara to Lake Erie. In 1833, workers completed an extension that stretched from Port Robinson south to Port Colborne (then called Gravelly Bay).

In a short time, the shipping industry wanted a larger waterway. The canal was greatly enlarged by 1845, and enlarged further by 1887. In 1912, the Canadian government began improvements that eventually resulted in the Welland Ship Canal of today. The canal officially opened on Aug. 6, 1932. It cost $130 million.

The canal can be used by the largest bulk carriers on the Great Lakes. Ships can sail through the canal in 8 hours or less. Carman Miller

Wellcome Trust is one of the world's largest foundations. Most of its contributions fund biomedical research at universities in the United Kingdom. It offers major funding to support research in areas such as *epidemiology* (the study of how diseases spread), cancer, heart disease, medical history, and veterinary medicine. The trust's Medicine in Society program provides opportunities for public debate on medical ethics.

The trust has been a leading source of funding for the Human Genome Project, an international effort to analyze the complete chemical instructions that control heredity in human beings. It also supports medical research in developing nations that deals with controlling disease and improving the delivery of local health care. It also provides resources for educators and students.

Sir Henry Wellcome, a British pharmaceutical company owner, founded the Wellcome Trust in his will in 1936. The trust's headquarters are in London.

See also **Foundations** (table).

Welles, Gideon (1802-1878), served as secretary of the Navy under Presidents Abraham Lincoln and Andrew Johnson. Although a Democrat for 30 years, Welles joined the Republican Party when it was organized in 1854. Lincoln, a Republican, made him Navy secretary at the beginning of the American Civil War in 1861. Welles worked to boost morale and create an efficient administration. Under his supervision, the Union Navy added about 600 ships and grew from 7,500 sailors to more than 50,000. It also set up a blockade along the Confederate coast and formed a fleet of gunboats and ironclad vessels on the Mississippi River. Welles vigorously upheld President Johnson's moderate policy toward the South after the war.

Welles was born on July 1, 1802, in Glastonbury, Connecticut. From 1826 to 1836, he edited the *Hartford* (Connecticut) *Times* and advised President Andrew Jackson on affairs in Connecticut. During the Mexican War (1846-1848), Welles was chief of the Bureau of Provisions and Clothing of the U.S. Navy Department.   James E. Sefton

Welles, Orson (1915-1985), was an actor and motion-picture director. While only in his early 20's, Welles was regarded as an important director of stage plays and radio series, in which he also performed. In 1938, his famous Halloween radio production of H. G. Wells's novel *The War of the Worlds* frightened many listeners by convincing them that Martians had actually invaded New Jersey. On the strength of this sensation, RKO studios hired Welles to write, direct, and act in his own films in Hollywood.

United Press Int.
Orson Welles

Welles's first film, *Citizen Kane* (1941), told the story of a powerful newspaperman, based on the life of publisher William Randolph Hearst. Polls of international film critics rank the film as one of the most important films in motion-picture history. *Citizen Kane* is regarded, especially for its camera and sound techniques, as perhaps the most influential film ever made in the United States.

Welles's next film, *The Magnificent Ambersons* (1942), is only partly his work. While he was abroad, RKO studios reedited the film and changed the ending. Thereafter, he wrote and directed only a few films in Hollywood, including *The Lady from Shanghai* (1948) and *Touch of Evil* (1958).

Welles acted in more than 60 films, often to finance his independent filmmaking projects in Europe. While in Europe, he directed and acted in two films based on plays by William Shakespeare—*Othello* (1952) and *Falstaff* (also called *Chimes at Midnight,* 1966). Welles was criticized for his flamboyance, but his artistic independence inspired many filmmakers. He was born on May 6, 1915, in Kenosha, Wisconsin.   Robert Sklar

Wellesley College is a privately controlled liberal arts college for women in Wellesley, Massachusetts. It grants bachelor's degrees. Wellesley is noted for its library collection, art collection, and science center. Henry Fowle Durant founded Wellesley College in 1870. It opened in 1875.   Critically reviewed by Wellesley College

Wellington (pop. 163,824, met. area pop. 339,747) is the capital and one of the largest cities of New Zealand. Wellington ranks as one of the country's chief seaports and manufacturing centers. It lies on the southern coast of the North Island (see **New Zealand** [political map]).

Wellington and the surrounding area make up one of New Zealand's most highly populated regions.

The port of Wellington handles foreign trade and also shipping and transportation between the North Island and the South Island, the largest islands of New Zealand. Factories in the Wellington area manufacture chemicals, clothing, electrical machinery, processed foods, and other products.

Wellington is the home of Victoria University of Wellington. Other places of interest include the Parliament buildings; two cathedrals; the Dominion Museum and National Art Gallery; the Michael Fowler Centre; and Te Papa, New Zealand's national museum.

British settlers founded Wellington in 1840. The capital was moved there from Auckland in 1865 because of Wellington's central location.   Brian Kitching

Wellington, Duke of (1769-1852), was a British soldier and statesman who was known as *The Iron Duke*. He became famous as the general who overcame the armies of the French Emperor Napoleon I in Spain and Portugal and helped defeat Napoleon at the Battle of Waterloo in 1815. Later, Wellington became a leader of the Tory Party and served as prime minister.

Young soldier. Wellington was born Arthur Wellesley on May 1, 1769, in Dublin, Ireland. He was educated at Eton College and at a military college in France. At 18, he entered the army. Wellesley rose rapidly and by 1796 reached the rank of colonel. He first saw combat in 1794 in Flanders. In 1796, his regiment was sent to India, where his brother Richard, second Earl of Mornington, was governor general. Due to Richard's political influence, Wellesley became a major general before he was 35. In 1803, he received command of the British forces in the Maratha War. Wellesley soon defeated the Maratha chiefs and firmly established British power in India.

Peninsular War. In 1805, Wellesley returned to Britain. He was elected the next year to Parliament. Two years later, he was appointed chief secretary of Ireland. While there, he worked for new laws that would establish fair rents for tenants. He also laid the foundation for organization of the Irish police.

In 1808, Spain revolted against Napoleon, and the British sent troops there to help the Spanish. Wellesley was promoted to lieutenant general and took command of one of the British divisions fighting in the peninsula of Spain and Portugal. At first, many people believed Wellesley was put in command for political reasons. But he soon showed his military skill. Three weeks after landing in Portugal, he defeated the French in the Battle of Vimeiro and forced them to leave Portugal.

In 1809, Wellesley took command of all British forces in the Peninsular War. He fought many battles with the help of Spanish forces and a Portuguese army that was organized by Britain. His small army won many victories. Slowly, he drove the French forces from the peninsula. In April 1814, he won the Battle of Toulouse in France. But before he could penetrate farther into France, Napoleon gave up his throne and the fighting ended. Wellesley returned to Britain in triumph and was given the title of Duke of Wellington.

Victory at Waterloo. In July 1814, Wellington was appointed ambassador to France. The next year, he represented Britain at the Congress of Vienna, though the Congress had completed most of its work before he arrived (see **Vienna, Congress of**). He was at Vienna when the Congress heard that Napoleon had formed another army. Wellington signed the declaration naming Napoleon "the enemy and disturber of the peace of the world," and commanded the allied forces in the Netherlands. At the Battle of Waterloo, he fought Napoleon himself for the first time. In this battle, Wellington's troops and Prince Gebhard von Blücher's Prussian army crushed Napoleon's forces (see **Blücher, Gebhard L. von**). After that, Wellington headed the army that occupied France for a short time. See **Waterloo, Battle of**.

Political career. In 1818, Wellington returned to the United Kingdom and held various government and diplomatic posts. He became commander in chief of the army in 1827, but resigned in 1828 to become prime minister.

Wellington belonged to the Tory Party, but he angered many in his party by pushing through the Catholic Emancipation Act. This act allowed Roman Catholics to hold seats in Parliament and most other government offices. The British demanded parliamentary reform, and Wellington's opposition to a reform bill made his government unpopular. In 1830, he was forced to resign.

In late 1834, Wellington briefly served as prime minister after Viscount Melbourne resigned. He then served as foreign secretary during Sir Robert Peel's administration of 1834-1835. Seven years later, he became a member of Peel's second government and again served as commander in chief of the army. He retired in 1846. His opposition to reform made him unpopular at times. But by the time of his death, he had become a father figure known simply as "the Duke" and one of the United Kingdom's most famous national heroes.   Philip Dwight Jones

Wells, H. G. (1866-1946), was a famous English novelist, historian, science writer, and author of science-fiction stories. Wells's novel *Tono-Bungay* (1909) best reveals his varied talents. The novel, a story of the dishonest promotion of a patent medicine, contains social criticism tinged with satire. In it, Wells described trips in airplanes and submarines at a time when such journeys seemed like science fiction.

Herbert George Wells was born in Bromley, Kent (now part of London). He drew on his lower-middle-class background in some of his finest novels, including *Kipps* (1905) and *The History of Mr. Polly* (1909). His training as a scientist is reflected in his imaginative science-fiction stories. *The Time Machine* (1895) describes the adventures of a man who can transport himself into the future. Wells wrote about an invasion from Mars in *The War of the Worlds* (1898) and described a fictional utopia in *The Shape of Things to Come* (1933).

Wells supported social reform in the novel *The New Machiavelli* (1911), in the nonfiction study *The Work, Wealth and Happiness of Mankind* (1932), and in other books. Wells's *The Outline of History* (1920), a story of the development of the human race, shows his knowledge of biology and his liberal attitude in politics. With his son Geoffrey and Sir Julian Huxley, Wells wrote *The Science of Life* (1929-1930), a four-volume discussion of the principles of biology. Wells told his life story in *Experiment in Autobiography* (1934).   Sharon Bassett

Wells-Barnett, Ida Bell (1862-1931), was an American journalist and reformer. She was known chiefly for her campaign against the lynching of blacks during the late 1800's and early 1900's (see **Lynching**). Many blacks were lynched without even a trial after being accused of a crime, and others were lynched for no apparent reason at all. Wells-Barnett worked to expose such killings and to establish laws against lynching.

Ida Wells was born a slave in Holly Springs, Mississippi. She moved to Memphis in 1884. In 1889, she became part-owner and a reporter for *Free Speech*, a Memphis newspaper. In 1892, after three of her friends were hanged in Memphis, she began to investigate lynchings and other violence against blacks. Her work led to the founding of many antilynching organizations.

She moved to Chicago in 1894 and the next year married Ferdinand L. Barnett, a lawyer and journalist. In 1909, Wells-Barnett helped found the National Association for the Advancement of Colored People (NAACP). She also took part in the campaign to give women the right to vote.   Otey M. Scruggs

Wells, Fargo & Company was an early American express and banking organization. Henry Wells and William G. Fargo founded the company in 1852. They planned an express service from San Francisco to New York City, with the American Express Company serving as eastern representative. In 1866, Benjamin Holladay sold his overland mail and stagecoach business to Wells, Fargo & Company, which soon became the most powerful firm in the Far West. The company established a monopoly over the stagecoach business.

Wells, Fargo & Company carried passengers, freight, and mail. It specialized in shipping gold and silver from western mines. The Wells Fargo Nevada National Bank (now Wells Fargo Bank) was formed in 1905. In 1918, Wells, Fargo & Company merged its express operations with two other major express companies to form the American Railway Express Company. Today, Wells, Fargo & Company and its subsidiaries provide a large network of banking and financial services.   Dan L. Flores

See also **Fargo, William George**.

Welsh. See **Wales** (Language).

Welsh corgi. See **Cardigan Welsh corgi; Pembroke Welsh corgi**.

Welsh springer spaniel is a breed of dog that closely resembles its relative, the English springer span-

WORLD BOOK photo by E. F. Hoppe

The Welsh springer spaniel has a keen sense of smell.

iel. The Welsh springer spaniel is a little smaller, and its coat is always red and white. The dog has a keen sense of smell and is often used to retrieve game on land or in the water. Unless the Welsh springer spaniel is trained well, it may be headstrong and independent.

Critically reviewed by the Welsh Springer Spaniel Club of America

Welsh terrier is one of the oldest English breeds of dogs. It has been known in Wales for several hundred years. It is closely related to the original black and tan terrier of England. The Welsh looks like a small-sized Airedale, with its wiry coat of deep red and jet-black markings. It has a long head and powerful jaws. This hearty hunting terrier weighs about 20 pounds (9 kilograms). The Welsh terrier originally was bred for use in fox-hunting. See also **Dog** (picture: Terriers).

Critically reviewed by the Welsh Terrier Club of America

Welty, Eudora, *yoo DOHR uh* (1909-2001), was an American short-story writer and novelist known for her searching studies of small-town life in the South. She lived in Mississippi all of her life, and her affection for the South can be seen in her work.

Welty's style combines delicacy with shrewd, robust humor. The mixture of realism and fantasy in some of her stories gives them an almost mythical quality. Her major themes extend beyond the South—loneliness, the pain of growing up, and the need for people to understand themselves and their neighbors.

Welty's short stories appear in *The Collected Stories of Eudora Welty,* published in 1980. Her longer fiction consists of the novelettes *The Robber Bridegroom* (1942) and *The Ponder Heart* (1954) and the novels *Delta Wedding* (1946), *Losing Battles* (1970), and *The Optimist's Daughter* (1972). She received the 1973 Pulitzer Prize for *The Optimist's Daughter.* Her essays and reviews appear in *The Eye of the Story* (1978). She described the influence of her family and surroundings on her writing in *One Writer's Beginnings* (1984). Her *Complete Novels* and *Stories, Essays, and Memoir* were published in 1998. Welty was born in Jackson, Mississippi.   Noel Polk

Welwitschia, *wehl WIHCH ee uh,* also called *tumboa,* is a peculiar plant that grows in the sandy deserts of southwestern Africa. The Welwitschia resembles a giant,

Michael Fogden, Bruce Coleman Inc.

The Welwitschia resembles a giant, flattened mushroom. It bears two leaves that split into long, ribbonlike shreds.

flattened mushroom. Its short, woody trunk rises from a large taproot and spreads like a tabletop to a width of 5 to 6 feet (1.5 to 1.8 meters). The plant bears a single pair of leathery, green leaves that spread over the ground. The leaves are 2 to 3 feet (61 to 91 centimeters) wide and often twice as long. They grow in length for the life of the plant. Older plants appear to have many leaves because hot winds, blowing sand, and age split the two leaves into long, ribbonlike shreds.

Each year, stiff, jointed stemlike growths from 6 to 12 inches (15 to 30 centimeters) long develop at the point where the leaves join the trunk. These growths bear small, erect flower spikes called *cone clusters.* Welwitschia plants are either male or female. Male plants produce small cones. Female plants bear larger cones that are bright scarlet. The cones are pollinated by insects. Welwitschia plants grow slowly and often live 1,000 to 2,000 years. The plant was named for Friedrich Welwitsch, an Austrian botanist of the 1800's.

Michael G. Barbour

Scientific classification. The Welwitschia belongs to the division Gnetales. Its scientific name is *Welwitschia mirabilis.*

Wen is a *cyst* (growth) in the skin. The skin contains *sebaceous glands* that secrete oil to lubricate the skin. A wen forms when these secretions collect inside a sebaceous gland. Wens may appear on any part of the skin except the soles of the feet or the palms of the hands. Wens usually appear on the scalp, face, or shoulder. They grow slowly, forming round or oval lumps, from the size of a pea to that of a walnut. Wens are soft and painless. They hold a yellowish-white matter, which may have a rancid odor. Wens may become infected, causing inflammation and pain. Any lump or growth in the skin should be seen promptly by a doctor.

David T. Woodley

Wentworth, Thomas. See **Strafford, Earl of.**

Werewolf, according to superstition, is a person who changes into a wolf. The word comes from the Old English term *werwulf,* meaning *man-wolf.* Werewolves appear in many old stories. In some tales, they turn themselves into wolves by putting on a wolf skin, by drinking water from a wolf's footprint, or by rubbing a magic ointment on their bodies. In other stories, they are transformed by someone else's magic power.

The werewolves in most stories try to eat people. The people who are threatened by werewolves use various methods to bring them back to human form. These methods include saying the werewolf's real name, hitting the werewolf three times on the forehead, and making the sign of the cross. According to the stories, one way to find out a werewolf's identity is to wound it and later look for a human with similar wounds.

Stories about werewolves have been most common in Europe. Tales from other parts of the world tell of people who turn into various other kinds of animals.

The technical word for werewolf is *lycanthrope.* This word comes from *Lycaon,* the name of a king in Greek mythology who was turned into a wolf by the god Zeus. *Lycanthropy* is a form of mental illness in which a person imagines he or she is a wolf.   Alan Dundes

Wergeland, *VAIR guh lahn,* **Henrik Arnold** (1808-1845), was a Norwegian author and fervent nationalist. He became an early supporter of Norwegian political independence from Sweden, which controlled Norway from 1814 to 1905. He also encouraged Norwegians to seek cultural independence from Sweden and Denmark. Along with Henrik Ibsen and other writers, he played a major part in the development of a separate Norwegian culture. Wergeland wrote poetry, drama, and prose, but his poems are his greatest works. They include *Creation, Man, and Messiah* (1830) and *The Jew* (1842). Wergeland was born in Kristiansand, Norway. Byron J. Nordstrom

Werner, *VEHR nur,* **Abraham Gottlob,** *AH brah hahm GOHT lohp* (1749-1817), a German geologist, formulated a theory on the origin of the earth that was widely accepted in his time. Werner believed all rocks of the earth were formed from a giant ocean. Scientists accepted this theory for years until it was proven that some rocks were formed by the cooling of hot lava from volcanoes. Werner also introduced a system of identifying and classifying rocks and created new methods of describing minerals.

Werner taught at the Freiberg School of Mines in Freiberg from 1775 until his death. Students came from throughout Europe to hear him explain complex ideas in a simple way. His lectures helped geology gain respect as an important area of study. Rachel Laudan

See also **Geology** (The rock dispute).

Weser River, *VAY zuhr,* is an important German waterway. Its main headwater, the Werra, rises on the southwestern slopes of the Thüringian Forest in central Germany. The Weser winds 430 miles (700 kilometers) to its mouth at the North Sea near Bremerhaven. For location, see **Germany** (physical map). In 1894, its channel was deepened from the mouth to Bremen, about 45 miles (72 kilometers) to the south, so that large ships could sail to Bremen. Hugh D. Clout

Wesley, Charles (1707-1788), a clergyman of the Church of England, was a founder of Methodism and shared its leadership with his brother John. Charles is best known as the author of more than 7,000 hymns, many of which are still sung in Christian worship. They include "Hark, the Herald Angels Sing," "Christ the Lord Is Risen Today," and "Jesu, Lover of My Soul."

Wesley was born in Epworth, Lincolnshire. Like his brother, he was educated at Christ Church College at Oxford University in the 1720's. There he met with small groups of other students for methodical study, spiritual devotion, and practical good works. These activities earned them the nickname "Methodist." For the next 20 years, Charles helped his brother shape the Methodist movement. He was a vigorous evangelical preacher and wrote about 480 of the 525 hymns in the Methodist *Collection of Hymns* (1780), widely regarded as a spiritual classic. After his marriage in 1749, Charles settled into parish ministry, though he continued to be a close adviser of his brother. David Lowes Watson

See also **Methodists; Wesley, John.**

Wesley, John (1703-1791), a clergyman of the Church of England, was a founder of Methodism. He was the foremost leader in England of the Evangelical Revival, a movement in Protestant Christianity during the 1700's that emphasized personal faith and practical good works. In carrying out his evangelical mission, Wesley traveled about 250,000 miles (400,000 kilometers) and preached over 40,000 sermons, often as many as 4 in a day. His concern for the poor led him to provide loan funds, establish homes for widows and orphans, extend ministries to prisons and the armed forces, and open free medical dispensaries.

Early years. Wesley was born in Epworth in Lincolnshire. He was the 15th of 19 children born to Susanna Wesley and her husband, Samuel, an Anglican clergyman. Both parents were firmly committed to the Church of England, yet came from Nonconformist families who had separated from the Church of England. This background gave the young Wesley a deep sense of two traditions in English religious thought. One was the importance of the organized church, with its rules and teachings. The other was the vitality of Puritan inward religion, with its focus on a direct relationship with God.

Wesley was admitted to Christ Church College at Oxford University in 1720 and was ordained a priest in the Church of England in 1728. He returned to Oxford in 1729 as a fellow of Lincoln College. There he became spiritual adviser to some students, including his brother Charles, who gathered in small groups to help each other with study, devotions, and practical good works. They were ridiculed by other students as "The Holy Club" and "Bible Moths," but the nickname that prevailed was "Methodists." Their practice of accountability in small groups for the spiritual life of all their members became the basic structure of the later Methodist movement.

While Wesley was a missionary to Georgia from 1735 to 1737, he was influenced by the Moravians, a German church that stressed personal faith and disciplined Christian living. Its influence on Wesley led to a spiritual crisis that was not resolved until he returned to England. In London on May 24, 1738, he attended a small religious meeting. There, according to his *Journal,* his heart was "strangely warmed" as he experienced the inward assurance of faith that so impressed him about the Moravians.

Leadership of the Methodist societies. Wesley increasingly assumed a leadership role in the Evangelical Revival. In 1739, at the invitation of George Whitefield, another prominent evangelist, he began to preach in the open air. For a number of years, he was joined in this activity by his brother Charles. Their "field preaching" became characteristic of Methodism, drawing large crowds. Those who responded to their message joined societies patterned on the religious societies of the Church of England dating back to the late 1600's.

Wesley's genius lay in organizing the Methodist societies into a movement. In 1743, he drew up a set of General Rules, which required members to attend weekly "class meetings." At the meetings, each member was asked to give an account of his or her discipleship according to well-defined guidelines. Wesley gave considerable responsibility to the leaders of these classes, who became a crucial link in the authority he exercised over the movement. Wesley also adopted *lay* (unordained) preachers as his assistants

Detail of painting (1766) by Nathaniel Hone; National Portrait Gallery, London

John Wesley

and helpers, and in 1744 he started an annual conference to consult on matters of doctrine and practice. The minutes of these meetings, along with Wesley's *Letters* and detailed *Journal,* may be the fullest record of any religious movement. They were published as part of a 34-volume edition of *The Works of John Wesley* (1976-   ).

Wesley's evangelical message created controversy. It was opposed by many Anglican clergy as religiously fanatical and politically disruptive. The Calvinist wing of the Evangelical Revival criticized it as being too universal and putting too much emphasis on good works.

Formation of the Methodist Church. Wesley wanted Methodism to remain a reforming movement within the Church of England, and resisted separation from the church throughout his life. The issue was forced, however, by the need to provide for those who belonged to Methodist societies in the newly founded United States. In 1784, Wesley ordained Methodist preachers for North America, a step that led to the formation of the Methodist Episcopal Church, and then of the Methodist Church worldwide.   David Lowes Watson

See also **Hymn** (Words and music); **Methodists; Wesley, Charles; Whitefield, George.**

Additional resources

Collins, Kenneth J. *A Real Christian: The Life of John Wesley.* Abingdon, 1999.
Monk, Robert C. *John Wesley: His Puritan Heritage.* 2nd ed. Scarecrow, 1999.

Wesleyan Church is a religious denomination that was founded in 1968. It was formed by the merger of two American churches, the Wesleyan Methodist Church and the Pilgrim Holiness Church. The Wesleyan Methodist Church had been established in 1843, and the Pilgrim Holiness Church in 1897. Many beliefs of the Wesleyan Church are based on doctrines set forth by the Dutch theologian Jacobus Arminius and the English minister John Wesley. The church conducts missionary work in Africa, Asia, Australia, Latin America, the Pacific Islands, and the Caribbean region. In the United States, it operates four universities, an academy, and a children's home that includes a home for unwed mothers. The church operates a Bible college in Canada. Wesleyan churches are in more than 70 countries. The church's International Center is in Indianapolis. See also **Arminius, Jacobus; Wesley, Charles; Wesley, John.**

Critically reviewed by the Wesleyan Church

West, in international relations. See **Cold War.**

West, Benjamin (1738-1820), was an American painter who became famous for his large pictures of historical subjects. West taught many of the finest early American painters. His studio in London became a "school" for many American artists, including Ralph Earl, Samuel F. B. Morse, Charles Willson Peale, Rembrandt Peale, and John Trumbull.

West was born on Oct. 10, 1738, in Springfield, Pennsylvania. He went to Italy when he was 21, and studied and copied the Roman sculptures and Renaissance and Baroque paintings there for three years. West settled in London in 1763. In the early 1770's, he gained fame for his paintings *The Death of General Wolfe* and *Penn's Treaty with the Indians.* In 1772, King George III of England made West his official painter of history. In 1792, West was elected the second president of the Royal Academy of Arts, which he had helped establish in 1768.

He died on March 11, 1820.   Elizabeth Garrity Ellis

See also **Monroe, James** (picture: Elizabeth Kortright Monroe); **United States, History of the** (picture: Early colonists); **Wolfe, James** (picture).

West, Jerry (1938-   ), became one of the greatest all-around players in basketball history. West was drafted by the Minneapolis Lakers of the National Basketball Association (NBA) in 1960. He went with the franchise when it shifted to Los Angeles that year and won fame for his scoring ability, ball handling, and defensive skills. He retired as a player in 1974. Jerry Alan West was born on May 28, 1938, in Chelyan, West Virginia, near Charleston. He played at the University of West Virginia from 1956 to 1960.

West was head coach of the Lakers from 1976 to 1979. He served as general manager from 1982 to 2000. West became president of basketball operations for the Memphis Grizzlies of the NBA in 2002.   Bob Logan

West, Jessamyn (1902-1984), was an American author. Her first and most famous book is *The Friendly Persuasion* (1945). In a series of sketches, it describes the rural life of a Quaker family in the mid-1800's.

West was a Quaker, and Quaker ideals of brotherhood can be found throughout her work. Her first novel, *The Witch Diggers* (1951), is a symbolic story set on a poor farm in southern Indiana. *Except for Me and Thee* (1969) is a novel about characters who appeared in *The Friendly Persuasion. Collected Stories of Jessamyn West* was published in 1986, after her death. West also wrote screenplays, including one for the film *Friendly Persuasion* (1956). She was born on July 18, 1902, in Jennings County, Indiana.   Noel Polk

West, Mae (1892-1980), was an American actress who became famous for the humorous, bawdy sexuality of her stage and motion-picture performances. The success of her films *She Done Him Wrong* and *I'm No Angel* (both 1933) resulted in the Motion Picture Production Code to regulate the content of movies. To avoid having her material banned by the film censors, West spoke in double meanings, often cleverly parodying attitudes on sex. She became famous for such suggestive lines as "Come up and see me some time."

Mary Jane West was born on Aug. 17, 1892, in the Brooklyn section of New York City. She worked in vaudeville and stage appearances from the age of 5. Her hit stage appearances in the 1920's brought her to Hollywood. In the first of her 12 films, *Night After Night* (1932), she displayed the wit and skill with racy wisecracks that won her world fame. West's other films include *Belle of the Nineties* (1934) and *My Little Chickadee* (1940). She wrote an autobiography, *Goodness Had Nothing to Do with It* (1959). West died on Nov. 22, 1980.

Rachel Gallagher

See also **Fields, W. C.** (picture).

West, Nathanael (1903-1940), was an American novelist noted for a brilliant but bitter view of modern American life. He published only four short novels before he was killed in an automobile accident. *Miss Lonelyhearts* (1933) is a grim satire about a newspaperman who is assigned to write a column advising people on their problems. *The Day of the Locust* (1939) is a fantastic and sometimes nightmarish satire of life in Hollywood, where West wrote screenplays.

West was born in New York City. His real name was

Nathan Wallenstein Weinstein. He wrote his first novel, *The Dream Life of Balso Snell,* in the mid-1920's. It was published in 1931. West also wrote *A Cool Million* (1934), a parody of a "rags to riches" story. West's reputation developed only after his death.   Victor A. Kramer

West, Rebecca (1892-1983), was a British novelist, literary critic, and journalist. West analyzed the political and psychological reasons people betray their countries in *The Meaning of Treason* (1947, revised as *The New Meaning of Treason,* 1964) and *A Train of Powder* (1955). *Black Lamb and Grey Falcon* (1941) is a penetrating study of the history of Yugoslavia and other Balkan lands.

West's first book of literary criticism, *Henry James* (1916), describes the importance of James in shaping the modern novel. Her antiwar novel *The Return of the Soldier* (1918) shows James's influence in its emphasis on psychological motives. The powerful novel *The Judge* (1922) is set in Edinburgh, Scotland, during the struggle for women's right to vote. West's autobiographical novel *The Fountain Overflows* (1956) was followed by two sequels published after her death, *This Real Night* (1984) and the unfinished *Cousin Rosamund* (1985). Another novel published after her death, *Sunflower* (1986), describes her relationships with author H. G. Wells and newspaper tycoon Lord Beaverbrook.

West was born on Dec. 21, 1892, in London. Her given and family name was Cicely Isabel Fairfield. She became interested in women's rights and took the pen name Rebecca West from the heroine of Henrik Ibsen's drama *Rosmersholm.* In 1959, she was made a Dame Commander of the Order of the British Empire and became known as Dame Rebecca West.   Jane Marcus

West, The. In American history, the *frontier* (unsettled area) usually lay to the west of settled regions. For this reason, the terms *west* and *frontier* came to have the same meaning. To the first colonists, the frontier lay beyond the Appalachian Mountains. Later, pioneers who lived in the Midwest considered the plains and mountains farther west to be the frontier. See also **Pioneer life in America; Western frontier life in America; Westward movement in America.**   Jerome O. Steffen

West, The, in international relations. See **Cold War.**

West African Conference. See **Berlin Conference.**

West Bank is a territory in the Middle East that lies between Israel and Jordan. It covers about 2,270 square miles (5,880 square kilometers) and has more than 2 million people. Most of them are Palestinians.

Historically part of Palestine, the West Bank was annexed by Jordan in 1950. In 1967, Israel defeated Jordan, Egypt, and Syria in a war and captured the West Bank. In 1993, a peace process began between Israeli and Palestinian leaders, and the next year, Israel began withdrawing from the West Bank. But the two sides have not reached a final agreement. In 2002, Israel reoccupied much of the West Bank. See the *History and government* section of this article for more details.

East Jerusalem is the West Bank's largest city. But Israel, which includes West Jerusalem, does not consider East Jerusalem part of the West Bank. After the 1967 war, Israel made East Jerusalem a part of Israeli Jerusalem. But other countries do not recognize Israeli control.

People. Most West Bank Palestinians live in villages. About 12 percent of the Palestinians live in crowded refugee camps, where a United Nations (UN) agency provides schools and other services. Israelis make up about 15 percent of the West Bank's population. Many of them live in settlements built by the Israeli government.

Most West Bank Palestinians wear Western-style clothing. Older men may also wear a traditional *keffiyeh,* or headcloth. Women generally dress more conservatively than American and European women do. Beautifully embroidered dresses, for which the area is well known, are still made for wearing on special occasions. Israeli settlers generally wear Western-style clothing.

West Bank cooking is similar to that of other Arab lands. Dishes include *kibbeh* (ground lamb) and *tabbouleh* (a salad made of ground wheat, onion, lemon juice, parsley, and mint). *Baklava,* or *baklawa* (a thin pastry layered with honey and chopped nuts), and *halva,* or *halwa* (ground sesame seeds and honey), are desserts.

West Bank Palestinians speak Arabic. English is the most common second language. Most Palestinians are Muslims who belong to the Sunni division of Islam. About 8 percent of the people are Christians, chiefly members of the Eastern Orthodox or Eastern Catholic churches. The Israelis are Jewish and speak Hebrew.

Education. The West Bank has five private colleges and universities. Many well-educated Palestinians have found jobs outside of the territory.

Land and climate. The West Bank is hilly with generally thin, stony soil. Only about one-fourth of the land is suitable for farming. The highlands that cover most of the West Bank have mild summers and occasional freezing temperatures and snow in winter. In the east, the Jordan River Valley has mild winters and hot summers, with temperatures reaching 120 °F (49 °C) and higher.

Much of the West Bank receives little rainfall. Only 2 to 8 inches (5 to 20 centimeters) of rain falls annually in the Jordan River Valley. Agriculture there depends on irrigation. Some areas of the highlands receive 25 inches (64 centimeters) or more of rain a year. The West Bank's main river is the Jordan. The Dead Sea, the only lake, is on the southeast border. Its shore, which lies about 1,310 feet (399 meters) below sea level, is the lowest

© Richard Elkins, Gamma/Liaison

The West Bank is a barren land in the Middle East. The Dead Sea, *shown here,* is the region's only lake. The Dead Sea's extreme saltiness enables swimmers to float with ease.

West Bank

▬▬	International boundary
───	Road
───	Railroad
⊛	National capital
•	Other city or town
+	Elevation above sea level

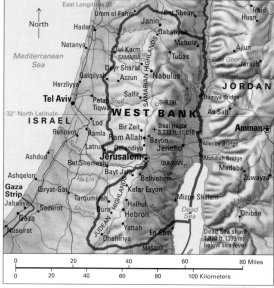

WORLD BOOK maps

place on Earth's surface.

Economy. The West Bank has a developing economy. It has a small amount of fertile land. Its only important natural resource is stone quarried for use as building material. Agriculture, which centers on the growing of citrus fruits and olives, is the most important economic activity. But water shortages limit expansion of agricultural production. The few industries are small. They include crafts, food processing, and textiles.

The West Bank has a fairly good road system but no railroads. An airport is in Qalandiya. Several Arabic newspapers are published. Radio and TV programs in the West Bank originate in Israel, Jordan, and Syria.

History and government. In the 1200's B.C., the Israelites settled in the West Bank. The Philistines settled there at about the same time. Later, the area was ruled by the Assyrians, Babylonians, Persians, and Romans.

In the A.D. 600's, Arab Muslim armies conquered the West Bank. The territory was part of a series of Muslim empires almost continuously from then until the defeat of the Ottoman Empire in World War I in 1918. In 1920, as an element of a post-World War I international agreement, the West Bank became part of the British mandate of Palestine. According to the mandate, the United Kingdom was to help Jews in Palestine establish a Jewish homeland. In 1947, the UN voted to divide the mandate into an Arab state and a Jewish state. The Palestinian Arabs rejected this plan. Their Arab allies attacked Israel in May 1948, the day after that country was established as a Jewish state. Jordan occupied the West Bank when the war ended in 1949. It annexed the territory in 1950.

In 1967, Israel defeated Jordan, Egypt, and Syria in a war. It captured the West Bank, as well as the Arab lands of the Gaza Strip, Golan Heights, and Sinai Peninsula. In 1974, King Hussein of Jordan gave up his government's responsibility for the West Bank to the Palestine Liberation Organization (PLO). In 1988, Jordan ended its financial and administrative support of the West Bank. Later that year, the PLO declared an independent Palestinian state in the West Bank and Gaza Strip. But Israel continued to occupy and, in effect, govern both territories. In the late 1980's, violence erupted between Israeli troops and Palestinian protesters in the occupied territories.

Beginning in 1993, Israel and the PLO signed several agreements that led to Israel's withdrawal from parts of the West Bank and Gaza Strip. As the Israelis withdrew, the areas came under Palestinian control. In 1996, Palestinians elected a legislature and president for these areas. But by the late 1990's, Israel still occupied over half of the West Bank. In 2000, Israeli and Palestinian leaders failed to reach a final peace settlement. Later that year, violence again erupted between Palestinians and Israeli forces. The struggle involved attacks on Israelis by Palestinian suicide bombers and several Israeli military strikes in the West Bank and Gaza Strip. In 2002, Israel reoccupied most West Bank cities. That same year, Israel began building a barrier designed to separate most of the West Bank from Israel.   Christine Moss Helms

See also **Arab-Israeli conflict; Hebron; Jericho; Jordan** (History); **Palestine; Palestinian Authority.**

West Highland white terrier is the only all-white breed of Scottish terriers. The breed was developed

WORLD BOOK photo by E. F. Hoppe

The West Highland white terrier is a faithful pet.

from the white puppies in litters of cairn, Scottish, and Skye terriers. It carries its tail high and its ears straight up. It has a wiry coat about 2 inches (5 centimeters) long. The dog weighs from 13 to 19 pounds (6 to 9 kilograms).

Critically reviewed by the American Kennel Club

West Indies are an island chain that divides the Caribbean Sea from the rest of the Atlantic Ocean. The islands stretch about 2,000 miles (3,200 kilometers) from near southern Florida to Venezuela's northern coast.

Three main island groups make up the West Indies. They are (1) the Bahamas in the north, (2) the Greater An-

The West Indies are islands of great natural beauty. Sandy beaches and tall palm trees line the coasts of many islands. This picture shows a secluded beach on the island of Barbados. The West Indies extend from near southern Florida to the northern coast of Venezuela.

Andy Levin, Black Star

tilles near the center, and (3) the Lesser Antilles in the southeast. The Bahamas consist of about 3,000 small islands and reefs. The Greater Antilles include the large islands of Cuba, Jamaica, Hispaniola, and Puerto Rico. Politically, Hispaniola is divided into the Dominican Republic and Haiti. The Lesser Antilles are smaller islands southeast of Puerto Rico. They are divided into two groups, the Leeward Islands and the Windward Islands. All the West Indian islands except the Bahamas are sometimes called the Antilles. The warm sunny climate, beautiful beaches, and tropical scenery of the West Indies attract large numbers of tourists.

The first inhabitants of the West Indies were American Indians. In 1492, Christopher Columbus became the first European to reach the islands, when he landed on an island believed to be present-day San Salvador in the Bahamas. He called them the Indies because he believed they were the East Indies islands of Asia. The islands were later given the name West Indies to distinguish them from the Asian islands. After Columbus visited the region, various European countries gained control of West Indian islands. Today, most of the islands make up, or form part of, independent nations. The rest are associated with the United Kingdom, France, the Netherlands, or the United States. For lists of the independent nations and the other political units of the West Indies, see the *tables* in this article.

People

Population and ancestry. The West Indies have a population of about 38 million. Nearly a third of the people live on Cuba, the largest of the West Indian islands. Some West Indian islands are among the world's most densely populated places.

A majority of the people of the West Indies are descendants of black Africans who were brought to the islands as slaves to work on sugar cane plantations. Most of the rest are of mixed black and European ancestry, or have British, Dutch, French, Portuguese, or Spanish ancestry. Some people are descended from farmworkers, mainly East Indians and Chinese, who arrived in the 1800's, after slavery was abolished. The area's original Indian population has died out, except for a small group of Carib Indians on Dominica.

Languages. The many languages and dialects spoken in the West Indies reflect the cultural heritage of the Eu-

ropean groups that colonized the area. For example, most of the people of Cuba, the Dominican Republic, and Puerto Rico speak Spanish. Dutch is the chief language of Aruba and the Netherlands Antilles. French is the official language of Haiti, Guadeloupe, and Martinique. English is the main language of the rest of the West Indies. Many West Indians use a *patois* (dialect) that mixes African languages and mainly English or French. A dialect called *Papiamento,* which is a combination of chiefly Dutch, English, Portuguese, and Spanish, is widely used in Aruba and the Netherlands Antilles.

People of the West Indies

Most people of the West Indies are descended from black Africans or Europeans. Some have Asian ancestry. These pictures give an idea of the varied ancestry of the area's people.

Fred Ward, Black Star
Spanish descent

Nicholas Devore III, Bruce Coleman Inc.
Black African descent

Trinidad & Tobago Tourist Board
East Indian descent

Porterfield-Chickering, Photo Researchers
Dutch descent

Independent countries of the West Indies

Map key	Name	Area		Population	Capital	Official language	Date of independence
		In mi²	In km²				
C 7	**Antigua and Barbuda**	171	442	78,000	St. John's	English	1981
A 3	**Bahamas**	5,358	13,878	320,000	Nassau	English	1973
D 7	**Barbados**	166	430	271,000	Bridgetown	English	1966
B 2	**Cuba**	42,804	110,861	11,334,000	Havana	Spanish	1898
D 7	**Dominica**	290	751	72,000	Roseau	English	1978
C 4	**Dominican Republic**	18,730	48,511	8,887,000	Santo Domingo	Spanish	1844
E 7	**Grenada**	133	344	102,000	Saint George's	English	1974
C 4	**Haiti**	10,714	27,750	7,636,000	Port-au-Prince	French	1804
C 2	**Jamaica**	4,243	10,990	2,669,000	Kingston	English	1962
C 6	**St. Kitts and Nevis**	101	261	37,000	Basseterre	English	1983
D 7	**St. Lucia**	208	539	163,000	Castries	English	1979
D 7	**St. Vincent and the Grenadines**	150	388	116,000	Kingstown	English	1979
E 7	**Trinidad and Tobago**	1,981	5,130	1,317,000	Port-of-Spain	English	1962

Dependencies in the West Indies

Map key	Name	Area		Population	Status
		In mi²	In km²		
C 6	**Anguilla**	37	96	13,000	British overseas territory; some self-government
E 4	**Aruba**	75	193	115,000	Self-governing part of the Netherlands
C 2	**Cayman Islands**	100	259	43,000	British overseas territory
C 7	**Guadeloupe**	658	1,704	442,000	Overseas department of France
D 7	**Martinique**	425	1,100	391,000	Overseas department of France
C 6	**Montserrat**	39	102	5,000	British overseas territory
E 5;C 6	**Netherlands Antilles**	308	798	222,000	Self-governing part of the Netherlands
C 5	**Puerto Rico**	3,515	9,103	3,944,000	United States commonwealth
B 4	**Turks and Caicos Islands**	166	430	19,000	British overseas territory
C 6	**Virgin Islands (U.S.)**	132	342	112,000	U.S. organized unincorporated territory
C 6	**Virgin Islands, British**	59	153	26,000	British overseas territory; some self-government

Each country and dependency in the West Indies has a separate article in World Book..
Populations are 2004 estimates based on figures from official government and United Nations sources.

Way of life. About 60 percent of the people of the West Indies live in urban areas, and about 40 percent live in rural areas. Most cities and towns in the West Indies lie along the coasts. These modern urban centers include such large cities as Havana, Cuba; San Juan, Puerto Rico; and Santo Domingo, Dominican Republic. They also include smaller towns, such as Bridgetown on Barbados and Roseau on Dominica. Many urban people work in business or government offices, stores, small factories, or in services related to tourism. The urban areas attract many rural people seeking a better way of life. But many of these people end up in crowded slums.

The urban areas have a wide variety of housing, including shacks, modern suburban homes, high-rise apartments, and mansions.

The West Indies have few natural resources except for their land, so farming is an important way of life. Many people work on large sugar cane plantations that belong to wealthy landowners. Some people own or rent small plots of land on which they raise crops and livestock. Many families must struggle to produce enough food for their own needs. Most of the rural people live in small, one- or two-room wooden houses.

Because of the warm weather, clothing in the West

Spence McConnell, Bruce Coleman Inc.

A crowded street market in Port-au-Prince, Haiti, features food, clothing, and household goods. Outdoor markets are common in many cities and towns in the West Indies.

M. Timothy O'Keefe, Bruce Coleman Inc.

Many rural houses in the West Indies are one- or two-room wooden structures. The house shown here is in Jamaica. Most rural West Indians make their living as farmers.

West Indies

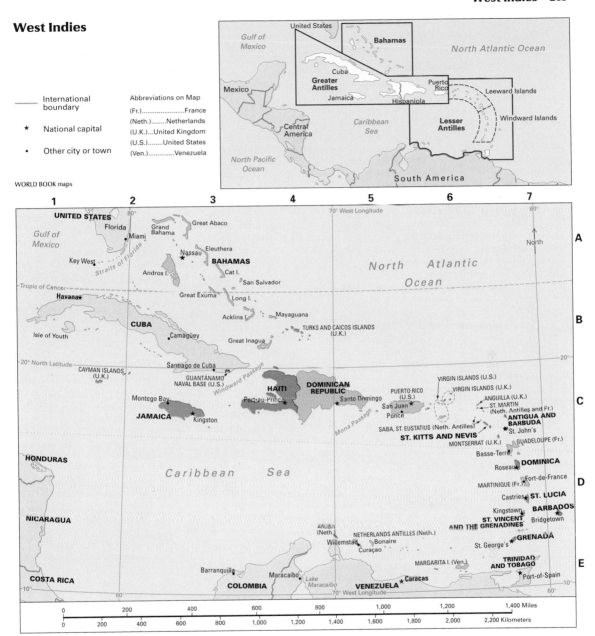

——	International boundary	Abbreviations on Map
★	National capital	(Fr.)....................France
		(Neth.)........Netherlands
		(U.K.)...United Kingdom
•	Other city or town	(U.S.)........United States
		(Ven.).............Venezuela

WORLD BOOK maps

Indies tends to be light and loose. Hats are popular because they provide protection from the sun. The diet of most West Indians includes rice, beans, goat stew, pork, fish, and such tropical fruits as bananas, oranges, papayas, and plantains. Soft drinks, beer, and rum rank as favorite beverages.

Religion. Most West Indians are Christians. Roman Catholicism is the main religion on the Spanish- and French-speaking islands. The English- and Dutch-speaking islands have a mixture of Catholics and Protestants. Small groups of Hindus, Jews, and Muslims also live in the West Indies. On several of the islands, people practice traditional African religions. Voodoo, one of the best known of these, is widespread on Haiti. Ras Tafari,

a religious group that worships former Emperor Haile Selassie I of Ethiopia as God, has numerous followers on Jamaica and several other islands. See **Voodoo.**

Education. Government-sponsored elementary and secondary education is available throughout the West Indies. But schools in rural areas often face shortages of teachers and equipment, and many students drop out and get jobs to help support their families. The West Indies have a number of colleges and universities, but many students go abroad to college. Many islands have technical schools that prepare people for careers in agriculture, engineering, tourism, and other fields.

Recreation. Popular sports in the West Indies include baseball, basketball, cricket, soccer, and track and field. Music is a favorite form of recreation. Most people enjoy performances of traditional songs and dances, and festivals are widely celebrated.

Land and climate

The West Indies cover a land area of about 91,000 square miles (235,000 square kilometers). The region's islands are spread out over a huge crescent more than 2,000 miles (3,200 kilometers) long. The islands are part of an underwater mountain chain that linked North and South America in prehistoric times. Many of the islands were formed by volcanoes. Others were formed after wind and rain wore down the mountain peaks. These islands are mostly flat strips of coral and limestone.

Volcanic mountains rise on a number of the islands. Several volcanoes have erupted in the last 500 years. They include Mount Pelée on Martinique, Soufrière on Basse-Terre Island in Guadeloupe, and another volcano called Soufrière on Saint Vincent. Other islands have boiling sulfur springs and inactive volcanic craters. Duarte Peak in the Dominican Republic on Hispaniola is the highest peak in the West Indies. It rises 10,417 feet (3,175 meters) above sea level. Fertile lowlands and sandy beaches line the coasts of many islands.

The West Indies have a number of fine harbors, and many islands have numerous bays and inlets along their coasts. Swift-flowing rivers run on many islands, but most can only be navigated by small boats. The Puerto Rico Trench, which lies off the northern coast of Puerto Rico, is one of the deepest spots in all the world's oceans. It descends to 28,232 feet (8,605 meters) below the ocean's surface.

Plant and animal life. Lush tropical vegetation covers many of the islands of the West Indies. Mangrove swamps, shrubs, grasses, and cactuses are common. The region's many flowering plants include bougainvillea, hibiscus, orchid, and poinsettia. Palms and citrus trees flourish.

Bats, frogs, lizards, rodents, and many species of birds live on the islands. There are no large wild animals. Dolphins, tropical fish, and such game fish as barracuda, marlin, and sailfish thrive in the blue-green waters surrounding the West Indies.

Climate. The islands of the West Indies have a warm, tropical climate. Steady ocean winds keep temperatures mild all year. Temperatures average about 80 °F (27 °C) in the summer and about 75 °F (24 °C) in the winter.

Rainfall in the West Indies ranges from 20 inches (50 centimeters) a year in some places to as much as 200 inches (500 centimeters) a year in mountainous areas. Most islands have alternate wet and dry seasons, with heavy showers common during the wet season. Hurricanes frequently strike the region, chiefly in late summer and early fall. They often cause severe damage.

Economy

Agriculture and tourism rank as the chief economic activities of the West Indies. Farming employs more than 40 percent of the work force. About 40 percent of the employed people work in government, tourism, or other service jobs. Most of the rest work in manufacturing, mining, or fishing. Unemployment is a problem.

Agriculture. Sugar cane is the area's leading crop. It is grown chiefly for export on large plantations. Other export crops include bananas, cacao (used to make chocolate), citrus fruits, coffee, tobacco, and spices. Farmers grow beans, carrots, sweet potatoes, tomatoes, and other crops throughout the West Indies. They also raise cattle, goats, pigs, and other livestock. However, many islands cannot produce enough to feed their people and must import food.

Tourism. More than 8 million people visit the islands each year to enjoy the sunny climate, beaches, and scenery. Many people tour the islands on cruise ships.

Manufacturing in the West Indies includes the production of cement, clothing, electrical parts, pharmaceuticals, plastics, and rum. Oil refineries on Curaçao process oil from Venezuela and other countries.

Mining is relatively unimportant in most of the West Indies. There are some important deposits of oil, natural gas, and asphalt on Trinidad. Jamaica is a leading producer of bauxite. Cuba and the Dominican Republic have large deposits of iron ore and nickel.

Fishing. Bonitos, sharks, tuna, and such shellfish as clams, crabs, and lobsters live in the waters surrounding the West Indies. Almost all the fish that are caught are sold in markets in the West Indies.

Trade. The main exports of the West Indies include assembled goods, bananas, petroleum products, rum, and sugar. Imports include food, manufactured products, and raw materials. Canada, the United Kingdom, and the United States are the area's main trading partners. A number of West Indian countries belong to the Caribbean Community and Common Market (CARICOM), an economic union that encourages trade among its members.

Transportation and communication. Most major West Indian cities have an international airport. Regional airlines serve smaller islands. Cargo and passenger ships from around the world visit West Indian ports. Paved roads link major cities with rural areas on most islands. Satellites beam radio and television programs from Europe and the United States to the West Indies. Most of the islands have at least one daily newspaper.

History

Early days. Ciboney Indians were the first inhabitants

Fred Ward, Black Star

A Cuban farmworker gathers sugar cane by hand. Sugar cane is the most important crop of the West Indies. It is grown chiefly on large plantations.

of the West Indies. They began living there in prehistoric times. Arawak Indians from South America moved to the West Indies between about 200 B.C. and A.D. 1000. They eventually settled in the Greater Antilles. About A.D. 1300, the Arawak were followed by the more warlike Carib Indians, who populated most of the Lesser Antilles. Both groups grew crops. The people also fished, hunted, and gathered wild plants for food.

The colonial period. Christopher Columbus landed on an island believed to be San Salvador in the Bahamas in 1492. During the next 10 years, he reached, and claimed for Spain, almost all the West Indian islands. The Spanish set up the first permanent European settlement in the West Indies in 1496 at Santo Domingo on Hispaniola. The search for gold and other riches drew thousands of Europeans to the region. In the early 1500's, Spaniards founded colonies on Cuba, Jamaica, and Puerto Rico. They enslaved the Indians and forced them to work in gold mines. Disease and overwork and other harsh treatment killed almost all the Indians.

Other Europeans learned of the wealth of the West Indies. Pirates from England, France, and the Netherlands attacked Spanish ships and ports and stole valuable cargo. In the 1600's, the Danes, Dutch, English, and French set up colonies on the smaller islands. In 1670, the English gained formal possession of Jamaica. The French took control of the western third of Hispaniola in 1697.

In the late 1600's and 1700's, the colonial powers gained great wealth from sugar cane grown in the West Indies. The Europeans brought millions of black African slaves to the islands to work on plantations.

Independence movements. During the 1800's, revolutions weakened colonial control on several islands. In 1804, Haiti became the first independent nation in the West Indies after slaves on Hispaniola, led by Toussaint L'Ouverture and others, rebelled against their French rulers. The Dominican Republic broke off from Haiti and declared independence in 1844. Slavery was abolished in all of the West Indies by the late 1800's. The plantation system then became much less profitable because plantation owners lost most of their cheap labor. As a result European interest in the West Indies declined.

The United States began playing an active role in the West Indies in 1898. In that year, a revolution in Cuba drew the United States into the Spanish-American War against Spain. After the United States won the war, Cuba became independent and Puerto Rico became a U.S. colony. In 1917, the United States purchased what are now the U.S. Virgin Islands from Denmark.

Dictators controlled Cuba, the Dominican Republic, and Haiti during much of the first half of the 1900's. In 1959, Fidel Castro overthrew the government of Cuba and established a Communist state.

Many islands of the West Indies have become independent or have gained more control over their own affairs since 1945. Both the Netherlands Antilles and Puerto Rico gained almost complete self-government in the early 1950's. Ten British colonies formed the West Indies Federation in 1958. They were (1) Antigua, (2) Barbados, (3) Dominica, (4) Grenada, (5) Jamaica, (6) Montserrat, (7) St. Christopher-Nevis-Anguilla, (8) St. Lucia, (9) St. Vincent, and (10) Trinidad and Tobago. The federation was dissolved in 1962 after Jamaica and Trinidad and Tobago became independent.

In the late 1960's, Antigua, Dominica, Grenada, St. Christopher-Nevis-Anguilla, St. Lucia, and St. Vincent became states associated with the United Kingdom. Together, the six states were called the West Indies Associated States. By the early 1980's, all of the West Indies Associated States except for St. Christopher-Nevis-Anguilla had become independent nations. In 1980, Anguilla officially became a separate British dependency. The rest of the state became independent in 1983 as a nation called St. Christopher and Nevis. This nation is now known as St. Kitts and Nevis.

The West Indies today face a number of economic and social problems, including overcrowding, poverty, and limited resources. Large numbers of West Indians cannot find jobs or must work for low wages. Many people leave the islands in search of jobs. West Indian governments are trying to develop new industries to lessen dependence on agriculture and tourism. Such regional economic organizations as the Caribbean Development Bank and CARICOM are also working to stimulate industrial growth.   Gerald R. Showalter

Related articles in *World Book.* See the separate articles on countries and other political units in the West Indies listed in the table in this article. See also:

British West Indies	Leeward Islands	Walcott, Derek
French West Indies	Maroons	Windward Islands
Grenadines	Naipaul, V. S.	

West Nile virus is a microscopic organism that has caused outbreaks of deadly disease in horses, birds, and human beings. The virus is named for a province in Uganda where it was first discovered in 1937. Since the 1950's, the virus has caused disease outbreaks in Africa, the Middle East, Australia, and parts of Europe. In 1999, scientists detected the virus for the first time in the Western Hemisphere after hundreds of birds were found dead throughout the northeastern United States. Since then, health officials have detected the virus in birds and people throughout the United States.

In most cases, the virus causes mild, flulike symptoms, such as fever and headache. In the elderly or people with weakened immune systems, however, the virus can cause *encephalitis* (inflammation of the brain), and occasionally convulsions, coma, or even death. People with severe disease require hospitalization.

The virus is transmitted from infected birds to human beings and other animals through the bites of mosquitoes. There is no known cure or vaccine for West Nile virus. Scientists are concerned that as the virus spreads throughout North America it will become a serious threat to public health.

People can reduce their risk of exposure to West Nile virus by avoiding areas where mosquitoes are present, wearing protective clothing, and using insect repellents. Public health officials use pesticides to eliminate the mosquitoes that carry the virus and drain standing pools of water where mosquitoes breed.   W. Ian Lipkin

West Point, New York, a United States military reservation, has served as the site of the U.S. Military Academy since 1802 (see **New York** [political map]). The reservation stands on a plateau above the west bank of the Hudson River. It also includes Constitution Island, which lies in the river. The island is the site of several forts from the Revolutionary War in America (1775-1783). See also **United States Military Academy.**

Bryan Allen, Shostal

The Allegheny Mountains cut through eastern West Virginia. Scenic mountains, steep hills, and narrow valleys cover almost all of the state, which has some of the nation's most rugged terrain.

West Virginia   *The Mountain State*

West Virginia, in the Appalachian Highlands, has some of the most rugged land in the United States. The state has few large areas of level ground, except for strips of valley land that lie along the larger rivers. Mountain chains cover the eastern and central sections of West Virginia. Steep and rolling hills and narrow valleys make up the region west of the mountains. The extreme ruggedness of the land gives West Virginia its nickname, the *Mountain State.*

The beautiful mountain scenery of this rugged state attracts many visitors. Forests of valuable hardwood trees grow on the mountain slopes, and vast mineral deposits lie under the ground. West Virginia is one of the nation's leading producers of coal. Coal deposits lie under about two-thirds of the land. West Virginia industries are based on coal and other important mineral resources found in the state. These resources include clay,

The contributors of this article are Stephen W. Brown, Professor of History at West Virginia Institute of Technology; and Kenneth C. Martis, Professor of Geography at West Virginia University.

limestone, natural gas, petroleum, salt, and sand. However, West Virginia's economic base is shifting. Today, service industries are growing rapidly and form the most important part of the economy.

Industrial cities line the banks of the broad Ohio River, which forms West Virginia's western border. Wheeling, Weirton, and other northern river cities produce iron and steel. Chemical plants operate in the Ohio and Kanawha river valleys. West Virginia's capital, Charleston, is in the Kanawha Valley. The Charleston area is a manufacturing center for chemicals and metal products. Huntington, Parkersburg, and many other cities have large plants that manufacture glassware and pottery.

West Virginia was part of the state of Virginia until the Civil War. Virginia joined the Confederate States in 1861. But the people of the northwestern counties remained loyal to the Union. They formed a new government, patterned after Virginia's, and broke away from the rest of the state. West Virginia became a separate state in 1863. The hardy independence of West Virginians is reflected in the state's motto, *Mountaineers Are Always Free.*

Lee Balterman from Marilyn Gartman

Coal mining is West Virginia's most important mining activity. Soft coal deposits lie under about two-thirds of the state.

Interesting facts about West Virginia

WORLD BOOK illustrations by Kevin Chadwick

Weirton, in the Northern Panhandle of West Virginia, is the only city in the United States that borders two other states while touching its own state on more than one side. Weirton extends to Ohio on the west and Pennsylvania on the east. West Virginia surrounds it on the north and south.

The glass marble manufacturing center of the United States is located in West Virginia. A few factories in the Parkersburg area make most of the nation's glass marbles.

Glass marbles

A huge chandelier hangs in the golden dome of the state capitol in Charleston. The chandelier has 10,080 hand-cut Bohemian crystals. It is 8 feet (2.4 meters) in diameter, weighs 2 short tons (1.8 metric tons), has 96 lights, and hangs from a 54-foot (16.5-meter) gold-plated chain.

West Virginia was the first state to levy a sales tax. The tax, enacted in 1921, was based on the gross receipts of the firms doing business in the state.

The town of Romney changed hands between Union and Confederate forces 56 times during the Civil War. West Virginia was the site of many battles during the war.

Romney

Rural Free Delivery originated in West Virginia. Postmaster General William L. Wilson introduced the idea to his home state. On Oct. 1, 1896, rural carriers began working out of post offices in Charles Town, Halltown, and Uvilla.

Bill Barley, Shostal

Downtown Charleston lies along the banks of the Kanawha River. Charleston is the capital and largest city of West Virginia. It ranks as the state's leading center of industry and trade.

West Virginia in brief

Symbols of West Virginia

The state flag, adopted in 1929, bears the state coat of arms. The state seal, which incorporates the coat of arms, was adopted in 1863. The design on the front includes a miner and a farmer. The rock between them shows the date of West Virginia's statehood. In the foreground, rifles symbolize the willingness to fight for freedom. The landscape on the back of the seal includes an oil derrick, a log cabin, sheep and cattle, a factory, a railroad, and wooded mountains.

State flag

State seal

West Virginia (brown) ranks 41st in size among all the states and 12th in size among the Southern States (yellow).

Charleston has housed the State Capitol since 1885 and from 1870 to 1875. Wheeling was the state capital from 1863 to 1870 and from 1875 to 1885.

General information

Statehood: June 20, 1863, the 35th state.
State abbreviations: W. Va. (traditional); WV (postal).
State motto: *Montani Semper Liberi* (Mountaineers Are Always Free).
State song: "The West Virginia Hills," Words by Ellen King; music by H. E. Engle (one of three state songs).

Land and climate

Area: 24,231 mi² (62,759 km²), including 145 mi² (375 km²) of inland water.
Elevation: *Highest*—Spruce Knob, 4,861 ft (1,482 m) above sea level. *Lowest*—240 ft (73 m) above sea level along the Potomac River in Jefferson County.
Record high temperature: 112 °F (44 °C) at Martinsburg on July 10, 1936, and at Moorefield on Aug. 4, 1930.
Record low temperature: −37 °F (−38 °C) at Lewisburg on Dec. 30, 1917.
Average July temperature: 72 °F (22 °C).
Average January temperature: 32 °F (0 °C).
Average yearly precipitation: 44 in (112 cm).

Greatest north-south distance 237 mi (381 km)

Highest elevation ●

Lowest elevation ●

Greatest east-west distance 265 mi (426 km)

Important dates

Germans from Pennsylvania established a settlement at New Mecklenburg (now Shepherdstown).

The counties of western Virginia refused to secede from the Union with Virginia.

 1600's   1727   1742   1861

West Virginia's Indian population began to decline due to wars and disease.

John P. Salling and John Howard discovered coal on the Coal River.

State bird
Cardinal

State flower
Rhododendron

State tree
Sugar maple

People

Population: 1,808,344
Rank among the states: 37th
Density: 75 per mi² (29 per km²), U.S. average 78 per mi² (30 per km²)
Distribution: 54 percent rural, 46 percent urban
Largest cities in West Virginia

Charleston	53,421
Huntington	51,475
Parkersburg	33,099
Wheeling	31,419
Morgantown	26,809
Weirton	20,411

Source: 2000 census.

Population trend

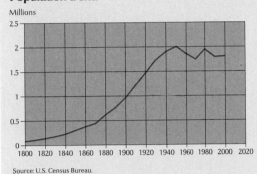

Millions

Source: U.S. Census Bureau.

Year	Population
2000	1,808,344
1990	1,793,477
1980	1,950,258
1970	1,744,237
1960	1,860,421
1950	2,005,552
1940	1,901,974
1930	1,729,205
1920	1,463,701
1910	1,221,119
1900	958,800
1890	762,794
1880	618,457
1870	442,014
1860	376,688
1850	302,313
1840	224,537
1830	176,924
1820	136,808
1810	105,469
1800	78,592
1790	55,873

Economy

Chief products

Agriculture: broilers, beef cattle, hay, turkeys, milk.
Manufacturing: chemicals; primary metals; wood products, fabricated metal products; transportation equipment; stone, clay, and glass products.
Mining: coal, natural gas.

Gross state product

Value of goods and services produced in 2000: $42,269,000,000. *Services* include community, business, and personal services; finance; government; trade; and transportation, communication, and utilities. *Industry* includes construction, manufacturing, and mining. *Agriculture* includes agriculture, fishing, and forestry.

Source: U.S. Bureau of Economic Analysis.

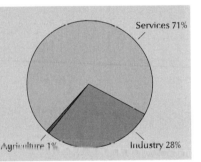

Services 71%

Agriculture 1%

Industry 28%

Government

State government

Governor: 4-year term
State senators: 34; 4-year terms
State delegates: 100; 2-year terms
Counties: 55

Federal government

United States senators: 2
United States representatives: 3
Electoral votes: 5

Sources of information

For information about tourism, write to: West Virginia Division of Tourism and Parks, 90 MacCorkle Avenue SW, South Charleston, WV 25303. The Web site at www.callwva.com also provides information.
For information on the economy, write to: West Virginia Development Office, Capitol Complex, Building 6, Room 553, 1900 Washington Street East, Charleston, West Virginia 25305-0311.
The state's official Web site at www.state.wv.us provides much data on West Virginia's economy and government. The site of the Division of Culture and History, www.wvculture.org, shows information on the state's historical resources and historic sites.

West Virginia became the 35th state on June 20.

The National Radio Astronomy Observatory began operating at Green Bank.

| 1863 | 1919-1921 | 1959 | 1985 |

Miners fought with mine guards, police, and federal troops in a dispute over organizing unions.

West Virginia established a state lottery.

Population. The 2000 United States census reported that West Virginia had 1,808,344 people. The population had increased by less than 1 percent over the 1990 figure, 1,793,477. The population grew again in the 1990's after economic problems had contributed to its decline during the 1980's. According to the 2000 census, West Virginia ranks 37th in population among the 50 states.

About 42 percent of West Virginia's people live in metropolitan areas. The areas around Charleston, Huntington, Parkersburg, and Wheeling are Metropolitan Statistical Areas (see **Metropolitan area**). Three other metropolitan areas also extend into West Virginia. For the names and populations of these areas, see the *Index* to the political map of West Virginia.

More than half of the people of West Virginia live in rural areas. The state has about 200 cities, towns, and vil-lages with populations of less than 2,500. Many were once coal-mining towns and trading centers for farm areas. West Virginia's large cities lie in river valleys, where the land is least hilly. They are centers for the chemical, iron, and steel industries. Charleston, Huntington, Parkersburg, and Wheeling are the largest cities.

Almost all the people of West Virginia were born in the United States. Many are of German, Irish, Scotch-Irish, English, African, or American Indian descent. Many immigrants came to West Virginia during the late 1800's and early 1900's to work in the state's coal mines.

Schools. Pioneer children in the region that became West Virginia attended classes in log buildings. These buildings served both as schools and as churches. As was typical of Virginia, of which West Virginia was then a part, parents paid schoolteachers in cash, in farm

Population density

The most densely populated areas of West Virginia are the northern and southwestern parts of the state. Much of the mountainous southeastern part of the state is thinly populated.

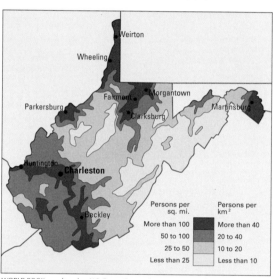

WORLD BOOK map; based on U.S. Census Bureau data.

Gary T. Truman

An art and craft fair in Ripley features modern artwork and traditional West Virginia crafts. The blacksmith shown in this picture is demonstrating the use of a hammer and tongs.

Stephen J. Shaluta, Jr., West Virginia Division of Tourism

Skiing in West Virginia's mountains provides recreation for residents and visitors. A ski lift takes skiers up a mountain slope at Canaan Valley State Park, near Red Creek, *shown here.*

products, and with "bed and board." In 1810, the Virginia legislature created a literary fund for the education of poor children.

The legislature passed a law in 1829 providing for free district schools in counties that wished to establish them. Few schools, however, were set up because most state and county officials believed parents should pay to educate only their own children.

West Virginia established a free school system in 1863, after it became a state. The constitutions of 1863 and 1872 provided limited tax funds to support the schools. In 1876, Alexander L. Wade of Monongalia County developed a graded school plan, which was adopted in West Virginia and in many other states. In 1933, the state's 398 school districts were replaced with 55 county systems.

Today, a nine-member state Board of Education administers the public schools. The governor appoints its members to nine-year terms. The board appoints a state superintendent of schools, who supervises the public school system. Children age 6 through 15 must attend school. For the number of students and teachers in West Virginia, see **Education** (table).

Libraries. A subscription library was operating in Wheeling as early as 1808. Members of this library contributed money to buy books, which they could use without charge. Public libraries were not common until after 1900. A state library commission was established in 1929 to help regulate and expand library services.

Today, many public library systems serve the people. Bookmobiles provide service for areas that lack libraries. The West Virginia University Library houses the West Virginia Regional History Collection of manuscripts and books. The Rosanna A. Blake Library at Mar-

shall University in Huntington is a collection of materials on the history of the Confederate States of America.

Museums. The West Virginia State Museum is in the Cultural Center at the Capitol Complex in Charleston. The Sunrise Museum in Charleston has an art museum, a science hall, and a planetarium. Art museums include the Huntington Museum of Art, Parkersburg Art Center in Parkersburg, and the Oglebay Institute's Mansion Museum in Wheeling. Museums at the Harpers Ferry National Historical Park feature displays on the American Civil War (1861-1865) and the 1859 armory raid by American abolitionist John Brown.

West Virginia University

West Virginia University is located in Morgantown. Woodburn Hall, *shown here,* is one of the oldest buildings on campus.

Marshall University

The Marshall University campus is located in Huntington. The school, established in 1837, is one of the state's two oldest universities.

Universities and colleges

This table lists the universities and colleges in West Virginia that grant bachelor's or advanced degrees and are accredited by the North Central Association of Colleges and Schools.

Name	Mailing address	Name	Mailing address
Alderson-Broaddus College	Philippi	Ohio Valley College	Vienna
Appalachian Bible College	Bradley	Salem International University	Salem
Bethany College	Bethany	Shepherd College	Shepherdstown
Bluefield State College	Bluefield	West Liberty State College	West Liberty
Charleston, University of	Charleston	West Virginia State College	Institute
Concord College	Athens	West Virginia University	*
Davis & Elkins College	Elkins	West Virginia University Institute	
Fairmont State College	Fairmont	of Technology	Montgomery
Glenville State College	Glenville	West Virginia Wesleyan	
Marshall University	Huntington	College	Buckhannon
Mountain State University	Beckley	Wheeling Jesuit University	Wheeling

*Campuses at Morgantown and Parkersburg.

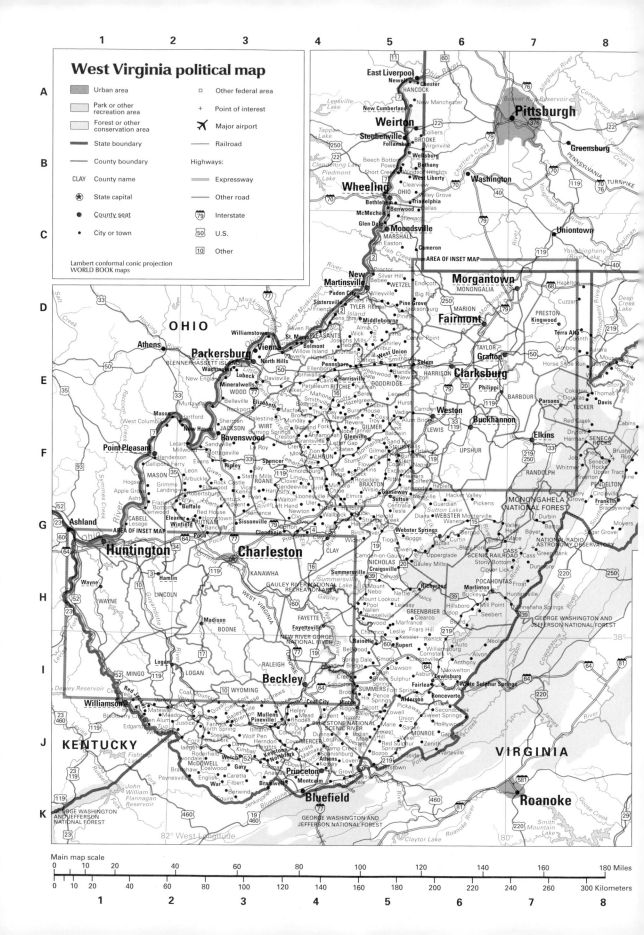

West Virginia map index

Metropolitan areas

Counties

Cities, towns, and villages

Beautiful scenery, mineral springs, and a variety of wildlife attract tourists, campers, hunters, and fishing enthusiasts to the mountains of West Virginia. The state's Allegheny Mountains offer alpine and Nordic skiing. Kayakers, canoeists, and white water rafters enjoy such rivers as the New, the Gauley, the Cheat, and the Tygart Valley. West Virginia's state parks and forests attract hikers and outdoor recreation enthusiasts. Tours of orchards, glass factories, and an exhibition coal mine of-

fer glimpses into some of the industries that are important to the state.

The Mountain State Forest Festival, held early in October at Elkins, is among the most colorful annual events in West Virginia. Most of the festival takes place on the campus of Davis and Elkins College. Highlights of the festival include jousting tournaments, wood-chopping and sawing contests, and archery and shooting exhibitions.

Sternwheel Regatta in Charleston

Stephen J. Shaluta, Jr., West Virginia Division of Tourism

Places to visit

Following are brief descriptions of some of West Virginia's many interesting places to visit:

Beckley Exhibition Coal Mine, at New River Park in Beckley, is a restored mine first operated in the late 1800's. Visitors can take a riding tour of the mine and view exhibits at the Coal Museum. A coal company house, mine superintendent's home, and a one-room schoolhouse are also at the site.

Blennerhassett Island, in the Ohio River near Parkersburg, was the site of a mansion built by Harman Blennerhassett about 1800. Blennerhassett, with Aaron Burr and others, was suspected of planning an independent government in the southwestern region of the United States. A reconstruction of the mansion has been built over the original foundation.

Cass, in Pocahontas County, has a state-owned scenic railroad powered by steam locomotives. Trains run through beautiful mountain country on the tracks of a former logging railroad.

Charles Town, the county seat of Jefferson County, was founded in 1786 by Charles Washington, younger brother of George Washington. A jury at the Jefferson County Courthouse found John Brown guilty of murder and treason after his 1859 raid on Harpers Ferry. A stone marker designates the site of the John Brown Gallows. Several historic homes stand in the area around Charles Town. Harewood was built about 1770 for George Washington's brother Samuel. Dolley Payne Todd and James Madison were married in this house in 1794. Charles Washington built Mordington, or "Happy Retreat," about 1780. Bushrod Washington, grandnephew of the president, built Claymont Court in 1820.

Jackson's Mill, near Weston, was the family farm where the Confederate General Stonewall Jackson spent his boyhood. In

1921, this area became the first state 4-H Club camp to be established in the United States.

National Radio Astronomy Observatory, in Green Bank, is a center for the study of radio waves from space. During the summer, visitors at the observatory may inspect radio telescopes that measure the waves, and view a film about the observatory's work.

New River Gorge Bridge, on U.S. 19 near Fayetteville, is the world's longest steel arch span bridge. A visitor center provides a scenic overview and an audio-visual presentation.

West Virginia Independence Hall-Custom House, in Wheeling, was the site of statehood conventions which led to the founding of West Virginia in 1863. Visitors can view exhibits detailing the movement for statehood.

National forests and parklands. Monongahela National Forest lies entirely within West Virginia, in the eastern part of the state. Parts of George Washington and Jefferson national forests extend into West Virginia from Virginia. The town of Harpers Ferry is famous in Civil War history. Harpers Ferry National Historical Park lies on the boundary between West Virginia and Maryland, as does the nearby Chesapeake and Ohio Canal National Historical Park. Bluestone National Scenic River, Gauley River National Recreation Area, and New River Gorge National River are in the southern part of West Virginia.

State parks and forests. West Virginia has 38 state parks and 9 state forests. Among the best-known state parks is Blackwater Falls, near Davis. There, sparkling water tumbles 63 feet (19 meters) over a rocky ledge. For information on the parks and forests of West Virginia, write to Division of Tourism and Parks, 90 MacCorkle Ave., SW, South Charleston, WV 25303.

Ron Snow, West Virginia Department of Commerce
Mountain State Forest Festival in Elkins

Annual events

January-May
Alpine Festival in Davis (March); Feast of the Ramson in Richwood (April); House and Garden Tour in Martinsburg (April); Dogwood Festival in Huntington (April); Strawberry Festival in Buckhannon (May); Webster County Woodchopping Festival (May); Vandalia Gathering in Charleston (May).

June-August
Folk Festival in Glenville (June); Mountain State Art and Craft Fair in Ripley (July); plays about West Virginia history at Grandview Park (June through Sunday before Labor Day); Appalachian String Band Music Festival at Camp Washington Carver (August); Augusta Heritage Festival in Elkins (August); Cherry River Festival in Richwood (August); West Virginia State Fair in Lewisburg (August); Sternwheel Regatta in Charleston (late August and early September).

September-December
Hardy County Heritage Weekend in Moorefield (September); King Coal Festival in Williamson (September); Preston County Buckwheat Festival in Kingwood (September); West Virginia Oil and Gas Festival in Sistersville (September); Black Walnut Festival in Spencer (October); Mountain State Forest Festival in Elkins (October); Winter Festival of Lights in Wheeling (early November-early January).

Harpers Ferry National Historical Park

Jeff Gnass, West Stock

Jodi Cobb, Woodfin Camp, Inc.

White water rafting on the New River

Land regions. In most places, West Virginia's boundaries follow the courses of rivers or the peaks of mountain chains. For this reason, the state has crooked boundaries. A narrow strip of West Virginia called the *Northern Panhandle* extends northward between Ohio and Pennsylvania. Another extension of West Virginia runs northward and eastward between Maryland and Virginia. It is called the *Eastern Panhandle.*

West Virginia has few large areas of level ground. Low mountains cover much of the eastern third of the state. Spruce Knob, the highest point in West Virginia, rises 4,861 feet (1,482 meters) above sea level near the eastern border. The widest valleys lie near the Ohio River in the west, and in parts of the Eastern Panhandle between the Allegheny and Blue Ridge mountains.

West Virginia has two main land regions: (1) the Appalachian Ridge and Valley Region, and (2) the Appalachian Plateau.

The Appalachian Ridge and Valley Region covers a wide strip of West Virginia along the state's eastern border. The Allegheny Mountains of this region belong to the Appalachian Mountain system. They form part of a series of long ridges and valleys that run from northeast to southwest across several eastern states. These mountains are made of folded layers of *sedimentary rock* (rock formed from deposits laid down by ancient rivers and seas). Erosion has worn down the softer layers, forming long parallel ridges of harder rock with valleys in between. Most streams and rivers run along the valleys between the ridges. A few streams cross the ridges in *water gaps* (breaks in the ridges). Water gaps occur where weak rock was worn away, or where streams cut through hard rock as nature lifted and folded it. Caves and underground streams are common throughout the region. Forests cover the mountainsides.

The *Allegheny Front* marks the western limits of the region. The Allegheny Front occurs where the sharply folded rock layers of the Appalachian Ridge and Valley Region meet the more gently folded layers of the Appalachian Plateau. The front appears in some places as a high, rugged *escarpment* (slope). In southern West Virginia, it becomes lost in the roughness of the southern Allegheny Mountains.

The Blue Ridge Mountains lie along the eastern borders of the Appalachian Ridge and Valley Region. These mountains are made of *igneous rock* (rock formed by the cooling of hot, melted material) and *metamorphic rock* (rock changed by heat and pressure).

The Appalachian Plateau covers the entire state west of the Appalachian Ridge and Valley Region. The plateau has a rugged surface. Streams have carved narrow valleys, leaving flat-topped uplands and rounded hills. The slopes are steep, especially in the west. Many peaks in the northeastern part of the region rise more than 4,000 feet (1,200 meters) above sea level.

Most of West Virginia's coal, salt, petroleum, and natural gas deposits are found in the Appalachian Plateau. Nearly all the state's larger cities lie in the wider river valleys of this region.

Rivers and lakes. The Ohio River flows along the western boundary of West Virginia for over 275 miles (442 kilometers). It provides a route to the Mississippi River and the Gulf of Mexico. The major rivers of the Appalachian Plateau flow northwestward into the Ohio. The

Stephen J. Shaluta, Jr., West Virginia Department of Commerce

Blackwater Falls tumbles 63 feet (19 meters) over a rocky ledge in Blackwater Falls State Park, near Davis. West Virginia has preserved its wilderness in many state parks and forests.

Land regions of West Virginia

WORLD BOOK map

Map index

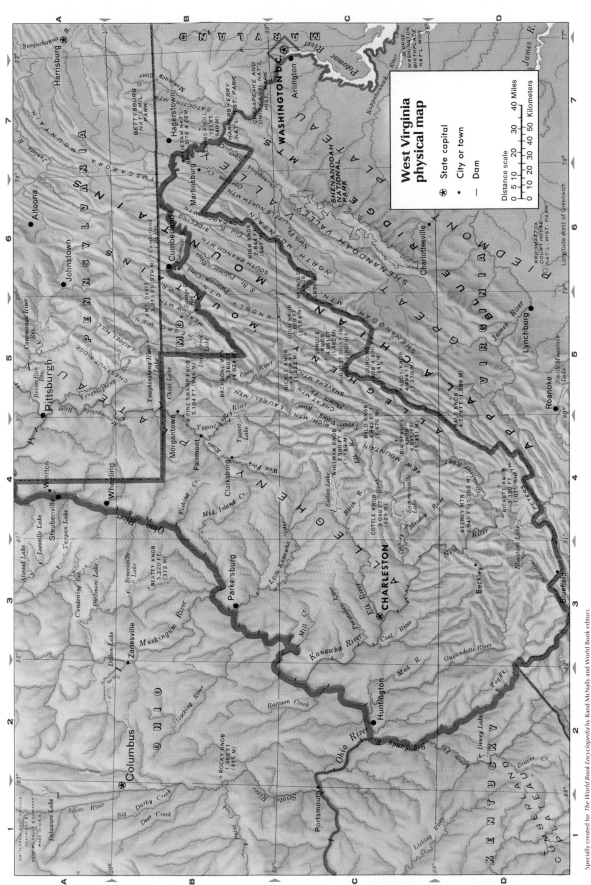

West Virginia physical map

⊛ State capital

• City or town

— Dam

Distance scale

0 5 10 20 30 40 Miles

0 10 20 30 40 50 Kilometers

Specially created for *The World Book Encyclopedia* by Rand McNally and World Book editors

The Kanawha River Valley, near Pliny, cuts through West Virginia's Appalachian Plateau region. The state's widest valleys lie in the western part of this region.

© Gary T. Truman

Kanawha River is the Ohio's largest tributary in West Virginia. The Kanawha and New rivers and their branches drain a large portion of the state. The Big Sandy, Guyandotte, and Little Kanawha rivers also flow into the Ohio River.

The Monongahela River begins near the northern border of West Virginia. It flows northward through Pennsylvania and helps form the Ohio River at Pittsburgh. The Monongahela and its branches, including the Cheat, Tygart Valley, and West Fork rivers, form the main drainage system of north-central West Virginia. A separate system drains the Eastern Panhandle. The Shenandoah and other rivers in that region flow northward and eastward into the Potomac River.

West Virginia has no large natural lakes. Dams and reservoirs have been built to hold back water during flood seasons and to release it during periods of low flow. The reservoirs serve as lakes for fishing and recreation.

Plant and animal life. Forests cover about four-fifths of West Virginia. The most important trees are beech, cherry, hickory, maple, oak, and poplar. Evergreen trees, including hemlock, red spruce, and white pine, grow on mountain ridges and plateaus. Evergreens also grow in river gorges.

The river valleys of West Virginia bloom with wild flowers from early spring to late fall. Bloodroot and hepaticas blossom beneath dogwood, redbud, white-blossomed hawthorn, and wild crab-apple trees. Azaleas and rhododendrons bloom in late spring and early summer. In autumn, the fields glow with asters, black-eyed Susans, and goldenrod.

White-tailed deer and black bears live in the mountains. Small woodland animals include gray and red foxes, minks, opossums, and raccoons. Many kinds of fish, including bass, trout, and walleyed pike, are found in the rivers and streams.

Climate. West Virginia has warm summers and moderately cold winters. The valleys are usually warmer than the mountains. Maximum summer temperatures average over 85 °F (29 °C), but in the mountains, they are

from 5 to 10 degrees Fahrenheit (3 to 6 degrees Celsius) cooler. Minimum winter temperatures average about 25 °F (−4 °C) in the central and northeastern mountains, and nearly 30 °F (−1 °C) in the south and southwest. The state's highest recorded temperature, 112 °F (44 °C), occurred at Moorefield on Aug. 4, 1930, and at Martinsburg on July 10, 1936. West Virginia's lowest recorded temperature, −37 °F (−38 °C), was set at Lewisburg on Dec. 30, 1917.

Rainfall is plentiful in all parts of the state. It is heaviest in the southern mountains, and lightest in the upper Potomac River valley in the east. The ample rainfall benefits West Virginia's agriculture and industry, but it also creates problems. Summer thunderstorms sometimes cause flash floods that damage property in valley settlements. Heavy winter and spring floods occur in the lower river valleys of West Virginia. Thick fogs often cover the valleys.

The southwest has the lightest snowfall—less than 20 inches (51 centimeters) a year. The mountains sometimes get as much as 100 inches (250 centimeters) of snowfall annually.

Average monthly weather

	Charleston					Elkins				
	Temperatures				Days of rain or snow		Temperatures				Days of rain or snow
	°F High	°F Low	°C High	°C Low			°F High	°F Low	°C High	°C Low	
Jan.	46	27	8	−3	18	Jan.	43	22	6	−6	18
Feb.	49	28	9	−2	14	Feb.	44	21	7	−6	16
Mar.	57	33	14	1	16	Mar.	52	27	11	−3	17
Apr.	68	42	20	6	15	Apr.	63	36	17	2	15
May	77	50	25	10	14	May	72	45	22	7	14
June	85	60	29	16	11	June	79	54	26	12	15
July	87	64	31	18	12	July	83	57	28	14	14
Aug.	86	62	30	17	10	Aug.	81	56	27	13	12
Sept.	81	56	27	13	9	Sept.	76	50	24	10	10
Oct.	71	44	22	7	9	Oct.	65	38	18	3	11
Nov.	57	35	14	2	11	Nov.	52	29	11	−2	13
Dec.	48	29	9	−2	13	Dec.	43	22	6	−6	16

Average January temperatures
West Virginia has moderately cold winters. The southwestern section usually averages above freezing.

Average July temperatures
The state has warm summers, with the west and east being the hottest. The central mountains are milder.

Average yearly precipitation
Rain is plentiful throughout the state. It is the heaviest in the mountains and lighter on the east and west borders.

WORLD BOOK maps

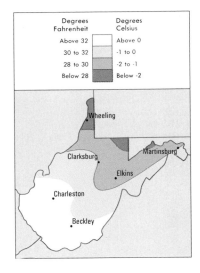

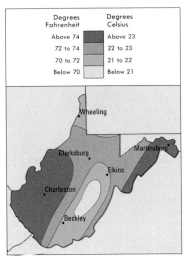

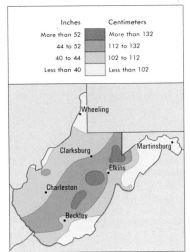

Economy

West Virginia's economy is shifting from a historical dependence on mining and manufacturing to an emphasis on service industries. Service industries, taken together, provide the greatest portion of West Virginia's *gross state product*—the total value of goods and services produced in a year. Service industries include such activities as education, health care, and retail trade.

Chemical manufacturing and coal mining continue to play major roles in West Virginia's economy. The Ohio and Kanawha river valleys are major centers of the nation's chemical industry. West Virginia is also a leading coal producer. But the increasing use of machines in the coal industry has reduced jobs. Jobs have also been lost due to the decline of West Virginia's steel and glass industries. The state's economy has begun to diversify into new kinds of manufacturing and tourism.

Natural resources. Few areas of similar size have so great a variety of resources as West Virginia. These resources include mineral deposits, timber, scenic recreational areas, and abundant rainfall.

Minerals are West Virginia's most valuable natural resources. Deposits of *bituminous* (soft) coal lie under about two-thirds of the state. Most of the coal deposits are in a broad belt that covers all of the southern and central counties. Fields of natural gas and petroleum-bearing sands are found in the western half of the state. Brine and rock salt come from the Ohio and Kanawha river valleys. Limestone is found in the mountains along the eastern border. Sand used in glassmaking comes from several north-central counties and from the Eastern Panhandle. Other products mined in West Virginia include clay, sandstone, and shale.

Soils. The most fertile soils in West Virginia are in the river valleys. Some of the sandy soils that cover the rest of the state contain natural lime that makes the land es-

Production and workers by economic activities

Economic activities	Percent of GSP* produced	Employed workers Number of people	Employed workers Percent of total
Community, business, & personal services	18	263,600	29
Manufacturing	16	84,600	10
Government	16	151,600	17
Wholesale & retail trade	15	192,800	22
Finance, insurance, & real estate	11	46,900	5
Transportation, communication, & utilities	11	44,900	5
Mining	7	26,300	3
Construction	5	48,900	6
Agriculture	1	29,900	3
Total	**100**	**889,500**	**100**

*GSP = gross state product, the total value of goods and services produced in a year.
Figures are for 2000.
Source: *World Book* estimates based on data from U.S. Bureau of Economic Analysis.

pecially good for grain crops and fruit trees.

Service industries account for the largest part of the gross state product of West Virginia. Most of the service industries are concentrated in the state's metropolitan areas. Several service industries benefit from the many tourists who visit the state's recreation areas, historic sites, and other attractions.

Community, business, and personal services contribute more to the gross state product and employ more people than any other service industry in West Virginia. Community, business, and personal services include such establishments as private health care, law

Coal barges move through the Greenup Locks on the Ohio River. West Virginia ranks among the nation's leading coal-mining states. Minerals are its most valuable natural resources.

Eric Carle, Shostal

firms, repair shops, and hotels. Tourists participating in such activities as skiing and whitewater rafting bring millions of dollars to the state. This group also includes the state's fast-growing information technology sector. Most of these high-tech firms are concentrated in the Interstate 79 corridor from Morgantown to Clarksburg.

Wholesale and retail trade ranks second. Wholesale trade takes place when a buyer purchases goods directly from a producer. The wholesale trade of groceries, coal, and other products is important to the state. Leading types of retail businesses include department stores, food stores, and service stations.

Government ranks third. Government services include public schools and hospitals. State government offices are based in Charleston, the state capital.

Ranking next among the state's service industries are (1) finance, insurance, and real estate and (2) transportation, communication, and utilities. These groups contribute equal amounts to the gross state product.

Real estate is a major contributor to the economy because of the large sums of money involved in the selling and leasing of property. Charleston and Huntington are the chief financial centers.

Rail and water transportation are of major importance to the state's economy because they transport coal, chemicals, and other goods from production sites to markets. Trucking companies are also an important part of the transportation sector. Telephone companies are

Economy of West Virginia

This map shows the economic uses of land in West Virginia and where the state's leading farm, mineral, and forest products are produced. Major manufacturing centers are shown in red.

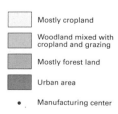

☐ Mostly cropland

▨ Woodland mixed with cropland and grazing

▩ Mostly forest land

▩ Urban area

• Manufacturing center

• Mineral deposit

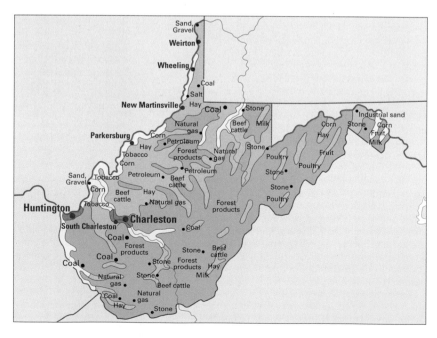

the major part of the communications sector. Utility companies supply electric, gas, and water service. Further information about transportation and communication appears later in this section.

Manufacturing. Products made in West Virginia have a *value added by manufacture* of about $9 billion a year. This figure represents the increase in value of raw materials after they have become finished products.

Chemicals are West Virginia's leading manufactured product by far. The chemical industry operates chiefly in the Kanawha and Ohio river valleys. It uses coal, natural gas, oil, and salt found in the region. Factories in Charleston, New Martinsville, Parkersburg, and South Charleston make adhesives, industrial chemicals, pharmaceuticals, and plastics.

Primary metals rank second in terms of value added by manufacture. This industry centers in the Northern Panhandle. Steel mills line the banks of the Ohio River near Wheeling and Weirton. Weirton manufactures tin plate and sheet steel, and Wheeling produces structural steel. Aluminum is produced in Ravenswood.

Wood products rank third among the state's manufactures. Lumber is the leading type of wood product.

Transportation equipment ranks next. Major automobile parts manufacturers operate factories in the state. The production of aerospace parts is a growing part of this sector.

Stone, clay, and glass products rank fifth in terms of value added. The state is well-known for its glassware and pottery. Table glassware is manufactured in many towns in the state. Other glass products include blown glass, bottles, crystalware, plate glass, stained glass, and structural glass. Most of the pottery plants are in Hancock County, although a few operate elsewhere along the Ohio River. They produce such products as chinaware, firebrick, paving brick, porcelain, and tile.

Other goods made in West Virginia include fabricated metal products and food products. West Virginia's leading types of fabricated metal products include cutlery, pipes, stampings, structural metal, and tools. Baked goods and soft drinks are the main food products made in West Virginia.

Mining. Coal is West Virginia's major mined product. The state ranks among the leaders in coal production. Coal accounts for about 75 percent of West Virginia's mining income. Bituminous coal is the only type of coal mined in the state. About two-thirds of it comes from underground mines. The rest comes from surface mines. About two-thirds of the state's land has coal beneath it. The southern part of West Virginia has the largest coal reserves. Much of the coal mined in the state is exported to other countries.

Coal is mined in 29 of West Virginia's 55 counties. Boone, Kanawha, Marshall, Mingo, and Monongalia counties rank among the state's leading coal-producers.

Certain kinds of coal from the southern part of the state are low in sulfur. Since the enactment of the Federal Clean Air Act of 1990, these coals have been in high demand. The low-sulfur coals have excellent heating and steam-producing qualities and are rich in such by-products as coal tar and creosote.

Coal companies have made increasing use of advanced mining technology to improve efficiency. This has resulted in a need for fewer workers. Thus, some coal-mining regions of West Virginia have high unemployment rates.

Among West Virginia's other mined products, natural gas is the most important, accounting for more than 20 percent of the state's mining income. Natural gas fields lie under most of the western part of the state. Much of the natural gas is piped to cities, where it is used to heat buildings. Some of the gas is converted to liquid form and transported by train or truck. Empty natural gas wells serve as storage places for gas from Louisiana, Oklahoma, or Texas. Pipelines carry the gas to West Virginia, where it is stored in the empty wells during the summer for use locally and in the northeastern states during the winter, primarily for heating.

Ron Simms, West Virginia Chamber of Commerce

A glassmaker demonstrates his craft to a tour group in a factory in Williamstown. West Virginia is famous for its glassware and pottery.

West Virginia also mines petroleum, crushed stone, salt, and sand and gravel. The northwestern part of the state produces the most petroleum. The petroleum is piped to a refinery at Newell for processing into gasoline, fuel oil, and other products. Limestone is the main source of crushed stone in West Virginia. The eastern part of the state has most of the limestone quarries. Crushed stone is used mainly to make roadbeds.

Miners produce large quantities of salt from deep underground mines in Marshall County. The salt is removed from the mines by forcing water into the salt beds to dissolve the salt and pumping out the brine.

Most of West Virginia's sand and gravel is obtained by dredging operations in the Ohio River. Sand and gravel is used mainly to make concrete. A mountain near Berkeley Springs contains sand that is excellent for making glass.

Agriculture. Farmland covers about a fourth of West Virginia's area. The state has about 21,000 farms.

Livestock and livestock products provide about 85 percent of the farm income in West Virginia. *Broilers* (chickens from 5 to 12 weeks old) are the state's most valuable farm product. Beef cattle rank as the state's second most valuable farm product. Most cattle ranches lie in the river valleys of the Appalachian Plateau. Dairy products and turkeys are also important sources of farm income for the state.

Crops account for about 15 percent of West Virginia's farm income. Hay is the most valuable field crop in West Virginia. Almost all the hay is fed to cattle. Corn and tobacco rank next in value. Much of the corn comes from the Ohio and Potomac river valleys. The lower Ohio Valley provides large amounts of tobacco.

West Virginia fruit growers raise large crops of apples and peaches. The easternmost part of West Virginia is one of the best apple-growing regions in the United States. Farmers in West Virginia were the first to grow the Grimes Golden and Golden Delicious apples.

Electric power. Almost all of West Virginia's electric power comes from steam plants that burn coal. Plants that burn petroleum or natural gas produce only a small amount of the state's power. The potential of the state's rivers and streams as a source of hydroelectric power has been largely untapped. But some communities are considering developing new water power projects.

Transportation. Much of the transportation in the state runs along the divides and valleys of the state's major streams. Herds of buffaloes opened trails along the waterways while migrating westward. Later, Indian war parties followed the same paths. Early settlers followed these trails and improved them for wagons. Many settlers traveled on trails along the Ohio River. Most communities developed along railroad lines built in the late 1800's. Paved highways were developed in the 1920's.

West Virginia has about 36,000 miles (58,000 kilometers) of roads and highways. The West Virginia Turnpike runs 88 miles (142 kilometers) between Charleston and Princeton. The state's rugged terrain long hampered efforts to develop a comprehensive road system. But the completion of the interstate highway system in West Virginia has improved transportation within the state.

Eleven rail lines provide freight service in West Virginia. Passenger trains serve about 10 cities. Charleston has West Virginia's busiest airport.

West Virginia has more than 400 miles (660 kilometers) of navigable waterways. Ships and barges on West Virginia rivers carry chemicals, coal, lumber, oil, sand, steel, and other bulky products. During the 1930's, the federal government built a series of locks and dams on the Ohio River and its branches. These locks and dams improved the rivers of West Virginia for barge traffic. The United States Army Corps of Engineers has continued to develop the state's waterways.

Communication. The state's first newspaper, the *Potowmak Guardian and Berkeley Advertiser,* appeared in Shepherdstown in 1790. The state now has about 100 newspapers, about 20 of which are dailies. The *Intelligencer,* founded in 1852 in Wheeling, is still being published. Other dailies published in West Virginia include *The* (Beckley) *Register-Herald,* the *Charleston Gazette,* the *Charleston Daily Mail, The* (Huntington) *Herald-Dispatch, The* (Morgantown) *Dominion Post, The Parkersburg News,* and the *Wheeling News-Register.* West Virginia publishers also produce about 35 periodicals.

The state's first radio station, WSAZ, began broadcasting from Huntington in 1923. WSAZ-TV, the first television station, started operations in Huntington in 1949. Today, West Virginia has about 125 radio stations and 10 television stations. Cable TV systems and Internet providers serve several of the state's communities.

Government

Constitution. West Virginia adopted its first constitution in 1863, when it became the 35th state in the Union. The state is now governed by its second constitution, adopted in 1872. The Constitution has been amended more than 50 times. Constitutional amendments may be proposed in either house of the State Legislature. They must be approved by a two-thirds majority of both houses, and then by a majority of the voters. The Constitution may also be revised by a constitutional convention. Before a convention can be called, it must be approved by a majority of the legislators and the voters.

Executive. The governor of West Virginia is elected to a four-year term and may serve any number of terms, but not more than two terms in succession. The heads of many state administrative departments are appointed

by the governor. Other top state officials include the secretary of state, auditor, treasurer, attorney general, and commissioner of agriculture. Each of these officials is elected to a four-year term.

Legislature of West Virginia consists of the Senate and House of Delegates. The voters of each of the state's 17 senatorial districts elect two senators to four-year terms. The House of Delegates has 100 members. They serve two-year terms. Each of the state's 56 delegate districts elects from 1 to 7 delegates, depending on the population of the district.

The Legislature meets every year. Regular sessions usually begin on the second Wednesday of January. However, in the year after an election for governor is held, the Legislature immediately adjourns until the second Wednesday of February. Regular sessions last 60 days. The governor may call special sessions or may be required to call them by a vote of the Legislature.

Courts. The highest court in West Virginia is the Supreme Court of Appeals. It has five justices elected to 12-year terms. Every year, the court chooses a chief justice from among its members. The state is divided into 31 judicial circuits. Each circuit has a circuit court with one or more judges elected to eight-year terms. The circuit courts have jurisdiction in civil cases and cases involving felonies and misdemeanors.

Each West Virginia county has one or more magistrate courts. The magistrate courts hear civil cases that involve amounts of money of $5,000 or less, and misdemeanor cases that are not handled by the circuit courts. Their judges, called magistrates, are elected to four-year terms.

Local government. Each of West Virginia's 55 counties elects a circuit clerk and a county clerk. All counties elect three county commissioners except for Jefferson County, which elects five. All of these officials serve six-year terms. Other elected county officials include a prosecuting attorney, sheriff, and assessor. These officials serve four years.

A 1936 amendment to the state Constitution gives West Virginia cities with populations of more than 2,000 the right to adopt or change their own charters. This right is called *home rule.* Only 10 West Virginia cities have taken advantage of the home-rule law. The majority of these cities have a council-manager form of government. Most of the state's other cities have a mayor-

Gerald S. Ratliff, West Virginia Chamber of Commerce

The West Virginia House of Delegates meets in the State Capitol in Charleston. Its 100 members serve two-year terms.

council government. West Virginia's home-rule cities are not so independent as home-rule cities of other states. This is because West Virginia courts continue to uphold the right of the State Legislature to control many city affairs.

Revenue. Taxes account for about half of the state government's *general revenue* (income). Most of the rest comes from federal grants and other U.S. government programs. West Virginia's most important sources of tax revenue are a general sales tax and a personal income tax. Other sources of tax revenue include taxes on motor fuels, corporate income, mining production, motor vehicle licenses, insurance premiums, and tobacco products.

Politics. Since 1864, West Virginia has divided its vote about equally between Republicans and Democrats in state elections. From 1896 to 1928, the Republicans won every state election except one. The Democrats won control of the state in 1932 and held it until 1956. Since then, both Democratic and Republican candidates have won the governorship. Democrats have usually won control of the State Legislature. Since the early 1930's, West Virginia voters have greatly favored Democratic presidential candidates over Republican presidential candidates. For West Virginia's voting record in presidential elections, see **Electoral College** (table).

The governors of West Virginia

	Party	Term
Arthur I. Boreman	Republican	1863-1869
Daniel D. T. Farnsworth	Republican	1869
William E. Stevenson	Republican	1869-1871
John J. Jacob	Democratic	1871-1877
Henry M. Mathews	Democratic	1877-1881
Jacob B. Jackson	Democratic	1881-1885
Emanuel W. Wilson	Democratic	1885-1890
Aretas B. Fleming	Democratic	1890-1893
William A. MacCorkle	Democratic	1893-1897
George W. Atkinson	Republican	1897-1901
Albert B. White	Republican	1901-1905
William M. O. Dawson	Republican	1905-1909
William E. Glasscock	Republican	1909-1913
Henry D. Hatfield	Republican	1913-1917
John J. Cornwell	Democratic	1917-1921
Ephraim F. Morgan	Republican	1921-1925
Howard M. Gore	Republican	1925-1929
William G. Conley	Republican	1929-1933
Herman G. Kump	Democratic	1933-1937
Homer A. Holt	Democratic	1937-1941
Matthew M. Neely	Democratic	1941-1945
Clarence W. Meadows	Democratic	1945-1949
Okey L. Patteson	Democratic	1949-1953
William C. Marland	Democratic	1953-1957
Cecil H. Underwood	Republican	1957-1961
William Wallace Barron	Democratic	1961-1965
Hulett C. Smith	Democratic	1965-1969
Arch A. Moore, Jr.	Republican	1969-1977
John D. Rockefeller IV	Democratic	1977-1985
Arch A. Moore, Jr.	Republican	1985-1989
Gaston Caperton	Democratic	1989-1997
Cecil H. Underwood	Republican	1997-2001
Bob Wise	Democratic	2001-

Indian days. The first Indians of the West Virginia area, known as Early Hunters, arrived about 14,000 years ago. They were nomadic hunters of large game. Woodland Indian societies, which existed between about 1000 B.C. and A.D. 1700, included mound builders. Mound builders constructed hundreds of burial mounds in the Ohio and Kanawha river valleys. One of the largest and most famous is Grave Creek Mound, at Moundsville (see **Mound builders**).

West Virginia's Indian population was highest from about A.D. 1000 through the 1500's. The population began declining in the 1600's. Many Indians were killed or driven out during tribal wars involving the Iroquois, Cherokee, and Shawnee. Epidemics of smallpox and other diseases also killed many Indians. By the time white settlers arrived in the 1700's, the Indian population had declined sharply.

White settlement. The area that became West Virginia formed part of the Virginia Colony. King James I of England granted that colony to the Virginia Company of London, a business group, in 1606. White settlement began in what is now West Virginia in the 1700's. A white settlement may have existed at Shepherdstown as early as 1717. It is known that Germans from Pennsylvania settled there in 1727. They called their settlement New Mecklenburg. One of the early settlers in the West Virginia region was Morgan Morgan, who arrived at Bunker Hill about 1731. Other settlements were soon founded, especially by Germans and by Scotch-Irish from what is now Northern Ireland. Most of the pioneers were farmers who settled in the Eastern Panhandle and the valleys of the Greenbrier River and the upper Monongahela River. In 1742, the explorers John Peter Salling (also spelled Salley) and John Howard discovered the great coal resources of West Virginia.

Indians often attacked the settlers, who were taking over Indian hunting grounds. During the 1750's and early 1760's, they destroyed most of the West Virginia settlements. Hoping to satisfy the Indians, King George III of Britain issued the Proclamation of 1763. This law forbade settlements west of the Alleghenies until treaties could be made with the Indians. Under treaties signed in 1768 and 1770, the Cherokee and Iroquois gave up their claims to lands between the Allegheny Mountains and the Ohio River. Settlers poured into the area. But Shawnee Indians and their allies in the area believed their claims to land had been ignored, and they attacked settlers. These clashes led to Lord Dunmore's War in 1774. The war's only major battle occurred at Point Pleasant, where the Indians were defeated.

Before the Revolutionary War in America (1775-1783), land speculators tried to establish a new colony called Vandalia. The colony, with Point Pleasant as its capital, was to include most of what is now West Virginia west of the Alleghenies, plus southwestern Pennsylvania and eastern Kentucky. The Revolutionary War wrecked these plans. The Virginia Colony, which still included West Virginia, became the state of Virginia in 1788. Later, the Continental Congress rejected a proposed 14th state known as Westsylvania, which included much of Vandalia.

Between 1777 and 1782, during the Revolutionary War, West Virginia settlers faced frequent Indian raids. For protection, the settlers relied on defenses that included Fort Henry at Wheeling and Fort Randolph at Point Pleasant.

Early industries. In 1794, Peter Tarr built the first iron furnace west of the Alleghenies near Weirton. About 1808, Samuel Jackson constructed an iron works at Ice's Ferry on the Cheat River. During the War of 1812 (1812-1815), Tarr supplied cannonballs used by Oliver Hazard Perry in his victory over the British on Lake Erie in 1813. Jackson's iron works supplied nails used in building Perry's ships. Before the War of 1812, West Virginians had relied heavily on imports of manufactured products from Britain. The war cut off trade with Britain, and manufacturing increased in West Virginia to make up for the loss. Wheeling became an important industrial center in the early 1800's.

Abundant natural resources added to the growth of industry. Salt production in the Kanawha Valley made it one of the nation's salt-making centers in the early 1800's. Coal mines supplied fuel for salt production and iron manufacturing. In 1841, William Tompkins successfully used natural gas as a fuel at his salt furnaces.

Sectional strife. During the early 1800's, serious differences developed between eastern and western Virginia. Eastern Virginia was a region of large tobacco plantations worked by slave labor. In contrast, small self-sufficient family farms dotted most of western Virginia. The interests of the planters and the farmers often conflicted. The eastern planters controlled the state government and used it for their own advantage. Western Virginians protested such state policies as taxation, voting requirements, and legislative representation.

Western demands led to two important conventions to consider constitutional changes. In a convention held in 1829 and 1830, eastern delegates blocked major changes in the constitution. Some western leaders called for the separation of the western counties from Virginia. The Reform Convention of 1850 and 1851 granted most western demands for political reforms. But it shifted more of the tax burden to the west and failed to deal with several economic concerns. In 1852, Joseph Johnson, a resident of Harrison County in the west, became the first popularly elected governor of Virginia. Even so, serious discontent in western Virginia continued.

The Civil War and statehood. The slavery question further divided eastern and western Virginians. In 1847, the *Ruffner Pamphlet,* written by a member of a prominent Kanawha Valley slaveholding family, called for an end to slavery west of the Blue Ridge Mountains. Disputes over slavery reached a climax in 1859. In that year, John Brown and his followers seized the federal arsenal at Harpers Ferry to protest slavery (see **Brown, John**).

The American Civil War began on April 12, 1861. On April 17, the Virginia Secession Convention voted to leave the Union and join the Confederacy. Most of the delegates from present-day West Virginia opposed secession. Westerners held conventions in Wheeling in May and June, where they declared that all state offices held by secessionists were vacant. The conventions set up the Reorganized Government of Virginia, with its capital in Wheeling. The Reorganized Government supported the Union during the Civil War.

In August 1861, western Virginians began the process of separating from Virginia and creating a new state to

Historic West Virginia

Point Pleasant • Harpers Ferry Green Bank •

Mound builders of various Indian groups built hundreds of burial mounds in the Ohio and Kanawha river valleys.

At the Battle of Point Pleasant in 1774, colonial troops defeated the Shawnee and their allies. As a result, the Indians remained neutral for the first two years of the Revolutionary War in America.

Several western counties that sided with the Union separated from Virginia at the beginning of the Civil War and formed their own government. They later became West Virginia.

John Brown, a famous abolitionist, captured the U.S. arsenal at Harpers Ferry in 1859 as part of an unsuccessful plan to start a rebellion of slaves.

Green Bank, the home of a National Radio Astronomy Observatory facility, opened in 1959.

Important dates in West Virginia

WORLD BOOK illustrations by Kevin Chadwick

1660's Large numbers of Indians in what is now West Virginia died during wars and disease epidemics.

1727 Germans from Pennsylvania established a settlement at New Mecklenburg (now Shepherdstown).

1742 John P. Salling and John Howard discovered coal on the Coal River.

1754-1755 The French and Indians defeated troops led by George Washington and General Edward Braddock.

1773 Plans for Vandalia, a 14th American colony—which would have included West Virginia—collapsed as the Revolutionary War approached.

1775 Gas was discovered near Charleston.

1836 The first railroad reached the state at Harpers Ferry.

1859 John Brown and his followers raided the federal arsenal at Harpers Ferry.

1861 The counties of western Virginia refused to secede with Virginia. These counties organized a separate government that supported the Union.

1863 West Virginia became the 35th state on June 20.

1872 The people ratified the present state constitution.

1919-1921 Labor disputes in Logan and Mingo counties led to conflicts between labor and management.

1924 John W. Davis of Clarksburg received the Democratic nomination for President of the United States. He was defeated by Republican Calvin Coolidge in the general election.

1954 The West Virginia Turnpike, connecting Charleston and Princeton, opened.

1959 The National Radio Astronomy Observatory began operating at Green Bank.

1968 Explosions and fire in a coal mine at Farmington took 78 lives. The disaster led to new mine safety laws.

1972 The Buffalo Creek Flood, one of the worst in West Virginia history, resulted in over 100 deaths near Man.

1985 The West Virginia legislature established a state lottery to help raise money for the state.

be known as Kanawha. A constitutional convention met from November 1861 to February 1862 and wrote a constitution for the new state, with the name changed to West Virginia. After receiving approval from the U.S. Congress and President Abraham Lincoln, West Virginia was admitted to the Union as the 35th state on June 20, 1863.

Although West Virginia was a Union state, its location as a borderland between the North and South resulted in divided loyalties. Some of its people favored the Confederacy. During the Civil War, neighbors and family members sometimes fought on opposite sides. The exact number of West Virginians who served in the war is unknown, but Unionists are believed to have outnumbered Confederates by a large margin. The most famous soldier from the state was Confederate General Stonewall Jackson.

An estimated 632 Civil War military actions took place in West Virginia. The Battle of Philippi on June 3, 1861, is sometimes called the first land battle of the war. Union armies captured the Monongahela and Kanawha valleys in the first year of the war. Many of the later military actions involved quick raids. With a victory in the Battle of Droop Mountain in 1864, Union forces gained control of most of West Virginia.

The Civil War ended in 1865. It had produced deep hatreds, some of which remained long after the conflict. Following the war, Radical Republican administrations took away political rights of approximately 15,000 West Virginians who had supported the Confederacy. Conditions resulting from the war played a part in the development of some family feuds, including the famous Hatfield-McCoy feud on the West Virginia-Kentucky border.

In 1870, Democrats won the governorship and most seats in the state legislature. They restored the political rights the Radical Republicans had taken away. They also wrote the state's present constitution, which the voters approved in 1872. Wheeling, which was in the heart of Republican territory, served as the first state capital. Following the Democratic victories of 1870, the capital was transferred to Charleston. Wheeling became the capital again in 1875. But two years later, the people voted to make Charleston the permanent capital. The move back to Charleston took place in 1885.

Industrial growth. When West Virginia entered the Union, about 90 percent of its people were farmers. In the last decades of the 1800's, however, the state experienced an industrial revolution based on coal, timber, oil,

Tent colonies such as Red Jacket, shown above in 1920, housed striking coal miners who were locked out of their company-owned homes. During the late 1800's and early 1900's, miners engaged in a bitter struggle to win higher wages and better working conditions.

natural gas, and other resources. New industries developed in part due to the building of railroads into most parts of the state. By 1900, coal had become the state's leading industry. West Virginia was one of the nation's top oil-producing states in the late 1800's and early 1900's. Israel C. White of West Virginia became a world-famous oil geologist. From 1906 to 1924, the state led the nation in natural gas production. West Virginia's extensive forests provided wood for large-scale timber and lumber development.

In the 1900's, West Virginia's resources helped increase manufacturing in the state. The production of chemicals, glass, and iron, steel, and other metals gained importance. Wheeling and Weirton became iron and steel centers. Chemical industries developed in the Kanawha and Ohio valleys. The Kanawha Valley became one of the chemical centers of the world. The presence of rich silica sands, natural gas, and limestone contributed to the development of the glass industry. A glass plant operated in nearly every major town. The invention of a bottle-making machine and other devices by Michael J. Owens of West Virginia further aided glass production in the state. The participation of the United States in World War I in 1917 and 1918 generated manufacturing needed to produce war supplies.

Labor developments. The needs of industry led to a large wave of immigration into West Virginia in the late 1800's and early 1900's. Coal companies recruited workers from European countries, especially Italy, Hungary, and Poland. Glass making in the Kanawha Valley attracted skilled workers from Belgium. African Americans left Southern states for jobs in the state's mines.

Labor disputes about wages, hours, and working conditions became common and sometimes led to violence. In 1877, a railroad strike that began at Martinsburg became the first U.S. nationwide industrial strike. Labor made some of its earliest gains through the organization of craft unions. The West Virginia Federation of Labor, organized in 1903, included 270 craft unions by 1914.

In the 1880's, most of West Virginia's nonunion workers were coal miners. In 1897, the United Mine Workers of America (UMWA) held a large rally at Wheeling. There, it attempted—without much success—to organize West Virginia miners. Coal mine operators fought back by using court injunctions, mine guards, special police, and other methods. In 1902, with the help of Mary Harris Jones—called "Mother Jones"—the UMWA organized miners in the Kanawha Valley.

In 1912 and 1913, when Kanawha mine operators refused to renew contracts, miners on Paint Creek and Cabin Creek went on strike. During the conflict, 12 miners and 4 company guards were killed at Mucklow (now Gallagher, near Montgomery). Governor William E. Glasscock imposed martial law twice to try to halt the conflict. After Governor Henry D. Hatfield took office in 1913, the union and the operators agreed to a new contract. The contract provided a nine-hour workday and the right to organize workers.

Labor unrest occurred in Logan and Mingo counties between 1919 and 1921, when operators attempted to prevent unionization of their mines. About 5,000 miners from the Kanawha Valley prepared to march on Logan. Governor John J. Cornwell persuaded most of them to return home. Other miners gave in when Cornwell threatened to call in federal troops.

In 1920, clashes at Matewan between miners and agents employed by operators led to the deaths of seven company detectives, two union members, and the town's mayor. The incident is called the Matewan Massacre. In August 1921, approximately 5,000 miners, angry over continued violence, gathered at Marmet for a protest march on Logan. Between 1,200 and 1,300 state police, deputy sheriffs, armed guards, and others stopped the marchers at Blair Mountain, near the Boone-Logan county line. A battle raged for four days. At the request of Governor Ephraim Morgan, 2,100 federal troops were sent to Blair Mountain. The federal forces included a chemical warfare unit and bomber and fighter planes. Faced with that situation, the miners surrendered. Later, 543 people were indicted on charges that included murder, treason, and carrying guns.

Union membership dropped sharply after 1921. However, the federal government's National Industrial Recovery Act (NIRA) of 1933 established the right of labor unions to bargain collectively. NIRA, later replaced by the Wagner Act, also established minimum wages, shortened workdays, and improved working conditions.

An era of change. The Great Depression of the 1930's brought economic hardship to West Virginia and the rest of the country. The United States entered World War II in 1941. From then until the war ended in 1945, manufacturing boomed as the state helped provide supplies for the war effort. During the 1950's, West Virginia entered a period of economic change. Coal production declined as many industries that used coal for power switched to other energy sources. New mining machines reduced the need for workers. As jobs disappeared, large numbers of people left the state. From 1950 to 1970, the population declined by 13 percent.

West Virginia's severe economic problems attracted national attention to its Democratic presidential primary election of 1960. John F. Kennedy defeated Hubert H. Humphrey, the leading Democratic candidate. Kennedy's stunning victory was the turning point in his successful bid for the nomination. He became president in 1961. From 1961 to 1969, the administrations of Kennedy and his successor, Lyndon B. Johnson, promoted economic programs that brought some improvements to West Virginia's economy. Also, during the 1970's, international oil shortages and high prices aided the coal industry. The state's population increased by about 12 percent during the decade.

Recent developments. The economic upturn of the 1960's and 1970's was reversed during the 1980's. West Virginia suffered high unemployment. The population declined by about $7\frac{1}{2}$ percent between 1980 and 1990.

The 1990's brought some signs of economic development, however. After several years of decline, coal production increased in 1990. From 1990 to 2000, the state's population increased by about 1 percent. The state's timber industry expanded, and tourism increased. Robert C. Byrd of West Virginia served as chairman of the United States Senate Appropriations Committee from 1988 to 1995. In that post, he helped the state win federal projects that created many jobs. The projects included a Federal Bureau of Investigation (FBI) fingerprint center at Clarksburg, federal highway construction, and water development projects.   Stephen W. Brown and Kenneth C. Martis

Study aids

Related articles in *World Book* include:

Biographies

Boyd, Belle
Brown, John
Buck, Pearl S.
Byrd, Robert Carlyle
Cornstalk
Davis, Henry G.
Davis, John W.

Jackson, Stonewall
Kenna, John E.
Pierpont, Francis H.
Reuther, Walter P.
Vance, Cyrus R.
Washington, George
Yeager, Charles E.

Cities and towns

Charleston
Harpers Ferry

Huntington
Wheeling

White Sulphur
    Springs

Physical features

Allegheny Mountains
Kanawha River
Monongahela River

Ohio River
Potomac River

Other related articles

Civil War

Virginia (History)

Outline

I. **People**
   A. Population
   B. Schools
II. **Visitor's guide**
   A. Places to visit
   B. Annual events
III. **Land and climate**
   A. Land regions
   B. Rivers and lakes
IV. **Economy**
   A. Natural resources
   B. Service industries
   C. Manufacturing
   D. Mining
V. **Government**
   A. Constitution
   B. Executive
   C. Legislature
   D. Courts
   E. Local government
   F. Revenue
   G. Politics
VI. **History**

C. Libraries
D. Museums

C. Plant and animal life
D. Climate

E. Agriculture
F. Electric power
G. Transportation
H. Communication

Questions

What were some of the reasons that led West Virginia to separate from Virginia?
Which economic activity employs the most people in West Virginia?
What two well-known varieties of apples were first grown in West Virginia?
How did West Virginia's 1960 Democratic presidential primary election gain national importance?
How does West Virginia rank among the states in coal production?
How has the nature of West Virginia's land influenced the state's economy?
What are West Virginia's main land regions?
How did the National Industrial Recovery Act (NIRA) of 1933 help West Virginia workers?
What is West Virginia's most important field crop?
What cities have served as West Virginia's capital?

Additional resources

Level I

Di Piazza, Domenica. *West Virginia.* 2nd ed. Lerner, 2002.
Fazio, Wende. *West Virginia.* Children's Pr., 2000.
Hoffman, Nancy. *West Virginia.* Benchmark Bks., 1999.

Level II

Bastress, Robert M. *The West Virginia State Constitution.* Greenwood, 1995.
Bickley, Ancella R., and Ewen, L. A., eds. *Memphis Tennessee Garrison: The Remarkable Story of a Black Appalachian Woman.* Ohio Univ. Pr., 2001.
Giesen, Carol A. B. *Coal Miners' Wives: Portraits of Endurance.* Univ. Pr. of Ky., 1995.
Rice, Otis K., and Brown, Stephen W. *West Virginia.* 2nd ed. Univ. Pr. of Ky., 1993.
Salstrom, Paul. *Appalachia's Path to Dependency: Rethinking a Region's Economic History, 1730-1940.* Univ. Pr. of Ky., 1994.
Thomas, Jerry D. *An Appalachian New Deal: West Virginia in the Great Depression.* Univ. Pr. of Ky., 1998.
Valentine, Fawn. *West Virginia Quilts and Quiltmakers.* Ohio Univ. Pr., 2000.
Williams, John A. *West Virginia: A History.* 2nd ed. W. Va. Univ. Pr., 2001.

West Virginia University is a coeducational institution in Morgantown and Parkersburg, West Virginia. It is the *land-grant university* of West Virginia (see **Land-grant university**). The university has colleges of agriculture and forestry, arts and sciences, business and economics, creative arts, engineering, human resources and education, law, and mineral and energy resources. In addition, it has schools of dentistry, journalism, medicine, nursing, pharmacy, physical education, and social work, and a center for extension and continuing education. Courses of study lead to bachelor's, master's, and doctor's degrees. West Virginia University was founded in 1867.   Critically reviewed by West Virginia University

Westcott, Edward Noyes (1846-1898), wrote the novel *David Harum,* published shortly after his death on March 31, 1898. The story deals with a shrewd and humorous small-town banker in upstate New York. The novel and dramatic adaptation were extremely popular. Will Rogers starred in a film version of the novel. Westcott was born on Sept. 27, 1846, in Syracuse, New York, where he became a successful banker. He wrote *David Harum* while dying of tuberculosis.   Bert Hitchcock

Westergaard, Harald Malcolm (1888-1950), a distinguished American civil engineer and mathematician, became noted for his applications of mathematical analysis in the solution of engineering problems. He developed methods for the design of dams and of pavements for roads, bridges, and airports. Westergaard was born on Oct. 9, 1888, in Copenhagen, Denmark, and came to the United States in 1914. He died on June 22, 1950.   Joseph W. Dauben

Westermarck, Edward Alexander (1862-1939), was a Finnish anthropologist. Before reaching the age of 30, he wrote his major work, *The History of Human Marriage* (1891). He was a professor at the University of London from 1907 to 1930. During this time, he wrote several works on marriage, the history and development of morals, and customs in Morocco. Westermarck was born on Nov. 20, 1862, in Helsinki.   David B. Stout

Western. See Westerns.

Western Australia is the largest state in area in Australia. This vast region covers the western third of the continent. Perth is its capital and largest city.

Land and climate. Western Australia covers 975,100 square miles (2,525,500 square kilometers) in the western part of Australia (see **Australia** [political map]). Mountain ranges include the Hamersley Range in the northwest, the Darling Range along the southwestern coast, the Stirling Range farther south, and vast ranges in the Kimberley area of the north. The Ashburton, Fortescue, Gascoyne, and Murchison rivers flow across the western part of the state during the wet season, from November until March. The Great Sandy Desert lies in the north, and the Great Victoria Desert covers part of the southeast. The Gibson Desert lies between them.

Temperatures in central Western Australia range from 80 to 90 °F (27 to 32 °C) in January and average about 60 °F (16 °C) in July. January temperatures in the north average 97 °F (36 °C), and July temperatures average about 86 °F (30 °C). Temperatures in the south vary from 70 to 80 °F (21 to 27 °C) in January to 60 °F (16 °C) in July. Less than 10 inches (25 centimeters) of rain falls annually in the central area. From 10 to 20 inches (25 to 51 centimeters) falls north and south of this region. Most coastal areas get 20 to 40 inches (51 to 100 centimeters).

People. The 2001 Australian census reported that Western Australia had 1,851,252 people. About 3 percent of the state's people are of Aboriginal descent. About two-thirds of the state's population was born in Australia.

All children ages 6 to 15 must attend school. The University of Western Australia, Murdoch University, Curtin University of Technology, Edith Cowan University, and the University of Notre Dame Australia are in Perth.

Economy. Iron ore is the most important mineral in Western Australia. Other minerals include bauxite, coal, gold, mineral sands, and nickel. There are oil and gas fields in the north and northwest. The state's most fertile regions are in the southwest. The chief crops include wheat, barley, oats, and fruits.

Many people work in heavy industries, such as metal refining. Others work in gold fields, iron ore mines, farmlands, or service industries. Kalgoorlie is a chief center of the state's mining industry. Other occupations include dairying, fishing, and stock raising.

Railroads and airlines link the state with the rest of the country. The state owns more than 4,380 miles (7,050 kilometers) of railroads. One of the world's longest stretches of track without branches or rail connections extends about 1,000 miles (1,600 kilometers) from Kalgoorlie to Port Augusta, South Australia. There are about 91,300 miles (146,930 kilometers) of roads.

Government. The British Crown appoints a governor for the state. A premier heads the government, assisted by a Cabinet of ministers. The state Parliament has two houses called the Legislative Assembly and the Legislative Council. The members of the Legislative Assembly, elected by popular vote, serve four years. Each member represents one electoral district. Election to the Legislative Council is based on a system called *proportional representation.* This system gives a political party a share of seats according to its share of the total votes cast. Council members serve four-year terms.

WORLD BOOK map

**Location of
Western Australia**

History. In 1616, the Dutch explorer Dirk Hartog became the first recorded European to sight Western Australia's coast. A military settlement was made at King George Sound in 1826. Full colonization began in 1829. That year, Captain James Stirling founded the Swan River settlement and the towns of Perth and Fremantle. In 1901, Western Australia became one of the Australian Commonwealth's six original states.   Zoltan Kovacs

See also **Perth.**

Western Church was a name given to the Roman Catholic Church after the Great Schism of the 800's to distinguish it from the Eastern Orthodox Church. See also **Roman Catholic Church.**

Western European Union (WEU) was a defense alliance that included members of the European Union (EU) and the North Atlantic Treaty Organization (NATO). The EU is a political and economic organization of Western European nations. NATO is the main military alliance of Western countries, including the United States. The WEU worked to strengthen NATO. The United Kingdom, France, Italy, Belgium, the Netherlands, Luxembourg, and West Germany formed the WEU in 1955. In 1988, Spain and Portugal joined. In 1990, newly united Germany replaced West Germany as a WEU member. Greece joined the WEU in 1992. In the late 1990's, the EU began planning to develop its own military.

Stuart D. Goldman

© James L. Stanfield, National Geographic Society

Western Australia has vast areas of dry land through which transportation is difficult. Trucks pulling trailers carry cattle and other freight great distances through the areas. Such vehicles are called *road trains.*

Western frontier life in America

Western frontier life in America marks one of the most exciting chapters in American history. The settlement of the West represented the dreams of gold-hungry prospectors, and of homesteaders whose back-breaking labor transformed barren plains into fields of grain. It is the story of cowboys and the open range. It is the drama of Indians and outlaws, of the trains and stagecoaches they attacked, and of the citizens who brought order to the frontier. It is a living tradition that symbolizes to men and women everywhere the American achievement of taming a wild and beautiful land.

The far western frontier appeared about 1850, and vanished about 1890. Adventurous settlers had crossed the Appalachian Mountains during the 1700's and come through the Cumberland Gap in the 1770's. They built homes along the Mississippi River a few years later. Traders and scouts reached the Pacific Coast in the early 1800's, and settlers arrived in the 1840's. But the area between the Missouri River and the Rocky Mountains did not attract many settlers until the 1860's. The final period of western settlement lasted from then to 1890. For the complete story of western expansion in the United States, see **Westward movement in America.**

The western frontier produced many colorful figures. Some, such as Jesse James and Billy the Kid, symbolize outlaws who "died with their boots on." Others, such as Pat Garrett, gained fame as fearless defenders of law and order. "Buffalo Bill" Cody—scout, Indian fighter, and showman—probably did more than anyone else to create interest in the old West. Other figures, though less well-known, did more to develop the area itself. Charles Goodnight, a fiery rancher and cattle breeder, helped settle the Texas range. Granville Stuart of Montana, who had been an illiterate prospector, became U.S.

Early settlers in the Far West crossed the plains to Oregon or California. Their high Conestoga wagons had already become museum pieces by the time of the last frontier.

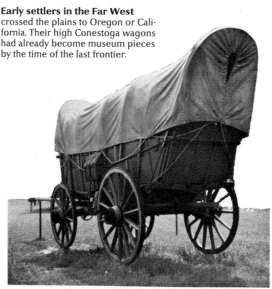

Tom Hollyman, courtesy *Holiday,* © 1955 Curtis Publishing Co.

minister to Paraguay and Uruguay. Adolph Sutro, a German immigrant, built a vast tunnel through Nevada's Comstock Lode, and was later mayor of San Francisco.

The West promised to satisfy the needs and dreams of immigrants fresh from Europe as well as those of thousands of Americans unhappy with their life in the East. Some went west to find adventure, others to find happiness in the green valleys or among the tall mountains. Many sought wealth, but only a few were lucky. The West was a place where American Indians fought to keep their land, where accidents were common, and where hard work was the rule for all. Life on the western frontier seems colorful when we look back on it today. But the people who settled there found it difficult and dangerous—and even dull at times.

Building the frontier

For many years, the land on the western side of the Mississippi River formed the frontier of American settle-

Courtesy J. B. Lippincott Company from *Frederic Remington* by Harold McCracken

A stagecoach roars across the desert with Indian attackers in close pursuit. In *Downing the Nigh Leader,* the American artist Frederic Remington caught the drama and excitement that symbolize "the Wild West" to people throughout the world.

ment. Only a few thousand settlers had moved to Texas and California in the early 1800's. Land was still plentiful in the East, and treaties with the Indians forbade white settlements in many areas of the West. But, after 1850, many causes led to westward expansion. During the Civil War (1861-1865), the Union government encouraged mining, because the valuable ores helped pay for the war. The Homestead Act of 1862 provided cheap farm land for new settlers, as did gifts of huge tracts of land to the railroads. At the same time, thousands of Europeans wanted to come to America. Revolutionary movements had failed in many countries. Poor harvests caused famines in Ireland. The Scandinavian nations had become overpopulated. Government agents increased their persecution of the Jews in Russia, Poland, and other areas of central Europe.

The land between the Missouri River and the Pacific Coast forms two great belts, running roughly north and south. The grasslands of the Great Plains stretch west from the Missouri River to the Rocky Mountains. Beyond the plains, from the Rockies to the Pacific Coast, lies a belt of land with many mountain ranges and several valleys. Because the Far West had many land regions and climates, it developed on several frontiers.

The rush to the west affected both belts of land, but it touched the Far West first. Settlers began moving to the Oregon region in large numbers in the early 1840's. In 1848, the Oregon Territory was established. California boomed with the discovery of gold at Sutter's mill in 1848, and it became a state in 1850. Washington also was settled before the Civil War. Congress created the Washington Territory in 1853.

The search for gold and silver attracted thousands of miners to the western mountains following the rush to California in 1849. At first, they mined in the Sierra Nevada mountains east of Sacramento. However, gold in this area became difficult to mine by the middle 1850's. So the prospectors moved eastward looking for *strikes,* or discoveries.

Several areas became important mining centers during the period from 1856 to 1875. The first was southern Arizona, where silver was found south of Tucson. Other silver discoveries were made there in the following years, including the giant strike in 1877 at Tombstone.

The next strike came in the Rocky Mountains west of Denver. It drew a great rush of fortune seekers, who vowed to reach "Pikes Peak or Bust." Central City and Leadville grew up almost overnight in Colorado. A third area centered on Virginia City in western Nevada, and encouraged further discoveries in the desert valleys and mountains. Both these areas began as gold fields. But black sand in Colorado and blue clay in Nevada clogged the machines the early miners used. The mines did not become profitable until mining companies found that the sands and clays had rich silver deposits.

Another mining region, in Idaho, Montana, and Washington, led to the settlement of such towns as Lewiston, Ida.; Helena, Mont.; and Walla Walla, Wash. The last great gold rush in the United States took place in the Black Hills of South Dakota in 1874 and 1875. Deadwood, founded in 1876, gained fame as one of the last frontier mining camps.

East meets West. The swarm of miners into the West showed the need for better transportation. Thousands of new settlers ran short of supplies. Prospectors could mine gold with pick, shovel, and pan, but silver-mining companies needed heavy machinery to dig the ore, and some means of shipping it to smelters. Such needs encouraged companies to build transcontinental railroad networks. Two companies began the first of these railroad systems in the early 1860's. Starting from the east was the Union Pacific, with Irish laborers who established such towns as Cheyenne and Laramie, Wyo.

The Central Pacific line, coming from the west, had thousands of Chinese in its road gangs. The two sets of tracks met at Promontory, near Ogden, Utah, in 1869. Other lines soon followed, including the Southern Pacific and the Atchison, Topeka, and Santa Fe. See **Railroad** (History; picture: The meeting of two railroads).

With the railroads to supply them, settlers had little fear of waterless deserts or hostile Indians. The growth of railroads almost led to the extermination of the bison, or American buffalo. Millions of these animals had roamed throughout the West, but hunters soon killed most of them. The hunters killed for buffalo hides, but seldom for meat.

The cattle boom. With the railroads came the period of "the cattle kingdom" on the Great Plains. Ranching started in southern Texas, where farmers raised longhorn cattle from Mexico. The ranchers branded the cattle to show ownership, and guarded them on horseback as they roamed the range. By the end of the Civil War, the number of cattle had increased, and people in the North had money to buy beef.

The era of the long drive, or trail drive, began when the ranchers saw that they could sell cattle in the East if they could get the animals to the railroads. A favorite route led along the Chisholm Trail, which ran from southern Texas to Abilene, Kan. Farther west, the Western Trail led to Dodge City, Kan. Millions of cattle plodded along these trails, sometimes as many as 4,000 in a single herd.

The open range did not last long. By 1885, overstocking had ruined many ranchers. They had more cattle than the land could support. Fierce blizzards in the winter of 1886-1887 spelled the end for many more. In a series of *range wars,* ranchers tried to keep out *nesters,* or permanent settlers. But the open range had disappeared, and the cattle boom came to an end.

Homesteading on the Great Plains had attracted few settlers before the Civil War. This was the land that novelist Hamlin Garland brought to life in his books and

Railroads helped tame the West. The train below ran out of Virginia City, Nev., on the Virginia & Truckee line.

The Western Pacific Railroad Company

Sunday Morning in the Mines by Charles Nahl. Permanent
Collection E. B. Crocker Art Gallery, Sacramento, California

In the gold fields, some miners spent Sunday reading the Bible or washing their clothes. Others wrestled or took part in horse racing.

short stories. It is often called "the land of the straddle-bug." In the 1840's and 1850's, *locators,* or land sales agents, picked the best farms on the grassy plains. They marked their claims with *straddlebugs,* three boards fastened together like tepee poles.

However, when *homesteaders,* or farmers, arrived later with their families, they often found themselves in trouble. They had little protection against the Plains Indians. When they rode horses, they could not use the long rifles they had carried in the woods back East. Also, water and trees were scarce in this region. When spring and late summer rains were scanty, crops withered and died. Farmers had difficulty finding wood for shelter, fuel, and fences.

New developments in the 1870's made it possible for eager settlers to farm the grasslands. Barbed wire, patented in 1873, provided the first cheap substitute for wood fences. Windmills solved the problem of bringing up water that lay far underground. Agricultural experts worked out methods of farming that would work in the dry climate (see **Dry farming**). With improved machinery, farmers could cultivate large areas. The railroads offered cheap land to homesteaders. Thousands of settlers moved into Kansas, Nebraska, and the Dakotas. The government opened a large section of Indian Territory in 1889, and the Oklahoma Territory was born (see **Indian Territory**). So much of the Far West had filled up by 1890 that the Census Bureau declared in a report that a definite frontier no longer existed.

Life on the frontier

The people of the western frontier formed a varied mixture. Americans streamed west from the East Coast, the Middle West, and the South. Some who had committed crimes went west because they wanted to get as far away from the law as possible. Others found life boring in the East, and wanted to try something new and different. Professional people and merchants cared for the needs of growing communities. Land speculators hoped to make quick fortunes. But most settlers were farmers, laborers, unskilled mechanics, miners, and former soldiers. Many of these pioneers saw the West as a place of opportunity for themselves and their children. They were willing to risk their lives to be part of the development of this region.

Large numbers of blacks moved to the frontier to escape the prejudice they had experienced in the East and South. Thousands of black homesteaders settled in California, Kansas, Nebraska, and Texas during the second half of the 1800's. Some of the best-known cowboys of that period were African Americans. A ranch hand named Nat Love gained fame for horsemanship and other skills on cattle drives. Bose Ikard, a former slave, was foreman of one of the largest ranches in Texas. Black soldiers in the U.S. Army fought Indians on the frontier.

Many other groups also lived in the Far West. Mexicans had settled in the Southwest and California since the 1700's. Indians furnished cheap labor. Basques from France and Spain herded sheep (see **Basques**). Scandinavians and other Europeans bought farms on the Great Plains. Miners came from England and Wales to join the search for precious metals. Chinese came to build the railroads, then drifted to mining camps where they ran laundries, restaurants, and small shops.

Most frontier people fell into two classes, *solid folk* and *boomers.* The solid folk settled down if they liked the life, or went home if they did not. Boomers were always heading for a new boom town. They seldom stayed long enough to make much money, and squandered their earnings in high living. Even among the steady people, few came to stay, as settlers had stayed on the land east of the Missouri River. Most of them wanted to get rich and go home.

The frontier was a man's world, and favored the jack-of-all-trades. Wyatt Earp was a law officer, buffalo hunter, stagecoach driver, and gambler. Hank Monk, a famous stagecoach driver, also mined, and rode the pony express. George Jackson, credited with discovering gold in the Rockies, had been a sheepherder, prospector, farm hand, miner, and roustabout, and later became a businessman.

Food on the frontier was usually simple. Flour served as the basic food, because it was nourishing and did not spoil. The people used it in sourdough biscuits and bread, and in *flapjacks,* or pancakes. Other important foods included dried beans; game, such as bison, deer, elk, antelope, and wild fowl; and preserved meats such as bacon, salt pork, and *jerky,* or dried meat. Ranchers could always eat beef, and sheep raisers had mutton. Frontier people rarely ate fresh fruit and vegetables or dairy products. Even cowboys did not milk cows.

People on the frontier had no need for fancy cooking—the men were too busy, and women were scarce. Meat with biscuits or flapjacks provided a feast. Old Len Martin of Carson City, Nev., declared while stewing a chicken that there was no sense "picking a chicken too darned close—anybody that don't like the feathers can skim 'em off."

Clothing had to be practical, and most people wore the same plain garments day after day. Men wore cowhide boots; woolen trousers or overalls; a wool shirt; a jacket or vest; and a felt hat. Some had socks. A man often wore a red bandanna handkerchief around his neck to protect himself from the dust and cold. Women wore sunbonnets and simple calico and gingham dresses. Cowboys wore leather *chaps* to protect their legs from brush. Cowboy hats, called *sombreros,* had a wide brim to shield the eyes, and a deep crown so that the hat would not blow off. Some men bought deerskin clothes from the Indians. Wealthy men and women bought clothes from New York City, London, or Paris.

Many frontiersmen, particularly outlaws and law-enforcement officers, carried weapons. Especially popular were Winchester rifles; Colt revolvers, including the famous six-shooter; and Bowie knives (see **Handgun** [picture]; **Bowie knife**).

Amusements on the frontier varied with the area and the type of settler. Homesteading families on the plains met for square dances, holiday celebrations, and house-raising or corn-husking bees. Miners and cowboys enjoyed spending their leisure time drinking and gambling in the saloons that sprang up in every town. Dance halls called *hurdy-gurdies* attracted many people, although men often had to dance with each other, because women were scarce. Informal rodeos featured expert horsemanship and other cowboy skills (see **Rodeo**). Throughout the West, people enjoyed horse races, shooting contests, and wrestling and boxing matches. In larger towns, settlers welcomed traveling dramatic groups and vaudeville shows. They applauded such famous performers as Edwin Booth, Laura Keene, and Helena Modjeska.

Religion came to the western frontier even before most white settlers arrived. In the early 1800's, Catholic and Protestant missionaries such as Father Pierre De Smet and Marcus Whitman had pushed into the Far West to convert the Indians (see **De Smet, Pierre Jean; Whitman, Marcus**). But new settlements often grew up far from the missions, and people had to rely on traveling preachers called *circuit riders* to perform religious services. These men rode about constantly. When they arrived in a town, they preached sermons and con-

Library of Congress

Virginia City bustled with activity in the 1860's. The town perched 6,500 feet (1,980 meters) high in the Sierra Nevada, close to Mt. Davidson, site of the fabulous Comstock Lode.

ducted marriages, baptisms, and other services for people who had sometimes waited many weeks. Among farm families on the plains, circuit riders set up Sunday schools and held summer camp meetings.

Frontier towns sprang up almost overnight. An early arrival in Bovard, Nev., told how he passed through the town in the morning and noticed four or five tents. When he returned in the afternoon, Main Street was 1 mile (1.6 kilometers) long and business was booming in a string of tent saloons. Some towns, such as Butte, Mont., started as shipping points for ore. Others, including Wichita, Kan., boomed as cattle transport centers. Many, such as Tombstone, Ariz., grew up around mines. Transportation centers usually grew and prospered. But most mining camps became ghost towns of rubble and sagebrush after the ores had been worked out or metal prices fell.

Most frontier towns provided few comforts. Miners often slept outdoors in summer, and built a dugout or crude shack in the winter. They might have a tent or make a shelter out of rocks, empty bottles, or packing cases. Two early settlers in Treasure City, Nev., collected all the rocks they could find for shelter against the winter. The next spring, they discovered that the walls were high-grade silver ore worth $75,000!

House furnishings were simple and often homemade. Miners needed blasting powder more than fine dishes. They papered their shacks with newspapers to make them warmer. Today, visitors can sometimes still read about events in a ghost town on the walls of its crumbling buildings. A few wealthy people shipped in furniture, tableware, and wallpaper at great expense. If a town became fairly permanent, the people built board sidewalks on each side of the dirt streets, lined with poles and stakes for hitching posts. Square false fronts made small buildings look impressive.

Life in frontier towns was difficult. People often lacked conveniences, and even necessities. Usually the only water available in mining camps was warm and dirty. Sometimes people hauled water a great distance and sold it for several dollars a barrel. In many areas on the plains, no trees grew.

Because of such shortages, western towns often grew

A teamster who "struck it rich" built this mansion near Virginia City. The teamster, whose name was Sandy Bowers, later went "ter Yoorup" to spend his fortune.

in groups, such as the one built around Virginia City, Nev. The rich silver and gold mines of the Comstock Lode centered around Virginia City, but the town had no wood or water. Other towns grew up nearby to supply these needs. Empire became a smelter town on the Carson River; Washoe, near the Sierra Nevadas, supplied fuel; and Reno grew up where the local railroad joined the main line of the Central Pacific.

During the 20-year period between 1860 and 1880, the Comstock Lode yielded more than $300 million worth of ore. Because of this great wealth, all the comforts of the day soon appeared in Virginia City. At first, supplies came in by muleback, a few at a time. When a road was built, slow freight wagons brought supplies. Finally, a railroad served the town with several trains a day. By 1876, Virginia City had 23,000 people, 20 laundries, 54 dry-good stores, 6 churches, and 150 saloons. The vice president of the express company built a four-story French-style mansion. An opera house and several theaters presented Italian light operas, vaudeville, lectures, and even Shakespeare's plays. The miners' union had a library. A local newspaper, the *Territorial Enterprise,* employed a young reporter who wrote under the name of Mark Twain. At any time, a person might find silver ore in the basement and be worth $1 million the next day. People had to be careful that they and their children did not fall into a neighbor's new mine.

Life in the country resembled that in the towns, except that settlers found it harder to obtain supplies. Prospectors roamed about with supplies loaded on a burro or two, but they had to return to a mining camp when they ran short. Country life on the frontier usually meant living on a ranch or a farm.

Ranches usually lay in mountain valleys watered by melting snow, or in broad uplands that had some moisture. Most ranches consisted only of a few simple buildings and some *corrals* (cattle pens) surrounded by high, strong fences made of stakes and poles. The grassland of the open range provided pastures. The *Texas house,* two log cabins joined by a roofed space, developed into the ranch-style house of today. The rancher used one cabin for cooking and eating, and the other for sleeping. As the ranch grew, the rancher might build a house for

the family, a cookshack, and a bunkhouse for the *hands* (cowboys).

Cattle ranchers let their herds graze on the open range, so they needed few buildings and no fences. But they did need cowboys to turn the cattle out to graze in spring, and move them to rich mountain pastures. Cowboys constantly guarded the herds against mountain lions and bands of rustlers. In the spring and fall, all the ranchers in an area held a *roundup* to gather in the cattle. Cowboys had already marked the grown cattle by branding them or cropping their ears. People from each ranch sorted out these cattle by their markings. New calves followed their mothers. Then cowboys cropped the calves' ears or branded them with the owner's mark.

Cowboys also drove herds to *cattle towns,* or *cow towns,* to be shipped east on the railroads. On the long drive, cattle moved in long lines, with riders ahead, behind, and on both sides. A *chuck wagon* carried food for the cowboys, and a *wrangler* took care of extra horses. When all went well, the cattle moved slowly but steadily. But they sometimes *stampeded* when they were afraid to swim a river, or were frightened by Indians or rustlers. After a few months, the drive plodded into a cattle town such as Abilene or Dodge City, where cowboys loaded the cattle into freight cars. For a description of cowboys and their work, see **Cowboy; Ranching**.

Farms, unlike ranches, depended on the soil, not the grass. Farmers plowed the grass under and raised grain, mainly wheat. Grasshoppers, hot winds, and prairie fires often made life hard for settlers on the plains. So did the ranchers, who resented the barbed-wire fences that destroyed the open range. Bloody fights developed in the range wars, or barbed-wire wars, that followed. Farmers fenced in watering places or blocked trails, then ranchers cut the wires. Barbed wire finally won, and farms spread farther and farther out over the rich grasslands of the Great Plains.

Life on the plains resembled that of pioneers east of the Missouri River. But there was a basic difference. While the farmer in Ohio might have too many trees, the

Texas Longhorns, an oil painting on canvas by Tom Lea; Dallas Museum of Art, gift of *LIFE* magazine

Texas longhorn cattle, hardy and fierce, were descended from wild cattle brought to America by the Spanish. Ranch owners branded them or notched their ears to identify them.

farmer on the plains usually had no wood at all. The western farmer's land has often been called *the sod-house frontier,* because so many settlers built houses of dirt and sod. Farmers plowed furrows of sod and cut them crosswise into blocks about 1 foot (30 centimeters) square. They piled rows of sod blocks on top of each other to make walls, and covered them with a thatch roof. Sometimes they brought wood with them and built a frame to support the roof, or found a little wood nearby. A sod house remained warm in winter and cool in summer, but it had many disadvantages. Dirt sifted down on the food, crumbled from the walls, and rose from the clay floor. Rats and mice lived in the thatch, and snakes and gophers often dug tunnels through the walls or floor. For fuel, the farmer used twigs, grass, corncobs, peat, and buffalo *chips,* or manure. Later, settlers often improved their *soddies* by whitewashing the walls and hauling in lumber for doors and ceilings.

Transportation and communication

Transportation varied with the area and the means at hand. Until the railroads appeared, travel was always slow and uncomfortable, and often dangerous. Roads were few and bad, and schedules were irregular.

Most people traveled by stagecoach. A group of passengers could defend themselves more easily against Indians or bandits than a person alone. One famous line, the Butterfield Overland Mail, ran four coaches weekly between St. Louis and San Francisco. The coaches bumped along day and night, covering about 100 miles (160 kilometers) in 24 hours. The passengers, grimy with dust in summer and shivering with cold in winter, tried to sleep on the hard seats. Crude wood or adobe "stations" every 10 miles (16 kilometers) or so provided food for both passengers and horses. Travelers faced the constant danger of Indian attack and bad weather. Traveling alone was even more dangerous, but people in a hurry rode horseback. Settlers moving with their families traveled in wagons.

Wagon trains served as the best means of hauling freight before railroads were built. They usually included about 25 heavy, high-wheeled wagons, each pulled by a team of 6 to 20 oxen or mules. People called *bullwhackers* or *mule skinners* drove the wagons and guarded the freight. The wagons lumbered along at 1 or 2 miles (1.6 or 3.2 kilometers) per hour, or about 100 miles (160 kilometers) in a seven-day week, because "there was no Sunday west of Omaha." The wagons hauled ore from mines and brought in mining machinery and blasting powder. They carried the food and water that made life possible in desert camps. If blizzards stopped them, the price of flour might soar to $100 a sack. Famous freight lines included Ben Holladay's Central Overland California and Pikes Peak Express Company, and the Wells, Fargo line (see **Wells, Fargo & Company**). Frontier people also used burros to carry goods. Some even used camels, imported from Asia because they could live on the desert (see **Camel**).

Communication. News traveled slowly, most of it by stagecoach. A letter took months to go from California to the Middle West, and snows in the mountains cut off almost all communication in winter.

The pony express carried the mail between St. Joseph, Mo., and Sacramento, Calif., a distance of almost 2,000 miles (3,200 kilometers). The service had about 80 riders. Pony-express riders generally made two runs a week over their part of the route in each direction. At first, it cost $5 to send $\frac{1}{2}$ ounce (14 grams) of mail by pony express, so that this volume of *The World Book Encyclopedia,* for example, would have cost more than $400 to send. Pony-express riders changed horses every 10 to 15 miles (16 to 24 kilometers), and new riders took over every 75 miles (121 kilometers). The pony express covered more than 200 miles (320 kilometers) a day, so that mail usually traveled from St. Joseph to Sacramento in about 10 days. The trip often took up to 15 days during winter. This remarkable system began in April 1860, but lasted only about 19 months. It was discontinued after the telegraph reached California in October 1861. See **Pony express**.

Law and order

Farm families on the frontier lived quietly, but crime troubled the mining camps and cattle towns. These isolated settlements sometimes had great wealth in precious metals and attracted people who came to cheat and steal. Others meant well but wanted to have a good time. A mixture of gambling, drinking, and firearms sometimes led to violence. But the West was far from the "wild" place pictured in legend and story.

Crime often resulted from the temptations of gold and silver. Miners who had *struck it rich* usually celebrated by getting drunk. Then they might be stabbed and robbed, or cheated in a poker game by a *cardsharp* who used a marked deck of cards. Gold and silver also tempted bandits, who followed shipments on their way to California or to the East. They picked a deserted spot in which to attack a wagon or stagecoach. Criminals also included *claim jumpers,* who illegally took over mine claims that belonged to someone else. *Confidence men* (swindlers) often sold worthless stocks. Many dealt in "salted" mines, selling worthless holes after putting in small amounts of good ore.

Horses, cattle, and sheep also provided a temptation for lawbreakers. The animals roamed great areas, and could be moved under their own power. Rustlers stole cattle, drove them to a *shebang* (hideout), and altered their brands. One valley in the Pahranagat Range of southeastern Nevada became a refuge for rustlers who roamed through Utah, Arizona, Nevada, and Idaho. A rider passing through the valley could count as many as 350 different brands on cattle stolen from as many ranches. One story tells of a sheriff who returned from such a robbers' roost looking triumphant. "Get your man?" somebody asked. "No," the sheriff replied, "but I rode plumb through the place without getting shot."

Disturbances also arose from the constant feuding between cattle ranchers and the sheep owners and farmers. The Lincoln County War inflamed New Mexico in 1878 as cattlemen and other groups fought for control of the county. Army troops and Governor Lew Wallace finally quieted the rival cattle ranchers. See **New Mexico** (Territorial days). In 1892, cattle ranchers in Johnson County, Wyoming, imported a trainload of gunmen to terrorize farmers. The army finally ended this Johnson County Cattle War after several killings on both sides. See **Wyoming** (The Johnson County War).

The *desperadoes* (outlaws) usually worked together

Jesse James, according to an old ballad, "killed many a man, and robbed the Glendale train." He and his gang terrorized Missouri for several years. This scene, painted in 1936 by Thomas Hart Benton, is from his mural *Social History of Missouri.* The mural appears in the State Capitol at Jefferson City.

Mural's outlaw panel; © T. H. Benton and R. P. Benton Testamentary Trusts/Licensed by VAGA, New York City; photo by Greg Leech, Missouri Department of Natural Resources

in gangs, such as those led by Henry Plummer, the Younger brothers, "the Dalton boys," and Frank and Jesse James. They robbed banks, trains, and stagecoaches throughout large areas. Sam Bass once stole $60,000 in gold from a single Union Pacific train traveling through Nebraska. Billy the Kid was said to have killed 21 men. Some of the most famous desperadoes were honest and kindly until drink or anger aroused them. Then they became killers. But even among lawbreakers, the code of the West demanded that people give each other a chance to defend themselves. A gunman who shot from behind or attacked an unarmed person was considered a coward. Outlaws who obeyed this code had many friends and admirers in spite of their crimes. They symbolized the independence and vitality of the West, and many legends grew up around them. Sooner or later most were shot or hanged.

Law enforcement. When Americans settled unorganized territory in the Far West, they brought with them federal, state, and local laws from their former homes. But these laws did not always help new communities. Often they did not take into account new and different situations, such as cattle rustling. Even when laws suited a community, enforcement was hard because of the great distances between settlements. For example, the sheriff at Pioche, Nevada, was responsible for law and order as far away as the mining camp of El Dorado, 300 miles (480 kilometers) distant. If the sheriff did capture a murderer, there was often no jail to hold the prisoner. And the outlaw's friends might kill innocent citizens to free the prisoner. Everyone had to be ready to "shoot it out." Judge Roy Bean, "the law west of the Pecos," held court in his saloon in Langtry, Texas, with the aid of a single law book and a six-shooter.

But law-abiding people lived in all parts of the frontier, and sooner or later they established order. The West often found law officers as fearless as the outlaws themselves. Many served as federal marshals. Tom Smith, the marshal of Abilene, Kansas, did not drink or swear, but he shocked a tough cattle town into behaving by knocking out armed men with his bare fists. The Texas Rangers also helped maintain law and order (see **Texas Rangers).**

The citizens themselves provided another answer to the problem of law enforcement. They banded together in groups of *vigilantes* to capture and punish criminals. Sometimes these groups killed innocent people in their haste, but most victims deserved the punishment they received. See **Vigilante.**

Indian fighting disturbed the frontier for many years. The federal government had reserved large areas of Western land for Indian use, but land-hungry white settlers constantly moved into these areas. Agents of the Indian Bureau tried to protect the Indians and to enforce laws for both Indians and whites. But most frontier troops, stationed in about 100 posts throughout the West, agreed with the claim many Westerners made that "the only good Indians are dead Indians." In 1864, an Army force killed more than 150 peaceful Indians near Sand Creek, Colorado. Such events, and the revenge they inspired, aroused the whole frontier. For the story of Indian wars in the West, see **Indian wars.**

An American tradition

The frontier is gone now. Most of its mining camps have become empty ghost towns. Other settlements of the wild West have grown into peaceful communities. Denver, Cheyenne, Boise, and Salt Lake City now stand where settlers once pitched their tents. But western frontier life left behind a great American tradition because of its dramatic appeal. Even before "Buffalo Bill" Cody organized his "Wild West Show" in 1883, the western frontier had captured the interest of people in all parts of the world. Books, stories, paintings, songs, plays, and motion pictures about the Old West still pour forth in a seemingly endless stream. Hundreds of works have appeared about Billy the Kid alone—including poems, novels, plays, ballets, and motion pictures. The West has also produced its own folklore heroes. Febold Feboldson performed amazing feats on the sod-house frontier of the Great Plains. Pecos Bill taught the cowboys all they knew, and even showed broncos how to buck. See **Feboldson, Febold; Pecos Bill.**

Many works of poor quality have strayed far from the truth, presenting only the most sensational parts of frontier life. But other works have artistic merit, and give a true picture of those who settled the West.

Literature. Most of the early writing about the West came from writers who had taken part in its development. Mark Twain's *Roughing It* became a frontier classic. Bret Harte's short stories and Joaquin Miller's poems found admirers in Europe as well as the United States. Owen Wister's novel about the West, *The Virginian,* stimulated much interest in the subject. Andy Adams, a cowboy, gave a truer picture of range life in *The Log of a Cowboy.* One of Emerson Hough's many novels, *The Covered Wagon,* became a popular motion picture. Hamlin Garland, with *A Son of the Middle Border,* and O. E. Rölvaag, with *Giants in the Earth,* immortalized the sod-house frontier. Zane Grey wrote over 50 colorful Western novels. Later books include Walter Van Tilburg Clark's *The Oxbow Incident,* Conrad Richter's *The Sea of Grass,* and A. B. Guthrie's *The Big Sky.*

Music of the West, like literature, has been mainly popular, rather than serious. Famous songs include "The Chisholm Trail," "The Lone Prairie," and "Streets of Laredo." Many of these ballads grew out of English or Spanish folk songs that the cowboys sang to quiet the cattle, or to help fill the long, lonely, empty hours.

Serious music with Western themes includes Giacomo Puccini's opera *The Girl of the Golden West,* Aaron Copland's ballets *Billy the Kid* and *Rodeo,* Ferde Grofé's *Grand Canyon Suite,* and Hershey Kay's ballet *Western Symphony.* One of the most popular of all American musical plays, *Oklahoma!,* by Richard Rodgers and Oscar Hammerstein II, tells how the cowboys clashed with the "hoe hands," or farmers.

Art. The color of the western landscape and the vigor of running horses, stampeding cattle, and rugged men have appealed to many artists. Frederic Remington, probably the most famous, painted and drew over 2,700 pictures of the West. Remington learned life on the frontier at first hand and preserved it in realistic paintings, sketches, and statues. Others who have painted the West include Charles Marion Russell and N. C. Wyeth. Many artists, including Thomas Hart Benton and Georgia O'Keeffe, have used western backgrounds. Will James, Tom Lea, Ross Santee, and others have illustrated their own books on the West.

Entertainment. Motion pictures and television have made western frontier life familiar to people everywhere. With cowboys and soldiers fighting outlaws and Indians, the "Western" offers endless opportunities for battles and thrilling chases through mountains and deserts. *The Squaw Man* of 1914, one of the first full-length films made in Hollywood, began a trend that continues today. William S. Hart, a typical two-gun cowboy, became a national hero. Other motion-picture cowboy idols have included Buck Jones, Tom Mix, Roy Rogers, John Wayne, and William Boyd, who made the first "Hopalong Cassidy" film in 1934. Many "Westerns" provide poor entertainment, but some have been fine motion pictures. Among these, such films as *Stagecoach* and *High Noon* achieved a high level. On the stage, Will Rogers gained fame as "the cowboy philosopher." Radio and television present hundreds of Western dramas every year. Rodeos, especially in the Western States, feature daring cowboys who ride bucking broncos and wild cattle. Thousands of people spend vacations on dude ranches, dressing like cowboys in settings that try to recapture a bygone era.   Odie B. Faulk

Related articles in *World Book.* See the articles on the various Western States, such as **Montana.** See also:

Famous westerners

Bass, Sam	Earp, Wyatt	Love, Nat
Bean, Judge Roy	Fargo, William G.	Masterson, Bat
Billy the Kid	Garrett, Pat	Oakley, Annie
Buffalo Bill	Hickok, Wild Bill	Starr, Belle
Calamity Jane	James, Jesse	

Other related articles

Boom town	L'Amour, Louis	Turner, Frederick J.
Circuit rider	Pioneer life in	
Comstock Lode	America	Vigilante
Cowboy	Pony express	Wells, Fargo &
Ghost town	Ranching	Company
Guthrie, A. B., Jr.	Rodeo	Westward movement in
Homestead Act	Texas Rangers	America
Indian wars		

Outline

I. Building the frontier
    A. The search for gold and silver
    B. East meets West
    C. The cattle boom
    D. Homesteading on the Great Plains

II. Life on the frontier
    A. The people   E. Religion
    B. Food   F. Frontier towns
    C. Clothing   G. Life in the country
    D. Amusements

III. Transportation and communication
    A. Transportation   B. Communication

IV. Law and order
    A. Crime   C. Indian fighting
    B. Law enforcement

V. An American tradition
    A. Literature   C. Art
    B. Music   D. Entertainment

Questions

Why was there so much crime on the western frontier? How did settlers enforce the law?

Why were traveling preachers called *circuit riders?*

What ended the period of the open range?

How did the first transcontinental railroad system affect the development of the western frontier?

Why was the western farmer's land often called "the sod-house frontier"?

What caused flour to become worth $100 a sack?

Why did some people import camels?

Why did some western towns grow up in groups?

Why was the pony express discontinued?

Additional resources

Level I

Duncan, Dayton. *People of the West.* Little, Brown, 1996. *The West: An Illustrated History for Children.* 1996.

Kalman, Bobbie. *Life in the Old West.* 11 vols. Crabtree Pub. Co., 1998-1999.

Level II

Jones, Mary E. *Daily Life on the Nineteenth Century American Frontier.* Greenwood, 1998.

Lamar, Howard R. *The New Encyclopedia of the American West.* Yale, 1998.

Luchetti, Cathy. *Children of the West.* Norton, 2001.

Ward, Geoffrey C. *The West.* 1996. Reprint. Back Bay Bks., 1999.

Western Hemisphere. See Hemisphere.

Western Reserve was a strip of land bordering Lake Erie in what is today Ohio. The strip extended westward about 120 miles (193 kilometers) from the northwestern border of Pennsylvania and covered 3,667,000 acres (1,483,982 hectares). It was part of a larger piece of land granted to the colony of Connecticut by King Charles II of England in 1662. This area stretched westward from the Atlantic Ocean to the Pacific Ocean. In 1786, Connecticut gave the new United States government all of this land except the Western Reserve.

In 1795, the Connecticut Land Company bought most of the Western Reserve for $1,200,000. In 1800, Connecticut and the U.S. government agreed to attach the land to the Ohio territory. The city of Cleveland was built on part of the Western Reserve.   William E. Foley

See also Cleveland.

Western Sahara, formerly Spanish Sahara, is an area located on the northwest coast of Africa. It lies between Morocco, Algeria, Mauritania, and the Atlantic Ocean (see Africa [political map]). The area belonged to Spain in the early 1500's and again from 1860 to 1976. Today, Morocco claims it. But some people who live in Western Sahara oppose the claim.

About 320,000 people live in the area. Most are Arabs or Berbers. The majority are nomads who move about constantly, seeking water and grass for their herds of camels, goats, and sheep. Some people fish for a living along the coast of the Atlantic Ocean.

Western Sahara covers about 102,700 square miles (266,000 square kilometers). Most of it is barren, rocky desert that gets little rainfall. Vegetation is scanty except for patches of coarse grass and low bushes near the coast. But the land yields large quantities of valuable chemicals called *phosphates,* which are used as fertilizers and in the manufacture of detergents.

Spain claimed the area in 1509. Morocco ruled it from 1524 until Spain regained control in 1860. Spain made the area one of its provinces—called the Province of Spanish Sahara—in 1958.

In 1976, Spain ceded Spanish Sahara to Morocco and Mauritania. The area came to be called Western Sahara. Morocco claimed the northern part, and Mauritania claimed the southern part. Algeria and an organization of people of Western Sahara called the Polisario Front opposed these claims and demanded independence for the area. The Polisario Front formed a government-in-exile for a nation in Western Sahara that it called the Saharawi Arab Democratic Republic (SADR).

Fighting broke out between Polisario Front troops and troops from Morocco and Mauritania. In 1979, Mauritania gave up its claim to Western Sahara and withdrew from the fighting. Morocco then claimed the part of Western Sahara that Mauritania had claimed. Fighting continued between the Polisario Front and Morocco. A United Nations-supervised cease-fire between Polisario Front forces and Moroccan forces was declared in late 1991. The cease-fire plan also called for a *referendum* (direct vote) to determine whether Western Sahara would become independent or part of Morocco. However, disagreements between Morocco and the Polisario Front over voter eligibility have repeatedly delayed the referendum.   Kenneth J. Perkins

See also **African Union.**

Western Samoa. See Samoa.

Western Union was the main provider of long-distance communications service in the United States during the second half of the 1800's. The company played a major role in communications well into the second half of the 1900's.

The company began in 1851 as the New York and Mississippi Valley Printing Telegraph Company. It soon gained control of major western telegraph routes through special agreements with railroad companies. In 1856, the company's name became Western Union Telegraph Company. In 1861, Western Union completed the first coast-to-coast telegraph line. By 1866, it had gained control of its major competitors and moved its headquarters from Rochester, New York, to New York City.

During the 1870's, Western Union made a number of important technological changes. The company introduced systems that could send more than one message at a time over one wire. These included the *quadruplex system,* which American inventor Thomas A. Edison developed to handle four messages at the same time. Edison and others also improved the company's *stock ticker service,* a telegraphic service that increased the speed of transmission of financial information from the New York Stock Exchange.

Western Union entered the telephone business in 1878. The company used telephone transmitters created by Edison and receivers developed by Elisha Gray, another American inventor. In 1879, however, Western Union sold its telephone business to the Bell Telephone Company. By the late 1890's, Western Union still controlled most of the telegraph industry, but long-distance telephone communication threatened to eliminate much of the telegraph business.

Western Union continued to play an important role in communications in the 1900's. In the 1940's, the company started to send messages via microwave radio beams relayed by a network of transmitting towers. In 1958, the company introduced Telex to the United States. This telegraphic system uses machines that resemble typewriters to send and receive messages. In the 1970's, the company began using satellites to send messages.

During the 1980's, Western Union gave up most of its communication business. In 1990, the company formed a subsidiary called Western Union Financial Services. In 1991, Western Union changed its name to New Valley Corporation, but it went bankrupt in 1993. However, Western Union Financial Services continued, and in 1995, it became a subsidiary of First Data Corporation. Today, it offers financial services, such as money transfers; and priority message services.   Paul B. Israel

See also **Telegraph; Telephone** (The Bell System).

Western Wall is a Jewish holy place located in Jerusalem. It is also called the *Wailing Wall*. During Roman times, it formed the western wall of the enclosure surrounding the courtyard of the Jews' holy Temple. The wall is about 160 feet (49 meters) long and about 40 feet (12 meters) high. Archaeologists have discovered that 19 rows of stones extend about 20 feet (6 meters) underground.

Beginning in the 700's, the Arabs who then ruled Jerusalem permitted Jews to assemble at the wall on the evenings before their Sabbath and before their feast days. In services at the wall, the Jews recalled their traditions and sufferings.

Jews continued to worship at the Western Wall after the British won control of Jerusalem during World War I (1914-1918). In 1948, Jordan captured the section of Jerusalem where the wall stood and prohibited Jews from the new state of Israel from using it. But the Jews regained access to the wall when Israel captured the Jordanian section of Jerusalem in the Arab-Israeli war of June 1967. Since then, it has become a place of pilgrimage and prayer, and a symbol of Jewish unity and survival.   Lawrence H. Schiffman

See also **Jerusalem** (Holy places; map; picture).

Westerns are works of literature and motion pictures that deal with the American West. These works typically explore the geography and history of the West and the lives of its inhabitants, especially pioneers, cowboys, and Indians.

Since the early 1800's, the West has exerted a powerful attraction on the imagination of Americans as well as people throughout the world. They have been fascinated by the vast open spaces, the rugged mountain ranges, and the long and powerful rivers of the West.

The stories written about the West often depict strong men—commonly frontiersmen and cowboys—as they challenge the wild land and violent weather. Many stories portray conflicts between pioneers moving West and the Indians settled in the region. For many people, the term *Western* suggests the novels of such authors as Zane Grey (*Riders of the Purple Sage,* 1912), A. B. Guthrie, Jr. (*The Big Sky,* 1947), Louis L'Amour (*Hondo,* 1953), and Larry McMurtry (*Lonesome Dove,* 1985).

Motion pictures have played an important role in establishing another common Western plot formula—the conflict between outlaws and the defenders of law and order. The first important motion picture, *The Great Train Robbery* (1903), was a Western. From the 1920's through the 1940's, hundreds of popular Western movies starred cowboy heroes, such as Gene Autry, Tom Mix, and Roy Rogers. More serious treatment of Western themes appeared in such movies as *High Noon* (1952) and *Shane* (1953). Director John Ford celebrated the grandeur of the Western landscape in *Stagecoach* (1939) and other films. Such stars as Gary Cooper and John Wayne defined the courageous hero of the West.

In the late 1900's, some films portrayed the West in less heroic terms, as in Clint Eastwood's *Unforgiven* (1992). The film *Dances with Wolves* (1990) brought new dignity to the treatment of the Indians in the history of the West.   Arthur R. Huseboe

There is a separate biography in *World Book* for each person discussed in this article. See also **Harte, Bret; Stegner, Wallace.**

Westinghouse, George (1846-1914), was an American inventor and manufacturer. He produced air brakes for railroad cars. His major inventions include a pipeline system that safely conducted natural gas into homes, and a type of gas meter. Westinghouse also introduced the use of alternating current for the transmission of electric power.

Westinghouse was born in Central Bridge, New York. As a boy, he worked in his father's machine shop. At 15 he invented a rotary engine. Westinghouse served in the Union Army and Navy during the American Civil War (1861-1865).

By 1866, Westinghouse had already perfected two inventions, a device for replacing derailed railroad cars and a railroad frog, which made it possible for a train to pass from one track to another. His perfection of an air brake in the late 1860's led to the formation of his first company, the Westinghouse Air Brake Company, in 1869. Westinghouse patented hundreds of inventions and organized over 50 companies. He was president of 30 corporations, including the Westinghouse Electric Company.   John H. White, Jr.

See also **Brake.**

Westminster Abbey is a great national church that stands near the Houses of Parliament in London. This world-famous church is one of the most beautiful in

A Western motion picture typically takes place during the late 1800's in the western United States. Most Westerns emphasize outdoor action. Many portray conflicts between cowboys and Native Americans. This scene appears in the classic Western *Stagecoach* (1939). Its director, John Ford, and star, John Wayne, were two of the great figures in the history of Western movies.

England. Westminster Abbey's official name is the Collegiate Church of Saint Peter. Its name of Abbey comes from the fact that it once served as the church of an ancient monastery.

Westminster Abbey marked the scene of many great events in English history. All the English rulers from the time of William the Conqueror, except Edward V and Edward VIII, were crowned there. In the chapel of Edward the Confessor stands the old Coronation Chair that dates from 1300. See **Coronation**.

Burial in Westminster Abbey is one of the greatest honors England can give. Many kings and queens are buried in the chapel of Henry VII. Political leaders and other important people of England are buried in other parts of the Abbey. The bodies of many of England's greatest poets lie in the Poets' Corner.

Westminster Abbey became the seat of a bishop in 1539. This act made the Abbey a cathedral. However, only this one bishop has ever served there. A dean has headed the Abbey from the time of Queen Elizabeth I to the present day.

Edward the Confessor built a church on the site of the Abbey between about 1042 and 1065. But the main part of the Abbey was begun in 1245 by Henry III. He made the Abbey one of the best examples of French Gothic architecture in England (see **Gothic art**). In the 1500's, Henry VII added the chapel that bears his name. The west towers were completed in 1740.

The floor plan of Westminster Abbey is in the shape of a Latin cross. The church is 513 feet (156 meters) long. The *transepts* (crossarms) extend 203 feet (62 meters). The *nave* (main hall) is 38 feet (12 meters) wide and 102 feet (31 meters) high. The twin towers on the west are 225 feet (69 meters) high. The square central tower barely rises above the roof.

Geoff Dore, Bruce Coleman Ltd.

Westminster Abbey in London is a national church of Britain. It was built in the French Gothic style of the 1200's.

Cloisters surrounding the Abbey date from the 1200's and 1300's. The chapter house was built in the 1200's. West of the main cloisters is the famous Jerusalem Chamber, which dates from the 1300's. Air raids in World War II damaged parts of the Abbey. A program designed to completely restore Westminster Abbey and maintain it began in 1953.   J. William Rudd

Westminster School is one of the oldest public schools of England. Elizabeth I founded it about 1560 as

part of Westminster Abbey. It is also called Saint Peter's College.

Westmoreland, William Childs (1914-   ), an American general, commanded United States forces in the Vietnam War from 1964 to 1968. He relied on ground operations that stressed the number of enemy dead over territory gained, a policy that became known as "search and destroy." In 1967, Westmoreland made several optimistic reports on United States progress in the war. But in early 1968, enemy attacks on the major cities of South Vietnam raised doubts about the war's outcome. Later that year, Westmoreland returned to the United States to serve as Army chief of staff. He retired in 1972.

In 1982, a CBS-TV documentary, "The Uncounted Enemy: A Vietnam Deception," charged that Westmoreland underestimated enemy strength in 1967 and 1968 to make it appear that U.S. forces were winning the war. Westmoreland sued CBS, claiming that its charges about the underestimated troop figures were false and had damaged his reputation. During the trial, some former high-ranking military officials supported the CBS charges. Soon afterward, Westmoreland and CBS officials reached an agreement to drop the suit. They issued statements pledging mutual respect for each other, but CBS also stood by its broadcast.

Westmoreland was born in Spartanburg County, S.C. He graduated from the United States Military Academy in 1936. During World War II (1939-1945), Westmoreland commanded artillery forces in North Africa, Sicily, and northern Europe. He led a paratroop regiment and became a brigadier general during the Korean War (1950-1953). He became a lieutenant general in 1963.

Allan R. Millett

Weston, Edward (1850-1936), an inventor and manufacturer, was noted for pioneering in the development of instruments used to measure voltage and current. Weston's instruments contributed to the development of the first electric light and power systems. He founded the Weston Electric Instrument Company in 1888.

Born near Wolverhampton, England, Weston moved to the United States in 1870. He entered the electroplating business, and developed an electroplating generator, an arc-lighting system, and an incandescent lighting system.   W. Bernard Carlson

Weston, Edward (1886-1958), was an American photographer. He produced dramatic pictures of people, landscapes, and such simple objects as sea shells, seaweed, and rocks. Many of Weston's photographs emphasize the forms and textures of objects and scenes from nature.

Weston was born in Highland Park, Ill. Early in his career, he won many awards for his photographs in the hazy, out-of-focus style that had become popular in the late 1800's. In the 1920's, however, Weston adopted the technique of *straight photography,* a style featuring focused, detailed photographs that portray subjects simply and directly. In 1932, he helped form a group of progressive photographers who promoted straight photography.

In 1937, Weston became the first photographer to win a Guggenheim Fellowship. The award is a grant given to scholars, scientists, and artists to advance their work.

Charles Hagen

Oil painting on wood panel (1821) by Thomas Birch; Wadsworth Atheneum, Hartford, Connecticut. Bequest of Mrs. Clara Hinton Gould

Covered wagons carried thousands of pioneers westward across the United States. The sturdy Conestoga wagon, *shown here,* was first built by German immigrants in the early 1700's.

Westward movement in America

Westward movement in America carried settlers across America, from the Atlantic Ocean to the Pacific Ocean. The westward movement began in the early 1600's with European settlements along the Atlantic Coast of North America. It continued until the late 1800's. By that time, the western frontiers of the United States had been conquered.

An abundance of land and other natural resources lured America's pioneers westward. Fur traders, cattle ranchers, farmers, and miners led the push to the west. Merchants and other business people followed. These hard-working men and women faced great dangers, endured severe hardships, and suffered loneliness and boredom in the hope of making a better life for themselves and their children. Some of them looked to the west for wealth or adventure. Others sought to improve their social position or increase their political power.

The pioneers struggled westward across hills, mountains, and prairies on foot and on horseback. Some floated through the Erie Canal on barges or traveled down rivers on flatboats and steamboats. Others crossed the rugged wilderness in covered wagons. For many pio-

Jerome O. Steffen, the contributor of this article, is Professor of History at the University of Oklahoma.

neers, the Cumberland Gap, the Oregon Trail, and other roads west became paths to opportunity.

The American frontier shifted westward in stages. The first American frontier ran along the Atlantic Coast. Settlers began to cross the Appalachian Mountains after territory west of the mountains came under British control in 1763. During the early 1800's, the next push westward took settlers into the Great Lakes region, the Mississippi River Valley, and the plains along the Gulf of Mexico. By the mid-1840's, adventurous pioneers had reached what are now California and Oregon in the Far West. The last frontier was the Great Plains between the Missouri River and the Rocky Mountains. The settlement of that region began in the 1860's.

In 1890, the U.S. Census Bureau reported that no frontiers remained in the United States. The pioneers had conquered the West.

For descriptions of the life of the people during this period, see **Colonial life in America; Pioneer life in America;** and **Western frontier life in America.**

The first frontiers

The earliest settlements. Colonists from England, the Netherlands, and other European countries began to settle along the Atlantic Coast of North America in the early 1600's. Jamestown, the first permanent English settlement in North America, was founded in Virginia in 1607. Other early settlements included St Marys City (now St. Mary's City) in Maryland; Plymouth and Boston in what is now Massachusetts; and New Amsterdam, which was the beginning of New York City.

The promise of owning land attracted many Europeans to the American Colonies. Some settlers were offered free land to develop. Others came as *indentured servants.* An indentured servant received free passage to America and food, housing, and clothing. In return, the servant agreed to work without wages for a specified period of time, usually four years. At the end of that period, indentured servants received their freedom. Beginning in 1619, black Africans also were brought to the colonies as indentured servants. Gradually, their periods of service were extended, and they began to be treated as slaves with no chance of freedom.

Some settlers came to America in search of religious freedom. Puritans, Quakers, and members of other groups sought to establish communities in which they could live according to their religious beliefs. Probably the best-known Puritans were the Pilgrims, who founded Plymouth Colony.

From the earliest settlements in Virginia and Maryland, colonists soon advanced inland along the valleys of the James, York, Rappahannock, and Potomac rivers. To the north, rich farmland drew settlers into the Connecticut, Merrimack, and Hudson river valleys. By the late 1600's, settlers had pushed as far west as the eastern edge of the Piedmont, the hilly uplands at the base of the Appalachian Mountains.

The Old West. Pioneers next moved into a region often called the Old West. It consisted of the Piedmont, the valleys of the Appalachians, and the back country of New England. In the Old West, fur traders offered Indians weapons and tools in exchange for deer hides, beaver pelts, and other skins and furs. Cattle owners in the

Important dates in the westward movement

1775 Daniel Boone opened the Wilderness Road, which aided the settlement of Kentucky.

1785 The Ordinance of 1785 provided an orderly system for surveying and selling government lands.

1787 The Northwest Ordinance provided government for the Northwest Territory.

1794 Victory over the Indians and a treaty with Britain brought peace to the Northwest Territory.

1795 The Pinckney Treaty with Spain opened the Mississippi River to American traders.

1803 The Louisiana Purchase opened a vast area beyond the Mississippi River to American settlers.

1804-1806 Lewis and Clark explored the northern part of the Louisiana Territory.

1825 The Erie Canal opened, providing improved transportation westward.

1845 The United States annexed Texas.

1846 Britain gave the United States the southern part of the Oregon region.

1846-1848 War with Mexico resulted in the acquisition of California and the Southwest.

1848 The discovery of gold in California inspired the gold rush.

1862 The Homestead Act promised free land to settlers in the West.

1869 The nation's first transcontinental rail system was completed.

1890 Settlement of the main areas of the Western United States brought an end to the frontier.

Southern Colonies found ample grazing lands in the Piedmont for their expanding herds, and cowboys led roundups and cattle drives. Farmers followed the fur traders and cattle ranchers into the Old West, settling in the Shenandoah Valley in Virginia and in the fertile hills and valleys of North and South Carolina.

Many kinds of people came to the Old West. Some owned small farms in the coastal lowlands but sought better land to the west. Others were the landless younger sons and daughters of established families in the East. These colonists were joined by new arrivals from Europe. For example, many German and Scotch-Irish immigrants fled hard times and religious persecution in Europe and settled in Pennsylvania during the early 1700's.

Settlers from different lands brought their own customs and way of life to the frontier. In the process, they helped create American culture. For example, Scandinavian settlers brought the log cabin to America. Other settlers copied the log cabin throughout the Old West. German gunsmiths in Pennsylvania adapted a European rifle to pioneer needs. The result—the Kentucky rifle—proved essential on the frontier for shooting game and for defense against wild animals.

Regional conflict. As each frontier became settled, tensions developed between western settlers and colonial governments in the east. The westerners resented paying taxes to distant governments that provided them with few benefits. The easterners viewed the west as a backwoods inhabited by people incapable of governing themselves. At times, disputes between the two groups turned violent. In 1764, Pennsylvania frontiersmen known as "the Paxton Boys" marched on Philadelphia, the colony's capital. But Pennsylvania statesman Benjamin Franklin persuaded them to turn back. In the Carolinas, a group of westerners known as the "Regulators" assembled to protest high taxes, insufficient representa-

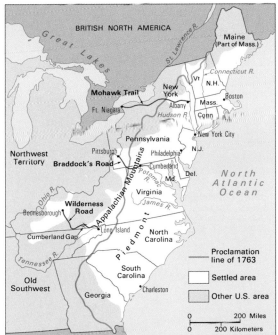

WORLD BOOK map

By 1790, the East Coast had been largely settled, and Americans had pushed beyond the Appalachians. Two new frontiers—the Northwest Territory and the Old Southwest—had opened.

tion in colonial government, and other injustices. A battle was narrowly avoided at the Saluda River in South Carolina in 1769. The Regulators fought and lost the Battle of Alamance in North Carolina in 1771.

The French and Indian War (1754-1763). The next frontier lay beyond the Appalachian Mountains. Both France and Britain claimed the territory between the Allegheny Mountains—a part of the Appalachians— and the Mississippi River. Their rivalry led to the French and Indian War between the French and the British, along with their Indian allies. The British defeated the French and gained nearly all of France's territory in North America.

The Proclamation of 1763. A vast territory west of the Appalachians lay open for settlement after the French and Indian War. However, Indians were prepared to defend their hunting grounds on that land. The British hoped to prevent costly Indian wars by keeping white settlers east of the Appalachians. For that reason, Britain issued the Proclamation of 1763. The proclamation drew a line through the mountains and forbade white settlements west of the line. It also ordered settlers already there to move back east and required traders in the region to have licenses. Investors in land, farmers, and traders—all eager to take advantage of the new territory—resented the restrictions.

Crossing the Appalachians. The Proclamation of 1763 halted westward expansion for only a short time. Investors and colonists clamored for more land as the population in the East increased and the amount of available farmland decreased. Treaties negotiated with the Indians in 1768 shifted the proclamation line westward and opened the way for the settlement of what are now West Virginia and southwestern Pennsylvania. Pioneers settled at Fort Pitt (now Pittsburgh) and in river valleys nearby.

Some pioneers marched farther west into what are now eastern Kentucky and Tennessee. Daniel Boone was one of the most famous of those adventuresome pioneers. In 1775, he led a group of woodsmen from Tennessee through the Cumberland Gap into Kentucky. The trail they carved out became known as the Wilderness Road (see **Wilderness Road**). In Kentucky, Boone founded a settlement called Boonesborough. Other pioneers, such as James Robertson and John Sevier, established frontier communities along the Holston, Watauga, and Clinch rivers in eastern Tennessee. By the time the Revolutionary War began in April 1775, this frontier region swarmed with land speculators and the settlers they had attracted.

The Revolutionary War (1775-1783). During the Revolutionary War, the British encouraged Indians to attack American settlements along the western frontier. Many western settlers fled back east. In 1778 and 1779, Virginia sent troops under Lieutenant Colonel George Rogers Clark to strike at the British. Clark captured several settlements under British control in what are now Illinois and Indiana. As a result of Clark's victories, the United States claimed the area between the Ohio River and the Great Lakes.

After the United States won its independence from Britain in 1783, it acquired British lands extending west to the Mississippi; north to Canada; and south to Florida, which was then a Spanish territory. Settled areas west of the Appalachians soon became part of the United States. Kentucky joined the Union in 1792, and Tennessee followed in 1796.

Reaching the Mississippi River

After the Revolutionary War ended in 1783, the westward movement carried settlers onto two new frontiers. They were the Old Northwest and the Old Southwest. The Old Northwest extended from the Ohio River north to the Great Lakes and from Pennsylvania west to the Mississippi River. The Old Southwest at first consisted of Kentucky and Tennessee. It gradually expanded south to the Gulf of Mexico.

The Ordinance of 1785. Congress, eager for revenue from the sale of land in the Old Northwest, adopted the Ordinance of 1785. That law required the government to survey the Old Northwest before selling the land to the public. The territory was divided into townships of 6 miles (9.7 kilometers) square. These townships were further divided into 36 sections, each 1 mile (1.6 kilometers) square, an area that equals 640 acres (259 hectares). The 640-acre units were then auctioned off to the public for a price of at least $1 an acre.

Few farmers could afford to buy as much as 640 acres. Land speculators, such as the Ohio Company and the Scioto Company, grabbed up most of the land. These companies then divided the land into smaller sections and sold them at a profit.

Townships and sections

The Ordinance of 1785 provided a framework for orderly settlement of the Northwest Territory. Its system of townships and sections prevented boundary disputes, and was used in surveying all the territories later acquired by the United States.

WORLD BOOK illustration by Sarah Woodward

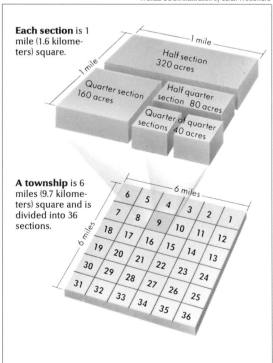

Each section is 1 mile (1.6 kilometers) square.

1 mile

1 mile

Half section 320 acres

Quarter section 160 acres

Half quarter section 80 acres

Quarter of quarter sections 40 acres

A township is 6 miles (9.7 kilometers) square and is divided into 36 sections.

6 miles

6 miles

6	5	4	3	2	1
7	8	9	10	11	12
18	17	16	15	14	13
19	20	21	22	23	24
30	29	28	27	26	25
31	32	33	34	35	36

Oil painting on canvas (1945) by Howard Chandler Christy (Ohio Historical Society)

Indians signed the Treaty of Greenville in 1795, opening up parts of Ohio and Indiana to pioneer settlement. The Indians were forced to sign many treaties, each time giving up more land.

The Northwest Ordinance of 1787 established a government for the Old Northwest, which then became known as the Northwest Territory. The ordinance also provided for the eventual division of the region into three to five states. Congress appointed the first officials of the territory—a governor, a secretary, and three judges. When the territory reached a population of 5,000 adult males, it could elect an assembly and send a nonvoting delegate to Congress. When any division of the territory reached a population of 60,000, it could apply for statehood.

The ordinances of 1785 and 1787 paved the way for full-scale migration to the west. The laws also established guidelines for the administration of all U.S. territories. Treaties with Britain and Spain further encouraged westward migration. Under the terms of the Jay Treaty, signed with Britain in 1794, the British agreed to abandon the military posts they still occupied in the Northwest Territory. In 1795, the United States signed the Pinckney Treaty with Spain, which then controlled Florida and the mouth of the Mississippi River. The treaty settled a dispute over the northern border of Florida, and it opened the Mississippi River to American traders.

Indian conflicts. America's rapid westward expansion led to warfare between white settlers and Indians. During the early 1790's, British traders in the Northwest Territory encouraged Indians to attack frontier settlements. The Indians in the Northwest twice fought off U.S. Army expeditions. But they were defeated by Major General Anthony Wayne at the Battle of Fallen Timbers near what is now Toledo, Ohio, in 1794. In the Treaty of Greenville, signed in 1795, the Indians gave up their claim to the southern two-thirds of what is now Ohio and the southeastern part of what is now Indiana. Pio-

neers rushed into the area. By 1800, the Ohio region had 45,000 settlers. In 1803, Ohio became the first section of the Northwest Territory to achieve statehood.

White settlers soon disregarded the line drawn by the Treaty of Greenville to separate their land from Indian land. As land-hungry pioneers advanced westward, the Indians were forced to sign many additional treaties, each time giving up more land. In the early 1800's, the Shawnee chief Tecumseh—aided by his brother, known as the Shawnee Prophet—tried to halt the invasion of white settlers. They worked to organize an alliance of Indian tribes from the Great Lakes to the Gulf of Mexico. But Tecumseh's plans for an alliance were largely destroyed when his forces were defeated at the Battle of Tippecanoe in the Indiana Territory in 1811.

The War of 1812 briefly interrupted America's westward expansion. During the war, many tribes in Tecumseh's alliance sided with the British against the United States. The Indians hoped that a U.S. defeat would allow them to keep their lands. However, two American victories hastened the downfall of Indian civilization east of the Mississippi River. In 1813, a combined British and Indian force suffered defeat at the Battle of the Thames in southern Canada. In 1814, Major General Andrew Jackson led soldiers to victory over the Creek Indians in the Battle of Horseshoe Bend in what is now Alabama.

By the mid-1800's, the U.S. government had moved almost all of the eastern Indians to the Indian Territory, an area set aside for the Indians west of the Mississippi River. That territory later became almost identical in area with present-day Oklahoma. Thousands of Indians died of starvation and disease on the march to the Indian Territory.

The Old Northwest. After the War of 1812, westward migration resumed at a brisk pace. By 1820, about

BRITISH NORTH AMERICA
Maine
Wisconsin Territory
Iowa Territory
New York
Vt.
N.H.
Boston
Albany
Mass.
Buffalo
Erie Canal
Conn. R.I.
Michigan
Detroit
New York City
Chicago
Pennsylvania
N.J.
Illinois
Indiana
Pittsburgh
Ohio
Cumberland
Md.
National Road
Cincinnati
Washington, D.C.
Del.
Vandalia
Ohio R.
Virginia
St. Louis
Louisville
Missouri
Kentucky
North Carolina
North Atlantic Ocean
Nashville
Tennessee
Arkansas
South Carolina
Natchez Trace
Georgia
Miss.
Alabama
REPUBLIC OF TEXAS
Natchez
Louisiana
New Orleans
Florida Terr.
Gulf of Mexico
0   400 Miles
0   400 Kilometers

☐ Settled area
☐ Other U.S. area

WORLD BOOK map

By 1840, pioneers had settled most of the land east of the Mississippi. Westward expansion had already carried many settlers across the river into Missouri, Arkansas, and Louisiana.

792,000 settlers had made their homes in the Old Northwest.

Pioneers headed to the Old Northwest over rough wagon roads and down the Ohio River. The Erie Canal, completed in 1825, provided another route westward, from the Hudson River to the Great Lakes. It also spurred the economic development of the Old Northwest. The canal allowed westerners to ship farm products efficiently and cheaply to the cities in the East. At the same time, Eastern cities could ship manufactured goods to the rapidly growing farm communities of the Northwest.

Steamboats and railroads encouraged further development of the Old Northwest during the next few decades. Pittsburgh, Louisville, Cincinnati, and other cities along the Ohio River became bustling centers of trade. Chicago and Detroit prospered along the Great Lakes.

The Old Southwest. The Adams-Onís Treaty, signed with Spain in 1819, gave the United States Florida and the southern strip of Alabama and Mississippi. Thousands of settlers poured into Florida. Pioneers also streamed onto the plains bordering the Gulf of Mexico that formed part of the Old Southwest.

Most of the settlers of the Old Southwest were cotton farmers. Farmers rushed first into western Georgia and then into Alabama and Mississippi after the federal government took over Indian lands in those states. Steamboats and an expanding network of roads sped the journey westward. Such cities as Natchez, Miss., New Orleans, and St. Louis prospered along the Mississippi River.

The best lands in the Old Southwest were held largely by plantation owners, unlike in the Old Northwest where small farms dotted the land. Plantation own-

ers dominated social and political life in most of the Old Southwest. As a result, the region developed an economy that depended almost entirely on cotton, and it experienced little industrial growth.

Exploring and settling the Far West

Settlers had begun to cross the Mississippi River by the 1820's. Yet American leaders misjudged the speed at which the nation was moving west. In 1801, President Thomas Jefferson foresaw a far distant time when the continent would be settled from coast to coast. However, pioneers reached California and other regions of the Far West during the 1840's.

The Louisiana Purchase. American settlement of the Far West began after President Thomas Jefferson purchased the Louisiana Territory from France in 1803. For about $15 million, the United States gained 827,987 square miles (2,144,476 square kilometers) of land. The purchase extended U.S. borders from the Mississippi River to the Rocky Mountains.

Before 1801, Spain had controlled the Louisiana Territory. The Spanish posed little threat to U.S. trade and westward expansion. But France, a more powerful and aggressive country, gained control of the territory in 1801. Jefferson feared French interference with U.S. trade along the Mississippi River and through the port of New Orleans. The Louisiana Purchase removed a possibly dangerous enemy from the western border of the United States.

Exploration. In 1803, Jefferson chose Meriwether Lewis, an Army captain, and William Clark, a former Army officer, to lead an expedition to explore the new territory. Jefferson wanted Lewis and Clark to trace the source of the Missouri River. He hoped that the explorers would find a water route from the Missouri to the Pacific Ocean. Jefferson also wanted the expedition to report on the natural resources and to establish friendly relations with Indians in the region.

In 1804, Lewis and Clark moved up the Missouri and across the Rockies. They reached the Snake River in the Oregon region in 1805 and followed the Columbia River to the Pacific. The expedition did not find a practical water route to the Pacific. But Lewis and Clark reported that the region was rich in furs, attracting fur traders and trappers to the area.

More government-sponsored expeditions followed the Lewis and Clark expedition. In 1806, Zebulon M. Pike, an Army officer, set out to explore the southern part of the Louisiana Purchase and gather information about neighboring Spanish territory. But he was captured by Spanish troops near the Rio Grande. After his release, Pike supplied the government with valuable information that later helped establish trade relations with Mexican settlements in the area. In 1820, Major Stephen H. Long led a small expedition up the Platte River to the Rocky Mountains. His report found the Great Plains unfit for settlement because it lacked trees and water. Long labeled the region the *Great American Desert*.

John C. Frémont, an Army surveyor, explored much of the Far West. Beginning in 1842, he led a series of expeditions that surveyed the Oregon Trail and mapped much of the Great Basin region between the Rockies and the Sierra Nevada. Frémont published a report on California, which drew many settlers to the region.

Fur traders and trappers also contributed greatly to the exploration of the Far West. Such well-known "mountain men" as Jim Bridger, Kit Carson, Thomas Fitzpatrick, and Jedediah Smith mapped many areas of the Rockies as they searched for beaver. Carson and Fitzpatrick served as guides on Frémont's expeditions. Bridger established a trading post that helped supply travelers along the Oregon Trail in what is now Wyoming. Jedediah Smith traveled more of the Far West than anyone of his time. In 1824, he used South Pass to cross the Rockies. It then became the route of many travelers. In 1826, Smith made the first overland trip to California.

The Santa Fe Trail. During the 1820's, traders also developed a trade network in the Southwest. In 1821, the trader William Becknell blazed the Santa Fe Trail, which extended from Independence, Mo., to Santa Fe in what is now New Mexico. New Mexico was then a province of Mexico. Another branch of the trail, opened in 1822, cut across the Cimarron Desert. It became the more popular route. Caravans of covered wagons journeyed to Santa Fe loaded with manufactured goods to exchange for Mexican silver, furs, and mules. The Santa Fe trade boosted Missouri's economy. It also made traders and explorers aware that Mexico had only a weak hold on New Mexico and its other northern provinces.

Texas. In the early 1820's, the Mexican government gave Stephen F. Austin, a pioneer from Missouri, permission to establish a colony in Texas. Texas belonged to Mexico as a result of the Adams-Onís Treaty of 1819, which defined the western border of the United States. The treaty drew a boundary line that zigzagged northwest from the Gulf of Mexico to the Pacific Ocean.

By 1835, American settlers outnumbered Mexicans in Texas, which made it difficult for Mexico to govern the territory. That year, the Texans rebelled. Texas gained its independence after its army, led by Samuel Houston, defeated the Mexicans at the Battle of San Jacinto in April 1836. Texas was an independent republic until December 1845, when the United States annexed Texas and made it a state.

The Oregon Trail. As Texans fought for their independence, other Americans looked to the Oregon region with great anticipation. Fur traders and missionaries were the first white settlers to reach the Pacific Northwest. Their glowing reports of fertile valleys attracted thousands of people to the region after 1835. Settlers followed the Oregon Trail. It began at Independence, Mo., and wound westward for about 2,000 miles (3,200 kilometers) across the Great Plains and the Rocky Mountains to the rich valleys of the Oregon region. Pioneer farmers, cattle ranchers, and sheep ranchers journeyed westward along the trail. The first large group of settlers, about 1,000, made the trip in 1843.

Travel on the Oregon Trail required strength and endurance. But the trek was not so lonely or dangerous as described in Western legend. The trail was crowded with wagon trains, army units, missionaries, hunting parties, traders, and even sightseeing tours. Some travelers complained that they sometimes had to stop early in the day to find a good campsite ahead of the crowd. Others spoke of the need to wear masks for protection against the dust kicked up by the heavy traffic. Stories about great numbers of pioneers killed by hostile Indians were also exaggerated. Of the 10,000 deaths that oc-

curred on the trail from 1835 to 1855, only 4 percent resulted from Indian attacks. Such diseases as cholera and smallpox and firearms accidents were the chief causes of death on the trail.

The flood of immigrants to Oregon helped America achieve its territorial ambitions. Since the late 1700's, Britain and the United States had had overlapping claims in the Oregon region. The two countries signed a treaty in 1818, agreeing that citizens of both nations could occupy the disputed area. By 1846, however, the growing number of American settlers in the Oregon region caused the British to abandon their hopes of keeping the area. Thus, in the Oregon Treaty of 1846, Britain gave up its claim to all of the Oregon territory south of the 49th parallel, except for Vancouver Island. That line later became the boundary between the United States and Canada.

The Southwest. In the Southwest, a border dispute led to war between the United States and Mexico in 1846. The Treaty of Guadalupe Hidalgo, signed in 1848, ended the Mexican War. The treaty gave the United States more than 525,000 square miles (1,360,000 square kilometers) of land. That huge territory covered all of present-day California, Nevada, and Utah; most of Arizona; and parts of Colorado, New Mexico, and Wyoming. In 1853, in the Gadsden Purchase, the United States bought from Mexico a strip of land that makes up southern Arizona and New Mexico. That purchase was made in part to provide a good southern route for a transcontinental railroad.

By the 1840's, many Americans believed that it was the destiny of the United States to rule all North America. Those Americans felt they had a mission to spread democracy to the West. The belief in the nation's inevitable expansion became known as the *doctrine of manifest destiny.* It encouraged America's bold and confident expansion westward.

Utah. Utah became the home of the Mormons, who came there in search of religious freedom. The Mormons had met hostility from non-Mormons in communities from New York to Illinois. In 1846, Brigham Young began leading Mormon settlers west from Illinois. In 1847, a small advance party established a settlement on the shores of the Great Salt Lake in Utah. Within 10 years, about 100 Mormon settlements had been established in what are now California, Idaho, Nevada, Utah, and Wyoming. One of the most remarkable chapters in the westward movement occurred from 1856 to 1860, when about 3,000 Mormons walked across the Great Plains to Utah, pushing their few belongings in handcarts. The Mormons survived in the desert because they successfully irrigated the parched land. By 1852, they had dug about 1,000 miles (1,600 kilometers) of irrigation ditches. See **Mormons** (The Mormons in Utah).

California. Reports of fertile valleys and a mild climate attracted a steady stream of pioneers to California during the early 1840's. In 1848, gold was discovered along the American River at Sutter's Mill, near what is now Sacramento. News of the discovery spread rapidly, and by 1849, eager gold seekers began pouring into California. The gold rush attracted "Forty-Niners" from all parts of the world. The population of California exploded from about 15,000 in early 1848 to more than 100,000 by the end of 1849. During that time, San Fran-

Oil painting on canvas (1865) by A. D. O. Bowere; National Cowboy Hall of Fame

Eager prospectors flocked to California after the discovery of gold in 1848. Many miners remained in the Far West, greatly contributing to the permanent settlement of the area.

cisco, the gateway to the gold fields, grew tremendously. It changed from a small town to a bustling city almost overnight.

Most people heading for California followed the Oregon Trail across the Rockies and then branched off to the south along the California Trail. Others chose more southerly routes, such as the Santa Fe, Gila River, and

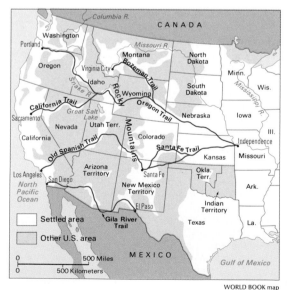

WORLD BOOK map

By 1890, settlements had spread throughout the Great Plains and Far West, though large areas were thinly populated. That year, the government reported that no frontiers were left.

Old Spanish trails. Some sailed the Atlantic Ocean south to the Isthmus of Panama, where they crossed over land to the Pacific Ocean and continued the sea voyage to San Francisco. From 1848 to 1855, more than 100,000 people traveled to the mining frontiers by the Panama route. Gold seekers also reached California by sailing around the southern tip of South America.

According to western tradition, miners caught up in gold fever either struck it rich or died in poverty. However, most prospectors did not fit that image. The majority searched for gold for several years and then returned home to their former occupation. Some stayed on in California and became farmers, ranchers, and merchants, greatly contributing to the permanent settlement of the area. Thus, gold rushes helped develop mining regions, though they did not last long in any one area. The process was repeated as prospectors carried their search elsewhere. Gold and silver rushes occurred in Nevada and Colorado in 1859. Gold rushes also drew miners to what is now Montana in 1862 and to what is now South Dakota in 1875.

Settling the Great Plains

The vast Great Plains between the Missouri River and the Rockies remained unsettled until the 1860's. But as the government gained control of Indian lands on the Plains, cattle ranchers and farmers rushed in. By 1890, the conquest of the West had drawn to a close.

The last Indian wars. After the Civil War ended in 1865, the U.S. Army began to round up the last Indian tribes that freely roamed the western plains. Land-hungry pioneers and expanding railroads wanted to move into the Great Plains from the east. Prospectors searching for gold and silver advanced from the west. But the

Plains Indians fought fiercely to keep their hunting grounds and to avoid being confined on reservations.

A series of bitter Indian wars occurred from the 1860's until 1890. The Sioux rose up in the mid-1860's, when the government built forts to protect the Bozeman Trail. That route, used by miners, ran through Sioux hunting grounds in Wyoming. Fighting broke out again after the discovery of gold in 1874 brought miners into Sioux territory in the Black Hills of South Dakota. To the south, some members of the Arapaho, Cheyenne, Comanche, Kiowa, and other Plains Indian tribes rebelled against moving to reservations in 1868. Indian hostilities in the south erupted again in 1871 and reached a climax in the Red River War of 1874-1875.

One by one, the various Plains Indian tribes were forced to sign treaties that opened their lands to white settlement. The Indians were then resettled on cramped reservations. The last major battle between the Plains Indians and whites occurred in 1890. That year, the U.S. Army massacred as many as 300 Sioux at Wounded Knee Creek in South Dakota.

Cattle frontiers. The Great Plains opened to settlers as the government defeated the Plains Indians. Ranchers moved in first. Ranching started in Texas, and it soon turned the Great Plains into a vast cattle empire.

The westward expansion of the railroads contributed to the rise of the cattle industry. Railroads provided transportation to markets in the East. By 1867, the railroad had extended west to Abilene, Kans., which became the first of the western cattle towns. That year, 35,000 cattle arrived in Abilene. By 1871, more than 600,000 cattle entered Abilene. Texas ranchers hired cowboys to drive their herds to the railroads. The cowboys followed the Chisholm Trail, the Western Trail, and other cattle trails north. Herds of livestock soon rumbled into such Kansas cattle towns as Ellsworth, Newton,

Wichita, Caldwell, and perhaps the most famous of all, Dodge City.

These boisterous cattle towns gave rise to many western legends about gunfighters and such law officers as Wild Bill Hickok, Wyatt Earp, and Bat Masterson. Although cowboys engaged in much merrymaking after the long cattle drives, reports of violence in these communities have been greatly exaggerated. From 1870 to 1885, only 45 violent deaths were recorded in all of the cattle towns together.

Ranching and the railroads quickly spread from Texas north and west into Colorado, Wyoming, Montana, and Oregon. In 1869, the Union Pacific and Central Pacific railroads met at Promontory, Utah, providing the nation with its first transcontinental railroad. Many people in the East and in Europe invested money in ranching after hearing reports of the easy money to be made in the cattle industry. However, the resulting overproduction of cattle, the rising costs of ranching, and the severe winter of 1886-1887 combined to bring an end to the cattle boom in the mid-1880's.

Homesteading on the Great Plains. Farmers known as *homesteaders* followed the cattle ranchers onto the Great Plains. The Homestead Act, passed by Congress in 1862, encouraged farmers to move west. This act gave 160 acres (65 hectares) of free land to any person who had lived on the land and improved it for five years. Many farmers came to the Great Plains because they no longer believed the Great American Desert image. The westward expansion of the railroad also was an important factor. The railroads offered land for sale and provided transportation for the western farmer's products.

Inventions of the 1870's also contributed to the successful settlement of the Great Plains. The lack of trees and water on the Plains presented difficulties for the western farmer. But barbed wire, first sold in 1874, pro-

Capture and Death of Sitting Bull (1890), a lithograph by Kurz and Allison; Denver Public Library

Advancing settlers fought the Indians for control of the Great Plains after the end of the Civil War in 1865. By 1890, the U.S. Army had defeated most of the Plains Indians.

vided a cheap substitute for the wood fence. Improved windmills allowed settlers to bring up water from far underground, and they became common sights on small farms by the 1890's. In addition, improvements in farm machinery produced more efficient plows and other machines that enabled the Plains farmer to cultivate large areas.

Closing of the frontier. The surge of eager homesteaders across the Great Plains left only the Indian Territory untouched. But white settlers demanded that the government make this area—now Oklahoma—available to them. In 1889, the government opened a large section of the Indian Territory that was not assigned for reservations. A wild land rush followed as thousands of pioneers scrambled for the best lots. Similar land rushes occurred in following years as more and more of the Indian Territory was opened to white settlement. But the conquest of the West had drawn to a close. In 1890, the Census Bureau declared in a report that no frontiers remained in the United States. The population west of the Mississippi River had grown remarkably—from 6,877,000 in 1870 to 16,775,000 in 1890.

Results of the westward movement

Patterns of migration. For almost 300 years, the westward movement influenced American history. However, the westward flow of people was not constant. Migration halted when Indian hostilities or wars with other nations made the frontiers unsafe. But once peace was restored, pioneers resumed their westward march. People also tended to migrate during prosperous times, when money was available. During periods of depression, migration often slowed to a trickle. Sometimes, as in the case of the Great Plains, technology spurred settlement. The invention of barbed wire and improvements in the windmill and in farm machinery helped open the Great Plains to settlers.

The frontier influence. The frontier was more than a place on a map. It was an experience that shaped many American institutions and ideas. The frontier environment presented challenges that produced creative solutions. For example, frontier settlements were much less complex than the established communities of the East. As a result, pioneers set up simple forms of government that met frontier needs. Similarly, the elaborate social customs of the East gave way to the simpler pleasures of barn dances and cornhusking contests.

The frontier experience promoted democracy. Established leaders rarely migrated from the East, and so the frontier brought a wide range of people into government. Class lines also blurred in frontier societies. It became difficult to distinguish a permanent upper or lower class because anyone might strike it rich or suffer a setback. The frontier's abundant resources were equally available to all.

The frontier experience also encouraged the development of certain "American" characteristics. Frontiers were isolated places, and so pioneers had to make many items they might otherwise have traded for or bought. They built their own houses and barns and produced their own food. They made their own candles, clothing, furniture, pots, tools, and other necessities. As jacks of all trades, pioneers became inventive and self-reliant. In addition, frontiers offered opportunities for success to those who worked hard. As a result, pioneers tended to be optimistic about the future and concerned with material wealth. Boastfulness and self-confidence emerged as frontier traits as well.

Unfortunately, the pioneers also became extremely wasteful because they lived among such plentiful natural resources. Pioneers cut down vast areas of forests, lost large amounts of gold and other minerals in careless mining operations, and exhausted the soil.

The continual pursuit of a better life made Americans more restless than their European ancestors. The French historian Alexis de Tocqueville remarked that in America "a man builds a house to spend his old age, and he sells it before the roof is on. . . . He brings a field into tillage and leaves other men to gather the crops; he embraces a profession and gives it up; he settles in a place, which he soon afterwards leaves to carry his changeable longings elsewhere." As people moved from place to place, they lost their attachment to a specific region. They began to identify more with the nation as a whole and to see themselves as "Americans." In that way, the westward movement promoted nationalism. Many historians believe that such frontier traits as nationalism, inventiveness, and optimism survive in the American character today.   Jerome O. Steffen

Related articles in *World Book.* See the *History* section of the various state articles, such as **Texas** (History). See also:

Leaders of the westward movement

Austin, Stephen Fuller	Houston, Sam
Boone, Daniel	Lee, Jason
Bridger, Jim	Lewis, Meriwether
Carson, Kit	Long, Stephen Harriman
Chouteau, Jean Pierre	McLoughlin, John
Chouteau, René Auguste	Pike, Zebulon Montgomery
Clark, George Rogers	Putnam, Rufus
Clark, William	Ross, Alexander
Colter, John	Sevier, John
Crockett, Davy	Smith, Jedediah Strong
Fargo, William George	Sublette, William Lewis
Fitzpatrick, Thomas	Whitman, Marcus
Frémont, John Charles	Young, Brigham
Gist, Christopher	

Early trails

Boston Post Road	Natchez Trace
Bozeman Trail	National Road
Chisholm Trail	Oregon Trail
El Camino Real	Santa Fe Trail
Mohawk Trail	Wilderness Road

Other related articles

Astoria	North West Company
Colonial life in America	Northwest Ordinance
Donner Pass	Northwest Territory
Forty-Niners	Ohio Company
Franklin, State of	Pioneer life in America
French and Indian wars	Public lands
Gold rush	Scout
Homestead Act	Turner, Frederick Jackson
Hudson's Bay Company	United States, History of the
Indian wars	(Expansion; pictures)
Lewis and Clark expedition	Watauga Association
Louisiana Purchase	Western frontier life in
Mexican War	America

Outline

I. The first frontiers
   A. The earliest settlements
   B. The Old West

C. Regional conflict
D. The French and Indian War (1754-1763)
E. The Proclamation of 1763
F. Crossing the Appalachians
G. The Revolutionary War (1775-1783)
II. Reaching the Mississippi River
A. The Ordinance of 1785
B. The Northwest Ordinance
C. Indian conflicts
D. The Old Northwest
E. The Old Southwest
III. Exploring and settling the Far West
A. The Louisiana Purchase
B. Exploration
C. The Santa Fe Trail
D. Texas
E. The Oregon Trail
F. The Southwest
G. Utah
H. California
IV. Settling the Great Plains
A. The last Indian wars
B. Cattle frontiers
C. Homesteading on the Great Plains
D. Closing of the frontier
V. Results of the westward movement
A. Patterns of migration
B. The frontier influence

Questions

Who were the "mountain men"?
What were the ordinances of 1785 and 1787?
Why did Indian wars break out on the Great Plains?
What American characteristics did people develop while living on the frontier?
How did the War of 1812 affect westward migration?
What routes did the Forty-Niners follow to California?
Why was the Erie Canal important to both the East and the West?
What inventions aided the settlement of the Great Plains?
Why did Britain issue the Proclamation of 1763?
What land did the United States gain as a result of the Mexican War?

Additional resources

Level I

Kimball, Violet T. *Stories of Young Pioneers in Their Own Words.* Mountain Pr. Pub. Co., 2000.
McNeese, Tim. *Americans on the Move.* 8 vols. Crestwood Hse., 1993.
Stefoff, Rebecca. *The Opening of the West.* Benchmark Bks., 2003.
Torr, James D., ed. *Westward Expansion.* Greenhaven, 2003.
Uschan, Michael V. *Westward Expansion.* Lucent Bks., 2001.

Level II

McLynn, Frank. *Wagons West.* Grove Pr., 2002.
Stegner, Page. *Winning the Wild West.* Free Pr., 2002.
Wexler, Alan. *The Atlas of Westward Expansion.* Facts on File, 1995.
Wexler, Sanford. *Westward Expansion.* Facts on File, 1991.

Wet milling. See Corn (The wet-milling industry).

Wetland is an area of land where the water level remains near or above the surface of the ground for most of the year. Wetlands occur throughout the world and support a wide variety of plants and animals.

The major types of wetlands include *bogs, fens, marshes,* and *swamps.* Bogs and fens are most common in cold climates and are characterized by extensive deposits of partially decayed plant material called *peat.* Bogs have highly acidic soils. The soils of fens are not highly acidic. Mosses are abundant in both bogs and fens. Marshes and swamps usually lack peat deposits and occur in both warm and cold climates. Marshes are found in the shallow waters of lakes and streams. Cat-tails, horsetails, bulrushes, and other nonwoody plants are common in marshes. Swamps tend to develop in areas that are not permanently flooded. Trees and shrubs are the most prominent plants in swamps. Coastal wetlands, such as salt marshes and tropical mangrove swamps, are exposed to a mixture of fresh water and salt water.

Many kinds of animals inhabit wetlands. They include a wide variety of birds and insects; amphibians, such as frogs and salamanders; and such reptiles as alligators, snakes, and turtles. Many mammals, including beavers, muskrats, and otters, also live in wetlands.

Wetlands play an important role in nature. In addition to being a habitat for many plants and animals—particularly many endangered species—wetlands help to control flooding because they retain large amounts of water. The water stored by wetlands also serves as a source of replenishment for ground water supplies. In addition, people use wetlands for fishing, hunting, and nature study.

Many wetlands throughout the world have been destroyed by human activities. Almost half the wetlands in existence at the time the United States was first settled have been destroyed. Since the early 1970's, however, awareness of the ecological and economic value of wetlands has steadily increased. In the United States, various federal and state programs have been designed to preserve the remaining wetlands. But a significant number of wetlands continue to be destroyed. Eric F. Karlin

See also Bog; Marsh; Peat; Peat moss; Swamp.

Weyden, Rogier van der. See Van der Weyden, Rogier.

Weyerhaeuser, *WY ur HOW zur,* **Frederick** (1834-1914), was the leading American lumber executive of his time. He came to the United States from Germany at the age of 18. In 1856, he went to work for a lumber firm in Rock Island, Illinois. Four years later, Weyerhaeuser and his brother-in-law, Frederick Denkmann, bought the mill. In 1870, they joined 16 other lumber firms and formed the Mississippi River Logging Company.

The new company floated rafts of logs down northern tributaries to the Mississippi. There, the logs were cut into lumber, which the firm sold in the Midwest. Through the years, Weyerhaeuser and his associates bought more and more woodland in the Midwest. In 1900, they incorporated the Weyerhaeuser Timber Company to purchase large areas of timberland in the Pacific Northwest. Weyerhaeuser became president of the firm. He was born on Nov. 21, 1834, in Niedersaulheim, Germany, near Mainz. Barry W. Poulson

See also Forest products (table).

Weymouth, *WAY muhth,* Massachusetts (pop. 53,988), is on an inlet of Massachusetts Bay, about 12 miles (19 kilometers) southeast of Boston (see **Massachusetts** [political map]). Industries in Weymouth produce electronic equipment, *resins* (materials used especially in making plastics), and sheet metal. The Abigail Adams House, birthplace of the wife of President John Adams, is in Weymouth. The town is the second oldest settlement in Massachusetts. Only Plymouth is older.

Weymouth was founded in 1622 and incorporated in 1635. Weymouth claims it originated the New England town meeting form of government (see **Town meeting**). Laurence A. Lewis

James Hudnall

A mother whale and her calf remain close together for at least a year. This baby humpback whale is resting on its mother's back as she swims along just beneath the surface of the water.

Whale

Whale is a huge sea animal that looks much like a fish. But whales are not fish. They belong instead to the group of animals called *mammals.* Other mammals include chimpanzees, dogs, and human beings. Like these mammals, whales have a highly developed brain and are among the most behaviorally complex of all animals.

Most whales are enormous. One kind, the blue whale, is the largest animal that has ever lived. Blue whales can grow up to 100 feet (30 meters) long and weigh over 150 short tons (135 metric tons). But some kinds of whales are much smaller. Belugas and narwhals, for example, grow only 10 to 15 feet (3 to 5 meters) long.

Whales have the same basic shape as fish, but they differ from fish in many ways. The most visible difference is the tail. Fish have *vertical* (up and down) tail fins, but whales have sideways tail fins. Fish breathe by

Bernd Würsig, the contributor of this article, is Professor of Marine Mammalogy and Director of the Marine Mammal Research Program at Texas A&M University.

means of gills, which absorb dissolved oxygen from water. Whales, on the other hand, have lungs and must come to the surface to breathe. But they can hold their breath for long periods. One kind of whale, the sperm whale, can hold its breath up to 2 hours.

Like other mammals, whales give birth to live young and feed them with milk produced by the mother's body. Most fish, however, lay eggs and do not feed their offspring. Whales are also *warm-blooded*—that is, their body temperature remains about the same regardless of the temperature of their surroundings. Almost all fish are *cold-blooded.* Their body temperature changes with changes in the temperature of the water.

Through the ages, whales have gradually lost some of the characteristics of mammals. For example, hair covers the bodies of most mammals. But whales have only a few stiff hairs on the head. Most mammals also have four legs. A whale has no hind legs. The only traces of them that remain are two tiny hipbones. In addition, the front legs have developed into flippers, which help a whale steer and keep its balance.

People have hunted whales since prehistoric times. In early days, people killed whales for their meat and for whale oil, which they used as a fuel for lamps and for cooking. Until the 1970's, whale oil and other parts of whales were used to make a variety of products, such as cosmetics, fertilizer, glue, medicines, and soap. Today, some people in Japan, as well as native peoples in Arctic regions, still eat whale meat.

Whaling fleets killed huge numbers of whales and endangered some species' survival in the 1900's. Therefore, the International Whaling Commission, a group of major whaling countries, imposed a *moratorium* (temporary halt) on commercial whaling. The United States government forbids the import of whale products.

Whales belong to a group of mammals called *cetaceans* (pronounced *sih TAY shuhnz).* This name comes from a Latin word meaning *large sea animal.* Scientists have identified at least 75 kinds of cetaceans. They divide the various kinds into two major groups— *baleen whales,* which do not have teeth, and *toothed whales,* which have teeth.

Kinds of baleen whales

Baleen whales have no teeth. Instead, they have hundreds of thin plates in the mouth. They use these plates to strain out food from the water. The plates are called *baleen* or *whalebone* and consist of the same material as human fingernails. The baleen hangs from the whale's upper jaw. The inside edges of the plates have brushlike fibers that filter out the food. Large baleen whales feed mainly on *plankton*—drifting masses of tiny aquatic organisms. Smaller baleen whales feed on plankton as well, but some species also eat schools of small fish.

Scientists divide whales into four groups. These groups are: (1) right whales; (2) pygmy right whales; (3) gray whales; and (4) rorquals.

Right whales have a thick, solid body and a huge head. The head of most right whales makes up about a third of the total body length. Right whales swim slowly, averaging about 3 miles (4.8 kilometers) per hour. They feed by swimming into a mass of plankton with their mouths open. Water flows through the baleen, and plankton becomes entangled in the baleen fibers. There are two main kinds of right whales: (1) bowhead whales and (2) black right whales.

Bowhead whales, also called *Greenland right whales,* have the longest baleen of all baleen whales. They have a highly arched mouth suited to the huge baleen, which may grow as long as 13 feet (4 meters). Bowhead whales are black with white areas on the chin. Some also have whitish patches on the belly and around the flippers and tail. They measure up to 60 feet (18 meters) long and live

William A. Watkins, Woods Hole Oceanographic Institution

A baleen whale has no teeth. Instead, it has hundreds of thin plates called *baleen.* Baleen whales, such as this black right whale, use these plates to filter out food from the water.

only in the Arctic Ocean.

Black right whales usually are called simply *right whales.* Compared with bowhead whales, they have shorter baleen and a less highly arched mouth. They are black, and some have white areas on the belly. Right whales live in all the oceans and may grow up to 60 feet (18 meters) long. They have a calluslike area called a *bonnet* on the snout, and other such areas around the snout, chin, and eyes. These areas are called *callosities.*

Pygmy right whales resemble right whales, but they grow no longer than 20 feet (6 meters). These animals rank as the smallest of all baleen whales. Unlike bowhead and black right whales, pygmy right whales have a *dorsal* (back) fin. They live south of the equator and probably feed only on plankton.

Gray whales live in the North Pacific Ocean. Their skin is gray, with white blotches, some of which are shellfish called *barnacles.* On the lower back, they have a series of low humps. The whales may be up to 43 feet (13 meters) long. They eat small animals living on the sandy ocean bottom. The whales suck up sand and mud and use their coarse, relatively short baleen to strain out the animals. They also feed on plankton and small fish.

Rorquals are baleen whales that have long grooves on the throat and chest. These grooves may number from 10 to 100 and are 1 to 2 inches (2.5 to 5 centimeters) deep. They enable a rorqual to open its mouth extremely wide and gulp enormous quantities of food and water. Rorquals lunge quickly forward into their prey. As the whale closes its mouth, its tongue forces the water out of the mouth through the baleen. The food becomes trapped inside the baleen and is swallowed.

All rorquals have a dorsal fin and so are sometimes called *finback whales.* Most have a long, streamlined shape and can swim faster than other whales.

There are six kinds of rorquals. They are (1) blue whales; (2) Bryde's (pronounced *BRIHD ihs)* whales; (3) fin whales; (4) humpback whales; (5) minke whales; and (6) sei *(say)* whales.

Blue whales are the largest animals that have ever lived. They may grow up to 100 feet (30 meters) long and can weigh more than 150 tons (135 metric tons). They are speckled blue-gray and white but appear evenly blue

WORLD BOOK illustration by Marion Pahl

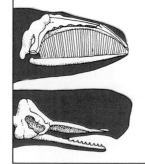

Baleen consists of thin plates that hang from the upper jaw of baleen whales. Baleen is made of the same type of material as human fingernails.

Peglike teeth grow from the lower jaw of nearly all species of toothed whales. Most species of dolphins and porpoises have teeth in the upper jaw as well.

Some kinds of whales

The illustrations on this page and the following page show some of the major kinds of baleen and toothed whales. Baleen whales include nearly all the extremely large types of whales. Among toothed whales, only the sperm whale can compare in size with baleen whales. Unlike baleen whales, the various kinds of toothed whales differ greatly in both size and appearance.

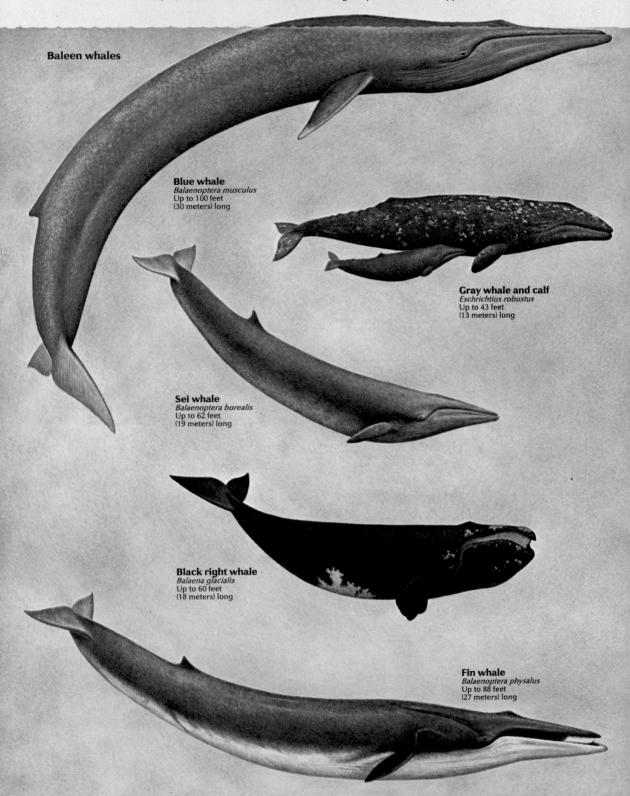

Baleen whales

Blue whale
Balaenoptera musculus
Up to 100 feet
(30 meters) long

Gray whale and calf
Eschrichtius robustus
Up to 43 feet
(13 meters) long

Sei whale
Balaenoptera borealis
Up to 62 feet
(19 meters) long

Black right whale
Balaena glacialis
Up to 60 feet
(18 meters) long

Fin whale
Balaenoptera physalus
Up to 88 feet
(27 meters) long

WORLD BOOK illustration by Harry McNaught

Bowhead whale
Balaena mysticetus
Up to about 60 feet
(18 meters) long

Minke whale
Balaenoptera acutorostrata
Up to 33 feet
(10 meters) long

Humpback whale
Megaptera novaeangliae
Up to 62 feet
(19 meters) long

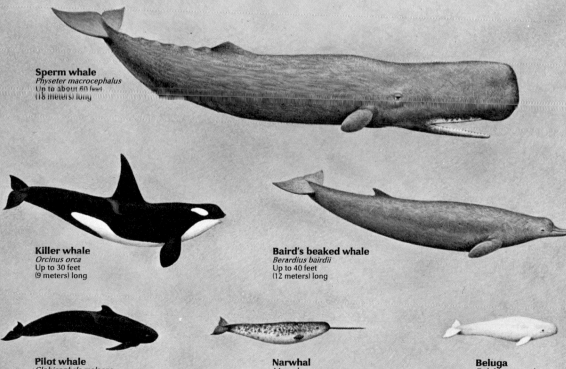

Toothed whales

Sperm whale
Physeter macrocephalus
Up to about 60 feet
(18 meters) long

Killer whale
Orcinus orca
Up to 30 feet
(9 meters) long

Baird's beaked whale
Berardius bairdii
Up to 40 feet
(12 meters) long

Pilot whale
Globicephala melaena
Up to 21 feet
(6 meters) long

Narwhal
Monodon monoceros
Up to 17 feet
(5.2 meters) long

Beluga
Delphinapterus leucas
Up to 17 feet
(5.2 meters) long

underwater. Some have growths of tiny yellowish organisms called *diatoms* on the belly. Blue whales live in
all the oceans but are classified as endangered species.
They feed almost entirely on small shrimplike animals
called *krill,* which are part of the plankton.

Bryde's whales live only in tropical and subtropical
seas. They are dark gray and reach about 45 feet (14 meters) in length. Unlike other rorquals, Bryde's whales eat
mainly small fish and squid.

Fin whales are dark gray on top and light gray or
whitish below. They have whitish baleen on the front
right side of the mouth, but the baleen is darker on the
left side of the mouth and in the back. The lower jaw is
white on the right side and dark gray or brownish-black
on the left. Fin whales grow up to 88 feet (27 meters)
long and live in all the oceans. Fin whales eat krill and
other shellfish and small fish.

Humpback whales grow up to 62 feet (19 meters) and
are chubby compared with other rorquals. The humpback whale's most outstanding feature is its exceptionally long flippers, which may be a third as long as its body.
The body is black on top and white underneath. Wartlike knobs cover the head. Humpback whales live in all
the oceans and often swim in coastal waters. They feed
on krill and small fish.

Minke whales, the smallest of the rorquals, measure
no more than 33 feet (10 meters) long. They are black or
dark gray on top and lighter below. Minke whales dwell
in all the seas. Those in the Southern Hemisphere feed
mainly on krill. Those in the Northern Hemisphere also
eat small fish.

Sei whales look much like small fin whales, except the
lower jaw is dark gray on both sides. They may grow up
to 62 feet (19 meters) long. Sei whales live in all the
oceans and are usually found in deep, temperate waters.
They feed on fish, squid, and tiny shellfish such as krill.

Kinds of toothed whales

Unlike baleen whales, toothed whales have teeth.
There are about 65 kinds of toothed whales. They differ
greatly in size, in shape, and in the number of teeth they
have. Most toothed whales eat fish or squid. However,

Bruce Coleman Inc.

Toothed whales, like this killer whale, use teeth only to capture
prey, not to chew it. They swallow their food whole.

the diet of some toothed whales might also include
octopus, cuttlefish, starfish, or crab.

Scientists divide the various kinds of toothed whales
into five groups: (1) sperm whales; (2) beaked whales; (3)
belugas and narwhals; (4) dolphins and porpoises; and
(5) river dolphins. Most people do not consider dolphins
and porpoises to be whales. But scientists classify them
as toothed whales because they have the same basic
body features as other toothed whales.

Sperm whales are by far the largest toothed whales.
Males become about one-third larger than females,
growing to about 60 feet (18 meters) long. Sperm whales
range in color from brownish-black to dark gray. They
have a huge, square-shaped head. It makes up about a
third of the total body length. The lower jaw is long and
extremely thin. It has 18 to 25 peglike teeth on each side.
The teeth fit into sockets in the toothless upper jaw.

Almost all sperm whales live only in tropical and *temperate* (mild) waters, though mature males spend the
summer in polar seas. They dive to great depths for
food, which consists mainly of large squid. They also eat
certain fishes, such as cod, skate, barracuda, and shark.
The sperm whale has two smaller relatives, the pygmy
and the dwarf sperm whales. The pygmy sperm whale
grows to about 11 feet (3.4 meters) long and the dwarf
sperm whale to about 9 feet (2.7 meters).

Beaked whales have a beaklike snout and only two
or four teeth in the lower jaw. Most have no upper
teeth. Some kinds of beaked whales grow only about 12
feet (3.7 meters) long, but others reach 42 feet (13 meters). Beaked whales live in all the oceans and feed mainly on squid and fish. There are 18 known species of
beaked whales. Most species live in deep waters and do
not approach boats. As a result, scientists know less
about beaked whales than any other kind of whale.

Belugas and narwhals usually measure 13 to 17 feet
(4 to 5.2 meters) long. Narwhals and most belugas live in
the Arctic, but some belugas are found farther south.
Belugas and narwhals eat mostly fish, squid, crab, and
shrimp. Belugas are white or yellow-tan when fully
grown and are often called *white whales.* The name beluga comes from the Russian word *belukha,* which
means white. They have 32 to 40 teeth. Narwhals are
grayish on top and whitish underneath and have dark
brown spots over the entire body. They have only two
teeth. The teeth of female narwhals usually remain
buried in the upper jaw. Among most males, the left
tooth develops into a spiral tusk up to 9 feet (2.7 meters)
long.

Dolphins and porpoises live in all the oceans. Most
porpoises grow 4 to 7 feet (1.2 to 2.1 meters) long. Dolphins usually range from 4 to 30 feet (1.2 to 9 meters)
long. The largest dolphins include killer whales and
pilot whales.

River dolphins, unlike other cetaceans, usually live in
the muddy waters of such rivers as the Amazon in South
America, the Ganges in India, the Indus in Pakistan, and
the Yangtze in China. They normally measure 5 to 8 feet
(1.5 to 2.4 meters) and have a long beak and poorly developed eyesight.

The bodies of whales

Several features of the whale body suggest that
whales are closely related to hoofed mammals, particu-

The body of a female fin whale

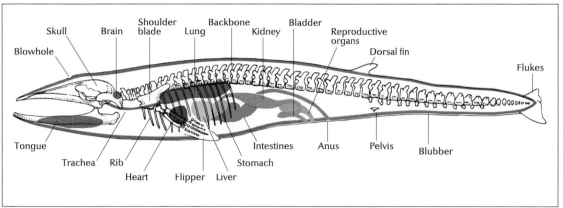

Skull · Brain · Shoulder blade · Lung · Backbone · Kidney · Bladder · Reproductive organs · Dorsal fin · Flukes · Blowhole · Tongue · Trachea · Rib · Heart · Flipper · Liver · Stomach · Intestines · Anus · Pelvis · Blubber

WORLD BOOK illustration by Marion Pahl

larly split-hoofed mammals, such as cattle and deer. Some scientists believe that whales developed from primitive meat-eating mammals. The oldest whale fossil yet discovered dates from about 50 million years ago. However, scientists think that whales probably began to develop as early as 70 million years ago.

Whales basically have the same body features as other mammals. But whales have many special characteristics suited to living in water. Also, living in water enables them to reach enormous sizes. A land animal can grow only so big before its bones and muscles can no longer support its body weight. But the *buoyancy* (lift) of water helps support a whale's body and makes it possible for whales to grow far larger than any land animal.

Body shape. Whales have a highly streamlined shape, which enables them to swim with a minimum of resistance. Their shape resembles that of fish. But a whale's powerful tail fins, called *flukes,* are horizontal instead of vertical like the tail fins of a fish. A whale propels itself by moving its flukes up and down. Most fish swim by swinging their tail fins from side to side.

The ancestors of whales lived on land and had four legs. But after these animals moved into the sea, their body features gradually changed. Over millions of years, the front legs developed into flippers and the hind legs disappeared. A whale uses its flippers to help in steering and in keeping its balance.

Skeleton. A whale's backbone, ribcage, and shoulder blades resemble those of other mammals. The absence of hind legs, however, distinguishes the whale from most other mammals. Two small bones buried in the hip

muscles are all that remain of the whale's hind legs.

Almost all mammals have seven neck vertebrae. But in whales, these vertebrae are greatly compressed into a short length or joined together into one bone. This feature keeps the head from moving about as a whale swims. It also contributes to the whale's streamlined shape by joining the head directly to the body.

Skin and blubber. Whales have smooth, rubbery skin that slips easily through the water. Most mammals are covered with hair, which holds warm air next to the body. Whales, however, do not have a coat of hair to provide them with insulation. A few bristles on the head are all the hair that whales have.

Beneath the skin, whales have a layer of fat called *blubber,* which keeps them warm. Actually, rorquals have more difficulty getting rid of excess heat than keeping warm. Their blubber, therefore, never grows more than about 6 inches (15 centimeters) thick. In contrast, right whales may have a layer of blubber up to 20 inches (50 centimeters) thick. Whales can live off their blubber for a long time. Large baleen whales, for example, feed very little for about eight months while migrating and breeding. In addition, blubber is lighter than water, so it increases the buoyancy of whales.

Respiratory system. Like all other mammals, whales have lungs. They must therefore come to the surface regularly to breathe. Baleen whales usually breathe every 5 to 15 minutes, but they can go as long as 40 minutes without breathing. A sperm whale can hold its breath up to 2 hours.

Whales can go for long periods without breathing for

WORLD BOOK illustration by Marion Pahl

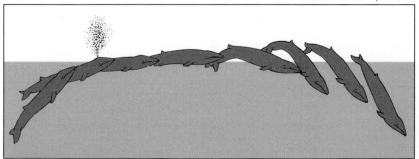

A rapid forward roll enables a whale to surface, breathe, and begin a new dive in one continuous motion. This movement gives the whale only about two seconds to exhale and inhale. Some kinds of whales throw their *flukes* (tail fins) clear of the water when beginning a deep dive.

Jen and Des Bartlett, Bruce Coleman Inc.

Impressive leaps from the water are performed by some species of whales. Scientists call this behavior *breaching*. The right whale shown above is breaching off the coast of Argentina.

several reasons. Their muscles store much more oxygen than do those of other mammals. Humans, for example, store only about 13 percent of their oxygen supply in the muscles, compared with about 41 percent for whales. During a dive, a whale's body greatly reduces the blood flow to the muscles but keeps a normal flow to the heart and brain. The heartbeat also slows, which helps save oxygen. After a dive, a whale must take several breaths to recharge its tissues with oxygen.

When a whale comes up to breathe, it rolls forward as it breaks the surface. This movement gives the whale only about two seconds to blow out and breathe in up to 2,100 quarts (2,000 liters) of air. Whales breathe through nostrils, called *blowholes,* at the top of the head. Toothed whales have one blowhole, but baleen whales have two. Powerful muscles and valves open the blowholes wide for whales to breathe, and then the openings snap tightly shut.

When a whale exhales, it produces a cloud called a *blow* or *spout.* The blow consists chiefly of water vapor and air that contains little oxygen. It may also include mucus and oil droplets. Experts can identify the species of a whale by the height and shape of its blow. Blows range in height from about 6 feet (1.8 meters) in humpback whales to 25 feet (8 meters) in blue whales. Right whales have a double V-shaped blow, and rorquals have a pear-shaped one. Sperm whales blow forward and to the left.

Senses. Whales have no sense of smell, but they have good eyesight and a well-developed sense of taste. All whales also have well-developed senses of touch and hearing. Their keen hearing provides them with much information about their surroundings. They can hear an extremely wide range of sounds, including low- and high-pitched sounds far beyond the range of human hearing. Whales can also tell from what direction a sound is coming underwater.

Toothed whales produce sounds within the *nasal sac system,* a series of air-filled pouches below the blowhole. The whales locate underwater objects by listening for the echoes produced when objects reflect the sounds. From the echoes, they determine the distance to an object and the direction in which it lies. This method of navigation is called *echolocation.* Biologists believe that baleen whales are not able to echolocate.

The life of whales

Reproduction. Most kinds of whales mate during a specific season. The male, called a *bull,* and the female, called a *cow,* engage in courting as part of the mating process. During courting, the whales may stroke each other with their flippers. Males may jostle aggressively as they compete for females. One male may mate with several females during a breeding season. Similarly, a female may mate with several males.

The pregnancy period varies from species to species, but in most kinds of whales it lasts 10 to 12 months. A female sperm whale, however, carries her baby 15

Paul Thomas, Black Star

A visible cloud called a *spout* is produced when a whale exhales through its *blowhole,* or nostril, *left.* Toothed whales have one blowhole. Baleen whales have two.

A whale's short, wide nasal passage, *below,* helps the whale breathe quickly.

WORLD BOOK illustration by Marion Pahl

The birth of a whale, such as that of the bottle-nosed dolphin shown here, occurs tailfirst. In many cases, other female whales help the mother while she gives birth.

A newborn whale begins swimming immediately, but it depends on its mother for food and protection. As soon as it is born, the mother helps it to the surface to take its first breath.

months. In almost all cases, a whale has only one baby, called a *calf,* at a time. Twins rarely occur. One or more females may help the mother during birth. Whales are already giants at birth. Newborn blue whales, for example, average about 2 tons (1.8 metric tons) in weight and 23 feet (7 meters) in length. As soon as the baby is born, the mother nudges it to the surface to take a first breath.

The mother whale is highly protective of her baby and stays close to it for at least a year. Like all other mammals, whales nurse their young. The female has special breast muscles that pump milk into the baby's mouth. Whale milk is highly concentrated and much richer in fat, protein, and minerals than the milk of land mammals. This rich food helps the calves grow amazingly fast. Baby blue whales gain about 200 pounds (91 kilograms) per day. Young blue and fin whales nurse up to seven months. Most other whales nurse for about a year. Sperm whales and pilot whales may nurse their young, at least occasionally, for three years or more.

Group life. Whales live in groups called *herds, pods,* or *schools.* Toothed whales appear to be more socially organized than baleen whales. However, scientists do not know enough about the social behavior of baleen whales to make a definitive comparison. Toothed whales, especially female offspring of the same mother, often live together for many years or for life. Many species of dolphins swim in herds of 1,000 or more. Most dolphin schools consist of animals of both sexes and a variety of ages. Other species, such as sperm whales, form all-male groups and groups consisting of several females and young calves. Most adult killer whales live in pods with their young.

Most baleen whales live alone or in small groups. The young usually stay with their mothers for a year or less. Baleen whales sometimes gather in large groups at their feeding or breeding grounds.

Whales communicate with one another by making a wide variety of sounds called *phonations.* Large baleen whales can produce sounds that are too low-pitched for people to hear. Toothed whales can produce sounds that are too high for human ears. Whales can easily hear these sounds over great distances. Microphones have picked up the deep moans of blue whales at a distance of over 50 miles (80 kilometers). Scientists believe that whales use these phonations to keep group members in contact with one another and to coordinate group activities.

The best-known whale sounds are the songs of the humpback whales. Each song consists of a series of sounds that lasts up to 20 minutes and is then repeated. All male humpback whales living in the same area produce basically the same song, but the songs of humpbacks of different areas vary greatly. The songs change gradually from year to year. Humpbacks produce their songs in the areas where they meet during breeding season. Scientists think that male humpbacks use the songs to maintain a certain distance from other males.

Migrations. Most kinds of baleen whales migrate between polar and tropical regions. The cold waters of the Arctic and Antarctic are rich with plankton. The whales spend the summer in these areas, feeding and storing up blubber. As winter approaches, the polar waters freeze over and the whales move to warmer seas. There they mate, and the females that are already pregnant give birth. The warm waters may provide a comfortable environment for the babies. In the tropics, adult whales live mostly off their blubber because food is scarce. Mother whales convert part of their blubber into milk for the babies. By late spring, whales return to the polar feeding area.

Two kinds of baleen whales do not make long migrations. Some Bryde's whales live in the tropics the year around, and bowhead whales never leave the Arctic. Most species of toothed whales also do not migrate. Belugas and narwhals stay in Arctic waters. Most sperm whales live only in tropical or temperate seas. Older, larger males spend the summer in polar waters.

Life span. The life span of whales ranges from 15 years for the common porpoise to 60 or more years for killer, bowhead, and sperm whales. Human beings and large sharks account for many whale and dolphin deaths.

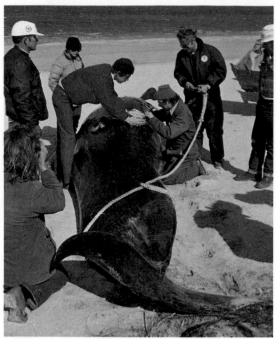

Larry Smith, Black Star

Scientists examine a beached whale that died after stranding itself ashore. Studies of beached whales and of whales killed by whalers provide most of our knowledge about whale anatomy.

Killer whales, which are dolphins, occasionally attack young whales, smaller dolphins, and weak or diseased baleen whales. Whales that escape human actions and large predators die of parasite infections, other diseases, or old age.

Some whales die after stranding themselves on a beach. In some cases, a whale swims ashore alone. In other instances, an entire school of whales becomes stranded. Only toothed whales beach themselves in groups. People often return beached whales to the sea, but most swim back onto the beach. Stranded whales cannot live long. Out of water, the whales quickly overheat and die unless people help them.

Scientists do not know for certain what causes beachings, but they have proposed a number of explanations. Some suggest that parasites in the whales' ears or brains interfere with the animals' ability to echolocate. Others suggest that gently sloping beaches reflect sounds over the heads of the whales. As a result, the whales are not warned that they are swimming onto a beach. Some scientists think whales navigate by sensing the earth's natural magnetic field. These scientists believe machine-made magnetic waves may confuse or misguide the animals, causing them to beach. Still other scientists think that a variety of these and other causes may be responsible for beachings.

The early days of whaling

The first whalers. People began to hunt whales in prehistoric times. At first, they simply killed and ate whales that had become stranded on beaches. People who lived in what is now Norway were probably among the earliest whalers to seek out and kill whales in the

sea. Norwegian rock carvings about 4,000 years old show a variety of whaling scenes. The earliest written record of Norwegian whaling dates from about A.D. 890,

The Basque people of southern France and northern Spain established the first large whaling industry in Europe. During the 900's, the Basques began to hunt baleen whales in the Bay of Biscay, which lies west of France and north of Spain. They hunted near the shore from small open boats. The whalers maneuvered their boat close enough to a whale so that one of them could harpoon it. A rope connected the harpoon to the boat. In time, the whale became exhausted. The whalers then killed it with sharp lances and towed the body to shore for processing.

During the 1200's, the Basques began to equip large sailing ships for whaling voyages. Each ship carried several small whaleboats from which the whalers set out to kill whales. After killing a whale, the whalers brought it alongside the ship. Then with long-handled knives, they peeled off the blubber in strips as the body turned over and over in the water. The crew used ropes to lift the blubber onto the ship. The whalers removed the baleen from the whale and discarded the rest of the body.

The whalers stored blubber and baleen on the ship until they had a full load. The ship then returned to shore, where the blubber was cooked to make oil. The Basques burned whale oil in lamps and used baleen in such articles as corsets, dress hoops, and whips.

The Basques chiefly hunted one type of whale, which became known as the *right whale.* The Basques considered it the right, or correct, whale to hunt because it swims slowly, floats when dead, and has great quantities of baleen. After right whales became scarce in the Bay of Biscay, the Basque whalers ventured farther out to sea. During the 1500's, their voyages even carried them as far as the coast of Newfoundland.

The growth of European whaling. Many European nations began whaling during the 1600's. Dutch and English explorers reported that the Arctic waters were filled with whales. Bowhead whales were especially plentiful around Svalbard, a group of islands north of Norway. Svalbard became the main center of Arctic whaling. The Dutch and the English in particular developed profitable whaling industries there. At first, they employed Basques to kill and cut up the whales, but they soon learned to do these jobs themselves. By 1720, whalers had killed most of the whales around Svalbard and moved on to other areas of the Arctic.

American whaling. The first American whalers were Indians, who hunted from shore in much the same way as the early Basques. During the early 1600's, the American colonists began to hunt right whales off the Atlantic coast. In 1712, a ship hunting for right whales was carried far from land by a storm. The ship came upon a school of sperm whales, killed one, and brought it back to port. This chance event began the sperm-whaling industry in America.

Shore-based whaling for right whales declined in the 1700's, but sperm whaling developed into a major industry by the end of the century. By 1800, Americans were hunting sperm whales throughout the Atlantic Ocean and in the South Pacific Ocean.

Whalers obtained three valuable substances from sperm whales. The most important was *sperm oil,* which came from the head and the blubber. People used the oil as a fuel for lamps and as a lubricant. Whalers also took another oil called *spermaceti* from the sperm whale's head. This oil became the chief ingredient in candles. The third substance, called *ambergris,* came from the intestines of sperm whales. It was used as a base for expensive perfumes.

The American sperm-whaling industry had its greatest prosperity from about 1820 to 1850. During this period, it employed more than 70,000 people and killed about 10,000 whales annually. The whaling fleet consisted of over 730 ships, which sailed all the oceans. Much whaling took place in the Pacific Ocean, and San Francisco became a major whaling port. By this time, many voyages lasted as long as four to five years.

The decline of American sperm whaling began with the California gold rush in 1849. Many crew members of whaling ships deserted to search for gold. But the American Civil War (1861-1865) dealt the most severe blow to the whaling industry. During the war, Southern ships sank many whaling vessels. Whaling began to revive after the war, but the birth of the U.S. petroleum industry posed a new threat. Petroleum products soon replaced sperm oil as a fuel for lamps and spermaceti as a base for candles. American sperm whaling declined throughout the late 1800's and early 1900's. After 1925, all that remained of the industry were a few shore-based whaling operations along the Pacific coast.

Modern whaling

Hunting techniques. During the 1860's, a Norwegian whaling captain named Svend Foyn invented a new type of harpoon and a gun to fire it. His harpoon was tipped with a bomb that would explode inside the whale and cause death much sooner than an ordinary harpoon. Foyn mounted the harpoon gun on the bow of another

of his inventions—a steam-powered whaling boat. This *catcher boat* could travel much faster than the sailing ships and small open boats that whalers had used previously. Foyn's boat and harpoon enabled whalers to hunt rorquals, whose great speed and power had formerly protected them from whalers. About 1900, whalers began to hunt the enormous rorqual populations in the waters surrounding Antarctica.

By 1925, whalers also had developed the *factory ship.* A factory ship was a huge vessel that was served by a fleet of catcher boats and was equipped to process a wide variety of whale products. A modern factory ship fleet included up to 12 diesel-powered catcher boats and a crew of about 400. Spotters in airplanes or helicopters helped the whalers in their search for whales. In addition, the ships had sonar to trace whales underwater. These advanced techniques enabled the crew of a catcher boat to track down and kill any whale that they spotted. After harpooning a whale, the whalers pumped air into its body cavity to keep it afloat. Later, the catcher boats or special *buoy boats* towed the whales to the factory ship. An iron claw was attached to the whale's flukes, and the animal was hauled onto the ship.

Modern whaling techniques proved highly effective. As a result, more whales were killed during the first 40 years of the 1900's than during the preceding four centuries. The number of whales killed worldwide peaked in 1962, when 66,000 were killed. Excessive killing, however, greatly reduced the world's whale populations and jeopardized the survival of some species. By 1980, the whale catch had decreased to about 15,000.

Processing whale products. Processing began after a whale had been hauled aboard a factory ship or to a shore-based factory. First, workers called *flensers* used long knives to cut slits along the whale's body. The flensers then peeled off the whale's blubber and cut it

Detail of *Panorama of a Whaling Voyage Round the World* (about 1847), a painting by Benjamin Russell and Caleb P. Purrington; New Bedford Whaling Museum, New Bedford, Mass.

American whaling flourished throughout the first half of the 1800's. The scene above shows hunters killing right whales off the northwest coast of North America in the 1840's.

Modern whaling vessels enabled whalers to kill and process whales efficiently. In the picture at the left, taken during the 1970's, a Soviet *factory ship* tows a dead whale to be processed on board. *Catcher boats,* such as the one on the right, were used to chase down and kill the whales.

Matt Herron, Black Star

up. The blubber then was placed in cookers, which removed the oil. After the blubber was peeled off, workers called *lemmers* cut up the rest of the body. They cut the meat to be sold as human food into large chunks and froze it. The bones, the rest of the meat, and some internal organs were cooked to make such products as cattle feed and fertilizer. Today, people in Japan eat the meat of whales killed for scientific use.

The future of whales

Many larger kinds of whales face an uncertain future. Whalers have killed so many blue, bowhead, humpback, and right whales that those species have been threatened with extinction. Overhunting also has greatly reduced the number of fin and sei whales.

In 1946, the major whaling countries formed the International Whaling Commission (IWC) to protect whales from overhunting and to regulate the whaling industry. For many years, the IWC established unrealistically high *quotas* (limits) on the number of whales that could be killed. During the 1960's and 1970's, it reduced quotas, banned the hunting of several whale species, and limited the use of factory ships. In 1979, the IWC created the Indian Ocean Whale Sanctuary, which banned all commercial hunting of whales in the Indian Ocean.

In 1982, the IWC voted for a *moratorium* (temporary halt) on commercial whaling, beginning with the 1985 and the 1986 hunting seasons. By 1988, all nations had halted commercial whaling. In 1992, Iceland, Greenland, Norway, and the Faroe Islands formed the North Atlantic Marine Mammal Commission (NAMMCO) as an alternative to the IWC. These nations felt IWC restrictions were too severe. In 1993, Norway resumed commercial hunting of minke whales. In 1994, the IWC strengthened its

efforts to protect whales by setting up the Southern Ocean Whale Sanctuary. This sanctuary would ban commercial whaling in most of the world's oceans south of 40° south latitude.

The United States has strongly opposed commercial whaling. In 1971, the U.S. government ordered an end to commercial U.S. whaling and outlawed the importation of whale products. Federal law also calls for *sanctions* (penalties) against any nation that disregards IWC rules.

Public opinion in the United States, Canada, and some European countries has been strongly opposed to commercial whaling. In 1973, antiwhaling groups agreed to *boycott* (refuse to buy) products from Japan and the Soviet Union until those countries stopped commercial whaling. Public opinion also played a major role in the passage of the IWC moratorium. After Norway resumed commercial whaling in 1993, some consumer groups in Europe and the United States boycotted Norwegian products.

The IWC permits native peoples who have traditionally depended on whales for food to continue hunting whales. These peoples include the Inuit (sometimes called Eskimos) of Alaska, Greenland, and Russia. They eat whale blubber, meat, and skin. The commission regulates which whales these people may hunt and the hunting methods used. The IWC also permits the killing of whales for scientific research, a practice that has stirred controversy.

Most biologists believe that all species of large baleen whales have been saved for the present. However, complete protection of endangered baleen species must continue for a long time to allow them to recover from years of extreme overhunting. Even with protection, some species may not be able to recover. For example, the right whale has been fully protected since 1935, but it has not yet made a significant comeback.

Many smaller toothed whales, especially dolphins and porpoises, remain threatened. Many whales die after becoming accidentally trapped in huge nets set for fish. Many are also deliberately killed for use as fishing bait and food. Some toothed whale populations have decreased because people have polluted ocean waters with chemicals and other substances. Human activities have also caused river dolphins, harbor porpoises, and some coastal dolphins to become seriously endangered.

Every year, the number of people in the world increases about $1\frac{1}{2}$ percent, and so the demand for food rises constantly. This fact may threaten the survival of whales. If the population does not level off, people may compete with whales for food from the sea. Some nations have already begun fishing for krill, the main food of whales in Antarctic waters.   Bernd Würsig

Scientific classification. Whales belong to the order Cetacea, which is divided into two suborders. Toothed whales form the suborder Odontoceti. Baleen whales make up the suborder Mysticeti.

Related articles in *World Book* include:

Ambergris	Fin whale	Narwhal
Blubber	Gray whale	Pilot whale
Blue whale	Greenpeace	Porpoise
Bowhead whale	Humpback whale	River dolphin
Bryde's whale	Killer whale	Sei whale
Cetacean	Krill	Sperm whale
Dolphin	Minke whale	Spermaceti

Outline

I. Kinds of baleen whales
  A. Right whales
      C. Rorquals
  B. Gray whales
II. Kinds of toothed whales
  A. Sperm whales
      D. Dolphins and porpoises
  B. Beaked whales
      E. River dolphins
  C. Belugas and narwhals
III. The bodies of whales
  A. Body shape
      D. Respiratory system
  B. Skeleton
      E. Senses
  C. Skin and blubber
IV. The life of whales
  A. Reproduction
      C. Migrations
  B. Group life
      D. Life span
V. The early days of whaling
  A. The first whalers
  B. The Basque people
  C. The growth of European whaling
  D. American whaling
VI. Modern whaling
  A. Hunting techniques
  B. Processing whale products
VII. The future of whales

Questions

Why can whales grow far larger than any land animal?
What are the two major groups of whales?
In what ways do whales differ from fish?
How do whales communicate with one another?
What functions does blubber serve for a whale?
Why do beached whales die?
What events led to the decline of American whaling?
What has been done to protect whales from extinction?
What were some uses of whale products?

Additional resources

Level I
Collard, Sneed B., III. *A Whale Biologist at Work.* Watts, 2000.
Currie, Stephen. *Thar She Blows: American Whaling in the Nineteenth*

Century. Lerner, 2001.
Greenaway, Theresa. *Whales.* Raintree Steck-Vaughn, 2001.
Greenberg, Daniel A. *Whales.* Benchmark Bks., 2000.

Level II
Carwardine, Mark. *Whales, Dolphins, and Porpoises.* 1995. Reprint. Dorling Kindersley, 2000.
Martin, Stephen. *The Whales' Journey.* Allen & Unwin, 2001. The lives of humpback whales.
Mawer, Granville A. *Ahab's Trade: The Saga of South Seas Whaling.* 1999. Reprint. Allen & Unwin, 2000.
Würtz, Maurizio, and Repetto, Nadia. *Whales and Dolphins.* Thunder Bay Pr., 1999.

Whale shark is the largest living fish. It is known to reach a length of at least 40 feet (12 meters). Whale sharks are found in tropical oceans throughout the world. Scientists know little about these sharks because they are so rare. A few whale sharks have been kept alive and studied in enormous aquariums in Japan.

Whale sharks are dark gray to reddish-brown with large white spots on the upper side of the body. They are pale white or yellow underneath. They have broad, flat heads with a wide mouth. Adult whale sharks have more than 300 rows of tiny, hooked teeth and a row of replacement teeth behind these. The sharks feed mainly on plankton. Whale sharks lay eggs the size of footballs. Newly hatched young are about 2 to 3 feet (60 to 90 centimeters) long.

Despite their size, whale sharks are harmless to people. However, boats sometimes accidentally ram large whale sharks, causing considerable damage to both the shark and the boat.   John E. McCosker

Scientific classification. The whale shark belongs to the whale shark family, Rhincodontidae. Its scientific name is *Rhincodon typus.*

Wharton, Edith (1862-1937), was an American author. She became known for her psychological examination of characters faced with changes in the moral and social values of middle-class and upper-class society. Her novels and short stories provide numerous expert characterizations of complex men and women.

Wharton's best-known novels focus on New York society during the 1800's and early 1900's. She won the 1921 Pulitzer Prize for fiction for *The Age of Innocence* (1920). This novel provides a questioning view of aristocratic New Yorkers during the 1870's. Her other novels include *The House of Mirth* (1905), *Ethan Frome* (1911), *The Reef* (1912), *The Custom of the Country* (1913), *Summer* (1917), *Old New York* (1924), and *The Mother's Recompense* (1925). She wrote about 85 short stories.

Wharton was born Jan. 24, 1862, in New York City into a socially prominent and wealthy family. Her given and family name was Edith Newbold Jones. She began writing as an adolescent but stopped in her late teens. After marrying Edward Wharton in 1885, she lived a fashionable life, mostly in Europe. Eventually, she started writing again, beginning with poems and short stories. But nervous ailments forced her to take rest cures. After her health improved, Wharton also began writing novels.

As she became a best-selling novelist, Wharton supported herself and her husband. After they divorced in 1913, she moved to France. Wharton was friends with many writers, including the American novelist Henry James, who stimulated her work. She wrote an autobiography, *A Backward Glance* (1934). Wharton died on Aug. 11, 1937.   Linda Wagner-Martin

Wheat

A field of ripened wheat is golden-brown. Wheat fields cover more of the world's farmland than any other food crop.

J. C. Allen & Son

Wheat is the world's most important food crop. Hundreds of millions of people throughout the world depend on foods made from the *kernels* (seeds or grains) of the wheat plant. The kernels are ground into flour to make breads, cakes, cookies, crackers, macaroni, spaghetti, and other foods.

Wheat is a member of the grass family. It belongs to the group of grasses called *cereals* or *cereal grains.* Other important cereals include rice, corn, barley, sorghum, oats, millet, triticale, and rye.

Wheat covers more of the earth's surface than any other food crop. The leading wheat-producing countries include Canada, China, France, India, Russia, and the United States. The world's farmers grow about 20 billion bushels of wheat a year. This amount could fill a freight train stretching around the world about $2\frac{1}{2}$ times. A bushel of wheat weighs 60 pounds (27 kilograms).

Long before the beginnings of agriculture, people gathered wild wheat for food. Scholars believe that about 11,000 years ago people in the Middle East took the first steps toward agriculture. Wheat was one of the first plants they grew. In time, farmers raised more grain than they needed to feed themselves. As a result, many people did not have to produce their own food and were freed to develop other useful skills. These changes led to the building of towns and cities, the expansion of trade, and the development of the great civilizations of ancient Egypt, India, and Mesopotamia.

Early farmers probably selected kernels from their best wheat plants to use as seeds for planting the next crop. In this way, certain desired qualities were passed on from one generation of wheat to the next. Such practices resulted in the gradual development of improved kinds of wheat. During the 1900's, scientists developed many new wheat varieties that produce large amounts of grain and can resist cold, disease, insects, and other crop threats. As a result, wheat production rose dramatically.

Uses of wheat

Food for people. Wheat is the most important food for more than a third of the world's people. In many areas of the world, wheat appears in some form at nearly every meal. Wheat is eaten chiefly in bread and other foods prepared from wheat flour. People also eat wheat in macaroni, spaghetti, and other forms of *pasta* and in breakfast cereal.

Wheat flour is excellent for baking because it contains a protein substance called *gluten* that makes dough elastic. This elasticity allows dough containing yeast to rise. About two-thirds of all the wheat flour milled is used by commercial bakers to bake bread, buns, cakes, cookies, crackers, pies, rolls, and other goods. In addition, wheat flour and baking mixes containing wheat flour are sold for use at home.

To produce wheat flour, millers grind the wheat kernels into a fine powder. Wheat kernels are rich in *nutri-*

Lavoy I. Croy, the contributor of this article, is Professor of Agronomy at Oklahoma State University.

ents (nourishing substances), including protein, starch, vitamin E, and the B vitamins—niacin, riboflavin, and thiamine. The kernels also contain such essential minerals as iron and phosphorus.

Whole wheat flour is made from the entire kernel. It therefore contains the nutrients found in all parts of the kernel. To produce white flour, however, millers grind only the soft, white inner part of the kernel, which is called the *endosperm*. The endosperm contains the gluten and nearly all the starch in the kernel. But white flour lacks the vitamins and minerals found in the *bran*—the kernel's tough covering—and the *germ,* which is the *embryo* (undeveloped stage) of a new wheat plant inside the kernel. In the United States, Canada, and many other countries, millers and bakers add B vitamins and iron to most white flour to increase its food value. Such flour is called *enriched flour.* See **Flour.**

Pasta. Wheat is the chief ingredient in macaroni, spaghetti, and other forms of pasta. Most pasta is made from *semolina*—the coarsely ground grain of durum wheat. Manufacturers of pasta products add water and other ingredients to the semolina to form a thick paste or dough. They force this paste through machines that form it into macaroni, noodles, spaghetti, and other shapes. See **Pasta.**

Breakfast foods. Many breakfast foods are made with wheat. Ready-to-eat breakfast cereals containing wheat include bran flakes, puffed wheat, shredded wheat biscuits, and wheat flakes. Cooked breakfast cereals made with wheat include cracked wheat, farina, malted cereals, rolled wheat, and whole wheat meal.

Livestock feed. Some wheat germ and bran that remain after white flour is milled are used in feeds for poultry and other livestock. Farm animals also eat wheat when it is economical to feed it to them.

Other uses. Wheat is also the source of certain substances that are used to improve the nutritional value or

Food value of whole-grain wheat

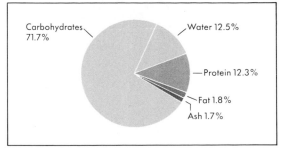

Source: *Composition of Foods—Raw, Processed, Prepared,* Agriculture Handbook No. 8, Agricultural Research Service, U.S. Department of Agriculture. Data are for hard, red winter wheat.

flavor of foods. Vitamin-rich wheat germ and wheat germ oil are added to some breakfast cereals, specialty breads, and other foods. Glutamic acid obtained from wheat is used in making *monosodium glutamate* (*MSG*). Monosodium glutamate is a salt that has little flavor of its own, but it brings out the flavor of other foods. See **Monosodium glutamate.**

The stems of wheat plants are dried to make straw, which can be woven into baskets and hats, made into strawboard for boxes, or used as fertilizer. Industry uses the outer coatings of wheat kernels to polish metal and glass. Adhesives made from wheat starch hold layers of plywood together. Alcohol made from wheat is used as a fuel and in manufacturing synthetic rubber and other products.

The wheat plant

Young wheat plants have a bright green color and look like grass. The mature plants grow 2 to 5 feet (0.6 to 1.5 meters) tall. They turn golden-brown when ripe.

Structure. The main parts of a mature wheat plant are the roots, stem, leaves, and head. Wheat has two

WORLD BOOK photo by Ralph J. Brunke

Foods made with wheat are a major part of the diet for over a third of the world's people. Such foods include bread, cake, breakfast cereal, cookies, crackers, and pasta.

J. C. Allen & Son

Feed for farm animals often contains wheat. The feed may include the wheat germ and bran that remain after white flour is milled, or it may contain wheat unsuitable for milling.

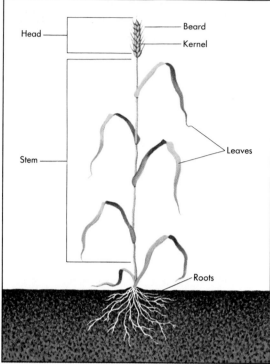

The wheat plant grows up to 5 feet (1.5 meters) high and turns golden-brown when ripe. The head of the plant holds from 30 to 50 kernels of grain. Many kinds of wheat have bristly hairs, called *beards* or *awns*, which extend from the head.

types of roots, primary and secondary. Three to five primary roots grow out of the seed, about $1\frac{1}{2}$ to 3 inches (3.8 to 7.6 centimeters) below the surface of the soil. These roots usually live for only six to eight weeks. As the stem begins to grow out of the soil, the secondary roots form just below the surface. They are thicker and stronger than the primary roots and anchor the plant securely in the soil. Most of the root system lies in the upper 15 to 20 inches (38 to 50 centimeters) of soil. But if the soil is loose, the root system may extend as deep as 7 feet (210 centimeters).

Most wheat plants have a main stem and several additional stalks, called *tillers.* Each leaf of a wheat plant has a sheath and a blade. The sheath wraps around the stem or tiller. The blade, which is long, flat, and narrow, extends from the top of the sheath. Each blade is on the opposite side of the stem from the blade that is just below it.

A wheat head, also called a *spike,* forms at the top of each main stem and tiller. The head is composed of a many-jointed stem. The head carries clusters of flowers, called *spikelets,* which branch off from each joint. Each primary spikelet contains a wheat kernel wrapped in a husk. Many kinds of wheat have bristly hairs, called *awns* or *beards,* which extend from the spikelets. A typical wheat spike bears 30 to 50 kernels.

A wheat kernel is usually $\frac{1}{8}$ to $\frac{3}{8}$ inch (3 to 9 millimeters) long. It has three main parts—the bran, the endosperm, and the germ. The bran, or seed coat, covers the

surface of the kernel. The bran has several layers and makes up about 14 per cent of the kernel. Inside the bran are the endosperm and the germ. The endosperm forms the largest part of the kernel—about 83 per cent. The germ makes up only about 3 per cent of the kernel. It is the part of the seed that grows into a new plant after sowing.

Growth and reproduction. A wheat kernel begins to absorb moisture and swell shortly after planting. The primary roots appear, and the stem starts growing toward the surface of the soil. One to two weeks later, the young plant appears above the ground. In less than a month, leaves appear and the tillers and secondary roots begin to grow.

In spring when conditions are favorable, stems *elongate* (lengthen) from the leaf sheaths. Heads appear on the tillers soon afterward. A few days after the spike emerges from the sheath, the flowers are pollinated and develop into wheat kernels. Usually, each wheat flower pollinates itself. Occasionally, however, pollen from one flower is carried by the wind and fertilizes another flower.

Wheat becomes fully ripe about 30 to 60 days after flowering, depending on the weather. During the ripening period, the kernels increase in size and gradually harden. The entire plant becomes dry and turns golden-brown. Ripe kernels may be white, red, yellow, or even purple, depending on the variety of wheat.

Kinds of wheat

There are several ways of classifying wheat. Wheats can be broadly grouped into winter wheats and spring wheats. Scientists classify wheat according to its species and variety. In addition, the government in many wheat-producing countries has introduced market classes to simplify wheat sales.

Winter wheats and spring wheats are grouped by their growing season. The kind of wheat planted depends primarily on the climate. Winter wheats are grown in milder climates than spring wheats. In general, winter wheats produce higher yields.

Winter wheat is planted in the fall and harvested the following spring or summer. It reaches the stage when

Cross section of kernel of wheat

WORLD BOOK illustration by Emily McGowan

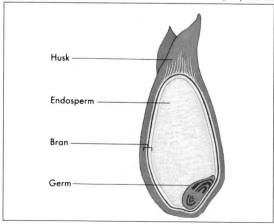

tillers form and then stops growing as cold weather arrives. The plants resume growing when warm weather returns in the spring. Winter wheat needs such a period of cold weather, with short days and long nights, to flower. If winter wheat is planted in the spring, it ordinarily will not *head* (produce a crop).

Spring wheat is grown in areas with extremely cold weather. It is planted in the spring of the year and becomes fully ripe that summer.

Species of wheat. Scientists have identified about 30 species of wheat, based on differences in such traits as appearance and growth patterns. Only three of these species—*common wheat, club wheat,* and *durum wheat* —are commercially important in the United States. Moreover, some scientists consider club wheat to be a part of common wheat, not a separate species. Scientists also disagree about the classification of several other species.

Common wheat is also called *bread wheat.* It is the most widely grown wheat species in the world. The kernels of common wheat may be red, *amber* (yellowish-brown), white, purple, or blue. They range in texture from hard to soft. Common wheat includes both winter and spring wheats. It is grown on the prairies of the central United States and Canada and in most major wheat-producing areas of the world.

Club wheat is closely related to common wheat. Its kernels are white or red and are usually soft in texture. In the United States, club wheat is grown mainly in the Pacific Northwest. Club wheat may be of the winter or spring type.

Durum wheat has hard kernels that are white, red, amber, or purple. Ground durum wheat holds together well when made into a paste. For this reason, durum wheat is used in pasta products. In North America, most durum wheat is of the spring wheat type and is grown in Minnesota, the Dakotas, and southern Canada.

Some species of wheat

Common name	Latin name	Common name	Latin name
Club	*Triticum compactum*	Persian	*T. carthlicum*
Common or Bread	*T. aestivum*	Polish	*T. polonicum*
		Shot	*T. sphaerococcum*
Cone, Poulard, or Rivet	*T. turgidum*	Spelt	*T. spelta*
Durum	*T. durum*	Wild einkorn	*T. boeoticum*
Einkorn	*T. monococcum*	Wild emmer	*T. dicoccoides*
Emmer	*T. dicoccon*		

Varieties of wheat. Each wheat species is divided into many varieties. These varieties differ in such characteristics as grain yield; growing time; grain protein content; and the ability to resist cold, drought, disease, and insect pests.

More than 40,000 varieties of wheat have been produced in the world. Scientists keep seeking new varieties with the most desirable combination of characteristics. In laboratories at agricultural experiment stations, seed companies, and universities, scientists breed new varieties by a process called *crossing.* In crossing, pollen from one variety is used to fertilize plants of another variety. The offspring form a new variety with some characteristics of both parent varieties. The offspring with the most desirable characteristics are grown for several generations to ensure that the new variety is pure and has acceptable characteristics.

Commercial classes of wheat. The United States Department of Agriculture (USDA) divides wheat into seven market classes based on such qualities as the color and texture of the kernels. These classes are (1) hard red winter wheat, (2) soft red winter wheat, (3) hard red spring wheat, (4) durum wheat, (5) red durum wheat, (6) white wheat, and (7) mixed wheat.

The USDA market classes help the government regu-

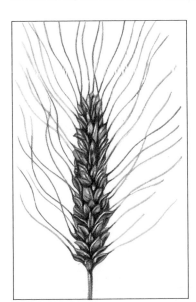

Common wheat, the most widely grown wheat species, includes both winter and spring types.

Club wheat has a short, thick head that is usually nonbearded. It includes both winter and spring types.

Durum wheat is usually bearded and has hard kernels. Most durum wheat in North America is spring wheat.

late the quality of wheat sold in the United States. They also help milling companies and exporters select the grain they purchase. Each class has different characteristics and uses. In general, hard wheats have more protein than soft wheats do. Hard red wheats make excellent bread flour. Soft red wheats are used for cakes, cookies, and pastries. Durum wheats are purchased to make pasta products. White wheats are soft and best suited for breakfast foods and pastries. Mixed wheats consist of wheats from two or more classes.

How wheat is grown

Wheat grows in a wide range of climates and soils. But a good wheat crop requires suitable weather and proper soil. To achieve the highest yields, wheat farmers must use high-quality seed that is free from disease. Farmers also must plant and harvest the wheat at just the right time. In addition, they must protect the growing crop from damage caused by diseases and pests.

The basic steps for growing wheat are much the same all over the world. However, wheat farms differ in size and levels of *mechanization* (work done by machinery). In many nonindustrial countries, wheat farmers use animals to pull their plows across small plots. They also may plant and harvest their crops by hand. In industrialized countries, nearly all the wheat is grown on large farms with the aid of tractors and specialized machinery. This section describes how wheat is grown on a large, mechanized farm.

Climate conditions. Fairly dry and mild climates are the most favorable for growing wheat. Extreme heat or cold, or very wet or very dry weather will destroy both spring and winter wheat. Weather conditions, including temperatures and rainfall, influence when wheat is planted. Planting seeds too early or too late reduces the yield. Late planting of winter wheat also increases the chance of damage from cold.

Farmers plant winter wheat in time for the young plants to become hardy enough to survive the winter cold. Winter wheat is planted as early as September 1 in Montana and as late as November 1 in Texas, where cold weather arrives much later. In northern winter wheat areas, farmers may plant wheat in *furrows* (narrow channels) a few inches deep. These furrows fill with blowing snow, which acts like a blanket and protects the plants from extreme cold.

Spring wheat is exposed to fewer weather hazards because it has a far shorter growing period than winter wheat does. Farmers in northern Nebraska and South Dakota may plant spring wheat in early March. Farmers to the north—in Minnesota and North Dakota—may wait until mid-April to plant spring wheat.

Soil conditions. Wheat grows best in the kinds of soil called *clay loam* and *silt loam* (see **Loam**). The soil should contain much decayed *organic* (plant and animal) matter to provide food for the wheat plants. If the soil lacks some nutrients, a farmer may add these in the form of fertilizer.

In many parts of the world, farmers grow wheat on the same land every year. After many years, such land may lack the nutrients needed to produce a good crop. In addition, erosion by wind or water can remove nutrients from the soil. Farmers commonly have samples of soil tested to determine if the soil has the necessary nutrients. Such tests also indicate the amount of acid in the soil. If soil becomes too acid, wheat will not grow well and may not even sprout. Farmers can add fertilizer and lime to the soil to restore nutrients and reduce acidity.

Some farmers do not plant wheat on the same land every year. They may plant wheat in rotation with such crops as clover, corn, oats, soybeans, or timothy. This practice returns nutrients to the soil and helps control diseases and pests. In regions with little rainfall, farmers may plant a field every other year. Between wheat crops, they leave the field *fallow* (unplanted) so that it can store moisture.

Preparing the soil. Wheat farmers prepare fields for the next crop by plowing. They begin plowing as soon

Shostal

Plowing the field is the first step in preparing the soil for planting wheat. The plow turns and loosens the earth to aid in planting. Plowing also makes it easier for the seeds to sprout and grow.

Planting wheat requires from $\frac{1}{2}$ bushel to 2 bushels of seeds per acre (1.2 to 4.9 bushels per hectare). A machine called a *drill, left,* drops the seeds into the ground and covers them with soil.

as possible after harvest. Plowing breaks up the soil surface and allows moisture to soak into the ground where it is stored for the next crop. It also buries weeds and the remains of the previous crop. This plant matter releases nutrients as it decays. In areas that suffer from erosion, farmers use a plow that loosens the soil but leaves plants on the surface. These plants help reduce erosion.

Just before planting wheat, farmers prepare the seedbed with a device called a *spring-tooth harrow.* Harrows have sharp metal spikes that break up chunks of earth into small pieces that can pack closely around the wheat seeds.

Planting. Farmers use a tractor-drawn machine called a *drill* to plant wheat seed. The drill digs furrows just deep enough to plant the seeds. At the same time, it drops the seeds, one by one, into the furrows and covers the seeds with soil. Some drills also drop a small amount of fertilizer with the seed. Drills can be set to plant the desired number of seeds per acre. Seeding rates range from about $\frac{1}{2}$ bushel per acre (1.2 bushels per hectare) in dry regions to about 2 bushels per acre (4.9 bushels per hectare) in moist regions. With a large drill, a farmer can plant more than 200 acres (81 hectares) of wheat a day.

Care during growth. Growing wheat can suffer damage from diseases, insect pests, and weeds. Wheat farmers employ various practices to help prevent such damage.

Controlling diseases. The most destructive wheat disease is *rust.* This disease is caused by a fungus that grows on the wheat plant and produces small, rust-colored spots on the leaves, stems, and heads. The spots later turn brown. The fungi draw food and water from the wheat plant. This action may prevent the kernels from developing. There are two types of rust, leaf rust and stem rust. To protect their wheat crops, farmers often destroy nearby barberry plants, on which the stem rust fungus must live during some stages of its growth. Some varieties of wheat are resistant to certain kinds of

rust. Breeders continue to develop more varieties of wheat that can resist rust. See **Rust.**

Another serious fungus disease that harms wheat kernels is *smut.* The two main kinds that attack wheat are *bunt* (also called *stinking smut*) and *loose smut.* Wheat kernels infected with bunt fill with a black mass of smut spores. These infected kernels are called *smut balls.* When smut balls break, they release a rotten, fishy odor. If smut balls break during harvesting, the spores spread and contaminate thousands of other kernels. If infected kernels are sown, the next crop also will be damaged. In wheat plants infected with loose smut, black smut spores replace both the kernels and the husks. Wind carries these spores to other wheat plants, spreading the disease. Farmers can control both kinds of smut by treating the seeds before planting or by spraying their crop with a chemical that kills the spores. Some varieties of wheat can resist smut infection. See **Smut.**

Several other diseases attack wheat, but in most cases they do not cause widespread damage. They include *flag smut, glume blotch, leaf blotch, scab, take-all, black chaff,* and *mosaic.*

Controlling insect pests. Insects damage about 10 per cent of the United States wheat crop every year. More than 100 different kinds of insects attack wheat. Some, including grasshoppers and locusts, eat the stems and leaves of the wheat plant. Wireworms, cutworms, and some other insects eat the roots and seeds or cut the wheat stem at the surface of the soil. Still other insects, including Hessian flies, suck sap from the stems. Insects that damage wheat also include army worms, cereal leaf beetles, greenbugs, jointworms, wheat stem sawflies, and wheat stem maggots. Grain weevils and Angoumois grain moths attack stored wheat grain.

Some varieties of wheat are resistant to Hessian flies and wheat stem sawflies. Farmers can control other insect pests by using insecticide sprays. Planting winter wheat after the Hessian flies that hatch in the fall have died also helps farmers to reduce the crop damage caused by this insect pest.

J. C. Allen & Son

Harvesting wheat is often done with a machine called a *combine*. The combine cuts the stalks and *threshes* the wheat—that is, separates the kernels from the rest of the plant.

Controlling weeds. Weeds rob wheat plants of moisture and nourishment. This loss reduces grain yields. Certain weeds can spoil a wheat crop. For example, wild garlic and wild onions give wheat an odor that makes it unfit for use as flour. Other weeds that cause serious damage to wheat crops include Canada thistle, cheat, field bindweed, Russian thistle, wild morning glory, wild mustard, and wild oats. Careful preparation of the seedbed helps prevent the growth of weeds. If weeds become a problem among growing wheat plants, farmers may apply chemicals that have been approved for such use by government agencies.

Harvesting. Farmers harvest wheat as soon as possible after it has ripened, before bad weather can damage the crop. Wheat is ready for harvest when moisture makes up no more than 14 percent of the weight of the kernel. To check for ripeness, farmers may take a sample to a grain storage elevator for moisture testing. Farmers also may test wheat by biting a kernel or breaking it with their fingernails. When ready for harvest, the kernels are hard and brittle and break with a sharp, cracking sound.

Large mechanized farms use huge, self-powered machines called *combines* to harvest wheat. Combines cut the stalks and *thresh*—that is, separate the kernels from the rest of the plant. In North America, large teams of combines follow the wheat harvest north from Texas to Canada. These combine teams move from field to field, operating day and night to harvest the wheat on time.

Where wheat is grown

The world's leading wheat-producing countries in-

Harvesttime around the world

Harvesting the world's wheat crop takes place all year. Each month, wheat is gathered and threshed somewhere in the world, as shown below.

January: Argentina, Australia, Chile, and New Zealand.
February: Chile, Myanmar, New Zealand, and Uruguay.
March: India and upper Egypt.
April: Lower Egypt, India, Iran, Mexico, and Morocco.
May: Algeria, China, Japan, Spain, and Southwestern United States.
June: China, southern France, Greece, Italy, Portugal, Spain, Tunisia, Turkey, and the United States south of about 40° north latitude.
July: Bulgaria, Croatia, southern England, France, Germany, Hungary, Kazakhstan, Moldova, Romania, Russia, Serbia and Montenegro, Ukraine, and Northern United States.
August: Belgium, Canada, Denmark, northern England, Kazakhstan, Moldova, the Netherlands, Russia, Ukraine, and Northern United States.
September and October: Parts of Canada, Kazakhstan, Russia, Scandinavian countries, and Scotland.
November: Argentina, Brazil, Venezuela, and South Africa.
December: Argentina and Australia.

clude Canada, China, France, India, Russia, and the United States. Some countries produce more wheat than their own people consume. Farmers in these countries depend heavily on export sales. The United States leads all other countries in exports of wheat and wheat flour. Argentina, Australia, Canada, and France also export large amounts of wheat. China is one of the world's leading importers of wheat.

Asia. In China, farmers grow wheat in many areas of the country, primarily on the North China Plain in the east. Most of China's farmers plant winter wheat. In some irrigated fields, they plant such crops as corn, cotton, or soybeans between the rows of wheat before the wheat is ready for harvest.

Farmers in Kazakhstan and central Russia grow softer varieties of spring wheat. The growing region is on a level prairie with deep, fertile soils. This area, called the Black Earth Belt, extends about 2,000 miles (3,200 kilometers) from the Danube River Basin in eastern Europe across northern Kazakhstan and into central Russia.

India, Pakistan, and Turkey are also among the major wheat-producing countries of Asia. Farmers plant winter wheat across much of northern India just after the summer rains stop.

Europe. Farmers in Moldova, Ukraine, and the European part of Russia grow hard red winter wheat. Other wheat-producing countries of Europe include France, Germany, Italy, and the United Kingdom.

North America. In the United States, the many varieties of wheat are planted at different times and in different areas, depending on the climate. In the southern Great Plains—Texas, Oklahoma, Kansas, Colorado, and Nebraska—farmers grow hard red winter wheat. In Minnesota and the northern Great Plains—South Dakota, North Dakota, and Montana—farmers plant hard red spring wheat. Winters in this region are often too cold for winter wheat. Spring durum wheat is also grown widely in the northern Great Plains. Smaller amounts of winter durum wheat are planted in Arizona and California.

In the Midwest and the East—in such states as Missouri, Illinois, Indiana, Ohio, and Pennsylvania—farmers

Wheat-producing areas of the world

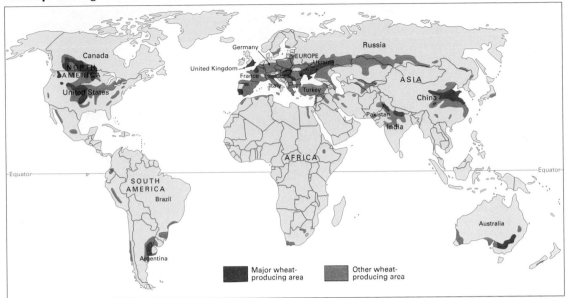

Major wheat-producing area

Other wheat-producing area

WORLD BOOK map

commonly plant soft red winter wheat. White wheat is grown in Michigan and New York.

In the western United States, the chief wheat-producing areas are the Columbia River Valley and the uplands of Washington, Oregon, and Idaho. This region has deep, fertile soils that hold water well. Most of the wheat grown is white wheat. White wheat also is grown in California.

In Canada, most wheat is grown in the Prairie Provinces—Saskatchewan, Alberta, and Manitoba. Nearly all of Canada's crop is hard red spring wheat, though some other wheats, especially durum, are also grown.

South America. The primary wheat-growing area in South America is the *Pampa*—a fertile plain in Argentina. Hard red winter wheat is grown on huge, mechanized plantations in the Pampa.

Australia. Farmers in Australia grow wheat in the southern part of the country. Nearly all of Australia's crop is white spring wheat.

Marketing wheat

Transporting and storing wheat. After the harvest, most farmers haul their wheat by truck to a country grain elevator for storage. Each truck empties its load of grain into a pit. A conveyor belt then scoops up the grain, carries it to the top of the elevator, and dumps it into a tall storage bin. Country elevators dry and clean the grain they receive and provide farmers with marketing information. Country elevators assign the grain to one of six grades, based on its weight and quality. The grades have different uses, and wheat is marketed on the basis of its grade. Country elevators receive most of their wheat directly from farmers, but some of the wheat may come from smaller country elevators.

From the country elevator, wheat travels by truck or railroad boxcar to a terminal elevator located in a large grain market or shipping center. Different lots may be combined at the terminal elevator to produce blends

needed by flour mills. If the grain is to be exported, the United States Department of Agriculture inspects and grades it. Terminal elevators commonly hold from 1 million to 10 million bushels of wheat, though some can hold much more. See **Grain elevator.**

From the terminal elevator, some wheat is loaded into huge ships for export. Much of the remainder is carried by truck, rail, or barge to mills for grinding into flour. The rest is shipped to other processors to be used in

Leading wheat-growing countries

Bushels of wheat grown in a year

Country	Bushels
China	3,312,100,000 bushels
India	2,583,500,000 bushels
United States	1,972,000,000 bushels
Russia	1,613,000,000 bushels
France	1,239,900,000 bushels
Germany	771,500,000 bushels
Canada	739,200,000 bushels
Australia	722,900,000 bushels
Turkey	704,700,000 bushels
Pakistan	691,900,000 bushels

One bushel equals 60 pounds (27.2 kilograms).
Figures are for a three-year average, 2001-2003.
Source: Food and Agriculture Organization of the United Nations.

animal feed or other industrial products. For a description of flour milling, see **Flour** (How white flour is milled).

Buying and selling wheat. In the United States, milling companies buy some wheat directly from farmers. Most often, however, country elevators buy the farmers' wheat. Most wheat stored in grain elevators is sold through a *commodity exchange* or *grain exchange.* The Chicago Board of Trade and the Kansas City (Missouri) Board of Trade are two large grain exchanges. An exchange itself does not buy or sell any wheat. It is an organized market where people who want to buy a *commodity* (good) meet those who want to sell it. These traders include farmers, representatives of grain elevators and flour mills, and exporters. In addition, some traders are *speculators*—that is, they buy and sell a commodity in the hope of making a profit without actually exchanging the commodity itself.

Buyers may purchase wheat already in storage. The larger exchanges also have a *futures market* where traders make contracts to buy and sell wheat at a specified price and future date. The futures market helps milling companies and other processors by assuring them a steady supply of grain at prices determined well in advance of delivery. See **Commodity exchange.**

A government agency, the Canadian Wheat Board (CWB), markets wheat in Canada. The CWB represents farmers, consumers, and the government. It buys and sells wheat at prices established by the government, establishes quotas for purchases from wheat farmers, and regulates exports. Wheat farmers are paid when they deliver their crop to a country elevator. The farmers' wheat is then pooled and sold by the wheat board. The farmers may receive an additional payment after the crop has been sold. Under this system, all farmers receive the same price for wheat of similar quality, and they are guaranteed a fair share of the market.

Controlling wheat production. Worldwide wheat production varies greatly from year to year, depending on weather and the amount of land planted. In years of high production, many countries may harvest more wheat than they can use. They can either store the sur-

Leading wheat-growing states and provinces

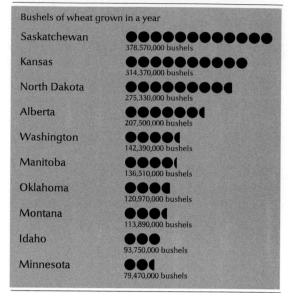

Bushels of wheat grown in a year

Saskatchewan	378,570,000 bushels
Kansas	314,370,000 bushels
North Dakota	275,330,000 bushels
Alberta	207,500,000 bushels
Washington	142,390,000 bushels
Manitoba	136,510,000 bushels
Oklahoma	120,970,000 bushels
Montana	113,890,000 bushels
Idaho	93,750,000 bushels
Minnesota	79,470,000 bushels

One bushel equals 60 pounds (27.2 kilograms).
Figures are for a three-year average, 2000-2002.
Sources: U.S. Department of Agriculture; Statistics Canada.

Wheat-producing areas in North America

Wheat is grown in large quantities in the United States and Canada. Spring wheat is raised in the northern Great Plains states and in the Prairie Provinces. Severe winters prevent planting in both these regions in the fall. The winter wheat belt extends from the southern Great Plains states through the eastern United States.

Spring wheat

Major producing area

Other producing area

Winter wheat

Major producing area

Other producing area

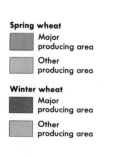

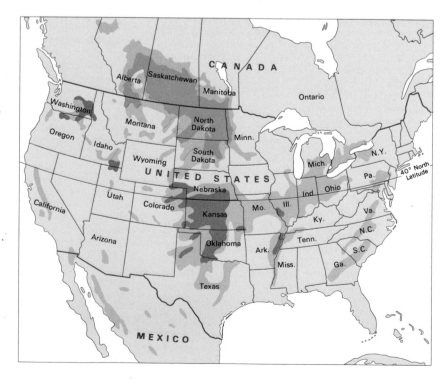

WORLD BOOK map

A country elevator stores wheat after it has been harvested. The elevator cleans the wheat and grades its quality. Grain is bought or sold on the basis of its grade.

plus or sell it to countries that need wheat. As countries try to unload their surplus, the price of wheat tends to drop. Sometimes, the price falls far below the farmers' cost of growing the wheat. If wheat prices remain low, farmers may decide to plant less wheat or switch to another crop. Then, in years of low production, there may be too little wheat to feed the people.

In many countries, the government has farm programs aimed at matching production levels with expected market demand, thus preventing large surpluses or shortages. Some governments support wheat prices by guaranteeing to buy surplus wheat at a "target" price if the market price falls below that price. The government may store the surplus wheat and sell it later when the price rises.

Other government programs aim at increasing or reducing the acreage planted, depending on the country's needs. The United States, for example, has a wheat surplus year after year. From 1962 to 1973 and again in the late 1970's, the U.S. government tried to limit the amount of land planted in wheat by paying farmers to leave fields unplanted. It offered a payment-in-kind (PIK) program in 1983 and 1984. Under this program, farmers who restricted their acreage could receive payment in surplus wheat that the government had stored from previous years. Farmers could sell this wheat or store it. A modified PIK program began in 1986. This new program allowed farmers to receive payment in other commodities besides wheat.

History

Origins. Scientists believe that wild relatives of wheat first grew in the Middle East. Species from that region—wild einkorn, wild emmer, and some wild grasses—are the ancestors of all cultivated wheat species. At first, people probably simply gathered and chewed the kernels. In time, they learned to toast the grains over a fire and to grind and boil them to make a porridge. Frying such porridge resulted in flat bread, similar to pancakes. People may have discovered how to make yeast bread after some porridge became contaminated by yeast.

Wheat was one of the first plants to be cultivated. Scientists think that farmers first grew wheat about 11,000 years ago in the Middle East. Archaeologists have found the remains of wheat grains dating from about 9,000 B.C. at the Jarmo village site near Damascus, Syria. They also have found bone hoes, flint sickles, and stone grinding tools that may have been used to plant, harvest, and grind grains.

The cultivation of wheat and other crops led to enormous changes in people's lives. People no longer had to wander continuously in search of food. Farming provided a handier and more reliable supply of food and enabled people to establish permanent settlements. As grain output expanded, many people were freed from food production and could develop other skills. With the improvement of agricultural and processing methods, people in some areas grew enough grain to feed people in other lands. In this way, trade developed. Thriving cities replaced tiny villages. These changes helped make possible the development of the great ancient civilizations.

The spread of wheat farming. By about 4,000 B.C., wheat farming had spread to much of Asia, Europe, and northern Africa. New species of wheat gradually developed as a result of the accidental breeding of cultivated wheats with wild grasses. Some of the new wheats had qualities that farmers preferred, and so those kinds began to replace older wheats. Emmer and einkorn were cultivated widely until durum wheat appeared about 500 B.C. By about A.D. 500, common wheat and club wheat had developed.

Wheat was brought to the Americas by explorers and settlers from many European countries. In 1493, Christopher Columbus introduced wheat to the New World on his second trip to the West Indies. Wheat from Spain reached Mexico in 1519 and Argentina by 1527. Spanish

At a grain exchange, traders buy and sell wheat and other crops. The traders include farmers, representatives of grain elevators and flour mills, and exporters.

missionaries later carried wheat with them to the American Southwest. In Canada, French settlers began growing wheat in Nova Scotia in 1605.

English colonists planted wheat at Jamestown, Va., in 1611 and at Plymouth Colony in New England in 1621. But the New England colonists had less luck with wheat than with the corn the Indians gave them. Colonists from the Netherlands and Sweden had more success growing wheat in New York, New Jersey, Delaware, and Pennsylvania.

Wheat farming moved westward with the pioneers. Wheat grew well on the Midwestern prairies, where the climate was too harsh for many other crops. Large shipments of wheat traveled to markets in the East by canal and railroad. By the 1860's, Illinois, Indiana, Iowa, and Ohio had become leading wheat-producing states.

The introduction of winter wheat gave the U.S. wheat industry a major boost. In the 1870's, members of a religious group called the Mennonites immigrated from Russia to Kansas. They brought with them a variety of winter wheat called Turkey Red, which was extremely well suited to the low rainfall on the Great Plains. Turkey Red and varieties that were developed from it soon were planted on nearly all the wheat farms in Kansas and nearby states. Many present-day varieties of wheat grown in the United States can be traced to Turkey Red.

The mechanization of wheat farming. From the beginnings of agriculture until the early 1800's, there was little change in the tools used for wheat farming. For thousands of years, farmers harvested wheat by hand with a sickle or a scythe. The stalks were then tied into bundles and gathered into piles to await threshing. To thresh the grain, livestock trampled the stalks or farmers beat the stalks with a hinged stick called a *flail.* After the grain was loosened from the stalks, the wheat was tossed into the air. The chaff blew away, leaving the kernels behind. This process was called *winnowing.* Much grain spoiled because it took so long to harvest and thresh it.

Machines that were developed in the 1800's made wheat farming far more efficient. The American inventor Cyrus McCormick patented the first successful reaping machine in 1834. By the 1890's, most reapers had an attachment that tied the stalks in bundles. Also in 1834, two brothers from Maine, Hiram and John Pitts, built a threshing machine. The thresher could do in a few hours the work that once took several days. A combined harvester-thresher, or combine, was developed in the 1830's by Hiram Moore and John Haskall of Michigan. However, most farmers continued to use separate reapers and threshers. During the 1920's, a shortage of farm labor coupled with improvements in combines led more farmers to use them.

Until the late 1800's, most farm equipment was powered by farm animals or human labor. During the 1880's, steam engines gradually replaced the animals that pulled most farm machinery in the United States. By the early 1920's, internal-combustion engines were used to power tractors and other farm machines.

Mechanization has greatly reduced the amount of human labor needed to grow wheat. Before 1830, it took a farmer more than 64 hours to prepare the soil, plant the seed, and cut and thresh 1 acre (0.4 hectare) of wheat. Today, it takes less than 3 hours of labor. Mechanization has also enabled farmers to cultivate much larger areas. Using hand tools, a farm family can grow

The Library of Congress

A steam-powered threshing machine, *above,* was used by wheat farmers of the late 1800's and early 1900's. The machine separated the kernels from the stalks and blew the husks from the kernels. Threshers were so expensive that a group of farmers bought and shared one machine.

WORLD BOOK photo by Ted Streshinsky

New varieties of wheat have enabled many countries to increase grain production. American agricultural scientist Norman E. Borlaug, *above in yellow cap,* won the 1970 Nobel Peace Prize for research that led to high-yield wheat varieties.

about 2.5 acres (1 hectare) of wheat. But with modern machinery, the same family can farm about 1,000 acres (405 hectares).

Breeding new varieties of wheat. Some of the most important advances in the history of wheat resulted from the scientific breeding of wheat begun during the 1900's. By developing new varieties of wheat, plant breeders greatly increased the yield of wheat per acre or hectare of land. Some varieties have higher yields because they can resist diseases or pests. Others mature early, enabling the grain to escape such dangers as early frosts and late droughts. Breeders also developed plants with strong stalks that can support a heavy load of grain. Many high-yield varieties require large amounts of fertilizers or pesticides.

During the mid-1900's, agricultural scientists led a worldwide effort to boost grain production in developing countries. This effort was so successful that it has been called the *Green Revolution.* Its success depended primarily on the use of high-yield grains. In 1970, American agricultural scientist Norman E. Borlaug was awarded the Nobel Peace Prize for wheat research that led to the development of these varieties. See **Borlaug, Norman E.**

The Green Revolution reduced the danger of famine in many developing countries. It helped these countries become less dependent upon imported wheat for their growing population. It also helped focus attention on obstacles to increasing the world's food supply. For example, water supplies are often limited and soils are of poor quality. Many farmers cannot afford irrigation systems or the large amounts of fertilizers and pesticides the new grains require. In some developing countries,

grain can be damaged or spoiled by insects, rodents, poor transportation, and poor distribution systems. Finally, in many countries, the population is growing faster than the food supply, offsetting the gains achieved by the Green Revolution.   Lavoy I. Croy

Scientific classification. Wheat belongs to the grass family, Poaceae or Gramineae. It makes up the genus *Triticum.*

Related articles in *World Book* include:

Enemies of wheat

Army worm	Grasshopper	Mosaic disease
Chinch bug	Hessian fly	Rust
Grain weevil	Locust	Smut

Growing and harvesting wheat

Agriculture	Kansas (picture)
Alberta (picture)	McCormick, Cyrus Hall
Combine	North Dakota (picture)
Dry farming	Reaper
Farm and farming	Saskatchewan (picture)
Grain elevator	Threshing machine

Products from wheat

Bran	Food (picture)	Pasta
Bread	Gluten	Starch
Flour		

Other related articles

Borlaug, Norman E.	Grain
Commodity exchange	Grass
Food supply	Triticale

Outline

I. Uses of wheat
  A. Food for people
  B. Livestock feed
  C. Other uses
II. The wheat plant
  A. Structure
  B. Growth and reproduction
III. Kinds of wheat
  A. Winter wheats and spring wheats
  B. Species of wheat
  C. Varieties of wheat
  D. Commercial classes of wheat
IV. How wheat is grown
  A. Climate conditions   D. Planting
  B. Soil conditions   E. Care during growth
  C. Preparing the soil   F. Harvesting
V. Where wheat is grown
  A. Asia
  B. Europe
  C. North America
  D. South America
  E. Australia
VI. Marketing wheat
  A. Transporting and storing wheat
  B. Buying and selling wheat
  C. Controlling wheat production
VII. History

Questions

What part of the wheat kernel is used in making white flour?
Why do some farmers plant wheat in rotation with other crops?
What are *tillers?*
Which three major wheat-farming machines were developed during the 1830's?
What are the three leading wheat-producing countries?
When and where do scientists think people first grew wheat?
What was the *Green Revolution?*
How many kernels does a typical head of wheat have?
What is a *grain exchange?*
How is the development of ancient civilizations linked to the history of wheat?

Wheatley, Phillis (1753?-1784), was the first important black American poet. She was brought to Boston on a slave ship when she was about 8 years old. John Wheatley, a wealthy merchant tailor, bought Phillis as a servant for his wife.

The Wheatleys taught Phillis to read and write. She also studied geography, history, and Latin. She began to write poetry when she was about 14. In 1773, she visited England, where her *Poems on Various Subjects, Religious and Moral* was published that year.

Wheatley was deeply religious. Some of her poems expressed her satisfaction at becoming a Christian in American society. She also wrote about more worldly issues, as in "To the Right Honorable William, Earl of Dartmouth" (1773). In this poem, Wheatley contrasted her status as a slave with the demand of the American Colonies for independence. After returning from England, Wheatley was freed and married John Peters, a free black man. Her reputation as a poet soon declined, and she died virtually unknown.   Jerome Loving

Wheatstone, Sir Charles (1802-1875), was a British physicist and inventor. He became best known for his work in electric telegraphy and on electric measuring devices. These devices include the "Wheatstone bridge," which he did not invent but improved, and the rheostat, which he invented. See **Rheostat; Telegraph** (Development of the telegraph); **Wheatstone bridge.**

Wheatstone experimented on the speed of electricity in wires, and suggested that electricity be used to send messages. With W. F. Cooke, he patented an electric telegraph in 1837, about the same time that Samuel Morse developed his telegraph in the United States. Wheatstone's device was widely used in Great Britain. He also did important research in acoustics and conducted experiments on underwater telegraphy.

Wheatstone was born in Gloucester. He became professor of experimental philosophy at King's College, London, in 1834.   David F. Channell

Wheatstone bridge is a type of electric circuit used to determine an unknown *resistance* (see **Electric cir-**

cuit [Circuit mathematics]). It consists of four resistors whose arrangement is usually represented by the figure of a diamond.

Two of the circuit's resistors have known resistances. They come together at an angle and form the top half of the diamond. In the lower half, a resistor representing an unknown resistance is connected to a variable resistor that can be adjusted to a known resistance. A device called a *galvanometer*, which measures current, is connected to the top and bottom corners of the diamond to bridge the two halves of the circuit. The other corners are connected to a battery, which produces a current through the resistors. The variable resistor is adjusted until the voltage at the top and bottom corners of the circuit are equal. At this point, the galvanometer shows no current flow, and the circuit is said to be *balanced*. The unknown resistance can then be determined by using the following formula:

$$R_x = \left(\frac{R_2}{R_1} \right) R_v$$

The unknown resistance (R_x) is found by multiplying the ratio of the two known resistances (R_1 and R_2) by the variable resistance (R_v).   Robert B. Prigo

Wheel and axle is a mechanical device used in lifting loads. It is one of the *six simple machines* developed in ancient times and ranks as one of the most important inventions in history. The simplest wheel and axle has a cylinder and a large wheel, fastened together and turning on the same axis. The wheel and axle is a first-class lever (see **Lever**). The center of the axle (the cylinder) corresponds to the fulcrum. The radius of the axle corresponds to the load arm. The radius of the wheel corresponds to the force, or effort, arm to which force is applied. Sometimes a crank is used instead of a wheel.

The advantage of a wheel and axle is that it can lift heavy loads with little effort on our part. The following law gives the ratio between the two: *The force applied multiplied by the radius of the wheel equals the load multiplied by the radius of the axle.* To reduce this to a formula, let *F* stand for force; *R* for the radius of the wheel; *L* for the load; and *r* for the radius of the axle.

$$F \times R = L \times r, \text{ or } \frac{L}{F} = \frac{R}{r}$$

The mechanical advantage of a machine is always the ratio of the load (*L*) to the force (*F*) (see **Machine** [Mechanical advantage]). Let us use an example in which the radius of the wheel (*R*) is 10 inches, the radius of the axle (*r*) is 1 inch, and the load (*L*) is 20 pounds. If there were no friction, the formula would be $\frac{20}{F} = \frac{10}{1}$. Since $10F=20$, the force needed would be the same as that normally used to lift a mere 2 pounds. The mechanical advantage, the ratio of *L* to *F*, would be $\frac{20}{2}$, or 10.

Uses of the wheel and axle. In the ordinary windlass used for raising water from a well, a crank replaces the wheel. The hand applies the effort to the crank. The weight of the bucket of water is the load. In a grindstone, the radius of the wheel is usually longer than the crank handle, because speed is needed as well as force. Sometimes teeth or cogs may be placed around the edge of the wheel, as in a cogwheel, or on the sprocket wheel of a bicycle.   W. David Lewis

See also **Ratchet; Windlass; Work.**

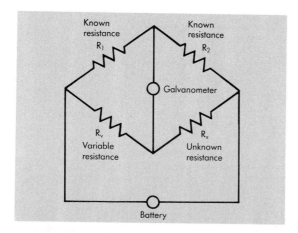

A Wheatstone bridge is an electric circuit used to measure an unknown resistance. A battery produces a flow of current through the circuit, and a variable resistor is adjusted until the galvanometer shows no current flow. The unknown resistance then can be calculated using a mathematical formula.

Wheelbarrow is a device for moving loads. It consists of a tub or box mounted on a wheel with two handles that extend under the body and join on the axle of the wheel. Wheelbarrows may be made of wood, plastic, or metal. They usually have rubber tires.

The wheelbarrow is a second-class lever (see **Lever**). It helps people lift loads with less effort. The longer the handles of the wheelbarrow, the less force required to lift a given load. Robert C. Post

Wheeler, Burton Kendall (1882-1975), a Montana Democrat, served in the United States Senate from 1923 until 1947. In 1924, he ran unsuccessfully for vice president on the Progressive Party ticket (see **Progressive Party**). He helped expose the scandals during the presidential administration of Warren G. Harding. Wheeler was an extreme isolationist before World War II (1939-1945). In 1962, he published his autobiography, *Yankee from the West.* He was born in Hudson, Massachusetts.

David E. Kyvig

Wheeler, Joseph (1836-1906), was an American soldier who served in campaigns against the Indians before he joined the Confederate Army in 1861. During the American Civil War (1861-1865), he served as a cavalry general at the Battle of Shiloh and in campaigns in Tennessee and Georgia. After the war, Wheeler practiced law in Alabama and served several terms as a Democratic U.S. congressman between 1881 and 1900. He commanded U.S. forces during the Spanish-American War of 1898 and in the Philippine Insurrection of 1900.

Wheeler was born near Augusta, Georgia, and graduated from the U.S. Military Academy. A statue of him represents Alabama in Statuary Hall.

Steven E. Woodworth

Wheeler, William Almon (1819-1887), served as vice president of the United States from 1877 to 1881 under President Rutherford B. Hayes. He also served as a Republican from New York in the U.S. House of Representatives from 1861 to 1863 and from 1869 to 1877. As a congressman, he devised the Wheeler Adjustment in 1874 to settle a disputed election in Louisiana.

Wheeler opposed the so-called Salary Grab Act of 1873, by which members of Congress granted themselves and other government officials pay increases. Wheeler refused to profit from the additional income. He bought government bonds, and then had the bonds canceled.

Wheeler was born in Malone, New York. He was a successful lawyer and businessman. James E. Sefton

See also **Vice President of the United States** (picture).

Wheeling (pop. 31,419; met. area pop. 153,172) is an industrial city on the Ohio River in northern West Virginia (see **West Virginia** [political map]). The city has an area of about 11 square miles (28 square kilometers). It includes Wheeling Island in the Ohio River. Wheeling is the seat of Ohio County. The Wheeling metropolitan area includes Belmont County in Ohio.

Wheeling lies on a level plain, which rises to steep hills, along the Ohio River. A scenic plaza was built in the heart of the business district. Two bridges connect Wheeling Island with the rest of the city. Wheeling Downs, which features dog races, occupies one end of the island. Wheeling has two principal parks and several neighborhood parks. Oglebay Park, a 1,400-acre (567-hectare) recreational area, lies outside the city.

Wheeling has about 40 public schools. Other educational institutions include Wheeling Jesuit University; West Virginia Northern Community College; Mount de Chantal Academy for Girls; and Linsly School, a preparatory school. West Liberty State College is nearby.

Wheeling lies near West Virginia's great coal- and natural-gas-producing region, and these minerals furnish power for many of the city's industries. Wheeling's most important products include aluminum, bronze, chemical products, garments, glass, iron and steel, metal stampings, plastics, and tin plate. The city is also a coal shipping center.

Tourism is the most important industry in Wheeling, which attracts visitors with its parks, historic sites, and local events. "Jamboree USA," a weekly country music show at Wheeling's Capitol Music Hall, is broadcast in the United States and Canada. A Winter Festival of Lights is held from early November to early January. Wheeling has two modern hospitals and is a medical center for the surrounding region.

Colonel Ebenezer Zane and his brothers founded Wheeling in the winter of 1769-1770. They came from the south branch of the Potomac Valley in Virginia to settle a claim at the city's present site. Other settlers soon joined them, and in 1774 they erected Fort Fincastle. In 1776, they changed the fort's name to Fort Henry in honor of Patrick Henry. Wheeling was laid out in 1793, incorporated in 1806, and first chartered as a city in 1836. The National Road, now U.S. Highway 40, reached the Ohio River at Wheeling in 1818.

During the American Civil War (1861-1865), Wheeling was the headquarters of Virginians who opposed secession from the Union. Union supporters organized the state of West Virginia in Wheeling on June 20, 1863, and the city served as the state capital from 1863 to 1870 and from 1875 to 1885. Wheeling has a city-manager form of government. Mack H. Gillenwater

Wheelwright, William (1798-1873), an American businessman, did much to develop transportation and communication in South America. In 1823, his ship was wrecked near Buenos Aires, Argentina, and he decided to settle in South America. He was appointed U.S. consul at Guayaquil, Ecuador, in 1824. He later moved to Valparaíso, Chile, and in 1840 set up a steamship line to serve the western coast of South America.

Wheelwright discovered coal and copper deposits in Chile and built one of the first railroads in South America, from the mines to the coast. He built other railroads in Chile and Argentina, and developed the port of La Plata. He also built the continent's first telegraph line. He was born in Newburyport, Massachusetts.

Michael L. Conniff

Whelk is a term for any of dozens of species of sea snail. Whelks include some of the world's largest snails. They grow from 4 to 10 inches (10 to 25 centimeters) in length. Whelks live in coastal waters throughout much of the world.

Like most snails, whelks have a soft body inside a protective spiral shell. The shell has an opening called an *aperture* on one side. Most whelk shells have the aperture on the right side, but some have the opening on the left. A whelk defends itself against enemies by retracting into its shell and closing the aperture with a hard, lidlike plate called the *operculum*. The operculum is attached to a large, muscular organ known as the *foot,* which the whelk uses to crawl about. Some people consider the foot of certain whelk species a delicacy.

Whelks feed on worms, clams, or dead fish. They eat with a tonguelike mouth part called the *radula,* which has several long rows of teeth. Female whelks package their fertilized eggs into capsules that protect the developing snails until they hatch.   Linda S. Eyster

Scientific classification. Whelks belong to several snail families, including Buccinidae and Melongenidae.

See also **Snail.**

Whetstone is any abrasive stone, natural or artificial, that is used for grinding and sharpening. Artificial abrasives, such as silicon carbide and aluminum oxide, are most often used. At one time a fine-grained variety of quartz, called *novaculite,* was used for grindstones. Its uniform hard grains made it capable of grinding quickly and withstanding wear.   Mihir K. Das

Whig Party was a name applied to political parties in England, Scotland, and America. *Whig* is a short form of the word *whiggamore,* a Scotch word once used to describe people from western Scotland who opposed King Charles I of England in 1648.

In the late 1600's, Scottish and English opponents of the growing power of royalty were called Whigs. The Whigs maintained a strong position in English politics until the 1850's, when the Whig progressives adopted the term Liberal. See **United Kingdom** (History).

In the American Colonies, the Whigs were those people who resented British control and favored independence from Britain. The term was probably first used in New York City about 1768. The Whigs supported the Revolutionary War in America. British loyalists, called *Tories,* opposed the Whigs in the struggle (see **Tory Party**). The terms *Whig* and *Tory* fell into disuse after the colonies won their independence.

The Whig Party of the 1800's began to take shape about 1832. Political groups that opposed Andrew Jackson and his theories started to combine and unify themselves into a political party. These groups included the National Republicans, certain conservative factions of the Democratic-Republican Party, and some former members of the Anti-Masonic Party. Some of the political leaders of the Whig Party included such well-known National Republicans as Henry Clay, Daniel Webster, and John Quincy Adams. Soon many wealthy Southern cotton planters joined in protest against the democratic, leveling doctrines of the Jacksonians. In the north and east, many factory owners also joined the group because it supported a protective tariff. First as the National Republicans and later under the name of Whigs, these groups advocated new and broader activities for both state and national governments.

The first program of the Whigs followed Henry Clay's "American System." It included a proposal for a high protective tariff to encourage the growth of American industry. Clay wanted to distribute to the states money received from the sale of federal lands, so that they would construct new transportation systems of canals and highways. Clay argued that Western and Southern farmers and Eastern manufacturers formed a natural and interdependent economic unit that would furnish markets for each other, if they were connected with good transportation facilities.

When Jackson and his followers came out against the United States Bank, Clay immediately supported it. The Whigs soon adopted an advanced financial program calling for federal control of the banking system in the interest of sound currency. They also wanted to ensure a supply of credit adequate to meet the increasing demands from expanding commercial interests in the East and from the moving frontier in the West. Clay opposed Jackson with this program in the presidential election of 1832, but Clay was defeated. In 1836, the Whig Party nominated William Henry Harrison, Hugh White, and Daniel Webster for the presidency. But the Democratic candidate, Martin Van Buren, won easily.

In the 1840's, many able leaders joined the party. They included Horace Greeley, editor of the New York *Tribune;* William H. Seward of New York; and Edward Everett, the Whigs' most brilliant orator.

The Whigs nominated William Harrison as their presidential candidate in 1840. He won the election but died after serving only one month in office. Vice President John Tyler followed Harrison as president. Tyler had received the nomination for vice president mainly to attract the Southern votes. Actually, Tyler was not a Whig, and he opposed the Whig program. His opposition as president weakened the Whig strength.

In 1844, the Whigs renominated Henry Clay for the presidency, but he lost again. One reason for his defeat lay in his refusal to take a position on slavery. This cost Clay many Northern Whig votes. In the election of 1844, the Whigs for the first time presented a real political program. The program included a high tariff, regulated currency, and a single term for the presidency.

Decline of the Whigs. The Whigs managed to win the presidency with the popular Zachary Taylor in 1848. Four years later they tried to repeat the victory with General Winfield Scott. But the Democratic candidate, Franklin Pierce, defeated him. In 1856, a Whig convention backed Millard Fillmore, the unsuccessful Know-Nothing candidate for the presidency.

The Whig Party had already begun to break into sectional groups over the question of slavery. The Kansas-Nebraska Bill of 1854 split the party still further. Most Northern Whigs joined the new Republican Party. Many Southern Whigs returned to the Democratic Party. The remaining Whigs joined the Constitutional Union Party by 1860.   Donald R. McCoy

See also the separate articles for the various Whig leaders mentioned in this article, such as **Clay, Henry.**

Whiplash is a term commonly used to describe a type of injury to the neck. This kind of injury results from a sudden blow that throws the head rapidly backward and forward. Such a blow can damage the muscles and ligaments that hold the bones in the neck. A whiplash injury typically causes pain and stiffness in the neck, and often in the shoulders. It frequently produces severe headaches. Most whiplash injuries occur in car accidents. Raised headrests and the use of safety belts greatly reduce the chance of such injuries.

In many cases of whiplash, the victim does not experience pain until several hours after the injury occurs. The pain generally is most severe during the next several days. Wearing a padded collar to stabilize the neck, use of heat and massage, and taking mild pain medicines can help reduce the discomfort. Emotional upset due to

WORLD BOOK illustration by David Cunningham

Whiplash most often occurs as the result of a car accident. When the car is struck from the front or the rear, the sudden force throws the head rapidly backward and forward.

whiplash injury can make the condition worse, so doctors often reassure victims that the pain will diminish.

In most cases of whiplash injury, X rays do not show damage to the muscles and ligaments of the neck. As a result, it is difficult to determine the exact cause of the pain and the amount of disability that the injury produces.   Richard D. Penn

Whippet is a medium-sized hound with great speed. The whippet's lean, muscular form gives it the appearance of a small greyhound. A whippet weighs from 18 to 23 pounds (8 to 10 kilograms) and stands $17\frac{1}{2}$ to $22\frac{1}{2}$ inches (44 to 57 centimeters) high. Whippets have a short coat that may be any color or combination of colors. The dogs have a long, lean head, arched muscular back, and a long, tapering tail.

Whippets are popular dogs for hunting rabbits and for racing. The dogs are able to run as fast as 35 miles (56 kilometers) per hour.

Critically reviewed by the American Whippet Club

See also **Dog** (picture: Hounds).

Whipping post is a post to which persons are tied when being whipped as a form of punishment. Such beatings once took place in public. Most villages in England and the American Colonies had whipping posts in their public squares. The posts were often set up with another device called the *stocks* (see **Stocks**).

Today, few persons are sentenced to be whipped. Fines and prison terms have replaced physical beating as forms of punishment in most countries. British law allowed whipping until 1948, and Canada abolished the whipping penalty in 1972. Delaware, the last state of the United States that allowed physical beating, prohibited the punishment in 1972. Whipping is still a legal punishment in some countries, including Singapore and such Muslim nations as Iran, Pakistan, and Saudi Arabia.

Marvin E. Wolfgang

Whipple, William (1730-1785), was a New Hampshire signer of the Declaration of Independence. He served as a delegate to the provincial congress of New Hampshire in 1775 and to the Continental Congress from 1776 to 1779. He fought as a brigadier general in the Revolution-

ary War in America (1775-1783). Whipple served in the state assembly from 1780 to 1784 and as financial receiver for New Hampshire from 1782 to 1784. He was a justice of the Supreme Court of New Hampshire from 1782 until his death. Whipple was born on Jan. 14, 1730, in Kittery, Maine. He was a sea captain and successful merchant.   Gary D. Hermalyn

Whippoorwill is a North American bird named for its odd, whistling call, which sounds like "whip-poor-will, whip-poor-will." The whippoorwill lives in the eastern, central, and southern parts of the United States. It also is found as far north as southeastern Canada and as far south as Mexico and Honduras. The whippoorwill spends the winter along the Gulf Coast, in Mexico, and in Central America.

Ron Willocks, Animals Animals

A whippoorwill has spotted brown feathers that blend with its woodland habitat and help protect the bird from enemies.

The whippoorwill is about 10 inches (25 centimeters) long. Its spotted, brown feathers make the bird hard to see in the heavily wooded areas in which it lives. During the day, the whippoorwill usually rests on the ground or perches lengthwise on a log. It flies mostly at night. The bird uses its wide mouth rimmed with long bristles to catch flying insects. The female whippoorwill lays her two eggs among the leaves on the ground. The whippoorwill and its relatives, the *chuck-will's widow* and the *poorwill,* often help farmers. These birds eat insects, including those that harm crops.   Bertin W. Anderson

Scientific classification. The whippoorwill belongs to the goatsucker family, Caprimulgidae. It is *Caprimulgus vociferus.*

See also **Bird** (picture: Birds' eggs).

Whirligig. See Water beetle.

Whirlpool is a mass of water which spins around and around rapidly and with great force. A whirlpool may form in water for several reasons. It may occur when the water current strikes against a bank which has a peculiar form. It may also occur when opposing currents meet, and it may be caused by the action of the wind. Rocks or tides may get in the way of an ocean current. Whirlpools often form as a result.

There are several well-known whirlpools. One is the whirlpool in the gorge below Niagara Falls. This whirlpool was caused by the wearing away of a side basin out of the line of the river's course. The Maelstrom, which is off the coast of Norway, is formed by rocks and tides that oppose the current. The Charybdis, between

Sicily and Italy, is formed by winds, which act against the tidal currents. During storms the whirlpools become violent and dangerous to ships.   Mark A. Cane

See also **Maelstrom; Niagara River** (Description).

Whirlwind is a whirling mass of air. Whirlwinds include cyclones, dust devils, hurricanes, tornadoes, typhoons, and waterspouts. For more information about these types of whirlwinds, see the separate articles on each of them in *World Book.*

Whiskey is an alcoholic beverage made from such grains as barley, corn, rye, and wheat. It is one of the leading alcoholic beverages in the United States.

Whiskey is made by a process called *distilling.* Distillers first grind the grains and cook them in water, forming a mash. This process changes the starch in the grain to sugar. Next, yeast is added and the mixture *ferments.* Fermentation changes the sugar to ethyl alcohol. The mash then is heated, giving off alcohol vapors. Distillers collect the vapors and cool them. The cooling vapors liquefy as whiskey.

Whiskey ages about 2 to 12 years in wooden barrels, where it develops flavor and an amber color. Before distillers bottle the whiskey, they add distilled water, diluting most beverages to between 80 and 100 *proof.* Proof signifies the percentage of alcohol in a beverage. In the United States, proof equals twice the amount of alcohol. Thus a beverage that is 100 proof is 50 percent alcohol.

Whiskeys differ according to the grain used, the proof of the beverage, and the aging conditions. The most common whiskeys made in the United States are *blended whiskey, bourbon, Tennessee whiskey,* and *rye.* Rye is made from a mash of mostly rye grains. Bourbon is made from a mash of mostly corn. Tennessee whiskey is similar to bourbon but is filtered through charcoal before aging. Blended whiskey is at least 20 percent *straight whiskey,* blended with other whiskeys or with pure ethyl alcohol and water. Straight whiskeys include bourbon and rye that have been stored at no more than 125 proof in charred new oak barrels for at least two years.

Imported whiskeys include *Canadian whisky, Irish whiskey,* and *Scotch whisky.* Canadian whisky is a blend made from corn, rye, wheat, and barley malt. Irish whiskey and Scotch whisky are made mostly from barley. Scotch whisky, also called *Scotch,* tastes smoky because it is made from malt that has been dried over peat fires.

F. A. Meister

See also **Alcoholic beverage; Distilling.**

Whiskey Rebellion of 1794 was brought about by a United States tax in 1791 on whiskey makers. The rebellion tested the use of federal power to enforce a federal law within a state. Farmers in western Pennsylvania led the uprising. They and farmers in other frontier regions found it profitable to turn much of their corn and rye crop into whiskey. They could ship whiskey to markets more profitably than they could bulky grain, because frontier transportation facilities were poor.

The federal tax law permitted government agents to enter homes and collect from small whiskey producers. Frontier farmers assembled quickly to protest the law and threatened tax inspectors. Congressional amendments soon removed the tax from the smallest stills. This change satisfied many farmers in Virginia and North Carolina. However, whiskey makers in Pennsylvania con-

tinued to refuse to pay the federal whiskey tax.

In the summer of 1794, the federal government ordered the arrest of the Pennsylvania ringleaders and their removal to Philadelphia. Rebel farmers in western Pennsylvania prevented the arrests. The rebels exchanged gunfire with government representatives, burned property of tax inspectors, and marched on Pittsburgh. Several people were killed and wounded before President George Washington raised an army of nearly 13,000 soldiers who put down the rebellion. Two rebels were convicted of treason, but they were later pardoned.   Edward K. Muller

See also **Washington, George** (Whiskey Rebellion).

Whiskey Ring was a group of whiskey distillers and United States government officials who cheated the government out of millions of dollars in federal liquor taxes during the 1870's. Secretary of the Treasury Benjamin H. Bristow exposed the conspiracy in 1875. The Whiskey Ring became the most notorious and extensive of a number of scandals that plagued the presidency of Ulysses S. Grant.

The Whiskey Ring began in St. Louis, Mo. Grant had appointed a long-time acquaintance, General John D. McDonald, as collector of internal revenue in the district that included St. Louis. McDonald accepted bribes from distillers to excuse them from paying the federal tax on whiskey. Tax collectors in Chicago, Milwaukee, and other cities also took payoffs from distillers. The ring even involved Grant's trusted adviser Orville E. Babcock and other important government officials. The President, however, seemed never to realize the seriousness and extent of the frauds.

The trials of the conspirators demanded much of Grant's attention during his last two years in office and resulted in many convictions. The ringleaders received only mild punishment, however. Babcock, Grant's private secretary, was acquitted after the President went to great lengths to protect him.   Michael Perman

Whistle is a device that makes a sound when air or steam is forced through it. Most whistles consist of a tube that has a hole in its side with a lip or a sharp edge on it. The air or steam that is blown in one end of the tube goes into a swirling motion when it strikes the lip. This motion first compresses and then expands the air, causing a sound.

Steam whistles are seldom used today. Steam locomotives once used them. But today's diesel locomotives use various types of air horns, some of which sound like steam whistles. Police officers and sports officials blow small air whistles.   Carol E. Stokes

Whistler, James Abbott McNeill (1834-1903), was a famous American artist. He spent most of his life in Europe. Whistler's paintings, flamboyant manner, clever wit, and quarrelsome nature made him an international celebrity. His best-known painting is *Arrangement in Gray and Black No. 1: Portrait of the Artist's Mother* (1872), commonly called *Whistler's Mother.* Its flattened forms, *monochrome* (single-color) tone, and unsymmetrical composition are characteristic of Whistler's style. He was influenced by Japanese artists who used similar techniques in woodcuts.

Whistler named many of his paintings for types of musical compositions, such as nocturnes and symphonies. He believed paintings, like music, should be ab-

Whistler's Mother ranks among the world's most famous portraits. The formal name of the painting is *Arrangement in Gray and Black No. 1: Portrait of the Artist's Mother*. Whistler painted the picture in London in 1872. He posed his mother against a gray wall. The small painting on the wall and the curtain enhance the harmony of the composition.

Orsay Museum, Paris (Art Resource)

stract. They should not describe objects or tell stories, but respond to the imagination of the artist. Whistler also felt forms in a painting are more important than the subject.

The British art critic John Ruskin criticized one of Whistler's most abstract paintings, *Nocturne In Black and Gold—The Falling Rocket* (about 1874). Ruskin declared that Whistler had flung "a pot of paint in the public's face."
Whistler sued Ruskin for libel and defended his theories on art in court. He won the case but got less than a penny in damages. The cost of the lawsuit forced him into bankruptcy. But it gave desirable publicity to his belief that art should be created for its own sake rather than for a moral purpose. Whistler included excerpts from his defense in a book of his collected writings, *The Gentle Art of Making Enemies* (1890).

In addition to his paintings, Whistler became well known for his prints and interior decorations. Whistler created approximately 440 etchings, including many illustrations of Venice and the River Thames. The most famous example of Whistler's interior decoration is the Peacock Room, which he designed for a house in London. The room is now in the Freer Gallery in Washington, D.C.

Self-portrait (1859), a dry point engraving, Art Institute of Chicago, Clarence Buckingham Collection

James A. M. Whistler

Whistler was born in Lowell, Massachusetts. In 1843, he moved with his family to St. Petersburg, Russia, where his father directed construction of a railroad. He returned to the United States in 1849. In 1851, Whistler entered the U.S. Military Academy at West Point. He was expelled in 1854 for academic reasons. He then worked for a few months as a chartmaker for the U.S. Coast and Geodetic Survey, where he received fine training in the technique of etching. In 1855, Whistler went to Paris to study art. He moved to London in 1859 and spent most of the rest of his life there.   Alison McNeil Kettering

See also **Impressionism** (American impressionism); **Ruskin, John.**

White. See Color.

White, Alfred Holmes (1873-1953), pioneered in the development of engineering as a profession in the United States. He spent most of his career at the University of Michigan, where he organized one of the first chemical engineering programs in the United States. White also wrote several early textbooks for the field. His work with the American Institute of Chemical Engineers and other organizations helped set formal standards for American engineering education. White was born on April 29, 1873, in Peoria, Illinois.   Terry S. Reynolds

White, Bill (1934-   ), served as president of the National Baseball League from 1989 to 1994. In that position, White was the highest-ranking African American executive of a major U.S. professional sports league.

White played in the National League for 13 seasons, beginning with the New York (now San Francisco) Giants in 1956. He spent most of his playing career as a first baseman for the St. Louis Cardinals, retiring in 1969 with a lifetime batting average of .286. In 1971, White became a broadcaster of New York Yankees games, a job he held until he was named National League president. William DeKova White was born on Jan. 28, 1934, in Lakewood, Florida. Donald Honig

White, Byron Raymond (1917-2002), was an associate justice of the Supreme Court of the United States from 1962 to 1993. President John F. Kennedy appointed him to succeed Justice Charles E. Whittaker, who had retired. White was deputy attorney general at the time of his appointment.

White sided with liberals in supporting school desegregation and *affirmative action* (see **Affirmative action**). However, he took conservative positions on a number of other issues. For example, White opposed court decisions that strengthened safeguards designed to assure that people accused of a crime are treated fairly. He also objected to the belief that the U.S. Constitution guarantees individuals a right to privacy. Thus, White opposed decisions that declared certain state laws against abortion invalid. He also wrote a majority opinion upholding a state law that made homosexual acts a crime.

White was born on June 8, 1917, in Fort Collins, Colorado. He graduated from the University of Colorado and from Yale Law School. He won national fame and the nickname "Whizzer" as an all-American halfback at Colorado. He played professional football to help finance his law studies. After completing law school, White served as a law clerk to Chief Justice Fred M. Vinson. He joined a Denver law firm in 1947 and became a partner in 1950. White was appointed deputy attorney general in 1961. He died on April 15, 2002. Owen M. Fiss

White, E. B. (1899-1985), was an American author. He was known chiefly as an essay writer, but he also wrote poetry and children's books. His essays, which deal with both serious and light subjects, have a clear, witty style. White wrote in an informal, personal manner.

White wrote three children's books. *Stuart Little* (1945), *Charlotte's Web* (1952), and *The Trumpet of the Swan* (1970). In these books, which deal with friendship and love, the animals talk and act like people (see **Literature for children** [picture: *Charlotte's Web*]). Collections of White's writings include *Letters of E. B. White* (1976), *Essays of E. B. White* (1977), and *Poems and Sketches of E. B. White* (1981). White wrote about such topics as baseball, farming, marriage. and his life in Maine.

Elwyn Brooks White was born on July 11, 1899, in Mount Vernon, New York. He started writing for *The New Yorker* magazine in 1925 and strongly influenced its literary style. White's collection *Writings from The New Yorker, 1925-1976* was published in 1990. He won a Pulitzer Prize special citation in 1978 for his writings.
Marcus Klein

White, Edward Douglass (1845-1921), served as chief justice of the United States from 1910 to 1921. In 1894, he was appointed an associate justice of the Supreme Court of the United States. White became best known for his dissent in the case declaring the national income tax unconstitutional, and for his antitrust decisions requiring the dissolution of the Standard Oil and American Tobacco companies.

White was born on Nov. 3, 1845, in Lafourche Parish, Louisiana. A statue of him represents Louisiana in the U.S. Capitol. Jerre S. Williams

White, Edward Higgins, II (1930-1967), in 1965 became the first United States astronaut to leave his craft while in outer space. The spacewalk lasted 21 minutes and took place on June 3, 1965, during a four-day flight made by White and James A. McDivitt. White and astronauts Virgil Grissom and Roger Chaffee died on Jan. 27, 1967, when a flash fire swept through their Apollo spacecraft. The fire occurred during a test at Cape Kennedy (now Cape Canaveral), Florida.

White was born on Nov. 14, 1930, in San Antonio. He graduated from the U.S. Military Academy in 1952 and went into the Air Force. In 1959, he earned a master's degree in aeronautical engineering from the University of Michigan. Lillian D. Kozloski

See also **Space exploration** (picture: The first U.S. astronaut to walk in space).

White, Hugh Lawson (1773-1840), an American statesman and jurist, was a Whig Party candidate for president of the United States in 1836. In that year, Vice President Martin Van Buren ran as President Andrew Jackson's hand-picked successor on the Democratic ticket. The Whigs ran three presidential candidates—Senator Daniel Webster; former Senator William Henry Harrison; and White, who had been a senator since 1825. White won in only two states, Georgia and Tennessee. Van Buren won the presidency.

White was born on Oct. 30, 1773, in Iredell County, North Carolina. He moved to Tennessee, where he became a judge, state senator, and U.S. district attorney. He was a U.S. senator from 1825 to 1840. James C. Curtis

White, John. See Lost Colony.

White, Patrick (1912-1990), an Australian novelist, won the 1973 Nobel Prize for literature. He became the first Australian writer to receive this high award. White wrote emotionally complex and stylistically rich fiction. He often used the *stream of consciousness* technique, which describes in detail the thoughts of the characters.

The major characters in White's novels tend to be isolated from those around them and draw, for the most part, on their own inner resources. He gained world recognition with his fourth novel, *The Tree of Man* (1955), which focuses on an Australian family. *Voss* (1957) describes an explorer's expedition across Australia in the mid-1800's. White's other novels include *Riders in the Chariot* (1961), *The Eye of the Storm* (1973), and *A Fringe of Leaves* (1977). White wrote an autobiography, *Flaws in the Glass* (1982). He also wrote plays, poetry, and stories. Patrick Victor Martindale White was born on May 28, 1912, in London, England. Michael Seidel

White, Peregrine (1620-1703), was the first English child born in New England, on the *Mayflower* in Cape Cod Bay on Dec. 17, 1620. His father, William, died soon afterward. His mother, Susanna, then married Edward Winslow, becoming both the first mother and the first bride in Plymouth. Peregrine White became a captain of militia and settled in nearby Marshfield. James Axtell

White, Stanford (1853-1906), was a leading American architect. He was a partner in McKim, Mead, and White, a famous American architectural firm of the late 1800's and early 1900's. White helped found the firm in 1879 with Charles Follen McKim and William Rutherford Mead. White's works were especially noted for their ornamentation and rich texture.

White designed country houses, churches, housing

projects, and office buildings. He collaborated with the American sculptor Augustus Saint-Gaudens on a number of monuments. White's designs include the Tiffany Building (1906), the Washington Arch (1889-1895), the Judson Memorial Church (1891), and the campus of what is now the Bronx Community College of the City University of New York (1892-1901). All these projects were built in New York City.

White was born in New York City. He began his career as an assistant to the American architect Henry Hobson Richardson. White was shot to death by Harry K. Thaw, the jealous husband of Evelyn Nesbit, one of White's friends. White's murder and Thaw's trial created a sensation in the United States.   Leland M. Roth

White, Walter Francis (1893-1955), was an American civil rights leader. White served as secretary of the National Association for the Advancement of Colored People (NAACP) from 1931 until his death. He fought to eliminate the lynching of blacks during the 1920's and 1930's. White's book *Rope and Faggot* (1929) was a powerful attack on lynching. White received the Spingarn Medal in 1937 for promoting the rights of blacks.

White was born on July 1, 1893, in Atlanta. He described his struggles against racial prejudice in his autobiography, *A Man Called White* (1948). White also wrote two novels that dealt with race relations, *Fire in the Flint* (1924) and *Flight* (1926).   Edwin H. Cady

White, William Allen (1868-1944), was a Kansas newspaper editor whose influence was felt throughout the United States. Major newspapers reprinted editorials that he published in his small-town newspaper, the *Emporia* (Kansas) *Gazette*. White won the Pulitzer Prize for editorial writing in 1923. His autobiography won a Pulitzer Prize in 1947.

White was born on Feb. 10, 1868, in Emporia. He studied at Emporia College and the University of Kansas, but left to become a journalist. He bought the *Gazette* in 1895. In 1896, White wrote an editorial, "What's the Matter with Kansas?" criticizing the Populist movement, which had widespread support in Kansas. The article made White famous, and he became the voice of Republicans in the Midwest.

By 1901, White had become a supporter of Theodore Roosevelt and a Progressive (see **Progressive Era**). White's editorials then favored election reform, the investigation of oil and railroad monopolies, and other Progressive causes. In 1940, he worked for American support of the nations fighting Germany.

Lee B. Jolliffe

White blood cell. See Blood.

White dwarf is a kind of star that has run out of fuel. A typical white dwarf has about 60 percent as much *mass* (amount of matter) as a medium-sized star, such as the sun, but is no larger than a small planet, such as the earth. Thus, its density is about 18 tons per cubic inch (1 metric ton per cubic centimeter). A white dwarf is the last stage in the life of most stars—those that have no more than about eight times the mass of the sun. The sun itself will eventually become a white dwarf.

A white dwarf is not actually white. Its color depends on its temperature. The hottest white dwarfs are violet, and the coolest are a deep red. A white dwarf sends out only about $\frac{1}{1,000}$ as much light as the sun. As a result, no white dwarf is visible to the unaided eye.

During most of a star's early lifetime, it produces energy by means of *nuclear fusion,* a joining of two atomic nuclei to produce a single nucleus. Fusion takes place in the star's core and occurs in several steps, some of which release energy. The main fusion fuels are hydrogen and helium nuclei. When most of the fuel has fused, the star swells to many times its original size, becoming a *red giant.* Later, it throws off its outer layers, leaving only the core—the white dwarf. The white dwarf then cools and changes color. After billions of years, it stops glowing, ending its life as a *black dwarf.*   Paul J. Green

See also **Star** (Intermediate-mass stars; Binary stars).

White-eye is the name of a group of small, active songbirds found mainly in Africa, southern Asia, Australia, and New Zealand. The birds get their name from the circle of bright white feathers that surround the eyes of most species in the group. Their other feathers are dull

WORLD BOOK illustration by John Dawson

Indian white-eyes live in southern Asia. Like most species of white-eyes, they have white feathers around the eyes. White-eyes huddle close together on branches when resting.

shades of green, yellow, gray, and tan. White-eyes average from 4 to $5\frac{1}{2}$ inches (10 to 14 centimeters) in length and have long, thin bills.

There are about 85 species of white-eyes. They live in open, shrubby, and sparsely wooded areas. These birds are usually found in flocks. The flocks continually move from tree to tree, feeding on insects, berries, fruits, and flower nectar. White-eyes seem to enjoy touching each other. They huddle close together on branches when resting, and members of the flock will often *preen* (groom) each other with their bills.

White-eyes build cuplike nests of tightly woven plant fibers, usually in the forks of branches. The female lays from 2 to 4 eggs, which normally hatch in 11 to 13 days. Often, several adult white-eyes feed the young.

For small birds, white-eyes have been exceptionally successful at reaching oceanic islands and establishing themselves there. Most of the islands in the Indian Ocean have at least one species of white-eye. Although white-eyes are useful to people because they eat insect pests, they also can be a nuisance because they destroy fruit crops.   David M. Niles

Scientific classification. White-eyes make up the white-eye family, Zosteropidae.

White heart. See Dutchman's-breeches.

Karen A. McCormack

The north portico of the White House faces Pennsylvania Avenue in Washington, D.C.

White House is the official residence of the president of the United States. The president lives and works in the world-famous mansion in Washington, D.C. The White House contains the living quarters for the Chief Executive's family and the offices in which the president and staff members conduct official business of the United States. Some of the most important decisions in history have been made there.

The White House contains 132 rooms. It stands in the middle of a beautifully landscaped 18-acre (7.3-hectare) plot at 1600 Pennsylvania Avenue (see **Washington, D.C.** [map]). The building was popularly known as the *White House* during the 1800's. However, the official name of the building was first the *President's House* and then the *Executive Mansion* until 1901. That year, President Theodore Roosevelt authorized *White House* as the official title.

The White House is a popular tourist attraction, and millions of people have enjoyed tours of the parts of the mansion open to the public. Tickets for tours are available through members of Congress.

Outside the White House

The main building is 175 feet (53 meters) long and 85 feet (26 meters) high. A wide curved *portico* (porch) with Ionic columns two stories high stands on the south side of the mansion. A square portico on the north side of the mansion is the main entrance. Two long, low galleries extend from the building's east and west sides. The terraced roof covering them forms a promenade on the first floor. Facilities for the White House press

corps are under the west terrace. A theater is under the east terrace.

The east and west wings stand at the end of the terraces. The west (executive) wing contains the president's office, an oval-shaped room called the Oval Office. It also contains the offices of the presidential staff and the Cabinet room. The east wing includes the offices of the president's military aides.

The south lawn contains many trees and shrubs planted by former occupants of the White House. For example, the south portico is shaded by magnificent magnolia trees which were planted by President Andrew Jackson.

Inside the White House

Public rooms. Tourists enter the White House through the east wing. Most visitors are shown only five rooms on the first floor of the mansion. However these rooms represent the elegance and beauty of the entire interior.

The State Dining Room at the west end of the main building can accommodate as many as 140 dinner guests at one time. It was remodeled in 1902.

The Red Room is furnished in the style of the period from 1810 to 1830. The walls are hung with red silk.

The Blue Room is the main reception room for guests of the president. The furnishings of the room represent the period between 1817 and 1825. President James Monroe, who occupied the White House during these years, ordered much of the furniture now in this oval room.

Drawing by Robert W. Nicholson, National Geographic Society;
copyrighted by the White House Historical Association

These models show the back of the White House and the main rooms of the building's interior.

Ground floor
1. Library
2. Ground Floor Corridor*
3. Vermeil Room
4. China Room

5. Diplomatic Reception Room
6. Map Room

First floor
7. East Room*

8. Green Room*
9. Blue Room*
10. South Portico
11. Red Room*
12. State Dining Room*

13. Family Dining Room
14. Cross Hall*
15. Entrance Hall*

*Open to the public

Lorenzo S. Winslow, Architect

This model shows the original main building and the two wings added later.

1. East wing
2. Movie theater for family

3. Main building
4. White House press facilities

5. President's office
6. Executive wing

Inside the
White House

The Diplomatic Reception Room, *above,* serves as the entrance to the White House for official functions. The wallpaper in this oval room was printed in France in 1834.

The Red Room, *above,* is furnished in the American Empire style, popular between 1810 and 1830. The walls are hung with red silk edged with gold trim. The Red Room serves as a parlor.

All photographs by the National Geographic Society, ©The White House Historical Association

The State Dining Room, *left,* is the scene of the President's official banquets. Its tables can accommodate 140 guests for a state dinner.

The Blue Room, *above,* is an oval drawing room. It serves as the main reception room for guests of the President. President James Monroe ordered many of the furnishings in the room.

The Green Room, *above,* is decorated in the style popular between 1800 and 1814. A light green silk material covers the walls. The Green Room, like the Red Room, is a parlor.

The library, *left,* is decorated chiefly in the style of the early 1800's. The crystal chandelier once belonged to the family of American novelist James Fenimore Cooper. The carpet was made in the mid-1800's in Tabriz, Iran.

The Green Room has been restored in the style of the years between 1800 and 1814. Its walls are covered with a light green silk moire. Its furniture is in the style of Duncan Phyfe, a noted American furniture maker of the late 1700's and early 1800's.

The East Room is the largest room in the White House, 79 feet (24 meters) long and $36\frac{3}{4}$ feet (11.2 meters) wide. Guests are entertained in the East Room after formal dinners. It is at the end of the first floor. The East Room was remodeled in 1902.

Private rooms. The president, the president's family, their guests, and the President's staff use many other rooms in the White House every day. The ground floor contains the Diplomatic Reception Room, used as the entrance for formal functions; the kitchen; the library; and offices of the White House physician and curator.

The second floor contains the living quarters of the president and the president's family. The Lincoln Bedroom, the Treaty Room, and the Queen's Room are also on that floor. The third floor contains guest rooms and staff quarters. The White House also has a private bowling alley, swimming pool, and movie theater.

History of the White House

The original building was begun in 1792. It was designed by James Hoban, an Irish-born architect. Hoban's design was selected in a competition sponsored by the federal government. It showed a simple Georgian mansion in the classical Palladian style of Europe in the 1700's. He modeled the design after Leinster House, the meeting place of the Irish Parliament, in Dublin, Ireland.

1807

1814

The White House changed appearance several times during the 1800's. It was almost completely rebuilt following a fire in 1814. The photograph of the White House about 1860 was taken by Mathew Brady, the famous Civil War photographer. It may be the first photograph of the White House.

From the book *The White House* by Amy La Follette Jensen, published by McGraw-Hill Book Co., Inc.; Brady-Handy Collection

1848

1860

President and Mrs. John Adams became the first occupants of the White House in 1800. But work on the White House had not yet been completed, and they suffered many inconveniences. Mrs. Adams used the East Room to dry the family laundry.

The White House became more comfortable and beautiful during the administration of Thomas Jefferson. With the aid of architect Benjamin H. Latrobe, Jefferson carried out many of the original White House plans, and added terraces at the east and west ends.

A new building. British forces burned the mansion on Aug. 24, 1814, during the War of 1812. President James Madison and his wife, Dolley, were forced to flee. The White House was rebuilt and President and Mrs. James Monroe moved into it in 1817. The north and south porticos were added in the 1820's.

President Theodore Roosevelt had the building repaired in 1902. He rebuilt the east terrace and added the executive wing adjacent to the west terrace.

President Franklin D. Roosevelt enlarged the west wing. An indoor swimming pool was added there. The east wing was also expanded.

Rebuilding and redecorating. The White House underwent extensive repairs from 1948 to 1952, during the presidency of Harry S. Truman. Workers used concrete and steel to strengthen the dangerously weakened structure of the Executive Mansion. The third floor was converted into a full third story, and a second-story balcony was added to the south portico for the president's private use. The basement was expanded, and the total number of rooms was increased from 125 to 132.

But the historic rooms familiar to the American public remained basically unchanged until the administration of John F. Kennedy. In 1961, Mrs. Kennedy appointed a Fine Arts Committee to restore the White House interior to its original appearance. The White House Historical Association was chartered in 1961 to publish guide books on the mansion and to acquire historic furnishings for the White House. A library committee was formed to stock the White House library with books representing American thought throughout the country's history.

More major changes in the building's historic rooms occurred during the administration of Richard M. Nixon. Beginning in 1970, Mrs. Nixon continued Mrs. Kennedy's efforts to restore the White House interior in an early 1800's *motif* (theme).   Clement Ellis Conger

Related articles. See the section on Life in the White House in articles on the presidents. Other related articles in *World Book* include:

First ladies
President of the United States (The life of the president; pictures)
Secret Service, United States
White House hostesses

Additional resources

Clinton, Hillary Rodham. *An Invitation to the White House.* Simon & Schuster, 2000.
Monkman, Betty C. *The White House.* Abbeville, 2000.
Patterson, Bradley H., Jr. *The White House Staff.* Brookings, 2000.
Seale, William, ed. *The White House.* Northeastern Univ. Pr., 2002.
Whitcomb, John and Claire. *Real Life at the White House.* Routledge, 2000.

White House conference is a national meeting that the president of the United States calls to talk about issues facing the American people. Community leaders, concerned citizens, and various experts attend the conferences, which may last three or four days, to discuss the topics and recommend action. White House conferences have dealt with such issues as child care, drug abuse, the economy, education, family life, and nutrition. Other topics have included aging, civil rights, disabled people, highway safety, and libraries. Each conference reports to the president, and the president usually speaks at a major session of the conference.

In organizing most White House conferences, the president appoints a governing committee and an executive director, who heads the conference staff and directs the selection of delegates. The president will sometimes request that governors call state conferences on a particular issue before a large national conference is held. Recommendations from state conferences are forwarded to the national meeting.

There have been more than 60 White House conferences, most of which have been held since 1945. President Theodore Roosevelt called the first conference in 1908 to discuss conservation of natural resources. The next year, Roosevelt authorized the Conference on Dependent Children. This conference of 216 delegates led to the formation in 1912 of the Children's Bureau, now part of the Department of Health and Human Services.

Some topics have become the subject of repeated and expanded conferences. Besides Roosevelt, Presidents Woodrow Wilson, Herbert Hoover, Franklin D. Roosevelt, Harry S. Truman, Dwight D. Eisenhower, Richard M. Nixon, and Ronald Reagan all held conferences on children and youth. Conferences on aging occurred in 1950, 1961, 1971, and 1981.   *Thomas E. Cronin*

White House hostesses are the women who receive and entertain the guests of the president of the United States, in place of the president's wife. Most White House hostesses assisted a president whose wife was deceased or too ill to handle social functions. The wives of presidents are called *first ladies* (see **First ladies of the United States**).

The paragraphs below list presidents who had White House hostesses. The presidents' names are followed by the dates of their terms, the reasons White House hostesses were needed, and then the names of the hostesses and their relationships to the presidents. An asterisk (*) after a hostess's name means a picture of her appears in the *World Book* article on the president she served.

Thomas Jefferson (1801-1809). Wife deceased. Hostesses: Martha Randolph* (daughter) and Dolley Madison (wife of James Madison, Jefferson's secretary of state).

Andrew Jackson (1829-1837). Wife deceased. Hostesses: Emily Donelson* (niece) and Sarah Yorke Jackson (daughter-in-law).

Martin Van Buren (1837-1841). Wife deceased. Hostess: Angelica Singleton Van Buren* (daughter-in-law).

William H. Harrison (1841). Wife ill. Hostess: Jane Irwin Harrison* (daughter-in-law).

John Tyler (1841-1845). First wife died in 1842; remarried in 1844. Hostesses between marriages: Priscilla Cooper Tyler (daughter-in-law) and Letitia Tyler Semple (daughter).

Zachary Taylor (1849-1850). Wife ill and disliked social functions. Hostess: Mary Elizabeth Bliss* (daughter).

Millard Fillmore (1850-1853). Wife ill. Hostess: Mary Abigail Fillmore (daughter).

Franklin Pierce (1853-1857). Wife grief-stricken during first half of term due to son's death. Hostess at that time: Abby Kent Means (wife's aunt).

James Buchanan (1857-1861). Never married. Hostess: Harriet Lane* (niece).

Andrew Johnson (1865-1869). Wife ill. Hostess: Martha Patterson* (daughter), when mother unable to host.

Chester A. Arthur (1881-1885). Wife deceased. Hostess: Mary Arthur McElroy* (sister).

Grover Cleveland (1885-1889 and 1893-1897). Unmarried until 1886. Hostess until marriage: Rose Cleveland (sister).

Woodrow Wilson (1913-1921). First wife died in 1914; remarried in 1915. Hostesses between marriages: Margaret Wilson* (daughter) and Helen Woodrow Bones (cousin).

Kathryn Kish Sklar

White Mountains are part of the Appalachian Mountain system. They stretch from western Maine across north-central New Hampshire. The mountains received their name because many high peaks are treeless and appear remarkably white when covered with snow. The whiteness becomes impressive in the spring and fall when snow does not cover the lower elevations. See **New Hampshire** (physical map).

The White Mountains cover about 1,000 square miles (2,590 square kilometers). The terrain is rugged and heavily forested. Most of the area is in the White Mountain National Forest. The natural beauty of the region draws many summer tourists, and heavy winter snowfall provides excellent skiing.

The mountains include a number of ranges. The most famous is the Presidential Range, which has the highest peaks in New England. Eight of the 86 peaks in this range bear the names of United States presidents—Adams, Eisenhower, Jackson, Jefferson, Madison, Monroe, Pierce, and Washington. Mount Washington is the highest peak in the northeastern United States. It has an elevation of 6,288 feet (1,917 meters).

Glaciers deepened a number of passes, known as "notches." Profile Mountain in Franconia Notch once included a famous New Hampshire landmark—the Old Man of the Mountain, or Great Stone Face. Erosion had carved the profile of a man's face on a cliff there. But the rock formation fell away in 2003.

Mount Washington is famous for extreme and rapidly changing weather conditions. The Mount Washington Observatory there keeps daily weather records. On April 12, 1934, the observatory recorded a wind of 231 miles (372 kilometers) per hour, the highest wind speed ever recorded on Earth.   *Robert L. A. Adams*

See also **Mount Washington; New Hampshire** (pictures).

White Russia. See **Belarus.**

White Sands Missile Range, New Mexico, is the main missile testing site of the United States Army. The range covers about 2 million acres (800,000 hectares) in south-central New Mexico. This area is almost as large as the states of Connecticut and Rhode Island combined. The range extends 120 miles (193 kilometers) from north to south, and 40 miles (64 kilometers) from east to west. The headquarters of the range are 27 miles (43 kilometers) east of Las Cruces.

The Army established the White Sands Proving Ground in 1945 and renamed it in 1958. The United States tested its first missiles there in 1945, shortly before the end of World War II. They were V-2 missiles captured from the Germans. The first atomic bomb was exploded in July 1945 at Trinity Site, on the eastern side of the range.   *Thomas S. Grodecki*

White Sands National Monument is in southern New Mexico. It contains great deposits of wind-blown gypsum sand. In bright light, the sands resemble a vast snowfield. The monument was established in 1933. For its area, see **National Park System** (table: National monuments).

White Sea is an arm of the Arctic Ocean. It reaches into northwestern Russia. For location, see **Russia** (terrain map). The White Sea is called *Beloye More* in Russian. The Onega, Dvina, and Mezen' rivers flow into the White Sea. Arkhangelsk is the largest city on this sea. The White Sea is icebound from September until June, but shipping is heavy in summer. The Dvina, Volga, and Dnieper rivers link the sea to the Caspian and Black seas. The Norwegian explorer Ottar discovered the White Sea in the A.D. 800's.   Leslie Dienes

White shark, also called *great white shark,* is one of the most dangerous sharks to human beings. Several white shark attacks on people occur each year, particularly along the coasts of California, Oregon, and South Australia. White sharks can grow to more than 21 feet (6.4 meters) in length. They live in coastal areas of cool oceans throughout the world. Unlike most other sharks, white sharks have warm blood and warm muscles. These characteristics make them faster and stronger than most other sharks. White sharks have sharp, triangular teeth with jagged edges and can rip chunks of flesh from seals and sea lions, two of their favorite prey.

Scientists think that white sharks attack humans because people look like seals to the sharks, especially when a person swims at the surface or floats on a surfboard. Many people survive an attack even though the first bite may be very damaging. Scientists believe victims can survive because of the way white sharks usually hunt any large prey. The shark stalks and then surprises its prey from behind and beneath, taking one huge bite from the body. The shark then waits for the victim to bleed to death before eating it. By waiting, the shark avoids possible injury from the claws and teeth of a struggling seal or sea lion. But this delay gives human victims a chance to be saved and to get medical treatment once on shore.

Sport and commercial fishing have seriously reduced the number of white sharks in many parts of the world.

WORLD BOOK illustration by Colin Newman, Bernard Thornton Artists
The white shark may attack human beings.

Some countries have laws that protect white sharks.
          John E. McCosker

Scientific classification. The white shark belongs to the mackerel shark family, Lamnidae. Its scientific name is *Carcharodon carcharias.*

See also **Shark** (picture: The mouth of a white shark).

White Sulphur Springs, West Virginia (pop. 2,315), is a famous health resort named for its mineral springs. It lies about 120 miles (193 kilometers) east of Charleston, the state capital (see **West Virginia** [political map]). The city has a mayor-council government.

Settlers first came to the region about 1750. Fashionable people of the Old South visited the springs as early as 1779. After the resort became famous, its *President's Cottage* served as the summer home of Presidents Martin Van Buren, John Tyler, and Millard Fillmore. During the Civil War, soldiers fought the Battle of Dry Creek near the resort.   Rebecca Sarver

Whitefield, *HWIHT feeld,* **George** (1714-1770), was an Anglican preacher and evangelist. In Britain, Whitefield played an important part in the founding of Methodism. In the American Colonies, he became a leader of a series of religious revival movements called the Great Awakening (see **Great Awakening**).

Whitefield was born on Dec. 27, 1714, in Gloucester, England. In the early 1730's, Charles and John Wesley, the founders of Methodism, influenced him. Whitefield experienced a religious conversion in 1735 that changed his life. He was ordained an Anglican deacon in 1736 and became known for his bold, dramatic, and severely challenging preaching. Some Anglican ministers accused him of disrupting their congregations and refused to let him preach in their churches. Whitefield began to preach outdoors and attracted large crowds. His success influenced John Wesley to begin outdoor preaching, which became typical of the Methodists.

Between 1738 and 1770, Whitefield visited America seven times. There he angered some ministers who resented his attacks on the lack of interest in the spiritual life. These ministers also denied their pulpits to Whitefield, so he again turned to outdoor preaching. His preaching made him one of the best known religious figures in colonial America.   Mark A. Noll

Whitefish is the name of a group of fishes that live in fresh water. Whitefish are found in many lakes and streams in the northern regions of North America, Europe, and Asia. They are related to trout and salmon, but they have larger scales than those fish. They also have smaller teeth than trout and salmon. Some whitefish are toothless. Whitefish are among the most important freshwater food fishes.

The *lake whitefish,* which lives in North American lakes and rivers, is the most valuable species. It has a long body, a cone-shaped snout, and a forked tail. It lacks teeth, and its upper jaw projects beyond the lower jaw. Most lake whitefish weigh about 4 pounds (1.8 kilograms). But individuals weighing up to 20 pounds (9 kilograms) have been caught in the Great Lakes. The fish eat insects and shellfish and usually live in deep water.

The *lake herring,* also called *cisco,* is another type of whitefish. It is found in the Great Lakes and is a valuable food fish. It is more abundant than the lake whitefish. Another excellent food fish is the *mountain whitefish.* It lives in mountain lakes and streams in the Western

United States. The *round whitefish* lives in the lakes of New England and the Adirondacks, in the Great Lakes, and in rivers and streams in northern Canada. This fish also is commercially valuable. David W. Greenfield

Scientific classification. Whitefish belong to the trout family, Salmonidae. The scientific name for the lake whitefish is *Coregonus clupeaformis,* and the lake herring is *C. artedii.* The mountain whitefish is *Prosopium williamsoni,* and the round whitefish is *P. cylindraceum.*

See also **Fish** (picture: Fish of temperate fresh waters).

Whitefly is the name of about 1,200 species of tiny insects that damage plants. Whiteflies stunt plant growth and limit fruit production by sucking sap from the leaves. They also secrete a sticky substance that causes an unsightly mold to grow on fruits. In addition, some species spread viruses.

A type of whitefly called the *silverleaf whitefly* has severely damaged crops in south-central California's Imperial Valley. This whitefly measures only about $\frac{1}{10}$ inch (2.5 millimeters) long. The insects have been difficult to control because they resist most pesticides and have few natural predators. They feed on many different plants, including broccoli, citrus fruits, cotton, lettuce, and melons. A species called the *greenhouse whitefly* infests tomatoes and other plants in greenhouses and gardens throughout North America.

WORLD BOOK illustration by John F. Eggert
Whitefly

The female whitefly lays her eggs on the underside of a plant's leaves. The eggs hatch into wingless young called *nymphs* or *crawlers.* The nymphs stick their mouthparts into a leaf vein and remain there, sucking out the sap, until they mature. The adult whiteflies also feed on plants occasionally. E. W. Cupp

Scientific classification. Whiteflies make up the whitefly family, Aleyrodidae, in the order Hemiptera.

Whitehead, Alfred North (1861-1947), was an English mathematician and philosopher. His writings did much to narrow the gap between philosophy and science. Whitehead's works reflect his firsthand knowledge of science, his philosophical insight, and his imaginative writing style. He thought scientific knowledge, though precise, is incomplete. It must be supplemented, he said, by philosophical principles and insights of poets.

Whitehead was born on Feb. 15, 1861, in Ramsgate. He taught at Cambridge University and London University until 1924, when he joined the faculty of Harvard University. Whitehead's writings on mathematics, logic, and the theory of knowledge laid the groundwork for his philosophical classic, *Process and Reality* (1929). This book explains that process and growth are the fundamental ideas which lead us to understand God, nature, and our own experiences. Whitehead also wrote *Principia Mathematica* (with Bertrand Russell, 1910-1913) and *Science and the Modern World* (1925). Whitehead died on Dec. 30, 1947. John E. Smith

Whitehorse (pop. 19,058) is the capital and chief distribution and communication center of the Canadian territory of Yukon. Whitehorse lies on the west bank of the Yukon River, 111 miles (179 kilometers) north of Skagway, Alaska. It is on the Alaska Highway. For the location of Whitehorse, see **Yukon** (map).

Most of Whitehorse's workers hold jobs in government, tourism, and trade. The city also provides services and support to the mining industry. Mining products are shipped from Whitehorse to outside markets. The city has regional headquarters of the Royal Canadian Mounted Police and many federal government agencies. Lake trout and grayling swim in neighboring streams and lakes. The region has bears, moose, and other game.

Airlines link Whitehorse with cities in Canada and the United States. A dam built above Whitehorse Rapids in 1959 to furnish power has created a lake in Miles Canyon. Many gold seekers came past Whitehorse in the rush of 1897-1898. Whitehorse was named for the Yukon River rapids, which resemble the mane of a white horse. Patricia Living

Whitewash is a white mixture made from whiting, glue, water, common salt, flour, and unslaked lime. It is used as a coating on outside walls of basements and lighthouses, and on fences and other structures where paint is too expensive to be practical. A heavy coating of whitewash on rough plaster, concrete, or wood helps protect against moisture and dirt. George J. Danker

Whiting. See Chalk.

Whitman, Marcus (1802-1847), was an American pioneer, doctor, and missionary among Indians in what is now the Pacific Northwest of the United States. He also helped settle the region.

Whitman was born on Sept. 4, 1802, in Rushville, New York. He practiced medicine for eight years. In 1835, Whitman was appointed to serve as a Presbyterian physician to the Oregon country by the American Board of Commissioners for Foreign Missions. Whitman traveled to the Pacific Northwest in 1836 with his wife, Narcissa, and missionaries William H. Gray and Henry and Eliza Spalding. The group drove a cart as far as Fort Boise, Idaho, thus opening part of the Oregon Trail. The trail began in Independence, Missouri, and became the longest overland route used in westward expansion of the United States.

The Whitmans founded a mission near the site of the present-day city of Walla Walla, Washington. In 1842, Whitman left for Boston to persuade the board to keep his mission open. He also sought to promote settlement in the Pacific Northwest. He returned in 1843 with about 900 settlers. In 1847, an epidemic of measles among new settlers in Whitman's community caused the death of many Indian children. Some Cayuse Indians, who probably believed their children were poisoned, killed the Whitmans and 12 others later that year, on Nov. 29, 1847. A statue of Whitman in the U.S. Capitol represents the state of Washington. Robert C. Carriker

See also **Whitman, Narcissa; Whitman Mission National Historic Site.**

Whitman, Narcissa (1808-1847), was a missionary teacher to the Indians of the Pacific Northwest. Born in Prattsburg, New York, she married missionary Marcus Whitman in 1836. She was one of the first white women to journey overland to the Northwest. The couple began a mission among the Cayuse Indians at Waiilatpu, in what is now Washington. Indians killed the Whitmans and 12 other people on Nov. 29, 1847. See also **Whitman, Marcus.**   Robert C. Carriker

Whitman, Walt (1819-1892), was an American poet who wrote *Leaves of Grass*. This collection of poems is considered one of the world's major literary works.

Whitman's poems sing the praises of the United States and of democracy. The poet's love of America grew from his faith that Americans might reach new worldly and spiritual heights. Whitman wrote: "The chief reason for the being of the United States of America is to bring about the common good will of all mankind, the solidarity of the world."

Whitman may have begun working on *Leaves of Grass* as early as 1848. The book's form and content were so unusual that no commercial publisher would publish it. In 1855, he published the collection of 12 poems at his own expense. In the preface, Whitman wrote: "The United States themselves are essentially the greatest poem." Between 1856 and 1892, Whitman published eight more revised and enlarged editions of his book. He believed that *Leaves of Grass* had grown with his own emotional and intellectual development.

His work. Beginning students of Whitman will find it easiest to study the poems separately. They should try to understand each poem's imagery, symbolism, literary structure, and unity of theme.

"Song of Myself," the longest poem in *Leaves of Grass*, is considered Whitman's greatest. It is a lyric poem told through the joyful experiences of the narrator, simply called "I," who chants the poem's 52 sections. Sometimes "I" is the poet himself—"Walt Whitman, an American." In other passages, "I" speaks for the human race, the universe, or a specific character being dramatized. Like all Whitman's major poems, "Song of Myself" contains symbols. For example, in the poem he describes grass as a symbol of life—"the babe of vegetation," "the handkerchief of the Lord/A scented gift and remembrancer designedly dropt."

"Out of the Cradle Endlessly Rocking" tells of a man recalling a boyhood experience in which a mockingbird lost its mate in a storm at sea. The memory of the bird's song teaches the man the meaning of death and thus the true vocation of a poet: to celebrate death as merely part of the cycle of birth, life, death, and rebirth.

Whitman wrote "When Lilacs Last in the Dooryard Bloom'd" on the death of Abraham Lincoln. Lincoln died in April, a time of rebirth in nature. As his coffin is transported from Washington, D.C., to Springfield, Illinois, it passes the young wheat, "every grain from its shroud in the dark-brown fields uprisen." Whitman says that each spring the blooming lilac will remind him not only of the death of Lincoln, but also of the eternal return to life. The evening star Venus symbolizes Lincoln, who has "droop'd in the western sky."

In "Passage to India," Whitman sees achievements in transportation and communication as symbols of universal brotherhood. Individuals are to be united with themselves and then with God, the "Elder Brother."

A group of Civil War poems called "Drum Taps" describes battlefield scenes and Whitman's emotions during wartime. "O Captain! My Captain!," another poem on Lincoln's death, is Whitman's most popular poem, but differs from his others in rhyme and rhythm. The "Chil-

Detail of an oil painting on canvas
Pennsylvania Academy of Fine Arts, Philadelphia

A portrait of Walt Whitman was painted by American artist Thomas Eakins in 1888 while Whitman was living in Camden, N.J.

dren of Adam" poems defend the sacredness of sex. The "Calamus" poems praise male companionship.

Whitman wrote in a form similar to *thought-rhythm,* or *parallelism.* This form is found in Old Testament poetry. It is also found in sacred books of India, such as the *Bhagavad-Gita,* which Whitman may have read in translation. The rhythm of his lines suggests the rise and fall of the sea he loved so much. This structure is better suited to expressing emotion than to logical discussion.

In general, Whitman's poetry is idealistic and romantic while his prose is realistic. His best prose is in a book of essays, mostly autobiographical, called *Specimen Days* (1882). Whitman's essay "Democratic Vistas" (1871) deals with his theory of democracy and with the creation of a democratic literature.

His life. Walter Whitman was born on May 31, 1819, in West Hills, Long Island, New York, and grew up in Brooklyn. He worked as a schoolteacher, printer, and journalist in the New York City area. He wrote articles on political questions, civic affairs, and the arts. Whitman loved mixing in crowds. He attended debates, the theater, concerts, lectures, and political meetings. He often rode on stagecoaches and ferries just to talk with people.

During the Civil War, Whitman was a government clerk and a volunteer assistant in the military hospitals in Washington, D.C. After the war, he worked in several government departments until he suffered a stroke in 1873. He spent the rest of his life in Camden, New Jersey, where he continued to write poems and articles. See **Camden.**

Whitman believed that the vitality and variety of his life reflected the vitality and variety of American democracy during his time. Most critics accept this view of the man and his poems. However, some insist Whitman was not a prophetic spokesman, but simply a powerful and unusual lyric poet.   Jerome Loving

Additional resources

Loving, Jerome. *Walt Whitman.* Univ. of Calif. Pr., 1999.
Meltzer, Milton. *Walt Whitman.* 21st Century Bks., 2002.

Whitman Mission National Historic Site is in southeastern Washington. It includes the site of an Indian mission and school established in 1836 by Marcus Whitman and his wife. The mission was a landmark on the Oregon Trail, and the school was the first mission school in the Pacific Northwest. The mission was made a national monument in 1936 and became a national historic site in 1963. For area, see **National Park System** (table: National historic sites).

Critically reviewed by the National Park Service

Whitney, Eli (1765-1825), an American inventor, is best known for his cotton gin. This invention provided a fast, economical way to separate the cotton seeds from the fibers. Whitney's cotton gin made cotton growing profitable and quickly helped the United States become the world's leading cotton grower. Whitney also became a manufacturer of muskets and other weapons.

Early life. Whitney was born on Dec. 8, 1765, in Westborough, Massachusetts. Even as a boy, he had mechanical skill. He made a violin when he was 12 and established a nail-making business when he was still a teen-ager. From 1783 to 1789, Whitney taught at a grammar school. He entered Yale College in 1789 and graduated three years later.

In 1792, Whitney went to Savannah, Georgia, to teach and study law. But he found that someone had taken the teaching job he expected to get. He then met Catherine Littlefield Greene, the widow of a hero of the Revolutionary War in America, General Nathanael Greene. She invited Whitney to be her guest while he studied law. Whitney wanted to be "worth his keep" and began fixing things around the house. His mechanical skill impressed her. One night, guests discussing green-seed cotton said they could not grow it profitably because of the time it took to clean. Mrs. Greene said, "Mr. Whitney can make a machine to clean it." By April 1793, Whitney had built the cotton gin. It could clean as much cotton in a day as 50 people could working by hand.

Brown Bros.

Eli Whitney

The cotton gin. In 1794, Whitney obtained a patent for his cotton gin. With the financial backing of a partner, Phineas Miller, Whitney began to make cotton gins in New Haven, Connecticut. But soon the business had problems. It could not make cotton gins fast enough to meet the demand. In addition, other manufacturers had been producing imitations of Whitney's cotton gin. Whitney sued them. He won after years of court trials. However, the life of his patent had almost expired, and the U.S. Congress refused to renew it.

Arms manufacturer. During the years he fought for his patent, Whitney also made arms for the U.S. government. In 1798, the Department of the Treasury gave him a contract to produce 10,000 muskets.

Whitney probably knew about existing French and American techniques for the mass production of muskets. As a result, he built a number of machines to help produce standard, interchangeable parts for the arms he was making. Some scholars credited him for the invention of a milling machine that made standard parts for weapons and that led to mass production. But no evidence exists that he invented such a machine or that he perfected the manufacture of interchangeable parts. However, Whitney was the best-known promoter of the "interchangeable system." R. Douglas Hurt

See also **Agriculture** (picture: The cotton gin); **Cotton gin; Mass production.**

Additional resources

Bagley, Katie. *Eli Whitney.* Bridgestone, 2003. Younger readers.
Green, Constance M. *Eli Whitney and the Birth of American Technology.* 1956. Reprint. Addison-Wesley, 1997. A standard work on Whitney's influence.

Whitney, Mount. See Mount Whitney.

Whitney Museum of American Art in New York City presents American art of all periods, with emphasis on the work of living artists. The permanent collection contains about 8,500 paintings, sculptures, prints, and drawings. Temporary exhibitions present historical surveys and comprehensive exhibits of major artists of the 1900's, as well as group shows introducing young and relatively unknown artists to a larger audience.

The museum's Film and Video Department has played a major role in the growing importance of video and film as art forms. The New American Film and Video Series presents programs of independent films and videotapes. Since 1973, the museum has established branches in New York City and Stamford, Connecticut.

The museum was founded in 1930 by Gertrude Vanderbilt Whitney, a patron of American art.

Critically reviewed by the Whitney Museum of American Art

Whittier, John Greenleaf (1807-1892), was an American poet. His best-known poems fall into two groups— those attacking slavery, and those praising the charms of New England country life. Whittier's simple, direct, and sometimes sentimental style has made his poems, such as "Maud Muller" (1854).

Whittier was born on Dec. 17, 1807, in Haverhill, Massachusetts. His parents were Quaker farmers. Whittier's poetry shows the influence of his Quaker religion and rural New England background, and he is often called the "Quaker poet." The Scottish poet Robert Burns also influenced Whittier. Like Burns, Whittier wrote ballads on rural themes. But his poetry lacks the wit of Burns's work.

From 1833 to 1863, Whittier was active in politics and the antislavery movement. He called for the abolition of slavery in newspaper articles and while serving in the Massachusetts legislature in 1835. The abolitionist cause also dominated his poetry. In "Massachusetts to Virginia" (1843), he criticized the slave state, Virginia, for betraying the Founding Fathers' democratic principles and love of liberty.

Whittier's finest political poem is "Ichabod" (1850), a lyric. "Ichabod" comes from the Hebrew word meaning *inglorious.* It criticizes

Brown Bros.

John Greenleaf Whittier

Senator Daniel Webster for his role in the passage of the Compromise of 1850. Whittier objected to the compromise because it required that runaway slaves be returned to their owners. But he used a dignified, restrained tone that makes "Ichabod" seem less an attack on Webster than an expression of sympathy for him.

In two ballads, "Skipper Ireson's Ride" (1857) and "Telling the Bees" (1858), Whittier showed his interest in the people, customs, legends, and settings of New England. These features appear in his masterpiece, "Snow-Bound" (1866), an affectionate description of Quaker life. The long poem tells of a family marooned in their farmhouse by a blizzard.   Jerome Loving

See also **Frietchie, Barbara; Liberty Party.**

Additional resources

Higginson, Thomas W. *John Greenleaf Whittier.* 1902. Reprint. Reprint Services, 1992.
Pickard, Samuel T. *Life and Letters of John Greenleaf Whittier.* 2 vols. Rev. ed. 1907. Reprint. M.S.G. Hse., 1969.
Woodwell, Roland H. *John Greenleaf Whittier.* HPL Pr., 1985.

WHO. See **World Health Organization.**

Who, The, became one of the most popular British groups in rock history. It originally consisted of guitarist Peter Townshend (May 19, 1945-   ), principal vocalist Roger Daltrey (March 1, 1944-   ), bass player John Entwistle (Oct. 9, 1944-June 27, 2002), and drummer Keith Moon (Aug. 23, 1947-Sept. 7, 1978). Kenney Jones became the drummer after Moon died from a drug overdose. In 1989, Simon Phillips replaced Jones. Townshend wrote most of The Who's music.

The Who was formed in London in 1964. The group soon became famous for its energetic concert performances, which often ended with the performers destroying their instruments and equipment on stage. The group's album *A Quick One* (U.S. title *Happy Jack,* 1966), featured its first attempt at rock opera. In the late 1960's, The Who was among the first rock groups to record "concept albums" tied together by a story line or theme. The album *The Who Sell Out* (1967) was the group's first concept album. Probably the most popular of these albums is the rock opera *Tommy* (1969). It was made into a film starring Daltrey in 1975.

In 1979, The Who was featured in two motion pic-

Mickey Adain, Star File
The Who became one of the most popular and influential British groups in the history of rock music. It originally consisted of, *left to right,* John Entwistle, bass player; Roger Daltrey, vocalist; Keith Moon, drummer; and Peter Townshend, guitarist.

tures. One was *Quadrophenia,* based on a 1973 Who album of the same name. The other was *The Kids Are Alright,* a history of the group. In 1982, The Who disbanded, but the members regrouped in 1989 for their "25th Anniversary" tour.   Don McLeese

See also **Townshend, Peter.**

Whooper. See **Whooping crane.**

Whooping cough, *HOO pihng,* also called *pertussis,* is a serious, highly contagious disease of the respiratory system. The name *whooping cough* comes from the high-pitched, whooping noise victims make when they try to catch their breath after severe coughing attacks. Whooping cough occurs worldwide, mainly among infants and young children. It is caused by a bacterium called *Bordetella pertussis.*

From the 1950's through the 1970's, the number of cases and the severity of whooping cough declined sharply in the United States and many other countries. These changes resulted from the widespread use of pertussis vaccine and from improvements in the standard of living and in health care.

In the early and mid-1980's, however, the percentage of young children in the United States who received the vaccine declined. As a result, the number of cases of whooping cough in the United States more than tripled from 1980 to 1986.

Symptoms of whooping cough progress through three stages. These stages, in order of development, are (1) the catarrhal stage, (2) the paroxysmal stage, and (3) the convalescent stage.

During the catarrhal stage, which lasts from one to two weeks, symptoms resemble those of the common cold. Victims have trouble breathing, due to inflammation and an increase of mucus in the nose and throat. They cough and have a fever. At this stage, the disease is highly contagious. It spreads through the spray of bacteria-filled droplets from the victim's nose and mouth. The catarrhal stage generally lasts from one to two weeks.

The paroxysmal stage, during which the "whoop" occurs, is the most serious phase of the disease. It generally lasts from two to three weeks. In this stage, severe coughing *paroxysms* (attacks) occur first at night, then later during both the day and night. Victims often spit up thick globs of mucus following these coughing spells. Infants often swallow the mucus and then vomit, which can cause dehydration and weight loss. The attacks can lead to inadequate oxygen circulation, which can cause convulsions. Other complications may include pneumonia or collapse of the lungs. Victims of whooping cough, especially infants under 6 months of age, may die during the paroxysmal stage.

During the convalescent stage, coughing, spitting up mucus, and vomiting begin to lessen. Victims show general improvement and finally return to a normal state of health. Full recovery may take weeks or months.

Treatment and prevention. Physicians use the antibiotic erythromycin to treat whooping cough. If given in the catarrhal stage, this drug can halt the illness or lessen its severity. After the paroxysmal stage begins, treatment centers on helping the patient breathe freely and on limiting the number of severe coughing attacks.

Immunization of infants and young children with pertussis vaccine protects them from whooping cough. For a recommended schedule of whooping cough immunizations, see **Immunization** (table: Recommended immunization for children in the United States). Physicians prescribe erythromycin to help prevent the development of whooping cough in unvaccinated people who have been exposed to the disease.   Michael G. Levitzky

Whooping crane is one of the rarest birds of North America. It is a symbol of wildlife conservation. Whooping cranes, also called *whoopers,* are named for their loud, buglelike call. Whooping cranes are the tallest birds in North America. They stand about 5 feet (1.5 meters) tall and have long legs and a long neck. The adults are white, with black-tipped wings and a patch of bare, red skin on their heads. Whoopers less than a year old are rust colored. See **Crane** (picture).

Wild whooping cranes breed in marshy areas of Wood Buffalo National Park in the Northwest Territories of Canada. They make nests of piles of grasses or other plants. The female usually lays two eggs, but only one chick survives in most cases. Whoopers migrate about 2,500 miles (4,000 kilometers) to Aransas National Wildlife Refuge in Texas for the winter. Their food in winter includes clams, crabs, and crayfish. However, scientists know little about what they eat during the rest of the year.

Whoopers once nested between Louisiana and Canada. They began to die out during the 1800's, when increasing numbers of settlers disturbed their habitats. By 1941, only 15 whoopers remained in the flock that migrated between Canada and Texas. Another 6 whoopers lived in Louisiana, but these birds died out by 1948.

Whooping cranes are protected by international law from shooting and other harm by people. The birds' breeding and wintering grounds are protected refuges, and the whoopers are closely watched during their migrations. This protection helped increase the size of the flock that was wintering in Texas.

In further efforts to save the species, biologists remove one egg from some of the whooper nests in Canada. Some of these eggs are artificially incubated to start a captive flock, which eventually produces eggs and offspring. Beginning in 1975, some of the removed eggs were transferred to the nests of sandhill cranes at Grays Lake National Wildlife Refuge in Idaho. The sandhill cranes acted as foster parents by hatching and raising the young whooping cranes. However, biologists were disappointed when this flock of whoopers did not begin breeding, and the program was discontinued in 1989.

In 1993, biologists began a program to release young whooping cranes at the Kissimmee Prairie in south-central Florida. This program eventually established a resident flock of whoopers in Florida, thus eliminating the hazards of long-distance migration for these birds. During migration, young whooping cranes are often killed when they fly into electrical or telephone wires.

In 2001, scientists used a special aircraft to lead a small flock of whooping cranes in an experimental migration. The cranes migrated from Wisconsin to the Chassahowitzka National Wildlife Refuge along the west coast of Florida. They then migrated back to Wisconsin unassisted in 2002. This small flock later grew and became an established migratory flock.   Eric G. Bolen

Scientific classification. The whooping crane belongs to the crane family, Gruidae. Its scientific name is *Grus americana.*

See also **Bird** (Endangered species).

Wichita, *WIHCH uh TAW* (pop. 344,284; met. area pop. 545,220), is the largest city in Kansas. It serves as a major manufacturing center and as the distribution center for a large farm region that produces dairy products, grain, and livestock. Wichita is called the *Air Capital of the World.* It ranks as the world's largest producer of general aviation aircraft. These aircraft include small planes that are used for business, recreation, and flight training.

Wichita lies in south-central Kansas where the Arkansas and the Little Arkansas rivers meet. For location, see **Kansas** (political map). The city is named after the Wichita Indians.

The city covers 123 square miles (319 square kilometers) and is the county seat of Sedgwick County. About half of Wichita lies east of the Arkansas River, and about half lies west of the river. The main business and industrial districts are in the area located east of the river.

Century II, a cultural-convention center, covers 5 acres (2 hectares) east of the river in the heart of downtown Wichita. This project includes an auditorium, a concert hall, convention and exhibition halls, and a theater. The A. Price Woodard, Jr., Memorial Park, with its fountains, trees, waterfalls, and an outdoor amphitheater, lies between Century II and the river. Expo Hall, which provides additional convention space, was completed in 1986. Wichita's old city hall, completed in 1892, still stands in the downtown area. Its architectural design and towers attract many tourists. Today, the building houses the Wichita-Sedgwick County Historical Museum.

Economy. Wichita is the largest manufacturing center in Kansas. There are almost 700 manufacturing plants in the metropolitan area. The production of business and defense aircraft is the major industry. A major aircraft producer, Boeing Company, is the largest private employer in Kansas. Wichita is also the petroleum capital of Kansas. Oil fields lie just outside the city, and many oil companies have offices or refineries in Wichita. Other industries produce chemicals, camping and recre-

© Joel Satore, *The Wichita Eagle*

Wichita is the largest city in Kansas. Its annual events include the Old Town Chili Cook-Off, *shown here.* This event is held in the city's downtown area.

ational equipment, metal products, computers, specialty equipment, and plastics.

Wichita is a regional medical center. The city has nine hospitals, including one operated by the Department of Veterans Affairs. Wichita lies in a rich, wheat-growing area, and Wichita's flour mills grind more wheat than any other Kansas city.

Four railroads serve the city, and truck lines also operate there. Wichita Mid-Continent Airport is southwest of the downtown area of the city. Wichita has one daily newspaper, the *Wichita Eagle*. Six television stations and more than 25 radio stations broadcast from the area.

Education and cultural life. Wichita's public school system includes about 85 elementary schools and 9 high schools. The city also has about 25 parochial and private schools.

Wichita State University is the third largest school of higher education in the state. The university is known for its National Institute for Aviation Research and its speech pathology and audiology program. Heartspring, formerly called the Institute of Logopedics, is a nationally known school that serves children with communication disorders. Friends University and Newman University (formerly Sacred Heart College) are also in Wichita. The city's public library system consists of a central library and several branches. The Wichita Symphony Orchestra performs at the Century II Concert Hall. The professional Music Theatre of Wichita stages five musicals each summer.

The Old Cowtown Museum re-creates frontier Wichita of the 1870's. The city has three art museums—the Wichita Center for the Arts, the Wichita Art Museum, and the Ulrich Museum of Art at Wichita State University. The Wichita Art Museum houses the famous Roland P. Murdock Collection, one of the nation's largest collections of American art.

Wichita's public park system includes about 80 parks. Pawnee Prairie, the largest park in the city, covers 700 acres (280 hectares). Chisholm Creek Park includes native and restored prairie habitats. The Sedgwick County Zoo lies on the northwest border of the city.

Government. Wichita has a council-manager form of government. The six city council members and a mayor are elected to four-year terms. The council appoints a city manager who is the administrative head of the city government.

History. Traders first entered the area in 1863 to trade with the Plains Indians. The city's name came from the Wichita Indians. This Oklahoma tribe was moved to the area in 1864 by the United States government during the American Civil War (1861-1865). In 1870, the settlement was incorporated as a town. The Wichita and Southwestern Railroad (now part of the Burlington Northern Santa Fe Corporation) began to serve Wichita in 1872, and the town soon became an important shipping point for cattle. Cowboys drove Texas longhorn cattle along the Chisholm Trail, fattened them on Kansas grass, and shipped them from Wichita to distant markets.

During the late 1880's, Wichita became known for its cowboys, dance halls, gambling, and saloons. Wyatt Earp, the famous frontier lawman, served as a peace officer in the town in the mid-1870's. Although Wichita gained attention for lawlessness, the people also built churches, a library, schools, and some industry, including a brick plant and a meat-packing plant.

Wichita received a city charter in 1886. The community's population grew from 4,911 in 1880 to 23,853 in 1890. Much of this growth resulted from land speculation.

The discovery of oil in the Wichita area during the early 1900's brought further growth. The city's population rose from 24,671 in 1900 to 111,110 in 1930. In 1919, Wichita's first airplane manufacturing company built its factory. Wichita soon became the nation's aircraft production center. The city won fame for its pioneers in the industry, including Walter H. Beech, Clyde V. Cessna, and Lloyd C. Stearman.

The prospering aircraft and oil industries helped Wichita avoid hard times during the 1930's. The rest of the Kansas region suffered during those years from dust storms and the Great Depression.

During World War II (1939-1945), Wichita's three airplane factories produced more military aircraft than any other U.S. city. After the war, Wichita continued to rank among the leading producers of jet bombers for the Air Force. In 1951, McConnell Air Force Base opened in Wichita. Aircraft production soared again during the Korean War (1950-1953).

In 1987, the Epic Center, the tallest building in Kansas, was completed in Wichita. The 22-story building rises 325 feet (99 meters). Also in 1987, a 10-acre (4-hectare) botanical complex called Botanica opened.

The city's economy grew during the early 1960's, when Learjet Corporation built a plant there. This plant helped Wichita become the world's largest producer of general aviation aircraft. In the mid-1970's, the city's aircraft industry grew tremendously. Growth continued until the 1980's, when there was a sharp decline in general aviation sales worldwide. But Wichita remained the world's leading producer of general aviation aircraft through the 1980's and continued to do so in the 1990's.

Allan B. Tanner

For the monthly weather in Wichita, see **Kansas** (Climate). See also **Kansas** (pictures).

Wichita Falls, *WIHCH uh TAW,* Texas (pop. 104,197; met. area pop. 140,518), is a center for services and trade in north-central Texas and southwestern Oklahoma. The city lies on the Wichita River near the Texas-Oklahoma border. For location, see **Texas** (political map).

Wichita Falls serves as a center of government, agriculture, oil production, and manufacturing. Sheppard Air Force Base is one of the city's leading employers. Wichita Falls also has more than 125 small manufacturing firms. The products of these firms include automobile parts, fiberglass, glass, hand tools, jet engine parts, and washing machines. The city is the home of Midwestern State University.

Wichita Falls was founded in 1879. It was named for the Wichita Indians and for the falls of the Wichita River, which no longer exist.

The arrival of the railroad in 1882 encouraged growth of the city. The first major oil deposit in north Texas was discovered near Wichita Falls in 1910, and the community became a boom town several years later. A tornado hit Wichita Falls in 1979, killing 42 people and destroying more than 3,000 homes.

Since the early 1990's, the Wichita Falls downtown area has been a focus for renovation. Projects completed include a library, arts center, museum, and coliseum.

Wichita Falls is the county seat of Wichita County. It has a council-manager form of government.

Carroll Wilson

Wicker is a small, flexible branch or twig, usually of willow, that can be woven to make baskets, furniture, and other objects. The term *wicker* also refers to any basketlike furniture or accessory. Some wicker objects are woven from such plant materials as bamboo, cane, rattan, and reed, and from artificial fibers.

Wicker furniture is made by weaving the material around a sturdy frame. Wicker is loosely woven and allows air to circulate, making such furniture especially suitable for hot areas. In addition, wicker is lightweight and extremely durable. Some pieces have lasted more than 100 years. Wicker furniture was originally used outdoors. Today, however, this type of furniture is popular indoors as well.

Wicker chairs were made in ancient Egypt. During the 1800's, wicker chairs and tables became popular in Europe and the United States. Each piece was handmade and took several days to complete. As the costs of labor and materials rose, manufacturers sought less expensive ways of making wicker objects. They developed an artificial fiber from specially treated twisted paper. They also began to weave wicker on looms. Today, however, some wicker objects are still made by hand, mostly in Asian countries.

Jim L. Bowyer

Wien. See Vienna.

Wiener, *WEE nuhr,* **Norbert** (1894-1964), was an American mathematician who did fundamental work in the analysis of numerical information. He developed techniques that could be used to analyze data transmitted by radio to separate useful information from undesired disturbances.

Wiener also led in the study of similarities in how nervous systems and machines perform the functions of communication and control. He originated the term *cybernetics* for this field and used the term as the title of a book he published in 1948.

Wiener was born in Columbia, Missouri, on Nov. 26, 1894. He received a Ph.D. degree from Harvard University at the age of 18. He taught at the Massachusetts Institute of Technology from 1919 to 1960. Wiener died on March 18, 1964.

Arthur Gittleman

See also **Cybernetics.**

Wiesbaden, *VEES BAHD uhn* (pop. 266,623), is a German resort city 6 miles (10 kilometers) northeast of Mainz. It is in a valley on the southern slope of the Taunus Mountains (see **Germany** [political map]). In 1946, it became the capital of the state of Hesse, which was formed in 1945. The tourist trade is an important source of income. Many mineral springs in and around Wiesbaden attract visitors. The springs in the area were known to the Romans, and many relics of the Roman period have been discovered there. The city's Latin name was *Aquae Mattiacorum,* which means *waters of the Mattiaci* (a German tribe). Its German name, *Wiesbaden,* means *baths on the meadows.*

John W. Boyer

Wiesel, *wee ZEHL,* **Elie,** *EHL ee* (1928-), an American author, became a leading spokesman for people who survived Nazi concentration camps during World War II (1939-1945). He was a prisoner at camps where the Nazis murdered millions of European Jews. Wiesel dedicated his life to describing the horrors he witnessed and to helping victims of oppression and racism. He won the 1986 Nobel Peace Prize.

Eliezer Wiesel was born on Sept. 30, 1928, in Sighet, Romania. In 1944, he was sent with his family and the town's other Jews to a camp at Auschwitz (now Oświecim), Poland, near Kraków. He was later sent to a camp at Buchenwald, Germany, near Weimar. Wiesel's parents and a sister died at these camps. After Buchenwald was liberated in 1945, Wiesel settled in France. He later studied philosophy at the University of Paris, became a journalist, and moved to the United States. In 1976, Wiesel became a professor of humanities at Boston University. President Jimmy Carter appointed him chairman of the President's Commission on the Holocaust in 1979. In 1980, Wiesel was named head of the United States Holocaust Memorial Council.

Wiesel's first book, *Night* (1958), is a memoir of his experiences in the concentration camps. *Dawn* (1960) and *The Accident* (1961) are novels about survivors of the Holocaust. Wiesel's other books include *The Jews of Silence* (1966), *A Beggar in Jerusalem* (1968), and *The Testament* (1980).

Michael Berenbaum

Wiesenthal, *VEE zehn TAHL,* **Simon** (1908-), is an Austrian Jew who helped bring more than 1,100 Nazi war criminals to justice. In 1961, he founded the Jewish Documentation Center in Vienna, Austria. The center, which Wiesenthal directed until 2003, collected evidence about the murders of approximately 6 million Jews and millions of other persons by the Nazis during World War II (1939-1945). It also gathered information on the location of Nazis who had avoided capture. Wiesenthal helped bring to trial such former Nazi officers as Adolf Eichmann, who directed the removal of Jews to concentration camps, and Karl Silberbauer, who arrested Anne Frank (see **Frank, Anne**).

Wiesenthal was born on Dec. 31, 1908, in Buchach, near Lvov, in what is now Ukraine. He was trained as an architect and engineer. Nearly all of Wiesenthal's relatives were killed by the Nazis during World War II, while he worked as a slave laborer in a number of concentration camps.

Leon A. Jick

Wig is a false covering of hair for the head. The name comes from the word *periwig.* The custom of wearing wigs dates back to ancient times. Egyptian mummies have been found with them. The ancient Greeks and Romans wore them. In the 1600's, the French made wigs fashionable. Wigs then became large, heavy, and expensive. Usually they were powdered white. Wigs were worn by nobles, courtiers, ministers, judges, doctors, and professional people. English judges began wearing wigs in the early 1700's and still wear them today. Wigs were fashionable in colonial America and became popular in the 1960's and 1970's. They are also worn by people who are bald. Quality wigs are made of the best grade of human and artificial hair. Some wigs are made with a netting that allows the wearer's hair to be drawn through the net to mix with the hair of the wig.

Franz J. Singer

See also **Colonial life in America** (Clothing); **Hairdressing** (with pictures).

Wigeon, *WIHJ uhn,* is the name of three species of medium-sized ducks that breed in temperate regions of Europe, North America, and South America. Wigeons measure about 20 inches (50 centimeters) long. They have a thin, bluish bill and a white patch on the shoulder of the wing. Wigeons inhabit lakes and river deltas.

The *American wigeon,* also called the *baldpate,* is found in Canada and much of the United States. The male American wigeon has a distinctive whistling call and a white forehead and crown. The female has white markings on the underwing.　　Rodger D. Titman

Scientific classification. Wigeons belong to the family Anatidae. The American wigeon is *Anas americana.*

See also **Bird** (picture: Birds of inland waters).

Wiggin, Kate Douglas (1856-1923), was an American writer of books for children. She is best remembered for her novel *Rebecca of Sunnybrook Farm* (1903). Rebecca Randall, the bright young heroine, leaves Sunnybrook Farm to live with her mother's sisters after her father's death. The novel's characters, places, and events are taken from Wiggin's childhood and later life in Maine. Her other notable children's novels include *The Birds' Christmas Carol* (1887) and *Mother Carey's Chickens* (1911). Wiggin also wrote books for adults and an autobiography, *My Garden of Memory* (1923).

Wiggin was born on Sept. 28, 1856, in Philadelphia. In 1878, she helped establish in San Francisco the first free kindergarten west of the Rocky Mountains.

Virginia L. Wolf

Wigglesworth, Michael (1631-1705), was a Puritan pastor, doctor, and poet of colonial New England. He is best known for his somber poem *The Day of Doom: or, A Poetical Description of the Great and Last Judgment* (1662). Wigglesworth believed that many people were disobeying God and that God judged both individuals and nations. He wrote *The Day of Doom* as a warning to the New England colonists. His crude but dramatic ballad presented theology to the colonists in a form they could easily read and memorize. *The Day of Doom* became a best seller. Wigglesworth was born on Oct. 18, 1631, in England. He moved to America with his parents at age 7. In 1656, he settled in Malden, Massachusetts, and served as minister and physician.　　Mark A. Noll

Wight, *wyt,* **Isle of,** lies off the southern coast of England (see **England** [terrain map]). A strait called *The Solent* separates the island from the mainland county of Hampshire. Ferries and hovercraft provide transportation between the island and the mainland. The island covers 147 square miles (381 square kilometers) and has a population of 132,719.

The Isle of Wight is famous for its mild, sunny climate and its scenery, which attracts tourists. The island's administrative center is Newport. Cowes, its leading port, is known for its sailing and yacht races. Many people work on farms or in light industry.　　D. Ian Scargill

Wigner, Eugene Paul (1902-1995), was an American theoretical physicist. He shared the 1963 Nobel Prize in physics with J. Hans Jensen and Maria Goeppert Mayer for his research on the use of a property known as *symmetry* in theories of the atom and the nucleus. He also worked with a team of scientists who in 1942 produced the first nuclear chain reaction. In 1958, he won the Atomic Energy Award Commission's Enrico Fermi Award, and he shared the 1959 Atoms for Peace Award with Leo Szilard. He became a lecturer at Princeton University in 1930 and later became a professor there.

Wigner was born Nov. 17, 1902, in Budapest, Hungary. In 1937, he became a United States citizen.　　Richard L. Hilt

Wigwam is the name for a kind of dwelling used by the Algonquian-speaking Indians of the Eastern Woodlands. In the East, the foundation was usually made of light poles tied together with bark, forming an oval-shaped dome. The dwelling was covered with layers of bark or reed mats, laid on like shingles. Other wigwams had a rectangular frame and gabled roof. Some northern Algonquian Indians used a cone-shaped tent. See also **Indian, American** (pictures).　　W. Roger Buffalohead

Wilberforce, Samuel (1805-1873), was an important figure in the Anglican Church in England. He held several major church offices, including bishop of Oxford, dean of Westminster, and Chaplain of the House of Lords. Wilberforce played a mediating role during a conflict between two groups within the church—the Anglo-Catholics and the Evangelicals. Anglo-Catholics wanted to reestablish ties with Roman Catholicism without accepting the authority of the pope. The Evangelicals stressed conversion, strict morality, and social action. As Chaplain of the House of Lords, Wilberforce used his considerable influence in an attempt to bring about prison reform and measures dealing with the abuse of women and children.

Wilberforce was born on Sept. 7, 1805, in Clapham, near London. He was ordained a priest in 1829. His father, William, an English statesman, played a crucial role in the abolition of slavery in British territories.

Charles H. Lippy

Wilberforce, William (1759-1833), was a leader in the fight to abolish the slave trade and slavery in the British Empire. In 1780, he entered Parliament and became a leading Tory, noted for his eloquence. In 1789, Wilberforce led a campaign against the British slave trade. A bill to end this trade passed in the House of Commons in 1792 but failed in the House of Lords. When such a bill finally became law in 1807, Wilberforce turned against the foreign slave trade. He retired from Parliament in 1825 but continued to support the campaign against the foreign slave trade. After 1823, Wilberforce supported the emancipation of the slaves in the United Kingdom's colonies. He was born on Aug. 24, 1759, in Hull, England, and studied at Cambridge University.

Howard Temperley

Wilberforce University is a private coeducational liberal arts university in Wilberforce, Ohio. It is affiliated with the African Methodist Episcopal Church. The university has divisions of business and economics, engineering and computer science, humanities, natural science, and social science. Courses lead to the bachelor's degree. All students alternate periods of study on the campus with periods of work at approved off-campus jobs. Wilberforce University was founded in 1856 and is the oldest predominantly black private university in the United States.　　Critically reviewed by Wilberforce University

Wilbur, Richard (1921-　　), is an American poet. He won Pulitzer Prizes in poetry for *Things of This World* in 1957 and *New and Collected Poems* in 1989. He was cowinner of the 1971 Bollingen Prize for poetry for *Walking to Sleep.* Wilbur received a one-year appointment as poet laureate of the United States in 1987.

Wilbur often uses myth and philosophy to illuminate ordinary experience. His poems see the dark side of human failure redeemed by a respect for intelligence, artistry, and "the things of this world." Wilbur's poems are often formal in style, have a musical quality, and are witty and mentally stimulating. From his first published work, *The Beautiful Changes* (1947), to *Advice to a Prophet* (1961), Wilbur tried to show how the mind and the senses can enrich understanding of the world.

Wilbur was born on March 1, 1921, in New York City. He wrote a children's book, *Loudmouse* (1963). *Responses* (1976) is a collection of essays and literary criticism. *The Catbird's Song* (1997) is a book of prose writings. Wilbur gained acclaim for his translations of comedies by the French playwright Molière and of tragedies by the French playwright Jean Racine.   Bonnie Costello

Wild ass. See Donkey; Onager.

Wild barley. See Foxtail barley.

Wild boar. See Boar, Wild.

Wild canary. See Goldfinch.

Wild carrot, also called *Queen Anne's lace,* is a member of the carrot family that grows wild. The cultivated carrot that people eat has a European and Asiatic origin.

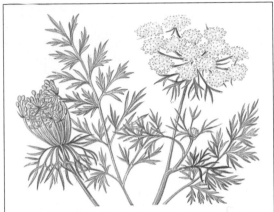

WORLD BOOK illustration by Christabel King

The wild carrot is also known as *Queen Anne's lace* because of the plant's lacy clusters of small white or yellowish flowers.

In North America, many carrot plants grow wild as common weeds. The plants were called *Queen Anne's lace* because of their lacy clusters of small white or yellowish flowers. The wild carrot grows to 3 feet (91 centimeters) tall. No part of the plant should be eaten as food. But the roots and seeds are sometimes boiled to make a tea that is used as a folk medicine for the kidneys and intestines.

Albert Liptay

Scientific classification. The wild carrot belongs to the parsley family, Umbelliferae. Its scientific name is *Daucus carota.*

Wild rice, also called *Indian rice,* is an aquatic grass that produces a cereal grain. It is not related to rice.

In North America, the most important species of wild rice is *northern wild rice.* Its stalks grow from 4 to 8 feet (1.2 to 2.4 meters) high. The grain, which is high in protein and vitamins, is on the heads of the stalks.

Northern wild rice is an *annual,* which means each plant lives only one year. It grows in shallow streams, rivers, and lakes of the central United States and central Canada. It also is cultivated commercially, notably in Minnesota and Wisconsin, in artificial paddies. Much of the grain is sold for livestock feed. American Indians harvested wild rice by bending the stalks over the edge of a boat and beating the grains loose with sticks. Today, most wild rice is harvested mechanically.   James E. Simon

Scientific classification. Wild rice is in the grass family, Poaceae or Graminaae. Northern wild rice is *Zizania palustris.*

Wildcat is a name generally given to small, wild members of the cat family. The true wildcat lives in Europe, Asia, and Africa. It is an extremely vicious animal and generally larger and stronger than the domestic cat. It has yellowish to grayish fur and black streaks around the body, legs, and tail.

Two species of wildcats live in North America. They have longer bodies, longer legs, and shorter tails than domesticated cats. They prowl mainly at night. Their ears have tufts of fur on them, and their coats vary in color and thickness. One species, called the *Canadian lynx,* has a long, gray coat. It ranges across the Northern United States, Alaska, and Canada. The other species, often called the *bobcat,* has short, yellowish-brown fur, covered with dark spots and other markings. It ranges from southern Canada south through Mexico. A variety of wildcat called the *Egyptian cat* is believed to be the ancestor of the common house cat.   Duane A. Schlitter

Scientific classification. Wildcats belong to the cat family, Felidae. The European species is *Felis silvestris.* Bobcats are *Lynx rufus.* The Canadian lynx is *L. canadensis.*

See also **Bobcat; Serval.**

Wildcat bank was the name for unstable banking institutions that issued paper money called *wildcat currency.* They operated under state charters, particularly in the South, during the early and middle 1800's. Wildcat banks became especially numerous and irresponsible after President Andrew Jackson's successful struggle against the Second Bank of the United States.

The Bank of the United States used its influence to restrain state banks from issuing more paper money, or *wildcat currency,* than their assets would justify. In 1833, Jackson succeeded in withdrawing government deposits from the bank. His victory so crippled the bank that it could no longer restrain the state banks. Many banks, especially those in the South and West, then issued unreasonably large amounts of paper money and lent it freely on the flimsiest security.

As a result, this caused a money inflation, followed by a period of wild speculation in Western land. Jackson then issued his famous *Specie Circular,* ordering government agents to accept nothing but gold and silver in payment for public lands. Many of the wildcat banks were unable to meet the demands made on them and failed abruptly. These bank failures contributed to the serious financial panic in 1837.   James C. Curtis

See also **Jackson, Andrew** (The money surplus); **Van Buren, Martin** (The Panic of 1837).

Wilde, *wyld,* **Oscar** (1854-1900), was an author, playwright, and wit. He preached the importance of style in both life and art, and he attacked Victorian narrow-mindedness and complacency.

Wilde was born on Oct. 16, 1854, in Dublin, Ireland. His full name was Oscar Fingal O'Flahertie Wills Wilde. At 20, he went to study at Oxford University where he distinguished himself as a scholar and wit. He soon became a well-known public figure, but the period of his true achievement did not begin until he published *The Happy Prince and Other Tales* in 1888. In these fairy tales and fables, Wilde found a literary form well-suited to his talents. Wilde's only novel, the ingenious *Picture of Dorian Gray* (1890), is an enlarged moral fable. It describes a man whose portrait ages and grows ugly as a reflection of his moral corruption while his actual appearance remains the same. The book seems to show the destructive side of a devotion to pleasure and beauty similar to Wilde's own.

Brown Bros.

Oscar Wilde

Wilde's plays taken together are his most important works. *Lady Windermere's Fan* (1892), *A Woman of No Importance* (1893), and *An Ideal Husband* (1895) combine the then-fashionable drama of social intrigue with witty high comedy. In each play, Wilde brings together an intolerant young idealist and a person who has committed a social sin in the past. They meet in a society where appearances are everything. The effect is always to educate the idealists to their own weaknesses and to show the need for tolerance and forgiveness.

In *The Importance of Being Earnest* (1895), his masterpiece, Wilde departed from his standard formula by combining high comedy with farce. The characters take insignificant things seriously while casually dismissing important concerns. The result is a satire on the shallowness of British society and its focus on good breeding and proper formalities. Almost every line in the play is an *epigram* (clever saying). Wilde also wrote *Salomé* (1893), a one-act Biblical tragedy, in French.

In 1895, Wilde was at the peak of his career and had three hit plays running at the same time. But in that year he was accused of having homosexual relations with Lord Alfred Douglas by Douglas's father, the Marquess of Queensberry. As a result, Wilde became involved in a hopeless legal dispute, and he was sentenced to two years in prison at hard labor. From his prison experiences came his best poem, *The Ballad of Reading Gaol* (1898), and a remarkable autobiographical document sometimes called *De Profundis*.

Wilde left England after his release. Ruined in health, finances, and creative energy, but with his wit intact, he died in France three years later.   Gerald M. Berkowitz

Additional resources

Belford, Barbara. *Oscar Wilde*. Random Hse., 2000.
Ellmann, Richard. *Oscar Wilde*. Vintage Bks., 1988.
Raby, Peter, ed. *The Cambridge Companion to Oscar Wilde*. Cambridge, 1997.

Wildebeest. See Gnu.

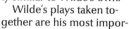

Wilder, *WYL duhr,* **Billy** (1906-2002), was a leading motion-picture director, producer, and writer. His movies combine technical skill, witty dialogue, and a cynical realism about human behavior. Wilder often worked with other writers on his scripts. His films vary in tone. They include the romantic comedies *Major and the Minor* (1942) and *Sabrina* (1954); the tragic *Double Indemnity* (1944), *The Lost Weekend* (1945), *Sunset Boulevard* (1950), and *Witness for the Prosecution* (1958); the seriocomic *A Foreign Affair* (1948), *Stalag 17* (1953), and

The Apartment (1960); and the satirical *Some Like It Hot* (1959), *One, Two, Three* (1961), *The Fortune Cookie* (1966), and *The Front Page* (1974). Wilder won Academy Awards as best director for *The Lost Weekend* and *The Apartment*. He also shared an Oscar for best screenplay for *The Apartment* with his long-time collaborator, I. A. L. Diamond.

Wilder was born Samuel Wilder on June 22, 1906, in Vienna, Austria. He came to the United States in 1934 and became a U.S. citizen in 1940.   Gene D. Phillips

Wilder, L. Douglas (1931-   ), the first elected black governor in the United States, was the chief executive of Virginia from 1990 to 1994. Wilder, a Democrat, defeated his Republican opponent, former state Attorney General J. Marshall Coleman, in the 1989 election.

Lawrence Douglas Wilder was born on Jan. 17, 1931, in Richmond, Virginia. Wilder graduated from Virginia Union University with a bachelor's degree in chemistry. He won a Bronze Star for bravery during the Korean War (1950-1953). Wilder earned a law degree in

A. Tannenbaum, Sygma

L. Douglas Wilder

1959 from Howard University and became a successful trial lawyer in Richmond. In 1969, Wilder became the first black elected to the Virginia Senate since 1877, when federal control ended after the American Civil War. In 1985, he was elected lieutenant governor of Virginia.   Guy Halverson

Wilder, *WYL duhr,* **Laura Ingalls,** LAWR uh *IHNG guhlz* (1867-1957), was an American author of books for children. She is best known for her series of nine novels called the "Little House" books. Most of the series is loosely based on her experiences growing up in the Midwest in the 1870's and 1880's. The series has been praised as a vivid literary saga of the American frontier. The "Little House" stories have a chronological pattern and follow Laura from her childhood wilderness home to her final home with her husband, Almanzo Wilder. The stories show the importance of a closely knit family, and they are filled with humor and tenderness.

Laura Ingalls was born on Feb. 7, 1867, in Pepin, Wisconsin. She lived a rugged pioneer life with her family as they moved from place to place. She described her childhood in the first "Little House" book, *Little House in the Big Woods* (1932). In 1885, she married Almanzo Wilder, who came from an old established family in New York. *Farmer Boy* (1933) is the story of his childhood. *These Happy Golden Years* (1943) unites the families with the marriage of Laura and Almanzo.

Harper & Bros.

Laura Ingalls Wilder

The other books in the series are *Little House on the Prairie* (1935), *On the Banks of Plum Creek* (1937), *By the Shores of Silver Lake* (1939), *The Long Winter* (1940), *Little Town on the Prairie* (1941), and *The First Four Years* (published in 1971, after the author's death). *West from Home* (1974) is a collection of letters Laura wrote to Almanzo in 1915 while she was visiting her daughter in San Francisco.   Jill P. May

See also **Laura Ingalls Wilder Award.**

Wilder, Thornton Niven (1897-1975), was an American playwright and novelist. He won Pulitzer Prizes in both fields—in 1928 for his novel *The Bridge of San Luis Rey* (1927) and in 1938 and 1943 for the plays *Our Town* (1938) and *The Skin of Our Teeth* (1942).

Wilder achieved his first success with *The Bridge of San Luis Rey,* a short novel that describes how fate influences human existence. He based two novels, *The Woman of Andros* (1930) and *The Ides of March* (1948), on ancient Roman sources. In the novel *Heaven's My Destination* (1935), Wilder created an ironic portrait of an American salesman. Wilder's longest and most complex novel, *The Eighth Day* (1967), deals with life in a Midwestern American city about 1900. Wilder's essays and other nonfiction were collected in *American Characteristics* (published in 1979, after his death).

Wilder began writing for the stage in 1915. In a 1941 essay, he wrote that "… the theater carries the art of narration to a higher power than the novel or the epic poem." Two collections of his early one-act plays were published as *The Angel That Troubled the Waters* (1928) and *The Long Christmas Dinner* (1931). Wilder's masterpiece is *Our Town* (1938), a sensitive drama about life and death in a New England village. He revised his 1938 farce *The Merchant of Yonkers* under the title *The Matchmaker* (1955). This comedy, in turn, was adapted into the musical *Hello, Dolly!* (1964). In *The Skin of Our Teeth,* Wilder wrote an expressionist fantasy about humanity's ability to survive even its own follies. Wilder was born in Madison, Wisconsin.   Barbara M. Perkins

Wilderness, Battle of the. See Civil War (Battle of the Wilderness).

Wilderness Road was an important pioneer road. In March 1775, the American pioneer Daniel Boone and a party of woodsmen began to cut a trail. Their route began at the Holston River in what is now Tennessee, passed through the Powell River Valley, crossed the Cumberland Mountains through Cumberland Gap, and ended in what is today central Kentucky. Boone and his followers built a settlement called *Boonesborough* at the trail's end near present-day Lexington. Another branch of the Wilderness Road led to Harrodsburg.

The road was the only usable route through the mountains to Kentucky. It was a rocky trail threatened by unfriendly Indians. By 1800, about 200,000 settlers had traveled the road.   William E. Foley

See also **Boone, Daniel** (The Wilderness Road).

Wildlife conservation is the wise management of natural environments for the protection and benefit of plants and animals. Some species of plants and animals have become extinct because of natural causes. However, in modern times, the activities of human beings and human population growth have increased the danger for wildlife. As a result, some species have declined greatly in numbers and others are now extinct. Thus, human beings created the need for conservation.

Throughout history, wildlife has suffered because of human beings and their activities. Increasingly efficient weapons, such as bows, rifles, and shotguns, enabled people to kill game with growing ease. With such weapons, hunters have killed off some species of animals. People also have cleared forests, drained swamps, and dammed rivers to clear the way for agriculture and industry. These activities have seriously harmed or destroyed large areas of plant and wildlife habitat. Human beings may also disrupt the natural processes of the habitats that remain. These disruptions affect the diversity and size of living populations in the habitats. Many such habitats are small and no longer connected to vast *ecosystems* (communities of living organisms and their physical environment). Environmental pollution has also affected many wild species.

Various species had become extinct even before people appeared on the earth. In the past, however, other species developed and replaced those that died off, and the total variety of life did not diminish. Today, human activities kill off species with no hope for their replacement, and so the variety of life decreases.

Since about 1600, many kinds of wildlife have become extinct. In North America, such species include the Carolina parakeet, the passenger pigeon, the California grizzly bear, and a birch that once grew in Virginia.

Beginning in the late 1800's, growing concern for the world's vanishing wildlife has led to increased conservation action. The governments of many nations have passed protective laws and set aside national parks and other reserves for wildlife. Such efforts have saved the American bison, the pronghorn, and many of the rare plants found on the Hawaiian and Galapagos islands.

But several hundred species of animals and thousands of species of plants still face the danger of extinction. Such animals include the Asiatic lion, the Bengal tiger, the blue whale, the mountain gorilla, the whooping crane, the California condor, and all the Asian rhinoceroses. Plants that are facing extinction include the black cabbage tree, the Ozark chestnut, the St. Helena redwood, and several kinds of California manzanitas.

Values of wildlife conservation. If people ignore the need for wildlife conservation, today's endangered species will soon become extinct. Many other species will also face extinction. If this happens, human beings will lose much of great value that cannot be replaced. Wildlife is important to people for four main reasons: (1) beauty, (2) economic value, (3) scientific value, and (4) survival value.

Beauty. Every kind of animal and plant differs from every other kind and thus contributes in a special way to the beauty of nature. Most people feel that such beauty enriches their life. It also heightens the enjoyment of camping and other forms of outdoor recreation.

Economic value. Wild species of animals and plants provide many valuable substances, such as wood and other plant products, fibers, meat and other foods, and skins and furs. The financial value of wild species is important to the economies of many nations. In industrialized nations, the recreational viewing of animals at zoos and wildlife refuges is also a source of revenue.

Scientific value. The study of wildlife provides valuable knowledge about various life processes. Such study has helped scientists understand how the human body functions and why people behave as they do. Scientists have also gained medical knowledge and discovered important medical products by studying wildlife. In addition, by observing the effect of environmental pollution on wild animals, scientists have learned how pollution affects human life.

Survival value. Every species of wildlife plays a role in helping maintain the balanced, living systems of the earth. These systems must continue to function if life is to survive. Thus, the loss of any species can threaten the survival of all life, including human beings.

Classifications of scarce wildlife. Three main classifications are commonly used for animals and plants that face possible extinction: (1) endangered, (2) vulnerable, and (3) lower risk.

Endangered species face the most serious threat of extinction. They require direct human protection for survival. The California condor is endangered because only about 180 birds of this species still exist, most of them in captivity. In 1987, wildlife biologists captured what was then the last remaining wild California condor. Since then, more than 150 California condors have been born and raised in captivity, and scientists have released some of these birds into the wild in California and Arizona.

Vulnerable species, also known as *threatened species,* are generally abundant in some areas, but they face serious dangers nevertheless. These dangers may result from unfavorable changes in the environment. They also may be due to extensive hunting, fishing, or trapping, or even to collecting by hobbyists. The gray wolf, a vulnerable species, is plentiful in some places. But its overall numbers worldwide are threatened by hunting, trapping, and poisoning.

Lower risk species, also known as *rare species,* have small populations. They often live in restricted geographical areas, but their numbers are not necessarily decreasing. For example, the rare bristlecone pine trees grow only at high altitudes in the western United States. But their survival is not seriously threatened.

Methods of wildlife conservation. The method used to protect wildlife depends on the source of the danger to the species. Much wildlife can be helped by ensuring that their environment provides enough food, water, and shelter. This method, *habitat management,* involves such action as soil conservation, good forestry practices, and water management.

Many species of wildlife are threatened because humans have destroyed their habitats. For example, people have drained swamps and marshes and converted them into farmland. The wetland habitats that remain have been further degraded due to factors caused by human activity. These factors include the redirecting of surface water away from wetland sites, reduction of ground water levels, sedimentation, toxic chemicals, and isolation from other wetlands. Poor farming practices also may destroy land, or the spread of cities and industries may pave over former wildlife habitats. Pollution may poison the air, water, plants, and animals. To save wildlife habitats, people must control pollution and set aside areas in which wild animals and plants can survive.

An animal threatened by too much hunting can be protected by laws that forbid or regulate such killing.

These laws may specify when a certain species may be hunted or how many of the species may be killed. Laws can also protect plants endangered by overcollection. If an entire habitat requires protection, the area may be made a national park or wildlife refuge. In some cases, predatory animals that kill an endangered species must be controlled until the endangered animal has increased in numbers. On the other hand, a species may become too numerous. When this happens, the animal may threaten its own survival—or the survival of other species—by eating too much of the food supply. This problem has occurred with elk and hippopotamuses in national parks. The numbers of such a species must then be reduced, either by controlled hunting or by restoring its natural enemies where they have become scarce.

If a species can no longer survive in its natural environment, it may be raised in captivity and then released into a protected area. This method saved the Hawaiian goose. Likewise, conservationists hope to save the black-footed ferret. This small mammal once lived in the Great Plains, but its population declined sharply during the 1900's. Scientists captured all known ferrets in the 1980's and began breeding them in captivity. In 1991, they began releasing the ferrets into the wild, where these animals have established new breeding populations.

A species threatened by disease may be helped by sanitation measures in its habitat. Rare plants can be maintained in botanical gardens, or their seeds can be saved in seed banks for future planting.

The success of wildlife conservation depends on a knowledge of the *ecology* of a species and the forces at work in a habitat. In other words, it requires an understanding of the way in which a species lives and how it relates to everything in its environment. See **Ecology**.

History. The first wildlife conservation probably occurred among prehistoric peoples. These peoples may have limited their hunting to preserve the supply of wild animals they needed for food. Rulers of ancient civilizations set up the first game reserves—as their personal hunting grounds—and medieval European kings continued this practice. These kings also forbade hunting by anyone other than a member of the ruling class. But such action resulted from a ruler's love of hunting as a sport, rather than any awareness of the need for conservation. Certain forests were protected for religious reasons, and others were preserved for their value in providing timber to build ships.

During the 1600's and 1700's, the British colonies in America passed laws to protect wildlife. But most colonists ignored these laws. Effective wildlife conservation in the United States began in the late 1800's. Congress established Yellowstone National Park, the world's first national park, in 1872. In 1903, President Theodore Roosevelt established Pelican Island, in Florida, as the nation's first federal wildlife refuge. Also in the late 1800's, many states began to pass—and enforce—game laws. Beginning in the 1890's, millions of acres of forests were protected by the national forest system.

Congress set up the National Park System in 1916 under the direction of the National Park Service, an agency of the Department of the Interior. In 1940, the government created the Fish and Wildlife Service in the same department. The service manages the federal wildlife refuges, which in 1966 were organized into the National Wildlife Refuge System. Many private wildlife conservation organizations have been founded since 1900. They include the National Audubon Society and the National Wildlife Federation.

Wildlife protection has a long history in Europe. In Italy, for example, what is now Gran Paradiso National Park has been a wildlife sanctuary since 1856. Australia set up its first national park in 1879. Canada created its first national park, Hot Springs Reservation (now called Banff National Park), in 1885. In 1898, the Sabi Game Reserve (now part of the Great Limpopo Transfrontier Park) was created in what is now South Africa. This reserve was the start of Africa's extensive network of national parks and game reserves. The first South American and Asian national parks were created in the early 1900's.

International cooperation in wildlife conservation began on a worldwide scale after the birth of the United Nations (UN) in 1945. The Food and Agriculture Organization of the United Nations (FAO) and the United Nations Educational, Scientific and Cultural Organization (UNESCO) set up wildlife conservation programs. In 1948, UNESCO helped establish the International Union for the Protection of Nature. In 1956, the name of this organization was changed to the International Union for the Conservation of Nature and Natural Resources (IUCN). The IUCN then started to gather information on the world's endangered species. It publishes this data in its *Red Data Book.* In 1961, the IUCN helped set up the World Wildlife Fund (now also called World Wide Fund for Nature). This fund raises money for conservation.

Wildlife conservation today. More than 37,000 protected areas exist worldwide. The majority of them are less than 4 square miles (10 square kilometers) in size. Most countries also have laws that protect wildlife. The U.S. National Park System has about 200 protected areas with significant wildlife habitats. The U.S. National Wildlife Refuge System includes more than 500 refuges.

State and federal laws also protect wildlife in the United States. For example, the Endangered Species Act of 1973 protects rare wildlife from being hunted, collected, or otherwise threatened. Among other things, the act prohibits federal projects, such as the construction of dams, that would destroy an area where an endangered species lives. In 1978, the act was amended to permit the exemption of certain federal projects.

A specialized profession has developed to serve the needs of wildlife conservation. Many universities have programs to train ecologists and conservation, fishery, and wildlife biologists. These specialists manage natural environments for the benefit of plants and animals.

But despite the many conservation efforts, the future remains uncertain for the world's wildlife. The continued growth of the human population, the destruction and disruption of wildlife habitats, and the spread of environmental pollution present an increasing threat to the survival of wild species.　　Leigh H. Fredrickson

Related articles in *World Book* include:

Adamson, Joy	Conservation
Animal (The future of animals)	Elephant (Protecting elephants)
Audubon Society, National	
Balance of nature	Endangered species
Bird (Bird study and protection)	Fish and Wildlife Service
	Fishing industry
Biodiversity	Fossey, Dian

Galdikas, Biruté	National Wildlife Federation	Poaching
Greenpeace		Seal (People and seals)
Izaak Walton League of America	National Wildlife Refuge System	Sierra Club
	Nature Conservancy	Spotted owl
Leopold, Aldo		WWF
National park		

Additional resources

Claggett, Hilary D., ed. *Wildlife Conservation.* H. W. Wilson, 1997.
Cohen, Daniel. *The Modern Ark: Saving Endangered Species.* Putnam, 1995. Younger readers.
Dobson, Andrew P. *Conservation and Biodiversity.* Scientific Am. Lib., 1996.
Manning, Phillip. *Islands of Hope: Lessons from North America's Great Wildlife Sanctuaries.* J. F. Blair, 1999.

Wilhelm, *VIHL hehlm,* or in English, William, was the name of two German emperors.

Wilhelm I (1797-1888) became king of Prussia and the first emperor of modern Germany. During the revolution of 1848, Wilhelm lost popularity because he opposed constitutional reform. He was forced to leave the country, but he soon came back and put down an uprising in Baden. In 1858, Wilhelm became regent in place of his brother, Frederick William IV, who was suffering from mental disorders. He was proclaimed king of Prussia and given the title Wilhelm I in 1861. He supported the policies of his prime minister, Otto von Bismarck, who brought about three wars while unifying the German states (see **Bismarck, Otto von**). During the Franco-Prussian War in 1871, Wilhelm became *kaiser* (emperor) of a united Germany (see **Franco-Prussian War**).

Wilhelm was born in Berlin on March 22, 1797, and died there on March 9, 1888. He was the second son of Frederick William III, king of Prussia. Trained as a soldier from his early youth, Wilhelm fought in the war of 1814 and 1815 against Napoleon I. See also **Prussia**.

Wilhelm II (1859-1941) was the last emperor of Germany. The Hohenzollern dynasty, which had ruled Prussia since 1701, ended with him (see **Hohenzollern**). Wilhelm was the kaiser during World War I (1914-1918). He received blame for the war, but historians now believe that Russia and Austria were equally guilty in starting it.

Wilhelm, the grandson of Wilhelm I, was born in Berlin on Jan. 27, 1859. He was the oldest son of Emperor Frederick III and Princess Victoria, daughter of Queen Victoria of England. George V of England and Nicholas II of Russia, who fought against him during World War I, were his cousins. His education emphasized military training and made him friendly to the aristocratic military class. Wilhelm had a paralyzed left arm. He hid this weakness and ruled as the most powerful figure in Germany.

Wilhelm came to the throne in 1888 after the 100-day reign of his father. Bismarck was still chancellor and prime minister, but Wilhelm dismissed him in 1890. Under Wilhelm's reign, Germany prospered. He encouraged manufacturing and trade. He gained colonies in Africa and the Pacific Ocean, and he built up the army and navy until they were among the world's greatest. His program of colonial, naval, and foreign trade expansion brought Germany into conflict with the United Kingdom.

In 1890, Wilhelm broke the old Prussian alliance with Russia. This diplomatic blunder forced Germany in 1914 to fight a two-front war and led that nation to ultimate defeat (see **Germany** [History]). Early in November 1918, several revolts broke out and the German Navy mutinied. On November 7, the prime minister demanded that Wilhelm give up his throne. Wilhelm abdicated two days later. He fled to the Netherlands, which was neutral. For more than 20 years he lived in comfortable exile at Doorn.   Gabriel A. Almond

Wilhelmina, WIHL hehl MEE nuh (1880-1962), became queen of the Netherlands in 1890 when her father, William III, died. Her mother, Queen Emma, ruled as regent until 1898. In 1901 Wilhelmina married Henry, Duke of Mecklenburg-Schwerin. Germany invaded the Netherlands in 1940, during World War II, and tried to capture Wilhelmina. But she escaped to London and directed the Netherlands forces against both Germany and Japan. After the war, her people joyfully welcomed Wilhelmina home. She celebrated her Golden Jubilee in August 1948 and then gave up her throne to her daughter, Juliana (see **Juliana**). Wilhelmina was born at The Hague, the Netherlands.   Jane K. Miller

Wilkes, Charles (1798-1877), was an American explorer and naval officer. From 1838 to 1842, he led a United States Navy expedition that proved Antarctica was a continent. Wilkes was also a key figure in the Trent Affair, which was a naval incident that almost made Britain an ally of the Confederacy in the Civil War (1861-1865).

Wilkes was born in New York City. In 1840, the Wilkes expedition sailed more than 1,500 miles (2,400 kilometers) along the coast of Antarctica. Wilkes became the first person to recognize Antarctica as a continent and not just a huge ice pack. In 1842, the Navy court-martialed Wilkes on numerous charges, but found him guilty only of illegally whipping members of his crew. He served on special duty from 1843 to 1861, mainly writing reports on his expedition's findings.

The Trent Affair began in November 1861, when Wilkes seized Confederate diplomatic agents James Mason and John Slidell from the British ship *Trent* near Cuba. This act violated the principle of freedom of the seas. Northerners considered Wilkes a hero, but the U.S. government in time released the two agents. See **Trent Affair**.   Gabor S. Boritt

Wilkins, Sir Hubert (1888-1958), was an Australian explorer, scientist, aviator, and photographer. He won fame for his air explorations in the Arctic and Antarctic.

Wilkins learned to live in the Arctic while on an expedition under explorer Vilhjalmur Stefansson from 1913 to 1916. Wilkins led a natural history expedition into northwestern Australia for the British Museum between 1923 and 1925. In 1928, after two unsuccessful attempts, he and Carl Ben Eielson became the first to fly an airplane across the Arctic Ocean from Point Barrow, Alaska, to Spitsbergen in the Arctic Ocean, a distance of 2,200 miles (3,540 kilometers). King George V of the United Kingdom knighted Wilkins that year.

Later in 1928, Wilkins led an Antarctic expedition and made the first Antarctic airplane flights while surveying the Antarctic Peninsula. In 1931, he tried, but failed, to reach the North Pole in the submarine *Nautilus*. He managed explorer Lincoln Ellsworth's Antarctic expeditions from 1933 to 1936, and served as a United States government adviser from 1942 to 1958.

George Hubert Wilkins was born in Mount Bryan East, in the state of South Australia.   William Barr

See also **Eielson, Carl Ben.**

Wilkins, Mary Eleanor. See Freeman, Mary Eleanor Wilkins.

Wilkins, Maurice Hugh Frederick (1916-   ), is a British biophysicist. He shared the 1962 Nobel Prize for physiology or medicine with biologists James D. Watson of the United States and Francis H. C. Crick of the United Kingdom. Wilkins performed X-ray studies on *deoxyribonucleic acid* (DNA), the substance that transmits genetic information from one generation to the next. This work led Watson and Crick to create a model of the molecular structure of DNA.

Wilkins worked on the World War II Manhattan Project that developed the atomic bomb. He turned to biophysics research after the war. Working at King's College in London, Wilkins became an authority on the structure of nucleic acids. Wilkins was born in Pongaroa, New Zealand.   Alan R. Rushton

Wilkins, Roy (1901-1981), was a noted black American leader and was often called "Mr. Civil Rights." Wilkins served as executive secretary of the National Association for the Advancement of Colored People (NAACP) from 1955 to 1977. He helped direct the fight for equal rights and opportunities for blacks. In 1964, Wilkins was awarded the Spingarn Medal for his work in civil rights.

Wilkins was born in St. Louis, Missouri, the grandson of a slave. He graduated from the University of Minnesota. Wilkins worked for a black newspaper, the *Kansas City Call*, before joining the NAACP in 1931. He edited the NAACP magazine *The Crisis* from 1934 to 1949.
      Carl T. Rowan

Will, in law, is a document that disposes of a person's property after the person's death. The person who makes the will is called the *testator,* if a man, and the *testatrix,* if a woman. Personal property left by will is called a *bequest,* or a *legacy.* Real estate left by will is called a *devise.*

Most wills are prepared by lawyers, who can make sure that the formal legal requirements for wills are satisfied. Wills must be in writing and signed by the testator or testatrix and, usually, two or three witnesses.

Each state of the United States and each province of Canada has laws governing wills. Some laws require that a will be witnessed. Other laws do not. The number of witnesses required may also vary. Many states do not allow witnesses to get any benefits under a will. Some states accept a *holographic* will, or one prepared in a person's own handwriting and unwitnessed.

A person may die *intestate* (without a valid will). The person's property then descends, according to state law, to the individual's spouse and relatives. If the person is not survived by a spouse or relatives and leaves no valid will, the individual's property may *escheat* (transfer) to the state in which the person lived.

Administration. People may dispose of their property in any way they choose. But in most states, the spouse of the testator or testatrix cannot be completely disinherited. In Louisiana, the children of the testator or testatrix must also receive a share of the estate. The will usually names some person as an *executor.* The executor must see that the provisions of the will are carried out. If no executor has been named, the court that has jurisdiction over estates may appoint an *administrator,* whose duties are the same as those of an executor. For the faithful performance of their duties, executors must give a *bond* (written pledge to pay money) or provide for *surety* (a person who agrees to pay if the executor cannot). If an executor does not faithfully carry out the provisions of the will, the bond is forfeited. Usually, the giving of a bond may be waived if the will so provides.

Estate plan. It is desirable that people who own considerable property have an estate plan in which the will is only a part. If a person owns more than a certain amount of property upon death, both the government of the state where the person lives and the U.S. government will collect an estate tax. A properly drawn estate plan may save many thousands of dollars that otherwise would have to be paid in estate taxes.

Codicil is an addition made after a will has been prepared that changes the will in some way. People may alter or destroy their wills at any time. Such alteration will be legal provided that the will maker is of sound mind and the alteration was not caused by undue influence from parties interested in the change. The codicil must be made according to the formalities required by state law just as the will must be. If the will must be witnessed by two people, then the codicil must be witnessed by two people.   William M. McGovern

See also **Executor; Legacy; Probate.**

Will-o'-the-wisp is a ghostly, bluish light sometimes seen over marshes and graveyards. Scientists believe it is caused by the natural burning of *methane* (marsh gas) produced by decaying plants. Will-o'-the-wisp is also called *jack-o'-lantern, foxfire,* and *ignis fatuus,* a Latin term that means *foolish fire.* Will-o'-the-wisp often seems to move away or vanish when approached. It was once thought to be a spirit that enjoyed misleading travelers. People who followed such a light would suddenly find themselves hopelessly lost in a swamp. In several English legends, the hero turns one of his garments inside out to magically end the power of will-o'-the-wisp. Other traditions speak of will-o'-the-wisp as the soul of a dead person. See also **Methane.**   Alan Dundes

Willamette River, *wih LAM iht,* rises in the Cascade Mountains and Coast Range of west-central Oregon. It flows northward for about 190 miles (306 kilometers) and empties into the Columbia River. For the location, see **Oregon** (physical map). The Willamette Valley is the richest farming area in Oregon. Oceangoing ships can sail up the river for 12 miles (19 kilometers) to Portland, Oregon's largest city. Locks at Willamette Falls allow small boats to travel upstream as far as Eugene.

Keith W. Muckleston

Willard, Emma Hart (1787-1870), was an early American supporter of higher education for women. Her efforts advanced that movement in the United States. She also wrote a volume of poems that included "Rocked in the Cradle of the Deep" (1830).

Willard was born in Berlin, Connecticut, and started teaching school there at the age of 16. In 1809, she married John Willard, who helped her establish a girls' boarding school at Middlebury, Vermont, in 1814. In 1819, she founded a girls' seminary at Waterford, New York. It was moved to Troy, New York, in 1821. The school, the Troy Female Seminary, later became famous as the Emma Willard School. Willard strongly supported the establishment of public schools, and she educated hundreds of teachers in her schools for girls.

Glenn Smith

Willard, Frances Elizabeth Caroline (1839-1898), was an American educator and social reformer. She organized the temperance movement on the plan by which it attained national prohibition (see **Prohibition**). She served as president of the Woman's Christian Temperance Union (W.C.T.U.) from 1879 until her death, and made the W.C.T.U. a national organization (see

Brown Bros.

Frances E. Willard

Woman's Christian Temperance Union). In 1883, Willard founded a world temperance union. She was also a strong advocate of woman suffrage.

Willard was born on Sept. 28, 1839, at Churchville, New York. She served as president of the Evanston (Illinois) College for Ladies. When the college merged with Northwestern University, Willard became the dean of the Woman's College.

A statue of Frances Willard represents the state of Illinois in Statuary Hall in the United States Capitol in Washington, D.C.   Louis Filler

Willemstad, *VIHL uhm STAHT* or *WIHL uhm STAHT* (pop. 50,000), is the capital of the Netherlands Antilles. It lies on the southwest coast of the island of Curaçao (see **Venezuela** [political map]). St. Anna Bay divides the city into two sections, Punda and Otrabanda.

Willemstad has two of the oldest Jewish landmarks in the Western Hemisphere—a cemetery established in 1659 and a temple built in 1732. Many houses in Willemstad are built in traditional Dutch style, and many are painted in pastel colors.

Arawak Indians were the first inhabitants of what is now Willemstad. The city was founded by the Dutch in 1634. Since 1915, it has been a center for the refining and shipping of crude oil. Willemstad is the southeast Caribbean's center for warehousing, shipping, banking, and property investment.   Gustavo A. Antonini

Willet is a large shore bird of North and South America. In eastern North America, the willet breeds along the Atlantic Coast and in the West Indies. In winter, it migrates as far south as northern Brazil. In western North America, the willet nests away from the shore, breeding from Manitoba to Nevada. It winters along the Pacific Coast from Oregon to northern Chile.

The willet is about 16 inches (41 centimeters) long and appears almost completely gray. When the bird is in flight, its wings and tail display striking patterns of black and white markings. The willet's long bill is straight

© WORLD BOOK illustration by Malcolm Ellis, Bernard Thornton Artists

Willet

and slender, enabling the bird to search in mud and sand for snails, clams, worms, and small crabs. The willet's loud cry when startled into flight is considered bothersome by hunters because it alerts nearby birds. For this reason, the willet has earned the nickname "tattler."   Peter G. Connors

Scientific classification. The willet belongs to the sandpiper family Scolopacidae. Its scientific name is *Catoptrophorus semipalmatus.*

William, of Germany. See **Wilhelm.**

William I (1772-1843) was the first king of the present-day kingdom of the Netherlands. He was the son of William V, Prince of Orange, the last Netherlands governor, or *stadholder,* who lost his throne to the French in 1795. William I joined the Prussian Army against Napoleon I, and in 1806 lost the German duchy of Nassau. He regained Nassau in 1815, but then he traded it for the duchy of Luxembourg at the Congress of Vienna.

The congress made William king of the new Kingdom of the Netherlands, which included Belgium and the Grand Duchy of Luxembourg. In 1830, Belgium demanded its independence, which was recognized in 1839. Because of trouble within the country, William gave up the Netherlands throne in 1840, in favor of his son William II.   Jane K. Miller

William I, Prince of Orange (1533-1584), was the father of the Dutch Republic. The prince was known as *William the Silent* because of his cautious nature.

William was born in Dillenburg, near Wetzlar, Germany. His parents were Lutherans, but William became a Roman Catholic to please Emperor Charles V, who had taken a liking to him. He put William in command of troops on the French frontier in 1555. In 1555 and 1556, Charles gave up rule of the Low Countries (mainly Belgium and the Netherlands) and Spain to his son Philip II. Philip tried to increase control of the Low Countries. When he also tried to stamp out the Protestant religion there, William joined the Protestant Church. He led a rebellion against Spain in 1568. William tried to unite all the Low Countries in the revolt, but he failed. In 1579, the seven northern provinces formed a league that later became the Dutch Republic. In 1581, Philip put a price on William's head. In 1584, an insane assassin killed him.

Jane K. Miller

William I, the Conqueror (1027?-1087), was the first Norman king of England. He took power in 1066, following his army's victory over the Anglo-Saxons of England. As king, William maintained tight control over the country's central government.

William was born at Falaise, in the Normandy region of northwestern France. He was the son of Robert I, Duke of Normandy, and inherited Normandy in 1035, at about the age of 8. During his youth, there were many disorders. In 1047, William put down a great rebellion at the battle of Val-ès-dunes, near Caen, with the aid of his lord, King Henry I of France. From that time on, William ruled Normandy with an iron hand.

William claimed that King Edward the Confessor of England promised him succession to the English throne because he was Edward's nearest adult heir. However, Edward's brother-in-law Harold became king in 1066 through a deathbed grant by Edward and election by the nobles.

William promptly prepared to invade England. But be-

fore William could sail, the king of Norway invaded northern England. King Harold hurried north and defeated the Norwegian invaders. William landed before Harold could return to defend the southern coast. The Normans destroyed the Anglo-Saxon army and killed Harold at the Battle of Hastings on Oct. 14, 1066.

On Christmas Day, 1066, William was crowned king. William then put down local rebellions. He took lands from those who resisted him. He kept some of these lands for himself and gave the rest to his followers in return for military service. To emphasize the lawfulness of his crown, William confirmed the laws of Edward the Confessor and kept all the powers of the Anglo-Saxon monarchy. He levied *Danegeld,* the only national tax on landed property in all of Europe at that time. At Salisbury in 1086, he made all the landholders swear allegiance directly to him as king.

William was devout, firm in purpose, and unchanging in gaining his ends. His greatest monument is *Domesday Book,* a survey of the land and principal landholders of his realm.   Joel T. Rosenthal

See also **Bayeux Tapestry; Domesday Book; Harold II (of England); Hastings, Battle of; Norman Conquest**

Additional resources

Ashley, Maurice. *The Life and Times of William I.* 1973. Reprint. Cross River, 1992.
Douglas, David C. *William the Conqueror.* Univ. of Calif. Pr., 1964. A classic work.
Green, Robert. *William the Conqueror.* Watts, 1998. Younger readers.

William II (1057?-1100) became king of England in 1087. He was the son of William I, the Conqueror. William II was called Rufus, meaning *red,* because of his ruddy complexion. He was an effective and powerful ruler. But his personal morality and his infringements on church rights led the clergy to denounce him and have given him a bad reputation among historians.

In 1088, several powerful Norman barons revolted against William. He put down the revolt and thus strengthened his position as king. Later, he gained control of Normandy by financing the crusading ventures of his brother Robert, Duke of Normandy. He also invaded Scotland and brought it under his control in 1097.

William's reign was marked by a bitter quarrel with the Roman Catholic Church. After the archbishop of Canterbury died in 1089, William did not appoint a replacement so that he could collect the district's revenues for himself. When William fell seriously ill in 1093, he welcomed Anselm as archbishop in order to atone for his sins. But when he recovered his health, he forced Anselm into exile. An arrow shot by a fellow hunter killed William while he was hunting. The clergy refused to give him a church funeral.   Joel T. Rosenthal

William III (1650-1702), also known as William of Orange, became King of England, Scotland, and Ireland in 1689. William was *stadholder* (governor) of the Netherlands when prominent English leaders became dissatisfied with King James II of England and invited William to intervene. William then invaded England and, without bloodshed, gained control of the country in what became popularly known as the Glorious Revolution. William also helped lead European opposition to King Louis XIV of France.

William was born in The Hague, the Netherlands. He

was the son of a Dutch nobleman, William II, Prince of Orange, and Mary, the oldest daughter of King Charles I of England. In 1672, after France had invaded the Netherlands, William was elected governor of the Netherlands for life and entrusted with its defense. His efforts to block French aggression became a lifelong task.

In 1677, William married his cousin Mary Stuart. Her father became King James II of England in 1685. William hoped to obtain England's support against France. But James II, a Roman Catholic, remained friendly to Louis XIV, also a Catholic. William and Mary were Protestants.

In 1688, James II had a son whom he planned to raise as a Roman Catholic. Key English political leaders who opposed James realized that England would remain under Catholic rule after James's death. Most people in England and Scotland were Protestants. Several English political and religious leaders then invited William to invade England. Later that year, William landed in England and permitted James II to flee to France.

In 1689, William and Mary became king and queen and accepted what became known as the Bill of Rights. This document guaranteed the people certain basic rights and limited the power of the monarchy. William never became popular with his English, Scottish, or Irish subjects, but he presided over the stabilization of England's society and economy. He also permitted development of England's parliamentary system of government and made the nation's law courts independent of the monarch. Near the end of his life, William played a leading role in the creation of the coalition of European powers that opposed France in the War of the Spanish Succession (1701-1714).   Richard L. Greaves

See also **Bill of Rights; Glorious Revolution; Mary II.**
William IV (1765-1837) was king of the United Kingdom from 1830 to 1837. He became king after his brother George IV died. William ruled in one of the most important periods in British history. During his reign, Parliament passed the Reform Act of 1832, which gave the right to vote to more British than ever before. In 1833, Parliament abolished slavery in the British Empire.

William was born on Aug. 21, 1765, in London. He was the third son of King George III. At the age of 13, William began a long career in the British Royal Navy. During his reign, he became known as the "Sailor King." He also ruled the German territory of Hanover from 1830 to 1837. His niece Victoria succeeded him.   James J. Sack

William, Prince (1982-   ), is a grandchild of Queen Elizabeth II of the United Kingdom. His father is Charles, Prince of Wales, the heir apparent to the British throne. William's mother was Diana, Princess of Wales. As the older of Prince Charles's two sons, Prince William is second only to his father in the line of succession to the throne. William Arthur Philip Louis Windsor was born on June 21, 1982, in London.

Prince William attended Ludgrove Preparatory School, in Berkshire. He then attended Eton, one of the leading private sec-

© Ian Jones, Liaison Agency
Prince William

ondary schools in the United Kingdom. In 2001, he entered the University of St. Andrews in Scotland.

Prince William's younger brother is Prince Harry. The brothers endured the divorce of their parents in 1996 and the death of their mother in 1997.   Howard Timms
William and Mary. See **William III; Mary II.**
William and Mary, College of, is a coeducational, state-supported university in Williamsburg, Virginia. It was founded in 1693 by King William III and Queen Mary II of England and is the second oldest institution of higher education in the United States. Harvard University, founded in 1636, is the oldest. In 1779, the College of William and Mary became the first college in the United States to offer professional training in law.

Courses lead to bachelor's, master's, and doctor's degrees. Areas of study include the arts and sciences, business administration, and education. The Marshall-Wythe School of Law offers the Master of Law and Taxation and the Doctor of Jurisprudence degrees. Graduate programs are also offered at the School of Marine Science at Gloucester Point, Virginia.

Famous former students of the university include Thomas Jefferson, James Monroe, John Tyler, and John Marshall. George Washington received his surveyor's license from William and Mary in 1749. He served as its chancellor from 1788 until his death in 1799.

Phi Beta Kappa, an honorary scholastic society, was founded at William and Mary in 1776 (see **Phi Beta Kappa**). The honor system was founded there in 1779. William and Mary was the first U.S. college to have an elective system of study (1779), a school of modern languages (1779), and a school of modern history (1803).
Critically reviewed by the College of William and Mary
William of Ockham, *AHK uhm* (1284?-1347?), also spelled *Occam*, was an English philosopher and theologian. He was the most influential scholastic thinker of the 1300's (see **Scholasticism**). His attitudes toward knowledge, logic, and scientific inquiry played a major part in the transition from medieval to modern thought.

Ockham believed that the primary form of knowledge came from experience gained through the senses. He based scientific knowledge on such experience and on self-evident truths—and on logical propositions resulting from those two sources.

In his writings, Ockham stressed the Aristotelian principle that "entities must not be multiplied beyond what is necessary." This principle became known as *Ockham's Razor.* In philosophy, according to Ockham's Razor, a problem should be stated in its basic and simplest terms. In science, the simplest theory that fits the facts of a problem is the one that should be selected.

Ockham was born in southern England. He joined the Franciscans and became prominent in that religious order. Ockham studied at Oxford University and then taught theology. In 1324, Pope John XXII called him to Avignon, France, to answer charges of *heresy* (teaching false doctrine). But he was never formally condemned. Ockham became involved in a controversy over the poverty of Jesus and His apostles in which he wrote critically, and brilliantly, against the pope, who excommunicated him. Ockham's political writings propose a view of human rights and limited government that anticipate much of modern political thought.   Timothy B. Noone
William of Orange. See **William III.**

William the Silent. See William I, Prince of Orange.

Williams, Bert (1874?-1922), was a great African American comedian. Surviving photographs show Williams's gift for comic facial expression. Recordings preserve his dry, biting humor in songs, many of which he wrote. His best-known songs are "Jonah Man," "Woodman, Woodman, Spare that Tree," and his theme song, "Nobody."

Egbert Austin Williams was probably born in Nassau, Bahamas, and was brought to the United States as a child. He began his career in minstrel shows, a form of entertainment featuring black musicians or white musicians with blackened faces, performing black music. Because of his light skin, Williams darkened his face with burnt cork for performances, a practice he followed for the rest of his career.

About 1893, Williams formed a vaudeville comedy team with George Walker. The two appeared in and often coauthored musical comedies intended for black audiences. Williams and Walker starred in *In Dahomey,* the first musical written and performed by blacks to play in a regular New York City theater when it opened there in 1903. Williams later became the first black entertainer featured in an otherwise all-white show, the 1910 edition of the *Ziegfeld Follies.*   Gerald Bordman

Williams, Daniel Hale (1856-1931), an American doctor, pioneered in surgery on the human heart. In 1893, he became the first surgeon to repair a tear in the *pericardium* (sac around the heart). Williams, a black, helped improve medical opportunities for black people. In 1891, he founded Provident Hospital in Chicago, the country's first interracial hospital and training school for black nurses and interns. Later, he established a nursing school for blacks at Freedman's Hospital in Washington, D.C. He established surgical clinics at Meharry Medical College, Nashville, Tennessee.

Williams was born on Jan. 18, 1856, in Hollidaysburg, Pennsylvania. He graduated from Chicago Medical College (now Northwestern University Medical School) in 1883 and began his Chicago practice. He was the only black original member of the American College of Surgeons, which was founded in 1913.   Daniel J. Kevles

Williams, Emlyn (1905-1987), was a Welsh actor and playwright. Williams also gained wide recognition for his concert readings from the works of the English author Charles Dickens and the Welsh poet Dylan Thomas.

Williams became best known for his autobiographical play *The Corn Is Green* (1938). This drama depicts his life as a poor boy in a Welsh village. Williams also wrote *Night Must Fall* (1935), a popular suspense thriller. Williams's performance as the charming but insane young murderer in this drama also brought him fame as an actor. His other plays include *The Light of Heart* (1940), *Accolade* (1950), and *Someone Waiting* (1953).

George Emlyn Williams was born on Nov. 26, 1905, in Mostyn, near Prestatyn. He wrote two autobiographies. *George: An Early Autobiography* (1961) describes his childhood and his years at Oxford University. *Emlyn* (1973) tells about his early career in the theater. Williams died on Sept. 25, 1987.   Mardi Valgemae

Williams, Hank (1923-1953), was a country and western singer and composer. His songs helped country music spread from the rural South and Southwest to other regions of the United States. Williams's best-known songs include "Cold, Cold Heart" (1951), "Jambalaya"

(1952), and "Your Cheatin' Heart" (1953).

Hiram Williams was born on Sept. 17, 1923, in Georgiana, Alabama. He taught himself to play the guitar when he was 8 years old. At 14, he formed a band, the Drifting Cowboys. The band began to perform on radio the next year. In 1947, Williams started recording in Nashville, Tennessee, the center of country music. There he achieved his greatest popularity through recordings and radio performances, particularly on "The Grand Ole Opry" program. Williams died of a heart ailment at the age of 29 while traveling to a performance. Williams's son, Hank Williams, Jr., also became an important country music singer and composer.   Lydia Dixon Harden

See also **Country music** (picture).

Williams, Ralph Vaughan. See Vaughan Williams, Ralph.

Williams, Robin (1952-   ), is an American actor and comedian known for his skill at improvising and his frantic comic style. Williams first gained fame for his sometimes eccentric comedy in nightclubs and on TV. He later won respect as a versatile, serious film actor.

Williams was born on July 21, 1951, in Chicago. He began his show business career as a stand-up comedian in clubs in San Francisco and Los Angeles. His big break came in 1978 when he made a guest appearance on the hit TV series "Happy Days" as a space alien named Mork. The success of the character led to Williams's starring in the TV comedy series "Mork and Mindy" (1978-1982).

Williams has played a wide variety of characters, including the title character in *Popeye* (1980). He received an Academy Award for best supporting actor for *Good Will Hunting* (1997). He was also nominated for his acting in *Good Morning Vietnam* (1987), *Dead Poets Society* (1989), and *The Fisher King* (1991). Williams's other major films include *The World According to Garp* (1982), *Moscow on the Hudson* (1984), *Cadillac Man* (1990), *Awakenings* (1990), *Mrs. Doubtfire* (1993), *The Bird Cage* (1996), *Patch Adams* (1998), *Insomnia* (2002), and *One Hour Photo* (2002). He was also the voice of the genie in the animated film *Aladdin* (1992).   Louis Giannetti

Williams, Roger (1603?-1683), was a clergyman, a founder of the colony of Rhode Island in America, and a strong supporter of religious and political liberty. He believed that people have a right to complete religious freedom, rather than mere religious toleration that can be denied at the government's will. Williams helped establish a complete separation of church and state for Rhode Island. This example contributed greatly to the system of separation that was later adopted by framers of the Constitution of the United States.

Early life. Williams was born in London, the son of a merchant tailor. As a youth, he became a scribe for Sir Edward Coke, a noted English lawyer and judge. Coke helped Williams enter Cambridge University, where he received a bachelor's degree in 1627. In 1629, Williams became a chaplain in the household of a wealthy Puritan lord. The Puritans were Protestant reformers who advocated simpler forms of worship and stricter morals. By that time, Williams had become a religious Nonconformist—that is, he did not agree with principles of England's official church, the Church of England. At the time, King Charles I and William Laud, bishop of London, were persecuting those who dissented from the Church of England. Williams associated with Nonconformists who were anxious to settle in New England, an area of English colonies in America. In 1629, Williams married Mary Barnard. They had six children.

In Massachusetts. Williams and his wife moved to Massachusetts Bay Colony in America in 1631. Williams refused an invitation to become the minister of the Puritan church in Boston because he opposed its ties to the Church of England. Williams and his wife moved to Plymouth Colony but returned to Massachusetts Bay Colony in 1634, when Williams became the minister of the Puritan church at Salem. There, many people accepted his desire to have a church that was independent of the Church of England and free from governmental interference in religious matters.

By this time, Williams had gained a reputation as a troublesome person. He argued that the royal charter did not justify taking land that belonged to the Indians, and he declared that people should not be punished for religious differences. Officials of Massachusetts Bay Colony acted to send Williams back to England. But he fled into the wilderness in early 1636. The Narragansett Indians provided Williams with land, and he founded Providence, later the capital of Rhode Island.

In Rhode Island. Williams established a government for Providence based on the consent of the settlers and on complete freedom of religion. In 1643, the Puritan colonies—Massachusetts Bay, Plymouth, Connecticut, and New Haven—organized the New England Confederation. The confederation denied membership to Providence and the other towns in Rhode Island because of disagreement with their system of government and of religious freedom. To safeguard Rhode Island liberties and lands, Williams visited England in 1643 and secured a charter from the English government. Under this charter, Rhode Island adopted a system of government that included frequent elections, a flexible constitution, and *home rule* (local self-government). Williams revisited England in 1651 to save the colony from a rival claim.

Williams's most famous work, *The Bloudy Tenent of Persecution* (1644), was published during his first visit to England. The book upheld his argument for the separation of church and state. He wrote it as part of a long dispute with John Cotton, a Puritan leader of Massachusetts Bay Colony. In the work, Williams explained his belief that the state's intervention in religious matters spoiled the worship of God and ruined true religion.

From 1654 to 1657, Williams was president of the Rhode Island colony. In 1657, he contributed to Rhode Island's decision to provide refuge for Quakers who had been banished from other colonies, even though he disagreed with their religious teachings.

Williams earned his living by farming and trading with the Indians. He knew the Indians well and compiled a dictionary of their language. He often acted as a mediator between them and the other colonies. But he served as a captain of the Providence militia and fought against the Indians during King Philip's War (1675-1676).

Williams died in 1683 and was buried with military honors. Rhode Island later placed a statue of him in the U.S. Capitol.   J. Stanley Lemons

See also **Rhode Island** (History).

Additional resources

Gaustad, Edwin S. *Liberty of Conscience: Roger Williams in America.* 1991. Reprint. Judson Pr., 1999.
Spurgin, Hugh. *Roger Williams and Puritan Radicalism in the English Separatist Tradition.* Edwin Mellen Pr., 1989.

Williams, Serena (1981-   ), is a dominant player in women's professional tennis. She won the 1999 United States Open at the age of 17, becoming the first African American woman to win a grand slam event since Althea Gibson of the United States won what is now the U.S. Open in 1958. Williams won the French Open, United States Open, and Wimbledon singles titles in 2002, and the Australian Open and Wimbledon singles titles in 2003. She defeated her older sister Venus in the finals of all five tournaments.

With Venus, Serena won the doubles titles at the French Open and U.S. Open in 1999, at Wimbledon in 2000 and 2002, and at the Australian Open in 2001 and 2003. Teaming up with Venus, she won a gold medal in women's doubles at the 2000 Summer Olympic Games.

Williams was born on Sept. 26, 1981, in Saginaw, Michigan, and grew up in Compton, California. She began playing tennis at about age 5 under the guidance of her father, Richard. Williams turned professional in 1995.
          Dave Nightingale

See also **Tennis** (picture: The Williams sisters).

Williams, Ted (1918-2002), was one of the greatest hitters in baseball history. Williams batted .406 in 1941 and was the last player to reach .400 in the major leagues. Williams won six American League batting titles and had a lifetime batting average of .344. He led the American League in home runs four times, in runs batted in four times, and in runs scored six times. Williams also had a career total of 2,019 walks, second only to Babe Ruth. Williams hit 521 home runs during his career.

Theodore Samuel Williams was born on Aug. 30, 1918, in San Diego, California. He was an outfielder with the Boston Red Sox for 19 seasons from 1939 through 1960. His career was interrupted twice by military service as a Marine Corps pilot. He missed the 1943, 1944, and 1945 seasons during World War II and most of the 1952 and 1953 seasons during the Korean War. Williams was elected to the National Baseball Hall of Fame in 1966. From 1969 through 1972, he was manager of the Washington Senators and the Texas Rangers. Williams died on July 6, 2002.   Dave Nightingale

See also **Baseball** (picture: Ted Williams).

Williams, Tennessee (1911-1983), was an American playwright whose dramas portray the loneliness and isolation of life. He is best known for two plays, *The Glass Menagerie* (1945) and *A Streetcar Named Desire* (1947). In both plays, Williams portrayed the confrontation between a sensitive and poetic individual and the brutality and coarseness of modern life.

In *The Glass Menagerie,* a narrator, Tom Wingfield, re-creates his memories of his sister, Laura, and of his mother, Amanda. Laura, a cripple, escapes into a fantasy world of old phonograph records and the glass animals in her "menagerie." Amanda's harsh practicality is balanced by romanticized memories of her Southern girlhood. Tom dreams of adventure and finally runs away from his family to join the merchant marine.

In *A Streetcar Named Desire,* Blanche DuBois, an aging Southern belle who lives in a world of illusion, seeks shelter from her troubled past. She goes to live in New Orleans with her sister Stella and Stella's brutal and cynical husband, Stanley Kowalski. Stanley symbolizes harsh realism and a new working class South without traditional Southern courtesy and refinement. The play won a Pulitzer Prize in 1948.

Williams's play *Cat on a Hot Tin Roof* (1955) won a Pulitzer Prize in 1955. His other plays include *Summer and Smoke* (1948), *The Rose Tattoo* (1951), *Sweet Bird of Youth* (1959), and *The Night of the Iguana* (1961).

Thomas Lanier Williams was born on March 26, 1911, in Columbus, Mississippi. He chose Tennessee as a pen name. He also wrote poetry, fiction, and memoirs. He died on Feb. 25, 1983.   Albert Wertheim

See also **Drama** (Later United States drama).

Williams, Venus (1980-   ), is an African American professional tennis star. She turned professional at age 14. Her powerful serve, speed, and ground strokes made her a dominant player by the end of the 1990's.

Williams reached the finals of the United States Open in 1997 and the semifinals in 1999, losing in both tournaments to top-seeded Martina Hingis. But Williams won the U.S. Open in 2000 and 2001. In the 2001 victory, she defeated her younger sister, Serena, in the finals. Venus also won the All-England (Wimbledon) Championship in 2000 and 2001. She and Serena won the women's doubles titles at the French Open and U.S. Open in 1999, at Wimbledon in 2000 and 2002, and at the Australian Open in 2001 and 2003. At the 2000 Summer Olympic Games, Venus won the gold medal in women's singles and, teaming up with Serena, a gold medal in doubles.

Venus Ebone Starr Williams was born on June 17, 1980, in Lynwood, California. She grew up in Compton, California. Venus won her first professional tournament in 1998.   Dave Nightingale

See also **Tennis** (picture: The Williams sisters).

Williams, William (1731-1811), was a Connecticut signer of the Declaration of Independence. He was a delegate to the Continental Congress from 1776 to 1778, and a delegate to the Congress of the Confederation in 1783 and 1784. He helped frame the Articles of Confederation and served in the Connecticut convention that ratified the United States Constitution in 1788. Williams was born in March or April, 1731, in Lebanon, Connecticut. He died on Aug. 2, 1811.   Gary D. Hermalyn

Williams, William Carlos (1883-1963), was an important American poet. Williams wrote about American themes in the language of common speech. His poetry sought to discover the essence of everyday objects and experiences. Williams composed in free verse, allowing the subject matter—and his feelings about it—to determine the form of his poems.

Williams was born Sept. 17, 1883, in Rutherford, New Jersey. He received an M.D. degree from the University of Pennsylvania Medical School in 1906. In 1910, he established a family practice in his hometown. He lived there the rest of his life, writing poems in the mornings and evenings about the people and events he observed.

Williams felt that poetry should see "the thing itself without forethought or afterthought but with great intensity of perception." In such poems as "Spring and All" and "The Red Wheelbarrow," he emphasized the overlooked beauty of the world around us. He also called attention to the power of language. He loved to play with language, revealing words as things in themselves.

Williams's work is notable for its humanity. His poetry takes ordinary people seriously. In this quality, it differs from the abstract or intellectual poetry of his time. Williams expressed his concern for people in such poems as "Tract" and "To Elsie."

Williams's short poems are collected in the two-volume *Collected Poems of William Carlos Williams* (1986-1988). In *Paterson* (1946-1958), his major long poem, his themes come together in an experimental epic about a typical American city. His other writings are collected in *Selected Essays* (1954), *The Farmers' Daughters: The Collected Stories* (1961), and *Many Loves and Other Plays* (1961). His *Autobiography* was published in 1951. He died on March 4, 1963.   Steven Gould Axelrod

Williamsburg (pop. 11,998) is a historic city that lies on a peninsula in Virginia between the James and York rivers (see **Virginia** [political map]). Williamsburg is a famous tourist attraction because the city's Historic Area looks much as it did during colonial times. More than 80 original buildings, including many homes, have been restored to appear as they did in the 1700's. In addition, over 400 structures, including public buildings, have been reconstructed on their original foundations.

Williamsburg was the capital of the Virginia Colony from 1699 to 1776 and of the Commonwealth of Virginia from 1776 to 1780. During colonial times, the city was a major cultural, political, and social center.

Many principles of self-government were established in Williamsburg. In 1765, the statesman Patrick Henry delivered a speech against the Stamp Act in the Williamsburg Capitol. There, the colonists adopted the Virginia Declaration of Rights in 1776. This document included the guarantees of liberty that became models for the Bill of Rights of the U.S. Constitution.

Early days. In 1633, English colonists founded the settlement that later became Williamsburg. They chose the site because it had fewer mosquitoes and better soil drainage for crops than did the area around Jamestown, Virginia, the first permanent English settlement in America. They called their community Middle Plantation because it lay in the middle of the peninsula. The College of William and Mary, the second oldest university in the United States, was founded in Middle Plantation in 1693. Only Harvard University is older.

In 1699, the colonists renamed their settlement Williamsburg in honor of King William III of England. Also in 1699, the capital of the Virginia Colony was moved to Williamsburg after a fire destroyed Jamestown. Williamsburg received a city charter in 1722.

Williamsburg was the most important city in the Virginia Colony. Twice a year, plantation owners and their families went to the city to attend sessions of the General Court, Virginia's highest court. On these occasions, called *publick times,* Virginians also conducted business and attended auctions, balls, fairs, horse races, and other social events. The colony's first newspaper, the *Virginia Gazette,* was published in Williamsburg in 1736.

Virginia became one of the first colonies to vote for independence from Britain. It passed the Virginia Resolution for American Independence in Williamsburg in May 1776. In 1780, during the Revolutionary War, the Virginians moved their capital from Williamsburg to Richmond. The westward shift of Virginia's population made the more central location of Richmond desirable. The people also feared that British warships might at-

© Richard Nowitz, Corbis

A wigmaker's shop is one of several colonial craft shops that visitors may tour in Williamsburg. Men in the American Colonies copied from Europe the fashion of wearing wigs, which they powdered white.

© Kelly/Mooney Photography from Corbis

A maker of musical instruments carves the neck of a violin in a Williamsburg craft shop. Workers in the historic shops wear traditional colonial clothing.

Colonial Williamsburg Foundation

Duke of Gloucester Street is lined with restored homes and shops that show how Williamsburg looked during the 1700's. The street is in the city's large Historic Area.

tack Williamsburg from the James River.

Williamsburg declined in importance and population after the Revolutionary War. Its economy came to depend largely on the College of William and Mary. In 1862, during the Civil War, the Battle of Williamsburg was fought east of the city. The city changed little during the 1800's and early 1900's.

Restoration. In 1926, philanthropist John D. Rockefeller, Jr., became interested in restoring and preserving the colonial appearance of the city. The idea came from W. A. R. Goodwin, minister of Williamsburg's Bruton Parish Church. Rockefeller provided the money that set up The Colonial Williamsburg Foundation.

Williamsburg today. Today, the Historic Area of Williamsburg covers more than 170 acres (69 hectares). Eleven major historic buildings and many colonial craft shops are open to the public daily. Guides escort visitors through the buildings. Craftworkers demonstrate

such colonial skills as barrelmaking, cabinetmaking, and blacksmithing, and trained *character interpreters* act out scenes and characters from the period. The guides, craftworkers, and interpreters are all in colonial costume. The furnishings of the homes, public buildings, and shops in Williamsburg make up one of the finest collections of American and English antiques in the United States. The DeWitt Wallace Decorative Arts Museum displays furniture, ceramics, silver, paintings, prints, textiles, and costumes. The Abby Aldrich Rockefeller Folk Art Museum has one of the most important folk art collections in the United States.

Among the tourist attractions near Williamsburg is Carter's Grove, a plantation mansion completed in 1755. Carter's Grove also features a reconstructed slave quarter from the 1700's. The Colonial National Historical Park includes much of Jamestown Island, several historic Yorktown homes, the Yorktown battlefield, and a scenic parkway that connects these sites with Williamsburg. Jamestown, Williamsburg, and Yorktown form what is often called the "historic triangle" of Virginia. Also near Williamsburg is Busch Gardens Williamsburg, an amusement park.

Williamsburg covers about 9 square miles (23 square kilometers), almost five times its area in colonial times. Many modern housing developments surround the city. Williamsburg has a council-manager government. The people elect the five members of the council to two-year terms. Williamsburg is the seat of James City County.   Critically reviewed by The Colonial Williamsburg Foundation

See also **Colonial life in America** (pictures); **Virginia** (picture).

Additional resources

Alter, Judy. *Williamsburg.* Compass Point, 2003. Younger readers.
Kopper, Philip. *Colonial Williamsburg.* Rev. ed. Abrams, 2001.

Williamson, Hugh (1735-1819), a scientist, writer, doctor, and politician, was a North Carolina signer of the Constitution of the United States. Williamson was one of the most outspoken delegates at the Constitutional Convention of 1787. He played a key role in settling the dispute between large and small states over representation in Congress. Later, Williamson helped win *ratification* (approval) of the Constitution by North Carolina.

Williamson was born in West Nottingham Township, in Chester County, Pennsylvania, on Dec. 5, 1735. He was educated at the College of Philadelphia. Although first trained as a minister, he later studied medicine in Scotland and the Netherlands. He began his medical practice in Philadelphia and joined the scientific circle around Benjamin Franklin. He assisted Franklin in experiments with electricity.

Williamson defended the rebellious acts of the New England Colonies to the British in his essay *The Plea of the Colonies* (1775). During the Revolutionary War in America (1775-1783), Williamson won distinction as an army doctor. In 1782, Williamson was elected to the North Carolina legislature. He served in the Congress of the Confederation from 1782 to 1785 and from 1787 to 1789, and in the U.S. House of Representatives from 1789 to 1793. He then retired to New York and devoted his time to scientific work and writing.   Joan R. Gundersen

Willingdon, Marquess of, *MAHR kwihs* (1866-1941), a British colonial official, was Canada's governor general from 1926 to 1931. He was the first Canadian governor general to represent the British monarch rather than the British government. Willingdon was born on Sept. 12, 1866, at Ratton, near Eastbourne, East Sussex. His given and family name was Freeman Freeman-Thomas. In 1900, he was elected to the British Parliament as a Liberal. He became an earl in 1931 and a marquess in 1936. In 1913, Willingdon was sent to India, where he served as governor of Bombay (now Mumbai) until the end of 1918 and as governor of Madras (now Chennai) from 1919 to 1924. He was *viceroy* (ruler) of India from 1931 to 1936. Willingdon did much to improve economic, political, and social conditions in India.   Jacques Monet

Willkie, Wendell Lewis (1892-1944), was the Republican candidate for United States president in 1940 when Franklin D. Roosevelt ran for a third term. Willkie was defeated, but he received over 22 million votes, 45 per-

cent of those cast. Senator Charles L. McNary of Oregon was his running mate for the vice presidency.

Having been a Democrat for most of his life, Willkie became a Republican in the mid-1930's. He rose to political prominence without the aid of a regular political organization, and most of his advisers were political amateurs. The chant "We want Willkie" from the galleries at the 1940 Republican National Convention forced many unwilling Republican leaders to give Willkie their party's nomination for U.S. president.

Harris & Ewing
Wendell L. Willkie

His life. Lewis Wendell Willkie was born on Feb. 18, 1892, in Elwood, Indiana. When he joined the Army during World War I, the Army mistakenly reversed his first and middle names. He accepted the change. He studied law at Indiana University. In 1929, he became legal adviser to the Commonwealth and Southern Electric Utilities Company. In 1933, he was elected the company's president. He fought a long legal battle against the Tennessee Valley Authority (TVA). But when in 1939 the U.S. Supreme Court refused to consider the constitutionality of the TVA's activities, he sold the properties of the Tennessee Electric Power Company, a subsidiary of Commonwealth and Southern, to the TVA for $78 million.

His public career. Willkie became prominent for his opposition to the New Deal of President Roosevelt. He favored many of its social reforms but opposed its business regulations. He favored removing controls and changing the tax system to encourage business expansion. He largely agreed with Roosevelt's foreign policy.

After the United States entered World War II in 1941, Willkie rallied his followers in a program of national unity. Roosevelt sent him on a number of visits to other countries as his unofficial envoy. After Willkie returned from an airplane trip around the world in 1942, he wrote the book *One World* (1943). In it, he outlined his ideas for international cooperation. Willkie entered the Wisconsin primary in 1944 as a candidate for the Republican nomination for president. He was defeated and retired from politics.   David E. Kyvig

See also **Roosevelt, Franklin D.** (Election of 1940).

Willow is a large group of graceful trees and shrubs that usually have slender branches and narrow leaves. There are about 300 species, and about 80 of them are native to North America. The smallest willow is a shrub about 1 inch (2.5 centimeters) high that grows in Arctic regions and above the timber line on mountains. The largest willows grow over 120 feet (37 meters) high.

Willows usually grow near water. Sometimes they are planted in damp regions so that their roots take up water and dry the soil. The roots interlace to form a tough network that holds the soil together and prevents soil erosion. Willows also are planted to provide shade and to protect fields from winds.

The twigs of the willow are soft and slender, and they bend easily. Because of this, the wood is used to make baskets and wicker furniture. The wood of some willows also produces a high grade of charcoal that once was used to make gunpowder. The bark yields a chemical that the human body converts to a *salicylate,* a group of compounds to which aspirin belongs. In the past, people in various parts of the world used willow bark to relieve pain and fever. Most willows have long, narrow leaves that taper to a point and have finely toothed edges. Some willows have small, oval-shaped leaves.

In early spring, willows produce upright clusters of tiny, yellowish-green flowers. These clusters are called *catkins* because they resemble a cat's tail. The female flower develops a flask-shaped pod that splits open and releases tiny seeds with white, silky, hairlike parts.

The *black willow* is an important tree in the eastern United States. It has rough, dark bark. Most willow lumber comes from the black willow. The lumber is used mainly for boxes, crates, and wicker furniture.

Wicker furniture and baskets are also made from young shoots of the shrubby *basket willow.* The basket willow was brought to North America from Europe and now grows in the northeastern United States.

The *white willow* is a popular decorative tree. The underside of its leaves looks white and silky. Thought to be native to China, the *weeping willow* has graceful, drooping branches. The *pussy willow* develops furry catkins. Its twigs are often used decoratively.   Linda B. Brubaker

Scientific classification. Willows belong to the willow family, Salicaceae. The scientific name for the black willow is *Salix nigra.* The basket willow is *S. viminalis,* the weeping willow is *S. babylonica,* the white willow is *S. alba,* and the pussy willow is *S. discolor.*

See also **Catkin; Osier; Pussy willow; Tree** (picture: Broadleaf trees of North America).

Willow herb. See Fireweed.

Wills, Helen Newington. See Moody, Helen Wills.

Willys, John North (1873-1935), was an American automobile manufacturer. Willys began selling bicycles in 1898 and soon added automobiles, including those of the small Overland Company. He took over that firm in 1907, reorganized it as the Willys-Overland Company, and developed it into a leading carmaker. In a recession in 1920, Willys lost control of the company, but he regained control the next year. Willys became United States ambassador to Poland in 1930. He resigned in 1932 to try to rescue Willys-Overland from a crisis brought on by the Great Depression, but he failed.

Willys was born on Oct. 25, 1873 in Canandaigua, New York . He died on Aug. 26, 1935.   Joel Webb Eastman

Wilmington (pop. 72,664; met. area pop. 586,216) is the largest city and chief manufacturing and financial center of Delaware. Leading chemical firms in the area include the DuPont Company, whose headquarters are in Wilmington. Wilmington is in the Brandywine Valley in northeast Delaware, where the Brandywine and Christina rivers join the Delaware River (see **Delaware** [political map]).

Description. Wilmington, the county seat of New Castle County, covers 16 square miles (41 square kilometers). It has a mayor-council form of government.

Tourist sites include Fort Christina State Park and Monument, Old Swedes Church, and a memorial to African American Medal of Honor winners. The Grand Opera House and the Playhouse in the Hotel du Pont present performing arts. The Riverfront Arts Center as well as a minor league baseball stadium are located on the waterfront of the Christina River.

Several museums are in or near the city. The Hagley Museum features exhibits of industries of the 1800's, including the original DuPont gunpowder mills. The Henry Francis du Pont Winterthur Museum has a collection of Early American furniture. Three du Pont family estates are open to the public. Other museums include the Delaware Art Museum and the Delaware Museum of Natural History. Schools in the area include Goldey-Beacom College, Widener University School of Law, Wilmington College, and campuses of Delaware Technical and Community College, Drexel University, Springfield College, and the University of Delaware.

Wilmington's chief employers are banks and chemical and pharmaceutical firms. Other economic activities include biotechnology and automobile manufacturing. The port on the Delaware River is a center for exporting and importing automobiles, fruit, lumber, and mineral products. Oceangoing ships dock there. Delaware Bay links the Delaware River and the Atlantic Ocean.

History. Delaware Indians lived in what is now the Wilmington area before European settlers arrived. In 1638, Swedish colonists arrived and planned to set up a fur-trading and shipping center along the river they named the Christina. The colonists chose a site with a natural wharf, and there they built Fort Christina. Dutch forces seized the settlement in 1655. The English captured it in 1664, and, in 1739, they named the settlement Wilmington in honor of the Earl of Wilmington.

In 1802, Éleuthère Irénée du Pont, a French chemist, built gunpowder mills near Wilmington. They grew into the DuPont Company. Many other firms also set up offices in the city during the 1800's and 1900's.

In the 1970's, a six-block mall was completed in downtown Wilmington. It includes many houses built in the 1700's, Old Town Hall and the Delaware Historical Society, branches of several colleges, a performing-arts center, and office buildings. Redevelopment projects in the 1980's included converting old mills on the Brandywine River into town houses. In the 1990's, the city revitalized the southern edge of the Christina River waterfront. See also **Delaware** (Visitor's guide; pictures).   David D. Oyler

Wilmot Proviso, *WIHL muht pruh VY zoh,* was an amendment proposed in 1846 that would have banned slavery in any territory acquired by the United States from Mexico. David Wilmot, a Democratic representative from Pennsylvania, offered the amendment to a bill proposed by President James K. Polk. Polk asked Congress to appropriate $2 million to negotiate peace with Mexico, then at war with the United States. He hoped to use this money as compensation for land the United States expected to acquire from Mexico. The Wilmot Proviso declared that slavery should be forbidden in any territory obtained with the money.

The House of Representatives approved the amendment on Feb. 15, 1847. But the Senate, where Southern representation was stronger, refused to pass it. For several years, the Wilmot Proviso was offered unsuccessfully as an amendment to many bills. It reopened the bitter debate over the issue of slavery in the territories. The issue was settled in 1862, when Congress banned slavery in any U.S. territory.   Dan L. Flores

Wilson, Angus (1913-1991), was a British author of novels and satirical short stories. His books deal with the deceptions that occur in human relationships, both public and private. Wilson compiled masses of detail to create a realistic atmosphere.

The heroes of his novels *Hemlock and After* (1952), *Anglo-Saxon Attitudes* (1956), and *The Middle Age of Mrs. Eliot* (1958) are all middle-aged or elderly. They are frustrated, confused, and bogged down in everyday detail. Wilson enlivened these dreary characters with brilliant, witty dialogue and sharp observations on society. His other novels include *The Old Men at the Zoo* (1961), *No Laughing Matter* (1967), *As If by Magic* (1973), and *Setting the World on Fire* (1980). *The Collected Stories of Angus Wilson* was published in 1987.

Wilson wrote several literary studies, including *The World of Charles Dickens* (1970) and *The Strange Ride of Rudyard Kipling* (1978). His criticism appears in *Diversity and Depth in Fiction* (1984).

Angus Frank Johnstone-Wilson was born on Aug. 11, 1913, in Bexhill-on-Sea, England. Queen Elizabeth II knighted him in 1981, and he became Sir Angus Wilson.
                                                                    Michael Seidel

Wilson, August (1945-   ), is a leading African American playwright. His major work is a cycle of plays that traces the black experience in America. The cycle, when completed, will consist of a play set in each decade of the 1900's. Wilson's powerful narratives are noted for their humor and dialogue, blending lively, colloquial phrases and poetic monologues.

In 1987, Wilson won a Pulitzer Prize for *Fences* (1985), a play about the struggles in 1957 of a black sanitation worker earlier denied a chance to play major league baseball. He won a second Pulitzer Prize in 1990 for *The Piano Lesson* (1987). In this drama, a brother and sister disagree over whether to sell or keep the family heirloom, a richly carved piano that is a symbol of the family's heritage of slavery. Both works are typical of Wilson's blend of the realistic with the fantastic or mystical.

The first play in Wilson's cycle was *Jitney* (1982), which describes the struggle of black taxi drivers in 1971. *Ma Rainey's Black Bottom* (1984), Wilson's first success, shows white promoters exploiting black recording artists in the 1920's. *Joe Turner's Come and Gone* (1986) tells of an embittered black man's search for his wife in 1911. The allegorical *Two Trains Running* (1990), set in 1969, focuses on characters in a restaurant discussing their fate. *King Hedley II* (2000) is set in the 1980's and tells the grim story of an ex-convict trying to build a better life for himself. Wilson was born on April 27, 1945, in Pittsburgh, Pennsylvania.   Thomas P. Adler

See also **Drama** (picture: African American playwrights).

Wilson, Edith Bolling (1872-1961), was one of the most influential first ladies in United States history. She was the second wife of Woodrow Wilson, who served as president from 1913 to 1921. Wilson's first wife, Ellen Axson Wilson, died in August 1914. Edith and the president met in March 1915 and married in December.

Edith Wilson became one of her husband's closest advisers. She went with him to Paris in 1918 to attend the peace conference after World War I. President Wilson suffered a paralytic stroke in October 1919. Edith Wilson believed he would more likely recover if he stayed in office than if he resigned. For many months, she decided who could see the president and what documents he

received. Critics scornfully called Edith Wilson "the first woman president." But she always denied having influenced government policy. She referred to the period of the president's illness as "my stewardship." From Woodrow Wilson's death in 1924 until she died in 1961, she worked to keep her husband's memory alive.

Culver Pictures
Edith Wilson

Edith Wilson was born in Wytheville, Virginia, on Oct. 15, 1872. Her maiden name was Bolling. With only two years of formal education, she became known for her intelligence and judgment. She married Norman Galt in 1896. Galt died in 1908.   Kendrick A. Clements

See also **Wilson, Woodrow.**

Wilson, Edmund (1895-1972), an American author, wrote about a wide variety of subjects. He became known for important works in literary criticism, Biblical studies, history, literature, and political science.

Wilson's many books reflect his broad interests. He learned Russian to do research on *Travels in Two Democracies* (1936). He mastered Hebrew to do research for *Scrolls from the Dead Sea* (1955). He showed his broad knowledge of cultural, social, and historical subjects in such books as *To the Finland Station* (1940), *Apologies to the Iroquois* (1960), and *Patriotic Gore: Studies in the Literature of the American Civil War* (1962).

Wilson's first work of literary criticism, *Axel's Castle* (1931), is a study of the symbolist movement in literature. *The Wound and the Bow* (1941) examines the writings of noted European and American authors. Many of Wilson's magazine essays and reviews were collected in *Classics and Commercials* (1950), *The Shores of Light* (1952), and *American Earthquake* (1958). Wilson wrote one novel, *I Thought of Daisy* (1929).

Wilson was born on May 8, 1895, in Red Bank, New Jersey. Wilson left over 2,000 pages of notes when he died. Five volumes of these notes were published as *The Twenties* (1975), *The Thirties* (1980), *The Forties* (1983), *The Fifties* (1986), and *The Sixties* (1993).   Victor A. Kramer

Wilson, Edward Osborne (1929-   ), is an American biologist known for his contributions to the study of animal societies. Wilson helped found the field of *sociobiology,* which studies the biological basis for the social behavior of animals. He argued that *genes* (hereditary material) heavily influence how species behave. Wilson made extensive studies of the social behavior of ants. He observed ant populations worldwide, discovering hundreds of new species. His work with ants also led him to learn how geography, or natural surroundings, plays a role in the formation of species. These and other findings by Wilson helped advance *biogeography,* the science of the distribution of living things.

Wilson was born on June 10, 1929, in Birmingham, Alabama. He received his Ph.D. degree from Harvard University in 1955. After spending one year studying ants in the tropics, Wilson joined the faculty at Harvard in 1956, becoming a full professor there in 1964. He has since held various teaching and research posts at Harvard and its Museum of Comparative Zoology.

Wilson's many books include *The Theory of Island Biogeography* (1967), written with the American ecologist Robert H. MacArthur, as well as *Sociobiology: The New Synthesis* (1975), *The Diversity of Life* (1992), *The Future of Life* (2002), and his autobiography, *Naturalist* (1994). Two of his works won the Pulitzer Prize for general nonfiction: *On Human Nature* (1978) and *The Ants* (1990), which he wrote with the German biologist Bert Hölldobler.   Keith R. Benson

Wilson, Ethel (1890-1980), was a Canadian author. Most of her novels and short stories are gentle, sympathetic treatments of people from humble backgrounds. Most of her novels are set in or around Vancouver, British Columbia. She described the city, its people, and the surrounding wilderness with wit and understanding.

Wilson's first novel was *Hetty Dorval* (1947). Her other novels include *The Innocent Traveller* (1949), *The Equations of Love* (1952), and *Love and Salt Water* (1956). Wilson's best-known novel, *Swamp Angel* (1954), tells the story of a middle-aged woman escaping a monotonous marriage to seek renewed contact with nature.

Wilson was born in Port Elizabeth, South Africa, and was raised in England and Vancouver. In 1937, she began to write short stories, which were collected in *Mrs. Golightly and Other Stories* (1961) and in *Ethel Wilson: Stories, Essays and Letters* (1987).   Laurie R. Ricou

Wilson, Harold (1916-1995), served as prime minister of the United Kingdom from 1964 to 1970 and from 1974 to 1976. He was also the leader of the British Labour Party from 1963 to 1976. Wilson was prime minister during times of great economic difficulty. His country faced inflation, strikes, low industrial production, and a deficit in its balance of payments. To try to solve these problems, Wilson's government devalued the British pound, raised taxes, and put a ceiling on prices and wages.

Wilson was born on March 11, 1916, in Huddersfield, Yorkshire, England. His full name was James Harold Wilson, but he was commonly known as Harold Wilson. Wilson graduated from Oxford University in 1937 and taught economics there for two years.

During World War II (1939-1945), Wilson served as an economist for the government. He was first elected to the House of Commons of Parliament in 1945. Also in 1945, Wilson became parliamentary secretary for the Ministry of Works. In 1947, he was named secretary of overseas trade. Later in 1947, he became president of the Board of Trade. He held that post until 1951. In 1954, he became a member of the Labour Party's parliamentary committee. He became the party's leader in 1963.

The Labour Party won the parliamentary elections in 1964, and Wilson became prime minister. His term ended in 1970, when the Conservative Party won the parliamentary elections. The Labour Party regained power in the 1974 elections, and Wilson became prime minister again. He resigned as prime minister and Labour Party leader in 1976. He was knighted that year and became Sir Harold Wilson. Wilson was in the House of Commons until 1983. He was then named a baron and became Lord Wilson and a member of the House of Lords.

    Richard Rose

Wilson, Henry (1812-1875), served as vice president of the United States from 1873 to 1875 under President Ulysses S. Grant. He was a Republican U.S. senator from Massachusetts from 1855 to 1873. Wilson, who had strong antislavery views, was chairman of the Senate Military Affairs Committee during the Civil War (1861-1865) and a "Radical Republican" during Reconstruction (see **Reconstruction**). He was involved in the Credit Mobilier scandal of 1872 (see **Credit Mobilier of America**).

Wilson was born Jeremiah Jones Colbath in Farmington, New Hampshire, on Feb. 16, 1812. He served in the Massachusetts legislature in the 1840's and early 1850's. Wilson was a member of the Whig Party, the Free Soil Party, and the American (or Know-Nothing) Party before he helped organize the Republican Party in 1854.

    James E. Sefton

See also **Vice president of the United States** (picture).

Wilson, James (1742-1798), a prominent Pennsylvania lawyer, was one of six people who signed both the Declaration of Independence and the Constitution of the United States. At the 1787 Constitutional Convention in Philadelphia, his influence was probably surpassed only by that of Virginia delegate James Madison. Wilson spoke 168 times at the convention. He also demonstrated his understanding of political theory in dealing with convention issues. Wilson argued for a strong national government whose authority would be based in the will of the people. He favored direct election of the chief executive and of both houses of the legislature. Wilson was largely responsible for Pennsylvania's *ratification* (approval) of the Constitution.

Wilson was born on Sept. 14, 1742, in Carskerdo, near St. Andrews, Scotland. He moved to America in 1765 and became a successful lawyer in Carlisle, Pennsylvania. Wilson was elected to the Second Continental Congress, which adopted the Declaration of Independence in 1776. He served in the Congress of the Confederation in 1783, 1785, and 1786. Wilson was appointed to the U.S. Supreme Court in 1789. In the 1793 case of *Chisholm v. Georgia,* he asserted the right of the court to decide cases brought against states.   Richard D. Brown

Wilson, Lanford (1937-   ), is a notable American playwright. Some of his dramas feature large numbers of characters on the margin of society, who suffer from alienation and seek a sense of community in urban America. Other plays center on several generations of a Midwestern family, who often try to discover a meaningful vocation in life.

Wilson won the 1980 Pulitzer Prize in drama for *Talley's Folly* (1979), a love story about Matt Friedman, a 42-year-old Jew, and Sally Talley, a 31-year-old non-Jew from a bigoted family. *The Fifth of July* (1978) also deals with the Talley family after the end of the Vietnam War. *Balm in Gilead* (1965) is a realistic portrait of life in an all-night New York City diner, while *The Hot l Baltimore* (1973) describes residents of a rundown New York hotel. The autobiographical memory play *Lemon Sky* (1970) tells how a father-son conflict leads to a family's disintegration. In *The Mound Builders* (1976), Wilson raises issues about the preservation of cultural heritage versus material progress. *Angels Fall* (1982) describes the reactions of people after a nuclear accident. *Burn This* (1987) focuses on the nature of artistic creativity. *Redwood Curtain* (1993) explores the impact of the Vietnam War on America in the early 1990's. Wilson was born on April 13, 1937, in Lebanon, Missouri. The town was the background for several of his plays.   Thomas P. Adler

**28th President of
the United States 1913-1921**

Taft
27th President
1909-1913
Republican

Wilson
28th President
1913-1921
Democrat

Harding
29th President
1921-1923
Republican

**Thomas R.
Marshall**
Vice President
1913-1921

Oil painting on canvas (1921) by Edmund Charles Tarbell; National Portrait Gallery, Smithsonian Institution, Washington, D.C.

Wilson, Woodrow (1856-1924), led the United States through World War I and gained lasting fame as a champion of world peace and democracy. Wilson was one of the most remarkable men in American history. Before reaching the height of popularity as a world statesman, he had achieved success in two other careers. First, as a scholar, teacher, and university president, he greatly influenced the course of education. Then, as a political leader, he brought successful legislative reforms to state and national government. Wilson would have won a place in history even if he had been active in only one of his three careers.

Wilson was first of all a scholar. Even his physical appearance was like the popular idea of a scholar. He was thin, of medium height, and wore glasses. His high forehead, firm mouth, and jutting jaw all gave signs of thoughtfulness and strength. He was also a strong leader as a teacher, university president, and statesman.

Wilson was a man of firm beliefs. When he made up his mind or felt his principles were at stake, he could be a difficult opponent. In his letters, he often said he was not able to establish close friendships. But in truth, he had a great capacity for warm friendship. His energy, magnetic personality, and high ideals won for him the loyalty of many friends and political supporters.

Historians consider Wilson one of the three or four most successful Presidents. They agree that, as a spokesman for humanity in a world crisis, he stood for integrity, purity of purpose, and responsibility. Not even Wil-

son's enemies suggested he was weak or stupid. They knew he was honest, and that not even friendship could turn him aside from what he thought was right.

A minority of the voters elected Wilson to the presidency in 1912. That year the Republicans split their votes between President William Howard Taft and former President Theodore Roosevelt. In 1916, the people reelected Wilson, partly because "He kept us out of war." Three months later, German submarines began unrestricted attacks on American ships. Wilson went before Congress and called for war. After the war ended in 1918, the President fought for a peace treaty that included a League of Nations. Wilson saw his dream of U.S. leadership of the League crumble in 1920 when Warren G. Harding was elected President. Harding opposed American membership in the new organization.

In many ways, the Wilson era separated an old America from the modern nation of today. In 1910, when Wilson was elected governor of New Jersey, Americans drove fewer than 500,000 automobiles. By 1920, toward the end of Wilson's presidency, more than 8 million cars, many of them Model T Fords, crowded the highways. Throughout this brief period of 10 years, the speeding-up in the nation's way of life could be seen in many ways. The electrical industry grew rapidly, skyscrapers rose in large cities, machinery revolutionized farm life, and good roads began to crisscross the country.

The period also brought further development of the great social changes that had been building in the nation since the late 1800's. After the Civil War ended in 1865, immigrants began pouring into the United States, especially from southern and eastern Europe and from Asia. Many settled in urban areas, causing cities to grow

John M. Mulder, the contributor of this article, is President of Louisville Presbyterian Theological Seminary. He is the author of Woodrow Wilson: The Years of Preparation.

World War I raged through Europe from 1914 to 1918.

The peace conference in 1919 led to the Treaty of Versailles.

The world of President Wilson

Major labor reforms were announced in 1914 by automobile manufacturer Henry Ford. He initiated the eight-hour work-day and established a minimum wage of $5 a day, double what skilled laborers had been earning.

Three amendments to the U.S. Constitution were ratified during Wilson's presidency. Amendment 17, ratified in 1913, provided for the direct election of U.S. senators by the voters of a state, rather than by state legislators. Amendment 18, ratified in 1919, instituted Prohibition. Women gained the right to vote as a result of Amendment 19, ratified in 1920.

The Panama Canal opened for shipping in 1914, though the official opening was delayed until 1920.

The first transcontinental telephone line was established between New York City and San Francisco in 1915.

Silent movies became a major form of entertainment. *The Birth of a Nation*, produced in 1916, was the first screen epic. Such movie stars as Charlie Chaplin, Douglas Fairbanks, Mary Pickford, and Buster Keaton enjoyed great popularity.

The Russian Revolution of 1917 toppled Czar Nicholas II and eventually led to the establishment of a Communist government under V. I. Lenin.

The Black Sox baseball scandal created a stir in 1920. Eight members of the Chicago White Sox were accused of purposely losing the 1919 World Series against the Cincinnati Reds, in return for money from gamblers.

Fears of Communism swept the nation around 1920. Police arrested many innocent people during the "Red Scare."

National Archives; *The Signing of Peace in the Hall of Mirrors, Versailles, 25th June, 1919,* oil painting by Sir William Orpen; by kind permission of the Trustees of the Imperial War Museum, London

dramatically. Between 1910 and 1920, city-dwellers became a majority in the United States for the first time. The nation also was becoming increasingly industrialized, with large corporations accumulating tremendous wealth and political power. In universities, the relatively new fields of sociology and psychology exposed serious social problems and explored human thought and behavior. Examples of changes in popular culture were the development of motion pictures and the popularity of jazz music, which first appeared on phonograph records in 1917. World War I revolutionized social life. It began a wave of such far-reaching changes as the prohibition of liquor, giving women the right to vote, and the migration of blacks from the South to the North.

Early years

Childhood. Woodrow Wilson was probably born on Dec. 29, 1856, at Staunton, Va. Confusion exists over the date because the family Bible shows it as "12 $\frac{3}{4}$ o'clock" at night on December 28. Wilson's mother said he was born "about midnight on the 28th." Wilson himself used

Important dates in Wilson's life

1856	(Dec. 29) Born at Staunton, Va.
1885	(June 24) Married Ellen Louise Axson.
1902	(June 9) Named president of Princeton University.
1910	(Nov. 8) Elected governor of New Jersey.
1912	(Nov. 5) Elected President of the United States.
1914	(Aug. 6) Ellen Wilson died.
1915	(Dec. 18) Married Edith Bolling Galt.
1916	(Nov. 7) Reelected President.
1919	(Sept. 26-Oct. 2) Suffered collapse and stroke.
1920	(Dec. 10) Awarded Nobel Peace Prize.
1924	(Feb. 3) Died in Washington, D.C.

December 28. He was the third of the four children of Joseph Ruggles Wilson and Janet "Jessie" Woodrow Wilson. The Wilsons named their first son Thomas Woodrow for his maternal grandfather. As a child, he was called "Tommy," but he dropped the name Thomas soon after he graduated from college.

Wilson's father, a Presbyterian minister, had grown up in Ohio. James Wilson, his grandfather, was a Scotch-Irish immigrant who had become a well-known Ohio newspaperman and legislator. Wilson's mother was born in Carlisle, England, near Scotland. Her Scottish father, also a Presbyterian minister, brought his family to the United States when Janet was 9.

An atmosphere of religious piety and scholarly inter-

Woodrow Wilson Birthplace Foundation

Wilson's birthplace in Staunton, Va., is a national historic site. The Wilsons moved to Georgia before Woodrow was 2.

ests dominated Wilson's early years. From the time of his birth, he lived among people who were deeply religious, believed in Presbyterian doctrines, and stressed the importance of education. Before Wilson was 2, his family moved to Augusta, Ga., where his father became pastor of a church. Between the ages of 4 and 8, Wilson lived in an atmosphere colored by the Civil War. His earliest memory was of a passer-by shouting in great excitement that Abraham Lincoln had been elected President and that war would follow. Years later, Wilson wrote about General William Sherman's famous march through Georgia saying, "I am painfully familiar with the details of that awful march." During the war, Joseph Wilson, a strong Southern sympathizer, turned his church into a hospital for wounded Confederate soldiers.

Education. Wilson did not begin school until he was 9, mainly because the war had closed many schools. Also, it seems likely that Wilson suffered from a type of *dyslexia* (reading disability) that he eventually outgrew. But Wilson's father taught the boy much at home. On weekdays, the minister would take him to visit a corn mill, a cotton gin, or some other plant. During the war, they visited ammunition factories and iron foundries. After these trips, Wilson always had to discuss what he had seen, because his father believed the exact expression of ideas was necessary for clear understanding. At home, the Wilsons read the Bible together every day, and gathered to sing hymns on Sunday evenings.

In 1870, Wilson's father became a professor in the Presbyterian theological seminary at Columbia, S.C. Three years later, when Wilson was 17, he entered Davidson College at Davidson, N.C. The school still suffered from the effects of the war. Davidson students had to carry their own water and firewood, as well as perform other chores. Wilson did well, and he enjoyed his freshman year at Davidson. But that year, his father was involved in a bitter dispute at the seminary. When he lost the fight, he resigned to serve as a minister in an important church in Wilmington, N.C. The Wilson family moved to Wilmington, and Woodrow stayed at home for a year. During that year, he decided to enter Princeton University (then called the College of New Jersey). He spent his time at home reading, learning shorthand, and preparing for his studies at Princeton.

In September 1875, Wilson enrolled in the college at Princeton. While there, he practiced public speaking, became a leader in debating, and read the lives of great American and British statesmen. During his senior year, he served as managing editor of the college newspaper, the *Princetonian.* In 1879, Wilson graduated 38th in a class of 106. He planned a career in public life.

In October, Wilson entered the University of Virginia Law School at Charlottesville, Va. He felt that law would provide the best path to the career he desired. Wilson took an active part in the university's debating societies. He withdrew from school in 1880 because of ill health.

Beginning career

Lawyer. In 1882, Wilson established a law office in Atlanta, Ga. He attracted few clients, and spent much of his time reading, writing newspaper articles, and studying political problems. By the spring of 1883, Wilson realized that he was not suited to be a lawyer. He decided to become a college teacher, and began graduate study in history and political science at Johns Hopkins University in Baltimore.

Graduate student. At Johns Hopkins, Wilson came into contact with brilliant, thoughtful men. He worked hard to improve his writing style and to master history and political science. In 1885, Wilson published his first book, *Congressional Government, A Study in American Politics.* Educators, lawmakers, and students praised his analysis of the federal government and of American legislative practices. Wilson later presented this study as his doctoral thesis, and Johns Hopkins awarded him the Ph.D. degree in June 1886.

Wilson's family. In 1883, Wilson made a business trip to Rome, Ga. There he met Ellen Louise Axson (May 15, 1860-Aug. 6, 1914), the daughter of a Presbyterian minister. They were married on June 24, 1885.

Mrs. Wilson became the most influential person in her husband's life. She appreciated his talents and greatness, and sympathized with his ideals. Mrs. Wilson had many literary and artistic interests. But she devoted most of her time to making a comfortable home where her husband could relax from the cares of his work.

The Wilsons had three daughters: Margaret Wilson (1886-1944), Jessie Woodrow Wilson (1887-1933), and Eleanor Randolph Wilson (1889-1967). Wilson was tender and affectionate, and enjoyed nothing more than rollicking with his children or telling them stories at the dinner table. Like his father, Wilson spent many evenings reading the works of British authors Sir Walter Scott, Charles Dickens, or William Wordsworth aloud to his family. He often played charades with his daughters, and once dressed up in a velvet curtain, feather scarf, and one of his wife's hats to look like an old lady.

Teacher. In the autumn of 1885, Wilson began a three-year period as associate professor of history at Bryn Mawr College, a woman's school in Bryn Mawr, Pa. He then became professor of history and political economy at Wesleyan University in Middletown, Conn. Wilson also coached football at Wesleyan, and developed one of the school's greatest teams. He told his players: "Go in to win. Don't admit defeat before you start." In 1889, Wilson published *The State,* one of the first textbooks in comparative government. In 1890, Princeton

Culver

Wilson and his first wife had three daughters. *Left to right* are Margaret, Mrs. Ellen Wilson, Eleanor, Jessie, and Wilson.

University invited him to become professor of jurisprudence and political economy.

University president

At Princeton, Wilson's reputation as a scholar and teacher grew steadily. He worked constantly to express his thoughts precisely in writing. He also became a popular and distinguished lecturer. On June 9, 1902, the Princeton trustees unanimously elected Wilson president of the university. Never before had anyone but a clergyman held this position. As soon as Wilson took office, he announced his intention to change Princeton from "a place where there are youngsters doing tasks to a place where there are men thinking." But his belief that "the object of a university is simply and entirely intellectual" met with opposition from some students devoted largely to social events and athletics.

Wilson helped reorganize the university's undergraduate course program. He introduced a new method of teaching which he called the *Preceptorial System.* He believed that this system, using individual instruction by tutors, would bring students and teachers into a closer relationship. He also believed it would help students organize scattered information from their undergraduate programs and from general reading.

Wilson's educational reforms won high praise from the few who understood them. But what brought the president of Princeton to public attention was his fight to reform the eating clubs. These organizations somewhat resembled the fraternities of other schools. Wilson felt that the clubs were undemocratic and detracted from the intellectual life of Princeton. Some people considered them to be centers of snobbery. Wilson wanted to replace the clubs by rebuilding the university with separate colleges, each arranged in a quadrangle around a central court. Each college would have its own dormitories, eating hall, master, and tutors. Wilson felt this arrangement, which became known as the *Quad Plan,* would stimulate intellectual life.

At first, many Princeton students, including members of the clubs, approved Wilson's idea. But the alumni disliked it because they enjoyed coming back to their clubs at reunions and football games. Bitter feelings were aroused. Finally, the board of trustees asked Wilson to withdraw his proposal. Twenty years later, Harvard and Yale both adopted a form of Wilson's Quad Plan. Princeton itself adopted the plan by the 1980's.

Wilson suffered a second defeat in the development of plans for Princeton's graduate school. He tried to integrate this school with the undergraduate college. He believed such a move would make the graduate school more responsive to his authority and establish it as the center of intellectual life on the campus. Andrew West, Dean of the Graduate College, opposed Wilson's plan. The two men even battled over the location of a proposed new building for the graduate school. The bitter fight ended in defeat when a graduate died and left a sum thought to be several million dollars to the graduate school on condition that West remain in charge.

Wilson's struggles at Princeton attracted wide public notice. Newspapers reported the argument over the Quad Plan as a fight by Wilson for democracy and against snobbery. He was pictured as a man who favored the common people against the rich and powerful. Such a picture was too simple, but it made him politically appealing.

Bettmann Archive

As president of Princeton from 1902 to 1910, Wilson gained nationwide attention for his efforts at educational and social reforms. He was viewed as a strong supporter of democracy.

Governor of New Jersey

James Smith, Jr., the Democratic Party boss in New Jersey, began to think of Wilson as a possible candidate for governor. The party's record was so bad that it needed a candidate whose honesty was above question. Colonel George B. M. Harvey, a party leader and the editor of *Harper's Weekly,* also became interested in Wilson. Smith and Harvey together could almost control the nomination, and they offered it to Wilson.

They timed their offer well. Because of his disappointments at Princeton, Wilson was ready to change careers. As a scholar in the field of government, he knew the facts of machine politics. He suspected that Smith planned to use him for some purpose of his own. But Wilson wanted to run for governor as the first step toward the White House, and Smith badly needed Wilson.

On Oct. 20, 1910, Wilson resigned from Princeton to campaign for governor. The power and eloquence of his campaign speeches stirred voters throughout the state. He was elected by the largest majority received by a Democrat in New Jersey up to that time.

Political reformer. Wilson at once made it clear that he wanted nothing to do with the political practices of the Democratic machine headed by Smith. Smith, who had previously served in the U.S. Senate, decided to run for that office again. At that time, senators were elected by the state legislatures. If no candidate received a majority of the votes in each house of a legislature, both houses met in joint session to elect a senator. Wilson's victory had given the Democrats a majority in the joint session of the New Jersey legislature. When Smith refused to withdraw, Wilson endorsed a rival candidate who won. A reporter wrote that Wilson had "licked the gang to a frazzle."

Meanwhile, Wilson was pushing a series of reforms through the legislature. These laws changed New Jersey from one of the most conservative states into one of the most progressive. During its first session, the legislature enacted the most important proposals of Wilson's campaign. It passed a primary-election law, a corrupt-practices act, a public-utilities act, an employers' liability law, various school-reform laws, and a law permitting cities to adopt the commission form of government. Wilson did not hesitate to break long-established customs. He hired a superintendent of schools from outside the state. He frequently asked the advice of members of the legislature, and turned up unexpectedly at some of their private meetings. He sometimes appealed directly to the people, to influence public opinion and put pressure on legislators and other officials.

Presidential candidate. Wilson's reforms in New Jersey brought him national attention at an opportune time. The progressive wing of the Democratic Party was seeking a presidential candidate to replace William Jennings Bryan, who had been defeated three times. By 1911, Wilson had clearly become a candidate for the nomination. He started speaking on national issues throughout the country, and progressive Democrats began to support him. Most importantly, Wilson won the confidence of Bryan, the party's official leader.

The Democratic national convention met at Baltimore in June 1912. Champ Clark of Missouri, Speaker of the House of Representatives, received a majority of the delegates' votes on the 10th ballot. Not since 1844 had a candidate who had gained a majority failed to go on and receive the two-thirds vote then necessary for nomination. But Wilson's followers stayed with him. On the 14th ballot, Bryan swung his support to Wilson. The old progressive rose dramatically in the crowded convention hall to explain his vote. He pointed out that Charles Francis Murphy, the boss of New York City's Tammany Hall machine, had thrown his support to Clark. He said he could never vote for Clark as long as the Speaker had Tammany's support. From this point on, Wilson gained slowly until the 46th ballot, when he won the nomination. The convention nominated Governor Thomas R. Marshall of Indiana for Vice President.

Wilson's nomination meant almost certain election, because the Republican Party was badly split. Conservative Republicans had renominated President William Howard Taft. Progressive Republicans then formed a new Progressive Party that nominated former President Theodore Roosevelt. In a series of campaign speeches, later published as *The New Freedom,* Wilson stirred the public with his understanding of national problems.

The popular vote, overwhelmingly for Wilson and Roosevelt, was a clear endorsement of a liberal reform program. Wilson received 435 electoral votes; Roosevelt, 88; and Taft, 8.

Wilson's first Administration (1913-1917)

Inauguration. During his inauguration on March 4, 1913, Wilson noticed that a wide space had been

Library of Congress
President-elect Wilson rode to his inauguration in 1913 in a horse-drawn carriage, with President Taft at his side.

cleared in front of the speaker's platform. He motioned to the police holding back the crowd and ordered: "Let the people come forward." His supporters said the phrase expressed the spirit of his Administration.

In his inaugural address, the President accepted the challenge of the November landslide that had also swept a Democratic Congress into office. "No one can mistake the purpose for which the nation now seeks to use the Democratic party," he declared. "It seeks to use it to interpret a change in its plans and point of view." Among the laws that needed to be changed, Wilson named those governing tariffs, industry, and the banking system.

Wilson was the last President to ride to his inauguration in a horse-drawn carriage. Neither he nor his wife liked large social affairs, so the Wilsons did not give an inaugural ball. On March 15, only 11 days after his inauguration, Wilson held the first regular presidential press conference. He felt that the people were entitled to reports on the progress of his Administration.

Legislative program. Wilson called Congress into special session on April 7, 1913, to consider a new tariff bill. For the first time since the presidency of John Adams, the President personally delivered his legislative requests to Congress. In October, Congress passed Wilson's first important reform measure, the Underwood Tariff Act. This law lowered rates on imports, and removed all of the tariffs from wool, sugar, iron ore, steel rails, and many other items. After signing the bill, Wilson remarked: "I have had the accomplishment of some-

Wilson's first election

Place of nominating convention	Baltimore
Ballot on which nominated	46th
Progressive opponent	Theodore Roosevelt
Republican opponent	William Howard Taft
Electoral vote*	435 (Wilson) to: 88 (Roosevelt) 8 (Taft)
Popular vote	6,293,152 (Wilson) to: 4,119,207 (Roosevelt) 3,486,333 (Taft)
Age at inauguration	56

*For votes by states, see **Electoral College** (table).

thing like this at heart ever since I was a boy."

On June 23, as Congress debated the tariff bill, Wilson presented his program for reform of the banking and currency laws. He spoke of this reform as "the second step in setting the business of this country free." Representative Carter Glass of Virginia introduced a bill to establish a central banking system. It was designed to provide a new currency and to help the flow of capital through 12 reserve banks, under the direction of a Federal Reserve Board. Congress debated the bill hotly for six months. In December, it passed the Federal Reserve Act basically in the form the President had recommended. Amendments also provided for exclusive governmental control of the Federal Reserve Board and for short-term agricultural credit through the new reserve banks. This act is regarded as the most far-reaching banking and currency bill in the nation's history. See **Federal Reserve System**.

Wilson also asked for a series of other reforms. In 1914, Congress established the Federal Trade Commission to investigate and stop unfair trade practices (see **Federal Trade Commission**). That same year, it passed the Clayton Antitrust Act, which increased the power of the federal government to police unfair practices of big business. In 1916, Wilson led Congress in adopting a series of reform measures. The Adamson Act established the eight-hour working day for railroad employees. The Child Labor Act, which limited children's work hours, began a new program of federal regulation of industry. Heavy taxes were placed on wealth. A tariff commission was established to "take the tariff out of politics." Other programs were started to improve rural education and rural roads.

Foreign affairs demanded much of the President's attention. He persuaded Congress to repeal the Panama Tolls Act, which had allowed American ships to use the Panama Canal toll-free when sailing between U.S. coastal ports. Wilson believed this law violated a treaty with Great Britain. The President also refused to approve a bankers' loan to China, and put himself on record against "dollar diplomacy." Wilson insisted that his party live up to its campaign promise of preparing the Philippines for independence. In 1916, Congress passed the

Puck, March 5, 1913

Revolutionary turmoil in Mexico was a problem Wilson inherited from Taft, as shown in this 1913 cartoon.

Jones Bill, which greatly increased Philippine self-government and made many reforms in the administration of the islands.

Crisis in Mexico. Relations between the United States and Mexico were frequently troubled during Wilson's first Administration. In 1913, the President told Congress that there could be no peace in Mexico while Victoriano Huerta ruled as dictator. Wilson declared that the United States "can have no sympathy with those who seek to seize the powers of government to advance their own personal interests or ambition." Wilson tried unsuccessfully to negotiate for Huerta's retirement. Then the President permitted the dictator's enemies, who had begun a revolution, to obtain arms in the United States. Wilson let the Mexican groups fight it out for a while. But when Huerta's forces arrested 14 American sailors who had gone ashore at Tampico, Mexico, the President struck hard. He refused to accept Huerta's apology, and demanded that Huerta publicly salute the American flag in Tampico. When Huerta refused, Wilson in April 1914 ordered American forces to occupy the Mexican port of Veracruz. Eighteen Americans were killed in the action.

At this point, Wilson accepted an offer of the ABC powers (Argentina, Brazil, and Chile) to arbitrate the dispute. A peaceful settlement was worked out. Huerta fled from Mexico, and Venustiano Carranza, the leader of the anti-Huerta rebels, became acting president of Mexico. Pancho Villa, one of Carranza's chief generals, then quarreled with his leader and led a revolution against him. Carranza's soldiers drove Villa into northern Mexico. From there, Villa's troops raided Columbus, N. Mex. Many Americans called for war, but Wilson would not yield to their pressure. "Watchful waiting" became his policy. He sent troops under General John J. Pershing to patrol the border. Then, in 1916, he ordered Pershing to pursue Villa deep into Mexico. Carranza warned that he would resist any further invasion. Fighting did occur,

Vice President and Cabinet

Vice President	* Thomas R. Marshall
Secretary of state	* William Jennings Bryan
	* Robert Lansing (1915)
	Bainbridge Colby (1920)
Secretary of the treasury	William Gibbs McAdoo
	Carter Glass (1918)
	David F. Houston (1920)
Secretary of war	Lindley M. Garrison
	Newton D. Baker (1916)
Attorney general	James C. McReynolds
	Thomas W. Gregory (1914)
	A. Mitchell Palmer (1919)
Postmaster general	Albert S. Burleson
Secretary of the Navy	Josephus Daniels
Secretary of the interior	Franklin K. Lane
	John B. Payne (1920)
Secretary of agriculture	David F. Houston
	Edwin T. Meredith (1920)
Secretary of commerce	William C. Redfield
	Joshua W. Alexander (1919)
Secretary of labor	William B. Wilson

*Has a separate biography in *World Book*.

and only a series of dramatic events in the late spring of 1916 averted open war. In 1917, Wilson officially recognized the government that had been established by a new constitution. But relations were never cordial with Mexico during the rest of the Wilson era. See **Mexico** (The revolution of 1910; The constitution of 1917).

Caribbean problems. Both Wilson and Secretary of State William Jennings Bryan spoke out against taking more land for the United States by the use of force. But their policies toward many small nations of Latin America and the Caribbean area did not differ much from those of previous Presidents. In 1914, Wilson and Bryan took over most of the control of revolution-torn Nicaragua. They sent troops in 1915 to occupy Haiti. A year later, the Dominican Republic was placed under American military government.

World War I begins. In August 1914, the outbreak of World War I stunned people everywhere. Most Americans joined in a single cry: "Let's stay out of it." Wilson proclaimed the neutrality of the United States. He said the nation "must be neutral in fact as well as in name . . . we must be impartial in thought as well as in action."

But neutrality became easier to think about than to maintain. On May 7, 1915, a German submarine torpedoed and sank the British passenger liner *Lusitania,* killing 128 Americans. This incident enraged some Americans, but Wilson remained calm. He began negotiations with the Germans and got them to order their submarines not to attack neutral or passenger ships. Angry people called Wilson "a human icicle" who did nothing to avenge the loss of American lives. But most Americans approved the President's fight for peace and neutrality.

UPI/Bettmann Newsphotos

Wilson's reelection campaign reminded voters of the various reforms his first Administration had achieved, and stressed the peace issue with such slogans as "He kept us out of war."

Life in the White House. With the help of her three daughters, Mrs. Wilson put her greatest efforts into making the White House as much like a private home as possible. She devoted herself to welfare work and to small groups interested in literature and art.

Then the Wilsons' family life changed radically. Within an eight-month period, from November 1913 to July 1914, two of the President's daughters were married, and Mrs. Wilson became ill. After a short illness, the President's wife died on Aug. 6, 1914. Wilson was so saddened by his wife's death that he nearly lost his will to live. Wilson's unmarried daughter, Margaret, and his first cousin, Helen Woodrow Bones, became hostesses for the President.

Remarriage. In March 1915, Wilson met Edith Bolling Galt (1872-1961), widow of a Washington jeweler. He fell in love with her almost at once, and sent long letters and flowers to her every day. They were married in her home in Washington on Dec. 18, 1915.

The second Mrs. Wilson was an intelligent and strong-minded woman. Wilson again found the happiness and security he had known with his first wife.

Election of 1916. In June 1916, the Democrats renominated Wilson and Marshall. The Republicans had healed the split in their party, and chose a ticket of Supreme Court Justice Charles Evans Hughes and former Vice President Charles W. Fairbanks. The war in Europe overshadowed all other issues in the campaign. Democrats sought votes for Wilson with the slogan, "He kept us out of war." Wilson himself appealed to those who favored peace, but he also stressed the reforms his Administration had accomplished.

On election night, the outcome was confused because of delays in receiving the election returns. Wilson went to bed believing Hughes had won. Many newspapers carried stories of Wilson's "defeat." But the final count in California gave the state to Wilson by about 3,400 votes. This insured his reelection.

Wilson's second Administration (1917-1921)

Declaration of war. During the next three months, Wilson devoted all his efforts to halting the fighting in Europe. But in February 1917, the Germans began unlimited submarine warfare against all merchant shipping,

Historical Pictures Service

Wilson's second wife was Edith Bolling Galt, a widow whom he married in December 1915, 16 months after the death of his first wife. Edith was a loving and devoted companion to him.

Wilson's second election

Place of nominating convention ......St. Louis
Ballot on which nominated 1st
Republican opponent ....Charles Evans Hughes
Electoral vote* ....277 (Wilson) to 254
(Hughes)
Popular vote ....9,126,300 (Wilson) to
8,546,789 (Hughes)
Age at second inauguration 60

*For votes by states, see **Electoral College** (table).

including American ships. The President immediately broke off diplomatic relations with Germany. Later that month, British agents uncovered a German plot to start a war between Mexico and the United States. German submarines began to attack U.S. ships without warning in March, and enraged Americans demanded war.

Wilson decided the United States could no longer remain neutral. On the evening of April 2, the President drove to the Capitol with an escort of cavalry. As he stepped before a joint session of Congress, his face was tense and white. He spoke in a voice heavy with feeling. He said actions by Germany were "in fact nothing less than war against the government and people of the United States." Thunderous applause greeted the President's words. Wilson asked Congress to declare war against Germany, declaring that "the world must be made safe for democracy."

Four days later, on April 6, 1917, Congress passed a joint resolution declaring war on Germany. For a complete discussion of the United States in the war, see **World War I** (The United States enters the war).

War leader. The President proved himself as great a leader in war as he had been in peace. His many speeches in support of the American and Allied cause stirred free people everywhere. Wilson stated the great issues of the war, and defined the aims for which the democracies fought. He also pointed out the necessity

Library of Congress
Wilson asked for a declaration of war in a speech before a joint session of Congress on April 2, 1917. Four days later, Congress passed a joint resolution declaring war on Germany.

Highlights of Wilson's Administration

1913 Wilson signed a bill creating an independent Department of Labor.
1913 Amendment 17 to the Constitution, providing for the election of U.S. senators by popular vote instead of by state legislatures, became law.
1913 Congress passed the Underwood Tariff Act and established the Federal Reserve System.
1914 Congress passed the Clayton Antitrust Act and created the Federal Trade Commission.
1914 Wilson emphasized U.S. neutrality after the outbreak of World War I in Europe.
1917 Congress approved the purchase of the Virgin Islands from Denmark.
1917 (April 6) Congress declared war against Germany.
1918 (Jan. 8) Wilson set forth the Fourteen Points.
1918 (Oct. 6–Nov. 11) Wilson negotiated the armistice with Germany.
1919 (Jan. 18–June 28) Wilson helped draft the Versailles Treaty at the Paris Peace Conference.
1919 Amendment 18 to the Constitution, banning the manufacture, sale, and transportation of alcoholic beverages, became law.
1920 Congress rejected the Versailles Treaty and American membership in the League of Nations.
1920 Amendment 19 to the Constitution, giving women the right to vote, became law.

of making a better world after the war. The American people rallied with great loyalty and patriotism. A crusading spirit, almost hysterical in its intensity, swept the nation. People sang "I'm a Yankee Doodle Dandy," "Over There," and other popular war songs. Well-known film stars, such as Mary Pickford and Charlie Chaplin, drew huge crowds to purchase Liberty bonds at rallies.

The Fourteen Points. Wilson delivered his most important speech on Jan. 8, 1918. In this address to Congress, he named Fourteen Points to be used as a guide for a peace settlement. Five of the points established general ideals. Eight points dealt with immediate political and territorial problems. The fourteenth point called for an association of nations to help keep world peace. The Fourteen Points are summarized as follows:

1. Open covenants of peace openly arrived at, with no secret international agreements in the future.
2. Freedom of the seas outside territorial waters in peace and in war, except in case of international action to enforce international treaties.
3. Removal of all possible economic barriers and establishment of equal trade conditions among nations.
4. Reduction of national armaments to the lowest point consistent with domestic safety.
5. Free, open-minded, and absolutely impartial adjustment of all colonial claims.
6. Evacuation of German troops from all Russian territory, an opportunity for Russia independently to determine its own political development and national policy, and a welcome for Russia into the society of free nations.
7. Evacuation of German troops from Belgium and the rebuilding of that nation.
8. Evacuation of German troops from all French territory and the return of Alsace-Lorraine to France.
9. Readjustment of Italian frontiers along the clearly recognizable lines of nationality.
10. Limited self-government for the peoples of Austria-Hungary.
11. Evacuation of German troops from Romania, Serbia, and Montenegro, and independence guaranteed for the Balkan countries.

Paris streets were mobbed with people waiting for Wilson to arrive for the peace conference of 1919. In France, Britain, and Italy, Wilson was hailed as a just and honorable leader.

The "Big Four" Allied leaders gathered at the peace conference. *Left to right* are David Lloyd George of Britain, Vittorio Orlando of Italy, Georges Clemenceau of France, and Wilson.

12. Independence for Turkey, but an opportunity to develop self-government for other nationalities under Turkish rule, and guarantees that the Dardanelles be permanently opened as a free passage to ships of all nations.

13. Independence for Poland.

14. "A general association of nations must be formed under specific covenants for the purpose of affording mutual guarantees of political independence and territorial integrity to great and small states alike."

Wilson's speech did much to undermine German morale during the final months of the war. It also gave the Germans a basis upon which to appeal for peace. On Nov. 9, 1918, only 10 months after the President had stated his Fourteen Points, Kaiser Wilhelm II gave up control of the German government. Two days later, an armistice that was negotiated by Wilson was proclaimed.

The peace settlement. After the armistice had been signed, Wilson decided to lead the United States delegation to the peace conference at Paris. He wanted to make certain that his Fourteen Points would be carried out. The President also thought the United States should

be represented by its political leader, as were Great Britain, France, and the other powers. Wilson appointed a peace delegation that included no member of the U.S. Senate and no influential Republicans. He was criticized for this, and later it helped cause the Senate to reject the treaty agreed upon at Paris.

Wilson knew the United States would be the only country represented at the peace table that wanted nothing for itself. He also believed he would be the only representative of the great powers who really cared about establishing an association of nations to prevent war. The President was determined to use his power and prestige to have the final peace settlement include a plan for a League of Nations.

Wilson was the first President to cross the Atlantic Ocean while in office. He landed at Brest, France, on Dec. 13, 1918, and the next morning rode through the streets of Paris. Never had the people of Paris given a king or emperor such a joyous reception. Banners welcomed "Wilson le Juste." From France, Wilson went to England, where he stayed at Buckingham Palace. In

---

Quotations from Wilson

The following quotations come from some of Woodrow Wilson's speeches and writings.

Uncompromising thought is the luxury of the closeted recluse.
Speech at the University of Tennessee, June 17, 1890

Big business is not dangerous because it is big, but because its bigness is . . . created by privileges and exemptions . . .
Acceptance speech, Democratic National Convention, 1912

Liberty is its own reward.
Speech in New York City, Sept. 9, 1912

We can afford to exercise the self-restraint of a really great nation which realizes its own strength and scorns to misuse it.
Message to Congress, Aug. 27, 1913

There must be, not a balance of power but a community of power; not organized rivalries but an organized, common peace. . . . It must be a peace without victory. . . . Victory would mean peace forced upon the loser . . . accepted in

humiliation. . . . It would leave . . . a bitter memory upon which terms of peace would rest, not permanently, but only as upon quicksand. Only a peace between equals can last.
Speech to the Senate, January 1917

There is one choice we cannot make . . . we will not choose the path of submission . . . The world must be made safe for democracy.
Speech before Congress, April 2, 1917

To conquer with arms is to make only a temporary conquest; to conquer the world by earning its esteem is to make a permanent conquest.
Speech to Congress, Nov. 11, 1918

. . . people call me an idealist. Well, that is the way I know I am an American. America is the only idealistic nation in the world.
Speech in Sioux Falls, S.D., Sept. 8, 1919

Rome, he met with Pope Benedict XV and became the first President to talk with a pope while in office. Everywhere he went in Europe, great crowds cheered him as the hope of humanity.

At the Paris Peace Conference, held from January to June, Wilson obtained only part of the treaty provisions he wanted. In order to win support for the League and other provisions in the Fourteen Points, he compromised on several major issues. Wilson's concessions weakened his moral position in the eyes of the world, though they insured establishment of the League of Nations. See **World War I** (The peace settlement); **League of Nations; Versailles, Treaty of.**

Opposition to the League. In February 1919, Wilson returned to the United States briefly to discuss the League and the peace treaty with the Senate. The Constitution required two-thirds approval by the Senate for the United States to adopt the treaty, which included the League. The President also hoped to quiet rising criticism throughout the country. Wilson's position was no longer strong politically. He had asked for the election of Democrats to Congress in 1918 as an indication of personal trust. But the voters had chosen more Republicans than Democrats.

Wilson soon discovered that he could not win Senate ratification of the League without some amendments to satisfy his critics at home. He went back to Paris in March 1919, and the conference delegates accepted several of these provisions. Wilson returned to the United States early in July with the text of the treaty. He found public debate on the peace terms in full swing, with mounting congressional opposition to the treaty and the League of Nations.

American opinion on the treaty was split into three groups. The isolationists, led by Senators William E. Borah, Hiram W. Johnson, and James A. Reed, stood firmly against any League. They argued that the United States should not interfere in "European affairs." The second group consisted of Wilson and his followers, who urged that the treaty be ratified with no important changes or compromises. The men in the largest group,

led by Senator Henry Cabot Lodge, took a middle ground between Wilson and the isolationists. They were ready to ratify the treaty with important changes. Some of these men, including Lodge, demanded changes that would reduce or eliminate America's obligations to the League.

Wilson's collapse. The President decided to take his case for the League to the American people—the method that had worked successfully for him in the past. On September 4, Wilson began a speaking tour through the Midwest and the West. His doctor had advised him against the trip, because his strenuous labors over the past several years had weakened his health. On September 25, Wilson spoke at Pueblo, Colo., urging approval of the League. That night, as his train sped toward Wichita, Kans., Wilson collapsed from fatigue and nervous tension. He canceled the remainder of his tour and returned to Washington. On October 2, the President suffered a paralytic stroke. Wilson had suffered strokes even before he became President. But in each case, he made a nearly complete recovery and almost no one knew of his condition.

Wilson was an invalid for the rest of his life, but he did not give up the presidency. The Constitution did not then state clearly who inherits executive power when a President becomes severely ill but does not die or resign. After October, Wilson left his bed only for simple recreation or for purely formal tasks. These greatly taxed his strength, and his wife guided his hand when he signed official documents. Wilson did not call a meeting of the Cabinet until April 13, 1920. Before that, the Cabinet met unofficially and carried on much of the routine work of government during Wilson's long illness.

From his sickbed, the President helplessly watched the losing fight for his treaty. Senator Lodge, chairman of the Senate Foreign Relations Committee, presented the treaty for vote in November 1919. He and his committee had added 14 reservations. The most important one declared that the United States assumed no obligation to support the League of Nations unless Congress specifically approved by joint resolution. Claiming that this reservation would destroy the League, Wilson instructed Senate Democrats to vote against approval of the treaty containing the Lodge reservations. As a result, the treaty failed to win two-thirds approval. The treaty came up for vote again in March 1920, but it failed.

Wilson insisted that the treaty and the League should be the chief issue of the 1920 presidential campaign. The Democratic platform endorsed the League, and the Republican platform opposed it. In the election, Warren G. Harding, the Republican nominee, overwhelmingly defeated James M. Cox, his Democratic opponent. As far as the United States was concerned, the League of Nations was dead.

On Dec. 10, 1920, Wilson was awarded the 1919 Nobel Peace Prize for his work in founding the League of Nations and seeking a fair peace agreement.

Last years

For almost three years after his term ended in March 1921, Wilson lived in quiet retirement in Washington. He formed a law partnership with Bainbridge Colby, his third secretary of state. Although Wilson had regained partial use of his arms and legs, his physical condition

UPI/Bettmann Newsphotos

Wilson toured the nation in 1919 to win public support for the League of Nations. But his collapse on September 25 cut short his efforts. He suffered a stroke in October.

did not permit any actual work. He saw an occasional movie or play, listened to books and magazines read aloud to him, and sometimes invited friends for lunch.

Wilson was confident that future events would prove him correct regarding the League and the peace terms. In his last public speech, to a group of friends outside his home on Armistice Day, 1923, he said: "I cannot refrain from saying it: I am not one of those who have the least anxiety about the triumph of the principles I have stood for. I have seen fools resist Providence before and I have seen their destruction, as will come upon these again—utter destruction and contempt. That we shall prevail is as sure as that God reigns."

Wilson continued to bear the crushing blows of defeat with dignity and calm. But he told his friends he was "tired of swimming upstream." On Feb. 3, 1924, he died in his sleep. Two days later, Wilson was buried in Washington Cathedral. He is the only president interred in Washington, D.C.   John M. Mulder

Related articles in *World Book* include:

Outline

Questions

Why was Wilson's election to the presidency in 1912 almost certain following his nomination?

What were Wilson's main reforms at Princeton University?

What brought Wilson to national attention as a presidential prospect?

What were the most important achievements in domestic affairs during his first administration?

What was one of Wilson's most valuable techniques for winning legislation that he wanted?

Why was Wilson's family life so important to him?

Why did Wilson personally attend the Paris Peace Conference in 1919?

Why do historians regard Wilson as one of the nation's greatest presidents?

What were his three main careers?

In what connection did Wilson make the statement: "Let the people come forward"?

Additional resources

Auchincloss, Louis. *Woodrow Wilson.* Viking Penguin, 2000.
Clements, Kendrick A. *Woodrow Wilson, World Statesman.* Rev. ed. Ivan R. Dee, 1999. *The Presidency of Woodrow Wilson.* Univ. Pr. of Kans., 1992.
Heckscher, August. *Woodrow Wilson.* Scribner, 1991.
Schraff, Anne E. *Woodrow Wilson.* Enslow, 1998. Younger readers.

Wilt occurs when the stems and leaves of a plant droop because they are not receiving enough water. In extreme cases, the leaves turn yellow and die. Common causes of wilt include drought and diseases caused by certain fungi and bacteria.

Fungi and bacteria cause wilt by plugging the *xylem vessels* of plants. Xylem vessels are channels that carry water from the roots to the leaves. The most common wilt-causing fungi are species in the groups *Fusarium* and *Verticillium. Fusarium* fungi cause wilt in many fruits and vegetables, including bananas, peas, and tomatoes. *Verticillium* fungi affect a wide variety of plants, including many flowers, crop plants, and trees. Dutch elm disease is a wilt disease that occurs when *Ceratocystis ulmi* fungus causes blockage of xylem vessels in elm trees. This fungus is spread by two kinds of beetles (see **Dutch elm disease**). Bacteria that cause wilt in plants include species in the groups *Pseudomonas* and *Erwinia.*

The best way to prevent wilt is to plant crop varieties resistant to wilt-causing fungi and bacteria. Once established, wilt can be hard to control. Crop rotation usually will not prevent fungal wilt because the fungi can survive in soil and on healthy plants. Trees with Dutch elm disease may need to be destroyed to keep the fungi from spreading to uninfected trees.   Joseph G. Hancock

Wimbledon. See Tennis.

Winchell, Walter (1897-1972), an American newspaperman and commentator, became important for making the gossip column a regular newspaper feature. His column, which focused on political and entertainment figures, became widely read and imitated. In the column, Winchell used a type of jargon that has been widely copied. He coined colorful words and phrases, such as "lohengrined" and "middle-aisled" for "married." He also had a popular radio show.

Winchell was born April 7, 1897, in New York City. He played in vaudeville before beginning to write for *The Vaudeville News* in 1920. His syndicated column about Broadway made him nationally known in 1929. He also appeared on TV. He retired in 1969 and died on Feb. 20, 1972.   Michael Emery

Winchester was the chief town of England in Anglo-Saxon times. It is the chief town in the district of Winchester, which has a population of 107,213. It is a religious, service, and light industrial center. It is also the administrative center of the county of Hampshire. Winchester is one of the most prosperous towns in the United Kingdom. It lies on the River Itchen in southern England (see **England** [political map]).

Both Alfred the Great and the Danish King Canute were buried at Winchester. After the Normans conquered England in 1066, Winchester continued to rival London as a trade and political center. William of Wykeham completed Winchester's famous cathedral in the 1300's. This cathedral, which is 556 feet (169 meters) long, is the longest church in England. William also founded Winchester College, one of the leading English public schools.   D. A. Pinder

Winchester College at Winchester, England, is one of the oldest and most prominent of the English public schools. England's "public schools" are not free schools. They are privately supported institutions for secondary education. William of Wykeham, bishop of Winchester, founded Winchester College in 1382, and it opened in 1394. The school's motto is "Manners Makyth Man." The college was originally established for 70 poor scholars, but greater numbers were gradually admitted. Winchester College was one of the first public schools to introduce science and mathematics courses.   P. A. McGinley

Winckelmann, *VIHNG kuhl MAHN,* **Johann Joachim,** *YOH hahn YOH ah kihm* (1717-1768), was a German scholar who has been called the father of both archaeology and art history. His work was the first systematic study of ancient Greek and Roman art. Winckelmann showed that art objects can reveal as much important information about the history of a culture as writings do. His belief in Greek art as an ideal greatly influenced many writers and artists of his time.

Winckelmann was born on Dec. 9, 1717, in Stendal, Prussia. As a boy, he learned Greek and Latin so he could read Homer and other ancient writers. Winckelmann later studied theology and medicine, but he earned his living as a teacher and a librarian.

In 1754 and 1755, Winckelmann studied art in Dresden. He then moved to Italy, where he did most of the work for which he became known. His reports of the excavations at the ancient Roman towns of Pompeii and Herculaneum were widely read. Art historians still use his principal work, *Geschichte der Kunst des Altertums (The History of Ancient Art,* 1764). Winckelmann died on June 8, 1768.   Richard G. Klein

Wind is air moving across Earth's surface. Wind may blow so slowly and gently that it can hardly be felt. Or it may blow so fast and hard that it smashes buildings and pushes over large trees. Strong winds can whip up great ocean waves that damage ships and flood land. Wind can blow away soil from farmland so crops cannot grow. Sharp grains of dust carried by wind wear away rock and change the features of land.

Wind is a part of weather. A hot, humid day may suddenly turn cool if a wind blows from a cool area to the hot area. Clouds with rain and lightning may form where the cool air meets the hot, moist air. Later, another wind may blow the clouds away and allow the sun to warm the land again. Wind can carry a storm great distances.

Winds are named according to the direction *from* which they blow. For example, an *east* wind blows from east to west. A *north* wind blows from north to south.

Causes of wind

Wind is caused by the uneven heating of the *atmosphere* (the air around Earth) by energy from the sun. The sun heats the surface of Earth unevenly. Air above hot areas expands and rises. Air from cooler areas then flows in to replace the heated air. This process is called *circulation.* The circulation over the entire planet is the *general circulation.* The smaller-scale circulations that cause day-to-day wind changes are known as *synoptic-scale circulations.* Winds that occur only in one place are called *local winds.*

General circulation produces average winds that occur over large sections of Earth's surface. These winds, called *prevailing winds,* vary with differences in latitude. Near the equator, heated air rises to about 60,000 feet

(18,000 meters). Surface air moving in to replace the rising air produces two belts of prevailing winds. These belts lie between the equator and about 30° north and south latitude. The winds there are called *trade winds* because sailors once relied on them in sailing trading ships.

The trade winds do not blow straight toward the equator. Instead, they blow somewhat from east to west. The westward part of their motion is caused by the spinning of Earth. Earth and the air around it rotate eastward together. Each point on Earth's surface travels around a complete circle in 24 hours. Points near the equator travel around larger circles than points near 30° north or south latitude, because Earth is larger at the equator. So, the points near the equator travel faster.

As air moves toward the equator, it reaches faster-moving points on Earth's surface. Since these surface points are moving eastward faster than the air, a person standing on Earth feels a wind blowing westward.

There are no prevailing winds near the equator and up to about 700 miles (1,100 kilometers) on either side of it, because the air rises there instead of moving across Earth. This calm belt is called the *doldrums.* Often the trade winds *converge* (come together) in a narrow zone called the *intertropical convergence zone* (ITCZ).

Some of the air that rises at the equator returns to Earth's surface at about 30° north and south latitude. Air moving downward there produces no wind. These areas are called the *horse latitudes,* possibly because many horses died on sailing ships that were stalled by the lack of wind there.

Two other kinds of prevailing winds result from the general circulation in the atmosphere. The *prevailing westerlies* blow somewhat from west to east in two belts between latitudes of about 30° and 60° north and south of the equator. These winds result from surface air moving away from the equator and reaching slower-moving points nearer the poles. Prevailing westerlies carry weather eastward across the northern United States and southern Canada. The *polar easterlies* blow somewhat from east to west in two belts between the poles and about 60° north and south latitude. Surface air moving away from the poles moves westward across faster-moving points nearer the equator.

Synoptic-scale circulations are air motions around relatively small regions of high and low pressure in the atmosphere. These regions form within the larger general circulation. Air flows toward low-pressure regions called *lows* or *cyclones.* Air flows away from high-pressure regions called *highs* or *anticyclones.* Viewed from above, the wind moves clockwise around a high and counterclockwise around a low in the Northern Hemisphere. These directions are reversed in the Southern Hemisphere.

Highs and lows generally move with the prevailing winds. As they pass a given spot on Earth, the wind direction changes. For example, a low moving eastward across Chicago produces winds that shift from southeast to northwest.

Local winds arise only in specific areas on Earth. Local winds that result from the heating of land during summer and the cooling of land during winter are called *monsoons.* They blow from the ocean during summer and toward the ocean during winter. Mon-

Beaufort wind scale

Beaufort number	Name	Miles per hour	Kilometers per hour	Effect on land
0	Calm	less than 1	less than 1	Calm; smoke rises vertically.
1	Light air	1-3	1-5	Weather vanes inactive; smoke drifts with air.
2	Light breeze	4-7	6-11	Weather vanes active; wind felt on face; leaves rustle.
3	Gentle breeze	8-12	12-19	Leaves and small twigs move; light flags extend.
4	Moderate breeze	13-18	20-28	Small branches sway; dust and loose paper blow about.
5	Fresh breeze	19-24	29-38	Small trees sway; waves break on inland waters.
6	Strong breeze	25-31	39-49	Large branches sway; umbrellas difficult to use.
7	Moderate gale	32-38	50-61	Whole trees sway; difficult to walk against wind.
8	Fresh gale	39-46	62-74	Twigs broken off trees; walking against wind very difficult.
9	Strong gale	47-54	75-88	Slight damage to buildings; shingles blown off roof.
10	Whole gale	55-63	89-102	Trees uprooted; considerable damage to buildings.
11	Storm	64-73	103-118	Widespread damage; very rare occurrence.
12-17	Hurricane	74 and above	119 and above	Violent destruction.

soons control the climate in Asia, producing wet summers and dry winters. A warm, dry, local wind that blows down the side of a mountain is called a *chinook* in the western United States and a *foehn* in Europe. These three local winds, as well as the harmattan and the sirocco, are discussed in articles listed in the *Related articles* at the end of this article.

Measuring wind

Two features of wind, its speed and its direction, are used in describing and forecasting weather.

Wind speed is measured with an instrument called an *anemometer*. Several kinds of anemometers are used today. The most common kind has three or four cups attached to spokes on a rotating shaft. The spokes turn the shaft as the wind blows. The wind speed is indicated by the speed of the spinning shaft.

In the United States, wind speeds are stated in miles per hour or in *knots* (nautical miles per hour). In many other countries, they are stated in kilometers per hour.

Wind direction is measured with an instrument called a *weather vane*. A weather vane has a broad, flat blade attached to a spoke pivoted at one end. Wind blowing on the blade turns the spoke so that the blade

lines up in the direction of the wind. The wind direction may be indicated by an arrow fastened to the spoke, or by an electric meter remotely controlled by the vane.

Wind directions are often indicated by using the 360 degrees of a circle. On this circle, north is indicated by 0°. An east wind blows from 90°, a south wind blows from 180°, and a west wind blows from 270°. Winds at various altitudes often differ in speed and direction. For example, smoke from a chimney may be blown northward while, at the same time, clouds higher in the sky are blown eastward.

Winds high above Earth's surface are measured by sending up helium-filled balloons. A balloon moves with the same speed and in the same direction as the wind. The balloon's motion is measured by sight or by radar. The balloon's altitude is sometimes determined by noting the atmospheric pressure, as measured by a barometer attached to the balloon. Cloud motions determined from satellites are also used to estimate winds, especially over the ocean, where few balloons are launched.

The Beaufort wind scale is a series of numbers, ranging from 0 to 17, that are used to indicate wind speeds. The Beaufort wind scale was devised in 1805 by British Rear Admiral Sir Francis Beaufort. He defined the

General circulation of air around Earth

Prevailing winds result from the general circulation of air around Earth. In this drawing, the circulation has been greatly simplified. At the equator, air is heated by the sun and rises, as shown by the blue arrows. In the upper atmosphere, this air flows away from the equator. When the air returns to Earth's surface, it flows across the surface, as shown by the black arrows. This moving surface air produces the six belts of prevailing winds around Earth. The turning of Earth causes the winds to blow toward the east in belts where the air moves away from the equator. In belts where the air moves toward the equator, the prevailing winds blow toward the west.

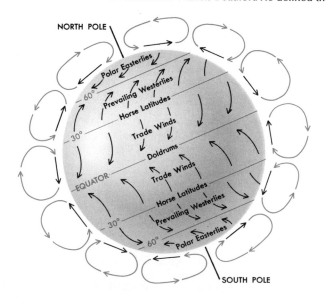

numbers in terms of the effect of various winds on sailing vessels. Today, the Beaufort scale is defined in terms of wind speeds measured 10 meters (about 33 feet) above the ground. The scale is sometimes used to estimate wind speeds, but the Beaufort numbers are little used in the United States. Margaret A. LeMone

Related articles in *World Book* include:

Air	Dune	Jet stream	Trade wind
Anemometer	Dust devil	Monsoon	Waterspout
Calms, Re-	Erosion	Norther	Weather
gions of	Foehn	Sirocco	Weather vane
Chinook	Harmattan	Squall	Wind chill
Climate	Horse lati-	Storm	Wind power
Cloud	tudes	Tornado	Wind shear
Cyclone	Hurricane		

Wind Cave National Park is a park in the rolling hills of southwestern South Dakota that surrounds one of the most unusual caves in the United States. Strong currents of wind that blow alternately in and out of the mouth of the cave suggested its name. In the cave, the wind is quiet, and the temperature remains a cool 53 °F (12 °C). The cave was formed as water slowly dissolved away layers of limestone.

Wind Cave has a series of strange boxwork and frostwork formations that are not found elsewhere in the United States. The boxwork formations are calcite crystal structures, which vary from bright yellow through pink and rich browns to deep blue. The frostwork is made up of many tiny white crystals along the ceilings and walls. Electric lights in the cave make the boxwork shine and the frostwork gleam.

Tom Bingham, a Black Hills pioneer, is credited with discovering the cave in 1881. While deer hunting, he heard a whistling sound coming from a clump of brush. Bingham discovered an opening in the rock, about 10 inches (25 centimeters) in diameter, from which a strong draft came. This opening is a few steps from the present entrance to the cave, which was built later.

The land around Wind Cave was made a national park in 1903. The park is about 10 miles (16 kilometers) north of Hot Springs, South Dakota. For the park's area, see National Park System (table: National parks). The surface area of Wind Cave National Park is a wildlife preserve for buffalo, deer, prairie dogs, pronghorn, and other animals. Critically reviewed by the National Park Service

Wind chill is a measure of how cold air cools the human body when the wind blows. Wind chill accounts for the fact that wind cools the body more effectively than still air does. The scientific term for *wind chill* is *wind chill equivalent temperature*. People also refer to it as the *wind chill index*.

In places that have low temperatures during winter, many weather reports include the wind chill. Reporting the wind chill helps people who plan to go outdoors judge the cooling effect of the air. For example, when the air temperature is 10 °F and the wind is blowing at 10 miles per hour (mph), the wind chill is −4 °F. Exposed skin will lose heat at the same rate as it would if the temperature were −4 °F and the air were motionless.

Wind chill cannot measure the body's heat loss precisely because it does not account for certain important factors. One such factor is body build. A person who is thinner than normal will lose more heat and feel colder than a stocky person.

The original wind chill measurements were based on experiments performed in Antarctica in the 1940's by the American explorers Paul A. Siple and Charles F. Passel. Siple and Passel measured the time required for 8.8 ounces (250 grams) of water in a plastic cylinder to freeze under various conditions of wind and temperature. Scientists used equations based on the experiments to create wind chill charts.

In the winter of 2001-2002, the National Weather Service of the United States and the Meteorological Services of Canada began to use new equations. Those equations are based on advances in scientific knowledge. They provide a more accurate measure of heat loss from the human face—the part of the body most often exposed to outdoor air during the winter. Joseph M. Moran

Wind instrument. See Music (Musical instruments).

Wind power is the energy associated with the air that moves over Earth's surface. The world's growing demand for energy threatens to exhaust the supply of such fuels as coal, oil, and natural gas. But wind is a *renewable* energy source that cannot be used up. In addition, wind provides clean, nonpolluting energy.

The *kinetic energy* (energy of movement) of wind throughout the world is estimated at more than 11 quadrillion *kilowatt-hours* per year. A kilowatt-hour is the amount of work done by 1,000 watts in one hour. If people could capture and use only 10 percent of the wind's kinetic energy, it would far exceed the world's yearly energy demand.

Devices that use wind power. People have harnessed the power of the wind to do work for thousands

Air temperature in degrees Fahrenheit																		
Calm	40	35	30	25	20	15	10	5	0	−5	−10	−15	−20	−25	−30	−35	−40	−45
5	36	31	25	19	13	7	1	−5	−11	−16	−22	−28	−34	−40	−46	−52	−57	−63
10	34	27	21	15	9	3	−4	−10	−16	−22	−28	−35	−41	−47	−53	−59	−66	−72
15	32	25	19	13	6	0	−7	−13	−19	−26	−32	−39	−45	−51	−58	−64	−71	−77
20	30	24	17	11	4	−2	−9	−15	−22	−29	−35	−42	−48	−55	−61	−68	−74	−81
25	29	23	16	9	3	−4	−11	−17	−24	−31	−37	−44	−51	−58	−64	−71	−78	−84
30	28	22	15	8	1	−5	−12	−19	−26	−33	−39	−46	−53	−60	−67	−73	−80	−87
35	28	21	14	7	0	−7	−14	−21	−27	−34	−41	−48	−55	−62	−69	−76	−82	−89
40	27	20	13	6	−1	−8	−15	−22	−29	−36	−43	−50	−57	−64	−71	−78	−84	91
45	26	19	12	5	−2	−9	−16	−23	−30	−37	−44	−51	−58	−65	−72	−79	−86	−93
50	26	19	12	4	−3	−10	−17	−24	−31	−38	−45	−52	−60	−67	−74	−81	−88	−95
55	25	18	11	4	−3	−11	−18	−25	−32	−39	−46	−54	−61	−68	−75	−82	−89	−97
60	25	17	10	3	−4	−11	−19	−26	−33	−40	−48	−55	−62	−69	−76	−84	−91	−98

Wind speed in miles per hour

Time in which frostbite occurs: ☐ 30 minutes ☐ 10 minutes ☐ 5 minutes

Wind chill equivalent temperatures

This chart shows how cold the wind makes the air feel, and it indicates the length of time human skin can be exposed to the air before frostbite develops.

Cynthia Cheak, Kenetech Corporation

Wind turbines are used in some parts of the world to generate electric current. The turbines shown here are among thousands set up in California's Altamont Pass, east of San Francisco.

of years. For example, the Egyptians used wind-powered sailing ships as early as 2800 B.C.

Windmills probably originated in Persia, now Iran, during the A.D. 600's. These devices convert a portion of the kinetic energy of the flowing air into *rotational* kinetic energy that turns a shaft. Most early windmills used this rotational energy to operate machinery to grind grain. But a windmill can also be used to drive other devices, such as a pump to lift water from a well.

Today, modern devices called *wind turbines* use rotational kinetic energy to drive electric power generators. Wind power was first used to generate electric power in Denmark in the 1890's. Windmills generated electric power in some rural communities of the United States in the early 1900's. An oil shortage in the 1970's focused greater attention on the idea of using the energy of the wind to generate electric power. By the 1990's, there were about 25,000 wind turbines operating in the world. However, these devices produced only about 0.1 percent of the world's electric power.

Challenges of using wind power. When a windmill or wind turbine is used to extract wind power, only part of the kinetic energy of the wind is transferred to the blades of the device. Scientists believe it is possible to extract only about 59 percent of the wind's kinetic energy. Modern wind turbines convert only about 40 percent of the energy of the wind that strikes their blades into useful rotational energy.

A number of other factors limit the extraction of power from the wind. These factors include practical limits on the size of wind power devices and the availability of land upon which to erect such devices. Another issue involves environmental concerns. Some people oppose the spread of wind power devices, saying that they pose a danger to birds that fly into the moving blades. Others complain that the devices are unsightly and create too much noise.

Because wind speeds vary greatly over the earth's surface, some sites are more suitable than others for wind power installations. In addition, wind does not blow at a constant speed, and at times it dies down completely. Thus, to ensure a reliable supply of electric power, wind turbines must be combined with either an energy storage system or a backup generator that uses a different energy source. Adel A. Ghandakly

See also **Turbine** (Wind turbines); **Windmill.**

Additional resources

Gipe, Paul. *Wind Energy Basics.* Chelsea Green, 1999.
Graham, Ian. *Wind Power.* Raintree Steck-Vaughn, 1999.
Hills, Richard L. *Power from Wind: A History of Windmill Technology.* 1994. Reprint. Cambridge, 1996.
Righter, Robert W. *Wind Energy in America: A History.* Univ. of Okla. Pr., 1996.

Wind shear is a sudden change of wind speed or direction over a short distance. Wind shear has caused numerous crashes or near-crashes of large airplanes. Milder wind shear causes "bumps" felt by passengers during take-off or landing.

Weather conditions that lead to wind shear include showers and thunderstorms. Wind shear can also develop when air flows over mountains or through cities.

Wind shear produced by a *microburst,* a downward flow of cool air, causes more airplane accidents than any other weather hazard. Microbursts often occur during showers and thunderstorms. The evaporation of rain or the melting and evaporation of snow or other ice particles cool the air in the microburst, making it heavier than the surrounding air. Raindrops or ice particles add weight to the air in the microburst. This air gains speed as it plunges to earth. When it hits the ground, it spreads in all directions like water from a faucet hitting the sink. Microbursts measure up to $2\frac{1}{2}$ miles (4 kilometers) across and last from 2 to 10 minutes.

When an airplane enters a microburst, it encounters a *head wind.* A head wind blows from the front to the back of the aircraft. Airflow increases over the wings, and the plane moves upward. The pilot may try to restore the aircraft to its previous path by leveling it and decreasing its speed. However, after the plane passes the downward air current at the center of the microburst, it enters a *tail wind.* A tail wind blows from the back to the front of the plane. Airflow decreases over the wings, and the airplane suddenly loses altitude. If the airplane is too close to the ground or moving too slowly when it enters the tail wind, it may crash.

Pilot education helps reduce airplane accidents from wind shear. Pilots learn to recognize and avoid microbursts. Machines called *flight simulators* that imitate an airplane in flight teach pilots how to react to a microburst.

Many major airports have wind shear detection systems that measure changes in wind speed and direction. If conditions seem dangerous, the control tower warns the pilots so they can postpone take-off or landing. A type of radar called *Doppler radar* is most effective because it can detect wind shear early. Doppler radar sends out radar waves that bounce off raindrops, ice particles, insects, or air currents. A change in wind speed or direction alters the frequency of the radar waves as they return to the radar antenna (see **Radar** [Doppler radar]).   Margaret A. LeMone

See also **Aerodynamics; Wind.**

Wind tunnel is a ground-based testing facility used to study the effects of wind, or airflow, on aircraft and other vehicles and structures. Wind tunnels are built in many shapes and for different purposes. Some of them are very large and can test full-sized experimental aircraft. But most wind tunnels test scaled-down models.

Most wind tunnels have a segment called the *test section* through which a stream of air is blown at an object at a uniform speed. Air pressure and temperature can be controlled as well. The air is generally blown by electric fans, but other devices, such as pressurized tanks, may be used. A large nozzle in front of the test section accelerates the air to the desired speed. After the wind passes through the test section, a duct called a *diffuser* slows down the airflow. The vehicle or structure being tested is secured by supports that extend from the ground or from behind the object. The supports are fastened to measuring devices outside the test section that record the force of the airflow on the vehicle or structure. Instruments also can measure surface pressure at many places on the object.

Wind tunnels in which the air speed is close to the speed of sound—that is, about 760 miles (1,225 kilometers) per hour—are called *transonic* tunnels. In *subsonic* tunnels, the air travels slower than the speed of sound. Wind tunnels in which air travels faster than the speed of sound are *supersonic* tunnels. In *hypersonic* tunnels, air speeds are at least five times as fast as sound.

Highly compressed air or other gases may be blown through wind tunnels to simulate various flight conditions. In some wind tunnels, very high or low temperatures can be achieved, enabling experts to study such subjects as aircraft icing and automobile performance in polar or tropical climates.   Allen Plotkin

See also **Aerodynamics; Airplane** (Design and testing); **Wright brothers.**

Windbreak. See **Shelterbelt.**

Windermere, *WIHN duhr MEER,* is the largest lake in England. This beautiful body of water lies in the county of Cumbria, in northwestern England. The lake forms part of the famous English Lake District (see **England** [terrain map]). The scenery surrounding Windermere inspired English romantic poets William Wordsworth, Robert Southey, and Samuel Coleridge. Wooded hills rise as much as 1,000 feet (300 meters) high around the lake. The small islands in the center of the lake form a picturesque group. Windermere covers 5.69 square miles (14.7 square kilometers) and is from 30 to 200 feet (9 to 61 meters) deep. Its greatest width is 1 mile (1.6 kilometers), and it is about $10\frac{1}{2}$ miles (16.9 kilometers) long. The River Leven flows from Windermere into Morecambe Bay.   M. Trevor Wild

Windflower. See **Anemone.**

Windhoek, *VIHNT hook* (pop. 160,000), is the capital and largest city of Namibia. It lies on a dry plateau near the center of the country. For location, see **Namibia**

(map). Windhoek serves as the commercial and administrative center of Namibia. A small technical college is in the city.

German soldiers established Windhoek in the late 1880's, when Germany occupied the surrounding area. South Africa conquered Namibia during World War I (1914-1918). After 1918, South Africa continued to control it, despite international protest, until 1990, when Namibia gained its independence.   Robert I. Rotberg

Windlass, *WIND lus,* is a simple machine used to lift weights and pull loads. It was once commonly used to hoist water from wells. The windlass is a form of the wheel and axle which raises a heavy load by the application of a small amount of force. The simple windlass consists of a cylinder which can be turned by a crank. A rope or chain is wound around this cylinder. In its use to lift water out of a well, a bucket fastened to the end of the rope or chain was lowered into a well and raised again by turning the crank. Modern forms of the windlass include drums and cables of cranes and elevators. Most modern forms are turned by machines rather than by hand.   Kurt M. Marshek

See also **Wheel and axle.**

Windmill is a machine that is operated by wind power. Windmills are used chiefly to provide power to pump water, grind grain, or generate electric power. Modern windmills used to produce electric power are called *wind turbines.*

Most windmills have a rotor of blades or sails that is turned by the wind. Typically, wind turbines have two or three blades, and other windmills have more. In most cases, the rotor is set on a horizontal shaft. The shaft is mounted on a tower, mast, or other tall structure. The shaft is turned by the movement of the rotor, and it transmits power, through a series of gears, to a vertical shaft. The shaft then transmits power to a water pump, flour mill, electric generator, or other device.

Windmills probably originated in the A.D. 600's in Persia, now Iran. These windmills had sails that revolved around a vertical axis. People used these windmills chiefly to grind grain.

By the 1100's, windmills had spread to Europe. About this time, inventors discovered that windmills produced more power if the sails or blades turned on a horizontal shaft. This discovery eventually led to the development of *Dutch windmills.* These windmills were widely used in the Netherlands to drain water from the land and to mill grain. Dutch windmills had four long arms, and cloth sails or wooden slats or shutters were mounted on the arms.

During the 1800's and

© Adam Woolfitt, Woodfin Camp, Inc.

A windmill is operated by the action of the wind on a wheel of blades or sails. This windmill provides power to pump water for cattle.

early 1900's, many *American windmills* were built throughout the United States to pump water. The rotor of these windmills had curved blades of wood or steel, and was mounted on a horizontal shaft. A vane on the end of the shaft opposite the rotor moved the rotor to face the wind.　　Mary Alexander Ilyin

See also **Environmental pollution** (Scientific efforts); **Turbine** (Wind turbines; History); **Wind power.**

Window is an opening in a wall or door to admit light and air into a closed space. The term may also refer to the glass placed over such an opening. One or more flat sheets of glass called *panes* cover most windows. Bars known as *mullions* hold the panes in place. The panes and mullions fit into a frame called a *sash.*

Some windows are designed to be permanently closed. There are two basic types of movable windows—*hinged* or *casement windows* and *double-hung windows.* Some hinged or casement windows have two sashes, one hinged to each side of the window. The sashes open inward or outward like a door. This was the first type of movable window. A double-hung window consists of two sashes hung one above the other. The lower sash slides upward on a track to let in air. The double-hung window was invented in the Netherlands about 1680 and rapidly became very popular.

Most windows are placed flat in a wall surface. However, there are also other designs. For example, *dormer windows* are cut through the roof of a building. *Bay windows, bow windows,* and *oriel windows* project out from a wall.

Until the 1800's, only small panes of glass could be manufactured. The invention of improved machinery in the 1850's permitted the production of large panes. This development had a major impact on the appearance and design of buildings. During the early and middle 1900's, huge panes of glass, often mirrored or tinted, became popular for large buildings. They are too large and heavy to be opened. But advancements in heating and air conditioning have made such windows practical.

In early times, people who lived in warm climates left windows uncovered. In cold climates, people put animal skins over windows for protection from the weather. People in the Far East used paper to cover windows.

During the Middle Ages, craftworkers invented stained glass for use in church windows. A stained-glass window consists of pieces of colored glass arranged to form figures and decorative patterns. Metal bands hold the pieces in place. Stained-glass windows made in tall, thin, pointed shapes are called *lancet* windows. Stained-glass windows made in a circular shape are called *rose windows.*　　William J. Hennessey

See also **Glass; Stained glass; Tracery.**

Windpipe. See **Trachea.**

Windsor, *WIHN zuhr,* is the name of the present royal family of the United Kingdom. The name *Windsor,* adopted in 1917, was taken from Windsor Castle, a royal residence. The new name was chosen to replace *Saxe-Coburg and Gotha,* which was abandoned during World War I (1914-1918) because of its German origin.

The Windsors are descended from the royal family known as the *House of Hanover. Elector* (ruler) George Louis of Hanover, a territory in Germany, became King George I of Britain (now the United Kingdom) in 1714. He was the second cousin and closest Protestant relative of

Britain's Queen Anne, who died that year. British law prohibited a Roman Catholic from being the nation's monarch. George's descendants ruled both Hanover and Britain. The last Hanoverian king, William IV, died in 1837. His niece Victoria became queen of the United Kingdom. But the rule of Hanover passed from the British royal family to Ernest Augustus, brother of William IV, because the laws of Hanover did not permit a woman ruler.

Victoria was the only child of Edward, Duke of Kent, fourth son of King George III, and of Victoria Maria Louisa, daughter of Francis, Duke of Saxe-Coburg and Saalfeld. Ernest, son of Francis, exchanged Saalfeld for Gotha in 1826 and founded the house of Saxe-Coburg and Gotha.

In 1840, Victoria married Albert, son of Ernest. Victoria's children took Albert's name. Edward VII, her son, was the first English king to bear the name *Saxe-Coburg and Gotha.* His son George V was the first to use the name *Windsor.* In 1960, Queen Elizabeth II announced that future generations, except for princes and princesses, will bear the name *Mountbatten-Windsor* in honor of her husband, Philip Mountbatten.

Queen Elizabeth and Prince Philip have four children. The children are Charles, Prince of Wales; Anne, Princess Royal; Andrew, Duke of York, and Prince Edward. Prince Charles is heir to the throne. His oldest son, Prince William, is next in line after Charles as heir.

James J. Sack

Related articles in *World Book* include:

Charles, Prince	Elizabeth II	Victoria
Edward VII	George V	Windsor Castle
Edward VIII	George VI	

Windsor, *WIHN zuhr,* Ontario (pop. 208,402; met. area pop. 307,877), is the southernmost city of Canada. It is the chief port of entry between Canada and the United States. Windsor lies on the southwest bank of the Detroit River, opposite Detroit (see **Ontario** [political map]). The Windsor-Detroit Tunnel and the Ambassador Bridge connect the two cities. The location of the city on one of the world's busiest inland waterways makes Windsor a major transportation center. Windsor leads all other Canadian cities in the production of automobiles and automotive products.

Description. Windsor covers 47 square miles (121 square kilometers). Windsor's metropolitan area covers 395 square miles (1,023 square kilometers). The city is the home of the St. Clair College of Applied Arts and Technology and the University of Windsor. Windsor's museums include the Art Gallery of Windsor and the Hiram Walker Historical Museum. The city is home to the Windsor Light Opera Association and the Windsor Symphony. Windsor has 1,387 acres (561 hectares) of parks, including about 95 acres (38 hectares) of riverfront parks.

Economy. Windsor's leading industry is the manufacture of transportation equipment, chiefly automobiles and automotive parts. This industry employs more than 25 percent of the city's workers. Windsor produces about 25 percent of Canada's automotive products and is sometimes called the *City That Put Canada on Wheels.* Many of Windsor's people work in Detroit offices and hospitals. They commute via the bridge or the tunnel that connects the two cities. Other leading industries include chemicals, food and beverages, and metal products. The city's harbor accommodates oceangoing ships.

Government and history. Windsor has a council-manager form of government. The city council consists of a mayor and 10 councillors, all of whom are elected to three-year terms. The council appoints a city manager.

Huron and Iroquois Indians lived in what is now the Windsor area before French explorers claimed it in the mid-1600's. The French government gave land to settlers who established a village there in the mid-1700's. English settlers arrived in the 1780's. A log ferryboat connected the village with Detroit, and in 1812 the people named their community The Ferry. They later changed its name to Richmond. In 1836, a dispute arose over whether to call it The Ferry, Richmond, or South Detroit. The people compromised by renaming it Windsor, the name of a borough near Richmond, England.

Windsor received a city charter in 1892. The Ford Motor Company produced the first Canadian-made car in Windsor in 1904. Two other U.S. automakers, the Chrysler and General Motors corporations, established plants in the city in 1920. Windsor annexed the towns of East Windsor, Sandwich, and Walkerville in 1935, and the city's population reached 100,000 that year. In the 1960's, Windsor annexed all or part of four other communities—Ojibway, Riverside, Sandwich East, and Sandwich West.

Windsor's Main Library opened in 1973. A number of expansion projects were also completed during the 1970's. These projects involved such institutions as Metropolitan General Hospital, the St. Clair College of Applied Arts and Technology, and the University of Windsor. In 1983, the Ouellette Avenue Mall was completed in Windsor's downtown section.   Donald G. Cartwright

Windsor, Duchess of. See Edward VIII.
Windsor, Duke of. See Edward VIII.
Windsor Castle is the principal residence outside of London of the rulers of Britain. The castle stands in Windsor, 21 miles (34 kilometers) west of London. William the Conqueror chose the site and built a castle there about 1070. The earliest parts of the present structure, however, were built during the reign of Henry III and Edward III. Later rulers added to the castle until it now covers 9 acres (3.6 hectares). Windsor Castle is located in the Home Park, which joins the Great Park south of Windsor. Queen Victoria and her husband are buried in the Home Park.

The dominant feature of the castle is the round *keep* (tower), which was completed in 1528. The keep is about 100 feet (30 meters) high. Fourteen other towers rise from the walls surrounding the castle.

The section west of the keep is called the Lower Ward. It contains St. George's Chapel (1473-1516). The chapel, with its elaborate fan-vaulted ceilings, is the most architecturally interesting building in the castle. In the chapel vault lie the bodies of Henry VIII, Charles I, William IV, George V, George VI, and other rulers of the country. The Albert Memorial Chapel also stands in the Lower Ward. Henry III began construction of this chapel, Henry VII rebuilt it, and Queen Victoria completed it in memory of her husband. King Edward VII was buried there in 1910. The Upper Ward, to the east of the central tower, contains the state apartments, built during the early 1800's.   J. William Rudd

Windsurfing is a common term for two similar water sports—*sailsurfing* and *sailboarding*. Both sports use a *sailboard,* which is a surfboard with a sail attached to a mast at the board's center. A sailsurfer rides like a surfer. A sailboarder sprints across flat water like a sailor. Therefore, sailsurfing needs waves, and sailboarding needs wind.

Most sailsurfing boards are no more than 7 feet (2.1 meters) long. A sailboard measures 10 to 12 feet (3.0 to 3.7 meters) long. The mast is attached to either kind of board by a universal joint. The universal joint allows the rider to turn the sail in any direction and thus steer the

F. Jalain, Explorer

Windsor Castle is the chief residence outside of London of the rulers of Britain. It stands in the town of Windsor, near London. The most notable architectural feature of the castle is the round *keep* (tower), which is shown at the far left.

© Darrell Jones, The Stock Market

Windsurfing includes the sport called *sailboarding, above,* in which individuals race wind-driven surfboards across flat water.

board. The sailboard was first patented in 1969.

Robert Sadler Clark

Windward Islands are a group of islands that lie in the southeastern West Indies. They stretch around the eastern end of the Caribbean Sea to South America (see **West Indies** [map]). The islands are so named because they are exposed to northeast trade winds. The Windward group consists of Dominica, Martinique, St. Lucia, Grenada, St. Vincent, and the Grenadine chain. Martinique is a French possession. St. Lucia and Dominica are independent nations. Grenada and part of the Grenadines form the independent nation of Grenada. St. Vincent and the rest of the Grenadines make up an independent nation called St. Vincent and the Grenadines.

The Windward Islands cover about 1,216 square miles (3,150 square kilometers) and have a population of about 695,000. Most of the people are of black African descent. The chief products include arrowroot, bananas, cocoa, cotton, mace, nutmeg, and sugar.

Arawak and Carib Indians were the first known inhabitants of the Windward Islands. The only remaining Carib Indians in the islands live in Dominica. Europeans settled in the Windward Islands in the early 1600's. Between 1763 and 1814, the islands, except for Martinique, became British colonies. Grenada became an independent nation in 1974. In 1978, Dominica gained its independence. St. Lucia and St. Vincent and the Grenadines became independent in 1979. Gerald R. Showalter

See also **Dominica; Grenada; Martinique; Saint Lucia; Saint Vincent and the Grenadines.**

Wine is an alcoholic beverage most often made from the juice of grapes. Wine also can be made from many other fruits, including apples and pears, and even from such plants as dandelions. Many wines retain the flavor and aroma of the fruit from which they were made. For thousands of years, people have used wine to complement meals and to celebrate. They have also used it in cooking and medicine and in religious ceremonies.

Types of wine. Wines can be divided into four categories: (1) table wines, (2) sparkling wines, (3) fortified wines, and (4) flavored wines. Alcohol makes up from 7 to 14 per cent of the volume of most wines. But fortified wines have from 18 to 24 per cent.

Table wines are the most commonly produced type

of wine. They are most often served with a meal. They may be grouped by color into red, white, and *rosé* (pink) wines. Crushed grapes produce a light green or yellow juice. The juice is tinted by contact with grape skins. In general, red and rosé wines are made from red or purple grapes, and white wines from white grapes. But a type of white wine called *blanc de noir* is made from red grapes. The grape skins have little contact with the juice, giving blanc de noir a paler color than rosé.

Wine drinkers describe a wine that lacks sweetness as *dry.* Most red table wines are dry. But white wines and rosé wines range from dry to sweet. Some white wines can be very sweet.

Sparkling wines, such as the champagne types, contain bubbles of carbon dioxide gas. People enjoy drinking sparkling wines on festive occasions.

Fortified wines have brandy or wine alcohol added to them. They tend to be sweeter than most other wines. For this reason, some people prefer to drink fortified wines with dessert or after a meal, while others choose to drink dry sherry or white port before dinner. The most popular fortified wines are port and sherry.

Flavored wines contain flavoring substances. For example, vermouth is a white wine flavored with herbs. Wine coolers are wines flavored with fruit juices. Most flavored wines are served alone or before a meal.

Where wine comes from. Most of the world's wine comes from grapes belonging to the species *Vitis vinifera,* which originated in the Middle East. Vinifera grapes are also known as European grapes. These grapes thrive in the vineyards of Europe and on the West Coast of the United States. Vinifera grapes produce their best wine when grown in regions that are cool but not cold. In the Eastern United States and in Canada, vinifera grapes have been crossbred with species native to North America, chiefly *Vitis labrusca* and *Vitis riparia.* These hybrid grapes can withstand cold climates better than European grapes can. But in many cases, hybrid grapes keep some of the flavor of the native grapes.

Robert Tixador, Agence Top

Wine is made from the juice of crushed grapes. Many European winemakers use a mechanical press like the one shown above to crush the grapes. The juice runs out the bottom of the press.

Grape juice becomes wine through the process of fermentation, which takes place in a large vat. Carbon dioxide escapes from the juice, causing a bubbling action, *above*.

David Moore, Colorific

Wine is aged in storage casks after it has fermented. Aging may take months or years, depending on the wine. A worker uses a device called a *wine thief* to take the wine from a cask to test it, *above*.

Grape species are made up of many varieties. In the United States, many wines take the name of the variety of grapes from which they are principally made. Such wines are often called *varietals*. Examples of varietal wines include Cabernet Sauvignon, Chardonnay, and Pinot Noir. According to U.S. law, a varietal made from vinifera grapes must contain at least 75 per cent of the variety after which it is named.

Most European wines are classified by the region they come from, such as Burgundy or Bordeaux in France or the valley of the Rhine River in Germany. Wines called *generics* sometimes take the name of a region in Europe, even though they may show little resemblance to wines from that region. A generic wine is usually a blend of several varieties of grapes.

Most nations produce some wine. The countries most famous for their wine include France, Italy, the United States, and Germany. Spain and Portugal also produce well-known wines.

Wines from France are famous because of French growing conditions and winemaking methods. The country's chief winemaking regions include Bordeaux, in southwestern France; Burgundy, in east-central France; and Champagne, east of Paris.

In the Bordeaux region, Cabernet Sauvignon and Merlot grapes go into making dry red wines. White Bordeaux wines come from Sémillon and Sauvignon Blanc grapes. Pinot Noir grapes form the basis of the red wines of Burgundy. White Burgundy wines come from Chardonnay grapes. Chardonnay and Pinot Noir grapes also form the basis of champagne, a sparkling wine of the Champagne region.

Wines from Italy. Grapevines grow throughout Italy. The red wines of the Piedmont region in northwestern Italy are known as Barolo and Barbaresco. They come from Nebbiolo grapes. Cortese grapes, also grown in the region, produce a crisp white wine called Gavi. Chianti, probably the most familiar Italian wine, comes mainly from Sangiovese grapes native to the regions of

Tuscany and Umbria in central Italy.

Wines from the United States. California produces about 90 per cent of the wine made in the United States. New York, Washington, Oregon, Virginia, and several other states also make wine. California wines are made from the same varieties of vinifera grapes as are European wines. California's chief grape-growing regions include the Napa and Sonoma valleys north of San Francisco Bay; the central coast; and the San Joaquin Valley, in the middle of the state.

Wines from Germany. Germany's distinctive white wines are produced mainly from Riesling grapes. Sylvaner grapes are also used to make white wine. Riesling and Sylvaner wines come from all of the country's winemaking regions, particularly those along the Rhine, Moselle (or Mosel), and Nahe rivers.

Wine styles from other countries include port and sherry. Port is a fortified wine that may be dark red or white. It was first made from grapes grown in the Douro Valley in northern Portugal. Sherry, a fortified white wine, ranges from pale gold to brown and from dry to sweet. The first sherry wines came from grapes grown in Jerez in southwestern Spain.

How wine is made. Winemaking requires a series of steps. Decisions made by the winemaker during each step influence the final "character" of the wine. A winemaker must first decide which grapes to use and when to harvest them. After the grapes are crushed, the juice is converted into wine through a process called *fermentation*. Wine is then aged until it is ready for drinking.

Harvesting the grapes. Grape growers harvest their crop as soon as the grapes have ripened, usually in the fall. Winemakers commonly measure ripeness by the amount of sugar in the grapes. They may also consider the grapes' acid content, flavor, and aroma. Workers pick grapes by hand or with mechanical harvesters that shake the fruit from the vine. The grapes then go to the winery for processing. The grape harvest is sometimes called the *vintage*. In some years, a favorable climate

Leading wine-producing countries

Amount of wine produced in a year

Italy	●●●●●●●●●●	1,612,100,000 gallons (6,102,400,000 liters)
France	●●●●●●●●●◖	1,550,100,000 gallons (5,867,600,000 liters)
Spain	●●●●●●◖	983,200,000 gallons (3,722,000,000 liters)
United States	●●●●◖	631,400,000 gallons (2,390,100,000 liters)
Argentina	●●●	394,600,000 gallons (1,493,900,000 liters)
Germany	●●◖	310,400,000 gallons (1,174,900,000 liters)
South Africa	●●	267,100,000 gallons (1,011,200,000 liters)
Australia	●◖	233,300,000 gallons (883,200,000 liters)

Figures are for a three-year average, 1999-2001.
Source: Food and Agriculture Organization of the United Nations.

produces grapes of especially high quality. Those vintage years are considered superior.

Preparing the juice. At the winery, a machine called a *crusher* breaks the grapes and removes them from their stems. The crushed grapes and their juice are called *must.* The length of contact between the juice and the skin affects the color of red wines and the taste of all wines. To make white wine, winemakers separate the skins and pulp from the juice. The juice then enters a tank or barrel for fermentation. In making red wine, the seeds and skins go into the fermentation tank with the juice. Stirring the mixture from time to time ensures that the color is extracted from the skins.

Fermentation is the chemical change in which yeast converts the sugar in grapes into alcohol. Some yeast grows naturally on the skins of grapes. Some European winemakers allow this yeast to conduct the fermentation. In the United States and most other countries, winemakers add selected yeasts to the must to begin fermentation. During fermentation, the yeast grows and changes sugars called *glucose* and *fructose* into ethanol, a type of alcohol, and carbon dioxide gas. The carbon dioxide is released as bubbles. The yeast also produces various by-products that may add to the wine's flavor and aroma.

Fermentation also releases heat. Most wineries refrigerate the must to keep its temperature constant during fermentation. Winemakers usually ferment juice for white wine at about 59 °F (15 °C) and juice for red wine at about 86 °F (30 °C). The temperature of the must influences the rate of fermentation, the retaining of grape aromas, and the formation of yeast by-products. It also determines the rate at which the color and flavor of the grape skins transfer into the wine. The fermentation of red wine takes from 4 to 6 days. White-wine fermentations last from 12 to 18 days.

Most red table wines and some white table wines undergo a second fermentation, by bacteria. This fermentation, called the *malolactic fermentation,* lowers a wine's acid content by converting a substance called *malic acid* into *lactic acid.*

Clarifying and aging the wine. A new wine appears cloudy after fermentation. Winemakers *clarify* (clear) the wine by removing particles of yeast and other unwanted substances. Such particles may be filtered out, allowed to settle naturally, or separated from the wine by a machine called a *centrifuge.* Wine may be further clarified, or *fined,* by adding certain solutions that reduce the content of unstable or unpleasant components.

After clarification, wine goes into wooden barrels or stainless steel tanks for aging. Wooden barrels contribute their own flavor to the wine. The size of the barrel, the age of the wood, the storage temperature and humidity, and the length of storage time all influence the extent of the aging process. Many wineries hold wine at a temperature close to freezing for one or more days so that a salt called potassium bitartrate will *precipitate* (separate) out of the wine. This prevents the salt from forming crystals in the wine after bottling.

Although some wines are soon ready for drinking, others must age a few years to soften harsh flavors and allow desirable flavors to develop. Wine is bottled after some aging, and it continues to age slowly in the bottle.

Fortified wines, such as port and sherry, are made by adding brandy to fermenting must. The brandy halts the fermentation by killing the yeast before all the sugar has turned into alcohol. The wine that results generally is sweet. Drier fortified wines are achieved by adding brandy near or at the end of fermentation. Sparkling wines are usually made by a second yeast fermentation of a table wine. This fermentation may take four to eight weeks. The bubbles of carbon dioxide produced by the fermentation are trapped in the wine.

History. The earliest references to wine date back about 5,000 years to civilizations in ancient Egypt and Babylon (now part of Iraq). Egyptian picture writing shows people harvesting and crushing grapes and storing wine in clay vessels. The Bible tells of winemaking in Canaan (later called Palestine). The ancient Greeks and Romans dealt extensively with wine in their paintings and writings. The Romans planted grapevines in regions they conquered, including what are now Austria, France, and Germany.

From about A.D. 500 to 1400, the spread of Christianity in Europe encouraged the growing of grapes to make the wines used in religious ceremonies. After the 1500's, European explorers and settlers introduced vinifera grapes to the lands now known as Argentina, Australia, Brazil, Chile, Mexico, New Zealand, South Africa, and the United States. Roger Boulton

See also **Grape; Europe** (picture: Grapes).

Winfrey, Oprah (1954-   ), is an American host and producer of one of the highest-rated television talk shows. Her sympathetic, natural, and sincere style has made millions of viewers worldwide watch "The Oprah Winfrey Show" regularly. Winfrey is one of the few women to head her own TV and film production studio, Harpo Productions. Winfrey is also an actress. She received an Academy Award nomination as best supporting actress for her film debut in *The Color Purple* (1985).

Oprah Gail Winfrey was born on Jan. 29, 1954, in Kosciusko, Mississippi. She was born to a single mother. Winfrey grew up in poverty. She later moved to the city of Nashville to live with her father. When she was 19 years old and a student at Tennessee State University,

Winfrey became the anchorwoman of a TV news broadcast in Nashville. She was the first African American woman and one of the youngest persons to anchor a newscast in Nashville.

Winfrey had her first major success in 1984 when she became host of "A.M. Chicago," a local TV talk show. The show was renamed "The Oprah Winfrey Show" in 1985 and became *syndicated* (broadcast nationally) in 1986. Winfrey has won numerous Daytime Emmy Awards as best talk show host.   Robert Feder

Harpo/King World
Oprah Winfrey

Wing. See Airplane (The wing); Aerodynamics; Bird (How birds move); Helicopter (Lift); Insect (Wings).

Wingate's Raiders were a group of Allied soldiers who fought behind Japanese lines in Burma during World War II. British Brigadier General Orde Charles Wingate organized the group, known as *Chindits,* from British, Burmese, and Nepalese troops in 1942. In 1943, the group entered Japanese-held territory, where it operated against enemy communications. The force suffered heavy losses, and its first campaign had only limited success. Wingate was promoted to major general and led a second similar campaign early in 1944.

Wingate died in an airplane crash in March 1944, but the Raiders continued to fight in Burma. Members of the group cut railroad lines, blew up bridges and highways, and destroyed Japanese military installations. They also supported the Allied advance into Burma led by U.S. General Joseph W. Stilwell.   James L. Stokesbury

See also **Commando.**

Winged Victory is a statue of Nike, the goddess of victory in Greek mythology. The marble sculpture is 8 feet (2.4 meters) high. It probably commemorates a sea victory. The dramatic statue shows a winged female figure alighting on the prow of a ship, presumably to crown the ship's commander. Her garments, wet with spray and blown by her flight, whip about her body.

The statue was discovered in 1863 on the Greek island of Samothrace. It was probably dedicated at the sanctuary of the Great Gods about 190 B.C. In the sanctuary, the Winged Victory was placed above a pool of water to simulate the sea. It now stands in the Louvre in Paris.   Marjorie S. Venit

Winkelried, *VIHNG kuhl REET,* **Arnold von,** *AHR nawlt fuhn,* is the legendary national hero of Switzerland. He was supposed to have brought victory to the Swiss in the battle of Sempach against the Austrians in 1386. According to legend, the Swiss were beginning to retreat when Winkelried, a Swiss soldier, dashed boldly into the Austrian ranks and seized with his bare hands as many enemy spears as he could reach. As he fell, pierced by the spears, he created a gap in the Austrian ranks. The Swiss rushed through the opening, and won the battle in hand-to-hand fighting.   Arthur M. Selvi

Winkle, Rip Van. See Rip Van Winkle.

Winnebago, Lake. See Lake Winnebago.

Winnebago Indians, *WIHN uh BAY goh,* were an eastern woodland tribe. The language of the Winnebago resembled that of the Sioux (see **Sioux Indians**). Tribal traditions say that at one time the Winnebago lived near the Missouri River, but that they were forced east and settled near Green Bay in Wisconsin. The tribe hunted buffalo, caught fish, and raised corn and squash. They built long lodges with arched roofs and arbors over the entrances. Chiefs, who were sometimes women, inherited their rank. Important tribal ceremonies included the Medicine Dance, organized around a secret society, and the Winter Feast, a war ceremony.

The Winnebago were nearly destroyed by the Illinois sometime before 1670. But small groups continued to live along Lake Winnebago and elsewhere in southern Wisconsin and northern Illinois. They were friendly to most nearby tribes, and to the French. During the Revolutionary War and the War of 1812, the Winnebago sided with Britain. Some Winnebago lived in a village, now called Prophetstown, on the Rock River in Illinois. The town was named after their leader, Wabokieshiek (White Cloud), who was called the Prophet. The Winnebago ceded their lands in Wisconsin and Illinois to the federal government in the 1830's. They were moved to Minnesota, then to South Dakota, and finally to Nebraska. Some of the Winnebago refused to leave Wisconsin and Minnesota, and they still live there. According to the 1990 United States census, there are about 7,000 Winnebago.   Robert E. Powless

See also **Nebraska** (History).

Winnemucca, *WIHN uh MUHK uh,* **Sarah** (1844?-1891), was an American Indian who won fame for her criticism of the government's mistreatment of her people. Winnemucca, a member of the Paiute tribe, began to speak out against the government as early as 1870. She later established two schools for Indian children.

Winnemucca, called *Thoc-me-tony* (Shell Flower) by the Paiute, was born near Humboldt Sink in what is now Nevada. During the late 1860's and the 1870's, she served as an interpreter, guide, and scout for various government officials. In the 1870's, she protested such abuses of the Paiute as seizure of their lands and an Army attack on a Paiute settlement.

In 1880, Winnemucca met on her people's behalf with President Rutherford B. Hayes. The next year, she lectured in Boston and other Eastern cities on the government's mistreatment of the Paiute. She also wrote a book called *Life Among the Paiutes: Their Claims and Wrongs* (1883). In 1881, Winnemucca opened a school for Indian children at Vancouver Barracks, an Army post in the Washington Territory (now Washington). She later founded a school for Paiute children near Lovelock, Nevada.   W. Roger Buffalohead

Winnetka Plan, *wuh NEHT kuh,* is a teaching plan designed to provide individualized instruction. It was developed in the public elementary and junior high schools of Winnetka, Illinois, after World War I (1914-1918). It influenced widely the growth of the progressive education movement. According to the plan, teachers deal with each pupil individually so that pupils can develop their own particular abilities at their own rate of speed. Pupils work alone in their regular studies, but take part in many group activities in which their achievements are not measured.   Douglas Sloan

Winnie-the-Pooh. See Milne, A. A.

The Winnipeg Art Gallery helps make the city one of the leading cultural centers of Canada. Winnipeg, the capital of Manitoba, lies in the southern part of the province.

The Winnipeg Art Gallery (Ernest Mayer)

Winnipeg, *WIHN uh PEHG,* is the capital of Manitoba and one of Canada's largest cities. It is Canada's main grain market and one of the nation's leading centers of culture, finance, and trade. More than half of Manitoba's people live in the city.

Winnipeg lies about 60 miles (97 kilometers) north of the Canadian-United States border and almost midway between the Atlantic and Pacific oceans. Its central location makes the city the chief transportation center linking eastern and western Canada. It is also a principal distribution point for goods traveling west from eastern Canada.

Winnipeg has the nickname *Gateway to the West.* The city was named after Lake Winnipeg, about 40 miles (64 kilometers) to the north. The word *Winnipeg* comes from the Cree Indian words *win-nipi,* meaning *muddy water.*

The city covers 180 square miles (465 square kilometers). Winnipeg lies at the junction of the Red and Assiniboine rivers in southern Manitoba.

Main Street, once an important settlers' trail, is Winnipeg's chief north-south street. Portage Avenue, the beginning of the old overland route between Winnipeg and Edmonton, Alberta, is the city's main east-west street.

The 33-story Toronto-Dominion Centre, Winnipeg's tallest structure, rises 413 feet (126 meters) at Main and Portage. The city's chief public buildings are in the nearby Civic Centre. The Manitoba Legislative Building stands on the Mall in a park on the north bank of the Assiniboine River.

Winnipeg's metropolitan area covers 1,603 square miles (4,151 square kilometers). The Winnipeg metropolitan area ranks as one of Canada's largest metropolitan areas in population. It is Manitoba's only Census Metropolitan Area as defined by Statistics Canada.

The people. More than 80 percent of Winnipeg's people were born in Canada, and most are of mixed European ancestry. About one-third of the city's people have British ancestors. The next largest ethnic groups are French people, Germans, and Ukrainians. The city also has a large number of Indians and *métis* (people of mixed Indian and white ancestry).

Economy. Winnipeg lies in the plains that cover part of southern Manitoba, a rich grain-growing region. The Winnipeg Commodity Exchange is Canada's major grain market. The Canadian Wheat Board and many grain companies have their main offices in Winnipeg. The Winnipeg Stock Exchange helps make the city a major financial center.

The city is also an important transportation center. A number of major nationwide trucking companies have their headquarters in Winnipeg. Canada's two transcontinental railroads—the Canadian National Railway and the Canadian Pacific Railway—and a United States railroad provide passenger service to the city. The Trans-Canada Highway and Manitoba's main highways pass through Winnipeg. Winnipeg International Airport is one of the busiest airports in Canada.

Facts in brief

Population: 619,544. *Metropolitan area population*—671,274.
Area: 180 mi² (465 km²). *Metropolitan area*—1,603 mi² (4,151 km²).
Altitude: 784 ft (239 m) above sea level.
Climate: *Average temperature*—January, −2 °F (−19 °C); July, 68 °F (20 °C). *Average annual precipitation* (rainfall, melted snow, and other forms of moisture)—21 inches (53 centimeters). For the monthly weather in Winnipeg, see **Manitoba** (Climate).
Government: Mayor-council. *Terms*—3 years for the mayor and 15 councilors.
Founded: 1870. Incorporated as a city in 1873.

Important products made by Winnipeg area factories include aerospace equipment, clothing, electronics, farm machinery, furniture, processed foods, and transportation equipment. The Royal Canadian Mint in Winnipeg supplies all Canadian coins and also coins money for foreign countries without mint facilities of their own.

Education. Winnipeg's public school system has about 255 elementary and high schools. The city also has about 40 parochial and private schools. Local property taxes provide the chief source of revenue for the public schools. The provincial government also provides some funds for school expenses.

The University of Manitoba was founded in Winnipeg in 1877. Other schools of higher education are the University of Winnipeg, in the downtown area; and Red River Community College, which provides training in technical and office skills.

Cultural life. Winnipeg is one of the chief cultural centers of Canada. The world-famous Royal Winnipeg Ballet, the Winnipeg Symphony Orchestra, and the Manitoba Opera Association perform in the Centennial Concert Hall. The hall is part of the Manitoba Centennial Centre, which also includes the Manitoba Theatre Centre, the Museum of Man and Nature, and a planetarium. The Winnipeg Art Gallery attracts many visitors. The city is also home to the Mennonite Heritage Centre and the Ukrainian Museum of Canada.

A public library system operates branches throughout the city. The Winnipeg Centennial Library is the main branch. The city has two daily newspapers, the *Winnipeg Free Press* and *The Winnipeg Sun*. About 5 television stations and about 10 radio stations serve Winnipeg, including one French-language television station and one multilanguage radio station.

Winnipeg has about 900 parks, squares, and athletic fields. Assiniboine Park, covering 375 acres (152 hectares), is the largest park. It includes beautiful gardens and a zoo. The Assiniboine Forest, a 692-acre (280-hectare) nature preserve, lies south of the park. The Winnipeg Blue Bombers of the Canadian Football League play their home games in Winnipeg Stadium.

Ross House, western Canada's first post office, is in downtown Winnipeg. It opened in 1855. Lower Fort Garry National Historic Park, north of Winnipeg, has the only stone fur-trading post still standing in North America. The post dates from the 1830's.

Government. Winnipeg has a mayor-council government. The voters in each of Winnipeg's 15 *wards* (voting areas) elect one councilor to the city council. The councilors serve three-year terms. The voters also elect a mayor to a three-year term as administrative head of the government. A five-member board of commissioners, including a chief commissioner, supervises various departments of the government. Property taxes provide about two-thirds of Winnipeg's revenue.

History. The Assiniboine and Cree Indians lived in what is now the Winnipeg area before the first whites arrived. In 1738, Sieur de La Vérendrye, a French-Canadian fur trader, became the first white person to reach what is now Winnipeg. He built Fort Rouge at the junction of the Red and Assiniboine rivers and traded for furs with the Indians. See **La Vérendrye, Sieur de**.

During the early 1800's, the Winnipeg area became the center of fur-trade rivalry between the North West Company and the Hudson's Bay Company. In 1812, Scottish and Irish farmers set up the area's first permanent settlement along the Red River (see **Manitoba** [The Red River Colony]). The Hudson's Bay Company absorbed its chief rival in 1821. That year, the company enlarged Fort Gibraltar, a post at the site of present-day Winnipeg,

City of Winnipeg

Winnipeg, a major transportation center, lies in southern Manitoba at the junction of the Red and Assiniboine rivers. The map shows the city and major points of interest.

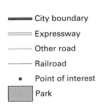

City boundary
Expressway
Other road
Railroad
▪ Point of interest
 Park

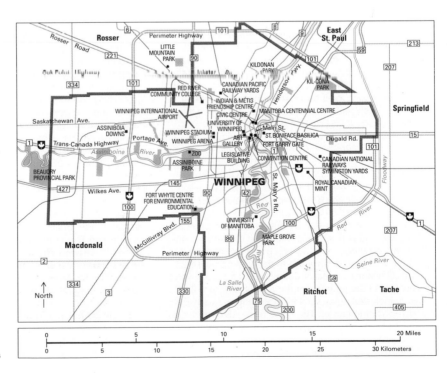

and renamed it Fort Garry. It rebuilt the fort in 1835 and called it Upper Fort Garry. A trading post north of Winnipeg was known as Lower Fort Garry. Upper Fort Garry became the center of the Red River settlement.

In 1870, Manitoba entered the Dominion of Canada. The Red River settlement was renamed Winnipeg that same year, and it became the capital of the new province. It was incorporated as a city in 1873. By then, it had about 1,900 people. In 1878, Manitoba's first railroad linked Winnipeg and St. Paul, Minnesota. The Canadian Pacific Railway connected Winnipeg with eastern Canada in 1881. The government's offer of free land in western Canada helped Winnipeg's population grow during the late 1800's.

During the early 1900's, large numbers of Europeans settled in Winnipeg. Industry grew rapidly in the city during this period, and Winnipeg became the manufacturing center of western Canada. The opening of the Panama Canal in 1914 slowed Winnipeg's expansion. Companies in eastern Canada could now send their products to the West more cheaply by ship through the canal than by railroad. Winnipeg's economy continued to suffer during the Great Depression of the 1930's.

During World War II (1939-1945), sharp increases in the demand for livestock, lumber, metals, and wheat brought prosperity back to Winnipeg. Between 1946 and 1950, about 200 industries began in Winnipeg. The city's population fell during the 1960's, partly because of a trend toward suburban living.

In 1960, the Manitoba legislature established the Metropolitan Corporation of Greater Winnipeg to administer a number of services for Winnipeg and 11 of its suburbs. These services included planning and zoning, public transportation, and water supply. Each municipality in the corporation also had its own governing council to administer local affairs.

In 1971, the Manitoba legislature combined Winnipeg and the suburbs into one municipality, the unified city of Winnipeg. The merger, which took effect on Jan. 1, 1972, greatly increased the city's area and population.

A downtown building boom began in the 1960's and 1970's. Tall apartment and office buildings and hotels replaced many old structures. New construction included the Winnipeg Convention Centre, which opened in 1975, and a system of enclosed walkways above the streets.

In 1981, the city, provincial, and federal governments launched the Winnipeg Core Area Initiative. Through this program, the three governments provided funds to improve education, social services, and economic development in a 10-square-mile (26-square-kilometer) area of the inner city. The Core Area initiative included renovation of historic office and warehouse buildings in the downtown Exchange district, and construction of a shopping and residential complex on Portage Avenue. The city, provincial, and federal governments also formed a public corporation to develop a 56-acre (23-hectare) historic area called the Forks. This area, which is located at the junction of the Assiniboine and Red rivers, includes many sites from Winnipeg's early days as a fur-trading center. The Forks opened to tourists in 1990, but development was to continue for many years.

John S. Brierley

Winnipeg, Lake. See Lake Winnipeg.

Winnipeg River is part of the Saskatchewan-Nelson river system that empties into Hudson Bay. The Winnipeg is 140 miles (225 kilometers) long. It rises in western Ontario and winds west, draining the Lake of the Woods. It empties into Lake Winnipeg, near the city of Winnipeg. Hydroelectric generating stations on the river supply some of Winnipeg's power. In pioneer days, the Winnipeg River was on the fur-trade route to the Northwest. See **Manitoba** (physical map). John S. Brierley

Winslow, Edward (1595-1655), was a founder of Plymouth Colony. He joined the Pilgrims in Leiden, the Netherlands, and came to Plymouth on the *Mayflower* in 1620. Winslow and Susanna White became the first couple to marry in the new colony. Winslow arranged the first treaty with the Indian chief Massasoit and explored and traded with the Indians. Winslow served as an assistant to the governor for 20 years and as governor of the colony for three. Winslow left Plymouth in 1646 and served in Oliver Cromwell's government in England. He was born in Droitwich, England. James Axtell

Winston-Salem (pop. 185,776) is a world tobacco center. It produces tobacco products and serves as a leaf-tobacco market. The city is located in northwestern North Carolina near the Blue Ridge Mountains (see **North Carolina** [political map]). With Greensboro and High Point, the city forms a metropolitan area with 1,251,509 people.

Winston-Salem also produces electronic equipment, fabrics, furniture, hosiery, and men's and boys' knitwear. The city is the home of Forsyth Technical Community College, Salem College, Wake Forest University, and Winston-Salem State University.

A group of Moravians founded Salem in 1766. Winston was founded in 1849 and consolidated with Salem in 1913. Winston-Salem is the seat of Forsyth County. It has a council-manager government. Jerry L. Surratt

Winter is the coldest season of the year. The Northern Hemisphere, the northern half of the earth, has winter weather during December, January, February, and early March. In the Southern Hemisphere, winter weather begins in late June and lasts until early September. For dates of the first day of winter and information about the position of the earth and sun during winter, see **Season**.

During winter, the polar region is especially cold because the sun does not rise there for weeks or months at a time. Cold, dry air moves south from this region, bringing cold weather. Storms move from west to east along the southern edge of the cold air. In the United States, winter storms produce large snowfalls in some areas. The most snow falls in the western mountains and in much of the northern region east of the Rocky Mountains. Many winter storms bring rain to warmer southern areas. The lowest winter temperatures usually occur in the middle of all continents. John E. Kutzbach

See also **December; January; February; March.**
Winter depression. See Seasonal affective disorder.
Winterberry, sometimes called *black alder,* is a shrub related to the American holly. Many winterberry plants grow in swamps and wet, wooded areas in eastern North America. The plant grows 6 to 12 feet (2 to 4 meters) tall. Its bright red berries appear in autumn.

Jerry M. Baskin

Scientific classification. The winterberry belongs to the holly family, Aquifoliaceae. Its scientific name is *Ilex verticillata.*

Wintergreen is a hardy woodland plant that bears white flowers. It grows in almost all parts of the Northern Hemisphere and received its name because its leaves remain green all winter. The name also applies to other plants of this type. The wintergreen is a low-growing shrub with creeping, or subterranean, stems. Its glossy oval leaves cluster at the top of short, erect reddish branches. Its attractive flowers are shaped like urns. The flowers cannot be seen easily because the plant's leaves hide them. The plant produces a bright red berry. Wintergreen provides a pleasant-smelling, pleasant-tasting oil. Wintergreen oil serves as a flavoring for candy, medicine, chewing gum, and tooth powder.

James L. Luteyn

Scientific classification. Wintergreen is in the heath family, Ericaceae. It is *Gaultheria procumbens.*

Winthrop, John (1588-1649), an American colonial leader, was a Puritan governor of the Massachusetts Bay Colony. He was appointed governor in 1629 by the Massachusetts Bay Company. In 1630, Winthrop sailed to Salem, a settlement in the colony, and led about a thousand English colonists to Massachusetts Bay. He succeeded John Endecott as governor and helped found Boston.

In 1631, the colony voted to allow Winthrop to remain as governor, a post he held numerous times during the rest of his life. As governor, Winthrop helped the colony maintain a certain amount of political independence from England. He also supported the banishment of Roger Williams and Anne Hutchinson from the colony. Williams and Hutchinson headed religious groups whose beliefs differed from the strict Puritanism of the colony's leaders.

Winthrop was born on Jan. 12, 1588, in Edwardstone, England, in the county of Suffolk. He attended Cambridge University and practiced law. A statue of him represents Massachusetts in the United States Capitol. Winthrop's son John Winthrop, Jr., served as colonial governor of Connecticut. John W. Ifkovic

Winthrop, John, Jr. (1606-1676), was a colonial governor of Connecticut. In 1662, he got a charter from King Charles II of England that gave Connecticut the right to govern itself and elect its own rulers. The charter served as Connecticut's constitution until 1818.

Winthrop was born on Feb. 12, 1606, in Groton, England, in the county of Suffolk. After studying law in London, he sailed to America in 1631. Winthrop was elected governor of Connecticut in 1657 and every year from 1659 until his death. He also practiced medicine; wrote on scientific subjects; established iron, lead, and salt works; and was a merchant and farmer. In 1663, he became the first North American to be elected to the Royal Society, an important scientific organization in England. Winthrop's father, John Winthrop, served as governor of the Massachusetts Bay Colony. John W. Ifkovic

Wintun Indians, *wihn TOON,* also spelled *Wintuan,* are a group of three tribes from the Sacramento Valley of north-central California. The tribes are the Wintu, Nomlaki, and Patwin. Their territory originally extended from the Sacramento River to the foothills of the California Coast Range and from the source of the Trinity River to the mouth of the Sacramento (see **California** [physical map]). Each village consisted of an extended family of 20 to 200 people led by a hereditary male chief. For food,

the Wintun hunted, fished, and gathered acorns. The Wintun had strong traditions of sacred song and dance. They took part in a religious revival called the Ghost Dance that began among the Paiute Indians in the late 1860's and quickly spread to other tribes.

In the early 1800's, Spanish missionaries and settlers took many Patwin to live at missions. A malaria epidemic killed large numbers of Wintun along the Sacramento River between 1830 and 1833. During the 1850's, white settlers and gold miners poured into Wintun lands. Fighting between Wintun and whites led to the Indians' being forced onto reservations by the United States government. Some escaped from the reservations. They worked for ranchers and lived in small communities called *rancherias.* About 1900, the government recognized the rancherias as Indian property. Today, many Wintun live throughout California, about 400 of them on or near rancherias. Victoria D. Patterson

Wire is a long, thin, flexible metal rod that has a uniform cross section. Only *ductile* metals, or metals that can be easily drawn out, can be used for making wire. The chief ductile metals are copper, steel, brass, tungsten, gold, silver, and aluminum.

How wire is made. From early ages until the 1300's, wire was made by hammering metal into plates. These plates were then cut into strips and rounded by beating. Then crude methods of "drawing" wire were introduced. Machine-drawn wire was first made in England in the mid-1800's. Today, all wire is machine-made. Steel or iron *billets,* 2-inch (5-centimeter) square blocks of metal, are heated and run through rollers that press them into smaller, longer shapes. They come out as long rods about $\frac{1}{4}$ inch (6 millimeters) in diameter. The rods are cast into coils and cleansed in sulfuric acid and water.

Pulling the rods through a series of tungsten carbide dies draws them out to form wire. The die has a funnel-like shape with a round opening smaller than the rod. The rod, which is pointed at one end by hammering, may be run into the die as thread runs through the eye of a needle. When the pointed end passes through the die, it is seized with a pair of pincers, which are operated mechanically or by hand, and drawn far enough to be attached to an upright drum. The drum rotates, pulling the wire through the die. The wire winds on the drum. Fine wire is drawn through a series of dies of continuously decreasing diameters. Drawn wire tends to harden, and so it is softened and made less brittle by being heated in a furnace. For drawing the finest wires, extremely hard dies made of diamonds are used.

Sizes of wire. The size of wire differs according to its gauge, or diameter. *American,* or *Brown and Sharpe,* is the standard gauge used in the United States for copper and other nonferrous wire. This gauge varies from No. 000000, which is 0.58 inch (15 millimeters) in diameter, to No. 51, which is 0.000878 inch (0.022301 millimeter). Sometimes other U.S. standards or the *imperial* gauge of England are used. France and Germany use gauges based on the millimeter. The *steel wire gauge* is the U.S. standard gauge for steel wire. Wire may be drawn through specially shaped dies to be made square, oval, flat, or triangular. But most wire is round.

Uses of wire. Manufacturers make telephone and electric-power wires of copper and aluminum, which are unusually ductile as well as good conductors of

How wire is made

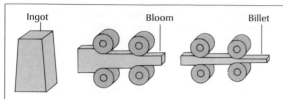

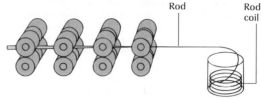

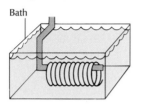

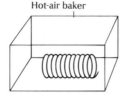

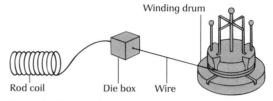

Rollers press an ingot of hot metal into a longer shape called a *bloom.* Further rolling of the bloom produces a bar called a *billet,* which is 2 inches (5 centimeters) square.

The billet passes through another series of rollers and comes out as a *rod* about $\frac{1}{4}$ inch (6 millimeters) in diameter. Machines cast the rod into a coil for easy handling.

The rod coil is cleansed in a bath of sulfuric acid and water. Then it is coated with lime. A hot-air baker dries the lime coating, which will act as a carrier for a lubricant.

The rod is lubricated and drawn through a die box onto a winding drum. As it passes through the funnellike die, the rod becomes longer and thinner until it is wire.

WORLD BOOK diagrams by Steven Liska

electricity. The very thin wires used in telescopes are made of platinum. People use wire in making nails, fences, watch springs, screens, and strings for musical and scientific instruments. Wire is also used in automobile springs, bolts, nuts, paper clips, screws, and staples. Magnet wire is used in generators and motors. Wire netting, gauze, and cloth are woven from wire. Wire ropes and cables consist of wires twisted together. Large suspension bridges are supported by steel-wire cables, which consist of many wires bunched together. Wire ropes are used in mining and oil drilling. *Optical fibers,* a type of wire made from glass, are used for high-speed data transmission.   Melvin Bernstein

Related articles in *World Book* include:
Annealing
Barbed wire
Cable
Copper (Copper wire)
Ductility
Fiber optics

Wire fox terrier is a popular breed of small, sturdy dogs. It has a rough, wiry, white coat, usually with patches of black or tan, or both black and tan. Its head is long and narrow with small ears that fall forward in a V shape. Its tail is short and erect. Wire fox terriers weigh about 15 to 19 pounds (7 to 9 kilograms). The American Kennel Club recognized the wire fox terrier as a breed in 1985. Until then, wire fox terriers and smooth fox terriers were regarded as a single breed, called *fox terriers* (see **Smooth fox terrier; Dog** [Terriers: picture]).

The wire fox terrier was developed in northern England in the late 1800's. It originally was used in fox-hunting to drive the fox from its hiding place. Wire fox terriers have remarkable endurance, excellent eyesight, and a keen sense of smell. They are friendly and good-tempered and make good pets. They also are excellent watchdogs.   Critically reviewed by the American Fox Terrier Club

Wire service. See News service.

Wirehaired pointing griffon is a hunting dog that originated in France and the Netherlands in the late 1800's. A good retriever, it shows where game is by pointing its body toward the game. It has a rough, steel-gray coat, with splashes of chestnut. The dog works deliberately, locating game by scent on the wind. Owners usually *dock* (cut off) about two-thirds of the tail. The wirehaired pointing griffon stands 19 to 23 inches (48 to 58 centimeters) high at the shoulder and weighs from 50 to 60 pounds (23 to 27 kilograms).

Critically reviewed by the American Kennel Club

WORLD BOOK photo by E. F. Hoppe

The wirehaired pointing griffon is a hunting dog.

Wireless communication involves sending and receiving information through the air or through space via electromagnetic waves, most often as radio waves. Wireless devices send and receive signals over distances ranging from a few feet or meters to thousands of miles or kilometers. Many people use such small wireless communication devices as cordless telephones, walkie-talkies, pagers, and cellular telephones. The military often uses larger wireless units that can be carried or mounted in vehicles. All communications to aircraft and sea vessels are wireless. Artificial satellites relay telephone calls in the form of microwave transmissions. The remote-control devices that control home electronic equipment use infrared light waves.

How wireless communication works. Essentially any information that people use can be transmitted wirelessly, including sound, text, still images, and video. A basic wireless communication system consists of three elements: (1) a transmitter, (2) a receiver, and (3) a wireless channel. The transmitter and receiver are electronic devices, and the wireless channel is the set of paths over which the signals travel to reach the receiver.

Unlike wire-based systems, wireless systems can function when the transmitter or receiver, or both, are moving. As the paths of the signals change, however, the signals can fade or become distorted. Thus, communication is generally less reliable over a wireless system than over a wire-based system.

The signals *propagate* (travel) via a *carrier wave.* This wave begins as a continuous wave pattern, but it is *modulated* (altered) in one or more of three ways to include a representation of the information. In *amplitude modulation* (AM), changes in the strength of the carrier wave represent the information. *Frequency modulation* (FM) varies the number of cycles per second of the carrier wave. *Phase modulation* (PM) alters the *phase* of the carrier wave by shifting a wave to its negative value, resulting in the periodic occurrence of two wave crests or troughs in a row rather than alternating crests and troughs. Information in *digital* (numeric) form may be sent via any of the three modulation methods.

History. Wireless communications began in the late 1880's when the German physicist Heinrich Hertz showed that electromagnetic waves existed and could be transmitted and received through the air. He thus proved theories proposed in the 1860's by the Scottish scientist James Clerk Maxwell. In 1891, Nikola Tesla, an American inventor from Austria-Hungary, invented the Tesla coil, a device that is still used in wireless communication. The Italian American inventor Guglielmo Marconi made one of the earliest long-distance wireless transmissions in 1895. Since the early 1980's, the number of wireless systems that use digital technology has greatly increased. David W. Matolak

Related articles in *World Book* include:

Cellular telephone	Marconi, Guglielmo	Remote control
Digital technology	Maxwell, James	Television
Hertz, Heinrich	Clerk	Tesla, Nikola
Rudolf	Radio	Walkie-talkie

Wiretapping usually means the interception of telephone conversations by a listening device connected to the telephone wire or placed nearby. The message may be heard live, or it may be recorded or transmitted to another location. Wiretapping is used in an investigative procedure called *audio surveillance.* The term *wiretapping* sometimes refers to the use of any electrical or electronic device to eavesdrop on private conversations. But the interception of nontelephone conversations is usually called *bugging* or *electronic eavesdropping.*

Sophisticated methods and devices allow eavesdropping in nearly any situation. Some types of microphones may be attached to a wall or door so that conversations can be overheard through the partition. Directional microphones may be beamed or focused to pick up conversations from long distances. Even greater distances can be overcome by concealed miniature microphones and transmitters that send messages to a radio receiver.

In most countries, the right of people to speak freely in their homes and businesses and in public places—without fear of eavesdroppers—is considered extremely important. Many nations, states, and provinces have passed laws restricting or prohibiting various types of electronic surveillance. But much illegal eavesdropping continues, both by individuals and by governments.

In the United States, the problem of wiretapping and electronic eavesdropping has become a controversial legal issue. There is much disagreement about (1) the constitutionality of electronic surveillance by law enforcement agencies and (2) methods of controlling government eavesdropping if it is permitted. But many Americans oppose wiretapping and bugging by either governments or private individuals. The wiretapping controversy began in 1928, when the Supreme Court of the United States ruled that wiretapping did not violate the Fourth Amendment to the Constitution. This amendment sets forth restrictions on search and seizure.

In 1934, Congress passed the Federal Communications Act, which bans the interception and public disclosure of any wire or radio communication. Based on this law, the Supreme Court ruled in 1937 that evidence obtained by wiretapping cannot be used in a federal court. Following this ruling, federal officials argued that the 1934 law did not prohibit wiretapping by the government so long as the evidence was not used in court. Since 1940, U.S. presidents have claimed constitutional power to order wiretaps in matters of national security.

In 1968, Congress passed a law permitting federal, state, and local government agencies to use wiretapping and bugging devices in certain crime investigations. Before undertaking such surveillance, an agency would have to obtain a court order. The law stated that nothing in it was intended to limit the president's constitutional authority to order wiretapping without court warrants in national security cases.

In the late 1960's and early 1970's, the executive branch broadly interpreted the national security provisions of the 1968 law. It conducted electronic surveillance without court approval on a number of domestic radicals it considered subversive. In 1972, the Supreme Court ruled that such surveillance without a court warrant was unconstitutional. Also in 1972, wiretapping of the Democratic Party's national headquarters became a main issue in the Watergate Scandal. Members of a committee working for the reelection of President Richard M. Nixon, a Republican, were involved in this wiretapping. See **Watergate.**

In 2001, Congress passed an antiterrorism bill called the USA PATRIOT Act. The act greatly expanded the government's powers to use wiretapping to defend against terrorism. George T. Felkenes

See also **Codes and ciphers; Warrant.**

Wireworm. See **Click beetle.**

Grant Heilman

Cows graze on a Wisconsin farm amid the state's rolling countryside. Farmers in Wisconsin raise thousands of herds of dairy cattle, earning the state the nickname of *America's Dairyland.*

Wisconsin *The Badger State*

Wisconsin is a Midwestern state of the United States that has long been famous for its dairy products. Thousands of herds of milk cows graze on the rich, green pastures of the rolling Wisconsin countryside. They make Wisconsin one of the nation's leading milk producers. The state also produces about a third of the country's cheese and about a fourth of its butter. This tremendous output of dairy products has earned Wisconsin the title of *America's Dairyland.* The processing of milk into butter, cheese, and other dairy products is a leading manufacturing activity in Wisconsin. Manufacturing is more important to Wisconsin's economy than it is to the economies of most other states.

Wisconsin is one of the leading states in the manufacture of machinery, food products, and paper products. The cities of southeastern Wisconsin produce construction cranes, engines, machine tools, and other machinery. Besides dairy products, the state's food products include canned and frozen vegetables, sausages, and beer. Northern Wisconsin has many paper mills.

Most of Wisconsin's workers are employed in service

The contributors of this article are Gary C. Meyer, Professor of Geography and Natural Resources at the University of Wisconsin at Stevens Point; and Benjamin D. Rhodes, Professor of History at the University of Wisconsin at Whitewater.

industries, which include education, finance, health care, and trade. The state's public university system is one of the largest in the nation. Milwaukee ranks as one of the Midwest's chief financial centers. Madison, Milwaukee, and La Crosse have major medical centers. Ports along Lake Michigan and Lake Superior handle both foreign and domestic trade.

The natural beauty and recreational resources of Wisconsin attract millions of vacationers every year. Wisconsin has about 15,000 lakes to delight swimmers, fishing enthusiasts, and boaters. Hikers and horseback riders follow paths through the deep, cool north woods of Wisconsin. Hunters shoot game animals in the forests and fields. In winter, sports fans enjoy skiing, tobogganing, and iceboating.

Wisconsin has won fame as one of the nation's most progressive states. An important reform movement called *Progressivism* started in Wisconsin during the early 1900's. The state began many educational, social, political, and economic reforms that were later adopted by other states and the federal government. Many of these reforms were sponsored by the La Follettes, one of the most famous families in American political history.

Wisconsin led the way to direct primary elections, regulation of public utilities and railroads, pensions for teachers, minimum-wage laws, and workers' compensa-

Buck Miller, Black Star

Grand Avenue Mall, in downtown Milwaukee, attracts many shoppers. Milwaukee is the largest city in Wisconsin.

Interesting facts about Wisconsin

WORLD BOOK illustrations by Kevin Chadwick

The first practical typewriter was invented by Christopher Latham Sholes, with the help of Carlos Glidden and Samuel W. Soule, in Milwaukee in 1867.

The first kindergarten in the United States was opened in 1856 in Watertown by Mrs. Carl Schurz. Schurz had been a pupil

First kindergarten

of Friedrich Fröbel, the father of the kindergarten movement, who started his first kindergarten in Germany in 1837.

The world's first plant to produce electricity from water power began operating in Appleton in 1882. The plant was built on the Fox River.

Malted milk was invented by William Horlick in 1887 in Racine.

The first woman commissioned by Congress to create a work of sculpture was Vinnie Ream of Madison. She was commissioned in 1866 to produce a statue of Abraham Lincoln when she was only 18 years old. The statue, completed in 1870, stands in the U.S. Capitol.

Malted milk

tion. Wisconsin also was the first state to end the death penalty for crime.

The first schools for training rural teachers were established in Wisconsin, as were the first vocational schools. The University of Wisconsin was one of the first universities to offer correspondence courses. The nation's first kindergarten began in Wisconsin. Wisconsin established the first library for state legislators.

Wisconsin has been a leader in the development of farmers' institutes and cooperatives, dairy farmers' associations, and cheese-making federations. It also played a major role in the founding of the Republican Party. One of the nation's first hydroelectric plants was installed in Wisconsin. Wisconsin was the first state to adopt the number system for marking highways. It passed the first law requiring safety belts in all new automobiles bought in the state.

Wisconsin is an Indian word. It has several possible meanings, including *gathering of the waters, wild rice country,* and *home land.* Wisconsin has been nicknamed the *Badger State,* and its people are known as *Badgers.* This nickname was first used for Wisconsin lead miners in the 1820's. Some of these miners lived in caves that they dug out of the hillsides. They reminded people of badgers burrowing holes in the ground.

Madison is the capital of Wisconsin. Milwaukee is the state's largest city.

Mercury Marine

Workers assemble outboard motors at a plant in Fond du Lac. Manufacturing is Wisconsin's leading economic activity.

Wisconsin in brief

Symbols of Wisconsin

The Wisconsin coat of arms appears on both the state flag and the state seal. On the coat of arms, a sailor and a miner support a shield with symbols of agriculture, mining, navigation, and manufacturing. A small United States shield symbolizes Wisconsin's loyalty to the Union. The badger above the shield represents Wisconsin's nickname—the *Badger State*. The flag was adopted in 1913, and the seal was adopted in 1881. The name *Wisconsin* and the year it became a state, *1848*, were added to the flag in 1981.

State flag

State seal

Wisconsin (brown) ranks 26th in size among all the states and 10th in size among the Midwestern States (yellow).

General information

Statehood: May 29, 1848, the 30th state.
State abbreviations: Wis. (traditional); WI (postal).
State motto: *Forward.*
State song: "On, Wisconsin!" Words by J. S. Hubbard and Charles D. Rosa; music by William T. Purdy.

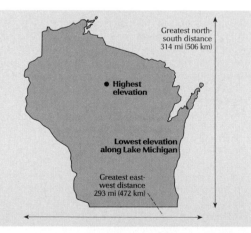

The State Capitol is in Madison, Wisconsin's capital since 1848. Territorial capitals were Belmont (1836), Burlington, now in Iowa (1837-1838), and Madison (1838-1848).

Land and climate

Area: 56,145 mi² (145,414 km²), including 1,831 mi² (4,741 km²) of inland water but excluding 9,355 mi² (24,229 km²) of Great Lakes water.
Elevation: *Highest*—Timms Hill, 1,952 ft (595 m) above sea level. *Lowest*—581 ft (177 m) above sea level along the shore of Lake Michigan.
Record high temperature: 114 °F (46 °C) at Wisconsin Dells on July 13, 1936.
Record low temperature: −55 °F (−48 °C) at Couderay on Feb. 4, 1996.
Average July temperature: 70 °F (21 °C).
Average January temperature: 14 °F (−10 °C).
Average yearly precipitation: 31 in (79 cm).

Greatest north-south distance 314 mi (506 km)

● **Highest elevation**

Lowest elevation along Lake Michigan

Greatest east-west distance 293 mi (472 km)

Important dates

Wisconsin became part of the United States.

Wisconsin became the 30th state on May 29.

| 1634 | 1783 | 1836 | 1848 |

Jean Nicolet, a French explorer, landed on the Green Bay shore.

Congress created the Wisconsin Territory.

State bird
Robin

State flower
Wood violet

State tree
Sugar maple

People

Population: 5,363,675
Rank among the states: 18th
Population density: 96 per mi² (37 per km²), U.S. average 78 per mi² (30 per km²)
Distribution: 68 percent urban, 32 percent rural
Largest cities in Wisconsin

Milwaukee	596,974
Madison	208,054
Green Bay	102,313
Kenosha	90,352
Racine	81,855
Appleton	70,087

Source: 2000 census.

Population trend

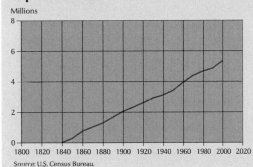

Source: U.S. Census Bureau.

Year	Population
2000	5,363,675
1990	4,891,769
1980	4,705,642
1970	4,417,821
1960	3,951,777
1950	3,434,575
1940	3,137,587
1930	2,939,006
1920	2,632,067
1910	2,333,860
1900	2,069,042
1890	1,693,330
1880	1,315,497
1870	1,054,670
1860	775,881
1850	305,391
1840	30,945

Economy

Chief products

Agriculture: milk, beef cattle, hogs, beets, cranberries, corn.
Manufacturing: machinery, transportation equipment, food products, fabricated metal products, paper products, electrical equipment.
Mining: crushed stone, sand and gravel.

Gross state product

Value of goods and services produced in 2000: $173,479,000,000.
Services include community, business, and personal services; finance; government; trade; and transportation, communication, and utilities. *Industry* includes construction, manufacturing, and mining. *Agriculture* includes agriculture, fishing, and forestry.

Source: U.S. Bureau of Economic Analysis.

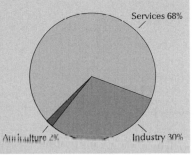

Services 68%
Agriculture 2%
Industry 30%

Government

State government

Governor: 4-year term
State senators: 33; 4-year terms
State representatives: 99; 2-year terms
Counties: 72

Federal government

United States senators: 2
United States representatives: 8
Electoral votes: 10

Sources of information

For information about tourism, write to: Wisconsin Department of Tourism, 201 W. Washington Avenue, P.O. Box 7976, Madison, WI 53707-7976. The Web site at www.travelwisconsin.com also provides information.
For information on the economy, write to: Wisconsin Department of Revenue, P.O. Box 8933, Madison, WI 53708.
The state's official Web site at www.wisconsin.gov/state/home also provides a gateway to much information on Wisconsin's economy, government, and history.

The state Legislature set up a teachers' pension and established a commission to settle labor disputes.

Wisconsin adopted a state lottery to increase government revenues.

1901   **1911**   **1932**   **1987**

Robert M. La Follette, Sr., became governor, and the Progressive Era began.

Wisconsin passed the first state unemployment-compensation act.

People

The University of Wisconsin at Madison is the largest of 13 universities in the extensive University of Wisconsin system. Agriculture Hall, *shown here,* is one of the main buildings on the Madison campus.

Michael Philip Manheim from Marilyn Gartman

The Green Bay Packers are Wisconsin's National Football League franchise. The Packers play home games at Lambeau Field in Green Bay.

Wisconsin Division of Tourism

Population density

About two-thirds of the people of Wisconsin live in metropolitan areas. Most of the urban population is concentrated in the southeastern part of the state.

Persons per sq. mi.	Persons per km²
More than 100	More than 40
50 to 100	20 to 40
25 to 50	10 to 20
Less than 25	Less than 10

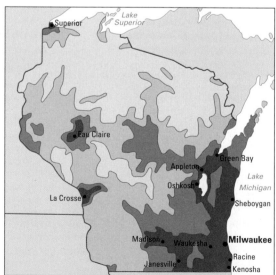

WORLD BOOK map; based on U.S. Census Bureau data.

Population. The 2000 United States census reported that Wisconsin had 5,363,675 people. The population had increased 9.5 percent over the 1990 figure, 4,891,769. According to the 2000 census, Wisconsin ranks 18th in population among the 50 states.

About two-thirds of Wisconsin's people live within the state's metropolitan areas. More than a fourth live in the metropolitan area of Milwaukee-Waukesha. There are 10 metropolitan areas that lie entirely within the state. One other area, La Crosse, extends partly into Minnesota. Two of Minnesota's metropolitan areas, Minneapolis-St. Paul and Duluth-Superior, extend into Wisconsin. For the populations of these metropolitan areas, see the *Index* to the Wisconsin political map.

Milwaukee, Wisconsin's largest city, is a leading center of manufacturing. Madison, the state's capital, is Wisconsin's second largest city. It is home to the oldest and largest campus of the University of Wisconsin. Other large Wisconsin cities are Green Bay, Racine, and Kenosha. All are important manufacturing and shipping centers.

About 97 of every 100 Wisconsinites were born in the United States. More than half of the state's people are of German descent. Milwaukee is a leading U.S. center of German American culture. Wisconsin's other large population groups include people of Irish, Polish, and English descent. About 6 percent of the state's people are African Americans.

The Milwaukee Public Museum is one of the finest natural history museums in the United States. These visitors are looking at one of the museum's life-sized replicas of dinosaurs.

Wisconsin Division of Tourism

Universities and colleges

This table lists the universities and colleges in Wisconsin that grant bachelor's or advanced degrees and are accredited by the North Central Association of Colleges and Schools.

Name	Mailing address	Name	Mailing address
Alverno College	Milwaukee	Milwaukee Institute of Art and Design	Milwaukee
Bellin College of Nursing	Green Bay	Milwaukee School of Engineering	Milwaukee
Beloit College	Beloit	Mount Mary College	Milwaukee
Bryant & Stratton College	Milwaukee	Northland College	Ashland
Cardinal Stritch University	Milwaukee	Ripon College	Ripon
Carroll College	Waukesha	Sacred Heart School of Theology	Hales Corners
Carthage College	Kenosha	St. Francis Seminary	St. Francis
Columbia College of Nursing	Milwaukee	St. Norbert College	De Pere
Concordia University Wisconsin	Mequon	Silver Lake College	Manitowoc
DeVry University	*	Viterbo University	La Crosse
Edgewood College	Madison	Wisconsin, Medical College of	Milwaukee
Lakeland College	Sheboygan	Wisconsin, University of	†
Lawrence University	Appleton	Wisconsin Lutheran College	Milwaukee
Maranatha Baptist Bible College	Watertown	Wisconsin School of Professional	
Marian College of Fond du Lac	Fond du Lac	Psychology	Milwaukee
Marquette University	Milwaukee		

* Campuses at Milwaukee and Waukesha.
† For campuses, see **Wisconsin, University of.**

Schools. Michael Frank, a newspaper editor in Southport (now Kenosha), led the movement for free schools in Wisconsin. In 1845, he started Wisconsin's first public school. The state Constitution, adopted in 1848, provided free schooling for all children in Wisconsin between the ages of 4 and 20. In 1856, Margaretha Meyer Schurz opened the first kindergarten in the United States in Watertown.

In 1891, the University of Wisconsin established one of the first correspondence schools in the United States. Wisconsin was also the first state to set up a system of state aid for industrial education. A 1911 law required all communities with populations of 5,000 or more to establish an industrial education board. Today, the state-supported Wisconsin Technical College System has over 45 campuses.

Wisconsin's public schools are directed by a nonpartisan superintendent of public instruction, who is elected to a four-year term. School attendance in the state is required of children from ages 6 through 17. For the number of students and teachers in Wisconsin, see **Education** (table).

Libraries. Wisconsin has about 450 public libraries. Wisconsin also has many college and university libraries and other special libraries serving industry, institutions, and government. The State Law Library was founded in Madison in 1836. State legislation authorizing free public libraries was passed in 1872. A reference library for legislators is in the state Capitol. It was founded in 1901 and was the first of its kind in the nation.

Today, the State Department of Public Instruction is responsible for the promotion and development of both public and school library service in the state. The Milwaukee Public Library is the largest public library in the state. The University of Wisconsin Library in Madison has a collection of materials on the history of books. The Beloit College Library houses a collection of works by Wisconsin authors. The State Historical Society in Madison has one of the nation's largest collections of books, newspapers, and manuscripts on United States history.

Museums. The Milwaukee Public Museum is Wisconsin's largest museum. It is among the finest natural history museums in the nation. The State Historical Museum in Madison features exhibits on the state's history. Wisconsin has some highly specialized museums, including the Houdini Historical Center in Appleton; the Circus World Museum in Baraboo; the Wisconsin State Agricultural Museum in Cassville; and the Experimental Aircraft Association AirVenture Museum in Oshkosh. Old World Wisconsin, near Eagle, honors the ethnic groups that settled the state. The Leigh Yawkey Woodson Art Museum, in Wausau, is known for its bird collection. Wisconsin has art museums in Beloit, Madison, Milwaukee, Oshkosh, and on university campuses.

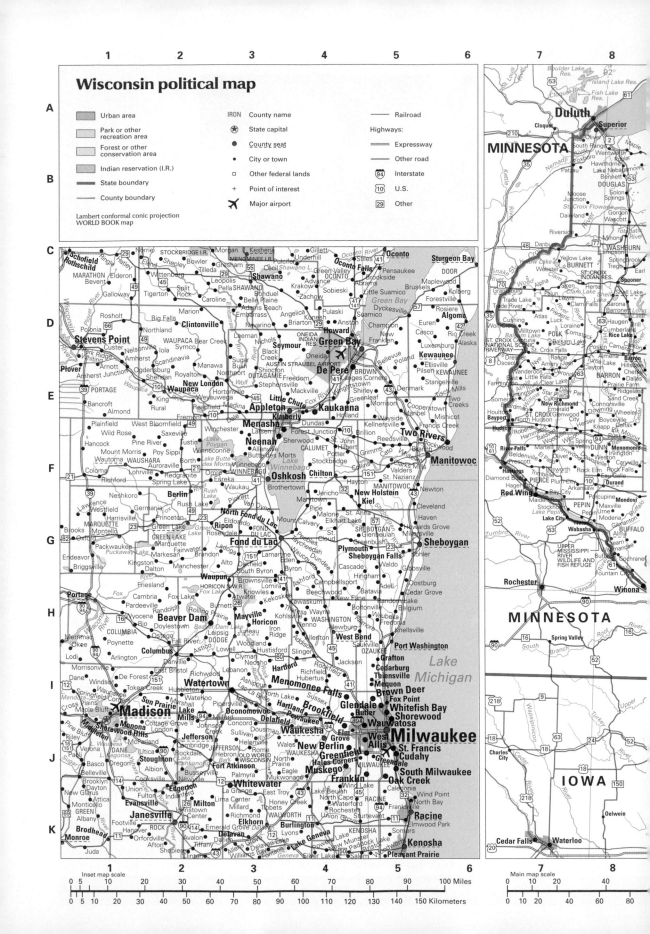

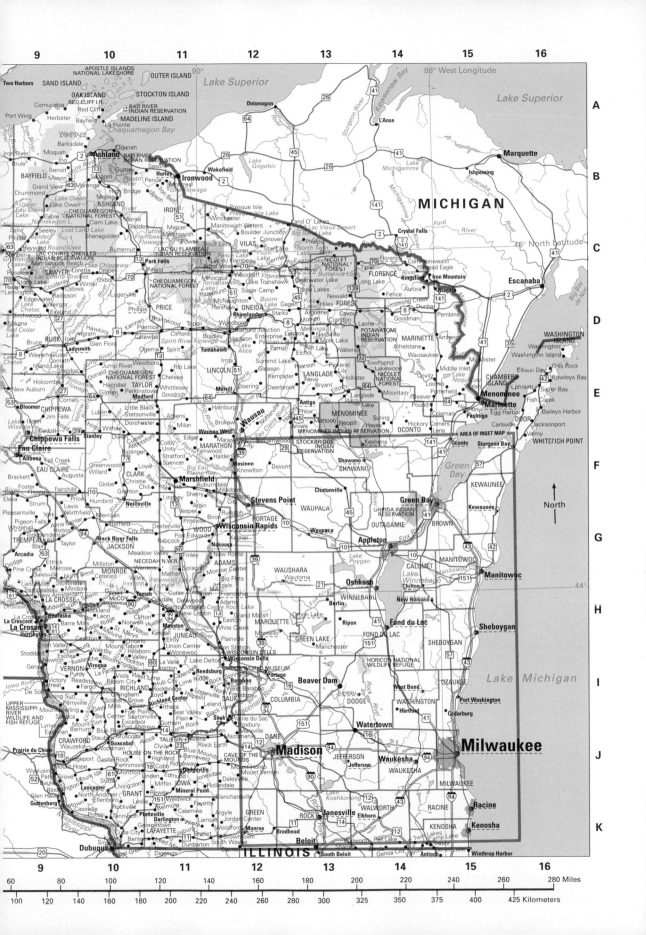

Wisconsin map index

Metropolitan areas

Counties

Cities and villages

*Does not appear on map; key shows general location.
†Census designated place—unincorporated, but recognized as a significant settled community by the U.S. Census Bureau.
°County seat.
Places without population figures are unincorporated areas.
Source: 2000 census.

Wisconsin's natural beauty has made it a favorite vacation spot with tourists in all seasons. Millions of people visit the state each year. Vacationers enjoy Wisconsin's sparkling lakes, rolling hills, quiet valleys, and cool, pine-scented breezes. In spring and summer, hikers and cyclists enjoy the countryside. The winters are ideal for cross-country skiing, skating, and snowmobiling. The state is host to the Birkebeiner, North America's largest cross-country ski race. The World Championship Snowmobile Derby takes place at Eagle River.

The city of Milwaukee offers a wide range of ethnic and music festivals. Summerfest, a music festival, offers live music of every type. Summer theaters in the state offer plays of all types, from off-Broadway to Shakespeare. During late July and early August, Wittman Field in Oshkosh becomes the busiest airport in the United States, as the Experimental Aircraft Association holds its annual Fly-In.

Door County peninsula, in the northeast part of the state, features about 250 miles (400 kilometers) of Lake Michigan shoreline. Wisconsin Dells, another popular vacation spot, offers scenic boat rides and large water theme parks. Many annual events celebrate the state's rich ethnic heritage and diversity.

Cameramann International, Ltd. from Marilyn Gartman

Door County, a popular vacation area

Places to visit

Apostle Islands, offshore from Bayfield, offer "deep-sea" fishing for trout and salmon. Visitors also enjoy camping, hiking, and sailing.

Cave of the Mounds, between Mount Horeb and Blue Mounds, has hundreds of colorful stone formations in the cavern's 14 rooms.

Circus World Museum, in Baraboo, has a large collection of equipment from U.S. circuses. Displays include items used by the Ringling brothers, who started their world-famous circus in Baraboo in 1884. Circus acts perform daily in summer.

Door County, on Door Peninsula, is a popular vacation spot. Tourists enjoy the picturesque countryside. Popular activities include camping, sailing, backpacking, and hiking.

House on the Rock is a 22-room home 11 miles (18 kilometers) north of Dodgeville. It sits atop a huge rock that rises 450 feet (137 meters). It has six fireplaces, seven pools, unique antiques, and the world's largest carrousel.

Old World Wisconsin, near Eagle, is an outdoor museum that contains a number of houses and other structures built by Wisconsin immigrants of the 1800's.

Pendarvis, in Mineral Point, is the site of several of the first permanent homes constructed in Wisconsin. These homes, built in the 1830's and 1840's, have been preserved and restored by the State Historical Society.

Taliesin, near Spring Green, is the site of the Hillside Home School built by U.S. architect Frank Lloyd Wright. The school, built of sandstone and oak, demonstrates Wright's philosophy that land, nature, and buildings should be treated as an organic whole.

Wisconsin Dells, in Adams, Columbia, Juneau, and Sauk counties, is one of the state's most beautiful regions. The Wisconsin River has cut a channel 7 miles (11 kilometers) long and 100 feet (30 meters) deep through soft sandstone. Weird formations have been carved out of the rock. They have such names as Devil's Elbow, Grand Piano, and Fat Man's Misery.

Parklands. The Ice Age National Scientific Reserve consists of several separate areas in southern and northwestern Wisconsin. The reserve is designed to preserve the features left on the land by the glaciers that once covered these parts of Wisconsin. The state also has a number of recreation areas managed by the National Park Service. For information on these areas, see the map and tables in the *World Book* article on **National Park System.**

National forests. Wisconsin's two national forests, covering nearly 2 million acres, were established in 1933. Chequamegon National Forest lies in north-central Wisconsin. This forest has more than 170 lakes within its borders. Nicolet National Forest, in northeastern Wisconsin, has over 260 lakes. Both national forests offer hunting, fishing, and skiing.

State parks and forests. Wisconsin has 45 state parks, 10 state forests, and 13 state trails. For information on the state parks and forests, write to Wisconsin Department of Tourism, Box 7976, Madison, WI 53707-7976.

Annual events

January-March
Winterfest in Milwaukee (January); World Championship Snowmobile Derby in Eagle River (January); Hot Air Affair Balloon Rally in Hudson (February); American Birkebeiner in Cable and Hayward (February); Milwaukee Journal Sentinel Sports Show (March).

April-June
Chocolate Festival in Burlington (May); Great Wisconsin Dells Balloon Rally (June); Walleye Weekend in Fond du Lac (June); World Championship Off-Road Races in Crandon (June); Summerfest in Milwaukee (June).

July-September
Art Fair on the Square in Madison (July); Great Circus Parade in Milwaukee (July); Lumberjack World Championships in Hayward (July); Experimental Aircraft Association Fly-In in Oshkosh (July); Wisconsin State Fair in Milwaukee (August); National Water Ski Show Championships in Janesville (August); Cranberry Festival in Warrens (September); Oktoberfest in La Crosse (September-October).

October-December
Colorama, statewide (October); Fall Flyway in the Great Horicon Marsh (October); World Dairy Expo in Madison (October); Holiday Folk Fair in Milwaukee (November).

Cameramann International, Ltd. from Marilyn Gartman

Experimental Aircraft Association Fly-In in Oshkosh

Wisconsin Division of Tourism

Ski-jumping tournament in Middleton

Joseph Rupp, West Stock

Rock climbing in Devil's Lake State Park

Hillstrom Stock Photo

A sightseeing boat in the Wisconsin Dells

The Mississippi River forms much of Wisconsin's western border with Minnesota and Iowa. Near Prairie du Chien, *above,* the river is broad and dotted with many islands.

Wisconsin is a land of rolling hills, ridges, fertile plains and valleys, and beautiful lakes. During the Pleistocene Epoch, which lasted from about 2 million to 11,500 years ago, a series of glaciers that began nearly 2 million years ago traveled over most of present-day Wisconsin. The glaciers scraped hilltops, filled in valleys, and changed most of the surface. As the ice melted and the glaciers wasted away, they left thick deposits of earth materials. These deposits blocked drainage of the water, causing lakes, marshes, and streams with falls and rapids. Glaciers do not appear to have touched southwestern Wisconsin. Much of this portion of the state is rough, with steep-sided ridges and deep valleys.

Land regions. Wisconsin has five major land regions. They are (1) the Lake Superior Lowland, (2) the Northern Highland, or Superior Upland, (3) the Central Plain, (4) the Western Upland, and (5) the Eastern Ridges and Lowlands, or Great Lakes Plains.

The Lake Superior Lowland is a flat plain that slopes gently upward toward the south from Lake Superior. The plain ends from 5 to 20 miles (8 to 32 kilometers) inland at a steep cliff.

The Northern Highland covers most of northern Wisconsin. It slopes gradually downward toward the south. The region is a favorite vacationland because of its heav-

ily forested hills and hundreds of small lakes. Timms Hill, the state's highest point, rises 1,952 feet (595 meters) above sea level in Price County.

The Central Plain curves across the central part of the state. Glaciers covered the eastern and northwestern parts of this region. Much of the southern portion was not touched by glaciers. In this southern portion, the Wisconsin River has carved the scenic gorge called the Wisconsin Dells.

The Western Upland is one of the most attractive parts of Wisconsin. Steep slopes and winding ridges, untouched by glaciers, rise in the southwestern part of the region. Limestone and sandstone bluffs of breathtaking beauty stand along the Mississippi River.

The Eastern Ridges and Lowlands region extends from the Green Bay area southward to Illinois. Gently rolling plains of glacial material partly cover limestone ridges that run from north to south. This region is Wiscon's richest agricultural section. It has the state's largest areas of high-grade soil, and its longest growing season.

Shoreline of Wisconsin extends 381 miles (613 kilometers) along Lake Michigan and 292 miles (470 kilometers) along Lake Superior. Bluffs and sandy beaches line the Lake Michigan shore. Lake Superior's shoreline also has sandy beaches, but fewer rugged bluffs. Wisconsin's largest ports include Ashland, Green Bay, Manitowoc, Milwaukee, and Superior.

Rivers, waterfalls, and lakes. An east-west *divide* cuts across northern Wisconsin. This ridge of land separates short rivers that enter Lake Superior—such as the Bad, Montreal, and Nemadji rivers—from the longer rivers that flow southward—such as the Flambeau and St. Croix. A north-south divide runs down the eastern third

Land regions of Wisconsin

LAKE SUPERIOR LOWLAND

NORTHERN HIGHLAND

CENTRAL

PLAIN

WESTERN UPLAND

EASTERN RIDGES AND LOWLANDS

St. Croix R.

Wisconsin R.

Black R.

Mississippi R.

WORLD BOOK map

Map index

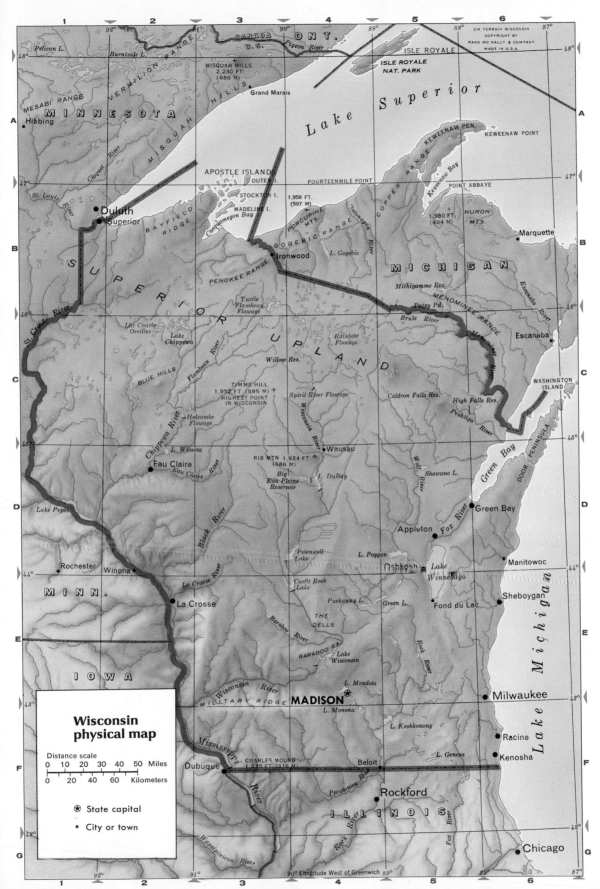

Wisconsin
physical map

Distance scale
0 10 20 30 40 50 Miles
0   20   40   60   Kilometers

⊛ State capital
• City or town

Specially created for *The World Book Encyclopedia* by Rand McNally and World Book editors

of the state. West of this divide, the rivers flow into the Mississippi. These rivers include the Black, Chippewa, La Crosse, St. Croix, and Wisconsin. Streams east of the divide empty into Lake Michigan directly or through Green Bay. These rivers include the Fox, Menominee, Milwaukee, Oconto, and Peshtigo.

Wisconsin has hundreds of waterfalls. The highest is Big Manitou Falls in Pattison State Park, in the extreme northwest. The falls, located on the Black River, drop more than 165 feet (50 meters).

Wisconsin has about 15,000 lakes. Lake Winnebago, the state's largest lake, covers 215 square miles (557 square kilometers). Green Lake, more than 237 feet (72 meters) deep, is the deepest lake. Other large natural lakes include Butte des Morts, Geneva, Koshkonong, Mendota, Pepin, Poygan, Puckaway, and Shawano. The chief artificially created lakes include Beaver Dam, Castle Rock, Chippewa, Du Bay, Flambeau, Petenwell, Wisconsin, and Wissota.

Average monthly weather

	Milwaukee					Green Bay			
	Temperatures			Days of rain or snow		Temperatures			Days of rain or snow
	F° High Low		C° High Low			F° High Low		C° High Low	
Jan.	29 15		−2 −9	10	Jan.	25 8		−4 −13	10
Feb.	32 17		0 −8	9	Feb.	26 9		−3 −13	9
Mar.	41 26		5 −3	11	Mar.	37 20		3 −7	11
Apr.	53 36		12 2	11	Apr.	52 32		11 0	11
May	64 45		18 7	13	May	65 44		18 7	12
June	75 55		24 13	11	June	75 54		24 12	11
July	81 61		27 16	9	July	81 59		27 15	10
Aug.	79 61		26 16	9	Aug.	79 57		26 14	10
Sept.	72 53		22 12	8	Sept.	70 50		21 10	9
Oct.	60 42		16 6	8	Oct.	58 39		14 4	8
Nov.	45 30		7 −1	10	Nov.	41 26		5 −3	9
Dec.	33 19		1 −7	10	Dec.	27 13		−3 −11	11

William Carter, Bruce Coleman Inc.

Horicon Marsh, north of Horicon, is a stopping place for thousands of Canada geese, ducks, and other waterfowl during their spring and fall migrations.

Plant and animal life. Forests cover almost half of Wisconsin. The state's softwood trees include balsam fir, hemlock, pine, spruce, tamarack, and white cedar. Hardwood trees include ash, aspen, basswood, elm, maple, oak, and yellow birch.

Blueberries, huckleberries, Juneberries, wild black currants, and other shrubs grow in parts of northern

Average January temperatures
Much of the state has long, severe winters. The southeastern section has the mildest temperatures in wintertime.

Average July temperatures
The southern and southwestern parts of the state have the warmest summers. The far north has the coolest summers.

Average yearly precipitation
Most of Wisconsin gets a fairly even amount of precipitation. The far north receives the heaviest snowfall.

WORLD BOOK maps

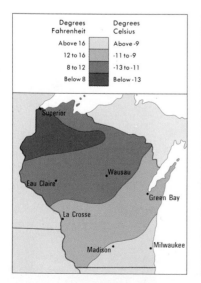

Degrees Fahrenheit	Degrees Celsius
Above 16	Above -9
12 to 16	-11 to -9
8 to 12	-13 to -11
Below 8	Below -13

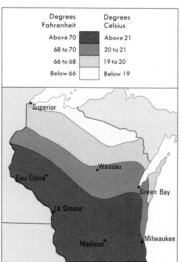

Degrees Fahrenheit	Degrees Celsius
Above 70	Above 21
68 to 70	20 to 21
66 to 68	19 to 20
Below 66	Below 19

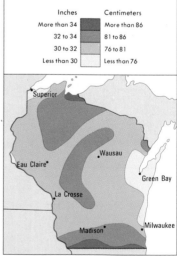

Inches	Centimeters
More than 34	More than 86
32 to 34	81 to 86
30 to 32	76 to 81
Less than 30	Less than 76

and central Wisconsin. Pink trailing arbutus blossoms over rocks and under trees in early spring. More than 20 kinds of violets bloom in all sections. In autumn, the Wisconsin countryside is a blaze of color. The red and gold tree leaves blend with brilliant asters, fireweeds, and goldenrods.

Bears, coyotes, deer, and foxes are found in Wisconsin's deep forests. Fur-bearing animals include beavers and muskrats. Badgers, gophers, and prairie mice scurry through the underbrush. Other animals found in Wisconsin include chipmunks, porcupines, raccoons, and woodchucks.

Wisconsin's northern lakes and streams abound with such game fish as bass, muskellunge, pickerel, pike, sturgeon, and trout. Game birds include ducks, geese, jacksnipes, partridges, pheasants, ruffed grouse, and woodcocks. Loons and other waterfowl breed on the northern lakes. The marshes shelter bitterns, black terns, and coots. Other birds that are found in Wisconsin include chickadees, nuthatches, robins, snipes, swallows, warblers, and wrens.

Climate. Wisconsin usually has warm summers and long, severe winters. Lake Michigan and Lake Superior make summers somewhat cooler and winters slightly milder along the shores. Average January temperatures range from 12 °F (−11 °C) in the northwest to 22 °F (−6 °C) in the southeast. Couderay recorded the lowest temperature, −55 °F (−48 °C), on Feb. 4, 1996. Average July temperatures range from 69 °F (21 °C) in the north to 73 °F (23 °C) in the south. The state's record high, 114 °F (46 °C), was set at Wisconsin Dells on July 13, 1936.

Wisconsin's *precipitation* (rain, melted snow, and other forms of moisture) averages about 31 inches (79 centimeters) a year. Annual snowfall averages from over 100 inches (250 centimeters) in northern Iron County to about 30 inches (76 centimeters) in southern Wisconsin.

Economy

Wisconsin's economy is full of contrasts. From the state's pastoral countryside to its many factories, Wisconsin's people find work in a wide range of industries. Manufacturing is the state's leading economic activity. Service industries, taken together, employ most of Wisconsin's people. These industries flourish in the state's cities and resort areas. Dairy products are important to the state's agriculture and manufacturing industries.

Natural resources of Wisconsin include rich soil, plentiful water, minerals, and vast forests.

Soil. Southeastern, southern, and western Wisconsin are the state's best agricultural areas. These areas have mostly gray-brown forest soils. They also have scattered sections of dark prairie soils. In northern Wisconsin, soils are less fertile and often contain too much acid.

Water. Wisconsin has 1,690 square miles (4,377 square kilometers) of inland water in addition to its outlying waters of Lake Michigan and Lake Superior. These two Great Lakes and the Mississippi River provide inexpensive transportation. Wisconsin's thousands of lakes help make the state a popular vacation area. Rainfall is abundant, and little water is needed for irrigation.

Minerals. Almost every Wisconsin county has sand and gravel. Stone, including dolomite and granite, is also valuable. Dolomite is found mainly in the southern part of the state and granite in the central and northern sections. Iron ore is found in Jackson County, and there are large deposits also in Ashland and Iron counties. Deposits of lead and zinc are found in Grant, Iowa, and Lafayette counties. Sulfide deposits containing large amounts of copper and zinc are in Forest, Oneida, and Rusk counties. Few of the metal ore deposits are being actively mined. The state's other mined products include peat and quartzite.

Forests cover almost half the state. Hardwood trees make up about 80 percent of the forests. Most of the woodlands have second-growth trees. The most valuable hardwoods found in Wisconsin include ash, aspen, basswood, elm, maple, oak, and yellow birch. Softwoods include balsam fir, hemlock, pine, spruce, tamarack, and white-cedar.

Service industries account for the largest portion of Wisconsin's *gross state product*—the total value of all goods and services produced in a state in a year. Most of the state's service industries are concentrated in its metropolitan areas.

Community, business, and personal services form Wisconsin's leading service industry in terms of the gross state product. This group is also Wisconsin's leading employer. It consists of such businesses as private health care, law firms, hotels and resorts, and repair shops. Many of the resort areas are located along the shores of Wisconsin's lakes and in the northern woods.

Ranking next among the service industry groups are (1) wholesale and retail trade and (2) finance, insurance, and real estate. Each of these groups accounts for a roughly equal share of the gross state product.

Important wholesale trade products in Wisconsin include farm products, groceries, and machinery. Roundy's, one of the leading U.S. wholesale grocery compa-

Production and workers by economic activities

Economic activities	Percent of GSP* produced	Employed workers	
		Number of people	Percent of total
Manufacturing	25	632,600	19
Community, business, & personal services	18	957,900	27
Wholesale & retail trade	16	740,800	22
Finance, insurance, & real estate	16	231,000	7
Government	11	403,000	12
Transportation, communication, & utilities	7	156,100	4
Construction	5	176,500	5
Agriculture	2	139,000	4
Mining	†	3,800	†
Total	**100**	**3,440,700**	**100**

*GSP = gross state product, the total value of goods and services produced in a year.
†Less than one-half of 1 percent.
Figures are for 2000.
Source: *World Book* estimates based on data from U.S. Bureau of Economic Analysis.

Cameramann International, Ltd.

Dairy products are a major part of Wisconsin's economy. Swiss cheese is made at this factory in Monroe. Wisconsin ranks among the nation's top producers of milk, cheese, and butter.

nies, has its headquarters in Pewaukee. Major retail businesses include automobile dealerships, discount stores, and food stores.

The large sums of money involved in the buying and selling of homes and other property make real estate the largest part of the finance, insurance, and real estate industry. Milwaukee ranks as one of the Midwest's major financial centers. It is the home of Wisconsin's two largest banking companies, Marshall & Ilsley and Associated Banc-Corp. One of the biggest insurance companies in the United States, Northwestern Mutual Life, is also based there. Madison and Green Bay are also centers of finance.

Government ranks fourth among the state's service industries. Government services include the operation of public schools and hospitals, military establishments, and Indian reservations. The public school system employs many people. The University of Wisconsin is one of the largest university systems in the nation. Its medical center, near the Madison campus, is one of the

state's leading health care facilities. Several Indian reservations lie in the northern part of the state.

Transportation, communication, and utilities rank fifth among the service industries. Milwaukee is home to many shipping and trucking companies. Telephone companies are a major part of the communications sector. Utilities include electric, gas, and water service.

Manufacturing. Goods made in the state have a *value added by manufacture* of about $64 billion yearly. This figure represents the increase in value of raw materials after they become finished products.

Machinery is Wisconsin's leading manufactured product in terms of value added by manufacture. Southeastern Wisconsin is one of the leading U.S. centers of machinery production. The main types of machinery made in the state include engines and turbines, power cranes and other construction machinery, heating and cooling equipment, and metalworking machinery.

Transportation equipment is Wisconsin's second-ranking manufacture. Motor vehicles and motor vehicle parts are the main types of transportation equipment.

Food products are the state's third-ranking manufactured product. Wisconsin is a leading butter-producing state. Its cheese factories make about a third of the cheese produced in the United States. Wisconsin also ranks high among the states in the production of ice cream and evaporated and dried milk. Plants that process dairy products are located throughout most of the state. Cudahy, Green Bay, and Madison have large meat-packing plants. Factories in Green Bay and other cities can huge amounts of the state's vegetable and fruit crops. Milwaukee, La Crosse, and many other cities make beer, Wisconsin's leading beverage product.

Fabricated metal products, including knives and hardware, metal cans, and metal forgings and stampings, rank fourth in terms of value added. Many metal products are manufactured in the Manitowoc, Milwaukee, and Racine areas.

Paper products rank fifth in value added. Paper products made in Wisconsin include typing paper, cardboard boxes, tissue paper, paper bags, and adhesive tape. The leading paper-manufacturing areas are the lower Fox River Valley and the upper Wisconsin River

Wisconsin Division of Tourism

Paper mills operate in Wisconsin mainly in the lower Fox River Valley and the upper Wisconsin River Valley. Wisconsin is a leading manufacturer of paper and paperboard products.

Economy of Wisconsin

This map shows the economic uses of land in Wisconsin and where the state's leading farm, mineral, and forest products are produced. Major manufacturing centers are shown on the map in red.

Cropland mixed with grazing

Grazing land mixed with cropland and woodland

Mostly forest land

Urban area

● Manufacturing center

● Mineral deposit

WORLD BOOK map

Valley. Fort Howard Paper Company has its headquarters in Green Bay.

Electrical equipment ranks next among Wisconsin's manufactured products. Chief electrical products include distributing equipment, household appliances, industrial controls, and motors and generators. Johnson Controls, a leading manufacturer of environmental controls for buildings, is based in Milwaukee.

Other types of products manufactured in Wisconsin include chemicals, computer and electronic equipment, plastics and rubber products, primary metals, and printed materials. Important chemical products made in the state include cleaning products, paints, and pharmaceuticals. Medical instruments and microchips are among the state's chief types of electronic products. Packaging materials are a leading plastics product. Iron and steel foundries are an important part of the primary metals sector. Wisconsin's major cities produce newspapers and large quantities of printed materials for businesses.

Agriculture. Farms and pastures cover about half of Wisconsin's land area. The state has about 77,000 farms.

Dairying is Wisconsin's leading farming activity. The dairy industry started about 1870. It was encouraged through the efforts of many people, especially William Dempster Hoard. In 1872, Hoard helped organize the Wisconsin Dairymen's Association, which did much to improve and promote Wisconsin's dairy products. Later, it urged farmers to work together and to market their products cooperatively. Today, about 200 farm cooperatives have headquarters in Wisconsin (see **Cooperative**).

Wisconsin ranks among the leading states in milk production. Milk provides more than half the farm income. The state's largest concentration of dairy cattle is in the region between Green Bay and Monroe. The region around Eau Claire also has many dairy farms.

Beef cattle and hogs rank as Wisconsin's second and third most valuable livestock products, after milk. Southwestern Wisconsin has the largest concentration of cattle and hog farms. The southeastern part of the state is the most important region for egg and chicken farms.

Corn is Wisconsin's leading field crop. It is grown mostly in southern Wisconsin. Farmers in all regions of the state raise hay. Corn is fed to hogs, and corn, hay, and oats are fed to cattle. Other field crops raised in Wisconsin include soybeans, tobacco, and wheat.

Wisconsin is an important producer of vegetables and fruit. It leads the states in the production of beets and snap beans. Wisconsin is also a chief producer of cabbages, cucumbers, green peas, lima beans, potatoes, and sweet corn. Most of the vegetables are sent to canneries. Wisconsin ranks among the leading states in growing cranberries. The state's farmers also raise apples, raspberries, strawberries, and other fruits.

Mining. Sand and gravel and crushed stone account for most of Wisconsin's mining income. Both of these products are used primarily in the construction industry.

Electric power. Plants that burn coal provide about 70 percent of the electric power generated in Wisconsin. Nuclear plants supply about 20 percent. Most of the remaining power comes from hydroelectric plants and plants that burn natural gas or petroleum. One of the first hydroelectric plants in the nation was built in Appleton on the Fox River in 1882.

Transportation. Many of Wisconsin's first settlers traveled by boat up the Mississippi River. Later settlers also arrived overland by wagon or via Lake Michigan by ship. Mississippi River traffic declined with the growth of railroads. Great Lakes transportation increased following the opening of the St. Lawrence Seaway in 1959.

The first railroad in Wisconsin began service in 1851.

It ran between Milwaukee and Waukesha, a distance of about 20 miles (32 kilometers). Today, six railroads provide freight service in Wisconsin. Passenger trains serve about 10 cities.

Milwaukee has Wisconsin's busiest airport. Madison and Green Bay also have major airports.

Wisconsin has about 112,000 miles (180,000 kilometers) of roads and highways. In 1917, Wisconsin became the first state to adopt the number system for highways. Other states soon adopted the system.

Wisconsin's major ports are at Superior, Green Bay, and Milwaukee. Superior shares port facilities with Duluth, Minnesota. Green Bay handles mostly U.S. cargo. International cargo passes mainly through Milwaukee. A canal located at Sturgeon Bay links Green Bay and Lake Michigan. An automobile ferry operates between Manitowoc and Ludington, Michigan.

Communication. Wisconsin's first newspaper, the *Green-Bay Intelligencer,* was founded in 1833. Today, Wisconsin publishers issue about 400 newspapers, of which about 35 are dailies. Daily newspapers with the largest circulations include the *Green Bay Press Gazette,* the *Milwaukee Journal Sentinel,* and the *Wisconsin State Journal* of Madison. Wisconsin publishers also issue about 280 periodicals.

In 1853, the Wisconsin Press Association was founded. It was the nation's first state news service. The association, now the Wisconsin Newspaper Association, collects and distributes news among member newspapers. Its membership includes all of the state's daily newspapers, about 220 weeklies, and 40 college newspapers.

The history of radio in Wisconsin dates from 1909. That year, University of Wisconsin scientists conducted wireless experiments. The university radio station was licensed as 9XM in 1916, and the station became WHA in 1922. The state's first television station, WTMJ-TV, started broadcasting from Milwaukee in 1947. Wisconsin now has about 240 radio stations and 40 television stations. Cable and satellite television systems and Internet providers serve many communities statewide.

Government

Constitution. Wisconsin is still governed under its original Constitution, adopted in 1848. Only six other states are governed under older constitutions. An amendment to Wisconsin's Constitution may be proposed in either house of the state Legislature. The amendment then must be approved by a majority of each house in two successive legislative sessions. Next, it must be ratified by a majority of the electors who vote on the amendment in a statewide referendum. The Constitution may also be amended by a constitutional convention. A proposal to call such a convention must be approved by a majority of the Legislature and by a majority of the people voting on the proposal in a statewide referendum.

Executive. The governor of Wisconsin holds office for a four-year term and can serve an unlimited number of terms.

The lieutenant governor, secretary of state, attorney general, treasurer, and state superintendent of public instruction are also elected by the people to serve four-year terms. The governor of Wisconsin appoints the heads of most major agencies and more than 1,000 members of various state boards and commissions.

Legislature consists of a Senate of 33 members and an Assembly of 99 members. Voters in each of Wisconsin's 33 senatorial districts elect one senator to a four-year term. One representative from each of 99 districts is elected to the Assembly to serve a two-year term.

Regular sessions of the Legislature begin in January of odd-numbered years and meet for a two-year period. The governor may call a special session at any time during the period. There is no time limit on the legislative sessions. The governor may call special sessions of the Legislature. Such sessions also have no time limit.

Courts. The highest court in Wisconsin is the state Supreme Court. It has seven justices, elected to 10-year terms. The justice who has been on the court for the longest time usually serves as the chief justice.

Other Wisconsin courts include four district appellate and numerous circuit courts. The people elect the

Wisconsin Legislature

The Wisconsin Legislature consists of an Assembly of 99 members and a Senate of 33 members. The Assembly meets in chambers in the State Capitol in Madison, *shown here.*

judges of these courts to six-year terms. All Wisconsin judges are elected on *nonpartisan ballots* (ballots without political party labels). A number of local governments also have municipal courts.

Local government. Wisconsin has 72 counties. A board of elected supervisors governs each county in the state. The supervisors select one of their members as chairperson. Other elected county officials in Wisconsin include the sheriff, clerk, treasurer, register of deeds, clerk of circuit court, and district attorney. Nine Wisconsin counties elect a county executive.

Wisconsin law allows cities to operate under the mayor, manager, or commissioner form of government. A few cities have the manager form. But most have the mayor-council form of government. Elected boards of trustees govern Wisconsin's villages, and elected town boards of supervisors govern its towns. Some Wisconsin towns use the town meeting form of government. Voters in these towns assemble to elect officials, approve budgets, and do other business.

Revenue. Taxes account for about 60 percent of the state government's *general revenue* (income). Most of the rest of the general revenue comes from U.S. government grants and programs and state charges for goods and services. Revenue from taxes on motor vehicle fuels and motor vehicle licenses goes into special funds.

The individual income tax accounts for about 45 percent and the general sales tax for about 30 percent of all tax revenues. Other important sources of tax revenue include taxes on corporate income, public utilities, and tobacco products.

Politics. The Democratic Party's strength is centered in Milwaukee, Madison, and other urban areas. Republican strength lies mainly in rural and suburban areas.

Throughout most of its early history, Wisconsin strongly favored the Republican Party. In fact, a meeting at a Ripon schoolhouse in 1854 contributed to the founding of the national party. The Democratic Party gained strength in the 1950's and was the majority party from the 1970's through the 1980's.

In presidential elections, Wisconsin has supported the Republican candidate about twice as often as the Democratic candidate. In the 1924 presidential election, Wisconsin cast its votes for a native son, Senator Robert M. La Follette, Sr., who ran unsuccessfully as a Progressive. For the state's voting record in presidential elections since 1848, see **Electoral College** (table).

The governors of Wisconsin

	Party	Term		Party	Term
Nelson Dewey	Democratic	1848-1852	Emanuel L. Philipp	Republican	1915-1921
Leonard J. Farwell	Whig	1852-1854	John J. Blaine	Republican	1921-1927
William A. Barstow	Democratic	1854-1856	Fred R. Zimmerman	Republican	1927-1929
Arthur MacArthur	Democratic	1856	Walter J. Kohler, Sr.	Republican	1929-1931
Coles Bashford	Republican	1856-1858	Philip F. La Follette	Republican	1931-1933
Alexander W. Randall	Republican	1858-1862	Albert G. Schmedeman	Democratic	1933-1935
Louis P. Harvey	Republican	1862	Philip F. La Follette	Progressive	1935-1939
Edward Salomon	Republican	1862-1864	Julius P. Heil	Republican	1939-1943
James T. Lewis	Republican	1864-1866	Walter S. Goodland	Republican	1943-1947
Lucius Fairchild	Republican	1866-1872	Oscar Rennebohm	Republican	1947-1951
Cadwallader C. Washburn	Republican	1872-1874	Walter J. Kohler, Jr.	Republican	1951-1957
William R. Taylor	Democratic	1874-1876	Vernon W. Thomson	Republican	1957-1959
Harrison Ludington	Republican	1876-1878	Gaylord A. Nelson	Democratic	1959-1963
William E. Smith	Republican	1878-1882	John W. Reynolds	Democratic	1963-1965
Jeremiah McLain Rusk	Republican	1882-1889	Warren P. Knowles	Republican	1965-1971
William D. Hoard	Republican	1889-1891	Patrick J. Lucey	Democratic	1971-1977
George W. Peck	Democratic	1891-1895	Martin J. Schreiber	Democratic	1977-1979
William H. Upham	Republican	1895-1897	Lee S. Dreyfus	Republican	1979-1983
Edward Scofield	Republican	1897-1901	Anthony S. Earl	Democratic	1983-1987
Robert M. La Follette, Sr.	Republican	1901-1906	Tommy G. Thompson	Republican	1987-2001
James O. Davidson	Republican	1906-1911	Scott McCallum	Republican	2001-2003
Francis E. McGovern	Republican	1911-1915	Jim Doyle	Democratic	2003-

History

Indian days. The Winnebago, Dakota, and Menominee Indians lived in the Wisconsin region when the first white explorers came in the early 1600's. These Indians were skilled craftworkers. They lived in lodges made of bark, saplings, and rushes. They fished and hunted, and grew corn, beans, and squash. The Winnebago lived in the area between Green Bay and Lake Winnebago. The Dakota lived in the northwestern part of the region. The Menominee lived west and north of Green Bay.

Many other tribes moved into the Wisconsin area during the later 1600's. Some had been driven from their eastern homes by white people. Others fled into the region to escape the warring Iroquois League. The Chippewa came from the northeast and settled along the southern shore of Lake Superior. Other tribes came from the Michigan region. The Sauk settled west of Green Bay, the Fox along the Fox River, and the Ottawa along the southern shore of Lake Superior. The Kickapoo settled in the south-central area, and the Huron in the northwestern section. Bands of Miami and Illinois Indians spread along the upper Fox River. The Potawatomi camped in what is now Door County.

Exploration and settlement. In 1634, the French explorer Jean Nicolet became the first white person to set foot in the Wisconsin area. He landed on the shore of Green Bay while seeking a water route to China. Nicolet stepped ashore wearing a colorful robe and firing two pistols. According to tradition he was disappointed when Winnebago Indians, not Chinese officials, greeted him. Nicolet returned to New France (Quebec) and reported that America was far vaster than anyone had imagined.

About 25 years later, Pierre Esprit Radisson and Médard Chouart, Sieur des Groseilliers, explored the Wisconsin area while searching for furs. The first missionary to the Wisconsin Indians, Father René Ménard, arrived about 1660. He established a Roman Catholic mission near present-day Ashland. Father Claude Jean Allouez came to Wisconsin about 1665 and set up several missions. With the help of Father Louis André, he established a center for missionary work on the site of present-day De Pere. Other French explorers and missionaries who visited the area included Louis Jolliet, Father Jacques Marquette, and Robert Cavelier, Sieur de La Salle.

Struggle for control. From the time of Nicolet's visit, the French had friendly relations with most of the Wisconsin Indian tribes. But in 1712, a long war broke out between the French and the Fox Indians. Both the French and the Fox wanted control of the Fox and Wisconsin rivers, the region's chief water route. After many bloody battles, the French finally defeated the Fox in 1740. But the long war had weakened France's defenses in the region. France also lost the friendship of many former Indian allies.

In 1754, the French and Indian War began. This war was fought between Britain and France over rival claims in America. Britain won the war. Under the terms of the 1763 Treaty of Paris, France lost Canada and almost all its possessions east of the Mississippi River. Control of the Wisconsin region thus passed to the British. See **French and Indian wars** (The French and Indian War).

English fur traders took over the fur-trading posts of the French. In 1774, the British passed the Quebec Act. Under this act, Wisconsin became part of the province of Quebec. The Quebec Act was one of the causes of the revolt by the American colonies against Britain in 1775. The 1783 Treaty of Paris ended the American Revolutionary War. Under the treaty, Britain gave up all its territory east of the Mississippi and south of the Great Lakes. The Wisconsin region then became part of the United States.

Territorial days. Wisconsin formed part of the Indiana Territory from 1800 to 1809, part of the Illinois Territory from 1809 to 1818, and part of the Michigan Territory from 1818 to 1836. Settlement of southwestern Wisconsin began during the 1820's. This region had rich deposits of lead ore. In the 1820's, the demand for lead for use in making paint and shot rose sharply. Lead miners from nearby states and territories poured into the region, and the population boomed. Some of the miners lived in shelters they dug out of the hillsides. These miners were nicknamed *Badgers,* which, in time, became the nickname of all Wisconsinites.

The Indians made their last stand in Wisconsin against white people in the Black Hawk War of 1832. The Sauk Indians of northwestern Illinois had been pushed across the Mississippi River into Iowa by the arrival of white settlers. Black Hawk, a Sauk leader, wanted to return to his homeland and grow corn. In April 1832, he led a thousand Indians back across the Mississippi. The white settlers panicked, and volunteer militia and regular troops were called out. Black Hawk's Indians retreated into Wisconsin, where several bloody battles were fought. When the war ended in August, only about 150 Indians were left.

On April 20, 1836, Congress created the Wisconsin Territory. The territorial legislature met temporarily in Belmont and later in Burlington (now in Iowa). The first meeting in Madison, the capital of the territory and later of the state, took place in 1838. The Wisconsin Territory included parts of present-day Minnesota, Iowa, and North and South Dakota. President Andrew Jackson appointed Henry Dodge as the first territorial governor. Congress created the Iowa Territory in 1838. Wisconsin's western boundary then became the Mississippi

River, with a northward extension to Lake of the Woods in present-day Minnesota. About a third of the present state of Minnesota remained part of Wisconsin until 1848.

Statehood. Wisconsin joined the Union as the 30th state on May 29, 1848. Its boundaries were set as they are today. The people had already approved a constitution. They elected Nelson Dewey, a Democrat, as the first governor. In 1840, 30,945 white people lived in Wisconsin. By 1850, the population had soared to 305,391. Newcomers came from other parts of the United States and from other countries. All saw opportunities for a better life in frontier Wisconsin.

In 1854, Wisconsin citizens became aroused over the introduction of the Kansas-Nebraska Bill in Congress. This bill was designed to allow the new territories of Kansas and Nebraska to decide for themselves whether they wished to permit slavery. Most Wisconsinites opposed slavery and did not want it extended to new territories. A group of Wisconsinites held a protest meeting against the bill in Ripon in February 1854. This meeting contributed to the development of the Republican Party. See **Kansas-Nebraska Act.**

The Republican Party quickly became a powerful force in the North. Wisconsin's first Republican governor, Coles Bashford, took office in 1856. For the next hundred years, except for brief periods, the Republicans controlled the state government.

During the American Civil War (1861-1865), Wisconsin generals at various times commanded the Iron Brigade, one of the Union Army's outstanding fighting groups. The brigade consisted largely of Wisconsin regiments.

In 1871, Wisconsin was struck by the worst natural disaster in its history—the great Peshtigo forest fire. The summer and fall of 1871 were extremely dry, and many small fires broke out at various places in northeastern Wisconsin. Then, on the night of October 8, northeastern Wisconsin erupted in flame. The fire wiped out the town of Peshtigo and several villages. The fire also spread into Michigan. About 1,200 people were killed, 900 more than the number of people killed in the Great Chicago Fire, which occurred that same night. The fire destroyed more than $5 million worth of property.

The Progressive era. During the 1890's, a split developed in the Republican Party in Wisconsin. The party had been controlled by political bosses who represented lumber and railroad interests. Robert M. La Follette, Sr., a Madison lawyer and former U.S. congressman, began to lead a movement to overthrow the rule by bosses.

La Follette won the Wisconsin governorship in 1900. He was reelected in 1902 and 1904. Under "Fighting Bob," the state made important social, political, and economic reforms. La Follette's program was called *Progressivism.* La Follette set up a "brain trust" of University of Wisconsin professors and experts on government to advise him on state problems. The brain trust was part of the "Wisconsin Idea." This was the theory that the state should be served by its best minds and its best experts in legislation and administration. Measures adopted under La Follette included an inheritance tax, a railroad property tax, regulation of railroad rates and service, and a direct primary law (see **Primary election**). La Follette entered the U.S. Senate in 1906 and served

Historic Wisconsin

Jean Nicolet, the first explorer to enter Wisconsin, landed at Green Bay in 1634 while seeking a Northwest Passage to China.

The Black Hawk War was fought in Wisconsin in 1832. Chief Black Hawk and his Sauk Indians were defeated after many bloody battles.

"Battling Bob" La Follette of Wisconsin ran for President as the nominee of the Progressive Party in 1924.

The Peshtigo forest fire swept through northeastern Wisconsin on the night of Oct. 8, 1871. About 1,200 people were killed, 900 more than the number who died in the Great Chicago Fire, which occurred the same night.

The University of Wisconsin System, created in 1971, merged state facilities that include 13 universities, 14 two year campuses, and an extension system. Administrative offices are in Madison.

WORLD BOOK illustrations by Kevin Chadwick

Important dates in Wisconsin

1634 Jean Nicolet, a French explorer, landed on the Green Bay shore.

c. 1670 Fathers Claude Jean Allouez and Louis André founded a missionary center at De Pere.

1673 Louis Jolliet and Father Jacques Marquette traveled through the Wisconsin region.

1740 The French defeated the Fox Indians.

1763 England received the Wisconsin region from France under terms of the Treaty of Paris.

1783 Wisconsin became part of the United States.

1836 Congress created the Wisconsin Territory.

1848 Wisconsin became the 30th state on May 29.

1871 About 1,200 persons were killed in a forest fire that destroyed Peshtigo and nearby villages.

1872 William D. Hoard and others organized the Wisconsin Dairymen's Association.

1901 Robert M. La Follette, Sr., became governor, and the Progressive era began.

1911 The state legislature set up a teachers' pension, established a commission to settle labor disputes, and passed other progressive legislation.

1924 Robert M. La Follette, Sr., was defeated as the Progressive Party candidate for President of the United States.

1932 Wisconsin passed the first state unemployment-compensation act.

1958 Gaylord Nelson became the first Democrat to win election as governor since 1932.

1964 Wisconsin became the first state to have its legislative districts reapportioned by its supreme court.

1971 The state legislature created a state university system—the University of Wisconsin System.

1987 Wisconsin adopted a state lottery to increase government revenues.

there until 1925. See **La Follette** (Robert Marion La Follette, Sr.).

In 1911, the Wisconsin legislature passed the Workmen's Compensation Act to protect workers injured in accidents. That same year, the legislature established the Wisconsin Industrial Commission to enforce industrial safety codes. Both measures were inspired by Professor John R. Commons of the University of Wisconsin. Other progressive reforms approved by the 1911 legislature included a state income tax law, the state life insurance fund, and forest and waterpower conservation laws.

The La Follette Progressives. In 1924, La Follette ran for president as the Progressive Party candidate. President Calvin Coolidge, a Republican, won the election. La Follette received the electoral votes of only one state—Wisconsin. But he got almost 5 million popular votes. La Follette died in 1925, and his eldest son, Robert, Jr., was elected to fill his Senate seat.

In 1930, Philip F. La Follette, the youngest son of Robert M. La Follette, Sr., was elected governor. La Follette, a Republican, lost the governorship in 1932. But he was reelected in 1934 and 1936 as a Progressive. Much of the legislation enacted under La Follette sought to relieve the suffering caused by the Great Depression of the 1930's. In 1932, under his administration, the first state unemployment-compensation act was passed.

In the spring of 1938, La Follette tried to organize a new national third party, the National Progressives of America. But he won little support. The voters rejected La Follette in 1938 and elected Julius P. Heil, a Republican, as governor. Heil worked to cut government costs. He did away with many agencies that La Follette had set up while in office. Heil was reelected in 1940.

Changes in agriculture. After World War II (1939-1945), Wisconsin agriculture, long the state's top-ranking industry, began to decline in importance to the economy. At the same time, the importance of manufacturing increased. Heavy beef imports from other countries, in addition to low milk prices, hurt agriculture in the state. Changes in the American diet, with emphasis on low-calorie foods, lowered the demand for dairy products. Between 1951 and 1969, the number of Wisconsin dairy farms fell from about 132,000 to 63,000. A number of cheese factories, creameries, and other processing plants closed. Many small farms merged, and the use of farm machinery increased. All these changes reduced the need for farmworkers in Wisconsin, and the population began to shift from farms to cities.

Decline of La Follette Progressivism. By the mid-1940's, La Follette Progressivism had lost its strength. After 21 years in the U.S. Senate, Robert M. La Follette, Jr., lost the 1946 primary election to Republican Joseph R. McCarthy. McCarthy won election to the Senate that year. He later became one of the most controversial figures in American politics because of his unsupported charges that Communists dominated the U.S. Department of State.

In 1958, after 26 years of Republican or Progressive control of the state government, Democrat Gaylord A. Nelson won the governorship. He was reelected in 1960. In 1962, Wisconsin voters elected another Democratic governor, John W. Reynolds.

Political conflict. During the 1960's, Governors Nelson and Reynolds battled with the Republican-controlled legislature over *reapportionment* (redivision) of the state's legislative and congressional districts. The Wisconsin Constitution requires that the districts be redrawn every 10 years, if necessary, to provide fair representation. Both Nelson and Reynolds vetoed reapportionment bills passed by the legislature. They said the bills did not make the districts equal in terms of population. In 1963, the legislature passed a bill that reapportioned the state's 10 congressional districts. Reynolds signed this bill, but he and the legislature could not agree on a bill for the legislative districts. Finally, in 1964, the Wisconsin Supreme Court drew up a reapportionment plan. This was the first time any state supreme court had reapportioned a state legislature. The court's plan went into effect with the 1964 elections.

Tax increases. The need for money to pay for education, public welfare, and other programs resulted in state tax increases during the 1960's. The state legislature also passed a law, in 1961, that established the first sales tax in Wisconsin's history. In 1963, the legislature increased the number of items covered by the sales tax.

University expansion. In the mid-1900's, Wisconsin expanded its educational facilities. Between 1956 and 1970, the University of Wisconsin opened 15 new branches throughout the state.

Officials of the University of Wisconsin tightened their control over student activities in the 1970's. In 1969, following several student disorders on the Madison campus, the state legislature passed laws to control such disturbances. These laws established fines and imprisonment for campus misconduct. In 1971, the state legislature merged the University of Wisconsin and Wisconsin State University to form a state university system called the University of Wisconsin System.

The economy. In 1987, Wisconsin adopted a state lottery as a means of increasing government revenues. As the 1900's ended, manufacturing, with the help of the Wisconsin Department of Development, remained strong in the state. But agriculture continued to be vital to the economy. Although dairying still provided the most agricultural income, income from crops was increasing. However, farms in Wisconsin continued to decrease in number and increase in size.

The state was concerned with problems related to agriculture, such as the huge debt of its farmers. Wisconsin faced a number of other challenges. These problems included increasing costs for education, welfare, control of water pollution, and the purchase of land for recreational purposes.

School developments. In 1990, Wisconsin became the first state in the nation to adopt a school voucher program. In such a program, low-income families receive a coupon called a voucher that they can use for tuition. The Wisconsin program operated in Milwaukee and included public schools and nonreligious private schools. In 1995, the state expanded the program to allow vouchers at some religious schools in Milwaukee. Critics argued that such voucher use was unconstitutional because it was state funding of religious activities.

In 1998, the Wisconsin Supreme Court ruled that the inclusion of religious schools in the voucher program was not a violation of the Constitution. The court stated that the program's purpose was to offer a wide choice of schools, not to promote religion. The court pointed out that the government did not fund religious schools directly but gave vouchers to parents, who made their own choices. Gary C. Meyer and Benjamin D. Rhodes

Study aids

Related articles in *World Book* include:

Biographies

Andrews, Roy Chapman	Marquette, Jacques
Berger, Victor L.	McCarthy, Joseph R.
Black Hawk	Nicolet, Jean
Catt, Carrie Chapman	O'Keeffe, Georgia
Derleth, August	Proxmire, William
Ferber, Edna	Raskin, Ellen
Gale, Zona	Ringling brothers
Jolliet, Louis	Schurz, Carl
Kennan, George F.	Turner, Frederick J.
La Follette (family)	Welles, Orson
Laird, Melvin R.	Wilder, Thornton N.
Lunt, Alfred	Wright, Frank Lloyd

Cities

Green Bay   La Crosse   Madison   Milwaukee

History

Northwest Territory	Westward movement in
Republican Party	America
Sauk Indians	Winnebago Indians

Physical features

Great Lakes   Mississippi River   Wisconsin River

Outline

I. **People**
  A. Population
  B. Schools
  C. Libraries
  D. Museums
II. **Visitor's guide**
  A. Places to visit
  B. Annual events
III. **Land and climate**
  A. Land regions
  B. Shoreline
  C. Rivers, waterfalls, and lakes
  D. Plant and animal life
  E. Climate
IV. **Economy**
  A. Natural resources
  B. Service industries
  C. Manufacturing
  D. Agriculture
  E. Mining
  F. Electric power
  G. Transportation
  H. Communication
V. **Government**
  A. Constitution
  B. Executive
  C. Legislature
  D. Courts
  E. Local government
  F. Revenue
  G. Politics
VI. **History**

Questions

What was the greatest natural disaster in Wisconsin's history?
How many state constitutions has Wisconsin had in its history?
What portion of the cheese made in the United States does Wisconsin produce?
How did Wisconsin receive the nickname the *Badger State?*
What role did glaciers play in shaping Wisconsin's surface features?
What was the "Wisconsin Idea"?
Why was Jean Nicolet disappointed when he landed on the Green Bay shore in 1634?
What role did Mrs. Carl Schurz play in the history of education?
What are some of the reforms Wisconsin began that other states later adopted?
What are Devil's Elbow, Grand Piano, and Fat Man's Misery?

Additional resources

Level I
Barenblat, Rachel. *Wisconsin.* World Almanac, 2002.
Blashfield, Jean F. *Wisconsin.* Children's Pr., 1998.
Bratvold, Gretchen. *Wisconsin.* 2nd ed. Lerner, 2002.
Ling, Bettina. *Wisconsin.* Children's Pr., 2002.
Zeinert, Karen. *Wisconsin.* Benchmark Bks., 1997.

Level II
Birmingham, Robert A., and Eisenberg, L. E. *Indian Mounds of Wisconsin.* Univ. of Wis. Pr., 2000.
Bromberg, Nicolette. *Wisconsin Then and Now.* Univ. of Wis. Pr., 2001. A book of photographs.
Crawford, Robert F. *Walking Trails of Southern Wisconsin.* 2nd ed. Univ. of Wis. Pr., 2000.
The History of Wisconsin. 6 vols. Wis. Hist. Soc., 1973-1998.
Lefebvre, Mark. *Wisconsin.* 2nd ed. Graphic Arts Ctr., 1997.
Loew, Patty. *Indian Nations of Wisconsin.* Wis. Hist. Soc., 2001.
Nesbit, Robert C. *Wisconsin.* 2nd ed. Univ. of Wis. Pr., 1989.
Pederson, Jane M. *Between Memory and Reality: Family and Community in Rural Wisconsin, 1870-1970.* Univ. of Wis. Pr., 1992.
Unger, Nancy C. *Fighting Bob La Follette.* Univ. of N.C. Pr., 2000. A biography of the former Wisconsin governor and major political leader of the late 1800's and early 1900's.
Wyman, Mark. *The Wisconsin Frontier.* Ind. Univ. Pr., 1998.

Wisconsin, University of, is a coeducational state-supported educational system. Its official name is the University of Wisconsin System. It consists of 13 universities, 13 two-year campuses, and an extension system. The Wisconsin State Universities and the University of Wisconsin merged to form the system in 1971. The administrative offices are in Madison. Each university in the system is called the University of Wisconsin (UW) and has its location or campus name in its title.

UW-Madison has colleges of agricultural and life sciences, engineering, and letters and science; and schools of business, education, family resources and consumer sciences, law, medicine, nursing, pharmacy, and veterinary medicine. It grants bachelor's, master's, and doctor's degrees.

UW-Eau Claire has schools of arts and sciences, business, education, graduate studies, and nursing. It grants bachelor's and master's degrees.

UW-Green Bay has programs in business administration, humanities and fine arts, natural sciences, and professional studies. It grants bachelor's and master's degrees.

UW-La Crosse has colleges of arts, letters, and sciences, business administration, education, and health, physical education, and recreation. It grants bachelor's and master's degrees.

UW-Milwaukee has colleges of engineering and applied science and of letters and science. It has schools of allied health, architecture and urban planning, business administration, education, fine arts, graduate studies, library and information science, nursing, and social welfare. The school grants bachelor's, master's, and doctor's degrees.

UW-Oshkosh has colleges of business administration, education and human services, letters and science, and nursing. UW-Oshkosh grants bachelor's and master's degrees.

UW-Parkside, located between Kenosha and Racine, has schools of business, education, liberal arts, and science and technology. It grants bachelor's and master's degrees.

University of Wisconsin

Bascom Hall, on the University of Wisconsin-Madison campus, contains the main administrative offices, the business school library, faculty offices, and many classrooms.

UW-Platteville has colleges of agriculture; arts and sciences; business, industry, and communication; education; and engineering. It grants bachelor's and master's degrees.

UW-River Falls has colleges of agriculture, arts and sciences, and education. It grants bachelor's and master's degrees.

UW-Stevens Point has colleges of fine arts, letters and science, natural resources, and professional studies. It grants bachelor's and master's degrees.

UW-Stout at Menomonie has schools of education and human services, home economics, industry and technology, and liberal studies. It grants bachelor's and master's degrees.

UW-Superior has divisions of business and economics, education, fine and applied arts, humanities and social sciences, and sciences and mathematics. It grants bachelor's and master's degrees.

UW-Whitewater has colleges of the arts, business and economics, education, and letters and science. It grants bachelor's and master's degrees.

Critically reviewed by the University of Wisconsin System

Wisconsin River is a beautiful stream that rises in Lac Vieux Desert on the Michigan-Wisconsin boundary. It flows south to Portage, Wis., and then turns westward. The Wisconsin empties into the Mississippi River below Prairie du Chien. It is about 430 miles (692 kilometers) long. The river was an important waterway in pioneer days. Today, there are a number of power dams and reservoirs along the river, and the upper Wisconsin River Valley is a leading paper-producing area.

Near the town of Wisconsin Dells, the Wisconsin River forms one of the most scenic spots in North America. Here the stream has cut through the sandstone rock to a depth of about 150 feet (46 meters). It forms canyon walls cut in unusual shapes.   Gary C. Meyer

Wisdom tooth. See Teeth (Permanent teeth).

Wise, Isaac Mayer (1819-1900), a prominent American rabbi, is generally considered the pioneer of Reform Judaism in America. He founded the Hebrew Union College in Cincinnati for the training of rabbis, and was its president from the time of its organization in 1875 until his death. Wise also helped organize the Union of American Hebrew Congregations in 1873, and the Central Conference of American Rabbis in 1889. He served as president of the Conference for 11 years. He was born at Steingrub, Bohemia, and came to the United States in 1846.   Yosef Levanon

Wise, John (1652-1725), was a Congregational minister of colonial Massachusetts. He vigorously opposed actions by both church and government that he believed would deprive colonists of their rights and privileges.

In 1687, Wise led a protest against what he felt was an unfair tax levied by Sir Edmund Andros, the English colonial governor. In the early 1700's, Wise opposed an attempt by some Massachusetts clergymen, led by Increase and Cotton Mather, to organize themselves into associations. These associations would have taken over many functions previously controlled by individual churches. Wise argued that the associations would reduce the ability of local church members to direct their own affairs. His opposition led to the plan's defeat.

Wise was born in Roxbury, Mass. From 1680 until his death, he served as minister of a Congregational church in Ipswich, Mass.   Mark A. Noll

Wise, Stephen Samuel (1874-1949), was one of the best-known American Jewish leaders. He became noted for his liberalism and his wide activities in political and social life. He was born in Budapest, Hungary, and came to the United States in 1875. He was educated at the College of the City of New York and Columbia University. He founded the Free Synagogue in New York City in 1907, and served as its rabbi until his death. In 1922, he founded the Jewish Institute of Religion and served as its first president. He also helped organize the American Jewish Congress.

Wise was a champion of Zionism, and established the first section of the Federation of American Zionists (see **Zionism**). He wrote many books, including *How to Face Life* (1917) and *Child Versus Parent* (1922). He also edited the magazine *Opinion.*   Yosef Levanon

Wisteria, *wihs TIHR ee uh,* is the name of a group of thick-growing vines that bear large clusters of flowers. Wisterias belong to the pea family. The *Chinese wisteria* is often seen growing around homes in the United States. It is native to China. Other species of wisterias are native to the eastern part of the United States.

Wisterias are twining, climbing vines and may grow over 35 feet (11 meters) tall. The flowers may be bluish-

Derek Fell

A wisteria is a thick-growing vine that produces clusters of showy flowers. The flowers droop from a screen of foliage. The plant is often grown to cover walls and verandas.

lavender, pink, or white and resemble pea blossoms. The flower clusters are 1 to 2 feet (30 to 61 centimeters) long and drop from a heavy screen of foliage. The lacy leaves consist of 9 to 15 leaflets. Wisteria is an easy plant to grow in deep soil with plenty of moisture. Wisteria pods and seeds contain a poison that can cause severe stomach upset if eaten.

Scientific classification. Wisterias belong to the pea family, Leguminosae, or Fabaceae. The Chinese wisteria is *Wisteria sinensis.* Fred T. Davies, Jr.

Witan. See Witenagemont.

Witch. See Witchcraft.

Witch hazel, *HAY zuhl,* is a shrub or small tree used to make a soothing lotion. Witch hazel grows in the eastern United States and Canada. Its jointed, twisting branches point in all directions. The forked twigs have been used for divining rods, and the name *witch hazel* comes from this use by superstitious people. Witch hazel is also called *tobaccowood, spotted alder,* or *winterbloom.*

After the leaves have died, in October or November, witch hazel bears its flowers. They grow in feathery, golden clusters. The fruits do not ripen until the next

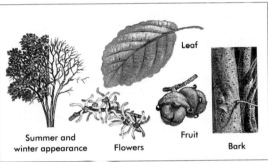

WORLD BOOK illustrations by John D. Dawson

Witch hazel has clusters of feathery, golden flowers.

year. Then the seeds shoot from their small woody capsules to a distance of several yards or meters.

Witch hazel lotion, or *hamamelin,* is a tonic and healing astringent, applied on the skin or taken internally. It is made by distilling the bark and leaves in alcohol. Doctors prescribe it for bruises, sprains, hemorrhoids, ulcers, bleeding, and skin troubles.

Scientific classification. Witch hazel makes up the witch hazel family, Hamamelidaceae. It is *Hamamelis virginiana.*

W. Dennis Clark

Witchcraft is commonly defined as the use of supposed magical powers to influence people and events. In this sense, it is known as *sorcery* and has been part of the folklore of many societies for centuries. Since the mid-1900's, Witchcraft has also come to refer to a set of beliefs and practices that some people consider a religion. Its followers sometimes call it Wicca, the Craft, the Wisecraft, or the Old Religion. However, many people, particularly conservative Christians, do not consider Witchcraft a religion as they understand the term.

Belief in witchcraft as sorcery exists around the world and varies from culture to culture. Historically, people have associated witchcraft with evil and usually have regarded a witch as someone who uses magic to harm

others, by causing accidents, illnesses, bad luck, and even death. However, some societies believe that witches also use magic for good, performing such actions as casting spells for love, health, and wealth. People around the world continue to practice witchcraft as sorcery, claiming to use magic for good or harm.

Unlike those who practice witchcraft as sorcery, the followers of Wicca believe in practicing magic only for beneficial purposes, not to harm. They worship a deity with male and female aspects, but they emphasize the female, or Goddess, side of the deity.

The term *witch* comes from the Old English word *wicca,* which is derived from the Germanic root *wic,* meaning to *bend* or to *turn.* By using magic, a witch is believed to change or bend events. Today, the word *witch* can be applied to a man or a woman. In the past, male witches were also called *warlocks* and *wizards.*

Witchcraft as sorcery

In folklore around the world, witches are believed to be masters of the supernatural world. They supposedly conjure and command spirits. They may have special helping spirits called *familiars,* who take the form of animals, particularly cats, snakes, owls, and dogs. In some tribal societies, a type of spell called *sending* involves the witch's familiar. In this type of spell, the witch instructs the familiar to carry out such commands as delivering a hex to a victim.

Some cultures believe witches have the power to *shape-shift* into animals. This power to change their shape enables them to travel about secretly. Witches also are said to be able to fly. They may fly under their own power, ride tools such as brooms or rakes, or ride magical animals.

Witches supposedly can control the weather. They are sometimes blamed for storms that damage dwellings or crops.

According to folklore, witches have great knowledge of how to make magical *potions* and *charms.* A potion is a drink that causes a desired effect in a person's behavior. A charm is a magical *incantation* (word or phrase) that helps to bring about a spell.

Witches also are believed to be able to see into the future. Some people believe that witches possess the *evil eye*—that is, the ability to kill by looking.

In many places around the world, witchcraft beliefs and practices have existed for centuries with little change. In many societies, it is believed that witches inherit their magical powers. Others believe that witches may be trained by local witches.

Witchcraft as a religion

The practice of Wicca—Witchcraft as a religion—developed in Britain in the mid-1900's. It flourishes primarily in English-speaking countries. The person most credited with the emergence of Wicca is Gerald B. Gardner, a British civil servant. Gardner had a lifelong interest in the *occult* (beliefs and practices involving magic or forces outside the natural world).

Organization and practices. Wicca has no central authority. Its followers, known as Witches, are loosely organized in groups called *covens.* Some covens are made up of only women or only men, and other covens are mixed. Many Witches do not join a coven but prac-

Selena Fox

An offering of fruits and vegetables is placed on a rock altar during an autumn thanksgiving festival. Modern witches honor the earth, the sun, and the seasons with special rituals.

tice alone as *solitaries.*

The practice of Wicca is controversial, primarily because many Christians find the idea of a religion based on witchcraft objectionable. Some Christians associate any form of witchcraft with the worship of evil powers. Others fear that Wicca might be tied to modern cults based on illegal drug use. Followers of Wicca deny any such connections.

Wicca is a re-creation of pagan, folk, and magical rites. Its primary sources are Babylonian, Celtic, Egyptian, ancient Greek, Roman, and Sumerian mythologies and rites. Wicca also borrows from other religions and mythologies, including Buddhism, Hinduism, and the rites of American Indians.

Essentially, Wicca is a fertility religion that celebrates the natural world and the seasonal cycles that are central to farming societies. It acknowledges the Goddess as the feminine side of a deity called God. Witches worship both Goddess and God in various personifications, including ancient gods and goddesses. Rites are tied to the cycles of the moon, which is the symbol of the power of the Goddess, and to the seasons of the year. Religious holidays are called *sabbats.* There are four major sabbats: Imbolc (February 1), Beltane (April 30), Lugnasadh or Lammas (July 31), and Samhain (October 31).

Most Witches practice in secrecy. Some do so because they believe that is the tradition. Others do so be-cause they wish to avoid persecution. Because of secrecy, it is difficult to estimate how many people practice Witchcraft as a religion.

Role of magic. Modern Witches practice magic, both for spell-casting and as a path of spiritual growth. Magic for spiritual growth is called *high magic* and is aimed at connecting a person to God or Goddess on a soul level.

Religious Witches say they perform magic for good and not for harm. They follow the Wiccan Rede, which is similar to the Golden Rule, "An' it harm none, do what ye will." Witches also believe in the Threefold Law of Karma, which holds that magic returns to the sender magnified three times. Thus, Witches say, evil magic only hurts the sender.

History

Ancient times. Witchcraft as sorcery has existed since humans first banded together in groups. Prehistoric art depicts magical rites to ensure successful hunting. Western beliefs about witchcraft as sorcery grew out of the mythologies and folklore of ancient peoples, especially the Greeks and Romans. Roman law made distinctions between good magic and harmful magic, and harmful magic was punishable by law. When Christianity began to spread, the distinctions vanished. Witchcraft came to be linked with worship of the Devil.

Middle Ages to the 1700's. In Europe, beginning in about the A.D. 700's, witchcraft was increasingly associated with *heresy* (rejection of church teachings). The Christian church began a long campaign to stamp out heresy. Beginning in the 1000's, religious leaders sentenced heretics to death by burning.

The Inquisition, which began about 1230, was an effort by the church to seek out and punish heretics and force them to change their beliefs. Eventually, the *secular* (nonreligious) courts as well as all Christian churches were involved in the persecution of witches. Especially after the 1500's, most people accused of witchcraft came to trial in secular courts. They were charged with human sacrifice and with worshiping the Devil in horrible rites.

Historians doubt that worship of the Devil was ever widespread, if indeed it even took place. But stories about it created a mood of fear and anxiety.

The witch hunt reached its peak in Europe during the late 1500's and early 1600's. Many victims, who were mostly women, were falsely accused of witchcraft. Many accused witches were tortured until they confessed. Then they faced imprisonment, banishment, or execution.

In the American Colonies, a small number of accused witches were persecuted in New England from the mid-1600's to the early 1700's. Some were banished and others were executed.

The most famous American witch hunt began in 1692 in Salem, Mass. There, a group of village girls became fascinated with the occult, but their games got out of hand. They began to act strangely, uttering weird sounds and screaming. Suspicions that witches were responsible for the girls' behavior led to the arrest of three women. More arrests followed, and mass trials were held. About 150 people were imprisoned on witchcraft charges. Nineteen men and women were convicted and hanged as witches. A man who refused to plead either innocent or guilty to the witchcraft charge was pressed to death with large stones.

The witchcraft scare lasted about a year. In 1693, the people still in jail on witchcraft charges were freed. In 1711, the Massachusetts colonial legislature made payments to the families of the witch-hunt victims.

Today, most historians agree that all the victims were falsely accused. The girls probably pretended to be possessed. Their reasons are unclear, though they may have been seeking attention.

Witchcraft in modern times. In 1939, Gerald B. Gardner became initiated into a coven of people who called themselves hereditary witches. They said they were practicing the Old Religion as it had been passed down to them through their families for many generations. They believed Witchcraft had been a religion since ancient times.

Gardner's coven was probably influenced by the writings of British anthropologist Margaret A. Murray. Writing in the 1920's, Murray had put forth the theory that witchcraft was an organized pagan religion that had originated as a pre-Christian fertility cult.

In the 1950's, Gardner published books about the ancient religious rituals of Witchcraft. He feared that Witchcraft was in danger of dying out, and he wanted to publicize it. He gathered information from his coven, but he also added material from such sources as European folklore, Eastern magic, and the writings of his friend Aleister Crowley. Crowley, a British writer, was known for his interest in spiritualism and the occult and for his writings on ceremonial magic. Gardner later collaborated with Doreen Valiente, whom he had initiated as a witch in 1953, in writing and revising the rituals. Valiente added an emphasis on the goddess that was missing in Gardner's work.

Gardner's books *Witchcraft Today* (1954) and *The Meaning of Witchcraft* (1959) became the basis for the modern religion of Witchcraft. The religion grew in popularity during the 1960's, in part because of its anti-establishment and feminist characteristics. The religion of Witchcraft spread from the United Kingdom to the rest of Europe and to the United States, Canada, Australia, and Asia.

As the religion was developing, however, Margaret Murray's theory came under criticism. Historians found no evidence of an ancient religion of witches. It became clear that Gardner had borrowed from other sources and had made exaggerated claims about a historical religion. Nevertheless, Witchcraft continued to grow as a religion. Its followers placed a greater emphasis on developing a goddess-worshiping religion out of the beliefs of pre-Christian and non-Christian religions.

Rosemary Ellen Guiley

Related articles in *World Book* include:

Evil eye	Mather, Cotton
Hecate	Salem witchcraft trials
Magic	Sewall, Samuel

Additional resources

Bartel, Pauline. *Spellcasters: Witches and Witchcraft in History, Folklore and Popular Culture.* Taylor Pub. Co., 2000.
Guiley, Rosemary E. *The Encyclopedia of Witches and Witchcraft.* 2nd ed. Checkmark, 1999.

Engraving (about 1520) by Albrecht Dürer

A witch rides a goat to a Witches' Sabbath in this engraving. For many centuries, witches were traditionally considered to be evil people, associated with the worship of the Devil.

Colored engraving (late 1800's) by Howard Pyle; Granger Collection

Colonial witchcraft trials were held in Salem, Massachusetts, in 1692. Many colonists believed evil spirits in the form of witches were tormenting them. Nineteen "witches" were hanged.

Witenagemot, *WIHT uh nuh guh мoнт,* means *a meeting of the witan* (or *wise men*) of Anglo-Saxon England. The witan were royal counselors, including bishops, abbots, earls, and *thanes,* or followers, who held important offices in the royal household or in local government. The king could summon anyone he wished to attend the witenagemot.

In early Anglo-Saxon history, the witan could dethrone a king or choose a new king in a disputed succession. But their role was more restricted during the 900's and 1000's. Throughout the Anglo-Saxon period, the king consulted his witan before taking important steps. He might seek their advice, for example, before issuing laws, granting lands, making war or peace, appointing bishops or earls, or deciding important lawsuits. The Normans who invaded England in 1066 had a similar institution, the *curia ducis* (duke's court). After 1066, the curia ducis and the witenagemot merged to form the *curia regis* (king's court). Emily Zack Tabuteau

Witherspoon, John (1723-1794), was a leader in American political, religious, and educational life. He served in the Continental Congress and signed the Declaration of Independence. Witherspoon was born in Scotland. He was a Presbyterian minister before coming to America in 1768 to become president of the College of New Jersey (now Princeton University). After the Revolutionary War in America (1775-1783), he continued his duties as college president. Glenn Smith

Witness is a person who gives testimony in a judicial, legislative, or administrative proceeding. Such testimony is given under oath, or, if the witness's religion forbids an oath, under affirmation. A witness may also be a person who signs a legal instrument, such as a will or deed, that another person executes in the presence of the witness.

A court witness is ordered to appear in court by a *subpoena,* which compels the person to attend and to give evidence. A person who fails to appear is liable to punishment for *contempt of court.* A witness who testifies untruthfully is guilty of the crime of *perjury,* and can be severely punished. Witnesses may legally refuse to testify against themselves or their spouses.

The question of who is suitable to serve as a witness is regulated by *rules of evidence.* The law considers certain people as unsuitable to give legal testimony. People who are insane and people who are too young to understand the nature of a binding oath are included in this class. Jack M. Kress

See also **Evidence; Oath; Perjury; Subpoena; Trial.**

Wittgenstein, *VIHT guhn ѕнтуν,* **Ludwig,** *LOOT vihk* (1889-1951), was one of the most important philosophers of the 1900's. His ideas greatly influenced two philosophical movements, called *logical positivism* and *linguistic analysis.*

In his later work, Wittgenstein suggested that most philosophical problems result because philosophers think most words are names. For example, philosophers have asked, "What is time?" and they have been puzzled because they could not find any thing named *time.* Wittgenstein said this is the wrong way to find out what time is. What is necessary is to determine how the word *time* is used in ordinary language. In the sentence, "It is time to go home," we know what *time* means, and so its meaning is not a problem. In general, the meaning of a term is determined by public standards of judgment, so a necessarily "private language" is impossible. Wittgenstein claimed that this way of viewing language "dissolves" many traditional problems of philosophy. His approach to language has greatly influenced scholars in many fields.

Wittgenstein was born in Vienna, Austria. He studied at Cambridge University in England and later taught there. He gained recognition for his books *Tractatus Logico-Philosophicus* (1921) and *Philosophical Investigations* (published in 1953, after his death). Karl Ameriks

Wizard. See Witchcraft.

Wizard of Oz. See Baum, L. Frank.

WMO. See World Meteorological Organization.

Wobblies. See Industrial Workers of the World.

Wodehouse, *WUD hows,* **P. G.** (1881-1975), was an English writer famous for his humorous novels and short stories. Nearly all his tales are set in England during the early 1900's. Wodehouse created many types of amusing characters, including silly young men, empty-headed young women, domineering older female relatives, and self-important businessmen. Two of his best-known characters are the dim-witted aristocrat Bertie Wooster and Wooster's valet, Jeeves. Wodehouse's clever, complex plots are filled with unlikely events.

Wodehouse wrote about 100 novels and books of short stories. He also worked with such famous composers as Jerome Kern and George Gershwin. He wrote lyrics for Kern's musical comedy *Leave It to Jane* (1917) and Gershwin's *Rosalie* (1928).

Pelham Grenville Wodehouse was born in Guildford, England, near London. The Nazis arrested him in France as an enemy alien in 1940, during World War II, and later detained him in Berlin. In 1941, while in German custody, Wodehouse made some controversial radio broadcasts in which he joked about his imprisonment. Many people in England considered him a traitor, but he was not formally accused. Wodehouse never returned to England. He moved to New York City in 1947 and became a United States citizen in 1956. Queen Elizabeth II knighted him in 1975. Michael Seidel

Woden. See Odin.

Wöhler, *WUR luhr* or *VUR luhr,* **Friedrich,** *FREE drihk* (1800-1882), a German chemist, in 1828 became the first person to make an organic substance (in this case urea) from inorganic chemicals. Organic substances consist primarily of carbon atoms linked together in chains or rings. Wöhler's experiments helped disprove the belief that organic substances could be formed only in the living bodies of animals or plants.

Wöhler isolated the element beryllium, and was one of the first people to isolate and describe the properties of aluminum (see **Aluminum** [The first aluminum]). Wöhler's studies with German chemist Justus von Liebig on benzoyl compounds played a major role in the development of organic chemistry. Wöhler was born in Frankfurt (am Main), Germany. Seymour Harold Mauskopf

See also **Chemistry** (picture).

Wojtyla, Karol Jozef. See John Paul II.

Wolcott, *WUL kuht,* **Oliver** (1726-1797), an American statesman, was a Connecticut signer of the Declaration of Independence. He also served as a member of Connecticut's convention to ratify the Constitution of the United States. He strongly supported ratification.

Wolcott was born in Windsor, Connecticut, and graduated from Yale College in 1747. He served several terms in the Connecticut legislature between 1764 and 1786. Wolcott was a delegate to the Continental Congress from 1776 to 1778 and a member of the Congress of the Confederation from 1781 to 1783. He served as governor of Connecticut from 1796 until his death.

Wolcott also became a military leader, rising to the rank of major general. He helped defend the Atlantic coast from British attack during the Revolutionary War in America (1775-1783).   John W. Ifkovic

Wolf is one of the largest members of the dog family. Wolves are expert hunters and prey chiefly on large hoofed animals, such as caribou, deer, elk, and moose. Many people fear wolves. They believe wolves attack human beings, and the animal's eerie howl frightens them. But wolves avoid people as much as possible and are rarely dangerous to human beings.

Most wolves belong to a species called the *gray wolf.* Two local names for gray wolves are the *timber wolf* and the *tundra wolf.* The timber wolf lives in wooded, subarctic regions. Some tundra wolves are also called Arctic wolves and are white. They make their homes on the treeless plains of the Arctic. Some zoologists believe that there is a separate species of wolf called the *red wolf.* This animal once lived throughout the southern United States. Today, however, only a few hundred red wolves remain, most of them in captivity.

Wolves can live in almost any climate, though they are seldom found in deserts or tropical forests. In ancient times, they roamed throughout the northern half of the world. But wherever large numbers of people settled, they destroyed wolves. As a result, wolves have disappeared from many areas. Today, most wolves live in sparsely populated northern regions, such as Alaska, Minnesota, Canada, China, and Russia. Small numbers of wolves still inhabit remote areas of such places as Greece, eastern Europe, France, India, Italy, the Middle East, Portugal, and Spain.

The body of a wolf

Wolves look much like large German shepherd dogs. But a wolf has longer legs, bigger feet, a wider head, and a long bushy tail. Most adult male wolves weigh from 75 to 120 pounds (34 to 54 kilograms). They measure from 5 to 6 $\frac{1}{2}$ feet (1.5 to 2 meters) long, including the tail, and are about 2 $\frac{1}{2}$ feet (76 centimeters) tall at the shoulder. Female wolves are smaller than the males.

The fur of a wolf varies in color from pure white in the Arctic to jet black in the subarctic forests. Most wolves have gray fur. Wolves of the northern and Arctic regions grow long, thick winter coats that protect them from the bitter cold.

A wolf has excellent senses of vision, smell, and hearing. These senses help the animal locate prey. A wolf can see and smell a deer more than 1 mile (1.6 kilometers) away. A wolf has 42 teeth, including 4 fangs at the front of the mouth that are used to wound, grab, and kill prey. The fangs may measure up to 2 inches (5 centimeters) long from root to tip. The small front teeth are used to nibble and pull at skin. The sharp side teeth cut easily through tough muscle. The flat back teeth crush thick bone so it can be swallowed.

The wolf has a large stomach and can eat as much as 20 pounds (9 kilograms) of food at one time. However, a wolf can go without food for two weeks or longer.

The life of a wolf

Wolves live in family groups called *packs.* Most packs have about 8 members, but some have more than 20. Zoologists believe pack members remain together because they have strong affection for one another. Most maturing wolves leave the pack and become *lone wolves.* A lone wolf travels alone until it finds a mate. These two may have pups and form their own pack.

Habits. Each wolf pack has a social order called a *dominance hierarchy.* Every member of the pack has a certain rank in the hierarchy. High-ranking members, called *dominant wolves,* dominate low-ranking members, known as *subordinate wolves.* A dominant wolf and a subordinate wolf show their rank almost every time they meet. The dominant wolf stands erect, holds its tail aloft, and points its ears up and forward. It may show its teeth and growl. The subordinate wolf crouches, holds its tail between its legs, and turns down its ears. It may also whine. See **Dominance** (picture).

Leonard Lee Rue III, Keystone

The timber wolf lives in forests of northern Asia, Europe, and North America. Most timber wolves have fur that is brown or gray or a mixture of those colors, but some have jet black coats.

Warren Garst, Van Cleve Photography

Young wolves learn some hunting skills by scuffling with one another. They begin to hunt with the pack when they are about 6 months old. This family of wolves includes a black pup.

A pack lives within a specific area called a *territory.* Wolves claim a territory by marking it with their scent. The leader of the pack urinates on rocks, trees, and other objects along the boundaries of the area. Other wolves can then recognize the boundaries. A pack does not allow other wolves to hunt in its territory. If wolves from another pack trespass, they may be attacked and killed.

Studies indicate that the size of the territory depends mainly on the availability of prey. If prey is scarce, the territory may cover as much as 800 square miles (2,100 square kilometers). If prey is plentiful, the area may be as small as 30 square miles (78 kilometers).

Young. Wolves mate during the winter. The female carries her young inside her body for about 63 days. She then gives birth to 1 to 11 pups in a sheltered area called a *den.* The den may be in a cave, a hollow log, an abandoned beaver lodge, or underground.

Wolf pups weigh about 1 pound (0.5 kilogram) at birth and are blind, deaf, and helpless. At first, they live on only the mother's milk. When the pups are about 3 weeks old, they begin to eat meat and to leave the den for short periods. Adult wolves provide the pups with meat. An adult eats much meat after killing an animal. To get some of this meat, the pups lick the mouth of the adult wolf. The adult coughs up the meat, and the pups eat it.

Wolf pups leave the den permanently when they are about 2 months old. The pups move to an unsheltered area that is called a *rendezvous site,* and they remain

Rolf O. Peterson

A wolf pack chases a moose through the snow. But the wolves may not be able to kill their prey after cornering it. Many animals are too strong for even a group of hungry wolves to kill.

there during the summer while the adults hunt and bring back food. In the fall, the quickly growing pups and the adults begin to hunt together as a pack.

How wolves hunt. When the members of a pack gather to begin a hunt, they greet each other and howl. Their howling may become very loud, and it warns other wolves to stay out of the pack's territory.

Wolves roam through their territory until they find prey. They then move in on the prey. They may inch closer to their prey, perhaps in single file. Then they break into a run, and the chase begins.

Wolves hunt and chase down many more animals than they can catch. Wolves eat almost any animal they can catch. Many of the animals they hunt, such as caribou and elk, are faster and stronger than wolves. Therefore, wolves must be quick, tireless, and clever to catch their prey.

Wolves hunt at any time of the day or night but tend to hunt more in the evening, night, and early morning. If wolves can catch their prey, they attack the rump or sides of the animal. They try to wound the animal and make it bleed until it weakens. Then they grab the victim by the throat or snout. Wolves can usually kill a large animal in only a few minutes. However, the entire hunt may take several hours. The wolves may give up the chase if the animal is strong, such as a healthy moose. They also may abandon the hunt if the animal is exceptionally fast.

Sick, injured, or aged animals that lag behind their herds make easy targets for wolves. The wolf helps strengthen the herds of its prey by killing such animals. An old or unhealthy animal can be a burden to its herd. For example, an aged caribou eats food that other caribou need to raise their young. A sick elk may infect other members of the herd. By eliminating such animals, wolves perform an important natural function.

Wolves and people

Many people despise the wolf because it kills other animals. Wolves provoke farmers and ranchers by destroying sheep, cows, and other livestock. Many hunters dislike the wolf because it kills game animals, such as elk and deer. These hunters mistakenly think that wolves wipe out game in certain areas. That is seldom true.

Fables and folklore also have contributed to the wolf's bad reputation. In many old sayings, the animal is a symbol of badness or evil. For example, "to keep the wolf from the door" means to prevent hunger or poverty. "A wolf in sheep's clothing" describes a person who acts friendly but has evil intentions. Fables pass on the misleading notion that wolves attack people. In the story of Little Red Riding Hood, a wolf threatens to eat a little girl.

Hatred and fear of wolves have led people to destroy large numbers of them. Government poisoning programs formerly helped exterminate wolves in the United States and other countries. *Bounties* (rewards) were sometimes offered for the deaths of wolves.

The United States government has classified the gray wolf as a threatened species in many states. The red wolf is classified as endangered in all the Southern States. Gray wolves have been reintroduced into the wild in Wyoming and Idaho, where they once roamed in great numbers. Red wolves have been reintroduced into the wild in North Carolina and Tennessee.

L. David Mech

Scientific classification. Wolves belong to the family Canidae. The scientific name for the gray wolf is *Canis lupus.* The red wolf is *C. rufus.*

Additional resources

Hampton, Bruce. *The Great American Wolf.* Henry Holt, 1997.
Steinhart, Peter. *The Company of Wolves.* 1995. Reprint. Random Hse., 1996.
Swinburne, Stephen R. *Once a Wolf: How Wildlife Biologists Fought to Bring Back the Gray Wolf.* Houghton, 1999. Younger readers.

Wolf, Tasmanian. See Tasmanian tiger.
Wolf fish. See Wolffish.
Wolfe, James (1727-1759), was the British general whose success in the Battle of Quebec in 1759 won Canada for Britain (now called the United Kingdom). His victory against the French came after several discouraging failures, due in part to his poor judgment. His greatness as a general has sometimes been exaggerated because of his dramatic death at the moment of victory.

Before the attack on Quebec, Wolfe moved his troops up the Saint Lawrence River to a landing well above the city. The troops moved down the river during the night of Sept. 12-13, 1759, to a point much nearer Quebec. They landed there and then climbed a steep bluff on the north side of the river to the plains outside the city walls. When General Montcalm, the French commander, discovered the British in the morning, he decided to fight on the site Wolfe had chosen.

The Battle of Quebec lasted less than 15 minutes. Wolfe was wounded twice, but he continued in command until a third bullet struck his lungs. He died just as the French troops were breaking. General Montcalm was also mortally wounded, and he lived only a few hours after the battle (see **Montcalm, Marquis de; Quebec, Battle of**).

Wolfe was born in the County of Kent, England. He joined the army when he was 14 and served in Flanders and Scotland. He became a brigadier during the Seven Years' War (also called the French and Indian War). In the war, in 1758, Wolfe served under Major General Jeffery Amherst in the Battle of Louisbourg (see **Amherst, Lord Jeffery; Louisbourg**).

Wolfe returned to Britain after that battle. William Pitt, who was then directing Britain's foreign affairs, chose Wolfe to command the expedition against Quebec. Wolfe's success there, at the cost of his life, permitted the British to seize Montreal in 1760 and to complete the conquest of Canada (see **Canada, History of** [British conquest and rule]).   Phillip Buckner

Wolfe, Thomas Clayton (1900-1938), was an American author who won fame for his autobiographical novels. Wolfe claimed that all great art was necessarily autobiographical. The story of his childhood and youth takes on a symbolic significance in his novels. His main character, under whatever name he appears, is a sensitive, worthwhile person who is, in essence, the author. Using this character, Wolfe treated a theme that is important to his work—the development of the artist in America.

Wolfe was born in Asheville, North Carolina. He graduated from the University of North Carolina in 1920 and then entered the Harvard University graduate school. Wolfe taught English at New York University between 1924 and 1930.

Maxwell E. Perkins, an editor at Scribner's publishers, was the most important influence in Wolfe's career. Wolfe wrote long rambling works, and Perkins helped him cut and organize the material. Wolfe's first novel was *Look Homeward, Angel* (1929). It was followed by a sequel, *Of Time and the River* (1935). After Wolfe's death, Edward Aswell, an editor at Harper publishers, edited his two other novels—*The Web and the Rock* (1939) and *You Can't Go Home Again* (1940). The character of Eugene Gant in the first two novels is modeled on Wolfe as a young man. The other two novels also draw on Wolfe's personal experiences. They concern a character called George Webber.

Oil painting on canvas (1770); Gift of the Duke of Westminster, National Gallery of Canada, Ottawa

The Death of General Wolfe, a famous painting by Benjamin West, shows Wolfe's death at the moment of victory in the Battle of Quebec.

Wolfe's writing has been criticized for its apparent lack of discipline and artistic control. Some critics believe that each novel is a torrent of undigested details and that Perkins's editing is responsible for whatever form the novels have. Wolfe seemed to support this view in *The Story of a Novel* (1936), in which he critically examined his own writings. However, later critics have stressed that Wolfe was more than a reporter. They note that he chose details and emphasized elements that make each of the episodes in his novels a dramatic unit.

Although Wolfe has been frequently criticized for excesses in language, at his best he wrote powerful prose that is often close to poetry. *The Notebooks of Thomas Wolfe* (1970) describes Wolfe's struggle to become a mature writer. *The Complete Short Stories of Thomas Wolfe* was published in 1987.   Noel Polk

Additional resources

Bloom, Harold, ed. *Thomas Wolfe.* Chelsea Hse., 1987.
Donald, David Herbert. *Look Homeward: A Life of Thomas Wolfe.* 1987. Reprint. Harvard Univ. Pr., 2002.
Teicher, Morton I. *Looking Homeward: A Thomas Wolfe Photo Album.* Univ. of Mo. Pr., 1993.

Wolfe, Tom (1931-   ), is an American journalist, essayist, novelist, and social commentator. Much of his work is an example of New Journalism, which mixes detailed reporting with controversial opinion.

Wolfe has written about many aspects of modern life and the arts. His first book, *The Kandy-Kolored Tangerine-Flake Streamline Baby* (1965), is a collection of essays about modern American life styles. *Radical Chic & Mau-Mauing the Flak Catchers* (1970) is a controversial description of a fund-raiser for the radical Black Panther Party at the home of symphony conductor Leonard Bernstein. *The Right Stuff* (1979) describes the selection, training, and daily lives of the first seven American astronauts. *The Painted Word* (1975) criticizes the pretensions Wolfe saw in modern art. *From Bauhaus to Our House* (1981) attacks modern architecture. *The Bonfire of the Vanities* (1987) is a novel about the very wealthy and the very poor in New York City. *A Man in Full* (1998) is a complex novel about politics and racial tensions in modern Atlanta.

Thomas Kennerly Wolfe, Jr., was born on March 2, 1931, in Richmond, Virginia. He has been a newspaper reporter and an editor for *New York* and *Esquire* magazines.   Barbara M. Perkins

Wolffish is the name of five species of aggressive ocean fish. Three species of wolffish live in the North Atlantic, and two inhabit the North Pacific. Wolffish get their name from their large, fanglike front teeth, which they use to tear apart their food. Their powerful jaws crush the shells of clams, crabs, and other hard-shelled animals they eat. Wolffish attack when threatened.

Wolffish may grow more than 5 feet (1.5 meters) long

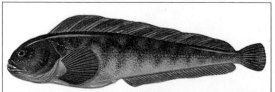

WORLD BOOK illustration by Colin Newman, Linden Artists Ltd.
A wolffish has powerful jaws and teeth.

and may weigh more than 40 pounds (18 kilograms). They are mainly brown or gray with dark vertical bands or dark spots on the body. Wolffish eggs are among the largest of known fish eggs, measuring about $\frac{1}{4}$ inch (6 millimeters) in diameter. A large female may lay as many as 40,000 eggs in round masses.

Wolffish are important food fish in North America, northern Europe, and northern Asia. Their strong, durable skin makes a good leather used for pouches, bookbindings, and other articles.   Tomio Iwamoto

Scientific classification. Wolffish belong to the family Anarhichadidae.

See also Fish (picture: Fish of coastal waters).

Wolfhound is the name of a family of dogs made up of three breeds—the *Irish wolfhound,* the *borzoi* or *Russian wolfhound,* and the *Scottish deerhound.* The Irish dog is the largest of all dogs, although not the heaviest. It was the companion of kings in ancient Ireland, and is still used for hunting.

The borzoi resembles the greyhound except for its long, luxuriant coat. This breed of wolfhound was developed by the Russian czars. The czars used these dogs to chase after wolves.

The Scottish deerhound descended from the staghound and other large breeds once used for stalking deer. It is a large, striking dog.

Critically reviewed by the American Kennel Club

See also **Borzoi; Dog** (picture: Hounds); **Irish wolfhound; Scottish deerhound.**

Wolfram. See Tungsten.

Wolfram von Eschenbach, *VAWL frahm fuhn EHSH uhn BAHK* (1170?-1220?), was a German knight and poet. His rhymed poem *Parzival* is considered a masterpiece of medieval literature.

Parzival is about a courageous boy who finds his way through ignorance to manhood and wisdom. During years of wandering, Parzival grows in purity and humility until God judges him worthy of the *Grail,* a holy stone that transmits God's will by a mysterious inscription. Wolfram based his poem on a French romance by Chrétien de Troyes. Richard Wagner based his opera *Parsifal* on Wolfram's work. Wolfram also wrote short poems and two unfinished verse epics—*Titurel* and *Willehalm.*

Little is known of Wolfram's life. He was born into a noble family in Bavaria and probably served as a knight under powerful lords.   James F. Poag

Wolframite, *WUL fruh myt,* is one of the two most important ores of tungsten. It consists of iron, manganese, oxygen, and tungsten, and its chemical symbol is $(Fe,Mn) WO_4$. Tungsten is a chemical element that is important in the production of electronic equipment and industrial tools (see **Tungsten**). The other chief tungsten ore is scheelite.

Wolframite is a black to brownish mineral. It is often found with quartz in veins that run in and around granite. Countries with wolframite deposits are Australia, Bolivia, China, and Portugal.   Robert B. Cook

Wollongong, *WOOL uhn GAWNG* (pop. 257,510), is an important industrial city along the southeast coast of Australia. It lies 51 miles (82 kilometers) south of Sydney, Australia's largest city. It is in the state of New South Wales. For the location of Wollongong, see **Australia** (political map). Wollongong has many historic buildings in the Georgian and Victorian styles of architecture that date from the 1840's. The city also has modern residential and commercial areas. It is the home of the University of Wollongong.

Wollongong's major industries include steel and iron production and coal mining. Wollongong is also a shipping center for products produced in the area.

Wollongong was first settled by Europeans in 1815. It became a town in 1859 but did not receive the status of a city until 1942. Alan Fitzgerald

Wollstonecraft, *WUL stuhn kraft,* **Mary** (1759-1797), a British author, was best known for her book *A Vindication of the Rights of Woman* (1792). This book was one of the first to claim that women should have equality with men. Wollstonecraft said that men considered women morally and mentally inferior to themselves. She argued that women could live happy, creative lives if they had better educational opportunities. She based her book on the democratic principles of the French Revolution (1789-1799) and on her own experiences.

Wollstonecraft was born in London. She educated herself by studying books at home. For a brief period, she and her sisters ran a school. From this experience, she wrote *Thoughts on the Education of Daughters* (1787). In this pamphlet, she criticized the cruel treatment of young girls that was common at the time. She also wrote other essays as well as stories and translations.

Bettmann Archive

Mary Wollstonecraft

In 1797, Wollstonecraft married William Godwin, a British political reformer. Their daughter, Mary Wollstonecraft Shelley, wrote the famous horror novel *Frankenstein* (1818). Cynthia F. Behrman

Wolsey, *WUL zee,* **Thomas Cardinal** (1473?-1530), was an English statesman who served as the principal adviser to King Henry VIII from 1514 to 1529. Wolsey was also a cardinal of the Roman Catholic Church.

Wolsey was born at Ipswich, England, and graduated from Magdalen College at Oxford University. In 1498, he was ordained a priest. He was made chaplain to the archbishop of Canterbury in 1501, and chaplain to the

English governor of Calais, a French city under English control, in 1503. Wolsey's Oxford friends and his own driving ambition helped his rapid rise to power. By 1507, he had become chaplain to King Henry VII. The king used Wolsey in diplomatic missions. In 1509, Wolsey became *dean* (head clergyman) of Lincoln Cathedral.

Oil painting (about 1600) by Sampson Strong; Christ Church College, Oxford, England

Thomas Cardinal Wolsey

After Henry VIII became king in 1509, he appointed Wolsey to his council. In 1513, Henry made Wolsey responsible for organizing a military campaign against France. In 1514, Wolsey was made bishop of Lincoln and then archbishop of York. Pope Leo X made him a cardinal in 1515. Wolsey loved display, power, and wealth. His income was many times larger than those of England's greatest nobles, and he lived in royal splendor.

Cardinal Wolsey used his abilities as a statesman and administrator mainly in managing foreign affairs. His foreign policy sought to settle disputes between the two major European rivals, France and the Holy Roman Empire, a German-based empire that also included Austria and parts of what are now Belgium, Italy, and the Netherlands. Wolsey worked to maintain peace and increase England's prestige.

Wolsey's greed and ambition earned him many enemies. But he held Henry VIII's confidence until he proved unable to persuade the pope to *annul* (declare invalid) Henry's marriage to his first wife, Catherine of Aragon. The king wanted to marry Anne Boleyn, who was a lady in Catherine's court. Wolsey's failure to obtain an annulment of the king's marriage resulted in Henry dismissing him in 1529.

Wolsey's fall from a position of great influence was sudden and complete. He was stripped of his property and most of his offices, remaining only archbishop of York. In 1530, he was accused of treason and ordered to London. On his journey to the capital, Wolsey fell ill and died. Richard L. Greaves

See also **Henry VIII.**

Wolverine, *WUL vuh REEN,* is a fur-bearing animal that lives in the northern woods and *tundras* (cold, treeless

James R. Simon, Van Cleve Photography

The wolverine lives in North America, northern Europe, and Asia. It is one of the most powerful animals of its size.

plains) of Europe, Asia, and North America. It is sometimes called the *glutton.* Adult wolverines measure about 3½ feet (110 centimeters) long and weigh up to 55 pounds (25 kilograms). They are somewhat bearlike in appearance, with a heavy body and short legs. The wolverine's long coat ranges from dark-brown to black, with a band of lighter-colored fur along its sides to the top of a bushy tail. The animal is extremely powerful for its size.

During the summer, wolverines feed chiefly on small and medium-sized mammals, birds, and plants. During the winter, they hunt reindeer and caribou. A wolverine kills such large prey by jumping on the animal's back and holding on until the animal falls. The wolverine will tear apart the body and hide the pieces until it can return to eat them. Wolverines also feed on the remains of reindeer and caribou that have been killed by wolves, bears, or other animals.

The wolverine is rare today. In the past, it was ruthlessly hunted for its fur and because it sometimes kills game animals and livestock.

Scientific classification: The wolverine belongs to the weasel family, Mustelidae. It is *Gulo gulo.*   Gary A. Heidt

Wolverine State. See Michigan.

Woman. See Human being; Women's movements.

Woman suffrage is the right of women to vote. Today, women in nearly all countries have the same voting rights as men. But they did not begin to gain such rights until the early 1900's, and they had to overcome strong opposition to get them. The men and women who supported the drive for woman suffrage were called *suffragists.*

In the United States

During colonial times, the right to vote was limited to adult males who owned property. Many people thought property owners had the strongest interest in good government and so were best qualified to make decisions. Most women could not vote, though some colonies gave the vote to widows who owned property.

By the mid-1700's, many colonial leaders were beginning to think that all citizens should have a voice in government. They expressed this belief in such slogans as "No Taxation Without Representation" and "Government by the Consent of the Governed."

After the United States became an independent nation, the Constitution gave the states the right to decide who could vote. One by one, the states abolished property requirements and, by 1830, all white male adults could vote. Only New Jersey gave women the vote, but in 1807, that state also limited voting rights to men.

Beginnings of the movement. Changing social conditions for women during the early 1800's, combined with the idea of equality, led to the birth of the woman suffrage movement. For example, women started to receive more education and to take part in reform movements, which involved them in politics. As a result, women started to ask why they were not also allowed to vote.

One of the first public appeals for woman suffrage came in 1848. Two reformers, Lucretia Mott and Elizabeth Cady Stanton, called a women's rights convention in Seneca Falls, N.Y., where Stanton lived. The men and women at the convention adopted a Declaration of Sen-

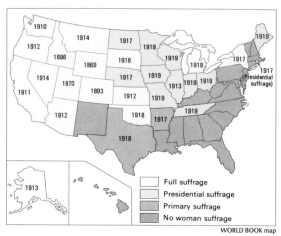

WORLD BOOK map

Woman suffrage existed in three forms before it became law throughout the United States in 1920—voting in all elections, voting only in presidential elections, or voting only in primary elections. The dates shown are the years in which these states granted women the right to vote.

timents that called for women to have equal rights in education, property, voting, and other matters. The declaration, which used the Declaration of Independence as a model, said, "We hold these truths to be self-evident: that all men and women are created equal. . . ."

Suffrage quickly became the chief goal of the women's rights movement. Leaders of the movement believed that if women had the vote, they could use it to gain other rights. But the suffragists faced strong opposition.

Most people who opposed woman suffrage believed that women were less intelligent and less able to make political decisions than men. Opponents argued that men could represent their wives better than the wives could represent themselves. Some people feared that women's participation in politics would lead to the end of family life.

Growth of the movement. The drive for woman suffrage gained strength after the passage of the 15th Amendment to the Constitution, which gave the vote to black men but not to any women. In 1869, suffragists formed two national organizations to work for the right to vote. One was the National Woman Suffrage Association, and the other was the American Woman Suffrage Association.

The National Woman Suffrage Association, led by Stanton and another suffragist named Susan B. Anthony, was the more radical of the two organizations. Its chief goal was an amendment to the Constitution giving women the vote. In 1872, Anthony and a group of women voted in the presidential election in Rochester, N.Y. She was arrested and fined for voting illegally. At her trial, which attracted nationwide attention, she made a stirring speech that ended with the slogan "Resistance to Tyranny Is Obedience to God."

The American Woman Suffrage Association, led by the suffragist Lucy Stone and her husband, Henry Blackwell, was more conservative. Its main goal was to induce individual states to give the vote to women. The two organizations united in 1890 to form the National

American Woman Suffrage Association. The Woman's Christian Temperance Union and other organizations also made woman suffrage a goal.

During the early 1900's, a new generation of leaders brought a fresh spirit to the woman suffrage movement. Some of them, including Carrie Chapman Catt and Maud Wood Park, were skilled organizers who received much of their support from middle-class women. These leaders stressed organizing in every congressional district and lobbying in the nation's capital. Other leaders, including Lucy Burns, Alice Paul, and Stanton's daughter Harriot E. Blatch, appealed to young people, radicals, and working-class women. This group of leaders devoted most of their efforts to marches, picketing, and other active forms of protest. Paul and her followers even chained themselves to the White House fence. The suffragists were often arrested and sent to jail, where many of them went on hunger strikes.

Action by individual states. In 1869, the Territory of Wyoming gave women the right to vote. The Utah Territory did so a year later. Wyoming entered the Union in 1890 and became the first state with woman suffrage. Colorado adopted woman suffrage in 1893, and Idaho adopted it in 1896. By 1920, 15 states—most of them in the West—had granted full voting privileges to women. Twelve other states allowed women to vote in presidential elections, and two states let them vote in primary elections.

The 19th Amendment. A woman suffrage amendment was first introduced in Congress in 1878. It failed to pass but was reintroduced in every session of Congress for the next 40 years.

During World War I (1914-1918), the contributions of women to the war effort increased support for a suffrage amendment. In 1918, the House of Representatives held another vote on the issue. Spectators packed the galleries, and several congressmen came to vote despite illness. One congressman was brought in on a stretcher. Representative Frederick C. Hicks of New York left his wife's deathbed—at her request—to vote for the amendment. The House approved the amendment, but the Senate defeated it. In 1919, the Senate finally passed the amendment and sent it to the states for approval.

By late August 1920, the required number of states had ratified what became the 19th Amendment. The amendment says, "The right of citizens of the United States to vote shall not be denied or abridged by the United States or by any state on account of sex."

In other countries

In 1893, New Zealand became the first nation to grant women full voting rights. In 1902, Australia gave women the right to vote in national elections. Other countries that enacted woman suffrage during the early 1900's included Canada, Finland, Germany, Sweden, and the United Kingdom. During the mid-1900's, China, France, India, Italy, Japan, and other nations gave women the right to vote. By 1990, women had the right to vote in almost every country where men had the right. Some countries still did not allow many or all of the people to vote. Only Kuwait extended the vote to men but not to women.   Anne Firor Scott

Related articles in *World Book* include:
Anthony, Susan B.   Blatch, Harriot E. S.

Catt, Carrie Chapman
Davis, Paulina Wright
Duniway, Abigail J. S.
Kelley, Florence
League of Women Voters
Lockwood, Belva A. B.
Mansfield, Arabella Babb
McClung, Nellie
Morris, Esther H.
Mott, Lucretia C.

Pankhurst, Emmeline G.
Paul, Alice
Rose, Ernestine P.
Shaw, Anna Howard
Spencer, Anna G.
Stanton, Elizabeth Cady
Stone, Lucy
Thomas, Martha Carey
Willard, Frances E. C.
Woodhull, Victoria C.

Additional resources

Baker, Jean H., ed. *Votes for Women: The Struggle for Suffrage Revisited.* Oxford, 2002.
Bjornlund, Lydia D. *Women of the Suffrage Movement.* Lucent Bks., 2003. Younger readers.
Haesly, Richard, ed. *Women's Suffrage.* Greenhaven, 2002.
Hannam, June, and others, eds. *International Encyclopedia of Women's Suffrage.* ABC-CLIO, 2000.
Stalcup, Brenda, ed. *Women's Suffrage.* Greenhaven, 2000.

Woman's Christian Temperance Union (WCTU)

is a nonprofit organization that works to lessen social problems. The organization's official name is the National Woman's Christian Temperance Union. It is also commonly called the WCTU. One of the WCTU's chief aims is to educate people, especially youths, on the harmful effects of alcohol, narcotic drugs, and tobacco. The WCTU has helped enact state laws requiring public schools to teach about such effects.

The WCTU's programs also promote good citizenship, child welfare, and world peace. In addition, the WCTU takes leading roles in other areas that deal with humanitarian concerns. These areas include child abuse and equal justice for women and minority groups.

The WCTU has headquarters in Evanston, Illinois. It has branches in all the states of the United States and in Puerto Rico and the Virgin Islands. It was founded in 1874. The WCTU developed out of the Women's Temperance Crusade of 1873. During this campaign, women church members went into saloons, sang hymns, prayed, and asked the saloonkeepers to stop selling liquor. The Temperance Crusade swept over 23 states, and resulted in the closing of thousands of places that sold liquor throughout the nation.

Members of the Temperance Crusade attending the Chautauqua Sunday School Assembly in 1874 discussed the need for a national temperance organization. These discussions resulted in the organization of the National Woman's Christian Temperance Union in November 1874 at Cleveland, Ohio. The WCTU's first president was Annie Wittenmyer, and the second was the noted educator and reformer, Frances E. Willard (see **Willard, Frances E.**).

The organization grew rapidly, and its influence increased with its growth. It worked through schools, churches, and other groups. Finally the 18th Amendment to the Constitution of the United States (passed in 1919) prohibited the manufacture, import, export, and sale of alcoholic beverages. This amendment remained in force from 1920 until 1933, when the 21st Amendment repealed it. See **Prohibition.**

In 1883, Willard founded the first international organization for women, called the World's Woman's Christian Temperance Union.

Critically reviewed by the National Woman's Christian Temperance Union

See also **American Council on Alcohol Problems.**

Woman's Relief Corps, National, is the oldest woman's patriotic organization in the United States. In July 1883, it was voted the official auxiliary of the Grand Army of the Republic, an organization of veterans of the Union Army in the American Civil War (1861-1865). The Grand Army of the Republic operated until 1956. The Woman's Relief Corps has thousands of members. Members do not have to be descendants of Civil War veterans.

The Woman's Relief Corps was formed to aid and memorialize the Grand Army of the Republic and to perpetuate the memory of its dead. Today, the organization also works to assist veterans of later U.S. wars. Members promote patriotism and take part in child welfare work. Headquarters are in Springfield, Illinois.

Critically reviewed by the National Woman's Relief Corps

Womb. See Uterus.

Wombat is a stocky, burrowing mammal of Australia. Wombats measure up to 4 feet (1.2 meters) long and weigh from 30 to 75 pounds (14 to 34 kilograms). There are two main kinds—the *common wombat* and the *hairy-nosed wombat.* The common wombat lives in coastal forests and feeds mostly on grass, small bushes, and roots. It has thick brown fur. Two species of hairy-nosed wombats live on the Australian plains and eat mainly

Eric Worrell, Photographic Library of Australia

Wombats are stocky, burrowing animals of Australia. The *common wombat, shown here,* has thick brown fur and small ears.

grass. Both species have gray fur and white hairs on the nose. Hairy-nosed wombats were once widespread but now inhabit only small areas of land. People have killed many of the animals because they damage crops.

Wombats are *marsupials.* Like other marsupials, wombats give birth to tiny, poorly developed young. The offspring are carried in a pouch on the mother's belly and remain there for at least six months. Unlike most other marsupials, the wombat has a pouch that opens toward the rear of its body. Michael L. Augee

Scientific classification. Wombats belong to the family Vombatidae. The scientific name for the common wombat is *Vombatus ursinus.* The two species of hairy-nosed wombats are *Lasiorhinus latifrons* and *L. krefftii.*

Women's American ORT is an affiliate organization of the Organization for Rehabilitation through Training (ORT). ORT is the world's largest independent network of vocational education and technical training. It was

founded in Russia in 1880 to teach trades and agricultural skills. Today, the organization operates hundreds of schools and training projects throughout the world and teaches thousands of students at the primary, secondary, and college levels. ORT offers a wide range of courses, from apprenticeship programs that teach basic skills to advanced courses in computer science, electronic engineering, and robotics.

Women's American ORT has thousands of members in the United States. It is concerned with a variety of domestic issues, including the quality of public education, the adjustment of refugees to a new culture, literacy, and equal opportunities for women. Headquarters are in New York City. Critically reviewed by Women's American ORT

Women's Bureau is an agency of the United States Department of Labor. It develops policies and programs to improve the welfare and status of women in the work force. The bureau is chiefly a fact-finding, service, and promotional agency. It does not administer any laws.

The Women's Bureau conducts research and develops programs to find ways of improving job opportunities for women and girls, especially in fields that have not traditionally been open to them. It encourages improved vocational counseling, better job-training programs, and continuing education for women. It works for the expansion of child care and other supportive services. The bureau also promotes legislation to improve the status of women and to eliminate sex discrimination in the workplace. It conducts or sponsors various studies and publishes its findings.

The bureau provides assistance to individuals; employers; labor unions; schools; employment agencies; federal, state, and local government agencies; and international organizations. Congress established the bureau in 1920. Critically reviewed by the Women's Bureau

Women's Clubs, General Federation of, is a women's volunteer service organization that trains women to be effective community leaders. It has more than 1 million members worldwide in more than 20 countries. Members work to support the arts, education, the environment, and international peace efforts.

The organization was founded in 1890 by New York newspaperwoman Jane Cunningham Croly. International headquarters are in Washington, D.C.

Critically reviewed by the General Federation of Women's Clubs

Women's Equal Rights Amendment. See Equal Rights Amendment.

Women's International Bowling Congress (WIBC) regulates women's organized bowling competition. It has over 1 million members and ranks as one of the largest women's sports organizations in the world. It includes both amateurs and professionals.

The WIBC establishes and enforces rules for leagues and tournaments and for bowling equipment. It also issues and regulates bowling center certificates to approved centers of the WIBC and the American Bowling Congress (ABC). The WIBC presents awards for outstanding achievements, and promotes interest in bowling. It conducts the annual WIBC Championship Tournament and the WIBC Queens Tournament, an event for only the top women bowlers.

The WIBC was founded in 1916. It has headquarters in Greendale, Wisconsin.

Critically reviewed by the Women's International Bowling Congress

Bettmann Archive

Penelope Breese, Gamma/Liaison

Women's movements have led to greater social, economic, and political rights for women. In the early 1900's, *left,* women marched for the right to vote. Since the 1960's, women have demonstrated for equal pay and job opportunities, and for child care and other social programs, *right.*

Women's movements

Women's movements are group efforts, chiefly by women, that seek to improve women's lives or the lives of others. Probably the best-known women's movements are those that have engaged in political efforts to change the roles and status of women in society. Such political movements by women on their own behalf are often referred to as *feminist movements* (see **Feminism**). Women's groups also have worked to help others, primarily through religious and charitable activities. Whether political, religious, or charitable, women's movements have sought to achieve greater social, economic, and political involvement for women.

Throughout history, women have usually had fewer rights and a lower social status than men. The traditional role of wife and mother dominated, and most women's lives centered around their households. Women's movements first developed during the 1800's in the United States and Europe and then spread to other parts of the world. The first women's movements arose largely in response to the coming of modern urban and industrial society. The industrial age brought about great economic and political changes, creating upheaval in women's traditional roles and causing women to question their status and situation. This first wave of women's movements concentrated primarily on gaining voting rights for women.

A second wave of women's movements emerged during the 1960's, another period of great political and social change in many areas of the world. These contemporary women's movements have sought greater equality for women in the family, in the workplace, and in political life.

Women's movements have enabled large groups of women to question and determine their rights and responsibilities. The specific goals and methods of these movements have varied from one time and place to another, depending on local customs regarding the treatment of women, on national political values, and on economic conditions. But in almost every case, women's movements have won greater freedom for women to act as self-sufficient individuals, rather than as dependent wives or daughters.

Women's status through the ages

Origins of women's traditional roles. Throughout history, most societies have held women in an inferior status compared to that of men. This situation was often justified as being the natural result of biological differences between the sexes. In many societies, for example, people believed women to be naturally more emotional and less decisive than men. Women were also held to be less intelligent and less creative by nature. But research shows that women and men have the same range of emotional, intellectual, and creative characteristics. Many sociologists and anthropologists maintain that various cultures have taught girls to behave according to negative *stereotypes* (images) of femininity, thus keeping alive the idea that women are naturally inferior.

There are, of course, certain physical differences between the sexes. From earliest times, the fact that women were the childbearers helped establish a division of tasks between women and men. In every society, only women bear children and nurse infants, leading to a tradition of women assuming most of the responsibility for child care. Men, by contrast, have been free to work at greater distances from their families. In early societies, this division of labor did not necessarily suggest inequality. But in more developed societies, a division of labor between women who worked mainly in the home and men who worked outside the home could give men economic superiority. A woman who stayed home came to depend on someone else—usually a man—to earn money for the necessities of life.

Women also differ physically from men in being, on average, smaller and less powerfully muscled. These physical differences helped define certain physically demanding or dangerous jobs as "men's work."

Eventually, the division of tasks that originally had been determined by physical differences became a matter of tradition. Consequently, even after machinery canceled out the advantage of male strength and after birth control gave women the means to regulate their childbearing, women continued to face barriers to entering many occupations.

The remainder of this section traces the status of women through history. It focuses on Western societies, because it is in these societies that women's movements first arose and have had their greatest impact to date.

In ancient societies, the lives of most women centered around their households. For example, in the Greek city-state of Athens from about 500 to 300 B.C., women raised children and managed the spinning, weaving, and cooking in the household. Wealthy women supervised slaves in these tasks, but they also did some of the work themselves. Respectable Athenian women seldom left their homes. Only men could purchase goods or engage in soldiering, lawmaking, and public speaking. The societies of ancient Egypt and of the Greek city-state of Sparta provided a rare contrast. Both Egyptian and Spartan women could own property and engage in business.

In ancient Rome, as in Athens, women's primary role was to manage household affairs. Women could not hold public office. Men dominated as head of the household. But the Romans developed a system of government based on the authority and leadership of a noble class that included not only statesmen and military leaders, but also the *matrons* (married women) of leading Roman families. For example, the Roman matron Cornelia, who lived during the 100's B.C., achieved fame and respect for her managerial skill, patriotism, and good works. In time, such upper-class women gained greater control over their property and over marriage decisions. However, even these women could not vote or hold public office.

During the Middle Ages, which began in the A.D. 400's and lasted about a thousand years, women's lives continued much as before. Like the Roman matrons, medieval noblewomen managed large households and supervised servants, oversaw gardens, attended to clothing and furnishings, and entertained guests. Many other women worked as cooks and servants, or worked in the pastures and fields of large estates.

However, two new roles for women did appear during the Middle Ages—the nun and the woman active in trade, either as an artisan or as a merchant. Convents flourished during the early Middle Ages. They offered primarily upper-class women an alternative to marriage and provided education, spiritual development, and control over extensive land. Beginning in the 1200's, women found increasing opportunities for independence as artisans and merchants in the medieval cities of England, France, Germany, and other western European lands.

From the Renaissance to the 1800's, fundamental changes in religious and political outlook took root, as leading thinkers began to emphasize the rights of the individual. The Renaissance was a period of great cultural and intellectual activity that spread throughout Europe from the 1300's to about 1600. The most significant intellectual movement of the Renaissance was *humanism,* which stressed the importance of human beings and their nature and place in the universe. Some humanists questioned certain traditional ideas about women, and favored better education and a more responsible family role for women.

The Reformation, the religious movement of the 1500's that gave rise to Protestantism, also encouraged a reassessment of women's roles. Protestant leaders permitted ministers to marry and began to picture marriage as a mutual relationship of spiritually equal partners. Husbands had less control over the lives of their wives. Protestants also began to view marriage and divorce as matters of individual choice rather than as the fulfillment of obligations to such authorities as parents and the church.

The Age of Reason—another period of great intellectual activity—swept Europe in the 1600's and 1700's. During this era, educated women participated in intellectual and political debates. In Paris, gatherings called *salons* promoted conversation and discussion among learned men and women. The salons widened these women's view of society and their possible roles in it.

Women's roles as workers also expanded during the Age of Reason. In western Europe and the American Colonies, women worked as innkeepers, landowners, midwives, printers, servants, teachers, and textile workers. But rural occupations continued to employ the largest group of female, and male, workers. Rural women toiled as laborers on large farms and in their own small gardens and cottages. Both urban and rural women engaged in knitting, sewing, and other home industries that made crucial contributions to household income.

The rise of women's movements

Forces of change. Several developments during the late 1700's and early 1800's set the stage for the rise of women's movements. The thinkers of the Age of Reason questioned established political and religious authority and stressed the importance of reason, equality, and liberty. The new intellectual atmosphere helped justify women's rights to full citizenship. On the eve of the French Revolution (1789-1799), the Marquis de Condorcet, a French philosopher, spoke in favor of women's right to vote. The British author Mary Wollstonecraft argued for women's rationality and equality with men in her book *A Vindication of the Rights of Woman* (1792).

In the American Colonies, the Revolutionary War (1775-1783), fought in the name of liberty and equality, raised the hopes of some women. Women supported the war with their sewing and farming, and by boycotting British goods and engaging in other forms of protest. Although neither the American nor the French revolutions increased women's rights, these conflicts gave new prominence to the idea of equality.

The spread of industrialization during the 1800's also affected women. The Industrial Revolution moved men's, women's, and children's work out of the home and into factories (see **Industrial Revolution**). Factory jobs offered working-class women an opportunity to earn wages. But if a woman was married, her husband legally controlled her earnings.

Industrialization had a different effect on middle-class women in small towns and cities. With the separation of work and home, these women lost a sense of useful involvement in productive work. They became regarded as "ladies" whose place was in the home, while their husbands provided the family income. Many of these women turned to such pursuits as needlework and craftwork—and to religious and charitable activities, as well.

The beginnings of women's movements. Before women's movements emerged, women began to form many kinds of groups based on common interests. After the French Revolution, for example, various women's political clubs took shape in both France and Great Britain. In the United States, women formed temperance societies, which campaigned to abolish alcoholic beverages, and missionary societies, which supported the spread of Christianity.

In the United States and Britain, two major types of women's movements gradually developed: (1) "social," or "domestic," women's movements and (2) "equal rights" feminist groups. Women's social movements carried out religious, charitable, and social activities. Equal rights feminists primarily worked to remove educational and political barriers to women and to change women's roles.

Before the Civil War (1861-1865), many American women's movements were of the social type. These included societies to promote temperance, to aid poor women and orphans, and to send missionaries to the Indians or to foreign lands. Women formed similar religious and charitable associations in Britain before 1860 and in other Western countries during the late 1800's.

Fewer groups were centered on gaining equal rights for women. But such groups had a clear goal to improve women's situation through such reforms as better education for girls, support for women's property rights, and voting rights for women.

Women's educational opportunities gradually expanded throughout the 1800's. In 1821, American teacher Emma Willard founded the Troy Female Seminary (now the Emma Willard School) in Troy, N.Y. Willard's school was one of the first institutions to offer girls a high-school education. In 1833, Oberlin Collegiate Institute (now Oberlin College) opened as the first coeducational college in the United States. By 1900, some major European and American universities were accepting women for advanced study and professional training.

Women's efforts to secure legal rights, particularly property rights, also brought reform. In the United States, many states enacted property laws during the 1840's and 1850's. Such laws allowed married women to make contracts, to own property, to control their own earnings, and to have joint custody of their children. For example, in 1848 a New York law gave married women the right to retain control of their own real estate and personal property. The new laws especially aided widowed, deserted, and mistreated wives. Similar legislation passed in Britain and other Western countries during the middle and late 1800's.

In 1848, social reformers Lucretia Mott and Elizabeth Cady Stanton organized the first women's rights convention in the United States in Seneca Falls, N.Y. The convention adopted a Declaration of Sentiments, which called for women to receive "all the rights and privileges which belong to them as citizens of the United States." National women's rights conventions met almost every year from 1850 until the onset of the Civil War in 1861. The delegates discussed the rights of women regarding divorce, guardianship of children, property control, voting, and other concerns.

Many of the equal rights feminists were also leaders in the movement to abolish slavery. During the Civil War, most women reformers devoted their efforts to supporting war activities.

The right to vote. The issue of *suffrage* (the right to vote) became increasingly important to women during the 1800's. In the United States, the cause of woman suffrage was championed by two key organizations: the National Woman Suffrage Association (NWSA) and the American Woman Suffrage Association (AWSA). Stanton and women's rights leader Susan B. Anthony led the NWSA, founded in 1869. The more radical organization of the two, the NWSA demanded equal education, equal employment opportunities, and voting rights for women immediately. Women's rights leader Lucy Stone, her husband, Henry Blackwell, and other reformers formed the AWSA, also in 1869. The more moderate AWSA supported gradual advances, such as limited suffrage for women in local elections.

In 1890, the two organizations joined to form the National American Woman Suffrage Association (NAWSA). *Suffragists* (supporters of woman suffrage) held conventions, waged state-by-state campaigns, and distributed literature to win support for their cause. New methods of campaigning used by British women suffragists—especially parades and outdoor speeches—spurred the drive for suffrage. Support from both social and equal rights women's movements proved necessary to the final suffrage victory. Women's social movements—temperance organizations, missionary societies, and progressive reformers—realized that they needed the vote to reach their goals. Equal rights feminists appealed to women laborers and to professional and college-educated women, all of whom had an interest in securing political power and more responsible and better-paying jobs. In 1920, the United States adopted the 19th Amendment to the Constitution, granting American women the right to vote.

Suffrage movements also arose in other Western countries during the 1800's and early 1900's. In 1893, New Zealand became the first nation to grant women full voting rights. Australia gave women the right to vote in federal elections in 1902. Swedish women with property could vote in city elections in 1862. Sweden granted women full suffrage in 1921. In Britain, the suffrage movement began in the 1860's, though women did not win full voting rights until 1928. See **Woman suffrage.**

Birth control also emerged as a woman's issue during the early 1900's. At that time, the distribution of birth control information was illegal in the United States. A number of social reformers supported birth control as a way to relieve poverty. Margaret Sanger, a trained nurse, led the birth control movement in the United States. By the 1920's, her work had helped make it possible for doctors to give out birth control information legally.

Decline after 1920. By 1920, the first wave of women's movements had peaked in the United States. With suffrage finally granted, many women assumed that the need for women's movements had disappeared. As a result, a period of relative inactivity followed. The NAWSA became the League of Women Voters and worked to educate women voters about current political issues. A few women, such as Frances Perkins, who served as secretary of labor under President Franklin D.

Roosevelt, were appointed to high public office.

In some countries, including Belgium, France, and Italy, the struggle for woman suffrage continued into the 1940's. But they, too, experienced little feminist activity after women gained the right to vote.

During World War II (1939-1945), several million American women took factory production jobs to aid the war effort. But after the war ended, these women were urged to leave the work force to make room for the returning servicemen. Society encouraged women to become full-time housewives. Devotion to home and family and the rejection of a career emerged as the ideal image for women. This view of womanhood, described by American author Betty Friedan in her book *The Feminine Mystique* (1963), all but replaced any organized struggle for women's rights until the 1960's.

Contemporary women's movements

In Western societies, a new wave of women's movements emerged during the 1960's. Civil rights protests in the United States, student protests around the world, and women's rebellion against the middle-class housewife's role contributed to this second wave of women's movements. It began with women's examination of their personal lives and developed into a program for social and political change. Women's groups discovered discrimination in the workplace, where women received less pay and fewer promotions than men. They also uncovered barriers to women seeking political office and to female students striving for high academic achievement.

Women's organizations. Two types of women's groups appeared in the United States during the 1960's. One type consisted of the small, informal women's liberation groups, which were first formed by female students active in the civil rights movement and in radical political organizations. These groups tended to be leaderless and focused on members' personal experiences. They emphasized self-awareness and open discussion to combat discrimination and to establish greater equality between men and women in marriage, child-rearing, education, and employment.

Large, formal organizations developed alongside the small women's liberation groups. These organizations, known as women's rights groups, campaigned for the passage and strict enforcement of equal rights laws. President John F. Kennedy's Commission on the Status of Women, founded in 1961, discovered a number of legal barriers to women's equality. It reported on laws that barred women from jury service, excluded women from certain occupations, and, in general, kept women from enjoying their full rights as citizens. In 1966, a number of feminist leaders formed the National Organization for Women (NOW) to fight sexual discrimination.

Other women's rights organizations also appeared. The Women's Equity Action League, founded in 1968, monitored educational programs to detect inequalities in faculty pay and promotion. The organization also drew attention to what was called the "chilly classroom climate," an environment that discouraged discussion and participation by female students. The National Women's Political Caucus, formed in 1971, focused on finding and supporting women candidates for political office. Concerned Women for America, founded in 1979,

stresses the preservation of traditional American values.

Other Western nations experienced a similar revival of women's movements. In Canada, for example, both women's liberation groups and women's rights organizations formed in the 1960's. The National Action Committee on the Status of Women, founded in 1972, is the largest women's organization in Canada.

Legal gains. The second wave of women's movements brought about many important legal gains for women. In the United States, several laws passed during the 1960's and 1970's aimed at providing equal rights for women. The Equal Pay Act of 1963 requires equal pay for men and women doing the same work. Title VII of the Civil Rights Act of 1964 prohibits job discrimination on the basis of sex as well as on the basis of color, race, national origin, and religion. Title IX of the Education Amendments of 1972 bans discrimination on the basis of sex by schools and colleges receiving federal funds. This law applies to discrimination in all areas of school activity, including admissions, athletics, and educational programs. The Equal Credit Opportunity Act took effect in 1975. It prohibits banks, stores, and other organizations from discriminating on the basis of sex or marital status in making loans or granting credit.

Court rulings have also expanded women's legal rights in the United States. Undoubtedly the most controversial such ruling was the 1973 Supreme Court decision in *Roe v. Wade,* which established women's unrestricted right to abortion during the first three months of pregnancy. NOW and a number of other women's groups have consistently opposed attempts at limiting women's legal access to abortion. Other women, however, favor tighter restrictions on the availability of abortion. See **Abortion.**

Not all efforts to broaden women's rights have been successful. In 1972, Congress passed the Equal Rights Amendment (ERA) and sent it to the states for ratification. The proposed amendment read: "Equality of rights under the law shall not be denied or abridged by the United States or any state on account of sex." Supporters of the ERA argued that the amendment would provide specific constitutional guarantees of equal treatment under the law, regardless of sex. Opponents, which included political activist Phyllis Schlafly and many other women, argued that passage of the ERA would require women to serve in the military and would deprive them

© Joseph Rodriquez, Black Star

The establishment of day-care centers, like this one in Sweden, is a goal of today's women's movements. Such child care programs help women obtain equal employment opportunities.

of the right to financial support from their husbands. The amendment failed to become part of the Constitution because only 35 of the necessary 38 states had approved it by the 1982 deadline.

Since the 1970's, women's groups in the United States have increasingly pushed for the enactment of social welfare legislation. Such laws provide benefits through family and community programs. Women need such programs if they are to have equal employment opportunities. Social welfare bills may concern preschool child care; before- and after-school programs for children; and parental leave from work for pregnancy, childbirth, or the care of sick family members. France, Sweden, and other European countries have instituted a number of such social welfare programs. In 1993, the U.S. Congress passed a law that requires companies with 50 or more employees to offer at least 12 weeks of unpaid leave to employees with a sick family member, a newborn infant, or a recently adopted child.

In Eastern Europe and the former Soviet republics. Many countries that underwent Communist revolutions or take-overs granted women equal rights and benefits in one stroke, often long before women in Western societies obtained such rights. In 1918, for example, the Soviet Union instituted maternity leave, government-funded child care, equal pay for equal work, equal education, and the right to hold any political office. Women gained similar rights in East Germany (now part of Germany) in 1949.

Beginning in the late 1980's, the Communists lost control of the governments of the Soviet Union and many Eastern European nations. In 1991, most of the Soviet republics declared their independence, and the Soviet Union was dissolved. Many women became concerned because economic reforms by the new Eastern European governments and former Soviet republics often included cuts in such programs as government-funded child care. In addition, unemployment caused by the economic reforms has affected more women than men in these countries.

Despite the gains made under Communism, women who do have jobs face a "double burden" as employment and household responsibilities have continued to fall heavily on women. Women's employment appears to have had less effect on men's roles in the formerly Communist countries than in Western nations. Husbands rarely help with shopping, cooking, and other household tasks. Also, women fill few important political offices at the national level. In business and commerce, few top managers are women. For these reasons, some women are working to generate Western-style women's movements in these countries.

In developing nations in Africa, Asia, and Latin America, few organized women's movements have emerged. In addition, vast cultural differences make it difficult to determine the direction women's movements may take in such nations. For instance, Muslim women in the Middle East and northern Africa come from a tradition where men's and women's activities have been strictly segregated and women have lived largely in seclusion. Women in eastern and western Africa, on the other hand, have a long history of social independence as food producers and traders.

Yet despite cultural differences, women in developing countries share some common concerns. Many women in these nations question whether modern economic development benefits them. During the 1970's and 1980's, several reports on the effects of economic development described women's loss of involvement in food production. Western experts often gave men the money and machinery to improve agricultural production, though women were traditionally the farmers. Men used the scarce resources to buy expensive equipment to produce and transport cash crops. As a result, women directed their efforts away from growing food for family use and the local market. Instead, they grew carnations, strawberries, and other cash crops that would bring in more money. Food shortages resulted.

Women working in industry also faced problems. Foreign-owned factories employed women in such industries as food processing, electronics, and textiles. But the women received low pay and little job security. In addition, they endured poor working conditions and heavy demands for high productivity and obedience.

The United Nations sponsored several conferences to examine women's living conditions around the world during its Decade for Women (1975-1985). At these conferences, women from the developing world expressed concern about food shortages, the poverty of women and children, and other issues. They have continued to stress the need for greater consideration of women's lives when working for economic development.

Impact of women's movements

Contemporary women's movements have had an impact on several levels of society in such Western countries as Canada, Sweden, and the United States. Women's groups have changed many people's views about male and female roles. These changes have affected the workplace, the family, and the way women live their lives. Through the vote, women's groups have influenced election results and government. They have also influenced legislation. Information about the legislative impact of women's movements appears in the section *Contemporary women's movements.*

On women's lives. The most notable single change in women's lives may be their growing participation in the paid labor force. In the United States, the percentage of employed women rose from 28 percent in 1940 to 57 percent in 1989. The contemporary women's movement contributed to an increasing acceptance of careers for all women, including mothers with young children. The proportion of married women with children under 18 and a job rose dramatically, from 18 percent in 1950 to 66 percent in 1988.

However, long-standing differences between the sexes in job opportunities and in earnings showed little sign of disappearing, even in such progressive nations as Sweden. The majority of women's work opportunities still fell within a narrow range of occupations, such as nursing, teaching, retail sales, and secretarial work. Largely because of lower pay in these "women's" jobs, women working full-time and the year around continued to earn less than men. In the United States, such women earned about 70 percent of what men earned in 1988. Furthermore, women throughout the world continued to face the "double burden" of being primary homemaker while working outside the home.

© James A. Sugar, Black Star

A woman commercial pilot holds a traditionally male job. Women's movements have changed attitudes about female and male roles, thereby increasing career opportunities for women.

On attitudes and values. Certain broad cultural changes have taken place that reflect new attitudes toward the roles of men and women. They also point to a growing equality between the sexes. Textbook publishers have adopted guidelines to eliminate language that uses male forms to represent everyone. For example, *fireman* becomes *firefighter,* and *policeman* becomes *police officer.* Women as well as men serve as anchors for television news shows. Several women have held the highest political office in their country, including Margaret Thatcher of the United Kingdom, Golda Meir of Israel, and Corazon Aquino of the Philippines. In the United States, the number of women in law and medicine rose dramatically. In high schools and colleges, women's studies courses in history, literature, and sociology have brought new attention to women's lives.

Changing attitudes about the roles of women and men have also affected the way people conduct their everyday lives. For example, many men now take a more active role in parenting. More husbands now join their wives in natural childbirth classes. Some men have taken parental leave from work or chosen to work part-time when they become new fathers.

Notable differences in outlook still exist between the sexes, however. In the early 1980's, U.S. elections revealed for the first time a "gender gap," where women followed a different voting pattern than men. Women's votes showed greater support for candidates favoring social programs and domestic spending, while more men voted for candidates favoring defense spending. A similar voting pattern has emerged in other countries, including Canada, Sweden, and the United Kingdom.

The final outcome of these changing attitudes and values has yet to be seen. But it appears likely that the blurring of distinctions between women's and men's roles and the trend toward greater equality of the sexes will continue.   Janet Zollinger Giele

Related articles in *World Book* include:

Leaders in women's movements

See the biographies listed at the end of **Woman suffrage.**
See also the following articles:

Adams, Abigail S.	Goldman, Emma	Sanger, Margaret
Beecher, Catharine Esther	Greer, Germaine	Steinem, Gloria
	Grimké (family)	Terrell, Mary C.
Besant, Annie W.	Heckler, Margaret M.	Truth, Sojourner
Blackwell, Antoinette B.		Walker, Mary E.
	Howe, Julia Ward	Wells-Barnett, Ida Bell
Bloomer, Amelia J.	Mill, Harriet Taylor	
Dickinson, Anna E.	Murphy, Emily G.	Willard, Emma H.
Friedan, Betty	O'Reilly, Leonora	Wright, Frances
Gilman, Charlotte Perkins		

Other related articles

Abortion	Equal Rights	Planned Parent-
Affirmative action	Amendment	hood Federa-
Alimony	Feminism	tion of America
Birth control	History (Approach-	Roe v. Wade
Civil Rights Act of 1964	es to history)	Sex discrimination
	Marriage	Sexual harassment
Day care	National Organiza-	Woman suffrage
Divorce	tion for Women	Women's Bureau
Domestic violence		

Outline

I. Women's status through the ages
    A. Origins of women's traditional roles
    B. In ancient societies
    C. During the Middle Ages
    D. From the Renaissance to the 1800's
II. The rise of women's movements
    A. Forces of change   C. The right to vote
    B. The beginnings of   D. Birth control
       women's movements E. Decline after 1920
III. Contemporary women's movements
    A. In Western societies
    B. In Eastern Europe and the former Soviet republics
    C. In developing nations
IV. Impact of women's movements
    A. On women's lives   B. On attitudes and values

Questions

Why did women's movements experience a decline after 1920?
What is the chief concern of women in developing nations?
How did the National Woman Suffrage Association and the American Woman Suffrage Association differ?
What was the role of women in ancient Athens?
How does social welfare legislation benefit women?
What two types of women's groups emerged in the United States during the 1960's?
How did the Industrial Revolution affect middle-class women?
What is the "double burden" that most women carry?
How do the Civil Rights Act of 1964 and the Education Amendments of 1972 affect women?
How has the "gender gap" affected voting patterns?

Additional resources

Brakeman, Lynne, and Gall, S. B., eds. *Chronology of Women Worldwide.* Gale Research, 1997.
Cullen-DuPont, Kathryn. *Encyclopedia of Women's History in America.* 2nd ed. Facts on File, 2000.
Howard, Angela M., and Kavenik, F. M., eds. *Handbook of American Women's History.* 2nd ed. Sage, 2000.
Nelson, Barbara J., and Chowdhury, Najma, eds. *Women and Politics Worldwide.* Yale, 1994.
Saari, Peggy, and others, eds. *Women's Chronology.* 2 vols. UXL, 1997. Younger readers.
Schenken, Suzanne O. *From Suffrage to the Senate: An Encyclopedia of American Women in Politics.* 2 vols. ABC-CLIO, 1999.
Zilboorg, Caroline C., and Gall, S. B., eds. *Women's Firsts.* Gale Research, 1997.

Women's rights. See Women's movements.

Wonder, Stevie (1950-   ), is an American composer, singer, and musician. A child prodigy, he recorded his first hit, "Fingertips" (1963), at the age of 13. Wonder has since matured into one of the most highly praised artists in popular music. He often uses his music as a force for social progress.

Wonder's compositions range in style from the rhythmic soul music of "Superstition" (1972) to the social realism of "Living for the City" (1973). He also wrote melodic ballads, such as "You Are the Sunshine of My Life" (1973). Wonder has incorporated Jamaican and African rhythms into his music. He paid tribute to the American composer Duke Ellington with the song "Sir Duke" (1977), one of his biggest hits. Wonder's other hits include "Uptight, Everything Is Alright" (1965), "My Cherie Amour" (1969), and "Isn't She Lovely" (1976). Wonder composed and recorded the music for the motion pictures *The Woman in Red* (1984) and *Jungle Fever* (1991). He won a 1984 Academy Award for his song "I Just Called to Say I Love You" from *The Woman in Red.*

Wonder was born on May 13, 1950, in Saginaw, Michigan. His given and family name is Steveland Judkins Morris. Wonder has been blind almost from birth.

Tony Korody, Sygma
Stevie Wonder

Since the early 1970's, Wonder's mastery of synthesizers and other instruments has made him almost a one-man band in the recording studio. He was elected to the Rock and Roll Hall of Fame in 1989.   Don McLeese

Wonders of the world. See Seven Natural Wonders of the World; Seven Wonders of the Ancient World.

Wood is a tough substance under the bark of trees, shrubs, and certain other plants. The physical properties of wood, plus its chemical composition, make it one of the most valuable natural resources. Wood is used in making thousands of products, including baseball bats, charcoal, furniture, lumber, musical instruments, paper, plywood, railroad ties, and rayon.

Wood's physical properties make it especially useful for construction work. It is tough, strong, and easy to handle. Wood also insulates well, does not rust, and resists high heat better than steel. However, wood shrinks and swells, depending on how much moisture it loses or absorbs. Every piece of wood has a distinctive—and different—pattern called the *figure.* The figure is a highly desirable feature of wood used for furniture, cabinets, and other fine wood products.

This article discusses the physical and chemical properties of wood. For additional information on wood and its many uses, see the *World Book* articles on **Forest products, Lumber,** and **Tree.**

Kinds of wood. There are two general kinds of wood, *softwood* and *hardwood.* These terms refer to the type of tree from which wood comes. They do not necessarily indicate the hardness of wood.

Softwood comes from cone-bearing trees, called *conifers.* Most conifers have needlelike, evergreen leaves. Common softwoods include cedar, Douglas-fir, hem-

Some types of wood   Wood is classified as *softwood* or *hardwood.* Softwoods are used chiefly for structural work. Hardwoods are used for furniture, floors, and paneling. Some popular hardwoods are shown here.

Chester B. Stem, Inc. (WORLD BOOK photos)

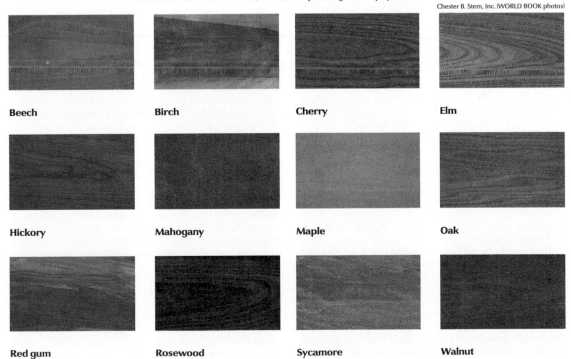

Beech

Birch

Cherry

Elm

Hickory

Mahogany

Maple

Oak

Red gum

Rosewood

Sycamore

Walnut

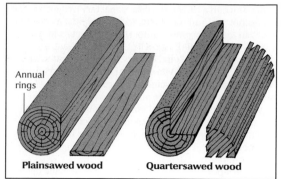

Annual rings

Plainsawed wood   **Quartersawed wood**

WORLD BOOK diagram by David Cunningham

Wood patterns are determined partly by the way logs are cut. Plainsawed wood is cut along the edges of a tree's annual rings, and quartersawed wood is cut through the rings.

lock, pine, redwood, and spruce. They can be easily sawed, planed, chiseled, and bored, and so they are good for construction purposes. They also supply most of the pulpwood used to make paper products.

Hardwood comes from broad-leaved trees. Most of these trees are *deciduous*—that is, they lose their leaves every autumn. Birch, elm, mahogany, maple, and oak are common hardwoods. Their rich and distinctive figures add to the beauty of furniture, paneling, and floors.

The composition of wood. Wood consists of tiny, tube-shaped cells that form layers of permanent tissue around a plant stem. The walls of wood cells are made of three chief substances—*cellulose, lignin,* and *hemicellulose.* Cellulose makes up about half of wood by weight. It is soft and consists of fibers. Cotton, for example, contains more than 95 percent cellulose. Lignin, on the other hand, is a heavy, solid material that is found between strands of cellulose and between the wood cells themselves. Lignin makes wood hard and stiff. Hemicellulose helps to hold cellulose strands together. Wood also contains substances called *extractives.* They include fats, gums, oils, and coloring matter.

The proportion of cellulose, lignin, hemicellulose, and extractives varies among different kinds of wood. The cellular structure also differs. These variations make some wood heavy and some light, some stiff and some flexible, and some plain and some colorful.

Manufacturers obtain useful chemicals and by-products from wood. These products include animal feeds, adhesives, lacquers, turpentine, plastics, photographic film, rayon, and artificial vanilla. Chemicals obtained from wood are used to give special properties to various materials, including explosives and concrete.

Wood figure is determined chiefly by the growth process of the tree. It results from combinations of color, luster, texture, and grain.

The color comes mainly from extractives. Uneven distribution of the extractives produces a *pigment figure,* found especially in ebony, rosewood, and walnut. Luster is the way wood reflects light. Many woods, including birch and pearwood, require a coat of varnish or another clear finish to bring out their luster. The texture of wood results from the structure of the cells. For example, beech, satinwood, and sycamore have small, closely spaced cells, which produce a fine texture. Other

woods, such as oak, ash, and elm, contain groups of large cells called *vessels* that produce areas of coarse texture and interesting patterns. The grain depends on the arrangement and direction of the cells. The figure is also determined by the way wood is sawed. There are two ways of cutting wood, *plainsawing* and *quartersawing.* Plainsawing produces oval and curved figures. Quartersawing gives wood a striped appearance.

In some woods, the figure depends on the part of the tree from which the wood is cut. Tree stumps and wartlike outgrowths called *burls* have attractive patterns. The most popular stumpwood is American walnut. Cherry and walnut have highly prized burls.   Douglass F. Jacobs

Related articles. See Forest products, Lumber, and **Tree** with their lists of *Related articles.* See also:

Cellulose	Lignum-vítae	Varnish
Furniture	Plywood	Wallboard
Lignin	Stain	Woodworking

Wood, Grant (1891-1942), was an American painter and printmaker known for his images of the rural Midwest. With Thomas Hart Benton and John Steuart Curry, Wood was a founder and leading figure in the *regionalism* movement that was prominent in American art during the 1930's. Wood primarily portrayed the people and landscape of Iowa, where he lived and taught most of his life. Wood believed that artists should remain in their home communities and paint from personal experience based on their local and national heritage.

Wood's most famous painting is *American Gothic* (1930), which portrays a Midwestern farmer and his daughter in front of their home. This painting is reproduced in **Painting** (The 1900's). In *The Midnight Ride of Paul Revere* (1931), Wood made good-hearted fun of Revere's legendary ride by moving it from New England to a hilly Iowa landscape. *Arbor Day* (1932) praises the values of domestic life in rural America.

Wood's paintings show the influence of German and Flemish art of the 1400's and 1500's in their realism, precise details, and enamellike surfaces. His compositions are based on simple shapes with sharp contours rendered in bright but earthy colors. Wood was born on Feb. 13, 1891, near Anamosa, Iowa.   Deborah Leveton

Wood, Leonard (1860-1927), was a United States soldier and colonial administrator. As military governor of Cuba from 1899 to 1902, he helped prepare Cubans for independence. Wood introduced political reforms based on U.S. laws and procedures. His troops trained and supervised Cubans in the building of roads and schools and in the cleaning of swamps and other mosquito-ridden areas to help stamp out yellow fever.

Wood was born on Oct. 9, 1860, in Winchester, New Hampshire. He graduated from Harvard Medical School in 1884 and soon afterward joined the Army Medical Corps. During the Spanish-American War of 1898, he was the first commander of the *Rough Riders,* a famous U.S. volunteer regiment. Theodore Roosevelt, who later led the regiment, served as his second-in-command.

Wood commanded the U.S. forces in the Philippines from 1906 to 1908. He helped modernize the U.S. Army as Army chief of staff from 1910 to 1914. In 1920, Wood sought the Republican presidential nomination without success. He served as governor general of the Philippines from 1921 until his death.   Lewis L. Gould

See also **Fort Leonard Wood.**

Wood-block print. See Block printing; Hokusai (picture); Japanese print.

Wood-burning stove. See Heating (Local heating devices).

Wood carving. See Woodcarving.

Wood duck is a colorful water bird that lives in forests of southern Canada and throughout wooded areas of the United States. Most wood ducks are found in the eastern half of North America, but some live along the Pacific Coast. The lowland forests along the Mississippi River provide excellent habitats for wood ducks.

Male wood ducks are the most colorful North American ducks. Their upper feathers glitter with green, blue, and purple. Underneath, the feathers are red, yellow, and white. Females are brown above and yellowish-brown and whitish below. Both males and females have crests extending back from the top of their heads. Wood ducks are about 20 inches (51 centimeters) long.

Wood ducks frequent ponds, swamps, and other wetlands near woods. They feed in shallow water on acorns, seeds, and insects. Wood ducks nest in tree cavities formed by woodpeckers and natural decay. Each female lays 10 to 15 eggs.

Wood ducks nearly became extinct in the early 1900's because of overhunting and the clearing of their forest habitats by people. Since then, conservation efforts have helped to increase the number of these birds.

Scientific classification. The wood duck is a member of the family Anatidae. It is *Aix sponsa.*   Eric G. Bolen

See also Duck (picture: A wood duck and her ducklings).

Wood louse, also called *sow bug,* is a small *invertebrate* (animal without a backbone) that lives on land. It belongs to a group of mostly marine animals known as *isopods.* Like its marine relatives, a wood louse has a flat, oval body that is divided into a number of segments. Special muscles enable the animal to roll up into a ball when disturbed.

Most wood lice live in dark, damp, humid places, such as under stones and

WORLD BOOK illustration by John F. Eggert
Wood louse

in bark. They come out only at night to feed. A few species live in the desert. They burrow deep into the sand to avoid daytime heat.

Scientific classification. The wood louse belongs to the subphylum Crustacea and the order Isopoda. The most common species are in the genera *Oniscus* and *Porcellio.*
P. A. McLaughlin

Wood nymph, an insect. See Butterfly (Satyrs and wood nymphs; pictures).

Wood pewee. See Pewee.

Wood pulp. See Paper; Forest products; Lumber (Introduction); Tree (Wood products).

Wood rat. See Woodrat.

Wood sorrel. See Shamrock.

Wood thrush. See Thrush.

Wood tick. See Tick; Rocky Mountain spotted fever.

Woodbine. See Honeysuckle; Virginia creeper.

Woodcarving is the act of creating figures or designs in wood by cutting or chiseling. Woodcarving is both a hobby and an art form. Some carving is performed on machines with cutters mounted on high-speed spindles. This article describes woodcarving by hand.

Most woodcarving is done with chisels of various sizes and shapes. Chisels have flat cutting edges. Other tools called *gouges,* have cutting edges that vary in shape from almost flat to deeply U-shaped. *Parting tools* have V-shaped cutting edges.

Woodcarvers can use a variety of methods. In *chip carving,* they cut patterns or designs into a wooden surface by removing small triangular slices of wood with a chisel or a knife or both. In *line* or *scratch carving,* carvers cut lines into the wood with a U-shaped gouge or a V-shaped parting tool. In *relief carving,* woodcarvers cut background wood away, leaving designs that project from the surface, which looks three-dimensional. Another woodcarving technique, *carving in the round,* involves making a free-standing object that can be viewed from any side, such as a statue or a bowl.

A number of woodcarvers have gained fame as artists. One of the best known was Grinling Gibbons, who worked in England during the late 1600's and early 1700's. Gibbons carved many beautiful interior decorations for chapels and libraries. Wilhelm Schimmel was a noted American woodcarver of the 1800's. Schimmel, a wandering folk artist, became especially famous for his crudely carved figures of eagles.   Harold L. Enlow

Related articles in *World Book* include:
Folk art   Furniture

Woodcarving tools include a variety of chisels and other cutting implements. A woodcarver uses the slanted cutting edge of a *skew chisel* to cut the outline of a design into a smooth surface (picture 1). A *bend gouge* with a U-shaped cutting edge is used to cut away wood near the edge of the design (picture 2). A carver deepens lines in the design with the V-shaped cutting edge of a *parting tool* (picture 3). The background area can be cut away with a *straight chisel* (picture 4).

WORLD BOOK illustrations by David Cunningham

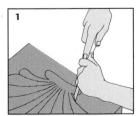

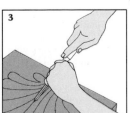

Indian, American (Carving)   Relief
Knife (picture: Kinds of knives)

Woodchuck, also called *ground hog,* is a small animal that belongs to the squirrel family. The woodchuck is a kind of marmot (see **Marmot**). Woodchucks live in Canada and in the eastern and midwestern United States. According to an old superstition, a person can tell when spring will come by watching what a woodchuck does on Ground-Hog Day, February 2 (see **Ground-Hog Day**).

Several subspecies of woodchucks live in North America. The woodchuck of Canada and the eastern United States is a typical subspecies. This woodchuck is about 2 feet (61 centimeters) long, including its bushy tail, and has a broad, flat head. Its coarse fur is grayish-brown on the upper parts of its body and yellowish-orange on the under parts.

Woodchucks dig complex burrows or dens that contain several compartments and may have several entrances. In winter, the woodchuck hibernates in a special den that has only one entrance.

When a woodchuck goes to look for food, it first sits up on its haunches at the entrance to its burrow. There,

Leonard Lee Rue III, Tom Stack & Assoc.

The woodchuck, also known as the *ground hog,* lives in Canada and the eastern and midwestern United States. Adult woodchucks eat grasses and other green plants.

it looks and listens for any sign of danger. This habit makes the woodchuck an easy target for hunters. Woodchucks eat such plants as alfalfa and clover. Some farmers consider woodchucks to be pests because they frequently destroy crops.

Woodchucks eat large amounts of food in the fall before hibernating. The extra food is changed to fat in their bodies, and the woodchucks live on this fat during their winter sleep. Female woodchucks give birth to four or five young in the spring.   Charles A. Long

Scientific classification. The woodchuck belongs to the squirrel family, Sciuridae. Its scientific name is *Marmota monax.*

Woodcock is the name of several species of birds that live in moist woods and sheltered marshes in many parts of the world. Woodcocks are mostly tan and brown, the colors of wood and dead leaves. These colors camouflage the bird in its surroundings and help protect it from enemies.

The *American woodcock* nests in the eastern half of the United States and southern Canada. It measures about 11 inches (28 centimeters) long and has a large

WORLD BOOK illustration by John F. Eggert

The American woodcock has a long bill.

body for its length. It has short legs and a long bill that it uses to search for earthworms in the mud. The American woodcock winters from Missouri to New Jersey and south to the Gulf Coast. It arrives north again in February or early March. The bird builds its nest of dry leaves on the ground.

Male woodcocks perform remarkable displays of courtship for the females on spring mornings or evenings. The male circles high in the air, then dives earthward, making whistling sounds with its feathers. It pulls out of the dive just before crashing, lands in a clearing, and gives a mating call. Many bird watchers visit the display sites of woodcocks to observe this ritual.
        Peter G. Connors

Scientific classification. Woodcocks belong to the family Scolopacidae. The scientific name for the American woodcock is *Scolopax minor.*

Woodcock, Leonard (1911-2001), was an American labor leader and diplomat. He served as president of the United Automobile Workers (UAW), one of the largest labor unions in the United States, from 1970 to 1977. From 1979 to 1981, Woodcock was U.S. ambassador to China.

Woodcock was a Detroit factory worker before he became a union organizer of the Congress of Industrial Organizations (CIO) in 1938. He joined the UAW staff in 1940. From 1947 to 1955, Woodcock held many leadership posts in the union. In 1955, he became a UAW vice president and the union's chief negotiator with the General Motors Corporation. In the early 1970's, Woodcock led a drive to establish national health insurance in the United States. He served on the U.S. Pay Board in 1971 and 1972. In 1977, President Jimmy Carter appointed Woodcock chief of the U.S. Liaison Office in Beijing, China. Woodcock was named ambassador to China in 1979, after the United States and China established full diplomatic ties. He was born in Providence, Rhode Island.
        Abraham J. Siegel

Woodcut is a print or design made from a block of wood. The block itself is also called a woodcut. Since the 1400's, artists have produced woodcuts that rank among the masterpieces of printmaking.

Artists make most woodcuts from pine blocks. The artist alters the surface by removing parts of the wood using chisels, gouges, and knives. The cutaway sections

Making a woodcut

Cutting

Inking

Printing

© Peter Gonzalez

An artist creates a woodcut by cutting away portions of a block of wood with sharp tools, *left.* To make a print of the picture, the uncut, raised surfaces of the block are coated with ink, *center,* and a sheet of paper is placed over the block. The paper is then rubbed with the back of a spoon or some similar object. The rubbing transfers the inked image onto the paper, *right.*

appear white in the final print, and the uncut parts produce the desired image. The artist coats the uncut parts, which stand in relief, with ink. A sheet of paper is then placed over the inked block and rubbed with the back of a spoon or with some similar implement. The rubbing transfers the inked image onto the paper. To make colored woodcuts, the artist uses colored ink and a number of separate blocks of wood, generally one for each color. Each block makes up a portion of the picture. The artist must cut the blocks so they appear in the correct *registration* (relationship to each other) in the completed woodcut.

Woodcuts were first used in Europe during the Middle Ages to print patterns on textiles. By the 1400's, artists made woodcuts to portray religious subjects, to decorate and illustrate books, and to make playing cards. In the late 1400's and early 1500's, the German artist Albrecht Dürer created woodcuts that achieved new heights of expression and technical skill. For examples of early woodcuts, see the *World Book* articles on **Bookplate, Card game, Literature for children** (picture: *The New England Primer),* and **Switzerland** (picture: The Battle of Sempach).

During the 1700's and 1800's, Japanese artists produced many outstanding woodcuts. These Japanese woodcuts are known as *ukiyo-e.* The ukiyo-e influenced such European artists as Edgar Degas, Edouard Manet, Henri de Toulouse-Lautrec, and Vincent van Gogh. The Europeans admired the Japanese woodcuts for their bold, flat shapes of brilliant color; delicate flowing lines; and superb composition. For examples of Japanese woodcuts, see **Japanese print, Drama** (Asian drama), **Hokusai,** and **Sharaku.**

During the early 1900's, expressionist artists created many fine woodcuts (see **Expressionism**). These artists included Ernst Ludwig Kirchner of Germany and Edvard Munch of Norway. Andrew J. Stasik, Jr.

See also **Baskin, Leonard; Bewick, Thomas; Dürer, Albrecht; Escher, M. C.; Ward, Lynd K.**

Wooden, John (1910-   ), was one of the greatest coaches in college basketball history. He coached the University of California at Los Angeles (UCLA) to a record 10 National Collegiate Athletic Association (NCAA) championships from 1964 to 1975. In that period, his teams won 335 games and lost 22. His teams won a record seven straight NCAA championships from 1967 to 1973. From 1971 to 1974, UCLA won 88 consecutive games, a college basketball record. He coached many all-Americans, including Kareem Abdul-Jabbar, Gail Goodrich, Bill Walton, and Sidney Wicks.

John Robert Wooden was born in Martinsville, Indiana, and graduated from Purdue University. He won all-America honors as a guard on the Purdue basketball team in 1930, 1931, and 1932. Wooden was basketball coach at UCLA from 1948 to 1975. He was the first man elected to the Naismith Memorial Basketball Hall of Fame as both a player and a coach. Bob Logan

Woodhull, Victoria Claflin (1838-1927), was the first woman to run for president of the United States. In 1872, she was the candidate of the new Equal Rights Party. Women's voting rights groups admired her stand in favor of allowing women to vote. However, they rejected Woodhull's candidacy because she also spoke for the right of women to have love affairs, whether married or not.

In 1870, Woodhull and her sister Tennessee Claflin established the first stock brokerage firm owned by women, near Wall Street in New York City. That same year, the two sisters founded a weekly newspaper. Both ventures did very well for several years.

Bettmann Archive

Victoria C. Woodhull

Victoria Woodhull was born in Homer, Ohio, near Utica. She received little formal education. Woodhull and her sister moved to England in 1877. Miriam Schneir

Woodpecker is a bird that uses its long, chisellike bill for drilling into trees. Woodpeckers bore holes in bark and wood to find food and build nests. These small- to medium-sized birds live in almost all parts of the world.

Body. Woodpeckers have several features that are especially useful to their way of life. Strong feet and sharp claws enable the birds to climb up and down tree trunks and to cling to bark. Most woodpeckers have two front toes and two hind toes, an arrangement that helps them to climb without falling backwards. Stiff tail feathers brace the birds against the tree trunk. Strong neck muscles propel the bird's head rapidly back and forth while it drills. Muscles on the head act as shock absorbers, protecting the skull from the impact of drilling.

Many woodpeckers are black and white or brown and white, and many are banded or spotted. Males of most species have some red feathers on their head.

Habits. Woodpeckers use their bill to probe bark and wood for the adult insects and insect larvae they eat. They draw the food out with an extremely long, sticky tongue that has a barbed tip. Some woodpeckers also catch insects on the ground or in the air. In addition, many woodpeckers eat fruit and nuts. The wood-boring insects that woodpeckers eat are available the year around. For this reason, few woodpeckers migrate.

For nests, woodpeckers dig holes in the trunks of trees or, sometimes, in the ground or in buildings. The nest may extend 6 to 18 inches (15 to 45 centimeters) below the entrance. It has no lining except for wood chips. A female woodpecker lays two to eight white eggs.

A woodpecker's call consists of a series of harsh notes. The birds also drum with their bills on dead branches or on anything hollow. They use this sound to advertise their presence and defend their territory. Except for nesting pairs, most woodpeckers live alone.

Woodpeckers occasionally damage buildings and trees when they dig holes in them. However, woodpeckers are mostly beneficial to human beings, feeding upon insects that damage timber and agricultural crops.

Kinds. There are about 200 species of woodpeckers, but only about 23 species live in North America. Their habitat ranges from evergreen forests to arid deserts.

The large *ivory-billed woodpecker* once lived in swampy forests of the southeastern United States. Logging has destroyed most of the bird's habitat, and scientists believe that the bird is either critically endangered or extinct. Some people mistake the male *pileated woodpecker* for the ivory-bill because both of these birds have red crests on their heads. The pileated woodpecker, however, remains fairly common in North American forests. The *acorn woodpecker* of the western United States drills holes for storing acorns, which it

M. Vinciguerra, N.A.S.

The male pileated woodpecker, *shown in the photograph,* is often mistaken for the ivory-billed woodpecker. It is found in eastern North America and in parts of the Northwest. Both sexes have a high crest on the head.

Ivory-billed woodpecker
Campephilus principalis
Once found in southeastern United States and Cuba, but now possibly extinct
Body length: 20 inches (51 centimeters)

Green woodpecker
Picus viridis
Found in Eurasian forests
Body length: 12 inches
 (30 centimeters)

Hairy woodpecker
Picoides villosus
Found in North America
Body length: 10 inches
 (25 centimeters)

WORLD BOOK illustrations
by Guy Coheleach

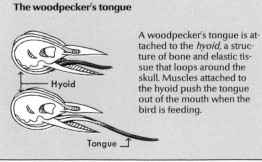

WORLD BOOK illustration by Marion Pahl

The woodpecker's tongue

A woodpecker's tongue is attached to the *hyoid,* a structure of bone and elastic tissue that loops around the skull. Muscles attached to the hyoid push the tongue out of the mouth when the bird is feeding.

Hyoid

Tongue

eats when other food is scarce. The *redheaded wood-pecker* of the eastern and midwestern United States has a bright-red head and neck. It also stores nuts and corn for the winter. *Flickers* are among the most common North American woodpeckers. They feed mainly on the ground and are especially fond of ants. Harlo H. Hadow

Scientific classification. Woodpeckers belong to the woodpecker family, Picidae. The ivory-billed woodpecker is *Campephilus principalis;* the pileated is *Dryocopus pileatus;* the acorn is *Melanerpes formicivorus;* and the redheaded is *M. erythrocephalus.*

See also **Bird** (picture: Birds of the desert); **Flicker; Sapsucker; Wryneck.**

Woodrat, also called *pack rat* or *trade rat,* is a native of North and Central America. It looks much like the house rat but has larger ears, softer fur, and a hairy, instead of a naked, scaly tail. The woodrat also has cleaner habits. It will not live in sewers and garbage dumps. Some western woodrats live in the mountains. Others live in the deserts. A female has one or two litters (3 to 6 young) a season. Woodrats are curious. They pick up and hide or carry home small articles that catch their fancy, such as silverware, nails, buckles, brightly colored stones, and even manure. This is why they got the name *pack rats.* Sometimes the animal will drop and leave behind something, in order to "pack off" a more attractive article. This accounts for its being called *trade rat.* Clyde Jones

Scientific classification. Woodrats belong to the family Cricetidae. They make up the genus *Neotoma.* The scientific name for one typical species is *N. floridana.*

Woods, Granville T. (1856-1910), was an African American inventor who obtained over 50 patents. His most significant invention, a railway telegraph system developed in 1887, allowed crew members on moving trains to communicate with one another and with railroad stations. It did much to help avoid train collisions.

Woods was born in Columbus, Ohio. He was mostly self-taught, but also took college engineering courses and worked as a railroad engineer. Woods received his first patent, for an improved steam boiler furnace, in 1884. His inventions included an egg incubator, an automatic air brake, a *galvanic* (electric) battery, a telephone transmitter, and devices for telegraphs and railway systems. Woods sold many inventions to such large companies as General Electric, Westinghouse Air Brake, and American Bell Telephone. Raymond W. Smock

Woods, Tiger (1975-   ), an American golfer, created a sensation in the sports world with his brilliant play. Woods is especially known for his long, accurate drives, but he has also gained praise for his complete game as well as his composure and his competitive intensity.

Woods became the youngest golfer to win the four Grand Slam tournaments during a career. Woods is also the first professional player to hold all four Grand Slam titles at the same time. The Grand Slam consists of the Masters, the U.S. Open, the Professional Golfers' Association (PGA) Championship, and the British Open. Woods holds or shares the record for the lowest total score for each tournament. He won the Masters in 1997, the youngest golfer and the first with African American heritage to win the tournament. Woods won the Masters again in 2001 and 2002. Woods also won the PGA title in 1999 and 2000, the U.S. Open in 2000 and 2002, and the British Open in 2000.

Woods first gained attention as an amateur golfer. He won the U.S. Junior Amateur Championship in 1991, 1992, and 1993. He also won the U.S. Amateur Championship in 1994, 1995, and 1996. He won the Division I men's title in the National Collegiate Athletic Association (NCAA) Championships in 1996 while attending Stanford University. Woods turned professional in 1996.

Woods was born on Dec. 30, 1975, in Cypress, California. His given name is Eldrick Woods. His father named him "Tiger" after an Army buddy. Woods had a great impact on golf internationally because of his diverse ethnic background, which is African American, American Indian, Chinese, European, and Thai. Marino A. Parascenzo

See also **Golf** (picture: Golf stars of today).

Woods Hole Oceanographic Institution is a private, nonprofit research center for marine science on Cape Cod, at Woods Hole, Massachusetts. It has a variety of laboratories onshore and several research vessels for exploring the oceans, including a small deep-diving submarine. Scientists at the institution pursue research in such fields as marine biology, chemistry, geology and geophysics, physics, and engineering. The institution awards doctor's degrees and offers programs for advanced undergraduates and postdoctoral students.

Critically reviewed by the Woods Hole Oceanographic Institution

Woodson, Carter Goodwin (1875-1950), is widely regarded as the leading writer on black history of his time. An African American, Woodson devoted his life to bringing the achievements of black people to the world's attention. His founding of the Association for the Study of Negro Life and History (now the Association for the Study of African-American Life and History) in 1915 has been called the start of the black history movement. The association began publishing *The Journal of Negro History,* a scholarly magazine, in 1916. The best known of Woodson's 16 books is *Negro in Our History* (1922).

Woodson was born in New Canton, Virginia. His parents were former slaves. Woodson received a Ph.D. degree in history from Harvard University. He won the Spingarn Medal in 1926. Richard Bardolph

See also **Black History Month.**

Woodstock festival was the most famous outdoor rock music concert of the 1960's. It was also known as the Woodstock Music and Arts Festival. The festival became a symbol of the "Woodstock Nation," a group of young people united by common beliefs, values, and lifestyles. These youths distrusted authority and standard American values, and they supported the freedom to openly experiment with drugs and sex.

Woodstock helped rock music become more popular and a bigger business than ever. The festival and the documentary film *Woodstock* (1970) promoted a new generation of performers whose music was more offbeat and varied than the hits played on Top 40 radio programs. Songs that the music industry considered uncommercial but that allowed musicians creative freedom of expression gained wide popularity as a result of the festival. Musical highlights of the festival included the Grateful Dead; Jimi Hendrix; Jefferson Airplane; Janis Joplin; Santana; and Crosby, Stills, Nash, and Young.

The Woodstock festival took place near Bethel in upstate New York on fields owned by a farmer named Max Yasgur. It had been planned to be held in Wallkill, New York, near Woodstock. However, promoters moved the

The Woodstock festival of 1969 attracted more than 300,000 rock fans. The famous three-day outdoor concert became a symbol of their generation for many young people, and it helped rock music become more popular than ever.

J. Dominis, The Image Works

event to Yasgur's fields after Wallkill residents objected. Over 300,000 rock fans, many of whom were students, hippies, and opponents of the Vietnam War, attended.

Woodstock ran from Aug. 15 to 17, 1969, which promoters called "Three Days of Peace and Music." The festival remained peaceful even though conditions created a potential for disaster. Rains drenched the crowd, and food and water supplies grew scarce. Despite the problems, the concertgoers kept a spirit of communal celebration and harmony.   Don McLeese

Woodsworth, James Shaver (1874-1942), was a Methodist minister and one of Canada's leading social reformers of the 1900's. He recommended many of the social welfare programs that Canada has adopted since World War II ended in 1945, including old-age pensions and unemployment relief.

Woodsworth was born near Toronto. In the early 1900's, he became known for his dedication to helping needy farmers and workers. Woodsworth strongly opposed violence, and during World War I (1914-1918), he spoke out against Canada's military draft. He participated in the Winnipeg General Strike of 1919, in which about 30,000 workers in Winnipeg struck for various rights. In 1921, Woodsworth won election to the Canadian Parliament as a member of the Manitoba Independent Labour Party. He served there until his death.

During 1932 and 1933, Woodsworth helped found the Co-operative Commonwealth Federation, Canada's former socialist party. He led the party (now the New Democratic Party) until 1940. He was the only member of the House of Commons who voted against Canada's entry into World War II in 1939.   Richard Allen

Woodwind instrument. See Music (Musical instruments [Wind instruments]; illustration); **Orchestra** (The musicians; illustration).

Woodworking is the forming and shaping of wood to make useful and decorative objects. It is one of the oldest crafts and ranks as a popular hobby and an important industry. A skilled woodworker with a well-equipped home workshop can build items as simple as a birdhouse or as complicated as decorative furniture. Tools for a workshop can be purchased at hardware and department stores. Lumber retail stores and hobby shops sell a wide variety of wood.

The construction industry employs carpenters who construct the wooden framework of buildings. Other kinds of woodworkers include *finish carpenters* and *cabinetmakers*. Finish carpenters do the inside trim work around windows, cabinets, and other features that must fit exactly. Cabinetmakers design, shape, and assemble furniture, built-in cabinets, and stairways.

This article discusses woodworking as a hobby. For details on woodworking in industry, see **Carpentry**.

The history of woodworking goes back to about 8,000 B.C., when people first used an ax as a woodworking tool. In the Middle Ages, woodworkers and other craftworkers formed organizations called *guilds*. The guilds were similar in some ways to today's labor unions.

In 1873, electric power was used to drive machine tools for the first time. Through the years came the development of the power tools now used for woodworking. The first practical hand drill was patented in 1917. By 1925, woodworkers could buy electric portable saws for their home workshop. Today, power tools can be used in most woodworking operations, but many people enjoy shaping wood with hand tools instead.

Steps in woodworking

Woodworking projects, together with plans for their construction, can be found in books, magazines, and manuals in bookstores and public libraries. There are five main steps in woodworking: (1) planning and design, (2) cutting, (3) drilling, (4) fastening, and (5) sanding and finishing.

Planning and design. Careful planning can prevent mistakes and save time and materials. A scale drawing of the object being built should be made before starting any woodworking project. This drawing includes the exact measurements of the object. The craftworker marks the measurements on the wood with a pencil and lists all the steps to be followed in the project.

A woodworking *tape* and *rule* are used to measure dimensions. A *square* can also be used for measuring and for making straight lines and angles. Various *gauges* make marks and parallel lines for the woodworker to follow when cutting joints and attaching hinges.

The parts of the finished object will fit together properly if the drawing has been prepared correctly and if measuring and construction have been done accurately. A well-designed object is both attractive and the right size for its purpose. For example, a birdhouse must have an entrance that is large enough for the birds that will use it.

Cutting wood to the right size and shape can be done with a variety of hand and power tools, including *saws, chisels,* and *planes.* The largest and most familiar handsaws are the *crosscut saw* and the *ripsaw.* Crosscut saws cut across the grain of the wood, and ripsaws cut with the grain.

Power tools can do a job far more quickly, easily, and accurately than hand tools. For example, a *circular saw* has a toothed disk that spins at great speed. Different blades can be attached for a variety of cutting operations, such as crosscutting and ripping.

A common hand tool for cutting joints is the *backsaw,* which has a thin rectangular blade for fine work. The blade has a metal bar along its back to make it stiff. Chisels, which can cut deeply into the surface of wood, can be used for making joints or for trimming and carving. A *portable electric router* has attachments called *bits* that can be used to trim or shape wood and to make joints and decorative cuts. A hand tool called a *coping*

Basic tools for woodworking Hobbyists use many of the woodworking tools pictured below. Although power tools can be used in any woodworking operation, many people prefer to shape wood with hand tools.

Measuring tools

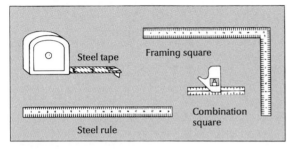

Steel tape
Framing square
Combination square
Steel rule

Drilling tools

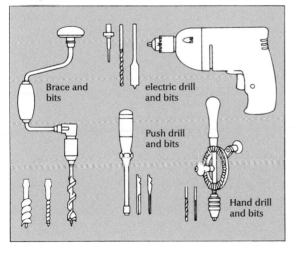

Brace and bits
electric drill and bits
Push drill and bits
Hand drill and bits

Cutting tools

WORLD BOOK illustrations by Dick Keller and William Graham

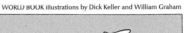
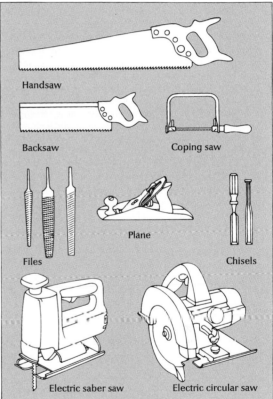

Handsaw
Backsaw
Coping saw
Plane
Files
Chisels
Electric saber saw
Electric circular saw

Fastening tools

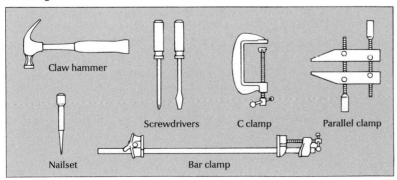

Claw hammer
Screwdrivers
C clamp
Parallel clamp
Nailset
Bar clamp

Sanding tools

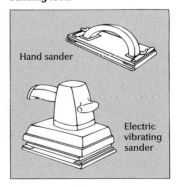

Hand sander
Electric vibrating sander

saw consists of a metal frame that holds a narrow blade used for cutting curves in wood. *Jigsaws* and *saber saws,* power tools that cut curves, have a thin blade that moves up and down at great speed.

Mechanical planes, called *jointers,* and hand planes have sharp blades that smooth and shape wood. A *wood-turning lathe* shapes wood into rounded forms by rapidly spinning it against a cutting edge held by the operator. A *file* shapes wood in places where a sharper cutting tool does not fit. Files can also sharpen tools.

Drilling enables a woodworker to connect sections of wood with *screws, metal plates,* and *hinges.* Drilling may also be required when constructing some *joints.* Braces and *hand drills* have bits to make holes of different sizes for various purposes. *Portable electric drills* and *drill presses* also use bits to drill holes. They have attachments for sanding and other purposes.

Fastening. Sections of wood are fastened together with metal fasteners, such as *screws* and *nails,* and with *adhesives.* Tools for fastening include *screwdrivers* and *hammers.* Screwdrivers insert screws that connect sections of wood and hold hinges and metal plates. Hammers drive in nails and other types of metal fasteners.

Gluing is one of the oldest methods of fastening sections of wood, and a variety of adhesives are used in woodworking. *Polyvinyl resin emulsion glue,* or white glue, can be applied directly from the bottle. It should not be used if it will come in contact with water or high temperatures. *Urea-formaldehyde resin glue* and *resorcinol formaldehyde resin glue* both must be mixed by the user. Urea glue can resist cold water for short periods, but it cannot withstand high temperatures. Resorcinol glue is waterproof and heat resistant. After gluing, wood should be put into *clamps* for as long as 12 hours. The length of time depends on the temperature, kind of wood, and type of glue. Clamping holds the wood in place and spreads the glue into the pores.

Sanding and finishing. Sanding removes tool marks and makes wood surfaces smooth for finishing. Sanding should not begin until the wood has been cut to its final size. Most *abrasive paper* manufactured for use by hand has rough particles of the minerals *flint* or *garnet.* *Aluminum oxide* is a common sanding material used in such machines as a *portable belt sander* or a *vibrating sander.* Portable belt sanders work better than vibrating sanders on large wood surfaces.

Woodworkers use a variety of *finishes* to protect wood and to bring out the beauty of the grain. A *stain* is a dye that colors wood without hiding the pattern and feel of the grain. *Paint* covers the grain of the wood and provides a color of its own. Varnish, shellac, and lacquer add a hard, glossy finish while exposing the beauty of the wood. *Wax* protects varnish and has a smooth, shiny finish when polished. *Enamel* is a type of glossy paint.

Tool care and safety

Tools are made to be safe when used correctly. They can be preserved—and accidents can be prevented—by using the right tools for the job and keeping them clean and sharp. A woodworker must use extra pressure with a dull tool, and injury could result if the tool slips. Many tools can be sharpened on the rough surface of an *oilstone.* A woodworker should not use broken or damaged tools because they will not work properly.

Whenever possible, a worker should hold wood in place with a vise or clamps, so that both hands are free to handle the tool being used. Floors should be kept clean of such substances as sawdust and finishing materials, which are slippery and also could catch fire. Safety glasses should always be worn during cutting and boring operations in order to protect the eyes from flying particles of wood. Loose clothing and jewelry that could get caught in a machine should not be worn in a woodworking area.

A craftworker can prevent accidents by holding a portable power tool until all the moving parts have stopped. A machine should never be left unattended while it is running. In addition, a machine should be disconnected when not in use. The hazard of receiving an electric shock can be reduced by connecting *ground wires* to machines that have not been previously grounded.

Wood for woodworking

Woodworkers classify wood as *hardwood* or *softwood,* depending on the type of tree from which it comes. Most hardwood trees are *deciduous*—that is, they lose their leaves every autumn. Most softwood, or *coniferous,* trees have narrow, pointed leaves and stay green the year around. This classification system does not indicate the hardness of wood, because various softwoods are harder than some hardwoods. However, the two types of wood have other characteristics that are important to the woodworker.

Hardwoods have beautiful grain patterns and can be used to make fine furniture. Some hardwoods have large pores and must be treated with a paste or liquid called *filler* before being covered with a finish. Wood to be finished with paint does not need a fancy grain to be attractive because the paint covers the pattern. Hardwoods used in woodworking include birch, mahogany, maple, oak, and walnut.

Most softwoods can easily be sawed, planed, chiseled, or bored. They are used mainly for structural work, but such softwoods as Douglas fir, ponderosa pine, redcedar, and white pine can be used for woodworking and furniture.

Hardwood or softwood can also be used to make a type of manufactured board called *plywood.* Plywood consists of an odd number of thin layers of wood glued together. This type of board is lightweight and strong and can be purchased in many sizes and wood patterns.

Alva H. Jared

See also **Plywood; Saw; Wood; Woodcarving.**

Additional resources

Level I
Chambers, Catherine. *Wood.* Raintree Steck-Vaughn, 1996.
McGuire, Kevin. *Woodworking for Kids.* Sterling Pub., 1993.

Level II
The Complete Book of Woodworking. Landauer Bks., 2002.
Guidice, Anthony. *The Seven Essentials of Woodworking.* Sterling Pub., 2001.
Salaman, R. A. *Dictionary of Woodworking Tools.* Rev. ed. Ed. by Philip Walker. 1990. Reprint. Astragal Pr., 1997.
Stankus, Bill. *How to Design and Build Your Ideal Woodshop.* Rev. ed. Popular Woodworking Bks., 2001.

Woody nightshade. See Bittersweet.
Woof. See Weaving.

Grant Heilman

Sheep shearers use power clippers to remove a fleece. An expert shearer can clip 200 or more sheep a day. In most parts of the world, sheep are sheared once a year.

Wool is a fiber that comes from the fleece of sheep and some other animals. It makes durable fabrics used in manufacturing blankets, clothing, rugs, and other items. Wool fabrics clean easily, and they resist wrinkles and hold their shape well. Wool also absorbs moisture and insulates against both cold and heat. All these features make wool popular for coats, sweaters, gloves, socks, and other clothing.

Wool fibers are nearly cylindrical in shape. Overlapping scales on the surface make the fibers mat and interlock under heat, moisture, and pressure. This property of wool fibers is called *felting*. Felting increases the strength and durability of wool fabrics. It also enables wool to be made into felt. See **Fiber** (picture: Wool and nylon fibers).

The guidelines of the United States Federal Trade Commission (FTC) define wool as the fiber from the fleece of sheep. Wool also includes such fibers as alpaca, from alpacas; camel's hair; cashmere, from Cashmere goats; mohair, from Angora goats; and vicuña, from vicuñas.

Worldwide production of raw wool totals about 5 billion pounds (2.3 billion kilograms) annually. The leading wool-producing nation is Australia. Every state in the United States produces some wool. Texas ranks as the leading producer.

Sources of wool. Almost all wool comes from sheep. These animals—and their wool—are classified into five groups, depending on the quality of the fleece. The five classifications of wool, listed here in order of quality, are (1) fine wool, (2) crossbred wool, (3) medium wool, (4) long wool, and (5) coarse wool, or carpet wool.

Fine-wooled sheep include the Merino and breeds with Merino ancestry, such as the Debouillet and the Rambouillet. These types of sheep produce the finest wool, which makes high-quality clothing.

Crossbred-wooled sheep, such as the Columbia and Corriedale, are crossbreeds of fine- and long-wooled breeds. Their wool is used for rugged clothing.

Medium-wooled sheep provide wool used in making industrial and upholstery fabrics. Cheviot, Dorset, Hampshire, Oxford, Polypay, Shropshire, Southdown, and Suffolk sheep are in this group.

Long-wooled sheep include the Cotswold, Leicester, Lincoln, and Romney. They produce wool used for carpets and industrial fabrics.

Coarse-wooled sheep include the Karakul and Scottish Blackface. The wool of these animals is used mostly for carpets and handicraft yarns.

Types of wool are determined by the quality of a sheep's fleece. The quality depends on the age and physical condition of the animal and by the climate in which it lives. An oily substance called *yolk* covers the fleece of a healthy sheep. Yolk consists of wool grease and *suint* (dried perspiration). It protects the sheep from rain and keeps the fleece from becoming matted.

Young sheep produce the best wool. The softest and finest wool, called *lamb's wool,* comes from 6- to 12-month-old sheep.

Sheep that have been slaughtered for their meat provide *pulled wool,* sometimes called *skin wool* or *slipe wool. Dead wool* comes from sheep that have died or are seriously ill. Fleeces soiled by manure or dirt are called *tag locks* in the United States and *stain pieces* in England and Australia.

In the United States, FTC guidelines classify wool into two categories. *Virgin wool,* also called *new wool,* has never been spun into yarn or made into felt. Some fabrics are made of fibers that have been reclaimed from previously spun or woven wool. *Recycled wool* is the name given to these products. Fabrics made from recy-

Leading wool-producing countries

Wool clipped from sheep in a year	
Australia	●●●●●●●●●●●● 1,512,400,000 pounds (686,000,000 kilograms)
China	●●●●●◖ 634,300,000 pounds (287,700,000 kilograms)
New Zealand	●●●●◖ 565,100,000 pounds (256,300,000 kilograms)
Iran	●◖ 162,900,000 pounds (73,900,000 kilograms)
United Kingdom	●◖ 142,600,000 pounds (64,700,000 kilograms)
Argentina	●◖ 133,000,000 pounds (60,300,000 kilograms)
Uruguay	● 122,100,000 pounds (55,400,000 kilograms)
South Africa	● 118,600,000 pounds (53,800,000 kilograms)
India	◖ 101,400,000 pounds (46,000,000 kilograms)
Sudan	◖ 100,300,000 pounds (45,500,000 kilograms)

Figures are for a three-year average, 1999-2001.
Source: Food and Agriculture Organization of the United Nations.

cled wool are sometimes called *shoddy.*

Processing of wool involves four major steps: (1) shearing, (2) sorting and grading, (3) making yarn, and (4) making fabric.

Shearing. Most sheep shearers use power shears, and experts can clip 100 or more animals a day. They remove the fleece in one piece so the various parts can be easily identified for sorting and grading. Different parts of a fleece vary in quality. For example, the best wool comes from the shoulders and sides of the sheep, while the poorest comes from the belly areas.

During the 1990's, researchers in Australia began to use a process that eliminates much of the hard work involved in shearing and produces higher quality wool. The process, known commercially as Bioclip, involves injecting sheep with a protein that causes them to naturally shed their fleece. This process must be further refined before it can gain widespread use.

In most parts of the world, sheep ranchers shear their animals once a year, in spring or early summer. But in some regions, the fleeces may be cut off twice yearly, with the second shearing occurring in the autumn.

Sorting and grading. Workers remove any stained, damaged, or inferior wool from each fleece and sort the rest of the wool according to the quality of the fibers. Wool fibers are judged not only on the basis of their strength, but also by their (1) *fineness* (diameter), (2) *length,* (3) *crimp* (waviness), and (4) color.

There are three ways to grade wool. The *blood* method involves comparing the fineness of the wool fibers with the fineness of Merino wool. The *count* method involves counting the number of *hanks*—that is, 560 yard (512 meter) lengths of worsted yarn—that can be spun from one pound of wool fiber. The most precise method involves measuring the fiber diameter in units called *microns.* A micron equals 0.001 millimeter ($\frac{1}{25,400}$ inch).

Fiber length is important in determining what processes will be used to make yarn and fabric. *Carding length fibers,* also called *clothing length fibers,* measure less than $1\frac{1}{2}$ inches (3.8 centimeters) long. *French combing length fibers* range from $1\frac{1}{2}$ to $2\frac{1}{2}$ inches (3.8 to 6.4 centimeters) in length. *Combing length fibers* are more than $2\frac{1}{2}$ inches (6.4 centimeters) long.

The natural crimp of wool provides the fibers with elasticity. This property enables wool fabrics to hold their shape after being stretched or twisted. The best wool fibers have many evenly spaced waves.

Most wool ranges in color from white to dark ivory. White wool is the most desirable because manufacturers may have to bleach darker wool before dying it.

Making yarn. Woolen mills scour the wool with detergents to remove the yolk and such impurities as dust and sand. Wool grease from the yolk is processed into lanolin, a substance used in hand creams and cosmetics.

After the wool dries, machines *card* it. This process involves passing the wool through rollers with thin wire teeth. The teeth untangle the fibers and arrange them into a flat sheet called a *web.* The carding machines then form the web into narrow ropes known as *slivers.*

After carding, the processes used in making yarn vary slightly, depending on the length of the fibers. Carding length fibers are used to make *woolen yarn.* Combing length and French combing length fibers are made into *worsted yarn.* The processes used for the two kinds of yarn are similar. But worsted slivers go through an additional step called *combing,* which removes impurities and short fibers.

After carding or combing, machines stretch and slightly twist the slivers to form thinner strands called *rovings.* Spinning machines then twist the rovings into yarn. Woolen yarn is bulky and fuzzy, with fibers that lie in different directions. Worsted yarn is smooth and

Burlington Industries, Inc.

Making wool yarn involves several steps. Carding machines, *left,* untangle the fibers and arrange them into a sheet called a *web.* Webs are formed into narrow ropes called *slivers, center.* Slivers are stretched into thinner strands, and spinning machines twist them into yarn, *right.*

Burlington Industries, Inc.

Wool fabrics are woven by large power looms, *shown here.* After a fabric has been made, it goes through various finishing processes to give it the desired appearance and strength.

highly twisted, and its fibers lie parallel.

Making fabric. Wool manufacturers knit or weave yarn into a variety of fabrics. They use woolen yarns in making flannel, homespun, melton, Saxony, Shetland, and tweed fabrics. Worsted yarns make such fabrics as broadcloth, crepe, gabardine, serge, sharkskin, twill, and whipcord. Almost all wool fabrics except felt are made from yarn (see **Felt**).

Wool may be dyed at various stages of the manufacturing process. Dyeing that takes place before the fibers are spun is called *stock dyeing* or *top dyeing.* Dyeing that occurs after the fibers have been spun into yarn is called *yarn dyeing, package dyeing,* or *skein dyeing.* If the dyeing takes place after the fabric has been woven, it is known as *piece dyeing.* Most fabrics with fancy designs are stock dyed or yarn dyed. Piece dyeing is used for solid-colored fabrics. See **Dye**.

All wool fabrics undergo finishing processes to give them the desired appearance and feel. The finishing of fabrics made of woolen yarn begins with *fulling.* This process involves wetting the fabric thoroughly with water and then passing it through rollers. Fulling makes the fibers interlock and mat together. It shrinks the material and gives it additional strength and thickness. Worsteds go through a process called *crabbing,* in which the fabric passes through boiling water and then cold water. This procedure strengthens the fabric.

Some wool fabrics tend to shrink when dry-cleaned. To prevent such shrinkage, some manufacturers preshrink the fabric. One popular process, called London Shrinking, uses water and pressure to shrink the fabric. After the various finishing processes, manufacturers cut

and sew the fabric into clothing and other products.

History. About 10,000 years ago, people in central Asia began to raise sheep for food and clothing. The art of spinning wool into yarn developed about 4000 B.C. and encouraged trade among the nations in the region of the Mediterranean Sea.

The first wool factory in England was established about A.D. 50 in Winchester by the Romans. The wool industry soon played a major part in England's economy. By 1660, the export of wool fabrics accounted for about two-thirds of England's foreign trade.

Merino sheep originated in Spain. In the early 1500's, explorers from Spain brought sheep to what is now the United States. England discouraged the wool industry's growth in the American Colonies so that the colonists would have to rely on English goods. But colonists smuggled sheep from England. By the 1700's, spinning and weaving were flourishing in the United States. The British began breeding Merinos in the late 1700's. In 1797, they brought 13 Merinos to Australia and started that country's Merino sheep industry.

In the 1800's, many pioneers brought sheep with them while traveling to the western United States. As a result, the production of wool and wool fabrics spread to nearly all parts of the United States.   John Carlson

Related articles in *World Book* include:

Alpaca
Camel
Cashmere
Cashmere goat
Goat
Guanaco
Lanolin
Llama
Mohair
Sheep
Vicuña
Weaving

Woolf, Virginia (1882-1941), was a major British novelist, critic, and essayist. She was a leading figure in the literary movement called *Modernism.* Woolf used a literary technique called *stream of consciousness* to reveal her characters' inner lives and to criticize the social system of the day. See **Novel** (New directions in the novel).

Woolf's most famous novel, *To the Lighthouse* (1927), examines the life of an upper-middle class British family. It shows the fragility of human relationships and the collapse of social values. The portrait of Mr. Ramsay in this novel may resemble Woolf's father, critic Leslie Stephen.

Woolf's other fiction includes the novels *Jacob's Room* (1922) and *Mrs. Dalloway* (1925), in which she studies the world of characters tragically affected by World War I. *Orlando* (1928) and *Flush* (1933) are fanciful biographies. In *The Waves* (1931), interior monologues reveal the personalities of the six central characters. Unlike other modernists, whose politics were right-wing and often profascist, Woolf was a feminist, socialist, and pacifist. She expressed her theories in the essays *A Room of One's Own* (1929) and *Three Guineas* (1938). Woolf's last novels, *The Years* (1939) and *Between the Acts* (1941), are as experimental as her earlier work.

Virginia Stephen was born in London. In 1912, she married editor and writer Leonard Woolf. She was part of the Bloomsbury Group, an informal group of intellectuals (see **Bloomsbury Group**). With her husband, she founded the Hogarth Press, which published works of noted modern writers. Her reputation has soared with the publication of several volumes of letters and diaries and her critical essays. Jane Marcus

Woolley, Sir Leonard (1880-1960), was a British archaeologist. He became known for his discoveries at Ur, a city in ancient Sumer (now part of Iraq). His findings revealed achievements of the Sumerians, who created one of the earliest civilizations over 5,000 years ago.

Between 1922 and 1934, Woolley directed excavations at Ur. He discovered geological evidence for a great flood, possibly the Flood described in the Bible. He also uncovered the royal cemetery, whose tombs contained bodies buried with objects made of precious metals.

Woolley, whose full name was Charles Leonard Woolley, was born in London and graduated from Oxford University. He led excavations in Britain, Italy, Turkey, Syria, and Iraq. He wrote more than 25 books, including *Spadework: Adventures in Archaeology* (1953) and *Excavations at Ur: A Record of 12 Years' Work* (1954). He was knighted in 1935. Richard G. Klein

Woolley, Mary Emma (1863-1947), was an outstanding American educator. She served as president of Mount Holyoke College from 1901 to 1937 and was president of the American Association of University Women from 1927 to 1933. Woolley was also active in world peace movements and public affairs. In 1932, she became the first woman to represent the United States at an international disarmament conference. Woolley was born in Norwalk, Connecticut. Albert E. Van Dusen

Woolly monkey is a type of large monkey that lives in the Amazon River Basin of South America. There are two species—the *common woolly monkey,* also called *Humboldt's woolly monkey,* and the *yellow-tailed woolly monkey.*

Woolly monkeys have thick, soft, dark fur. They live in groups of about 12 animals. They move through the trees, feeding mostly on fruit. Woolly monkeys spend most of their time sleeping, but they are playful when awake. They are known to greet each other by "kissing."

Adult woolly monkeys weigh from 10 to 20 pounds (4.5 to 9 kilograms). They measure 15 to 23 inches (38 to 58 centimeters) long, not including their 22- to 27-inch-(56- to 69-centimeter-) long tail, which can be used to grasp objects. The underside of the tail has no fur near the end. This area has ridges similar to human fingerprints and rough skin.

Woolly monkeys are threatened by the destruction of their rain forest home and by hunters who kill them for their meat. The yellow-tailed woolly monkey is extremely rare. Roderic B. Mast and Russell A. Mittermeier

Scientific classification. Woolly monkeys belong to the New World monkey family, Cebidae. The common woolly monkey is *Lagothrix lagothricha,* and the yellow-tailed is *L. flavicauda.*

See also **Monkey** (pictures).

Woollybear is a common name for the caterpillar stage of several species of tiger moths. Woollybears have a dense, stiff, hairlike coat. In North America, the most familiar of these caterpillars is the *banded woollybear,* the larva of the Isabella moth.

The banded woollybear is black on both ends and has a reddish-brown band around the middle. It feeds on plants and grows to about $1\frac{1}{2}$ inches (4 centimeters) in length. In autumn, the fully grown caterpillar finds a

E. R. Degginger, Color-Pic, Inc.

A woollybear has a dense coat of stiff hair.

sheltered spot, such as under bark or leaves. It remains there inactive during winter. In spring, it spins a loose cocoon of silk and hairlike parts around itself. An adult moth emerges from the cocoon after 3 to 4 weeks.

According to folklore, the coat of the banded woollybear can help forecast the severity of the coming winter. A narrow reddish-brown band on the coat is said to indicate a milder winter than a wide band. Scientists believe that the differences in the widths are related to current temperature and moisture conditions rather than to the outlook for cold weather. John R. Meyer

Scientific classification. Woollybears are in the tiger moth family, Arctiidae. The scientific name for the banded woollybear is *Pyrrharctia isabella.*

Woolrich, Cornell (1903-1968), was an American author of suspense fiction. Woolrich was known more for style, atmosphere, and breathless pace than for consistent and believable plots. He specialized in devices such as the race against time and situations in which a character mysteriously vanishes. His tales were made more suspenseful because the reader was never sure whether they would end happily.

Woolrich's best-known novels include *The Bride Wore Black* (1940), *The Black Curtain* (1941), *Black Alibi* (1942), and *The Black Path of Fear* (1944). One of his many short stories was adapted into the famous Alfred Hitchcock motion picture *Rear Window* (1954). Woolrich also wrote several books under the name William Irish, notably *Phantom Lady* (1942).

Woolrich was born in New York City. His full name was Cornell George Hopley-Woolrich. He began his literary career in the 1920's writing Jazz Age novels influenced by Amerian author F. Scott Fitzgerald. In the 1930's, Woolrich turned to writing crime fiction for *Black Mask* and other magazines that specialized in this type of writing. Woolrich was a solitary person who lived with his mother in residential hotels most of his life. Jon L Breen

Woolman, John (1720-1772), was a colonial American writer and Quaker minister. He worked to abolish slavery, relieve poverty, obtain better treatment for Indians, and end war.

Woolman was born on a farm near what is now Rancocas, New Jersey. He worked as a clerk until he was 22 years old, when he became a minister and a tailor. Woolman preached while traveling on foot from New England to North Carolina. He convinced Philadelphia Quakers at their yearly meeting in 1758 to resolve not to keep or deal in slaves. This resolution was the first of its kind in the American Colonies.

When he was about 36 years old, Woolman began to

write an account of his life and religious beliefs. His *Journal,* published in 1774, is noted for its sensitive descriptions of his feelings. Woolman also wrote essays condemning slavery and calling for better conditions for the poor. Edward W. Clark

Woolworth is the family name of two American businessmen who were brothers.

Frank Winfield Woolworth (1852-1919) was the principal founder in 1912 of the F. W. Woolworth Company, a chain of five-and-ten-cent stores. When he died, the chain had more than 1,000 stores. In 1913, he built the Woolworth Building in New York City. It was the tallest building in the world at that time.

Woolworth was born on April 13, 1852, in Rodman, New York, and he clerked in the village grocery store there. In 1878, while working for the firm of Moore & Smith in Watertown, New York, he suggested putting slow-moving goods on a counter and selling them for 5 cents. The venture was so successful that it was continued with new goods. Six store chains grew out of the 5-cent counter experiment. All of the chains were united in 1912 to form the F. W. Woolworth Company.

Charles S. Woolworth (1856-1947) was cofounder of the F. W. Woolworth Company. He served as vice president until 1919 and as chairman of the board until 1944, when he retired. He was born on Aug. 1, 1856, in Rodman, New York. Woolworth founded 15 stores, which he and his brother united with 581 other stores in 1912 to form the F. W. Woolworth Company. W. H. Baughn

Worcester, *WUS tuhr* (pop. 172,648; met. area pop. 511,389), is a leading New England industrial center and the second largest city of Massachusetts. Only Boston has more people. Worcester lies in central Massachusetts, about 40 miles (64 kilometers) west of Boston. For location, see **Massachusetts** (political map).

In 1673, settlers from eastern Massachusetts founded the village of Quinsigamond on the site of Worcester. In 1684, King Charles II of England canceled the Massachusetts Bay Colony's charter. This action so angered the people of Quinsigamond that they renamed their village Worcester. According to tradition, this name honored the Battle of Worcester (1651), in which Charles suffered a great defeat against England's Parliamentary leader Oliver Cromwell.

Worcester, the county seat of Worcester County, covers 38 square miles (98 square kilometers). Its manufacturing plants produce fabricated metals; printed materials; and chemicals, plastics, and abrasives. Worcester has several medical centers, which employ many of the city's people. It is the site of the Massachusetts Biotechnology Research Park, where many biotechnology companies have facilities. Airlines, railroad freight lines, and passenger trains serve the city.

The College of the Holy Cross, the oldest Roman Catholic college in New England, was founded in Worcester in 1843. The city is also the home of Assumption College, Clark University, Worcester Polytechnic Institute, Worcester State College, and the University of Massachusetts Medical School.

The Worcester Art Museum is known for its art objects from many periods of history. The John Woodman Higgins Armory Museum has an outstanding display of medieval and Renaissance armor. The American Antiquarian Society owns the largest collection of early American publications, including newspapers, sheet music, and children's books. The Ecotarium includes Gage Planetarium and a science museum and zoo. Also in Worcester are Mechanics Hall, the site of many cultural events; Centrum Civic Center; Worcester Convention Center; and Worcester Center, a three-level shopping complex.

Nipmuc Indians lived near the site of Worcester before white people built a village there in 1673. Indians destroyed that settlement and another one that was built in 1684. The whites settled Worcester permanently in 1713 and incorporated the settlement as a town in 1722. During the Revolutionary War in America (1775-1783), Worcester became the home of the *Massachusetts Spy,* a newspaper that became famous for its support of the colonists.

Manufacturing became important in Worcester after 1828, when the Blackstone Canal linked the town with Narragansett Bay, an arm of the Atlantic Ocean. Worcester received a city charter in 1848. Through the years, the growing number of industrial jobs in Worcester attracted thousands of immigrants.

The city's population reached a peak of 203,486 in 1950. During the last half of the 1900's, many middle-income families left Worcester and moved to the suburbs. Worcester has a council-manager form of government. Laurence A. Lewis

Word processing is the use of computers to type, edit, and print letters, reports, articles, and other documents. It has replaced typewriting for many tasks at home, in school, and in the office. Business people, authors, students, and lawyers turn to word processing as a tool for writing.

Two main types of equipment are used for word processing: (1) personal computers and (2) electronic typewriters. Personal computers need special instructions called *programs* or *software* to perform word processing. Electronic typewriters resemble electric typewriters but include a built-in specialized computer. This computer provides limited word processing capabilities, such as the ability to store and automatically type a small amount of text.

Personal computers display characters on a computer screen as the user types them. Words, lines, paragraphs, and pages can be added, deleted, moved, or copied with a few keystrokes or the click of a button on a *mouse* or some other handheld input device. Most word-processing programs enable the user to check for spelling errors. Many can check grammar in a limited way. Most can also sort and merge lists and perform limited mathematical computations. At the touch of a key, the user can print out an entire document. The computer can store documents on magnetic disks or other storage devices, so additional corrections or copies can easily be made later.

Personal computers are more powerful than electronic typewriters. They can also be programmed to do many things besides word processing. For example, a personal computer can exchange information with other computers over a network. But personal computers are generally more expensive than electronic typewriters.

Electronic typewriters can perform only the most basic word-processing functions, such as inserting, deleting, and underlining text. Most can also check for spelling errors. On many electronic typewriters, a small screen displays material as it is typed. Many electronic typewriters have a memory, but the amount of text it can store is much smaller than that which a personal computer can store.

History. In the mid-1970's, computer companies introduced *dedicated word processors,* relatively expensive computers that mainly performed word processing. In the 1980's, more versatile personal computers—and word processing programs for those computers—became common. Today, personal computers are the most widely used form of word processor.   M. David Stone

See also **Computer** (Applications software); **Desktop publishing; Office work** (Recording information); **Printer.**

Worden, Alfred Merrill (1932-   ), a United States astronaut, was the command module pilot on the Apollo 15 mission. The Apollo 15 mission was the first moon trip that was devoted primarily to scientific exploration.

During the Apollo 15 mission, from July 26 to Aug. 7, 1971, Worden orbited the moon in the command module Endeavour for six days. He took photographs, operated recording instruments, and launched an 80-pound (36-kilogram) subsatellite into lunar orbit. While Worden orbited the moon, astronauts David R. Scott and James B. Irwin explored the moon. During the return to Earth, Worden left the spacecraft for 20 minutes and took the first "walk" in deep space.

Worden was born on Feb. 2, 1932, in Jackson, Michigan. He entered the Air Force after graduating from the United States Military Academy in 1955. Worden was an astronaut from 1966 until 1972, when he took an administrative job in the space program.   James R. Hansen

Words. See Dictionary; Etymology; Language; Pronunciation; Semantics; Slang; Spelling; Vocabulary.

Wordsworth, William (1770-1850), is considered by many scholars to be the most important English Romantic poet. In 1795, Wordsworth met Samuel Taylor Coleridge. The two men collaborated on *Lyrical Ballads* (1798), a collection of poems frequently regarded as the symbolic beginning of the English Romantic movement. Wordsworth wrote most of the poems in the book. See **Romanticism.**

In the preface to the second edition of *Lyrical Ballads* (1800), Wordsworth outlined ideas about poetry that have since been identified with Romanticism. He argued that serious poems could describe "situations from common life" and be written in the ordinary language "really used by men." He believed such poems could clarify "the primary laws of our nature." Wordsworth also insisted that poetry is "emotion recollected in tranquility" and that a poet is "a man speaking to men," different from his fellows only in the degree of his sensitivity but not in any essential way.

Wordsworth has frequently been praised for his descriptions of nature. However, he rightly claimed that his primary interest was the "mind of man." In fact, a key section of his poem *The Prelude: or, Growth of a Poet's Mind* insists that love of nature leads to the love of humanity. His finest poems, including the "Lucy" lyrics (1798-1799), "Michael" (1800), "Resolution and Independence" (1802), and "The Solitary Reaper" (1807), dramatize how imagination creates spiritual values out of the memory of sights and sounds in nature.

Early life. Wordsworth was born on April 7, 1770, in Cockermouth, which is now in the county of Cumbria. His mother died in 1778, his father in 1783. Relatives provided for his education. Wordsworth entered Cambridge University in 1787, the year he wrote his first significant poem. During a summer vacation in 1790, he visited France, then in turmoil because of the French Revolution. After graduating from Cambridge in 1791, Wordsworth returned to France and became a supporter of the revolution. He returned to England in December 1792.

Although liberal in his youth, Wordsworth later became politically and religiously conservative. As a result, he was severely criticized by the English poets Lord Byron and Robert Browning and others as a traitor to his own youthful principles. Wordsworth was appointed poet laureate in 1843.

Later career. Wordsworth married Mary Hutchinson in 1802. They had five children. Wordsworth was deeply saddened by the drowning death of his brother John in 1805. His sadness was reflected in his poem "Elegiac Stanzas Suggested by a Picture of Peele Castle" (1806). This poem may have marked the end of Wordsworth's youthful creative period. It seems to reject his early optimistic belief, stated in "Tintern Abbey," that "nature never did betray the heart that loved her." In 1807, Wordsworth completed one of the most famous poems in English literature, "Ode: Intimations of Immortality." In this piece, Wordsworth praised childhood and urged individuals to rely on intuition.

Wordsworth's masterpiece is his long autobiographical poem, *The Prelude.* He wrote it between 1798 and 1805, but he continued to revise it for the rest of his life. The poem was published in 1850, shortly after his death on April 23 of that year. The revisions that Wordsworth made in *The Prelude* between 1805 and 1850 clearly indicate how his values changed as he aged. In its best passages, *The Prelude* achieves a remarkable combination of simplicity and grandeur.

Wordsworth wrote most of his best poetry before 1807. But he wrote several important works, notably *The Excursion* (1814), later. This long poem discusses virtue, education, and religious faith. Wordsworth also wrote 523 sonnets, many of which compare with those of the great English sonnet writers William Shakespeare and John Milton.   Frederick W. Shilstone

See also **Bryant, William Cullen; Coleridge, Samuel Taylor; Lake Poets; Poetry** (Rhythm and meter); **Romanticism.**

Additional resources

Gill, Stephen C. *William Wordsworth.* Oxford, 1989. *Wordsworth and the Victorians.* 1998. Reprint. 2001.
Johnston, Kenneth R. *The Hidden Wordsworth.* 1998. Reprint. Norton, 2001.
Noyes, Russell. *William Wordsworth.* Rev. ed. Twayne, 1991.

Work, in physics, is a result of a force moving an object through a distance against a resistance. Work is always done by some agent, such as a person or a machine. This agent produces the force that causes the movement.

Two factors determine the amount of work done. One factor is the amount of force applied. The other is the distance the object moves. In physics, work occurs only when the force is sufficient to move the object. In other words, work is a measure of what is done, not the effort applied in attempting to move the object. People do work when lifting, pushing, or sliding an object from one place to another. They do no work when holding an object without moving it, even though they may become tired. People also can do work when rotating an object. For example, a person who unscrews the lid of a milk jug does work. In this case, the resistance is the force of friction that the screw threads of the jug exert against the lid.

Scientists and engineers measure work in units that represent the measurement of both force and distance. In the inch-pound system of measurement customarily used in the United States, the *foot-pound* is the most commonly used unit of work. One foot-pound equals the work done when a force of 1 pound moves something a distance of 1 foot. So if a 50-pound object is lifted 4 feet, the work done is 200 foot-pounds. If a 4-pound object is lifted 50 feet, the work done is also 200 foot-pounds.

In the metric system, the unit of work is the *joule*. One joule is the amount of work done when a force of 1 *newton* moves something a distance of 1 meter (see **Newton**). Thus, 1 joule equals 1 *newton-meter*. One foot-pound equals 1.356 joules.

The calculation of work done during rotation is more complicated. However, this kind of calculation uses the same principles used to compute the amount of work done when an object is moved in a straight line.

The units used to measure work are also used to measure energy. Energy is the ability of something to do work (see **Energy**). The rate at which work is done is called *power*. In measuring power, the amount of time needed to do the work is considered along with force and distance. Power is measured in a unit called the *watt*. One watt equals one joule per second. See **Power; Watt.**   Gregory Benford

See also **Foot-pound; Joule; Thermodynamics.**

Workers' compensation is an insurance program that provides pay and medical help for workers who are injured on the job or become ill because of work conditions. Workers' compensation also provides benefits to the dependents of such workers in cases where death occurs. Loss of income due to accidents on the job has been a major problem of workers since the introduction of machine methods to industry. Today, most industrialized countries have laws or private programs for workers' compensation.

In the United States, almost all states require employers to provide workers' compensation coverage for employees. Federal laws provide such coverage for employees of the federal government and certain other workers.

Injured workers normally receive about two-thirds of their salary while disabled. However, most states limit the size of cash payments to any individual. Medical benefits are unlimited. Most states provide training in new jobs for workers who cannot continue in their old work because of injuries. Some states limit workers' compensation coverage for farm and domestic workers as well as for workers employed in small businesses. In most states, employers pay the full cost of workers' compensation benefits through taxes or insurance premiums. In a few states, such costs are financed with money from the state's general fund.

Each state administers its own compensation program, but the level of state agency involvement varies considerably among the states. Federal compensation programs are administered by the Office of Workers' Compensation Programs in the Department of Labor.

Employers' liability laws preceded workers' compensation laws. They made an employer responsible for injuries to workers caused by defective machinery or by negligence on the part of management. In 1880, Britain adopted one of the first such laws.

The first workers' compensation laws were passed in Germany in 1883. Austria passed similar laws in 1887. Norway, Finland, France, Denmark, and Britain passed such laws in the 1890's. During the early 1900's, most other European nations passed workers' compensation laws.

In the United States, Maryland passed the first state compensation law in 1902. But the U.S. Supreme Court declared the Maryland law and other compensation acts of that decade unconstitutional. The growth of workers' compensation coverage increased greatly after Congress passed the Federal Employees' Compensation Act of 1916. This law provided benefits for certain federal civilian workers, or their survivors, in connection with injuries or death on the job.

Ten states passed workers' compensation laws in 1911. Wisconsin was the first. In 1948, the last of the then 48 states enacted a workers' compensation program. Alaska and Hawaii had such laws when they became states in 1959. In several states, however, workers' compensation coverage by employers is voluntary. Average companies spend about an amount equal to about 2 percent of their payroll on workers' compensation protection.   Paul L. Burgess

Works Progress Administration, also called the WPA, was a United States government agency created in 1935 to provide paying jobs for unemployed workers. Most of these workers had lost their jobs during the *Great Depression,* a worldwide economic slump that began in 1929. The WPA was part of the *New Deal,* President Franklin D. Roosevelt's program of economic recovery during the depression. In 1939, the WPA was renamed the Work Projects Administration. Before the WPA was disbanded in 1943, it had provided some employment for about $8\frac{1}{2}$ million people.

Many WPA projects involved construction work. The agency hired workers to build roads, bridges, parks, airport runways, public swimming pools, and county fairgrounds. Most of these workers were men who were the sole wage earners in their families.

The WPA also created jobs in the arts. The agency hired actors, artists, musicians, and writers to produce stage plays, concerts, paintings, and post office murals. WPA writers created a series of books that recorded the histories of hundreds of American communities. Some WPA writers interviewed former black American slaves to record their memories.

Critics of the WPA charged that many of its projects involved work that did not really need to be done. But Roosevelt and his administrators believed that offering unemployed workers jobs and wages was better for the workers' morale than was simply giving them welfare checks.   William W. Bremer

The world—the planet Earth—is home to a great variety of peoples and nations. The land masses in this photo of Earth taken from outer space include Africa, the Arabian Peninsula, and Antarctica.

World

World is the planet Earth viewed especially as the home of human beings and other living things. Earth is just one of countless heavenly bodies in the universe. However, it is the only one known to support life.

People have always adapted to and modified their cultural and physical environments. Some human beings live with low levels of technology. They hunt wild animals and gather native plant products for food. They make clothing from hides or furs and build shelters with such resources as branches and other natural materials. Others cultivate plants and animals for food. Those who farm usually settle in one place and produce enough food to feed many others, thus supporting the emergence of villages, towns, and cities whose occupants must learn to live together peaceably. The growth of urban centers makes necessary the development of new occupations and forms of government.

Over time, people have achieved advanced levels of technology and complex forms of social organization. They have built thriving cities, developed great civilizations, and discovered ways to control and modify some forces of nature.

David Clawson, the contributor for this article, is Professor of Geography at the University of New Orleans in Louisiana.

The world's surface consists of water and land. Air surrounds the surface and extends far above it. Water—chiefly the oceans—covers 71 percent of the world's surface. All living things must have water to live, just as they must have air. People also use water for industry, irrigation, power, and transportation. In addition, the lakes,

Interesting facts about the world

Area of the world's surface is about 196,900,000 square miles (510,000,000 square kilometers).

Population of the world in 2004 totaled about 6,350,500,000.

Largest continent is Asia, which covers about 17,028,000 square miles (44,103,000 square kilometers).

Smallest continent is Australia, excluding the Pacific Islands, which covers about 2,989,000 square miles (7,741,000 square kilometers).

Largest country is Russia, which covers 6,592,850 square miles (17,075,400 square kilometers).

Smallest country is Vatican City. It has an area of only $\frac{1}{6}$ square mile (0.4 square kilometer).

Most populous country is China, which had approximately 1,319,377,000 people in 2004.

Least populous country, Vatican City, had only about 1,000 citizens in 2004.

Highest point in the world, Mount Everest in Asia, rises 29,035 feet (8,850 meters) above sea level.

Lowest point on land is the shore of the Dead Sea in Asia. It lies 1,310 feet (399 meters) below sea level.

Deepest point in the world's oceans is Challenger Deep, 35,840 feet (10,924 meters) below the surface of the Pacific Ocean southwest of Guam in the Mariana Trench.

oceans, and rivers provide fish and other foods.

The oceans separate huge land masses called *continents*. Most of the world's countries lie on the continents. Others are on islands. Each country has its own political and economic systems. However, countries cooperate with one another in many ways. For example, they make trade agreements and sign treaties intended to reduce the likelihood of war.

The physical features of a country strongly influence where the people of that country live. People can most easily grow food on plains or in river valleys, where much of the soil is rich and deep. Mountainous regions generally are less suitable for crop farming because the soil is thin and easily washed away by rainfall. Many of the world's biggest cities began as trading centers on lakeshores, riverbanks, and seacoasts. Thus, the majority of people live on flat, fertile plains and in large cities that border major water transportation routes.

More than 6 billion people live in the world. They are distributed unevenly over the land. Many areas are heavily populated. Other areas have no people at all. The population is increasing far more rapidly in some countries than in others.

All human beings belong to the same species, *Homo sapiens,* which means they have a common ancestry. But many groups of people have lived apart for so long that they have developed physical variations.

In the past, scholars used physical variations to classify people into races. The members of one race were thought to resemble one another more than they resembled the members of other races. Today, most *anthropologists* (scientists who study human beings) reject the idea that human beings can be biologically classified into races. However, people in numerous societies continue to view themselves and others as members of various races. See **Races, Human.**

Physical differences among people have often been confused with cultural differences, such as differences in language or religion. Physical and cultural differences have been a basis of discrimination and prejudice. At times, these differences have served as an excuse for slavery, violence, and war.

This article provides an overview of the world as the home of human beings. It briefly describes the world's nations, people, and surface features. For information on the world as a planet, see **Earth.** For the story of human history and progress, see **World, History of the.**

Nations of the world

The world has 193 independent countries and more than 40 dependencies. An independent country controls its own affairs. Dependencies are controlled in some way by independent countries. In most cases, an independent country is responsible for the dependency's foreign relations and defense, and some of the dependency's local affairs. However, many dependencies have complete control of their local affairs. Almost all of the world's people live in independent countries. Only about 12 million people live in dependencies.

The world's largest nation in area is Russia. It covers 6,592,850 square miles (17,075,400 square kilometers). The next four largest nations, in descending order, are Canada, China, the United States, and Brazil—and each covers more than 3 million square miles (8 million

square kilometers). Vatican City is the smallest independent country in the world, followed by Monaco, Nauru, Tuvalu, and San Marino. Each of these countries covers less than 25 square miles (65 square kilometers). Vatican City has an area of only $\frac{1}{6}$ square mile (0.4 square kilometer).

Throughout history, the political map of the world has changed repeatedly. The most important changes have resulted from major wars. During ancient times, such military leaders as Alexander the Great and Julius Caesar conquered many groups of people and established vast empires. Numerous empires rose and fell later in history, and boundaries changed again and again.

Beginning about 1500, many European nations established colonies in North America, South America, Asia, Africa, and Australia. Most national boundaries established by the ruling countries remained after the colonies gained their independence.

World War I (1914-1918) and World War II (1939-1945) resulted in many important changes on the world map. World War I led to the formation of a number of new nations in Europe, including Austria, Czechoslovakia, Hungary, and Yugoslavia. After World War II, several nations gained or lost territory. In addition, many new nations were established in Asia. In Africa, an independence movement swept the continent. More than 45 African colonies gained their independence in the middle and late 1900's. In 1991, the Soviet Union broke up into Russia and 14 other independent nations.

How nations are grouped. The nations of the world may be grouped in various ways. They may be grouped by region, such as the Middle East or Central America. People often call the countries of the Eastern Hemisphere the Old World and those of the Western Hemisphere the New World. In addition, countries are often identified by continent, such as African or Asian.

Economists generally divide the nations of the world into two groups—*developed countries* and *less developed countries*. Developed countries have a wide variety of industries and, in general, are wealthier than less developed countries. Less developed countries have few industries and have long depended on agriculture. Most of them are poor.

Developed nations include Australia, Canada, Japan, the United States, and most countries in western Europe. The majority of less developed countries are in Africa and Asia. Most industrial nations lie in the Northern Hemisphere.

Forms of government. Nearly all governments claim to be democracies. However, governments differ greatly in how closely they fulfill the democratic ideal of government by the people. In a democracy, the people elect representatives who make laws and govern the people according to those laws. Any qualified individual from among the people may run for office. The people's representatives may remove officials who behave improperly. Nations and governments can be classified as being more or less democratic, depending on the extent to which the people may take part in the process of government.

Democratic nations may be republics or constitutional monarchies. For example, the United States is a republic in which the president serves as head of state and head of government. The United Kingdom is a constitutional

Text continued on page 412b.

Political map of the world

This map shows each continent
in a different color. The
names of continents and
independent nations
are printed in
capital letters.

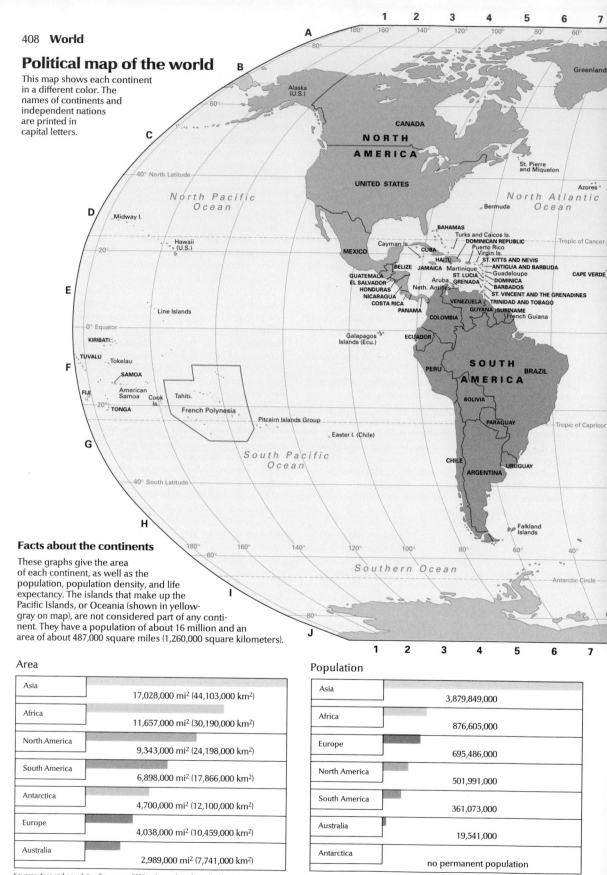

Facts about the continents

These graphs give the area
of each continent, as well as the
population, population density, and life
expectancy. The islands that make up the
Pacific Islands, or Oceania (shown in yellow-
gray on map), are not considered part of any continent. They have a population of about 16 million and an
area of about 487,000 square miles (1,260,000 square kilometers).

Area

Continent	Area
Asia	17,028,000 mi² (44,103,000 km²)
Africa	11,657,000 mi² (30,190,000 km²)
North America	9,343,000 mi² (24,198,000 km²)
South America	6,898,000 mi² (17,866,000 km²)
Antarctica	4,700,000 mi² (12,100,000 km²)
Europe	4,038,000 mi² (10,459,000 km²)
Australia	2,989,000 mi² (7,741,000 km²)

Population

Continent	Population
Asia	3,879,849,000
Africa	876,605,000
Europe	695,486,000
North America	501,991,000
South America	361,073,000
Australia	19,541,000
Antarctica	no permanent population

Sources: Area and population figures are 2004 estimates based on official government and United Nations sources. Life expectancy figures are Population Reference Bureau estimates for 2002.

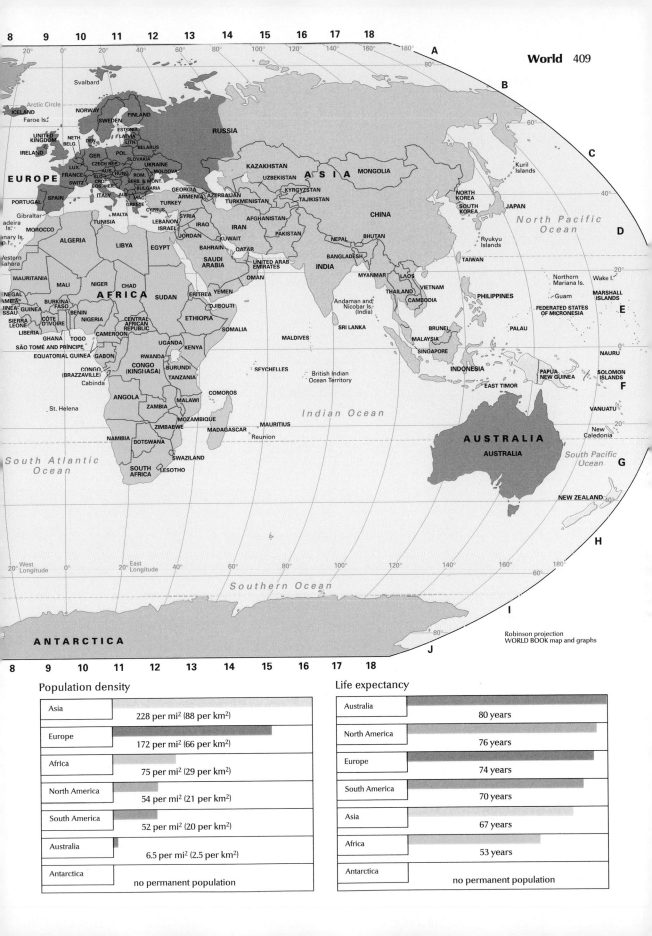

Population density

Asia	228 per mi² (88 per km²)
Europe	172 per mi² (66 per km²)
Africa	75 per mi² (29 per km²)
North America	54 per mi² (21 per km²)
South America	52 per mi² (20 per km²)
Australia	6.5 per mi² (2.5 per km²)
Antarctica	no permanent population

Life expectancy

Australia	80 years
North America	76 years
Europe	74 years
South America	70 years
Asia	67 years
Africa	53 years
Antarctica	no permanent population

Robinson projection
WORLD BOOK map and graphs

Independent countries of the world*

Name	Area In mi²	Area In km²	Rank in area	Population†	Rank in population	Capital	Map key
Afghanistan	251,773	652,090	40	25,150,000	43	Kabul	D 11
Albania	11,100	28,748	140	3,214,000	130	Tiranë	C 11
Algeria	919,595	2,381,741	11	32,480,000	34	Algiers	D 10
Andorra‡	181	468	177	71,000	184	Andorra la Vella	C 10
Angola	481,354	1,246,700	22	14,777,000	62	Luanda	F 10
Antigua and Barbuda	171	442	180	78,000	182	St. John's	E 6
Argentina	1,073,518	2,780,400	8	37,533,000	32	Buenos Aires	G 6
Armenia	11,506	29,800	138	3,465,000	126	Yerevan	D 13
Australia	2,988,902	7,741,220	6	19,541,000	54	Canberra	G 16
Austria	32,378	83,859	112	8,041,000	90	Vienna	C 10
Azerbaijan	33,436	86,600	111	8,232,000	89	Baku	D 13
Bahamas	5,358	13,878	155	320,000	167	Nassau	D 6
Bahrain	268	694	174	673,000	156	Manama	D 12
Bangladesh	55,598	143,998	92	131,035,000	9	Dhaka	D 14
Barbados	166	430	181	271,000	170	Bridgetown	E 7
Belarus	80,155	207,600	83	9,885,000	81	Minsk	C 12
Belgium	11,787	30,528	136	10,286,000	77	Brussels	C 10
Belize	8,867	22,965	147	259,000	171	Belmopan	E 5
Benin	43,484	112,622	99	7,007,000	96	Porto-Novo	E 10
Bhutan	18,147	47,000	128	2,312,000	138	Thimphu	D 14
Bolivia	424,164	1,098,581	27	9,069,000	83	La Paz; Sucre	F 6
Bosnia-Herzegovina	19,767	51,197	124	4,160,000	118	Sarajevo	C 10
Botswana	224,607	581,730	45	1,575,000	144	Gaborone	G 11
Brazil	3,300,171	8,547,403	5	177,971,000	5	Brasília	F 7
Brunei	2,226	5,765	162	352,000	166	Bandar Seri Begawan	E 15
Bulgaria	42,823	110,912	102	7,742,000	91	Sofia	C 11
Burkina Faso	105,792	274,000	73	12,988,000	66	Ouagadougou	E 9
Burundi	10,747	27,834	142	7,154,000	93	Bujumbura	F 11
Cambodia	69,898	181,035	87	13,210,000	65	Phnom Penh	E 15
Cameroon	183,569	475,442	52	16,191,000	58	Yaoundé	E 10
Canada	3,849,674	9,970,610	2	30,806,000	37	Ottawa	C 4
Cape Verde	1,557	4,033	164	473,000	162	Praia	E 8
Central African Republic	240,535	622,984	42	3,967,000	121	Bangui	E 10
Chad	495,755	1,284,000	20	8,899,000	84	N'Djamena	E 10
Chile	292,135	756,626	37	15,942,000	60	Santiago	G 6
China	3,692,671	9,563,974	3	1,319,377,000	1	Beijing	D 14
Colombia	439,737	1,138,914	25	44,847,000	27	Bogotá	E 6
Comoros	719	1,862	168	631,000	158	Moroni	F 12
Congo (Brazzaville)	132,047	342,000	63	3,401,000	129	Brazzaville	F 10
Congo (Kinshasa)	905,355	2,344,858	12	58,103,000	22	Kinshasa	F 11
Costa Rica	19,730	51,100	125	4,129,000	119	San José	E 5
Côte d'Ivoire (Ivory Coast)	124,504	322,463	68	17,381,000	57	Yamoussoukro	E 9
Croatia	21,829	56,538	123	4,385,000	115	Zagreb	C 10
Cuba	42,804	110,861	103	11,334,000	70	Havana	D 5
Cyprus	3,572	9,251	161	773,000	154	Nicosia	D 11
Czech Republic	30,450	78,866	114	10,262,000	78	Prague	C 10
Denmark	16,639	43,094	130	5,375,000	107	Copenhagen	C 10
Djibouti	8,958	23,200	146	658,000	157	Djibouti	E 12
Dominica	290	751	170	72,000	183	Roseau	E 6
Dominican Republic	18,730	48,511	127	8,887,000	85	Santo Domingo	E 6
East Timor	5,743	14,874	154	828,000	153	Dili	F 16
Ecuador	109,484	283,561	72	13,549,000	63	Quito	F 6
Egypt	386,662	1,001,449	29	72,534,000	16	Cairo	D 11
El Salvador	8,124	21,041	149	6,748,000	97	San Salvador	E 5
Equatorial Guinea	10,831	28,051	141	511,000	160	Malabo	E 10
Eritrea	45,406	117,600	98	4,037,000	120	Asmara	E 12
Estonia	17,413	45,100	129	1,309,000	149	Tallinn	C 11
Ethiopia	426,373	1,104,300	26	69,195,000	18	Addis Ababa	E 11
Fiji	7,056	18,274	151	881,000	152	Suva	F 1
Finland	130,559	338,145	64	5,214,000	109	Helsinki	B 11
France	212,935	551,500	47	59,579,000	20	Paris	C 10
Gabon	103,347	267,668	75	1,357,000	146	Libreville	F 10
Gambia	4,361	11,295	157	1,432,000	145	Banjul	E 9
Georgia	26,911	69,700	118	5,151,000	111	Tbilisi	D 12
Germany	137,847	357,022	62	81,886,000	14	Berlin	C 10
Ghana	92,098	238,533	79	20,087,000	51	Accra	E 9
Greece	50,949	131,957	94	10,953,000	73	Athens	D 11
Grenada	133	344	183	102,000	178	St. George's	E 6
Guatemala	42,042	108,889	104	12,606,000	68	Guatemala City	E 5

See footnotes at end of table on page 412.

Independent countries of the world* (continued)

Name	Area In mi²	Area In km²	Rank in area	Population†	Rank in population	Capital	Map key	
Guinea	94,926	245,857	76	8,648,000	87	Conakry	E	9
Guinea-Bissau	13,948	36,125	133	1,319,000	147	Bissau	E	9
Guyana	83,000	214,969	82	767,000	155	Georgetown	E	7
Haiti	10,714	27,750	143	7,636,000	92	Port-au-Prince	E	6
Honduras	43,277	112,088	100	7,028,000	95	Tegucigalpa	E	5
Hungary	35,920	93,032	108	9,770,000	82	Budapest	C	10
Iceland	39,769	103,000	105	287,000	169	Reykjavík	B	9
India	1,269,219	3,287,263	7	1,075,516,000	2	New Delhi	D	13
Indonesia	735,358	1,904,569	15	213,483,000	4	Jakarta	F	16
Iran	636,372	1,648,195	17	74,293,000	15	Tehran	D	12
Iraq	169,235	438,317	57	25,576,000	41	Baghdad	D	12
Ireland	27,133	70,273	117	3,875,000	123	Dublin	C	9
Israel	8,130	21,056	148	6,543,000	98	Jerusalem	D	11
Italy	116,340	301,318	70	57,231,000	23	Rome	C	10
Jamaica	4,243	10,990	159	2,669,000	135	Kingston	E	6
Japan	145,881	377,829	61	127,638,000	10	Tokyo	D	16
Jordan	35,467	91,860	110	5,506,000	105	Amman	D	11
Kazakhstan	1,052,090	2,724,900	9	14,879,000	61	Astana	C	13
Kenya	224,081	580,367	46	31,524,000	36	Nairobi	E	11
Kiribati	280	726	172	88,000	180	Tarawa	F	1
Korea, North	46,540	120,538	96	22,880,000	48	Pyongyang	C	16
Korea, South	38,328	99,268	107	47,986,000	25	Seoul	D	16
Kuwait	6,880	17,818	152	2,118,000	140	Kuwait	D	12
Kyrgyzstan	76,834	199,000	84	5,153,000	110	Bishkek	C	15
Laos	91,429	236,800	81	5,782,000	101	Vientiane	E	15
Latvia	24,942	64,600	121	2,367,000	137	Riga	C	11
Lebanon	4,015	10,400	160	3,718,000	124	Beirut	D	11
Lesotho	11,720	30,355	137	2,297,000	139	Maseru	G	11
Liberia	43,000	111,369	101	3,415,000	128	Monrovia	E	9
Libya	679,362	1,759,540	16	5,771,000	102	Tripoli	D	10
Liechtenstein‡	62	160	188	34,000	187	Vaduz	C	10
Lithuania	25,174	65,200	120	3,661,000	125	Vilnius	C	11
Luxembourg	998	2,586	166	458,000	163	Luxembourg	C	10
Macedonia	9,928	25,713	145	2,059,000	141	Skopje	C	10
Madagascar	226,658	587,041	44	17,856,000	56	Antananarivo	F	12
Malawi	45,747	118,484	97	11,293,000	72	Lilongwe	F	11
Malaysia	127,320	329,758	66	23,786,000	45	Kuala Lumpur	E	15
Maldives	115	298	185	303,000	168	Male	E	13
Mali	478,841	1,240,192	23	12,731,000	67	Bamako	E	9
Malta	122	316	184	396,000	165	Valletta	D	10
Marshall Islands	70	181	187	54,000	185	Majuro	E	18
Mauritania	395,955	1,025,520	28	2,995,000	132	Nouakchott	D	9
Mauritius	788	2,040	167	1,199,000	150	Port Louis	G	12
Mexico	756,066	1,958,201	14	103,011,000	11	Mexico City	D	4
Micronesia, Federated States of	271	702	173	135,000	176	Palikir	E	17
Moldova	13,070	33,851	135	4,251,000	117	Chisinau	C	11
Monaco‡	0.58	1.49	192	33,000	188	Monaco	C	10
Mongolia	604,829	1,566,500	18	2,484,000	136	Ulaanbaatar	C	15
Morocco	172,414	446,550	56	32,063,000	35	Rabat	D	9
Mozambique	309,496	801,590	34	19,614,000	53	Maputo	F	11
Myanmar	261,228	676,578	39	50,003,000	24	Yangon	D	14
Namibia	318,261	824,292	33	1,844,000	143	Windhoek	G	11
Nauru	8	21	191	13,000	191	—	F	18
Nepal	56,827	147,181	91	25,257,000	42	Kathmandu	D	14
Netherlands	16,033	41,526	131	16,087,000	59	Amsterdam	C	10
New Zealand	104,454	270,534	74	3,890,000	122	Wellington	G	18
Nicaragua	50,193	130,000	95	5,617,000	103	Managua	E	5
Niger	489,191	1,267,000	21	12,493,000	69	Niamey	E	10
Nigeria	356,669	923,768	30	136,769,000	8	Abuja	E	10
Norway	149,151	386,299	60	4,536,000	114	Oslo	B	10
Oman	119,499	309,500	69	2,887,000	133	Muscat	E	12
Pakistan	307,374	796,095	35	156,164,000	6	Islamabad	D	13
Palau	177	459	178	21,000	190	Koror	E	16
Panama	29,157	75,517	115	3,005,000	131	Panama City	E	5
Papua New Guinea	178,704	462,840	53	5,606,000	104	Port Moresby	F	17
Paraguay	157,048	406,752	58	6,057,000	100	Asunción	G	7
Peru	496,225	1,285,216	19	27,344,000	38	Lima	F	6
Philippines	115,831	300,000	71	82,351,000	12	Manila	E	16
Poland	124,808	323,250	67	38,466,000	31	Warsaw	C	10
Portugal	35,514	91,982	109	10,068,000	79	Lisbon	D	9

See footnotes at end of table on page 412.

(Table continued on page 412.)

Independent countries of the world* (continued)

Name	Area		Rank in area	Population†	Rank in population	Capital	Map key
	In mi²	In km²					
Qatar	4,247	11,000	158	600,000	159	Doha	D 12
Romania	92,043	238,391	80	22,206,000	49	Bucharest	C 11
Russia	6,592,850	17,075,400	1	141,802,000	7	Moscow	C 13
Rwanda	10,169	26,338	144	8,272,000	88	Kigali	F 11
St. Kitts and Nevis‡	101	261	186	37,000	186	Basseterre	E 6
St. Lucia	208	539	176	163,000	174	Castries	E 6
St. Vincent and the Grenadines	150	388	182	116,000	177	Kingstown	E 6
Samoa	1,093	2,831	165	176,000	173	Apia	F 1
San Marino‡	24	61	189	28,000	189	San Marino	C 10
São Tomé and Príncipe	372	964	169	160,000	175	São Tomé	E 10
Saudi Arabia	830,000	2,149,690	13	22,998,000	46	Riyadh	D 12
Senegal	75,955	196,722	85	10,403,000	75	Dakar	E 9
Serbia and Montenegro§	39,449	102,173	106	10,489,000	74	Belgrade	C 10
Seychelles	176	455	179	84,000	181	Victoria	F 12
Sierra Leone	27,699	71,740	116	5,261,000	108	Freetown	E 9
Singapore	239	618	175	4,305,000	116	Singapore	E 15
Slovakia	18,924	49,012	126	5,416,000	106	Bratislava	C 11
Slovenia	7,821	20,256	150	1,978,000	142	Ljubljana	C 11
Solomon Islands	11,157	28,896	139	509,000	161	Honiara	F 18
Somalia	246,201	637,657	41	10,352,000	76	Mogadishu	E 12
South Africa	471,445	1,221,037	24	44,552,000	28	Cape Town; Pretoria; Bloemfontein	G 11
Spain	195,365	505,992	50	39,878,000	29	Madrid	C 9
Sri Lanka	25,332	65,610	119	19,646,000	52	Sri Jayewardenepura Kotte	E 14
Sudan	967,500	2,505,813	10	34,056,000	33	Khartoum	E 11
Suriname	63,037	163,265	90	424,000	164	Paramaribo	E 7
Swaziland	6,704	17,364	153	1,030,000	151	Mbabane	G 11
Sweden	173,732	449,964	54	8,796,000	86	Stockholm	B 10
Switzerland	15,940	41,284	132	7,153,000	94	Bern	C 10
Syria	71,498	185,180	86	17,905,000	55	Damascus	D 11
Taiwan#	13,892	35,980	134	22,912,000	47	Taipei	D 16
Tajikistan	54,865	142,100	93	6,298,000	99	Dushanbe	D 14
Tanzania	341,217	883,749	32	38,493,000	30	Dodoma	F 11
Thailand	198,115	513,115	49	63,418,000	19	Bangkok	E 15
Togo	21,925	56,785	122	5,007,000	113	Lomé	E 9
Tonga	289	748	171	100,000	179	Nuku'alofa	F 1
Trinidad and Tobago	1,981	5,130	163	1,317,000	148	Port-of-Spain	E 6
Tunisia	63,170	163,610	89	9,898,000	80	Tunis	D 10
Turkey	299,158	774,815	36	71,455,000	17	Ankara	D 11
Turkmenistan	188,456	488,100	51	5,103,000	112	Ashgabat	D 13
Tuvalu	10	26	190	11,000	192	Funafuti	F 1
Uganda	93,065	241,038	78	26,418,000	39	Kampala	E 11
Ukraine	233,090	603,700	43	47,730,000	26	Kiev	C 11
United Arab Emirates	32,278	83,600	113	2,790,000	134	Abu Dhabi	D 12
United Kingdom	93,784	242,900	77	59,107,000	21	London	C 9
United States	3,615,275	9,363,520	4	291,575,000	3	Washington, D.C.	C 4
Uruguay	67,574	175,016	88	3,431,000	127	Montevideo	G 7
Uzbekistan	172,742	447,400	55	26,293,000	40	Tashkent	D 14
Vanuatu	4,706	12,189	156	211,000	172	Port-Vila	F 18
Vatican City‡	0.17	0.44	193	1,000	193	—	C 10
Venezuela	352,144	912,050	31	23,950,000	44	Caracas	E 6
Vietnam	128,066	331,689	65	82,280,000	13	Hanoi	E 15
Yemen	203,850	527,968	48	21,524,000	50	Sanaa	E 12
Zambia	290,587	752,618	38	11,320,000	71	Lusaka	F 11
Zimbabwe	150,872	390,757	59	13,524,000	64	Harare	G 11

*Each country listed has a separate article in *World Book.*
†Populations are 2004 estimates based on the latest figures from official government and United Nations sources.
‡Not on map; key shows general location.   §Formerly called Yugoslavia.   #Claimed by China.

Populated dependencies of the world*

Name	Area		Population†	Capital	Map key
	In mi²	In km²			
American Samoa (United States)	77	199	77,000	Pago Pago	F 1
Anguilla (United Kingdom)‡	37	96	13,000	The Valley (unofficial)	E 6
Aruba (Netherlands)	75	193	115,000	Oranjestad	E 6
Azores (Portugal)	868	2,247	242,000	Ponta Delgada	D 8
Bermuda (United Kingdom)	20	53	65,000	Hamilton	D 6

See footnotes at end of table.

Populated dependencies of the world*

Name	Area In mi²	In km²	Population†	Capital	Map key	
Cayman Islands (United Kingdom)	100	259	43,000	George Town	D	5
Channel Islands (United Kingdom)‡	76	197	144,000	St. Helier; St. Peter Port	C	9
Cook Islands (New Zealand)	93	240	21,000	Avarua	F	2
Easter Island (Chile)	47	122	3,000	—	G	5
Falkland Islands (United Kingdom)	4,699	12,170	2,000	Stanley	H	7
Faroe Islands (Denmark)	540	1,399	48,000	Tórshavn	B	9
French Guiana (France)	35,135	91,000	187,000	Cayenne	E	7
French Polynesia (France)	1,540	4,000	248,000	Papeete	F	2
Gaza Strip (§)‡	146	378	1,325,000	Gaza	D	11
Gibraltar (United Kingdom)	2.5	6.5	27,000	Gibraltar	D	9
Greenland (Denmark)	836,330	2,166,086	56,000	Nuuk	B	7
Guadeloupe (France)	658	1,704	442,000	Basse-Terre	E	6
Guam (United States)	209	541	165,000	Hagåtña	E	17
Madeira Islands (Portugal)	307	794	240,000	Funchal	D	9
Man, Isle of (United Kingdom)‡	221	572	78,000	Douglas	C	9
Martinique (France)	425	1,100	391,000	Fort-de-France	E	6
Mayotte (France)	144	373	186,000	Mamoudzou	F	12
Midway Island (United States)	2	5	400	—	D	1
Montserrat (United Kingdom)‡	39	102	5,000	—	E	6
Netherlands Antilles (Netherlands)	308	798	222,000	Willemstad	E	6
New Caledonia (France)	7,366	19,079	232,000	Nouméa	G	18
Niue Island (New Zealand)‡	100	260	2,000	—	F	1
Norfolk Island (Australia)‡	13	35	2,000	—	G	18
Northern Mariana Islands, Commonwealth of the (United States)	184	477	85,000	Saipan	E	17
Pitcairn Islands Group (United Kingdom)	17	44	50	—	G	3
Puerto Rico (United States)	3,515	9,103	3,944,000	San Juan	E	6
Reunion (France)	970	2,512	767,000	Saint-Denis	G	12
St. Helena Island Group (United Kingdom)	158	410	7,000	Jamestown	F	9
St.-Pierre and Miquelon (France)	93	242	7,000	St-Pierre	C	7
Tokelau (New Zealand)	4	10	1,000	—	F	1
Turks and Caicos Islands (United Kingdom)	166	430	19,000	Grand Turk	D	6
Virgin Islands (United Kingdom)	59	153	26,000	Road Town	E	6
Virgin Islands (United States)	132	342	112,000	Charlotte Amalie	E	6
Wake Island (United States)	3	8	100	—	E	18
Wallis and Futuna Islands (France)‡	106	275	16,000	Mata-Utu	F	1
West Bank (#)‡	2,270	5,879	2,313,000	—	D	11
Western Sahara (**)	102,700	266,000	283,000	—	D	9

*The dependencies listed are controlled in some way by the country shown in parentheses.
†Populations are 2004 and earlier estimates based on the latest figures from official government and United Nations sources.
‡Not on map; key shows general location.

§Administered by the Palestinian Authority; Israel controls external security and foreign affairs.
#Part of the West Bank is administered by the Palestinian Authority with external security and foreign affairs controlled by Israel; other parts are occupied by Israel.
**Occupied by Morocco; claimed by Morocco and by the Polisario Front.

© Mario Tama, Getty Images

A United Nations (UN) General Assembly session brings together delegates from nearly all the world's nations. The UN works to settle disputes among countries, to maintain world peace, and to help people to better their way of life.

© Dimitar Dilkoff, AFP/Getty Images

Voting is a right of the citizens of many countries. People vote to choose their leaders and to decide public issues. This woman is casting a vote in a presidential election in Skopje, Macedonia.

monarchy. A king or queen serves as head of state, and a prime minister serves as head of government. Other countries with democratic governments include Australia, Canada, Japan, New Zealand, most countries of Europe, and many of the less developed countries of Africa, Asia, and Latin America.

Many countries that claim to be democracies actually have an *authoritarian* government. In such countries, relatively few people have power, and most citizens play a limited role in making decisions. Authoritarian governments may rule by persuasion, force, or both. Communist Party organizations control authoritarian governments in China and a few other nations. Dictators supported by military forces rule other countries. Saudi Arabia and several other Middle Eastern monarchies have authoritarian governments.

Economic systems. Every country has an economic system to determine how to use its resources. The three main economic systems today are (1) capitalism, (2) Communism, and (3) mixed economies.

Capitalism is based on *free enterprise*—that is, most of the resources needed for production are privately owned. Individuals and private firms determine what to produce and sell, and how to use their income. Capitalist economic systems exist in Australia, Canada, New Zealand, the United States, and many countries of Europe. The role of capitalism is expanding in many less developed countries as well.

Communism traditionally has been based on government ownership of most productive resources. The government also plays a large role in deciding what goods to produce and how to distribute income. Communism was once the main economic system in the Soviet Union and many nations of Eastern Europe. However, these nations began to decrease government control over their economies in the late 1980's and early 1990's. Today, only a few countries claim to run their economies on Communist principles. Even China and other countries that are often thought of as Communist have loosened government control over economic activities.

Mixed economies combine both private and government control. Under a mixed economy, the government may own such industries as banks, railroads, and steel. However, other industries are privately owned. The government does some economic planning, but it also allows much private choice. Denmark, Norway, Sweden, and some less developed countries have mixed economies.

Cooperation among nations. Every nation depends on other nations in some ways. The interdependence of the entire world and its peoples is called *globalism*. Nations trade with one another to earn money and to obtain manufactured goods or the natural resources that they lack. Nations with similar interests and political beliefs may pledge to support one another in case of war. Developed countries may provide less developed countries with financial aid and technical assistance. Such aid strengthens trade as well as defense ties.

Several international organizations promote cooperation among countries. The United Nations (UN) is the largest such organization. Nearly all independent countries are UN members. The UN works mainly to settle disputes among nations and to promote world peace. It also has programs to aid needy people and to improve health and education, particularly in less developed countries.

Many international organizations are designed to encourage economic progress among member nations. Such groups stimulate trade among members by eliminating tariffs and other trade barriers within the organization. These groups include the European Union, the North American Free Trade Association (NAFTA), and the Southern Common Market (Mercosur).

People of the world

Population. By the early 2000's, the world's population reached about $6\frac{1}{3}$ billion. The yearly rate of population growth is about 1.2 percent. At that rate, the world's population would double in about 60 years.

If all the world's people were distributed evenly over the land, about 110 people would live on every square mile of land (43 on every square kilometer). However, the world's people are not distributed evenly, and so the *population density* (the average number of people in a specific area) varies greatly. Some regions, including Antarctica and certain desert areas, have no permanent

Modern manufacturing systems are used to produce consumer goods in many parts of the world. This man uses a mechanical arm to assemble a minivan at an automobile factory in Tokyo.

© Junko Kimura, Getty Images

settlers at all, while the populations of many urban areas continue to grow rapidly (see **City** [table: The 100 largest urban centers in the world]).

The most densely populated regions of the world are in Europe and in southern and eastern Asia. North America has heavy concentrations of people in the northeastern and central regions and along the Pacific coast. Africa, Australia, and South America have densely populated areas near the coasts. The interiors of those continents are thinly settled.

Just as the population density varies from one part of

the world to another, so does the rate of population growth. Less developed countries generally have higher average rates of increase than developed nations. Africa has a population growth rate of 2.3 percent yearly, the highest of all continents. South America has a 1.4 percent rate of increase, and Asia a 1.3 percent rate. North America's rate is 1.1 percent, and Australia's rate of increase is 1 percent. Europe's population is actually declining, losing 0.2 percent each year.

The world's largest countries in terms of population are China—which is the largest—and India. Each has

Where the people of the world live   This map shows how the world's population is distributed. About three-fourths of all people live in Asia and Europe. Regions with severe climates, such as desert areas, are thinly populated. The map also shows the location of some of the world's largest metropolitan areas.

WORLD BOOK map

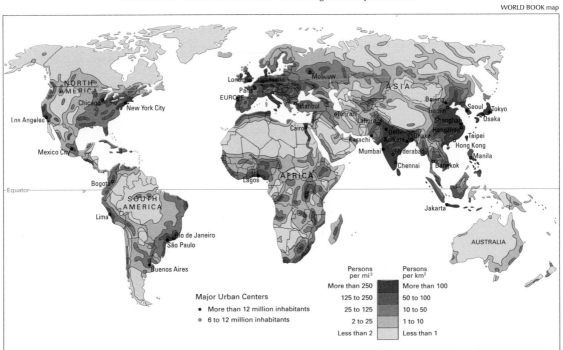

Major Urban Centers	Persons per mi²	Persons per km²
● More than 12 million inhabitants	More than 250	More than 100
○ 6 to 12 million inhabitants	125 to 250	50 to 100
	25 to 125	10 to 50
	2 to 25	1 to 10
	Less than 2	Less than 1

more than a billion people. The United States ranks as third largest, followed in descending order by Indonesia, Brazil, Pakistan, and Russia. Over half the world's total population lives in these seven nations. Vatican City has the smallest population of any of the world's nations. It has only about 1,000 people.

The growth and change of the world's population throughout history are described in the article **Population.** See also the articles on individual countries, states, and provinces for population details.

Languages. There are about 6,000 spoken languages in the world. But only about 10 of these are spoken by more than 100 million people. More people speak Mandarin Chinese than any other language. Arabic, Bengal, English, Hindi, Portuguese, Russian, and Spanish are among the other most-spoken languages.

Beginning in the late 1400's, Portugal and Spain, and then England and France, established colonies in various parts of the world. For this reason, Portuguese, Spanish, English, and French are now spoken in many nations outside their countries of origin. Portuguese became the main language of Angola, Brazil, and Mozambique. Spanish became the chief language throughout most countries of Latin America. English became the chief language in Australia, New Zealand, and the United States. It is also one of the main languages in Canada, India, and South Africa.

French, like English, is an important language of Canada. Most people in the province of Quebec speak French. French is also widely spoken in Algeria; Chad; Morocco; Senegal and some other countries in western Africa; and Vietnam.

For information about the development of the world's languages, see **Language.** See also the articles on individual countries for the most widely used languages in those nations.

Religions. The peoples of the world practice thousands of religions. Christianity has about 2 billion members, more than any other religion. Islam has more than 1.1 billion members, and Hinduism has about 800 million. Other major religions or belief systems of the world include the Bahá'í Faith, Buddhism, Confucianism, Jainism, Judaism, Shinto, Sikhism, and Taoism.

Christianity originated in the Middle East. Today, Christianity is the major religion in Australia, Europe, and the Western Hemisphere, which includes North America and South America. Islam also began in the Middle East and is now the chief religion throughout most of that area. It is also the major faith in Afghanistan, northern Africa, Bangladesh, Indonesia, Malaysia, Pakistan, and some Asian countries of the former Soviet Union. Hinduism, Jainism, and Sikhism have most of their followers in India, where the religions originated. Buddhism, which also developed in India, is the major religion of Sri Lanka and the mainland of southeastern Asia. Buddhism also has many followers in such countries as Japan and South Korea. Shinto is the native religion of Japan. The Bahá'í Faith originated in what is now Iraq.

Confucianism and Taoism are native belief systems of China. China's Communist government tolerates the practice of religion, with certain restrictions. Chinese people living in Taiwan also practice Confucianism and Taoism. Judaism originated in the Middle East. Today, the largest number of Jews live in France, Israel, Russia, and the United States. Thousands of local traditional re-

Growth of the world's population

The world's population grew slowly before A.D. 1. It then almost doubled by the year 1000. In the 1700's and 1800's improvements in agriculture, transportation, and communication improved living conditions and reduced death rates. Improvements such as these helped the world's population increase rapidly since 1800. At its present rate of growth, the world's population will double in about 60 years. Most of this growth will occur in less developed regions.

World population growth, 2000 B.C to A.D. 2000

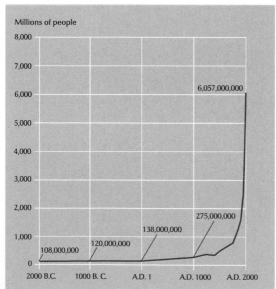

World population growth since 1800

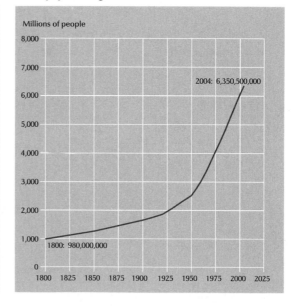

Source: WORLD BOOK estimates based on data from the United Nations.

ligions are practiced by ethnic groups in Africa, Asia, Australia, North America, South America, and the Pacific Islands.

For a description of major religions, see **Religion** and the separate articles on the various faiths. See also the *Religion* section of the country and continent articles.

Problems among the world's people. Through the years, human beings have made great progress in providing for their basic needs. Modern methods of producing food, clothing, and shelter have helped many people live more comfortably. Education has become available to more and more people, and scientists have discovered cures for many diseases.

But serious challenges still face the world's people. Millions of people in less developed countries lack adequate food, clothing, shelter, medical care, and education. Many people in developed countries, especially in large cities, suffer from poverty, unemployment, and discrimination. Numerous nations face the growing problem of environmental pollution. In addition, ethnic, political, and religious differences continue to lead to conflicts among the peoples of the world.

Physical features of the world

The surface area of the world totals about 196,900,000 square miles (510,000,000 square kilometers). Water covers about 139,700,000 square miles (362,000,000 square kilometers), or 71 percent of the world's surface. Only 29 percent of the world's surface consists of land, which covers about 57,200,000 square miles (148,000,000 square kilometers).

The physical geography of a specific region includes the region's surface features and climate. It also includes the soil, mineral deposits, plant and animal life, and other natural resources. Physical geography thus helps determine a region's economy and its people's way of life.

This section describes the two major surface features of the world: (1) water and (2) land.

Water. Oceans, lakes, and rivers make up most of the water that covers the surface of the world. The water surface consists chiefly of three large oceans—the Pacific, the Atlantic, and the Indian.

The Pacific Ocean is the largest. It covers 66 million square miles (171 million square kilometers), or about a third of the world's surface. The Atlantic Ocean is about half as large as the Pacific Ocean, and the Indian Ocean is slightly smaller than the Atlantic. These three oceans meet the Southern Ocean at 60° south latitude. In the north, the Atlantic Ocean meets the Arctic Ocean near Greenland; and the Pacific Ocean meets the Arctic Ocean in the Bering Strait, between Russia and Alaska.

The world's largest lake is the Caspian Sea, a body of salt water that lies between Asia and Europe east of the Caucasus Mountains. The Caspian covers about 143,250 square miles (371,000 square kilometers). The world's largest body of fresh water is the Great Lakes in North America. These five lakes—Erie, Huron, Michigan, Ontario, and Superior—are interconnected, and so they can be referred to as one body of water. Together, they cover 94,230 square miles (244,060 square kilometers).

The longest river in the world is the Nile in Africa, which flows 4,160 miles (6,695 kilometers). The second longest river, the Amazon in South America, is 4,000 miles (6,437 kilometers) long. Although it is shorter than the Nile, the Amazon carries a much greater volume of water—about one-fifth of all the water that empties into the world's oceans.

All living things need water to stay alive. People obtain drinking water from rivers, freshwater lakes, and wells. We also require water to maintain our way of life. We use water in our homes for cleaning and cooking. The manufacture of almost all our products requires water. In dry regions, farmers draw water from lakes, rivers, and wells to irrigate their crops. Lakes, oceans,

Text continued on page 418.

Physical map index

Physical map of the world

This map shows the world's chief physical features. Areas shown in shades of green generally have fertile soil and sufficient rainfall. Most of the world's people live in these areas.

Facts about the world's physical features

Land areas make up 29 percent of the world's surface. The four oceans cover 71 percent. The longest river and the largest desert are in Africa. Asia has the highest mountain.

The world's surface

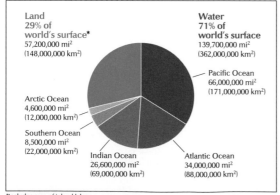

Land
29% of
world's surface*
57,200,000 mi²
(148,000,000 km²)

Water
71% of
world's surface
139,700,000 mi²
(362,000,000 km²)

Pacific Ocean
66,000,000 mi²
(171,000,000 km²)

Arctic Ocean
4,600,000 mi²
(12,000,000 km²)

Southern Ocean
8,500,000 mi²
(22,000,000 km²)

Indian Ocean
26,600,000 mi²
(69,000,000 km²)

Atlantic Ocean
34,000,000 mi²
(88,000,000 km²)

*Includes area of inland lakes.

Longest river on each continent

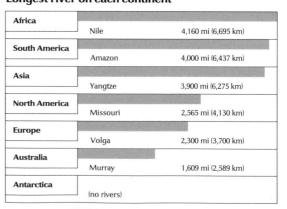

Africa	Nile	4,160 mi (6,695 km)
South America	Amazon	4,000 mi (6,437 km)
Asia	Yangtze	3,900 mi (6,275 km)
North America	Missouri	2,565 mi (4,130 km)
Europe	Volga	2,300 mi (3,700 km)
Australia	Murray	1,609 mi (2,589 km)
Antarctica	(no rivers)	

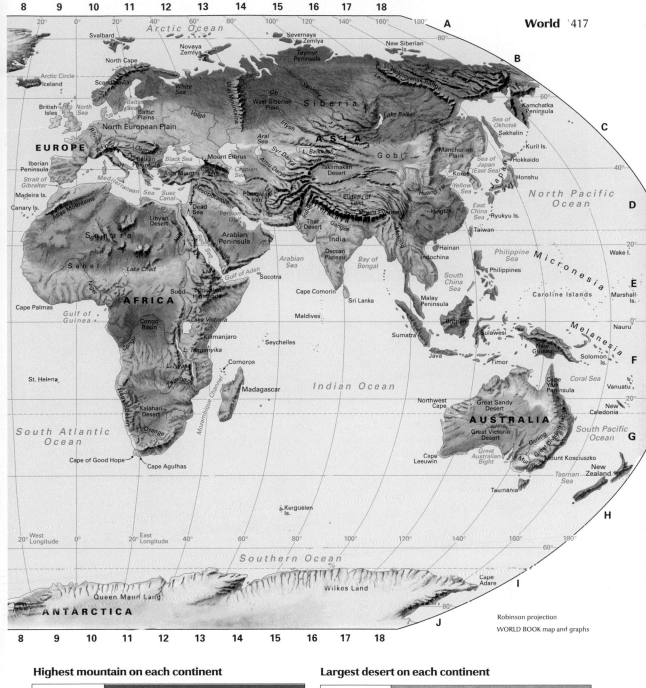

Robinson projection
WORLD BOOK map and graphs

Highest mountain on each continent

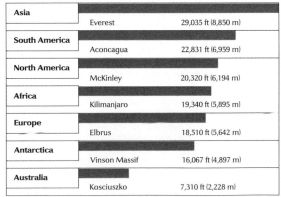

Asia	Everest	29,035 ft (8,850 m)
South America	Aconcagua	22,831 ft (6,959 m)
North America	McKinley	20,320 ft (6,194 m)
Africa	Kilimanjaro	19,340 ft (5,895 m)
Europe	Elbrus	18,510 ft (5,642 m)
Antarctica	Vinson Massif	16,067 ft (4,897 m)
Australia	Kosciuszko	7,310 ft (2,228 m)

Largest desert on each continent

Africa	Sahara	3,500,000 mi^2 (9,000,000 km^2)
Asia	Gobi	500,000 mi^2 (1,300,000 km^2)
Australia	Great Victoria	250,000 mi^2 (650,000 km^2)
South America	Atacama	140,000 mi^2 (360,000 km^2)
North America	Sonoran	120,000 mi^2 (310,000 km^2)
Europe	(no deserts)	
Antarctica	(no deserts)	

Air pollution is a serious world problem. A major form of environmental pollution, it is a health hazard for people in many of the world's urban areas. This photograph shows Mexico City amid a haze of smog.

© Susana Gonzalez, Getty Images

and rivers supply us with fish and other foods.

Water is also a source of power. The force of falling water from dams, rivers, and waterfalls can be used to generate hydroelectric power. In such countries as Brazil and Norway, hydroelectric power stations supply nearly all the electric power used in industry and homes.

The waters of the world also serve as major transportation routes. Every day, thousands of cargo ships cross the oceans, sail along seacoasts, and travel on inland waters. A nation's location along a seacoast can have a powerful influence on its progress and prosperity. Japan, the United Kingdom, the United States, and some other leading trading nations have long coastlines. Many of the world's major cities border important water transportation routes.

Land. The land area of the world consists of seven continents and many thousands of islands. Asia is the largest continent, followed by Africa, North America, South America, Antarctica, Europe, and Australia. Geographers sometimes refer to Europe and Asia as one continent called Eurasia.

The world's land surface includes hills, mountains, plains, plateaus, and valleys. Relatively few people live in mountainous areas or on high plateaus. Most such regions are too cold, dry, or rugged for commercial crop farming and other economic activities. But some mountains and high, grassy plateaus serve as grazing lands for cattle, sheep, and other livestock.

Mountainous areas have certain limitations. Nevertheless, many of the largest cities in regions near the equator, such as parts of Africa, Asia, and Latin America, are in high mountain valleys. Because certain diseases thrive in tropical lowlands, these mountain valleys are healthier for human occupation than the nearby tropical lowlands are. For example, malaria and yellow fever are more common in tropical regions with a low altitude than in tropical regions with a high altitude.

The majority of the world's people live on plains or in hilly regions. Except for some tropical lowlands, most plains and hilly regions have fertile soils and enough water for farming, manufacturing, and trade. Many areas less suitable for farming, particularly mountainous ar-

eas, have plentiful mineral resources. Some desert regions, especially in the Middle East, have large deposits of petroleum.

A region's natural resources influence its economic development. The Pampa, a grassy plain in central Argentina, has excellent pastureland for raising cattle and rich soil for growing wheat and other grains. Agricultural products make up Argentina's leading exports. The United Kingdom has relatively little farmland, but large deposits of coal and iron ore helped make the country an industrial power. Such countries as Canada, Russia, and the United States have various and abundant natural resources, which have greatly boosted their economies.

Threats to the environment. For hundreds of years, people have used the world's natural resources to make their lives more comfortable. However, these resources are not always used wisely. Many human practices threaten the environment.

Many water supplies have become polluted by sewage, industrial chemicals, and other wastes. The burning of fuel in motor vehicles, factories, and furnaces has caused severe air pollution in numerous cities. Many forest regions have been stripped of large areas of trees, resulting in soil erosion and the destruction of plant and animal life. Certain farming practices, including the use of chemical fertilizers and pesticides, have polluted the soil. Many farmers plant the same crop in a field year after year. This practice reduces the soil's fertility and increases the likelihood that plants will become diseased or infested with insects.

Since the mid-1900's, people have become increasingly aware of the need to protect and improve their natural environment. Local and national governments have passed laws to control the use of natural resources. But it takes many years to renew a water supply, grow a forest, or replace a layer of topsoil. People would need to practice wise resource management over extended periods to repair damage that has already occurred and to prevent future problems. David L. Clawson

Related articles in *World Book.* For detailed information about the physical world, see **Earth** and its list of *Related articles.* For the story of human history and progress, see **World, History of the;** and **Prehistoric people.** See also the lists of *Re-*

lated articles at the end of these articles. See also:

Continents

Africa
Antarctica
Asia
Australia

Europe
North America
South America

Countries

See the separate article on each country and dependency listed in the *Nations of the world* section of this article.

Regions

Arctic
Balkans
Central America
Far East

Latin America
Middle East
Pacific Islands
Southeast Asia

Geography

Climate
Desert
Geography
Island
Lake
Mountain
Ocean
Plain
Plateau
Rain
River
Seven Natural Wonders of the World
Valley
Volcano
Water
Waterfall
Weather

Government and economics

Capitalism
Communism
Democracy
Economics
Foreign aid
Government
Gross domestic product
International trade

Law
Multinational corporation
Poverty
Public health
Socialism
Standard of living
Trade

Organizations, agreements, and programs

See **United Nations** and the international organizations listed in its *Related articles*. See also the following articles:
Agency for International Development
African Union
Arab League
Asian Development Bank
Bank for International Settlements
CERN
Colombo Plan
Europe, Council of
European Free Trade Association
European Monetary System
European Space Agency
European Union
General Agreement on Tariffs and Trade
International Air Transport Association
International Bureau of Weights and Measures
International Confederation of Free Trade Unions
International Council of Scientific Unions
International Energy Agency
Mercosur
North American Free Trade Agreement
North Atlantic Treaty Organization
Organization for Economic Cooperation and Development
Organization of African Unity
Organization of American States
Organization of the Petroleum Exporting Countries

Strategic Arms Limitation Talks
Warsaw Pact

Other related articles

Agriculture
Anthropology
Art and the arts
Civilization
Clothing
Communication
Conservation
Culture
Developing country
Education
Energy supply
Environmental pollution
Food
Food supply
Geopolitics
Human being
Industry
International law

International relations
Invention
Irrigation
Language
Manufacturing
Medicine
Natural resources
Olympic Games
Peace
Population
Races, Human
Religion
Science
Shelter
Technology
Third World
Transportation
War

Outline

I. Nations of the world
   A. How nations are grouped
   B. Forms of government
   C. Economic systems
   D. Cooperation among nations
II. People of the world
   A. Population
   B. Languages
   C. Religions
   D. Problems among the world's people
III. Physical features of the world
   A. Water
   B. Land
   C. Threats to the environment

Questions

How does the geography of a region help determine how people in the region live?
How does an independent country differ from a dependency?
What threats to the environment have resulted from the unwise use of natural resources?
What three oceans make up most of the water surface of the world?
Which language is spoken by the largest number of people?
What are the three main economic systems practiced in the world today?
How do people use the world's water supplies?
What has caused the most important changes in the world's political map throughout history?
Why do most of the world's people live on plains or in hilly regions?
How do international organizations help countries cooperate with one another?

Additional resources

Level I
Lands and Peoples. 6 vols. Rev. ed. Grolier, 2003.
Mason, Antony. *People Around the World.* Kingfisher, 2002.
National Geographic World Atlas for Young Explorers. Rev. ed. National Geographic Soc., 2003.
The World Book Encyclopedia of People and Places. 6 vols. Rev. ed. World Book, 2004.

Level II
McCoy, John F., ed. *Geo-Data: The World Geographical Encyclopedia.* 3rd ed. Gale Group, 2003.
The Times Atlas of the World. 10th ed. Times Bks., 1999.
The World Factbook. Central Intelligence Agency, published annually.
The Worldwatch Institute. *State of the World.* Norton, published annually.

Art Resource

Ancient Egypt

Photoresources

The Golden Age of Greece

Giraudon from Art Resource

The Middle Ages

Human history is a dramatic story that began about 2 million years ago. It traces the experiences of human societies from the earliest times to the space age.

World history

World, History of the. People have probably lived on the earth about 2 million years. In the earliest days, human groups established small societies throughout much of the world. People started to use writing about 5,500 years ago. The period before people began to write is usually called *prehistory*.

Archaeologists have pieced together the story of prehistory by studying what the people left behind, including artwork, tools, ruins of buildings, fossils, and even their own skeletons. Such objects provide the main evidence of what prehistoric people were like and how they lived. For a description of life in prehistoric times, see the *World Book* article **Prehistoric people**.

The first traces of writing date from about 3500 B.C. From then on, people could record their own history. By writing down their experiences, they could tell future generations what they were like and how they lived. From these documents, we can learn firsthand about the rise and fall of civilizations and other important events. The history of the world—from the first civilizations to the present—is based largely on what has been written down by peoples through the ages.

The development of agriculture about 9000 B.C. brought about a great change in human life. Prehistoric people who learned to farm no longer had to migrate in search of food. Instead, they could settle in one place. Some of their settlements grew to become the world's first cities. People in the cities learned new skills and developed specialized occupations. Some became builders and craftworkers. Others became merchants and priests. Eventually, systems of writing were invented. These developments gave rise to the first civilizations.

For hundreds of years, the earliest civilizations had little contact with one another and so developed independently. The progress each civilization made depended on the natural resources available to it and on the inventiveness of its people. As time passed, civilizations advanced and spread, and the world's population rose steadily. The peoples of various civilizations began to exchange ideas and skills. Within each civilization, groups of people with distinctive customs and languages emerged. In time, some peoples, such as the Romans, gained power over others and built huge empires. Some of these empires flourished for centuries before collapsing. Great religions and later science and scholarship developed as people wondered about the meaning of human life and the mysteries of nature.

SCALA from Art Resource

The Renaissance

AP/Wide World

World War I

NASA

The space age

About 500 years ago, one civilization—that of western Europe—started to exert a powerful influence throughout the world. The Europeans began to make great advances in learning, the arts, science, and technology. The nations of Europe sent explorers and military forces to distant lands. They set up overseas colonies, first in the Americas and then on other continents, and conquered other regions. As a result, European customs, skills, political ideas, and religious beliefs spread across much of the world.

Today, the many peoples of the world continue to observe different cultural traditions. But they also have more in common than ever before. Worldwide systems of communications and transportation have broken down barriers of time and distance and rapidly increased the exchange of ideas and information between peoples. However far apart people may live from one another, they are affected more and more by the same political, economic, and cultural changes. In some way, almost everyone can now be affected by a war or a political crisis in a faraway land or by a rise in petroleum prices in distant oil-producing countries. The various cultures of the world are increasingly influencing one another. Much of world history is the story of the way different civilizations have come closer together.

About this article

Jerry H. Bentley, the contributor of this article, is Professor of History at the University of Hawaii and Editor of the Journal of World History. *He is the author of numerous historical works. They include* Old World Encounters: Cross-Cultural Contacts and Exchanges in Pre-Modern Times *and* Politics and Culture in Renaissance Naples.

The article traces the history of the world from ancient times to the present. The outline below gives the major sections of the article. Each section of the text includes a reference page that provides a timeline of major developments of the period, a map, and a table of important dates. World Book *also has many separate articles on important events and people in world history. Cross-references within this article refer the reader to other* World Book *articles for additional details on key topics. The* Study aids *section at the end of the article includes a listing of related articles. The section also provides a listing of selected outside resources for further reading on world history.*

Article outline

The civilization of ancient Egypt began to develop in the Nile River Valley about 3100 B.C. Agriculture thrived in the valley, where floodwaters of the Nile deposited rich soil year after year. The farming scenes shown here were painted on a tomb during the 1400's B.C.

For hundreds of thousands of years, prehistoric people lived by hunting, fishing, and gathering wild plants. Even small groups of people had to migrate constantly over large areas of land to find enough food. A group usually stayed in one place only a few days or a few weeks. The discovery of agriculture gradually ended the nomadic way of life for many people. After prehistoric men and women learned to raise crops and domesticate animals, they no longer had to migrate in search of food. They could thus begin to settle in villages.

Agriculture was developed at different times in different regions of the world. People in southwest Asia began to grow cereal grasses and other plants about 9000 B.C. They also domesticated goats and sheep at about that time, and they later tamed cattle. In southeastern Asia, people had begun cultivating rice by about 7000 B.C. People who lived in what is now Mexico probably learned to grow crops about 7000 B.C.

The invention of farming paved the way for the development of civilization. As prehistoric people became better farmers, they began to produce enough food to support larger villages. In time, some farming villages developed into the first cities. The plentiful food supplies enabled more and more people to give up farming for other jobs. These people began to develop the arts, crafts, trades, and other activities of civilized life.

Agriculture also stimulated technological and social changes. Farmers invented the hoe, sickle, and other tools to make their work easier. The hair of domestic animals and fibers from such plants as cotton and flax were used to make the first textiles. People built ovens to bake the bread they made from cultivated grain and learned to use hotter ovens to harden pottery. The practice of agriculture required many people to work together to prepare the fields for planting and to harvest

the crops. New systems of government were developed to direct such group activities.

The changes brought about by agriculture took thousands of years to spread widely across the earth. By about 3500 B.C., civilization began. It started first in southwest Asia. Three other early civilizations developed in Africa and in south and east Asia. All these early civilizations arose in river valleys, where fertile soil and a readily available water supply made agriculture easier than elsewhere. The valleys were (1) the Tigris-Euphrates Valley in southwest Asia, (2) the Nile Valley in Egypt, (3) the Indus Valley in what is now Pakistan, and (4) the Huang He Valley in northern China.

While large, complex civilizations were developing in the river valleys, agriculture also appeared in other parts of the world. Most people in Europe, central and southern Africa, southeastern Asia, central Mexico, and the Andean region of South America began to cultivate their food after about 2000 B.C. They did not immediately build complex civilizations like those of the river valleys, but they organized settled societies that later expanded and dominated large regions.

The Tigris-Euphrates Valley. One of the most fertile regions of the ancient world lay between the Tigris and Euphrates rivers in southern Mesopotamia (now Iraq). Silt deposited by the rivers formed a rich topsoil ideal for growing crops. By the 5000's B.C., many people had settled in villages in the lower part of the Tigris-Euphrates Valley, an area later called Sumer.

The Sumerians lived by farming, fishing, and hunting the wild fowl of the river marshes. They built dikes to control the flooding of the Tigris and Euphrates rivers and irrigation canals to carry water to their fields. By about 3500 B.C., some Sumerian farm villages had grown into small cities, which marked the beginning of

Major developments

WORLD BOOK illustration by Tak Murakami

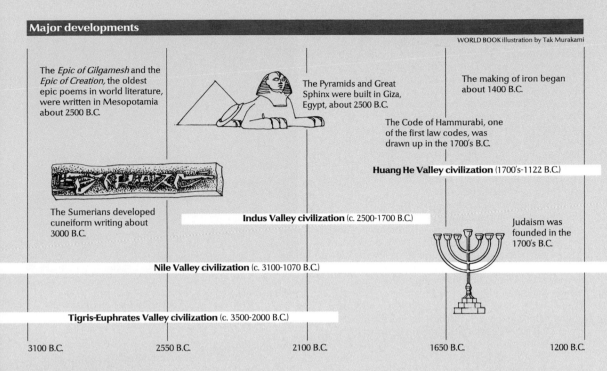

The *Epic of Gilgamesh* and the *Epic of Creation,* the oldest epic poems in world literature, were written in Mesopotamia about 2500 B.C.

The Pyramids and Great Sphinx were built in Giza, Egypt, about 2500 B.C.

The making of iron began about 1400 B.C.

The Code of Hammurabi, one of the first law codes, was drawn up in the 1700's B.C.

Huang He Valley civilization (1700's-1122 B.C.)

The Sumerians developed cuneiform writing about 3000 B.C.

Indus Valley civilization (c. 2500-1700 B.C.)

Judaism was founded in the 1700's B.C.

Nile Valley civilization (c. 3100-1070 B.C.)

Tigris-Euphrates Valley civilization (c. 3500-2000 B.C.)

3100 B.C.   2550 B.C.   2100 B.C.   1650 B.C.   1200 B.C.

The earliest civilizations arose in four river valleys in Asia and Africa between about 3500 B.C. and the 1700's B.C. The fertile soil of the valleys supported flourishing farming villages. Civilization began when such villages developed into cities.

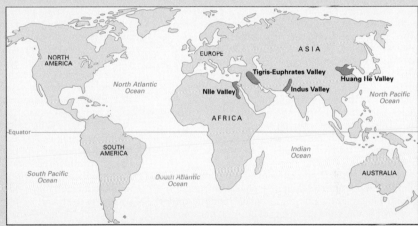

WORLD BOOK map

Important dates

c. 9000 B.C. The development of agriculture began with the growing of crops and the domestication of animals in southwest Asia.

c. 3500 B.C. A number of small cities, centers of the world's first civilization, appeared in Sumer, the lower part of the Tigris-Euphrates Valley.

c. 3500 B.C. The Sumerians invented the first form of writing. The Sumerian system was later simplified to produce wedge-shaped *cuneiform* writing, which spread throughout southwest Asia.

c. 3100 B.C. King Menes of Upper Egypt united Lower and Upper Egypt.

c. 3000-1100 B.C. The Minoan civilization on the island of Crete rose and fell.

c. 2500 B.C. The Indus Valley civilization began to flourish at Mohenjo-Daro and Harappa in what is now Pakistan.

2300's B.C. Sargon of Akkad conquered the Sumerians and united all Mesopotamia under his rule, creating the world's first empire.

1700's B.C. The Shang Dynasty began its rule in the Huang He Valley of China.

c. 1792-1750 B.C. Babylonia flourished under King Hammurabi.

1500's-c. 1100 B.C. The city of Mycenae was the leading political and cultural center on the Greek mainland.

c. 1595 B.C. The Hittites, a warlike people from what is now central Turkey, conquered the Babylonians.

c. 1500 B.C. The Aryans of central Asia began migrating to India.

the world's first civilization. A number of these cities developed into powerful city-states by about 3200 B.C.

The Sumerians produced one of the greatest achievements in world history. By about 3500 B.C., they had invented the first form of writing. It consisted of picture-like symbols scratched into clay. The symbols were later simplified to produce *cuneiform,* a system of writing that used wedge-shaped characters (see **Cuneiform**). Archaeologists have found thousands of clay tablets with Sumerian writings. These tablets show the high level of development of the Sumerian culture. They include historical and legal documents; letters; economic records; literary and religious texts; and studies in mathematics, astronomy, and medicine.

The Sumerians used baked bricks to build great palaces and towering temples called *ziggurats* in their cities. They believed that their gods lived on the tops of the ziggurats. Sumerian craftworkers produced board games, beautifully designed jewelry, metalware, musical instruments, decorative pottery, and stone seals engraved with pictures and inscriptions. The Sumerians invented the potter's wheel and were among the first people to brew beer and make glass. Their system of counting in units of 60 is the basis of the 360-degree circle and the 60-minute hour. For more information on the Sumerian civilization, see **Sumer**.

The Sumerian city-states had no central government or unified army and continually struggled among themselves for power. As time passed, they were increasingly threatened by neighboring Semitic peoples, who were attracted by the growing wealth of the Tigris-Euphrates Valley. During the 2300's B.C., a Semitic king, Sargon of Akkad, conquered Sumer. Sargon united all Mesopotamia under his rule, creating the world's first empire. The Akkadians combined Sumerian civilization with their own culture. Their rule lasted more than 60 years. Then invaders from the northeast overran the empire. These invaders soon left Mesopotamia, and Sumer was once again divided into separate city-states. One city-state, Ur, briefly controlled all the others. See **Sargon of Akkad**.

By about 2000 B.C., the Sumerians had completely lost all political power to invading Semites. Mesopotamia then broke up into a number of small kingdoms under various Semitic rulers. The city of Babylon became the center of one kingdom. The Babylonian rulers gradually extended their authority over all Mesopotamian peoples. The greatest Babylonian king was Hammurabi, who ruled from about 1792 to 1750 B.C. Hammurabi developed one of the first law codes in history. The famous Code of Hammurabi contained nearly 300 legal provisions, including many Sumerian and Akkadian laws. It covered such matters as divorce, false accusation, land and business regulations, and military service. See **Babylonia; Hammurabi**.

The Nile Valley. The civilization of ancient Egypt began to develop in the valley of the Nile River about 3100 B.C. Agriculture flourished in the valley, where the floodwaters of the Nile deposited rich soil year after year. Beyond the Nile Valley lay an uninhabited region of desert and rock. Egyptian culture thus developed with little threat of invasions by neighboring peoples.

Karachi Museum (SCALA from Art Resource)

A stone seal from the Indus Valley civilization has a carved figure of an animal and some writing. The seal, which is about 4,000 years old, was uncovered at Mohenjo-Daro, Pakistan.

During the 3000's B.C., Egypt consisted of two large kingdoms. Lower Egypt covered the Nile Delta. Upper Egypt lay south of the delta on the two banks of the river. About 3100 B.C., according to legend, King Menes of Upper Egypt conquered Lower Egypt and united the two kingdoms. Menes also founded the first Egyptian *dynasty* (series of rulers in the same family). The rulers of ancient Egypt were believed to be divine.

The ancient Egyptians invented their own form of writing—an elaborate system of symbols known as *hieroglyphics* (see **Hieroglyphics**). They also invented *papyrus,* a paperlike material made from the stems of reeds. The Egyptians developed one of the first religions to emphasize life after death. They tried to make sure their dead enjoyed a good life in the next world. The Egyptians built great tombs and *mummified* (embalmed and dried) corpses to preserve them. They filled the tombs with clothing, food, furnishings, and jewelry for use in the next world. The most famous Egyptian tombs are gigantic pyramids in which the kings were buried. The pyramids display the outstanding engineering and surveying skills of the Egyptians. The government organized thousands of workers to construct the pyramids, as well as temples and palaces, in the Egyptian cities. The cities served chiefly as religious and governmental centers for the surrounding countryside. Most of the people lived in villages near the cities.

Over the years, huge armies of conquering Egyptians expanded the kingdom's boundaries far beyond the Nile Valley. At its height in the 1400's B.C., Egypt ruled Syria, Lebanon, Palestine, and part of the Sudan. As a powerful state at the junction of Asia and Africa, Egypt played an important role in the growth of long-distance trade. Egyptian caravans carried goods throughout the vast desert regions surrounding the kingdom. Egyptian ships sailed to all the major ports of the ancient world. From other lands, the Egyptians acquired gems, gold, ivory, leopard skins, fine woods, and other rich materials, which they used to create some of the most magnificent art of ancient times.

Although the ancient Egyptians had contacts with other cultures, their way of life changed little over thousands of years. Their civilization gradually declined, and the Egyptians found it harder and harder to resist invaders who had greater vigor and better weapons.

Egyptian records from the 1200's and 1100's B.C. describe constant attacks by "sea peoples." These peoples may have come from islands in the Aegean Sea or from lands along the east coast of the Mediterranean Sea. After 1000 B.C., power struggles between rival Egyptian dynasties further weakened the kingdom.

For a detailed description of life in ancient Egypt, see **Egypt, Ancient.**

The Indus Valley. Historians have been unable to translate the writings left behind by the ancient civilization that arose in the valley of the Indus River and its tributaries. As a result, they have had to rely almost entirely on archaeological findings for information about the Indus culture. The ruins of two large cities—Mohenjo-Daro (also spelled Moenjodaro) and Harappa—tell much about the Indus civilization. Also, the remains of hundreds of small settlements have been discovered in the valley. Some of these settlements were farming villages, and others were seaports and trading posts.

Mohenjo-Daro and Harappa probably had more than 35,000 inhabitants each by about 2500 B.C. The people of the Indus Valley had a well-developed system of agriculture that provided food for the large population. They dug ditches and canals to irrigate their farms. The Indus cities had brick buildings and well-planned streets laid out in rectangular patterns. Elaborate brick-lined drainage systems provided sanitation for the towns. Craftworkers made decorated furniture, fine jewelry, metal utensils, toys, and stone seals engraved with animal and human forms. Inscriptions on these seals, as well as on some pottery and a few other objects, provide the only traces of Indus writing known at present.

Archaeologists have discovered that standardized sizes of bricks and uniform weights and measures were used throughout the Indus Valley. The Indus settlements traded with one another and with foreign cultures. Traces of seals used on goods from the Indus Valley have been found as far away as Mesopotamia. The Indus people probably also traded with people of central Asia, southern India, and Persia.

Between 2000 and 1750 B.C., the Indus Valley civilization began to decay. Scholars do not know why this process of decay took place. Changing river patterns may have disrupted the agriculture and economy of the region. Overuse of the land along the riverbanks also may have caused environmental damage that led to decreased agricultural production throughout the Indus Valley. By about 1700 B.C., the Indus civilization had disappeared.

For more information on what archaeologists have discovered about the ancient Indus Valley culture, see **Indus Valley civilization.**

The Huang He Valley. The earliest written records of Chinese history date from the Shang dynasty, which arose in the valley of the Huang He during the 1700's B.C. The records consist largely of writings scratched on animal bones and turtle shells. The bones and shells, known as *oracle bones*, were used in religious ceremonies to answer questions about the future. After a question was written on an oracle bone, a small groove or hole was made in the bone. The bone was then heated so that cracks ran outward from the groove or hole. By studying the pattern of the cracks, a priest worked out the answer to the question.

Thousands of oracle bones have been found. They provide much information about the ancient Chinese. Many of the bones record astronomical events, such as eclipses of the sun and moon, and the names and dates of rulers. The system of writing used by the Shang people had more than 3,000 characters. Some characters on the oracle bones resemble those of the present-day Chinese language.

Little remains of the cities of the Shang period. Most of the buildings were made of mud or wood and have long since crumbled away. However, the foundations of pounded earth survive and indicate that some of the cities were fairly large and surrounded by high walls. The people of the Shang period cast beautiful bronze vessels. They also carved marble and jade and wove silk. The Shang people had many gods. They attached great importance to ties of kinship and worshiped the spirits of their ancestors. They believed that their ancestors could plead with the gods on their behalf.

The Shang people were governed by a king and a hereditary class of aristocrats. The king and the nobility carried out religious as well as political duties. However, only the king could perform the most important religious ceremonies. The Shang leaders organized armies of as many as 5,000 men and equipped them with bronze weapons and horse-drawn war chariots. They used their armies to control the other peoples of the Huang He Valley. The Shang ruled much of the valley for about 600 years. For more information on the culture of the Shang, see **Shang dynasty.**

Palace of St. Michael and St. George, Corfu, Greece (Photoresources)

A bronze ceremonial vessel shows the skill of an ancient Chinese artist. The vessel dates from the Shang dynasty, which arose in the valley of the Huang He during the 1700's B.C.

Temple of Poseidon (400's B.C.), Paestum, Italy (Photoresources)

Greek civilization was the first advanced civilization on the European mainland. It became one of the most magnificent civilizations of ancient times and spread to other lands. Greek colonists built many temples, such as this one in southern Italy, in regions they settled.

From about 1200 B.C. to A.D. 500, Mesopotamia and Egypt were increasingly affected by the gradual growth of a new civilization in the basin of the Mediterranean Sea. Phoenicians and Greeks traded actively throughout the Mediterranean region, and they encouraged the development of a prosperous and productive society. From the 700's to the 200's B.C., Greeks linked Mediterranean lands and peoples. After the 200's B.C., Romans established an empire throughout the Mediterranean basin and much of Europe. The combined arts, philosophies, and sciences of ancient Greece and Rome provided much of the foundation of later European culture.

As the civilizations of ancient times grew and spread, they began to have certain features in common. By about A.D. 500, for example, all the major civilizations had learned how to make iron. The spread of such knowledge was helped by trade, conquest, and migration. Traders carried the products of one culture to other cultures. The soldiers of invading armies often settled in the conquered lands, where they introduced new ways of life. Groups of people migrated from one region to another, bringing the customs, ideas, and skills of their homelands with them.

The most important migrations in ancient times were made by peoples belonging to the Indo-European language groups. The Indo-European peoples once lived in the area north of the Black Sea, in southern Russia and the Ukraine. Sometime before 2000 B.C., large numbers of them began moving into Europe, into southwest Asia, and across the highlands of Persia to India. Many of the migrations resulted in the destruction of old states and the creation of new ones.

Civilizations of southwest Asia. For several hundred years following 1200 B.C., various Indo-European and Semitic peoples struggled for power in southwest Asia. One of the Semitic peoples, the Hebrews, founded a kingdom in what is now Israel about 1029 B.C. The Hebrews, later called Jews, established the first religion based on the belief in one God. Their faith, called Judaism, had a lasting influence on human history. Both Christianity, the most widespread religion of modern times, and Islam, the religion of the Muslims, developed from Judaism. See **Jews**.

During the 700's B.C., much of southwest Asia was conquered by the Assyrians, a northern Mesopotamian people. The cities of Nineveh and Assur on the upper Tigris River were the chief centers of their empire. The Assyrians often treated their subject peoples harshly. Conquered rulers were replaced by Assyrian governors who acted on orders from the central government in Nineveh. For more information, see **Assyria**.

In 612 B.C., the Semitic Babylonians and an Indo-European people called the Medes joined forces and destroyed Nineveh. The Assyrian Empire thus ended. The Medes then established the Median Empire, which included the area north of Mesopotamia (see **Media**). In Mesopotamia and to the west, the New Babylonian Empire, sometimes called the Chaldean Empire, came into being. Under its most famous ruler, Nebuchadnezzar II, Babylon became one of the most magnificent cities of the ancient world. Nebuchadnezzar probably built the Hanging Gardens, one of the Seven Wonders of the Ancient World (see **Seven Wonders of the Ancient World** [with picture]).

About 550 B.C., the Persians, led by Cyrus the Great, overthrew the Medes and established the Persian Empire. Cyrus went on to conquer Babylonia, Palestine, Syria, and all Asia Minor. Cyrus's son Cambyses added

Major developments

WORLD BOOK illustration by Tak Murakami

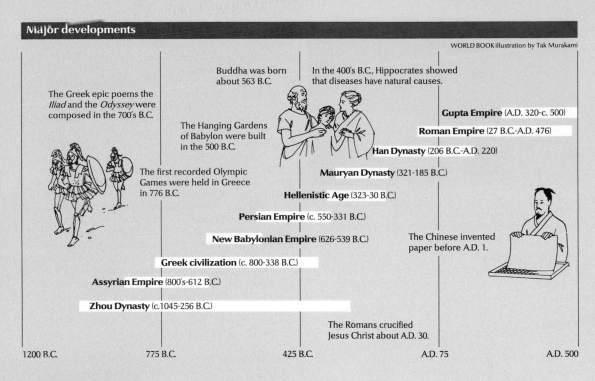

Buddha was born about 563 B.C.

In the 400's B.C., Hippocrates showed that diseases have natural causes.

The Greek epic poems the *Iliad* and the *Odyssey* were composed in the 700's B.C.

The Hanging Gardens of Babylon were built in the 500 B.C.

Gupta Empire (A.D. 320-c. 500)

Roman Empire (27 B.C.-A.D. 476)

Han Dynasty (206 B.C.-A.D. 220)

The first recorded Olympic Games were held in Greece in 776 B.C.

Mauryan Dynasty (321-185 B.C.)

Hellenistic Age (323-30 B.C.)

Persian Empire (c. 550-331 B.C.)

New Babylonian Empire (626-539 B.C.)

The Chinese invented paper before A.D. 1.

Greek civilization (c. 800-338 B.C.)

Assyrian Empire (800's-612 B.C.)

Zhou Dynasty (c.1045-256 B.C.)

The Romans crucified Jesus Christ about A.D. 30.

| 1200 B.C. | 775 B.C. | 425 B.C. | A.D. 75 | A.D. 500 |

Powerful empires emerged as civilization advanced and spread between 1200 B.C. and A.D. 500. The Roman Empire covered much of Europe, southwest Asia, and the north coast of Africa. The Han Dynasty of China and the Gupta Dynasty of India also built huge empires.

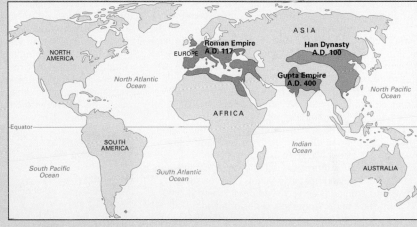

WORLD BOOK map

Important dates

1029 B.C. The Hebrews founded a kingdom in what is now Israel.

800's B.C. The Etruscans settled in west-central Italy.

750-338 B.C. Athens, Corinth, Sparta, and Thebes were the chief city-states of Greece.

c. 550 B.C. Cyrus the Great established the Persian Empire.

509 B.C. The people of Rome revolted against their Etruscan rulers and established a republic.

338 B.C. Philip II of Macedonia conquered the Greeks.

331 B.C. Alexander the Great won the Battle of Gaugamela, assuring his conquest of the Persian Empire.

221-206 B.C. The Qin Dynasty established China's first strong central government.

206 B.C.-A.D. 220 The Han Dynasty ruled China.

146 B.C. The Romans conquered Greece.

55-54 B.C. Julius Caesar led the Roman invasion of Britain.

27 B.C. Augustus became the first Roman emperor.

c. A.D. 250 The Maya Indians developed an advanced civilization in Central America and Mexico.

313 Constantine issued the Edict of Milan, which granted freedom of worship to Christians of the Roman Empire.

320 India began its golden age under the Gupta Empire.

395 The Roman Empire split into the East Roman, or Byzantine, Empire and the West Roman Empire.

476 The Germanic chieftain Odoacer overthrew Romulus Augustulus, the last emperor of the West Roman Empire.

British Museum, London (Photoresources)

Assyrian King Ashurbanipal and his queen are shown feasting in the royal garden on this stone carving. The carving, found at the king's palace in Nineveh, dates from the 600's B.C.

Egypt to the empire in 525 B.C. The Persians built excellent roads throughout their vast empire. They divided the empire into provinces, each governed by a Persian official. Unlike the Assyrians, the Persians allowed the conquered peoples to keep their own religions and traditions. See **Persia, Ancient**.

The Persian Empire lasted more than 200 years. Under Persian rule, Medes, Babylonians, Jews, and Egyptians were united for the first time. Although they still had different traditions and customs, they could no longer be thought of as belonging to separate civilizations. Another people who came under Persian control were the Phoenicians, who lived along the coasts of what are now Syria, Lebanon, and Israel. The Phoenicians were great explorers and traders who helped spread civilization among the peoples living in coastal areas along the Aegean Sea and in what is now Turkey. The Phoenicians developed an alphabet that became the basis of the Greek alphabet. All other Western alphabets, in turn, have been taken from the Greek. See **Phoenicia**.

The Greeks. The first major civilization in the region of Greece began to develop on Crete, an island in the Aegean Sea, about 3000 B.C. Scholars call this civilization the *Minoan* culture after Minos, the legendary king of the island (see **Minos**). The Minoans were skilled artists and architects and active traders. By about 2000 B.C., they had begun to build a series of magnificent palaces, the most elaborate of which was the Palace of Minos in the town of Knossos.

The Minoans traded with peoples in southwest Asia, Sicily, and Greece. Their trade routes provided an important link between the civilizations of southwest Asia and mainland Europe. Minoan culture flourished for about 500 years. It began to decline after 1450 B.C., when fire destroyed nearly all the towns on Crete. By about 1100 B.C., the culture had disappeared.

The most important early culture on the mainland of Greece centered on the southern city of Mycenae. The people of Mycenae were probably descendants of Indo-European peoples who had been migrating to Greece since about 2000 B.C. By the 1500's B.C., the Mycenaean culture had become rich and powerful. Mycenae was the leading political and cultural center on the Greek mainland until it collapsed in the early 1100's B.C. About

this time, nomadic peoples from the north began moving into Greece. Later Greeks called these people the Dorians. Historians are not sure what part the Dorians played in the fall of Mycenae.

Greek civilization developed between about 800 and 500 B.C. The first recorded Olympic Games were held for Greek athletes in 776 B.C., and the first surviving Greek inscriptions date from about 50 years later. The ancient Greeks settled in independent communities called *city-states*. Between 750 and 338 B.C., the chief city-states were Athens, Corinth, Sparta, and Thebes. The city-states were never united politically, and the people were divided into various groups. However, the Greeks were tied together by a common culture and language, and they thought of themselves as distinct from other peoples. The first democratic governments were established in the Greek city-states. Neither slaves nor women could vote, but more people took part in government in Greece than in any earlier civilization.

Greek culture gradually spread to other lands. The Greeks established many towns and trading posts in Sicily and in what are now southern Italy and Turkey. Greek colonists also founded settlements as far away as present-day Portugal, France, Libya, and India. Many Greeks served as craftworkers, teachers, and soldiers in the courts of foreign rulers.

From 500 to 479 B.C., the Greeks resisted invasions of Persian forces. Greek civilization then entered its Golden Age. Architects constructed masterpieces of classical beauty. Lasting works of art, literature, drama, history, and philosophy were produced. Greek scientists made great advances in mathematics, medicine, physics, botany, and zoology. During this period, Athens became the cultural center of the Greek world.

The achievements and growing power of Athens were the envy of the other Greek city-states. Hostility between the Athenians and their fellow Greeks led to the

Delphi Museum, Greece (Photoresources)

An ancient Greek dish portrays the god Apollo, patron of musicians and poets and the ideal of manly beauty. Greek culture thrived in the 400's B.C., the Golden Age of Greek civilization.

A famous Roman aqueduct, the Pont du Gard near Nîmes, France, stands as a reminder of one of the world's greatest empires. At its peak of power, in the A.D. 100's, the Roman Empire covered about half of Europe, much of southwest Asia, and the north coast of Africa.

bitter Peloponnesian War (431-404 B.C.). Athens lost the war. The victorious city-states soon started to quarrel among themselves, and Greece began to decline in power.

In 338 B.C., Philip II of Macedonia conquered the Greek city-states. His son, Alexander the Great, succeeded him in 336 B.C. Until his death in 323 B.C., Alexander expanded his empire through conquests of much of the civilized world from Egypt to the Indus River. Alexander helped spread Greek ideas and the Greek way of life into all the lands he conquered.

After Alexander died, his empire was divided among his generals. They continued to preserve Greek culture. The period after Alexander's death became known as the Hellenistic Age in the Mediterranean basin and southwest Asia. It lasted until the Romans took control, ending in Greece in 146 B.C. Egypt, the last major stronghold of the Hellenistic world, fell to the Romans in 30 B.C. See **Alexander the Great; Hellenistic Age.**

For a detailed description of life in ancient Greece, see **Greece, Ancient.**

The Romans. By the 500's B.C., Greek traders and colonists had established many settlements in Italy and Sicily. They carried Greek civilization directly to the mixed group of peoples living there, most of whom were descendants of Indo-European immigrants. These peoples included the Etruscans, who had settled in west-central Italy during the 800's B.C. In 509 B.C., the people of Rome, one of the cities under Etruscan control, revolted. The Romans gained their independence and declared Rome a republic.

For hundreds of years, Roman conquerors expanded the republic. By 290 B.C., Rome controlled most of Italy. It soon became one of the most powerful states of the western Mediterranean. During the 200's and 100's B.C., Rome defeated its only major rival, the former Phoenician colony of Carthage, in a series of struggles called the Punic Wars (see **Punic Wars**). As a result of the wars, Sicily and Spain became Roman provinces. Rome also expanded into the eastern Mediterranean. In 148 B.C., the Romans made Macedonia their first eastern province. Two years later, they conquered Greece. In 55 and 54 B.C., the Roman general Julius Caesar invaded Britain. Other conquests followed until the original city of Rome had grown into an enormous empire. At its height, in A.D. 117, the empire covered about half of Europe, much of southwest Asia, and the entire north coast of Africa.

Roman territory included all the Greek lands of the Hellenistic Age. The Romans imitated Greek art and literature, made use of Greek scientific knowledge, and based their architecture on Greek models. Educated people throughout the Roman Empire spoke Greek. By imitating Greek accomplishments, the Romans preserved and passed on much Greek culture that otherwise might have been lost.

The Romans also contributed their own achievements to the civilization they developed. They were superb engineers who constructed massive aqueducts and bridges, vast systems of roads, and monumental arches. The Romans developed an excellent legal system. Their legal code forms the basis of civil law in numerous

Detail of a mosaic (about 986-994) in Hagia Sophia, Istanbul, Turkey (Photoresources)

Constantine the Great was the first Roman emperor to become a Christian. He came to the throne in A.D. 306 and formed close ties between the Christian church and the Roman Empire.

European and Latin American countries, and many of its principles and terms are part of English and American common law. Latin, the language of the Romans, was the official language of the empire. It became the basis of French, Italian, Spanish, and other Romance languages of today.

The Romans excelled in the art of government. One of their most important achievements was the empire itself, which provided a stable framework of government for many peoples with widely different customs. The Romans showed respect for these customs and won the good will of many of the peoples they governed. Rome was a republic until 27 B.C., when Augustus took supreme power. Augustus and his successors retained republican titles and forms of government, but Rome actually became a monarchy ruled by emperors.

During the A.D. 100's and 200's, Rome was increasingly threatened by Germanic invaders in both the east and the west. As a result, the army became more and more powerful and began to play a major role in choosing Rome's emperors. One of the most important emperors the army helped bring to power was Constantine the Great, who came to the throne in 306. In 313, Constantine granted Christians of the Roman Empire freedom of worship. Christ had been born during the reign of the Emperor Augustus and was crucified by the Roman authorities in about A.D. 30, during the rule of Tiberius. The Romans had at times persecuted the Christians. However, after Constantine granted Christians legal recognition, a strong link was formed between the Christian church and the Roman Empire. Emperor Theodo-

sius I proclaimed Christianity the official religion of the empire in the late 300's.

A period of great disorder followed Constantine's death in 337. In 395, the Roman Empire split into two parts—the West Roman Empire and the East Roman, or Byzantine, Empire. The West Roman Empire soon fell to Germanic invaders, but the Byzantine Empire was to thrive for many years. For more information on the rise and fall of the Roman Empire, see **Rome, Ancient**.

The Mauryan Empire in India. About 1500 B.C., bands of Aryans, an Indo-European people, began migrating to India. The Aryans came from the plains of central Asia through the mountain passes of the Hindu Kush. By 1000 B.C., they had taken over most of the valley of the upper Ganges River in northern India.

The Aryans never migrated to southern India, but their influence gradually extended over the entire country and greatly affected Indian culture. Sanskrit, the language spoken by the Aryans, is the basis of languages still spoken in India. Hinduism, the religion of most Indians today, is rooted in Indo-European beliefs. The Aryans divided their society into four main social classes that became part of the *caste system* of Indian society. These four classes were priests and scholars; rulers and warriors; merchants and professionals; and laborers and servants. See **Caste**.

At various times in its history, the Aryan territory was divided into many states. In one state, a prince named Siddhartha Gautama was born about 563 B.C. Gautama abandoned a life of luxury to seek religious enlightenment. He became a great religious teacher known to his followers as *Buddha* (Enlightened One). Gautama's teachings are the foundation of Buddhism, one of the world's major religions. See **Buddhism**.

By about 300 B.C., much of India was united for the first time under one dynasty, the Mauryan. The Mauryan Empire reached its peak under Emperor Ashoka, who ruled during the 200's B.C. From his capital at Pataliputra (now Patna) in northern India, Ashoka controlled almost

Borromeo from Art Resource

A Hindu stone temple built during the A.D. 500's stands at Aihole, India, near Belgaum. It reflects a style of architecture that became popular under the Gupta dynasty.

The Great Wall of China was built to keep out invaders from the north. Most of the Great Wall was constructed after the A.D. 1500's. But as early as the 200's B.C., Emperor Shi Huangdi had ordered the linking of small walls built by local rulers.

A jade ornament of a bearded man dates from the Han dynasty, which ruled China from 206 B.C. to A.D. 220.

all India and part of central Asia. Ashoka supported Buddhism, which spread and prospered during his reign. He sent Buddhist missionaries to Ceylon (now Sri Lanka) and other countries. See **Ashoka; Mauryan Empire.**

The Mauryan dynasty ended with the assassination of its last emperor in 185 B.C. For most of the next 500 years, India was divided into small political units under no one ruler. In A.D. 320, a new dynasty, the Gupta, came to power in northern India. The Gupta dynasty lasted about 200 years. During the Gupta period, Indian civilization enjoyed a golden age of peace, good government, and cultural development. Beautiful cities arose, and universities were founded. Sanskrit literature, particularly drama, flourished during the Gupta era. The Gupta emperors were Hindus, but Buddhism also thrived under their rule. See **Gupta dynasty.**

The unification of China. About 1045 B.C., the Zhou people conquered the Shang from the west and established their own dynasty. The Zhou ruled until 256 B.C. The Zhou kings introduced the idea that they had been appointed to rule by Heaven. All later Chinese dynasties adopted that idea. From its beginning, the Zhou dynasty directly controlled only part of northern China. The rest of the kingdom consisted of semi-independent states. As time passed, the lords of these states grew increasingly powerful and so weakened the dynasty. In 771 B.C., the Zhou were forced to abandon their capital, near what is now Xi'an, and move eastward to Luoyang.

For hundreds of years after the Zhou moved their capital, fighting raged among the states for control of all

China. Efforts to restore order to Chinese society led to the birth of Chinese philosophy during this period. The great philosopher Confucius stressed the importance of moral standards and tradition and of a well-ordered society in which people performed the duties of their stations in life. See **Confucianism.**

In 221 B.C., the Qin (also spelled Ch'in) state defeated the last of its rivals to the east. The Qin created the first unified Chinese empire controlled by a strong central government. The name *China* came from the name of their dynasty. The first Qin emperor, Shi Huangdi, standardized weights and measures and the Chinese writing system. He also built extensive irrigation projects and ordered the construction of massive defensive walls in the northern and western parts of his realm.

The Qin dynasty lasted only until 206 B.C., when the Han dynasty began to take control of China. Under the Han emperors, Confucianism became the philosophical basis of government. Candidates for government jobs had to take a civil service examination based on Confucian ideals. Art, education, and science thrived during the Han period. By A.D. 1, the Chinese had invented paper. Sometime before A.D. 100, Buddhism was introduced into China from India.

Han China expanded southwest to what is now Tibet. Han warriors also conquered parts of Vietnam and Korea and overcame nomadic peoples in the north and west. Political struggles among the Han leaders led to the dynasty's collapse in A.D. 220. For the next 400 years, China was divided into warring states. See **Han dynasty.**

September by the Limbourg brothers, from the Duc de Berry's illuminated manuscript of the 1400's *Très Riches Heures;* Musée Condé, Chantilly, France (Giraudon from Art Resource)

European life in the Middle Ages centered on control of the land. Lords owned most of the land, which was farmed by their peasants. The lords lived in mighty castles like the one shown.

Various parts of the world gradually came more closely into contact with one another during the period from 500 to 1500. In fact, some regions came into contact with other regions for the first time. However, the various regions still remained largely independent of one another during most of that time, and their histories continued to progress along separate lines.

Great changes occurred in the old areas of civilization during the 1,000-year period. In western Europe, a number of separate states eventually arose from the disorder that followed the fall of the West Roman Empire. The East Roman, or Byzantine, Empire continued to survive and flourish. A new world religion, Islam, sprang up in Arabia and spread to many other parts of the world. Meanwhile, China continued to preserve its special way of life under a series of dynasties. Partly under influence from China, another Asian civilization appeared, that of Japan. In the Americas, civilizations developed without any outside influences.

In European history, the period between about 500 and 1500 is often referred to as the *Middle Ages* or the

medieval period. The word *medieval* comes from the Latin words *medium,* meaning *middle,* and *aevum,* meaning *age.* The terms *Middle Ages* and *medieval period* made sense to later Europeans who looked back on those years as a distinct period in the middle of their history between the civilizations of ancient Greece and Rome and the start of modern times. But the terms cannot be applied to world history as a whole because the histories of many parts of the world have no connection with ancient Greece and Rome.

Medieval Europe. By A.D. 400, many Germanic invaders and immigrants from the east had settled within the West Roman Empire. In 476, a Germanic chieftain named Odoacer overthrew the last emperor, Romulus Augustulus. By that time, Germanic conquerors had carved kingdoms out of all the West Roman provinces, where they displaced the framework of government created by the Romans.

Roman culture was not completely destroyed, however. Many Germanic rulers adopted some Roman customs and converted to Christianity. The Christian church became the most important civilizing force among the Germanic peoples. Its missionaries introduced them to Roman ideas of government and justice. Cathedrals and monasteries provided the main centers of learning and philosophy. The monks and the clergy helped continue the reading and writing of Latin and preserved many ancient manuscripts.

For hundreds of years after the fall of the West Roman Empire, the Germanic kings had great difficulty defending themselves against invaders. The invaders included Arabs from the south, Vikings from the north, and Magyars and Avars from the east. During these troubled times, a new military and political system known as *feudalism* developed in western Europe. Under this system, powerful lords—who owned most of the land—gave some of their holdings to less wealthy nobles in return for pledges of allegiance. These lesser nobles, called *vassals,* swore to fight for the lord when he needed their help. Peasants worked the fields of the lords and their vassals. By the 900's, most of western Europe was divided into feudal states. The feudal lords completely controlled their estates. Kings ruled only their own lands and vassals. See **Feudalism.**

During the 1000's, many lords established strong governments and achieved periods of peace under the feudal system. Trade revived along the old land routes and waterways used by the Romans. Towns sprang up and prospered along the trade routes. The peasants learned better farming methods and gained new farmland by clearing forests and draining swamps. The population rose. Learning and the arts thrived as trade brought increasing contact with the advanced Byzantine and Islamic civilizations. During the 1100's and 1200's, the first European universities were established.

The people of the medieval towns often supported the kings against the feudal lords. The townspeople agreed to pay taxes to the kings in return for protection and freedom. During the 1300's and 1400's, some kings became increasingly powerful and began to extend their authority over the feudal lords. By 1500, France, England, Spain, and Portugal had become unified

Major developments

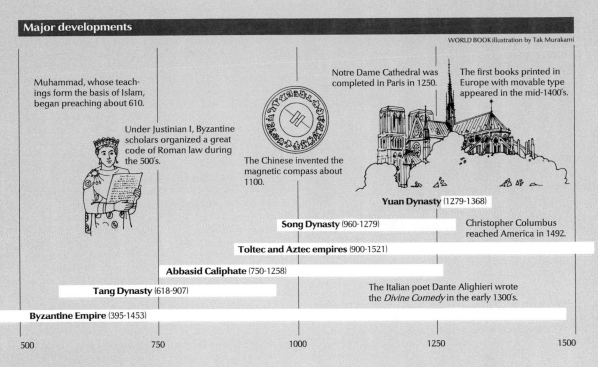

WORLD BOOK illustration by Tak Murakami

Muhammad, whose teachings form the basis of Islam, began preaching about 610.

Under Justinian I, Byzantine scholars organized a great code of Roman law during the 500's.

The Chinese invented the magnetic compass about 1100.

Notre Dame Cathedral was completed in Paris in 1250.

The first books printed in Europe with movable type appeared in the mid-1400's.

Yuan Dynasty (1279-1368)

Song Dynasty (960-1279)

Christopher Columbus reached America in 1492.

Toltec and Aztec empires (900-1521)

Abbasid Caliphate (750-1258)

Tang Dynasty (618-907)

The Italian poet Dante Alighieri wrote the *Divine Comedy* in the early 1300's.

Byzantine Empire (395-1453)

| 500 | 750 | 1000 | 1250 | 1500 |

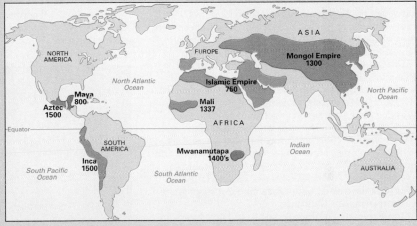

Between 300 and 1500, new civilizations appeared in Africa and the Americas. In southwest Asia, the Muslim Arabs rose to power and conquered a huge empire by the mid-700's. In the 1200's, Mongol warriors swept through Asia, creating one of the largest empires in history.

WORLD BOOK map

Important dates

300's-mid-1000's The Ghana Empire, the first great black empire in western Africa, existed as a trading state.

527-565 The Byzantine Empire reached its greatest extent under Emperor Justinian I.

622 Muhammad, prophet of Islam, fled from Mecca to Medina. His flight, called the *Hijra* or *Hegira,* marks the beginning of the Islamic calendar.

732 Charles Martel and the Franks defeated invading Muslims at the Battle of Tours in west-central France. The battle limited Muslim advances in Europe.

750 The Abbasids became the caliphs of the Islamic world.

800 Pope Leo III crowned Charlemagne, ruler of the Franks, emperor of the Romans.

c. 988 Vladimir I (also spelled Volodymyr) established Christianity among the East Slavs, ancestors of the Belarusian, Russian, and Ukrainian people.

1054 Rivalries between the church in Rome and the church in Constantinople resulted in their separation as the Roman Catholic Church and Eastern Orthodox Churches.

1192 Yoritomo became the first shogun to rule Japan. Shogun rule lasted until 1867.

1215 English barons forced King John to grant a charter of liberties called Magna Carta.

1279 The Mongols gained control of all China.

1300's The Renaissance began in Italy.

1368 The Ming Dynasty began its nearly 300-year rule of China.

1453 The Ottomans captured Constantinople (now Istanbul, Turkey) and overthrew the Byzantine Empire.

Detail of a painting (1400's) by Jean Mielot (Bettmann Archive)

Medieval monks like the one shown here copied many valuable manuscripts written by ancient Greek and Roman scholars. Their work helped preserve knowledge of ancient times.

nation-states ruled by monarchs. For more information about medieval Europe, see **Middle Ages.**

The Byzantine Empire was a continuation of the East Roman Empire. Its capital and military stronghold was Constantinople (now Istanbul, Turkey). The Byzantine rulers kept Roman governmental and legal traditions. However, the East Roman provinces had always been more influenced by Greek culture than by Latin culture. As a result, the Byzantines helped preserve ancient Greek language, literature, and philosophy.

Christianity flourished in the Byzantine Empire. The Byzantine church was the chief civilizing force among the Slavic peoples of southeastern Europe and Russia. Byzantine missionaries converted the Slavs to Christianity and invented a script in which the Slavic languages were written down. The church in Constantinople was united with the church in Rome for many years. But rivalries developed between the churches, and they drifted apart. The Western church eventually became known as the Roman Catholic Church. The Eastern Orthodox Churches developed out of Byzantine Christianity. See **Eastern Orthodox Churches.**

The Byzantine Empire reached its greatest extent under Emperor Justinian, who came to the throne in 527. His empire included Italy, much of southeastern Europe, part of Spain, much of southwest Asia, and lands along the north coast of Africa. At the command of Justinian, Byzantine scholars collected and organized the many laws of the ancient Romans. The resulting code of laws, called the *Justinian Code,* clarified the laws of the times and is today the basis of the legal systems of many countries (see **Justinian Code**). Art and architecture flourished during Justinian's reign. The Byzantines constructed domed cathedrals with ornately decorated interiors. One of these cathedrals is the magnificent Hagia Sophia built by Justinian in Constantinople. See **Byzantine art; Hagia Sophia.**

For hundreds of years, the Byzantine Empire protected western Europe from attacks from the east by nomadic peoples, Persians, and such Muslim invaders as

the Arabs and Ottomans. Starting in the 1000's, however, the Byzantine emperors fought a losing battle against the Muslims. By 1400, the Ottomans had taken much of southeastern Europe and all the Asian territories of the Byzantines. In 1453, the Ottomans captured Constantinople. This conquest brought to an end the last remnants of the old Roman Empire. See **Byzantine Empire.**

The Islamic world. In the 600's, Islam, a new religion based on the teachings of Muhammad, began in Arabia. Muhammad was born about 570 and grew up in Mecca, a major trading center on the Arabian Peninsula. At that time, many Arabs believed in nature gods and prayed to idols and spirits. But Muhammad urged the Arabs to worship one God. The Meccans rejected Muhammad's teachings and persecuted him and his followers. In 622, Muhammad and his disciples fled to the city of Medina (then called Yathrib). Muhammad's flight is called the Hijra, also spelled Hegira. The Muslim calendar is dated from the beginning of the year in which the Hijra took place. The people of Medina accepted Muhammad as God's messenger. By 630, Muhammad and his followers had captured Mecca.

After Muhammad's death in 632, authority to head the Islamic community passed to religious leaders later called *caliphs.* The first caliphs were members of Muhammad's family. Under their leadership, Islam became a great conquering force. The Muslim armies defeated the tribes of southern Arabia and then spread north to Palestine, Syria, Mesopotamia, and Persia. In 661, the caliphate passed to another family, the Umayyads, who established their capital at Damascus. The Umayyad ca-

SCALA from Art Resource

The Basilica of St. Mark in Venice, Italy, is one of the outstanding examples of Byzantine architecture in western Europe. The Roman Catholic church was built during the 1000's.

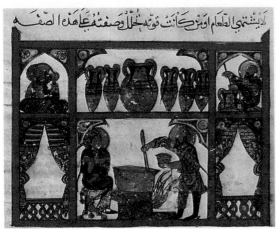

Illumination by an unknown Persian artist; Metropolitan Museum of Art, New York City (Werner Forman Archive)

A Muslim pharmacist is shown preparing a drug in an illustration from a medical book of the 1200's. Muslims, followers of Islam, contributed greatly to advances in science and the arts.

liphs led the Muslim Arabs to new victories. By the early 700's, the Arabs had conquered Rhodes, Sicily, northern Africa, and Afghanistan. Muslim forces had also pushed into Spain and India and reached the borders of China.

In 750, the Abbasids became the caliphs of the expanding Islamic world. They moved the capital to Baghdad. Under the Abbasids, Islamic civilization reached its greatest heights. Baghdad became a huge city, rivaling Constantinople in wealth and population. Islamic art and architecture flourished, and many Islamic academies and universities were founded.

As a result of their conquests, the Muslims had come into contact with Persian astronomy, history, and medicine; Indian mathematics; and Greek science and philosophy. The Arabs became learned in these fields and made significant contributions of their own in mathematics, medicine, astronomy, and other sciences. They also developed literature of their own in Arabic. Many ancient Greek texts were translated into Arabic and eventually introduced into western Europe.

The Abbasid caliphate declined during the 900's as peoples from central Asia began invading southwest Asia. Some of these peoples were Turks who had been converted to Islam. During the early 1300's, the Ottomans, who had settled in Anatolia (now Turkey), became the military leaders of the Islamic world. After the Ottomans seized Constantinople in 1453, they made the city the capital of their empire. By 1700, the Ottoman Empire covered southeastern Europe, southern Russia, part of northern Africa, and much of southwest Asia. See **Ottoman Empire.**

For more details on the history of the Islamic world, see **Muslims.**

China. From 500 to 1500, China had a highly productive agricultural economy. Food surpluses enabled craft-workers to produce high-quality silk and porcelain that became popular throughout much of the Eastern Hemisphere. Merchants flocked to China by camel caravan across central Asia, and mariners from as far away as In-

dia and Persia sailed to China through the Indian Ocean. During the Tang dynasty (618-907) and the Song dynasty (960-1279), China enjoyed great prosperity and cultural accomplishment.

The Tang and Song rulers continued to use the system of civil service examinations based on Confucianism that had begun hundreds of years earlier during Han times. Successful candidates for government office thus shared a common body of beliefs and a respect for traditional ways. Cities and towns grew rapidly during the Tang and Song periods. The Tang capital at Chang'an (now Xi'an) had a population of more than a million people. Literature, history, and philosophy flourished under the Tang and Song dynasties. During the Tang period, the Chinese invented gunpowder and block printing. Chinese inventions during the Song period included a type of handheld gun, the magnetic compass, and movable type for printing. See **Tang dynasty; Song dynasty.**

During the 1200's, Mongol warriors swept into China from the north. The Mongol leader Kublai Khan established the Yuan dynasty, which lasted from 1279 to 1368. The Mongol period marked the first time that all China had come under foreign rule. Kublai Khan encouraged commerce and cultural exchange with other peoples. During Yuan times, Europeans became increasingly interested in China as a result of the reports of travelers and traders. The most enthusiastic reports came from Marco Polo, a trader from Venice. Rebellions drove the Mongols from China during the mid-1300's. In 1368, Chinese rule was reestablished under the Ming dynasty, which held power until 1644. See **Mongol Empire.**

The rise of Japanese civilization. The development of Japanese civilization was greatly influenced by the neighboring Chinese culture. During the 500's, Confucianism and Buddhism reached Japan from China. The Japanese borrowed the Chinese system of writing and adopted some Chinese ideas of government and administration. Japanese government, like Chinese government, centered on an emperor. Beneath the emperor, Japanese society was divided into various *clans* (related families).

During the late 700's and early 800's, the Fujiwaras, an aristocratic clan, rose to power in Japan. The Fujiwaras

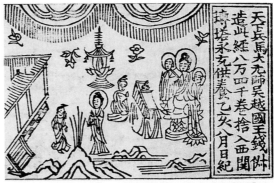

Denver Art Museum, Marion G. Hendrie Collection

A Chinese block print from 975 symbolizes China's technological progress. The Chinese invented block printing during the Tang dynasty, which ruled from 618 to 907.

Rival Japanese clans fought for control of the country's government during the 1100's. Members of the Minamoto family helped kidnap a Taira family emperor in 1160, *shown here,* but failed to gain power. Minamoto leaders finally won control of Japan in 1185. They later established a form of military government known as the *shogunate.*

Detail of *The Tale of the Heiji War Scroll* (mid-1200's), an ink painting with colors on paper by an unknown Japanese artist; Museum of Fine Arts, Boston (Gemini Smith)

gained control over the emperor and his court by intermarrying with the imperial family. Under the Fujiwaras, the court nobility enjoyed a life of splendor and luxury. The people of Japan began to cast off Chinese cultural influences. Some of the first masterpieces of Japanese literature were written during the Fujiwara era. The Japanese also produced fine ceramics and lacquerware and developed such arts as flower arranging, landscape gardening, and silk weaving. Japanese exports gradually began to appear in the markets of China and southeastern Asia. The Fujiwara clan ruled Japan about 300 years. During that time, the emperors lost all real power, though they still officially reigned.

During the 1000's, civil wars between rival nobles brought an end to Fujiwara rule. Another powerful clan, the Minamoto, seized control of the imperial court in 1185. The Minamoto leaders established a form of military government called the *shogunate.* The emperor remained in retirement, and a Minamoto *shogun* (military commander) ruled in his name (see **Shogun**). The Minamoto shogunate collapsed in the early 1300's, when Japan was again torn by violent civil wars. The wars slowed the growth of cities and towns and weakened the society. But Japan remained safe from attack by foreign powers because of its isolated island position. The Mongols tried to invade Japan in 1274 and 1281, but both attempts failed because of typhoons in the Sea of Japan. See **Japan** (History).

The age of invasions of India. After the Gupta Empire fell in about 500, India broke up into many small kingdoms. From then until the early 1500's, India suffered repeated invasions from the northwest. In the early 700's, Muslim invaders from Arabia swept across northwestern India but were eventually overcome by Indian forces. During the late 1100's, Muslim Turks from central Asia conquered the Indus Valley. By 1206, they had established a *sultanate* (government by a sultan) in Delhi. The Delhi Sultanate soon controlled all northern India. During the sultanate, many Muslims came to India to serve as soldiers, government officials, merchants, and priests. Muslim holy men converted many Indians to Islam. See **Delhi Sultanate**.

In 1398, a Mongol army raided India and captured Delhi. The Mongols soon withdrew, however. The sultanate regained Delhi, but the rest of the sultanate territory was split into kingdoms. In 1526, Babur, a Muslim

Eliot Elisofon, National Museum of African Art, Timbuktu, Mali

The Sankore Mosque in Timbuktu, Mali, became an important Islamic house of worship in the Mali Empire. During the 1200's, the Mali Empire emerged as the most powerful state in western Africa. The Mali Empire flourished until the 1400's.

Early civilizations in the Americas
were developed by the Maya Indians in
Mexico and Central America and by the
Inca Indians in Peru. The jade carving of a
Maya official dates from about 900. The
silver cup was made by an Inca artist in
about 1500.

British Museum, London (Photoresources)   Lee Boltin

prince from central Asia, invaded India and defeated the
forces of the last sultan of Delhi. Babur founded the
Mughal Empire and made himself emperor. By the time
Babur died in 1530, the Mughal Empire stretched from
Kabul In what is now Afghanistan to the mouth of the
Ganges River in what is now Bangladesh. See **Babur;
Mughal Empire.**

African civilizations. The Muslim Arabs completed
their conquest of northern Africa by 710. For hundreds
of years, the Islamic faith and culture spread to other
parts of Africa. Camel caravans that crossed the Sahara
brought northern Muslims into contact with western
Africa. Muslim traders who sailed the Indian Ocean converted the peoples living along the east coasts of what
are now Somalia, Kenya, and Tanzania. Black African empires developed and prospered along some of the major trade routes.

Islamic records provide information about the Ghana
Empire, the first great black empire in western Africa.
The empire existed from the 300's to the mid-1000's. The
Arabs called Ghana the "land of gold" because Ghanaian
traders supplied them with gold from regions south of
the empire. During the 1200's, an even bigger empire,
the Islamic Mali Empire, arose as the most powerful
state in western Africa. One of Mali's cities, Timbuktu,
became an important center of trade and Muslim culture. The Mali Empire began to break up during the
1400's. By 1500, most of it had come under the control of
the Songhai Empire. This empire, which was also Islamic, became powerful mainly by controlling trade across
the Sahara. Songhai lasted until 1591. See **Ghana Empire; Mali Empire; Songhai Empire.**

Islamic influence did not extend into southern Africa.
Much of the south was originally settled by peoples
who spoke Bantu languages. About the time of Christ,
these peoples began migrating southward from what is
now the border region between Nigeria and Cameroon.
Their migrations lasted over 1,000 years.

On the east coast of Africa, the Bantu peoples came
into contact with traders from the Persian Gulf region
who wanted to buy gold, copper, iron, ivory, and slaves.
Several large trading empires developed in southeastern Africa, but little is known about them. One empire,

the Mwanamutapa Empire, arose during the 1400's in
what are now Mozambique and Zimbabwe. The city of
Zimbabwe served as the empire's capital. During the
late 1400's, the Changamire Empire conquered the
Mwanamutapa and took over the capital. Massive towers and walls from a royal residence and burial place
built during Changamire times still stand on the site of
the city. See **Zimbabwe** (History).

Civilizations in the Americas. The first civilizations
in the Americas arose in Central America and in what
are now Mexico and Peru. The Maya Indians of Central
America and Mexico built a sophisticated agricultural
society. Between about 250 and 900, the Maya built religious centers consisting of palaces, pyramids, temples,
and terraces. The Maya studied astronomy, invented an
accurate yearly calendar, and developed an advanced
form of writing. For reasons still unknown, Maya civilization began to decline during the 900's. Many Maya sites
were abandoned. See **Maya.**

From about 900 to 1200, the Toltec Indians were the
dominant people in the central Mexican highlands. By
the early 1400's, the Aztec replaced the Toltec as the
most powerful people in central Mexico. The Aztec built
a magnificent capital city, Tenochtitlan, on the site of
present-day Mexico City and established a mighty empire. The Aztec devoted much of their time to religious
practices. Human sacrifice was a central feature of their
religion. The Aztec believed that the shedding of blood
was necessary for continued agricultural productivity.
See **Toltec Indians; Aztec.**

By the 1200's, civilization had made great advances in
Peru. Peruvian farmers were using bronze tools, and Peruvian stonemasons had become master builders. The
people used *quipu,* a cord with knotted strings of various lengths and colors, to keep records and send messages. During the 1300's and 1400's, the Inca Indians
gained control of the Peruvian civilization. By the early
1500's, the Inca ruled an empire that stretched between
what are now southern Colombia and central Chile. A
vast network of roads linked the distant provinces of the
empire. Conquered peoples were forced to help build
and maintain the roads, to raise crops for the Inca, and
to serve in the Inca army. See **Inca.**

Detail from *The Return of the Ambassadors* (1490's) by Vittore Carpaccio, Accademia, Venice (SCALA from Art Resource)

Renaissance artists and scholars developed bold new ideas that led to major achievements in architecture, painting, sculpture, and literature in western Europe from the 1300's through the 1500's. Venice, Italy, *shown here,* an early center of the Renaissance, attracted many visitors.

Great changes occurred in the course of world history between 1500 and 1900. The world's population rose dramatically, from about 450 million in 1500 to more than $1\frac{1}{2}$ billion by 1900. Cities and towns grew steadily. European civilization began to lead the world in economic and technological matters. A world in which civilizations developed largely independently of one another gradually gave way to the dominance of European civilization.

A number of factors contributed to the wide expansion of European influence. An age of European exploration during the 1400's and 1500's led to the founding of European colonies in Africa, Asia, and the Americas. Thousands of Europeans migrated to these colonies. Industrialization began in Europe during the 1700's, and the continent soon became the manufacturing center of the world. The European nations established more and more colonies overseas to serve as markets for their manufactured products and as sources of raw materials for industry. Growing trade with these colonies brought increasing wealth and power to the continent. Political rivalries among the European states also encouraged

them to expand their empires abroad. Advances in technology, such as better ships and weapons, helped the Europeans conquer new territories.

The Europeans often introduced their arts and technology and their systems of law, government, and education into the various areas where they settled. In this way, the ideas and skills of European civilization became more widespread than those of any other civilization in history.

The Renaissance. The transformation of European society began with the Renaissance, a period of intense cultural activity lasting from about 1300 to 1600. Scholars known as *humanists* were the intellectual leaders of the Renaissance. Most humanists were deeply pious and did not reject Christianity. But they did reject traditional medieval theology, which dealt with religious issues in a highly abstract manner, in favor of a more down-to-earth approach. They encouraged the study of Greek and Roman classics because they believed that the examination of ancient literature, history, and philosophy would lead to a deep understanding of human nature and human society. They also believed that by returning to the clas-

Major developments

WORLD BOOK illustration by Tak Murakami

Charles Darwin proposed his theory of evolution in 1859 in *The Origin of Species.*

European colonial expansion in Africa and Asia (1870-1914)

Latin American wars of independence (1791-1824)

French Revolution (1789-1799)

Revolutionary War in America (1775-1783.)

Industrial Revolution (1700-mid 1800's)

Nicolaus Copernicus proposed in 1543 that the sun is the center of the universe.

William Shakespeare wrote many of the world's greatest dramas between 1590 and 1616.

Michelangelo completed painting the ceiling of the Sistine Chapel in the Vatican in 1512.

Manchu rule of China (1644-1912)

Tokugawa shogunate in Japan (1603-1867)

Mughal Empire (1526-1707)

Voyages of discovery (1400's-1700's)

Ludwig van Beethoven composed many of his greatest symphonies between 1800 and 1815.

Ottoman Empire (1326-1922)

Renaissance (1300-1600)

Alexander Graham Bell invented the telephone in 1876.

| 1500 | 1600 | 1700 | 1800 | 1900 |

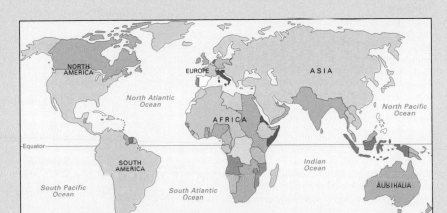

European colonial empires had spread over much of the world by the late 1800's. The largest empires of the period belonged to the United Kingdom, France, and Germany.

WORLD BOOK map

- Belgium
- France
- Germany
- Italy
- Netherlands
- Portugal
- Spain
- United Kingdom

Important dates

1500's The Reformation led to the birth of Protestantism.

1519-1521 Ferdinand Magellan commanded the first globe-circling voyage, completed in 1522 after his death.

1521 The Spanish conquistador Hernando Cortés defeated the Aztec Indians of Mexico.

1526 Babur, a Muslim prince, invaded India and founded the Mughal Empire.

1588 The Royal Navy of England defeated the Spanish Armada, ending the threat of Spanish invasion.

1644-1912 The Manchus ruled China as the Qing Dynasty.

1776 The 13 American Colonies adopted the Declaration of Independence, establishing the United States of America.

1789 The French Revolution began.

1815 Napoleon Bonaparte was defeated in the Battle of Waterloo, ending his attempt to rule Europe.

1853-1854 Commodore Matthew Perry visited Japan and opened two ports to U.S. trade.

1858 The United Kingdom took over the rule of India from the East India Company after the Indian Rebellion, also called the Sepoy Rebellion.

1865 Union forces defeated the Confederates in the American Civil War after four years of fighting.

1869 The Suez Canal opened.

1871 Germany became united under the Prussian king, who ruled the new empire as Kaiser Wilhelm I.

1898 The United States took control of Guam, Puerto Rico, and the Philippines following the Spanish-American War.

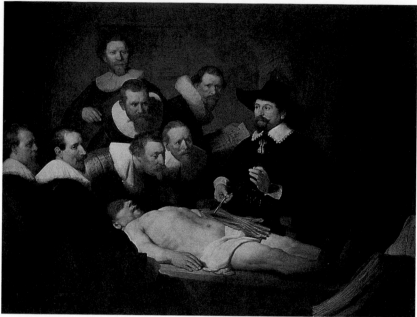

The Royal Gallery, The Hague (SCALA from Art Resource)

The study of the body led to important medical discoveries in Europe during the 1600's. The Dutch artist Rembrandt portrayed this study in his famous painting *Anatomy Lesson of Professor Tulp.*

sics, they could launch a new golden age of culture. See **Humanism.**

The Renaissance began in Italy in the early 1300's and spread throughout most of Europe during the 1400's and 1500's. Writers of the period described human feelings and situations that people could easily understand. Renaissance artists tried to capture the dignity and majesty of human beings in lifelike paintings and sculptures. Architects designed many buildings that incorporated elements of classical style. Many world masterpieces of architecture, literature, painting, and sculpture were created during the Renaissance. See **Renaissance.**

Other changes that occurred during the Renaissance affected the Christian church itself. During the early 1500's, a religious movement called the Reformation led to the birth of Protestantism. The Reformation followed many earlier attempts by religious reformers to correct abuses that had developed within the Roman Catholic Church. Beginning in 1517, Martin Luther, a German monk and theology professor, became the leader of the reform movement. Luther's criticisms gradually led him and his followers to break completely with the Catholic Church.

By 1600, reformers had established Protestant churches in about half of western Europe. Many Protestant groups emerged. The Protestant movement encouraged Roman Catholic leaders to work toward reform and renewal in their own church. This movement led to the Counter Reformation, which ended many abuses in the Roman Catholic Church and greatly strengthened the authority of the pope. Religious rivalries led to bitter conflicts and even religious wars. By the mid-1600's, however, Protestants and Catholics alike had become weary of conflict, and they began to move toward religious toleration. See **Reformation; Counter Reformation.**

The spread of new ideas during the Renaissance was made faster and easier by the invention of movable type in Europe in the mid-1400's. Most of the first printed books were classic Greek and Roman texts or religious books, particularly the Bible. But the Renaissance stimulated a renewed interest in scientific research and in the study of the natural world, and so books on scientific subjects began to appear by the late 1500's. During the 1600's, scientists developed the modern scientific method, with its emphasis on experimentation and careful observation. The invention of such instruments as the microscope and telescope contributed to a rapid growth in scientific knowledge. By 1700, new discoveries had revolutionized such fields as anatomy, astronomy, chemistry, and physics.

The age of exploration. A remarkable wave of European exploration had begun in the early 1400's. Portuguese explorers in search of an eastward sea route to Asia started to sail down the west coast of Africa. They gradually developed better navigational charts and improved the rigging of their sailing ships. By 1473, a Portuguese ship had crossed the equator, and another one had reached the Cape of Good Hope at the southern tip of Africa by 1487. Christopher Columbus, an Italian navigator in the service of Spain, reached America in 1492. In 1497 and 1498, a Portuguese explorer, Vasco da Gama, made the first voyage from Europe around Africa to India.

During the 1500's and 1600's, Europeans continued to gain geographical knowledge. In the early 1500's, Ferdinand Magellan, a Portuguese navigator in the service of Spain, set out on an expedition to sail around the world. Magellan was killed on the journey, but one of his ships completed the voyage. Sailors from France, England, and the Netherlands led the search for shorter routes to Asia—either a Northwest Passage across North America or a Northeast Passage north of Europe. Explorers slowly began to work their way through the land mass of America. See **Exploration** (The great age of European exploration).

The discovery of new territories provided opportunities for the expansion of European commerce. By 1700, Europeans were trading throughout the world, and some European lands had acquired colonial empires. The colonies provided Europeans with coffee, cotton fabrics, hardwoods, spices, sugar, and other products. New crops, such as potatoes and tobacco, were introduced into Europe from America. A large slave trade developed with Africa. In addition, a continuous flow of gold and silver from the New World enabled Europeans to increase their trade with India and China, where demand for the precious metals was high.

The colonization of America. The search for gold drew many of the first Spanish explorers and *conquistadors* (conquerors) to the New World. The most famous conquistador was Hernando Cortés. In 1519, he landed in Mexico, marched his army to the Aztec capital at Tenochtitlan, and took the Aztec emperor captive. The Aztec rebelled in 1520. They were finally defeated in 1521. Cortés then claimed Mexico for Spain. In 1533, another Spaniard, Francisco Pizarro, conquered the wealthy empire of the Inca Indians in Peru. See **Cortés, Hernando; Pizarro, Francisco.**

Except for members of the Spanish clergy, few Spaniards had respect for the Indians and their ways of life. They made the Indians give them a fortune in gold and other riches and forced them to work in their mines and on their plantations. Millions of Indians died of mistreatment or of smallpox and other diseases introduced to the Americas by the Spaniards.

Spanish rule rapidly expanded in the Americas. By 1700, Spain controlled Mexico, Central America, and most of South America. The Spaniards established cities and universities throughout their territory. European government, the Spanish language, and the Catholic Church became dominant in most of Latin America. The population of the colonies rose as more settlers arrived and the Indians acquired some resistance to European diseases. Many Spaniards and Indians intermarried, producing the beginning of a population of mixed ancestry. However, the ruling class of the colonies consisted only of people of unmixed European ancestry.

Much of Latin America had been colonized before the first lasting English settlement was established at Jamestown, Virginia, in 1607. By 1733, there were 13 English colonies, with a total population of about a million, along the Atlantic coast of North America. Many colonists were drawn to the New World by its economic opportunities, such as the availability of plentiful land. Some settlers, including Puritans, Quakers, and Roman Catholics, came to the English colonies to escape religious persecution. Most of the colonists were English. But other Europeans also came. In 1624, for example, the Dutch settled New Netherland, which included parts of what are now Connecticut, Delaware, New Jersey, and New York. Farther north, French colonists settled throughout the St. Lawrence River Valley.

The English colonists were soon able to grow enough food to support themselves. They also produced tobacco and other valuable exports to pay for imports from England. But unlike the Spanish colonies, the English colonies had no silver or gold. In addition, the English settlers in North America did not find densely populated Indian societies like those in Mexico and Peru. At first, the Indians and the settlers had friendly relations. But as more and more settlers claimed greater amounts of Indian hunting grounds, wars broke out between the two groups. See **Indian wars** (Colonial days).

The Islamic empires. Parts of Europe and Asia remained under control of the Ottoman Empire until the early 1900's. The Ottoman Empire never had a strong central government. Ottoman governors ruled the prov-

From the *Vallard Atlas;* The Huntington Library

An atlas printed in 1547 included this map of the Caribbean region. The map is fairly accurate, but it shows the region with North America at the bottom and South America at the top. An age of European exploration began during the 1400's. By 1700, the general outlines of most of the world's major land masses were known.

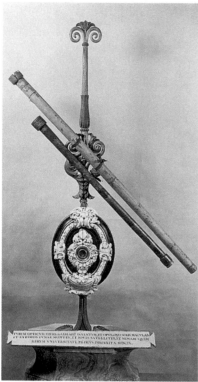

Museo della Scienza, Florence (SCALA from Art Resource)

Nachet Collection (Giraudon from Art Resource)

New scientific devices, such as the telescope and the microscope, contributed to a rapid growth of knowledge during the 1600's and 1700's. The two long tubes are telescopes used by the Italian astronomer Galileo, who made revolutionary discoveries in astronomy. The device on a wooden stand is a Dutch microscope made during the 1700's. It has three reflecting mirrors.

inces of the empire. Their chief tasks included collecting taxes and raising armies. But they interfered as little as possible in the lives of the conquered peoples. For example, Christians and Jews could practice their faiths as long as they paid their taxes. The subject peoples thus lived as separate communities and felt no loyalty to their Ottoman rulers. This lack of unity weakened the empire.

The Ottomans could not control some areas of their empire. Mesopotamia was especially difficult to govern. For nearly 200 years, this valley between the Tigris and Euphrates rivers was the site of warfare between the Ottomans and another Islamic power, Persia. A new dynasty, the Safavid, had developed in Persia in the early 1500's. The greatest Safavid king was Shah Abbas, who came to the throne in 1587. He successfully fought the Ottomans and Uzbek tribes from Turkestan. Shah Abbas and his successors strongly supported the development of the arts. Isfahan, which became the Safavid capital in 1598, was known as one of the world's most beautiful cities. Safavid power began to decline after Shah Abbas died in 1629. It ended in 1722, when armies from Afghanistan invaded Persia and captured Isfahan.

In addition to fighting the Ottomans, the Safavid rulers fought another great Islamic power, the Mughal Empire of India. The Mughal Empire reached its height under Akbar, who ruled from 1556 to 1605. Akbar controlled most of what are now northern and central India, Afghanistan, Bangladesh, and Pakistan. He ruled wisely, and his religious tolerance won the loyalty of many Hindus. The empire weakened under Akbar's successors.

Serious trouble developed during the reign of Aurangzeb, who became emperor in 1658. Aurangzeb reimposed a special tax on Hindus that had been abolished by Akbar and destroyed many of their temples. He also tried to force non-Muslims to convert to Islam. Partly as a result of Aurangzeb's policies and costly wars with Persia, the Mughal Empire began breaking up soon after his death in 1707. See **Akbar; Aurangzeb.**

At first, the spread of European influence affected the Islamic world little, though trade gradually increased between the European lands and the Islamic empires. But as the Islamic powers declined, the Europeans took advantage of the situation and began to assume control of Islamic lands. By 1900, European nations dominated most of the Islamic world. The French established themselves in northern Africa, and the Dutch took Indonesia. The United Kingdom occupied Egypt and the Sudan, set up an empire in India, and ruled Malaya. In the 1900's, Italy seized Ottoman territories in northern Africa and along the eastern shores of the Mediterranean Sea.

Developments in China and Japan. The Ming dynasty, which had come to power in China in 1368, began to decline during the 1500's. Rebellions in outlying provinces troubled the empire, and Indochina and other distant dependencies slipped out of its control. The Ming emperors looked down on all things foreign and regarded the European traders who visited China as inferiors. But some rights were granted to the Europeans as the Ming dynasty weakened. The Portuguese were allowed to establish a settlement at Macao, on the southeast coast of China, in 1557. A European community later grew up in the city of Canton (now called Guangzhou), a major center of foreign trade with China.

In 1644, the Ming asked the Manchus, a seminomadic people from Manchuria, for help in putting down rebellions within the empire. The Manchus then invaded China—but only to establish their own dynasty, the Qing, on the throne. The Manchus ruled China until 1912. They had great respect for Chinese civilization and did little to change Chinese life or government. The Manchu rulers pushed back Russian advances in the Amur River Valley, established control over Tibet, regained parts of Indochina, and added Korea to their territory. During the 1700's, contacts with Europeans multiplied, and Christian missionaries were welcomed at the Manchu capital, Beijing. The Manchus admired the Europeans' scientific knowledge and their skills in mapmaking and the manufacture of guns, but they did not wish to imitate European ways of life.

In Japan, the Tokugawa family seized power in 1603 and established the Tokugawa shogunate. The Tokugawas ruled for more than 250 years. They were determined to end the civil wars that had troubled the country for years and restore order to Japanese society. Under Tokugawa rule, Japan was divided into about 250 regions, each headed by a lord who swore allegiance to the shogun.

European traders and Christian missionaries had begun arriving in Japan during the 1500's. But the Tokugawa rulers feared that the missionaries might soon bring European armies with them to conquer Japan. In the early 1600's, they ordered all missionaries to leave the country. They also tried to force all Japanese converts to give up their new faith. Those who refused were persecuted or killed. By 1640, Christianity had been almost eliminated.

The Tokugawa rulers also believed that it was necessary to restrict contact with European merchants, who, it was believed, might serve the interests of European conquerors. In the 1630's, the government cut its ties with all European merchants except for a small community of Dutch traders, who had shown no interest in promoting Christianity or interfering in Japanese politics. The Dutch were permitted to live on the tiny island of Deshima in the harbor at Nagasaki. Although the Tokugawas sharply restricted Japanese trade with Europe, they permitted flourishing trade with China and Korea.

The rise of democracy and nationalism. During the 1700's and 1800's, most countries in the Western world were affected by two powerful political forces—democracy and nationalism. During this period, many peoples won the right to take part in their governments. Nationalistic feelings—particularly the desire of people who shared a common culture to be united as a nation—led to the formation of many new states.

In some areas, the movement toward democracy and nationalism triggered revolts against existing political systems. One of the most important revolts was the Revolutionary War in America. Relations between the United Kingdom and its colonies in America began to break down in the mid-1700's. The colonists, who had enjoyed a large degree of self-government, wanted even greater freedom. They resented efforts by the British government to tighten its control over the colonies. The Revolutionary War began in 1775. On July 4, 1776, the colonists issued the Declaration of Independence, in which they declared their freedom from British rule and the formation of a new nation, the United States of America. The British were defeated in the war, and in 1783, they acknowledged the independence of the colonies. The U.S. Constitution, adopted in 1788, officially established the new nation as a republic. See **Declaration of Independence**; **Revolutionary War in America**.

Another major revolution occurred in France. The

The French Revolution began on July 14, 1789, with an attack on the Bastille, *shown here.* This famous prison in Paris had come to symbolize the hated government of King Louis XVI. The French revolutionaries issued the Declaration of the Rights of Man and of the Citizen, a document that declared the equality of all citizens. The revolution lasted 10 years.

Smoking factory chimneys signaled the start of the Industrial Revolution in Europe during the 1700's. Industrialism reshaped European civilization and changed the lives of millions of people in many parts of the world.

Bettmann Archive

French Revolution lasted from 1789 to 1799. It began when King Louis XVI called a meeting of the Estates-General, the French national assembly, to solve the state's financial problems. Commoners in the Estates-General revolted and seized control of the government, declaring themselves the legal National Assembly of France. The Assembly adopted the Declaration of the Rights of Man and of the Citizen. This document set forth the principles of human liberty and the rights of individuals. The French nobles gave up most of their titles and special privileges. In 1792, the revolutionaries established the First French Republic. See **Rights of Man, Declaration of the; French Revolution.**

During the French Revolution, Napoleon Bonaparte, a professional soldier, began to attract notice as a successful general. In 1799, he overthrew the revolutionary government and seized control of France. Napoleon made himself emperor in 1804. Under his leadership, the French came to control most of western Europe. But Napoleon lost much of his army when he invaded Russia in 1812. In 1815, allied European forces crushed Napoleon in the Battle of Waterloo, ending his attempt to rule Europe. See **Napoleon I.**

From late 1814 through early 1815, European leaders held a series of meetings called the Congress of Vienna. By that time, the ideas of the French Revolution had spread throughout Europe. The great rulers at the congress feared the effects of these ideas and wanted to smother liberal and nationalistic feelings among their subjects. They restored monarchies in Italy, Spain, and several other countries where they had been overthrown by Napoleon. They also approved the restoration of the French monarchy. But the congress failed to halt the spread of liberalism and nationalism in the long run. See **Vienna, Congress of.**

By 1880, nearly every European nation had a constitution. In some, all adult males had received the right to vote. Germany and Italy, which had been divided into many small states, were each united as a nation under a constitutional monarchy. Many new nations with constitutional governments appeared in southeastern Europe

as the Ottoman Empire began to crumble. The United States had survived the crisis of its Civil War (1861-1865), when its unity as a nation had been at stake. By 1900, many people believed that democracy and nationalism would continue to spread and eventually solve all the world's political problems. But in some areas, these forces had already started to create new problems. Nationalism posed serious threats for Russia and Austria-Hungary, which governed peoples of many different nationalities. Quarrels among the new nations of southeastern Europe also threatened to disrupt peace.

The Industrial Revolution. During the 1700's and 1800's, the spread of power-driven machinery helped bring about a rapid growth of industry. Large factories replaced homes and small workshops as manufacturing centers. The use of the new machinery and the development of factories led to a huge increase in the production of goods. As industrial nations began exporting manufactured products and importing raw materials for their factories, a worldwide system of markets took shape. The Industrial Revolution began in the United Kingdom. By the mid-1800's, industrialization had become widespread in western Europe and the northeastern United States. Russia and Japan also began to develop their industries. See **Industrial Revolution.**

The Industrial Revolution transformed human life more dramatically than any other change since the development of agriculture. Before the Industrial Revolution, most Europeans lived in the countryside. Towns and villages served chiefly as market centers for the farmers. But as factories appeared, towns grew into industrial cities. People streamed into the cities to take factory jobs. Better transportation and communication between cities became necessary. Many railroads, roads, and waterways were built. By 1837, invention of the telegraph had furnished fast long-distance communication.

Industrialization brought many social changes. The middle class prospered and grew rapidly. Members of the middle class owned most of the factories, hired the workers, and operated the banks, mines, and railroads. They believed that business should be regulated by supply and demand, largely without government control. This idea forms the basis of *capitalism,* an economic system in which the chief means of production are privately owned. During the early 1800's, the United Kingdom began to develop the first capitalist economy. Capitalism soon spread to other industrial nations. See **Capitalism.**

Often, early factory workers were poorly paid and had to work long hours under unhealthful conditions. They could not form labor unions, and their working conditions were not regulated by law. In the growing industrial cities, housing could not keep up with the migration of workers from rural areas. Severe overcrowding resulted, and many people lived in extremely unsanitary conditions that led to outbreaks of disease. Unemployed workers rioted and destroyed machinery in an attempt to gain revenge against the factories they blamed for their joblessness. Employed workers joined in riots, went on strike, and formed illegal trade unions to fight for their rights.

Some people believed that the evils of industrialization resulted from capitalism. Socialism became the chief rallying point for many such people. The socialists wanted to put all industrial production under the workers' control. From that basic idea, Karl Marx, a German writer and social philosopher, developed the theories of Communism. He believed that workers would be driven by the march of history to rise up against the wealthy and to establish socialist economic systems and classless societies. By 1900, many European socialists had accepted Marx's ideas and belonged to political parties whose aim was the overthrow of the capitalist system. See **Communism** (Communism in theory); **Marx, Karl.**

During the 1800's, workers in many countries won the right to form labor unions. Laws regulating working conditions were passed in the United States and the United Kingdom during the 1840's. The United Kingdom and Germany pioneered in social legislation that provided accident, sickness, and unemployment insurance for industrial employees. By the late 1800's, most industrial nations had laws that regulated working conditions and raised the workers' standards of living.

Imperialism. The Industrial Revolution contributed to a great rise in *imperialism*—that is, the political or economic control of one country over others—during the 1800's. The industrialized nations acquired more and more colonies as they eagerly sought raw materials for their factories, markets for their manufactured goods, and opportunities for investment. Africa was one of the main areas of colonial expansion. By the late 1800's, Bel-

gium, France, Germany, Italy, Portugal, Spain, and the United Kingdom had divided up almost all of Africa. Only Ethiopia and Liberia remained independent.

European nations also took over large sections of southeastern Asia and many islands in the South Pacific Ocean. The only major Asian nations that remained independent were China, Japan, and Siam (now Thailand). However, China's government had weakened, and the country had given up Indochina and many of its other outlying dependencies to imperialist powers. After the British defeated the Chinese in the Opium War in 1842, China lost all real control over the presence of foreigners in its territory. Many Chinese ports were opened to foreign residence and trade. Japan began to develop into an industrial and military power in the 1860's and successfully resisted imperialist interference. By the early 1900's, Japan had become strong enough to seize parts of Chinese territory and to win a war against Russia over control of southern Manchuria and Korea.

In Latin America, a series of wars of independence during the early 1800's freed many colonies from European rule (see **Latin America** [The wars of independence]). The United States, backed by the United Kingdom, acted to protect the new Latin American republics against European attempts to reestablish colonial rule. In 1823, U.S. President James Monroe issued the Monroe Doctrine, which warned European powers not to interfere in the affairs of the Western Hemisphere.

The United States itself expanded into new areas during the 1800's. As a result of the Mexican War (1846-1848), it gained Mexican territory that now covers California, Nevada, Utah, and parts of four other states. In 1867, the United States purchased Alaska from Russia. Spain surrendered Guam, Puerto Rico, and the Philippines to the United States after losing the Spanish-American War in 1898.

Imperialism affected the colonized peoples in various ways. In some areas, it brought economic development and raised living standards by introducing European agricultural, industrial, and medical techniques. Colonial rule also ended local wars in numerous lands. However, many imperialist nations took advantage of their colonies by exporting natural resources without providing economic benefits in return to most of the people. Colonial administrations often cared little about local customs and destroyed old ways of life. As time passed, injustices under the imperialistic system triggered nationalistic feelings, resistance movements, and demands for self-government among the colonized peoples.

The world since 1900

Since 1900, the world has changed faster than ever before. The global population has risen much more rapidly than in any earlier period. The world had about $1\frac{2}{3}$ billion people in 1900, about $2\frac{1}{2}$ billion in 1950, and over 6 billion by the early 2000's. Industrial output has soared as more and more countries have become industrialized, and international trade has expanded enormously. Advances in science and technology have altered basic ways of life to an extent that would never

have been dreamed possible during the 1800's. The space age began in 1957, when the Soviet Union launched the first artificial satellite to circle Earth. In 1969, two United States astronauts became the first human beings to walk on the moon (see **Space exploration**).

The world has seen dramatic political changes since 1900. The large colonial empires of the 1800's have disappeared, and many new nations have emerged. Europe no longer dominates international affairs. After 1945, the United States and the Soviet Union ranked as the world's superpowers. But serious economic problems contributed to a sharp loss of Soviet power after 1985, and the Soviet Union dissolved in late 1991. Since 1900, world leaders have worked to establish institutions, such as the United Nations (UN), that strive to promote international health, peace, and prosperity.

The world's many peoples retain their unique beliefs and customs. But they increasingly trade with one another and share such cultural elements as clothing, food, and music. Migration has grown quickly since 1900 and has surged since the 1980's. Powerful political and economic forces operate globally, and events in one country can quickly affect faraway lands.

The world wars. War—fought on a greater scale than ever before—overshadowed world developments in the first half of the 1900's. World War I raged from 1914 to 1918, and World War II from 1939 to 1945.

World War I broke out chiefly because of competition for colonial and economic power among European nations; the desire of national groups to gain independence; and military alliances that divided Europe. In the war, the Allies, which included France, Italy, Russia, and the United Kingdom, fought the Central Powers, which included Austria-Hungary, Germany, and the Ottoman Empire. The United States joined the Allies in 1917. In November 1917 (October on the old Russian calendar), a revolution in Russia established a Communist dictatorship there, and Russia withdrew from the war. The Allies gained victory in 1918. The Treaty of Versailles, signed in 1919, ended the war with Germany (see **Versailles, Treaty of**). The Allies signed separate treaties with the other Central Powers. See **World War I.**

World War I was fought at a terrible cost. Millions of men, women, and children were killed, and whole cities were destroyed. The economic damage was huge. The war brought about many changes in the political map of Europe. For example, Austria-Hungary and the Ottoman Empire broke up into separate national states. In Germany, the Weimar Republic replaced the monarchy.

The Treaty of Versailles required Germany to disarm, give up much of its territory, and pay war damages to the Allies. These requirements weakened Germany and caused great economic hardship. The situation became worse after 1929, when the Great Depression caused economic problems throughout the world.

Many German people felt that the Treaty of Versailles was excessively harsh and unfair. Adolf Hitler, head of the Nazi Party, won support in Germany by claiming that the Jewish people were responsible for the country's defeat in the war and by promising to rebuild Germany as a mighty empire. In 1933, he became dictator of Germany. He soon began to whip up anti-Jewish sentiment and developed a plan to eliminate all Jews. See **Hitler, Adolf.**

In 1938, Hitler ordered German forces to seize Austria and part of Czechoslovakia. In March 1939, Hitler's forces took the rest of Czechoslovakia. On September 1, Germany invaded Poland and World War II began. Germany, Italy, Japan, and other Axis powers fought the Allies, which included Canada, China, France, the Soviet

© Hulton Archive/Getty Images

The United States dropped an atomic bomb on the Japanese city of Nagasaki on Aug. 9, 1945, during World War II. The explosion, *shown here,* killed about 40,000 people. Three days earlier, the United States had dropped an atomic bomb on Hiroshima.

Union, the United Kingdom, and the United States. The United States entered the war in 1941, after Japan attacked U.S. military bases at Pearl Harbor in Hawaii. The war in Europe ended with Germany's surrender in May 1945. In August 1945, U.S. planes dropped the first atomic bombs used in warfare on the Japanese cities of Hiroshima and Nagasaki. The next month, Japan signed the terms of surrender. See **World War II.**

The cost of World War II, both financially and in terms of human suffering and loss of life, was even greater than that of World War I. The political effects were also more sweeping. Europe lay in ruins. Allied forces occupied Germany, once Europe's strongest nation. The major European countries were too weak to keep their colonies. The United States and the Soviet Union emerged as the world's leading powers. Out of the horror of the war came attempts by nations to settle disputes peacefully. A new international organization, the United Nations, was established near the end of the war to provide a place where countries could work to resolve their differences (see **United Nations**).

The rise of Communism and the Cold War. The Communist movement achieved its first major success when the Bolsheviks came to power in Russia in 1917.

Major developments

WORLD BOOK illustration by Tak Murakami

Sigmund Freud developed psychoanalysis about 1900.

Alexander Fleming discovered penicillin in 1928.

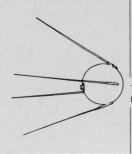

The Soviet Union launched the first artificial satellite in 1957.

The first computers were developed in the 1930's and 1940's.

Space age (1957-   )

The Wright brothers made the first successful airplane flights in 1903.

The British Broadcasting Corporation made the world's first TV broadcasts in 1936.

Vietnam War (1957-1975)

Korean War (1950-1953)

Biologists finished sequencing essentially the entire human genome in the early 2000's.

Albert Einstein published his special theory of relativity in 1905.

World War II (1939-1945)

Researchers developed the first successful recombinant DNA procedure in 1974.

World War I (1914-1918)

| 1900 | 1925 | 1950 | 1975 | 2000 |

The wealth of nations can be compared on the basis of each country's *gross national income* (GNI). The GNI is the value of all goods and services produced within a country in a year. The developing countries of Africa and Asia have the lowest GNI per person.

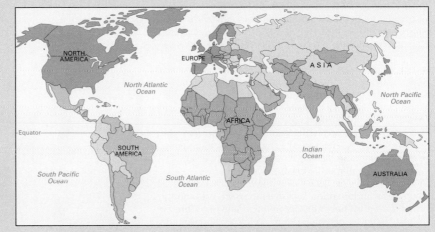

High GNI per person

Medium GNI per person

Low GNI per person

Very low GNI per person

WORLD BOOK map
Source: World Bank.

Important dates

1914 The assassination of Archduke Franz Ferdinand of Austria-Hungary started World War I.

1917 The Bolsheviks (Communists) seized power in Russia.

1933 Adolf Hitler became dictator of Germany.

1939 Germany invaded Poland, starting World War II.

1941 The Japanese attacked Pearl Harbor, and the United States entered World War II.

1945 The United Nations was established.

1945 The first atomic bombs used in warfare were dropped by U.S. planes on Hiroshima and Nagasaki.

1945 World War II ended in Europe on May 7 and in the Pacific on September 2.

1949 The Chinese Communists conquered China.

1950 North Korean Communist troops invaded South Korea, starting the Korean War.

1957 The Vietnam War started when South Vietnamese rebels attacked the U.S.-backed South Vietnamese government.

1969 U.S. astronauts made the first human moon landing.

1989-1990 Democratic reforms spread across Eastern Europe, and several non-Communist governments replaced Communist dictatorships.

1991 The Communist Party of the Soviet Union lost control of the Soviet government, and the Soviet Union ceased to exist.

2001 Terrorists crashed hijacked aircraft into the World Trade Center in New York City and the Pentagon Building outside Washington, D.C., killing about 3,000 people.

The movement grew quickly after World War II. In the late 1940's, the Soviet Union imposed Communist governments in most countries of Eastern Europe, which Soviet armies had seized from German control after World War II. Germany consisted of West Germany, governed by freely elected representatives, and Communist-controlled East Germany. Chinese Communists founded the People's Republic of China in 1949. In 1959, a Communist government came to power in Cuba, giving Communism a foothold in the Western Hemisphere. Communist movements also emerged in other Asian and Latin American countries.

Alarmed by Communist expansion, the United States and its allies began giving military and economic aid to non-Communist countries and pledged to help nations threatened by Communist take-overs. The struggle between the Communist world, led by the Soviet Union, and the non-Communist world, led by the United States, came to be called the Cold War. The United States and the Soviet Union formed armed coalitions to guard against military threats. The United States and its allies founded the North Atlantic Treaty Organization (NATO) in 1949. The Soviet Union and its allies responded by establishing the Warsaw Pact in 1955. See **Cold War.**

Cold War tensions increased in the 1950's and 1960's. The Korean War (1950-1953) began when troops from Communist-ruled North Korea invaded South Korea (see **Korean War**). Cold War incidents occurred at times in the divided German city of Berlin. In 1961, the Communists built the Berlin Wall between democratic West Berlin and Communist-ruled East Berlin to prevent East Germans from escaping (see **Berlin Wall**).

The most serious Cold War incident was the Cuban missile crisis of 1962. In October of that year, the United States learned that the Soviet Union had installed missiles in Cuba that could launch nuclear attacks on United States cities. The crisis passed after the Soviet Union and U.S. President John F. Kennedy agreed that the Soviets would remove their missiles from Cuba in return for the removal of U.S. nuclear missiles from Turkey and Kennedy's promise that the United States would not invade Cuba. See **Cuban missile crisis.**

The Vietnam War (1957-1975) grew out of Vietnam's struggle for independence from France and was another major contest between Communists and non-Communists. After France pulled out of Vietnam, the United States entered to aid the non-Communists, and the Soviets increased their support for the Communist side. The war ended in a Communist victory. See **Vietnam War.**

The birth of new nations. Large-scale colonialism ended in the 1950's and 1960's. After World War II, European nations had neither the money nor the will to continue to rule their colonies. Nationalistic feelings and demands for self-government had also been growing among colonial peoples in Africa and Asia. Colonized peoples organized independence movements and, in some places, fought bitter wars of liberation against colonial powers. From 1950 to 1980, over 45 colonies in Africa gained their freedom. Most European colonies in Asia, the Middle East, and the Pacific islands also became independent.

The end of colonialism complicated international poli-tics. No longer did a few Western nations dominate the world. Some new nations experienced conflicts that might not have occurred in the colonial era. For example, serious tensions and wars complicated relations between India and Pakistan, both formerly ruled by the United Kingdom. The formation of new nations also led to a large increase in the membership of the UN and greatly affected the balance of power in the UN. Many former colonies became part of a group of economically developing countries called the Third World. These countries had a majority of votes in the UN General Assembly. Many of them sought to develop policies that were independent of the Communist and non-Communist *blocs* (groups of nations). See **Third World.**

The new nations hoped independence would bring political stability and economic well-being. But most of them continued to face serious economic, political, and social difficulties. In some developing nations, religious or ethnic tensions have led to political division and civil conflict. Such grave problems as disease, food shortages, illiteracy, poverty, and rapid population growth have also troubled many of these countries. Most of the former colonies have had to depend on investment from wealthier countries to develop their economies. But this investment itself has frequently led to renewed political interference from the countries providing aid.

The end of the Cold War. Relations between Communist and non-Communist nations began to improve in the 1970's. Soviet and U.S. leaders embarked on a policy of *détente,* meaning a relaxation of political tensions. At the same time, the United States and China worked to

© Hulton Archive/Getty Images

Algerians celebrate their independence in the city of Algiers. Algeria gained its freedom from France on July 3, 1962. During the 1960's, European colonial rule ended in most of Africa.

The spread of television in the United States during the 1950's and 1960's had a huge impact on the way that people spent their leisure time and learned about the world. This photo shows an American family watching an address by United States President John F. Kennedy on television in the early 1960's.

establish normal diplomatic relations.

Cold War tensions fell even more sharply in the late 1980's. In 1987, Soviet leader Mikhail Gorbachev and United States President Ronald Reagan signed a treaty calling for the destruction of many United States and Soviet nuclear missiles. Tensions decreased further in 1989, when the Soviet Union withdrew military forces from Afghanistan, which the Soviet military had invaded in 1979.

Also in the late 1980's, Gorbachev worked to decentralize the Soviet economic system to improve the nation's poor economy. He also worked to increase democracy and freedom of expression in the Soviet Union. Gorbachev encouraged similar economic and political changes in Eastern Europe. As a result, non-Communist governments came to power in several Eastern European nations that had been Communist dictatorships since the late 1940's. In 1990, East Germany and West Germany were reunited.

The Communist Party of the Soviet Union lost control of the government in 1991, after conservative Communist officials tried to overthrow Gorbachev. The Soviet parliament suspended all Communist Party activities. By the end of 1991, most of the republics that made up the Soviet Union had declared independence, and the Soviet Union ceased to exist. The Cold War had ended.

Scientific and technological achievements. In the 1900's and early 2000's, advances in science and technology changed the world dramatically. Computers, lasers, plastics, and refrigerators were just a few inventions that transformed human life. Transportation underwent a revolution after people began to use petroleum as fuel. Ships, automobiles, and airplanes moved people and goods around the globe faster and more cheaply than ever before. Undersea cables, radio, television, communications satellites, and the Internet sped up the transmission of information.

Research into the structure of the atom led to the discovery of nuclear energy as a source of power. Remotely controlled space probes explored other planets and sent back data that helped scientists understand the origins and structure of the solar system.

In addition, the life expectancy of human beings rose. Antibiotics and other drugs helped physicians treat many diseases that could not be treated effectively before. Agricultural output soared as scientists developed better plants and effective fertilizers and pesticides. As a result, millions of people lived healthier, longer lives.

In some cases, human achievements created new problems. Nuclear research led to the creation of powerful weapons. A growing knowledge of the genetic makeup of human beings fueled debates about the ethical uses of such knowledge. The rapid growth of industrial technology created so great a demand for fuel that the world occasionally experienced fuel shortages. Extensive use of petroleum generated much pollution. By the late 1900's, there was mounting evidence that carbon dioxide emissions were contributing to a general warming of Earth's climate.

Increases in life expectancy contributed to overpopulation in many developing countries, where birth rates remained high and death rates fell. As population increased, people turned forestlands into cities, factories, and fields. This expansion caused the extinction of many animal and plant species after 1900. Fishing methods became so effective in the 1900's that some fish species became extinct, while others barely survived. See **Technology** (Challenges of technology).

A turbulent and interdependent world. The world remains politically divided. No war has broken out directly between major world powers since World War II ended in 1945, but fighting has gone on in some part of the globe almost every day since then.

For example, the Arab-Israeli conflict, which began in 1948 with the creation of Israel, has continued into the 2000's. This conflict is a struggle between the Jewish state of Israel and Arabs in the Middle East over a region known as Palestine. The two groups claim a right to the land, which contains sites holy to both Jews and Muslim Arabs. Thousands of people have died in the conflict, characterized by wars and terrorist activities.

From the 1950's to the 1970's, Cold War tensions fueled many conflicts. The collapse of the Soviet Union and the end of the Cold War led to a power vacuum in much of eastern Europe and central Asia. Tensions in those areas contributed to political division and violent conflicts between ethnic or religious groups.

Regional conflicts have occasionally broken out when local rulers have tried to extend their influence to neighboring areas. In 1991, for example, the United States, the United Kingdom, and other countries drove Iraq out of Kuwait after Iraq had invaded and occupied Kuwait in 1990 (see **Persian Gulf War of 1991**). In 1999, the United States and several European countries attacked Serbia. The move came after Serbian leader Slobodan Milošević ended self-rule in the province of Kosovo and deprived the province's ethnic Albanian majority of many rights.

In economics, the gulf between developing and developed countries has widened. About 60 percent of people in the Third World live in extreme poverty, while developed countries consume huge quantities of resources simply to provide luxuries. Agricultural production, banking systems, and industrial capacity are all strong in developed countries, but economic institutions are weak in many African and Asian nations.

Countries have increasingly joined forces to deal with problems that are too big for any one government to handle. Such problems include pollution and the reduction of natural resources. Many countries belong to international economic or political organizations that work to coordinate policies on important issues, deal with large-scale health problems, improve working conditions, increase trade, or stabilize the global economy.

Some developed countries also give financial and technical aid to developing nations.

The ability of people to travel more easily and rapidly than ever before between different parts of the world has helped the spread of diseases. For example, the HIV virus, which causes AIDS, began to spread from Africa to many parts of the world in the 1970's. By the early 2000's, AIDS had taken millions of lives. In 2003, the virus that causes Severe Acute Respiratory Syndrome (SARS) spread from China to other countries, causing a public health crisis.

The war on terrorism. Modern technology has also aided the spread of terrorism. After the Persian Gulf War of 1991, some Muslims (followers of the Islamic religion) objected to the presence of U.S. troops in Saudi Arabia, the site of Islam's holiest shrines. The Saudi-born millionaire and radical Osama bin Laden organized a terrorist group named al-Qa`ida. On Sept. 11, 2001, Qa`ida terrorists hijacked commercial jetliners and crashed them into the World Trade Center in New York City and the Pentagon Building near Washington, D.C. Another hijacked jet crashed in rural Pennsylvania. About 3,000 people of many nationalities died in the attacks. See **September 11 terrorist attacks.**

In response to the September 11 attacks, the United States led the United Kingdom and other nations in military action in southwest Asia. In Afghanistan, where bin Laden was based, United States-led forces destroyed many terrorist camps and overthrew the government of the Taliban—a radical Muslim group that supported bin Laden and al-Qa`ida. After the conflict, the UN aided the formation of a new national government in Afghanistan. However, it was clear that Afghanistan was only one of several countries that harbored terrorist groups and that the "war on terrorism" would probably continue into the future.

In 2003, U.S. President George W. Bush accused Iraqi leader Saddam Hussein of supporting international ter-

NASA

Walking in space was one of the most exciting achievements of the U.S. space program. The space age began in the mid-1900's and opened a new chapter in the history of exploration.

rorist groups and possessing weapons of mass destruction—that is, biological, chemical, or nuclear weapons. That year, the United States led forces from the United Kingdom, Australia, and other countries and overthrew Iraq's government. But by mid-2004, the U.S.-led coalition had found no weapons of mass destruction in Iraq (see **Iraq War**).

The growing ability of distant individuals, groups, and governments to interact directly has presented challenges and even dangers to the world's citizens. However, these global links hold strong potential to increase prosperity and the quality of life worldwide. Many leaders believe that change for the better will require not only a victory over terrorism but also a more equal distribution of wealth and resources among the nations and peoples of the world.   Jerry H. Bentley

Related articles in *World Book.* See the *History* section of country articles, such as **Argentina** (History), and separate articles: **Canada, History of; United States, History of the.** See also:

History of continents or regions

See the historical sections of the following articles:

Africa	Europe
Asia	Latin America
Balkans	Middle East
Central America	Pacific Islands

Early centers of civilization

Aegean civilization	Mesopotamia
Babylonia	Nubia
Egypt, Ancient	Sumer
Hittites	Troy
Indus Valley civilization	

The advance of civilization

Aksum	Kush	Parthia
Assyria	Kushan Empire	Persia, Ancient
Carthage	Lydia	Phoenicia
Chaldea	Macedonia (histor-	Phrygia
Etruscans	ical region)	Rome, Ancient
Greece, Ancient	Nok	Silk Road
Jews	Palestine	

The world from 500 to 1500

Aztec	Hundred Years' War	Maya
Benin	Inca	Middle Ages
Byzantine Empire	Kanem	Mongol Empire
Crusades	Knights and knight-	Muslims
Feudalism	hood	Songhai Empire
Ghana Empire	Kongo	Vikings
Holy Roman Empire	Mali Empire	

The spread of European civilization

Age of Reason	Reformation
Exploration	Renaissance
French Revolution	Revolution of 1848
Fur trade	Revolutionary War in America
Industrial Revolution	Seven Years' War
New France	Thirty Years' War
Ottoman Empire	Vienna, Congress of

The world since 1900

Cold War	September 11 terrorist
Great Depression	attacks
Holocaust	Space exploration
Iraq War	United Nations
Korean War	Vietnam War
Nuclear energy	World War I
Persian Gulf War of 1991	World War II

Other related articles

Archaeology	Painting
Architecture	Philosophy
Capitalism	Population
Civilization	Prehistoric people
Classical music	Religion
Colonialism	Science
Communism	Sculpture
Culture	Slavery
Democracy	Socialism
Developing country	Terrorism
Government	War
History	Women's movements
Indian, American	World
Law	Writing
Literature	

Outline

I. Early centers of civilization
  A. The Tigris-Euphrates Valley
  B. The Nile Valley
  C. The Indus Valley
  D. The Huang He Valley

II. The advance of civilization
  A. Civilizations of southwest Asia
  B. The Greeks
  C. The Romans
  D. The Mauryan Empire in India
  E. The unification of China

III. The world from 500 to 1500
  A. Medieval Europe
  B. The Byzantine Empire
  C. The Islamic world
  D. China
  E. The rise of Japanese civilization
  F. The age of invasions of India
  G. African civilizations
  H. Civilizations in the Americas

IV. The spread of European civilization
  A. The Renaissance
  B. The age of exploration
  C. The colonization of America
  D. The Islamic empires
  E. Developments in China and Japan
  F. The rise of democracy and nationalism
  G. The Industrial Revolution
  H. Imperialism

V. The world since 1900
  A. The world wars
  B. The rise of Communism and the Cold War
  C. The birth of new nations
  D. The end of the Cold War
  E. Scientific and technological achievements
  F. A turbulent and interdependent world
  G. The war on terrorism

Questions

How did the invention of farming pave the way for the development of civilization?

How did Chinese culture influence early Japanese civilization?

Why are people and nations tied together more closely now than ever before?

What contributions did the Aryans make to civilization in India?

What military and political system developed in western Europe after the fall of the West Roman Empire?

How did science and technology transform life in the 1900's?

What were some of the important accomplishments of the Sumerians? Of the Egyptians?

How did European leaders at the Congress of Vienna try to halt the spread of democracy and nationalism?

How was Greek culture preserved in the Roman Empire?

What were some factors that aided the spread of Western civilization after 1500?

Additional resources

Level I

Grant, Neil. *Oxford Children's History of the World.* Oxford, 2000.

Haywood, John. *World Atlas of the Past.* 4 vols. Oxford, 1999.

Heel, K. Donker van, ed. *The Illustrated Encyclopedia of World History.* Sharpe, 1997.

Kingfisher History Encyclopedia. Kingfisher Bks., 1999.

Somerset Fry, Plantagenet. *The Dorling Kindersley History of the World.* Dorling Kindersley, 1994.

Level II

Encyclopedia of World History. Facts on File, 2000.

Fromkin, David. *The Way of the World: From the Dawn of Civilizations to the Eve of the Twenty-First Century.* Knopf, 1998.

Mellersh, H. E. L., and Williams, Neville. *Chronology of World History.* 4 vols. ABC-Clio, 1999.

O'Brien, Patrick K., ed. *Atlas of World History.* Oxford, 1999.

Roberts, John M. *The Illustrated History of the World.* 11 vols. Oxford, 1999.

World Bank is an international organization that provides loans to governments and private firms for development projects, such as irrigation, education, and housing. It also grants loans to support government policies that it believes will strengthen a country's economy, such as lower import tariffs and more efficient judicial systems. The bank's official name is the International Bank for Reconstruction and Development.

Almost all countries are members of the World Bank. The bank gets most of its funds by borrowing in world financial markets. Its bonds are backed by the pledges of its members and by the loans it makes to governments and firms. The bank is an agency of the United Nations. Its headquarters are in Washington, D.C.

Plans for the World Bank were drawn up at an economic conference held in Bretton Woods, New Hampshire, in 1944. The bank began operating in 1946.

The International Development Association, established in 1960, is a World Bank affiliate that makes interest-free, long-term loans to impoverished countries. Another affiliate, the International Finance Corporation, was established in 1956 to encourage private firms to invest in less-developed countries.

The World Bank has faced criticism, especially in the United States. Critics note that the bank has had little success in persuading some developing countries to adopt the policies the bank believes would improve their economies. Critics also argue that the bank should not fund investment projects that can be financed by private loans.   Gary Hufbauer

See also **Bretton Woods; International Finance Corporation; International Monetary Fund.**

World Book Encyclopedia. See Encyclopedia *(World Book).*

World Council of Churches is a worldwide organization of hundreds of Protestant, Anglican, Old Catholic, and Orthodox churches. It works to promote cooperation and unity among all churches. Council churches have millions of members.

The Roman Catholic Church, though not a member of the council, works with the organization in some programs. The World Council of Churches has also opened discussions with such non-Christian groups as Buddhists and Muslims.

The activities of the council include education; worldwide missionary and evangelical work; aid to refugees, the sick, and underprivileged; and the promotion of world peace and social and interracial justice. The council was founded in 1948 in Amsterdam, the Netherlands. The council's headquarters are in Geneva, Switzerland, and in New York City.

Critically reviewed by World Council of Churches

World Court. See International Court of Justice.

World Cup is a tournament held every four years to determine the world's soccer championship. Tournaments are held for both men's and women's teams. Each team consists of all-star players who represent their country. The tournaments are supervised by the governing body of international soccer, the Fédération Internationale de Football Association (FIFA). The first men's World Cup was held in 1930. The first women's World Cup was held in 1991.

In the men's World Cup, elimination tournaments are held two years before the final competition. For the 2002 tournament, 188 teams began elimination competition in 2000. The elimination rounds are organized in six geographical zones. The tournament finals bring together 32 teams. The host country and the previous champion receive automatic berths. The other teams qualify through the elimination rounds.

The women's World Cup includes 16 teams for the finals. For the 1999 tournament, almost 75 teams entered the elimination competition for 15 places in the finals. The host country receives an automatic berth.

The finals are held at various sites throughout the host country. For early rounds, teams are organized into groups. As the competition progresses, teams are eliminated until two teams qualify for the final match. The televised men's final is the most popular single sports event in the world. For World Cup results, see **Soccer** (table: World Cup championship games).

There are also World Cup competitions in a number of other sports, including cricket, rugby football, and skiing. For information on the World Cup in skiing, see **Skiing** (Skiing as a sport).

Critically reviewed by the Fédération Internationale de Football Association

World Health Organization (WHO) is a specialized agency of the United Nations. It helps build better health systems, especially in developing countries.

WHO establishes standards in a variety of fields, such as food, biological and pharmaceutical goods, diagnostic procedures, and environmental health protection. It also helps name and classify diseases. Prevention of disease is a key goal of WHO. The agency works with governments to provide safe drinking water, adequate sewage disposal, and immunization against childhood diseases. WHO also identifies important research goals and organizes researchers worldwide to achieve them. WHO's headquarters are in Geneva, Switzerland. The organization was founded in 1948.

Critically reviewed by the World Health Organization

World Jewish Congress is an international association of Jewish communities and organizations. These groups work together to promote unity among Jews and to maintain Jewish cultural, religious, and social customs. The association also sponsors the Institute of Jewish Affairs in London, which conducts research into various problems facing Jews.

The association tries to protect the rights of Jews throughout the world. For example, it attempted to rescue Jews from Nazi persecution before and during

World War II (1939-1945). The congress later set up relief and rehabilitation programs for the victims. During the 1970's, the congress helped arrange the release of thousands of Jews from the Soviet Union.

The World Jewish Congress was founded in 1936. The organization has its headquarters in New York City.

Critically reviewed by the World Jewish Congress

World Medical Association is an organization of many of the world's national medical associations. Organized in 1947, the association has adopted an international code of medical ethics and several other ethical declarations and statements. Headquarters are in Ferney-Voltaire, near St.-Claude, France.

Critically reviewed by the World Medical Association

World Meteorological Organization (WMO) is a specialized agency of the United Nations. It helps form worldwide networks for the observation of weather, climate, water levels, and other physical conditions. WMO helps develop and manage early-warning systems for drought, cyclones, floods, ozone-layer depletion, and the movement of air pollution across national boundaries. WMO was founded in 1950 to replace the International Meteorological Organization, established in 1873. Headquarters are in Geneva, Switzerland.

Critically reviewed by the World Meteorological Organization

World Series. See Baseball (Major leagues).

World Trade Center was a building complex in New York City that was largely destroyed in the worst terrorist attack in United States history. The center originally consisted of seven buildings, including two 110-story towers that were among the world's tallest skyscrapers. On Sept. 11, 2001, terrorists in two hijacked commercial jetliners crashed the planes into the towers. Thousands of gallons of jet fuel fed raging fires that weakened the towers, causing both to collapse to the ground. The fires and destruction killed about 3,000 people and injured many others, and damaged or destroyed other buildings in the World Trade Center complex and nearby. That same day, a third hijacked plane crashed into the Pentagon Building, near Washington, D.C., and a fourth crashed into a field in Somerset County, Pennsylvania.

© Superstock

The twin towers of the World Trade Center were among the world's tallest buildings. In 2001, terrorists crashed hijacked airplanes into the 110-story towers, causing both to collapse.

Many U.S. government agencies and businesses and organizations involved in international trade had offices in the World Trade Center. About 50,000 people worked in the two towers. The center had been the target of an earlier terrorist attack in 1993, when a large bomb exploded in the complex's underground parking garage. The blast killed 6 people and injured more than 1,000 others. Four men, including Sheik Omar Abdel Rahman, an Egyptian Muslim cleric, were convicted of the bombing and sent to prison.

American architect Minoru Yamasaki designed the World Trade Center. Construction began in 1966. Tenants began to occupy One World Trade Center, at 1,368 feet (417 meters) the taller of the two towers, in 1970, and the 1,362-foot (415-meter) Two World Trade Center in 1972. The complex cost over $750 million to build.

See also **New York City** (picture); **September 11 terrorist attacks.**

World Trade Organization is an international organization that promotes trade in goods and services among nations. Most nations belong to the World Trade Organization, often called the WTO. The WTO's main responsibilities are to help members conclude trade negotiations and to act as a neutral judge in trade disputes. The WTO does not determine trade policies. Instead, it helps put into effect decisions made by members.

Except in special circumstances, a member country's export goods and services get the same treatment as those of any other WTO member. This treatment includes the same tariffs (import taxes) and other trade restrictions. A member nation must follow WTO guidelines on international trade. For example, a member nation must treat the exports of all WTO members equally. In case of disagreement over a trade issue, a member nation agrees to submit the case to a WTO committee for review. If the committee finds that a country has violated its WTO commitments, the country must either change its practices, offer compensation, or face increased taxes on its exports.

The World Trade Organization was founded in 1995. It absorbed the General Agreement on Tariffs and Trade (GATT), which covered trade in manufactured and agricultural goods. The WTO also regulates trade in services and in intellectual property, which includes such creations as books, computer software, and recordings.

Since the late 1990's, the WTO has come under increasing criticism. Some people argue that the WTO's power in deciding trade disputes limits national governments' economic and political independence and authority. Labor unions contend that the WTO focuses too much on expanding trade without considering whether workers are harmed in the process. Some environmentalists argue that the WTO weakens governments' policies to protect the environment. Still other critics assert that international trade in general takes unfair advantage of workers in the developing nations, and that the WTO is an agent of this abuse.

The WTO is one of three major organizations that oversee international economic relations among governments. The other two are the International Monetary Fund and the World Bank. WTO headquarters are in Geneva, Switzerland.   Michael O. Moore

See also **General Agreement on Tariffs and Trade; International Monetary Fund; World Bank.**

Bettmann Archive   Bettmann Archive

Soldiers headed for the battlefront at first welcomed the outbreak of World War I. The German soldiers at the left received flowers as they marched off to France. The French cavalrymen at the right confidently rode off to drive the Germans back. Each side expected quick victory.

World War I

World War I (1914-1918) involved more countries and caused greater destruction than any other war except World War II (1939-1945). An assassin's bullets set off the war, and a system of military *alliances* (agreements) plunged the main European powers into the fight. Each side expected quick victory. But the war lasted four years and took the lives of nearly 10 million troops.

Several developments led to the awful bloodshed of the Great War, as World War I was originally called. War plants kept turning out vast quantities of newly invented weapons capable of extraordinary slaughter. Military drafts raised larger armies than ever before, and extreme patriotism gave many men a cause they were willing to die for. Propaganda whipped up support for the war by making the enemy seem villainous.

On June 28, 1914, an assassin gunned down Archduke Francis Ferdinand of Austria-Hungary in Sarajevo, the capital of Austria-Hungary's province of Bosnia-Herzegovina. The killer, Gavrilo Princip, had ties to a terrorist organization in Serbia (now part of Yugoslavia). Austria-Hungary believed that Serbia's government was behind the assassination. It seized the opportunity to declare war on Serbia and settle an old feud.

The assassination of Francis Ferdinand sparked the outbreak of World War I. But historians believe that the war had deeper causes. It resulted chiefly from the growth of extreme national pride among various European peoples, an enormous increase in European armed forces, a race for colonies, and the formation of military alliances. When the fighting began, France, Britain, and Russia—who were known as the Allies—backed Serbia. They opposed the Central Powers, made up of Austria-Hungary and Germany. Other nations later

Edward M. Coffman, the contributor of this article, is Emeritus Professor of History at the University of Wisconsin-Madison and the author of The War to End All Wars: The American Military Experience in World War I.

joined the Allies or the Central Powers.

Germany won early victories in World War I on the main European battlefronts. On the Western Front, France and Britain halted the German advance in September 1914. The opposing armies then fought from trenches that stretched across Belgium and northeastern France. The Western Front hardly moved for $3\frac{1}{2}$ years in spite of fierce combat. On the Eastern Front, Russia battled Germany and Austria-Hungary. The fighting seesawed back and forth until 1917, when a revolution broke out in Russia. Russia soon asked for a truce.

The United States remained neutral at first. But many Americans turned against the Central Powers after German submarines began sinking unarmed ships. In 1917, the United States joined the Allies. U.S troops gave the Allies the manpower they needed to win the war. In the fall of 1918, the Central Powers surrendered.

World War I had results that none of the warring nations had foreseen. The war helped topple emperors in Austria-Hungary, Germany, and Russia. The peace treaties after the war carved new nations out of the defeated powers. The war left Europe exhausted, never to regain the controlling position in world affairs that it had held before the war. The peace settlement also created conditions that helped lead to World War II.

Causes of the war

The assassination of Archduke Francis Ferdinand triggered World War I. But the war had its origins in developments of the 1800's. The chief causes of World War I were (1) the rise of nationalism, (2) a build-up of military might, (3) competition for colonies, and (4) a system of military alliances.

The rise of nationalism. Europe avoided major wars in the 100 years before World War I began. Although small wars broke out, they did not involve many countries. But during the 1800's, a force swept across the continent that helped bring about the Great War. The force was *nationalism*—the belief that loyalty to a person's nation and its political and economic goals comes before any other public loyalty. That exaggerated form

Imperial War Museum

Robert Hunt Library

Destruction and death, instead of quick victory, awaited the warring nations in the long and brutal conflict. After fierce fighting in Belgium, the city of Ypres lay in ruins, *left.* Many men, like the French soldier on the right, met death in a trench along the Western Front.

of patriotism increased the possibility of war because a nation's goals inevitably came into conflict with the goals of one or more other nations. In addition, nationalistic pride caused nations to magnify small disputes into major issues. A minor complaint could thus quickly lead to the threat of war.

During the 1800's, nationalism took hold among people who shared a common language, history, or culture. Such people began to view themselves as members of a national group, or nation. Nationalism led to the creation of two new powers—Italy and Germany—through the uniting of many small states. War had a major role in achieving national unification in Italy and Germany.

Nationalist policies gained enthusiastic support as many countries in Western Europe granted the vote to more people. The right to vote gave citizens greater in-

The warring nations

The table below indicates the date on which each of the Allies and Central Powers entered World War I. More than 20 countries eventually joined the war on the Allied side. However, not all of them sent troops.

The Allies

Belgium (Aug. 4, 1914)
Brazil (Oct. 26, 1917)
British Empire
  (Aug. 4, 1914)
China (Aug. 14, 1917)
Costa Rica
  (May 23, 1918)
Cuba (April 7, 1917)
France (Aug. 3, 1914)
Greece (July 2, 1917)
Guatemala
  (April 23, 1918)
Haiti (July 12, 1918)
Honduras (July 19, 1918)
Italy (May 23, 1915)
Japan (Aug. 23, 1914)
Liberia (Aug. 4, 1917)
Montenegro
  (Aug. 5, 1914)

Nicaragua (May 8, 1918)
Panama (April 7, 1917)
Portugal (March 9, 1916)
Romania (Aug. 27, 1916)
Russia (Aug. 1, 1914)
San Marino
  (June 3, 1915)
Serbia (July 28, 1914)
Siam (July 22, 1917)
United States
  (April 6, 1917)

The Central Powers

Austria-Hungary
  (July 28, 1914)
Bulgaria (Oct. 14, 1915)
Germany (Aug. 1, 1914)
Ottoman Empire
  (Oct. 31, 1914)

terest and greater pride in national goals. As a result, parliamentary governments grew increasingly powerful.

On the other hand, nationalism weakened the eastern European empires of Austria-Hungary, Russia, and Ottoman Turkey. Those empires ruled many national groups that clamored for independence. Conflicts among national groups were especially explosive in the Balkans—the states on the Balkan Peninsula in southeastern Europe. The peninsula was known as the *Powder Keg of Europe* because tensions there threatened to ignite a major war. Most of the Balkans had been part of the Ottoman Empire. First Greece and then Montenegro, Serbia, Romania, Bulgaria, and Albania won independence in the period from 1821 to 1913. Each state quarreled with neighbors over boundaries. Austria-Hungary and Russia also took advantage of the Ottoman Empire's weakness to increase their influence in the Balkans.

Rivalry for control of the Balkans added to the tensions that erupted into World War I. Serbia led a movement to unite the region's Slavs. Russia, the most powerful Slavic country, supported Serbia. But Austria-Hungary feared Slavic nationalism, which stirred unrest in its empire. Millions of Slavs lived under Austria-Hungary's rule. In 1908, Austria-Hungary greatly angered Serbia by adding the Balkan territory of Bosnia-Herzegovina to its empire. Serbia wanted control of this area because many Serbs lived there.

A build-up of military might occurred among European countries before World War I broke out. Nationalism encouraged public support for military build-ups and for a country's use of force to achieve its goals. By the late 1800's, Germany had the best-trained army in the world. It relied on a military draft of all able-bodied young men to increase the size and strength of its peacetime army. Other European countries followed Germany's lead and expanded their standing armies.

At first, Britain remained unconcerned about Germany's military build-up. Britain, an island country, relied on its navy for defense—and it had the world's strongest navy. But in 1898, Germany began to develop a naval force big enough to challenge the British navy.

Important dates during World War I

1914

June 28	Archduke Francis Ferdinand was assassinated.
July 28	Austria-Hungary declared war on Serbia. Several other declarations of war followed during the next week.
Aug. 4	Germany invaded Belgium and started the fighting.
Aug. 10	Austria-Hungary invaded Russia, opening the fighting on the Eastern Front.
Sept. 6-9	The Allies stopped the Germans in France in the First Battle of the Marne.

1915

Feb. 18	Germany began to blockade Great Britain.
April 25	Allied troops landed on the Gallipoli Peninsula.
May 7	A German submarine sank the liner *Lusitania*.
May 23	Italy declared war on Austria-Hungary, and an Italian Front soon developed.

1916

Feb. 21	The Germans opened the Battle of Verdun.
May 31-June 1	The British fleet fought the German fleet in the Battle of Jutland.
July 1	The Allies launched the Battle of the Somme.

1917

Feb. 1	Germany resumed unrestricted submarine warfare.
April 6	The United States declared war on Germany.
June 24	American troops began landing in France.
Dec. 15	Russia signed an armistice with Germany, ending the fighting on the Eastern Front.

1918

Jan. 8	President Woodrow Wilson announced his Fourteen Points as the basis for peace.
March 3	Russia signed the Treaty of Brest-Litovsk.
March 21	Germany launched the first of its final three offensives on the Western Front.
Sept. 26	The Allies began their final offensive on the Western Front.
Nov. 11	Germany signed an armistice ending World War I.

Germany's decision to become a major seapower made it a bitter enemy of Great Britain. In 1906, the British navy launched the *Dreadnought,* the first modern battleship. The heavily armed *Dreadnought* had greater firepower than any other ship of its time. Germany rushed to construct ships like it.

Advances in *technology*—the tools, materials, and techniques of industrialization—increased the destructive power of military forces. Machine guns and other new arms fired more accurately and more rapidly than earlier weapons. Steamships and railroads could speed the movement of troops and supplies. By the end of the 1800's, technology enabled countries to fight longer wars and bear greater losses than ever before. Yet military experts insisted that future wars would be short.

Competition for colonies. During the late 1800's and early 1900's, European nations carved nearly all of Africa and much of Asia into colonies. The race for colonies was fueled by Europe's increasing industrialization. Colonies supplied European nations with raw materials for factories, markets for manufactured goods, and opportunities for investment. But the competition for colonies strained relations among European countries. Incidents between rival powers flared up almost every year. Several of the clashes nearly led to war.

A system of military alliances gave European powers a sense of security before World War I. A country hoped to discourage an attack from its enemies by entering into a military agreement with one or more other countries. In case of an attack, such an agreement guaranteed that other members of the alliance would come to the country's aid or at least remain neutral.

Although military alliances provided protection for a country, the system created certain dangers. Because of its alliances, a country might take risks in dealings with other nations that it would hesitate to take alone. If war

World War I battlefronts

The fighting in World War I spread from Western Europe to the Middle East. The key battles were fought along the Western Front, which stretched across Belgium and France, and along the Eastern Front, which seesawed across Russia and Austria-Hungary.

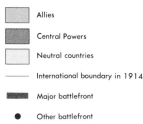

	Allies
	Central Powers
	Neutral countries
——	International boundary in 1914
▰▰	Major battlefront
●	Other battlefront

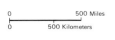

WORLD BOOK map

came, the alliance system meant that a number of nations would fight, not only the two involved in a dispute. Alliances could force a country to go to war against a nation it had no quarrel with or over an issue it had no interest in. In addition, the terms of many alliances were kept secret. The secrecy increased the chances that a country might guess wrong about the consequences of its actions.

The Triple Alliance. Germany was at the center of European foreign policy from 1870 until the outbreak of World War I. Chancellor Otto von Bismarck, Germany's prime minister, formed a series of alliances to strengthen his country's security. He first made an ally of Austria-Hungary. In 1879, Germany and Austria-Hungary agreed to go to war if either country were attacked by Russia. Italy joined the agreement in 1882, and it became known as the Triple Alliance. The members of the Triple Alliance agreed to aid one another in the case of an attack by two or more countries.

Bismarck also brought Austria-Hungary and Germany into an alliance with Russia. The agreement, known as the Three Emperors' League, was formed in 1881. The three powers agreed to remain neutral if any of them went to war with another country. Bismarck also persuaded Austria-Hungary and Russia, which were rivals for influence in the Balkans, to recognize each other's zone of authority in the region. He thus reduced the danger of conflict between the two countries.

Germany's relations with other European countries worsened after Bismarck left office in 1890. Bismarck had worked to prevent France, Germany's neighbor on the west, from forming an alliance with either of Germany's two neighbors to the east—Russia and Austria-Hungary. In 1894, France and Russia agreed to *mobilize* (call up troops) if any nation in the Triple Alliance mobilized. France and Russia also agreed to help each other if either were attacked by Germany.

The Triple Entente. During the 1800's, Britain had followed a foreign policy that became known as "splendid isolation." But Germany's naval build-up made Britain feel the need for allies. The country therefore ended its isolation. In 1904, Britain and France settled their past disagreements over colonies and signed the Entente Cordiale (Friendly Agreement). Although the agreement contained no pledges of military support, the two countries began to discuss joint military plans. In 1907, Russia joined the Entente Cordiale, and it became known as the Triple Entente.

The Triple Entente did not obligate its members to go to war as the Triple Alliance did. But the alliances left Europe divided into two opposing camps.

Beginning of the war

World War I began in the Balkans, the site of many small wars. In the early 1900's, the Balkan states fought the Ottoman Empire in the First Balkan War (1912-1913) and one another in the Second Balkan War (1913). The major European powers stayed out of both wars. But they did not escape the third Balkan crisis.

The assassination of an archduke. Archduke Francis Ferdinand, heir to the throne of Austria-Hungary, hoped that his sympathy for Slavs would ease tensions between Austria-Hungary and the Balkans. He arranged to tour Bosnia-Herzegovina with his wife, Sophie. As the

UPI/Bettmann Newsphotos

Archduke Francis Ferdinand of Austria-Hungary, *far right,* was shot to death on June 28, 1914, shortly after this photo was taken. His assassination triggered the outbreak of World War I.

couple rode through Sarajevo on June 28, 1914, an assassin jumped on their automobile and fired two shots. Francis Ferdinand and Sophie died almost instantly. The murderer, Gavrilo Princip, was linked to a Serbian terrorist group called the Black Hand.

The assassination of Francis Ferdinand gave Austria-Hungary an excuse to crush Serbia, its long-time enemy in the Balkans. Austria-Hungary first gained Germany's promise of support for any action it took against Serbia. It then sent a list of humiliating demands to Serbia on July 23. Serbia accepted most of the demands and offered to have the rest settled by an international conference. Austria-Hungary rejected the offer and declared war on Serbia on July 28. It expected a quick victory.

How the conflict spread. Within weeks of the archduke's assassination, the chief European powers were drawn into World War I. A few attempts were made to prevent the war. For example, Britain proposed an international conference to end the crisis. But Germany rejected the idea, claiming that the dispute involved only Austria-Hungary and Serbia. However, Germany tried to stop the war from spreading. The German *kaiser* (emperor), Wilhelm II, urged Czar Nicholas II of Russia, his cousin, not to mobilize.

Russia had backed down before in supporting its ally Serbia. In 1908, Austria-Hungary had angered Serbia by taking over Bosnia-Herzegovina, and Russia had stepped aside. In 1914, Russia vowed to stand behind Serbia. Russia first gained a promise of support from France. The czar then approved plans to mobilize along Russia's border with Austria-Hungary. But Russia's military leaders persuaded the czar to mobilize along the German border, too. On July 30, 1914, Russia announced it would mobilize fully.

Germany declared war on Russia on Aug. 1, 1914, in response to Russia's mobilization. Two days later, Germany declared war on France. The German army swept into Belgium on its way to France. The invasion of neutral Belgium caused Britain to declare war on Germany on August 4. By the time the war ended in November 1918, few areas of the world had remained neutral.

The Western Front. Germany's war plan had been prepared in 1905 by Alfred von Schlieffen. Schlieffen was chief of the German General Staff, the group of officers who provided advice on military operations. The Schlieffen Plan assumed that Germany would have to fight both France and Russia. It aimed at a quick defeat of France while Russia slowly mobilized. After defeating France, Germany would deal with Russia. The Schlieffen Plan required Germany to strike first if war came. Once the plan was set in motion, the system of military alliances almost assured a general European war.

The Schlieffen Plan called for two wings of the German army to crush the French army in a pincers movement. A small left wing would defend Germany along its frontier with France. A much larger right wing would invade France through Belgium; encircle and capture France's capital, Paris; and then move east. As the right wing moved in, the French forces would be trapped between the pincers. The success of Germany's assault depended on a strong right wing. However, Helmuth von Moltke, who had become chief of the General Staff in 1906, directed German strategy at the outbreak of World War I. Moltke changed the Schlieffen Plan by reducing the number of troops in the right wing.

Belgium's army fought bravely but held up the Germans for only a short time. By Aug. 16, 1914, the right wing of the German army could begin its pincers motion. It drove back French forces and a small British force in southern Belgium and swept into France. But instead of swinging west around Paris according to plan, one part of the right wing pursued retreating French troops east toward the Marne River. This maneuver left the Germans exposed to attacks from the rear.

Meanwhile, General Joseph Joffre, commander in chief of all the French armies, stationed his forces near the Marne River east of Paris and prepared for battle. Fierce fighting, which became known as the First Battle of the Marne, began on September 6. On September 9, German forces started to withdraw.

The First Battle of the Marne was a key victory for the Allies because it ended Germany's hopes to defeat France quickly. Moltke was replaced as chief of the German General Staff by Erich von Falkenhayn.

The German army halted its retreat near the Aisne River. From there, the Germans and the Allies fought a series of battles that became known as the Race to the Sea. Germany sought to seize ports on the English Channel and cut off vital supply lines between France and Britain. But the Allies stopped the German advance to the sea in the First Battle of Ypres in Belgium. The battle lasted from mid-October until mid-November.

By late November 1914, the war reached a *deadlock* along the Western Front as neither side gained much ground. The battlefront extended more than 450 miles (720 kilometers) across Belgium and northeastern France to the border of Switzerland. The deadlock on the Western Front lasted nearly $3\frac{1}{2}$ years.

The Eastern Front. Russia's mobilization on the Eastern Front moved faster than Germany expected. By late August 1914, two Russian armies had thrust deeply into the German territory of East Prussia. The Germans learned that the two armies had become separated, and they prepared a battle plan. By August 31, the Germans had encircled one Russian army in the Battle of Tannenberg. They then chased the other Russian army out of East Prussia in the Battle of the Masurian Lakes. The number of Russian *casualties*—that is, the number of men killed, captured, wounded, or missing—totaled about 250,000 in the two battles. The victories made heroes of the commanders of the German forces in the east—Paul von Hindenburg and Erich Ludendorff.

Austria-Hungary had less success than its German ally on the Eastern Front. By the end of 1914, Austria-Hungary's forces had attacked Serbia three times and been beaten back each time. Meanwhile, Russia had

The Western Front: 1914-1917

Fighting began in August 1914, when Germany invaded Belgium and France. The two sides were locked in trench warfare along the Western Front by year's end. The Western Front remained deadlocked for nearly $3\frac{1}{2}$ years.

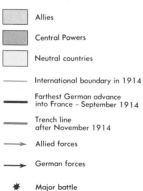

- Allies
- Central Powers
- Neutral countries
- —— International boundary in 1914
- —— Farthest German advance into France – September 1914
- —— Trench line after November 1914
- → Allied forces
- → German forces
- ✱ Major battle

WORLD BOOK map

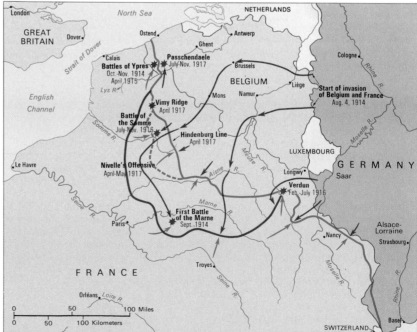

Weapons of World War I

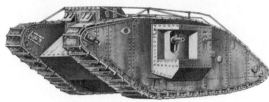

The tank was a British invention of World War I. Tanks were designed to rip through barbed wire and cross trenches. Crews inside gunned down the enemy. This MK IV tank first saw action in 1917.

The airplane was first used in combat during World War I. Airco D.H.4's, like this one, were highly regarded British bombers. The D.H.4 held a pilot and a gunner and carried bombs under its wings.

The machine gun made World War I more deadly than earlier wars. The gun's rapid fire slaughtered attacking infantrymen. The 8-millimeter Hotchkiss gun used by the French army is shown here.

The submarine proved its value as a warship in World War I. German submarines, like this UB II, challenged British sea power. They fired torpedoes that struck surface ships and then exploded.

WORLD BOOK illustrations by Tony Gibbons, Linden Artists Ltd.

captured much of the Austro-Hungarian province of Galicia (now part of Poland and Ukraine). By early October, a humiliated Austro-Hungarian army had retreated into its own territory.

Fighting elsewhere. The Allies declared war on the Ottoman Empire in November 1914, after Turkish ships bombarded Russian ports on the Black Sea. Turkish troops then invaded Russia. Fighting later broke out in the Ottoman territories on the Arabian Peninsula and in Mesopotamia (now mostly Iraq), Palestine, and Syria.

Britain stayed in control of the seas following two naval victories over Germany in 1914. The British then kept Germany's surface fleet bottled up in its home waters during most of the war. As a result, Germany relied on submarine warfare.

World War I quickly spread to Germany's overseas colonies. Japan declared war on Germany in late August 1914 and drove the Germans off several islands in the Pacific Ocean. Troops from Australia and New Zealand seized other German colonies in the Pacific. By mid-

1915, most of Germany's empire in Africa had fallen to British forces. However, fighting continued in German East Africa (now Tanzania) for two more years.

The deadlock on the Western Front

By 1915, the opposing sides had dug themselves into a system of trenches that zigzagged along the Western Front. From the trenches, they defended their positions and launched attacks. The Western Front remained deadlocked in trench warfare until 1918.

Trench warfare. The typical *front line trench* was about 6 to 8 feet (1.8 to 2.4 meters) deep and wide enough for two men to pass. Dugouts in the sides of the trenches protected men during enemy fire. *Support trenches* ran behind the front-line trenches. Off-duty soldiers lived in dugouts in the support trenches. Troops and supplies moved to the battlefront through a network of *communications trenches.* Barbed wire helped protect the front-line trenches from surprise attacks. Field artillery was set up behind the support trenches.

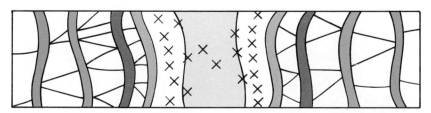

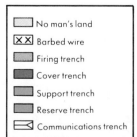

No man's land
☒☒ Barbed wire
Firing trench
Cover trench
Support trench
Reserve trench
Communications trench

A network of trenches snaked along the Western Front. No man's land separated opposing sides. Firing and cover trenches protected front-line soldiers from enemy fire. Communications trenches linked front lines with support and reserve troops at the rear.

Gernsheim Collection, Harry Ransom Humanities Research Center, University of Texas

Gas masks were worn by soldiers on the Western Front for protection against poisonous fumes. Germany was first to use poison gas, in April 1915 during the Second Battle of Ypres.

Between the enemy lines lay a stretch of ground called "no man's land." No man's land varied from less than 30 yards (27 meters) wide at some points to more than 1 mile (1.6 kilometers) wide at others. In time, artillery fire tore up the earth, making it very difficult to cross no man's land during an attack.

Soldiers generally served at the front line from a few days to a week and then rotated to the rear for a rest. Life in the trenches was miserable. The smell of dead bodies lingered in the air, and rats were a constant problem. Soldiers had trouble keeping dry, especially in water-logged areas of Belgium. Except during an attack, life fell into a dull routine. Some soldiers stood guard. Others repaired the trenches, kept telephone lines in order, brought food from behind the battle lines, or did other jobs. At night, patrols fixed the barbed wire and tried to get information about the enemy.

Enemy artillery and machine guns kept each side pinned in the trenches. Yet the Allies repeatedly tried to blast a gap in the German lines. Allied *offensives* (assaults) followed a pattern. First, artillery bombarded the enemy front-line trenches. The infantry then attacked as commanders shouted, "Over the top!" Soldiers scrambled out of trenches and began the dash across no man's land with fixed bayonets. They hurled grenades

into enemy trenches and struggled through the barbed wire. But the artillery bombardment seldom wiped out all resistance, and so enemy machine guns slaughtered wave after wave of advancing infantry. Even if the attackers broke through the front line, they ran into a second line of defenses. Thus, the Allies never cracked the enemy's defensive power.

Both the Allies and the Central Powers developed new weapons, which they hoped would break the deadlock. In April 1915, the Germans first released poison gas over Allied lines in the Second Battle of Ypres. The fumes caused vomiting and suffocation. But German commanders had little faith in the gas, and they failed to seize that opportunity to launch a major attack. The Allies also began to use poison gas soon thereafter, and gas masks became necessary equipment in the trenches. Another new weapon was the flame thrower, which shot out a stream of burning fuel.

The Battle of Verdun. As chief of the German General Staff, Falkenhayn decided in early 1916 to concentrate on killing enemy soldiers. He hoped that the Allies would finally lack the troops to continue the war. Falkenhayn chose to attack the French city of Verdun. He believed that France would defend Verdun to the last man. Fierce bombardment began on February 21.

Joffre, commander of the French armies, felt that the loss of Verdun would severely damage French morale. Through spring and summer, the French forces held off the attackers. As Falkenhayn predicted, France kept pouring men into the battle. However, Falkenhayn had not expected the battle to take nearly as many German lives as French lives. He halted the unsuccessful assault in July 1916. The next month, Hindenburg and Ludendorff—the two German heroes of the Eastern Front—replaced Falkenhayn on the Western Front. Hindenburg became chief of the General Staff. Ludendorff, his top aide, planned German strategy.

General Henri Pétain had organized the defense of Verdun and was hailed a hero by France. The Battle of Verdun became a symbol of the terrible destructiveness of modern war. French casualties totaled about 315,000 men, and German casualties about 280,000. The city itself was practically destroyed.

The Battle of the Somme. The Allies planned a major offensive for 1916 near the Somme River in

Imperial War Museum

A cry of "Over the top!" signaled the start of an assault. At the command, troops scrambled out of their trenches to begin the dash toward enemy trenches. The Canadian soldiers shown here were following an officer over the top during the Battle of the Somme in France in July 1916.

France. The Battle of Verdun had drained France. Thus, the Somme offensive became mainly the responsibility of the British under General Douglas Haig.

The Allies attacked on July 1, 1916. Within hours, Britain had suffered nearly 60,000 casualties—its worst loss in one day of battle. Fierce fighting went on into the fall. In September, Britain introduced the first primitive tanks. But the tanks were too unreliable and too few in number to make a difference in the battle. Haig finally halted the useless attack in November. At terrible cost, the Allies had gained about 7 miles (11 kilometers). The Battle of the Somme caused more than 1 million casualties—over 600,000 Germans, over 400,000 British, and nearly 200,000 French. In spite of the tragic losses at Verdun and the Somme, the Western Front stood as solid as ever at the end of 1916.

The war on other fronts

During 1915 and 1916, World War I spread to Italy and throughout the Balkans, and activity increased on other fronts. Some Allied military leaders believed that the creation of new battlefronts would break the deadlock on the Western Front. But the war's expansion had little effect on the deadlock.

The Italian Front. Italy had stayed out of World War I during 1914, even though it was a member of the Triple Alliance with Austria-Hungary and Germany. Italy claimed that it was under no obligation to honor the agreement because Austria-Hungary had not gone to war in self-defense. In May 1915, Italy entered World War I on the side of the Allies. In a secret treaty, the Allies promised to give Italy some of Austria-Hungary's territory after the war. In return, Italy promised to attack Austria-Hungary.

The Italians, led by General Luigi Cadorna, hammered away at Austria-Hungary for two years in a series of battles along the Isonzo River in Austria-Hungary. Italy suffered enormous casualties but gained very little territory. The Allies hoped that the Italian Front would help Russia by forcing Austria-Hungary to shift some troops away from the Eastern Front. Such a shift occurred, but it did not help Russia.

The Dardanelles. After World War I began, the Ottoman Empire closed the waterway between the Aegean Sea and the Black Sea. It thereby blocked the sea route

The Italian Front

Italy entered the war against Austria-Hungary in May 1915. In spite of many bitter battles, the Italians gained very little territory. But they wore down the armies of Austria-Hungary.

WORLD BOOK map

	Allies		Farthest Allied advance into Austria-Hungary
	Central Powers		Farthest advance of the Central Powers into Italy
	International boundary in 1914	✶	Major battle

to southern Russia. French and British warships attacked the Dardanelles, a strait that formed part of the waterway, in February and March 1915. The Allies hoped to open a supply route to Russia. However, underwater mines halted the assault.

In April 1915, the Allies landed troops on the Gallipoli Peninsula on the west shore of the Dardanelles. Troops from Australia and New Zealand played a key role in the landing. Ottoman and Allied forces soon became locked in trench warfare. A second invasion in August at Suvla Bay to the north failed to end the standstill. In December, the Allies began to evacuate their troops. They had suffered about 250,000 casualties in the Dardanelles.

Eastern Europe. In May 1915, the armies of Germany and Austria-Hungary broke through Russian lines in Galicia, the Austro-Hungarian province that Russia

Robert Hunt Library

Robert Hunt Library

Atop a rocky peak near Austria-Hungary's border, Italian troops prepared to do battle, *far left.* They first had to hoist artillery into position, *near left.* The rugged Alps hampered Italy's efforts to advance into Austria-Hungary.

had invaded in 1914. The Russians retreated about 300 miles (480 kilometers) before they formed a new line of defense. In spite of the setback, Czar Nicholas II staged two offensives to relieve the pressure on the Allies on the Western Front. The first Russian offensive, in March 1916, failed to pull German troops away from Verdun.

The second Russian offensive began in June 1916 under General Alexei Brusilov. Brusilov's army drove Austria-Hungary's forces back about 50 miles (80 kilometers). Within a few weeks, Russia captured about 200,000 prisoners. To halt the assault, Austria-Hungary had to shift troops from the Italian Front to the Eastern Front. The Russian offensive nearly knocked Austria-Hungary out of the war. But it also exhausted Russia. Each side suffered about a million casualties.

Bulgaria entered World War I in October 1915 to help Austria-Hungary defeat Serbia. Bulgaria hoped to recover land it had lost in the Second Balkan War. In an effort to aid Serbia, the Allies landed troops in Thessaloniki (Salonika), Greece. But the troops never reached Serbia. By November, the Central Powers had overrun Serbia, and Serbia's army had retreated to Albania.

Romania joined the Allies in August 1916. It hoped to gain some of Austria-Hungary's territory if the Allies won the war. By the end of 1916, Romania had lost most of its army, and Germany controlled the country's valuable wheat fields and oil fields.

The war at sea. British control of the seas during World War I caused serious problems for Germany. The British Navy blockaded German waters, preventing supplies from reaching German ports. By 1916, Germany suffered a shortage of food and other goods. Germany combated British seapower with its submarines, called *U-boats.* In February 1915, Germany declared a submarine blockade of the United Kingdom and Ireland and warned that it would attack any ship that tried to pass the blockade. Thereafter, U-boats destroyed great amounts of goods headed for the United Kingdom.

On May 7, 1915, a U-boat torpedoed without warning the British passenger liner *Lusitania* off the coast of Ireland. Among the 1,201 passengers who died were 128 Americans. The sinking of the *Lusitania* led U.S. President Woodrow Wilson to urge Germany to give up unrestricted submarine warfare. In September, Germany agreed not to attack neutral or passenger ships.

The warships that the British and the Germans had raced to build before World War I remained in home waters during most of the war. There, they served to discourage an enemy invasion. The only major encounter between the two navies was the Battle of Jutland. It was fought off the coast of Denmark on May 31 and June 1, 1916. Admiral Sir John Jellicoe commanded a British fleet of 150 warships. He faced a German fleet of 99 warships under the command of Admiral Reinhard Scheer. Despite the superior strength of the British, Jellicoe was cautious. He feared that he could lose the entire war in a day because the destruction of the British fleet would give Germany control of the seas. Both sides claimed victory in the Battle of Jutland. The United Kingdom lost more ships than Germany, but it still ruled the seas.

The war in the air. Great advances in aviation were made by the Allies and the Central Powers during World War I. Each side competed to produce better airplanes than the other side. Airplanes were used mainly

The Eastern Front

The Eastern Front swung back and forth until Russia agreed to stop fighting late in 1917. Under the Treaty of Brest-Litovsk, Russia gave much territory to Germany. To the south, the Central Powers had crushed Serbia in 1915 and Romania in 1916.

Allies

Central Powers

Neutral countries

International boundary in 1914

Farthest advance westward by Allies

Farthest advance eastward by Central Powers

Allied forces

Forces of the Central Powers

Major battle

World Book map

Robert Hunt Library

On the seas, Germany tried to starve Britain into surrender by sinking cargo ships headed for its ports. The ship shown here was torpedoed by the German submarine in the foreground.

to observe enemy activities. The pilots carried guns to shoot down enemy planes. But a pilot risked shooting himself if a bullet bounced off the propeller.

In 1915, Germany developed a machine gun timed to fire between an airplane's revolving propeller blades. The invention made air combat more deadly and led to *dogfights*—clashes between enemy aircraft. A pilot who shot down 5 or more enemy planes was called an *ace*. Many aces became national heroes. Germany's Baron Manfred von Richthofen, who was known as the Red Baron, shot down 80 planes, more than any other ace. Other famous aces included Billy Bishop of Canada, René Fonck of France, Edward Mannock of Great Britain, and Eddie Rickenbacker of the United States.

Aerial bombing remained in its early stages during World War I. In 1915, Germany began to bomb London and other British cities from airships called *zeppelins.* But bombing had little effect on the war.

The final stage

Allied failures. During 1917, French and British military leaders still hoped that a successful offensive could win the war. But German leaders accepted the deadlock on the Western Front and improved German defenses. In March 1917, German troops were moved back to a strongly fortified new battle line in northern France. It was called the Siegfried Line by the Germans and the Hindenburg Line by the Allies. The Siegfried Line shortened the Western Front and placed German artillery and machine guns to best advantage. It also led to the failure of an offensive planned by France.

General Robert Nivelle had replaced Joffre as commander in chief of French forces in December 1916. Nivelle planned a major offensive near the Aisne River and predicted he would smash through the German line within two days. Nivelle's enthusiasm inspired the French troops. Germany's pullback to the Siegfried Line did not shake Nivelle's confidence.

In April 1917, shortly before Nivelle's offensive began, Canadian forces seized a hill called Vimy Ridge. Many Allied troops had fallen in earlier attempts to dislodge

the Germans from that height in northern France.

Nivelle's offensive opened on April 16, 1917. By the end of the day, it was clear that the assault had failed. But fighting continued into May. Mutinies broke out among the French forces after Nivelle's offensive collapsed. The troops had had enough of the pointless bloodshed and the horrid conditions on the Western Front. They no longer had faith in their leaders. Men who had fought bravely for almost three years refused to go on fighting. Pétain, the hero of Verdun, replaced Nivelle in May 1917. Pétain improved the soldiers' living conditions and restored order. He promised that France would remain on the defensive until it was ready to fight again. Meanwhile, any further offensives on the Western Front remained Britain's responsibility.

General Haig was hopeful that a British offensive near Ypres would lead to victory. The Third Battle of Ypres, also known as the Battle of Passchendaele, began on July 31, 1917. For more than three months, British troops and a small French force pounded the Germans in an especially terrible campaign. Heavy Allied bombardment before the infantry attack began had destroyed the drainage system around Ypres. Drenching rains then turned the water-logged land into a swamp where thousands of British soldiers drowned. Snow and ice finally halted the disastrous battle on November 10. In late November, Britain used tanks to break through the Siegfried Line. But the failure at Ypres had used up the troops Britain needed to follow up that success.

In 1917, first France and then Britain thus saw their hopes for victory shattered. Austria-Hungary drove the Italians out of its territory in the Battle of Caporetto in the fall. A revolution in Russia made the Allied situation seem even more hopeless.

Imperial War Museum from Keystone

Military aviators played an important role in World War I. Pilots, such as these members of the British Royal Flying Corps, fought enemy planes in aerial battles called *dogfights*.

Bettmann Archive

War-weary Russian soldiers retreated in disorder in the summer of 1917 after learning that the Germans had smashed through their battle line. By year's end, Russia had quit fighting.

The Russian Revolution. The Russian people suffered greatly during World War I. By 1917, many of them were no longer willing to put up with the enormous casualties and the severe shortages of food and fuel. They blamed Czar Nicholas II and his advisers for the country's problems. Early in 1917, an uprising in Petrograd (now St. Petersburg) forced Nicholas from the throne. The new government continued the war.

To weaken Russia's war effort further, Germany helped V. I. Lenin, a Russian revolutionary then living in Switzerland, return to his homeland in April 1917. Seven months later, Lenin led an uprising that gained control of Russia's government. Lenin immediately called for peace talks with Germany. World War I had ended on the Eastern Front.

Germany dictated harsh peace terms to Russia in a peace treaty signed in Brest-Litovsk, Russia, on March 3, 1918. The Treaty of Brest-Litovsk forced Russia to give up large amounts of territory, including Finland, Poland, Ukraine, Bessarabia, and the Baltic States—Estonia, Livonia (now Latvia), and Lithuania. The end of the fighting on the Eastern Front freed German troops for use on the Western Front. The only obstacle to a final German victory seemed to be the entry of the United States into the war.

The United States enters the war. At the start of World War I, President Wilson had declared the neutrality of the United States. Most Americans opposed U.S. involvement in a European war. But the sinking of the *Lusitania* and other German actions against civilians drew American sympathies to the Allies.

Several events early in 1917 persuaded the United States government to enter World War I. In February, Germany returned to unrestricted submarine warfare, which it assumed might bring the United States into the war. But German military leaders believed that they could still win the war by cutting off British supplies.

They expected their U-boats to starve Britain into surrendering within a few months, long before the United States had fully prepared for war.

Tension between the United States and Germany increased after the British intercepted and decoded a message from Germany's foreign minister, Arthur Zimmermann, to the German ambassador to Mexico. The message, known as the "Zimmermann note," revealed a German plot to persuade Mexico to go to war against the United States. The British gave the message to Wilson, and it was published in the United States early in March. Americans were further enraged after U-boats sank several U.S. cargo ships.

On April 2, Wilson called for war, stating that "the world must be made safe for democracy." Congress declared war on Germany on April 6. Few people expected that the United States would make much of a contribution toward ending the war.

Mobilization. The United States entered World War I unprepared for battle. Strong antiwar feelings had hampered efforts to prepare for war. After declaring war, the government worked to stir up enthusiasm for the war effort. Government propaganda pictured the war as a battle for liberty and democracy. People who still opposed the war faced increasingly unfriendly public opinion. They could even be brought to trial under wartime laws forbidding statements that might harm the successful progress of the war.

During World War I, U.S. government agencies directed the nation's economy toward the war effort. President Wilson put financier Bernard M. Baruch in charge of the War Industries Board, which turned factories into producers of war materials. The Food Administration, headed by businessman Herbert Hoover, controlled the prices, production, and distribution of food. Americans observed "meatless" and "wheatless" days in order that food could be sent to Europe.

Manpower was the chief contribution of the United States to World War I. The country entered the war with a Regular Army of only about 128,000 men. It soon organized a draft requiring all men from 21 through 30 years old to register for military service. The age range was broadened to 18 through 45 in 1918. A lottery determined who served. Many men enlisted voluntarily, and women signed up as nurses and office workers. The

Granger Collection

A propaganda poster urged Americans to buy war bonds by showing the enemy as a vicious killer. *Hun* was a scornful term applied to Germans during World War I.

American gunners crawled through a war-torn area of northeastern France in the fall of 1918 during the last assault of World War I. The area lay between the Meuse River and the Argonne Forest. Almost a million U.S. troops took part in the assault, known as the Meuse-Argonne offensive.

National Archives

U.S. armed forces had almost 5 million men and women by the end of the war. Of that number, about $2\frac{3}{4}$ million men had been drafted. Few soldiers received much training before going overseas because the Allies urgently needed them.

Before U.S. help could reach the Western Front, the Allies had to overcome the U-boat threat in the Atlantic. In May 1917, Britain began to use a *convoy system,* by which cargo ships went to sea in large groups escorted by warships. The U-boats proved no match for the warships, and Allied shipping losses dropped sharply.

American troops in Europe. The soldiers sent to Europe by the U.S. Army made up the American Expeditionary Forces (AEF). General John J. Pershing, commander of the AEF, arrived in France in mid-June 1917. The first troops landed later that month. Pershing told U.S. military authorities that he needed 3 million American troops, a third of them within the next year. The American officials were shocked. They had planned to send only 650,000 troops in that time. In the end, about 2 million Americans served in Europe.

Britain, France, and Italy knew well how desperately they needed U.S. manpower by the fall of 1917. In November, the Allies formed the Supreme War Council to plan strategy. They decided to make their strategy defensive until U.S. troops reached the Western Front. The Allies wanted Americans to serve as replacements and fill out their battered ranks. But Pershing was convinced that the AEF would make a greater contribution by fighting as an independent unit. The argument was the major wartime dispute between the Europeans and their American ally. Pershing generally held firm, though at times he lent troops to France and Britain.

The last campaigns. The end of the war on the Eastern Front boosted German hopes for victory. By early 1918, German forces outnumbered the Allies on the Western Front. In spring, Germany staged three offensives. Ludendorff counted on delivering a crushing blow to the Allies before large numbers of American troops reached the front. He relied on speed and surprise.

Germany first struck near St.-Quentin, a city in the Somme River Valley, on March 21, 1918. By March 26, British troops had retreated about 30 miles (50 kilometers). In late March, the Germans began to bombard Paris with "Big Berthas." The enormous guns hurled shells up to 75 miles (120 kilometers). After the disaster at St.-Quentin, Allied leaders met to plan a united defense. In April, they appointed General Ferdinand Foch of France to be the supreme commander of the Allied forces on the Western Front.

A second German offensive began on April 9 along the Lys River in Belgium. British troops fought stubbornly, and Ludendorff called off the attack on April 30. The Allies suffered heavy losses in both assaults, but German casualties were nearly as great.

Germany attacked a third time on May 27 near the Aisne River. By May 30, German troops had reached the Marne River. American soldiers helped France stop the German advance at the town of Château-Thierry, less than 50 miles (80 kilometers) northeast of Paris. During June, U.S. troops drove the Germans out of Belleau Wood, a forested area near the Marne. German forces crossed the Marne on July 15. Foch ordered a counterattack near the town of Soissons on July 18.

The Second Battle of the Marne was fought from July 15 through Aug. 6, 1918. It marked the turning point of World War I. After winning the battle, the Allies advanced steadily. On August 8, Britain and France attacked the Germans near Amiens. By early September, Germany had lost all the territory it had gained since spring. In mid-September, Pershing led U.S. forces to easy victory at St.-Mihiel.

The last offensive of World War I began on Sept. 26, 1918. About 900,000 U.S. troops participated in heavy fighting between the Argonne Forest and the Meuse River. Ludendorff realized that Germany could no longer overcome the superior strength of the Allies.

The fighting ends. The Allies won victories on all fronts in the fall of 1918. Bulgaria surrendered on September 29. British forces under the command of General Edmund Allenby triumphed over the Ottoman army in Palestine and Syria. On October 30, the Ottoman Empire signed an armistice. The last major battle between Italy and Austria-Hungary began in late October in Italy. Italy, with support from France and Great Britain, defeated Austria-Hungary near the town of Vittorio Veneto. Austria-Hungary signed an armistice on November 3.

Germany teetered on the edge of collapse as the war continued through October. Britain's naval blockade had nearly starved the German people, and widespread discontent led to riots and rising demands for peace. Kaiser Wilhelm gave up his throne on November 9 and fled to the Netherlands. An Allied delegation headed by Foch met with German representatives in a railroad car in the Compiègne Forest in northern France.

In the early morning on Nov. 11, 1918, the Germans accepted the armistice terms demanded by the Allies. Germany agreed to evacuate the terrorities it had taken during the war; to surrender large numbers of arms, ships, and other war materials; and to allow the Allied powers to occupy German territory along the Rhine River. Foch ordered the fighting to stop on the Western Front at 11 a.m. World War I was over.

Consequences of the war

Destruction and casualties. World War I caused immeasurable destruction. Nearly 10 million soldiers died as a result of the war—far more than had died in all the wars during the previous 100 years. About 21 million men were wounded. The enormously high casualties resulted partly from the destructive powers of new weapons, especially the machine gun. Military leaders contributed to the slaughter by failing to adjust to the changed conditions of warfare. In staging offensives,

The Western Front: 1918

Germany staged three assaults from March to June of 1918. With American help, the Allies halted the German advance outside Paris in June. Thereafter, the Allies steadily drove the Germans back. An armistice ended the fighting on Nov. 11, 1918.

WORLD BOOK map

Allies		Farthest German advance in June 1918	
Central Powers		Allied forces	
Neutral countries		German forces	
International boundary in 1914		Major battle	

they ordered soldiers armed with bayonets into machine-gun fire. Only in the last year of the war did generals successfully use tanks and new tactics.

Germany and Russia each suffered about $1\frac{3}{4}$ million battle deaths during World War I—more than any other country. France had the highest percentage of battle deaths in relation to its total number of servicemen. It lost about $1\frac{1}{3}$ million soldiers, or 16 per cent of those mobilized. No one knows how many civilians died of disease, starvation, and other war-related causes. Some historians believe as many civilians died as soldiers.

Property damage in World War I was greatest in France and Belgium. Armies destroyed farms and villages as they passed through them or, even worse, dug in for battle. The fighting wrecked factories, bridges, and railroad tracks. Artillery shells, trenches, and chemicals made barren the land along the Western Front.

Economic consequences. World War I cost the fighting nations a total of about $337 billion dollars. By 1918, the war was costing about $10 million an hour. Nations raised part of the money to pay for the war through income taxes and other taxes. But most of the money came from borrowing, which created huge debts. Governments borrowed from citizens by selling war bonds. The Allies also borrowed heavily from the United States. In addition, most governments printed extra money to meet their needs. But the increased money supply caused severe inflation after the war.

The problem of war debts lingered after World War I ended. The Allies tried to reduce their debts by demanding *reparations* (payments for war damages) from the Central Powers, especially Germany. Reparations worsened the economic problems of the defeated countries and did not solve the problems of the victors.

World War I seriously disrupted economies. Some businesses shut down after workers left for military service. Other firms shifted to the production of war materials. To direct production toward the war effort, governments took greater control over the economy than ever before. Most people wanted a return to private enterprise after the war. But some people expected government to continue to solve economic problems.

The countries of Europe had poured their resources into World War I, and they came out of the war exhausted. France, for example, had lost nearly one-tenth of its work force. In most European countries, many returning soldiers could not find jobs. In addition, Europe lost many of the markets for its exports while producing war goods. The United States and other countries that had played a smaller role in the war emerged with increased economic power.

Political consequences. World War I shook the foundations of several governments. Democratic governments in Britain and France withstood the stress of the war. But four monarchies toppled. The first monarch to fall was Czar Nicholas II of Russia in 1917. Kaiser Wilhelm II of Germany and Emperor Charles of Austria-Hungary left their thrones in 1918. The Ottoman sultan, Muhammad VI, fell in 1922.

The collapse of old empires led to the creation of new countries in the years after World War I. The prewar territory of Austria-Hungary formed the independent republics of Austria, Hungary, and Czechoslovakia, as well as parts of Italy, Poland, Romania, and Yugosla-

National Archives

Cheering the end of World War I, a joyful crowd streamed through the streets of a French town on Nov. 11, 1918. The long, horrible war had taken the lives of nearly 10 million soldiers.

via. Russia and Germany also gave up territory to Poland. Finland and the Baltic States—Estonia, Latvia, and Lithuania—gained independence from Russia. Most Arab lands in the Ottoman Empire were placed under the control of France and Britain. The rest of the Ottoman Empire became Turkey. European leaders took national groups into account in redrawing the map of Europe and thus strengthened the cause of nationalism.

World War I gave the Communists a chance to seize power in Russia. Some people expected Communist revolutions to break out elsewhere in Europe. Revolutionary movements gained strength after the war, but Communist governments did not take hold.

Social consequences. World War I brought enormous changes in society. The death of so many young men affected France more than other countries. During the 1920's, France's population dropped because of a low birth rate. Millions of people were uprooted by the war. Some fled war-torn areas and later found their houses, farms, or villages destroyed. Others became refugees as a result of changes in governments and national borders, especially in central and eastern Europe.

Many people chose not to resume their old way of life after World War I. Urban areas grew as peasants settled in cities instead of returning to farms. Women filled

jobs in offices and factories after men went to war, and they were reluctant to give up their new independence. Many countries granted women the vote after the war.

The distinction between social classes began to blur as a result of World War I, and society became more democratic. The upper classes, which had traditionally governed, lost some of their power and privilege after having led the world into an agonizing war. Men of all classes had faced the same danger and horror in the trenches. Those who had bled and suffered for their country came to demand a say in running it.

Finally, World War I transformed attitudes. Middle- and upper-class Europeans lost the confidence and optimism they had felt before the war. Many people began to question long-held ideas. For example, few Europeans before the war had doubted their right to force European culture on the rest of the world. But the destruction and bloodshed of the war shattered the belief in the superiority of European civilization.

The peace settlement

The Fourteen Points. In January 1918, 10 months before World War I ended, President Woodrow Wilson of the United States proposed a set of war aims called the Fourteen Points. Wilson believed that the Fourteen Points would bring about a just peace settlement, which he termed "peace without victory." In November 1918, Germany agreed to an armistice. Germany expected that the peace settlement would be based on the Fourteen Points.

Eight of Wilson's Fourteen Points dealt with specific political and territorial settlements. The rest of them set forth general principles aimed at preventing future wars. The last point proposed the establishment of an international association—later called the League of Nations—to maintain the peace. See **Wilson, Woodrow** (The Fourteen Points).

The Paris Peace Conference. In January 1919, representatives of the victorious powers gathered in Paris to draw up the peace settlement. They came from 32 nations. Committees worked out specific proposals at the Paris Peace Conference. But the decisions were made by four heads of government called the Big Four. The Big Four consisted of Wilson, Britain's Prime Minister David Lloyd George, France's Premier Georges Clemenceau, and Italy's Prime Minister Vittorio Orlando.

The Paris Peace Conference largely disregarded the lofty principles of the Fourteen Points. The major European Allies had sacrificed far more than the Americans and wanted to be paid back. Wilson focused his efforts on the creation of the League of Nations. He yielded to France and Britain on many other issues.

In May 1919, the peace conference approved the treaty and presented it to Germany. Germany agreed to it only after the Allies threatened to invade. With grave doubts, German representatives signed the treaty in the Palace of Versailles near Paris on June 28, 1919. The date was the fifth anniversary of the assassination of Archduke Franz Ferdinand.

In addition to the Treaty of Versailles with Germany, the peacemakers drew up separate treaties with the other Central Powers. The Treaty of St-Germain was signed with Austria in September 1919, the Treaty of Neuilly with Bulgaria in November 1919, the Treaty

Military casualties in World War I (1914-1918)*

	Dead	Wounded
The Allies		
Belgium	14,000	44,700
British Empire	908,400	2,090,200
France	1,358,000†	4,266,000
Greece	5,000	21,000
Italy	650,000	947,000
Portugal	7,200	13,800
Romania	335,700†	120,000
Russia	1,700,000	4,950,000
Serbia and Montenegro	48,000	143,000
United States	116,516‡	234,428‡
The Central Powers		
Austria-Hungary	1,200,000	3,620,000
Bulgaria	87,500	152,400
Germany	1,773,000	4,216,000
Ottoman Empire	325,000	400,000

*Except for the United States, all figures are approximate.
†Includes missing.
‡Official U.S. government figure.
Source: U.S. War Department, Dec. 10, 1922.

of Trianon with Hungary in June 1920, and the Treaty of Sèvres with the Ottoman Empire in August 1920.

Provisions of the treaties that officially ended World War I stripped the Central Powers of territory and arms and required them to pay reparations. Germany was punished especially severely. One clause in the Treaty of Versailles forced Germany to accept responsibility for causing the war.

Under the Treaty of Versailles, Germany gave up territory to Belgium, Czechoslovakia, Denmark, France, and Poland and lost its overseas colonies. France gained control of coal fields in Germany's Saar Valley for 15 years. An Allied military force, paid for by Germany, was to occupy the west bank of the Rhine River for 15 years. Other clauses in the treaty limited Germany's armed forces and required the country to turn over war materials, ships, livestock, and other goods to the Allies. A total sum for reparations was not set until 1921. At that time, Germany received a bill for about $33 billion.

The Treaty of St.-Germain and the Treaty of Trianon reduced Austria and Hungary to less than a third their former area. The treaties recognized the independence of Czechoslovakia, Poland, and a kingdom that later became Yugoslavia. Those new states, along with Italy and Romania, received territory that had belonged to Austria-Hungary. The Treaty of Sèvres took Mesopotamia (later renamed Iraq), Palestine, and Syria away from the Ottoman Empire. Bulgaria lost territory to Greece and Romania. Germany's allies also had to reduce their armed forces and pay reparations.

The postwar world. The peacemakers found it impossible to satisfy the hopes and ambitions of every nation and national group. The settlements they drew up disappointed both the victors and the defeated powers.

In creating new borders, the peacemakers considered the wishes of national groups. However, territorial claims overlapped in many cases. For example, Romania gained a chunk of land with a large Hungarian population, and parts of Czechoslovakia and Poland had many Germans. Such settlements heightened tensions between countries. In addition, some Arab nations were bitter because they had failed to gain independence.

Certain borders created by the peace settlements made little economic sense. For example, the new countries of Austria and Hungary were small and weak and unable to support themselves. They had lost most of their population, resources, and markets. Austria's largely German population had wanted to unite with Germany. But the peace treaties forbade that union. The peacemakers did not want Germany to gain territory from the war.

Among the European Allies, Britain entered the postwar world the most content. The nation had kept its empire and control of the seas. But Britain worried that the balance of power it wanted in Europe could be upset by a severely weakened Germany and a victory by the Communists in a civil war in Russia. France had succeeded in imposing harsh terms on Germany—its traditional foe—but not in safeguarding its borders. France had failed to obtain a guarantee of aid from Britain and the United States in the event of a German invasion. Finally, Italy had gained less territory than it had been promised and felt it deserved.

In the United States, the Senate reflected public opinion and failed to approve the Treaty of Versailles. It thereby rejected President Wilson. The treaty would have made the United States a member of the League of Nations. Many Americans were not yet ready to accept

Europe and the Near East after World War I

World War I led to changes in many borders. Austria-Hungary and the Ottoman Empire split into national states. Russia and Germany gave up territory. Although several states won independence, most Arab lands in the Ottoman Empire were placed under French and British rule.

▓	German Empire
▒	Austria-Hungary
░	Russian Empire
□	Ottoman Empire
——	International boundary of newly created country
——	Other international boundary

0   500 Miles
0   500 Kilometers

WORLD BOOK map

the responsibilities that went along with their country's new power. They feared that the League of Nations would entangle the country in European disputes.

The Treaty of Versailles imposed harsher terms than Germany had expected. The responsibility of having accepted those terms weakened Germany's government. In the 1930's, a strongly nationalist movement led by Adolf Hitler gained power in Germany. Hitler promised to ignore the Treaty of Versailles and to avenge Germany's defeat in World War I. In 1939, Germany invaded Poland. World War II had begun.   Edward M. Coffman

Related articles in *World Book.* See the *History* section of articles on the countries that took part in World War I. See also the following articles:

Battle areas

Alsace-Lorraine	Jutland, Battle of	Verdun, Battles of
Balkans	Saar	Vimy Ridge, Battle
Flanders Field	Siegfried Line	of

Allied military biographies

Albert I	Kitchener, Horatio H.
Allenby, Lord	March, Peyton C.
Bishop, Billy	Mitchell, Billy
Byng, Julian H. G.	Pershing, John J.
Foch, Ferdinand	Pétain, Henri Philippe
Haig, Douglas	Pilsudski, Józef
Jellicoe, John R.	Rickenbacker, Eddie
Joffre, Joseph J. C.	York, Alvin C.

Allied civilian biographies

Asquith, Herbert H.	Nicholas II (czar)
Baruch, Bernard M.	Orlando, Vittorio E.
Borden, Sir Robert L.	Poincaré, Raymond
Clemenceau, Georges	Venizelos, Eleutherios
Hoover, Herbert C.	Wilson, Woodrow
Lloyd George, David	

Central Powers biographies

Hindenburg, Paul von	Wilhelm (II)
Ludendorff, Erich F. W.	Zeppelin, Ferdinand von

Other biographies

Atatürk, Kemal	Constantine I (of	Lenin, V. I.
Cavell, Edith L.	Greece)	Mata Hari
	Lawrence, T. E.	

Forces, materials, and weapons

Air force	Chemical-biological-radiolog-
Air Force, United States	ical warfare
Aircraft, Military	Coast Guard, United States
Airplane (History)	Code talkers
Airship	Codes and ciphers (History)
Army	Machine gun
Army, United States	Navy
Artillery	Navy, United States
Aviation	Submarine
Camouflage	Tank

Treaties

Saint Germain, Treaty of
Sèvres, Treaty of
Trianon, Treaty of
Versailles, Treaty of

Other related articles

Ace	Neutrality
American Legion	Red Cross
American Legion Auxiliary	Refugee
Fourteen Points	Selective Service System
League of Nations	Socialism (World Wars I and
Lusitania	II)
Mandated territory	Stars and Stripes

United States, History of the	Veterans Day
Unknown soldier	War crime

Outline

I. Causes of the war
  A. The rise of nationalism
  B. A build-up of military might
  C. Competition for colonies
  D. A system of military alliances

II. Beginning of the war
  A. The assassination of an archduke
  B. How the conflict spread
  C. The Western Front
  D. The Eastern Front
  E. Fighting elsewhere

III. The deadlock on the Western Front
  A. Trench warfare
  B. The Battle of Verdun
  C. The Battle of the Somme

IV. The war on other fronts
  A. The Italian Front
  B. The Dardanelles
  C. Eastern Europe
  D. The war at sea
  E. The war in the air

V. The final stage
  A. Allied failures
  B. The Russian Revolution
  C. The United States enters the war
  D. The last campaigns
  E. The fighting ends

VI. Consequences of the war
  A. Destruction and casualties
  B. Economic consequences
  C. Political consequences
  D. Social consequences

VII. The peace settlement
  A. The Fourteen Points
  B. The Paris Peace Conference
  C. Provisions of the treaties
  D. The postwar world

Questions

What were the four chief causes of World War I?

What country first used poison gas in World War I? What country first used tanks?

Which World War I heads of government made up the Big Four?

Which countries formed the Triple Entente? The Triple Alliance? How did the two alliances differ?

How did Germany combat British naval power during World War I?

What was the chief contribution made by the United States to World War I?

What was the Schlieffen Plan in World War I?

Why was the First Battle of the Marne a key Allied victory?

How did the Treaty of Versailles affect Germany?

Why did French troops mutiny in 1917?

How did Germany try to weaken Russia's war effort in 1917?

Additional resources

Burg, David F., and Purcell, E. L. *Almanac of World War I.* 1998. Reprint. Univ. Pr. of Ky., 2004.

Hamilton, Richard F., and Herwig, H. H., eds. *The Origins of World War I.* Cambridge, 2003.

Keegan, John. *The First World War.* Knopf, 1999. *An Illustrated History of the First World War.* 2001.

Palmer, Alan. *Victory, 1918.* Grove Pr., 2001.

Stevenson, David. *Cataclysm: The First World War as Political Tragedy.* Basic Bks., 2004.

Stewart, Gail B. *World War I.* 1991. Reprint. Blackbirch Pr., 2004. Younger readers.

Strachan, Hew. *The First World War.* Viking, 2004.

Zieger, Robert H. *America's Great War: World War I and the American Experience.* Rowman & Littlefield, 2000.

Süddeutscher Verlag

Imperial War Museum

The fighting fronts in World War II spread to nearly every part of the globe. In Europe and northern Africa, they included cities and desert wastes. Little remained standing in Tournai, Belgium, *left,* after a German bombing raid. Tank warfare kept armies on the run in Egypt, *right.*

World War II

World War II (1939-1945) killed more people, destroyed more property, disrupted more lives, and probably had more far-reaching consequences than any other war in history. It brought about the downfall of Western Europe as the center of world power and led to the rise of the Soviet Union. The development of the atomic bomb during the war opened the nuclear age.

The exact number of people killed because of World War II will never be known. Military deaths probably totaled about 17 million. Civilian deaths were even greater as a result of starvation, bombing raids, massacres, epidemics, and other war-related causes. The battlegrounds spread to nearly every part of the world. Troops fought in the steaming jungles of Southeast Asia, in the deserts of northern Africa, and on islands in the Pacific Ocean. Battles were waged on frozen fields in the Soviet Union, below the surface of the Atlantic Ocean, and in the streets of many European cities.

World War II began on Sept. 1, 1939, when Germany invaded Poland. Germany's dictator, Adolf Hitler, had built Germany into a powerful war machine. That machine rapidly crushed Poland, Denmark, Luxembourg, the Netherlands, Belgium, Norway, and France. By June 1940, the United Kingdom stood alone against Hitler. That same month, Italy joined the war on Germany's side. The fighting soon spread to Greece and northern

Africa. In June 1941, Germany invaded the Soviet Union. Japan attacked United States military bases at Pearl Harbor in Hawaii on Dec. 7, 1941, bringing the United States into the war. By mid-1942, Japanese forces had conquered much of Southeast Asia and had swept across many islands in the Pacific.

Germany, Italy, and Japan formed an alliance known as the Axis. Bulgaria, Hungary, Romania, and the German-created states of Croatia and Slovakia eventually joined the Axis. The United States, the United Kingdom, China, and the Soviet Union were the major powers fighting the Axis. They were called the Allies. The Allies totaled 50 nations by the end of the war.

In 1942, the Allies stopped the Axis advance in northern Africa, the Soviet Union, and the Pacific. Allied forces landed in Italy in 1943 and in France in 1944. In 1945, the Allies drove into Germany from the east and the west. A series of battles in the Pacific brought the Allies to Japan's doorstep by the summer of 1945. Germany surrendered on May 7, 1945, and Japan on Sept. 2, 1945.

An uneasy peace took effect as a war-weary world began to rebuild after World War II. Much of Europe and parts of Asia lay in ruins. Millions of people were starving and homeless. Europe's leadership in world affairs had ended. The United States and the Soviet Union had become the world's most powerful nations. But their wartime alliance broke down soon after the war. New threats to peace arose as the Soviet Union sought to spread Communism in Europe and Asia.

Causes of the war

Many historians trace the causes of World War II to problems left unsolved by World War I (1914-1918). World War I and the treaties that ended it also created new political and economic problems. Forceful leaders in several countries took advantage of those problems

James L. Stokesbury, the contributor of this article, is a former Professor of History at Acadia University and the author of A Short History of World War II.

to seize power. The desire of dictators in Germany, Italy, and Japan to conquer additional territory brought them into conflict with democratic nations.

The Peace of Paris. After World War I ended, representatives of the victorious nations met in Paris in 1919 to draw up peace treaties for the defeated countries. The treaties, known together as the Peace of Paris, followed a long and bitter war. They were worked out in haste by countries with opposing goals and failed to sat-

National Archives

Charles Kerlee from National Archives

Battlegrounds in Asia and the Pacific included tropical jungles and vast ocean spaces. Troops waded across muddy rivers and crawled through thick vegetation, *left,* in Southeast Asia and on Pacific islands. Planes based on aircraft carriers, *right,* did much of the fighting at sea.

isfy even the victors. Of all the countries on the winning side, Italy and Japan left the peace conference most dissatisfied. Italy gained less territory than it felt it deserved and vowed to take action on its own. Japan gained control of German territories in the Pacific and thereby launched a program of expansion. But Japan was angered by the peacemakers' failure to endorse the principle of the equality of all races.

The countries that lost World War I—Germany, Austria, Hungary, Bulgaria, and Turkey—were especially dissatisfied with the Peace of Paris. They were stripped of territory and arms and were required to make *reparations* (payments for war damages).

The Treaty of Versailles, which was signed with Germany, punished Germany severely. The German government agreed to sign the treaty only after the victorious powers threatened to invade. Many Germans particularly resented a clause that forced Germany to accept responsibility for causing World War I.

Economic problems. World War I seriously damaged the economies of European countries. Both the winners and the losers came out of the war deeply in debt. The defeated powers had difficulty paying reparations to the victors, and the victors had difficulty repaying loans from the United States. The shift from a wartime economy to a peacetime economy caused further problems. Many soldiers could not find jobs after the war.

Italy and Japan suffered from too many people and too few resources after World War I. They eventually tried to solve their problems by territorial expansion. In Germany, runaway inflation destroyed the value of money and wiped out the savings of millions of people. In 1923, the German economy neared collapse. Loans from the United States helped Germany's government restore order. By the late 1920's, Europe appeared to be entering a period of economic stability.

A worldwide business slump known as the Great Depression began in the United States in 1929. By the early 1930's, it had halted Europe's economic recovery. The Great Depression caused mass unemployment and spread poverty and despair. It weakened democratic

governments and strengthened extreme political movements that promised to end the economic problems. Two movements in particular gained strength. The forces of Communism, known as the Left, called for revolution by the workers. The forces of fascism, called the Right, favored strong national government. Throughout Europe, the forces of the Left clashed with the forces of the Right. The political extremes gained the most support in countries with the greatest economic problems and the deepest resentment of the Peace of Paris.

Nationalism was an extreme form of patriotism that swept across Europe during the 1800's. Supporters of nationalism placed loyalty to the aims of their nation above any other public loyalty. Many nationalists viewed foreigners and members of minority groups as inferior. Such beliefs helped nations justify their conquest of other lands and the poor treatment of minorities within their borders. Nationalism was a chief cause of World War I, and it grew even stronger after that war.

Nationalism went hand in hand with feelings of national discontent. The more people felt deprived of national honor, the more they wished to see their country powerful and able to insist on its rights. Many Germans felt humiliated by their country's defeat in World War I and its harsh treatment under the Treaty of Versailles. During the 1930's, they enthusiastically supported a violently nationalistic organization called the Nazi Party. The Nazi Party declared that Germany had a right to become strong again. Nationalism also gained strength in Italy and Japan.

The Peace of Paris established an international organization called the League of Nations to maintain peace. But nationalism prevented the League from working effectively. Each country backed its own interests at the expense of other countries. Only weak countries agreed to submit their disagreements to the League of Nations for settlement. Strong nations reserved the right to settle their disputes by threats or, if tough talk failed, by force.

The rise of dictatorships. The political unrest and poor economic conditions that developed after World War I enabled dictatorships to arise in several countries, especially in those countries that lacked a tradition of democratic government. During the 1920's and 1930's, dictatorships came to power in the Soviet Union, Italy, Germany, and Japan. They held total power and ruled without regard to law. The dictatorships used terror and secret police to crush opposition to their rule. People who objected risked imprisonment or execution.

In the Soviet Union, the Communists, led by V. I. Lenin, had seized power in 1917. Lenin set up a dictatorship that firmly controlled the country by the time he died in 1924. After Lenin's death, Joseph Stalin and other leading Communists struggled for power. Stalin eliminated his rivals one by one and became the Soviet dictator in 1929.

In Italy, economic distress after World War I led to strikes and riots. As a result of the violence, a strongly nationalistic group called the Fascist Party gained many supporters. Benito Mussolini, leader of the Fascists, promised to bring order and prosperity to Italy. He vowed to restore to Italy the glory it had known in the days of the ancient Roman Empire. By 1922, the Fascists had become powerful enough to force the king of Italy to appoint Mussolini prime minister. Mussolini, who took the title *Il Duce* (The Leader), soon began to establish a dictatorship.

In Germany, the Nazi Party made spectacular gains as the Great Depression deepened during the early 1930's. Many Germans blamed all their country's economic woes on the hated Treaty of Versailles, which forced Germany to give up territory and resources and pay large reparations. In 1933, Adolf Hitler, the leader of the Nazis, was appointed chancellor of Germany. Hitler,

who was called *der Führer* (the Leader), soon made Germany a dictatorship. He vowed to ignore the Versailles Treaty and to avenge Germany's defeat in World War I. Hitler preached that Germans were a "superior race" and that such peoples as Jews and Slavs were inferior. He began a campaign of hatred against Jews and Communists and promised to rid the country of them. Hitler's extreme nationalism appealed to many Germans.

In Japan, military officers began to hold political office during the 1930's. By 1936, they had strong control of the government. Japan's military government glorified war and the training of warriors. In 1941, General Hideki Tojo became premier of Japan.

Aggression on the march. Japan, Italy, and Germany followed a policy of aggressive territorial expansion during the 1930's. They invaded weak lands that could be taken over easily. The dictatorships knew what they wanted, and they grabbed it. The democratic countries responded with timidity and indecision to the aggression of the dictatorships.

Japan was the first dictatorship to begin a program of conquest. In 1931, Japanese forces seized control of Manchuria, a region of China rich in natural resources. Some historians consider Japan's conquest of Manchuria as the real start of World War II. Japan made Manchuria a puppet state called Manchukuo. In 1937, Japan launched a major attack against China. It occupied most of eastern China by the end of 1938, though the two countries had not officially declared war. Japan's military leaders began to speak about bringing all of eastern Asia under Japanese control.

The world at war: 1939-1945 Germany, Italy, Japan, and their Axis partners fought the United Kingdom, the Soviet Union, the United States, and the other Allies in World War II. This map shows the Allies and the lands controlled by the Axis nations at the height of their power. Few countries remained neutral.

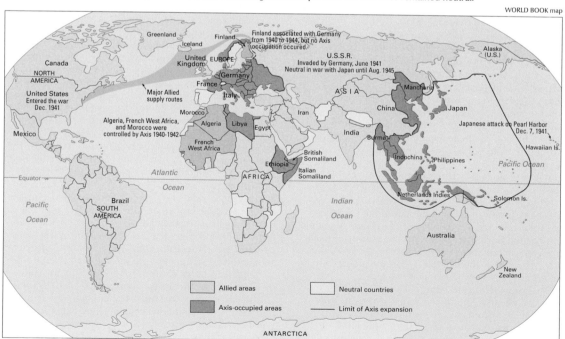

WORLD BOOK map

Italy looked to Africa to fulfill its ambitions for an empire. In 1935, Italian troops invaded Ethiopia, one of the few independent countries in Africa. The Italians used machine guns, tanks, and airplanes to overpower Ethiopia's poorly equipped army. They had conquered the country by May 1936.

Soon after Hitler took power, he began to build up Germany's armed forces in violation of the Treaty of Versailles. In 1936, Hitler sent troops into the Rhineland, a region of Germany along the banks of the Rhine River. Under the treaty, the Rhineland was to remain free of troops. In March 1938, German soldiers marched into Austria and united it with Germany. Many people in Germany and Austria welcomed that move.

The acts of aggression were easy victories for the dictatorships. The League of Nations proved incapable of stopping them. It lacked an army and the power to enforce international law. The United States had refused to join the League or become involved in European disputes. The United Kingdom and France were unwilling to risk another war so soon after World War I. They knew they would bear the burden of any fighting.

The aggressors soon formed an alliance. In 1936, Germany and Italy agreed to support one another's foreign policy. The alliance was known as the Rome-Berlin Axis. Japan joined the alliance in 1940, and it became the Rome-Berlin-Tokyo Axis.

The Spanish Civil War. A civil war tore Spain apart from 1936 to 1939. In 1936, many of Spain's army offi-

AP/Wide World

Members of the Nazi Party marched in a rally in Nuremberg, Germany, in 1938. Their banners bore the Nazi emblem, the *swastika.* The Nazi Party gained control of Germany in 1933.

The warring nations

The Allies

Argentina (March 27, 1945)
Australia (Sept. 3, 1939)
Belgium (May 10, 1940)
Bolivia (April 7, 1943)
Brazil (Aug. 22, 1942)
Canada (Sept. 10, 1939)
Chile (Feb. 14, 1945)
China (Dec. 9, 1941)
Colombia (Nov. 26, 1943)
Costa Rica (Dec. 8, 1941)
Cuba (Dec. 9, 1941)
Czechoslovakia
  (Dec. 16, 1941)
Denmark (April 9, 1940)
Dominican Republic
  (Dec. 8, 1941)
Ecuador (Feb. 2, 1945)
Egypt (Feb. 24, 1945)
El Salvador (Dec. 8, 1941)
Ethiopia (Dec. 1, 1942)
France (Sept. 3, 1939)
Greece (Oct. 28, 1940)
Guatemala (Dec. 9, 1941)
Haiti (Dec. 8, 1941)
Honduras (Dec. 8, 1941)
India (Sept. 3, 1939)
Iran (Sept. 9, 1943)
Iraq (Jan. 16, 1943)
Lebanon (Feb. 27, 1945)
Liberia (Jan. 26, 1944)
Luxembourg (May 10, 1940)
Mexico (May 22, 1942)

Mongolian People's Republic
  (Aug. 9, 1945)
Netherlands (May 10, 1940)
New Zealand (Sept. 3, 1939)
Nicaragua (Dec. 8, 1941)
Norway (April 9, 1940)
Panama (Dec. 7, 1941)
Paraguay (Feb. 8, 1945)
Peru (Feb. 11, 1945)
Poland (Sept. 1, 1939)
San Marino (Sept 24, 1944)
Saudi Arabia (March 1, 1945)
South Africa (Sept. 6, 1939)
Soviet Union (June 22, 1941)
Syria (Feb. 26, 1945)
Turkey (Feb. 23, 1945)
United Kingdom
  (Sept. 3, 1939)
United States (Dec. 8, 1941)
Uruguay (Feb. 22, 1945)
Venezuela (Feb. 16, 1945)
Yugoslavia (April 6, 1941)

The Axis

Bulgaria (April 6, 1941)
Croatia* (April 10, 1941)
Germany (Sept. 1, 1939)
Hungary (April 10, 1941)
Italy (June 10, 1940)
Japan (Dec. 7, 1941)
Romania (June 22, 1941)
Slovakia* (Sept. 1, 1939)

Dates are those on which each country entered the war.

*German-created state

Lee Lockwood, Black Star

Two European dictators, Adolf Hitler of Germany, *left,* and Benito Mussolini of Italy, *right,* dreamed of powerful empires. Their actions plunged much of Europe and Africa into war.

AP/Wide World

The glorification of military power accompanied the rise of a dictatorship in Japan during the 1930's. This military band was showered with confetti as it marched through Tokyo in 1937.

cers revolted against the government. The army rebels chose General Francisco Franco as their leader. Franco's forces were known as Nationalists or Rebels. The forces that supported Spain's elected government were called Loyalists or Republicans. The Spanish Civil War drew worldwide attention. During the war, the dictatorships again displayed their might while the democracies remained helpless.

Hitler and Mussolini sent troops, weapons, aircraft, and advisers to aid the Nationalists. The Soviet Union was the only power to help the Loyalists. France, Britain, and the United States decided not to become involved. However, Loyalist sympathizers from many countries joined the International Brigades that the Communists formed to fight in Spain.

The last Loyalist forces surrendered on April 1, 1939, and Franco set up a dictatorship in Spain. The Spanish Civil War served as a military proving ground for World War II because Germany, Italy, and the Soviet Union used it to test weapons and tactics. The war in Spain was also a rehearsal for World War II in that it split the world into forces that either supported or opposed Nazism and Fascism.

The failure of appeasement. Hitler prepared to strike again soon after Germany absorbed Austria in March 1938. German territory then bordered Czechoslovakia on three sides. Czechoslovakia had become an independent nation after World War I. Its population consisted of many nationalities, including more than 3 million people of German descent. Hitler sought control of the Sudetenland, a region of western Czechoslovakia where most of the Germans lived. Urged on by Hitler, the Sudeten Germans began to clamor for union with Germany.

Czechoslovakia was determined to defend its territory. France and the Soviet Union had pledged their support. As tension mounted, Britain's Prime Minister Neville Chamberlain tried to restore calm. Chamberlain wished to preserve peace at all cost. He believed that war could be prevented by meeting Hitler's demands. That policy became known as *appeasement*.

Chamberlain had several meetings with Hitler during September 1938 as Europe teetered on the edge of war. Hitler raised his demands at each meeting. On September 29, Chamberlain and French Premier Édouard Daladier met with Hitler and Mussolini in Munich, Germany. Chamberlain and Daladier agreed to turn over the Sudetenland to Germany, and they forced Czechoslovakia to accept the agreement. Hitler promised that he had no more territorial demands.

The Munich Agreement marked the height of the policy of appeasement. Chamberlain and Daladier hoped that the agreement would satisfy Hitler and prevent war—or that it would at least prolong the peace until Britain and France were ready for war. The two leaders were mistaken on both counts.

The failure of appeasement soon became clear. Hitler broke the Munich Agreement in March 1939 and seized the rest of Czechoslovakia. He thereby added Czechoslovakia's armed forces and industries to Germany's military might. In the months before World War II began, Germany's preparations for war moved ahead faster than did the military build-up of Britain and France.

Early stages of the war

During the first year of World War II, Germany won a series of swift victories over Poland, Denmark, Luxembourg, the Netherlands, Belgium, Norway, and France. Germany then attempted to bomb Britain into surrendering, but it failed.

The invasion of Poland. After Hitler seized Czechoslovakia, he began demanding territory from Poland. Great Britain and France pledged to help Poland if Germany attacked it. Yet the two powers could aid Poland only by invading Germany, a step that neither chose to take. Britain had only a small army. France had prepared to defend its territory, not to attack.

Great Britain and France hoped that the Soviet Union would help defend Poland. But Hitler and Stalin shocked the world by becoming allies. On Aug. 23, 1939, Germany and the Soviet Union signed a *nonaggression pact* —in which they agreed not to go to war against each other. They secretly decided to divide Poland between themselves.

On Sept. 1, 1939, Germany invaded Poland and began World War II. Poland had a fairly large army but little modern equipment. The Polish army expected to fight along the country's frontiers. However, the Germans introduced a new method of warfare they called *blitzkrieg* (lightning war). The blitzkrieg stressed speed and surprise. Rows of tanks smashed through Poland's defenses and rolled deep into the country before the Polish army had time to react. Swarms of German dive bombers

Ullstein Bilderdienst

Germany's *blitzkrieg* (lightning war) overran Poland at the outbreak of World War II. In Tczew, the people deserted the streets as German armored vehicles rumbled through, *above*.

and fighter aircraft knocked out communications and pounded battle lines.

The Poles fought bravely. But Germany's blitzkrieg threw their army into confusion. On Sept. 17, 1939, Soviet forces invaded Poland from the east. By late September, the Soviet Union occupied the eastern third of Poland, and Germany had swallowed up the rest.

The Phony War. Great Britain and France declared war on Germany on Sept. 3, 1939, two days after the invasion of Poland. But the two countries stood by while Poland collapsed. France moved troops to the Maginot Line, a belt of steel and concrete fortresses it had built after World War I along its border with Germany. Britain sent a small force into northern France. Germany stationed troops on the Siegfried Line, a strip of defenses Hitler built in the 1930's opposite the Maginot Line. The two sides avoided fighting in late 1939 and early 1940. Journalists called the period the Phony War.

The conquest of Denmark and Norway. Valuable shipments of iron ore from Sweden reached Germany

by way of Norway's port of Narvik. Hitler feared British plans to cut off those shipments by laying explosives in Norway's coastal waters. In April 1940, German forces invaded Norway. They conquered Denmark on the way. Britain tried to help Norway, but Germany's airpower prevented many British ships and troops from reaching the country. Norway fell to the Germans in June 1940. The conquest of Norway secured Germany's shipments of iron ore. Norway also provided bases for German submarines and aircraft.

Chamberlain, the champion of appeasement, resigned after the invasion of Norway. Winston Churchill replaced him as Britain's prime minister on May 10, 1940. Churchill told the British people he had nothing to offer them but "blood, toil, tears, and sweat."

The invasion of the Low Countries. The Low Countries—Belgium, Luxembourg, and the Netherlands—hoped to remain neutral after World War II began. However, Germany launched a blitzkrieg against them on May 10, 1940. The Low Countries immediately requested Allied help. But Luxembourg surrendered in one day, and the Netherlands in five days. British and French forces rushed into Belgium and fell into a German trap. As the Allied forces raced northward, the main German invasion cut behind them through the Belgian Ardennes Forest to the south. The Germans reached the English Channel on May 21. They had nearly surrounded Allied forces in Belgium.

King Leopold III of Belgium surrendered on May 28, 1940. His surrender left the Allied forces trapped in Belgium in great danger. They were retreating toward the French seaport of Dunkerque on the English Channel. Britain sent all available craft to rescue the troops. The rescue fleet included destroyers, yachts, ferries, fishing vessels, and motorboats. Under heavy bombardment, the vessels evacuated about 338,000 troops from May 26 to June 4. The evacuation of Dunkerque saved most of Britain's army. But the army left behind all its tanks and equipment. The remaining Allied troops in Dunkerque surrendered on June 4, 1940.

AP/Wide World

Keystone

The evacuation of Dunkerque rescued about 338,000 Allied soldiers in 1940. While the Germans attacked, every available British vessel, including small craft like those above, ferried the troops to safety. At the right, soldiers waded out to a ship.

World War II in Europe and northern Africa: 1939-1942

Germany's powerful war machine brought much of Europe under Axis control during the early stages of the war. By November 1942, Axis-controlled territory extended from Norway to northern Africa and from France to the Soviet Union. That month, Allied forces invaded northern Africa.

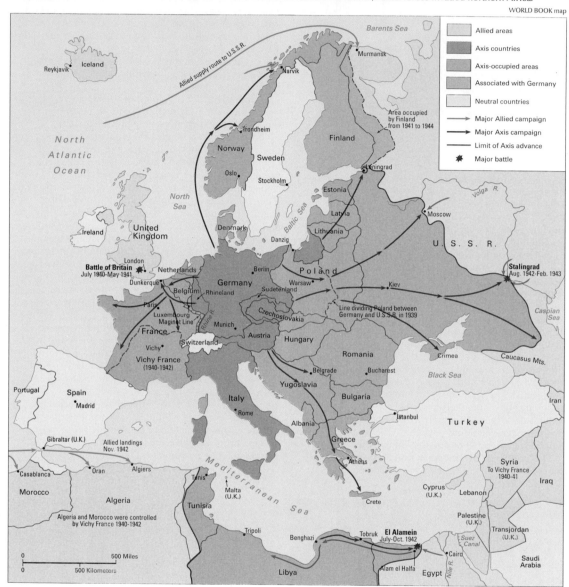

WORLD BOOK map

The fall of France. France had expected to fight along a stationary battlefront and had built the Maginot Line for its defense. But German tanks and aircraft went around the Maginot Line. The Germans passed north of the Maginot Line as they swept through Luxembourg and Belgium and into northern France in May 1940. They launched a major assault against France on June 5. The blitzkrieg sent French forces reeling backward. As France neared collapse, Italy declared war on France and the United Kingdom on June 10.

German troops entered Paris on June 14, 1940. The French government had already fled the capital. Paul

Reynaud had become premier of France in March. Reynaud wanted to fight on. But many of his generals and cabinet officers believed that the battle for France was lost. Reynaud resigned, and a new French government agreed to an *armistice* (truce) on June 22.

Under the terms of the armistice, Germany occupied the northern two-thirds of France and a strip of western France along the Atlantic Ocean. Southern France stayed in French control. The town of Vichy became the capital of unoccupied France. Marshal Henri Philippe Pétain, a French hero of World War I, headed the Vichy government. He largely cooperated with the Germans. Then in

Important dates in Europe and northern Africa: 1939-1942

1939

Sept. 1	Germany invaded Poland, starting World War II.
Sept. 3	Britain and France declared war on Germany.

1940

April 9	Germany invaded Denmark and Norway.
May 10	Germany invaded Belgium and the Netherlands.
June 10	Italy declared war on France and Great Britain.
June 22	France signed an armistice with Germany.
July 10	Battle of Britain began.

1941

April 6	Germany invaded Greece and Yugoslavia.
June 22	Germany invaded the Soviet Union.
Sept. 8	German troops completed the blockade of Leningrad, which lasted until January 1944.

1942

Aug. 25	Hitler ordered his forces to capture Stalingrad.
Oct. 23	Britain attacked the Axis at El Alamein in Egypt.
Nov. 8	Allied troops landed in Algeria and Morocco.

Mauritius, Black Star

After France fell, victorious German soldiers paraded down the Champs Élysées, the famous Paris boulevard. France's surrender in June 1940 left Britain alone to fight Germany.

November 1942, German troops occupied all France.

One of the French generals, Charles de Gaulle, had escaped to Britain after France fell. In radio broadcasts to France, he urged the people to carry on the fight against Germany. The troops who rallied around de Gaulle became known as the Free French forces.

The Battle of Britain. Hitler believed that Great Britain would seek peace with Germany after the fall of France. But Britain fought on alone. Hitler made preparations to cross the English Channel and invade southern England. Before the Germans could invade, however, they had to defeat Britain's Royal Air Force (RAF). The Battle of Britain, which began in July 1940, was the first battle ever fought to control the air.

In August 1940, the German air force, the Luftwaffe, began to attack RAF bases. Germany's aircraft out-numbered those of the RAF. But radar stations along England's coast provided warning of approaching German planes and helped the RAF intercept them.

Each side greatly overestimated the number of enemy planes it had shot down. By September 1940, the Luftwaffe mistakenly believed it had destroyed the RAF. The Germans then halted their strikes against RAF bases and began to bomb London and other civilian targets. They hoped to weaken civilian morale and force Britain to surrender. Air raids known as the Blitz took place nearly every night through the fall and the winter. In May 1941, Germany finally gave up its attempts to defeat Britain from the air.

Hitler's decision to end the attacks on the RAF enabled Britain to rebuild its air force. Britain's survival was immensely important later in the war because the country served as a base for the Allied *liberation* (freeing) of Europe from Nazi rule.

BBC Hulton from Bettmann Archive

UPI/Bettmann Newsphotos

The bombing of London, called the Blitz, began in September 1940 and caused much ruin, *left.* Londoners sought safety in subway tunnels during the nightly raids, *above.* In May 1941, Germany stopped trying to bomb Britain into surrendering.

World War II had become a global conflict by the end of 1941. Fighting spread to Africa, the Balkan Peninsula of southeastern Europe, and the Soviet Union. The Axis and the Allies also battled each other at sea. In December 1941, the United States entered the war.

Fighting in Africa. The Italians opened battlefronts in Africa at about the time of the Battle of Britain. Mussolini expected easy victories over the small British forces in British Somaliland (now northern Somalia) and Egypt. In August 1940, the Italians pushed eastward from Ethiopia and overran the forces in British Somaliland. The following month, Italian forces that were stationed in Libya invaded Egypt.

For two years, the fighting seesawed back and forth across Libya and Egypt. Britain fought to keep the Axis out of Egypt. Axis control of Egypt would have cut Britain off from oil fields in the Middle East and from the Suez Canal, the shortest sea route to Britain's empire in Asia. Britain struck back at the Italians in December 1940, sweeping them out of Egypt and back into Libya. However, an Italian invasion of Greece then drew part of Britain's force from Africa and ended the advance.

Early in 1941, Hitler sent tank units trained in desert warfare to help the Italians in northern Africa. The tank units, known as the Afrika Korps, were led by General Erwin Rommel. Rommel's clever tactics earned him the nickname "The Desert Fox." During the spring, Rommel recaptured the Libyan territory the Italians had lost and drove into Egypt. The British again pushed the Axis forces back into Libya. In May 1942, Rommel broke through British lines and reached El Alamein, only 200 miles (320 kilometers) from the Suez Canal.

However, the Germans did not save Mussolini's empire in eastern Africa. By May 1941, Britain had defeated the Italians in British Somaliland and Ethiopia.

Fighting in the Balkans. Hitler used threats to force Bulgaria, Hungary, and Romania into joining the Axis. Those countries supplied Germany with food, petroleum, and other goods. Yugoslavia's government signed an agreement with the Axis in March 1941. But Yugoslavia's armed forces rebelled and overthrew the government. An enraged Hitler ordered that Yugoslavia be crushed. German troops began to pour into the country on April 6. Yugoslavia surrendered 11 days later. During that time, Hitler had to rescue Mussolini's troops elsewhere on the Balkan Peninsula.

Mussolini had tired of playing Hitler's junior partner, and he badly wanted a victory to boost his standing. In October 1940, Italian forces based in Albania invaded Greece. They expected to defeat the poorly equipped Greek army easily. The Greeks fought fiercely, though they were greatly outnumbered. By December, they had driven the Italians out of Greece and had overrun part of Albania. Britain sent a small force to help Greece. But in April 1941, a much larger German force came to the aid of the Italians. By the end of April, the Axis controlled Greece.

British troops in Greece withdrew to the island of Crete in the Mediterranean Sea. On May 20, 1941, thousands of German paratroopers descended on Crete and seized an airfield. More German troops then landed. The first airborne invasion in history gave Germany an important base in the Mediterranean by the end of May.

The defeats in the Balkans were serious blows to Britain. However, some historians believe that the detours into Yugoslavia and Greece were costly for Hitler because they delayed his invasion of the Soviet Union. Hitler confidently predicted victory over the Soviet Union within eight weeks, and he had failed to prepare for a winter war.

Süddeutscher Verlag
Ullstein Bilderdienst

In the Battle of the Atlantic, German submarines, called *U-boats,* sank ships headed for Britain. Britain's survival depended on shipments across the Atlantic from North America. At the left, a U-boat surfaced to look for targets. At the right, a U-boat officer prepared to launch a torpedo.

The invasion of the Soviet Union. Germany and the Soviet Union proved to be uneasy partners. Hitler viewed the Soviet Union as Germany's chief enemy. He feared Soviet ambitions to expand in eastern Europe. Hitler also wanted control of Soviet wheat fields and oil fields. His 1939 nonaggression pact with Stalin served merely to keep the Soviet Union out of the war while Germany overran western Europe.

Stalin distrusted Hitler, and he sought to obtain more naval bases and to strengthen Soviet borders. In November 1939, the Soviet Union invaded Finland. The Finns surrendered in March 1940 after a fierce fight. In the summer, the Soviet Union seized the countries of Estonia, Latvia, and Lithuania along the Baltic Sea.

Germany's invasion of the Soviet Union, which was code-named Operation Barbarossa, began on June 22, 1941. It took the Soviet Union by surprise. German tanks smashed through Soviet battle lines. During the first few weeks of the campaign, the German armies encircled and killed or captured hundreds of thousands of Soviet troops. As the Germans advanced, the Soviet people destroyed factories, dams, railroads, food supplies, and anything else that might be useful to the enemy. The Germans appeared headed for victory by late July. They then began to make mistakes.

Hitler's generals wanted to press on to Moscow. But Hitler overruled them. Instead, he reinforced the German armies heading north toward Leningrad (now St. Petersburg) and south toward the Crimean Peninsula on the Black Sea. While the Germans wasted time transferring forces, Stalin brought in fresh troops. The German advance slowed in September, though the Germans took the city of Kiev. Heavy rains fell in October, and German tanks and artillery bogged down in mud.

By November 1941, the Germans had surrounded Leningrad and had begun to encircle Moscow. They reached the suburbs of Moscow by early December. The temperature then plunged to −40 °F (−40 °C). An unusually severe Soviet winter had begun early. German troops lacked warm clothing and suffered from frostbite. Their tanks and weapons broke down in the bitter cold. Winter had saved the Soviet Union.

The Battle of the Atlantic. Britain's survival in World War II depended on shipments of food, war materials, and other supplies across the Atlantic Ocean from North America. Throughout the war, Germany tried to destroy such shipments, while Britain struggled to keep its Atlantic shipping lanes open.

Germany's surface fleet was far too weak to challenge Britain's Royal Navy in battle during World War II. But individual German battleships attacked British cargo vessels. The Royal Navy hunted down and sank such raiders one by one. The biggest operation was against the powerful German battleship *Bismarck.* In May 1941, a fleet of British warships chased, trapped, and finally sank the *Bismarck* about 600 miles (970 kilometers) off the coast of France. Afterward, Germany rarely allowed its large warships to leave harbor.

The greatest threat to British shipping came from German submarines, called *Unterseeboote* or *U-boats.* The U-boats prowled the Atlantic, torpedoing any Allied cargo ships they spotted. The conquest of Norway and of France gave Germany excellent bases for its U-boats. To combat the U-boats, Britain began to use a *convoy system.* Under that system, cargo ships sailed in large groups escorted by surface warships. But Britain had few such ships available for escort duty.

From 1940 to 1942, Germany appeared to be winning the Battle of the Atlantic. Each month, U-boats sank thousands of tons of Allied shipping. But the Allies gradually overcame the U-boat danger. They used radar and an underwater detection device called *sonar* to locate German submarines. Long-range aircraft bombed U-boats as they surfaced. Shipyards in North America stepped up their production of warships to accompany convoys. By mid-1943, the Allies were sinking U-boats faster than Germany could replace them. The crisis in the Atlantic had passed.

The United States enters the war

After World War II began in Europe in 1939, President Franklin D. Roosevelt announced the neutrality of the United States. Canada declared war on Germany almost at once. As part of the British Commonwealth of Nations, it entered the war on Sept. 10, 1939, one week after Great Britain did.

The majority of people in the United States thought that their country should stay out of World War II. Yet most Americans hoped for an Allied victory. Roosevelt and other *interventionists* urged all aid "short of war" to nations fighting the Axis. They argued that an Axis victory would endanger democracies everywhere. *Isolationists,* on the other hand, opposed U.S. aid to warring nations. They accused Roosevelt of steering the nation into a war it was not prepared to fight.

All the countries in North and South America eventually declared war on the Axis. But only Brazil, Canada, Mexico, and the United States sent troops. The United States played a key role in the final Allied victory.

The arsenal of democracy. Roosevelt hoped to defeat the Axis powers by equipping the nations fighting them with ships, tanks, aircraft, and other war materials. Roosevelt appealed to the United States to become what he called "the arsenal of democracy."

At the start of World War II, U.S. neutrality laws forbade the sale of arms to warring nations. Congress soon changed the laws to help Britain and France. A new law permitted warring nations to buy arms for cash. But by late 1940, Britain had nearly run out of funds for arms. Roosevelt then proposed the Lend-Lease Act, which would permit him to lend or lease raw materials, equipment, and weapons to any nation fighting the Axis. Congress approved the act in March 1941. In all, 38 nations received a total of about $50 billion in aid under Lend-Lease. More than half the aid went to the British Empire and about a fourth to the Soviet Union.

Japan attacks. Japan, not Germany, finally plunged the United States into World War II. By 1940, Japanese

The attack on Pearl Harbor by Japanese planes on Dec. 7, 1941, drew the United States into World War II. The air raid crippled the U.S. Pacific Fleet. Within hours, 21 ships and more than 300 planes had been damaged or destroyed.

Bettmann Archive

forces were bogged down in China. The Chinese government, led by Chiang Kai-shek, had fled to central China. But China refused to give up. To force China to surrender, Japan decided to cut off supplies reaching China from Southeast Asia. Japan also wanted the rich resources of Southeast Asia for itself. Japan's military leaders spoke of building an empire, which they called the Greater East Asia Co-Prosperity Sphere.

The United States opposed Japan's expansion in Southeast Asia. In 1940, Japanese troops occupied northern Indochina (today part of Laos and Vietnam). In response, the United States cut off important exports to Japan. Japanese industries relied heavily on petroleum, scrap metal, and other raw materials from the United States. Tension rose after Japan seized the rest of Indochina in 1941. Roosevelt then barred the withdrawal of Japanese funds from American banks.

General Hideki Tojo became premier of Japan in October 1941. Tojo and Japan's other military leaders realized that only the United States Navy had the power to block Japan's expansion in Asia. They decided to cripple the U.S. Pacific Fleet with one forceful blow.

On Dec. 7, 1941, Japanese aircraft attacked without warning the U.S. Pacific Fleet at anchor in Pearl Harbor in Hawaii. The bombing of Pearl Harbor was a great success for Japan at first. It disabled much of the Pacific Fleet and destroyed many aircraft. But in the long run, the attack on Pearl Harbor proved disastrous for Japan. It propelled enraged Americans to arms.

The United States, Canada, and Great Britain declared war on Japan on Dec. 8, 1941. The next day, China declared war on the Axis. Germany and Italy declared war on the United States on December 11. World War II had become a global conflict.

The Allies Attack in Europe and Northern Africa

Allied defeats in Europe ended late in 1941. Soviet forces held off the German advance in eastern Europe in 1942 and won a major victory at Stalingrad in 1943. The Allies invaded northern Africa in 1942 and forced Italy to surrender in 1943. Allied troops swarmed ashore in 1944 in northern France in the largest seaborne invasion in history. Allied attacks from the east and the west forced Germany to surrender in 1945.

The strategy. Churchill, Roosevelt, and Stalin—the leaders of the three major Allied powers—were known during World War II as the Big Three. The Big Three and their military advisers planned the strategy that defeated the Axis. Churchill and Roosevelt conferred frequently on overall strategy. Stalin directed the Soviet war effort but rarely consulted his allies.

Roosevelt relied heavily on his military advisers, the Joint Chiefs of Staff. They consisted of General of the

Army Henry H. Arnold, commanding general of the Army Air Forces; General of the Army George C. Marshall, chief of staff of the Army; Fleet Admiral Ernest J. King, chief of naval operations; and Fleet Admiral William D. Leahy, Roosevelt's chief of staff. Churchill had a similar advisory body.

The main wartime disagreement among the Big Three concerned an Allied invasion of western Europe. Stalin constantly urged Roosevelt and Churchill to open a second fighting front in western Europe and thus draw German troops from the Soviet front. Both Roosevelt and Churchill supported the idea but disagreed on where and when to invade. The Americans wanted to land in northern France as soon as possible. The British argued that an invasion of France before the Allies were fully prepared would be disastrous. Instead, Churchill favored invading Italy first. His view won out.

Roosevelt and Churchill first met in August 1941 aboard ship off the coast of Newfoundland. They issued the Atlantic Charter, a statement of the postwar aims of the United States and the United Kingdom. After the Japanese attacked Pearl Harbor, Roosevelt and Churchill conferred in Washington, D.C. The two leaders felt that Germany was a nearer and a more dangerous enemy than Japan. They decided to concentrate on defeating Germany first.

In January 1943, Roosevelt and Churchill met in Casablanca, Morocco. They agreed to invade the Mediterranean island of Sicily after driving the Germans and Italians from northern Africa. At the conference, Roosevelt announced that the Allies would accept only *unconditional* (complete) surrender from the Axis powers. Churchill supported him.

Roosevelt and Churchill first met with Stalin in November 1943 in Tehran, Iran. The Big Three discussed plans for a joint British and American invasion of France in the spring of 1944. They did not meet again until Germany neared collapse. In February 1945, Roosevelt, Churchill, and Stalin gathered at Yalta, a Soviet city on the Crimean Peninsula. They agreed that their countries would each occupy a zone of Germany after the war. France was to occupy a fourth zone. At the Yalta Conference, Stalin pledged to permit free elections in Poland and other countries in eastern Europe after the war. He later broke that pledge. Roosevelt died in April 1945, two months after the Yalta Conference.

On the Soviet front. Soviet forces struck back at the Germans outside Moscow in December 1941. The Soviet troops pushed the invaders back about 100 miles (160

National Archives

The Big Three set overall Allied strategy. They were Soviet leader Joseph Stalin, *left;* U.S. President Franklin D. Roosevelt, *center;* and British Prime Minister Winston Churchill, *right.*

kilometers) from Moscow during the winter. The Germans never again came so close to Moscow as they had been in December 1941. However, the Soviet recovery was short lived.

In the spring of 1942, the Germans again attacked. They overran the Crimean Peninsula and headed eastward toward Soviet oil fields in the Caucasus region. Hitler ordered General Friedrich von Paulus to press on and to take the city of Stalingrad (now Volgograd). A savage five-month battle for Stalingrad began in late August. By September, German and Soviet soldiers were fighting hand to hand in the heart of the city.

Süddeutscher Verlag

Ullstein Bilderdienst

In the Soviet Union, winter weather and the determination of the army and the people slowed the German advance. German equipment broke down and had to be pushed through the snow, *left.* In the ruins of Stalingrad, *right,* Soviet soldiers fought the Germans building by building.

With winter approaching, Paulus asked permission to pull back from Stalingrad. Hitler ordered him to hold on and fight. Soviet troops counterattacked in mid-November. Within a week, they had trapped Paulus's army. The Luftwaffe promised to supply the army by air. But few supplies landed. Each day, thousands of German soldiers froze or starved to death. On Feb. 2, 1943, the last German troops in Stalingrad surrendered.

The Battle of Stalingrad marked a turning point in World War II. It halted Germany's eastward advance. About 300,000 German troops were killed or captured. An enormous number of Soviet soldiers also died.

In northern Africa. The Germans took a beating in northern Africa about the same time as their defeat at Stalingrad. In the summer of 1942, German and Italian forces led by Rommel faced the British at El Alamein, Egypt. General Harold Alexander and Lieutenant General Bernard L. Montgomery commanded the British forces in northern Africa.

Rommel attacked in late August 1942 at Alam el Halfa, south of El Alamein. The British halted the attack, partly because they had secretly learned of Rommel's battle plan. Churchill called for an immediate counterattack. But Montgomery refused to rush into battle before

World War II in Europe and northern Africa: 1943-1945

The Allies attacked the Axis in Europe after defeating it in northern Africa in May 1943. Italy surrendered in September 1943, two months after the invasion of Sicily. In June 1944, the Allies landed in northern France. Attacks from the east and west forced Germany to surrender in May 1945.

WORLD BOOK map

he was fully prepared. On October 23, Montgomery struck at El Alamein. He had broken through the enemy lines by early November. The Axis forces retreated toward Tunisia with the British in hot pursuit. The Battle of El Alamein, like the Battle of Stalingrad, marked a turning point in the war. In both battles, the Allies ended Hitler's string of victories.

Soon after the Battle of El Alamein, the Allies invaded French colonies in northern Africa. Allied troops commanded by Lieutenant General Dwight D. Eisenhower of the United States landed in Algeria and Morocco on Nov. 8, 1942. Vichy French forces in northern Africa fought back for a few days. They then joined the Allied side.

The Allies hoped to advance rapidly into Tunisia and thereby cut off the Axis forces from their home bases in Italy and Sicily. But Axis troops moved faster and seized Tunisia first. There, Rommel prepared for battle. American troops first engaged in combat with the Germans in February 1943 near Kasserine Pass in northern Tunisia. Rommel defeated the inexperienced Americans in hard fighting. But thereafter, the Allies steadily closed in. The last Axis forces in northern Africa surrendered in May. Rommel had already returned to Germany. By clearing the Axis forces from northern Africa, the Allies obtained bases from which to invade southern Europe.

The air war. Before World War II began, some aviation experts claimed that the long-range bomber was the most advanced weapon in the world. They believed that bombers could wipe out cities and industries and so destroy an enemy's desire and ability to go on fighting. Their theory was tested during World War II.

The first great air battle in history opened in 1940 between Germany's Luftwaffe and Britain's Royal Air Force. During the Battle of Britain, Marshal Hermann Goering, commander of the Luftwaffe, failed to defeat Britain from the air. RAF fighter planes, including Spitfires and Hurricanes, helped win the Battle of Britain by shooting down German bombers. By May 1941, the bombing of Britain had largely stopped. But RAF bombers pounded Germany until the end of the war.

Important dates in Europe and northern Africa: 1943-1945

1943

Feb. 2	The last Germans surrendered at Stalingrad.
May 13	Axis forces in northern Africa surrendered.
July 4	Germany opened an assault near the Soviet city of Kursk.
July 10	Allied forces invaded Sicily.
Sept. 3	Italy secretly surrendered to the Allies.
Sept. 9	Allied troops landed at Salerno, Italy.

1944

June 6	Allied troops landed in Normandy in the D-Day invasion of northern France.
July 20	A plot to assassinate Hitler failed.
Dec. 16	The Germans struck back at U.S. troops in the Battle of the Bulge.

1945

April 30	Hitler took his life in Berlin.
May 7	Germany surrendered unconditionally to the Allies in Reims, France, ending World War II in Europe.

Imperial War Museum

The air war against Germany was aimed at destroying its ability to keep on fighting. Bombers like this American B-17 struck factories, railroads, and other industrial targets.

At first, Britain's bombing campaign was costly and ineffective. The RAF relied on *area bombing* in the hope of hitting a target by plastering the area with bombs. It favored nighttime raids, which were safer than daytime raids. But pilots often missed their targets in the dark. In 1942, Britain turned to *saturation bombing* of German cities. About 900 bombers battered Cologne on May 30, 1942, in the first such massive raid.

The United States joined the air war against Germany in 1942. The American B-17 bomber carried a better bombsight than British planes. B-17's were known as Flying Fortresses because of their heavy armor and many guns, and they could take much punishment. For those reasons, the Americans favored *pinpoint bombing* of specific targets during daytime rather than area bombing at night. From 1943 until the end of the war, bombs rained down on Germany around the clock.

In spite of the massive bombardment, German industries continued to increase production, and German morale failed to crack. The air war achieved its goals only during the last 10 months of World War II. In that time, nearly three times as many bombs fell on Germany as in all the rest of the war. By the end of the war, Germany's cities lay in ruins. Its factories, refineries, railroads, and canals had nearly ceased to operate. Hundreds of thousands of German civilians had been killed. Millions more were homeless. The bomber had finally become the weapon its supporters had foreseen.

Germany's air defenses rapidly improved during World War II. The Germans used radar to spot incoming bombers, and they used fighter aircraft to shoot them down. In 1944, Germany introduced the first jet fighter, the Messerschmitt Me-262. The fast plane could easily overtake the propeller-driven fighters of the Allies. But Hitler failed to use jet fighters effectively, which kept Germany from gaining an advantage in the air war.

In 1944, Germany used the first guided missiles against Britain. The V-1 and V-2 missiles caused great

AP/Wide World

The campaign in Italy was a slow and bitter struggle against strongly defended German posts. The U.S. infantrymen above belonged to the 92nd Division, a black unit that served in Italy.

damage and took many lives. But the Germans introduced the weapons too late to affect the war's outcome.

The invasion of Italy. The Allies planned to invade Sicily after driving the Axis forces out of northern Africa. Axis planes bombed Allied ships in the Mediterranean Sea from bases in Sicily. The Allies wanted to make the Mediterranean safe for their ships. They also hoped that an invasion of Sicily might knock a war-weary Italy out of the war.

Allied forces under Eisenhower landed along Sicily's south coast on July 10, 1943. For 39 days, they engaged in bitter fighting with German troops over rugged terrain. The last Germans left Sicily on August 17.

Mussolini fell from power on July 25, 1943, after the invasion of Sicily. The Italian government imprisoned Mussolini, but German paratroopers later rescued him. Italy's new premier, Field Marshal Pietro Badoglio, began secret peace talks with the Allies. Badoglio hoped

to prevent Italy from becoming a battleground. Italy surrendered on September 3. However, Field Marshal Albert Kesselring, Germany's commander in the Mediterranean region, was determined to fight the Allies for control of Italy.

Allied forces led by Lieutenant General Mark W. Clark of the United States landed at Salerno, Italy, on Sept. 9, 1943. They fought hard just to stay ashore. Another Allied force had already landed farther south. The Allies slowly struggled up the Italian Peninsula in a series of head-on assaults against well-defended German positions. By early November, the Allies had nearly reached Cassino, about 75 miles (120 kilometers) south of Rome. But they failed to pierce German defenses there. Some of the most brutal fighting of World War II occurred near Cassino.

In January 1944, the Allies landed troops at Anzio, west of Cassino, in an effort to attack the Germans from behind. However, German forces kept the Allies pinned down on the beaches at Anzio for four months. Thousands of Allied soldiers died there.

The Allies finally broke through German defenses in Italy in May 1944. Rome fell on June 4. The Germans held their positions in northern Italy through the fall and winter. But in the spring, the Allies swept toward the Alps. German forces in Italy surrendered on May 2, 1945. Mussolini had been captured and shot by Italian resistance fighters on April 28.

D-Day. Soon after the evacuation of Dunkerque in 1940, Great Britain started to plan a return to France. In 1942, the United States and Britain began to discuss a large-scale invasion across the English Channel. That summer, the Allies raided the French port of Dieppe on the channel. The raiders met strong German defenses and suffered heavy losses. The Dieppe raid convinced the Allies that landing on open beaches had a better chance of success than landing in a port.

Throughout 1943, preparations moved ahead for an

U.S. Coast Guard

Hitting the beach, Allied infantrymen swarmed ashore along the Normandy coast of northern France on D-Day—June 6, 1944. It was the largest seaborne invasion in history. Hitler had boasted that German defenses along the coast could resist any attack. But he was wrong.

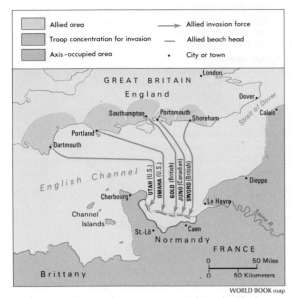

	Allied area	→	Allied invasion force
	Troop concentration for invasion	—	Allied beach head
	Axis-occupied area	•	City or town

The Normandy invasion on June 6, 1944, brought Allied forces ashore on five beaches, shown with their code names. Within a week, the Allies held the area outlined in blue.

WORLD BOOK map

U.S. Army

Talking to his men, General Dwight D. Eisenhower, commander of the Normandy invasion, wished paratroopers luck before they dropped behind German lines in France on D-Day.

invasion of northern France the following year. The invasion plan received the code name Operation Overlord. The Allies assembled huge amounts of equipment and great numbers of troops for Overlord in southern England. General Dwight D. Eisenhower was selected to command the invasion.

The Germans expected an Allied invasion along the north coast of France in 1944. But they were unsure where. A chain of fortifications, which the Germans called the Atlantic Wall, ran along the coast. Hitler placed Rommel in charge of strengthening German defenses along the English Channel. Rommel brought in artillery, mined the water and the beaches, and strung up barbed wire. The Germans concentrated their troops near Calais, at the narrowest part of the English Channel. But the Allies planned to land farther west, in a region of northern France called Normandy.

Eisenhower chose Monday, June 5, 1944, as D-Day—the date of the Normandy invasion. Rough seas forced him to postpone D-Day until June 6. During the night, about 2,700 ships carrying landing craft and 176,000 soldiers crossed the channel. Minesweepers had gone ahead to clear the water. Paratroopers dropped behind German lines to capture bridges and railroad tracks. At dawn, battleships opened fire on the beaches. At 6:30 A.M., troops from the United States, Britain, Canada, and France stormed ashore on a 60-mile (100-kilometer) front in the largest seaborne invasion in history.

D-Day took the Germans by surprise. But they fought back fiercely. At one landing site, code-named Omaha Beach, U.S. troops came under heavy fire and barely managed to stay ashore. Nevertheless, all five Allied landing beaches were secure by the end of D-Day. The Allies soon had an artificial harbor in place for unloading more troops and supplies. A pipeline carried fuel

across the channel. By the end of June 1944, about a million Allied troops had reached France.

The Allied forces advanced slowly at first. The Americans struggled westward to capture the badly needed port of Cherbourg. British and Canadian soldiers fought their way to Caen. The battle for Cherbourg ended on June 27. Caen, which the British hoped to capture on D-Day, fell on July 18. Near the end of July, the Allies finally broke through German lines into open country.

The drive to the Rhine. On July 25, 1944, Allied bombers blasted a gap in the German front near St.-Lô, about 50 miles (80 kilometers) southeast of Cherbourg. The U.S. Third Army under Lieutenant General George S. Patton plowed through the hole. The battlefield had opened up. During August, the Allies cleared the Germans out of most of northwestern France. Allied bombers hounded the retreating Germans.

Patton's army rolled eastward toward Paris. On Aug. 19, 1944, Parisians rose up against the occupying German forces. Hitler ordered the city destroyed. But his generals delayed carrying out the order. American and Free French forces liberated Paris on August 25.

In mid-August 1944, Allied forces landed in southern France. They moved rapidly up the Rhône River Valley. Meanwhile, Patton raced eastward toward the German border and the Rhine River. In late August, his tanks ran out of fuel. To the north, British forces led by Field Marshal Bernard L. Montgomery swept into Belgium and captured Antwerp on September 4. The Allies planned a daring airborne operation to carry them across the Rhine. On September 17, about 20,000 paratroopers dropped behind German lines to seize bridges in the Netherlands. But bad weather and other problems hampered the operation. It became clear that victory over Germany would have to wait until 1945.

Wild with joy, Parisians welcomed Allied troops as they rode down the Champs Élysées on Aug. 26, 1944. Paris had been freed the day before, after over four years of Nazi occupation.

Robert Capa, Magnum

Germany's generals knew they were beaten. But Hitler pulled his failing resources together for another assault. On Dec. 16, 1944, German troops surprised and overwhelmed the Americans in the Ardennes Forest in Belgium and Luxembourg. But the Germans lacked the troops and fuel to turn their thrust into a breakthrough. Within two weeks, the Americans stopped the Germans near the Meuse River in Belgium. The Ardennes offensive is also known as the Battle of the Bulge because of the bulging shape of the battleground on a map.

The Soviet advance. The Soviet victory in the Battle of Stalingrad ended Germany's progress in eastern Europe. After January 1943, Soviet soldiers slowly pushed the Germans back. Soviet forces had improved by 1943, and they greatly outnumbered the opposing German armies. Supplies poured into the Soviet Union from Britain and the United States, and Soviet factories had geared up for wartime production.

Nevertheless, the Germans returned to the offensive in July 1943 near the Soviet city of Kursk. They massed about 3,000 tanks for the assault. Soviet forces lay waiting for them. In one of the greatest tank battles in history, Soviet mines, tanks, antitank guns, and aircraft blew apart many German tanks. Hitler finally called off the attack to save his remaining tanks.

Soviet troops moved slowly forward during the summer and fall of 1943. In January 1944, a Soviet offensive ended the siege of Leningrad, which had begun in September 1941. Historians estimate that about 1.7 million Soviet citizens may have died in and around Leningrad during the siege, mostly from lack of food and heat. But the city never surrendered.

In June 1944, soon after the Normandy invasion, Stalin's armies attacked along a 450-mile (720-kilometer) front. By late July, Soviet troops had reached the outskirts of Warsaw. Poland's Home Army rose up against German forces in Warsaw on August 1. But Soviet troops refused to come to Poland's aid. Stalin permitted the Germans to destroy the Home Army, which might have resisted his plans to set up a Communist govern-

ment in Poland after the war. The Home Army surrendered after two months. More than 200,000 Poles died during the Warsaw uprising. Soviet forces entered Warsaw in January 1945.

Meanwhile, Soviet troops drove into Romania and Bulgaria. The Germans pulled out of Greece and Yugoslavia in the fall of 1944 but held out in Budapest, the capital of Hungary, until February 1945. Vienna, Austria's capital, fell to Soviet soldiers in April. By then, Soviet troops occupied nearly all of eastern Europe.

Victory in Europe. The Allies began their final assault on Germany in early 1945. Soviet soldiers reached the Oder River, about 40 miles (65 kilometers) east of Berlin, in January. Allied forces in the west occupied positions along the Rhine by early March.

British and Canadian forces cleared the Germans out of the Netherlands and swept into northern Germany. American and French forces raced toward the Elbe River in central Germany. Hitler ordered his soldiers to fight to the death. But large numbers of German soldiers surrendered each day.

As they advanced, the Allies discovered horrifying evidence of Nazi brutality. Hitler had ordered the imprisonment and murder of millions of Jews and members of other minority groups in concentration camps. The starving survivors of the death camps gave proof of the terrible suffering of those who had already died.

The capture of Berlin, then Germany's capital, was left to Soviet forces. By April 25, 1945, Soviet troops had surrounded the city. From a *bunker* (shelter) deep underground, Hitler ordered German soldiers to fight on. On April 30, however, Hitler committed suicide. He remained convinced that his cause had been right but that the German people had proven unworthy of his rule.

Grand Admiral Karl Doenitz briefly succeeded Hitler as the leader of Germany. Doenitz arranged for Germany's surrender. On May 7, 1945, Colonel General Alfred Jodl, chief of staff of the German armed forces, signed a statement of unconditional surrender at Eisenhower's headquarters in Reims, France. World War II had ended in Europe. The Allies declared May 8 as V-E Day, or Victory in Europe Day.

Imperial War Museum

Survivors of a Nazi death camp—some too weak to stand—provided proof of Nazi savagery. The Nazis imprisoned and murdered millions of Jews, Slavs, and members of other groups.

The Spitfire was an outstanding British fighter plane of World War II. Spitfires were noted for their speed, ability to make tight turns, and rapid climbing rate. Thus, they could outmaneuver most German fighters. In 1940, Spitfires helped defeat Germany in the Battle of Britain. A Spitfire IA is shown at the left.

The B-17 was a widely used U.S. bomber of World War II. B-17's became famous for daytime raids over Germany. They were called Flying Fortresses because of their heavy armor and many guns. The B-17G, *right,* carried 13 machine guns.

The DUKW, nicknamed "Duck," was an American six-wheeled truck that traveled over water and land. Ducks carried men and supplies from transport ships to enemy shores in *amphibious* (seaborne) landings. They were first used in the invasion of Sicily in July 1943 and later in amphibious operations in the Pacific.

The tank played a key role in combat in World War II. Germany, in particular, made use of the tank's mobility and firepower. In early victories, Germany massed its tanks and smashed through enemy battle lines in surprise attacks. The German Tiger, *right,* was a heavy tank that could outgun almost all Allied tanks.

The aircraft carrier was a floating airfield that became the backbone of the U.S. Navy during World War II. Carrier-based planes took part in many battles in the Pacific and helped defeat Japan. The irregular pattern on the U.S.S. *Wasp, below,* made it hard for enemy submarines to determine the ship's course.

WORLD BOOK illustrations by Tony Gibbons

The attack on Pearl Harbor on Dec. 7, 1941, left the U.S. Pacific Fleet powerless to halt Japan's expansion. During the next six months, Japanese forces swept across Southeast Asia and the western Pacific Ocean. Japan's empire reached its greatest size in August 1942. It stretched northeast to the Aleutian Islands of Alaska, west to Burma (now Myanmar), and south to the Netherlands Indies (now Indonesia). The Allies halted this expansion in the summer of 1942. They nibbled away at its empire until Japan agreed to surrender in August 1945.

Early Japanese victories. On Dec. 8, 1941, within hours of the attack on Pearl Harbor, Japanese bombers struck the British colony of Hong Kong on the south coast of China and two U.S. islands in the Pacific Ocean—Guam and Wake. The Japanese invaded Thailand the same day. Thailand surrendered within hours and began cooperating with the Japanese. Japanese troops took Hong Kong, Guam, and Wake Island by Christmas.

From Thailand, Japanese forces soon advanced into Malaya (now part of Malaysia) and Burma. Great Britain then ruled that region. The British wrongly believed that soldiers could not penetrate the thick jungles of the Malay Peninsula. They expected an assault by sea instead. But Japanese troops streamed through the jungles and rapidly overran the peninsula.

By late January 1942, the Japanese had pushed British forces back to Singapore, a fortified island off the Malay Peninsula. The Japanese stormed the island on February 8, and Singapore surrendered a week later. Japan captured about 85,000 soldiers, making the fall of Singapore Britain's worst military defeat ever. Japan then targeted the petroleum-rich Netherlands Indies, south of Malaya. Allied warships protected those islands. Japan's navy mauled the ships in February 1942 in the Battle of the Java Sea. The Netherlands Indies fell in early March.

Meanwhile, Japanese forces had advanced into southern Burma. China sent troops into Burma to help the United Kingdom hold onto the Burma Road. Weapons, food, and other goods traveled over that supply route from India to China. In April 1942, Japan seized and shut down the Burma Road. The Japanese had driven Allied forces from most of Burma by mid-May.

Only the conquest of the Philippines took longer than Japan expected. Japan had begun landing troops in the Philippines on Dec. 10, 1941. American and Philippine forces commanded by U.S. General Douglas MacArthur defended the islands. In late December, MacArthur's forces abandoned Manila, the capital of the Philippines, and withdrew to nearby Bataan Peninsula. Although suffering from malnutrition and disease, they beat back Japanese attacks for just over three months.

President Roosevelt ordered MacArthur to Australia, and he left the Philippines in March 1942. He promised the Filipinos, "I shall return." On April 9, about 75,000 exhausted troops on Bataan surrendered to the Japanese. Most of them were forced to march about 65 miles (105 kilometers) to prison camps. Many prisoners died of disease and mistreatment during what became known as the Bataan Death March. Some soldiers held out on Corregidor Island, near Bataan, until May 6. By then, the Japanese were victorious everywhere.

Japan's string of quick victories astonished even the Japanese. It terrified the Allies. The fall of the Netherlands Indies left Australia unprotected. The capture of Burma brought the Japanese to India's border. Australia and India feared invasion. Japanese planes bombed Darwin on Australia's north coast in February 1942.

The tide turns. Three events in 1942 helped turn the tide against Japan. They were (1) the Doolittle raid, (2) the Battle of the Coral Sea, and (3) the Battle of Midway.

The Doolittle raid. To show that Japan could be beaten, the United States staged a daring bombing raid on the Japanese homeland. On April 18, 1942, Lieutenant Colonel James H. Doolittle led 16 B-25 bombers in a surprise attack on Tokyo and other Japanese cities. The bombers took off from the deck of the *Hornet,* an aircraft carrier more than 600 miles (960 kilometers) east of Japan. The raid did very little damage. But it alarmed Japan's leaders, who had believed that their homeland was safe from Allied bombs. To prevent future raids, the Japanese determined to capture more islands to the south and the east and so extend the country's defenses. They soon found themselves in trouble.

UPI/Bettmann Newsphotos
American soldiers in the Philippines had to march to prison camps after they were captured by the Japanese in April 1942. Many died during what is known as the Bataan Death March.

Important dates in the Pacific: 1941-1942

	1941
Dec. 7	Japan bombed U.S. military bases at Pearl Harbor in Hawaii.
Dec. 8	The United States, the United Kingdom, and Canada declared war on Japan.
	1942
Feb. 15	Singapore fell to the Japanese.
Feb. 26-28	Japan defeated an Allied naval force in the Battle of the Java Sea.
April 9	U.S. and Philippine troops on Bataan Peninsula surrendered.
April 18	U.S. bombers hit Tokyo in the Doolittle raid.
May 4-8	The Allies checked a Japanese assault in the Battle of the Coral Sea.
June 4-6	The Allies defeated Japan in the Battle of Midway.
Aug. 7	U.S. marines landed on Guadalcanal.

The Battle of the Coral Sea. In May 1942, a Japanese invasion force sailed toward Australia's base at Port Moresby on the south coast of the island of New Guinea. Port Moresby lay at Australia's doorstep. American warships met the Japanese force in the Coral Sea, northeast of Australia. The Battle of the Coral Sea, fought from May 4 to 8, was unlike all earlier naval battles. It was the first naval battle in which opposing ships never sighted one another. Planes based on aircraft carriers did all the fighting. Neither side won a clear victory. But the battle halted the assault on Port Moresby and temporarily checked the threat to Australia.

The Battle of Midway. Japan next sent a large fleet to capture Midway Island at the westernmost tip of the Hawaiian chain. The United States had cracked Japan's naval code and thus learned about the coming invasion. Admiral Chester W. Nimitz, commander of the U.S. Pacific Fleet, gathered the ships that had survived the raid on Pearl Harbor and the Battle of the Coral Sea. He prepared to ambush the Japanese.

The Battle of Midway opened on June 4, 1942, with a Japanese bombing raid on Midway. Outdated U.S. bombers flew in low and launched torpedoes against Japanese warships. But Japanese guns downed most of the slow-moving planes. American dive bombers swooped in next. They pounded enemy aircraft carriers while their planes refueled on deck. During the three-day battle, the Japanese lost 4 aircraft carriers and more than 200 planes and skilled pilots. Japan sank 1 U.S. aircraft carrier and shot down about 150 U.S. planes.

The Battle of Midway was the first clear Allied victory over Japan in World War II. Aircraft carriers had become the most important weapon in the war in the Pacific. Japan's naval power was crippled by the loss of 4 of its 9 aircraft carriers.

Although Japan failed to capture Midway, it seized two islands at the tip of Alaska's Aleutian chain on June 7, 1942. The Americans drove the Japanese out of the Aleutians in the spring and summer of 1943.

The South Pacific. After the Battle of Midway, the Allies were determined to stop Japanese expansion in the South Pacific. In the battles that followed, American

World War II in Asia and the Pacific: 1941-1942 After Japan attacked Pearl Harbor on Dec. 7, 1941, its forces rapidly advanced across Southeast Asia and the Western Pacific Ocean. This map shows key battles in that campaign and the greatest extent of Japan's empire. The Allies halted Japan's expansion in the summer of 1942.

WORLD BOOK map

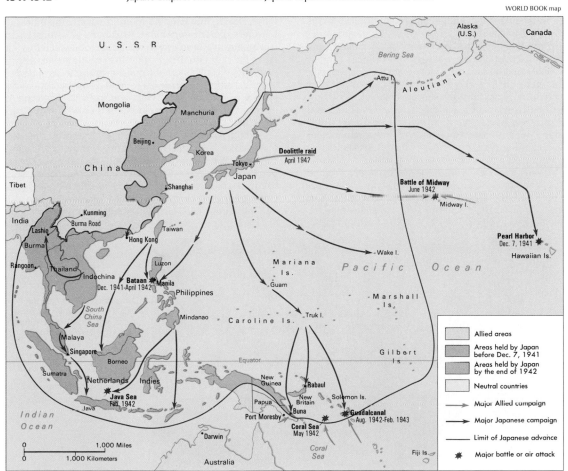

soldiers and marines fought many jungle campaigns on Pacific islands. The jungle itself was a terrifying enemy. Heavy rains drenched the troops and turned the jungle into a foul-smelling swamp. The men had to hack their way through tangled, slimy vegetation and wade through knee-deep mud. The Japanese hid everywhere, waiting to shoot unsuspecting servicemen. Scorpions and snakes were a constant menace. Malaria and other tropical diseases took a heavy toll.

The Americans also encountered Japan's strict military code in the South Pacific. The code required Japanese soldiers to fight to the death. Japanese soldiers believed that surrender meant disgrace, and the Allies rarely captured them alive. When cornered, the Japanese sometimes charged at Allied troops in nighttime suicide attacks. Rather than admit defeat, Japan's military leaders took their lives by stabbing themselves in the abdomen according to the tradition of *hara-kiri.*

The Allies developed two major campaigns against Japan in the South Pacific. One force under MacArthur checked the Japanese on New Guinea. Another force under Nimitz battled the Japanese in the Solomon Islands northeast of Australia. MacArthur and Nimitz aimed at taking the port of Rabaul on New Britain. Rabaul was Japan's chief base in the South Pacific. Japanese aircraft and warships attacked Allied ships from Rabaul, and Japan supplied other islands in the South Pacific from that base.

New Guinea. In the summer of 1942, Japanese troops began an overland drive across New Guinea's rugged, jungle-covered mountains to the Australian base of Port Moresby on the south coast. An Allied force made up chiefly of Australians quickly counterattacked. By November, the Japanese had been pushed back across the mountains. MacArthur then attacked Japanese positions along the north coast in a series of brilliant operations that combined air, sea, and land forces. Brutal fighting continued on New Guinea until mid-1944.

Guadalcanal. On Aug. 7, 1942, U.S. marines invaded the island of Guadalcanal in the first stage of a campaign in the Solomon Islands. The Japanese were building an air base on Guadalcanal from which to attack Allied

ships. The invasion took the Japanese by surprise. But they fought back, and a fierce battle developed.

The six-month battle for Guadalcanal was one of the most vicious campaigns of World War II. Each side depended on its navy to land supplies and troop reinforcements. In a series of naval battles, the Allies gained control of the waters surrounding Guadalcanal. They then cut off Japanese shipments. Until that time, Allied supplies had been short, and the marines had depended on rice captured from the enemy. By February 1943, the starving Japanese had evacuated Guadalcanal.

After taking Guadalcanal, American forces led by Admiral William F. Halsey worked their way up the Solomon Islands. In November 1943, the Americans reached Bougainville at the top of the island chain. They defeated the Japanese there in March 1944.

Rabaul. In the summer of 1943, Allied military leaders canceled the invasion of Rabaul. Instead, American bombers pounded the Japanese base, and aircraft and submarines sank shipments headed for Rabaul. About 100,000 Japanese defenders waited there for an attack that never came. The Allies spared many lives by isolating Rabaul rather than capturing it.

Island hopping in the Central Pacific. From late 1943 until the fall of 1944, the Allies hopped from island to island across the Central Pacific toward the Philippines. During the island-hopping campaign, the Allies became expert at *amphibious* (seaborne) invasions. Each island they captured provided a base from which to strike the next target. But rather than capture every island, the Allies by-passed Japanese strongholds and invaded islands that were weakly held. That strategy, known as *leapfrogging,* saved time and lives. Leapfrogging carried the Allies across the Gilbert, Marshall, Caroline, and Mariana islands in the Central Pacific.

Admiral Nimitz selected the Gilbert Islands as the first major objective in the island-hopping campaign. American marines invaded Tarawa in the Gilberts in November 1943. The attackers met heavy fire from Japanese troops in concrete bunkers. But they inched forward and captured the tiny island after four days of savage fighting. About 4,500 Japanese soldiers died defending

Department of Defense

Hugging the ground to avoid enemy gunfire, U.S. marines crawled over the sandy shores of Tarawa in the Gilbert Islands in November 1943. Lessons learned in the costly battle for Tarawa helped the Allies improve their seaborne landing techniques.

the island. Only 17 remained alive. More than 3,000 marines were killed or wounded in the assault. The Allies improved their amphibious operations because of lessons they had learned at Tarawa. As a result, fewer men died in later landings.

In February 1944, U.S. marines and infantrymen leaped north to the Marshall Islands. They captured Kwajalein and Enewetak in relatively smooth operations. Allied military leaders meanwhile had decided to bypass Truk, a key Japanese naval base in the Caroline Islands west of the Marshalls. They bombed Truk instead and made it unusable as a base.

The Americans made their next jump to the Mariana Islands, about 1,000 miles (1,600 kilometers) northwest of Enewetak. Bitter fighting for the Marianas began in June 1944. In the Battle of the Philippine Sea on June 19 and 20, Japan's navy once again attempted to destroy the U.S. Pacific Fleet. During the battle, which was fought near the island of Guam, the Allies massacred Japan's navy and destroyed its airpower. Japan lost 3 aircraft carriers and about 480 airplanes, or more than three-fourths of the planes it sent into battle. The loss of so many trained pilots was also a serious blow to Japan.

By August 1944, American forces occupied Guam, Saipan, and Tinian—the three largest islands in the Marianas. The occupation of the Marianas brought Nimitz's forces within bombing distance of Japan. Tojo resigned as Japan's prime minister in July 1944 after the loss of Saipan. In November, American B-29 bombers began using bases in the Marianas to raid Japan.

A final hop before the invasion of the Philippines took U.S. forces to the Palau Islands in September 1944. The islands lie between the Marianas and the Philippines. The attackers met stiff resistance on Peleliu, the chief Japanese base in the Palaus. About 25 per cent of the Americans were killed or injured in a month-long fight.

The liberation of the Philippines. The campaigns in New Guinea and the central Pacific brought the Allies within striking distance of the Philippine Islands. MacArthur and Nimitz combined their forces to liberate the Philippines. Allied leaders decided to invade the island of Leyte in the central Philippines in the fall of 1944.

The Allies expected the Japanese to fight hard to hold the Philippines. They therefore assembled the largest landing force ever used in the Pacific campaigns. About 750 ships participated in the invasion of Leyte, which began on Oct. 20, 1944. It had taken MacArthur more than $2\frac{1}{2}$ years and many brutal battles to keep his pledge to return to the Philippines.

While Allied troops poured ashore on Leyte, Japan's navy tried yet again to crush the Pacific Fleet. The Battle for Leyte Gulf, which was fought from Oct. 23 through 26, 1944, was the largest naval battle in history. In all, 282 ships took part. The battle ended in a major victory for the United States. Japan's navy was so badly damaged that it was no longer a serious threat for the rest of the war.

During the Battle for Leyte Gulf, the Japanese unleashed a terrifying new weapon—the *kamikaze* (suicide pilot). Kamikazes crashed planes filled with explosives onto Allied warships and died as a result. Many kamikazes were shot down before they crashed. But others

FPG

An attack by a Japanese *kamikaze* (suicide pilot) set this aircraft carrier aflame. In a last desperate effort to win the war, kamikazes crashed their planes onto Allied ships.

caused great damage. The kamikaze became one of Japan's major weapons during the rest of the war.

The fight for Leyte continued until the end of 1944. On Jan. 9, 1945, the Allies landed on the island of Luzon and began to work their way toward Manila. The city fell in early March. The remaining Japanese troops on Luzon pulled back to the mountains and went on fighting until the war ended.

About 350,000 Japanese soldiers died during the campaign in the Philippines. American casualties numbered nearly 14,000 dead and about 48,000 wounded or missing. Japan was clearly doomed to defeat after losing the Philippines. But it did not intend to surrender.

The China-Burma-India theater. While fighting raged in the Pacific, the Allies also battled the Japanese on the Asian mainland. The chief *theater of operations* (area of military activity) involved China, Burma (now Myanmar), and India. By mid-1942, Japan held much of eastern and southern China and had conquered nearly all Burma. The Japanese had closed the Burma Road, the overland supply route from India to China. China lacked equipment and trained troops and barely managed to go on fighting. But the Western Allies wanted to keep China in the war because the Chinese tied down hundreds of thousands of Japanese troops. For three years, the Allies flew war supplies over the world's tallest mountain system, the Himalaya, from India to China. The route was known as "the Hump."

China. By 1942, five years after Japan had invaded China, the opposing armies were near exhaustion. Japanese troops staged attacks especially to capture China's food supplies for themselves and to starve the country into surrender. As a result, millions of Chinese people died from lack of food during the war.

A struggle between China's Nationalist government, headed by Chiang Kai-shek, and Chinese Communists further weakened the country's war effort. At first, the Nationalist forces and the Communists had joined in fighting the Japanese invaders. But their cooperation gradually broke down as they prepared to fight each other after the war.

World War II in Asia and the Pacific: 1943-1945

From 1943 to August 1945, the Allies worked their way across the Pacific toward Japan. Allied forces on the Asian mainland recaptured Burma. This map shows the Allied route and gives the dates of key battles in the Pacific campaign. Japan still held much territory when it surrendered.

WORLD BOOK map

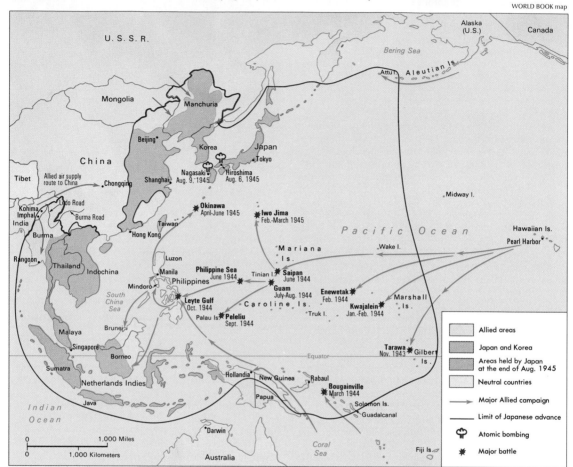

The United States sent military advisers as well as equipment to China. Colonel Claire L. Chennault, for example, trained pilots and established an air force in China. By the end of 1943, his pilots controlled the skies over China. But they could not help exhausted Chinese troops on the ground. Major General Joseph W. Stilwell served as Chiang's chief of staff and trained the Chinese army. Stilwell also commanded the U.S. forces in China and Burma.

Burma. The Allied campaign in Burma was closely linked to the fighting in China. From 1943 until early 1945, the Allies fought to recapture Burma from the Japanese and reopen a land route to China. But rugged jungle, heavy rains, and a shortage of troops and supplies hampered the Allies in Burma.

Admiral Louis Mountbatten of Great Britain became supreme Allied commander in Southeast Asia in August 1943. He directed several successful offensives in Burma in late 1943 and in 1944. By the end of 1944, Allied forces had battled their way through the jungles of northern Burma. They opened a supply route across northern

Burma to China in January 1945. Rangoon, Burma's capital, fell to the Allies in May. The Allies finally regained Burma after a long, horrible campaign.

India. India became an important supply base and training center for Allied forces during World War II. Japan's conquest of Burma in 1942 placed India in great danger. In early 1944, Japanese troops invaded India and encircled the towns of Imphal and Kohima just inside India's border. The British supplied the towns by air. The attackers finally began to withdraw from India late in June. Thousands of Japanese soldiers died of disease and starvation during the retreat.

Closing in on Japan. Superiority at sea and in the air enabled the Allies to close in on Japan in early 1945. By then, Japan had lost much of its empire, most of its aircraft and cargo ships, and nearly all its warships. Hundreds of thousands of Japanese soldiers remained stranded on Pacific islands by-passed by the Allies. American B-29 bombers were pounding Japan's industries, and American submarines were sinking vital supplies headed for Japan.

Important dates in the Pacific: 1943-1945

1943

Nov. 20	U.S. forces invaded Tarawa.

1944

June 19-20	A U.S. naval force defeated the Japanese in the Battle of the Philippine Sea.
July 18	Japan's Prime Minister Tojo resigned.
Oct. 20	The Allies began landing in the Philippines.
Oct. 23-26	The Allies defeated Japan's navy in the Battle of Leyte Gulf in the Philippines.

1945

March 16	U.S. marines captured Iwo Jima.
June 21	Allied forces captured Okinawa.
Aug. 6	An atomic bomb was dropped on Hiroshima.
Aug. 8	The Soviet Union declared war on Japan.
Aug. 9	An atomic bomb was dropped on Nagasaki.
Aug. 14	Japan agreed to surrender unconditionally.
Sept. 2	Japan signed surrender terms aboard the battleship U.S.S. *Missouri* in Tokyo Bay.

U.S. Air Force

Allied flights over the Himalaya, the world's tallest mountains, supplied China with war materials from 1942 to 1945. The dangerous air route from India to China was called "the Hump."

In January 1945, Major General Curtis E. LeMay took command of the air war against Japan. LeMay ordered more frequent and more daring raids. American bombers increased their accuracy by flying in low during nighttime raids. They began to drop *incendiary* (fire-producing) bombs that set Japanese cities aflame. A massive incendiary raid in March 1945 destroyed the heart of Tokyo. By the end of the month, about 3 million people in Tokyo were homeless.

Japan's military leaders went on fighting, though they faced certain defeat. The Allies decided they needed more bases to step up the bombing campaign against Japan. They chose the Japanese islands of Iwo Jima and Okinawa.

Iwo Jima lies about 750 miles (1,210 kilometers) south of Japan. About 21,000 Japanese troops were stationed there. They prepared to defend the tiny island from fortified caves and underground tunnels. Allied aircraft began bombarding Iwo Jima seven months before the invasion. American marines landed on Feb. 19, 1945, and made slow progress. The Japanese hung on desperately until March 16. About 25,000 marines—about 30 per cent of the landing force—were killed or wounded in the campaign for Iwo Jima.

Okinawa, the next stop on the Allied route toward Japan, lies about 350 miles (565 kilometers) southwest of Japan. Allied troops began to pour ashore on Okinawa on April 1, 1945. Japan sent kamikazes to attack the landing force. By the time the battle ended on June 21, kamikazes had sunk at least 30 ships and damaged more than 350 others. The capture of Okinawa cost the Allies about 50,000 casualties. About 110,000 Japanese died, including many civilians who chose to commit suicide rather than be conquered.

By the summer of 1945, some members of Japan's government favored surrender. But others insisted that Japan fight on. The Allies planned to invade Japan in November 1945. American military planners feared that the invasion might cost as many as 1 million U.S. lives. Some Allied leaders believed that Soviet help was needed to

AP/Wide World

Supplies poured ashore on Iwo Jima after U.S. marines secured beaches on the Japanese island in February 1945. The battle for Iwo Jima was one of the bloodiest campaigns of World War II.

UPI/Bettmann Newsphotos

An atomic blast demolished the center of Hiroshima, Japan, *above,* on Aug. 6, 1945. Japan agreed to surrender after a second atomic bomb was dropped on Nagasaki on August 9.

UPI/Bettmann Newsphotos

Japan's surrender on Sept. 2, 1945, ended World War II. General of the Army Douglas MacArthur, *far left,* signed for the Allies, and General Yoshijiro Umezu, *right,* for the Japanese army.

defeat Japan, and they had encouraged Stalin to invade Manchuria. However, the Allies found another way to end the war.

The atomic bomb. In 1939, the German-born scientist Albert Einstein had informed President Roosevelt about the possibility of creating a superbomb. It would produce an extremely powerful explosion by splitting the atom. Einstein and other scientists feared that Germany might develop such a bomb first. In 1942, the United States set up the Manhattan Project, a top-secret program to develop an atomic bomb. The first test explosion of an atomic bomb occurred in the New Mexico desert in July 1945.

Roosevelt died in April 1945, and Vice President Harry S. Truman became President of the United States. Truman met with Churchill and Stalin in Potsdam, Germany, in July, shortly after Germany's defeat. At the Potsdam Conference, Truman learned of the successful test explosion of the atomic bomb and informed the other leaders of it. The United States, Britain, and China then issued a statement threatening to destroy Japan unless it surrendered unconditionally. In spite of the warning, Japan went on fighting.

On Aug. 6, 1945, an American B-29 bomber called the *Enola Gay* dropped the first atomic bomb used in warfare on the Japanese city of Hiroshima. The explosion killed from 70,000 to 100,000 people, it is estimated, and destroyed about 5 square miles (13 square kilometers). After Japanese leaders failed to respond to the bombing, the United States dropped a larger bomb on Nagasaki on August 9. It killed about 40,000 people. Later, thousands more died of injuries and radiation from the two bombings. Meanwhile, on August 8, the Soviet Union declared war on Japan and invaded Manchuria. Soviet troops raced south toward Korea.

Victory in the Pacific. Although Japan's emperors had traditionally stayed out of politics, Hirohito urged the government to surrender. On August 14, Japan agreed to end the war. Some of the country's military leaders committed suicide.

On Sept. 2, 1945, representatives of Japan signed the official statement of surrender aboard the U.S. battleship *Missouri,* which lay at anchor in Tokyo Bay. Representatives of all the Allied nations were present. Truman declared September 2 as V-J Day, or Victory over Japan Day. World War II had ended.

The secret war

Throughout World War II, a secret war was fought between the Allies and the Axis to obtain information about each other's activities and to weaken each other's war effort. Codebreakers tried to decipher secret communications, and spies worked behind enemy lines to gather information. Saboteurs tried to disrupt activities on the home front. Many people in Axis-held territories joined undercover *resistance groups* that opposed the occupying forces. All the warring nations used propaganda to influence public opinion.

The Ultra secret. Soon after the outbreak of World War II, Britain obtained, with the help of Polish spies, one of the machines Germany used to code secret messages. In an outstanding effort, British mathematicians

and codebreakers solved the machine's electronic coding procedures. Britain's ability to read many of Germany's wartime communications was known as the Ultra secret. Ultra helped the Allies defeat Germany.

The Ultra secret played an important role in battle. During the 1940 Battle of Britain, for example, Ultra supplied advance warning of where and when the Luftwaffe planned to attack. Ultra also helped Montgomery defeat the Germans in Egypt in 1942 by providing him with Rommel's battle plan. The British carefully guarded the Ultra secret. They were extremely cautious about using their knowledge so that Germany would not change its coding procedures. The Germans never discovered that Britain had broken their code.

Spies and saboteurs were specially trained by the warring nations. Spies reported on troop movements, defense build-ups, and other developments behind enemy lines. Spies of Allied nations also supplied resistance groups with weapons and explosives. Saboteurs hampered the enemy's war effort in any way they could. For example, they blew up factories and bridges and organized slowdowns in war plants.

Germany had spies in many countries. But its efforts at spying were less successful in general than those of the Allies. The U.S. government set up a wartime agency called the Office of Strategic Services (OSS) to engage in spying and sabotage. The OSS worked closely with a similar British agency, the Special Operations Executive. The Soviet Union operated networks of spies in Allied nations as well as in Germany and Japan.

Resistance groups sprang up in every Axis-occupied country. Resistance began with individual acts of defiance against the occupiers. Gradually, like-minded people banded together and worked in secret to overthrow the invaders. The activities of resistance groups expanded as the war continued. Their work included publishing and distributing Illegal newspapers, rescuing Allied aircrews shot down behind enemy lines, gathering information about the enemy, and sabotage.

In such countries as France, Yugoslavia, and Burma, resistance groups engaged in *guerrilla warfare*. They organized bands of fighters who staged raids, ambushes, and other small attacks against the occupation forces.

All resistance movements suffered many setbacks. But they also achieved outstanding successes. For example, the French resistance interfered with German efforts to turn back the Allied invasion of Normandy in 1944. Norwegian resistance workers destroyed a shipment of *heavy water* headed for Germany. Heavy water is a substance needed in the production of an atomic bomb. Yugoslavia had the most effective resistance movement of all—the Partisans. With Allied help, the Partisans drove the Germans out of Yugoslavia in 1944.

Even in Germany itself, a small underground movement opposed the Nazis. In July 1944, a group of German army officers planted a bomb intended to kill Hitler. However, Hitler escaped the explosion with minor injuries. He ordered the plotters arrested and executed.

The risks of joining the resistance were great. A resistance worker caught by the Nazis faced certain death. The Germans sometimes rounded up and executed hundreds of civilians in revenge for an act of sabotage against their occupation forces.

Propaganda. All the warring nations used propaganda to win support for their policies. Governments aimed propaganda at their own people and at the enemy. Radio broadcasts reached the largest audiences. Motion pictures, posters, and cartoons were also used.

The Nazis skillfully used propaganda to spread their beliefs. Joseph Goebbels directed Germany's Ministry of Propaganda and Enlightenment, which controlled publications, radio programs, motion pictures, and the arts in Germany and German-occupied Europe. The ministry worked to persuade people of the superiority of German culture and of Germany's right to rule the world. After the war began to go badly for the Axis, the Germans

A U.S. government poster reminded Americans of the event that plunged them into war—Japan's attack on Pearl Harbor. All warring nations used propaganda techniques to stir patriotism.

claimed that they were saving the world from the evils of Communism.

Mussolini stirred the Italians with dreams of restoring Italy to the glory of ancient Rome. Italy's propaganda also ridiculed the fighting ability of Allied soldiers.

Japan promised conquered peoples a share in the Greater East Asia Co-Prosperity Sphere, which would unite all eastern Asia under Japanese control. Using the slogan "Asia for the Asians," the Japanese claimed that they were freeing Asia from European rule.

Nightly newscasts beamed by the British Broadcasting Corporation (BBC) to the European mainland provided truthful information about the day's fighting. The Nazis made it a crime for people in Germany and German-held lands to listen to BBC broadcasts.

The U.S. government established the Office of War Information (OWI) to encourage American support for the war effort. The agency told Americans that they were fighting for a better world. In 1942, the Voice of America, a government radio service, began broadcasting to Axis-occupied countries.

The warring countries also engaged in *psychological warfare* intended to destroy the enemy's will to fight. American planes dropped leaflets over Germany that told of Nazi defeats. The Axis nations employed English-speaking radio announcers whose programs were designed to weaken the morale of Allied soldiers. For example, Mildred Gillars, an American known as "Axis Sally," made broadcasts for Germany. The Japanese also used English-speaking female announcers, some of whom were referred to as "Tokyo Rose" by soldiers. Such broadcasts merely amused most troops.

National Archives

"Rosie the Riveter" became the humorous yet respectful name for the millions of American women who worked in defense plants during the war. This "Rosie" worked on an airplane assembly line.

World War II affected the civilian populations of all the fighting nations. But the effects were extremely uneven. Much of Europe and large parts of Asia suffered widespread destruction and severe hardship. The United States and Canada, which lay far from the battlefronts, were spared most of the horror of war. North America, in fact, prospered during World War II.

In the United States and Canada, most people fully backed the war effort. Nearly all Americans and Canadians despised Nazism and wished to defeat it. Americans sought also to avenge the bombing of Pearl Harbor.

Producing for the war. Victory in World War II required an enormous amount of war materials, including huge numbers of ships, tanks, aircraft, and weapons. The United States and Canada built many plants to manufacture war goods. They also turned old factories into war plants. For example, automobile factories began to produce tanks and aircraft.

The United States astonished the world with its wartime output. Roosevelt called for the production of 60,000 aircraft during 1942—a goal many industrialists believed was impossible to achieve. Yet U.S. war plants turned out nearly 86,000 planes the following year. Shipbuilding gains were just as impressive. For example, the time needed to build an aircraft carrier dropped from 36 months in 1941 to 15 months in 1945.

Canada also greatly expanded its output during World War II. Wartime expansion made Canada a leading industrial power by the war's end.

Millions of women in the United States and Canada joined the labor force during World War II, after men left for combat. Women worked in shipyards and aircraft factories and filled many jobs previously held only by men. The number of working women in the United States climbed from about 15 million in 1941 to about 19 million in 1945. Canadian women replaced men on farms as well as in factories. They helped raise the crops that fed Allied troops.

New opportunities opened up for American blacks

during World War II. In 1941, Roosevelt created the Fair Employment Practices Committee to prevent job discrimination in U.S. defense industries. Large numbers of Southern blacks moved to the North to work in war plants.

Mobilizing for the war. The United States introduced its first peacetime draft in September 1940. Under the draft law, all men aged 21 through 35 were required to register for military service. The draft was later extended to men 18 through 44. More than 15 million American men served in the armed forces during World War II. About 10 million were drafted. The rest volunteered. About 338,000 women served in the U.S. armed forces. They worked as mechanics, drivers, clerks, and cooks and also filled many other noncombat positions.

Canada also expanded its armed forces greatly during World War II. At the outbreak of the war, the Canadian government promised not to draft men for service overseas. Canada relied on volunteers for overseas duty until November 1944. By then, it suffered from a severe shortage of troops and began to send draftees overseas. More than a million Canadians, including about 50,000 women, served in the armed forces during the war.

Financing the war. The U.S. and Canadian governments paid for the costs of World War II in several ways. In one major method, they borrowed from individuals and businesses by selling them war bonds, certificates, notes, and stamps. The United States government raised nearly $180 billion from such sales. Canada's government also raised several billion dollars.

Taxes also helped pay for World War II. Income increased tremendously during the war years. As a result, revenue from income taxes soared. In the United States, the tax rate on the highest incomes reached 94 per cent.

AP/Wide World

Government rationing helped assure the fair distribution of scarce goods in the United States and Canada. Ration books enabled citizens to buy limited amounts of meat and other items.

AP/Wide World

The wartime confinement of Japanese Americans in relocation camps was a denial of their rights. It resulted from distrust of all Japanese after the attack on Pearl Harbor.

The government also taxed entertainment and such luxury goods as cosmetics and jewelry. Corporations paid extra taxes on higher-than-normal profits. Canadians also paid increased taxes during the war.

In spite of greater borrowing and higher taxes, the U.S. and Canadian governments spent more than they raised to pay for the war. In the United States, the national debt increased from about $49 billion in 1941 to $259 billion in 1945. Canada's national debt rose from $4 billion in 1939 to $16 billion in 1945.

Government controls over civilian life in the United States and Canada expanded during World War II. In both countries, the national government established various agencies to direct the war effort on the home front. The agencies helped prevent skyrocketing prices, severe shortages, and production foul-ups. The War Production Board, for example, controlled the distribution of raw materials needed by U.S. industries. The Office of Price Administration limited price increases in the United States. It also set up a *rationing program* to distribute scarce goods fairly. Each family received a book of ration coupons to use for purchases of such items as sugar, meat, butter, and gasoline.

Canada's government had even greater wartime powers. For example, the National Selective Service controlled Canada's work force. It forbade men of military age to hold jobs it termed "nonessential." Such jobs included driving a taxi or selling real estate. Canada's Wartime Prices and Trade Board determined wages and prices and set up a rationing program.

Treatment of enemy aliens. During World War II, the U.S. government classified more than a million newly arrived immigrants from Germany, Italy, and Japan as *enemy aliens.* However, only the Japanese were treated unjustly. After the bombing of Pearl Harbor, some Americans directed their rage at people of Japanese ancestry. In 1942, anti-Japanese hysteria led the U.S. government to move about 110,000 West Coast residents of Japanese ancestry to inland relocation camps. They lost their homes and their jobs as a result. About two-thirds of them were citizens of the United States. Canada also relocated about 21,000 people of Japanese ancestry during the war.

In Germany, most of the people greeted the start of World War II with little enthusiasm. But Germany's string of easy victories from 1939 to mid-1941 stirred support for the war. By the summer of 1941, the Germans did not expect the war to last much longer.

Civilian life. Food, clothing, and other consumer goods remained plentiful in Germany during the early years of the war. Imports poured in from Nazi-occupied countries of Europe. The Allied bombing of Germany got off to a slow start and did little damage at first.

Germany's situation had changed by late 1942. The armed forces bogged down in the Soviet Union, and there were fewer reports of German victories to cheer the people. Allied bombs rained down day and night on German cities. Consumer goods became scarce. Yet the people continued to work hard for the war effort.

The Nazi terror. Hitler's dreaded secret police, the Gestapo, ruthlessly crushed opposition to the Nazi Party. The Gestapo arrested anyone suspected of opposing Nazism in Germany and in German-held territories.

To free German men for combat, the Gestapo recruited workers from occupied countries. Millions of Europeans were eventually forced to work long hours under terrible conditions in German war plants. Many died of mistreatment or starvation.

The Nazis brutally persecuted several groups, including Jews, Gypsies, and Slavs. By 1942, Hitler had started a campaign to murder all European Jews. The Nazis rounded up Jewish men, women, and children from occupied Europe and shipped them in boxcars to concentration camps. Many Jews were mowed down by firing squads or killed in groups in gas chambers. Others died from lack of food, disease, or torture. Altogether, Hitler's forces killed approximately 6 million European Jews. About 4 million of these people died in concentration camps. The Nazis also slaughtered many Poles, Slavs, Gypsies, and members of other groups.

In other countries, conditions on the home front depended on the nearness of the fighting and on the length of the war effort. Conditions were especially difficult in the Soviet Union, where fierce fighting went on for nearly four years. Stalin ordered retreating Soviet soldiers to burn everything in their path that German troops could use for food or shelter. But that *scorched-earth policy* also caused great hardships for the Soviet people. Millions of Soviet civilians died of famine and other war-related causes. In Ukraine and areas occupied by the Soviet Union, many of the people at first welcomed the conquering German troops. They believed that the Germans would deliver them from Stalin's harsh rule. But the cruelty of the Nazi occupation forces turned the people against them. During World War II, civilians and soldiers in the Soviet Union fought the Germans with a hatred and determination seldom matched elsewhere in Europe.

The civilian population of Britain also united wholeheartedly behind the war effort. The people worked long hours in war plants and accepted severe shortages of nearly all goods. Prime Minister Churchill inspired the British people with his stirring words.

Life was especially hard in the countries under Nazi rule. Germany looted the conquered lands to feed its own people and fuel its war effort. Opponents of Nazism lived in constant fear of Gestapo brutality.

Japan came closest to collapse of all the warring nations. As the Allies closed in, they deprived Japan of more and more of the raw materials needed by the country's industries. American bombers pounded Japan's cities, and American submarines sank Japanese cargo ships. By 1945, hunger and malnutrition were widespread in Japan. But the Japanese people remained willing to make enormous sacrifices for the war effort.

Consequences of the war

Deaths and destruction. World War II took more lives and caused more destruction than any other war. Altogether, about 70 million people served in the armed forces of the Allied and Axis nations. About 17 million of them lost their lives. The Soviet Union suffered about $7\frac{1}{2}$ million battle deaths, more than any other country. The United States and Great Britain had the fewest battle deaths of the major powers. About 400,000 American and about 350,000 British military personnel died in the war. Germany lost about $3\frac{1}{2}$ million servicemen, and Japan about $1\frac{1}{4}$ million.

Aerial bombing during World War II rained destruction on civilian as well as military targets. Many cities lay in ruins by the end of the war, especially in Germany and Japan. Bombs wrecked houses, factories, and transportation and communication systems. Land battles also spread destruction over vast areas. After the war, millions of starving and homeless people wandered among the ruins of Europe and Asia.

No one knows how many civilians died as a direct result of World War II. Bombing raids destroyed many of the records needed to estimate those deaths. In addition, millions of people died in fires, of diseases, and of other causes after such essential services as fire fighting and health care broke down in war-torn areas.

The Soviet Union and China suffered the highest toll of civilian deaths during World War II. About 19 million Soviet civilians and as many as 10 million Chinese civilians died. Many of the deaths resulted from famine.

Displaced persons. World War II uprooted millions of people. By the war's end, more than 12 million *displaced persons* remained in Europe. They included orphans, prisoners of war, survivors of Nazi concentration and slave labor camps, and people who had fled invading armies and war-torn areas. Other people were displaced by changes in national borders. For example, many Germans moved into Poland, Czechoslovakia, and other lands in eastern Europe that the Nazis took over. After the war, those countries expelled these German residents.

To help displaced persons, the Allies established the United Nations Relief and Rehabilitation Administration (UNRRA). UNRRA began operating in 1944 in areas freed by the Allies from Nazi occupation. The organization set up camps for displaced persons and provided them with food, clothing, and medical supplies. By 1947, most of the displaced persons had been resettled. However, about a million people still remained in camps. Many had fled from countries in eastern Europe and refused to return to homelands that had come under Communist rule.

New power struggles arose after World War II ended. The war had exhausted the leading prewar powers of Europe and Asia. Germany and Japan ended the war in complete defeat, and Britain and France were severely weakened. The United States and the Soviet Union emerged as the world's leading powers. Their wartime alliance soon collapsed as the Soviet Union sought to spread Communism in Europe and Asia. The struggle between the Communist world, led by the Soviet Union, and the non-Communist world, led by the United States, became known as the Cold War.

The United States had fought the Axis to preserve democracy. After the war, Americans found it impossible to return to the policy of isolation their country had followed before the war. Americans realized that they needed strong allies, and they helped the war-torn nations recover.

World War II had united the Soviet people behind a great patriotic effort. The Soviet Union came out of the war stronger than ever before, in spite of the severe destruction it had suffered. Before the war ended, the Soviet Union had absorbed three nations along the Baltic Sea—Estonia, Latvia, and Lithuania. It had also taken parts of Poland, Romania, Finland, and Czechoslova-

Keystone

The human suffering caused by World War II was enormous. Cities lay in ruins, and millions of people had to be resettled. These homeless Germans reflected the widespread despair.

kia by mid-1945. At the end of the war, Soviet troops occupied most of eastern Europe. In March 1946, Churchill warned that an "iron curtain" had descended across Europe, dividing eastern Europe from western Europe. Behind the Iron Curtain, the Soviet Union helped Communist governments take power in Bulgaria, Czechoslovakia, Hungary, Poland, and Romania.

Communism also gained strength in the Far East. The Soviet Union set up a Communist government in North Korea after the war. In China, Mao Zedong's Communist forces battled Chiang Kai-shek's Nationalist armies. Late in 1949, Chiang fled to the island of Taiwan, and China joined the Communist world.

By 1947, Communists threatened to take control of Greece, and the Soviet Union was demanding military bases in Turkey. That year, President Truman announced that the United States would provide military and economic aid to any country threatened by Communism. American aid helped Greece and Turkey resist Communist aggression.

In 1948, the United States set up the Marshall Plan to help war-torn nations in Europe rebuild their economies. Under the plan, 18 nations received $13 billion in food, machinery, and other goods. The Soviet Union forbade countries in eastern Europe to participate in the Marshall Plan.

The nuclear age opened with the development of the atomic bomb during World War II. Many people believed that weapons capable of mass destruction would make war unthinkable in the future. They hoped that the world would learn to live in peace. But a race to develop ever more powerful weapons soon began.

At the end of World War II, only the United States knew how to build an atomic weapon. In 1946, the United States proposed the creation of an international

Military casualties in World War II (1939-1945)

	Dead	Wounded
The Allies		
Australia	23,365	39,803
Belgium	7,760	14,500
Canada	37,476	53,174
China	2,200,000	1,762,000
France	210,671	390,000
Poland	320,000	530,000
Soviet Union	7,500,000	5,000,000
United Kingdom*	329,208	348,403
United States	405,399	671,278
The Axis		
Austria	380,000	350,117
Bulgaria	10,000	21,878
Finland	82,000	50,000
Germany	3,500,000	7,250,000
Hungary	140,000	89,313
Italy	77,494	120,000
Japan	1,219,000	295,247
Romania	300,000	(†)

*Including colonials.
†Figure unavailable.
Source: James L. Stokesbury, author of *A Short History of World War II*.

agency that would control atomic energy and ban the production of nuclear weapons. But the Soviet Union objected to an inspection system, and the proposal was dropped. Stalin ordered Soviet scientists to develop an atomic bomb, and they succeeded in 1949. During the early 1950's, the United States and the Soviet Union each tested an even more destructive weapon, the hydrogen bomb.

People have feared a nuclear war since the nuclear age began. At times, Cold War tensions threatened to erupt into war between the two superpowers. But the terrifying destructiveness of nuclear weapons may well have kept them from risking a major war.

Establishing the peace

Birth of the United Nations (UN). Out of the horror of World War II came efforts to prevent war from ever again engulfing the world. In 1943, representatives of the United Kingdom, the United States, the Soviet Union, and China met in Moscow. They agreed to establish an international organization that would work to promote peace. The four Allied powers met again in 1944 at Dumbarton Oaks, an estate in Washington, D.C. The delegates decided to call the new organization the United Nations. In April 1945, representatives from 50 nations gathered in San Francisco, California, to draft a charter for the United Nations. They signed the charter in June, and it went into effect on October 24.

Peace with Germany. Before World War II ended, the Allies had decided on a military occupation of Germany after its defeat. They divided Germany into four zones, with the United Kingdom, the United States, the Soviet Union, and France each occupying a zone. The four powers jointly administered Berlin.

At the Potsdam Conference in July 1945, the Allies set forth their occupation policy. They agreed to abolish Germany's armed forces and to outlaw the Nazi Party. Germany lost territory east of the Oder and Neisse riv-

ers. Most of the region went to Poland. The Soviet Union gained the northeastern corner of this territory.

The Allies brought to trial Nazi leaders accused of war crimes. The trials exposed the monstrous evils inflicted

© Corbis/Bettmann Archive

The Nuremberg Trials brought many Nazi leaders to justice. Those tried included, *center row, left to right*, Hermann Goering, Rudolf Hess, Joachim von Ribbentrop, and Wilhelm Keitel.

by Nazi Germany. Many leading Nazis were sentenced to death. The most important war trials took place in the German city of Nuremberg from 1945 to 1949.

Soon after the occupation began, the Soviet Union stopped cooperating with its Western Allies. It blocked all efforts to reunite Germany. The Western Allies gradually joined their zones into one economic unit. But the Soviet Union forbade its zone to join.

The city of Berlin lay deep within the Soviet zone of Germany. In June 1948, the Soviet Union sought to drive the Western powers from Berlin by blocking all rail, water, and highway routes to the city. For over a year, the Western Allies flew in food, fuel, and other goods to Berlin. The Soviet Union finally lifted the Berlin blockade in May 1949, and the airlift ended in September.

The Western Allies set up political parties in their zones and held elections. In September 1949, the three Western zones were officially combined as the Federal Republic of Germany, also known as West Germany. In May 1955, the Western Allies signed a treaty ending the occupation of West Germany, and granting the country full independence. However, the treaty was not a general peace treaty because the Soviet Union refused to sign it. The Soviet Union set up a Communist government in its zone. In October 1949, the Soviet zone became the German Democratic Republic, also known as East Germany.

In September 1990, the Soviet Union and the Western Allies signed a treaty to give up all their occupation rights in East and West Germany. In October 1990, Germany was reunited as a non-Communist nation.

Peace with Japan. The military occupation of Japan began in August 1945. Americans far outnumbered other troops in the occupation forces because of the key role their country had played in defeating Japan. General MacArthur directed the occupation as supreme commander for the Allied nations. He introduced many reforms designed to rid Japan of its military institutions and transform it into a democracy. A constitution drawn up by MacArthur's staff took effect in 1947. The constitution transferred all political rights from the Japanese emperor to the people. In addition, the constitution granted voting rights to women, and denied Japan's right to declare war.

The Allied occupation forces brought to trial 25 Japanese war leaders and government officials who were accused of war crimes. Seven of these individuals were executed. The others received prison sentences.

In September 1951, the United States and most of the other Allied nations signed a peace treaty with Japan. The treaty took away Japan's overseas empire, although it permitted Japan to rearm. The Allied occupation of Japan ended soon after the nations signed the treaty. However, a new treaty permitted the United States to keep troops in Japan. China's Nationalist government signed its own peace treaty with Japan in 1952, and the Soviet Union and Japan also signed a separate peace treaty in 1956.

Peace with other countries. Soon after World War II ended, the Allies began to draw up peace treaties with Italy and the other countries that fought the Allies. The treaties limited the armed forces of the defeated countries and required them to pay war damages. The treaties also called for territorial changes. Bulgaria gave up territory to Greece and Yugoslavia. Czechoslovakia gained land from Hungary. Italy gave up land to France, Yugoslavia, and Greece. The country also lost its empire in Africa. Romania gained territory from Hungary, but in turn it lost land to Bulgaria and the Soviet Union.

James L. Stokesbury

Study aids

Related articles in *World Book.* See the *History* section of articles on countries that took part in World War II. Additional related articles in *World Book* include:

Battles

Bataan Peninsula	Midway Island
Chinese-Japanese wars	Okinawa
Corregidor	Pearl Harbor
Dunkerque	Russo-Finnish wars
Guam	Saipan
Iwo Jima	Stalingrad, Battle of
Leningrad, Siege of	Wake Island
Manila Bay	

Allied military leaders

Alanbrook, Lord	Montgomery, Bernard L.
Alexander of Tunis, Earl	Mountbatten, Louis
Arnold, Henry H.	Nimitz, Chester W.
Bradley, Omar N.	Patton, George S., Jr.
Chennault, Claire L.	Ridgway, Matthew B.
Clark, Mark W.	Roosevelt, Theodore, Jr.
Doolittle, James H.	Spaatz, Carl
Eisenhower, Dwight D.	Spruance, Raymond A.
Halsey, William F., Jr.	Stilwell, Joseph W.
Hobby, Oveta C.	Taylor, Maxwell D.
LeMay, Curtis E.	Tedder, Arthur W.
MacArthur, Douglas	Wainwright, Jonathan M.
Marshall, George C.	Zhukov, Georgi K.
McNaughton, Andrew G. L.	

Axis military leaders

Doenitz, Karl	Rommel, Erwin
Goering, Hermann W.	Yamamoto, Isoroku
Heydrich, Reinhard	Yamashita, Tomoyuki
Jodl, Alfred	

Allied political figures

Attlee, Clement R.	Haile Selassie I
Beneš, Eduard	Hull, Cordell
Chamberlain, Neville	Knox, Frank
Chiang Kai-shek	Molotov, Vyacheslav M.
Churchill, Sir Winston L. S.	Roosevelt, Franklin D.
Daladier, Édouard	Stalin, Joseph
De Gaulle, Charles A. J. M.	Tito, Josip Broz
Eden, Sir Anthony	Truman, Harry S.

Axis political figures

Bormann, Martin	Konoye, Prince	Ribbentrop,
Eichmann, Adolf	Fumimaro	Joachim von
Goebbels, Joseph	Laval, Pierre	Rosenberg, Alfred
Hess, Rudolf	Mussolini, Benito	Speer, Albert
Himmler, Heinrich	Pétain, Henri P.	Tojo, Hideki
Hirohito	Quisling, Vidkun	Tokyo Rose
Hitler, Adolf	A. L.	

Other biographies

Bonhoeffer, Dietrich	Krupp
Frank, Anne	Mauldin, Bill
Kaiser, Henry J.	Mercier, Desire Joseph

Miller, Dorie
Murphy, Audie

Pyle, Ernie
Schindler, Oskar

Wallenberg, Raoul

Conferences and treaties

Munich Agreement
Pan-American Conferences
Potsdam Conference

San Francisco Conference
Tehran Conference
Yalta Conference

Forces, materials, and weapons

Ace
Air force
Air Force, United
  States
Aircraft, Military
Aircraft carrier
Airplane
Amphibious
  warfare
Army
Army, United
  States
Aviation
Balloon (Balloons
  in war)
Bazooka
Blitzkrieg
Bomb
Bulldozer
Camouflage

Coast Guard,
  United States
Code talkers
Codes and ciphers
  (History)
Commando
Fifth column
Flying Tigers
Guided missile
Helmet
Hostage
Intelligence service
Jeep
Jet propulsion
Kamikaze
Lend-Lease
Marine Corps,
  United States
Mine warfare
Navy

Navy, United
  States
Night vision
  systems
Nuclear weapon
Propaganda
PT boat
Radar
Rationing
Remote control
Rocket
Savings bond
Seabees
Sonar
Submarine
Tank
Torpedo
Tuskegee Airmen
War correspond-
  ent
Warship

Organizations

American Legion
American Legion Auxiliary
AMVETS
Red Cross
Strategic Services, Office of

United Nations
United Service Organizations
Veterans of Foreign Wars of
  the United States

Other related articles

Alaska Highway
Asian Americans
  (Japanese in-
  ternment)
Atlantic Charter
Azores
Bismarck (ship)
Burma Road
Codes and ciphers
  (History)
Concentration
  camp
D-day
Draft, Military
Family (Changes)
Gestapo
Graf Spee

Hiroshima
Holocaust
Holocaust Memor-
  ial Museum,
  United States
Jews (The Holo-
  caust)
Katyn Massacre
Korean War
Lidice
Maquis
Mein Kampf
Neutrality
Nuremberg Trials
Partisans
Polish Corridor

Refugee
Reparations
Selective Service
  System
Socialism (World
  Wars I and II)
Spanish Civil War
Stars and Stripes
Underground
United States,
  History of the
Unknown soldier
V-E Day
V-J Day
War crime
World War I

Outline

I. Causes of the war
  A. The Peace of Paris
  B. Economic problems
  C. Nationalism
  D. The rise of
    dictatorships
  E. Aggression on the march
  F. The Spanish Civil War
  G. The failure of
    appeasement

II. Early stages of the war
  A. The invasion of Poland
  B. The Phony War
  C. The conquest of
    Denmark and Norway
  D. The invasion of
    the Low Countries
  E. The fall of France
  F. The Battle of Britain

III. The war spreads
  A. Fighting in Africa
  B. Fighting in the Balkans
  C. The invasion of the Soviet Union
  D. The Battle of the Atlantic

IV. The United States enters the war
  A. The arsenal of democracy

  B. Japan attacks

V. The Allies attack in Europe and northern Africa
  A. The strategy
  B. On the Soviet front
  C. In northern Africa
  D. The air war
  E. The invasion of Italy
  F. D-Day
  G. The drive to the Rhine
  H. The Soviet advance
  I. Victory in Europe

VI. The war in Asia and the Pacific
  A. Early Japanese victories
  B. The tide turns
  C. The South Pacific
  D. Island hopping in the Central Pacific
  E. The liberation of the Philippines
  F. The China-Burma-India theater
  G. Closing in on Japan
  H. The atomic bomb
  I. Victory in the Pacific

VII. The secret war
  A. The Ultra secret
  B. Spies and saboteurs
  C. Resistance groups
  D. Propaganda

VIII. On the home front
  A. In the United States
    and Canada
  B. In Germany
  C. In other countries

IX. Consequences of the war
  A. Deaths and destruction
  B. Displaced persons
  C. New power struggles
  D. The nuclear age

X. Establishing the peace
  A. Birth of the United Nations (UN)
  B. Peace with Germany
  C. Peace with Japan
  D. Peace with other countries

Questions

Why did Japan decide to cripple the U.S. Pacific Fleet at anchor in Pearl Harbor?

Which two battles marked a turning point for the Allies in the war against Germany?

What was *appeasement?* When did it become clear that that policy had failed?

What terrifying new weapon did Japan introduce in 1944 during the Battle for Leyte Gulf?

What was the largest seaborne invasion in history?

Which leaders shocked the world by becoming allies in 1939?

How did the United States help the Allies before it entered World War II?

How was the Battle of the Coral Sea unlike all earlier naval battles?

How did the bombing campaigns against Germany by the United States and the United Kingdom differ?

What was the Ultra secret? How did it help the United Kingdom win the battle of Britain?

Additional resources

Adams, Simon. *World War II.* Dorling Kindersley, 2000. Younger readers.

Dear, I. C., and Foot, M. R., eds. *The Oxford Companion to World War II.* 1995. Reprint. Oxford, 2001.

Keegan, John, ed. *World War II: A Visual Encyclopedia.* Sterling Pub., 1999.

Lyons, Michael J. *World War II.* 4th ed. Prentice Hall, 2004.

Ruggiero, Adriane. *World War II.* Benchmark Bks., 2003.

Schneider, Carl J. and Dorothy. *World War II.* Facts on File, 2003.

Schomp, Virginia. *World War II.* Benchmark Bks., 2002. Younger readers.

Vandiver, Frank E. *1001 Things Everyone Should Know about World War II.* Broadway Bks., 2002.

World Wide Web is a system of computer files linked together on the Internet. The Internet connects computers and computer networks around the world. The portion of the Internet not on the World Wide Web (often called the Web, for short) contains only text information. But the Web has *multimedia* capabilities—that is, its files include illustrations, sounds, and moving pictures in addition to text. The Web is made up of electronic addresses called *Web sites,* which contain *Web pages* that hold the multimedia information. Web sites and their pages reside in computers connected to the Internet.

Tim Berners-Lee, an English computer scientist at the European Organization for Nuclear Research (CERN) physics laboratory near Geneva, Switzerland, wrote the Web software in 1990. The Web became part of the Internet in 1991. The introduction of the Web helped make the Internet popular and easier to use.

Many computer users find the Web's multimedia content more attractive than text-only content. In addition, *Web browsers* make the Web easy to use. A Web browser is a software package used to locate and display information on the Web. To find information on other parts of the Internet requires complex software and knowledge of specific computer commands. A Web browser is easier to use because it employs a *graphical user interface*—a way of interacting with a computer using pictures as well as words. The pictures represent commands in a manner that is easy to understand. For example, a small picture of a printer represents the command to print a document. By clicking the computer's mouse on an element, the user gives the computer command represented by that element.

Another major feature of the Web is *hypertext.* Hypertext enables a user to jump from one document to another—even if the documents are stored on different parts of the Internet. For example, in a Web site concerning space exploration, the words *space shuttle* might be highlighted. Clicking on these words would bring information about the shuttle to the screen. Pictures, too, can be used as *hyperlinks* (hypertext links). Words and pictures that hyperlink to other documents are called *hot spots.* Hot spots and their hyperlinks are created by the author of a Web page.   Keith Ferrell

Related articles in *World Book* include:

Advertising (picture)	Newspaper (Online newspapers)
Berners-Lee, Tim	
E-commerce	Online service
Internet	Television (Web television)
Journalism (Online journalism; Journalism today)	Web site

World Wildlife Fund. See WWF.

World's fair is an international exposition that features exhibits dealing with commerce, industry, and science. Most fairs also offer entertainment and cultural activities and promote tourism in a region or country. Exhibitors include nations and private companies.

A world's fair runs for several months and attracts millions of visitors. Most fairs have been held in Europe and the United States. But fairs have also been held in Africa, Australia, Canada, India, Japan, and New Zealand.

The first world's fair was the Great Exhibition of 1851 in London. A huge glass and iron hall called the Crystal Palace housed exhibits of art, handicrafts, and machinery. New products on display included the reaper and the Colt revolver.

World's fairs are regulated by the Bureau of International Expositions (B.I.E.). The B.I.E. has established regulations that govern the frequency and duration of officially approved events. Under B.I.E. rules, only one major fair can be held each decade and it can last for no longer than six months. But the B.I.E. also approves smaller events that can be held more often.

Through the years, world's fairs have become a showcase for new inventions, new types of foods, and new kinds of art. Alexander Graham Bell's newly invented telephone was displayed at the Centennial Exposition in Philadelphia in 1876. Visitors at the 1904 Louisiana Purchase Exposition in St. Louis, Missouri, saw early types of automobiles and several new foods, including iced tea and the ice cream cone. Visitors to the New York World's Fair in 1939 and 1940 could see early versions of television.

A number of famous structures have been designed for world's fairs. The Eiffel Tower was erected for a world's fair in Paris in 1889. The Museum of Science and Industry in Chicago is housed in a building constructed for the World's Columbian Exposition in 1893. The Space Needle was built for the Century 21 world's fair in Seattle, Washington, in 1962.

Early world's fairs offered general exhibits. Modern fairs have had themes. The Century 21 fair emphasized exhibits about the dawn of the space age. The 1975 fair in Okinawa, Japan, featured the ocean environment. The 1982 fair in Knoxville, Tennessee, dealt with energy needs. The 1986 fair in Vancouver, Canada, centered on transportation. The 1988 fair in Brisbane, Australia, explored leisure in the age of technology. The 1990 fair in Osaka, Japan, focused on global environmental issues. The 1992 fair in Seville, Spain, celebrated the 500th anniversary of Christopher Columbus's voyage to America.

Michael R. Pender

See also **Architecture** (The Industrial Revolution); **Chicago** (A city reborn; picture); **Tennessee** (picture).

Worm is any of several kinds of animals that have a soft, slender body and no backbone or legs. There are thousands of kinds of worms. The largest species measure many feet or meters long, and the smallest ones cannot be seen without a microscope. Some worms live in water or soil. Many of these free-living worms eat small plants and animals, and others feed on decaying matter. Still other worms live as parasites in various animals and plants. They cause a number of diseases.

Many people believe that such wormlike animals as caterpillars and grubs are worms. But these animals are insects in their *larval* (juvenile) stage and do not resemble worms after they mature.

Most kinds of worms have a well-developed sense of touch. They also have special organs that respond to chemicals in their surroundings. Many species have a sense of sight, with eyes or eyespots on the head.

There are four main groups of worms: (1) flatworms, or *Platyhelminthes;* (2) ribbon worms, or *Nemertea;* (3) roundworms, or *Nematoda;* and (4) segmented worms, or *Annelida.* The study of worms is *helminthology.*

Flatworms are the simplest kinds of worms. Some of them look like oval leaves, and others resemble ribbons. Flatworms include both free-living species and parasitic species. Most free-living flatworms live in the sea. But many freshwater species live among algae and stones along the shores of lakes and ponds. These flatworms, called *planarians,* eat tiny animals. *Flukes* and *tapeworms* are parasitic flatworms that infect human beings and many other animals. In human beings, they cause serious blood and intestinal disorders.

Ribbon worms resemble flatworms, but many species are larger. Most ribbon worms live in the sea. A few grow several feet or meters long. Ribbon worms are also called *proboscis worms.* They have a long *proboscis* (tubelike structure) that they shoot out from their head to capture prey. They feed on animals, including other worms and mollusks.

Roundworms make up the largest group of worms. There are about 12,000 species. Roundworms have a long, cylindrical body that resembles a piece of thread. Some, including *filariae, hookworms,* and *trichinae,* are parasites that cause disease in human beings and other animals and in plants. Free-living roundworms live in water or in soil. They eat bacteria, fungi, and small plants and animals.

Segmented worms are the most highly developed worms. Their body consists of segments that give the worms a ringed appearance. This group includes *polychaete worms, oligochaete worms,* and *leeches.*

Polychaete worms, the largest group of segmented worms, live in the sea and along the shore. Many of these worms have *tentacles* (feelers) on their head and a pair of leglike projections called *parapodia* on each body segment. The parapodia are used in crawling. They have many *setae* (bristles) that help the worms grip the surface on which they are moving. Many polychaete worms live among algae or burrow in mud or sand. Some live in tubes attached to the sea floor. A worm makes its tube from sand or from material secreted by its body. Some polychaete worms eat small plants and animals. Others feed on plant and animal remains.

Oligochaete worms include earthworms and many freshwater species. They have a few setae but no parapodia. Most oligochaete worms eat decaying plant matter.

Leeches make up the smallest group of segmented worms. They grow from $\frac{3}{8}$ to 12 inches (1 to 30 centimeters) long and have a flat body with a sucker at each end. Most leeches live in water and feed on the blood of fish and other water creatures.   Robert D. Barnes

Related articles in *World Book* include:

Earthworm	Horsehair worm	Ribbon worm
Eelworm	Leech	Roundworm
Filaria	Lugworm	Tapeworm
Flatworm	Nematode	Trichina
Fluke	Pinworm	Vinegar eel
Hookworm	Planarian	

Worms, *vawrms* (pop. 71,827), is a historic town and river port in southern Germany. It lies on the west bank of the Rhine River. For location, see **Germany** (political map).

Worms has a magnificent cathedral that is a fine example of Romanesque architecture. The cathedral dates from the 1000's. A monument dedicated to the Protestant reformer Martin Luther stands in the city. It honors Luther's appearance before the Diet of Worms in 1521. The *diet* (assembly) issued the Edict of Worms, which proclaimed Luther a heretic. Worms is also the site of what may be Europe's oldest Jewish cemetery. The cemetery dates from the 1000's. Worms produces the famous Liebfraumilch wine. Its other economic activities include shipping and the manufacture of chemicals, furniture, leather goods, machinery, and textiles.

Roman soldiers built a fort on the site of what is now Worms in 14 B.C. During the Middle Ages, officials of the Holy Roman Empire held nearly 100 diets in Worms.
        Melvin Croan

Worms, Edict of, was a decree that declared Reformation leader Martin Luther a heretic and cast him and his followers outside the protection of the law. The de-

Some common worms   There are several thousand kinds of worms. These illustrations show representatives of each of the four major groups of worms. The sizes listed are approximate because many species can stretch to unusually great lengths. For example, bootlace worms are normally no more than $6\frac{1}{2}$ feet (2 meters) long. But scientists measured one bootlace worm that was stretched to nearly 90 feet (27 meters). The illustrations are not drawn to scale.

WORLD BOOK illustrations by Patricia J. Wynne

Flatworms (Platyhelminthes)

Planarian
Genus *Dugesia*
Up to $\frac{1}{2}$ inch
(1.3 centimeters) long

Tapeworm
Genus *Taenia*
Up to 100 feet
(30 meters) long

Liver fluke
Genus *Fasciola*
Up to 1 inch
(2.5 centimeters) long

Ribbon worms (Nemertea)

Bootlace worm
Genus *Lineus*
Up to $6\frac{1}{2}$ feet
(2 meters) long

Pink ribbon worm
Genus *Amphiporus*
Up to $3\frac{1}{8}$ inches
(8 centimeters) long

Roundworms (Nematoda)

Hookworm
Genus *Necator*
Up to $\frac{1}{2}$ inch
(1.3 centimeters) long

Vinegar eel
Genus *Turbatrix*
Up to $\frac{1}{10}$ inch
(2.4 millimeters) long

Segmented worms (Annelida)

Earthworm
Genus *Lumbricus*
Up to 12 inches
(30 centimeters) long

Clamworm
Genus *Nereis*
Up to 18 inches
(46 centimeters) long

Leech
Genus *Hirudo*
Up to 6 inches
(15 centimeters) long

cree was issued by a *diet* (assembly) of princes, nobles, and clergy at Worms, Germany, in May 1521.

The edict was an important instance of a civil body issuing a condemnation for the religious charge of heresy. Succeeding diets debated whether it should be enforced, and leagues of Roman Catholic and Protestant states were formed to defend each side of the question. The conflict did not end until the truce provided by the Peace of Augsburg in 1555.   Dale A. Johnson

See also **Luther, Martin** (The Diet of Worms); **Reformation** (Martin Luther).

Wormwood is a large group of plants that give off pleasant odors. Often the term applies to an entire group of about 250 different kinds of plants of the genus *Artemisia.* The wormwood shrub grows mostly in the Northern Hemisphere and is most abundant in arid regions. The most important wormwood in commercial use is a perennial plant that grows in Europe and North Africa. This kind supplies an essential oil used in the manufacture of absinthe and medicine. Europeans grow common wormwood, or *mugwort,* for seasoning and medicinal purposes. People in eastern Canada and the northeastern United States consider this plant a weed. Several kinds of shrubby wormwoods are called *sagebrush* in the western United States.   Lyle E. Craker

Scientific classification. Wormwood is in the composite family, Asteraceae or Compositae. The scientific name for the wormwood that yields oil for absinthe is *Artemisia absinthium.* The common wormwood is *A. vulgaris.* The common sagebrush is *A. tridentata.*

Worry. See Anxiety.

Worship. See Religion; Colonial life in America (Why the colonists came to America); **Freedom of religion; God; Idolatry; Prayer; Sun worship.**

Wotan. See Odin.

Wouk, *wohk,* **Herman** (1915-   ), is a popular American novelist and playwright. His most successful books are based on his experiences serving in the United States Navy during World War II (1939-1945).

Wouk won the 1952 Pulitzer Prize for fiction for *The Caine Mutiny* (1951). This novel tells about the conflict between Philip Queeg, the unstable captain of an American minesweeper in the Pacific Ocean, and his rebellious junior officers. Wouk adapted part of the novel for a play, *The Caine Mutiny Court-Martial* (1954).

In *The Winds of War* (1971) and *War and Remembrance* (1978), Wouk describes the effects of World War II on Victor Henry, an American naval officer, and his family. The two novels mingle fictional characters with historical figures against a background of major events of the period.

Wouk's other novels include *Aurora Dawn* (1947), *The City Boy* (1948), *Marjorie Morningstar* (1955), *Youngblood Hawke* (1962), *Don't Stop the Carnival* (1965), *Inside, Outside* (1985), and *The Hope* (1993). His other plays are *The Traitor* (1949) and *Nature's Way* (1957). He discusses Judaism in *This Is My God* (1959). Wouk was born in New York City.   Barbara M. Perkins

Wounded Knee, now a village on the Pine Ridge Sioux Indian Reservation of South Dakota, was the site of two famous events in American Indian history. The first was a massacre of Lakota Sioux Indians by United States Army troops in 1890. The second was the seizure of the village in 1973 by an armed group that included members of the American Indian Movement (AIM).

The 1890 massacre. On Dec. 28, 1890, a band of about 350 Lakota Sioux sought by the Army surrendered near Wounded Knee Creek. The band, consisting of about 120 men and 230 women and children, were followers of the Ghost Dance religion, which taught that God would restore the Indian world to the way it was before whites arrived. Army leaders feared the religion would lead to an Indian uprising. About 470 troops surrounded the Lakota band. As the troops began to disarm the band the next day, someone—whether an Indian or a soldier is uncertain—fired a shot. The troops then fired on the Lakota with rifles and powerful, rapid-shooting Hotchkiss guns. The Lakota warriors fought back but were greatly outgunned. Some experts estimate that up to 300 Lakota were killed in the massacre or died later from wounds received in it. The dead included many unarmed women and children. Twenty-five soldiers were killed, most of them by Army cross fire. The incident is known as the Massacre of Wounded Knee or the Battle of Wounded Knee. It was the last armed conflict between the Sioux and the Army.

The 1973 incident involved about 200 armed Indians. They occupied Wounded Knee in part to protest federal policies toward Indians. The occupation also resulted from a dispute over tribal leadership that broke out among the Oglala Lakota. The occupiers demanded the return of lands taken from Indians in violation of treaty agreements. During the occupation, several gunfights took place between the occupiers and federal authorities. The occupation lasted 71 days and led to 2 deaths and over 300 arrests.   Jo Allyn Archambault

See also **Ghost Dance.**

Wovoka, *woh VOH kuh* (1856?-1932), a Paiute Indian religious leader, founded the Ghost Dance religion of 1890 among the Plains Indians. While sick with a fever in the late 1880's, he dreamed that God taught him a dance. God told him to teach his people to live peaceably and love others. Then no Indian would ever grow old or suffer illness or hunger. All the dead Indians and buffalo would come back to life. By doing the dance, which white people called the Ghost Dance, the Indians would make these good times come sooner. Wovoka based his teachings on a similar Ghost Dance religion that was founded in the late 1860's but which had died out.

Wovoka's religion was adopted by many Plains tribes that had been forced onto reservations and suffered from hunger and disease. Whites had wiped out the buffalo, the Indians' chief source of food. Although the religion was nonviolent, United States Army leaders feared it would lead to an uprising by Sioux Indians in what is now South Dakota. The Army had Indian police try to arrest Sioux chief Sitting Bull, but he was killed in the attempt. Sitting Bull's death led eventually to the deaths of many other Indians at Wounded Knee Creek in 1890.

Wovoka was born in Nevada. He grew up in the home of a white settler named David Wilson, who called Wovoka Jack Wilson.   Jerome A. Greene

See also **Ghost Dance; Wounded Knee.**

WPA. See Works Progress Administration.

Wrangell-St. Elias National Park, *RANG guhl SAYNT uhl EYE uhs,* is the largest national park in the United States. Located in southeastern Alaska, it covers about

8,332,000 acres (3,372,000 hectares), or about 13,000 square miles (34,000 square kilometers). It is so vast that few tourists have ever visited its remote parts. For location, see **Alaska** (political map).

The park includes the country's greatest collection of mountains that stand more than 16,000 feet (4,880 meters) high. The tallest, Mount St. Elias, rises 18,008 feet (5,489 meters). The park also has the largest group of glaciers in North America. Animals that live in the park include black bears, grizzly bears, caribou, moose, Dall's sheep, mountain goats, minks, sea otters, and trumpeter swans. The area was established as a national monument in 1978 and became a national park in 1980.

Critically reviewed by the National Park Service

Wrasse, *ras,* is the name of a family of over 500 species of ocean fish. Many species live in tropical reefs of the Atlantic, Pacific, and Indian oceans. Others live in cool waters off Europe, North America, Australia, and New Zealand. The *California sheepshead,* for example, is a wrasse found in cool Pacific waters from the Gulf of California in Mexico to Monterey Bay in California.

Wrasses show a greater variety of size, shape, and color than any other fish family. They range in size from 2 inches (5 centimeters) to 6 feet (1.8 meters). Some wrasses are long and cigar-shaped, and others are short and oval in outline. Many wrasses go through rapid, but temporary, color changes.

Wrasses start off life as females, but some individuals of a species turn into males as they grow older. Their color and shape often change dramatically with growth and the shift of sexes. For example, a small, strikingly colored young wrasse may change into a drab, medium-sized female, which may in time change into a larger, colorful male.

Many of the larger wrasses feed on crabs, snails, and clams, which they crush with strong teeth in their throat. The *cleaner wrasse* feeds on parasites it picks off the skin, gills, and mouth of other—often much larger—fish. The fish being cleaned will open its mouth and gills and allow the cleaner wrasse to enter. Most wrasses spend the night buried in the sand.   Tomio Iwamoto

See also **Fish** (picture: A wrasse and a blenny).

Scientific classification. Wrasses belong to the family Labridae. The scientific name for the California sheepshead is *Semicossyphus pulcher.* The cleaner wrasse is *Labroides dimidiatus.*

Wren is the name of a group of small, energetic birds found in most parts of the world. These birds are extremely protective of their nests. Some wrens are known to enter nearby nests of other birds and pierce the eggs. Wrens eat insects and seeds that they find in under-

Bewick's wren
Thryomanes bewickii
Found from southern Canada to Mexico
Body length $5\frac{1}{2}$ inches (14 centimeters)

WORLD BOOK illustrations by Guy Tudor

Karl Maslowski, Photo Researchers

The house wren often builds its nest in a backyard birdhouse. The entrance is about the size of a quarter.

Winter wren
Troglodytes troglodytes
Found in the Northern Hemisphere
(Body length 4 to 5 inches)

Riverside wren
Thryothorus semibadius
Found in Costa Rica and Panama
(Body length $5\frac{1}{2}$ to $5\frac{3}{4}$ inches)

brush and tangled root growths. They sing melodiously, but can also make harsh, chattering sounds. There are 63 types of wrens, most of which live in Asia and the Americas. Only one kind lives in Europe.

A wren has a slender bill and rounded wings. Most wrens are brown and may be striped, spotted, or streaked with black or white. Wrens have short tails that they often hold upward.

The *house wren,* commonly known as the *jenny wren,* is the most familiar wren in North America. It is about 5 inches (13 centimeters) long. It often lives in cities, where many people build birdhouses for it. Gardeners value the house wren because it eats insects. The female house wren lays six to eight eggs a year. The eggs are white and speckled with brownish-red.

The largest wren in North America is the *cactus wren,* which grows to $8\frac{1}{2}$ inches (22 centimeters) long. This wren lives in dry regions of the southwestern United States and northern Mexico. Its back, wings, and tail are heavily streaked, and it has a broad stripe over each eye. The *rock wren* lives in the western section of the United States. It builds its nest under rocks in the dry foothills of the Rocky Mountains. Most rock wrens are gray-brown with cinnamon coloring near the tail. The *Carolina wren* lives in the southern part of the United States. Its back is rust-brown, and its belly is dull yellow. Most Carolina wrens nest around farm buildings.

Other wrens common in the United States are the Bewick's wren, winter wren, marsh wren, and sedge wren. The *Bewick's wren* lives near people's homes. It has a white-edged tail and white stripes over its eyes. The *winter wren* nests in the Northern United States and in Canada. Its songs echo through evergreen forests in these regions. The *marsh wren* nests in cattail marshes. The *sedge wren* prefers grassy marshes and meadows. The marsh wren, which is more common, has a gurgling song. The sedge wren's song is like the sound made by striking two pebbles together rapidly.

Edward H. Burtt, Jr.

Scientific classification. Wrens are in the wren family, Troglodytidae. The house wren is *Troglodytes aedon,* and the cactus wren is *Campylorhynchus brunneicapillus.*

See also **Bird** (pictures: Birds of brushy areas; Birds' eggs; table: State and provincial birds).

Wren, Sir Christopher (1632-1723), was an English architect, scientist, and mathematician. After the Great Fire of London in 1666, he redesigned part or all of 55 of the 87 churches that it destroyed. The most famous one is St. Paul's Cathedral (1675-1710). The grace and variety of many of Wren's church spires are still a feature of the London skyline. His other major buildings include the churches of St. Bride (about 1678) and St. James (about 1684); Royal Hospital, Chelsea (1682-1689); and Greenwich Hospital (about 1715).

Wren was born on Oct. 20, 1632, in the county of Wiltshire. His early interests and training were in science and mathematics. From 1641 to 1646, he attended Westminster School in London.The poet John Dryden and the philosopher John Locke were fellow students. Wren got his B.A. degree from Oxford University in 1651 and his M.A. degree there in 1653. In 1657, he was appointed professor of astronomy at Gresham College in London.

In 1661, King Charles II appointed Wren to the important architectural position of assistant surveyor general. Unlike other English architects of his day, Wren never went to Italy to study classical architecture. However, he did visit France in 1665, and the architecture he saw there can be seen in his work. Wren received many honors. He was recognized as a founding member of the Royal Society in 1660.   J. William Rudd

For a picture of the exterior of St. Paul's Cathedral, see **Architecture** (Baroque); for a picture of the interior of this cathedral, see **London** (Visitor's guide). See also **England** (The arts); **London** (Churches).

Additional resources

Downes, Kerry. *The Architecture of Wren.* Universe Bks., 1982.
Hart, Vaughan. *St. Paul's Cathedral.* Phaidon, 1995.
Tinniswood, Adrian. *His Invention So Fertile: A Life of Christopher Wren.* Oxford, 2001.

Wrestling, *REHS lihng,* is a sport in which two opponents try to *pin* (hold) each other's shoulders to a mat on the floor. Wrestlers use maneuvers called *holds* to grasp their opponents and control their movements.

Successful wrestling demands strength, speed, coordination, balance, physical conditioning, and knowledge of body leverage. A clever wrestler can often defeat a stronger and heavier opponent.

Eric Crichton, Bruce Coleman Ltd.

Wren's Greenwich Hospital is typical of the architect's style in its repetition of columns and arches. The buildings, which are located in Greenwich, a borough of London, now house the Royal Naval College.

There are more than 50 kinds of wrestling. Each has its own rules. Some kinds do not require a pin for victory. In Japanese *sumo,* for example, a wrestler tries to throw his opponent to the ground or force him outside a 15-foot (4.6-meter) circle.

Amateur wrestling

Amateur wrestling is a popular sport in schools in the United States and Canada. Every year, students in elementary school through college take part in wrestling matches. National and world championship competitions are held annually. Every four years, wrestlers compete in the Summer Olympic Games. Wrestlers from Western Hemisphere nations also meet at four-year intervals in the Pan American Games.

The Fédération Internationale de la Lutte Amateur (FILA) governs international amateur wrestling. USA Wrestling governs the sport in the United States. Although amateur wrestling traditionally is a sport for boys and men, FILA established separate competition for women's freestyle wrestling in 1988.

Chief forms of wrestling. The two most popular forms of wrestling in the world are *Greco-Roman* and *freestyle.* Freestyle is the older of the two forms and the most popular in North America. It resembles the style practiced by the ancient Greeks. The Greco-Roman style developed after the Romans conquered Greece and modified the Greeks' style. Greco-Roman is the more popular form throughout Europe. International competition, including the Olympics, is held in both freestyle and Greco-Roman.

Most of the rules and procedures in the two styles are the same. The main difference concerns the use of the legs. In freestyle, wrestlers may use the legs to grasp an opponent's arms or legs, or to trip or tackle an opponent's legs. In Greco-Roman, a wrestler cannot attack an opponent's legs or attack with his own legs. The legs may be used only for support, so upper body strength and leverage are the chief factors.

Cameramann International, Ltd.

Sumo is the traditional form of wrestling in Japan. A wrestler tries to throw his opponent to the ground or force him outside a circle. Sumo wrestlers weigh over 300 pounds (136 kilograms).

How points are scored in college competition

Individual match points

Near fall	2 or 3 points
Takedown	2 points
Reversal	2 points
Time advantage (1 minute)	1 point
Escape	1 point

Dual meet points

Fall	6 points
Forfeit	6 points
Default	6 points
Disqualification	6 points
Match termination (by 15 points)	4 points
Decision (by 10 points)	4 points
Decision (by less than 10 points)	3 points

Some international wrestling meets feature competition in a style called *sambo,* or *sombo,* which originated in the Soviet Union in the 1930's. Sambo is a blend of several forms of wrestling and the martial arts, especially judo.

High school and intercollegiate wrestling. There are 13 weight classes in high school wrestling in the United States. There are 10 intercollegiate classes. A wrestler may weigh no more than the weight in his class, though he may weigh less. High school weight classes range from 100 pounds to a heavyweight class of no more than 275 pounds. Intercollegiate classes range from 118 pounds to no more than 275 pounds.

High school matches are divided into three periods of two minutes each. Intercollegiate matches begin with a three-minute period. The remaining two periods last two minutes each. Matches take place on a cushioned mat with a wrestling area at least 32 feet (9.75 meters) square or 32 feet in diameter. At least 5 feet (1.5 meters) of mat must surround the wrestling area. The first period begins with the wrestlers standing and facing each other. The second period begins with one wrestler having a choice of top position, bottom position, or neutral position, or the wrestler can defer the choice to the opponent. For a description of these positions, see the illustrations of holds and positions in this article.

Wrestlers receive points for skillfully executing various holds and maneuvers. They may also win points if their opponent commits a technical error, uses an illegal hold, or breaks a rule. The match ends when a wrestler gains a fall by holding his opponent's shoulders to the mat. The opponent's shoulders must be held for two seconds in a high school match and for one second in an intercollegiate match. If no fall occurs, the wrestler with the most points wins by a *decision.* The referee is sometimes assisted by a second referee.

International competition. There are 10 weight classes in both freestyle and Greco-Roman wrestling in international competition, including the Olympics. They range from 105.5 pounds to a class of no more than 286 pounds. The participants in each weight class are paired using a blind draw within a bracket system. The athletes wrestle for the first six places. The top three receive medals.

Each match consists of one five-minute period, plus a three-minute overtime if neither wrestler has scored at least three points. The wrestlers start the match on their

Wrestling holds and positions   These illustrations show some basic holds and positions college wrestlers use. Most wrestling holds and positions are used to pin an opponent or to control his movements.

A match begins when the wrestlers approach each other from opposite sides of the mat. Each wrestler tries to outmaneuver his opponent in an effort to pin his shoulders.

The starting position, also called the referee's position, begins the second and third periods. One starting position is shown on the left, with the offensive man on top and the defensive man on the bottom. In the *optional starting position,* shown on the right, the offensive man is behind the defensive man. The wrestlers reverse positions to begin the third period.

A take down is awarded when one wrestler puts his opponent on the mat from a *neutral position*—that is, from a position in which neither wrestler had control.

University of Iowa

A ride is one of several methods by which a wrestler controls the movements of his opponent. An offensive wrestler rides his opponent by controlling a leg and an arm.

An escape occurs when the wrestler on the bottom gains a neutral position and the top wrestler has lost control of his opponent. The referee awards the escaping wrestler 1 point.

A near fall is a position in which the offensive wrestler has his opponent in a controlled pinning position for two seconds. The referee awards either 2 or 3 points.

A fall ends a match. To gain a fall, a wrestler must pin his opponent's shoulders to the mat while the referee counts a specific amount of time, 1 second in college competition.

feet, facing each other. Three officials direct each match. At least two of them must agree on a decision.

Professional wrestling

Professional wrestling has become more of an entertainment spectacle than a sport. Showmanship often replaces skill. Most matches take place in a roped and padded ring similar to a boxing ring. Many wrestlers wear fantastic costumes and use unusual names. Many matches pair a "hero" against a "villain," and they often appear to be violently attacking each other.

History

Wrestling dates back to prehistoric times. In French caves, drawings and carvings 15,000 to 20,000 years old show wrestlers in various positions. Wrestling was introduced into the Olympic Games in Greece in 708 B.C. In America, Indians wrestled before Europeans arrived in the New World.   Dan Gable

See also **Olympic Games** (table; wrestling).

Wright, Frances (1795-1852), was a lecturer and journalist who worked to promote human rights in the United States. She supported women's rights, the abolition of slavery, and public education for children.

Wright was born in Scotland and came to the United

States in 1824. In 1828 and 1829, she toured the country, lecturing to large, working-class audiences. Wright argued that depriving women of equal rights lowered the quality of life for all people. She shocked audiences by claiming that women had a right to receive information on birth control and to seek divorces. Wright criticized organized religions because she believed they discouraged people from thinking for themselves.

In 1825, Wright founded Nashoba, a model community near Memphis in which slaves worked to buy their freedom. Nashoba failed and closed in 1827. Wright then joined a community founded by the Welsh-born social theorist Robert Owen in New Harmony, Ind. Wright and Owen's son, Robert D. Owen, edited the New Harmony *Gazette,* a magazine. From 1829 to 1832, they edited the magazine *Free Enquirer* in New York City.

June Sochen

Bettmann Archive

Frances Wright

Wright, Frank Lloyd (1867-1959), was one of America's most influential and imaginative architects. In his career of almost 70 years, he created a striking variety of architectural forms. His works ranged from buildings typical of the late 1800's to ultramodern designs, such as his plan for a skyscraper 1 mile (1.6 kilometers) high.

Wright became internationally famous as early as 1910, but he never established a style that dominated either American or European architecture. His influence was great but generally indirect. It was spread as much by his speeches and writings as by his buildings and designs. His *Autobiography* (1932, revised 1943 and 1977), one of the great literary self-portraits of the 1900's, provides insights into his philosophy of architecture.

Early career. Wright was born on June 8, 1867, in Richland Center, Wisconsin. He studied engineering briefly at the University of Wisconsin in the mid-1880's. In 1887, Wright moved to Chicago, where he became a draftsman for Joseph Lyman Silsbee, a noted Midwestern architect. Wright designed his first building while working for Silsbee.

Later in 1887, Wright joined the staff of the famous Chicago architects Dankmar Adler and Louis Sullivan. He soon became their chief draftsman. Wright left Adler and Sullivan in 1893 to establish his own practice. Wright's work after 1893 reflected Sullivan's influence, especially in attempts to harmonize a building's form with its function. See **Sullivan, Louis H.**

Wright's first distinctive buildings were homes designed in his famous *Prairie style.* In a typical Prairie house, spaces inside the home expand into the outdoors through porches and terraces. Because of their low, horizontal form, the homes seem to grow out of the ground. This effect was emphasized by Wright's use of wood and other materials as they appear in nature.

Wright designed many Prairie houses in and around Chicago. The Willits House (1902) in Highland Park, Illinois, was shaped like a cross, with the rooms arranged so they seemed to flow into one another. The Robie House (1909-1910) in Chicago looks like a series of horizontal layers floating over the ground.

Wright's nonresidential designs of the early 1900's included the Larkin Soap Company administration building (1904-1906) in Buffalo, New York, and Unity Temple (1906-1908) in Oak Park, Illinois. The core of the Larkin building was a skylighted court. Unity Temple was one of the nation's first public buildings whose concrete construction formed part of its exterior. In most earlier concrete buildings, the concrete had been covered with

some other materials.

In 1910, a German publishing firm printed a luxurious volume of illustrations of Wright's drawings and plans. A second volume appeared in 1911. These books and later publications of Wright's works strongly influenced the development of architecture in Europe from about 1913 through the 1920's. European architects were especially impressed by Wright's complex use of cubic shapes.

Karsh, Ottawa

Frank Lloyd Wright

During the 1920's, Wright designed several houses in southern California that are noted for the use of precast concrete blocks. He also planned the Imperial Hotel complex (1915-1922) in Tokyo. The hotel was designed to withstand the earthquakes common in Japan and was one of the few undamaged survivors of a severe earthquake that struck Tokyo in 1923.

Later career. In 1932, Wright founded the Taliesin Fellowship. This fellowship was made up of architectural students who paid to live and work with Wright. They worked during the summer at Taliesin, Wright's home near Spring Green, Wisconsin. In winter, they worked at Taliesin West, Wright's home in Scottsdale, Arizona. Today, Taliesin and Taliesin West operate jointly as the Frank Lloyd Wright School of Architecture.

Wright's projects of the 1930's included the Kaufmann "Fallingwater" house (1936-1937) at Bear Run near Uniontown, Pennsylvania, and the Johnson Wax Company administration building (1936-1939) in Racine, Wisconsin. The Kaufmann house was dramatically perched over a waterfall and became a symbol for the general public of far-out modern architecture. The Johnson Wax building featured a smooth, curved exterior of brick and glass. The design expressed the streamlined style in automobiles and other products of the late 1930's. A laboratory tower designed by Wright was added later.

During his final years, Wright designed two of his most famous projects—the Guggenheim Museum (completed in 1959) in New York City and the Marin County (California) Civic Center. The interior of the museum is dominated by a spiral ramp that runs from the floor almost to the ceiling. The Civic Center is a series of long structures that connects three hills. About nine build-

Ed Kumler, Tom Stack & Assoc.

Wright's Marin County Civic Center was one of his final and most imaginative designs. This series of long structures connects several hills near San Francisco.

Wright's Robie House is an example of his Prairie style. He tried to blend the structure with its natural surroundings.

ings are planned for the center, which still has not been completed.   Leland M. Roth

For additional pictures of Wright's work, see **Architecture** (Frank Lloyd Wright); **Florida** (People); **Furniture** (Organic design); **United States** (The arts).

Additional resources

Levine, Neil. *The Architecture of Frank Lloyd Wright.* Princeton, 1996.
Middleton, Haydn. *Frank Lloyd Wright.* Heinemann Lib., 2002. Younger readers.

Wright, James Claude, Jr. (1922-   ), a Texas Democrat, served as speaker of the United States House of Representatives from 1987 to 1989. Wright resigned as speaker and as a member of Congress after the House Committee on Standards of Official Conduct accused him of breaking a number of House ethics rules.

One charge was that Wright had accepted about $145,000 worth of gifts from a Texas real estate developer who was in a position to benefit directly from legislation over which Wright had influence. The committee also accused Wright of earning more income from outside sources than House rules permitted. According to the committee, the extra income was disguised as earnings from the sale of Wright's book *Reflections of a Public Man* (1984). Wright denied that he had broken any House rules. But he resigned as speaker and gave up his seat in Congress. Before becoming speaker, Wright had served as majority leader of the House since 1976.

Wright was born on Dec. 22, 1922, in Fort Worth, Texas, and attended Weatherford College and the University of Texas. He left the university in 1941, during World War II, to enlist in the Army Air Forces. From 1947 to 1949, Wright served in the Texas House of Representatives. Then, at the age of 26, he was elected mayor of Weatherford, Texas. He was mayor until 1954, when he won election to the U.S. House of Representatives.

In Congress, Wright supported generous spending for defense and highway construction. He also favored water conservation.   Nancy Dickerson Whitehead

Wright, Richard (1908-1960), is often considered the most important African American writer of his time. He earned a reputation for artistic excellence and outspoken criticism of racial discrimination.

Wright gained his reputation as a result of four books written early in his career. *Uncle Tom's Children* (1938), in its first edition, consists of four stories set in the

South about black males who are victims of racial violence. Wright's first novel, *Native Son* (1940), tells the story of Bigger Thomas, a 19-year-old Chicago black who accidentally commits murder. Bigger is pursued, tried, and sentenced to death. The novel condemns the racial injustice that creates an environment forcing Bigger into crime. Wright warns that this environment threatens to produce new Biggers. Wright's *12 Million Black Voices* (1941) is a pictorial history of blacks in the United States. *Black Boy* (1945) is Wright's story of his childhood and youth in Mississippi and Tennessee.

Wright also wrote poetry, as well as nonfiction, about his ideas and experiences. *White Man, Listen!* (1957) is a collection of some of his essays. Wright explains why he abandoned Communism in an essay published in an anthology of writings by former Communists called *The God That Failed* (1949). He continued his autobiography in *American Hunger* (published in 1977 after his death). He was born on Sept. 4, 1908, near Natchez, Mississippi, and died on Nov. 28, 1960.   Nellie Y. McKay

Additional resources

Fabre, Michel. *The Unfinished Quest of Richard Wright.* Rev. ed. Univ. of Ill. Pr., 1992. *The World of Richard Wright.* Univ. Pr. of Miss., 1985.
Gates, Henry L., Jr., and Appiah, K. A., eds. *Richard Wright: Critical Perspectives Past and Present.* Amistad Pr., 1993.

Wright, Willard H. See Van Dine, S. S.
Wright brothers—Wilbur (1867-1912) and Orville (1871-1948)—invented and built the first successful airplane. On Dec. 17, 1903, they made the world's first flight in a power-driven, heavier-than-air machine near Kitty Hawk, North Carolina. With Orville at the controls, the plane flew 120 feet (37 meters) and was in the air 12 seconds. The brothers made three more flights that day. The longest, by Wilbur, was 852 feet (260 meters) in 59 seconds.

Besides the Wrights, four men and one boy witnessed the flights. One of the men snapped a picture of the plane just as Orville piloted it into the air. Only a few newspapers mentioned the event, and their stories were inaccurate. The Wrights continued to fly from a pasture near their hometown of Dayton, Ohio, but local newspapers remained uninterested. The Wrights issued a statement about their achievement to the press in January 1904. It received little attention. Octave Chanute, an American civil engineer, reported their success in an article appearing in the March 1904 issue of *Popular Science Monthly.* The first eyewitness report of a flight by the Wrights appeared in a magazine called *Gleanings in Bee Culture* in January 1905.

Despite some factual and accurate stories, the Wrights' achievement was practically unknown for five years. Most people at that time remained doubtful about flying machines. In any case, the Wrights preferred to work quietly, perfecting their airplane and developing flight technique. They believed that airplanes would eventually be used to transport passengers and mail. They also hoped airplanes might serve to prevent war.

Early life. Wilbur Wright was born on April 16, 1867, on a farm 8 miles (13 kilometers) from New Castle, Indiana, and Orville was born on Aug. 19, 1871, in Dayton, Ohio. Their father was a bishop of the United Brethren Church. The boys went through high school, but neither received a diploma. Wilbur did not bother to go to the

Underwood & Underwood

Orville Wright   **Wilbur Wright**

commencement exercises, and Orville took special subjects rather than a prescribed course in his final year. Mechanics fascinated them even in childhood. To earn pocket money they sold homemade mechanical toys. Orville started a printing business, building his own press. They later launched a weekly paper, the *West Side News,* with Wilbur as editor. Wilbur was 25 and Orville 21 when they began to rent and sell bicycles. Then they began to manufacture them, assembling the machines in a room above their shop.

Flying experiments. After reading about the death of pioneer glider Otto Lilienthal in 1896, the brothers became interested in flying. They began serious reading on the subject in 1899, and soon obtained all the scientific knowledge of aeronautics then available.

On the advice of the Weather Bureau (now the National Weather Service) in Washington, D.C., the Wrights selected for their experiments a narrow strip of sand called Kill Devil Hill, near the settlement of Kitty Hawk, N.C. In 1900, they tested their first glider that could carry a person. The glider measured 16 feet (5 meters) from wing tip to wing tip. They returned to Kitty Hawk in 1901 with a larger glider. They showed that they could control sidewise balance by presenting the tips of the right and left wings at different angles to the wind. But neither the 1900 nor the 1901 glider had the lifting power they had counted on.

The Wrights concluded that all published tables of air pressures on curved surfaces must be wrong. They set up a 6-foot (1.8-meter) wind tunnel in their shop and began experiments with model wings. They tested more than 200 wing models in the tunnel. From the results of their tests, the brothers made the first reliable tables of air pressures on curved surfaces. These tables made it possible for them to design a machine that could fly.

The brothers built a third glider and took it to Kitty Hawk in the summer of 1902. This glider, based on their new figures, had aerodynamic qualities far in advance of any tried before. With it, they solved most of the problems of balance in flight. They made nearly 1,000 glides in this model, and, on some, covered distances of more than 600 feet (180 meters). Their basic patent, applied for in 1903, relates to the 1902 glider.

First airplane. Before leaving Kitty Hawk in 1902, the brothers started planning a power airplane. By the fall of 1903, they completed building the machine at a cost of less than $1,000. It had wings $40\frac{1}{2}$ feet (12 meters) long and weighed about 750 pounds (340 kilograms) with the pilot. They designed and built their own lightweight gasoline engine for the airplane.

The Wrights went to Kitty Hawk in September 1903, but a succession of bad storms and minor defects delayed their experiment at Kill Devil Hill until December 17. They had reason to be sure of their eventual success because their gliders had proven their airplane's design and control system to be sound. The brothers had also become skilled pilots. Their understanding of aerodynamics and ability as pilots set them apart from most others who tried and failed to fly powered airplanes.

The Wrights continued their experiments at a field near Dayton in 1904 and 1905. In 1904, they made 105 flights, but totaled only 45 minutes in the air. Two flights lasted five minutes each. On Oct. 5, 1905, the machine flew 24.2 miles (38.9 kilometers) in 38 minutes 3 seconds. When the Wrights first offered their machine to the U.S. government, they were not taken seriously. But by 1908 they closed a contract with the U.S. Department of War for the first military airplane. Meanwhile, they resumed experimental flights near Kitty Hawk that newspapers reported at great length.

Immediately after these trials, Wilbur went to France, where he aroused the admiration and enthusiasm of thousands. He made flights to altitudes of 300 feet (91 meters) and more. He arranged with a French company for the construction of his machine in France. When he returned to the United States, he made demonstration flights from Governors Island, N.Y., around the Statue of Liberty, up to Grant's Tomb, and back.

While Wilbur was in France, Orville made successful flights in the United States. On the morning of Sept. 9, 1908, he made 57 complete circles at an altitude of 120 feet (37 meters) over the drill field at Fort Myer, Va. He remained in the air 1 hour 2 minutes and set several records the same day. On September 17, however, while he was flying at 75 feet (23 meters), a blade of the right-hand propeller struck and loosened a wire of the rear rudder. The wire coiled about the blade and snapped it

Culver

The Wright brothers' first airplane reached a speed of about 30 miles (48 kilometers) per hour on its first flight in December 1903.

across the middle. The machine became difficult to manage and plunged to the earth. Orville suffered a broken thigh and two broken ribs. His passenger, Lieutenant Thomas E. Selfridge, died within three hours of a fractured skull. This accident was the most serious in the Wright brothers' career. Orville reappeared at Fort Myer the next year, fully recovered. He completed official tests with no evidence of nervousness.

In August 1909, the Wrights closed a contract with some wealthy men in Germany for the formation of a German-Wright Company. Later that year, they formed the Wright Company in New York City to manufacture airplanes. They earned some money but were troubled with imitators, infringements on their patents, conflicting claims, and lawsuits. From 1910 to 1912, the Wrights gave flying lessons to several people who later became aviation leaders and famous exhibition pilots.

After Wilbur's death. Wilbur died of typhoid fever on May 30, 1912, just as the airplane was beginning to make great advances. Orville worked on alone, and in 1913 won the Collier Trophy for a device to balance airplanes automatically. He sold his interest in the Wright Company and retired in 1915.

Orville continued work on the development of aviation in his own shop, the Wright Aeronautical Laboratory. In 1929, he received the first Daniel Guggenheim Medal for his and Wilbur's contributions to the advancement of aeronautics. He died on Jan. 30, 1948. Wilbur was elected to the Hall of Fame for Great Americans in New York City in 1955, and Orville in 1965.

Orville sent the original plane flown near Kitty Hawk to the Science Museum in London in 1928. The Science Museum sent the plane to the United States in 1948, and it is now in the National Air and Space Museum in Washington, D.C. Basic principles of that plane are used in every airplane. The Kill Devil Hill Monument National Memorial in North Carolina became the Wright Brothers National Memorial in 1953.   Roger E. Bilstein

See also **Air Force, U.S.** (picture); **Aircraft, Military** (picture); **Airplane** (The Wright brothers; pictures); **Glider** (History; picture).

Additional resources

Freedman, Russell. *The Wright Brothers*. Holiday Hse., 1991. Younger readers.
Jakab, Peter L. *Visions of a Flying Machine: The Wright Brothers and the Process of Invention.* 1990. Reprint. Smithsonian Institution, 1997.

Wrist is the joint that connects the hand and the forearm. A person uses the wrist to move the hand up, down, and sideways. The word *wrist* also refers to an area of the upper part of the hand. This area includes eight small bones called *carpals.*

The carpal bones extend across the hand in two rows of four bones each. Strong tissues called *ligaments* bind the carpals in place, but they also permit movement. Three carpals of the upper row join the *radius,* one of the two bones of the forearm, to form the wrist joint. The *ulna,* the other bone of the forearm, does not connect with the carpals. It forms a joint with the radius just above the wrist. This joint permits the wrist to rotate and thus helps turn the palm of the hand up and down.

Cordlike tissues called *tendons* extend through the carpal area and connect the finger bones with muscles in the arm. When these arm muscles contract, they pull

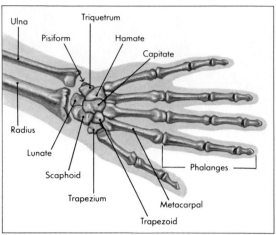

WORLD BOOK illustration by Lou Barlow

The wrist includes eight small, irregularly shaped bones located between the ulna and radius, the bones of the forearm, and the metacarpals, the bones of the palm.

the tendons and make the fingers move. The tendons on the palm side of the carpals bend the fingers. Those on the back of the hand straighten the fingers.

A fall on an outstretched arm may fracture one of the carpals, called the *scaphoid* bone, or the radius's lower end. Either injury is called a broken wrist. Many athletes suffer such fractures.   J. Donald Opgrande

See also **Carpal tunnel syndrome; Hand.**

Writ is generally used in its legal meaning to describe the written orders of a court of law. Many kinds of orders have specific names. For instance, if a court orders the sheriff to seize property that has been wrongfully taken, it gives the sheriff a *writ of replevin.* A *writ of habeas corpus* is designed to protect people taken into custody unlawfully. A *writ of error* is an order to a court to send records of a proceeding to a superior or appellate court, so that the judgment may be examined for errors of law. Early English-speaking people called anything in writing a writ. Even today, some people call the Bible the *Holy Writ.*   Paul C. Giannelli

Related articles in *World Book* include:

Attachment	Mandamus
Certiorari, Writ of	Subpoena
Habeas corpus	Summons
Injunction	

Writ of assistance was a general search warrant that permitted customs officers to enter premises in the daytime, using force if necessary, to search for goods imported illegally. The writs did not specify the place to be searched and were good for an unlimited time. But they expired six months after the death of a king. Writs were authorized for English customs officials in 1662. Courts in the American Colonies first issued them in the 1750's. The colonists strongly criticized the writs in the years before the Revolutionary War in America (1775-1783).

In 1761, James Otis of Boston tried to persuade the Superior Court of Massachusetts that writs of assistance violated "the fundamental principles of law." He failed. The controversy over such writs led to the prohibition of general warrants in the Fourth Amendment to the Constitution of the United States.   Pauline Maier

Writing, as a career, offers a range of personal rewards. It enables people to express themselves, as well as to entertain, inform, and influence others. With only a few tools—paper, a typewriter, a pencil, and often a personal computer—a writer can have an impact on the surrounding world. But most authors spend hundreds of hours perfecting their skills before they can sell any of their works.

There are two main kinds of writers, *staff writers* and *free-lance writers.* Staff writers are professional writers who work for a salary. Many earn a living as newspaper reporters or columnists. Others work as *technical writers,* who express the complex ideas of engineers and scientists in words that a nonexpert can understand. Many staff writers prepare documents for public agencies. Others work as editors for book publishers, magazines, or newspapers.

Free-lance writers get paid only if a publisher buys their work. Free-lancers write most books—both fiction and nonfiction—dramas, poems, screenplays, and short stories, as well as many magazine and newspaper articles. Many staff writers create free-lance material in addition to their regular work.

This article discusses the chief types of free-lance writing and tells how to submit works for publication. For some information on how to write, see *A Guide to Writing Skills* in the Research Guide/Index, Volume 22.

Preparing for a writing career. A person who wants to be a writer should set aside some time to write every day. Learning to express ideas clearly and effectively in writing takes a great deal of practice. Many experienced writers keep a journal. A journal can serve as a storehouse for information, observations, and ideas. It can also be a place to develop new material.

Beginning writers should read the many kinds of writing encountered every day and pay special attention to what they find most interesting. News items, feature stories, textbooks, cookbooks, repair manuals, poems, essays, short stories, novels, and plays differ in their methods of organizing and presenting material. A beginning writer who reads widely and carefully will develop an appreciation of different writing approaches and styles. In time, the writer can acquire a more flexible approach to his or her own work.

Successful authors write about subjects they know and understand. They sometimes take weeks or months revising or refining an article, poem, or story. Beginning writers usually benefit from finding one or more friendly critics who will read their work and discuss its strengths and weaknesses with them.

High schools and colleges offer many learning opportunities for young writers. Composition and literature courses can be helpful. Creative writing and journalism courses may further assist a beginning writer in developing his or her skills. Many students work on literary magazines, newspapers, or yearbooks published by their schools. They may write stories, edit articles, or gain other valuable experience.

Free-lance markets include book publishers, magazines, and newspapers. A reference book called *Writer's Market* lists the name, address, editorial needs, and policies of more than 5,000 magazines, publishers, and other literary markets. It also provides general information about methods of preparing a manuscript and the legal rights of authors and publishers. *Writer's Market* is revised annually and can be found in most public libraries. Articles in such monthly magazines as *The Writer* and *Writer's Digest* also offer helpful tips on how to write and sell manuscripts.

Some magazines welcome free-lance material. Many editors send a free copy of their magazine and a list of editorial guidelines to anyone who requests them. These materials can help free-lancers decide whether the content and style of their work would appeal to readers of a publication.

Some writers hire a *literary agent* to find markets for their works. An agent reads a client's manuscript and suggests ways to improve it. The agent then tries to sell the manuscript to a publisher. If the manuscript is sold, the agent receives a commission of 10 to 15 per cent of the author's income for that piece of writing. Beginning writers should try to sell their own works. Many agents work only with writers who have been recommended by editors or professional authors.

Nonfiction ranks as the largest market for free-lance writers. Book publishers buy about 10 times as many nonfiction manuscripts as novels. In most magazines, nonfiction articles greatly outnumber poems and short stories. Nonfiction articles range in length from a few hundred words to book length. Long articles may be *serialized* (published in installments) in a magazine.

Several kinds of publications accept nonfiction from free-lancers. General-interest magazines contain articles on current, popular subjects that appeal to a wide audience. Such magazines attract many professional writers. Readers of specialized publications share a common interest, such as a hobby, a political viewpoint, a specialized technical subject, or membership in a professional organization. Many beginners succeed in selling articles to these magazines, which attract relatively few well-known writers.

Writers should choose a topic that readers want to know more about. They may also select a topic that they care so much about they can make their readers care also. The writer should then choose a *format* (form of presentation) suited both to the subject and the kind of magazine that might publish the article. A beginning writer usually works up a topic and a way of presenting it alone. Later, the writer and an editor may cooperate on its revision. A free-lancer who writes about money might offer an article called "How to Find a Part-Time Job" to *Seventeen.* Another article, called "Stretching Your Food Dollars," might be sent to *Family Circle.* A writer should always use reliable sources so that the article presents accurate information.

Payment for nonfiction material varies widely. Specialized publications with a small readership usually offer lower payments than general-interest magazines with large readerships. Payment for a magazine article ranges from less than $100 to thousands of dollars. Book publishers usually pay authors a *royalty* (commission) of 10 to 15 per cent of the book's price for each copy sold.

Fiction sold by free-lance writers includes short stories of various kinds—adventure and confession tales, mysteries, romances, science fiction, and Westerns. Markets include many general-interest publications and fiction and literary magazines.

A writer who wants to write a novel should first

concentrate on writing the novel and then be concerned with selling it. But the writer may find it helpful to read other novels being written today and be familiar with books being issued by various publishers. In this way, a writer can learn which publishers are most likely to buy a particular kind of work.

Some writers submit an entire manuscript to a publisher. Others prefer to submit only the first few chapters of a novel, plus a one- or two-page summary of the plot. The length of time it takes editors to respond varies. A writer may inquire about the manuscript if there is no response after two or three months.

Poetry is one of the most challenging types of writing. It is also one of the lowest-paying. Some magazines only pay poets by giving them copies of the issues in which their work appears. Others pay a dollar or, more rarely, several dollars a line. Reading widely in modern poetry will stimulate many ideas. However, poems are not written by formula. Poems must come from the poet's own language, imagination, and experience.

Scriptwriting. Writing scripts for plays, movies, or television can bring great financial rewards. However, scriptwriting is an extremely competitive field in which relatively few people succeed. Scriptwriting can be less personal than other forms of writing. It may turn into a group project, with the actors and directors contributing to the completion of a script. Most plays produced on Broadway in New York City are written by established authors. Some off-Broadway and regional theaters have special programs to encourage the work of talented young playwrights. But most beginners have their works performed in school or community theaters. Many play producers and theaters list their interests and needs in *Writer's Digest* and such specialized publications as *The Dramatists Guild Quarterly, Information for Playwrights,* and *Scriptwriter News.*

Most professional and amateur productions pay the scriptwriter a percentage of the total box-office receipts as royalties. Royalties of 5 to 10 percent are common. Other forms of payment include buying the rights to the material and payment per performance.

Many motion-picture screenplays and television scripts are written by free-lance writers. Free-lancers should hire an agent to sell such material because movie and television producers rarely deal directly with an author. The size of the royalty depends on the writer's professional reputation and the quality of the script. Such publications as *Daily Variety, The Hollywood Reporter,* and *Scriptwriter News* help writers by reporting trends in the film and television industries.

Literature for children includes adventure stories, mysteries, and articles about folklore, nature, science, and famous people. Many children's magazines also buy quizzes, puzzles, and riddles. Articles and stories published in children's magazines are usually no more than 1,500 words long. Authors usually receive payment of about 4 cents per word or a single payment that is generally less than $100. Free-lance authors write nearly all of the juvenile books published yearly in the United States. Most publishing firms that specialize in children's books prefer to receive complete manuscripts.

Preparing and submitting a manuscript. All manuscripts should be neatly typed or printed from a computer. They should be on good-quality white paper, usu-

ally $8\frac{1}{2}$ by 11 inches (22 by 28 centimeters). The typist should doublespace and leave margins on the top, bottom, and sides of every page. Each page should be numbered, usually centered at the top of the page or toward the right margin. Often the first page is not numbered. The title and author's *by-line* should be centered halfway down the first page. A by-line shows the author's name as he or she wants it to appear in the published article or book. The writer should put his or her complete name, address, and phone number in the top corner of the first page. Many writers also put their last name by the page number on succeeding pages in case the manuscript gets divided up in an editor's office.

A writer may enclose a *cover letter* that briefly describes his or her qualifications for writing about the subject. A writer offering a literary work may wish to include just an introductory letter. Some editors prefer that free-lancers send a *query letter* that summarizes the manuscript before submitting the entire work. A writer should always enclose a stamped, self-addressed envelope for the editors to use to return the manuscript.

David Hamilton

Related articles in *World Book* include:

Autobiography	Ghost story	Novel
Biography	Literature	Poetry
Book	Literature for chil-	Publishing
Criticism	dren	Science fiction
Detective story	Magazine	Short story
Drama	Motion picture	Television (Writ-
Essay	(Development)	ers)
Fiction		

Additional resources

Burack, Sylvia K., ed. *The Writer's Handbook.* The Writer, frequently updated.
King, Stephen. *On Writing.* Scribner, 2000.

Writing is a system of human communication by means of visual symbols or signs. The earliest stages of writing date almost from the dawn of humanity. The first developed systems of writing appeared about 5,500 years ago, or possibly earlier, in Egypt and Mesopotamia. About 5,000 years ago, a developed writing system was used in Minoan Crete, and about 4,000 years ago, the Hittite people of Anatolia (modern Turkey) had a writing system. In China, bones dating from 3,500 years ago have been found which bear written inscriptions.

Counting devices have been used in all parts of the world. Such devices include sticks, pebbles, clay tokens, and strings. For example, a shepherd could record the exact number of sheep in his flock by cutting one notch in a stick for each sheep. He could also keep pebbles or clay tokens of about the same size and shape to represent the different kinds of animals in his care. The Inca of Peru tied knots in strings of various lengths and colors to keep accounts. These methods of counting could not easily be adapted to real writing.

Rock drawings conveyed a clearer meaning, but were not so useful for counting. A simple rock drawing was found near a dangerously steep trail in New Mexico. The design shows a mountain goat and a man riding a horse. The mountain goat stands on all fours, but the horse and rider are upside down. The design warns a horseman that a mountain goat can climb the rocky trail, but that his horse cannot.

Ideographs express an idea without any clear connection with any language. For example, a picture of a smiling face represents happiness. Any person can understand the idea of such a drawing, whether or not he or she speaks the language of the person who drew it. This way of expressing ideas, not necessarily in words, is called *ideography*. Pictures drawn for the purpose of communication differ only slightly from pictures drawn for artistic purposes. Communication pictures are simplified and stereotyped, and they have no details that are not needed as part of the communication.

Logographs. Human beings took the decisive step in developing real writing when they learned to express ideas indirectly. They did this by using signs that stood for the words in their language, not the ideas the words stood for. This kind of writing is called *logography.* To see how it works, take such a message as "The king killed a lion." In ideography, the message would include two drawings, one showing a man with the insignia of his office, such as a crown, holding a spear in his hand, and the other showing a lion. Logography, or word writing, would express the same message by signs that stand for the words themselves. One picture, of a man wearing a crown, stands for the word "king." A spear stands for the word "kill," and a drawing of a lion stands for "lion." If the king had killed three lions, the phrase "three lions" would be expressed in word writing by two signs, one standing for the numeral "three" and the other for "lion." In ideography, the message would have to contain pictures of three lions.

Early in the development of this kind of writing, the pictures became *conventional,* or simplified and formal. They often showed only a part for the whole, such as a crown for the word "king." But pictures cannot represent words like "the" or "a," nor can they represent grammatical endings like the "-ed" of "killed."

The Sumerians, who lived in southern Mesopotamia, were the first people to reach the stage of logographic writing, about 3500 B.C. They kept records with such simple entries as "10 arrows" and the sign for a personal name, or "5 cows" and the sign for another name. They could easily use signs for numbers and for items such as arrows or cows. But they had difficulty in writing names and abstract ideas.

Phonetization. To overcome these problems, the Sumerians found that they could use word-symbols of objects that were easy to picture, like "arrow," to stand for words that sounded similar, but were hard to picture. The sign for "arrow" could also stand for "life," because the word *ti* means both things in Sumerian. This principle of *phonetization,* often called the *rebus* principle, is the most important single step in the history of writing (see **Rebus**). If the arrow sign could stand for both "arrow" and "life," because they are both pronounced *ti,* why not use the arrow sign for the sound *ti* wherever it occurs, regardless of its meaning? The Sumerian language was made up largely of one-syllable words, so it was not difficult for the people to work out a *syllabary* of about one hundred phonetic signs.

Sumerian writing is called *logo-syllabic,* or word-syllabic. It uses both *logograms,* or word signs, and *syllabograms,* or syllabic signs. Logograms expressed most of the words in the language. Syllabograms expressed rare and abstract words and proper names. Sumerian writing gradually developed the wedgelike appearance we call *cuneiform.* The Babylonians and Assyrians took

cuneiform from the Sumerians, and the Hittites and other peoples learned it from them (see **Cuneiform**).

The Egyptians developed another important word-syllabic writing, *hieroglyphic,* about 3000 B.C. It resembled Sumerian in using word-signs but differed in the choice of syllabic signs. The Sumerians regularly indicated differences in vowels in their syllabic signs, but the Egyptians did not. The Hittites also had a writing of their own, *hieroglyphic Hittite,* that was related to some of the systems used in the lands around the Aegean Sea. See **Hieroglyphics**.

The Chinese, perhaps about 1500 B.C., began the most highly developed word writing in the world. The peoples of the Middle East usually had only a few hundred word signs, but the Chinese may have as many as 50,000. They use some of these signs for the syllables in proper names or in foreign words.

The alphabet. The older word-syllable systems were gradually simplified. From the complicated Egyptian system, the Semites of Syria and Palestine, especially the Phoenicians, developed simple systems of from 22 to 30 signs, each standing for a consonant followed by any vowel. The Japanese worked out a syllabic system with symbols for an initial consonant and different vowels. They also used many word symbols borrowed from Chinese. The Greeks were the first to evolve a system of vowel signs, creating the first alphabetic system of writing.   Harold Patrick Brent

Related articles. See the articles on letters of the alphabet. See also the following articles:

Aegean civilization	Egypt, Ancient (The	Manuscript
Alphabet	people)	Pictograph
Babylonia	Hittites	Rune
Chinese language	Inca	Sumer

Wrocław, *VRAWTS lahf* (pop. 643,600), is a city in Poland that serves as a rail center and river port. It lies in southwestern Poland on the Oder River (see **Poland** [political map]). Leading products of Wrocław include computers, machinery, and textiles. The city has two universities and a cathedral that dates from the 1100's. Wrocław became part of Poland in the 900's. Austria took over the city in 1526, and Prussia seized it in 1742. Wrocław became part of Germany in 1871. Its German name was *Breslau.* When World War II ended in 1945, Poland regained control of the city.   Janusz Bugajski

Wryneck, also called *snakebird,* is the name of two species of small birds. One species lives in Europe and one in Africa. Wrynecks nest in the hollows of trees. When disturbed, the bird thrusts its head and neck out of the nest and hisses. The bird's name comes from the twisting motion of its neck as it does this. The wryneck has brownish feathers marked with streaks and spots. The bird uses its long, slender tongue to reach into crevices for ants.

WORLD BOOK illustration by
Trevor Boyer, Linden Artists Ltd.

European wryneck

Scientific classification. Wrynecks make up the genus *Jynx* in the woodpecker family, Picidae.   Fred J. Alsop, III

Wu, *woo,* **Chien-shiung,** *chehn shung* (1912-1997), an American physicist, helped disprove the law of the conservation of parity (see **Parity** [physics]). For about 30 years, most physicists had accepted this law as a universal principle. But in 1957, Wu did an experiment that showed it to be incorrect. The law stated, in part, that electrons called *beta particles,* which are emitted by a radioactive nucleus, would fly off in any direction, regardless of the spin of the nucleus. Using atoms of cobalt-60, Wu showed that beta particles were more likely to be emitted in a direction that depended on the spin of the cobalt nuclei. Her experiment confirmed a theory proposed in 1956 by Chinese-born American physicists Tsung Dao Lee and Chen Ning Yang, who shared the 1957 Nobel Prize in physics for their work.

Wu was born on May 31, 1912, in Liuhe, China, near Shanghai. She moved to the United States in 1936 and received a Ph.D. degree from the University of California at Berkeley. Wu became a professor of physics at Columbia University in 1957.   Tian Yu Cao

Wu Daozi, *woo dow dzuh* (A.D. 700's), was a famous Chinese painter. His name is also spelled *Wu Tao-tzu.* He painted chiefly religious subjects on the walls of Buddhist and Taoist temples in the Chinese capital of Chang'an (now Xi'an). He usually worked on a large scale in black and white. His murals were destroyed, and we know his style only from descriptions and bad copies. He was born near Luoyang, in Henan.   Robert A. Rorex

Wu Tao-tzu. See Wu Daozi.

Wuchang. See Wuhan.

Wuhan, *woo hahn* (pop. 3,832,536), is the collective name for the adjacent cities of Hankou, Hanyang, and Wuchang in Hubei Province of China (see **China** [political map] for the location of Wuhan). The cities are considered a single political and economic unit. Wuchang lies on the south bank of the Yangtze River. Hankou and Hanyang are on the north bank. The Han River separates Hankou and Hanyang. The Han River bridge and ferries provide transportation between these two cities. The Yangtze bridge links Wuchang with Hanyang. Wuhan, an industrial center, was the birthplace of the Chinese Revolution in 1911.   Parris H. Chang

Wundt, *voont,* **Wilhelm,** *VIHL hehlm* (1832-1920), a German philosopher, became known as the father of modern psychology. He founded one of the first laboratories for experimental psychology in 1879. He believed the ways of studying psychology included both laboratory experimentation and *introspection* (self-observation). He was born on Aug. 16, 1832, in Neckarau, in Baden. See also **Psychology** (History).   Kenneth E. Clark

Wupatki National Monument, *wu PAT kee,* is in northern Arizona. It contains prehistoric dwellings, built by farming Indians. The Hopi Indians are believed to be partially descended from the Indians who built these dwellings. The monument was established in 1924. For its area, see **National Park System** (table: National monuments).   Critically reviewed by the National Park Service

WWF, formerly known as the World Wildlife Fund or the World Wide Fund for Nature, is one of the world's largest conservation organizations. Since it was founded in 1961, the organization has worked in over 100 countries to protect hundreds of plant and animal species and their habitats. The organization officially changed its name to WWF in 2001.

WWF campaigns to save such animals as the rhinoceros, tiger, elephant, and giant panda. The organization works to prevent the illegal use and trade of endangered species and their parts. These parts include tiger bone and rhinoceros horn. WWF has preserved vast areas of land and helped reduce exhaustion and pollution of natural resources. It campaigns about such issues as loss of fisheries, destruction of forests, and global warming.

The organization has more than 1 million members in the United States and about 5 million members worldwide. Its global headquarters are near Geneva, Switzerland.   Critically reviewed by WWF

Wyatt, *WY uht,* **Sir Thomas** (1503?-1542), was an English poet whose most important works are lyrics he wrote for lute accompaniment. Wyatt was active during the first phase of the English Renaissance. He adapted works by many writers, including the Italian Renaissance poet Luigi Alamanni. Wyatt and Henry Howard, Earl of Surrey, are credited with introducing Petrarch's sonnet techniques into English literature. Wyatt is usually linked in literary history with the Earl of Surrey because their poems were first published together in *The Book of Songs and Sonnets* (1557), usually called *Tottel's Miscellany.* See **Surrey, Earl of.**

Wyatt was born in Kent. He received a good education and traveled on the European continent as a diplomat for King Henry VIII. Wyatt wrote a satire on court life called *Mine Owne John Poins.*   John N. King

Wycherley, *WIHCH uhr lee,* **William** (1640?-1716), an English playwright, ranks with Sir George Etherege and William Congreve as a leading author of witty satires called *comedies of manners* during the Restoration period of English literature. Many of Wycherley's plays are brutally satiric, and his attitude toward people is often venomous and cynical.

Wycherley's first plays, *Love in a Wood* (1671) and *The Gentleman Dancing Master* (1672), are light comedies of intrigue. *The Country Wife* (1675) best reveals Wycherley's attitude toward his society and toward humanity. Most of the characters are fools, *cuckolds* (husbands of unfaithful wives), or comically shrewd seekers of sexual pleasures. *The Plain Dealer* (1676) is based partly on plays by William Shakespeare and Molière, but it is more savage in its presentation of humanity. Wycherley was born in the county of Shropshire.   Albert Wertheim

Wycliffe, *WIHK lihf,* **John** (1328?-1384), was a leading English philosopher in religion and politics during the late Middle Ages. His challenges to religious and political practices remained influential long after his death.

Wycliffe was educated at Oxford University and became a *master* (professor) there at Balliol College in 1360. At one time, he served as a parish priest, but he was best known as a professor of philosophy.

Wycliffe felt driven to become a reformer because of conditions in Europe during his time. An epidemic of plague, now known as the Black Death, killed between one-fourth and one-half of Europe's population in the middle to late 1300's. The Hundred Years' War between England and France began in 1337. Throughout the 1300's, violent struggles for power occurred between the popes and clergy on one side, and the kings and their nobles on the other. Both sides seemed corrupt and dominated by self-interest, and apparently neither cared about the common people.

The conditions in Europe raised many questions in people's minds. Was the pope lord over kings? Could a civil government punish a wicked bishop or priest? Could a civil government tax the church, or could the church demand that the government support it? Could church rulers or civil rulers make laws merely because they wished to, or did their laws have to be fair? Wycliffe dealt with these issues in his lectures and books. His chief political idea was summarized in the statement, "Dominion is founded in grace." He meant that unjust rulers could not claim that people must obey them because obedience was God's will. After Wycliffe applied this idea to the popes and bishops, he was tried several times in church courts. Each time, the English royal family saved him from condemnation.

By about 1371, Wycliffe had become a writer for the royal family and its supporters against the bishops and their followers. He evidently felt that there was more hope of reform from the royal family. Wycliffe tried to show that the claim to authority by popes and bishops was founded on false ideas of the superiority of priests over lay people. He denied the doctrine of transubstantiation, which he regarded as the basis of the clergy's claim to superiority. According to this doctrine, priests changed bread and wine into the body and blood of Jesus Christ during the Mass. In Wycliffe's later writings, he declared that the Bible, not the church, was the authority for Christian beliefs.

Wycliffe's followers, with his help and inspiration, translated the Bible into English about 1382. They completed an improved version about 1388, after his death. Wycliffe's followers, called *Lollards,* were severely persecuted in England (see **Lollards**). The upper classes felt that Wycliffe's ideas encouraged the poor to demand better lives.

Wycliffe's writings influenced a number of reformers, including John Hus of Bohemia. Many early English Protestants regarded the teachings of Wycliffe as forerunners of those of the Reformation. They considered Wycliff the first great English reformer.

Peter W. Williams

Wyeth, Andrew (1917-), probably ranks as the most popular American painter of his time. He is best known for his realistic and thoughtful pictures of people and places in rural Pennsylvania and Maine.

Wyeth's paintings show uncrowded rural scenes that are reminders of earlier American life. His works include pictures of old buildings with bare windows and cracked ceilings, and abandoned boats on deserted beaches. Such scenes portray the remains of past activity rather than the accomplishments of the present. Wyeth also depicts the people he knows. In 1986, he revealed a group of works representing a neighbor named Helga. She had been one of his favorite subjects for 15 years. An example of his portraits, *Albert's Son,* appears in the **Painting** article.

Wyeth paints in a style that follows the tradition of Thomas Eakins and Winslow Homer, two American realist painters of the late 1800's. His work is often extremely detailed. Wyeth paints in *egg tempera,* a medium that allows him to represent tiny details and gives his pictures a smooth, delicate surface. He also uses a water-color technique called *dry brush.*

Christina's World (1948) tempera on gessoed panel © Andrew Wyeth The Museum of Modern Art, New York City (photo © The Museum of Modern Art/Art Resource)

Wyeth's *Christina's World* shows the artist's disabled friend Christina Olson on her farm in Maine. The detailed realism and the haunting sense of loneliness are typical of Wyeth's style.

Wyeth was born on July 12, 1917, in Chadds Ford, Pennsylvania, near Philadelphia. His father, N. C. Wyeth, was a noted illustrator (see **Literature for children** [picture: Great illustrators of the 1900's]). He gave Andrew an appreciation of disciplined drafting skills. Andrew Wyeth's son Jamie is also a painter. Sarah Burns

Wyler, William (1902-1981), was a motion-picture director whose films have a high artistic quality and wide popular appeal. He won Academy Awards for his directing in *Mrs. Miniver* (1942), *The Best Years of Our Lives* (1946), and *Ben-Hur* (1959). His other important films include *Dodsworth* (1936), *Dead End* (1937), *Jezebel* (1938), *Wuthering Heights* (1939), *The Letter* (1940), *The Little Foxes* (1941), *The Heiress* (1948), *Roman Holiday* (1953), *The Desperate Hours* (1955), *Friendly Persuasion* (1956), *The Big Country* (1958), and *Funny Girl* (1968).

Wyler was born on July 1, 1902, in Mulhouse, France. His real name was Willy Wyler. He was a film publicist in Europe before coming to Hollywood in 1920 as an assistant director. Wyler directed his first motion picture in 1925. He became a United States citizen in 1928. Wyler died on July 29, 1981. Gene D. Phillips

Wylie, Elinor (1885-1928), was an American poet. Her style is noted for its rich, exact vocabulary and its brilliant word pictures. Wylie experimented widely in traditional verse forms, and was equally skilled using such forms as blank verse and the sonnet. Her goal as a poet was the refinement of verse technique.

Wylie had a short but brilliant literary career. She became known in 1921 with the publication of her first major collection, *Net to Catch the Wind.* She wrote three more volumes of poetry: *Black Armour* (1923), *Trivial Breath* (1928), and *Angels and Earthly Creatures* (published in 1929, after her death). Wylie also wrote four novels, all with historical backgrounds. The best known is *Jennifer Lorn* (1923).

Wylie was born on Sept. 7, 1885, in Somerville, New Jersey. Her maiden name was Elinor Hoyt. She wrote under the name of her second husband, Horace Wylie. In 1923, she married her third husband, William Rose Benét. After her death, Benét edited Wylie's *Collected Poems* (1932) and *Collected Prose* (1933). Wylie died on Dec. 16, 1928. Bonnie Costello

See also **Benét, William Rose.**

John M. Burnley, Bruce Coleman Inc.

The Teton Mountains rise sharply from a beautiful valley called Jackson Hole in northwestern Wyoming. The Grand Teton peak, *center,* rises to a height of 13,770 feet (4,197 meters). The majestic mountains are a feature of Grand Teton National Park.

Wyoming *The Equality State*

Wyoming is a state of the United States that is famous for the beauty of its mountains. The peaks of the Rocky Mountains tower over the landscape. They provide the setting for the world's oldest national park—Yellowstone. Wyoming also has the first national monument in the United States, Devils Tower, and the first national forest, Shoshone. Another famous scenic wonder, Grand Teton National Park, includes some of the West's most beautiful mountains. Millions of tourists visit Wyoming each year to enjoy the state's scenery and historic places.

Not all of Wyoming is mountainous. Between the mountain ranges in the state lie broad, flat, treeless basins. Some of these basins are dotted with rugged, lonely towers of rock called *buttes.* In the eastern part of

The contributors of this article are Ronald E. Beiswenger, Professor of Geography at the University of Wyoming; and Phil Roberts, Assistant Professor of History at the University of Wyoming.

the state, a flat, dry plain stretches westward toward the mountains.

Much of Wyoming's wealth comes from its land. About 50 percent of the state's land is used for grazing. Thousands of oil wells dot the prairies. Visitors to Wyoming may see a white-face steer cropping the grass near a pumping oil well. Petroleum, natural gas, coal, and other mineral products make Wyoming an important mining state.

Most of Wyoming's workers are employed in service industries. Service industries include such activities as education, health care, and retail trade.

The federal government owns almost half the land in Wyoming. Since the state depends mostly on its land, this makes the government especially important in Wyoming's economy. Federal agencies control grazing, logging, and mining activities that take place on the government land. The U.S. Air Force operates a nuclear missile base just outside Cheyenne, the state capital.

Wyoming has attracted travelers since the earliest

Interesting facts about Wyoming

The world's largest bronze bust, a likeness of Abraham Lincoln, is located near Laramie. University of Wyoming sculptor Robert Russin created the bust, which weighs 3 short tons (3.2 metric tons). It is 12 feet (3.8 meters) tall and rests on a stone base 30 feet (9 meters) high.

Independence Rock is a granite boulder located near Casper. It rises to a height of 193 feet (59 meters) and covers 27 acres (11 hectares). The rock is called the "Register of the Desert." More than 5,000 pioneers have carved their names on the rock, some as long ago as the early 1800's.

It took four treaties for the United States to get the land that makes up Wyoming, more than for any other state.

Independence Rock

The National Elk Refuge

The National Elk Refuge, near Jackson, was established in 1912. It was the first big-game refuge created before the animals to be protected were considered endangered. The refuge covers about 25,000 acres (10,000 hectares). From 7,000 to 8,000 elk feed there each winter. The first national forest, Shoshone, and the first national park, Yellowstone, are also in Wyoming.

Ranchers round up cattle on a Wyoming range. Ranching ranks as the leading agricultural activity in the state. About 50 per cent of Wyoming's land is used to graze cattle and sheep.

days of white settlement. Three of the great pioneer trails cross Wyoming. The California, Mormon, and Oregon trails all took the covered wagons through South Pass. This pass became famous as the easiest way for the pioneers to travel across the mountains.

Millions of people have crossed Wyoming, but relatively few have stayed. The 1980 United States census reported that Wyoming had fewer people than any other state except Alaska. The 1990 census showed that Alaska had passed Wyoming, leaving Wyoming last among the states in population. Wyoming's largest city, Cheyenne, has only about 50,000 people.

The word *Wyoming* comes from a Delaware Indian word meaning *upon the great plain.* Wyoming is nicknamed the *Equality State* because Wyoming women were the first in the nation to vote, hold public office, and serve on juries. In 1870, Wyoming's Esther H. Morris became the nation's first woman justice of the peace. In 1924, Wyoming voters elected the first woman governor, Nellie Tayloe Ross.

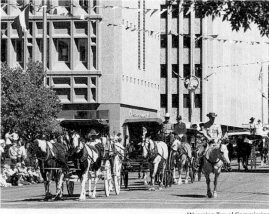

Frontier Days, Wyoming's most popular annual event, takes place during late July in Cheyenne. The festival has been held each year since 1897. Cheyenne is the capital of Wyoming.

Wyoming in brief

Symbols of Wyoming

The state flag, adopted in 1917, shows the seal on a buffalo to represent the branding of livestock. The red border symbolizes Indians and the blood of the pioneers. On the state seal, adopted in 1893, the woman and the motto symbolize equal rights in Wyoming, the first state to grant unrestricted civil and political rights to women. A cowboy and a miner represent the state's important livestock and mining industries.

State flag

State seal

Wyoming (brown) ranks ninth in size among all the states and fourth among the Rocky Mountain States (yellow).

General information

Statehood: July 10, 1890, the 44th state.
State abbreviations: Wyo. (traditional); WY (postal).
State motto: *Equal Rights.*
State song: "Wyoming." Words by Charles E. Winter; music by G. E. Knapp.

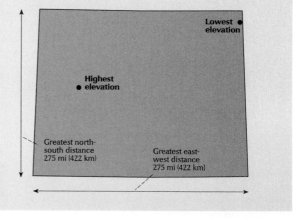

The State Capitol is in Cheyenne, the capital of Wyoming since 1869.

Land and climate

Area: 97,818 mi² (253,349 km²), including 714 mi² (1,848 km²) of inland water.
Elevation: *Highest*—Gannett Peak, 13,804 ft (4,207 m) above sea level. *Lowest*—Belle Fourche River in Crook County, 3,100 ft (945 m) above sea level.
Record high temperature: 115 °F (46 °C) at Basin on Aug. 8, 1983.
Record low temperature: −66 °F (−54 °C) at Moran, near Elk, on Feb. 9, 1933.
Average July temperature: 67 °F (19 °C).
Average January temperature: 19 °F (−7 °C).
Average yearly precipitation: 13 in (33 cm).

Lowest elevation

Highest • elevation

Greatest north-south distance 275 mi (422 km)

Greatest east-west distance 275 mi (422 km)

Important dates

Robert Stuart discovered South Pass, which became an important pioneer route across the Rocky Mountains.

The Union Pacific Railroad entered Wyoming.

| 1807 | 1812 | 1834 | 1867 | 1872 |

John Colter explored the Yellowstone area.

William Sublette and Robert Campbell established Fort William (later Fort Laramie).

Yellowstone became the first national park.

State bird
Meadowlark

State flower
Indian paintbrush

State tree
Cottonwood

People

Population: 493,782
Rank among the states: 50th
Density: 5 per mi² (2 per km²), U.S. average 78 per mi² (30 per km²)
Distribution: 65 percent urban, 35 percent rural

Largest cities in Wyoming

Cheyenne	53,011
Casper	49,644
Laramie	27,204
Gillette	19,646
Rock Springs	18,708
Sheridan	15,804

Source: 2000 census.

Population trend

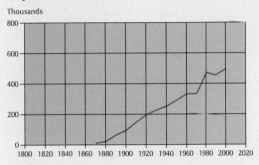

Thousands

Source: U.S. Census Bureau.

Year	Population
2000	493,782
1990	453,588
1980	469,557
1970	332,416
1960	330,066
1950	290,529
1940	250,742
1930	225,565
1920	194,402
1910	145,965
1900	92,531
1890	62,555
1880	20,789
1870	9,118

Economy

Chief products

Agriculture: beef cattle, hay, hogs, sugar beets.
Manufacturing: chemicals, petroleum products, food and beverage products.
Mining: petroleum, coal, natural gas.

Gross state product

Value of goods and services produced in 2000: $19,293,000,000. *Services* include community, business, and personal services; finance; government; trade; and transportation, communication, and utilities. *Industry* includes construction, manufacturing, and mining. *Agriculture* includes agriculture, fishing, and forestry.

Source: U.S. Bureau of Economic Analysis.

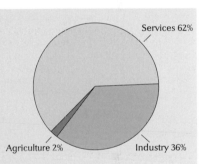

Services 62%

Agriculture 2%

Industry 36%

Government

State government

Governor: 4-year term
State senators: 30; 4-year terms
State representatives: 60; 2-year terms
Counties: 23

Federal government

United States senators: 2
United States representatives: 1
Electoral votes: 3

Sources of information

For information about tourism, write to Wyoming Travel and Tourism, I-25 and College Drive, Cheyenne, WY 82002. The Web site at wyomingtourism.org also provides information.
For information on the economy, write to: Wyoming Business Council, 214 West 15th St., Cheyenne, WY 82002.
The state's official Web site at www.state.wy.us also provides a gateway to much information on Wyoming's economy, government, and history.

Wyoming became the 44th state on July 10.

Fire damaged large areas of Wyoming's Yellowstone National Park.

| 1883 | 1890 | 1925 | 1988 |

The state's first oil well was drilled in the Dallas Field near Lander.

Nellie Tayloe Ross became the first woman governor in the United States.

Population. The 2000 United States census reported that Wyoming had 493,782 people. The population had increased about 9 percent over the 1990 figure, 453,588. According to the 2000 census, Wyoming ranks 50th in population among the 50 states.

Only 30 percent of Wyoming's people live in metropolitan areas. This percentage is the smallest among the 50 states. Wyoming has two metropolitan areas, the Casper metropolitan area and the Cheyenne metropolitan area. For their populations, see the *Index* to the political map of Wyoming.

Most of Wyoming's cities are small compared with those in other states. Cheyenne, the capital and largest city, and Casper, the second largest city, both have only about 50,000 people. The next three cities, in order of size, are Laramie, Gillette, and Rock Springs. About a third of the people live in cities and towns along a single major highway and rail line in southern Wyoming.

About 89 out of 100 people in Wyoming are non-Hispanic whites. About 6 percent of the state's people are Hispanic Americans. American Indians make up about 2 percent of Wyoming's population.

Schools. The first school in Wyoming was founded at Fort Laramie in 1852. William Vaux, the chaplain of the fort, started the school. In 1860, a school was built at Fort Bridger.

In 1869, the territorial legislature passed a law providing tax support for schools. There were district schools in many communities after 1870. The first high school in Wyoming opened in Cheyenne in 1875.

Wyoming's public school system is supervised by an elected state superintendent of public instruction. An 11-member board of education makes school policies. The governor, with the approval of the senate, appoints board members to six-year terms.

Children are required to attend school either from age 7 through 15, or until they complete the eighth

Population density

Wyoming is one of the most sparsely populated states. Thirty percent of the people live in metropolitan areas— the lowest percentage of metropolitan area dwellers among the 50 states.

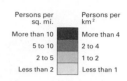

Persons per sq. mi.	Persons per km²
More than 10	More than 4
5 to 10	2 to 4
2 to 5	1 to 2
Less than 2	Less than 1

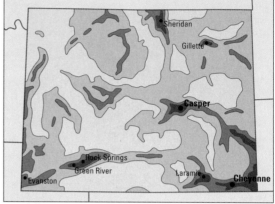

WORLD BOOK map; based on U.S. Census Bureau data.

grade. Wyoming has one of the highest percentages in the United States of people who can read and write. For the number of students and teachers in Wyoming, see **Education** (table).

The University of Wyoming is the state's only university. It is accredited by the North Central Association of Colleges and Schools. The university was founded in Laramie in 1886 and is state supported. Wyoming also has seven community colleges.

Libraries and museums. In 1886, Wyoming's territo-

Wyoming map index

rial legislature passed laws providing for a system of free county libraries. Today, each of Wyoming's 23 counties has a public county library. The Wyoming Territorial Library was established in Cheyenne in 1871. It is now called the Wyoming State Library. The chief libraries at the University of Wyoming include the Brinkerhoff Geology Library, the George William Hopper Law Library, the Science Library, and the William Robertson Coe Library.

Outstanding museum collections in the state include the exhibits at the Wyoming State Museum and the Cheyenne Frontier Days Old West Museum, both in Cheyenne; the Fort Caspar Museum in Casper; the Fort Bridger State Historic Site in Fort Bridger; the Wyoming Pioneer Museum in Douglas; and the National Museum of Wildlife Art in Jackson Hole. The Centennial Complex at the University of Wyoming in Laramie includes the American Heritage Center, which has a strong collection on Western history; and the university's Art Museum, which features items from many cultures and periods.

The University of Wyoming Geological Museum has collections of fossils, minerals, and rocks; and exhibits about prehistoric times.

Other museums have exhibits about particular areas or points of interest. For example, the Fort Laramie National Historic Site has relics from the days of the old pioneer wagon trains. The Jackson Hole Historical Society and Museum in Jackson has displays about the area's early days. The National Park Service maintains exhibits at several visitor centers in Yellowstone National Park. It also operates the Colter Bay Visitor Center and Indian Arts Museum in Grand Teton National Park.

The Buffalo Bill Historical Center in Cody displays possessions of the famous hunter and showman Buffalo Bill Cody. Also in the center are the Cody Firearms Museum, which has a collection of more than 5,000 firearms; the Draper Museum of Natural History; the Plains Indian Museum; and the Whitney Gallery of Western Art, which features paintings and sculpture by famous Western artists.

University of Wyoming in Laramie is the state's only university. Robert Russin's sculpture *The Family, center,* stands on the main quadrangle of the campus.

University of Wyoming

Kendrick	.B 13	McKinley	.G 14	Oriva	.C 13	Ryan Park	.J 12	Tower Junction	.E 2
Keystone	.J 12	McKinnon†	.49 .J 6	Orpha	.F 14	Saddle String	.C 11	Turner Flat	177 .F 5
Kinnear	.F 8	Medicine Bow	774 .H 13	Osage†	.215 .D 15	Sage	.I 5	Ucross	.B 12
Kirby	.57 .D 9	Meeteetse	.351 .C 8	Oshoto	.B 14	St. Stephens	.F 9	Ulm	.B 12
Kirtley	.F 16	Meriden	.I 16	Otto	.C 9	Salt Wells	.I 8	Upton	.872 .C 15
La Barge	.431 .H 6	Merna	.F 6	Pahaska	.B 6	Sand Draw	.F 9	Urie	.J 6
La Grange	.332 .J 16	Midvale	.E 9	Parkerton	.F 13	Saratoga	.1,726 .J 12	Uva	.J 15
Lake Junction	.G 2	Midwest	.408 .E 12	Parkman†	.137 .A 11	Savageton	.D 13	Valley	.C 7
Lamont	.H 11	Milford	.F 8	Patrick Draw	.I 9	Savery	.J 11	Van Tassell	.18 .G 16
Lance Creek†	.51 .F 15	Millis	.J 4	Pavillion	.165 .E 8	Seminoe Dam	.H 11	Verne	.I 6
Lander°	.6,867 .F 8	Mills	.2,591 .F 12	Pedro	.D 16	Shawnee	.G 15	Verona	.B 12
Laramie°	.27,204 .J 14	Moneta	.F 10	Piedmont	.I 5	Shell	.B 10	Veteran†	.28 .H 16
Leefe	.I 4	Moorcroft	.807 .C 15	Pine Bluffs	.1,153 .J 16	Sheridan°	.15,804 .B 11	Walcott	.I 12
Leiter	.B 12	Moose	.J 1	Pinedale°	.1,412 .F 7	Shirley Basin	.G 13	Waltman	.F 11
Leo	.H 12	Moran		Pine Haven	.222 .C 15	Shoshoni	.635 .E 9	Wamsutter	.261 .I 10
Leroy	.J 5	Junction	.I 2	Point of Rocks†	.3 .I 8	Sinclair	.423 .I 11	Wapiti	.B 7
Lightning Flat	.A 14	Morrisey	.E 16	Powder River†	.51 .F 11	Slater†	.82 .H 15	Warren AFB†	.4,440 .J 15
Linch	.E 13	Morton	.F 8	Powell	.5,373 .B 8	Smoot†	.182 .G 5	Wendover	.G 15
Lindbergh	.J 16	Morton	.F 14	Quealy	.I 7	South Pass City	.G 8	West Thumb	.G 2
Lingle	.510 .H 16	Moskee	.C 16	Ralston†	.233 .B 8	South		Weston	.B 14
Little America†	.56 .I 6	Mountain Home	.K 13	Ranchester	.701 .B 11	Torrington	.H 16	Westvaco	.I 7
Lonetree†	.61 .J 6	Mountain		Ranchettes†	.4,869 .J 15	Spotted Horse	.B 13	Wheatland°	.3,548 .H 15
Lost Cabin	.E 10	View	.1,153 .J 6	Rawlins°	.8,538 .I 11	Story†	.887 .B 11	Whitman	.F 16
Lost Springs	.1 .F 15	Mountain		Recluse	.B 13	Sundance°	.1,161 .C 16	Wildcat	.B 13
Lovell	.2,281 .B 9	View†	.103 .F 12	Red Buttes†	.439 .J 14	Sunrise	.G 15	Willwood	.B 8
Lox	.F 11	Muddy Gap	.G 11	Redbird	.E 16	Sunshine	.D 8	Wilson†	.1,294 .J 1
Lucerne†	.525 .D 9	Natrona	.F 12	Red Desert	.I 9	Superior	.244 .J 8	Winchester†	.60 .D 9
Lusk°	.1,447 .F 16	Neiber	.D 9	Reliance†	.665 .J 7	Sussex	.D 12	Wind River	.F 8
Lyman	.1,938 .J 6	Newcastle°	.3,065 .D 16	Riner	.I 10	Sweetwater		Wind River	
Lysite	.E 10	New Haven	.B 15	Riverside	.59 .J 12	Station	.G 9	Indian	
Madison		Node	.F 16	Riverton	.9,310 .F 9	Table Rock†	.82 .I 9	Reservation	.23,245 .E 8
Junction	.F 1	Norris Junction	.F 1	Riverview	.E 16	Ten Sleep	.304 .D 10	Wolf	.B 11
Mammoth	.A 5	Nugget	.I 5	Robertson†	.59 .J 5	Teton Village†	.175 .J 1	Woods	
Manderson	.104 .C 10	O'Donnell	.B 8	Rochelle	.E 15	Thayne	.341 .F 5	Landing	.100 .J 13
Manville	.101 .F 15	Old Faithful	.G 1	Rock River	.235 .I 13	Thermopolis°	.3,172 .E 9	Worland°	.5,250 .D 10
Marbleton	.720 .G 6	Opal	.102 .I 6	Rock Springs	.18,708 .I 7	Thornton	.C 15	Wright	.1,347 .D 14
Marse	.H 5	Orchard		Rockypoint	.B 14	Tie Siding	.J 14	Wyarno	.B 12
Mayoworth	.D 12	Valley	.J 15	Rolling Hills	.449 .F 13	Tipton	.I 9	Wyodak	.C 14
McFadden	.I 13	Orin	.G 14	Rozet	.C 14	Torrington°	.5,776 .H 16	Yoder	.169 .H 16

*Does not appear on map; key shows general location.
†Census designated place—unincorporated, but recognized as a significant settled community by the U.S. Census Bureau.
°County seat.
Places without population figures are unincorporated areas.
Source: 2000 census.

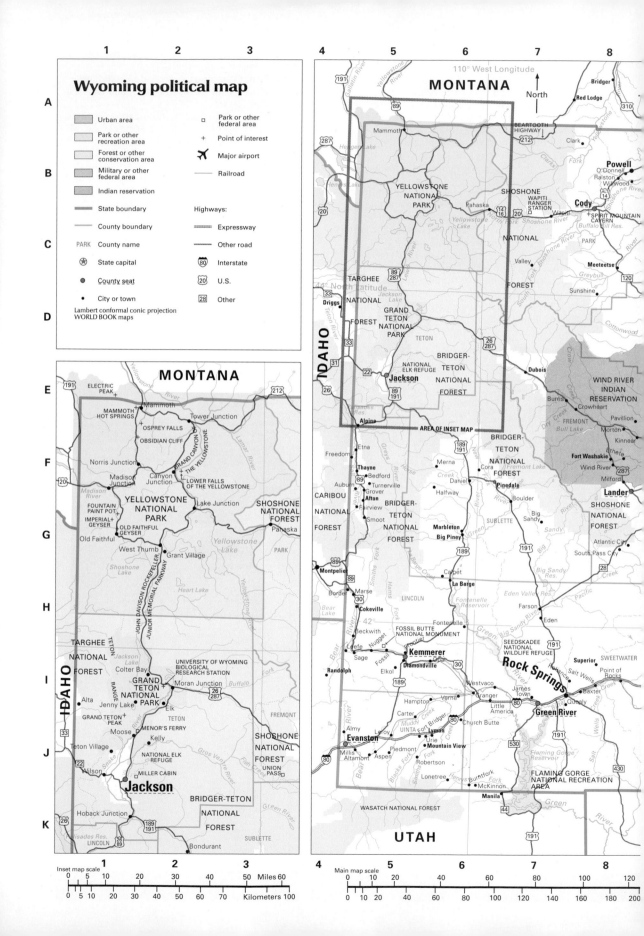

Wyoming political map

Legend:

- Urban area
- Park or other recreation area
- Forest or other conservation area
- Military or other federal area
- Indian reservation
- □ Park or other federal area
- + Point of interest
- ✈ Major airport
- State boundary
- County boundary
- PARK County name
- ★ State capital
- ● County seat
- • City or town
- Railroad

Highways:
- ▬ Expressway
- ▬ Other road
- 80 Interstate
- 20 U.S.
- 28 Other

Lambert conformal conic projection
WORLD BOOK maps

Inset map scale
0 5 10 20 30 40 50 Miles 60
0 5 10 20 30 40 50 60 70 Kilometers 100

Main map scale
0 10 20 40 60 80 100 120 Miles
0 10 20 40 60 80 100 120 140 160 180 200 Kilometers

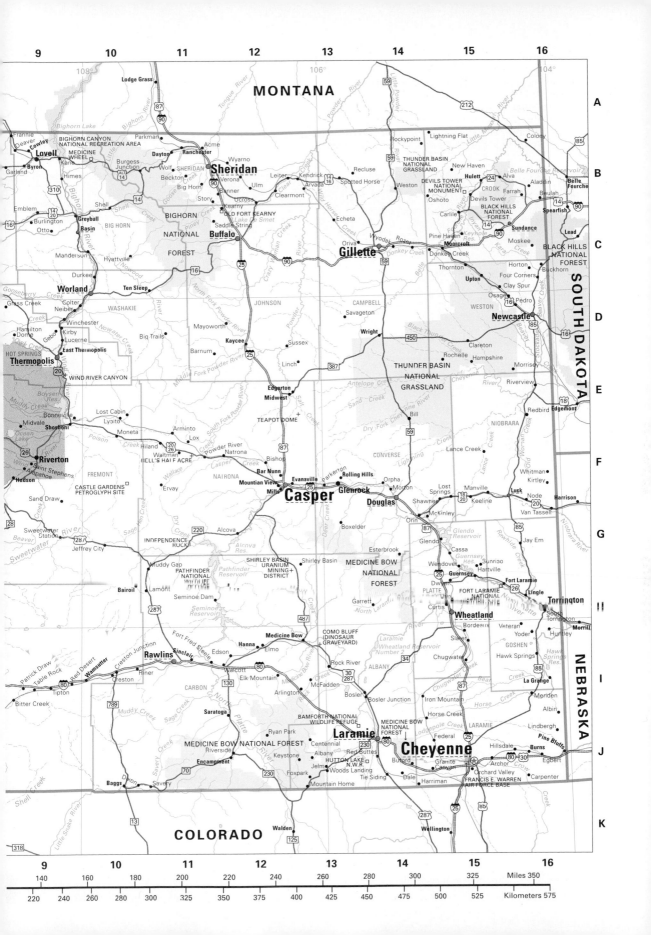

Wyoming's tourist attractions rank among the most spectacular in the nation. Each year, several million people visit the state. Yellowstone and Grand Teton national parks are the chief attractions. They have beautiful mountain scenery and many kinds of animals. Wilderness trails challenge the hiker's skill. Visitors also come to Wyoming to hunt big game animals or to fish in the lakes and streams. In 1904, the Eaton Ranch, near Sheridan, became the first dude ranch in the West.

Wyoming's most popular annual event is the Frontier Days celebration in Cheyenne, which has been staged since 1897. The celebration is held for 10 days in July.

Artstreet

Devils Tower National Monument

Larry Beck

Green River Rendezvous in Pinedale

Places to visit

Following are brief descriptions of some of Wyoming's many interesting places to visit:

Devils Tower National Monument, in northeastern Wyoming, is a volcanic tower that stands 867 feet (265 meters) above its base. In 1906, United States President Theodore Roosevelt established Devils Tower as the nation's first national monument.

Fort Laramie National Historic Site, near the town of Fort Laramie, was a fur-trading center and later a military post. The fort helped protect pioneer wagon trains on the Oregon Trail. A number of the original buildings at Fort Laramie have been restored.

Fossil Butte National Monument, 10 miles (16 kilometers) west of Kemmerer, has the fossilized remains of fishes and plants that lived in the water which covered the area about 50 million years ago.

Grand Teton National Park lies in northwestern Wyoming. The majestic Teton Mountains rise sharply from the floor of a beautiful valley called Jackson Hole. One of the nation's most popular ski resorts lies in the Jackson Hole region of the park. Several lakes lie along the east side of the mountains. Visitors can see many kinds of wild animals, which are protected there. See **Grand Teton National Park.**

National Historic Trails Interpretive Center, in Casper, documents the westward movement in America. It interprets the story of people traveling along the Oregon, Mormon Pioneer, California, and Pony Express trails in the 1800's.

Wildlife refuges. Wyoming has six major wildlife refuge areas where visitors can watch animals and birds in their natural surroundings. The largest area is the National Elk Refuge near Jackson. Federal waterfowl refuges include Pathfinder north of Rawlins, Bamforth and Hutton Lake near Laramie, and Seedskadee near Green River.

Wind River Canyon, south of Thermopolis, offers motorists a scenic drive between the Bridger and Owl Creek mountains. Cliffs rise 2,000 feet (610 meters) above the river. The canyon walls are interesting because of the rock formations exposed where the river cut through the mountains.

Yellowstone National Park, in northwestern Wyoming, is the world's oldest national park and one of the largest ones in the nation. Its spectacular beauty and unusual attractions were recognized by early explorers.

Yellowstone became a national park in 1872. The most notable features of the park include the world's largest geyser area, spectacular towering waterfalls, hot springs, deep canyons, and excellent fishing. See **Yellowstone National Park.**

National forests. Five national forests in Wyoming provide timber and serve as recreation areas. Shoshone, in northwestern Wyoming, is the largest forest. Other forests entirely in Wyoming are Bighorn, near Sheridan, and Medicine Bow, near Laramie.

Wyoming shares two of its national forests with bordering states. The Black Hills forest is shared with South Dakota and Bridger-Teton with Idaho.

State parks. Wyoming has a number of historic sites, parks, and recreation areas. For information on the state parks and facilities in Wyoming, write to Director, State Parks and Historic Sites, Barrett Building, 3rd floor, Cheyenne, WY 82002.

Annual events

January-April
Cutter (horse-drawn sleigh) races near Afton, Big Piney, Jackson, Pinedale, and Saratoga (February); Wyoming State Winter Fair in Lander (January).

May-August
Chugwater Chili Cookoff (June); Woodchopper's Jamboree Encampment (mid-June); Pioneer Days in Lander (July 1-4); Rodeos in Buffalo, Cody, Sheridan, and other towns (July 4); Jubilee Days in Laramie (first week of July); Green River Rendezvous in Pinedale (second Sunday in July); Central Wyoming Fair in Casper (mid-July); Indian Sun Dances in Ethete and Fort Washakie (late July); Cheyenne Frontier Days (late July); Indian pageant in Thermopolis (early August); Wyoming State Fair in Douglas (late August).

September-December
Cowboy Days Rodeo in Evanston (Labor Day); Jackson Hole Fall Arts Festival (mid-September and early October).

Wyoming Travel Commission

Frontier Days Rodeo in Cheyenne

Tom Stack & Associates

Indian dance at Frontier Days

John Running, Black Star

Old Faithful geyser in Yellowstone National Park

Geri Wright, Bruce Coleman Inc.

Cutter race in Jackson Hole

Land regions. Wyoming lies where the Great Plains meet the Rocky Mountains. The Continental Divide winds through Wyoming from the northwest corner to the south-central edge of the state (see **Continental Divide**). Water on the east side of the divide flows to the Atlantic Ocean. Water on the west side goes into the Pacific Ocean. Wyoming has an average elevation of 6,700 feet (2,042 meters), and is higher than any other state except Colorado. Wyoming has three major land regions: (1) the Great Plains, (2) the Rocky Mountains, and (3) the Intermontane Basins.

The Great Plains cover the eastern part of the state. This region is part of the vast interior plain of North America that stretches from Canada to Mexico. In Wyoming, short-grass prairie covers much of the land and provides good grazing for cattle and sheep. Cottonwoods and shrubs grow along the rivers. Little rain falls on the plains, but irrigation has turned portions of this region into valuable farmland.

A portion of the famous Black Hills lies in the northeastern part of the state. About a third of the Black Hills area is located in Wyoming, and the rest is in South Dakota.

The Rocky Mountains sweep across Wyoming in huge ranges, most of which extend from north to south. In the north, the Bighorn Mountains form the front range of the mountain area. The Laramie Range stretches north from Colorado. Between these two front ranges lies a wide plateau. In the 1800's, pioneers traveled westward on trails through this area. The Absaroka Range rises along the east side of Yellowstone National Park. The rugged Wind River Range to the south includes nine peaks that tower above 13,000 feet (3,960 meters). Among them is the highest mountain in Wyoming, 13,804-foot (4,207-meter) Gannett Peak. The Granite Mountains extend eastward from near the southern tip of the Wind River Range. The Gros Ventre, Salt River, Snake River, Teton, and Wyoming ranges are near the western border. The scenic Teton Mountains rise nearly straight up for more than 1 mile (1.6 kilometers) from the Jackson Hole Valley. Other major mountain ranges include the Medicine Bow and Sierra Madre in southern Wyoming.

There is one special link between the flat land of the plains and the heights of the mountains. It is in southeastern Wyoming, where a narrow finger of land rises gently from the plains to a point high in the Laramie Mountains. Along the slope are major rail and highway routes that quickly bring a traveler from the plains to the mountains. This slope, sometimes called the *Gangplank,* is only about 100 yards (91 meters) wide.

The Intermontane Basins include several fairly flat areas between Wyoming's mountain ranges. The word *intermontane* means *between mountains.* The major basins include the Bighorn and Powder River basins in the north, and the Wind River Basin in central Wyoming. The Green River, Great Divide, and Washakie basins are in southwestern Wyoming.

The basins are mostly treeless areas that get less rainfall than the mountains. Short grasses and other low plants make most of the basins good areas for grazing sheep and cattle. The Great Divide Basin is an exception. It lies along the Continental Divide, but has no drainage of water either to the Atlantic or the Pacific. The divide splits and runs around the 3,000 square miles (7,800 square kilometers) of this basin. The little rain that falls there soaks quickly into the dry ground. A part of the Great Divide Basin and the area to the south of it are sometimes called the *Red Desert.* Pronghorns and wild

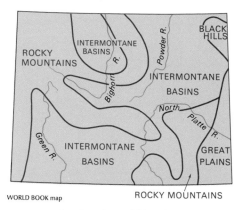

WORLD BOOK map

Land regions of Wyoming

Map index

*Does not appear on the map; key shows general location.

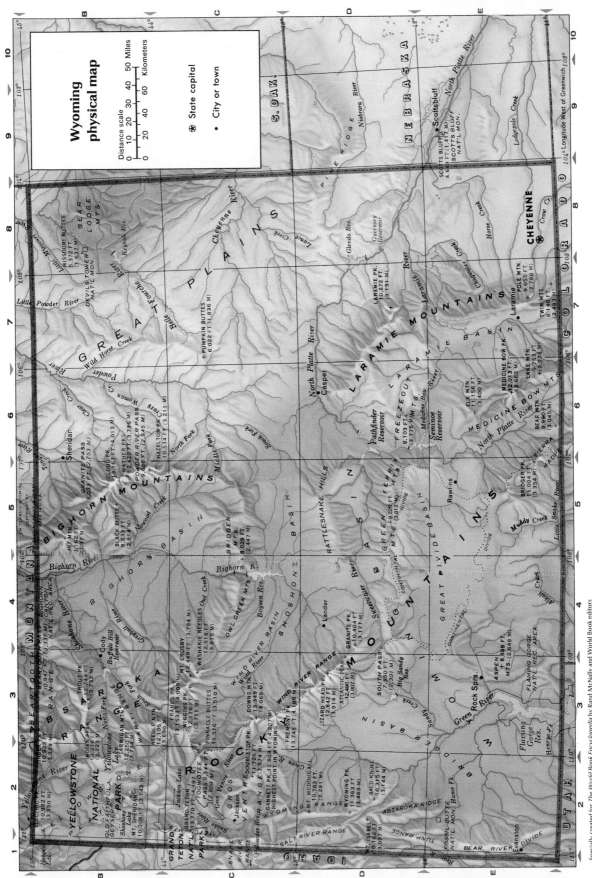

Wyoming physical map

Distance scale

⊛ State capital

• City or town

Miles: 0 10 20 30 40 50

Kilometers: 0 20 40 60

S. DAK.

NEBRASKA

COLORADO

UTAH

IDAHO

MONTANA

104° Longitude West of Greenwich 103°

BEARTOOTH MONTAINS

YELLOWSTONE NATIONAL PARK

Yellowstone River

Harebell Lake

Heart Lake
10,992 FT. (3,350 M)

INDEX PK.
11,820 FT. (3,329 M)

BEARTOOTH PASS
10,947 FT. (3,337 M)

ABSAROKA RANGE

TROUT PK.
12,244 FT. (3,732 M)

Old Faithful Geyser

Yellowstone Lake

Shoshone Lake

Shoshone River

North Fork

LARGMAN MTN.
12,305 FT.

MT. SHERIDAN
10,308 FT. (3,142 M)

GRAND TETON NATIONAL PARK

GRAND TETON
13,770 FT. (4,197 M)

Jackson Lake

Jackson Lake

TETON RANGE

Snake River

SNAKE RIVER RANGE

SALT RIVER RANGE

Greys River

GROS VENTRE RANGE

MT. ISABEL
10,162 FT. (3,097 M)

FOSSIL BUTTE NAT'L. MON.

TUNP RANGE

Evanston

BEAR RIVER DIVIDE

Bear Riv.

Henry's Fk.

Green River

DOUBLETOP PK.
11,725 FT.

GANNETT PK.
13,804 FT. (4,207 M) HIGHEST POINT IN WYOMING

WIND RIVER RANGE

TOGWOTEE PASS
9,544 FT. (2,909 M)

WIGGINS PK.
12,176 FT. (3,711 M)

FRANCS PK.
13,153 FT. (4,009 M)

Gros Ventre River

MT. McDOUGAL
10,763 FT. (3,281 M)

WYOMING PK.
11,363 FT. (3,463 M)

BALD KNOLL
10,315 FT. (3,144 M)

Greys River

ABSAROKA RIDGE

FREMONT PK.
13,745 FT. (4,189 M)

ATLANTIC PEAK
12,490 FT. (3,807 M)

WIND RIVER BASIN

LIZARD HEAD PK.
12,842 FT. (3,914 M)

DOWNS MTN.
13,349 FT. (4,069 M)

PINNACLE BUTTES
11,516 FT. (3,510 M)

NEEDLE MTN.
12,105 FT. (3,690 M)

WAPITI RANGE

South Fork

MT. CROSBY
12,449 FT. (3,794 M)

WASHAKIE NEEDLES
12,518 FT. (3,815 M)

Owl Creek

OWL CREEK MTS.

Wind River

SHOSHONE BASIN

Bighorn R.

BRIDGER MTS.
8,029 FT. (2,447 M)

Lander

GRANITE PK.
10,404 FT. (3,171 M)

SOUTH PASS
7,550 FT. (2,301 M)

Big Sandy Res.

Sandy Creek

GREAT DIVIDE BASIN

CONTINENTAL DIVIDE

ROCK

MOUNTAINS

Rock Sprs.

Green River

ASPEN MTS.
8,688 FT. (2,648 M)

FLAMING GORGE NAT'L. REC. AREA

Flaming Gorge Res.

Muddy Creek

Little Snake River

SIERRA MADRE

BRIDGER PK.
11,004 FT. (3,354 M)

Rawlins

GREEN FERRY MTS.
9,225 FT. (2,812 M)

ATLANTIC RIM

DIVIDE

CONTINENTAL DIVIDE

Sweetwater River

RATTLESNAKE HILLS

SHOSHONE BASIN

Boysen Res.

WIND RIVER CANYON

Bighorn River

Bighorn R.

Greybull River

NoWood Creek

Greybull River

BIGHORN MOUNTAINS

BIGHORN BASIN

Cody

Buffalo Bill Reservoir

Shoshone River

North Fork

BLACK BUTTE
9,233 FT. (2,814 M)

HUNT MTN.
10,162 FT. (3,097 M)

CLOUD PK.
13,167 FT. (4,013 M)

MATHER PKS.
12,420 FT. (3,786 M)

POWDER RIVER PASS
9,666 FT. (2,945 M)

HAZELTON PK.
10,534 FT. (3,211 M)

GRANITE PASS
9,033 FT. (2,753 M)

Sheridan

Tongue River

Tongue Riv.

Goose Cr.

Clear Creek

Powder River

Crazy Woman Cr.

Middle Fork

North Fork

South Fork

Little Powder River

Wild Horse Creek

GREAT PLAINS

Belle Fourche River

DEVILS TOWER NAT'L. MON.

MISSOURI BUTTES
5,372 FT. (1,637 M)

BEAR LODGE MTS.

Little Missouri River

Little Powder River

PUMPKIN BUTTES
6,022 FT. (1,836 M)

North Platte River

Casper

North Platte River

Pathfinder Reservoir

Seminoe Reservoir

FREEZEOUT MTS.

Medicine Bow River

MEDICINE BOW MTS.

ELK MTN.
11,156 FT. (3,400 M)

MEDICINE BOW PK.
12,013 FT. (3,662 M)

LAKE MTN.
9,753 FT. (3,045 M)

BEAR MTN.
9,990 FT. (3,045 M)

North Platte River

LARAMIE MOUNTAINS

LARAMIE BASIN

LARAMIE PK.
10,272 FT. (3,131 M)

Laramie River

Laramie River

Laramie

POLE MTN.
9,055 FT. (2,760 M)

TWIN MTS.
8,146 FT. (2,483 M)

Chugwater Creek

Cheyenne River

Lance Creek

PINE RIDGE

Niobrara River

Lodgepole Creek

Horse Creek

Crow Cr.

CHEYENNE ⊛

Guernsey Reservoir

Glendo Res.

Keyhole Res.

SCOTTS BLUFF
4,649 FT. (1,417 M)

SCOTTS BLUFF NAT'L. MON.

Scottsbluff

David R. Frazier

Yellowstone Lower Falls tumbles 308 feet (94 meters) into the Grand Canyon of Yellowstone National Park. The beautiful canyon reaches a depth of about 2,000 feet (610 meters).

horses feed on the thinly scattered plant growth and sagebrush. Sometimes sheep are grazed there.

Rivers and lakes. Parts of three great river systems start in the mountains of Wyoming. These three river systems are the Missouri, the Colorado, and the Columbia.

The tributaries of the Missouri flow both north and east. The Yellowstone, Clarks Fork, Bighorn, Tongue, and Powder rivers flow north. The Cheyenne, Niobrara, and North Platte rivers flow east.

The Green River, the major source of the Colorado River, rises in the Wind River Mountains and flows south across western Wyoming into Utah. The Snake River is part of the Columbia River system. This river starts in the Absaroka mountains in Yellowstone Park. It flows into Grand Teton National Park, then turns west into Idaho. The Snake leaves Wyoming through a magnificent canyon that cuts through three mountain ranges. The Snake River is joined by the Salt River and eventually reaches the Columbia. Bear River, in the southwestern corner of Wyoming, flows into the Great Salt Lake of Utah.

Average monthly weather

	Cheyenne						Sheridan				
	Temperatures				Days of rain or snow		Temperatures				Days of rain or snow
	F.°		C°				F.°		C°		
	High	Low	High	Low			High	Low	High	Low	
Jan.	37	14	3	−10	7	Jan.	33	7	1	−14	8
Feb.	40	16	4	−9	6	Feb.	36	11	2	−12	9
Mar.	44	20	7	−7	9	Mar.	43	20	6	−7	12
Apr.	54	29	12	−2	10	Apr.	56	31	13	−1	11
May	63	37	17	3	13	May	66	40	19	4	13
June	74	47	23	8	11	June	75	48	24	9	11
July	83	54	28	12	11	July	86	55	30	13	7
Aug.	81	53	27	12	10	Aug.	84	53	29	12	7
Sept.	72	43	22	6	7	Sept.	73	43	23	6	8
Oct.	60	33	16	1	6	Oct.	61	32	16	0	7
Nov.	47	23	8	−5	6	Nov.	46	21	8	−6	8
Dec.	40	17	4	−8	5	Dec.	37	12	3	−11	8

Average January temperatures

Wyoming's winters are cold and dry. The western and south-central parts have the coldest temperatures.

Average July temperatures

The state has mild and sunny summers. The eastern and central sections generally have the warmest temperatures.

Average yearly precipitation

Precipitation varies widely in Wyoming. The Bighorn Basin is dry but the northwestern mountains get heavy snows.

WORLD BOOK maps

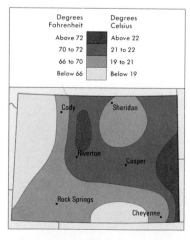

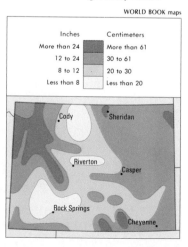

Many rivers have cut beautiful canyons, and some plunge over steep cliffs in spectacular waterfalls. The most interesting canyons include the Laramie River Canyon, the Grand Canyons of the Snake and the Yellowstone, Platte River Canyon, Shoshone River Canyon, and the Wind River Canyon. The most dramatic waterfalls are the Upper and Lower falls of the Yellowstone River.

Wyoming has hundreds of clear, cold, mountain lakes. Among the largest are Fremont, Jackson, Shoshone, and Yellowstone lakes. The major artificially created lakes include Big Sandy, Boysen, Buffalo Bill, Glendo, Guernsey, Keyhole, Pathfinder, and Seminoe reservoirs. Two new dams outside the state formed major lakes in Wyoming. Yellowtail Dam in Montana created a large lake in the northeastern part of Wyoming. Flaming Gorge Dam in Utah backs up water of the Green River 30 miles (48 kilometers) inside Wyoming.

Plant and animal life. Forests cover nearly a sixth of Wyoming's land. The chief commercial trees are Douglas-fir, Engelmann spruce, lodgepole pine, and ponderosa pine. Other trees include subalpine fir, aspen, and cottonwood.

Bluegrass, wheat grass, tufted fescues, and redtops grow on much of the state's approximately 50 million acres (20 million hectares) of grazing lands. Cactus and sagebrush are found in the drier regions. Areas of Wyoming with poor soil produce greasewood brush, which is used as firewood. Mountain wildflowers found in the state include the arnica, buttercup, evening star, five-finger, flax, forget-me-not, goldenrod, saxifrage, sour dock, and windflower.

Wyoming's most common larger animals include black bears, elk, mule deer, and pronghorns. Moose are common in the state's northwestern forests, and mountain sheep live among the rocky peaks of the higher mountains. Grizzly bears, lynxes, and mountain lions are sometimes seen. Some of the smaller fur-bearing animals include beavers, martens, raccoons, and otters.

Pronghorns are common in the open areas of the basins. Other animals in the basin areas include badgers, cottontail and jack rabbits, coyotes, foxes, skunks, and wildcats. Game birds include ducks, geese, grouse, pheasants, sage hens, and wild turkeys. Wyoming also is the home of bald and golden eagles. The bald eagle builds its nest in tall pines near mountain streams or lakes. The golden eagle usually chooses a home farther from water.

Climate. Wyoming has a dry, sunny climate. Winters are cold and the summers are warm. The dry air makes the climate more comfortable than the temperatures would indicate. Differences in altitude create large differences in temperature in various parts of the state. At Casper, in central Wyoming, the average January temperature is 22 °F (−6 °C), and the average July temperature is 71 °F (22 °C). Near Yellowstone Lake, at a higher elevation, the January average is 12 °F (−11 °C), and the July average is 59 °F (15 °C). In Wyoming's high mountains, freezing temperatures can occur any time of the year.

Wyoming's highest recorded temperature was 115 °F (46 °C) at Basin on Aug. 8, 1983. Moran, near Elk, had the lowest temperature, −66 °F (−53 °C), on Feb. 9, 1933.

The average annual *precipitation* (rain, melted snow, and other forms of moisture) ranges from about 5 inches (13 centimeters) at Hyattville in the Bighorn Basin to about 50 inches (130 centimeters) in the Yellowstone Park area. Snowfall varies from 15 to 20 inches (38 to 51 centimeters) in the Bighorn Basin to about 260 inches (660 centimeters) in the northwestern mountains.

On the Great Plains, and in some open areas of southern Wyoming, the wind blows during the afternoons, usually from the west or southwest. If dry snow is on the ground, the wind may whip it into a *ground blizzard.* A person cannot see straight ahead in the swirling snow, even though the sky may be blue and the sun shining.

Economy

Service industries, taken together, make up the largest part of Wyoming's *gross state product*—the total value of all goods and services produced in a state in a year. However, Wyoming's economy depends heavily on its land. The land provides the state's most important product—coal. Coal, natural gas, petroleum, and other mined products account for about a fourth of the gross state product. Wyoming's land also provides grazing for cattle and sheep. Most of the state's manufacturing plants process the products of Wyoming's mines, farms, and forests. Millions of tourists come to Wyoming to enjoy its scenic beauty. These visitors spend nearly $2 billion annually.

Government plays an important part in Wyoming's economy. The federal government owns about half of the state's land. The government controls grazing, logging, and mining rights in this huge area, which includes national forests and parks, Indian lands, and other public lands.

Natural resources. Wyoming's most important natural resources are mineral deposits, grazing land, scenery, wildlife, and water.

Soil. Wyoming does not have large areas of fertile soil. Much of the state has sandy soil formed from sandstone rock that lies beneath the surface. The most fertile soils of Wyoming are those deposited in the major river valleys by floodwaters. Wind-blown dirt called *loess* also has formed fertile soil in some areas.

Minerals. Wyoming's reserves of bentonite clay, coal, petroleum, sodium carbonate, and uranium rank among the nation's largest. The mineral reserves are found mostly in the basin areas of the state.

Many of the petroleum and natural-gas reserves occur in an underground region called the *Overthrust Belt.* This region lies beneath southwestern Wyoming and parts of neighboring states. About 40 percent of Wyoming has coal under it. Most of Wyoming's coal is found in the northeastern part of the state. Trona, a material containing sodium carbonate, is found in southwestern Wyoming. The state's largest uranium deposits are in the Powder River, Shirley, and Wind River basins. Bentonite is a clay used in oil drilling and in the manufacture of chemical products. The largest reserves of bentonite are in the northeast and north-central sections.

Wyoming also has agate and jade. Other mined products include building stone, gold, gypsum, and limestone.

Forests cover about 11 million acres (4 $\frac{1}{2}$ million hectares), or more than a sixth of Wyoming's land. Most of the forests grow in the mountain areas. About two-fifths of the forests are available for commercial use. About 2 $\frac{2}{3}$ million acres (1.1 million hectares) have been set aside in parks and other reserves. The federal government controls about three-fourths of the commercial forestland in Wyoming. The chief commercial trees are lodgepole pine, Engelmann spruce, and ponderosa pine. Other trees in Wyoming include subalpine fir, aspen, cottonwood, and Douglas-fir.

Service industries account for the largest portion of Wyoming's gross state product. Most of the service industries are concentrated in Casper, Cheyenne, and Laramie, the state's largest cities.

Most important among Wyoming's service industry groups are (1) government and (2) transportation, communication, and utilities. These groups contribute a roughly equal amount to the state's gross state product.

Government includes public schools and hospitals and military establishments. A large number of people are employed in Wyoming's public schools and universities. State government offices are based primarily in Cheyenne. Warren Air Force Base lies just outside Cheyenne. The base is the control center for a large network of long-range nuclear missiles. The federal government also operates Yellowstone National Park and Grand Teton National Park, both of which provide hundreds of seasonal jobs.

Pipeline companies are a major part of the transportation sector. Pipelines carry Wyoming's large oil and gas output to processing and distribution sites. Railroad companies transport other mined products and farm goods. Telephone companies are the most important part of the communications sector. Utility companies supply electric, gas, and water service. More information about transportation and communication appears later in this section.

Finance, insurance, and real estate rank third. Real estate is important because of the large sums of money involved in the selling and leasing of houses and other buildings. Casper and Cheyenne are the leading financial centers. The state's largest bank is Wells Fargo Bank Wyoming.

Both (1) community, business, and personal services and (2) wholesale and retail trade contribute about the same amount to Wyoming's gross state product. But community, business, and personal services employ more people. This group includes private health care, hotels and ski resorts, law firms and engineering companies, and repair shops. Tourism growth in Wyoming has benefited the state's hotels, dude ranches, and ski resorts.

The wholesale trade of petroleum is important to the state. Automobile dealerships, grocery stores, and restaurants are the leading types of retail businesses.

Mining provides a larger portion of the gross state product in Wyoming than in any other state. Coal, petroleum, natural gas, trona, and bentonite are the state's leading mined products.

Wyoming is the leading state in coal production and ranks among the leaders in petroleum and natural gas.

Changes in the prices of any of these products have a large impact on Wyoming's overall economy.

Almost all of Wyoming's coal is obtained from surface mines. These mines provide a variety of coal called *subbituminous*. Campbell County provides most of Wyoming's coal. Sweetwater and Converse counties produce most of the remaining coal.

Large petroleum deposits lie in several parts of Wyoming. The leading oil-producing counties are Campbell, Park, Sweetwater, and Uinta. The oil companies that produce the most petroleum in Wyoming are BP, Chevron-Texaco, and Marathon.

Natural gas, like petroleum, is found in several parts of the state. Southwestern Wyoming is the leading area for natural gas production.

Among Wyoming's other mined products, sodium carbonate-containing trona is the most important. It is used to manufacture glass, soap, and paper. All of the trona comes from Sweetwater County. Wyoming is also a major producer of bentonite and other clays. The state also produces crushed stone, gypsum, and sand and gravel.

Manufacturing in Wyoming makes up a smaller percentage of the gross state product than in most other states. Goods manufactured in Wyoming have a *value added by manufacture* of about $1 $\frac{1}{2}$ billion a year. Value added by manufacture represents the increase in value of raw materials after they become finished products.

The production of chemicals and related products is Wyoming's most important manufacturing activity. Soda ash is the state's chief chemical product. It is manufactured from local deposits of trona.

Petroleum refining ranks second among Wyoming's manufacturing activities. Casper and Sinclair have large oil refineries. Refineries also are located near Cheyenne and Newcastle.

Other products made in Wyoming include fabricated metal products, food products, machinery, nonmetallic mineral products, and wood products. Metal containers, structural metals, and machine shops are key parts of the fabricated metals sector. The state's most important

Production and workers by economic activities

Economic activities	Percent of GSP* produced	Employed workers	
		Number of people	Percent of total
Mining	24	19,400	6
Government	14	64,100	20
Transportation, communication, & utilities	14	17,200	5
Finance, insurance, & real estate	12	21,300	6
Community, business, & personal services	11	83,200	25
Wholesale & retail trade	11	66,600	20
Manufacturing	7	13,600	4
Construction	5	24,900	8
Agriculture	2	18,400	6
Total	100	328,700	100

*GSP = gross state product, the total value of goods and services produced in a year.
Figures are for 2000.
Source: *World Book* estimates based on data from the U.S. Bureau of Economic Analysis.

Economy of Wyoming

This map shows the economic uses of land in Wyoming and where the leading farm, mineral, and forest products are produced. The urban areas, shown on the map in red, are the important manufacturing centers.

Cropland mixed with grazing

Mostly grazing land

Mostly shrubland

Mostly forest land

Mostly unproductive land

• Manufacturing center

• Mineral deposit

WORLD BOOK map

food products include dairy products, refined sugar, and soft drinks. Casper, Gillette, and Powell produce machinery. Cement and ready-mix concrete are the state's main nonmetallic mineral products. Hulett, Laramie, Sheridan, and many other cities have sawmills.

Agriculture. Farms and ranches cover about half of Wyoming. The state has about 9,200 farms and ranches.

Livestock and livestock products account for about 70 percent of Wyoming's total agricultural income. Cattle ranching is by far the most important agricultural activity in Wyoming. Most beef cattle are raised in eastern Wyo-

David R. Frazier

Drilling for oil is one of the most important mining activities in Wyoming. The state ranks among the nation's leading producers of both petroleum and natural gas.

ming. Other livestock products in Wyoming include hogs, milk, sheep, and wool. Wyoming is among the leading states in the production of sheep and wool. About half of Wyoming's land is used to graze cattle and sheep. This includes vast amounts of federal government land leased to ranchers.

Crops provide about 30 percent of Wyoming's farm income. The state's most valuable field crops are grown on irrigated land. The leading crops are barley, beans, corn, hay, sugar beets, and wheat. Hay is grown chiefly as feed for livestock, especially cattle. Certified seed potatoes, which must be unusually free of disease, are raised in Goshen and Laramie counties. Farmers use dry farming methods on the Great Plains (see **Dry farming**). The most important crops raised on farms in the Great Plains include hay, and wheat and other grains.

Electric power. Coal-burning power plants generate more than 95 percent of the state's electric power. Major plants operate near Gillette and in Glenrock, Kemmerer, Rock Springs, and Wheatland. Water power provides most of the rest of Wyoming's electric power.

Transportation. Wyoming has about 27,000 miles (43,500 kilometers) of roads and highways. Jackson has the state's busiest airport. Wyoming's first railroad was the Union Pacific. It was built across the territory in 1867 and 1868. Today, three rail lines provide Wyoming with freight service to other states. No local passenger trains serve Wyoming.

Communication. The first newspaper in Wyoming was the *Daily Telegraph,* published at Fort Bridger in 1863. Today, Wyoming has about 50 newspapers, including 8 dailies. Newspapers with the largest circulations include the *Star-Tribune* of Casper and the *Wyoming Tribune-Eagle* of Cheyenne. Wyoming publishers also produce about 65 periodicals.

Wyoming's first radio station, KDFN (now KTWO), began broadcasting at Casper in 1930. The first television station was KFBC-TV (now KGWN-TV) in Cheyenne, which started operating in 1954. Today, the state has about 70 radio stations and 15 television stations. Cable TV systems serve several Wyoming communities.

Constitution. Wyoming is still governed under its original Constitution, which was adopted in 1889. *Amendments* (changes) to the Constitution must be approved by a majority of the people voting in that particular election. Amendments may be proposed by a two-thirds vote of both houses of the Legislature, or by a constitutional convention. Such a convention must be approved by two-thirds of the members of each house of the Legislature, and by a majority of the voters.

Executive. The people of Wyoming elect the governor to a four-year term. The governor may serve no more than two terms during a 16-year period. Much of the governor's power lies in the right to appoint other important state officials, including the attorney general and the heads of numerous state agencies.

The voters elect four other high state officials to four-year terms. These are the secretary of state, auditor, treasurer, and superintendent of public instruction. They have the same term limitations as the governor.

Wyoming does not have a lieutenant governor. If the governor dies or resigns, the secretary of state serves as governor until a new governor is elected.

Legislature consists of a 30-member Senate and a 60-member House of Representatives. Senators are elected to four-year terms and may serve no more than three terms during a 24-year period. Representatives are elected to two-year terms and may serve no more than six terms during a 24-year period.

The two houses of the Legislature meet each year. General sessions begin on the second Tuesday of January in odd-numbered years. Budget sessions begin on the third Monday in February in even-numbered years. The Legislature may not meet more than 40 legislative days in any year or more than 60 days in each two-year period. The governor may call special sessions.

Courts. The highest court in Wyoming is the Supreme Court. It has five justices who are appointed to serve eight-year terms. These justices elect one of their number to serve as the chief justice. The Supreme Court usually hears only appeals from the lower courts.

Most major civil and criminal trials in the state are held in district courts. Wyoming has nine judicial districts, each with either one or two district judges. District judges are appointed to six-year terms. The governor appoints all judges of the Supreme Court and district courts. The governor chooses them from nominees of the Wyoming Judicial Nominating Commission. At the next election, voters then choose whether or not to have the judges stay in office. Other courts in Wyoming include county courts, police courts, municipal courts, and justice-of-the-peace courts.

Local government. Wyoming has 23 counties, each governed by a board of three or five commissioners. The commissioners are elected to four-year terms. Most Wyoming cities have a mayor-council government. By state law, a community must have at least 4,000 residents to be classified as a city. Wyoming's cities are called first-class cities. Communities with populations between 150 and 4,000 are called towns.

Revenue. Taxes account for about 35 percent of the state government's *general revenue* (income). Most of

Wyoming State Capitol

The Wyoming House of Representatives meets in the State Capitol in Cheyenne. Its 60 members serve two-year terms. The Wyoming Senate has 30 members who serve four-year terms.

The governors of Wyoming

	Party	Term		Party	Term
Francis E. Warren	Republican	1890	Leslie A. Miller	Democratic	1933-1939
Amos W. Barber	Republican	1890-1893	Nels H. Smith	Republican	1939-1943
John E. Osborne	Democratic	1893-1895	Lester C. Hunt	Democratic	1943-1949
William A. Richards	Republican	1895-1899	Arthur Griswold Crane	Republican	1949-1951
DeForest Richards	Republican	1899-1903	Frank A. Barrett	Republican	1951-1953
Fenimore Chatterton	Republican	1903-1905	C. J. Rogers	Republican	1953-1955
Bryant B. Brooks	Republican	1905-1911	Milward L. Simpson	Republican	1955-1959
Joseph M. Carey	Democratic	1911-1915	J. J. Hickey	Democratic	1959-1961
John B. Kendrick	Democratic	1915-1917	Jack R. Gage	Democratic	1961-1963
Frank L. Houx	Democratic	1917-1919	Clifford P. Hansen	Republican	1963-1967
Robert D. Carey	Republican	1919-1923	Stanley K. Hathaway	Republican	1967-1975
William B. Ross	Democratic	1923-1924	Edgar J. Herschler	Democratic	1975-1987
Frank E. Lucas	Republican	1924-1925	Mike Sullivan	Democratic	1987-1995
Nellie Tayloe Ross	Democratic	1925-1927	Jim Geringer	Republican	1995-2003
Frank C. Emerson	Republican	1927-1931	Dave Freudenthal	Democratic	2003-
Alonzo M. Clark	Republican	1931-1933			

the rest comes from federal grants and other U.S. government programs. The leading sources of tax revenue are a tax on mineral production and a sales tax. Wyoming collects no personal or corporate income taxes.

Politics. In state and local elections, Republicans have won two-thirds of the contests since 1890. The cities of southern Wyoming have traditionally been a major source of Democratic strength. Republicans usually receive more votes from the northern counties, which are largely rural.

In presidential elections, Wyoming has voted for Republican candidates more than twice as often as for Democratic candidates. For Wyoming's electoral votes and voting record, see **Electoral College** (table).

History

Indian days. The first people who lived in the Wyoming area were Indian hunters of at least 11,000 years ago. Later, huge herds of buffaloes roamed the prairies. This rich source of meat attracted many Indians to the area. When white people arrived they found Arapaho, Bannock, Blackfeet, Cheyenne, Crow, Shoshone, Sioux, and Ute Indians living in what is now Wyoming.

Exploration. French trappers may have entered the Wyoming region in the mid-1700's. However, exploration of the area did not begin until after 1800. The United States bought most of the region from France in 1803, as part of the Louisiana Purchase. After that, American trappers came to the area to find furs. In 1807, a trapper named John Colter became the first white man to travel across the Yellowstone area. Five years later, in 1812, Robert Stuart and a party of fur traders from Oregon discovered a relatively easy way across the mountains through South Pass. They did not cross the pass, but the pass later became important in pioneer travel to the West.

During the 1820's and 1830's, the fur trade became more highly organized. General William Ashley established an annual *rendezvous* (gathering) of trappers. At these gatherings, Ashley's fur company traded ammunition, food, and other supplies for furs. The first rendezvous took place in 1825 on the Green River, near the present Wyoming-Utah border. The yearly rendezvous became important to the trappers not only for trading, but also for exchange of news and as an enjoyable social event.

A trapping and trading party of more than a hundred men came to the Wyoming area in 1832. The group was led by Captain Benjamin L. E. de Bonneville. Bonneville's party discovered an oil spring in 1833 in the Wind River Basin. In 1834, traders William Sublette and Robert Campbell established Fort William in what is now eastern Wyoming. This fort, later called Fort Laramie, was the area's first permanent trading post. In 1843, the famous Western scout and trapper Jim Bridger—with his partner, Louis Vásquez—founded Fort Bridger in southwestern Wyoming.

After trading posts were established, the rendezvous became less important. The last of these colorful gatherings was held in 1840.

In 1842 and 1843, Lieutenant John C. Frémont explored the Wind River Mountains. His party was guided by the famous scout Kit Carson. After Frémont made his report, Congress voted in 1846 to establish forts along the Oregon Trail to protect settlers moving west. In 1849, the government bought Fort William. This fort, also known as Fort John, was renamed Fort Laramie by the army.

At various times, parts of what is now Wyoming were in the territories of Louisiana, Missouri, Nebraska, Oregon, Washington, Idaho, Utah, and Dakota. Part of southern Wyoming, south of the 42nd parallel, belonged to Spain from the 1500's to the 1800's. Mexico claimed it in the early 1800's, but lost it to the Republic of Texas in 1836. This area became part of the United States in 1845 when Texas joined the Union.

The great trails. By the mid-1840's, pioneers were streaming west through the Wyoming area on three famous trails. These were the California Trail, the Mormon Trail to Utah, and the Oregon Trail to the Pacific Northwest. All three trails took South Pass through the mountains. Beyond South Pass, the Oregon Trail turned northwest, and the Mormon and California trails went southwest. Settlers moving across southern Wyoming

Emigrant Train Fording Medicine Bow Creek, Rocky Mountains (1870), an oil painting on canvas by Samuel Colman; Bennington Museum, Bennington, Vt. (Gail McCullough)

Pioneers traveling west passed through Wyoming in great numbers during the mid-1800's. This painting depicts a wagon train crossing the Medicine Bow River in southeastern Wyoming.

used the Overland (Cherokee) Trail, which joined other trails at Fort Bridger. Thousands of settlers traveled through Wyoming, but few of them stayed.

The Plains Indians often assisted early wagon trains by pointing out grazing lands and watering areas. The various tribes often traded with the travelers.

Indian and settler conflicts. By 1849, the Sioux and other tribes were becoming alarmed at the growing number of settlers crossing traditional Indian land. The white settlers killed or frightened away the game. Their carelessness with fire caused roaring blazes on the prairie, and their diseases killed or crippled countless Indians. Fighting broke out between the Indians and the settlers, and the United States Army often had to step in. The conflicts resulted in the deaths of many more Indians than settlers.

Gold was discovered in Montana in the 1860's, and settlers began moving north up the Bozeman Trail to Montana. This trail crossed the Powder River Basin, a different area of the Indian land. The tribes fought with new fury.

To keep the Bozeman Trail open, the army built Fort Phil Kearny near the Bighorn Mountains in the summer of 1866. The Sioux hated this fort. Led by Red Cloud, they put war parties around it in what was called the *Circle of Death.* During the first six months, about 150 men were killed. Captain W. J. Fetterman and 81 of his men died in a single battle. Finally, in 1868, Red Cloud and other Indian leaders signed a treaty. The army agreed to give up Fort Phil Kearny and two other forts and leave northeastern Wyoming to the Indians. In return, the Indians agreed not to interfere with the construction of the Union Pacific Railroad through southern Wyoming.

A troubled peace lasted until 1874, when prospectors discovered gold in the Black Hills of South Dakota just east of Wyoming. Thousands of white people violated the treaty by moving into the area. The Sioux considered the Black Hills sacred, and they fought the new invasion. Sioux and Cheyenne warriors won two bitter battles with U.S. soldiers in what is now Montana. However, the Indian force broke up to flee from other troops. Some Indians went to Canada, and others agreed to move to reservations. Serious Indian fighting ended in the sum-

mer of 1876, and Wyoming settlers finally had peace.

Territorial progress. Even before the Indian troubles ended, southern Wyoming was developing rapidly. The foundations for Wyoming's minerals industry had been laid long before the area became a territory. In 1833, the Bonneville party greased its wagon axles at a spot where oil seeped from the ground in the Wind River Basin. Jim Bridger sold oil at his fort, and pioneers mixed it with flour to use as axle grease.

Gold was found at South Pass in 1842. However, the discovery aroused little interest. In 1867, a more promising gold strike attracted many prospectors to the area. Several boom towns, such as Atlantic City and South Pass City, sprang up.

The Union Pacific Railroad entered the area in 1867. Towns were founded as the "end of track" moved west. Cheyenne, Laramie, Rawlins, Rock Springs, Green River, and Evanston grew up in turn. Towns also appeared along the route of the great trails. In 1868, Congress created the Territory of Wyoming. President Ulysses S. Grant appointed Brigadier General John A. Campbell as the first governor of the territory.

On Dec. 10, 1869, the territorial legislature granted women the right to vote, hold office, and serve on juries. The new law was the first of its kind in the United States. Women first served on juries in 1870, in Laramie. That same year, Esther H. Morris of South Pass City became the nation's first woman justice of the peace.

Wyoming's tourist industry got its start during the territorial days. In 1872, Congress created Yellowstone National Park, the nation's first national park. The park immediately attracted tourists.

In 1883 and 1884, interest in oil was revived because of profitable drilling elsewhere. The first successful well was drilled in 1883 in the Dallas Field, near Lander. Plans were made for exploration of several areas near Casper, but the industry developed slowly, and several years passed before oil activity prospered.

Ranching supported the new territory's economy. Large numbers of cattle were driven north from Texas to Wyoming. Wealthy ranchers controlled huge areas and ruled the affairs of the territorial government.

By 1885, however, cattle prices had dropped. In addi-

Bureau of American Ethnology, Smithsonian Institution

Wind River Indian Reservation was presented to the Shoshoni Indian Chief Washakie in 1868 by the U.S. government. The Shoshoni received the reservation in return for their friendliness to white people and their help in fighting tribes hostile to settlers. W. H. Jackson took this picture in 1870. His photographs form a vivid record of Wyoming history during the late 1800's.

Historic Wyoming

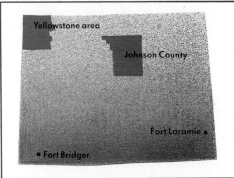

Yellowstone was established as the first national park in 1872. John Colter explored the area in 1807.

The Johnson County War broke out in 1892 between owners of large ranches and smaller operators. Large ranchers and their hired gunmen killed two men.

Fort Laramie and Fort Bridger offered protection and supplies for weary pioneers. Thousands of travelers crossed the state in covered wagons on overland trails between 1840 and 1870.

The Treaty of Fort Laramie in 1868 brought temporary peace with the Sioux when they agreed to limit their lands.

Nellie Tayloe Ross was elected governor of Wyoming in 1925, becoming the first woman governor in the U.S.

Important dates in Wyoming

WORLD BOOK illustrations by Kevin Chadwick

1807 John Colter explored the Yellowstone area.

1812 Robert Stuart discovered South Pass across the Rocky Mountains.

1833 Captain Benjamin L. E. de Bonneville mapped the Wyoming area and discovered oil east of the Wind River Mountains.

1834 William Sublette and Robert Campbell established Fort William (later Fort Laramie).

1843 Scout Jim Bridger established Fort Bridger.

1867 The Union Pacific Railroad entered Wyoming.

1868 Congress created the Territory of Wyoming. Its first coal mines began operation in Carbon and Sweetwater counties.

1869 The Wyoming territorial legislature gave women the right to vote and hold elective office.

1872 Yellowstone became the first national park.

1883 Wyoming's first oil well was drilled in the Dallas Field.

1890 Wyoming became the 44th state on July 10.

1892 The Johnson County War broke out after a dispute over cattle rustling.

1906 President Theodore Roosevelt made Devils Tower the first national monument.

1910 Engineers completed Shoshone (now Buffalo Bill) Dam.

1925 Nellie Tayloe Ross became the first woman governor in the United States.

1929 Grand Teton became a national park.

1938-1939 Engineers completed Alcova and Seminoe dams.

1951-1952 Major uranium deposits were found in several parts of Wyoming.

1960 The nation's first operational intercontinental ballistic missile base opened near Cheyenne.

1965 Minuteman missile installations were completed near Cheyenne.

1988 Fires damaged large areas of Yellowstone National Park.

tion, there was a severe shortage of grass for grazing. In 1887, thousands of cattle died in the howling blizzards and freezing temperatures of a bitterly cold winter. Many ranchers were ruined financially and lost much of their political power.

Statehood. Wyoming became the 44th state of the Union on July 10, 1890. Francis E. Warren, a Republican, became the first state governor on September 11. He resigned in November after being elected to the U.S. Senate. Settlers flocked to Wyoming, and trouble started almost immediately. Many settlers built homes on the prairie and tended small herds of cattle. Powerful cattlemen who had used the range for years grew angry when the settlers began fencing their small ranches. Many of the cattlemen who had financial problems blamed their hardship on the small ranchers. They accused these small outfits of fencing the land and *rustling* (stealing) cattle from established ranches to build their herds. The Wyoming Stock Growers Association, an organization controlled by the "cattle barons," hired detectives to protect its interests.

The Johnson County War. Violence broke out in north-central Wyoming in 1892. The established cattlemen were convinced that their herds were being looted. They had no proof to identify the rustlers, but they had strong suspicions. The operators of the large ranches prepared a list of suspects and decided to kill the men on the list. They brought in about 25 gunmen from Texas and made up a force of about 55 men. This force, called the Invaders, was formed in Cheyenne and secretly left for Johnson County. Along the way, the Invaders encountered two men who were allies of the small ranchers at a cabin of the KC Ranch near Buffalo. The two men were killed by the Invaders.

Information about the killings reached Buffalo, the seat of Johnson County, and a group of armed men was formed to stop the Invaders. The two forces met on the TA Ranch, but federal troops arrived in time to prevent a bloody battle. The Invaders were taken to Cheyenne for trial. However, important witnesses failed to appear at the trial. The Invaders were released, and the "war" ended.

Trouble again broke out on the range in the early 1900's. Cattlemen and sheepmen argued over grazing rights. The cattlemen claimed that their animals would not feed on land that had been grazed by sheep. A feud developed as the number of sheep increased. The climax came when cattlemen killed three sheepmen near Ten Sleep in 1909. But tempers cooled, and sheep became an important Wyoming product.

Progress as a state. After 1900, Wyoming's population grew rapidly. The Homestead acts of 1909, 1912, and 1916 provided large areas of free land for settlers under certain conditions. The construction of dams along major streams brought irrigation water to some areas of the prairie. Crops grown on this land increased the agricultural wealth of the state. In 1906, President Theodore Roosevelt made Devils Tower the first national monument. Tourism became more important as railroads and improved roads made it easier for people to reach such scenic areas as Yellowstone National Park and Jackson Hole.

Wyoming's first oil boom came in 1912 in the Salt Creek Field north of Casper. Oil companies built pipe-

lines and refineries to handle the crude oil. By 1918, Casper had become a bustling center of business and finance.

In 1924, Wyoming voters elected the nation's first woman governor, Nellie Tayloe Ross. In 1933, Ross became the first woman director of the U.S. Mint.

Wyoming faced deep economic hardships well before the Great Depression of the 1930's began. Unstable economic conditions in Wyoming during the early 1920's included the failure of many banks, which became a nationwide feature of the Great Depression in the next decade. During the depression years of the 1930's, Wyoming's economy was helped by increasing oil production and by various government construction projects. These included the Kendrick Project, which provided both irrigation water and new hydroelectric capacity. The project, on the North Platte River, included Alcova, Kortes, and Seminoe dams.

The mid-1900's. Wyoming's economy boomed during World War II (1939-1945). The war brought great demands for the state's coal, lumber, meat, and oil. Economic development continued after the war, and tourism increased.

New industrial growth in Wyoming resulted from the mining of two minerals, trona and uranium. Sodium carbonate, the key ingredient of trona, has many uses in the chemical industry and in the manufacture of glass.

Oil drilling in southwestern Wyoming had shown that trona lay over 1,500 feet (457 meters) under the surface of the earth in the Green River Basin. A mine shaft was sunk there in 1947, and mining of trona began. Output increased rapidly during the 1950's. During the 1960's, two chemical companies built huge plants near the town of Green River to be used for the mining of trona and the production of sodium carbonate.

The first major uranium discovery in Wyoming occurred in 1951. Large deposits of uranium were found in the Powder River area. After the findings were published early in 1952, uranium was discovered in many areas throughout the state. By the late 1950's, Wyoming ranked third among the states in known uranium reserves.

Many companies expanded their operations in Wyoming during the 1960's. A steel company built a new iron ore processing plant near Sunrise. Another firm revived the ghost town of Atlantic City by opening an iron mine and building a processing plant there. Trona operations near Green River continued to grow. Oil and natural gas exploration also expanded, with the greatest activity in the Powder River Basin. Electric companies built generating plants that use Wyoming's huge coal deposits as fuel. The plants are at Glenrock, Kemmerer, Rock Springs, and Wheatland. Coal production dropped during the 1950's after railroad locomotives switched from coal to diesel power, but it began to rise again in the 1960's.

In 1960, Wyoming became the headquarters of the first operational long-range missile squadron in the United States. This squadron ranks as one of the largest missile installations in the world. The control center for the missile squadron is Francis E. Warren Air Force Base located just outside Cheyenne.

Recent developments. Between 1970 and 1980, Wyoming's population grew by about 42 percent, one of the highest rates in the nation. Large numbers of people moved to Wyoming to work in the state's rapidly developing mining industries. An Arab oil embargo in 1973 and 1974 reduced supplies, and raised prices, of petroleum in the United States and other countries. Wyoming's coal industry then grew as alternate energy sources were required. New coal mines were opened, and abandoned mines were reopened. The boom in coal helped lead to other economic growth in the state.

Wyoming's sudden population growth caused housing shortages and other problems in mining communities. During the 1970's, the state legislature approved new taxes on minerals to provide funds to help communities deal with their problems.

Wyoming began experiencing economic problems during the 1980's. Important uranium discoveries in Canada and Australia reduced the demand for Wyoming's uranium. Also, the nuclear energy industry, which uses uranium, has continued to develop slowly in the United States. Many Wyoming uranium mines and mills closed down. Americans also became more conservation-minded and reduced their use of coal and oil.

In the 1990's, Wyoming's production of coal and some other minerals increased. Tourism also grew in the state in the 1990's, benefiting the economy. Today, state leaders are trying to find ways to broaden the economy and make it less dependent on mineral production.

During the 1980's, Alaska passed Wyoming in population, leaving Wyoming last among the 50 states. Wyoming grew in population during the 1990's but still ranked last among the states in the 2000 census.

Ronald E. Beiswenger and Phil Roberts

Study aids

Related articles in *World Book* include:

Biographies

Bridger, Jim
Laramie, Jacques
Morris, Esther H.
Pollock, Jackson
Ross, Nellie Tayloe
Simpson, Alan K.
Spotted Tail
Washakie

Cities

Casper   Cheyenne   Laramie

History

Bozeman Trail
Homestead Act
Indian, American
Indian wars (Wars on the Plains)
Oregon Trail
Pony express
Western frontier life in America

Physical features

Black Hills
Devils Tower National Monument
Fossil Butte National Monument
Grand Teton National Park
Great Plains
Rocky Mountains
Teton Range
Yellowstone National Park
Yellowstone River

Other related articles

Cowboy
Ranching
Wyoming, University of

Outline

I. **People**
   A. Population
   B. Schools
   C. Libraries and museums
II. **Visitor's guide**
   A. Places to visit
   B. Annual events
III. **Land and climate**
   A. Land regions
   B. Rivers and lakes
   C. Plant and animal life
   D. Climate
IV. **Economy**
   A. Natural resources
   B. Service industries
   C. Mining
   D. Manufacturing
   E. Agriculture
   F. Electric power
   G. Transportation
   H. Communication
V. **Government**
   A. Constitution
   B. Executive
   C. Legislature
   D. Courts
   E. Local government
   F. Revenue
   G. Politics
VI. **History**

Questions

What three famous pioneer routes crossed Wyoming in the mid-1800's? How did the passage of the pioneers disturb the Plains Indians?

What part of what is now Wyoming once belonged to the Republic of Texas?

What was the first U.S. national park? How did its establishment affect Wyoming?

Why was the construction of the Union Pacific Railroad during the 1860's important to the development of cities in Wyoming?

Why was the result of Wyoming's election for governor in 1924 so unusual?

What is Wyoming's leading mineral product?

What Wyoming tourist attraction became the first U.S. national monument?

Why is Wyoming nicknamed the *Equality State*?

Who were the Invaders?

What was a fur trappers' *rendezvous*?

Additional resources

Level I

Baldwin, Guy. *Wyoming.* Benchmark Bks., 1999.
Fontes, Justin and Ron. *Wyoming.* World Almanac, 2003.
Frisch, Carlienne A. *Wyoming.* 2nd ed. Lerner, 2002.
Kent, Deborah. *Wyoming.* Children's Pr., 2000.
Maynard, Charles W. *Fort Laramie.* PowerKids Pr., 2002.

Level II

Cawley, Gregg, and others. *The Equality State: Government and Politics in Wyoming.* 4th ed. Eddie Bowers Pub., 2000.
Knight, Dennis H. *Mountains and Plains: The Ecology of Wyoming Landscapes.* 1994. Reprint. Yale, 1996.
Larson, Taft A. *History of Wyoming.* 2nd ed. Univ. of Neb. Pr., 1978.
Melford, Michael. *Big Sky Country.* Rizzoli, 1996. A book of photographs.
Murray, Robert A. *The Bozeman Trail.* Pruett, 1988.
Pitcher, Don. *Wyoming.* 5th ed. Avalon Travel, 2003. A travel guide.
Preston, Thomas and Elizabeth. *The Double Eagle Guide to Western State Parks.* Vol. 2, *Rocky Mountains: Colorado, Montana, Wyoming.* 2nd ed. Discovery Pub., 1997.
Roberts, Phil, and others. *Wyoming Almanac.* 4th ed. Skyline West, 1996.
Smith, Duane A. *Rocky Mountain West: Colorado, Wyoming, and Montana, 1859-1915.* Univ. of N. Mex. Pr., 1992.
Smith, Phyllis. *Bozeman and the Gallatin Valley: A History.* Two Dot, 1997.
Stamm, Henry E. *People of the Wind River: The Eastern Shoshones, 1825-1900.* Univ. of Okla. Pr., 1999.
Wyoming Atlas and Gazetteer. 3rd ed. DeLorme, 2001.

Wyoming, University of, is a state-supported coeducational school in Laramie, Wyo. It has colleges of agriculture, arts and sciences, business, education, engineering, health sciences, and law; a graduate school; and Army and Air Force ROTC units. Courses lead to bachelor's, master's, and doctor's degrees.

The University of Wyoming is noted for its geology program, its American Studies program, and its large manuscript and printed collections on the history of the Western United States. The school has an astronomical observatory and an atmospheric monitoring station in the Medicine Bow Mountains. It also has a biological research station at Jackson, and five agricultural substations in the state. The University of Wyoming was founded in 1886.

Critically reviewed by the University of Wyoming

Wyoming Valley is a section of northeastern Pennsylvania 3 to 4 miles (5 to 6 kilometers) wide and about 20 miles (32 kilometers) long. It lies along the north branch of the Susquehanna River near Wilkes-Barre. The valley has rich deposits of *anthracite* (hard coal).

The Wyoming Valley is a historic gateway to central Pennsylvania from New England and New York. Many settlers entered the valley during colonial days. In the 1770's, it became the center of a boundary controversy between Connecticut and Pennsylvania. Congress settled the dispute in favor of Pennsylvania. In 1778, the Wyoming Valley was the scene of a bloody massacre (see **Wyoming Valley Massacre**).

Wyoming Valley Massacre, one of many tragedies of the American Revolutionary War, occurred in what is now Luzerne County, Pennsylvania. In 1778, it was an incorporated county in the colony of Connecticut. At that time, most of the inhabitants of the Wyoming Valley believed in the American cause of independence from Great Britain. However, some residents of the Wyoming Valley were Tories, and they remained loyal to Great Britain.

As the war went on, the Tories were driven out of the community, and joined other Tory and Indian bands. In the summer of 1778, these bands attacked Wyoming Valley. The inhabitants fled for safety to Forty Fort, near the site of the present city of Wilkes-Barre, Pa. About 300 men defended the fort. An army of 800 fighters, led by a British officer, opposed them. Six hundred of the attackers were Indians.

On July 3, the two groups met in a hard-fought battle. The attackers defeated the settlers, and killed more than two-thirds of them. The Indians tortured many of them to death. The survivors were left to find their way to the nearest settlements, and many of them died before they could reach help. The attackers completely destroyed the village and left the rest of the valley in ruins.

John W. Ifkovic

Wyss family, *vees,* wrote *The Swiss Family Robinson,* a popular children's adventure story about a shipwrecked family. Johann David Wyss (1743-1818), a Swiss pastor, made up the story to tell his four young sons. He wrote it down for the family, and he and his son Johann Emmanuel (1782-1837) illustrated it. Years later, another son, Johann Rudolf (1781-1830), rediscovered the story. He revised it and, in 1812 and 1813, had it published. He and his father are each sometimes considered the author.

In *The Swiss Family Robinson,* the Robinson family struggles to survive alone on an island. They learn that they must work together, rather than separately. Young readers especially enjoy the book because the four Robinson sons behave—and misbehave—like real children. The book shows the influence of *Robinson Crusoe* (1719), a novel about a shipwrecked man on an island. This novel, by the English author Daniel Defoe, was extremely popular at the time. See **Robinson Crusoe**.

Johann Rudolf Wyss was a professor and a scholar of Swiss folklore. He wrote the words to a popular Swiss patriotic song. He, Johann Emmanuel Wyss, and their father were all born in Bern.   Marilyn Fain Apseloff

Wyszyński, *vih SHIHN skee,* **Stefan Cardinal** (1901-1981), was the head of the Roman Catholic Church in Poland from 1948 until his death. He became an archbishop in 1948 and a cardinal in 1953. Several months after Wyszyński became a cardinal, Poland's Communist government imprisoned him for opposing its antireligious policies.

Wyszyński led the opposition to the government from 1956, when he was released from prison, until his death. However, he followed a policy of compromise. For example, he spoke out for religious freedom and other personal rights. But he avoided open conflict with the Communists, especially when he thought it might lead to Russian intervention in Poland. During the 1970's, his policies helped improve relations between the church and the government.

Keystone
Cardinal Wyszyński

Wyszyński was born in Zuzela, near Warsaw. He was ordained a priest in 1924 and earned a doctorate in sociology from Catholic University in Lublin. He took part in the movement against the Nazi occupation of Poland during World War II (1939-1945).   Adam Bromke

Wythe, *wihth,* **George** (1726-1806), an American statesman, was a signer of the Declaration of Independence. He was also a well-known lawyer and judge and a supporter of political leader Thomas Jefferson and other distinguished Virginians. He wrote the original Virginia protest against the Stamp Act in 1764. It was so passionate that it had to be rewritten in a milder style.

Wythe served in the Second Continental Congress in 1775 and 1776. Later he helped draft the Virginia Constitution. He became a judge of the court of chancery of Virginia in 1778, and, in 1786, he became chancellor of the state. In 1787, he supported *ratification* (approval) of the United States Constitution while participating in the Constitutional Convention.

Wythe was born at Back River, Va., and attended the College of William and Mary. He became a lawyer in 1747 and entered the Virginia House of Burgesses in 1754. In 1779, Wythe was appointed to the nation's first law professorship. The professorship was established that year at William and Mary by Thomas Jefferson.

Robert A. Becker

See also **Jefferson, Thomas** (Early life).

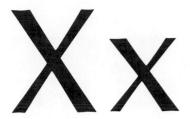

X is the 24th letter of our alphabet. It probably developed from a letter called *samekh* used by the Semites, who once lived in Syria and Palestine. Historians are not sure what symbol the Semites used for this letter. About 1000 B.C., the Phoenicians developed a symbol that looks like a support for their letter *samekh.* The Greeks later took this symbol into their alphabet. It could represent the sounds of *kh* or *ks.*

Uses. *X* or *x* is about the 23rd most frequently used letter in books, newspapers, and other printed material in English. *X,* used alone or in combination with other letters, often stands for the word *Christ,* as in *Xmas. X* is the Roman numeral for *ten. X* is used in physical science and in mathematics to denote an unknown quantity, or a quantity that was at first unknown, as in *X ray.* In arithmetic problems, *x* is the sign of multiplication. In describing measurements, *x* represents the word *by,* as in *9′ x 12′,* or *nine by twelve feet.*

Pronunciation. In English, *x* has six sounds: *ks,* as in *six; gz,* as in *examine; ksh,* as in *luxury; gzh,* as in *luxurious; sh,* as in *anxious;* and *z,* as in *xylophone.* In some cases, such as *luxury,* the *x* is not voiced. In *luxurious,* the *x* is voiced. In Spanish, *x* may be pronounced as the English *s* or as the English *h.* In most other European languages, *x* has the same sounds as it has in English. See **Pronunciation.**   Marianne Cooley

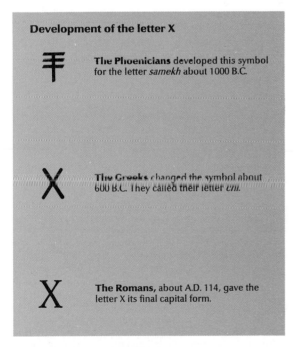

Development of the letter X

The Phoenicians developed this symbol for the letter *samekh* about 1000 B.C.

The Greeks changed the symbol about 600 B.C. They called their letter *chi.*

The Romans, about A.D. 114, gave the letter X its final capital form.

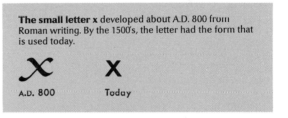

The small letter x developed about A.D. 800 from Roman writing. By the 1500's, the letter had the form that is used today.

A.D. 800   Today

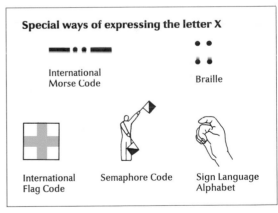

Special ways of expressing the letter X

International Morse Code

Braille

International Flag Code

Semaphore Code

Sign Language Alphabet

Common forms of the letter X

Handwritten letters vary from person to person. *Manuscript* (printed) letters, *left,* have simple curves and straight lines. Cursive letters, *right,* have flowing lines.

Roman letters have small finishing strokes called *serifs* that extend from the main strokes. The type face shown above is Baskerville. The italic form appears at the right.

Sans-serif letters are also called *gothic letters.* They have no serifs. The type face shown above is called Futura. The italic form of Futura appears at the right.

Computer letters have special shapes. Computers can "read" these letters either optically or by means of the magnetic ink with which the letters may be printed.

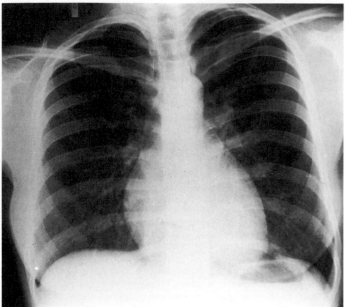

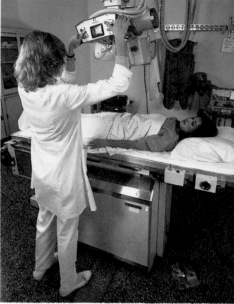

Saint Mary of Nazareth Hospital Center   © Larry Mulvehill, Photo Researchers

A chest X ray, *left,* reveals the shadows of the heart, the lungs, and the ribs. It can help physicians detect lung disease, broken bones, and other abnormal conditions inside a patient's body. X-ray pictures are produced by an X-ray machine, *right,* operated by a technologist.

X rays are one of the most useful forms of energy. Their main uses have been in the field of medicine. X rays find wide use in medicine because they can pass through flesh and produce photographic images of what lies beneath the skin. X rays also have many uses in science. For example, researchers who investigate the structure of solid materials use X rays to determine the arrangement of atoms in crystals. Astronomers study X rays generated by stars and other heavenly objects to learn about the objects' structure and temperature.

The German physicist Wilhelm C. Roentgen discovered X rays in 1895. He called them *X rays* because at first he did not understand what they were. *X* is a scientific symbol for the unknown.

Scientists now know that X rays are one of several forms of *electromagnetic radiation.* Another form of such radiation is visible light. The various forms can be distinguished by their *wavelength,* the distance between successive crests of their waves. From the shortest wavelength to the longest, electromagnetic radiation consists of gamma rays, X rays, ultraviolet rays, visible light, infrared rays, and radio waves. Wavelength is related to energy: the shorter the wavelength, the higher the energy. Thus, X rays have a shorter wavelength, but more energy, than do waves of visible light.

X rays can produce biological, chemical, and physical changes in the substances they enter. For this reason, X rays can be dangerous. In human beings, an overdose of X rays may cause cancer, skin burns, anemia, or other serious conditions. But physicians also use X rays to treat cancer. X rays kill cancer cells more readily than they kill normal cells.

In X-ray machines used in medicine and science, a special tube that resembles a television picture tube produces X rays. Scientists also use intense, narrow beams of X rays generated by devices called *synchrotrons.* In nature, extremely hot stars and other heavenly objects *emit* (send out) X rays.

Uses of X rays

In medicine, health workers use X-ray machines to make *radiographs* (X-ray pictures) of the bones and internal organs of the body. Radiographs help physicians detect injuries and diseases, such as broken bones or tumors, inside a patient's body. Dentists take X-ray pictures to reveal cavities in teeth.

Because X rays can harm living tissue, health workers who use them in diagnostic work give their patients only as much radiation as necessary. In addition, the workers shield parts of the body not being examined. For example, a dental technician lays a lead apron on a patient's body before taking X rays of the patient's teeth.

A health worker produces a radiograph by passing a beam of X rays through the patient's body onto a sheet of photographic film or a special plastic that is sensitive to X rays. The patient's bones absorb more rays than do the muscles or internal organs, and so the bones cast the sharpest shadows on the film or plastic. Because a radiograph is a photographic negative, the shadows of the bones show up as light areas. Other parts of the body allow more X rays through than the bones do and so cast shadows in varying shades of gray.

In another process, called *digital imaging,* detectors measure the X rays that pass through the body and send this information to a computer. The computer converts the data into an image that is displayed on a monitor.

A machine called a *computed tomographic scanner* or *CT scanner* uses X-rays to produce cross-sectional images of a patient's body. The machine shoots a pencil-thin beam of X rays at the body from many angles. Detectors measure the rays that pass through and send the measurements to a computer. The computer then uses the measurements to create the images.

In industry, inspectors use X rays to examine products made of various kinds of materials, including aluminum, steel, and other cast metals. Radiographs reveal cracks and other defects inside the products. Workers also use X rays to check the quality of mass-produced products, such as computer chips and other small electronic devices. Scanners at airports use X rays to check baggage for weapons or bombs.

In crystal research, X rays help scientists determine the arrangement of atoms that make up crystals. The atoms in crystals are arranged in planes, with regular spacing between the planes. *Crystallographers* (scientists who study crystals) pass a beam of X rays through a crystal. The planes act as tiny mirrors, *diffracting* (spreading out) the rays into a geometric pattern. Each type of crystal produces a different diffraction pattern. Mathematical analysis of such patterns can reveal the precise geometric arrangement of atoms in different crystals. Scientists also use X rays to study the structure and makeup of complex biological molecules known as *enzymes* and *proteins.*

In astronomy, scientists study X rays emitted by extremely hot objects, including tremendous clouds of gas, *supernovae* (exploding stars), the centers of certain galaxies, and disks of gas that orbit about *black holes.* A black hole is an invisible object with such powerful gravitational force that not even light can escape its surface. An X ray's energy depends on the energy of its source, so astronomers can use information gathered by the detectors to determine the temperatures of the various sources. Because the atmosphere absorbs X rays approaching Earth from cosmic sources, scientists use devices mounted on spacecraft to detect the rays.

Characteristics of X rays

Wavelength. X rays have longer wavelengths than gamma rays and shorter wavelengths than ultraviolet rays. Scientists working in different fields define the ranges of wavelength differently. In general, however,

the ranges for X rays span a band from about 0.01 to 10 *nanometers* (nm). One nanometer is one billionth of a meter, equal to $\frac{1}{25,400,000}$ inch. By comparison, the wavelengths of visible light range from about 400 to 700 nm.

Some scientists refer to X rays with wavelengths shorter than 0.1 nm as *hard X rays* because of their great penetrating power. Longer X rays are known as *soft X rays.* Many scientists who use X rays in their work measure wavelengths in *angstrom units.* One angstrom unit equals 0.1 nanometer.

Penetrating power. The penetrating power of X rays is a result of their high energy. Because the energy of X rays is second only to that of gamma rays, only gamma rays have greater penetrating power than X rays.

Any form of electromagnetic radiation will penetrate matter until something in the matter absorbs its energy. In the case of X rays, the absorbing objects are negatively charged particles of matter known as *electrons.* In an atom, one or more electrons orbit a central nucleus. The nucleus consists of one or more positively charged *protons* and an approximately equal number of *neutrons,* which have no net charge. In a complete atom, the number of electrons equals the atom's *atomic number*—the number of protons in the nucleus. Elements whose atoms have high atomic numbers therefore absorb more X rays than do elements with low atomic numbers.

Lead, which has an atomic number of 82, absorbs more X rays than do most other substances. For this reason, lead is often used to make X-ray shields. The metal beryllium, with an atomic number of only 4, absorbs few X rays. This metal is therefore used to make small exit windows in X-ray tubes.

The penetrating power of X rays has affected the design of mirrors used in X-ray telescopes. Only X rays that strike a mirror almost parallel to its surface will reflect strongly from it. The mirror reflects these X rays at a small angle called a *grazing incidence angle.* The reflection of a ray at a grazing incidence is like the skipping of a stone off the surface of a pond. To focus X rays via grazing incidence, X-ray mirrors have a curved design. They consist of tapered tubes that are nested within one another. The rays enter the mirror almost parallel to the axis of the tubes and reflect off the inner surfaces of the tubes.

WORLD BOOK diagram

How an X-ray tube works

Electric current flows through a connection called the *cathode,* heating it. The heated cathode releases electrons. A voltage applied across the cathode and a connection called the *anode* forces electrons to strike a tungsten target, where they produce X rays. The rays exit through a window and can go on to produce an image of what lies beneath a patient's skin.

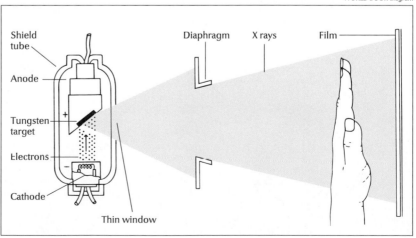

Shield tube
Anode
Tungsten target
Electrons
Cathode
Thin window
Diaphragm
X rays
Film

The ability of X rays to change substances that they penetrate is also a result of their high energy. When an electron in an atom absorbs energy, it moves to an orbit farther from the atom's nucleus. If the electron absorbs enough energy, it actually leaves the atom. If the atom had been complete—with equal numbers of protons and electrons—it becomes an *ion* (an electrically charged atom) when the electron leaves it. The process in which an electron absorbs energy and leaves an atom is known as *ionization.* This process affects the ability of the atom to maintain its position and function in a substance. Chemical bonds may be broken, and the shape of molecules may be changed. Thus, if enough ionization occurs in an object—or in living tissue—damage results.

How X rays are produced

In X-ray tubes. An X-ray tube works by accelerating a beam of electrons to extremely high speeds and directing them into a piece of solid material called a *target.* The target material absorbs most of the energy of the electrons and converts it to heat. But some of the energy becomes X rays by either of two processes. One process produces what physicists call *bremsstrahlung* (pronounced *BREHM shtrah lung)*—the German word for *braking radiation.* The other process generates *characteristic X rays.*

Bremsstrahlung. The process that produces bremsstrahlung makes use of a fundamental characteristic of charged particles that are in motion: When such a particle changes direction, it emits electromagnetic radiation. The wavelength of the radiation depends on the energy of the particle and on how sharply the particle's path bends—the higher the energy and the sharper the bend, the shorter the wavelength.

In an X-ray tube, electrons in the beam change direction after the beam has entered the target. The bending occurs because objects with opposite electric charges attract each other. When an electron in the beam passes near a target nucleus, protons in the nucleus attract the electron. Targets are made of materials whose atoms have high atomic numbers, so their nuclei have large numbers of protons. As a result, the attraction between the electron and the protons is extremely strong. The path of the electron therefore bends sharply.

Characteristic X rays. The second process begins when an electron in the beam transfers much of its energy to an electron in a target atom. The electrons in the target atom orbit the nucleus in groups called *shells.* Electrons with the lowest energy are in the shell that is closest to the nucleus. Electrons with successively higher energies are in shells that are farther and farther from the nucleus. In the target atom, the electron that absorbs the energy is usually in the closest shell, and it absorbs so much energy that it leaves the atom.

After this electron departs, another electron in the target atom tends to take its place. But the replacement electron is in a shell that is farther from the nucleus than the departed electron had been. Therefore, to replace the departed electron, the replacement electron must give up the difference in energy between the two shells. It does so by emitting electromagnetic radiation in the form of an X ray. The energy of the X ray is characteristic of the target atom. That is, target atoms of a given chemical element emit X rays that have the same energy.

Synchrotron radiation. The most intense beams of X rays produced in machines come from synchrotrons. These are large machines—the biggest synchrotron radiation source designed to produce X rays measures 4,710 feet (1,436 meters) in circumference. This machine is the Super Photon Ring-8 GeV (SPring-8) machine, near Osaka, Japan.

A synchrotron consists of straight and curved sections arranged in a ring. In the straight sections, radio waves accelerate a beam of electrons or other charged particles to high speeds. Electromagnets in the curved sections guide the beam around the ring. This method of guidance works because a charged particle will change its direction when it crosses a *magnetic field* (a region in which the force of magnetism can be detected). When a particle changes direction, it also emits electromagnetic radiation known as *synchrotron radiation.*

Scientists built the first synchrotrons in the 1940's to study subatomic particles. In those machines and in sim-

Argonne National Laboratory

A huge "X-ray machine" called the Advanced Photon Source (APS) accelerates subatomic particles to nearly the speed of light, then uses powerful magnets to force the particles to produce intense beams of X rays. The APS operates at Argonne National Laboratory near Chicago.

ilar machines built since then, the particle beam strikes a target. The resulting impacts break particles away from the target or produce new particles. Special devices detect the particles that fly away from the points of impact. Physicists then study the information provided by the detectors. Synchrotron radiation plays no role in such experiments. In fact, it is unwanted because the machine must make up for the energy that is radiated away.

Synchrotron radiation has proved useful to crystallographers and other scientists who investigate the structure of matter. It has been so useful that, since the 1970's, scientists have built machines just to produce synchrotron radiation in the ultraviolet and X-ray ranges. There are now about 50 such synchrotron sources.

The radiation comes from *insertion devices* (ID's) mounted in some of the straight sections. An ID consists mainly of two sets of several permanent magnets. Each set is arranged so that magnetic south poles alternate with magnetic north poles. One set is mounted above the beam path, and the other is below the path. When an electron beam passes through the magnetic fields, the electrons change direction again and again. Each time they do so, they emit synchrotron radiation.

In outer space, the main sources of X rays are very hot objects. The X rays originate in the vibrations of atoms. The atoms of any object vibrate at various speeds. Each time an atom vibrates back and forth, some of its energy of motion is transferred to one or more electrons. The electrons then return to their former energy levels by emitting electromagnetic radiation. The more rapid the vibration, the shorter the wavelength of the emission. The object therefore emits radiation at various wavelengths. But some of these wavelengths carry more of the total energy that is emitted by the object than do the other wavelengths. The higher the temperature, the shorter are the wavelengths that carry the most energy.

Celestial objects with temperatures of about 1 million °C have peak wavelengths in the ultraviolet range but are also powerful emitters of X rays. One leading type of X-ray emitter is an *X-ray binary,* which consists of two stars that orbit each other at close range. One of the stars is a normal star and the other is a *neutron star,* the smallest and densest kind of star known. The tremendous gravitational force of the neutron star pulls matter off the normal star. This matter forms a large disk around the neutron star. Friction heats the disk to more than 1 million °C, and so it emits X rays.

David E. Moncton

Related articles in *World Book* include:

Angiography	Particle accelerator
Astronomy (X-ray astronomy)	Radiation
Atom (The forces within an atom)	Radiology
Bragg, Sir William Henry	Roentgen, Wilhelm C.
Computed tomography	Siegbahn, Karl M. G.
Fluoroscopy	Teeth (Dental checkups; picture)
Moseley, Henry Gwyn-Jeffreys	Telescope (Other telescopes)

Additional resources

McClafferty, Carla K. *The Head Bone's Connected to the Neck Bone: The Weird, Wacky, and Wonderful X-Ray.* Farrar, 2001.
Tucker, Wallace H. and Karen. *Revealing the Universe: The Making of the Chandra X-Ray Observatory.* Harvard Univ. Pr., 2001.

Xavier, *ZAY vee uhr,* **Saint Francis** (1506-1552), was a Jesuit missionary. He is called the "Apostle of the Indies."

Most of his work was done in Asia.

Saint Francis Xavier was born Francisco de Xavier on April 7, 1506, near Sangüesa, Spain. His study in Paris brought him acquaintance with Ignatius of Loyola, with whom he helped to found the Society of Jesus. He went with Ignatius to Italy, doing hospital and missionary work, and was ordained a priest in 1537. He remained in Rome as secretary to the Jesuit society until 1540.

The next year, Xavier was sent by John III of Portugal to spread Christianity in the Portuguese possessions in India. He landed in Goa, on the Malabar Coast, in 1542. His preaching in Travancore, in Melaka, and in Japan gained many converts to the Roman Catholic Church. In 1551, the Vatican named him provincial of the province of India.

Xavier planned a mission to China but died on the island of Shangchuan while trying to gain admission to the mainland. His body lies in a shrine in Goa. He was declared a saint in 1622.

Many miracles were credited to Xavier. He was one of the greatest missionaries and explorers in the Far East. Xavier's converts numbered in the hundreds of thousands. Wherever the missionary worked, he left well-organized Christians. His feast day is December 3.

James A. De Jong

See also **Japan** (Warring states period); **Jesuits.**

Xenon, *ZEE nahn* or *ZEHN ahn,* is a chemical element that makes up about 1 part in 20 million of the earth's atmosphere. The British chemists Sir William Ramsay and Morris W. Travers discovered xenon in 1898 (see **Ramsay, Sir William**). Industry uses xenon in filling flash lamps and other powerful lamps.

Xenon is a colorless, odorless, tasteless gas. It is obtained from liquid air. It does not react readily with other substances. Xenon is classed as a *noble gas* (see **Noble gas**). The chemical symbol for xenon is Xe. Xenon has an *atomic number* (number of protons in its nucleus) of 54. Its *relative atomic mass* is 131.293. An element's relative atomic mass equals its *mass* (amount of matter) divided by $\frac{1}{12}$ of the mass of an atom of carbon 12, the most abundant form of carbon. Xenon may be condensed to a liquid that boils at −107.1 °C and freezes at −111.9 °C. It forms compounds with two chemical elements, fluorine and oxygen. Frank C. Andrews

Xenophon, *ZEHN uh fuhn* (430?-355? B.C.), was a Greek soldier, historian, and writer. His most important contributions are books about the Greek philosopher Socrates and about Greek history.

Xenophon was born in Athens of a noble family. He studied under Socrates but was more interested in military subjects than in philosophy.

In 401 B.C., Xenophon and other Greek adventurers fought in the Battle of Cunaxa in Persia. The Greeks formed part of an army led by the Persian prince Cyrus the Younger, who wanted to seize the throne of Persia from his brother Artaxerxes II. Cyrus was killed in the battle, and all the Greek commanders were killed soon afterward. Thus, the remaining Greeks—about 10,000—were stranded without a commander in a strange country. They chose Xenophon to lead their retreat. Xenophon described this 1,500-mile (2,400-kilometer) march in his book *Anabasis.*

After returning home, Xenophon became a close friend and admirer of King Agesilaus of Sparta, under whom he served in Asia and in Greece. The Spartans rewarded Xenophon by granting him an estate near Olympia in Elis. The Eleans later drove him from his estate. Xenophon then moved to Corinth, where he died.

Xenophon's book *Hellenica* is the major source for Greek history from 411 to 362 B.C. His *Memorabilia* and *Apology* tell much about Socrates. Xenophon's *Constitution of Sparta* and his eulogy of Agesilaus are vital to the understanding of Sparta.   Donald Kagan

Xenotransplant, *ZEHN oh TRANS plant,* is the transfer of cells, tissues, or organs from one species into another. Medical researchers are actively investigating the use of nonhuman animal organs to replace diseased or damaged organs in human beings. Xenotransplant surgery has not been successful in human beings, but scientists hope they will one day help save human lives by increasing the supply of organs available for transplant.

Scientists have experimented with xenotransplants using organs from baboons and chimpanzees, but most believe pigs are a better choice. Pig organs are about the same size as adult human organs and, because pigs are raised for food, most people can accept killing them to save human lives.

The immune system normally rejects transplanted organs. An organ from another species causes a strong reaction called *hyperacute rejection.* The transplanted organ becomes a black, swollen mass and dies in minutes. To prevent rejection, scientists are experimenting with *transgenic* pigs, created by injecting human genes into pig embryos. Transgenic pigs have organs coated with human proteins that trick the human immune system into mistaking them for human organs. Scientists are also experimenting with pigs which lack genes that produce proteins which prompt rejection in human beings.

Many medical experts are concerned that xenotransplants will allow animal viruses to spread to people. Pigs naturally carry several viruses that could be transformed and infect human beings through transplanted organs. These viruses may endanger the organ recipient and could possibly infect others.   Arlene J. Klotzko

See also **Organ donation; Transplant.**

Xerography. See Copying machine (Electrostatic copying).

Xerox Corporation, *ZIHR ahks,* is one of the world's largest manufacturing companies. It developed the first automatic copier that makes dry copies of printed or written materials on ordinary paper. Xerox makes equipment for the production and distribution of documents, black-and-white or color, in paper and electronic form.

The corporation was founded in 1906 as The Haloid Company, a manufacturer of photocopying and photographic papers. In 1947, Haloid licensed patents for *xerography,* a process for making copies without ink or pressure, from Chester F. Carlson, the inventor of the process. The company perfected xerography in 1959 with its development of the Xerox 914, the first automatic, plain-paper office copier. The corporation, which has headquarters in Stamford, Connecticut, took its present name in 1961.   Critically reviewed by the Xerox Corporation

See also **Copying machine.**

Xerxes I, *ZURK seez* (519?-465 B.C.), ruled the Persian Empire from 486 B.C. until his death. He succeeded his father, Darius I, and spent several years trying to achieve his father's goal of conquering Greece. But Xerxes failed to do so, and his struggles against the Greeks greatly weakened the Persian Empire's influence and power.

During the early years of his reign, Xerxes put down revolts in the Persian provinces of Babylonia and Egypt. Then he began to assemble a huge land and sea force to invade Greece. This force included more than 180,000 men drawn from all over the empire, which then stretched as far west as Libya and as far east as the Indus River in what is now Pakistan.

In 480 B.C., Xerxes led his army against a Greek force in a mountain pass at Thermopylae, northwest of Athens. The Greeks, led by troops from Sparta, held back the Persians until a traitor told Xerxes of another way through the mountains. The Persians attacked the Greeks from the rear and defeated them. The people of Athens then abandoned their great city. Xerxes burned many temples and other buildings in Athens.

Soon afterward, the Greeks and Persians fought in the Bay of Salamis. The Greeks had fewer ships but were better trained than the Persians for maneuvering in the small bay. Xerxes watched from a hillside on shore as the Greeks crushed his fleet. Then he fled to his western capital in Asia Minor (now Turkey).

In 479 B.C., Persian forces attacked the Greeks at Plataea, west of Athens, and were again defeated. In 467 or 466 B.C., Greek soldiers and seamen defeated Persian forces again at the mouth of the Eurymedon River, on the southern coast of Asia Minor. As a result a group of Persian nobles murdered Xerxes.   Jack Martin Balcer

See also **Thermopylae.**

Xhosa, *KOH suh,* are a black people whose ancestors moved into southern Africa by the 1500's. More than half of the approximately 5 million Xhosa live in the Eastern Cape Province of South Africa.

Most Xhosa once tended cattle and raised crops for a living. The wealth of each group depended on how many cattle it owned. The Xhosa did not kill their cattle for food, though they sacrificed some of the animals during religious ceremonies.

Xhosa men traditionally practiced *polygyny,* the custom of having more than one wife at a time. A typical household consisted of a man, his wives and unmarried children, and his married sons and their families. Household members lived in a cluster of small cone-shaped houses with thatched roofs. Since 1900, this traditional way of life has mostly disappeared among the Xhosa.

Large numbers of British and Dutch settlers migrated to southern Africa during the 1800's, and the Xhosa were defeated in war by the British in the late 1800's. Their defeat, loss of grazing land, and poverty forced many Xhosa to migrate to towns or farms where they worked for whites. Today, many Xhosa live in urban areas. Many others work on white-owned farms. The Xhosa and other nonwhite groups in South Africa have suffered severe discrimination at the hands of South African whites.

Between the mid-1980's and mid-1990's, conflict between the Xhosa and a rival ethnic group, the Zulu, led to much violence and thousands of deaths among the two groups in South Africa. Much of the fighting had taken place between supporters of the African National Congress, many of whom are Xhosa, and members of the Inkatha Freedom Party, most of whom are Zulu.

Wade C. Pendleton

See also **Apartheid; Zulu.**

Xi Jiang, *shee jee ahng,* or West River, is a major transportation route in southern China. The Xi Jiang, also spelled Hsi Chiang, rises on the border of Yunnan and Guizhou provinces. It flows southeast for about 1,650 miles (2,655 kilometers) before it empties into the Zhu Jiang (Pearl River). The Zhu Jiang is an *estuary* (river mouth) that separates mainland China from Hong Kong. Guangzhou, one of China's largest cities, lies on the delta formed by the Xi Jiang and smaller rivers. Ships can sail 230 miles (370 kilometers) up the Xi Jiang to the city of Wuzhou. For the location of the Xi Jiang, see **China** (terrain map).   James A. Hafner

Xiamen, *shee ah muhn* (pop. 639,436), is a seaport on the coast of Fujian Province in southeast China (see **China** [political map]). Xiamen is also known as *Amoy* (pronounced *uh moy).* The name Amoy is based on the pronunciation of the city's name in the South Fujian dialect. Xiamen has a fine harbor and was once the center of China's tea trade.

In the 1600's, Portuguese traders traded with Xiamen, but the Chinese drove them out because they mistreated the people. In 1842, a treaty with the United Kingdom opened Xiamen and four other ports to British trade (see **Treaty port**). British citizens and other foreigners living in Xiamen gained special rights. In 1943, the United Kingdom and the United States gave up these special privileges, and other countries followed their example. Before World War II (1939-1945), Xiamen had a flourishing trade. In the early 1980's, the Chinese government set up the Xiamen Special Economic Zone to attract foreign investment. Trade began to flourish once again.

Opposite Xiamen is Gulangyu, an island where many wealthy Chinese have their homes. From the port of Xiamen, numerous Chinese from Fujian have gone to various countries in Southeast Asia. Most of the "overseas Chinese" in Southeast Asia speak the South Fujian dialect.   Parris H. Chang

Xi'an, *shee ahn* (pop. 2,872,539), also spelled Xian or Sian, is the capital and largest city of the Shaanxi Province in China. For location, see **China** (political map). The city is a major tourist center. Its attractions include many ancient towers, temples, and pagodas, and the nearby tomb of Emperor Shi Huangdi, who ruled China in the 200's B.C. Near the tomb, archaeologists have discovered burial pits with thousands of life-sized clay statues of soldiers and horses (see **Archaeology** [picture: An army of life-sized statues]).

Xi'an is an important center for industry and technology. It produces chemical products, computer equipment, electronic instruments, machinery, paper, textiles, and transportation vehicles.

The Zhou dynasty founded its capital near what is now Xi'an in about 1045 B.C. The area served almost continuously as the capital of succeeding dynasties for more than 2,000 years.   Parris H. Chang

Xinjiang, *shihn jee ahng,* also spelled *Sinkiang,* is a region in western China. For its location, see **China** (political map). The Chinese government rules Xinjiang but calls the area an *autonomous* (self-governing) region.

Much of Xinjiang is a desolate, thinly populated land of deserts and mountains. The region covers about 17 percent of China's land but has only about 1 percent of its population. Most of Xinjiang's 15 million people live on or near natural or artificially created oases.

A majority of the region's people are non-Chinese in origin. Turkic people called Uygurs make up about half of the population. Other groups include people of Kazakh and of Kyrgyz ancestry. Xinjiang was on the Silk Road, an old trade route that connected the Middle East and Europe with China. Many Middle Eastern people settled in Xinjiang, and Middle Eastern influences became strong. Islam—the chief religion of the Middle East—is also the chief religion of Xinjiang. The language and clothing of the people, and the region's architecture and music, also show Middle Eastern influences.

Herding and farming are important economic activities in Xinjiang. Herders raise cattle, sheep, goats, and other animals. Farmers grow corn, cotton, fruits, rice, and wheat. Xinjiang's vast mineral resources include coal, iron ore, oil, and uranium. Factories in Ürümqi, Xinjiang's capital, make farm machinery and cement.

China first ruled Xinjiang during the Han dynasty (206 B.C.-A.D. 220). After periods of Uygur and Mongol rule, Xinjiang came under Chinese control again during the Manchu (Qing) dynasty (1644-1912). In 1884, China made it a province.

Gerald Cubitt, Bruce Coleman Ltd.

A Xhosa boy herds cattle in the Eastern Cape Province of South Africa. Some of the Xhosa still farm for a living. Many others have moved into urban areas. More than half of the approximately 5 million Xhosa live in the Eastern Cape Province.

Xinjiang shared a 2,000-mile (3,200-kilometer) border with the Soviet Union before that country broke up in 1991. Several border disputes with the Soviet Union caused tension in Xinjiang. Russia, Kazakhstan, Kyrgyzstan, and Tajikistan are the former Soviet republics that border Xinjiang.   Norma Diamond

See also **Turkestan.**

Xmas. See **Christmas** (introduction).

Xochimilco. See **Lake Xochimilco**

Xunzi, *shyoon dzuh* (340?-245? B.C.), also spelled *Hsun Tzu,* was an influential Chinese philosopher best known for his belief that human nature is basically evil. He considered himself a follower of the philosophy of Confucianism. However, his view of human nature differed from that of most Confucianists.

According to Xunzi, the evil tendencies of human beings can be controlled only through education and moral guidance. He believed that people can be taught to perform good deeds and obey the moral laws of their society. Xunzi emphasized the importance of cultural traditions and their role in maintaining social order. His ideas are presented in the book *Xunzi* (or *Hsun-tzu),* most of which he wrote himself.

Xunzi was born in the state of Zhao, in what is now Shanxi Province. Nothing is known of his early life. From about 278 to 265 B.C., he was the most honored philosopher in the state of Qi, which had an academy of scholars. He held government posts in Qi and several other states.   David R. Knechtges

See also **Confucianism** (Early Confucianism).

Xylem. See **Stem; Tree** (Trunks and branches; picture).

Xylophone, *ZY luh fohn,* is a percussion instrument that consists chiefly of a number of bars arranged on a frame like the keys of a piano. Most xylophones have 44 bars with a range of $3\frac{1}{2}$ octaves. The majority of xylophones have bars made of rosewood, but some have plastic bars. A musician strikes the instrument's bars

Northwestern University (WORLD BOOK photo by Ted Nielsen)

The xylophone has two rows of bars arranged on a frame. A musician strikes the bars with mallets. A metal tube called a *resonator* lies beneath each bar and amplifies the sound.

with a mallet to produce a hard, brittle sound. A hollow metal tube called a *resonator* lies beneath each bar. The resonators amplify the sounds that are produced when the bars are struck. Variations in tone quality may be produced by using different types of plastic or rubber mallets.

No one knows exactly where or when the xylophone originated, but prehistoric peoples used some form of the instrument. During the 1500's in Europe, the xylophone was called the *Strohfiedel* because the bars were placed on belts made of straw. The German word *stroh* means *straw.* The word *fiedel* means *fiddle.* Musicians now play the xylophone in bands, orchestras, and small musical groups.   John H. Beck

XYZ Affair was the name given to a controversial exchange of diplomatic proposals between France and the United States in 1797. Relations between the two nations were strained at the time. The exchange included outrageous demands from France. The three French agents who made these demands became known as X, Y, and Z. The XYZ Affair led to fighting at sea between the United States and France, though war was never declared.

The XYZ incident occurred while France was at war with Britain. The British had captured many French ships during that war. As a result, France depended on American ships to carry on the trade between France and the United States. But the French became enraged at the Americans in 1796, when the U.S.-British Jay Treaty took effect. This treaty failed to guarantee American rights to trade with France. The French then began to seize American ships and cargoes. The French government also refused to receive the United States minister, General Charles Cotesworth Pinckney, who had been appointed by President George Washington.

The next president, John Adams, tried to avoid war by sending a special mission to France. He appointed two distinguished political leaders, John Marshall and Elbridge Gerry, to join Pinckney and settle the dispute. The French foreign minister, Prince Talleyrand, tried to stall the negotiations. He believed that a political dispute in the United States between the pro-French Republicans (later called Democratic-Republicans) and the pro-British Federalists was weakening the American ambassadors' bargaining position. Talleyrand appointed three agents to deal with the Americans sent by Adams. The agents told the Americans that before Talleyrand would see them, they would have to pay him a bribe of $250,000, loan France $12 million, and apologize for pro-British policies.

Adams reported France's demands to Congress. Republican Party congressmen asked to see the letters sent home by the American ambassadors as proof that the French had acted badly. Adams gave them the correspondence but substituted the letters X, Y, and Z for the actual names of the French agents. Thus, these events became known as the XYZ Affair.

Adams then asked Congress for money to prepare for war and gave American ships permission to fire on French ships. In 1800, after two years of naval conflict, a second American mission to France obtained a peace settlement.   Jerald A. Combs

See also **Adams, John** (Difficulties with France); **Gerry, Elbridge; Marshall, John; Pinckney, Charles C.; Talleyrand.**

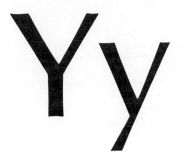

Y is the 25th letter of our alphabet. It came from a symbol used by the Semites, who once lived in Syria and Palestine. They named it *waw,* their word for *hook,* and adapted an Egyptian *hieroglyphic* (picture symbol). *Waw* was also the origin of F, U, V, and W. The Greeks later took the symbol into their alphabet, and gave it its capital Y form. They called it *upsilon.* The Romans used the letter when writing words taken from Greek. See **Alphabet.**

Uses. *Y* or *y* is about the 17th most frequently used letter in books, newspapers, and other printed material in English. *Y* represents the word *young* in many abbreviations, such as *YMCA* for *Young Men's Christian Association.* In archaic words, such as *ye* in *Ye Olde Tea*

Shoppe, y represents a discarded Anglo-Saxon character called *thorn.* The thorn resembled *y* in appearance, and had the sound of *th.* In chemistry, *Y* represents the metallic element *yttrium.*

Pronunciation. *Y* or *y* may be either a vowel or a consonant. In English, a person pronounces the consonant *y* by placing the front of the tongue near the hard palate, and then gliding the tongue into position to make the sound of the vowel that follows. The velum, or soft palate, is closed, and the vocal cords vibrate. As a vowel, the letter *y* may have the sound of long *i* as in *my* and *fly;* that of short *i* as in *myth* and *nymph;* that of *u* as in *myrtle;* or that of long *e* as in *baby.* See **Pronunciation.**   Marianne Cooley

Development of the letter Y

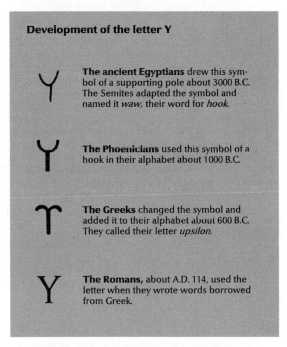

The ancient Egyptians drew this symbol of a supporting pole about 3000 B.C. The Semites adapted the symbol and named it *waw,* their word for *hook.*

The Phoenicians used this symbol of a hook in their alphabet about 1000 B.C.

The Greeks changed the symbol and added it to their alphabet about 600 B.C. They called their letter *upsilon.*

The Romans, about A.D. 114, used the letter when they wrote words borrowed from Greek.

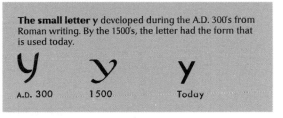

The small letter y developed during the A.D. 300's from Roman writing. By the 1500's, the letter had the form that is used today.

A.D. 300   1500   Today

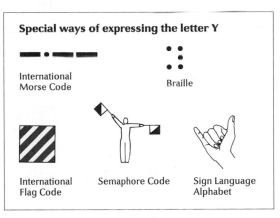

Special ways of expressing the letter Y

International Morse Code

Braille

International Flag Code

Semaphore Code

Sign Language Alphabet

Common forms of the letter Y

Handwritten letters vary from person to person. *Manuscript* (printed) letters, *left,* have simple curves and straight lines. Cursive letters, *right,* have flowing lines.

Roman letters have small finishing strokes called *serifs* that extend from the main strokes. The type face shown above is Baskerville. The italic form appears at the right.

Yy Yy

Sans-serif letters are also called *gothic letters.* They have no serifs. The type face shown above is called Futura. The italic form of Futura appears at the right.

Computer letters have special shapes. Computers can "read" these letters either optically or by means of the magnetic ink with which the letters may be printed.

Y-Teens is a program for members of the Young Women's Christian Association who are of junior high or high school age. The program aims to serve the educational, health, recreational, and social needs of teenage women. Members work to promote understanding among all people and to end racism. Y-Teens began as the Little Girls' Christian Association in Oakland, California, in 1881. It was a model for other girls' clubs across the United States. In 1918, the program became known as Girl Reserves, and its name was changed to Y-Teens in 1947. Headquarters are in New York City.

Critically reviewed by the Young Women's Christian Association

Yablonovyy Mountains, YAHB luh nuh VOY, lie in southeastern Siberia, in Russia. The name of the range is also spelled *Yablonoi* (pronounced YAHB luh NOY). For location, see **Russia** (terrain map). The range extends northeast from northern Mongolia for about 1,000 miles (1,600 kilometers) until it joins the Stanovoy Mountains. The Yablonovyy range is the dividing line between the rivers that flow into the Arctic Ocean and those that flow into the Pacific. Mount Sokhondo (8,199 feet, or 2,499 meters) is the highest peak. The Yablonovyy Mountains are the source of many minerals. Craig ZumBrunnen

Yahweh. See Jehovah.

Yak, yak, is a wild ox of Asia. It inhabits the cold, dry plateaus of Tibet, often over 16,000 feet (4,870 meters) above sea level. The wild yak stands over 6 feet (1.8 meters) high at the shoulders. But it carries its head low with the nose almost touching the ground. It may weigh from 1,100 to 1,200 pounds (499 to 544 kilograms). The yak is covered with black or brownish-black hair. The hair is especially long and silky on shoulders, flanks, and tail. In spite of its bulk. the yak can slide down icy slopes, swim swift rivers, and cross steep rock slides. If forced to defend itself, it charges furiously. The animal is in danger of extinction due to excessive hunting.

The domestic yak, often called the *grunting ox* because of the sounds it makes, is the result of many generations of careful breeding. It is often white or piebald instead of black like the wild yak. Smaller and much more docile than the wild yak, it is useful in many ways. As a pack animal, it can carry a heavy load 20 miles (32 kilometers) a day. In Tibet, the yak carries travelers and mail. It provides rich milk. Its flesh is dried or roasted for

Lynn M. Stone, Animals Animals
The yak of Asia is a relative of the American bison. Although big and bulky, the yak is agile.

food. The soft hair of the domestic yak is used to make cloth, and the coarser hair for mats and tent coverings. Saddles, whips, boots, and other articles are made from the hide. The bushy tail of the domestic yak is used as a fly chaser at ceremonial processions in India, and as an ornament for a tomb or shrine. C. Richard Taylor

Scientific classification. The yak belongs to the bovid family, Bovidae. It is *Bos grunniens.*

Yale, Elihu, EHL uh HYOO (1649-1721), was an official of the East India Company and a benefactor of Yale University. During 27 years' service in India, from 1672 to 1699, he acquired a large fortune and became governor of Fort Saint George in Madras.

After returning to England, Yale made numerous gifts to churches, schools, and missionary societies. He donated books and many other valuable goods to the Collegiate School, founded in 1701 by the Congregationalists in Connecticut. In 1718, in recognition of his generosity, the trustees renamed the school Yale College. Yale was born on April 5, 1649, in Boston. He was taken to England at the age of 3. He joined the East India Company in 1670. Robert H. Bremner

Yale, Linus, LY nuhs, **Jr.** (1821-1868), an American inventor and manufacturer, developed key locks and combination locks whose methods of operation are still used. He specialized in bank locks and won fame as an expert on these devices by picking the "unpickable" locks of rival manufacturers. In 1861, he patented a pin-tumbler cylinder lock, one of the most secure key-operated locks ever invented. This lock was among the first to be mass-produced. In 1868, Yale and two partners founded Yale Lock Manufacturing Company in Stamford, Connecticut. Yale was born on April 4, 1821, in Salisbury, New York. See also **Lock.** W. Bernard Carlson

Yale University is a coeducational, privately endowed, nonsectarian school in New Haven, Connecticut. Chartered in 1701, Yale is the third oldest institution of higher learning in the United States. Only Harvard University and the College of William and Mary are older.

Yale graduates have always played a major role in American life. Many graduates have become leaders in government, business and industry, the arts, and community services. The presidents of about 90 U.S. universities and colleges graduated from Yale. Yale's Web site at www.yale.edu presents information about the school.

The Yale campus covers about 175 acres (71 hectares). Connecticut Hall, built in 1752, is the oldest building. This red brick building is the only structure left on the campus from colonial days. Famous American architects have designed many newer buildings at Yale, including a science center.

First-year students live on the *Old Campus,* the site of the original school. Sophomores, juniors, and seniors live in 12 residential colleges. Each college houses about 360 students and some faculty members. Each college has its own library, common rooms, and dining hall. The colleges compete with each other in several sports. The residence plan started in 1933 through the gifts of Edward S. Harkness, a Yale graduate.

The Yale library, with more than 9 million volumes, ranks as one of the largest libraries in the world. Yale's Beinecke Rare Book and Manuscript Library was dedicated in 1963. This facility is one of the largest buildings in the world devoted to rare books and manuscripts.

Yale's Peabody Museum of Natural History is one of the oldest university-related museums in the United States. It has many world-famous fossil exhibits. The Yale University Art Gallery is the oldest university art museum in the nation. The Yale Center for British Art has an excellent collection of British paintings and drawings, and related books and papers.

The *Yale Daily News,* established in 1878, is the oldest college daily newspaper in the United States. The *Yale Literary Magazine,* founded in 1836, was the first undergraduate magazine published in the United States.

Educational system. Yale has 12 divisions, each under the supervision of its own dean and faculty. The divisions of the university include Yale College; the graduate school; and the schools of art, architecture, divinity, drama, forestry, law, medicine, music, nursing, and organization and management.

The Corporation of Yale University governs the school. The corporation consists of the university president, the governor and lieutenant governor of Connecticut, and 16 *fellows* (trustees).

History. Yale was founded in 1701, when 10 Connecticut clergymen met in the village of Branford and made a gift of books to found a college. Later that year, the General Assembly of Connecticut approved a charter for the *Collegiate School.* From 1702 to 1707, classes met in the home of Rector Abraham Pierson at Killingworth (now Clinton).

Classes were held in Milford and then Saybrook before the school moved to New Haven in 1716. Two years later, the school's only college building was still unfinished due to lack of funds. Elihu Yale, a retired merchant in London, gave money to the school in 1718 (see **Yale, Elihu**). Yale is sometimes called *Old Eli.* The same year, the school adopted its present name in honor of Yale. The undergraduate school, known as Yale College, was open only to men until 1969.

Critically reviewed by Yale University

See also **Connecticut** (picture); **Library** (picture: A rare-book collection).

Yalta, *YAWL tuh* or *YAHL tah* (pop. 89,000), is a city in Ukraine. It lies on the southern coast of the Crimean Peninsula, along the Black Sea. For location, see **Ukraine** (political map). Yalta is a popular health resort and vacation area. It has a mild climate and mineral-rich sea air. The city is a busy seaport and a center for the production of wine, fruits, and tobacco.

Yalta was originally a Greek colony. The colony later fell under the control of Italy and then Turkey. Yalta became a part of Russia in 1783. In 1945, during World War II, Allied leaders met in the city for the Yalta Conference. For details of the meeting, see **Yalta Conference**.

Jaroslaw Bilocerkowycz

Yalta Conference was one of the most important meetings of key Allied leaders during World War II (1939-1945). These leaders were President Franklin D. Roosevelt of the United States, Prime Minister Winston Churchill of the United Kingdom, and Premier Joseph Stalin of the Soviet Union. Their countries became known as the "Big Three." The conference took place at Yalta, a famous Black Sea resort in the Crimea, from Feb. 4 to 11, 1945. Over time, decisions made there regarding divisions in Europe have stirred bitter debates.

When the meeting began, the Soviet Union held the

strongest European military position. Soviet armies occupied much of Eastern Europe, and they were preparing to enter Berlin, Germany. The agenda at the Yalta Conference included the major problems in a postwar Europe.

Roosevelt, Churchill, and Stalin agreed on several points. These were (1) to accept the structure of a world peacekeeping organization that was to become the United Nations; (2) to reestablish order in Europe and to help the defeated countries create democratic governments; (3) to divide Germany into four zones that would be occupied by the United Kingdom, the United States, the Soviet Union, and France; (4) to support the Soviet-backed government and hold free elections in Poland, and to extend the Soviet Union's territory into Poland; and (5) to force Germany to give the Soviet Union equipment and other resources to make up for Soviet losses. The Soviet Union also agreed to enter the war against Japan in exchange for control of the Kuril Islands, the southern half of Sakhalin Island, and two strategic ports.

After the war, critics said Roosevelt had "sold out" Eastern Europe and had given too much to the Soviet Union. But most modern scholars believe the conference produced a traditional and balanced settlement. They argue that the Soviet Union held the superior military and political position in Eastern Europe and yet made the greatest concessions at the conference. Stalin failed to win demands for huge sums of money from Germany to pay for tremendous war losses and for a shift of the German-Polish border westward. Most scholars also believe the Soviet Union's domination of Eastern Europe resulted from earlier and later events, not from decisions made at the Yalta Conference.

Diane Shaver Clemens

Yalu River, *YAH LOO,* rises from the highest peak of the Changbai Shan, or Long White Mountains, in northeastern China. It forms most of the boundary between China and North Korea as it flows 500 miles (800 kilometers) to the Yellow Sea. See **China** (terrain map).

The river became important during the Korean War (1950-1953). Chinese troops crossed the Yalu in October 1950 to aid North Korea in the war. James A. Hafner

Yam is a major food crop in many tropical countries. The edible part of the yam plant is its *tuber.* This enlarged portion of the plant's stem grows underground and stores food for the plant. The tuber contains a large amount of starch and water, and some sugar. Some tubers contain poisons that may cause illness if they are not destroyed by cooking. The tubers of some wild yams produce compounds called *saponins* that can be used to make cortisone and certain other drugs.

The word *yam* is commonly used to refer only to yam tubers. Some yams weigh as much as 100 pounds (45 kilograms) and measure as long as 6 feet (1.8 meters). Their flesh is white or yellow. Yams are often confused with sweet potatoes, because some sweet potatoes produce storage roots that are similar to yam tubers (see **Sweet potato**).

Yam plants are climbing vines. Their stems bear small green flower clusters. Yams require hot, moist weather and a long growing season. About 21 million tons (19 million metric tons) of yams are grown for food each year. Western Africa produces about half of this crop. Yams also grow in India and in the countries of South-

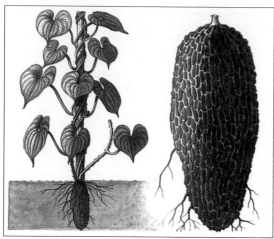

WORLD BOOK illustration by Jill Coombs

The yam is a major crop in many tropical countries.

east Asia and the Caribbean Sea. The United States grows no yams due to the cold climate and short growing season. Conrad K. Bonsi and Bobby R. Phills

Scientific classification. Yams belong to the yam family, Dioscoreaceae. Common edible yams include *Dioscorea alata* and *D. rotundata.*

Yam bean. See Jicama.

Yamamoto, *YAH muh MOH toh,* **Isoroku,** *EE soh ROH koo* (1884-1943), commanded the Japanese combined fleet at the time of the attack on Pearl Harbor in 1941, during World War II. He was one of Japan's great admirals, with a long and distinguished career in war and peace. He opposed the policies that led to war with the United States. But he sponsored the plans for the Pearl Harbor attack as Japan's only chance of victory in the war in the Pacific. Yamamoto was born on April 4, 1884, in Nagaoka. He was killed in 1943 when his plane was shot down in the South Pacific. Jeffrey E. Hanes

Yamashita, *YAH mah SHEE tah,* **Tomoyuki,** *TAW maw YOO kee* (1885-1946), a Japanese general in World

War II (1939-1945), was executed for "violation of the laws of war." A brilliant field commander, Yamashita advanced rapidly in Korea and Manchuria. He became famous for the campaign against Malaya and Singapore in 1942. Later, he served in Manchuria until he took charge of the defense of the Philippines in 1944. Yamashita was born on Nov. 8, 1885, in Kochi prefecture. Marius B. Jansen

Yamato period. See Kofun era.

Yamoussoukro, *YAH moo SOO kroh* (pop. 106,786), is the official capital of Côte d'Ivoire. The city stands in the south-central part of the country, also called Ivory Coast. For location, see **Côte d'Ivoire** (map).

Félix Houphouët-Boigny, who in 1960 became the first president of Côte d'Ivoire, was born in Yamoussoukro about 1905. At that time, Yamoussoukro was just a village. As president, Houphouët-Boigny decided to make Yamoussoukro the nation's capital. Throughout the 1960's and 1970's, it received the largest share of urban development funds outside of Abidjan, which was the capital at that time. The National Assembly officially designated Yamoussoukro the capital of Côte d'Ivoire in 1983. Today, the city has wide boulevards; modern hotels, offices, and apartment buildings; and a lavish presidential palace. The basilica of Our Lady of Peace, a Roman Catholic church, is the largest Christian church in Africa and one of the largest in the world.

Despite Houphouët-Boigny's wishes, few government offices moved from Abidjan, the former capital, to Yamoussoukro. Houphouët-Boigny died in 1993 and was buried in Yamoussoukro. Thomas J. Bassett

Yamuna River, *YUH muh nuh,* in northern India, is one of the most important branches of the Ganges River. The Yamuna rises in the Himalaya and flows southeastward for almost 900 miles (1,400 kilometers). It empties into the Ganges at the city of Allahabad. Two canals, one leading westward and one leading eastward, irrigate about 12,000 square miles (31,100 square kilometers) of farmland in the river valley. H. J. McPherson

Yancey, *YAN sih,* **William Lowndes,** *lowndz* (1814-1863), an American statesman, was often called "The Orator of Secession." He served in the United States House of Representatives as a Democrat from Alabama from

© AFP/Getty Images

Yamoussoukro is the official capital of Côte d'Ivoire. Félix Houphouët-Boigny, the first president of Côte d'Ivoire, decided to have Yamoussoukro, which was his birthplace, replace Abidjan as the nation's capital. Among the buildings he had constructed in Yamoussoukro was a lavish presidential palace, *shown here.*

1844 to 1846. After leaving Congress, Yancey devoted himself to arousing the South to defend its rights.

Yancey's "Alabama Platform" demanded that Southerners have the right to take their slaves into Western territories. He opposed the Compromise of 1850. In 1858, he tried to organize a League of United Southerners to work for Southern rights in both the Democratic and Republican parties.

Yancey opposed Stephen A. Douglas's candidacy for the Democratic presidential nomination in 1860 and supported John C. Breckinridge. He drew up Alabama's Secession Ordinance. After the American Civil War began in 1861, he served as a Confederate commissioner to Europe and a Confederate senator from Alabama. Yancey was born in Warren County, Georgia. He practiced law and edited a newspaper in Greenville, South Carolina, before moving to Alabama.   Thomas L. Connelly

Yang, *yahng,* **Chen Ning** (1922-   ), a Chinese-born physicist, shared the 1957 Nobel Prize in physics with Tsung Dao Lee (see **Lee, Tsung Dao**). They received the award for their contributions to the laws of fundamental particles. They disproved the law of *conservation of parity,* which concerned the physical interactions of fundamental nuclear particles. Yang was born in Hefei, Anhui, China. He was a staff member at the Institute for Advanced Study in Princeton, New Jersey, from 1949 to 1965. He became director of the Institute for Theoretical Physics at State University of New York at Stony Brook in 1965. See also **Parity.**   Tian Yu Cao

Yangcheng. See **Guangzhou.**

Yangon (pop. 1,315,964; met. area pop. 2,452,881) is the capital and largest city of Myanmar. It is also the country's chief port and industrial center. Yangon, also spelled *Rangoon,* lies in southern Myanmar on both banks of the Yangon River. It is about 20 miles (32 kilometers) north of the Gulf of Martaban, an arm of the Indian Ocean. For Yangon's location, see **Myanmar** (map).

Yangon has many Buddhist temples. The most famous is the Shwe Dagon pagoda, which dates from ancient times. The city has a national museum and a number of parks and lakes. It is the home of the University of Yangon, the Yangon Institute of Technology, and the Institute of Medicine.

Many of Yangon's people work for the government. The city's industries include shipbuilding, oil refining, and the milling of rice and wood.

Rice and teakwood are Yangon's principal exports. Yangon's factories manufacture pottery and cloth made of cotton and silk.

In the A.D. 500's, a settlement called Dagon occupied the area that is now Yangon. Dagon was a small town until the 1750's, when Alaungpaya, a Burmese king, founded the city and named it Yangon. The British captured Yangon in 1825 during the First Anglo-Burman War, but they did not occupy the city until after the Second Anglo-Burman War in 1852. Fire destroyed Yangon in 1851, but the city was soon rebuilt. Yangon remained under British occupation until the Japanese drove them out during World War II. In 1948, Myanmar—then called Burma—gained independence. Yangon's population has grown rapidly since 1948.   David P. Chandler

Yangtze River, *yahng dzuh,* also called Yangtze Kiang, is the world's third longest river. Only the Nile and Amazon rivers are longer. It is China's longest and most important river. To many Chinese, the Yangtze is known as the *Chang Jiang,* or *long river.*

The Yangtze River rises in the Tanggula Mountains of Qinghai Province, about 16,000 feet (4,880 meters) above sea level, and follows an irregular 3,900-mile (6,275-kilometer) course to the East China Sea. The waterway flows east, southeast, and then south into the province of Yunnan. From there, it turns northeast across Sichuan Province. It then flows east through central China and enters the East China Sea. For the location of the Yangtze River, see **China** (terrain map). The Yangtze and its branches drain about 700,000 square miles (1,800,000 square kilometers).

The high mountains at the Yangtze's source cause it to flow rapidly for most of its length. In places, mountains more than 1 mile (1.6 kilometers) high form the river's banks. The great gorges in the river's upper reaches above Yichang make it one of the most beautiful waterways in the world.

About half of China's ocean trade is carried over the Yangtze and its branches. Ocean steamers can travel upstream to Wuhan, 680 miles (1,090 kilometers) by river from the coast. Smaller boats can go 1,000 miles (1,600 kilometers) farther inland.

Thousands of Chinese live on the Yangtze on sailing craft called *junks.* Among the great cities along the Yangtze River are Shanghai, Nanjing, Anqing, and Chongqing. Occasional summer floods temporarily force many people from their homes.

In 1994, construction began in the area above Yichang on the Three Gorges Dam. When completed, the dam is expected to control flooding along the Yangtze and generate large amounts of hydroelectric power. Plans include the creation of Three Gorges Lake, a reservoir that

© Cavendish, Reflex from Picture Group

Yangon is Myanmar's capital and largest city. In this picture, lines of traffic jam a Yangon boulevard. The Sule Pagoda, *left,* rises in the background.

will extend from the dam site hundreds of miles west to Chongqing.　　James A. Hafner

See also **Three Gorges Dam.**

Yankee. People of other countries often call any person from the United States a Yankee. In the southern United States, the word *Yankee* means a Northerner, or someone who comes from north of Mason and Dixon's Line. But most of the people of the United States use the word *Yankee* to mean a New Englander.

People often say that someone is "shrewd as a Yankee" or "clever as a Yankee." The people of early New England had to develop great shrewdness and cleverness as they struggled to make homes and create industries in the rocky wilderness. "Yankee peddlers" roamed far and wide through early American communities, selling the articles made by Yankee craftworkers. These peddlers won a great reputation for getting high prices.

No one is sure where the word *Yankee* came from. Some dictionaries say it came from the Scottish word *yankie,* which means *clever woman.* Other dictionaries say it came from *Yengee,* an American Indian pronunciation of the word *English* or of the French word for *English,* which is *Anglais.* The most likely explanation is that the word comes from *Janke,* the Dutch equivalent of the English name Johnny. A pirate nicknamed Janke sailed in American waters in the 1680's. English colonists in New York spelled his name as it sounded to them, *Yankey,* and applied it to New Englanders as an insult for their sharp trading practices.

Perhaps the first person to use the word *Yankee* in a positive way was Jonathan Hastings, a farmer of Cambridge, Massachusetts. He used the word in the early 1700's to express the idea of excellence, speaking of a "Yankee good horse" or "Yankee cider." Harvard students who hired horses from Hastings began to use the expression. The word was widely used during the Revolutionary War in America (1775-1783), when British soldiers made fun of New England troops by calling them Yankees. During the American Civil War (1861-1865), Confederate soldiers called Federal troops Yankees. When United States troops arrived in Paris in 1917, the French press hailed them as Yankees or Yanks. Europeans have continued to use the word as a name for American soldiers.　　Fred W. Anderson

See also **Yankee Doodle.**

Yankee Doodle is a song that has been popular in the United States since the 1700's. Music historians disagree about the song's origin, but they know that its melody and words have changed over time. In 1767, American composer Andrew Barton used "Yankee Doodle" in his opera *The Disappointment.* The song must have been well known by that time because Barton did not write out the music. He simply directed the performers to sing his words to the tune of "Yankee Doodle."

Through the years, different words have been sung with the "Yankee Doodle" melody. In the late 1700's, people sang variations of the following words:

> Yankee Doodle came to town
> Upon a little pony,
> He stuck a feather in his hat
> And called it macaroni.

At that time, the word *macaroni* referred to young men in London who dressed and behaved extravagantly.

In England in the 1800's, children sang "Yankee Doodle" with words from a nursery rhyme that begins:

> Lucy Locket lost her pocket,
> Kitty Fisher found it;
> Nothing in it, nothing in it,
> But the binding round it.

During colonial times, British soldiers sang "Yankee Doodle" to poke fun at troops from New England. But instead of taking offense, American soldiers liked the song. During the Revolutionary War in America (1775-1783), patriots sang "Yankee Doodle" in their camps and whistled it in battle. According to tradition, American bands played "Yankee Doodle" when the British surrendered at Yorktown, Virginia, in 1781.

In 1890, American composer John Philip Sousa published a version of "Yankee Doodle" in a collection of patriotic songs. Sousa's "Yankee Doodle" is the version most people know today.　　Valerie Woodring Goertzen

Yanomami Indians, *YAH nuh MAH mee,* of South America live in rain forests and scattered grasslands along the Brazil-Venezuela border. Until the late 1900's, they were the largest American Indian group whose way of life had been relatively unchanged by contact with Western culture. The group's name is also spelled *Yanoama, Yanomama,* and *Yanomamö.*

There are about 20,000 Yanomami. Their communities range in size from a single extended family to about 300 people. In most cases, the entire community lives in a large circular structure made of poles and thatch. The Yanomami have gardens where they grow a number of food crops. But the main crop is a type of banana called the *plantain.* Traditional Yanomami also travel several months each year hunting animals and gathering wild plant foods. Intense wars have broken out between some Yanomami groups. Anthropologists have offered a number of possible reasons for this warfare, including scarcity of game, competition over women, and competition for Western manufactured goods.

Missionaries began entering Yanomami areas around 1950. But some Yanomami groups had no direct contact with the outside world until the early 1990's. Since the 1950's, increased contact with Western culture has brought deadly epidemics and social and environmental disruption to the Yanomami. The governments of Brazil and Venezuela have taken limited steps to protect Yanomami lands from invasion by outsiders.　　R. Brian Ferguson

Yaoundé, *yah oon DAY* (pop. 653,670), is the capital of Cameroon. It lies on a plateau in the southern part of the country. For location, see **Cameroon** (map). The city is in the most densely populated region of Cameroon. It is important as the country's center of government, but it has little industry. The University of Yaoundé is the country's only university. The city has an international airport. Railroads connect Yaoundé with Douala, the country's largest city and leading port, and with many other cities.

The Germans founded Yaoundé in 1888. In 1922, the city became the capital of a French territory called French Cameroun. It remained the capital when French Cameroun became the independent nation of Cameroon in 1960.　　Immanuel Wallerstein

See also **Cameroon** (picture).

Yap Islands, *yahp* or *yap,* is an island group in the western Pacific Ocean. Located in the Caroline Island chain, they form the Yap State of the country of the Federated States of Micronesia (FSM). For location, see **Micronesia, Federated States of** (map). The Yap Islands include four large islands and 10 smaller islands. The main islands are Yap (the largest), Gagil-Tamil, Map, and Rumung. The island group covers 39 square miles (101 square kilometers) and has a population of about 5,200. The islands are composed of ancient crystalline rocks and have a rugged surface. Long, narrow channels separate the islands. Coral reefs surround them. One large break in the reefs allows small vessels to enter a natural harbor.

The people of the Yap Islands are Micronesians. Most of them make a living by farming. Taro, bananas, yams, coconuts, and tropical fruits are the main crops. Fishing is also important. Some people are employed by the government.

Spaniards first discovered and controlled Yap. In 1899, Spain sold the islands to Germany. In 1905, Yap became internationally important as a cable station between the United States, the Netherlands Indies (now Indonesia), and Japan.

After World War I ended in 1918, the League of Nations put Yap under Japanese mandate. The United States protested this action. In 1921, the United States and Japan signed a treaty by which the United States recognized the Japanese mandate. In return for this recognition, Japan granted the United States equal rights to cable and radio service through Yap, and also allowed United States citizens free entry there.

During World War II (1939-1945), the Japanese used the island group as a naval and air base. American troops occupied Yap after the war ended. In 1947, the United Nations made the United States trustee of the islands as part of the Trust Territory of the Pacific Islands. In 1978, the Yap Islands and other Carolines formed the Federated States of Micronesia, a political unit that had self-government but remained under U.S. control. In 1986, FSM became an independent country in free association with the United States.   Robert C. Kiste

See also **Caroline Islands; Pacific Islands, Trust Territory of the.**

Yaqui Indians, *YAH kee,* are a tribe that lives in Mexico, Arizona, and California. They are noted for their religious ceremonies, which blend concepts of Roman Catholicism with ancient tribal customs. On holy days, the Yaqui perform ancient dances and rituals in honor of Jesus Christ, the Virgin Mary, and tribal patron saints.

The ancient Yaqui lived along the Yaqui River in northwestern Mexico. They raised beans, corn, and squash. They also hunted game and gathered wild plants. The Yaqui lived in small, scattered villages and had no central government.

Yaqui warriors defeated the Spanish invaders who entered their territory in 1533 and 1609. In 1610, the Yaqui made a treaty with the Spaniards and asked for Jesuit missionaries to settle in their villages.

The Yaqui wanted the Jesuits to teach them how to raise wheat, fruit, and livestock. The Jesuits arrived in 1617, and the Yaqui lived prosperously for the next 120 years. The Indians learned the Roman Catholic religion and blended it with their own culture. The Jesuits also helped the Yaqui organize the villages into eight towns, which became centers of religion and government.

In the 1730's, many Yaqui became dissatisfied with the Jesuits and the Spanish colonial government. Some of them sought independence. The tribe fought Spanish and Mexican troops in a series of wars that lasted until the 1900's. During these wars, the Mexican government forced many Yaqui to leave their homeland and settle in other parts of Mexico. Some of the Yaqui fled Mexico to live in the United States. There are now about 40,000 Yaqui in Mexico. According to the 2000 United States census, there are about 15,000 Yaqui.   Don D. Fowler

Yard is a unit of length in the inch-pound system of measurement customarily used in the United States. One yard is equal to 3 feet, or 36 inches. One yard equals exactly 0.9144 meter.

Yates, Elizabeth (1905-2001), was an American author. Yates wrote fiction and nonfiction for both children and adults. She was best known for her biographies for young readers and for her historical fiction.

Yates won the 1951 Newbery Medal for *Amos Fortune, Free Man* (1950). The book traces the life of an African who was brought to America as a slave at the age of 15, and who bought his freedom when he was 50 years old. In *The Lighted Heart* (1960), Yates described her experiences with her husband's blindness. Her other children's books include *Carolina's Courage* (1964) and *Sound Friendships* (1987). She also wrote three volumes of autobiography: *My Diary—My World* (1981), *My Widening World* (1983), and *One Writer's Way* (1984). Yates was born in Buffalo, New York, on Dec. 6, 1905.
          Kathryn Pierson Jennings

Yawning is the act of opening the mouth wide, or *gaping*. The usual yawn is due to drowsiness or fatigue. It is a sign that the body needs sleep. Yawning is an involuntary reflex. After the act has started, it is almost impossible to stop it. The mouth can be held closed, but the yawning muscles still contract.

People and animals yawn when oxygen is slowly cut off from them, and when the muscles are thoroughly relaxed. People who yawn often are probably not getting enough oxygen. They may need better ventilation, or exercise. They will generally stop yawning if they drink a beverage, or bathe their face with cold water. Scientists are not sure what part of the nervous system controls yawning, but it may be the *mesencephalon* (midbrain) in the brain. One purpose of yawning may be to awaken a person by stretching the muscles, helping the blood to circulate, and by increasing the amount of inhaled air.
          Charles W. Cummings

Yaws, also called *frambesia, fram BEE zhuh,* is a disease that attacks chiefly children of humid tropical regions. Various kinds of *lesions* (skin eruptions) appear and disappear during the course of the disease, which may last several years. Yaws attacks the skin, cartilage, and bones, but it causes death in only rare cases.

Bacteria called *spirochetes* cause yaws. The spirochetes resemble those that cause syphilis, but yaws is not a sexually transmitted disease. The spirochetes enter the body through a break in the skin. In most cases, a person catches yaws from contact with an infected person. Three to four weeks after infection, a small, yellow-red, pimplelike lesion forms where the spirochetes entered the body. Other lesions, some resembling raspberries, break out weeks or months later. Painful sores often form on the soles of the feet and make walking difficult. Still later, lesions may develop. The disease may gradually destroy the cartilage of the nose and cripple bones and joints. It can be cured by treatment with penicillin.   Felipe Kierszenbaum

Yazoo Fraud was a crooked land deal in Georgia in 1795. Georgia's General Assembly sold a large area of state-owned land on the Yazoo River to speculators for far less than it was worth. This land is now part of Mississippi and Alabama.

Most of the Georgia legislators were bribed to sell the land. When the people of Georgia protested, the legislature passed a Rescinding Act to take back the land in 1796. The Supreme Court of the United States ruled in 1810 that the Rescinding Act was unconstitutional. But by this time, Georgia had sold the land to the federal government. See **Georgia** (Early statehood).

William E. Foley

Yeager, *YAY guhr,* **Charles Elwood** (1923-   ), was the first person to fly an aircraft faster than the speed of sound. He achieved this on Oct. 14, 1947, in a Bell X-1 rocket airplane. He set another record on Dec. 12, 1953, by flying $2\frac{1}{2}$ times the speed of sound in a Bell X-1A.

Yeager was born on Feb. 13, 1923, in Myra, West Virginia. During World War II (1939-1945), he served as a fighter pilot. In 1975, he retired from the military with the rank of brigadier general. In 1986, he was named to the presidential commission investigating the accidental destruction of the space shuttle Challenger.

Richard P. Hallion

Year is the time the earth takes to make one complete revolution around the sun. There are two different kinds of years which astronomers use. The *solar, equinoctial,* or *tropical* year is the time between two passages of the sun through the March equinox. In the Northern Hemisphere, this equinox is called the *vernal equinox.* This year is 365 days, 5 hours, 48 minutes, and 46 seconds long and is used for all practical and astronomical purposes. It is the basis of our common or calendar year.

The *sidereal* year is made up of 365 days, 6 hours, 9 minutes, and 9.5 seconds. This is the time it takes the earth to return to the same place in its orbit, with reference to the fixed stars. The sidereal year is longer than the solar year because of the *precession of the equinoxes.* The sidereal year is seldom used except in the calculations of astronomers.

The calendar year is only 365 days long, and so we have to add an extra day every four years to correct the difference in time between the calendar year and the solar year. This fourth year is called *leap year,* and the extra day is February 29. Adding an extra day every fourth year makes the average calendar year 11 minutes, 14 seconds too long. So, the day is not added in the century years, except in those divisible by 400. The years 1700, 1800, and 1900 had only 365 days. The year 2000 had 366 days.

Today, the *leap second* corrects for differences in the earth's rate of rotation from year to year. It is usually added to or subtracted from the last minute of the year.

The *lunar year* is made up of 12 lunar months. The ancient Greeks used this year. It contained 354 days.

In most Western nations, the calendar year begins on January 1. During the Middle Ages, however, most European nations considered March 25, Annunciation Day, to be the first day of the calendar year. By 1600, most of them had adopted the Gregorian calendar, which recognized January 1 as the beginning of the year.

The church calendar, which is used in the Roman Catholic and in most Protestant churches, is regulated partly by the solar and partly by the lunar year. This causes a difference between the fixed feast days, which always fall on the same day every year, and movable feasts such as Easter, whose dates vary from year to year. The fixed feast days are determined by the solar year, and the movable feast days, by the lunar year.

In the early ancient Roman calendar, the year began on March 1. Later, the Romans used January 1 as the new year. The Jewish year begins near the September equinox, which is known as the *autumnal equinox* in the Northern Hemisphere. The Islamic year is based on the changing of the phases of the moon and lasts 354 days. Therefore, the beginning of the Islamic year continually falls earlier in the seasons. Thirty Islamic years make up a cycle during which there are 11 leap years at irregular intervals.   James Jespersen

Related articles in *World Book* include:

A.D.	Christian Era	Olympiad
B.C.	Equinox	Season
Calendar	Leap year	

Yeast is a single-celled organism that bakers put into dough to make it rise. It is also used in the production of beer, wine, and other alcoholic beverages. The yeasts used commercially consist of masses of the microscopic yeast organisms. There are about 600 species of yeasts, but only a few are used commercially.

In early times, people made bread, beer, and wine without understanding the role yeasts played in their production. In the 1600's, Dutch scientist Anton van Leeuwenhoek first observed yeast cells. Then, in 1860, French scientist Louis Pasteur confirmed that live yeast organisms caused the fermentation of wine and beer.

Yeasts belong to a group of simple organisms known as *fungi,* which exist almost everywhere in nature, including the air. Yeasts reproduce rapidly, and they grow especially well in substances containing sugar. Yeast cells reproduce by *fission* (splitting in two) or by *budding.* In budding, part of the cell wall of the yeast swells and forms a new growth called a *bud.* The bud then breaks off and becomes an independent cell.

How yeast is used. Yeast fungi lack chlorophyll, the green matter that green plants use to make their own food. Therefore, yeasts must rely on other sources for food. They feed on sugar from a variety of natural sources, including fruit, grain, and nectar, and also from molasses. Yeast cells produce chemicals called *enzymes,* or *ferments,* that break down their food. Some species of yeast break down sugar into alcohol and carbon dioxide. This process, called *fermentation,* plays an important part in making bread, beer, and wine.

In breadmaking, a commercial yeast called *baker's yeast* is used as a *leaven,* a substance that makes dough rise. Bread dough is made by mixing such basic ingredients as flour, water or milk, salt, and yeast.

Since sugar is needed for fermentation, bakers add to dough certain enzymes that convert some of the starch in the flour into sugar. In addition, bakers may hasten fermentation by adding sugar to the dough. The yeast then breaks down the sugar into alcohol and carbon dioxide gas. The bubbles of this gas are trapped by a

How yeast makes bread dough rise

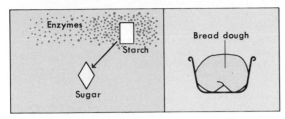

Enzymes are added to bread dough at the beginning of the breadmaking process. The enzymes convert starch into sugar.

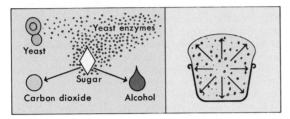

Yeast releases enzymes that break down the sugar into alcohol and carbon dioxide gas. The gas bubbles make the dough rise.

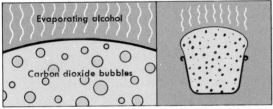

WORLD BOOK diagrams by Steven Liska

During baking, the alcohol evaporates. The gas bubbles remain trapped in the bread and give it a light, airy texture.

substance in the dough called *gluten* (see **Gluten**). As the gas expands, the gluten stretches, causing the dough to rise. The alcohol produced by fermentation evaporates in baking. Baking also destroys the yeast.

The yeast used in winemaking acts on the sugar in grapes and other fruits to produce alcohol and carbon dioxide gas through fermentation. In most wines, the gas is allowed to escape into the air. But in some champagnes and other sparkling wines, the gas is retained to provide the beverages' characteristic bubbles.

Another type of commercial yeast, called *brewer's yeast,* cannot act directly on the grain used in the brewing of beer. Brewers must first convert the starch in the grain into sugar by means of a process called *malting.* The yeast is then added to convert the sugar to alcohol. Gas formed during fermentation is pumped off the beer and later added back to the beer to carbonate it.

Other uses of yeast fungi include the production of a dietary supplement called *single cell protein* (SCP). Some species of yeasts produce large amounts of a particular vitamin and are used in the commercial production of that vitamin. Other species, such as the yeasts used in brewing, can absorb and store vitamins from their food. People may eat these yeasts as vitamin supplements. Certain kinds of yeast fungi can produce large amounts of such useful substances as fat, glycerol, industrial alcohol, and various enzymes. The yeasts are used in the commercial production of these substances.

How yeast is made. Before the commercial production of yeast in the 1880's, yeast fungi from the air leavened the bread that people baked. Homemakers prepared a dough and left it uncovered, and yeasts landed on it and began the fermentation process. Later, excess yeast from the beer and winemaking industries was used in breadmaking. This yeast is called *barm.* When the production of baker's yeast first became an industry, manufacturers grew yeast fungi on malted grain.

Today, baker's yeast is produced on molasses, which consists mostly of sugar. Baker's yeast is manufactured in two forms—as a moist, compressed cake and as dried grains. Cakes of yeast are made up of live, active yeast cells. The yeast cells in dried yeast are alive but not active. Dried yeast must be mixed with warm water before the yeast fungi can grow. Yeast cakes must be refrigerated, but they spoil after about six weeks. Dried yeast need not be refrigerated, but it lasts longer under refrigeration.   Arthur J. Ashe, III

See also **Bread; Brewing; Fermentation.**

Yeats, *yayts,* **William Butler** (1865-1939), an Irish poet and dramatist, won the 1923 Nobel Prize for literature. Many critics consider him the greatest poet of his time. Yeats led the Irish Literary Revival, a movement of the late 1800's and early 1900's that stimulated new appreciation of traditional Irish literature. The movement also encouraged the creation of works written in the spirit of Irish culture, as distinct from English culture.

Yeats developed elaborate theories about history as a recurring cycle of events. He expressed his views about history and life through the use of old Irish tales and the facts and legends of Irish history. His views also reflect his belief in the supernatural. Yeats published his theories in *A Vision* (1925), a book that can help with the interpretation of some of his more difficult poems.

Yeats was born in Dublin and lived in London for part of his childhood. He spent many holidays in Sligo, a county in western Ireland that he loved and often wrote about. In 1898, he joined the authors Lady Gregory and Edward Martyn in establishing the Irish Literary Theatre. It was reorganized in 1904 as the Abbey Theatre, which became world famous.

The Irish Literary Theatre was founded partly to support Irish nationalism by encouraging the writing and production of plays about Irish life. The theater

Ewing Galloway

William Butler Yeats

performed most of Yeats's 26 plays, and he served until his death as one of the directors who managed the institution. The theater's first production was Yeats's *The Countess Cathleen,* written in 1891. This play was inspired in part by the author's love for Maud Gonne, a beautiful Irish nationalist leader. She became the subject of many of his plays and love lyrics.

Yeats's verse, unlike that of most poets, improved as

he grew older. He wrote much of his best work in the last 10 years of his life. His most important works were published in *Collected Plays* (1952) and *The Poems: A New Edition* (1984). *Memoirs,* containing autobiographical writings, was published in 1973.   Lorraine Weir

Additional resources

Brown, Terence. *The Life of W. B. Yeats.* Blackwell, 1999.
Foster, R. F. *W. B. Yeats: A Life.* Oxford, 1997. Covers the period 1865-1914.
McCready, Sam. *A William Butler Yeats Encyclopedia.* Greenwood, 1997.

Yekaterinburg, *yuh KAT uhr ihn BURG* (pop. 1,270,700), is a trading and manufacturing center in the Ural Mountains of Russia (see **Russia** [political map]). Yekaterinburg is a railroad center and the largest city in the Urals. It has a machine-building industry.

After the Russian Revolution, the Bolsheviks imprisoned Czar Nicholas II and his family at Yekaterinburg and killed them there on July 17, 1918. The city was renamed Sverdlovsk in 1924, when Russia was a republic of the Soviet Union. It was renamed Yekaterinburg in 1991, shortly before the Soviet republics became independent.   Roman Szporluk

Yellow fever is a virus disease carried by certain mosquitoes. The virus damages many body tissues, but especially the liver. As a result of this damage, the liver cannot function properly and yellow bile pigments gather in the skin. These pigments make the skin look yellow and give the disease its name.

In most cases, the *Aëdes aegypti* mosquito carries the yellow fever virus from one person to another. Some monkeys and sloths may also be infected. When the mosquito bites an infected person or animal, the virus enters the insect's body, where it develops rapidly. After 9 to 12 days, the bite of the mosquito can produce yellow fever. A mosquito that becomes infected with the virus can transmit the disease for the rest of its life.

Symptoms. The first stage of yellow fever begins from three to six days after a person has been bitten. The victim develops a fever, headache, and dizziness, and the muscles ache. In many individuals, the disease progresses no further. In others, however, the fever drops for a day or two and then rises steeply. The skin turns yellow, and the patient's gums and stomach lining bleed.

Many patients recover from this stage. But some become delirious and go into a coma. Death follows the coma in most cases. Only from 2 to 5 percent of all cases of yellow fever result in death, though the figure may be higher during an epidemic. Patients who recover have lifelong immunity to the disease.

Prevention. Yellow fever was once widespread throughout Central America, parts of South America, Africa, and some tropical islands. Occasional outbreaks of the disease continue to occur in jungle areas, especially in South America. However, yellow fever is under control in most urban areas. A United States Army physician, William Gorgas, developed mosquito control measures that eliminated the disease as a major health menace in the Panama Canal Zone. The disease can also be prevented with a vaccine developed in 1937 by Max Theiler, a South African research physician.

The conquest of yellow fever was one of the great achievements of modern medicine. In 1881, Carlos Fin-

lay, a Cuban physician, suggested that a mosquito transmitted the disease. Walter Reed, a U.S. Army doctor, proved that yellow fever was carried by a mosquito. Reed suggested that the cause was a microorganism. In 1927, three research physicians proved that the microorganism was a virus.   A. William Holmes

Related articles in *World Book* include:

Finlay, Carlos Juan
Gorgas, William C.
Lazear, Jesse W.
New Orleans (The *Paris of America*)

Panama Canal (Victory over disease)
Reed, Walter
Tennessee (Reconstruction)

Yellow jacket is a type of small wasp with black-and-yellow markings. Some people mistakenly call yellow jackets "bees," but they actually are related to hornets. Like hornets, yellow jackets make their nests of paper. They form the paper by chewing up old wood and plant fibers. The nests consist of numerous hexagonal cells inside a thick paper covering. Most yellow jackets nest underground, but sometimes nests can be found hanging in trees or bushes, or within hollows in old stumps or the walls of buildings.

Yellow jackets eat primarily to feed their young. After feeding, the adult *regurgitates* (spits up) the food for the young. Most species prey on insects. They consume large numbers of flies, caterpillars, and other pests. Some species feed chiefly on dead animal matter, such as sandwich meats and decaying fish. Yellow jackets also feed on sweet, sugary substances, such as ripe fruit and soft drinks. Such feeding habits often make yellow jackets a nuisance at picnics and campsites.

Like honey bees and ants, yellow jackets live in communities made up of *queens* (mated females), *workers* (unmated females), and males. Males and queens do not sting, but workers will vigorously defend a nest if it is disturbed, often stinging repeatedly. People are sometimes stung when they run lawn mowers over hidden nests. Some people are strongly allergic to the proteins in a yellow jacket's *venom* (poison). If stung, they may require immediate medical attention.   Robert W. Matthews

WORLD BOOK illustration by Oxford Illustrators Limited

Queen yellow jacket

Scientific classification. Yellow jackets belong to the family Vespidae. Two common North American species are *Vespula pennsylvanica* and *V. maculifrons.*

See also **Hornet; Wasp.**

Yellow-poplar, also called *tuliptree* and *tulip-poplar,* is the tallest broadleaf tree in the eastern United States. In forests, it may grow 200 feet (60 meters) high, and its trunk may be 5 to 10 feet (1.5 to 3 meters) thick at the base. The yellow-poplar is a valuable North American hardwood and grows from New England southward to Florida and westward to Louisiana and Arkansas. It is the state tree of Indiana, Kentucky, and Tennessee.

The showy yellow blossoms of the yellow-poplar resemble tulips, and are an important source of pollen for

© Yeager and Kay, Photo Researchers

A yellow-poplar blossom resembles a yellow tulip flower. The blossoms are an important source of pollen for bees.

bees. Its distinctive leaves are smooth, notched at the tip, and long-stemmed. The *sapwood* (outer wood) is whitish. The *heartwood* (inner wood) is sunshine-yellow to pale tan. The wood is used chiefly for furniture, veneer, boxes, and baskets.   Kenneth R. Robertson

Scientific classification. The yellow-poplar belongs to the magnolia family, Magnoliaceae. Its scientific name is *Liriodendron tulipifera.*

See also **Tree** (Familiar broadleaf and needleleaf trees [picture]).

Yellow River. See **Huang He.**

Yellow Sea is an arm of the Pacific Ocean that extends inland for about 400 miles (640 kilometers) between the east coast of China and Korea (see **China** [political map]). The Chinese named this area the *Huang Hai* (Yellow Sea) because the waters along the banks are a yellow, muddy color. The Huang River carries deposits of yellow earth *(huangtu)* to the Yellow Sea. The sea is about 300 feet (91 meters) deep in its deepest part. It covers 480,000 square miles (1,243,194 square kilometers). Qingdao lies on China's coast on the southern shore of the Shandong Peninsula. Lüshun and Dalian are at the southern end of China's Liaodong Peninsula. The Korea Strait connects the Yellow Sea with the Sea of Japan (also called the East Sea). At the north, the Yellow Sea forms Laizhou Bay, the Bo Gulf, the Liaodong Gulf, and Korea Bay.

David A. Ross

Yellowhammer is a popular name for the *northern flicker,* a North American woodpecker. It is about 12 to 14 inches (30 to 36 centimeters) long and has a brown back and an ashy-gray head. The undersides of its wings have yellow patches. The bird ranges from the northern forests of Alaska and Canada south through the eastern United States to the Gulf of Mexico. It spends much of its time on the ground, searching for insects. It is the state bird of Alabama. The *great crested flycatcher,* a North American bird, is sometimes called a *yellowhammer.* The name also refers to a species of bunting found in Europe and Asia.   Sandra L. Vehrencamp

Scientific classification. The northern flicker, or yellowhammer, is a member of the woodpecker family, Picidae. Its scientific name is *Colaptes auratus.*

See also **Flicker; Bird** (picture: Birds of forests and woodlands [Yellow-shafted flicker]).

Yellowknife (pop. 16,541) is the capital and largest city of Canada's Northwest Territories. The city lies on the shores of Yellowknife Bay, a projection at the northern end of Great Slave Lake. For location, see **Northwest Territories** (map). Yellowknife is a mining center. Its industries include gold mining, prospecting, transportation, and tourism. Yellowknife was founded in the mid-1930's and incorporated as a city in 1970.

G. Peter Kershaw

Yellowlegs is the name of two species of shore birds that have black and white markings and long yellow legs. The *greater yellowlegs* measures about 15 inches (38 centimeters) in length, and the *lesser yellowlegs* is a little over 10 inches (25 centimeters) long. Both can be seen along shores, ponds, and marshes when they fly north in spring. They nest in northern North America. In winter, they fly as far south as southern Chile in South America. Yellowlegs lay four buff or tan eggs. They have a flutelike whistle that hunters imitated to lure them to decoys. At one time they became rare because so many

WORLD BOOK illustration by John Dawson

The yellowlegs is named for its long yellow legs. In spring, it can be seen along shores, ponds, and marshes.

people hunted them. Now, federal laws protect them and they are again becoming common.   Fritz L. Knopf

Scientific classification. Yellowlegs belong to the family Scolopacidae. The scientific name for the greater yellowlegs is *Tringa melanoleuca.* The lesser yellowlegs is *T. flavipes.*

Yellowstone National Park, the oldest national park in the world, is famous for its many natural wonders. The park has more geysers and hot springs than any other area in the world. Yellowstone's scenic attractions include deep canyons, thundering waterfalls, sparkling lakes, and vast evergreen forests broken by rolling meadows. Yellowstone is also one of the largest wildlife preserves in the United States. It has a greater concentration of large and small animals than any other area in the United States except Alaska. Bears, elk, and *bison* (American buffaloes) roam the park, and bald eagles, trumpeter swans, and white pelicans nest there.

Yellowstone lies in the northwest corner of Wyoming and spreads into Idaho and Montana. The park covers 2,200,000 acres (898,000 hectares). A series of high plateaus extends across the park, and mountains rise along Yellowstone's northern, eastern, and western boundaries. The highest point, Eagle Peak, rises 11,358 feet

Yellowstone's natural wonders include sparkling lakes and hot spring terraces. Yellowstone Lake, *left,* is the largest high-altitude lake in North America. The gently flowing waters of Minerva Terrace, *right,* deposit minerals that build up large rock terraces, one above the other.

(3,462 meters) in the Absaroka Range in the east.

Most of Yellowstone's landscape was created by volcanic eruptions more than 60,000 years ago. A large mass of molten rock still lies beneath the surface of the park. This rock, called *magma,* furnishes the heat for the park's geysers and hot springs. Yellowstone has more than 200 active geysers and thousands of hot springs.

The government established Yellowstone in 1872. It was named for the yellow rocks that lie along the part of the Yellowstone River that is north of the park. Over $2\frac{1}{2}$ million people visit Yellowstone yearly. Most of them drive through the park, but many explore large wilderness areas that can be reached only by foot or on horseback. The park has more than 350 miles (560 kilometers) of roads and over 1,200 miles (1,900 kilometers) of trails.

Touring Yellowstone

There are five entrances into Yellowstone National Park—two from Wyoming and three from Montana. Each entrance road connects with the Grand Loop, a 142-mile (229-kilometer) road that leads to major points of interest. The Grand Loop consists of the southern Lower Loop and the northern Upper Loop.

The Lower Loop. The west entrance road joins the Lower Loop at Madison Junction. Southbound, the Lower Loop leads to several geyser basins. The Lower Geyser Basin includes the Fountain Paint Pots, a series of hot springs and bubbling pools of mud called *mudpots* or *paintpots.* The mudpots are formed by steam and other gases that rose from holes in the ground and changed the surrounding rock into clay. Minerals in the clay give the mud various colors. Great Fountain Geyser, also in the Lower Geyser Basin, erupts from the center of a large pool. The bursts of water from this geyser sometimes spout 200 feet (61 meters) above the pool.

Grand Prismatic Spring, in Midway Geyser Basin, is the largest hot spring in Yellowstone. Its pool, which has

Yellowstone National Park

	Park boundary
	State boundary
	Road
▪	Point of interest

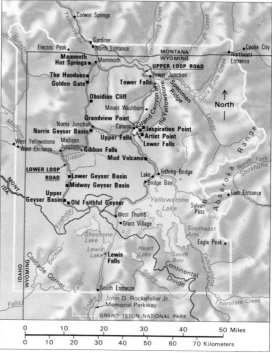

a deep blue center ringed with pale blue, measures 370 feet (113 meters) in diameter. Small water organisms called *algae* give the pool its color.

The Upper Geyser Basin has a large group of geysers. In most years, Old Faithful, the most famous geyser in the park, erupts about every 76 minutes. The actual intervals between eruptions vary from about 30 to 120 minutes. The geyser sends a stream of boiling water more than 100 feet (30 meters) into the air (see **Wyoming** [picture]). Other geysers include Castle, Giantess, Grand, and Grotto. Morning Glory Pool, one of the basin's most beautiful hot pools, resembles the morning-glory flower in color and shape.

Yellowstone Lake, which lies 7,733 feet (2,357 meters) above sea level, is the largest high-altitude lake in North America. It measures about 20 miles (32 kilometers) long and 14 miles (23 kilometers) wide. The lake has a shoreline of about 110 miles (180 kilometers). Geysers and hot springs occur along the shore at West Thumb. The Lower Loop follows the shoreline for 21 miles (34 kilometers), providing a view of the lake's islands and the rugged mountains of the Absaroka Range.

The Grand Canyon of the Yellowstone cuts across the landscape for about 20 miles (32 kilometers). This canyon reaches a depth of about 1,200 feet (370 meters) in some places. The Yellowstone River runs through the canyon, creating two waterfalls. The Lower Falls plunges 308 feet (94 meters) and the Upper Falls 109 feet (33 meters) into the canyon. Views of the canyon are especially beautiful from Artist Point, Grandview Point, and Inspiration Point. See **Yellowstone River.**

The Upper Loop leads north from Canyon with a climb through the mountains of the Washburn Range. Mount Washburn rises 10,243 feet (3,122 meters) on the east. Specimen Ridge, which can be seen from the road leading to the northeast entrance, has some of the park's most famous petrified forests. The trees there were buried during volcanic eruptions about 50 million years ago by mudflows and streams carrying suspended earth and ash. Minerals from the mud and water seeped into the trees and turned them into stone.

At Mammoth Hot Springs, beautiful terraces are formed by gently flowing waters. The waters deposit a form of limestone called *travertine,* building large terraces one above the other. Algae and bacteria give some terraces various colors. Minerva Terrace and Opal Terrace are among the most beautiful in the area. The terraces change through the years as the waters deposit calcium carbonate, a mineral that builds up the formations. Some springs die, and the terraces become gray and lifeless. The Hoodoos are the remains of old hot-spring terraces broken up by landslides.

Obsidian Cliff is a mountain of black glass that was formed by molten lava. Rootless vegetation called *lichens* now cover the glass in many places.

Norris Geyser Basin consists of hundreds of geysers, hot springs, and pools. It is the hottest and most active thermal area in Yellowstone. The temperature of the water in some of the springs reaches more than 400 °F (200 °C). Several geysers may erupt at the same time.

Plants and wildlife

Evergreen forests and mountain meadows cover most of Yellowstone. The most abundant tree is the lodgepole pine. Forests of Douglas-fir, Engelmann spruce, limber pine, and subalpine fir grow in some areas. During the summer, the mountain meadows display a variety of wildflowers, including the fringed gentian, Indian paintbrush, monkey flower, and mountain bluebell.

More than 275 species of birds and nearly 50 kinds of other animals live in the park. Trumpeter swans, blue herons, white pelicans, bald eagles, and gulls feed on fish in its lakes and rivers. These fish include cutthroat trout, grayling, mountain whitefish, and rainbow trout.

Elk are the most common of the large animals in the park. Approximately 31,000 elk live in the park in summer. About half of them stay there through the winter, but the rest wander south to warmer areas. Yellowstone has about 2,400 bison. These animals were widely hunted in the United States during the 1800's. The protection provided by the park helped save them from being killed off completely. Other large animals in Yellowstone include black bears, grizzly bears, moose, mule deer, bighorn sheep, and cougars.

In Yellowstone, the balance of nature is maintained through natural controls such as disease, weather, and competition for food (see **Balance of nature**). For example, if the park's elk population becomes too large, many of the animals die during winters when food is scarce. In addition, park regulations protect the animal and plant life from human interference. The feeding of bears is prohibited not only because it is dangerous but because it disrupts their natural feeding habits.

Recreational activities

More than 1,200 miles (1,900 kilometers) of trails provide a wide choice of hiking routes through Yellowstone. Park naturalists offer guided hikes and evening campfire programs. TW Services, Inc., has a program of bus tours, horseback trips, stagecoach rides, and cookouts in summer.

Fishing in the park's rivers and lakes is controlled by special regulations, and a permit is required. Hunting and the use of firearms are prohibited. Boats and canoes may be used on most of the lakes. Visitors must obtain a permit to use any type of boat or canoe.

Campgrounds are located at Canyon, Madison Junction, Mammoth, Norris Junction, and other sites. A few major sites, including Canyon, Old Faithful, Mammoth, and Lake, have cottages, cabins, and hotels. Visitors who want to camp in the wilderness must have a permit.

During the winter, a heavy snow covers the park. All park roads, except the one connecting the north and northeast entrances, are closed. Snowmobiles may be used on the park's roads, which are left unplowed but are groomed for snowmobile traffic. Cross-country skiers and snowshoers can travel over the park's trails.

Information may be obtained by writing Superintendent, P.O. Box 168, Yellowstone National Park, WY 82190.

History

Yellowstone's landscape was shaped by the action of volcanoes and glaciers through millions of years. A large mass of magma, which lies about 1 to 2 miles (1.6 to 3.2 kilometers) below the surface of the park, has erupted more than 27 times during the past 2 million years.

A major volcanic eruption occurred in the Yellowstone area about 2 million years ago. About 600,000 years ago, another explosion of magma and gas created much of Yellowstone's present-day geography. The eruption produced the Yellowstone Caldera, which is a huge crater about 47 miles (76 kilometers) long and 28 miles (45 kilometers) wide. Yellowstone Lake now occupies part of this crater.

Glaciers once covered much of the area. The last ones melted about 8,500 years ago and filled Yellowstone Lake. Outflow from the lake drained northward and helped shape the Grand Canyon of the Yellowstone.

One Indian tribe, the Sheepeaters, is known to have lived in the area of the present-day park. Other tribes, including the Bannock, the Crow, and the Blackfeet, crossed the area to hunt bison and elk.

The U.S. government obtained the Yellowstone region in 1803 as part of the Louisiana Purchase. John Colter, a member of the Lewis and Clark expedition, was the first white person to see Yellowstone. He traveled alone on foot through the area in 1807 (see **Colter, John**). Many trappers explored the area in the 1830's and 1840's. They returned with stories of spouting geysers, hot springs, and mudpots.

In 1870, General Henry D. Washburn, the surveyor general of the Montana Territory, led an expedition to check out the reports of the trappers. In 1871, a government expedition led by Ferdinand V. Hayden, a geologist, documented the unusual features of the area.

In 1872, Congress passed a bill to establish the park and preserve its natural resources. Civilian superintendents administered the park for the first few years, but they were unable to stop widespread hunting and trapping there. The Army took over control of the park in 1886 and began to protect the wildlife. A detachment of cavalry occupied the park until 1916, when Congress established the National Park Service. Today, the National Park Service manages Yellowstone. A superintendent, appointed by the director of the park service and assisted by rangers, naturalists, and a maintenance staff, administers the park. Park headquarters are located at Mammoth.

In 1988, fires raged in Yellowstone. In keeping with park policy, the fires were allowed to burn naturally. The blaze burned large areas of forests and meadows, which have since begun their natural cycle of regeneration.

Critically reviewed by Yellowstone National Park

See also **National park** (picture: The Grand Canyon of the Yellowstone).

Additional resources

Bauer, Erwin A. and Peggy. *Yellowstone.* Rev. ed. Voyageur Pr., 1999.
Magoc, Christopher J. *Yellowstone: The Creation and Selling of an American Landscape, 1870-1903.* Univ. of N. Mex. Pr., 1999.
Meagher, Mary, and Houston, D. B. *Yellowstone and the Biology of Time: Photographs Across a Century.* Univ. of Okla. Pr., 1998.

Yellowstone River rises near the Continental Divide in northwestern Wyoming and flows north into Yellowstone National Park. For location, see **Wyoming** (physical map). There it forms Yellowstone Lake, which covers 137 square miles (355 square kilometers) at an elevation of 7,731 feet (2,356 meters). The lake is one of the largest high-elevation lakes in North America. North of the lake, the river plunges 109 feet (33 meters) over its upper falls and 308 feet (94 meters) over its lower falls into Yellow-

stone Canyon. Then it flows northeast across the Great Plains of Montana. The Yellowstone flows a total distance of 671 miles (1,080 kilometers) and joins the Missouri River on the Montana-North Dakota line. See also **Montana** (picture).   Ronald E. Beiswenger

Yellowthroat is the name of a group of North American birds with bright orange-yellow throats. There are about 13 species. The *common yellowthroat* is about 5 inches (13 centimeters) long and has an olive-green back. The face of the male has a black mask with a white border above it. Common yellowthroats breed throughout North America. They spend the winter from northern California to South Carolina and Central America. The birds live in wet grassy or marshy areas, where they can hide among the tall reeds. They nest on or near the ground. The female usually lays four eggs.

Belding's yellowthroat has solid yellow underparts and a yellow border on the black mask of the male. It

Tom Edwards, Animals Animals

The yellowthroat is about as big as a small wren. It lives in wet areas among tall reeds, where it can hide easily.

lives in wetlands of Baja California, Mexico.

Sandra L. Vehrencamp

Scientific classification. Yellowthroats belong to the subfamily Parulinae in the emberizid family, Emberizidae. The scientific name for the common yellowthroat is *Geothlypis trichas.* Belding's yellowthroat is *G. beldingi.*

Yeltsin, Boris Nikolayevich (1931-   ), was president of Russia from 1991 to 1999. He took office when Russia became independent following the collapse of the Soviet Union in 1991. In 1990 and 1991, while Russia was still a republic of the Soviet Union, he headed the Russian republic's legislature. Yeltsin played a major role in the breakup of the Soviet Union. In December 1991, Yeltsin and the presidents of the Soviet republics of Belarus and Ukraine formed the Commonwealth of Independent States (C.I.S.). They declared the Soviet Union had ceased to exist. The Soviet Union's leader, Mikhail S. Gorbachev, resigned, and the Soviet Union was dissolved.

Yeltsin was born in Sverdlovsk (now Yekaterinburg). In 1955, he graduated from Ural Polytechnic Institute. He joined the

© G. De Keerle, Gamma/Liaison

Boris Yeltsin

Communist Party in 1961. He became head of the local party in Sverdlovsk in 1976 and, in 1985, chief of the party organization in Moscow and a member of the party's ruling Politburo. The party removed Yeltsin from these posts in 1987 because of his radical policies and his criticism of Gorbachev's more cautious ones. In 1989, Yeltsin won a seat in the new Soviet national legislature. In 1990, he resigned from the Communist Party.

In August 1991, a group of conservative Soviet Communist officials staged a coup against Gorbachev. Yeltsin led opposition to the coup. The coup failed after three days. Yeltsin's role in defying the coup earned him increased power and prestige both at home and abroad.

As president, he supported major economic reforms, including a move to free enterprise. Yeltsin and his program faced opposition from Russia's increasingly antireform parliament. In a referendum of April 1993, a majority of voters expressed confidence in Yeltsin and his program for economic change. But opposition in parliament continued. In September 1993, Yeltsin dissolved parliament. In December, voters elected a new parliament and approved a new constitution. Yeltsin remained president. In 1996, he was elected to a second term.

Russia's transition to a market economy proved difficult, and Yeltsin maneuvered to maintain control of the country. In 1998, he abruptly fired his prime minister, Viktor S. Chernomyrdin. Over the next year and a half, Yeltsin appointed and then dismissed three different prime ministers. In 1999, the State Duma considered impeaching Yeltsin for a number of his actions. The Duma voted against impeachment.

In August 1999, Yeltsin appointed Vladimir V. Putin as prime minister. On the last day of 1999, Yeltsin resigned and named Putin acting president. Stuart D. Goldman

Yemen is a country in the southern part of the Arabian Peninsula. The Gulf of Aden borders Yemen on the south and the Red Sea on the west. Most of the people of Yemen are Arab Muslims.

Sanaa is Yemen's capital and largest city. Aden is an important port and oil center. Most of Yemen is hot and dry, though there are a few fertile areas where the land can be farmed. The high interior of northwestern Yemen is the most beautiful and best-cultivated part of Arabia.

Most of the workers in Yemen are farmers or craftworkers, but employment in modern businesses is growing. The country is famous for its Mocha coffee. Yemeni craftworkers have been famous for their textiles, leatherwork, and ironwork since ancient times.

In 1990, two nations—Yemen (Aden), also called South Yemen or Southern Yemen; and Yemen (Sanaa), also known as North Yemen or Northern Yemen—merged to form Yemen. Yemen's full name in Arabic, the country's official language, is Al-Jumhuriyah al Yamaniyah (the Republic of Yemen).

Government

National government. A president heads the government of Yemen. The president is elected by the people to a seven-year term and can be reelected only once. The president appoints a vice president, cabinet members, and a prime minister. Parliament consists of a House of Representatives and a Shura Council. The people elect the 301 members of the House of Representatives to six-year terms. The president appoints the 111 members of the Shura Council.

Local government. Yemen has 18 governorates, headed by governors appointed by the president. The governorates have smaller divisions called districts. Members of the governorate and district councils are

Facts in brief

Capital: Sanaa.
Official language: Arabic.
Area: 203,850 mi² (527,968 km²). *Coastline*—about 1,020 mi (1,642 km).
Elevation: *Highest*—12,336 ft (3,760 m). *Lowest*—sea level.
Population: *Estimated 2004 population*—21,524,000; density, 106 per mi² (41 per km²); distribution, 74 percent rural, 26 percent urban. *1994 census*—14,587,807.
Chief products: *Agriculture*—coffee, fruits, grains, khat, vegetables. *Manufacturing*—building materials, handicrafts. *Mining*—petroleum.
Flag: Red, white, and black horizontal stripes. See Flag (picture: Flags of Asia and the Pacific).
Money: *Basic unit*—rial. One hundred fils equal one rial.

Sanaa is the capital of Yemen. The city is enclosed by a wall. Traffic enters and leaves through one of eight gates.

Yemen

▬▬	International boundary
⌒⌒	Road
⌒⌒	Seasonal stream
✪	National capital
•	Other city or town
+	Elevation above sea level

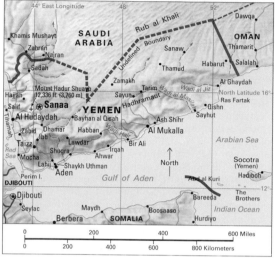

WORLD BOOK maps

elected by the people. The president appoints city mayors.

People

Most of Yemen's people are Arabs. The rest are Pakistanis, Eritreans, Somalis, or Indians. Most of the people are Muslims of the Zaydi or Shafii sects. The Zaydis live in northwestern Yemen. They have long been associated with the government and the military. The Shafii sect has a powerful merchant class. The division between the politically powerful Zaydis and the wealthy Shafiis has caused bitterness between them. Clan relationships are also very important to most Yemenis. Feuds between rival clans divide many areas of the country.

Way of life. Most people of Yemen make a living as farmers or herders. Farmers grow crops in the highland valleys and scattered oases. Herders raise sheep in the drier regions. Many people make a living by doing craftwork. These workers produce handicrafts in small, one-room shops. They make such articles as inlaid *jambiyas* (daggers), wooden chests, brassware, and jewelry.

On the coasts and on Socotra Island, many people live by fishing. The men spear fish near the shore from dugout canoes called *sambugs,* or net them in deeper water from single-sail *dhows.*

Many of Yemen's young men leave the country to seek work. Most of them are employed in Saudi Arabia or other countries of the Arabian Peninsula.

Some city people reside in modern houses or apartment buildings, and many others live in one-story brick houses. Some farm families live in towns, such as Sayun, that have mud-brick houses three or four stories high. Others live in small villages close to the land they farm.

Near the Red Sea coast, many people live in straw huts.

Food and clothing. Rice, bread, vegetables, lamb, and fish are the chief foods in Yemen. The national dish is a spicy stew called *salta.*

Almost all the men of Yemen and many of the women chew the leaves of a plant called the *khat* (also spelled *kat* or *qat).* These leaves contain a stimulant, and they produce a mild intoxication or *euphoria* (feeling of well-being). Groups of men and groups of women get together most afternoons for a session of khat chewing.

Some Yemenis, especially those in the cities, wear Western-style clothing. Many others wear more traditional Arab clothing. The men's garments include cotton breeches or a striped *futa* (kilt). Many men wear skull-caps, turbans, or tall, round hats called *tarbooshes.* Many women wear long robes, black shawls, and veils.

Education. Less than half the people of Yemen 15 years of age or older can read and write. For the country's literacy rate, see **Literacy** (table: Literacy rates). Public schools exist in cities and larger towns. In rural areas, most education takes place in Muslim religious schools. Yemen's first university, the University of Sanaa, was established in 1970. Another university is located in Aden.

Land

Yemen has flat land along the west and south coasts and high land inland. Beyond the inland hills and cliffs stretches the Rub al Khali (or Empty Quarter), a sandy desert that extends into Saudi Arabia.

The coastal plain along the Red Sea is called the *Tihamah.* It extends inland from the Red Sea for 20 to 50 miles (32 to 80 kilometers). The Tihamah is hot and humid, and few people live there. Temperatures range from 68 to 130 °F (20 to 54 °C).

A few rocky hills border the Tihamah on the east.

Robert Harding Picture Library

Aden has many streets lined with traditional Arab-style buildings. The city is an important port and oil center.

© Michael Jenner, Robert Harding Picture Library

The Hadhramaut region of central Yemen is one of the parts of the country that have some fertile areas. But most of Yemen is hot and dry.

Then, cliffs rise steeply. Rains have cut into the cliffs, forming deep valleys called *wadis.*

East of the cliffs is an area called the High Yemen. Broad valleys and plateaus lie 6,000 feet (1,800 meters) above sea level. They are surrounded by steep mountains that rise as high as 12,336 feet (3,760 meters). The high altitude makes the region much cooler than the Tihamah. East of the mountains, the land slopes toward the desert of Saudi Arabia.

The coastal plain along the Gulf of Aden is mostly sand but has a few fertile areas. It varies from about 5 to 10 miles (8 to 16 kilometers) in width.

A dry, hilly plateau borders the Gulf of Aden coastal plain. The plateau is cut by wadis that have some rich farmland. For example, the land between Sayun and Tarim in the Hadhramaut region in eastern Yemen is a farming area. The desert lies north of the plateau.

Rainfall averages 5 inches (13 centimeters) in Aden on the south coast. The High Yemen gets 10 to 15 inches (25 to 38 centimeters) of rain a year. It is not uncommon for desert areas to receive no rain for five years or more.

Economy

Much of the economy of Yemen depends on extensive foreign aid and on the wages sent home by the many Yemenis who work in other parts of the Arabian Peninsula. Farming and the petroleum industry also contribute to Yemen's income.

The hills and highlands of northwestern Yemen are the most productive farming area. Farmers raise such food grains as wheat, barley, and *durra* (a sorghum). They also raise a variety of fruits, including apricots, bananas, citrus fruits, grapes, papayas, and pomegranates. They grow beans, lentils, onions, and tomatoes in gardens. People on the Tihamah raise durra and some dates and cotton. Agriculture in southern Yemen is limited to the few areas with underground water for irrigation. Farmers grow three or four crops a year of barley, millet, sesame, sorghum, and wheat. Since the early 1980's, the Yemenis have worked to turn desert areas into farmland by means of dams, irrigation, and other water and agricultural development projects.

Khat is the leading cash crop of Yemen. It comes from the leaves of a woody shrub that grows in the highlands. Coffee is another important cash crop. Coffee plants grow on terraces cut into the hills. Ancient *aqueducts* (water channels) carry water to the terraces.

Aden's oil refinery and port provide Yemen with much of its income. The oil refinery processes oil shipped from other countries, mostly those on the Persian Gulf. Ships of many nations use the port for refueling, repairs, and transferring cargoes.

Until the early 1980's, Yemen had almost no other industry. But large petroleum deposits were found in the northwestern part of the country, and petroleum mining is growing in importance. Construction is also a growing industry. Construction projects include new factories, hotels, office buildings, schools, and roads.

Many goods in the country are still made by hand. The people weave and dye cloth, and make rope, glassware, harnesses, saddles, and pottery. They sell their goods in the village *bazaars* (marketplaces).

Trucks and automobiles provide most of the land transportation in Yemen. But many people still use camels, donkeys, and horses.

History

According to Arab tradition, Semitic people invaded what is now northwestern Yemen about 2000 B.C. They brought farming and building skills to the herders who lived there. About 1400 B.C., an important trade route began forming. Caravans carrying pearls and spices passed through Yemen. Cities, castles, temples, and dams were built during this time. The Queen of Sheba ruled Yemen during the 900's B.C.

Yemen's prosperity ended in the A.D. 300's. Local chieftains fought among themselves, and Abyssinia (Ethiopia) invaded Yemen. The next 1,300 years were marked by fighting between Yemeni tribes and religious groups, and against invading Egyptians and Turks. In the 600's, the Prophet Muhammad's son-in-law, Ali, introduced Islam to the people. In A.D. 897, an *imam* (ruler) became the political and religious leader of Yemen.

The Ottoman Empire, centered in Asia Minor (now Turkey), took over Yemen in 1517, and it had varying degrees of control for more than 400 years. The Treaty of Lausanne ended Turkish rule in 1924. By that time, the Turks were holding only northwestern Yemen. The rest of the country had been taken over by the British. The land freed from the Turks was called Yemen, though it was only part of what is now the country of Yemen. It later became Yemen (Sanaa), and the land under British control became Yemen (Aden).

Formation of Yemen (Aden). The United Kingdom seized Aden in 1839, after people from the town robbed a wrecked British ship. Aden became an important refueling stop for British ships going to India by way of the Suez Canal and Red Sea. Aden was ruled from British India until 1937, when it became a British crown colony.

To protect Aden from take-over by the Ottomans, the United Kingdom extended its control to the tribal states in the region around Aden. The United Kingdom signed treaties with the tribal leaders, promising protection and aid in return for loyalty. The region came to be known as the Aden Protectorate.

In 1959, six tribal states in the protectorate formed the Federation of the Arab Emirates of the South. The United Kingdom signed a treaty with the federation, promising to grant independence. The date for independence was later set for 1967. Meanwhile, the British controlled the federation's foreign policy and provided military protection and economic aid. In 1962, the name of the federation was changed to the Federation of South Arabia. By 1965, Aden and all but four of the tribal states in the protectorate had joined the federation.

In the early 1960's, the United Kingdom tried to form a representative government that would rule the federation after independence. But radical Arab nationalist leaders in Aden and tribal leaders in the protectorate both wanted to rule. The radicals began a terror campaign against the British and the tribal leaders. Two radical groups, the National Liberation Front (NLF) and the Front for the Liberation of Occupied South Yemen (FLOSY), also fought each other.

In late 1967, the federation government collapsed. The United Kingdom announced that it would withdraw its troops and give power to any group that could set up a government. The NLF emerged as the most powerful group in the federation. On Nov. 30, 1967, the last British troops were withdrawn, and the NLF formed a government. The NLF proclaimed the federation an independent country—the People's Republic of South Yemen. In 1970, the name was changed to the People's Democratic Republic of Yemen. The country was often referred to as Yemen (Aden), South Yemen, or Southern Yemen.

After independence, the NLF became the National Front, which merged with several smaller political groups in 1975 and formed the United Political Organization National Front (UPONF). In 1978, the groups that made up UPONF reorganized as the Yemeni Socialist Party (YSP). The leaders of Yemen (Aden) favored some political principles of Karl Marx, one of the founders of Communism. Yemen (Aden) developed strong ties with the Soviet Union, Cuba, and other Communist countries. These countries provided much aid to Yemen (Aden).

In 1986, civil war broke out in Yemen (Aden) between the government and a group holding more extreme Marxist views than those held by the government. The extreme group won and took control of the government.

Formation of Yemen (Sanaa). On Sept. 26, 1962, military officers supported by Egypt overthrew the ruling imam in what is now northwestern Yemen—then called Yemen—and set up a republic. The officers named the country the Yemen Arab Republic. It became informally known as Yemen (Sanaa), North Yemen, or Northern Yemen. The imam's forces—called *royalists*—fought from their bases in the mountains to try to regain control of the government. They were supported by Saudi Arabia. But the republicans, supported by Egypt, ruled most of Yemen (Sanaa). The fighting ended in 1970. The republicans set up a new government that included republicans and royalists. In 1974, army leaders took control of the government of Yemen (Sanaa). They were conservatives who opposed Communism.

Unification. In September 1972, strained relations between Yemen (Aden) and Yemen (Sanaa) led to fighting along the border they shared. But an Arab League mission was able to bring about a cease-fire. In October, representatives of the two countries signed a peace agreement and an agreement on eventual unification. Committees were set up to discuss details of the unification. But continued fighting through the 1970's interrupted the talks. Yemen (Aden) also was involved in fighting

with Oman, its eastern neighbor. These clashes went badly for Yemen (Aden), and in the 1980's it adopted a more peaceful foreign policy.

Unification talks between Yemen (Aden) and Yemen (Sanaa) continued through the 1980's, and the two countries increasingly cooperated in economic and administrative matters. In 1990, they officially merged and became the country of Yemen. But disagreements between supporters of the united country's president, who was from North Yemen; and its vice president, from South Yemen, led to a civil war between northerners and southerners in May 1994. The fighting caused thousands of deaths and much destruction. Troops loyal to the president won the war in July, and the country remained united. Robert Geran Landen

See also **Aden; Sanaa.**

Yen is the monetary unit of Japan. Coins in denominations of 5, 10, 50, 100, and 500 yen are commonly used. Paper money is printed in denominations of 1,000; 5,000; and 10,000 yen. The *sen* and *rin,* smaller denominations of the yen, were removed from circulation in 1954 but are used as units for calculation. R. G. Doty

Yenisey River, *YEN uh SAY,* flows through Siberia, a part of Russia (see **Russia** [terrain map]). The Yenisey travels 2,543 miles (4,093 kilometers) from its origin in the Sayan Mountains of southern Siberia to its mouth on the Arctic coast. After the river leaves the mountains, it flows north. It enters the Kara Sea through an *estuary* (broad river mouth) about 200 miles (320 kilometers) east of the Gulf of Ob (Obskaya Guba). Ocean steamers go 400 miles (640 kilometers) up the river to Igarka, a lumber port. There are two hydroelectric stations along the river. Craig ZumBrunnen

Yeoman, *YOH muhn,* was a *retainer* (dependent) of a feudal lord during the late Middle Ages in England. In the early 1400's, the name was used for officials in the households of nobles and for small freeholders and farmers on a feudal manor. By the Tudor period (1485-1603), yeomen had become an independent class of small landowners and farmers. They were superior in status to ordinary villagers and workers but ranked below gentlemen and squires. During the late 1700's, men of this class formed their own cavalry groups, called *yeomanry.* The yeomanry were officially organized by an Act of Parliament in 1794.

In 1485, King Henry VII organized the Yeomen of the Guard, who formed a bodyguard to the monarch of England. Today, the Yeomen still serve as royal bodyguards on formal occasions, but their duties are purely ceremonial. Enlisted men wear colorful costumes—and carry weapons—that date back to the late 1400's and the 1500's. According to tradition, a visiting grand duke in 1669 was astonished by the large amounts of beef that the Yeomen Warders of the Tower of London consumed. He nicknamed them *beefeaters,* which they are still called today. See **Tower of London.**

An appointment to the Yeomen of the Guard is honorary. Members are chosen from the officers and enlisted men of the United Kingdom's regular armed forces. In the United States Navy, petty officers performing clerical work have the rating of yeoman. Richard P. Abels

Yerevan, *YEHR uh VAHN* (pop. 1,114,000), is the capital and largest city of Armenia. Its name is also spelled *Erevan.* Yerevan lies on the Razdan River (see **Armenia**

[map]). Yerevan is an important cultural and scientific center. It has a university and several colleges, libraries, museums, theaters, and scientific research institutes. The city's products include chemicals, clothing, food, liquor, machinery, and synthetic rubber.

Archaeological evidence suggests that a fortress was built at what is now Yerevan in the 780's B.C. From the A.D. 1400's to the 1800's, Yerevan stood on the border of the rival Persian and Ottoman powers, and was frequently destroyed.   Leslie Dienes

See also **Armenia** (picture: Armenian shoppers).

Yerkes, *YUR keez,* **Robert Mearns,** *murnz* (1876-1956), was an American psychologist known for his research on the behavior of apes. His most important book is *The Great Apes: A Study of Anthropoid Life* (1929), which his wife, the botanist Ada Watterson Yerkes, helped him write. The book describes the anatomy, behavior, and intelligence of chimpanzees, gorillas, and other apes. During 1923 and 1924, Yerkes raised two chimpanzees in his home. He wrote *Almost Human* (1925) and coauthored *Chimpanzee Intelligence and Its Vocal Expressions* (1925) based on this experience.

In 1929, Yerkes founded an ape-breeding colony and research facility in Orange Park, Florida. He also became the center's first director. It is now in Atlanta, Georgia, and is called the Yerkes Primate Research Center.

Yerkes was born on May 26, 1876, in Breadysville, near Hatboro, Pennsylvania. He taught psychology at Harvard University from 1902 to 1917 and at Yale University from 1924 to 1944.   Donald Symons

Yerkes Observatory, *YUR keez,* is an astronomical observatory operated by the University of Chicago in Williams Bay, Wisconsin. It houses three telescopes. Two are reflecting telescopes, one with a mirror 41 inches (104 centimeters) in diameter and the other with a mirror 24 inches (61 centimeters) in diameter. The third is a refracting telescope with a lens 40 inches (102 centimeters) in diameter. The refracting telescope, the largest of its kind in the world, is 63 feet (19 meters) long. A dome 90 feet (27 meters) in diameter protects it.

Yerkes Observatory is famous for its accurate measurements of the distances of stars. These measurements were first made by the American astronomer Frank Schlesinger. The observatory's first director, George E. Hale, achieved advances in solar physics. The observatory is also noted for its studies of infrared radiation, interstellar matter, stellar *photometry* (light measurement), stellar spectra, and theoretical astrophysics. Yerkes is the administrative headquarters for the Center for Astrophysical Research in Antarctica, a National Science Foundation center. Hale founded the observatory in 1895 with a large donation from Chicago businessman Charles T. Yerkes.   Critically reviewed by Yerkes Observatory

See also **Hale, George Ellery.**

Yeti. See Abominable Snowman.

Yevtushenko, *YEHV too SHEHNG koh,* **Yevgeny,** *yehv GEH nee* (1933-   ), is a Russian poet. Most of his works are directed toward people who grew up in the Soviet Union after World War II ended in 1945. He is a master of technique and uses straightforward language.

Yevtushenko became famous in the West as one of the first Soviet writers to criticize Soviet society. He won worldwide fame with "Babi Yar" (1961), a tribute to Soviet Jews massacred by the Nazis in 1941 (see **Babi Yar**). The

poem was remarkable for its open attack on anti-Semitism, a topic avoided by most Soviet writers. His works include a novel in verse and prose, *Wild Berries* (1981); the long poem *Fuku* (1985); and *The Collected Poems, 1952-1990* (1991). Yevtushenko was born on July 18, 1933, in Zima, near Irkutsk.   Anna Lisa Crone

Yew is the name of a group of evergreen trees and shrubs. The leaves of yews are flat, pointed needles, dark green on top and pale green beneath. They spread apart in two rows along the stem. A yew's scaly bark has reddish-brown coloring. The purplish-black seeds possess scarlet coverings, making them resemble small olives. The bark, needles, and seeds of yews are poisonous. In some cases, yew trees grow large and live for hundreds of years.

Yews have tough, elastic wood. The heartwood possesses an orange-red color and a grain almost as beautiful as that of mahogany. People use polished yew wood in the manufacture of tables.

Yews grow around the world. The *English yew* is found in Europe, Asia, and Africa. Many yews stand near the English Channel, where the chalky soil seems to further their growth. In the Middle Ages, English archers made excellent longbows out of yew wood. Yew trees have often grown in English churchyards. Branches of

© Earl Kubis, Tom Stack & Assoc.

The American yew, or *ground hemlock,* grows in North America. People often use its branches for Christmas decorations.

the trees served as funeral decorations, and were twined into wreaths for the heads of the mourners. For this reason, the yew has often symbolized sadness.

The tall *western,* or *Pacific, yew* grows in western North America. People use its wood for cabinetwork and canoe paddles. Another North American species, the *American yew* or *ground hemlock,* is a low, straggling shrub. The Asian *Japanese yew* grows more in the form of a shrub.   James D. Mauseth

See also **Conifer; Plant** (picture: Japanese yew); **Taxol.**

Scientific classification. Yews belong to the family Taxaceae. The scientific name for the English yew is *Taxus baccata.* The western yew is *T. brevifolia,* the American yew is *T. canadensis,* and the Japanese yew is *T. cuspidata.*

Yi dynasty. See Korea, History of (The Choson dynasty).

Yiddish language is a language of European Jews and their descendants. Yiddish has been the language of the *Ashkenazim* for about 1,000 years. The Ashkenazim are Jews primarily of central and eastern European origin. Yiddish is generally classified as a Germanic language, like English, German, Dutch, and the Scandinavian tongues—Icelandic, Danish, Norwegian, and Swedish. However, Yiddish is written in Hebrew characters from right to left like Hebrew and Aramaic, two Semitic languages used by the Jews.

Yiddish developed among Jews who spoke Judeo-Old-French and Judeo-Old-Italian, Jewish dialects of the medieval French and Italian languages. These Jews migrated to German-speaking regions and later eastward to Slavic lands, including Poland and Russia. Yiddish developed from the resulting blend of medieval German city dialects with French, Italian, Slavic, and Hebrew-Aramaic elements. Yiddish became the most widely spoken of all Jewish languages. It is estimated that almost 90 percent of the Jews in Europe spoke Yiddish during the late 1800's and early 1900's.

A highly developed Yiddish culture emerged over the centuries. This culture was expressed in folklore and folk songs, religious and political publications, educational institutions, theater, and motion pictures. Most important, Yiddish culture gave birth to a rich and important literature. The Nazis, during their rule in Germany from 1933 to 1945, effectively destroyed European Yiddish civilization.

Millions of Yiddish-speaking European Jews immigrated to the United States and Canada during the late 1800's and the early 1900's. Their language was influenced by English and, in turn, Yiddish contributed many words to the American language. Some words taken from Yiddish include *bagel, kibitz,* and *klutz.*

Dorothy S. Bilik

See also **Yiddish literature.**

Additional resources

Blech, Benjamin. *The Complete Idiot's Guide to Learning Yiddish.* Alpha Bks., 2000.
Bluestein, Gene. *Anglish/Yinglish: Yiddish in American Life and Literature.* 2nd ed. Univ. of Neb. Pr., 1998.
Rosten, Leo C. *The Joys of Yiddish.* 1968. Reprint. Pocket Bks., 2000.

Yiddish literature is the literature of Jews who write and speak the Yiddish language. Yiddish literature originated in the late 1200's and reached its peak in the late 1800's and early 1900's.

The earliest Yiddish literature took the form of explanations, interpretations, and translations of the Hebrew Bible and other traditional religious and ethical writings. The invention of the printing press had an enormous effect on this literature in the 1500's. Many guides to morals and customs, religious poetry, prayer books, and poems on Biblical subjects were published beginning in the mid-1500's. Perhaps the most important and popular work of this period was the *Tsenerene,* or *Women's Bible* (1590). Although a few Yiddish writers produced knightly romances, historical poems, and other nonreligious works, until the 1800's Yiddish literature focused primarily on ethical and religious subjects.

Three important Yiddish writers appeared in the late 1800's and early 1900's. They were Mendele the Bookseller, the pen name of Shalom Jacob Abramovich; Isaac Leib Peretz; and Sholem Aleichem, the pen name of Shalom Rabinowitz. The novels, stories, and plays of these writers are rooted in the world of the *shtetl* (small Jewish town). Their works typically describe social conflicts within the community and the challenges from the non-Jewish world to traditional Jewish life.

Between the end of World War I in 1918 and the start of World War II in 1939, Yiddish literature flourished in such eastern European cities as Moscow; Warsaw, Poland; Vilnius, Lithuania; and Kiev, Ukraine, then part of the Soviet Union. New York City also became an important center, especially for Yiddish poetry. Outstanding writers of the period included Sholem Asch, Israel Joshua Singer, Moshe Kulbak, and David Bergelson in Eastern Europe; and Moshe Leib Halperin and Mani Leib in the United States. Many Yiddish writers were among the 6 million Jews killed by the Nazis during the Holocaust (1939-1945). The government of the Soviet Union often imprisoned Yiddish writers. Many, including Bergelson, were executed in 1952.

Interest in Yiddish literature has increased in the late 1900's, partly because of the availability of good translations. In addition, such writers as Jacob Glatstein, Chaim Grade, and Isaac Bashevis Singer kept the Yiddish literary tradition alive. In 1978, Singer, the younger brother of Israel Joshua Singer, became the first Yiddish writer to receive the Nobel Prize for literature. The United States and Israel are the main centers for Yiddish literature today.   Dorothy S. Bilik

See also **Asch, Sholem; Sholem Aleichem; Singer, Isaac Bashevis; Yiddish language.**

YMCA. See Young Men's Christian Association.

YMCA Adventure Guides is a national program of parent-and-child activities in the United States sponsored by the Young Men's Christian Association (YMCA). The program seeks to foster understanding and companionship between children who are 5 to 9 years old and their parents. The YMCA Adventure Guides program emphasizes the role of parents as guides in a child's life.

Adventure Guides (parents) and *Explorers* (children) meet regularly in small community groups called *Circles.* The Circle provides structure, support, and a sense of community for all group activities. Group activities commonly include camping, service projects, arts and crafts, music, and storytelling. In many cases, multiple Circles join together to participate in *Expedition* adventures. Some Expedition adventures specifically involve certain other family members.

A central theme of the YMCA Adventure Guides is the compass. The four directions of the compass represent the four essential parts of the YMCA Adventure Guides program: (1) family, (2) nature, (3) community, and (4) fun. Family, at the north point of the compass, serves as the focal point of the program. The program's motto is *Friends Forever.*

The YMCA Adventure Guides program was founded in 2003. It replaced the Y-Indian Guides as the central parent-and-child program of the YMCA. The Y-Indian Guides program had operated since 1926.

Critically reviewed by the YMCA of the USA

Yo-yo is a small toy that has been popular in the United States and Europe since the 1930's. It consists of two round, flat pieces of wood or plastic joined at the center by a small peg. A string is attached to the peg and winds around it. The player ties the free end of the string to one finger. The yo-yo spins in and out of the hand as the string unwinds and rewinds. Players can perform tricks with the yo-yo because the string is looped around the peg rather than permanently attached. The loop permits the yo-yo to spin in place.

The word *yo-yo* originated in the Philippines and means "come back." People in the Philippines used the yo-yo as both a weapon and a toy. In the West, people have had toys like yo-yos for at least 3,000 years. In the late 1920's, the name *yo-yo* became associated with an improved yo-yo developed in the United States by Donald F. Duncan. Rachel Gallagher

Yoga is a term that has two meanings. It is both (1) a school of thought in the Hindu religion and (2) a system of mental and physical exercise developed by that school. Followers of the yoga school, who are called *yogis* or *yogins*, use yoga exercise to achieve their goal of isolation of the soul from the body and mind. A large number of non-Hindus in Western countries practice some form of yoga exercise in hope of improving their health and achieving peace of mind. The word *yoga* means *discipline* in Sanskrit, the classical language of India.

According to the yoga school, every human being consists of *prakrti* and *purusha*. Prakrti includes a person's body, mind, and *ego* (conscious self). Purusha is pure, empty consciousness—the soul. The yoga school teaches that the soul is completely separate from the rest of a person, but that the person does not realize it. Human beings suffer because they wrongly believe that their soul is bound to their body and mind. The yoga school, through yoga exercise, aims to give people *prana* (understanding) of the meaning of their soul. After a person has obtained this understanding, his or her soul will gain *moksha* (release) from the *samsara* (cycle of rebirth) in which Hindus believe.

A yogi, under the guidance of a *guru* (teacher), goes through eight stages of training on the way to *moksha*. The yogi learns: (1) disciplined behavior, called *yama;* (2) positive values *(niyama);* (3) bodily postures, such as the lotus position *(asana);* (4) control of breathing *(pranayama);* (5) control of the senses *(pratyahara);* (6) fixing of the mind on a chosen object *(dharana);* and (7) meditation *(dhyana)*. The eighth stage, called *samadhi*, is a state of concentration in which yogis realize that their soul is pure and free, and empty of all content. A yogi who has completed these eight stages has reached *kaivalya*. Kaivalya is total isolation of the soul from the body, from all other souls, and from all of nature.

Various forms of yoga have become popular in the United States and Europe. *Transcendental Meditation* is a simplified version of the yoga of Hinduism. *Bhakti-yoga* involves the dedication of all actions and thoughts to a chosen god. Members of the Hare Krishna movement practice bhakti-yoga by dedicating themselves to the god Krishna. *Hatha-yoga,* which stresses difficult bodily postures and breathing techniques, has become popular as a method of gaining better health. People also study hatha-yoga for the unusual control some yogis develop over such functions as metabolism and blood flow. Charles S. J. White

See also **Hinduism; Meditation.**

Additional resources

Gates, Rolf, and Kenison, Katrina. *Meditations from the Mat: Daily Reflections on the Path of Yoga.* Anchor Bks., 2002.
Khalsa, Shakta K. *Yoga for Women.* DK Pub., 2002.
Lalvani, Vimla. *Classic Yoga for Stress Relief.* Sterling Pub., 1999.
Luby, Thia. *Children's Book of Yoga.* Clear Light Pub., 1998.
Younger readers. *Yoga for Teens.* 2000.

Yogurt, also spelled *yoghurt,* is a smooth, semisolid dairy product made from milk. It has a high acid content and thick curd. Yogurt ranks as a popular food in many parts of the world. People in Iran, Turkey, and some other countries of the Middle East have eaten yogurt for thousands of years. Yogurt consumption in the United States increased considerably in the late 1900's.

Yogurt may be made from the milk of buffaloes, cows, goats, or other cud-chewing animals. In the United States, commercial yogurt is made from cows' milk. Yogurt makers add two types of bacteria to milk to make yogurt. These bacteria, called *Lactobacillus bulgaricus* and *Streptococcus thermophilus,* multiply at carefully controlled temperatures and cause milk to *ferment* (ripen). During the fermentation process, the bacteria change *lactose* (milk sugar) into *lactic acid.* Lactic acid causes fluid milk to thicken, resulting in yogurt.

The high acid content of yogurt gives the product a sour taste that many people enjoy. However, many others prefer yogurt that has been sweetened with fruit flavoring. Yogurt has the same nutritional elements as milk. Some unflavored yogurt contains only a few calories per serving and is popular for low-calorie diets.

Some people make yogurt at home. They use commercial yogurt or bacteria from special laboratories to start fermentation. Several firms manufacture yogurt-making machines for home use. Michael F. Hutjens

Yokohama, *YOH kuh HAH muh* (pop. 3,426,506), is a Japanese port and a major center of commerce and industry. Among the cities of Japan, only Tokyo has more people. Yokohama lies about 20 miles (32 kilometers) south of Tokyo, on the island of Honshu (see **Japan** [political map]). Yokohama is the capital of Kanagawa Prefecture. A prefecture is a political unit in Japan.

Yokohama covers 163 square miles (421 square kilometers) on the western shore of Tokyo Bay and on the slopes of the surrounding hills. Downtown Yokohama occupies a triangular plain. The plain is bordered by narrow streams on two sides and by the bay on the third side. Residential areas of the city lie among the hills.

Yokohama has a number of gardens, libraries, parks, and theaters. Universities in the city include Kanagawa University, Kanto Gakuin University, Yokohama Municipal University, and Yokohama National University.

The city faces such problems as air and water pollution and lack of space. Overcrowded harbor conditions led to the construction of a pier that opened in 1970. The pier has special loading and unloading machinery to speed the handling of cargo.

Yokohama is Japan's largest port in terms of cargo value. Ships leaving the city carry many products manufactured in Tokyo and other nearby industrial regions. Rail lines link Yokohama with such other major cities as Kobe, Osaka, and Tokyo. Shipbuilding is a major industry in Yokohama. The city's factories also make such products as automobiles, chemicals, electrical equipment, iron and steel, and machinery.

Until 1854, the area that is now Yokohama was little more than a seashore with a few houses. That year, Commodore Matthew C. Perry of the U.S. Navy signed an agreement with the Japanese opening Japan to trade with the United States. Traders from a number of countries established offices in Yokohama in 1859. In time, Yokohama became a major seaport.

The city has twice been almost destroyed. On Sept. 1, 1923, one of the worst earthquakes in history killed over 23,000 Yokohamans. In 1945, during World War II, U.S. bombers dropped thousands of fire bombs on Yokohama. The city later was rebuilt a second time.

In 1973, a Yokohama law took effect that regulates new construction. It requires that no structure be built that allows sunlight to fall on the surrounding neighborhood less than four hours a day.   Kenneth B. Pyle

Yokuts Indians, *YOH kuhts,* are a group of tribes who once lived in south-central California, in the San Joachin Valley and the foothills of the Sierra Nevada mountains. Traditionally, the Yokuts lived in tribes of about 350 people. Each tribe had its own name, dialect, and territory. The tribes were divided into clans, each of which had a bird or other animal as a *totem* (emblem). Each clan inherited certain tribal offices, with the highest-ranking chief being the head of the Eagle clan.

The main foods of the Yokuts were fish, waterfowl, shellfish, roots, and seeds. In addition, many Yokuts ate salmon, acorns, and deer. The valley Yokuts used a tough-stemmed plant called *tule* for food and to make baskets, houses, boats, mats, and clothing.

Spanish explorers first encountered the Yokuts in 1772. At that time, there were between 18,000 and 50,000 Yokuts. In 1833, a malaria epidemic killed about 75 percent of the Yokuts. The gold rush of 1849 brought many white settlers into Yokuts territory, forcing the tribes off their traditional lands. In 1873, the Tule River Reservation was established for the Indians.

Today, about 1,200 Yokuts live on the reservation or in *rancherias* (protected areas) or towns near Fresno. Many of them work in logging or farming. They maintain some of their traditional culture by continuing such activities as acorn gathering, basket making, and community celebrations.   Victoria D. Patterson

Yom Kippur, *YOHM kih POOR,* is the Jewish day of atonement and the most important and sacred Jewish holy day. It falls in September or October, in the Jewish month of Tishri. It lasts from sunset on the ninth day of Tishri until three stars appear after the tenth day.

Jews observe Yom Kippur as a day of fasting and worship. On this day, devout Jews think of their sins, repent, and ask forgiveness from God and from other people. In ancient times, the high priest held a service in the Temple in Jerusalem and sacrificed certain animals as a ceremonial offering. The service, part of the process of repentance and atonement, was the main event of the day. Today, Jews fast, perform no work, and attend services in the synagogue or temple. The laws about Yom Kippur are found in Leviticus 16; 23:26-32; 25:9; and in Numbers 29:7-11. See also **Scapegoat.**   B. Barry Levy

Yonkers, New York (pop. 196,086), part of the New York City metropolitan area, is an important manufacturing center. Yonkers lies between the Bronx and Hudson rivers. For location, see **New York** (political map).

Yonkers covers 18 square miles (47 square kilometers). The city is the home of St. Joseph's College, and Sarah Lawrence College is in nearby Bronxville. Museums include Philipse Manor Hall and the Hudson River

Museum. Yonkers has many manufacturing plants. The chief products include chemicals, corn syrup and molasses, and electronic parts for aircraft and spacecraft.

Manhattan Indians once lived in the area that is now Yonkers. In 1646, Adriaen Van der Donck, a Dutch nobleman, received a land grant that included the site. He built a sawmill near the junction of the Nepperhan and Hudson rivers, where he could use the Nepperhan's water power. Van der Donck was called *De Jonkheer* (young gentleman). The settlement around the mill was known as De Jonkheer's land and, later, as Yonkers.

In 1693, a merchant named Frederick Philipse gained possession of much of the Yonkers area. He rented land to farmers, and, by the 1800's, the community consisted chiefly of farmers. The Hudson River Railroad opened in 1849, which encouraged the development of new industries in the area. Elisha G. Otis opened an elevator manufacturing shop in Yonkers in 1853, and his business grew into a leading industry (see **Otis, Elisha Graves**). Yonkers became a village in 1855 and a city in 1872. Industrial expansion continued in Yonkers in the early 1900's. Newly created manufacturing jobs attracted many immigrants.

In 1983, the Otis elevator factory closed. Yonkers has a council-manager government.   John Kenneth White

York was one of England's largest provincial cities from the Middle Ages until the Industrial Revolution of the 1700's and early 1800's. It stands at the junction of the rivers Ouse and Foss (see **England** [political map]). York is the center of the *unitary authority* (local government area) of York, which has a population of 181,131.

Romans founded York and called it *Eboracum.* York Minster Cathedral is one of the finest English churches. It was badly damaged by fire in 1984. Repairs of the damage were completed in 1988. The archbishop of York is second in authority to the archbishop of Canterbury in the Church of England. York's historic sites attract many tourists. The city is famous for its museums, which include the National Railway Museum and the Viking Museum.   M. Trevor Wild

York is a branch of the English royal family of Plantagenet. The House of York won the English throne from the House of Lancaster during the Wars of the Roses (1455-1485). Members belonging to the House of York ruled England for most of the period from 1461 to 1485.

Richard, Duke of York and leader of the Yorkist party, was the richest nobleman in England. He was descended through his mother from the third son of King Edward III. Henry VI, the reigning king, was descended in a line of males from Edward III's fourth son, John of Gaunt, Duke of Lancaster. Because the Duke of York was descended from an older son, he claimed that he had a better right to the throne than Henry VI.

Open warfare broke out in 1455, when Henry VI was defeated at the first battle of St. Albans. In December 1460, the Duke of York was killed at the Battle of Wakefield. But, the following year, King Henry's forces were decisively beaten, and York's oldest son was crowned Edward IV, the first Yorkist king. Edward lost his throne in 1470 but regained it in 1471 after the battles of Barnet and Tewkesbury. He ruled until 1483. He was succeeded by his 12-year-old son, Edward V. Shortly afterward, the boy's uncle, Richard, Duke of Gloucester, seized the crown as Richard III. He imprisoned Edward and his younger brother. The boys were never heard of again.

In 1485, Henry Tudor, Earl of Richmond, a descendant of the House of Lancaster, defeated and killed Richard III at Bosworth Field. He was crowned Henry VII, first ruler of the Tudor dynasty. Henry married Edward IV's daughter, Elizabeth, and so at last united the rival houses of Lancaster and York.   Ralph A. Griffiths

Related articles in *World Book* include:

Edward IV	Henry VI (of Eng-	Lancaster
Edward V	land)	Richard III
	Henry VII	Wars of the Roses

York, Alvin Cullum (1887-1964), an outstanding American soldier of World War I (1914-1918), killed more than 20 Germans and forced 132 others to surrender on Oct. 8, 1918. York was a member of a patrol sent to silence German machine-gun nests. He shot about 25 soldiers and forced a German major to order the entire group to surrender. York received the Medal of Honor for his deed. Marshal Ferdinand Foch of France called it "the greatest thing accomplished by any private soldier of all the armies of Europe." Although he became famous as Sergeant York, he was a corporal at the time of his feat.

United Press Int.

Alvin C. York

York was born in Fentress County, Tennessee, and grew up on a mountain farm. He developed amazing marksmanship with the rifle and pistol while a boy. He became deeply religious and sought exemption from the draft because he believed war was wrong. But he was denied exemption.   Christopher R. Gabel

York, Cape. See Cape York.

Yorkshire terrier is a breed of toy dog that weighs 4 to 7 pounds (1.8 to 3.2 kilograms). Weavers in northern England developed the breed in the 1850's. They wanted a dog bold enough to kill rats, but small enough to be carried in a pocket. The dog has long, silky hair. Its coat is steel-blue with golden-tan.

Critically reviewed by the Yorkshire Terrier Club of America

See also **Dog** (picture: Toy dogs).

Yorktown, Virginia, is a historic village on the York River (see **Virginia** [political map]). In 1781, Lord Cornwallis surrendered to General George Washington at Yorktown in the last major battle of the Revolutionary War. During the 1700's, Yorktown served as a major tobacco port. Today, several historic homes in Yorktown are part of Colonial National Historical Park. This park includes the Yorktown Battlefield and much of Jamestown Island.   Will Molineux

Yorktown, Battle of. See Revolutionary War in America (Surrender at Yorktown; picture).

Yoruba, *YOH ru bah,* are a group of people who inhabit southwestern Nigeria and parts of Benin and Togo. More than 17 million Yoruba live in these areas. They speak a language called Yoruba, which belongs to the Niger-Congo family of African languages.

Many Yoruba make their living mainly by farming. Large numbers of them live in cities and work on family-owned farms in surrounding areas. Many other Yoruba sell craftwork items, including handwoven cloth, metalwork, and pottery. Women control the sale of crafts, farm products, and imported goods in the lively local markets. Still other Yoruba work in technical jobs, in business, or in such professions as law and medicine.

The Yoruba practice several religions. Most Yoruba are Christians or Muslims. Others believe in the group's traditional religion. This religion centers on a supreme god and over 400 spirits called *orishas,* each with its own cult and priests.

Traditional Yoruba society included city-states, which consisted of towns, villages, and the surrounding farms and forests. Some city-states were ruled by a king called an *oba,* who was believed to be divine. Others were governed by chiefs or by the heads of large family groups. Some city-states became large kingdoms, the most powerful of which were Ife and Oyo.

From the late 1400's to the 1800's, Europeans sold many Yoruba as slaves to the Americas. During the late 1800's, the British conquered the Yoruba homeland. They established Christianity and European education among the Yoruba. During the 1900's, Yoruba farmers became important producers of cacao, from which chocolate is made. The Yoruba helped Nigeria win its independence in 1960 and have played leading roles in the nation since. Yoruba civilization also has influenced art, music, and religion in the Americas.   Dan R. Aronson

See also **Ife**; **Nigeria** (People; History); **Soyinka, Wole**.

Yosemite Falls, *yoh SEHM ih tee,* in California's Yosemite National Park, is one of the world's highest waterfalls. It is formed by Yosemite Creek as it plunges 2,425 feet (739 meters) down a rock wall. Yosemite Falls has three parts: Upper Falls, 1,430 feet (436 meters) high; the intermediate cascade, 675 feet (206 meters); and Lower Falls, 320 feet (98 meters). See also **Waterfall** (table; picture).   Tom L. McKnight

Yosemite National Park, *yoh SEHM ih tee,* is a great wilderness in east-central California. It is in the Sierra Nevada, about 200 miles (320 kilometers) east of San Francisco (see **California** [political map]). It has about 700 miles (1,100 kilometers) of trails. Most of the trails lead to the "High Sierra," a region of sparkling lakes, rushing streams, and jagged mountain peaks. The park's Yosemite Museum has a collection of Indian displays and exhibits of the area's wildlife. For the area of the park, see **National Park System** (table: National parks).

More than 60 kinds of animals and more than 200 species of birds live in the forests and mountains. Bears and deer are numerous. Yosemite has more than 30 kinds of trees and more than 1,300 varieties of plants. There are three groves of the famous *Sequoiadendron giganteum* or *Big Trees.* The best known is the Mariposa Grove, 35 miles (56 kilometers) south of Yosemite Valley. It includes the Grizzly Giant Tree, whose base measures more than 34 feet (10 meters) in diameter.

In 1864, Congress gave Yosemite Valley to California for use as a public park and recreation area. John Muir, a naturalist, first saw the area in the 1860's. His reports of the beauties of the region aroused interest. Congress created Yosemite National Park in 1890. But it did not include Yosemite Valley and the Mariposa Grove. California ceded these areas back to the federal government, and they were added to the park in 1906. The park has

Gene Ahrens, Bruce Coleman Ltd.

Upper and Lower Yosemite Falls are a scenic attraction in Yosemite National Park. They rank among the 10 highest waterfalls in North America. The two falls and the cascade that connects them have a combined height of 2,425 feet (739 meters).

many tourist accommodations. Skiing is popular in the High Sierra. Other activities include horseback riding, fishing, golf, tennis, hiking, and swimming.

Yosemite Valley. Much of the park's most spectacular scenery is in the Yosemite Valley. The valley lies at a 4,000-foot (1,200-meter) elevation in the heart of the park. A group of explorers on their way to the Pacific Coast in the 1830's were probably the first white people to see the valley. But white people did not enter it until 1851. In that year, the Mariposa Battalion, a volunteer fighting force, set out to capture a group of Yosemite Indians. Tenaya, the Yosemite chief, had been leading raids on white settlers in the foothills of the Sierra Nevada. He was captured but eventually was allowed to return to the valley, which was named for his tribe.

Millions of years ago, California's Sierra Nevada was formed by a gradual series of earth upheavals. As the mountains rose, the westward-flowing Merced River accelerated to torrential speed and carved the narrow, V-shaped Merced Canyon. Later, massive glaciers flowed down the canyon. The glaciers ground and polished the canyon to a smooth U-shaped valley, nearly 1 mile (1.6 kilometers) wide and almost 1 mile deep in places. Tributary streams did not carve their canyons as deep as Merced Canyon. Glaciers sheared off these canyons, leaving them as "hanging valleys." Today, the world's greatest concentration of free, leaping waterfalls pours from these valleys.

Waterfalls. Bridalveil Fall is the first waterfall seen by most Yosemite visitors. It graces the southern wall of the valley with a 620-foot (189-meter) descent. The Illilouette Falls also tumbles over the side of the valley. Yosemite Falls is formed by Yosemite Creek, leaping free from its hanging valley 2,425 feet (739 meters) above the valley floor. The Upper Falls is 1,430 feet (436 meters) high, and

the Lower Falls measures 320 feet (98 meters) high. The cascades between the two tumble another 675 feet (206 meters). The total height is about $\frac{1}{2}$ mile (0.8 kilometer).

Vernal and Nevada falls pour over giant steps formed by glaciers. Vernal Falls, 317 feet (97 meters) high, is famous for the rainbows that sparkle in the heavy mist at its base. About 1 mile (1.6 kilometers) upstream is 594-foot (181-meter) Nevada Falls. Indians named it *squirming fall* because a curving rock causes the water to twist as it descends. Some of the park's falls burst forth during the high-water season in spring. These include the slender 1,612-foot (491-meter) Ribbon Falls; the erratic Sentinel Falls, which drops 2,000 feet (610 meters); and the 1,170-foot (357-meter) Silver Strand Falls.

Rock masses. A number of rock masses rise sharply from the valley floor. The Half Dome rises about 8,800 feet (2,700 meters) at the head of the valley. El Capitan, which is a gigantic mass of unbroken granite, rises vertically about 3,600 feet (1,100 meters) above the canyon. From Glacier Point, one can look down more than 3,000 feet (910 meters) into the valley. Cloud's Rest, the highest point in Yosemite Valley, stands about 9,900 feet (3,000 meters) above the valley floor.

Hetch Hetchy Valley lies in the northwestern part of the park. It was carved by the Tuolumne River and ancient glaciers in much the same manner as Yosemite Valley. A reservoir covers the valley floor. The Grand Canyon of the Tuolumne River is above Hetch Hetchy, to the east. The river rushes through the canyon, dropping 4,000 feet (1,200 meters) in 4 miles (6 kilometers). It creates many cascades and waterfalls, including the Waterwheel Falls, a series of pinwheels of water. Some pinwheels rise as high as 40 feet (12 meters). Pinwheels are formed when the river, cascading down a steep granite apron, strikes rocky obstructions.

The Tuolumne River flows through Tuolumne Meadows, a vast grassland. The meadows have an elevation of about 8,500 feet (2,590 meters). Tourists camp there, and the area is also used as a base camp by mountain climbers. Tenaya Lake, near the meadows on Tioga Road, is the largest of the more than 300 lakes in Yosemite.

Transportation. Yosemite is a year-round park. Most roads remain open in the winter. But snows close roads in the High Sierra region from about midautumn until late spring. In August 1990, fires destroyed part of the park. Roads were blocked, and the park was closed for 10 days. Critically reviewed by the National Park Service

Related articles in *World Book* include:
Bridalveil Fall   Muir, John   Yosemite Falls
California (picture)   Ribbon Falls

Young, Andrew Jackson, Jr. (1932-   ), was the first African American to serve as United States ambassador to the United Nations (UN). He held the post from 1977 to 1979. Young became known for his outspoken comments on world affairs. He strongly supported black majority rule in Africa. Young served as mayor of Atlanta, Georgia, from 1981 to 1989.

Young was born in New Orleans. He graduated from Howard University and from the Hartford Theological Seminary. In 1955, Young was ordained a minister in what is now the United Church of Christ. He served as pastor of several churches in Alabama and Georgia.

In 1960, Young joined the Southern Christian Leadership Conference (SCLC), a civil rights organization led by

Martin Luther King, Jr. Young became one of King's chief aides and served as executive director of the SCLC from 1964 to 1970. He was jailed in Selma, Alabama, and St. Augustine, Florida, for taking part in civil rights demonstrations.

Young, a Democrat from Georgia, won election to the U.S. House of Representatives in 1972. He was the first black elected to Congress from the South since 1901. He held the seat until President Jimmy Carter appointed him to the UN. In 1978, Young received the Spingarn Medal for his work in domestic and international affairs. In 1990, he ran unsuccessfully as a candidate for governor of Georgia. In 2000 and 2001, Young served as head of the National Council of Churches. Nancy Dickerson Whitehead

© Frank Capri, SAGA/Archive Photos
Andrew Young, Jr.

Young, Brigham (1801-1877), led the Mormons from Illinois to what is now Utah, and established their church there. Young was the second president of the Mormon church, which is officially called the Church of Jesus Christ of Latter-day Saints. He became the Mormon leader in 1844, after Joseph Smith, the church founder, was shot to death. Young was a tireless worker. A strong will, engaging personality, and deep convictions made him an outstanding leader.

Early life. Young was born on June 1, 1801, in Whitingham, Vermont. His father, a farmer, had fought under George Washington during the Revolutionary War. In 1804, Young's father took the family to western New York. Young spent most of his early years on his father's farm. He attended school only about 12 days. As a young man, he worked as a painter, glazier, and carpenter. In 1829, Young settled in Monroe County, New York, near Joseph Smith's home. He studied Smith's religious teachings and was baptized into the church in 1832. In 1833, he joined the Mormon settlement at Kirtland, Ohio.

Mormon leader. The Kirtland community broke up, and non-Mormons (called "gentiles" by the Mormons) drove them from Independence, Missouri, in the 1830's. Young, Smith, and other church members then settled in Far West, Missouri. Anti-Mormonism also developed there, and non-Mormons imprisoned Smith and other leaders on what Mormons believe were false charges in 1838. But Young led between 5,000 and 8,000 Mormons to safety in Illinois.

Young was one of the church's most successful missionaries. From 1839 to 1841, as a missionary in the United Kingdom he converted many people to his faith and arranged for them to come to the United States. Young was preaching in New England in 1844 when Joseph

Brigham Young

Smith was shot by a mob at Carthage, Illinois. Young hurried back to Illinois. Young made a powerful speech that rallied members of the church. He was the undisputed leader of the Mormons from then until his death.

Settles in Utah. Non-Mormons forced the Mormons to leave Illinois in 1846. Starting in midwinter, Young led his followers on a long journey across the Mississippi River and through Iowa to the region near present-day Omaha, Nebraska. But Young decided that there could be no lasting peace for his people until they were completely separated from the gentiles. So, in 1847, Young led an advance party of 148 Mormon settlers west to a previously planned refuge in the Great Basin. When the group arrived in the Great Salt Lake valley in what is now Utah, Young said, "This is the right place. Drive on." He supervised the migration of thousands of other Mormons to the valley. Young was formally elected president of the Mormon church in 1847.

The Mormons prospered in Utah. Under Young's leadership, they developed irrigation techniques, and parts of the barren desert blossomed into rich and fruitful land. The U.S. government established the Territory of Utah in 1850 and made Young its first governor. Young still found time to direct missionary work and set up hundreds of Mormon settlements in the West.

But the move to Utah did not end the Mormons' troubles. Gentiles came to the territory, and some who opposed them held political posts under the United States government. False reports circulated that the church was in rebellion against the government. These reports alarmed the federal government. In 1857, President James Buchanan replaced Young with a gentile governor and sent troops to Utah. The Mormons prepared to defend themselves, and the Utah War (also called the Mormon War) followed. But, no battles were fought between the Mormons and the federal troops. Though the Mormons raided some troop wagon trains as a delaying action, they then temporarily abandoned Salt Lake City to the army. The troops established a camp near the western mountains. Young and the federal troops discussed peace terms in the winter of 1857 and 1858. The hostilities ended in 1858 when Young accepted the new governor and President Buchanan fully pardoned all concerned. Though Young stepped down as governor, he remained Utah's most powerful man until his death.

Young's place in history. Critics have accused Young of intolerance to opposition. Many people opposed his practice of polygamy. Young took a number of wives, 16 of whom bore him children. But Young's leadership and pioneering efforts rank him as one of the most important colonizers of the American West. Mormon history records that Young brought 100,000 people to the mountain valleys, founded more than 200 cities, towns, and villages, and established many schools and factories. A statue of Young represents Utah in Statuary Hall in the U.S. Capitol in Washington, D.C.

Critically reviewed by the Church of Jesus Christ of Latter-day Saints

See also **Community of Christ; Mormons; Smith, Joseph; Utah.**

Additional resources

Arrington, Leonard J. *Brigham Young.* 1985. Reprint. Univ. of Ill. Pr., 1986.
Simon, Charnan. *Brigham Young.* Children's Pr., 1998. Younger readers.

Young, Coleman Alexander (1918-1997), won election as the first African American mayor of Detroit in 1973. Young, a Democrat, defeated Detroit police commissioner John F. Nichols. At the time, blacks made up about half of the city's population. Young won support from more than 90 percent of the black voters and about 10 percent of the white voters. He took office in 1974 and was reelected four times, serving as Detroit's mayor until 1993.

Young was born on May 24, 1918, in Tuscaloosa, Alabama. In the early 1920's, his family moved to Detroit, where he graduated from high school. During World War II (1939-1945), Young served in the Army Air Corps.

During the late 1940's and early 1950's, Young organized labor unions in Detroit and worked to protect the civil rights of black workers. He later became active in the Democratic Party and, in 1960, won election as a delegate to the Michigan Constitutional Convention. From 1964 to 1973, he served in the Michigan Senate. Young became the first black member of the Democratic National Committee in 1968.   Alton Hornsby, Jr.

Young, Cy (1867-1955), was one of the greatest right-handed pitchers in the history of baseball. Young won a record 511 major league games from 1890 through 1911. He also holds the record for the most innings pitched (7,356), the most complete games (753), and the most losses (313). Young pitched for the Cleveland Spiders, St. Louis Nationals, Boston Red Sox, Cleveland Indians, and Boston Braves.

Young was born on March 29, 1867, in Gilmore, Ohio. His full name was Denton True Young. He received the nickname "Cy" after a catcher said he was "as fast as a cyclone." He was elected to the National Baseball Hall of Fame in 1937. At the end of each season, the Cy Young Award is given to the outstanding pitcher in the National League and the American League.   Dave Nightingale

Young, Edward (1683-1765), was a poet of the Augustan age in English literature. His later verse was part of a trend away from the witty, imitative poetry of that time to the more passionate, imaginative poetry of the Romantic period.

Two works established Young's reputation. *The Complaint: or Night Thoughts on Life, Death, and Immortality* (1742-1745) is a series of nine meditative blank verse poems defending Christianity against freethinkers. This work became popular throughout Europe. *Conjectures on Original Composition* (1759) is a critical essay claiming that originality in literature is superior to the imitation of ancient writers.

Young was born in Upham, near Winchester, the son of a *rector* (clergyman in charge of a parish). In 1730, he became rector at Welwin in Hertfordshire. Young held this position until his death.   Gary A. Stringer

Young, John Watts (1930-   ), is a United States astronaut. He made six space flights from Earth and one liftoff from the surface of the moon. On March 23, 1965, Young and Virgil I. Grissom made the first flight in the Gemini program. They circled Earth three times and became the first space pilots to change their orbit.

Young and Michael Collins flew the Gemini 10 space mission from July 18 to 21, 1966. They performed two *rendezvous* (meetings) with unoccupied spacecraft.

Young, Eugene A. Cernan, and Thomas P. Stafford went into orbit around the moon during the Apollo 10

space flight of May 18 to 26, 1969. Young remained in orbit in the command module while Cernan and Stafford flew to within 10 miles (16 kilometers) of the moon in the lunar module. This mission was the final preparation for the first moon landing two months later.

From April 16 to 27, 1972, Young commanded the Apollo 16 flight to the moon. He and Charles M. Duke, Jr., explored in the Descartes region of the moon's central highlands.

Young commanded the first space shuttle flight from April 12 to 14, 1981. He and Robert L. Crippen orbited Earth more than 36 times in the shuttle Columbia and then piloted the vehicle to a landing. He also commanded the ninth space shuttle flight from Nov. 28 to Dec. 8, 1983. During this flight, the astronauts aboard Columbia conducted scientific experiments in Spacelab, a European-built space laboratory.

Young was born on Sept. 24, 1930, in San Francisco. He graduated from the Georgia Institute of Technology in 1952. He joined the Navy that year and became a test pilot. He became an astronaut in 1962.   Lillian D. Kozloski

See also **Astronaut.**

Young, Lester Willis (1909-1959), a tenor saxophonist, developed one of the most imitated styles in jazz history. More than any other jazz instrumentalist, Young was responsible for the transition from the "hot jazz" style in the 1930's to the more relaxed, behind-the-beat approach usually known as "cool." He did his best work while playing with the Count Basie band from 1936 to 1940. His solos on "Oh, Lady Be Good" (1936) and "Lester Leaps In" (1939) as well as his background playing for singer Billie Holiday were especially influential.

Young was born on Aug. 27, 1909, in Woodville, Mississippi. He was nicknamed "Prez." He played with King Oliver, Walter Page, and Fletcher Henderson before joining Basie. In the 1940's and 1950's, Young often played on "Jazz at the Philharmonic" concert tours. The last years of his life were tragic. He became mentally ill and was often hospitalized.   Frank Tirro

Young, Whitney Moore, Jr. (1921-1971), was an American civil rights leader. He served as the executive director of the National Urban League from 1961 until his death. Young helped thousands of African Americans obtain jobs. He started on-the-job training programs, and established Head Start and tutoring centers.

Young was born on July 31, 1921, in Lincoln Ridge, Kentucky. He graduated from Kentucky State College (now Kentucky State University) and earned a master's degree at the University of Minnesota. From 1947 to 1953, he worked for the Urban League in St. Paul and Omaha. Young was dean of the Atlanta University School of Social Work from 1954 to 1960. He taught at the University of Nebraska School of Social Work and served on federal commissions concerned with social welfare or race relations. Young wrote several books, including *To Be Equal* (1964).   C. Eric Lincoln

Young Men's Christian Association (YMCA) is one of the largest nonprofit voluntary organizations in the world. It serves about 30 million members in more than 120 countries. The World Alliance of YMCA's, an international YMCA organization, has headquarters in Geneva, Switzerland.

In the United States, about 17 million people participate annually at over 2,400 local YMCA branches, units, camps, and centers. Membership and services are open to people of all ages, religions, races, and incomes. Women and girls make up about 45 percent of those involved in the YMCA. About half of those served are under the age of 18.

All YMCA branches share the same basic goals. These goals are: (1) promoting healthy lifestyles, (2) strengthening the modern family, (3) developing leadership qualities in youth, (4) increasing international understanding, and (5) assisting in community development.

The association promotes its values through a variety of programs, such as health and fitness programs, child care, senior citizens' activities, and international education and exchange. Some YMCA's have residential and hotel facilities. YMCA's also offer employment, adventure, and leadership programs for teen-agers. The YMCA sponsors programs to fight juvenile delinquency. Other activities include refugee resettlement programs and educational programs for the disabled.

Volunteer board members from the local community control each individual YMCA. The national headquarters, called the YMCA of the USA, works closely with local YMCA's to discover successful program ideas at the local level and spread these ideas nationally. The YMCA of the USA has national offices in Chicago. It publishes a bimonthly magazine, *Discovery YMCA.*

In Canada, more than 60 YMCA's provide programs for communities throughout the country. More than a million persons, almost half of whom are women and girls, take part in these programs. Most Canadian YMCA's provide programs in six areas: (1) adult education, (2) camping and outdoor education, (3) community and youth services, (4) guidance and counseling, (5) health and physical education, and (6) institutional services, such as residences and cafeterias.

Each YMCA is managed by its own board of directors or governors. In 1912, the existing YMCA's established the National Council of YMCA's of Canada in order to help individual YMCA's achieve their goals through collective action. The council's main office is in Toronto.

History. The YMCA was founded in London in 1844 by a young British clerk named George Williams. Williams wanted to provide young clothing store clerks from the countryside with a place in London where they could read the Bible, relax, and find out about decent lodging. The YMCA movement traveled overseas to the United States and Canada in 1851. In that year, Thomas Sullivan, a missionary and retired sea captain, founded a YMCA in Boston. A group of young men formed a YMCA in Montreal at the same time.

Exercise and gymnastics became part of the American YMCA during the second half of the 1850's. The first YMCA swimming pool opened in the Brooklyn area of New York City in 1856. In 1891, a physical education instructor named James Naismith invented the game of basketball at the School for Christian Workers (now Springfield College) in Springfield, Massachusetts. The school was associated with the YMCA. The original teams consisted of nine players and used peach baskets as goals. In 1895, another physical education instructor, W. G. Morgan, invented volleyball at the Mount Holyoke, Massachusetts, YMCA because he believed that basketball was too strenuous for businessmen.

The San Francisco YMCA admitted the association's first women members in 1874. The YMCA introduced the ideas of night school and junior college. It also assisted with the formation of other major voluntary groups, such as Boy Scouts, Camp Fire USA, and the United Service Organizations (USO).

Critically reviewed by the YMCA of the USA

See also **HI-Y club; YMCA Adventure Guides.**

Young Women's Christian Association (YWCA) is one of the world's oldest and largest multiracial women's organizations. The YWCA is open to women and girls of all faiths and backgrounds. The organization tries to meet its members' needs with a program that combines services and social action. It works to eliminate racism and to increase the power of women, minority groups, and young people. The YWCA provides services and training that help women become equal partners with men in the continual development of their nations.

The YWCA has more than 25 million members and participants in more than 100 countries, including the United States and Canada. This total includes men and boys, who may become YWCA associates. The organization has thousands of national and local staff members and volunteer workers. The YWCA cooperates with, but is not related to, the Young Men's Christian Association (YMCA).

Programs. The YWCA conducts programs in thousands of locations throughout the United States—in cities, towns, and rural communities; and on college campuses. Local YWCA's offer a wide range of activities and services. They feature child-care centers, classes on various subjects, discussion programs, food services, and health education. They also provide counseling, job placement services, leadership training programs, recreational activities, and residential facilities.

The YWCA of the United States sponsors programs to fight crime and delinquency. Many local YWCA's have a Y-Teen program for teen-age members (see **Y-Teens**).

In Canada, YWCA's provide services in nine provinces and in the Northwest Territories. Canadian YWCA's offer programs and services that are similar to those offered by YWCA's in the United States.

History. In 1855, a group of women in London led by Emma Robarts organized a young women's association. The purpose of the association was to find housing for nurses who had returned from the Crimean War (1853-1856). At about the same time, another women's group in London organized prayer circles. The two groups united in 1877 as the Young Women's Christian Association.

In the United States, The Ladies' Christian Association, an organization similar to the London groups, was founded in New York City in 1858. The first Young Women's Christian Association was organized in Boston in 1866. The movement grew rapidly, especially in industrial cities, where the YWCA provided housing for single working women. Later, the YWCA became active at colleges. The first student YWCA in the United States was founded in 1873 at Illinois State Normal University (now Illinois State University) in Normal, Illinois. Separate organizations arose in the Midwest and in the East. In 1906, these organizations united as the Young Women's Christian Associations of the United States of America. The YWCA of the United States has headquarters in New York City.

The first YWCA in Canada was established in Saint John, New Brunswick, in 1870. The organization's purpose was to help meet the needs of young working women. In 1893, local YWCA's established the national organization, the YWCA of Canada. The main office of the YWCA of Canada is in Toronto.

The YWCA's of both Canada and the United States are members of the World YWCA. The association has headquarters in Geneva, Switzerland.

Critically reviewed by the Young Women's Christian Association

Youngstown (pop. 82,026) is an industrial city in northeastern Ohio (see **Ohio** [political map]). With Warren, it forms a metropolitan area with 594,746 people. Youngstown has many parks and recreation areas. Mill Creek Park covers more than 2,300 acres (931 hectares) and is one of the nation's most beautiful natural parks. Youngstown institutions include the Youngstown Public Library and its branches, Youngstown State University, Butler Institute of American Art, Stambaugh Auditorium, Youngstown Symphony Center, and the Youngstown Playhouse.

Youngstown has foundries, machine shops, metal fabricators, and mill equipment suppliers. Its factories produce aluminum products, automotive parts, light bulbs, electronic equipment, office equipment, paints, paper products, plastics, rubber goods, and textile products.

Youngstown was settled in 1797 and named in honor of John Young of New York, who bought the site of the future city from the Connecticut Land Company. The town was incorporated in 1848. For many years, it was a leading steel-producing city in the United States. Its first steel mill was built in 1891. By the 1930's, it ranked third in steel production among U.S. cities. In the late 1970's, a number of economic factors made the production of steel in the Youngstown mills unprofitable. As a result, all the city's steel mills closed between 1977 and 1981. Youngstown is the seat of Mahoning County and has a mayor-council form of government.   Richard J. Hopkins

Youth. See Adolescent.

Youth for Christ International is a nonprofit organization specializing in teen-age evangelism. Founded in 1944, it has local groups in the United States, Canada, and about 100 other countries. Its local interdenominational groups sponsor youth rallies, high school clubs, and camps designed to supplement the work of local churches. The organization's world office is in Singapore. The U.S. headquarters are in Denver, Colorado.

Critically reviewed by Youth for Christ International

Youth hostel, *HAHS tuhl,* is an inexpensive overnight accommodation for travelers who belong to hosteling associations. The major hosteling association, the International Youth Hostel Federation (IYHF), coordinates a system of more than 4,000 hostels in over 60 countries. The IYHF often uses the name Hostelling International. The IYHF's *affiliate* (branch organization) in the United States is Hostelling International-USA. Its Canadian affiliate is Hostelling International-Canada. The Youth Hostels Association (England and Wales) and the Scottish Youth Hostels Association coordinate systems of hostels throughout the United Kingdom. Both youths and adults can belong to hosteling associations.

Generally, each hostel has dormitory-style sleeping quarters, a common kitchen, and a lounge for socializing and relaxing. Large hostels in major cities offer addi-

tional facilities. On-site managers supervise each hostel, but visitors prepare their own meals and maintain their quarters themselves. Many hostels are close enough together that members can walk or cycle from one to the next. Many hostels occupy historic buildings.

Richard Schirrmann, a German schoolteacher, developed the youth hostel idea. He founded the first hostel in Altena, Germany, near Lüdenscheid, around 1910. His plan became popular and quickly spread to most European countries.

The first youth hostel in North America was established by two Canadian teachers, Mary and Catherine Barclay, in 1933. It was a tent at Bragg Creek, Alberta, Canada. Two American Scout leaders, Isabel and Monroe Smith, introduced the first hostel in the United States, at Northfield, Massachusetts, in 1934.

Critically reviewed by Hostelling International-USA

Youville, *YOO vihl,* **Saint Marguerite d'** (1701-1771), was the first native-born Canadian to be honored as a saint by the Roman Catholic Church. She was *canonized* (declared a saint) in 1990. Marguerite founded the Grey Nuns, a religious order, to care for the poor. The nuns also nursed the elderly, orphans, and smallpox victims, as well as soldiers wounded in the Seven Years' War, also called the French and Indian War (1754-1763).

D'Youville was born in Varennes, near Montreal, on Oct. 15, 1701. Her given and family name was Marie-Marguerite Dufrost de Lajemmerais. In 1722, she married François d'Youville. He died in 1730. In 1737, she and three companions began to house and care for ill and needy women. Their work was scorned and they were falsely accused of intoxication, resulting in the nickname "tipsy nuns." In 1747, she was named director of the General Hospital in Montreal. She received permission from King Louis XV of France to found the Grey Nuns in 1753. The name referred to the color of their clothing. Her feast day is October 16.   Marilyn J. Harran

Ypres, *EE pruh* (pop. 35,434), is a Belgian city in West Flanders, in the Dutch-speaking part of the country. For location, see **Belgium** (political map). The city's Dutch name is Ieper (pronounced *EE puhr).* Linen and lace are made in Ypres from the flax of Flanders.

Ypres became famous as a center of the textile industry about 1300. At that time, its population was about 20,000, almost as great as London's. In World War I, Ypres was the scene of severe fighting, and it was almost destroyed. It was rebuilt, but again became a battleground during World War II.   Aristide R. Zolberg

Ytterbium, *ih TUR bee uhm,* is a soft silvery metal. Small amounts of ytterbium are used in metallurgical and chemical experiments. In 1878, the Swiss chemist Jean de Marignac gave the name *ytterbium* to a substance that he found in a mineral called *yttria.* In 1907, the French chemist Georges Urbain separated de Marignac's substance into two chemical elements, *lutetium* and *ytterbium.* Several minerals, such as monazite, gadolinite, and xenotime, contain ytterbium.

Ytterbium is a rare-earth element. The chemical symbol for ytterbium is Yb. Its *atomic number* (number of protons in its nucleus) is 70. Ytterbium's *relative atomic mass* is 173.04. The relative atomic mass of an element equals its *mass* (amount of matter) divided by $\frac{1}{12}$ of the mass of carbon 12, the most abundant form of carbon. Ytterbium melts at 819 °C and boils at 1196 °C. It has a density of 6.973 grams per cubic centimeter at 25 °C (see **Density**).   Larry C. Thompson

See also **Lutetium; Rare earth.**

Yttrium, *IHT ree uhm,* is a silvery-white metallic element. It has a number of important uses, particularly in the electronics industry. For example, the compound yttrium oxide forms the basis of the phosphors used in color televisions to reproduce red. This compound is also used to produce two kinds of crystals called *garnets.* One type of garnet acts as a microwave filter in radar, and the other serves as an imitation diamond. Yttrium is also used in lasers and in the manufacture of certain chemicals, glass, and ceramics.

Yttrium resembles the rare-earth elements and it occurs in nearly all rare-earth minerals (see **Rare earth**). The metal is obtained commercially from monazite sand.

Yttrium has the chemical symbol Y. Its atomic number is 39, and its atomic weight is 88.90585. The metal melts at 1522 °C (±8 °C) and boils at 3338 °C. The Swedish chemist Carl Gustav Mosander discovered yttrium in 1843 in the mineral *yttria.*   R. Craig Taylor

Yuan, *yoo AHN,* is the monetary unit of China. In Taiwan, people refer to the New Taiwan dollar as a yuan. China uses the yuan as its basic unit of currency. It is divided into 10 *chiao,* each worth 10 *fen.* In 1914, China established the yuan as a silver coin with 23.4934 grams of pure silver. The yuan now circulates as paper money. The official name of the Chinese currency is the *renminbi.*   R. G. Doty

Yuan dynasty. See China (Mongol rule; map).

Yucatán Peninsula, *yoo kuh TAN* or *yoo kuh TAHN,* includes the southeastern Mexican states of Campeche, Quintana Roo, and Yucatán; Belize; and part of El Petén, a department of Guatemala. The peninsula separates the Gulf of Mexico from the Caribbean Sea. It covers over 75,000 square miles (194,000 square kilometers).

The peninsula is a low, rolling tableland of coral and limestone covered by a thin layer of soil. It has a hot, humid climate. Tropical rain forests cover the lowlands. Quintana Roo and Belize lie along the eastern coast of the peninsula. The state of Yucatán is in the peninsula's northern part. The state of Campeche lies south and west of Yucatán. Part of El Petén in Guatemala is inland in the peninsula's southern part. The chief cities include Mérida, capital of Yucatán; Campeche, capital of Campeche; and Progreso, Yucatán, the peninsula's chief port. Cancún, in Quintano Roo, is a popular resort area.

WORLD BOOK maps

The Yucatán Peninsula divides the Gulf of Mexico and the Caribbean Sea. It lies in southeastern Mexico, northern Guatemala, and Belize.

Most of the people, called *Yucatecos,* are descendants of the Maya Indians who lived in Yucatán hundreds of years before the Spaniards arrived. Ancient ruins of the Maya civilization have been found in Yucatán (see **Maya**). Most Yucatecos are farmers. Northern Yucatán is one of the chief henequen-raising areas of the world. Henequen is used in making twine. Other crops of the Yucatán Peninsula include cacao, coffee, corn, cotton, sugar cane, and tobacco.

Francisco Fernández de Córdoba, a Spaniard, came to the peninsula in 1517. By 1542, Francisco de Montejo the Younger had set up Spanish rule over half of Yucatán and established the cities of Campeche and Mérida. Some of the Indians became slave laborers on henequen plantations. In the 1800's and 1900's, the Indians revolted many times against the Mexican government. Salvador Alvarado and Felipe Carillo, who served as governors of Yucatán in the early 1900's, introduced many reforms. See also **Belize; Chichén Itzá.**   Roderic A. Camp

Yucca, *YUHK uh,* is the name of a group of shrubs or trees of the agave family. The yucca plant has a striking appearance. It is an evergreen plant and does not shed its leaves each year.

Some yucca plants have short stems and others have tall woody and scaly trunks. The leaves of the yucca plants are usually pointed, stiff, and narrow, with sawlike or fibrous edges. They grow along the stem or in clusters at the end of a stem. The yucca plant has flowers shaped somewhat like bells. Certain varieties of the yucca have whitish-green flowers, while others have white or cream-colored flowers. These flowers grow in a cluster on a stem which springs up from the center of a cluster of leaves. Some of these flowers give off a strong fragrance when they open at night. The yucca has large fruits that may be either fleshy or dry. They contain many small, flat, black seeds. The yucca is pollinated by the female yucca moth, which carries pollen from one yucca to another. See **Flower** (Cross-pollination).

Yuccas grow most abundantly in the southern and southwestern parts of the United States. They also grow in the desert highlands and plateaus of Mexico. Most of the species are low shrubs. But in deserts of the southwestern United States, and in Mexico, there are several species that become large, picturesque trees. Joshua Tree National Park in California contains important collections of yucca trees. The popular northern species of yucca is called *Adam's needle.*

The Indians found many uses for yucca plants. They made rope, sandals, mats, and baskets from the leaf fibers. They ate the buds and flowers raw or boiled. The Indians dried the fleshy fruits and ate them during the winter. They also made a fermented drink from the fruits. The roots and stems of the yucca make a soap. Some kinds of yucca are known as *soapweed.* Yuccas serve as decorative plants in gardens and are often grown as border plants.   Philip W. Rundel

Scientific classification. Yuccas belong to the agave family, Agavaceae. The scientific name for the Joshua tree is *Yucca brevifolia.* Another common species, *Y. baccata,* is found in the dry areas of the United States and Mexico. The soapweed, *Y. glauca,* is found from New Mexico to the Dakotas. The Adam's needle yucca is *Y. filamentosa.*

See also **Flower** (picture: Interesting facts about flowers); **Spanish bayonet.**

Yugoslavia was a country in the Balkan peninsula of Europe from 1918 to 2003. The country brought together the various ethnic groups of the region under one government. After World War II (1939-1945), Yugoslavia became a Communist country.

In the early 1990's, fighting between ethnic groups and the collapse of Communism split Yugoslavia into several smaller countries. Bosnia-Herzegovina, Croatia, Macedonia, and Slovenia each declared independence. The two remaining parts, Montenegro and Serbia, formed a new Yugoslavia. In 2003, the country revised its constitution and changed its name to Serbia and Montenegro. See **Serbia and Montenegro.**

Land of the South Slavs. Groups of Slavs began to move into the Balkans in the A.D. 500's. They migrated from what are now southern Poland and Russia and became known as *South Slavs.* Each Slavic group formed its own independent state. For example, the Croats established Croatia, and the Serbs founded Serbia.

By the mid-1400's, foreign powers controlled nearly all the lands of the South Slavs. In the 1800's, Austria-Hungary began ruling Croatia and Slovenia. In 1878, after the Ottoman Empire ended, Serbia gained independence and Bosnia-Herzegovina came under control of Austria-Hungary. During the 1800's and early 1900's, a movement to unite the South Slavs gained strength.

On June 28, 1914, Gavrilo Princip, a Serb from Bosnia-Herzegovina, assassinated Archduke Franz Ferdinand of Austria-Hungary in Sarajevo, Bosnia-Herzegovina's capital. Austria-Hungary accused Serbia of planning the killing and declared war on it, which marked the start of World War I. Austria-Hungary was defeated in 1918. The South Slavs were then free to form their own state.

A new nation called the Kingdom of the Serbs, Croats, and Slovenes formed in 1918. It consisted of Bosnia-Herzegovina, Croatia, Dalmatia, Montenegro, Serbia, and Slovenia. King Peter I of Serbia became king. Peter died in 1921, and his son became King Alexander I.

Problems soon developed. The Slovenes and Croats believed the Serbs had too much power. They demanded greater control over their local affairs. It also proved difficult to unite the kingdom's many ethnic groups.

The nation's 1921 Constitution created a constitutional monarchy. But in 1929, King Alexander abolished the Constitution and began to rule as a dictator. He named the country Yugoslavia and tried to unite the different nationalities by enforcing the use of one language, Serbo-Croatian. He created new political divisions that ignored the ethnic groups' historical borders. Alexander's actions worsened relations between the groups. He was assassinated in 1934 by a Macedonian from Bulgaria who was supported by Croatian revolutionaries.

Alexander's 11-year-old son, King Peter II, was too young to rule. Alexander's cousin, Prince Paul, ruled in the boy's place. Under Paul, an agreement was made to establish an *autonomous* (self-governing) Croatia, but not all Serbs accepted the arrangement.

World War II began in 1939 as a struggle between the Axis powers, led by Germany and Italy, and the Allies, which included the United Kingdom and France. Yugoslavia was unprepared for war, so its government tried to remain neutral. Under pressure from Germany, the Yugoslav government joined the Axis on March 25, 1941. But the Yugoslav army rebelled. The army over-

threw Paul's government, and 17-year-old Peter took the throne. On April 6, Germany invaded Yugoslavia. The Yugoslav army surrendered 11 days later. Peter fled to London and formed a government-in-exile.

German and other Axis troops occupied Yugoslavia. Croatia was proclaimed an independent state, but it was controlled by the Axis. Croatia's leader, Ante Pavelic, ordered the killing of many Jews, Roma (sometimes called Gypsies), and Serbs. A resistance movement against Axis occupation spread among the Yugoslav peoples. Some joined the *Partisans,* a group led by Josip Broz Tito and the Communist Party. Others joined the *Chetniks,* headed by Draža Mihajlović. The Partisans wanted to form a Communist government. The Chetniks supported the government of King Peter.

The two resistance groups fought each other, as well as the occupation forces. At first, the Allies provided the Chetniks with weapons and supplies. But they switched their support to the Partisans in 1943 because Tito's forces were more effective against the Axis.

Communist rule. The Partisans quickly gained the support of the Yugoslav peoples. The Communists set up a temporary government in Jajce (now in Bosnia-Herzegovina) in November 1943. Aided by Allied troops, the Partisans freed Belgrade from occupation in 1944. The Communists then began to govern from the capital. By the time World War II ended in Europe in May 1945, Tito and the Communists firmly controlled Yugoslavia.

On Nov. 29, 1945, Yugoslavia became a republic called the Federal People's Republic of Yugoslavia. The monarchy was abolished, and King Peter never returned to Yugoslavia. The 1946 Constitution organized Yugoslavia as a *federal* state—that is, one where each republic largely controlled its own affairs. The six republics were Bosnia-Herzegovina, Croatia, Macedonia, Montenegro, Serbia, and Slovenia. Kosovo and Vojvodina became *autonomous* (self-ruling) provinces of Serbia.

Only one political party, the Communist Party, was permitted. The government took control of farms, factories, and other businesses. The Communists began changing Yugoslavia from an agricultural country into an industrial nation. Opponents of the Communist government were either imprisoned or exiled. Mihajlović was executed in 1946. The Roman Catholic archbishop of Zagreb, Alojzije Stepinac, resisted the Communist take-over. He was imprisoned on false charges of having aided Germany and Italy during World War II.

Yugoslavia was a close Soviet ally, but Tito refused to let the Soviet Union control the country. In June 1948, Soviet dictator Joseph Stalin broke off relations with Yugoslavia. The Cominform, a group of Communist nations, expelled Yugoslavia and withdrew all aid. Yugoslavia turned to the United States and other Western nations for help. In 1951, the United States began providing Yugoslavia with economic aid. Later, the United States also granted military assistance.

After the split with the Soviet Union, Yugoslavia began to develop its own style of Communist government. In 1955, two years after Stalin's death, Soviet and Yugoslav leaders reopened relations. But Tito refused to take sides in the Cold War, a political rivalry between Communist nations and Western democracies. Instead, he became a leading speaker for uncommitted nations.

In 1971, a 23-member council called the *Presidency*

was established to head the Yugoslav government. A new constitution in 1974 reduced the Presidency to nine members. Tito remained the country's top leader as head of the council until he died in May 1980. Then, the eight members of the Presidency, one from each republic and province, took turns serving one-year terms as head of the council. Until 1989, the leader of Yugoslavia's Communist Party also held a seat on the council but did not take a turn as head of the Presidency.

Political changes and ethnic tensions. The Yugoslav economy started to decline in the late 1970's, and the country began to experience severe inflation and other economic problems. A serious economic gap grew between the country's developed republics, such as Croatia and Slovenia, and its less developed republics, such as Macedonia and Montenegro.

In the late 1980's, Communism was losing its grip on power across Eastern Europe, and many people in Yugoslavia called for a multiparty political system. In January 1990, Yugoslavia's Communist Party voted to end its monopoly on power in the country. Each of Yugoslavia's republics held multiparty elections in 1990. Non-Communist parties won a majority of seats in the parliaments of Bosnia-Herzegovina, Croatia, Macedonia, and Slovenia. In Serbia and Montenegro, the Communist parties, now known as Socialist parties, won majorities.

For years, tension had existed between Yugoslavia's ethnic groups, especially between Serbs and Croats and between Serbs and ethnic Albanians. In the 1960's, some Croats and Slovenes began to call for independence. Their demands grew in the 1980's. Croatia and Slovenia charged that Serbia, which had the most influence in the national government, sought to control the other republics. Demands for independence also increased among ethnic Albanians in Kosovo during the 1980's.

The breakup of Yugoslavia. In 1989, Slobodan Milošević, a supporter of Serbian unity and of expanding Serbian borders, became Serbia's president. Under him, Serbia stripped Kosovo and Vojvodina of autonomy and, in 1990, dissolved Kosovo's government.

In May 1991, Serbia blocked the election of a Croat scheduled to become head of the Presidency under the system of annual rotation. Partly as a result, Croatia and Slovenia declared their independence in late June. Fighting then broke out between ethnic Serbs in Croatia and the Croat militia. In September 1991, Macedonia declared its independence. In January 1992, a cease-fire between Serbian and Croatian forces ended most fighting. But Serbian forces still held some Croatian land.

In March 1992, a majority of Bosnian Muslims and ethnic Croats in Bosnia-Herzegovina voted for independence from Yugoslavia in a *referendum* (direct vote). Ethnic Serbs boycotted the referendum. Fighting then broke out between Serbs who claimed part of the republic and Muslims and Croats. Serbs soon gained control of about two-thirds of the republic.

In April 1992, Serbia and Montenegro formed a new Yugoslavia. In late 1995, the Croatian government and the leaders of the Croatian Serbs made peace. They agreed to a plan that would gradually reunite land still held by Croatian Serbs with the rest of Croatia. Also in late 1995, representatives of Bosnia, Croatia, and Serbia signed a peace plan for Bosnia. The plan called for dividing Bosnia into two parts, one to be ruled by a Muslim-Croat federation and the other by Bosnian Serbs.

Kosovo crisis. In 1997, Milošević ended his second term as Serbia's president. Yugoslavia's parliament then elected him president of Yugoslavia, though some members boycotted the vote.

In early 1998, Yugoslavia received international criticism after Serbian police attacked villages in the province of Kosovo, killing dozens of people and burning many homes. Milošević said the police attack was a crackdown on the rebel Kosovo Liberation Army, which demanded independence for the province. Fighting began between the Serbian and rebel forces. Serbian forces destroyed villages in the province and drove many of Kosovo's Albanians from their homes.

The North Atlantic Treaty Organization (NATO) sponsored peace talks in early 1999, but Serbian delegates rejected the peace plan. In March, NATO began air strikes against military targets in Yugoslavia to force the government to accept the peace plan. But Serb attacks continued, and hundreds of thousands of people fled Kosovo. In June, Serbian military commanders agreed to withdraw forces from Kosovo. NATO stopped the bombing and sent an international peacekeeping force to Kosovo. Refugees returned to Kosovo, but tensions ran high between Serbs and Albanians in the province.

The end of Yugoslavia. As opposition to Milošević's rule grew, the government seized or interfered with opposition newspapers and broadcasters, and protesters met stiff resistance from police forces. A series of assassinations and attempted assassinations targeted mainly foes of Milošević.

In a presidential election in September 2000, Vojislav Koštunica, leader of the Democratic Opposition party, won the majority of the votes. Milošević claimed that Koštunica had not won by a large enough majority and that a run-off election was necessary. The opposition claimed victory, and protesters demanding Milošević's resignation filled the streets of many of Serbia's major cities. Police forces were overwhelmed by the size of the protests, and Milošević was ousted from power.

WORLD BOOK map

Yugoslavia from 1946 to 1991 was a federal state with six republics. In 1991 and 1992, four republics (tan) declared independence. Serbia and Montenegro (yellow) formed a new Yugoslavia.

In 2002, the leaders of Montenegro, Serbia, and Yugoslavia formed plans to create a new constitution for Yugoslavia and to rename the country Serbia and Montenegro. The plans sought to address the concerns of Montenegro's independence movement, which demanded more self-rule for their republic. Early in 2003, the parliaments of each province and of Yugoslavia approved the new constitution, and Yugoslavia officially became Serbia and Montenegro.   Sabrina P. Ramet

Related articles. See **Serbia and Montenegro** and its list of *Related articles.* See also:

Alexander I	Kosovo	Serbia
Balkans	Macedonia	Slovenia
Bosnia-Herze-	Milošević,	Tito, Josip Broz
govina	Slobodan	World War I
Croatia	Montenegro	World War II

Additional resources

Lampe, John R. *Yugoslavia as History.* 2nd ed. Cambridge, 2000.
Meier, Viktor. *Yugoslavia.* Routledge, 1999.
Ramet, Sabrina P. *Balkan Babel: The Disintegration of Yugoslavia from the Death of Tito to the Fall of Milošević.* 4th ed. Westview, 2002.

Yukawa, *yoo KAH wah,* **Hideki,** *hee deh kee* (1907-1981), a Japanese theoretical physicist, won the 1949 Nobel Prize in physics, the first Japanese to be honored with a Nobel Prize. Yukawa received the award for a theory he published in 1935. His theory predicted the existence of the subatomic particles now known as *mesons* (see **Meson**). The meson was first discovered in 1947.

In the 1930's and 1940's, scientists studying the atom were puzzled by how the nucleus holds together. Yukawa's theory concluded that protons and neutrons in the nucleus attract one another by exchanging mesons.

Hideki Ogawa was born on Jan. 23, 1907, in Tokyo. He changed his name to Hideki Yukawa in 1932. He studied at Kyoto Imperial University (later renamed Kyoto University) and became a professor there in 1939. From 1948 to 1949, he was a professor at Columbia University in New York City. Yukawa served as director of the Research Institute for Fundamental Physics (now the Yukawa Institute for Fundamental Physics) at Kyoto University. He died on Sept. 8, 1981.   Richard L. Hilt

Yukon, *YOO kahn,* is a *territory* (political unit) in northwest Canada. It is part of a vast subarctic region, with long, cold winters and short, cool summers. The Yukon territory is sparsely populated due to its harsh climate and rugged terrain. Yukon has rich mineral deposits and magnificent scenery. Many prospectors hurried to the region during the Klondike Gold Rush in 1897 and 1898. Today, mining remains an important industry. Tourism and government services are also important to the economy.

Yukon is one of Canada's three territories. The other two are the Northwest Territories and Nunavut. Whitehorse is Yukon's capital and largest city.

The land and its resources

Location, size, and description. Yukon covers 186,661 square miles (483,450 square kilometers) in the shape of a rough triangle. The base rests on the border of British Columbia, and the peak on the Arctic Ocean. Alaska lies to the west of the territory, and the Northwest Territories lies to the east.

Ranges of the largest mountain system of North America almost entirely cover the Yukon territory. The

Richard Hartmier, Hot Shots

Spectacular mountains and unspoiled wilderness areas make Canada's Yukon a popular spot for tourists. Outdoors enthusiasts enjoy hiking and fishing in the territory.

Rockies form part of this system but spread out into smaller chains in the southeast, near the Liard River. The highest peaks rise in the Saint Elias Mountains in the southwest. Mount Logan (19,551 feet, or 5,959 meters), in this range, is the highest point in Canada.

The territory derives its name from the Yukon River. The word *Yukon* probably had its origin in the Gwich'in Indian word *Youcon (greatest* or *big river).* The Yukon River drains more than half of the territory. Most of the rest is drained into the Mackenzie River through the Peel and Liard river systems.

Natural resources. The territory has large deposits of asbestos, coal, copper, gold, lead, nickel, silver, and zinc. Valuable forests of white spruce cover much of the land. Other trees include birch, fir, pine, and poplar.

Varieties of numerous fur-bearing animals live in the territory of Yukon. Animals of the region include bears, caribou, Dall's sheep, elk, moose, mountain goats, and

Facts in brief

Capital: Whitehorse.
Government: *National*—members of the Senate, 1; members of the House of Commons, 1. *Territorial*—members of the Legislative Assembly, 18.
Area: 186,661 mi² (483,450 km²), including 1,730 mi² (4,481 km²) of inland water. *Greatest distances*—north-south, 666 mi (1,072 km); east-west, 600 mi (966 km). *Coastline*—213 mi (343 km).
Elevation: *Highest*—Mount Logan in the Saint Elias Mountains, 19,551 feet (5,959 meters) above sea level. *Lowest*—sea level, along the Beaufort Sea.
Population: *2001 census*—28,674; distribution, 59 percent urban, 41 percent rural; population density, 15 per 100 mi² (6 per 100 km²).
Chief products: *Fishing industry*—salmon, whitefish. *Fur industry*—beaver, lynx, marten, wolf, wolverine. *Manufacturing*—fabricated metal products, food products, printed materials. *Mining*—gold, natural gas, sand and gravel.

Yukon

National park (N.P.)

Boundary
Road
Railroad
★ Capital
• Other city or town
+ Elevation above sea level

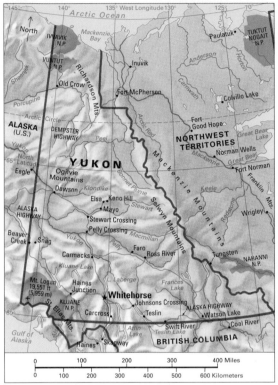

WORLD BOOK maps

wolves. Among the game birds are grouse, ptarmigan, and waterfowl. Rare gyrfalcons and peregrine falcons also live in the territory. Grayling, northern pike, lake and rainbow trout, salmon, and whitefish swim in the territory's streams and lakes.

Climate. Yukon has cold winters and cool summers. Average January temperatures are −2 °F (−19 °C) at Whitehorse and −16 °F (−27 °C) at Dawson. The coldest temperature ever recorded in the territory was −81 °F (−63 °C), at Snag Airport near the Alaska border on Feb. 3, 1947. Summer temperatures average from 50 °F (10 °C) in the north to 60 °F (16 °C) in the south. The territory's record high temperature, 97 °F (36 °C), occurred in Mayo on June 14, 1969. Annual snowfall varies from 28 inches (70 centimeters) in the north to more than 79 inches (200 centimeters) in the south. Rainfall averages from 4 to 10 inches (9 to 26 centimeters) per year.

The people

Most Yukoners have some British ancestry. More than 6,000 people are classified as American Indians. Almost all the people speak English. French is the native language of about 900 Yukoners. Tlingit and Gwich'in, two Indian languages, are spoken in some of the villages.

About two-thirds of the territory's people live in Whitehorse, the capital. Other Yukon communities include Dawson, Watson Lake, Faro, Ross River, and Haines Junction.

Most people live in modern houses. Electric heaters, oil, and wood are used to heat houses. The burning of wood has caused air pollution problems in some suburbs of Whitehorse. Daily airline and trucking services bring perishable foods and other goods to the territory.

Economy

Service industries, as a group, contribute more to Yukon's economy than any other economic activity. Important community, business, and personal services in the territory include health care, education, and the op-

© Wayne Towriss

Whitehorse is the capital and largest city of the Yukon territory. It lies on the Yukon River, near mountainous land that is rich in minerals. The city is also the distribution and communication center of Yukon.

eration of restaurants and hotels. Government services employ about a third of the work force.

Every year, about 300,000 people travel across Yukon on the Alaska Highway. The Yukon section is regarded by many to be the most scenic part of the highway. Tourists also visit the territory to see scenes of the Klondike Gold Rush. Dawson has preserved many landmarks of that era. Many visitors to Yukon have read the works of the poet Robert William Service, who wrote his first famous works in Whitehorse. Whitehorse's tourist attractions include the MacBride Museum, the Yukon Beringia Interpretive Centre, and the S.S. *Klondike,* an old Yukon paddlewheeler.

Kluane National Park lies in southwestern Yukon. Ivvavik National Park lies at the northern tip of the territory. Vuntut National Park is just south of Ivvavik. Spending by tourists contributes heavily to the service industries.

Mining. Yukon's mining industry is based largely on the production of metal ores. The value of Yukon mineral production often varies greatly from year to year because the price of metal ores is unstable. When the value of a particular metal is low, mines that produce that type of ore may close. But when metal prices rise, many of these mines reopen.

After a large zinc and lead mine at Faro was closed in the late 1990's, gold replaced zinc as Yukon's leading mineral. Other mined products in Yukon include silver, and sand and gravel. Natural gas production began to contribute significantly to the economy in the early 1990's.

Agriculture. Because of the short summer, most farmers plant only quick-growing vegetables. Several farmers have market gardens, and others grow hay. Excellent vegetables are grown in greenhouses during the long hours of sun in the spring and summer. Some farmers raise livestock, and the territory has a number of commercial egg producers.

Manufacturing. Yukon has several small manufacturing industries. Goods manufactured there have a *value added by manufacture* of about 8 million Canadian dollars a year. This figure represents the difference between the value of raw materials and the value of finished products made from them. Yukon's manufactures include printed materials, fabricated metal products, and processed foods, especially fish. Other industries include breweries and wood product manufacturers.

Fishing industry. A small amount of commercial fishing for salmon takes place in the territory. It occurs mainly on the Yukon river system.

Fur industry. Some of Yukon's people make a living as trappers. The chief animals trapped, in order of value, are martens, wolverines, lynxes, wolves, and beavers.

Electric power. About 90 percent of Yukon's electric power comes from hydroelectric sources. The rest comes mainly from generators burning fossil fuels.

Transportation and communication. Airlines connect Yukon with Alaska, Alberta, British Columbia, and the Northwest Territories. The Alaska Highway extends for about 600 miles (970 kilometers) through the territory. The 450-mile (725-kilometer) Dempster Highway links Yukon with Inuvik in the Northwest Territories.

The Canadian Broadcasting Corporation (CBC) has a radio station at Whitehorse. Automatic relays transmit its programs to the entire territory. Three other radio stations also serve Whitehorse. Live CBC television service reaches nearly all Yukon communities via satellite. Most areas also have access to telephone, high-speed Internet, and cable television services. Two newspapers publish in Whitehorse and one in Dawson.

Education and social services

Education. The territorial government operates the school system. Whitehorse schools offer a full range of public and private education programs. Thirteen rural communities have schools that provide kindergarten through grade 9 education, and some also include grades 10 through 12. Yukon College, in Whitehorse, is the only school of higher education. It has satellite campuses in 12 communities.

Social services. Resident doctors live in Dawson, Faro, Watson Lake, and Whitehorse. Resident dentists have offices in Whitehorse and visit other settlements periodically. Dawson, Mayo, Watson Lake, and Whitehorse have hospitals. Nursing stations serve other settlements.

Symbols of Yukon

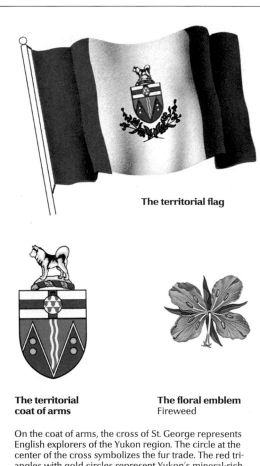

The territorial flag

The territorial
coat of arms

The floral emblem
Fireweed

On the coat of arms, the cross of St. George represents English explorers of the Yukon region. The circle at the center of the cross symbolizes the fur trade. The red triangles with gold circles represent Yukon's mineral-rich mountains. The wavy stripes represent its rivers. The malamute dog was important in Yukon history. The coat of arms was adopted in 1956, the territorial flag in 1968.

Government

The Canadian government appoints a commissioner to serve as the formal head of government for the territory of Yukon. The commissioner acts on recommendations from an Executive Council (cabinet), whose members direct government departments. A premier presides over the council and is the actual head of the territorial government. The premier belongs to the 18-member elected Yukon Legislative Assembly and is the head of the party that holds the most seats in the Assembly. The Assembly is the territory's lawmaking body. The territorial government deals with such regional matters as education, natural resources, public works, social services, and taxation. The people elect one representative to the Canadian House of Commons. The territory is also represented by one member in the Canadian Senate.

History

Indians have lived in the Yukon area since prehistoric times. In the 1840's, Robert Campbell, a British fur trader of the Hudson's Bay Company, became the first white person to explore the Yukon region. Campbell built a trading post on the Pelly River at Fort Selkirk in 1848. But Chilkat Indians looted and burned the post a short time later. The Yukon area was a part of the company's fur-trading empire until 1870, when the company began moving its operations farther east. In 1895, the Yukon region was made a district of the North West Territories.

On Aug. 17, 1896, George W. Carmack and his Indian friends Skookum Jim and Tagish Charlie made a gold strike on Bonanza Creek. This led to the Klondike Gold Rush of 1897 and 1898. The creek is a tributary of the Klondike River, near the present site of Dawson. Thousands of prospectors poured into the Yukon region when news of the discovery spread. These miners were often rough and unruly. At the beginning of the gold rush, a detachment of the North-West Mounted Police entered the region to preserve order.

At the height of the Klondike Gold Rush in 1898, an estimated 35,000 people lived in Yukon. Records show that 7,080 boats passed down the Yukon River in 1898, carrying 28,000 people. Approximately 5,000 people came to the territory by other routes.

The influx of people caused by the gold rush increased the Yukon region's political importance. In 1898, the region became a territory of Canada, and Dawson became its capital. Simple methods of hand mining produced $22,275,000 of gold in 1900. A fleet of gold dredges soon began digging gold. Dredges still dig gold from the deposits.

After much of the surface ore had been exhausted, many prospectors left the Klondike area. Whitehorse had railroad service. Because of this, it became the distributing point for the territory and grew more rapidly than Dawson. Whitehorse became the capital in 1953.

In 1979, the federal government transferred authority over a number of local matters from the commissioner to the elected council. These areas included education and taxation. During the early 1980's, the economy declined, mostly due to low metal prices. But by the end of the 1980's, the territory's economy had improved because of higher metal prices and the addition of new businesses and new jobs.

For many years, Indians in the Yukon territory have pushed for self-government and have sought title to their traditional lands. In 1995, federal laws went into effect which granted self-government to some Yukon Indians and settled their land claims.   Mary Walden

Related articles in *World Book* include:

Alaska Highway	McLaughlin,	Service, Robert W.
Klondike	Audrey M.	Whitehorse
	Mount Logan	Yukon River

Yukon River is one of the longest rivers in North America. It rises in far northwestern British Columbia, Canada. It flows across Canada's Yukon territory and Alaska in the United States. About two-thirds of the river's course is in Alaska, and about one-third is in Canada. The river's total length is 1,979 miles (3,185 kilometers). It drains over 330,000 square miles (855,000 square kilometers). About half of this area lies in Alaska.

The Yukon is navigable for almost its entire length. Before the late 1940's, wood-burning stern-wheelers traveled from its mouth to Dawson in the Yukon territory. The Yukon was the principal transportation route during the early mining days of Alaska and the famous Klondike Gold Rush in the Yukon territory. But decreased mining activities and the convenience of air transportation have made shipping by boat unprofitable. Villagers that live along the river still use boats to transport freight and other necessities. The Yukon is frozen up to seven months of the year. Many of the small tributaries contain gold-bearing gravels. The eastern part has hot springs.

The course of the Yukon. The Yukon River originates from a series of small lakes in northwestern British Columbia. It flows northwest and joins the Pelly River at Fort Selkirk, Yukon. The Yukon continues past Dawson and crosses the United States-Canada border near Eagle, Alaska. The river continues to flow northwest to Fort Yukon, where it begins flowing southwest. The Yukon then curves and flows northwest to the Bering Sea. The Yukon Valley is divided into two regions, the Upper

Brown Bros.

Rugged miners packed their belongings in sleds and hurried to the gold fields during the Klondike Gold Rush in 1897.

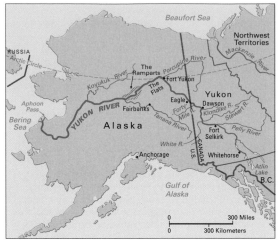

Location of the Yukon River

WORLD BOOK map

Yukon and the Lower Yukon.

Upper Yukon. The principal tributaries of the Upper Yukon are the Pelly, White, Stewart, Klondike, and Forty-Mile rivers. The first important discoveries of gold in this region were made on Forty-Mile Creek in 1895. Dawson, one of the largest settlements on the Upper Yukon, and the capital of the Yukon territory until 1953, stands where the Klondike and Yukon rivers meet.

After flowing northwest for 450 miles (724 kilometers), the Yukon turns almost at right angles and flows southwest for 200 miles (320 kilometers) through the famous "Flats." These are level areas of sand bars and low islands, covered with spruce, willow, and birch. There, the river channel constantly shifts, and at seasons of high water it increases from a normal width of 10 miles (16 kilometers) to more than 40 miles (64 kilometers). The "great bend" of the Yukon is about 3 miles (4.8 kilometers) north of the Arctic Circle.

The "Flats" end at the Ramparts, a gorge that extends 110 miles (177 kilometers) to the mouth of the Tanana River. In this part, the Yukon Valley is 1 to 3 miles (1.6 to 4.8 kilometers) wide. The Tanana, the Yukon's largest tributary entirely in Alaska, flows northwest for about 400 miles (640 kilometers), roughly parallel to and about 125 miles (201 kilometers) west of the Upper Yukon.

Lower Yukon. The Ramparts gorge ends at the Tanana's mouth. The Yukon River then enters a lowland about 25 miles (40 kilometers) wide. From this point to the sea, 800 miles (1,300 kilometers) away, the river valley is never less than 2 miles (3.2 kilometers) wide.

The Yukon delta covers nearly 9,000 square miles (23,000 square kilometers). The river has more than 20 outlets over 600 feet (180 meters) wide. But most of them are shallow and filled with sand bars. Steamers enter the delta through the Aphoon Pass, which is only 4 feet (1.2 meters) deep at low water. Claus-M. Naske

Yule is another word for Christmas. *Yuletide* means the Christmas season. The origin of the word *Yule* probably goes back to a pre-Christian harvest festival held in November. Germanic tribes called Goths used the word *qiul* or *hiul* for *wheel*. Some scholars suggest that yule refers to the annual revolution, or wheel, of the sun.

When Christian culture advanced northward, the customs of the harvest festival became part of Christmas.

The burning of the Yule log was a popular custom that survived into Christian times. On Christmas Eve, a huge log, often an oak, was brought in and lit with much celebrating. A torch from the previous year's log was used to light the new fire. Each night until the feast of Twelfth Night, the log would be burned for a while. The ashes and charcoal were used during the year to ward off evil and even to cure cattle diseases. Robert J. Myers

Yuma, *YOO muh* (pop. 77,515; met. area pop. 160,026), is a commercial center in southwestern Arizona. It lies on the Colorado River, near where Arizona, California, and Mexico meet (see **Arizona** [political map]).

Yuma has a hot, dry climate that once made farming in the area difficult. But irrigation systems built since the early 1900's have turned the desert that once surrounded the city into rich farmland. The area's major crops include alfalfa, citrus fruits, cotton, lettuce, and wheat. A U.S. Marine Corps air station and the Yuma Proving Ground—a U.S. Army testing area—are near Yuma. Agriculture, government and military agencies, and tourism each provide many jobs for Yuma's people.

Yuma was founded in 1854 at a popular spot for crossing the Colorado River. It was originally called Colorado City and, later, Arizona City. In 1873, it was renamed Yuma, after the Yuma Indians (also called the Quechan Indians). In the late 1800's, Yuma served as a shipping center for goods entering Arizona by way of the Colorado River. From 1876 to 1909, it was the site of the Arizona Territorial Prison. The prison buildings still stand, and the grounds are now a state historical park.

Yuma is the seat of Yuma County. It has a council-manager form of government. For the monthly weather, see **Arizona** (Climate). Cathy Carrithers Everett

Yuma Indians. See Quechan Indians.

Yurok Indians, *yoo RAHK,* originally lived in northern California, along the Klamath River and the Pacific coast. Most Yurok still live there.

The chief foods of the Yurok were acorns, which they ground into meal and boiled, and salmon. The Yurok also ate deer and other game, bulbs, seeds, and berries. Food from the ocean included fish, shellfish, seaweed, and such animals as sea lions and whales.

The Yurok paid great attention to wealth and social position, which were inherited. Valuable possessions included white deerskins, obsidian blades, headdresses made of woodpecker scalps, and strings of *dentalia* (tooth) shells. The dentalia strings were used as money, with the value determined by the length of the shells.

The gold rush that began in 1849 brought many white settlers to California. Many Yurok died in fighting with the settlers. In the 1850's and 1860's, the United States government forced the Yurok to move to the Hoopa Valley near McKinleyville, California. In 1876, the area was formally established as the Hoopa Valley Reservation. The traditional Yurok homeland along the Klamath River was added to the reservation in 1891. Almost 100 years later, in 1988, the Klamath River area became the separate Yurok Reservation. According to the 2000 U.S. census, the reservation has a population of about 1,100. Today, many Yurok work in logging, fishing, or farming.

Victoria D. Patterson

YWCA. See Young Women's Christian Association.

Zz

Z is the 26th and last letter in our alphabet. Historians believe that it came from a symbol used by the Semites, who once lived in Syria and Palestine. They named it *zayin* and adapted an Egyptian *hieroglyphic* (picture symbol) for an arrowlike object. The Greeks later made the symbol the sixth letter of their alphabet, and called it *zeta*. They gave it the capital Z form that we use. The Romans used *z* only when writing words borrowed from Greek, and moved the letter to the end of their alphabet. In Canada and the United Kingdom, *z* is called *zed*. In some English dialects, it is called *izzard*. See **Alphabet**.

Uses. *Z* or *z* is the letter least frequently used in books, newspapers, and other printed material in English. *Z* is often used to denote the last of anything, as in the phrase "from A to Z." *Z* is used to denote *atomic number* in chemistry and *zenith distance* in astronomy. *Zone* and *zero* are also represented by *z*.

Pronunciation. In English, a person pronounces the normal consonant *z* sound, as in *zone*, by placing the tongue blade near the edges of the upper front teeth, with a narrow chink left over the tip. The velum, or soft palate, is closed, and breath is expelled through the chink and against the front teeth. The vocal cords vibrate. The letter *z* may also have a *zh* sound in English as in *azure* or *glazier*. In German, *z* has a *ts* sound. In most of the other European languages, *z* sounds are like those in the English language. See **Pronunciation**.

Marianne Cooley

Development of the letter Z

The ancient Egyptians drew this symbol of an arrow about 3000 B.C.

The Semites simplified the Egyptian symbol about 1500 B.C. They named the letter *zayin,* their word for *weapon.*

The Phoenicians used this symbol of a weapon about 1000 B.C.

The Greeks changed the symbol about 600 B.C. and made it the sixth letter of their alphabet. They called it *zeta*.

The Romans used the letter Z when they wrote words borrowed from Greek about A.D. 114.

The small letter **z** developed during the A.D. 800's from Roman writing. By the 1500's, the letter had the form that is used today.

A.D. 800   Today

Special ways of expressing the letter Z

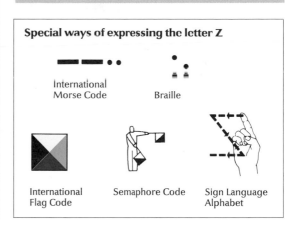

International Morse Code

Braille

International Flag Code

Semaphore Code

Sign Language Alphabet

Common forms of the letter Z

Handwritten letters vary from person to person. *Manuscript* (printed) letters have straight lines, *left,* and simple curves. Cursive letters, *right,* have flowing lines.

Roman letters have small finishing strokes called *serifs* that extend from the main strokes. The type face shown above is Baskerville. The italic form appears at the right.

Sans-serif letters are also called *gothic letters*. They have no serifs. The type face shown above is called Futura. The italic form of Futura appears at the right.

Computer letters have special shapes. Computers can "read" these letters either optically or by means of the magnetic ink with which the letters may be printed.

Zagreb, *ZAH grehb* (pop. 950,000), is the capital and largest city of Croatia. It lies on the banks of the Sava River in northern Croatia (see **Croatia** [map]).

Zagreb is Croatia's chief industrial center. Factories in the city produce chemicals, leather, machinery, paper, and textiles. Museums in Zagreb include the Museum of Art and Handicrafts, the Archaeological Museum, and the Ethnographical Museum. The University of Zagreb was established in the city in 1669.

Historical records mention Zagreb for the first time in 1094, when it became the seat of a Roman Catholic bishopric. In the 1800's, Zagreb became an important political, scientific, and literary center for Croats. In 1918, Croatia became part of the new Kingdom of the Serbs, Croats, and Slovenes, later renamed Yugoslavia. In 1991, war broke out between Croats and Serbs in Croatia after Croatia declared its independence. Tens of thousands of people fled to Zagreb after their villages were destroyed in the fighting.   Sabrina P. Ramet

See also **Croatia** (picture).

Zaharias, *zuh HAIR ee uhs,* **Babe Didrikson,** *bayb DIHD rihk suhn* (1911?-1956), is generally considered the greatest woman athlete in sports history. She gained her most enduring fame in golf and track and field, but she also competed in basketball, baseball, pocket billiards, tennis, diving, and swimming. In a 1932 track and field meet, she set four world records in three hours. At the 1932 Olympic Games, she set world records in the 80-meter hurdles, the javelin throw, and the high jump.

Didrikson began concentrating on golf in the early 1930's. Her style of play dramatically changed women's golf. Her powerful swing, low scores, and showmanship attracted many new fans to the sport. She won the U.S. Women's Amateur tournament in 1946. In 1946 and 1947, she won 17 tournaments in a row, including the 1947 British Women's Amateur. She became the first American to win this event. Didrikson turned professional in 1947. She was one of the founders of the Ladies Professional Golf Association (LPGA). She won the U.S. Women's Open in 1948, 1950, and 1954. The 1954 victory came a year after she had cancer surgery.

Wide World
Babe Didrikson Zaharias

Mildred Ella Didrikson was born in Port Arthur, Texas. She was nicknamed Babe after baseball slugger Babe Ruth because of the many home runs she hit playing baseball as a child. She married George Zaharias, a wrestler, in 1938.   Marino A. Parascenzo

See also **Olympic Games** (picture: Early women Olympic stars).

Additional resources

Freedman, Russell. *Babe Didrikson Zaharias.* Clarion, 1999.
Johnson, William O., and Williamson, N. P. *Whatta-gal! The Babe Didrikson Story.* Little, Brown, 1977.
Wakeman, Nancy. *Babe Didrikson Zaharias.* Lerner, 2000. Younger readers.

Zaire. See Congo (Kinshasa).

Zambezi River, *zam BEE zee,* is the fourth longest river in Africa. Only the Nile, Congo, and Niger rivers are longer. The Zambezi rises in Zambia, near the border between Congo (Kinshasa) and Angola. The river follows a winding 1,700-mile (2,736-kilometer) course, separating Zambia from Zimbabwe and crossing Mozambique to empty into the Mozambique Channel (see **Africa** [map]). The Zambezi has many branches and drains over 500,000 square miles (1,300,000 square kilometers).

The upper course of the river lies in level land, where the water supply depends on equatorial rains that fall from October to March. From this plateau, the Zambezi plunges to a lower level over Victoria Falls, a mighty cataract of water. A hydroelectric plant has been in operation there since 1938. Kariba Dam, completed in 1959, lies in Kariba Gorge, about 200 miles (320 kilometers) downstream. It forms a lake that covers 2,000 square miles (5,200 square kilometers).

Early geographers knew of the Zambezi region, probably through Arab traders. The first European to explore the Zambezi River was David Livingstone. He explored the river in the 1850's and 1860's.   Hartmut S. Walter

See also **Stanley and Livingstone; Victoria Falls.**

Zambia, *ZAM bee uh,* is a country in south-central Africa. It ranks as one of the world's largest producers of copper. Zambia exports copper to many parts of the world and gains much income from the exports.

Zambia takes its name from the Zambezi River, which forms most of the country's southern border. Victoria Falls, one of the world's most beautiful waterfalls, lies on the river. The great Kariba Dam, one of the world's largest hydroelectric projects, and Kariba Lake also are on the river, serving both Zambia and Zimbabwe.

Zambia was formerly a British protectorate called Northern Rhodesia. From 1953 to 1963, it formed part of the Federation of Rhodesia and Nyasaland with Nyasaland (now Malawi) and Southern Rhodesia (now Zimbabwe). Zambia became an independent nation in 1964. Lusaka is its capital and largest city.

Government. A president serves as head of state and government and is the most powerful official in Zambia. The National Assembly, the country's legislature, consists of 150 members. The president appoints a vice president and a Cabinet to help run the day-to-day affairs of the government. The people of Zambia elect the president and the Assembly members to five-year terms. The two largest political parties in Zambia are the Movement for Multiparty Democracy (MMD) and the United National Independence Party (UNIP).

The country is divided into nine provinces. Each province is administered by a minister of state.

People. Most Zambians are black Africans who speak Bantu languages (see **Bantu**). There are more than 70 ethnic groups represented and eight major local languages spoken in Zambia. Many people also speak English, the official language. In remote parts of the country, village life goes on much as it has for hundreds of years. The people live in circular, grass-roofed homes and raise food crops on the surrounding land. The development of mining has caused thousands of Zambians to move to mining towns.

Corn is the main food. A favorite dish is *nshima,* a thick porridge made from corn. The people plant their crops in November and December.

The majority of Zambians are Christians, but traditional local beliefs still have a strong hold on the village people. However, the use of traditional medicine, and old customs such as *polygyny* (marrying several wives) and *bride price* (paying the parents for a bride), are slowly dying out in the towns.

Most Zambian children attend elementary school, but only a fifth go to high school. Zambia's only university, the University of Zambia, was founded in 1965. Zambia also has several trade and technical schools.

Land. Most of Zambia is flat and covered with trees and bushes. It lies on a plateau about 4,000 feet (1,200 meters) above sea level. The plateau is broken by the 7,000-foot (2,100-meter) Muchinga Mountains in the northeast. In the south, the trees are smaller, and there are large open areas. The Zambezi River flows south through western Zambia and forms much of the southern border. Every year, it floods a broad, sandy plain in Western Province in the southwest.

Because of its altitude, Zambia has a milder climate than might be expected. The hot season lasts only from September through November. Midday temperatures then range between 80 and 100 °F (27 and 38 °C). From November through April, Zambia has a rainy season. Violent storms flood the rivers by March. From May through August, temperatures range from 60 to 80 °F (16 to 27 °C). Northern Zambia gets about 50 inches (130 centimeters) of rainfall a year. The south gets 20 to 30 inches (51 to 76 centimeters).

Economy. Copper accounts for about half of Zambia's export earnings. Four large copper mines and several smaller mines lie in an area called the *copper belt,* along Zambia's border with Congo (Kinshasa). Valuable amounts of cobalt are obtained as by-products of copper mining. Zambia has a lead and zinc mine at Kabwe, and coal deposits near Kariba Lake. The production of

Facts in brief

Capital: Lusaka.
Official language: English.
Official name: Republic of Zambia.
Area: 290,587 mi² (752,618 km²). *Greatest distances*—east-west, 900 mi (1,448 km); north-south, 700 mi (1,127 km).
Population: *Estimated 2004 population*—11,320,000; density, 39 per mi² (15 per km²); distribution, 62 percent rural, 38 percent urban. *2000 census*—10,285,631.
Chief products: *Agriculture*—cassava, corn, millet, sorghum grain, sugar cane. *Fishing*—perch, whitebait. *Manufacturing and processing*—cement, copper products, flour, wood products. *Mining*—copper, cobalt.
Flag: The flag has an orange eagle in the upper right corner over three vertical stripes of red (for freedom), black (for the people), and orange (for mineral wealth) on a field of green (for natural resources). See **Flag** (picture: Flags of Africa).
Money: *Basic unit*—kwacha. One hundred ngwee equal one kwacha.

copper products is the country's most important manufacturing activity. Corn is the most important farm product. Other leading crops include cassava, coffee, millet, sorghum, sugar cane, and tobacco.

Zambia has no outlet to the sea. Railroads connect the country with seaports in Angola, Mozambique, and Tanzania. The railroad to Angola passes through Congo (Kinshasa), and the one to Mozambique passes through Zimbabwe. The railroad to Tanzania was built in the early 1970's with millions of dollars of aid from China.

History. In 1851, the Scottish missionary David Livingstone crossed the Zambezi from the south. He spent nearly 20 years exploring the region.

In the late 1800's, Cecil Rhodes's British South Africa Company made treaties with African chiefs in the area. In 1897, the company named the area Northern Rhodesia to distinguish it from the region south of the Zam-

WORLD BOOK maps

Zambia

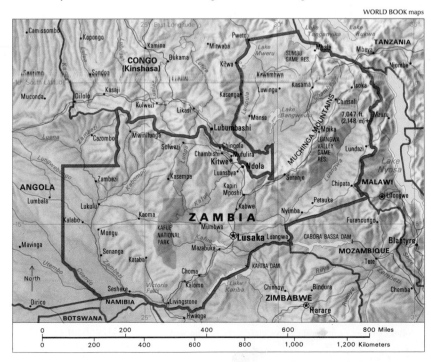

National park or reserve

International boundary

Road

Railroad

⊛ National capital

· Other city or town

+ Elevation above sea level

bezi, which it called Southern Rhodesia.

In 1924, the British government took over the administration of Northern Rhodesia and appointed a governor. Copper had been mined in the area for hundreds of years. The discovery of large copper ore deposits in the late 1920's brought a rush of Europeans to the area. Ten years later, mining was an important industry.

After World War II ended in 1945, the Europeans asked the United Kingdom for greater control of the government. Many wanted to merge Northern and Southern Rhodesia. The Africans of Northern Rhodesia opposed these demands. But in 1953, the United Kingdom formed a federation of Northern Rhodesia, Southern Rhodesia, and Nyasaland. The Africans opposed the federation because the European minority controlled the government in Southern Rhodesia. The United Kingdom dissolved the federation in 1963. On Oct. 24, 1964, Northern Rhodesia became the independent nation of Zambia. Kenneth Kaunda was elected president in 1964. He served in that position until 1991. In 1972, the UNIP became the only legal political party in Zambia.

Southern Rhodesia came to be called Rhodesia after the federation was dissolved. In 1965, Rhodesia declared its independence in defiance of the United Kingdom. Relations between Zambia and Rhodesia became strained because Rhodesia's white minority government refused to give the African majority a greater say in government.

Zambia experienced major economic problems in the late 1900's. Its economy suffered from low market prices for copper and a reduction in copper ore reserves. In 1980, blacks gained control of Rhodesia's government, and the country's name was changed to Zimbabwe. Relations then improved between Zambia and Zimbabwe.

Opposition parties became legal in 1990. MMD leader Frederick Chiluba defeated Kaunda in the 1991 presidential election and was reelected president in 1996. In 2001, Levy Mwanawasa of the MMD was elected president. Also in the early 2000's, a severe drought led to widespread food shortages in Zambia.   James Pletcher

Related articles in *World Book* include:

Bemba	Lake Bangweulu	Victoria Falls
Kaunda, Kenneth D.	Lusaka	Zambezi River

Robert Harding Picture Library Ltd.

Lusaka, Zambia's capital and commercial center, is a modern city with tall buildings and busy streets.

Zanzibar, *ZAN zuh BAHR* (pop. 157,634), is a historic seaport city on the west coast of Zanzibar Island. The city of Zanzibar is the seat of government for the Zanzibar island group, part of Tanzania (see **Tanzania** [map]). The island group consists of Zanzibar Island, Pemba Island, and a few other islands. Zanzibar's main exports are cloves and clove oil. In Stone Town, the city's old section on the sea, ornate buildings line narrow, winding streets. Large apartment buildings tower over the city's Ng'ambo section, inland from Stone Town.

In the early 1800's, the sultan of Oman, who controlled much of East Africa's coast, established his capital in Zanzibar. He built an economy based on clove plantations and the slave and ivory trades. The sultan's palace still stands in Stone Town.   Garth A. Myers

Zanzibar, *ZAN zuh bahr,* is a group of islands that is part of Tanzania. The islands lie in the Indian Ocean, about 25 miles (40 kilometers) off the east coast of the African mainland. The two main islands are Zanzibar Island (known locally as Unguja) and Pemba Island. The capital and largest city of the island group is the city of Zanzibar, on the west coast of Zanzibar Island. The region of Zanzibar has its own president and legislature and exercises some control over its own affairs.

The islands have a tropical climate with an average temperature of about 80 °F (27 °C). Heavy rains fall from March to May, and there is lighter rain from October to December. The rest of the year is mostly dry.

Most Zanzibaris have African ancestry. Arabs and Indians are the largest minority groups. Many residents have mixed African and Arab ancestry. Swahili (also called Kiswahili) is the main language. Nearly all Zanzibaris are Muslims.

Zanzibar has long been a major trading center. Agriculture and fishing are important to the local economy. The islands are often called the "spice isles" because they are among the world's largest producers of cloves. Zanzibaris also grow bananas, cassava, coconuts, limes, mangoes, pineapples, plantains, rice, tangerines, and other fruits and vegetables. Since the 1990's, tourism has been a significant economic activity.

Zanzibar was part of an ancient network that linked traders from eastern and central Africa with those from Arabia and the Red Sea and Indian Ocean regions. This network existed as early as the A.D. 100's and extended along much of the east African coast. In the 1800's, Zanzibar became the center of a trade in slaves and ivory from eastern Africa. The slaves were sold mainly in the Caribbean, Brazil, Indian Ocean islands, and Arabia. In the 1830's, the sultan of Oman moved his capital to the town of Zanzibar. Afterward, many people from Oman, Yemen, and India immigrated to the islands. The United Kingdom made the islands a British protectorate in 1890. In 1963, Zanzibar gained independence from the British. In 1964, it merged with Tanganyika, on the African mainland, to form the nation of Tanzania.   Laura Fair

See also **Tanzania; Zanzibar** (city).

Zapata, *sah PAH tah,* **Emiliano,** *EH mee LYAH noh* (1879-1919), was a leader of the Mexican Revolution, which began in 1910. His main goal was to gain land for the people. Zapata refused to lay down his arms until revolutionary leader Francisco Madero distributed land. In 1911, unhappy with Madero's gradual reforms, Zapata issued a program of immediate land reform known as the "Plan de Ayala." He also refused to recognize the authority of Victoriano Huerta, who overthrew Madero in 1913. In 1914, Zapata occupied Mexico City with Pancho Villa. Zapata was murdered by Colonel Jesús Guajardo in 1919. He was born on Aug. 8, 1879, in Anenecuilco, Morelos. See also **Mexico** (The Constitution of 1917).

W. Dirk Raat

Zapatista Army of National Liberation, ZAH pah TEES tah, commonly called the Zapatistas, is a group that seeks increased political rights for Mexico's native Indian population. The Zapatistas take their name from Emiliano Zapata, who fought for Indian land rights during the Mexican Revolution of 1910. A key Zapatista leader is a non-Indian who goes by the name Subcomandante Marcos.

The Zapatistas came to prominence on Jan. 1, 1994, when Mayan Indians seized control of several towns in the southern Mexican state of Chiapas. The Zapatistas demanded improved living conditions for all of Mexico's Indians. At first, the Mexican army tried to crush the rebellion through force. But protests in Mexico and other countries led Mexico's government to declare a cease-fire on Jan. 12, 1994. In 1996, the Zapatistas and the Mexican government signed an agreement on Indian rights. The government failed to carry out the agreement. A version of the accord that had been extensively amended by the Mexican Congress became law in 2001. The Zapatistas did not support the law. Neil F. Harvey

See also **Zapata, Emiliano.**

Zapotec Indians, ZAH puh tehk, developed an empire in what is now the state of Oaxaca in southern Mexico from about 1500 B.C. to A.D. 750. There, they built their capital city, Monte Albán, on a mountaintop. The city had a ceremonial district that included temples and a ball court. The Zapotec also produced the earliest written texts in Middle America. They carved on stone slabs records of conquests, sacrifices, and relations with other peoples. After the disintegration of their empire, the Zapotec abandoned Monte Albán. However, a number of smaller Zapotec kingdoms developed. Mixtec Indians gained control of several of these kingdoms by conquering or marrying into Zapotec ruling families. Some kingdoms were conquered by the Aztec Indians.

Thousands of Zapotec still live in the state of Oaxaca and speak Zapotec dialects. Most are farmers. Some Zapotec are also skilled potters and weavers. Their products are sold worldwide. William O. Autry

See also **Monte Albán; Rivera, Diego** (picture).

Zaragoza. See Saragossa.

Zarathustra. See Zoroastrianism.

Zebra is a striped member of the horse family. There are three species—the *common zebra, Grevy's zebra,* and the *mountain zebra.* They live in herds in the deserts and grasslands of eastern and southern Africa.

A zebra has alternating white and black or dark brown stripes. Each of the three species of zebras has a distinctive stripe pattern. In addition, much like fingerprints in human beings, no individual zebra's stripes are identical to those of another zebra. The stripes may help to keep herds of zebras together. Experiments have shown that, from birth, zebras are attracted to objects with stripes. Zebras with abnormal stripe patterns are usually not allowed in the herd and seldom survive.

A zebra eats grass. It may also eat bark, leaves, buds, fruits, and roots. A zebra spends most of its time eating.

Zebras' main enemies include lions, hyenas, leopards, and cheetahs. Zebras protect themselves from predators by keeping together in the herd. At least one herd member remains alert to danger at all times. A zebra's large ears rotate to locate sounds, and its night vision is as good as an owl's. If attacked, a zebra usually tries to flee. Zebras can run at speeds of up to 40 miles (65 kilometers) per hour. Zebras may live up to 22 years in the wild.

A zebra herd may range in size from a few individuals to several hundred. Most herds include smaller groups that consist of a male, several females, and their young. Young males often form herds with no females.

Although zebras seldom fight, competition among males for a particular female during the breeding season may become intense and involve pushing, biting, and kicking. Females become sexually mature at the age of 3 and may reproduce throughout the rest of their life. Most males begin mating at about 5 years of age.

The female zebra carries a single young, called a *foal,* in her body for about a year before giving birth. A newborn foal weighs 70 to 80 pounds (32 to 36 kilograms). It

Giuseppe Mazza

Zebras live in eastern and southern Africa. Most female zebras have one young, called a *foal,* every spring. The foal can stand within an hour after birth and will grow quickly. No individual zebra's stripes are identical to those of another zebra.

can stand within an hour after birth. In a few days, the young zebra begins eating grass. It may gain up to 1 pound (0.45 kilogram) a day for the next two months.

Zebras face an uncertain future in the wild. They must compete with ranchers and farmers for grazing land and scarce water resources. Many zebras have been killed for their meat and their hides. Only the common zebra is still numerous. Both Grevy's zebra and the mountain zebra are endangered. A fourth kind of zebra, the *quagga,* became extinct in the late 1800's.   Reginald A. Hoyt

Scientific classification. Zebras belong to the genus *Equus* in the horse family, Equidae. The scientific name for the common zebra is *Equus burchelli.*

Zebra mussel is a freshwater, Eurasian shellfish that is a major pest in North America. In parts of the Great Lakes, millions of zebra mussels clog pipes that provide water for drinking, irrigation, and industrial uses. They also cover boat bottoms, piers, fish traps and nets, and marker and navigation buoys. In addition, zebra mussels cover native freshwater mussels and smother them, resulting in the elimination of native mussels from some regions. The explosive growth of zebra mussels may threaten the food supply of many species of fish and shellfish native to the Great Lakes.

Zebra mussels grow to about 2 inches (5 centimeters) long, and many have stripes. Each mussel attaches to a hard surface by producing sticky tufts of *byssal threads.* Zebra mussels feed on tiny floating organisms called *plankton.* The mussels themselves are eaten by several species of fish and diving ducks.

Zebra mussels are native to the area around the Caspian and Black seas. They were first found in North America in 1987. Their larvae had been unintentionally released into the Great Lakes in *ballast water* (the water kept in the hold of a ship to keep the vessel stable). By 1994, zebra mussels had spread to all the Great Lakes, the Hudson and Mississippi rivers, and the Arkansas River as far west as Oklahoma. Biologists believe they eventually will spread to more than half the lakes and rivers of North America.   James T. Carlton

Scientific classification. Zebra mussels are in the family Dreissenidae in the class Bivalvia. The two species found in North America are *Dreissena polymorpha* and *D. bugensis.*

Zebulun, *ZEHB yuh luhn,* was the name of one of the 12 tribes of Israel. In the 1100's B.C., Zebulun, with neighboring tribes, played a leading part in the defeat of the Canaanites by Deborah and Barak (Judges 4-5). Later, it was a part of the northern kingdom of Israel. In 733 B.C., Zebulun was taken by the Assyrians with the rest of Galilee. Jesus Christ's home, Nazareth, lay in what had once been the tribe's territory. Zebulun was named for the 10th son of Jacob, the 6th and youngest born to him by Leah (Genesis 30:20). The tribe claimed that it descended from him.   H. Darrell Lance

Zechariah, *zehk uh RY uh,* **Book of,** is a book of the Old Testament or Hebrew Bible. It is named for a prophet who lived in Jerusalem and prophesied from 520 to 518 B.C. Chapters 1-8 are usually attributed to Zechariah himself. Chapters 9-14 are considered a slightly later collection written anonymously.

The Book of Zechariah elaborates on a plan to rebuild a temple and reestablish a community for the Israelites returning from exile. In the first section (1:1-8:23), a series of visions and oracles help the Israelites understand and

accept the new form of government by high priest and governor that Persia had permitted. Central to the plan was the recently refounded Temple of Yahweh that dominates all the visions and oracles. The second section (9:1-14:21) focuses on the struggle in the Jewish community after the Persian Empire experienced rebellions in Babylon and Egypt by 450 B.C.   Eric M. Meyers

Zedillo Ponce de León, *say DEE yoh PAWN say day lay OWN,* **Ernesto** (1951-   ), was president of Mexico from 1994 to 2000. A member of the powerful Institutional Revolutionary Party (PRI), he succeeded Carlos Salinas de Gortari.

Shortly after Zedillo became president, Mexico faced a severe economic crisis. In response, Zedillo's administration adopted an emergency economic plan that included a reduction in government spending and an increase in taxes. These measures, combined with an international aid package, helped the economy recover.

Zedillo also took a number of steps to reform Mexico's political system. In 1999, for example, he ordered that a primary be held to select the PRI presidential candidate. It was the first time voters, rather than the current president, chose the candidate. Zedillo's reforms helped make possible the presidential victory in 2000 by opposition candidate Vicente Fox Quesada. This victory ended the PRI's 71-year rule of Mexico.

Zedillo was born on Dec. 27, 1951, in Mexico City. He graduated in 1972 from Mexico's National Polytechnic Institute. He earned a Ph.D. degree in economics at Yale University in 1981. Upon returning to Mexico, he became an economist for Mexico's central bank.

Zedillo was secretary of planning and budget from 1988 to 1992 and then became secretary of public education. He resigned that post in late 1993 to manage the campaign of Luis Donaldo Colosio, the PRI presidential candidate. Colosio was assassinated in March 1994, and Zedillo was named the new candidate.   Roderic A. Camp

Zeeman, *ZAY mahn,* **Pieter,** *PEE tuhr* (1865-1943), a Dutch physicist, became known for his discoveries in spectroscopy, the study and analysis of spectra of light. In 1896, he discovered what is now called the *Zeeman effect,* the splitting of spectral lines by a magnetic field (see **Zeeman effect**). The theory for this phenomenon was developed by Hendrik A. Lorentz, and the two scientists shared the 1902 Nobel Prize in physics for their work (see **Lorentz, Hendrik A.**). Through the Zeeman effect, astronomers measure the strength of the magnetic field on the surface of stars. Zeeman was born on May 25, 1865, in Zonnemaire, in Zeeland, the Netherlands.   Bruce R. Wheaton

Zeeman effect, *ZAY mahn,* is an influence that magnetism has on light. The effect changes the color of the light *emitted* (sent out) by atoms. Scientists can use the light to measure the strength of the magnetism. Dutch physicist Pieter Zeeman first observed the effect in 1896.

The parts of an atom that actually emit light are negatively charged particles called *electrons.* An electron emits light when it jumps from a higher energy level to a lower energy level. The color of the light depends on the difference between the levels. The atoms in a substance will emit light when they are given enough energy—for example, by heating the substance.

You can study the light emitted by a particular kind of atom by using a prism to break the light into different colors. The colors appear as bright lines called *spectral lines*. The Zeeman effect is the splitting of a single spectral line into two or more lines. This effect occurs when a substance emitting light is placed in a *magnetic field*. A magnetic field is the influence that a magnet or electric current creates in the region around it.

The Zeeman effect occurs because electrons have magnetism resulting from their charge and motion. The effect occurs when the magnetic fields created by electrons of a particular kind of atom interact with the external magnetic field. Depending on how an electron is oriented, this interaction may increase or decrease the electron's energy slightly. Each new energy level makes a different spectral line. In this way, a single spectral line splits into two more lines when atoms are in a magnetic field.   Richard Wolfson

Zen is an East Asian form of Buddhism. Zen Buddhism is practiced primarily in Japan and has greatly influenced Japanese culture. Since the mid-1900's, Zen has gained many followers in the United States.

The goal of Zen is the attainment of a state of spiritual enlightenment called *satori*. Zen Buddhists believe meditation is the key to achieving satori. There are two major schools of Zen, *Rinzai* and *Soto*. Followers of Rinzai meditate on the meaning of baffling riddles called *koans* while sitting cross-legged. People who practice Soto meditate in the same position. They also read from the sacred works of Mahayana Buddhism, another East Asian form of the religion. Zen Buddhists believe physical labor contributes to the attainment of enlightenment. They work closely with a teacher called the *master*, who guides their search for satori.

Zen developed in China, where it is called Chan. According to legend, an Indian monk named Bodhidharma first taught its principles in China in the A.D. 500's. Two Japanese priests, Eisai and Dogen, introduced Chan into Japan. Eisai founded the Rinzai school in the 1100's, and Dogen established the Soto school in the 1200's. Zen quickly became a major religious and cultural force in Japan.   Frank E. Reynolds

See also **Buddhism** (Zen); **Meditation**.

Additional resources

Dumoulin, Heinrich. *A History of Zen Buddhism*. 1963. Reprint. Munshiram Manoharial, 2000.
Ferguson, Andrew. *Zen's Chinese Heritage*. Wisdom, 2000.
Smith, Jean. *The Beginner's Guide to Zen Buddhism*. Bell Tower, 2000.
Tanahashi, Kazuaki, and Schneider, T. D., eds. *Essential Zen*. 1994. Reprint. DIANE, 1999. Selected readings.

Zenger, *ZEHNG uhr,* **John Peter** (1697-1746), gained the first major victory for freedom of the press in the American Colonies. Political opponents of British governor William Cosby established Zenger as printer of the *New-York Weekly Journal* in 1733. These opponents, including Chief Justice Lewis Morris, belonged to the Popular Party and used the *Journal* to oppose the Government Party. In 1734, when Cosby abruptly dismissed Morris from his office, the *Journal* criticized Cosby severely. Zenger shielded Cosby's enemies by refusing to reveal who had written the critical articles.

Because they could find no one else to prosecute, the British arrested Zenger and tried him in 1735 for criminal libel. Zenger's lawyers were disbarred, and he was left almost defenseless. Finally, Andrew Hamilton, a famous Philadelphia lawyer, came to New York to aid Zenger. Hamilton gave a powerful speech that persuaded the jury to find Zenger "not guilty" by arguing that Zenger had printed the truth, and that truth is not libelous. After the trial, Zenger published *A Brief Narrative of the Case and Tryal of John Peter Zenger* (1736).

Zenger was born in Germany and came to New York at the age of 13. He was apprenticed to a printer and set up his own printing shop in 1726.   Jethro K. Lieberman

See also **Freedom of the press** (In the United States).

Zenith, *ZEE nihth,* in astronomy, is any point directly above a person on the earth. Zeniths lie on the *celestial sphere,* which can be pictured as an imaginary sphere that encloses the universe. A point directly below a person on the earth is called a *nadir* (see **Nadir**).

Astronomers speak of two kinds of zeniths, *astronomical zeniths* and *geocentric zeniths.* An astronomical zenith is determined by gravity. It is any point where an extended *plumb line* would intersect the celestial sphere. A geocentric zenith is determined by geometry. It is any point where a line drawn from the earth's center through a person on its surface would intersect the celestial sphere. The angular distance of a star or other celestial body from a zenith is called the *zenith distance.* This information can be used to describe the position of such an object.   Lee J. Rickard

Zeno of Citium, *ZEE noh, SIHSH ee uhm* (335?-265? B.C.), was the founder of Stoic philosophy in Athens. He was born in Citium on the island of Cyprus. It is reported that he was originally a merchant, but was shipwrecked and lost all his property traveling to Athens in 314 B.C. He stayed there and took up the study of philosophy, meeting his students on a *stoa* (porch), from which the name *stoic* came (see **Stoic philosophy**).

Zeno taught that it is foolish to try to shape circumstances to our desires. The world process is not like a blindly running machine. Instead, a divine intelligence guides and governs it, and directs all things ultimately toward what is good. Wise people will "follow nature" and fit their desires to the pattern of events. They will find happiness in freedom from desire, from fear of evil, and in knowing that they are in tune with the divine purpose directing all things. The Stoic philosophy spread to Rome and flourished there for several centuries after the birth of Christ.   S. Marc Cohen

Zeno of Elea, *ZEE noh, EE lee uh* (490?-430 B.C.), was a Greek philosopher who lived in the Greek colony of Elea in southern Italy. He defended the doctrine of his teacher, the philosopher Parmenides, who believed that what exists is one, permanent, and unchanging (see **Parmenides**). Zeno tried to prove that motion, change, and *plurality* (reality consisting of many substances) are impossible. Zeno used a method of arguing called *reductio ad absurdum.* By this method, he would derive impossible conclusions from the opinions of his opponents.

Zeno is believed to have devised at least 40 arguments, but only 8 have survived. His four *paradoxes* concerning motion make up his most famous surviving arguments. In one of these paradoxes, Zeno argued that a runner can never reach the end of a race course. He stated that the runner first completes half of the course, then half of the remaining distance, and so on infinitely without ever reaching the end. Zeno's apparently simple arguments raise profound issues about time, space, and infinity. These issues continue to interest philosophers and scientists.   S. Marc Cohen

Zeolite, *ZEE uh lyt,* is any of a group of crystalline mineral compounds whose framework of atoms forms microscopic tunnels and "rooms." The internal structure of zeolites makes them useful as filters and *catalysts.* Catalysts are substances that speed up a chemical reaction without being consumed by the reaction. Zeolites, one of the most abundant kinds of minerals, are made of silicon, oxygen, and aluminum and other metals.

Researchers have also developed synthetic zeolites, which contain such substances as phosphorus and sulfur. Industry uses more synthetic zeolite catalysts than any other kind of catalyst. The petroleum industry uses synthetic zeolite catalysts to break down large molecules and to produce gasoline from methyl alcohol. Other uses of synthetic zeolites include the treatment of liquid nuclear waste, soil improvement, and water purification and softening.   Galen D. Stucky

Zephaniah, *zehf uh NY uh,* **Book of,** is a book of the Hebrew Bible, or Old Testament. It is named for the prophet Zephaniah, whose ministry in the Kingdom of Judah probably occurred between about 630 and 625 B.C. During Zephaniah's ministry, Palestine was invaded by the Scythians, a barbarian people. Zephaniah equated their arrival with God's judgment on Judah and on all humanity. He stated, however, that God's wrath was principally directed against Judah so that people might repent. Zephaniah forecast a destructive "Day of the Lord," when the wicked would be punished. This theme is a central element in Biblical prophecy. The prophet predicted that a faithful few would be spared God's anger and be preserved in Jerusalem and in the rest of Judah. There God would gather them and they would accept His rule.   Eric M. Meyers

See also **Bible** (Books of the Hebrew Bible).

Zeppelin. See Airship (The Zeppelins).

Zeppelin, *ZEHP uh lihn* or *TSEHP uh LEEN,* **Ferdinand von** (1838-1917), was a famous German pioneer in lighter-than-air vehicles. He designed aircraft that were primarily gas bags, supported internally by a light framework. Engines powered and controlled his aircraft. These aircraft soon were named after him. Germany used zeppelins in air raids against the British during World War I. These attacks were the first planned air raids against a civilian population (see **Airship**).

Zeppelin was born in Constance, Baden, on July 8, 1838. He was trained to be an army officer. He visited the United States during the Civil War and went up in balloons with the Union forces. The balloons convinced him of the value of aircraft. He served in the Franco-Prussian War in 1870. After his retirement in 1891, he devoted himself to aeronautics. He had spent most of his savings when Kaiser Wilhelm II became interested in his work and offered financial support.   Richard P. Hallion

Zero, in arithmetic, is the name of the digit 0, sometimes called *naught* or a *cypher.* It is used to indicate the absence of quantity. A zero is needed in a positional numeral system, such as the familiar decimal system commonly used by most people today. In a *positional* system, the *position,* or place, of a digit determines the digit's value. Thus, in the numeral 246, the digit 2 stands for two hundreds, the digit 4 stands for four tens (or

forty), and the digit 6 stands for six units, or ones. The numeral represents the number 246. In order to write the number 206, a symbol is needed to show that there are no tens. The digit 0 serves this purpose. Zero added to or subtracted from a number gives the original number. A number multiplied by zero gives zero. Division by zero is undefined. Zero is an even number.

On most scales, zero marks the starting point or the neutral position. Positive numbers are placed to the right or above zero, and negative numbers are placed to the left or below zero. But on some scales, zero is set arbitrarily. For example, on a Celsius thermometer, zero is set at the temperature at which water freezes.

There is evidence that the Maya of Central America were using symbols for zero by about A.D. 250 and that the Hindus had developed such a symbol by the late 800's. The Hindu symbol spread from India and was adopted in Europe during the late 1400's. The word *zero* probably came from *ziphirum,* a Latinized form of the Arabic word *sifr. Sifr* is a translation of the Hindu word *sunya* (void or empty).   Robert M. Vancko

See also **Decimal system.**

Zeus, *zoos,* was the ruler of the gods in Greek mythology. Zeus was a sky and weather god, especially associated with rain, thunder, and lightning. The Greeks believed he was all-knowing and all-seeing. The Greeks considered Zeus a father figure and a protector, especially of guests and strangers. The Roman god Jupiter was equivalent to Zeus (see **Jupiter**).

Zeus was the son of Cronus and Rhea, members of an earlier race of ruling gods called the Titans. Zeus and the other children of Cronus defeated the Titans. Zeus then took Cronus's place and ruled from his home on Mount Olympus. He headed a family of 12 major gods and goddesses called the Olympians. Some lesser gods also lived on Olympus. Zeus's brothers were the gods Hades and Poseidon. Hades ruled the underworld, and Poseidon ruled the seas. The goddesses Demeter, Hera, and Hestia were Zeus's sisters.

At the time Zeus was introduced in Greece, the religion of that area was based on fertility. Each community had a major fertility goddess and a male god associated with her. Zeus eventually took the place of many of these male gods, and became the husband or lover of the goddesses. Later, Hera became Zeus's wife, and other goddesses took a lesser status.

Zeus had many love affairs with goddesses and mortal women and fathered many children. His children included the goddess Aphrodite; the gods Apollo, Dionysus, and Hermes; and the mortal heroes Perseus and Heracles (*Hercules* in Latin). Zeus alone gave birth to the goddess Athena.

In art, Zeus is depicted as bearded and majestic, often holding a thunderbolt. The eagle and the oak tree were symbols associated with Zeus.   F. Carter Philips

There is a separate article in *World Book* for each mythological figure mentioned in this article. See also **Mount Olympus; Mythology** (picture: The Greek gods).

Zhao Ziyang, *jow zu yahng* (1919-   ), also spelled *Chao Tzu-yang,* served as general secretary of the Chinese Communist Party from November 1987 until June 1989. He had been acting general secretary since January 1987. As general secretary, Zhao held the highest post in the Communist Party, which controls China's government. But at the time, Deng Xiaoping was the country's most influential leader (see **Deng Xiaoping**). Zhao was dismissed from his post in June 1989 after he showed support for a protest in favor of increased democracy in China (see **China** [Deng Xiaoping]).

Zhao was born on Oct. 17, 1919, in Henan (Honan) Province. He joined the Communist Party in 1938. He rose through the ranks and, in 1965, was given the party post of first secretary of Guangdong (Kwangtung) Province. He was removed from office in 1967 during China's Cultural Revolution (see **China** [The Cultural Revolution]). Zhao regained his post in 1971. In 1975, he became the Communist Party's first secretary of Sichuan (Szechwan) Province and helped improve the economy there. Zhao's work in Sichuan helped him advance rapidly in the Communist Party and the government. From 1980 to 1989, Zhao was a member of China's most powerful policymaking body—the standing committee of the Communist Party's Politburo. In 1980, he became premier of China. The premier heads the operations of the government. Zhao held that post until he became general secretary in 1987.   Arif Dirlik

Zhou dynasty, *joh,* also spelled *Chou,* was a Chinese *dynasty* (family of rulers) that governed from about 1045 B.C. to 256 B.C. It was China's longest-ruling dynasty.

The dynasty began when the Zhou tribes conquered the ruling Shang dynasty from the west. Zhou rulers set up a society with three classes—aristocrats, commoners, and slaves. The commoners farmed their own land and that of the aristocrats. Zhou rulers divided the kingdom into many states. A local chief headed each state but enforced the central government's rules.

A weak Zhou ruler was overthrown by his enemies in 771 B.C. The dynasty then moved its capital east from Hao (near what is now Xi'an) to Luoyang. The move marked the beginning of the *Eastern Zhou period.* During this period, cities grew, a merchant class developed, and the use of money replaced *barter* (trade). The famous philosophers Confucius and Laozi developed their ideas during this time (see **Confucius; Laozi**).

The Zhou central government gradually lost power to its large states, and the dynasty finally ended in 256 B.C. Seven large states controlled China until 221 B.C., when the Qin dynasty took over.   Eugene Boardman

Zhou Enlai, *joh ehn ly* (1898-1976), also spelled *Chou En-lai,* became premier and foreign minister of China in 1949, when the Communists won control of the country. He was replaced as foreign minister in 1959 but until his death remained China's most influential spokesman in international affairs.

Zhou was born in Jiangsu (Kiangsu) Province. He attended schools in China, Japan, and France, and he became a spokesman for the international Communist movement. In 1931, Zhou joined Mao Zedong, leader of the Chinese Communists. Zhou took part in the *Long March* of 1934 and 1935, when Mao led the Communists 6,000 miles (9,700 kilometers)

Audrey Topping, Rapho Guillumette
Zhou Enlai

across China. Zhou was a leader in the conflict with the Nationalists for control of China in the 1940's. As premier, he became Mao's spokesman in foreign affairs. In 1972, for example, Zhou held meetings with Richard M. Nixon, the first United States president to visit China while in office. Zhou died on Jan. 8, 1976.   Arif Dirlik

Zhuangzi, *jwahng dzuh,* also spelled *Chuang Tzu,* was a Chinese philosopher of the 300's B.C. He ranks with Laozi (Lao Tzu) as the most important figure in the development of the philosophy called Taoism. Zhuangzi probably wrote parts of a book called the *Zhuangzi,* which was named after him. The book's wit and imaginative style make it one of the greatest works of Chinese literature. The *Zhuangzi* also helped shape the branch of Buddhism called Chan (Zen).

The *Zhuangzi* teaches the mystical doctrine that all things come together in an indefinable harmony called the *Tao* (Way). The book urges that people live spontaneously, calmly accepting inevitable changes—even death. One passage asks: "How do I know hating death is not like having strayed from home when a child and not knowing the way back?"   N. Sivin

See **Laozi; Taoism.**

Zhukov, *ZHOO kawf,* **Georgi Konstantinovich,** *gay AWR gih KAWN stahn TEE nah vihch* (1896-1974), became a Soviet military hero during World War II (1939-1945). He organized the defense of Moscow and Leningrad (now St. Petersburg) in 1941 and the Soviet victory at Stalingrad (now Volgograd) in 1942 and 1943. He led the Soviet forces that captured Berlin in 1945. Zhukov became a marshal—the highest rank in the Soviet army—in 1943.

Soviet dictator Joseph Stalin feared Zhukov's popularity after the war and assigned him to minor posts. Stalin died in 1953, and Zhukov rose to the post of defense minister in 1955. Zhukov helped Nikita S. Khrushchev increase his power in the Communist Party in 1957. Khrushchev made Zhukov a member of the Presidium (later called the Politburo), the highest Soviet governing body, but came to fear his influence. Khrushchev removed him from his high positions later that year. Zhukov was born on Dec. 1, 1896, in Strelkovka, near Moscow. He fought in World War I (1914-1918).   Albert Marrin

Ziegfeld, *ZIHG fehld,* **Florenz** (1867-1932), was an American theater producer. He became famous for a series of musical revues, called the *Ziegfeld Follies,* which he presented annually from 1907 to 1927.

The *Ziegfeld Follies* featured a chorus line of beautiful women in lavish costumes performing in extravagant settings. Many Ziegfeld beauties became motion-picture stars, including Marion Davies, Irene Dunne, and Paulette Goddard. Ziegfeld introduced many famous entertainers in the revues, notably Eddie Cantor, Fanny Brice, Will Rogers, W. C. Fields, and Bert Williams. Ziegfeld commissioned such composers as Irving Berlin and Jerome Kern to provide songs for the *Follies.* Ziegfeld also produced numerous musical comedies, such as *Rio Rita* (1927), *Show Boat* (1927), and *Rosalie* (1928). He was born in Chicago on March 21, 1867, and died on July 22, 1932.   Daniel J. Watermeier

Ziggurat. See **Architecture** (Mesopotamian).

Zimbabwe, *zihm BAH bway,* is a landlocked country in southern Africa. Most of the country is a high plateau. Zimbabwe lies in the tropics but has a pleasant climate

Zimbabwe

◼ National park (N.P.)

▬ International boundary
▬ Road
▬ Railroad
⊛ National capital
• Other city or town
+ Elevation above sea level

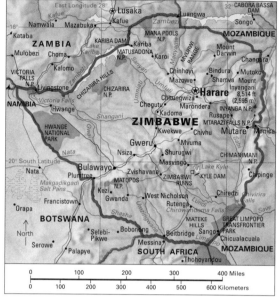

WORLD BOOK maps

because of the high altitude. Zimbabwe's beautiful scenery includes the famous Victoria Falls on the Zambezi River along the country's northern border. Harare is the capital and largest city.

Since the late 1800's, the area that is now the country of Zimbabwe has had a troubled political history. The vast majority of Zimbabwe's people are black Africans, but whites controlled the government and economy from about 1890 to 1979. During the last decade of white

Facts in brief

Capital: Harare.
Official language: English.
Area: 150,872 mi² (390,757 km²). *Greatest distances*—east-west, 515 mi (829 km); north-south, 470 mi (756 km).
Population: *Estimated 2004 population*—13,524,000; density, 90 per mi² (35 per km²); distribution, 68 percent rural, 32 percent urban. *1997 census*—11,789,274.
Chief products: *Agriculture*—cattle, coffee, corn, cotton, sugar, tea, tobacco, wheat. *Manufacturing and processing*—chemicals, clothing and footwear, iron and steel, metal products, processed foods, textiles. *Mining*—asbestos, chromite, coal, copper, gems, gold, nickel.
National anthem: "Ngaikomborerwe Nyika yeZimbabwe" ("Blessed be the Land of Zimbabwe").
Flag: The flag has seven horizontal stripes of green, yellow, red, black, red, yellow, and green. A white triangle on the left contains a yellow Great Zimbabwe bird on a red star. See **Flag** (picture: Flags of Africa).
Money: *Basic unit*—Zimbabwe dollar. One hundred cents equal one dollar.

rule, black nationalists in Zimbabwe—then called Rhodesia—engaged in guerrilla warfare against the government. At the same time, the nation's economy was crippled by international trade *sanctions* (restrictions).

In the face of mounting opposition at home and abroad, white Rhodesians finally agreed to give political power to the blacks. The first black-majority government was elected in 1979. However, many blacks rejected this government because they felt it was unrepresentative and allowed whites to retain many special privileges.

Widespread guerrilla violence continued until late 1979, when the government and the rebels signed a peace treaty. The government agreed to hold new elections in February 1980. The political party of Robert Mugabe, one of the rebel leaders, won a large majority of votes in these elections. Mugabe then became prime minister of the independent republic of Zimbabwe.

Government. An executive president, who heads Zimbabwe's government, is elected by the people to a six-year term. This official appoints two vice presidents and a Cabinet to carry out government operations.

A 150-member House of Assembly is Zimbabwe's parliament. Of the members, 120 are elected by the people, 12 are appointed by the president, 8 are provincial governors, and 10 are traditional chiefs of Zimbabwe. The members of the House serve five-year terms.

People. About 98 percent of Zimbabweans are black Africans. About 1 percent are whites. The rest are Asians and *Coloureds* (people of mixed ancestry). About two-thirds of the blacks live in rural areas. Most of the whites, Asians, and Coloureds live in cities and towns. The largest black ethnic group in Zimbabwe is the Shona (often called the Mashona). The Ndebele (often called the Matabele) is the next largest group. The Shona speak the Chishona language. The Ndebele speak isiNdebele.

Most blacks in Zimbabwe are farmers. Most raise only enough food for their families. Their main crop, corn, is pounded into flour to make a dish called *sadza*.

The white population of Zimbabwe includes farmers and business and professional people. Before the early 2000's, many black people worked on commercial farms owned by white people. In the early 2000's, Zimbabwe's government seized most of the white-owned farms, saying it intended to redistribute the land to black people. Many of the black farm workers became unemployed.

Land. Most of Zimbabwe is a high, rolling plateau from 3,000 to 5,000 feet (910 to 1,500 meters) above sea level. The High Veld, a central plateau, crosses the country from northeast to southwest. The Middle Veld lies on either side of the High Veld. The Low Veld consists of sandy plains in the Zambezi, Limpopo, and Sabi river basins. Mount Inyangani (8,514 feet, or 2,595 meters) is Zimbabwe's highest point.

Zimbabwe's summer lasts from October to April and is hot and wet. The winter, from May to September, is cool and dry. Temperatures in the country range between 54 and 85 °F (12 and 29 °C), and rainfall varies from 15 inches (38 centimeters) a year in the west to 50 inches (130 centimeters) in the east.

Economy. Commercial agriculture is the largest employer in Zimbabwe. The country's chief agricultural exports include beef, coffee, tea, flowers, and tobacco. Zimbabwe also produces large quantities of corn, vegetables, and fruits for domestic use. Zimbabwe is an important producer of asbestos, coal, gold, nickel, and other minerals. Textiles and food processing are among the most important manufacturing industries.

The Kariba Gorge hydroelectric complex on the Zambezi is one of the world's largest. Its dam forms Kariba Lake, which covers 2,000 square miles (5,200 square kilometers). Its power plant supplies electric power to most of Zimbabwe. It is operated by Zimbabwe and Zambia.

History. Ancient paintings and tools made by the San (Bushmen) people have been found in Zimbabwe. These discoveries indicate that people have lived in the region for thousands of years. By the A.D. 800's, people were mining minerals for trade. Shona people began their rule about A.D. 1000. They built a city called Zimbabwe, or Great Zimbabwe. The word *zimbabwe* means *house of stone* in the Shona language. The city's ruins lie near Masvingo. They include a tower 30 feet (9 meters) high and part of a wall 800 feet (240 meters) around. The structures were made of huge granite slabs, most of which were fitted together without mortar.

During the 1400's, a branch of the Shona, called the Karanga, established the Mwanamutapa Empire. This empire included most of what is now Zimbabwe. At eastern African ports, the Karanga traded ivory, gold, and copper for porcelain from China and cloth and beads from India and Indonesia.

The Rozwi, a southern Karanga group, rebelled in the late 1400's and founded the Changamire Empire. This empire became stronger than the Mwanamutapa Empire, and the Rozwi took over the city of Zimbabwe. The Rozwi built the city's largest structures. The Changamire Empire was prosperous and peaceful until Nguni people from the south defeated much of the empire in the 1830's. The city was abandoned after the fall of the Changamire Empire.

Portuguese explorers introduced Christianity to what is now Zimbabwe in the 1500's. But few people accepted Christianity until the late 1800's. In 1888, Lobengula, the Ndebele ruler, signed an agreement that granted mineral rights in the area under his control to the British South Africa Company. This company was controlled by the British financier Cecil Rhodes. By 1893, the British South Africa Company occupied most of the region. In 1895, this company named its territory Rhodesia.

The British South Africa Company crushed black

African uprisings in 1896 and 1897, and reports of gold brought more Europeans to the area. In 1897, the United Kingdom recognized Southern and Northern Rhodesia as separate territories. In 1922, the white settlers of Southern Rhodesia (now Zimbabwe) voted for self-government, and Southern Rhodesia became a self-governing British colony in 1923. In 1953, the United Kingdom set up the Federation of Rhodesia and Nyasaland, which included Southern Rhodesia, Northern Rhodesia (now Zambia), and Nyasaland (now Malawi).

In 1961, the United Kingdom and Southern Rhodesia approved a new constitution. But the leading black African party boycotted the first election, because it felt too few blacks could vote. The government later banned two black parties, the Zimbabwe African People's Union (ZAPU) and the Zimbabwe African National Union. Both demanded a greater part in government for blacks.

The Federation of Rhodesia and Nyasaland was dissolved in 1963. In 1964, Northern Rhodesia became the independent nation of Zambia, and Nyasaland became independent as Malawi. Southern Rhodesia became known as Rhodesia. Its government demanded independence in 1964. The United Kingdom declared that Rhodesia must first guarantee the black majority a greater voice in the government. Rhodesian talks with the United Kingdom finally broke down. On Nov. 11, 1965, Prime Minister Ian Smith declared Rhodesia independent. The United Kingdom called Rhodesia's action illegal and banned all trade with Rhodesia. Rhodesia rejected British proposals for a settlement. In 1966, the United Nations (UN) imposed economic sanctions against Rhodesia. Most countries then stopped or reduced their trade with Rhodesia.

In 1969, Rhodesian voters—mostly whites—approved a new constitution designed to prevent the black African majority from ever gaining control of the government. The Constitution took effect in 1970. Rhodesia declared itself a republic on March 2, 1970. But no country recognized its independent status. Led by the United Nations, many countries continued to apply political and economic pressure to end white rule in Rhodesia.

In 1971, the United Kingdom and Rhodesia reached an agreement that included provisions to gradually increase black representation in the government. But most Rhodesian blacks opposed the pact, and it did not take effect. In the early 1970's, fighting erupted between government troops and black guerrillas in Rhodesia. In 1974, the two sides agreed to a cease-fire.

In 1976, fighting again broke out between Rhodesian government troops and black guerrillas. Mozambique and other black African nations joined in the demand for an end of white rule in Rhodesia. Clashes between Rhodesian government troops and troops of Mozambique broke out near the border between the countries.

In the late 1970's, Rhodesia's white rulers, led by Prime Minister Smith, began making plans to establish a new government with a majority of black leaders. In 1978, the whites reached an agreement with conservative black leaders to form a government. Voting procedures were changed to allow all people 18 years old or over to vote. Previously, strict economic and educational requirements had prevented most blacks from voting. Elections in April 1979 resulted in a government with a majority of black leaders. Abel T. Muzorewa, a Method-

Cameramann International, Ltd. from Marilyn Gartman

Harare is the capital and largest city of Zimbabwe. Modern high-rise hotels and office buildings line the wide streets in Harare's downtown area.

ist bishop, became the first black prime minister. But many blacks rejected the new government as unrepresentative, and no other country officially recognized it.

Widespread fighting between black guerrillas and the government went on until September 1979, when the United Kingdom arranged a peace deal. Both sides finally agreed to the formation of a new government. In elections in February 1980, the Zimbabwe African National Union-Patriotic Front (ZANU-PF) party won a majority of the seats in the House of Assembly. Robert Mugabe, the party's leader, became prime minister. On April 18, 1980, the British recognized the country's independence, and Rhodesia's name was officially changed to Zimbabwe. Most countries and the United Nations soon recognized the new government and lifted the remaining trade sanctions against the nation. After the blacks gained control of the government, many whites left the country.

In 1981, fighting broke out between the national army and guerrilla forces formerly aligned with ZAPU. In 1982, Mugabe dismissed ZAPU leader Joshua Nkomo from his Cabinet. Clashes between the guerrillas and the army continued until 1984. Mugabe's party won the 1985 national elections. In 1987, the office of prime minister was abolished and replaced with the office of executive president. Parliament elected Mugabe to the new office. In 1989, Mugabe's ZANU-PF and Nkomo's ZAPU formally merged under the name ZANU-PF. In 1990 and 1996, the voters reelected Mugabe president.

In 2000, supporters of Mugabe began squatting on hundreds of white-owned farms. Many of them were veterans of Zimbabwe's war of independence. They attacked the landowners, forcing many to flee. The struggles over land, along with drought conditions, led to a drop in farm production and, in turn, widespread food shortages. Mugabe remained president after winning a disputed election in 2002. Later that year, his government ordered about 3,000 white farmers to leave their land. The government then seized the white-owned farms for redistribution to black people.　　　John D. Metzler

Related articles in *World Book* include:

Bulawayo	Mugabe, Robert G.	Victoria Falls
Harare	Rhodes, Cecil J.	Zambezi River

Zinc, a chemical element, is a shiny, bluish-white metal. It is important in industry. Zinc can be worked into almost any shape using conventional metalworking methods. Such metals as iron and steel can be *galvanized*—that is, coated with zinc—to prevent rusting. Galvanized

Leading zinc-mining countries

Tons of zinc produced in a year

China
1,764,000 tons (1,600,000 metric tons)

Australia
1,674,000 tons (1,519,000 metric tons)

Peru
1,165,000 tons (1,057,000 metric tons)

Canada
1,113,000 tons (1,010,000 metric tons)

United States
928,000 tons (842,000 metric tons)

Figures are for 2001.
Source: U.S. Geological Survey.

metal is used to make roof gutters and tank linings. Zinc is also used in electric batteries. Plants and animals require zinc for normal growth and healing. Zinc is also a component of the hormone insulin.

Zinc can be combined with other metals to form many *alloys* (mixtures). For example, brass is an alloy of copper and zinc. Bronze is copper, tin, and zinc. Nickel silver is copper, nickel, and zinc. Zinc is also used in *solders* (easily melted alloys used for joining metals). Zinc and its alloys are used in *die-casting* (forming objects from liquid metal in molds), *electroplating* (coating an object by using an electric current), and *powder metallurgy* (forming objects from metal powder). Since 1982, United States pennies have been made from a predominantly zinc alloy coated with a layer of copper.

Moist air *tarnishes* (discolors) zinc with a protective coating of zinc oxide. Once a thin layer of this coating forms, air cannot tarnish the zinc below it. White, powdery zinc oxide is used in making cosmetics, plastics, rubber, skin ointments, and soaps. It is also used as a pigment in paints and inks. Zinc sulfide, a compound of zinc and sulfur, glows when ultraviolet light, X rays, or *cathode rays* (streams of electrons) shine on it. It is used on luminous dials for clocks and to coat the inside of television screens and fluorescent lamps. When mixed with water, zinc chloride, a compound of zinc and chlorine, protects wood from decay and insects.

Pure zinc is never found in nature. It occurs combined with sulfur in a mineral called *sphalerite* or *zinc blende*. Other zinc-containing minerals are *calamine, franklinite, smithsonite, willemite,* and *zincite.* Zinc is hard and brittle at room temperature. It is taken from its ores by heating them in air to convert them to zinc oxide. The oxide is heated with carbon to produce zinc.

Zinc's chemical symbol is Zn. Its *atomic number* (number of protons in its nucleus) is 30. Its *relative atomic mass* is 65.39. An element's relative atomic mass equals its *mass* (amount of matter) divided by $\frac{1}{12}$ of the mass of carbon 12, the most abundant form of carbon. Zinc melts at 419.58 °C and boils at 907 °C. Alloys containing large amounts of zinc have been found in prehistoric ruins. In the 100's B.C., the Romans made brass coins from ores containing zinc and copper. The first complete study of zinc was published in 1746 by Andreas Sigismund Marggraf, a German chemist.　　　Raymond E. Davis

See also **Alloy; Galvanizing; Sphalerite.**

Zinjanthropus is the old name for a humanlike creature that lived about 1,750,000 years ago in Africa. In 1967, *Zinjanthropus* was renamed *Australopithecus boisei.* See **Australopithecus; Leakey, Mary Douglas.**

Zinnemann, *ZIHN uh muhn,* **Fred** (1907-1997), was a motion-picture director whose films are noted for their skillful character portrayal. He won Academy Awards for *From Here to Eternity* (1953) and *A Man for All Seasons* (1966). His other major films include *The Seventh Cross* (1944), *The Search* (1947), *The Men* (1950), *High Noon* (1952), *The Nun's Story* (1958), *The Sundowners* (1960), and *Julia* (1977). His central characters often come into conflict with their communities because of the characters' determination to follow their own consciences. His short films *That Mothers Might Live* (1938) and *Benjy* (1950) won Academy Awards.

Zinnemann was born on April 23, 1907, in Vienna, Austria. He learned film techniques while working in

Paris. He moved to Hollywood in 1929. *A Life in the Movies* (1992) is his autobiography.   Gene D. Phillips

Zinnia, *ZIHN ee uh,* is the name of a group of flowering plants, some of which are commonly grown in gardens. There are about 25 species. Zinnias are native to the southwestern United States, Central America, and South America. They are also cultivated in Europe.

Mexican zinnia

Narrow-leafed zinnia

WORLD BOOK illustrations by Lorraine Epstein

Zinnias are popular garden flowers.

Zinnias grow from about 4 inches (10 centimeters) to over 3 feet (90 centimeters) tall. Zinnia blossoms consist of many small flowers of two types—small, tube-shaped *disk flowers* of varying colors grouped in the center and petallike *ray flowers* around the edge. The ray flowers can be white, pink, red, orange, yellow, and even green.

Some zinnias are *annuals* and live for one year. Others are *perennials* and bloom more than once. Zinnias grow best in a warm, sunny climate and deep, sandy soil. The seeds should be planted in early spring after the danger of frost has passed. The seeds can also be planted inside in late winter and transplanted outside in spring. Zinnias flower in midsummer to late summer.   David J. Keil

Scientific classification. Zinnias make up the genus *Zinnia* in the composite family, Asteraceae or Compositae. The three species most commonly cultivated are the common zinnia, *Z. elegans;* the Mexican zinnia, *Z. haageana;* and the narrow-leafed zinnia, *Z. angustifolia.*

See also **Flower** (picture: Garden annuals).

Zion, *ZY uhn,* is a word with many different meanings. It comes from the Hebrew word *Tsiyōn.* Originally, it was the name of a hill in the city of Jerusalem. After the Israelites captured the city from the Jebusites, Zion became the place where the royal palace of King David stood and where Solomon later built the Temple. It was the seat of Jewish worship and government. The name Zion also refers to the Israelites themselves. After their exile from the Holy Land, the word Zion meant to them their homeland, with Jerusalem, the Temple, and all Palestine's ancient glory. Among Christians, the name Zion means the church ruled by God, or a heavenly city or heavenly home. See also **Zionism.**   Gary G. Porton

Zion National Park lies in southwestern Utah. It has many colorful canyons, some of which are extremely narrow and have steep, plunging walls. Rock formations range in color from dark red and orange to light purple and pink. These colors change continuously as the light changes. Wild plants and such animals as mule deer and bats flourish there. Zion Canyon is the main feature of the park. It is about 10 miles (16 kilometers) long and

from $\frac{1}{2}$ mile (0.8 kilometer) to less than 50 feet (15 meters) wide. Its walls tower as high as 3,000 feet (910 meters), in some places almost straight up and down. The canyon contains many unusual rock formations.

The park was set aside in 1909 as Mukuntuweap National Monument. In 1918, the park was enlarged and in 1919 it became Zion National Park. Zion National Monument, a vast area of rugged land adjoining the park, was added in 1956. For the park's area, see **National Park System** (table: National parks). For location, see **Utah** (political map).   Critically reviewed by the National Park Service

Zionism is a movement to establish a Jewish national state in Palestine, the ancient Jewish homeland. Active Zionism began in the late 1800's and led to the establishment of Israel in 1948. Zionists revived the Jewish national language and culture and set up the political and social institutions needed to re-create national Jewish life. Zionism supports various projects in Israel and acts as a cultural bridge between Israel and Jews in other countries. *Zion* is the poetic Hebrew name for Palestine.

Movement to Palestine. Anti-Semitism in Europe in the late 1800's and early 1900's spurred the creation of the Zionist movement. Responding to the *pogroms* (riots against the Jews) in Russia, groups of Jewish youths calling themselves *Hoveve-Zion* (Lovers of Zion) formed a movement in 1882 to promote immigration to Palestine. They started what was called *practical Zionism,* which established Jewish settlements in Palestine. Theodor Herzl, an Austrian journalist, developed *political Zionism,* which worked for political recognition of the Jewish claim to a Palestine homeland.

Herzl was a reporter at the famous trial in 1894 of Alfred Dreyfus, a French army officer falsely convicted of treason. The Dreyfus affair convinced Herzl that if anti-Semitism could be an active force in a country as enlightened as France, Jews could not assimilate in non-Jewish society. To him, the only remedy was to create an independent Jewish state.

Herzl organized the Zionist movement on a worldwide scale at the First Zionist Congress in Basel, Switzerland, in 1897. In the early 1900's, however, many Jews, including the extremely religious and those who sought full assimilation, opposed the new movement.

The Balfour Declaration. In 1917, the United Kingdom issued the Balfour Declaration, which pledged British support for the establishment of a Jewish homeland in Palestine. About the same time, the United Kingdom freed Palestine from Ottoman control. The Balfour Declaration was included in the *mandate* (order to rule) over Palestine that the League of Nations awarded the United Kingdom in 1920. The mandate gave the Jewish Agency the responsibility for Jewish immigration. The Jewish community in Palestine grew significantly in the 1920's and 1930's. It developed various economic, political, and cultural institutions.

Arabs opposed a Jewish state in Palestine, and severe fighting broke out several times in the 1920's and 1930's. Assuming from earlier British promises to them that Palestine would be an Arab state, Arab leaders demanded an end to Jewish immigration and land purchase.

In 1939, the British began to set limits on Jewish immigration to Palestine. Palestine's Jews fought against the restrictions, which they felt kept many Jews from fleeing increasing persecution in Europe.

After World War II ended in 1945, the Zionists wanted to establish a Jewish state immediately to provide a homeland for survivors of the *Holocaust.* The Holocaust was the mass murder of European Jews and others by the Nazis. But Arabs continued to oppose the creation of a Jewish state in Palestine. In 1947, the United Kingdom submitted the problem to the United Nations (UN). The UN voted to partition Palestine into an Arab and a Jewish state. In 1948, the Zionists proclaimed the state of Israel. For information on the history of Israel, see **Israel** (History).
                    Marsha Rozenblit

Related articles in *World Book* include:

Arab-Israeli conflict	Israel
Balfour Declaration	Jews (The Zionist movement)
Hebrew literature	Palestine
Herzl, Theodor	Weizmann, Chaim

Additional resources

Medoff, Rafael, and Waxman, C. I. *Historical Dictionary of Zionism.* Scarecrow, 2000.
Wigoder, Geoffrey, ed. *New Encyclopedia of Zionism and Israel.* 2 vols. Fairleigh Dickinson, 1994.

ZIP Code is a code system used to speed the sorting and delivery of mail in the United States. The name stands for *Zone Improvement Plan.*

The ZIP system uses five numerals that appear after an address. In the ZIP number 22207, for example, the first numeral—2—designates one of 10 geographic areas. Area 2 consists of the District of Columbia, Maryland, North Carolina, South Carolina, Virginia, and West Virginia. The second two numerals—22—indicate a metropolitan area or sectional center. In this case, the mail is going to the Arlington area of Virginia. The last two numerals—07—represent a small town or delivery unit from which the mail will be delivered. In 1983, the Postal Service introduced a voluntary nine-number ZIP Code. High-volume business mailers that use this code receive a discount on their mailing rate.

The Post Office Department (now the United States Postal Service) introduced the ZIP Code in 1963. At that time, mail volume in the United States had increased almost 900 percent since 1900. The mail had also become more widely used for business correspondence.

In 1963, the Post Office Department introduced two-letter abbreviations for states and some other areas. These abbreviations enable companies using mechanized addressing systems to save space by putting a ZIP Code on the same line of an address as the city and state. For the two-letter state abbreviations, see **Postal Service, United States** (table).

The ZIP Code especially speeds up the handling and delivery of *bulk mail* (a huge number of identical pieces). Several other nations also use code systems.
                    Critically reviewed by the United States Postal Service

Zipper is a term often used to mean any kind of slide fastener. Most zippers have two rows of metal or plastic teeth that interlock. Each tooth has a raised dome on top and a hollow on the bottom. A slide draws the teeth together and meshes the domes into the hollows. The teeth can only be locked or unlocked in sequence. They remain locked until the slide is drawn back. Some zippers have plastic spirals instead of rows of teeth.

In 1893, Whitcomb L. Judson of Chicago patented an early form of the slide fastener, which used hooks and eyes. In 1917, Gideon Sundback obtained a patent on a

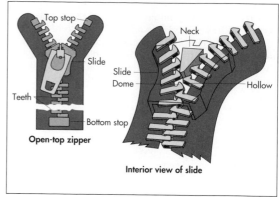

WORLD BOOK illustrations by Bensen Studios

A meshed-tooth zipper has two rows of teeth that are joined or separated by a *slide.* When the slide is pulled up, its curved sides push the teeth together so that the dome of one tooth locks into the hollow of the opposite tooth. Pulling the slide down unlocks the teeth by forcing a V-shaped wedge called a *neck* between the teeth. The teeth may be metal or plastic. They are designed to lock and unlock only in sequence.

new type of hookless slide fastener, which used meshed teeth like modern zippers. These zippers were mostly used in small personal items, such as tobacco pouches and gloves, and in flying suits for the United States Navy during World War I (1914-1918). In 1923, the B. F. Goodrich Company gave the trade name *Zipper* to rubber boots with slide fasteners. Zippers became common in everyday clothing during the 1930's.   Valerie Steele

Zircon, *ZUR kahn,* is a mineral composed chiefly of the elements silicon, oxygen, and zirconium. It is a *silicate* and has the chemical formula $ZrSiO_4$ (see **Silicate**). Zircon contains smaller amounts of other elements, including hafnium, iron, and the rare earths. Some zircons also contain the radioactive elements thorium and uranium. Zircon crystals may be reddish-brown, yellow, green, blue, or colorless. They resemble prisms with pyramid-shaped ends. The crystals occur in alkali basalts, granites, and other *igneous rocks* (see **Igneous rock**). Zircon is resistant to weathering, so it is also found in gravel and sand produced by the erosion of igneous rock.

Zircon is the world's main source of zirconium and hafnium. These metals are used in the ceramics industry and in making parts for nuclear reactors. Large zircon crystals are used for jewelry (see **Gem** [picture]). Zircon is a December birthstone.   Robert W. Charles

Zirconium, *zur KOH nee uhm,* is a grayish-white metal. It is found in nature as the silicate mineral *zircon* and the oxide mineral *baddeleyite.*

Zirconium is used to make the cores of nuclear reactors because it resists corrosion and does not readily absorb neutrons. *Zircaloy* is an important alloy developed for such nuclear applications as a coating for fuel parts. Baddeleyite can withstand extremely high temperatures. It is used for laboratory *crucibles* (melting pots for metals) and the linings for furnaces.

Zirconium's chemical symbol is Zr. Its *atomic number* (number of protons in its nucleus) is 40. Its *relative atomic mass* is 91.224. An element's relative atomic mass is its *mass* (amount of matter) divided by the mass of carbon 12, the most abundant form of carbon. Zirconium melts at 1857 °C and boils at 4200 °C. At 25 °C, its density is 6.51 grams per cubic centimeter (see **Density**). Martin Heinrich Klaproth, a German chemist, isolated the oxide of zirconium from zircon in 1789. Metallic zirconium was first prepared in 1824 by Jöns J. Berzelius, a Swedish chemist. *S. C. Cummings*

Zither is a stringed musical instrument commonly found in Austria and southern Germany. It consists chiefly of a flat, wooden box with 30 or more strings stretched along its length. The zither is placed on a table when played. The five strings nearest the musician provide the melody. The other strings are used for accompaniment. The player strums the melody strings with a ring-shaped *plectrum* (pick) worn on the thumb of the right hand. The second, third, and fourth fingers on that hand pluck chords. The left hand presses the melody strings against a fingerboard with *frets* (ridges) to select the pitch. *André P. Larson*

Roland Klotz

The zither

Zodiac, *ZOH dee ak,* is a band-shaped section of the sky that contains 12 special constellations. It extends about 9 degrees on either side of the *ecliptic,* the yearly path the sun seems to follow in relation to other stars.

The zodiac in astrology. The zodiac has special meaning to people who follow *astrology,* the belief that the stars and other heavenly bodies influence people's lives. Astrologers divide the zodiac into 12 equal parts called *signs,* named after the zodiac's 12 constellations.

The 12 signs—and the 12 constellations—are Aries, Taurus, Gemini, Cancer, Leo, Virgo, Libra, Scorpio, Sagittarius, Capricorn, Aquarius, and Pisces.

Astrologers believe that each person comes under the special influence of a particular zodiac sign, depending on the person's birth date. For example, anyone born from March 21 to April 19 has Aries as his or her sign and is called "an Aries." Astrologers think that people born under each sign have certain characteristics. An Aries, for example, is supposed to be bold, energetic, and strong-willed. But scientists and many other people consider astrology to be no more than a superstition.

The origin of the zodiac. Prehistoric people probably noticed that the seasons changed every year when certain groups of stars reached certain positions in the night sky. These early people may have invented the constellations by giving the groups names that could be represented by human, animal, or other figures. The outlines of the figures, drawn over maps of the night sky, would have helped the people identify and remember the groups. The word *zodiac* comes from an ancient Greek word meaning *circle of animals.*

Over thousands of years, the constellations have changed their positions in the sky with respect to the *celestial equator,* an extension of the earth's equator into space. For this reason, people have identified different constellations at different times. According to some historians, the constellations of the zodiac were named in three stages. Gemini, Virgo, Sagittarius, and Pisces were named during the 5000's B.C., when these constellations appeared at the ecliptic in spring, summer, autumn, and winter, respectively. The first farmers in the Middle East may have looked for those four constellations as markers for the change of seasons.

By the 2000's B.C., the ancient Egyptians and Mesopotamians had probably identified the constellations Taurus, Leo, Scorpio, and Aquarius as seasonal markers. Aries, Cancer, Libra, and Capricorn may have

The signs of the zodiac Astrologers believe that everyone is influenced by a particular sign, depending on his or her birthday. The chart below shows the dates and some characteristics associated with each sign.

WORLD BOOK diagram by Dick Keller

been added in the 1000's B.C. The earliest known horoscope to mention all 12 signs of the zodiac dates from about the 400's B.C.

The Eastern zodiac, also called the Chinese zodiac, is a set of symbols used since ancient times in China, Japan, Korea, and some other Asian countries. The Eastern zodiac does not involve constellations and has no historical connection with the Western zodiac. Both zodiacs, however, consist of 12 symbols. And in both, according to popular belief, the symbol a person is born under influences the person's character and fate.

The 12 symbols of the Eastern zodiac are animals. The zodiac matches the animals to years that repeat in a 12-year cycle. The years 1984 and 1996, for example, were years of the rat. The 12 animals, in chronological order, are the rat, ox, tiger, rabbit (or hare), dragon, snake, horse, sheep, monkey, rooster (or cock), dog, and pig (or boar).   Alexander A. Gurshtein

See also **Astrology; Birthstone; Constellation; Horoscope; House** (in astrology); and the articles on each sign of the zodiac, such as **Aries.**

Zodiacal light, *zoh DY uh kuhl,* is a cone-shaped glow of faint light that is seen soon after twilight and just before dawn. The zodiacal light is brightest near the sun and shades off gradually. It can easily be traced halfway across the sky. It brightens again in an area just opposite the sun called the *Gegenschein,* which means *counterglow.* The zodiacal light is so named because it is seen against the zodiacal constellations that lie along the *ecliptic,* the sun's apparent path through the sky in relation to other stars. The accepted explanation of the light is that large numbers of small particles of material scattered about the inner solar system reflect sunlight and become visible when the sky is dark. These dust particles are believed to be debris from comets and asteroids.   Lee J. Rickard

Zola, *ZOH luh,* **Émile,** *ay MEEL* (1840-1902), made Naturalism the leading form of literature in France in the late 1800's. He described life as he saw it, and his books and his life demonstrate his courage, intelligence, and sense of justice. Zola's open letter *J'accuse* (1898) helped win a new trial for Alfred Dreyfus, a French army officer unjustly convicted of spying. Zola was convicted of libel after publication of the letter. He fled to England for a year, but he later became a national hero for his part in the affair. Zola also tried to win acceptance for artist Édouard Manet and other Impressionist painters who broke with artistic tradition.

Zola was born on April 2, 1840, in Paris. He began his career as a journalist and novelist in the 1860's. His first novel of merit was *Thérèse Raquin* (1867). After the Franco-Prussian War of 1870, he started working on a long series of novels, *The Rougon-Macquart.* Zola subtitled the series the "natural and social history of a family in the Second Empire." Each of the 20 novels in the series describes the adventures of one or several members of the Rougon-Macquart family, and each treats a different profession, trade, or class of society.

The Belly of Paris (1873), the third volume in the series, gives a vivid picture of the central markets of Paris. *The Grog Shop* (1877) is a terrifying portrait of the effects of alcoholism on industrial workers in Paris. *Nana* (1880), a study of prostitution and other vice, caused a scandal when it was published. *Germinal* (1885) is probably

Zola's best novel and perhaps the finest novel ever written on the life of miners. *The Crash* (1892) describes France's defeat by Germany in 1870.

Zola wrote a second series, *The Three Cities,* dealing with religious and social problems. A third series, *The Four Gospels,* was still unfinished at his death.

In his fiction, Zola tried to practice the scientific method. He argued that the novels of *The Rougon-Macquart* showed the effects of heredity and environment on society. However, the scientific basis of Zola's work is weak. But he used the documentary style skillfully and his novels are still valid portraits of various aspects of French life from 1860 to 1890.

Each of Zola's major novels is dominated by a symbol, such as the mine in *Germinal.* His style is somewhat heavy, but he excelled in writing descriptions, especially of crowds. Zola's characters often lack complexity, but they perform vividly in dramas of death and destruction.

Zola wrote several works of criticism defending the Naturalist movement. These include *The Experimental Novel* (1880), *The Naturalistic Novelists* (1881), and *Naturalism in the Theater* (1881).   Thomas H. Goetz

See also **Naturalism; Dreyfus affair.**

Zone Improvement Plan (ZIP). See ZIP Code.

Zone melting is a method of removing impurities from solid materials that are used in industry and in research. Germanium metal was the first material to be refined commercially using this procedure. Germanium can be purified by zone melting until it contains only 1 atom of an impurity in every 10 billion atoms. If a boxcar of sugar were this pure, it would contain only one grain of impurity. Extremely pure germanium and other substances are used in making semiconductor electronic devices, such as transistors and integrated circuits.

The apparatus used for zone melting consists of a row of ring-shaped heaters that move slowly along a tube containing the solid to be purified. Each heater melts a narrow band of the material, forming a liquid "zone" that moves along with the heater. After each heater passes, the liquid cools and freezes. The impurities tend to stay in the liquid zone and are carried to one end of the tube. The material melts again when the next heater passes, and it becomes purer with each melting and freezing.   David C. Armbruster

Zoning is a procedure that controls the use of land. Local legislative bodies pass laws that divide a town, city, or county into zones for commercial, industrial, residential, or other types of development. These laws generally limit building and lot dimensions in each zone. Many regulations require certain building features and limit the number and location of parking and loading areas and the use of signs. Other regulations provide space for schools, parks, or other public facilities.

Zoning helps city planners bring about orderly growth and change. It controls population density and helps create attractive, healthful residential areas. It also helps assure property owners and residents that the characteristics of nearby areas will remain stable.

People have regulated land use since ancient times. Zoning became increasingly important as population and industry grew in urban areas. In 1916, New York City enacted the first major zoning ordinance in the United States. Today, many cities around the world have zoning regulations.   Jack Meltzer

Ron Garrison, Zoological Society of San Diego

A zoo gives people a chance to see many kinds of animals they might never see otherwise. Many zoos keep their animals in spacious outdoor and indoor exhibits, and offer visitors guided tours. At the San Diego Zoo, *shown here,* zoogoers can tour the zoo in special double-decker buses.

Zoo

Zoo is a place where people keep and display animals. Visiting zoos is a popular recreational and educational activity throughout the world. Almost every large city has at least one zoo, and many smaller communities also have one. Many zoos have beautiful gardens and tree-lined paths leading from one animal display to another. The word *zoo* is short for *zoological garden.*

Zoos vary in the type of animals they keep. Many large zoos keep mammals, birds, reptiles, and fish from all over the world. Some even have collections of interesting insects. Smaller zoos may have animals from just one part of the world, or just one type of animal. Zoos that have only fish and aquatic mammals, which live in water, are called aquariums. Some zoos display only animals from the region where the zoo is located.

Jack Hanna, the contributor of this article, is the Director of the Columbus Zoological Gardens in Ohio and the author of several children's books about animals and zoos. He frequently appears on television shows to increase public awareness of wildlife and conservation.

Zoos range in size from hundreds of acres or hectares to only a few. But size alone does not determine the quality or importance of a zoo. The best zoos are those that have healthy, well-tended animals and displays that help visitors learn about each animal's natural behavior and its role in the environment.

Modern zoos have become refuges for some *species* (types) of animals that are in danger of *extinction* (dying out) in the wild. Many human activities threaten the survival of wild species, especially the destruction of *habitats* (natural environments). Most animals are specially suited to live in a certain environment and cannot survive when their habitat is destroyed. Zoos are becoming increasingly active in the struggle to save the world's vanishing wildlife.

The importance of zoos

Zoos are important centers for (1) recreation and education, (2) wildlife conservation, and (3) scientific studies.

Recreation and education. People of all ages enjoy viewing animals they would probably never see other-

Michael Nichols, Magnum

At a children's zoo, youngsters can touch and sometimes even feed a variety of animals. In this picture, two girls pet a reptile in the children's zoo at the Audubon Park Zoo in New Orleans.

wise. In the United States and Canada, zoos attract millions of visitors every year. Zoos also help people understand how animals live. In addition, zoos teach people about the problems facing wildlife and about conservation.

In many zoos, trained workers give visitors brief talks and provide guided tours. Many zoos have education departments that conduct lectures, classes, and group programs for children and adults. Some zoos offer summer day camps and junior zookeeper programs that give youngsters opportunities to help care for the animals. In addition, zoos publish magazines, pamphlets, and other materials that describe their activities. Some zoos even produce television programs.

Wildlife conservation has become one of the most important jobs of zoos. Zoos breed many endangered species to increase their numbers. Such captive breeding in zoos has helped save several species from extinction, including the European bison; the *nene,* also known as the Hawaiian goose; and the Arabian *oryx,* a type of antelope.

Zoos throughout the world trade and lend animals to one another to avoid *inbreeding* (breeding animals that are closely related to each other). Inbreeding can produce birth defects and can eventually weaken an entire population. A number of zoo associations share breeding information through the International Species Information System (ISIS), a computerized inventory of hundreds of thousands of animals cared for by zoos throughout the world. ISIS also maintains records on the ancestors of the animals to more accurately track the genetic background of the living animals.

The American Zoo and Aquarium Association sponsors the Species Survival Plan (SSP), a long-term plan to save some of the most seriously endangered species. Many major zoos in the United States and other countries participate in the SSP. There are dozens of SSP programs, each focusing on a different species or group of species. Participating zoos keep careful records of each animal's family lines and physical characteristics. Zoos use this information to determine which males and females to breed together. The goal is to develop healthy

populations of animals that can someday be returned to the wild.

Zoos also participate in conservation projects outside their walls. For example, many zoos sponsor efforts to preserve the natural habitats of threatened species, such as the Asian bamboo forests of the giant panda and the South American tropical rain forests of the *lion tamarin,* a species of small monkey.

Scientific studies. Zoos provide scientists with living laboratories in which to study animals. By treating diseased animals and by studying animals that have died, zoo veterinarians and other scientists have developed and improved medical equipment, drugs, and surgical techniques for animals.

Scientists called *zoologists* study animals in zoos, as well as in the wild, to learn about animal behavior, such as hunting, eating, breeding, and caring for the young. Such research helps zoos know how to better care for their animals and how to make their exhibits as natural as possible. This knowledge is especially important for breeding because many animals will only reproduce if they are healthy and living in natural surroundings.

Scientific progress in breeding techniques has greatly reduced the need to move animals from zoo to zoo for mating. Researchers can freeze the sperm and embryos of various species. The frozen material can be shipped to another zoo for use in *artificial insemination,*

WORLD BOOK photo

Tigers and deer at the Milwaukee County Zoo live in areas that are side by side. A deep moat, which visitors cannot see, prevents the tigers from attacking the deer.

embryo transfer, and other breeding techniques (see
Breeding [Animal breeding]).

Displaying animals

In the past, zoos kept their animals in rows of mostly
bare cages made of concrete and steel bars. Often, the
cages were arranged in no particular order.

Today, animal displays are far different. Zoos have replaced most old-fashioned cages with natural-looking
enclosures that give animals greater liberty to lead normal lives. Both the layout of the zoo and the design of
the exhibits teach visitors about animals.

Layout of a zoo. Many zoos group their animals
mostly by type. For example, lions, tigers, and other
large cats may be kept in the same building or in nearby
outdoor exhibits. Animals from similar climates, such as
warm tropical areas or chilly polar regions, are often
housed together. Zoos also group animals by the continent where they naturally live, such as Africa or Asia.

Another grouping method is by the animals' natural
habitat, such as the East African *savanna* (grassland with
scattered trees) or the Australian desert. In habitat
groupings, many animals appear to be living together.
However, animals that would attack each other are kept
apart by empty *moats* (deep, wide pits) or by hidden
fences.

Many zoos contain a *children's zoo,* where boys and
girls can pet and even feed tame animals. Some children's zoos give city youngsters an opportunity to see
farm animals. Many children's zoos feature baby animals.

Exhibits. Most modern exhibits, both indoors and
outdoors, are *naturalistic*—that is, they resemble the animal's natural habitat. Such exhibits contain rock formations, pools, grass, trees, shrubs, and places for the
animals to take shelter or hide. Heating coils may be
concealed in artificial rocks or trees to attract the animals to locations where they can be seen by visitors.

Many animals become bored if they have nothing to
do. To combat boredom, exhibits may provide climbing
structures and toys that encourage active behavior. Giant ice cubes keep polar bears occupied. Rhinoceroses
and elephants seem to enjoy rolling in shallow pools of
mud. In addition, keepers often hide meals in shrubs,
trees, and other places so that the animals must search
for the food just as they would in the wild. A stimulating
environment is especially important to apes, elephants,
and other intelligent species. In some zoos, chimpanzees may keep busy for hours probing artificial ter-
mite mounds filled with honey, cereal, or other treats.

Barriers. Zoos use a variety of barriers to keep animals in their exhibits. One widely used naturalistic barrier is a moat surrounding the display area. Moats enable
zoos to safely keep bears, lions, tigers, and other large
animals in spacious outdoor settings.

Zoos also use barriers that are almost invisible, such
as glass or a net of thin wire. Through underwater viewing windows, visitors can watch such animals as polar
bears and hippopotamuses swimming or observe beavers building a dam. A zoo may cover a huge bird shelter, complete with trees and plants, with a wire net.

Controlled environments. Indoor exhibits enable zoos
to reproduce the environmental conditions that some
animals need to stay healthy. For example, penguins

Interesting facts about zoo animals

A polar bear's coat sometimes looks green instead of white.
Each hair of a polar bear's coat is hollow. The air in the middle of
each hair helps keep the bear warm. Sometimes, green *algae*
(simple plantlike organisms) grow in the hollows and the green
color shows through.

A giraffe's tongue is up to
21 inches (53 centimeters)
long. A giraffe uses its tongue
to reach high into trees for
leaves and tender branches.
The outer part of the tongue is
purplish-blue. The dark pigment may help protect the
tongue from sunburn.

The fierce-looking gorilla
is actually a gentle, peaceful
animal. A gorilla will not hurt
a human being unless the gorilla or its family is threatened
or attacked. The animal's fero-
cious "King-Kong" reputation
is just a movie myth.

WORLD BOOK illustration by Colin Newman,
Bernard Thornton Artists

An elephant uses its trunk as a human being uses hands
and arms. An elephant's trunk has about 40,000 muscles. It is
strong enough to lift a 600-pound (270-kilogram) log. Yet the tip
of the trunk has enough flexibility to grasp a single peanut.

Snakes in zoos sometimes eat only once a month. Their
meals last a long time because snakes, which are cold-blooded,
do not use much food energy to maintain a steady body temperature. The bodies of cold-
blooded animals are warm
when their surroundings are
warm, and cool when their
surroundings are cool. Also,
snakes use little energy because they stay inactive for
long periods and live off their
body fat.

**Flamingos need a special
diet** to maintain the bright
pink and red colors of their
feathers. In zoos, these birds
may receive reddish foods
such as shrimp and some-
times even liquid red dye.

When a dolphin dives, its
lungs collapse and its heart
beats slower. These actions allow the animal's body to adjust to the increasing pressure
of the water as the dolphin dives deeper.

WORLD BOOK illustration by Colin Newman,
Bernard Thornton Artists

from the Antarctic need cold air. Other creatures may
require moist air, dry air, or regular rain showers.

One special indoor exhibit is for *nocturnal* animals,
which are active at night. Zoos display such nocturnal
animals as owls, bats, and raccoons under a blue light
or other dim light, which seems like darkness to the animals. But visitors can clearly see the animals going
about their normal nighttime activities. At night, a bright
light causes the animals to sleep as if it were day.

With modern technology, a number of zoos have created vast enclosures that imitate scorching deserts,
frigid polar regions, and other natural habitats. Such exhibits house a variety of mammals, fish, birds, reptiles,

An underwater viewing window enables zoogoers to observe the activities and graceful movements of fish and aquatic mammals beneath the water. At the left, a woman meets a nurse shark close up in a viewing tunnel at the Sydney Aquarium in Australia.

Sydney Aquarium

and insects that would naturally live in the environment. A number of zoos, for example, have large indoor exhibits that reproduce steamy tropical rain forests. These exhibits house trees, cliffs, and waterfalls in structures several stories tall. Machines produce a foglike mist. Elevated walkways allow zoogoers to stroll among the treetops and view several types of primates, birds, and other animals that live in the trees.

Cageless zoos. Drive-through zoos keep their animals in outdoor settings without cages, though predators and prey are kept apart. Visitors view the animals while riding through the zoo in their automobile or aboard a bus or a train.

Wild-animal parks resemble drive-through zoos because the animals are not caged. But these parks are larger than most drive-through zoos and are more interested in breeding animals, especially endangered species, than in exhibiting them. Such parks provide the natural surroundings many animals need to mate successfully and raise offspring. The San Diego Wild Animal Park, the first such establishment in the United States, opened in 1972. In this enormous zoo, which covers about 2,200 acres (900 hectares), groups of rhinoceroses, giraffes, deer, antelope, zebras, and many other species roam over large areas under the close watch of zoo workers. Visitors ride a special train that travels through the park. The train's route skirts the areas where animals live, thus disturbing the herds as little as possible.

Caring for zoo animals

Zoo animals receive daily care, special diets, and regular medical attention.

Daily care. Trained workers called *keepers* take care of the animals' daily needs. In large zoos, each keeper usually looks after just one type of animal. The keepers clean the animals' enclosures. They feed the animals and watch for changes in behavior, eating habits, and overall appearance that may be signs that an animal is sick or injured. Keepers also provide companionship for the animals. Many types of animals, including monkeys and apes, become fond of their keepers and develop special relationships with them.

Diet. An appropriate diet is vital in keeping zoo animals healthy. The kinds and amounts of food different creatures require vary greatly.

Zoo kitchens stock a wide assortment of basic foods, including fruits, vegetables, meat, fish, dairy products, cereals, seeds, grains, and hay. They also have such unusual items as rats, mice, brine shrimp, crickets, worms, and snakes. Many animals enjoy grazing on the leaves of freshly cut branches. In addition, zoos use large quantities of prepared pellets, seed mixes, and other foods made especially for animals. Zoos also use vitamins and mineral supplements to ensure a nutritious diet for each animal.

Some animals require exactly the type of food they would eat in the wild. For example, koalas will eat only certain kinds of eucalyptus leaves. Giant pandas must have bamboo. Zoos ship in these foods from wherever they are grown or grow the foods themselves.

In zoo kitchens, keepers, nutritionists, and other trained workers prepare balanced meals for each animal in whatever form the animal will eat. Some animals eat their food just as it comes. But for many animals, zoo workers must peel, chop, combine, and even cook foods. Some animals, including certain birds and small mammals, eat several meals each day. Other animals, such as some species of snakes, eat only once every few weeks.

A zoo animal's diet varies under certain circumstances. For example, pregnant females and mothers nursing their young require special food. Animals may also need special diets for gaining or losing weight, for breeding, or for health problems.

Some zoos sell food pellets that visitors may distribute to certain animals. The zoo controls the amount of food provided so the animals are not overfed. Except for such pellets, visitors should not feed zoo animals. Candy, popcorn, and similar foods can make an animal sick. Thoughtless visitors often throw wrappers or other trash to the animals. If an animal swallows this trash, it could become ill and might even die.

Medical care. Most large zoos employ one or more full-time veterinarians. Smaller zoos often have part-time veterinarians. The doctor visits regularly and treats sick or injured creatures. Many animals receive routine vaccinations to protect them from diseases.

Before examining or treating an animal, the doctor may inject the animal with tranquilizers or drugs that temporarily paralyze the patient. After the drugs take effect, the doctor can examine and treat the animal without danger of injury to either the doctor or the animal.

Many large zoos have their own hospitals with operating rooms, X-ray machines, and laboratories. Some zoos have *quarantine* areas where newly acquired animals or those with contagious diseases are kept apart from the other animals to prevent the spread of disease.

How zoos operate

Many zoos are owned and operated by local governments. Some zoos are owned by individuals or nonprofit corporations. In the United States, zoos must be licensed by the U.S. Department of Agriculture.

In the United States and Canada, a number of zoos are members of the American Zoo and Aquarium Association. The association requires its members to maintain high standards of animal care and management. All member institutions must pass an inspection every five years.

Funding. Zoo operations are funded by several sources. Many zoos receive funds from local governments. Most zoos charge admission fees. Other money comes from food and gift shop sales, fund-raising events, donations, "adopt-an-animal" programs, membership fees, and grants from foundations and corporations.

Zoo workers. A zoo is similar to a small town and needs many types of workers to operate smoothly. A *director* is the head of the zoo. A *curator* manages the care of zoo animals and supervises the people who work with the animals. Large zoos may have more than one curator, each overseeing a particular group of animals. Keepers take care of the animals, and veterinarians provide medical care. Zoo scientists study the animals and do research.

Most zoo jobs that involve working with animals require a college degree. Keepers and curators often study biology or zoology. Zoo scientists usually have training in such fields as animal behavior, genetics, anthropology, nutrition, reproductive science, or veterinary technology. Some veterinary schools offer training

Michael Nichols, Magnum

An indoor rain forest exhibit at the Henry Doorly Zoo in Omaha, Nebraska, re-creates the vegetation and humid climate of a tropical rain forest inside an eight-story structure. Visitors stroll among the treetops on elevated walkways and view primates, birds, and other animals.

in wild-animal medicine. Some zoos provide internships for students at the graduate and undergraduate levels.

Many people who have jobs at zoos do not work directly with the animals. Large numbers of employees are involved in administration, office work, fund-raising, security, and maintaining the grounds and buildings. In addition, zoos may rely on volunteer workers to sweep sidewalks, help keepers watch animals, guide tours, and perform many other important jobs.

Obtaining animals. Most zoo animals are born in captivity. A smaller and smaller number of zoo animals are captured in the wild by hunters.

A zoo's director and curators usually decide which animals the zoo needs. Zoos often get animals to fill a gap in their collection, such as when an animal dies. To obtain animals, zoos deal directly with one another, buying, trading, or lending stock. Zoos also buy animals from professional animal dealers. The American Zoo and Aquarium Association and animal dealers circulate lists of what each zoo needs and what species are available.

The United States government severely restricts the importing of many animals, especially endangered species and those that may transmit diseases. Animals that enter the United States from zoos outside the country or from the wild must be *quarantined* (kept in isolation) for a time to be sure they are disease-free.

When an animal first comes to a zoo, it must adjust to its new keepers, its exhibit mates, and its surroundings. Keepers watch the newcomers carefully so that they do not hurt themselves or harm other animals.

History

Early zoos. People have put wild animals on display since ancient times. One of the earliest known zoos was established by Queen Hatshepsut of Egypt about 1500 B.C. About 500 years later, the Chinese emperor Wen Wang founded the Garden of Intelligence, an enormous zoo that covered nearly 1,500 acres (610 hectares). Between 1000 and 400 B.C., rulers in northern Africa, India, and China established many small zoos that were designed to display their wealth and power.

In ancient Greece, rulers and nobles kept private zoos for their own enjoyment. Scholars visited such zoos to study the animals. The Romans also had many private zoos. In addition, the Romans kept a large collection of wild animals used in bloody fights in large outdoor theaters such as the Colosseum. During the Middle Ages, from about the A.D. 400's through the 1400's, many European rulers and nobles maintained private zoos.

By the end of the 1400's, global exploration and an increased interest in learning promoted the popularity of zoos in Europe. Explorers returned from the New World with strange creatures for European zoos. In 1519, Spanish explorers discovered a huge zoo built by the Aztec Indians in what is now Mexico.

During the next 250 years, several zoos were established in Europe. Some of them were merely small exhibits called *menageries.* These consisted of a few bears, lions, or tigers kept in small, gloomy cages or in pits. Only the nobility were allowed to visit most of these exhibits.

The first modern zoos. Over the years, menageries were replaced by larger collections of animals that received better care. These facilities not only displayed animals but also served as centers of research. They developed into the first modern zoos.

The oldest zoo still in existence is the Schönbrunn Zoo, which was founded in Vienna, Austria, in 1752. The Madrid Zoo in Spain was established in 1775. The Paris Zoo, the third oldest zoo in continuous operation, dates from 1793. The Berlin Zoo, which became a leader in research on animal behavior, opened in Germany in 1844.

The development of zoos in the United States began

Jim Tuten, Earth Scenes

Inside a zoo kitchen, trained workers peel, chop, combine, and even cook foods for the animals. Zoo kitchens stock a wide variety of fruits, vegetables, seeds, and many other types of foods. Each animal receives nutritionally balanced meals.

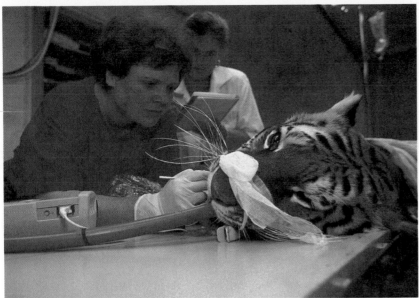

Regular medical treatment helps keep zoo animals healthy. In this photograph, a veterinarian gives a Siberian tiger a dental checkup. Before an examination, doctors often tranquilize the animal to eliminate the danger of injury to either the medical personnel or the animal.

Metropolitan Toronto Zoo

with the chartering of the Philadelphia Zoological Society in 1859. But the American Civil War (1861-1865) delayed construction of the zoo, which did not open until 1874. In 1889, Congress established the National Zoological Park in Washington, D.C. This zoo is the only one that is operated by the United States government. In Canada, the first zoo opened in Halifax, Nova Scotia, in 1847.

The evolution of zoos. In 1907, Carl Hagenbeck, a German animal dealer and zoo owner, developed the moat technique of displaying animals. The idea gradually spread to zoos throughout the world, improving the life of zoo animals and the experiences of visitors. Zoos began replacing barred cages with larger, more natural enclosures. The first children's zoo in the United States opened at the Philadelphia Zoo in 1938.

By the 1940's, zoologists recognized that many species of animals faced extinction in the wild. Zoos realized they could help preserve some of these species and began developing the first breeding programs. Before this time, most zoos had tried to display at least one member of as many different species as possible. Few zoos owned more than one or two animals of a rare species. Today, many zoos keep family groups and breeding populations.

Current issues. Some animal welfare groups criticize the treatment of animals in zoos. Some people are especially opposed to keeping large sea mammals, such as whales and dolphins, in captivity. They claim that these creatures fare poorly even under the best zoo conditions. Some animal rights activists call for all zoos to be shut down. They believe people have no right to keep animals in captivity.

Zoo officials stress the importance of zoos in conservation and science. They agree that substandard zoos should improve their treatment of animals but point out that many zoos meet high standards of care.

Jack Hanna

Related articles in *World Book* include:

Aquarium, Public
Endangered species
Hagenbeck, Carl
National Zoological Park
Veterinary medicine
Wildlife conservation
Zoology

Outline

I. The importance of zoos
  A. Recreation and education
  B. Wildlife conservation
  C. Scientific studies
II. Displaying animals
  A. Layout of a zoo
  B. Exhibits
  C. Cageless zoos
III. Caring for zoo animals
  A. Daily care
  B. Diet
  C. Medical care
IV. How zoos operate
  A. Funding
  B. Zoo workers
  C. Obtaining animals
V. History

Questions

What is an aquarium?
What are some ways that zoos help conserve wildlife?
Why do zoos try to prevent inbreeding among their animals?
How have zoos changed in the way they display their animals?
How do zoos help keep their animals amused?
What is the job of a zoo *curator?* Of a *keeper?*
What are some ways that zoos keep animals in their exhibits?
What is the oldest zoo in the United States?
What are some animals that zoos have saved from extinction?
Where does a zoo get new animals?

Additional resources

Benyus, Janine M. *Beastly Behaviors: A Zoo Lover's Companion.* Addison-Wesley, 1992.
Koebner, Linda. *Zoo Book.* 1994. Reprint. St. Martin's, 1997.
Nichols, Michael, and others. *Keepers of the Kingdom: The New American Zoo.* Lickle Pub., 1996.
Shepherdson, David J., and others, eds. *Second Nature: Environmental Enrichment for Captive Animals.* Smithsonian Institution, 1997.
Yancey, Diane. *Zoos.* Lucent Bks., 1995. Younger readers.

Zoogeography. See Geography (Physical geography).

Zoological garden. See Zoo (with pictures); San Diego (picture).

Zoology, *zoh AHL uh jee,* is the study of animals. Zoologists try to answer many questions about animals. For example, they conduct research to determine how animals carry out the activities of their lives. They also study how different species are related to one another and how species have *evolved* (changed over long periods). Zoologists observe the ways animals interact with one another and their environment. They also try to find out how people and animals affect one another.

The study of zoology has benefited people in many ways. Human beings and animals have many similar body parts and body functions. As a result, zoology forms a basis for understanding human medicine and other health-related fields. Some animals, such as certain insects and worms, can be harmful to people. Zoological research has led to better methods of dealing with such animals. Zoological studies also have helped in the management of wildlife and other natural resources and in the breeding of domestic animals.

What zoologists study

No one knows for certain how many kinds of animals there are in the world. More than 1 million species have been identified, and new ones are discovered every year. No zoologist can know more than a small part of all that is known about animals. As a result, most zoologists specialize in a certain area of study.

Many branches of zoology deal with a particular kind of animal. For example, *entomology* is the study of insects, the largest group of animals. *Mammalogy* deals with mammals, those animals that have hair and that feed their babies on the mother's milk. *Ichthyology* is the study of fish. A zoologist in any of these fields might spend a lifetime studying a single species of animal.

Other areas of zoology deal with certain characteristics that many animals have in common. *Taxonomy* is the study of naming and classifying animals. As part of their work, taxonomists establish relationships among different animal groups. For instance, they have shown that bats are more closely related to mice and other mammals than they are to birds. *Comparative anatomy* is the study of differences and similarities in the body structures of different animals. A comparative anatomist might compare the circulatory systems of sharks, frogs, and cats. *Paleontology* is the study of prehistoric organisms. Paleontologists and comparative anatomists have made important contributions to knowledge about the evolution of many animals.

Zoologists who study *embryology* deal with the formation and development of organisms from fertilized eggs to birth. *Physiology* is the study of the functions of animals. Physiologists may observe how the heart pumps blood, how nerves transmit impulses, and how muscles contract.

Other areas of zoology include *genetics, molecular biology,* and *ecology.* Genetics is the study of *heredity,* the passing on of characteristics from parents to their young. Molecular biology examines the structure and function of proteins and other large molecules essential to life. These two fields of zoology are important in breeding livestock and in understanding certain human diseases. In addition, through genetic engineering, scientists have been able to alter the *genes* (units of heredity) of various organisms (see **Genetic engineering**). *Ecology* is the study of the relationship of organisms to their environment. A knowledge of ecology helps in managing the limited resources of the earth without harming plant and animal populations.

How zoologists work

Many zoologists work in modern laboratories at universities, research centers, zoos, and museums. Other zoologists do *field studies* in the outdoors. These studies might be performed in a wildlife refuge, at the North Pole, in the jungle, at sea, or anywhere else animals live.

Like other scientists, zoologists conduct research by gathering information in an orderly way. Zoologists often begin their research with an observation that arouses different thoughts as to its meaning. For example, a zoologist working in a laboratory might notice that some rats are much smaller than others. Following this observation, the zoologist would attempt to explain why the rats are smaller by making a scientific guess called a *hypothesis.* The zoologist might hypothesize that the small rats lacked a substance that affects normal growth.

After making the hypothesis, the zoologist would test the hypothesis by a series of experiments. In this example, the zoologist might compare the blood of both groups of rats to see if any substance was missing in the blood of the smaller rats. Suppose, in this case, that a substance called growth hormone was absent in the small rats. Additionally, injections of growth hormone restored normal growth in the rats. At this point, the zoologist would develop a theory that would state a connection between this substance and growth. For example, the zoologist might state that growth hormone is necessary for normal growth in rats. Testing the theory in different situations for long periods of time might prove or disprove the theory.

When a zoologist adds to the knowledge of zoology, he or she writes a report of the findings. Such reports are published in scientific journals that are read by zoologists and other interested people.

History

People have always been curious about animals. Prehistoric people had an interest in those animals that were useful as food or clothing, as well as those that were dangerous. Early cave paintings show some of these animals.

During the 300's B.C., the Greek philosopher Aristotle described the structures and habits of animals found in Greece. He is sometimes called the father of zoology. Galen, a Greek physician, studied anatomy and physiology in the A.D. 100's. He made observations of dissected animals and experimented with living animals. Galen's work greatly influenced the early medical profession.

During the 1500's, Andreas Vesalius, an anatomist born in present-day Belgium, argued against Galen in *On the Structure of the Human Body* (1543). This book contained the first detailed portrayal of the human body. Many of Vesalius's observations are still accepted today. The development of the compound microscope in the 1500's and 1600's led to many discoveries. Cells, bacteria, and protozoans were observed for the first time.

Many zoological discoveries occurred in the 1700's and 1800's. In 1758, the Swedish naturalist, Carolus Linnaeus, published a classification system for animals. The system enabled all scientists to use a universally accepted name for each animal that had been discovered. In the early 1800's, Baron Cuvier of France made important contributions to paleontology and comparative anatomy. Cuvier concluded that several animals had become extinct. See **Classification, Scientific.**

Until the end of the 1700's, most people believed that each species of life had remained unchanged and no new species had appeared since the world began. In 1809, the Chevalier de Lamarck, a French naturalist, proposed a theory of evolution of new species based on the influence of the environment. For example, Lamarck said that giraffes had developed long necks by stretching for leaves. Long necks, he said, would then be passed on to the next generation of giraffes. Discoveries in genetics later showed that Lamarck was wrong. But his ideas influenced many scientists, among them the British naturalist Charles Darwin. Darwin made tremendous contributions to zoology. In 1859, he published *The Origin of Species,* one of the most influential zoology books ever written. In it, Darwin presented the theory of *natural selection* to explain how evolution works. See **Evolution; Natural selection.**

Important findings have continued to occur in zoology since 1900. Many of them were made in the areas of genetics, physiology, developmental biology, and *neurobiology* (the study of the nervous system). An important area of zoology that developed in the mid-1900's is *ethology,* the study of animal behavior.

Today, molecular biology and conservation biology have become increasingly significant branches of zoology. Molecular biology has enabled scientists to learn much more about the genetic makeup of animals. Scientists have even learned to develop *clones,* or genetic copies, of certain animals. Conservation biologists work to conserve animal species threatened with extinction. Many zoologists in this field try to get these animals to breed in captivity. As more species have become threatened, such work has grown increasingly important.

Careers in zoology

Zoology offers a broad range of career opportunities. The majority of these careers require a college education. In addition to zoology courses, students who wish to become zoologists must take courses in mathematics, chemistry, and physics. Many students also study computer science and statistics. Zoology careers usually require further training in graduate or professional school.

Many zoologists teach and conduct research in colleges and universities. Others work in zoos and museums. Many scientists with zoological training work to make more food available for people. These agricultural scientists work with cattle, hogs, sheep, and other farm animals. They use genetic engineering, selective breeding, and other methods to produce more and bigger animals for food. Zoologists with special training in fishery biology try to improve the production of fish for food.

Some zoologists work with animals in the field. These zoologists include game wardens, park managers, and ethologists. Manufacturers sometimes hire zoologists to test the effect that a product, such as a fertilizer or insecticide, will have on animals in their natural environment. Zoologists also may work as writers, illustrators, or photographers.　　Lawrence C. Wit

Related articles. See **Animal** and its list of *Related articles.* See also the following:

Biographies

Broom, Robert	Hamilton, William	Morris, Desmond
Cuvier, Baron	Donald	Schaller, George B.
Frisch, Karl von	Huxley, Thomas H.	Swammerdam, Jan
Goodall, Jane	Leakey, Meave	Tinbergen, Niko-
Haeckel, Ernst H.	Gillian	laas
	Lorenz, Konrad	Vesalius, Andreas

Branches of zoology

Anatomy	Ethology	Ornithology
Biochemistry	Genetics	Paleontology
Biophysics	Herpetology	Pathology
Ecology	Histology	Physiology
Embryology	Morphology	

Other related articles

Classification,	Evolution	Taxidermy
Scientific	Fauna	Zoo

Additional resources

Grzimek, Bernhard. *Grzimek's Animal Life Encyclopedia.* 17 vols. 2nd ed. Gale Group, 2003, 2004.
Hickman, Cleveland P., and others. *Integrated Principles of Zoology.* 12th ed. McGraw, 2004.

Zoroastrianism, *zawr oh AS tree uh nihz uhm,* is a religion founded between 1400 and 1000 B.C. by a Persian prophet named Zoroaster. *Zoroaster* is the Greek form of the Persian name *Zarathustra,* which means *He of the Golden Light.*

Beliefs. Zoroastrianism teaches a belief in one god, Ahura Mazda, who created all things. Devout people must seek and obey Ahura Mazda, who will judge everyone at the end of worldly time after their bodies have been resurrected.

The heart of Zoroastrianism is the belief in a battle between good and evil. Zoroaster taught that the earth is a battleground where a great struggle is taking place between Spenta Mainyu, the spirit of good, and Angra Mainyu, the spirit of evil. Ahura Mazda calls upon everyone to fight in this struggle, and each person will be judged at death on how well he or she fought. Each person should be dedicated to fighting for good thoughts, good words, and good deeds.

Zoroaster composed several hymns called *Gathas* that were collected in a sacred book called the *Avesta.* These hymns are the only record of what Zoroaster believed, in his own words. Some scholars believe that traces of Zoroaster's theology can be found in the concept of Satan as the personification of evil (Angra Mainyu). They also find similarities between the Zoroastrian belief in Fravashirs (guardian spirits) and the angels of Western religions.

History. Little is known about Zoroaster's life. Scholars believe that he lived between 1400 and 1000 B.C. in what is now northeastern Iran. However, Zoroastrian tradition

A winged god named Ahura Mazda is the symbol of Zoroastrianism. He was the chief god of the ancient Persians.

teaches that he lived between the early 600's and the mid-500's B.C. He left his home in search of religious truth. After wandering and living alone for several years, he began to have revelations at the age of 30. In a vision, he spoke with Vohu Manah, a figure who represented the Good Mind. In the vision, Zoroaster's soul was led in a holy trance into the presence of Ahura Mazda.

In the years after his revelations, Zoroaster composed the *Gathas* and spread the teachings of Ahura Mazda. Zoroaster's conversion of Vishtaspa, a powerful ruler, strengthened the new religion. According to the Avesta, Zoroaster was assassinated at the age of 77.

Zoroastrianism thrived in Persia from about 550 to 330 B.C., when the religion seems to have lost some of its vitality. The Muslim conquest of Persia in the mid-A.D. 600's led to a further decline in the practice of Zoroastrian rites and rituals. However, several groups continued to observe the religion's traditions. These groups have carried the faith into the present in Iran, India, and other countries. In India, the followers are called Parsis. Modern Zoroastrians read from the *Avesta,* practice traditional purification habits, and attend rituals at fire temples. Fire is important in Zoroastrianism as a symbol of Ahura Mazda.   Robert William Smith

See also **Persia, Ancient** (Religion); **Magi; Mithra.**

Zouaves, *zoo AHVZ,* were soldiers of certain light infantry regiments in the French Army who wore distinctive Oriental-style uniforms. The name *Zouave* came from that of the *Zouaoua* tribe of Kabyles in Algeria, where the French first recruited Zouaves in 1830. At first, these regiments consisted mainly of Algerians. Later, Frenchmen joined the Algerian regiments. Finally, the army separated the Zouaves into French and Algerian regiments. The Algerian regiments were called *Turcos.* The Zouaves fought with Free French forces in North Africa during World War II (1939-1945).

Zouave regiments were also formed in the Union and Confederate armies during the American Civil War (1861-1865). These regiments, which consisted of American volunteers, also wore Oriental-style uniforms. See **Civil War, American** (Mobilizing for war [illustration: Uniforms of the Civil War]).   John W. Gordon

Zucchini, *zoo KEE nee,* is a type of squash that resembles a cucumber. Zucchini are cylindrical, and most have shiny green skin, though some varieties are golden colored. Their flesh is greenish-white. People eat zucchini raw in salads, including the skin. Zucchini also are eaten cooked and are used in making a kind of bread. They are low in calories, but they are a good source of calcium, vitamin C, thiamine, riboflavin, and niacin. The term *zucchini* means *little squashes* in Italian. It was first used in California for a type of Italian or Spanish squash.

Zucchini are popular garden vegetables and grow well in climates with at least two months of warm weather. Zucchini are planted from seeds after all danger of frost has passed for the season. The vegetables grow on a bush that has a short stem and large leaves. Zucchini are picked when they are 6 to 8 inches (15 to 20 centimeters) long and their rind is still tender.   W. E. Splittstoesser

See also **Squash.**

Scientific classification. Zucchini belong to the family Cucurbitaceae. They are *Cucurbita pepo.*

Zukerman, *ZOO kur mahn,* **Pinchas,** *PIHNG kuhs* (1948–   ), is an Israeli-born violinist, violist, and con-

ductor of international fame. His performances are distinguished by his unique interpretations of the standard repertoire as well as less familiar music.

Zukerman was born on July 16, 1948, in Tel Aviv. He began studying at the Israel Conservatory at age 8. He went to New York City in 1962 to study on an American-Israel Cultural Foundation scholarship. His effortless technique distinguished him as a natural player early in his career. From 1965 to 1969, he studied music at the Juilliard School in New York City. He made his New York debut as a violinist in 1969. Zukerman first appeared as a conductor in 1974 with the English Chamber Orchestra and the Aspen Chamber Symphony. He became a U.S. citizen in 1976. Zukerman served as director of the St. Paul Chamber Orchestra in Minnesota from 1980 to 1987. He became the music director of the National Arts Centre Orchestra of Canada in 1998.   Stephen Clapp

Zulu, *ZOO loo,* are one of the main Bantu-speaking peoples of Africa. About 7 million Zulu live in the Republic of South Africa, mostly in the province of KwaZulu-Natal. They make up the largest language group in that country. Many Zulu live in urban areas. For many years, the Zulu and other black South Africans have suffered severe discrimination at the hands of South African whites.

During the early 1800's, a Zulu king named Shaka led his nation in a series of military conquests. In 1838, the Zulu clashed with invading white settlers called *Boers.* The Zulu remained independent until the British conquered them in 1879.

Before the British conquest, the Zulu were farmers and cattle herders. They lived in cone-shaped houses made of finely matted reeds and straw. They arranged these houses in circles to form villages. The Zulu had a powerful monarch and a well-disciplined army.

Zulu men have traditionally practiced *polygyny,* the custom of having more than one wife at a time. A traditional Zulu family consists of a man, his wives, his unmarried children, and his married sons and their wives and children. In urban areas, however, polygyny is becoming rare, and most families are much smaller.

Between the mid-1980's and mid-1990's, conflict between the Zulu and the Xhosa, another black ethnic group, led to much violence and thousands of deaths in South Africa. Much of the fighting occurred between Inkatha Freedom Party members, most of whom are Zulu, and African National Congress supporters, many of

WORLD BOOK illustration by James Teason

A single plant produces many zucchini squash.

whom are Xhosa. Many people believe the Inkatha group represents a revival of Zulu nationalism.

Pierre L. van den Berghe

Related articles in *World Book* include:

Africa (picture: Traditional African dancing)	Bantu Inkatha Freedom Party	Shaka South Africa Xhosa

Zuni Indians, ZOON *yee* or ZOO *nee,* are a tribe that lives in northern New Mexico near the Arizona border. They are one of several tribes of Pueblo Indians. According to the 1990 United States census, there are about 8,000 Zuni. Many tribal members live in the pueblo village of Zuni, which the tribe has inhabited since about A.D. 1000. Many Zuni are farmers. The Zuni are known for their silver, coral, and turquoise jewelry. Many Zuni live in traditional houses of stone. Others live in modern houses.

The Zuni religion is one of the most complex native religions in the Southwest. It centers around six cults, each with its own rituals. One colorful Zuni ceremony is the *Shalako.* It is held annually between Thanksgiving and mid-December to celebrate the arrival of winter.

The Zuni are descended from a prehistoric group called the Anasazi. In 1539, the first Spanish expedition to enter New Mexico met the Zuni. The explorers were searching for the fabled *Seven Cities of Cíbola,* which were believed to be rich in gold (see **Cíbola, Seven Cities of**). The Zuni resented the invasion by foreigners. They killed one of the explorers, a black guide named Estevanico (see **Estevanico**). The Spanish adventurer Francisco Coronado came seeking the Seven Cities in 1540 and instead found six Zuni villages.

The Zuni came under U.S. authority after the Mexican War ended in 1848. That year, the United States acquired land from Mexico, including regions that later became parts of Arizona and New Mexico. In 1969, the tribe established the Zuni Comprehensive Development Plan to create jobs and improve education and living conditions. In 1970, it became the first tribe to contract with the federal government to run programs organized by the U.S. Bureau of Indian Affairs. Alfonso Ortiz

Zunz, *tsoonts,* **Leopold** (1794-1886), has been called the founder of modern Jewish scholarship. He was the first scholar to use scientific methods to study the religious and cultural traditions of Judaism.

Zunz tried to reform Jews politically and religiously. He believed that if the Jews integrated themselves into the community life of Europe, anti-Semitism would disappear. Zunz helped form the Society for Jewish Culture and Science, which existed from 1819 to 1824. The society aimed to hasten the Jews' entry into European culture. The society also promoted the "Science of Judaism," a method of studying Judaism that tried to bridge the Jewish and non-Jewish worlds. Zunz was born on Aug. 10, 1794, in Detmold, Germany. Yosef Levanon

Zurbarán, *THUR bah RAHN* or *zur bah RAHN,* **Francisco de** (1598-1664), was a famous Spanish artist. Zurbarán was one of the most skillful interpreters of the monastic life, the Counter Reformation, and religious aspirations of Spain in the 1600's (see **Counter Reformation**). His subjects included meditating monks, saints, and Christian legends. His most effective paintings have only one or two figures placed in dreamlike landscapes or set against neutral dark backgrounds. An example,

Saint Serapion, appears in the **Painting** article.

Zurbarán's style is characterized by precise outlines, dramatic modeling in light and shade (called *tenebrism),* and intense realism. Zurbarán was a great painter of still-life subjects, such as earthenware jugs. His attention to the surface details and textures of objects carried over into his figure painting. His images of saints often seem to be portraits of real people in ordinary dress.

Zurbarán was born on Nov. 7, 1598, in the region of Extremadura. He painted his finest works for monasteries in Seville, Jerez, and Guadalupe between 1629 and 1640. His works strongly influenced painting in Spain's American colonies. Marilyn Stokstad

See also **Moors** (picture).

Zurich, *ZUR ihk* (pop. 360,980; met. area pop. 976,719), is the largest city in Switzerland and the capital of the *canton* (state) of Zurich. It is a major manufacturing and commercial center. Zurich lies on Lake Zurich, along the Limmat River (see **Switzerland** [political map]).

Zurich has many architectural treasures. These include two medieval churches, the Grossmünster and the Fraumünster; beautifully restored houses used by associations of craftworkers called *guilds;* and the Baroque *Rathaus* (town hall). Bahnhofstrasse, a famous avenue, is flanked by stone palaces built in the 1800's that house Swiss banks, insurance companies, luxury stores, and fancy hotels. Zurich's schools include the Swiss Institute of Technology and the University of Zurich, the largest university in Switzerland.

Products made in Zurich include machine tools, paper, radios, and textiles. The city is one of the world's financial centers and a hub of the international gold trade. People from many countries deposit money in Zurich's banks (see **Switzerland** [Banking]).

According to archaeological evidence, a prehistoric settlement existed near Zurich, on the lake. The Romans built a fort at Zurich, possibly in the late A.D. 100's. In 1351, Zurich united with other Swiss areas in a political

Shostal

The stately Grossmünster Church in Zurich, built between the 1000's and 1200's, towers over the Limmat River. Many architectural landmarks in Zurich date from the Middle Ages.

alliance called the Swiss Confederation, which became modern Switzerland. New textile manufacturing and machine industries contributed to Zurich's growth in the 1800's. As the city grew, it expanded from the area around Lake Zurich and the Limmat River to neighboring valleys.   Heinz K. Meier

Zweig, *zwyg* or *tsvyk,* **Stefan** (1881-1942), was an Austrian writer of psychological novels, stories, biographies, and poems. His best-known stories include *Amok* (1922), *Conflicts* (1927), and *Beware of Pity* (1939). Some of his best biographies are *Romain Rolland* (1921), *Marie Antoinette* (1932), and *Erasmus of Rotterdam* (1934).

Zweig was born on Nov. 28, 1881, in Vienna, Austria. The Nazis forced him to leave Austria because of his Jewish ancestry, and from 1934 to 1940 he lived in London. Depressed over world affairs, he and his wife committed suicide in Brazil. He described the tragic conflicts of his life in his autobiography, *The World of Yesterday* (published in 1943, after his death).   Jeffrey L. Sammons

Zwilich, *ZWIHL ihk,* **Ellen Taaffe,** *EHL ehn tayf* (1939-   ), an American composer, became the first woman to win the Pulitzer Prize in music. She won the 1983 prize for her *Symphony No. 1* (originally titled *Three Movements for Orchestra,* 1982). The work is noted for its imagination touched with humor. Zwilich writes skillfully for individual instruments, and her works have a clear structure. Her other orchestral compositions include *Prologue and Variations* (1983), *Celebration for Orchestra* (1984), and *Symbolon* (1988). She has also written chamber music and vocal music.

Ellen Taaffe was born on April 30, 1939, in Miami, Florida. She studied at Florida State University and then moved to New York City, where she played violin in the American Symphony Orchestra from 1965 to 1972. In 1969, she married Joseph Zwilich, a violinist in the Metropolitan Opera orchestra. She then studied at the Juilliard School, where her teachers included the composers Elliott Carter and Roger Sessions. Zwilich received a doctorate in 1975, the first woman to receive such a degree from the school.   Richard Jackson

Zwingli, *ZWIHNG lee* or *TSVIHNG lee,* **Huldreich,** *HUL drykh* (1484-1531), was a leader of the Protestant Reformation. His career centered in Switzerland, but he influenced the Reformation in Germany, the Netherlands, and England.

His life. Zwingli was born on Jan. 1, 1484, in the Wildhaus Valley near St. Gall, Switzerland. In 1506, he was ordained a Catholic priest. By 1514, Zwingli had become a follower of the Dutch humanist Desiderius Erasmus. He studied Erasmus's edition of the Greek text of the New Testament and adopted the program of the Christian humanists for reforming the church. This program tried to follow what the humanists felt was the simple faith of the New Testament and of the early Christians.

In 1518, Zwingli was chosen to be a priest of the cathedral in Zurich. He became a forceful reform preacher, following the views of Erasmus. Soon he read works by the reformer Martin Luther. By 1520, Zwingli had worked out a Protestant theology unlike that of Luther.

After the Catholic bishop of Zurich tried to silence Zwingli, the civil magistrates took charge of all the city's religious affairs. In 1523, the magistrates called a public meeting to decide between Catholicism and Zwingli's new Protestantism. The decision favored Zwingli's new

theology. During the next two years, the magistrates abolished religious images, such as statues; adopted a Protestant liturgy; closed the monasteries; and substituted the Lord's Supper for the Mass. By 1528, the major German-Swiss cities had followed Zurich's lead. Rural areas remained Catholic. In 1531, Zwingli, serving as a chaplain with the Protestant troops, died during a war with Catholics.

His ideas. Zwingli agreed with other early reformers on many issues. These issues included salvation by faith rather than by good works, the supremacy of the Bible as the sole authority for Christianity, and the universal priesthood of all believers. The concept of universal priesthood declared that all believers were considered priests because they helped bring God's grace to others. Catholic priests were set apart from lay people by their power to perform the sacraments.

Luther and Zwingli disagreed on certain points, especially the Lord's Supper. Luther believed Jesus Christ was really present in this sacrament, though not in the same way the Catholic Church taught. Zwingli considered the Lord's Supper a thanksgiving to God for grace already given in other ways, especially through God's gift of the Gospel.

Luther was mainly concerned about individual salvation. Zwingli, however, had greater concern about what he called the "renaissance of Christendom." By this he meant the total rebirth of humanity and society.

Zwingli became active in politics and in social reform. He supported radical changes in the church and worked successfully for the right of the people to control the church.   Peter W. Williams

See also **Luther, Martin; Reformation** (Zwingli and the Anabaptists).

Zworykin, *ZWAWR uh kihn,* **Vladimir Kosma,** *VLAD uh MEER KAHZ muh* (1889-1982), was a Russian-born American physicist and electronics engineer. He was responsible for many advances in radio, television, and the electron microscope.

Zworykin came to the United States in 1919. In 1920, the Westinghouse Electric Company hired him as a research engineer for the radio tube department. Zworykin invented the *iconoscope* and the *kinescope* in 1923. The iconoscope was the first successful television camera tube, and the kinescope was an early version of the television picture tube. While at Westinghouse, Zworykin studied physics at the University of Pittsburgh. He received a Ph.D. degree from the university in 1926.

In 1929, Zworykin joined the Radio Corporation of America (RCA) as director of electronics research. That same year, he demonstrated the first practical, all-electronic television. While at RCA, he also helped develop the electron microscope. He became vice president of RCA in 1947. The U.S. government gave Zworykin the National Medal of Science, the nation's highest science award, in 1966.

Zworykin was born on July 30, 1889, in Murom, Russia. He graduated from the Petrograd Institute of Technology in 1912 with a degree in electrical engineering. He then studied in Paris, where he did research on X rays with physicist Paul Langevin. Zworykin returned to Russia when World War I began in 1914.   Richard L. Hilt

See also **Electronics** (picture: Vladimir K. Zworykin).

Zygote. See **Fertilization.**